ANTITRUST LAW, POLICY AND PROCEDURE

**MICHIE CONTEMPORARY
LEGAL EDUCATION SERIES**

Antitrust Law, Policy and Procedure

Cases, Materials, Problems

Fourth Edition

E. Thomas Sullivan
Dean and Professor of Law
University of Minnesota

Herbert Hovenkamp
Ben V. and Dorothy Willie Professor
of Law
University of Iowa

LEXIS® LAW PUBLISHING
CHARLOTTESVILLE, VIRGINIA

LEXIS® LAW PUBLISHING
P.O. Box 7587, Charlottesville, VA 22906-7587

Law School Publications
Phone: 800/446-3410, ext. 5578 or 804/961-5578
E-mail: llplawschool@lexis-nexis.com

Customer Service
Phone: 800/533-1646
E-mail: customer.support@bender.com

1319412

To Susan and Beverly

Preface to the Fourth Edition

This Fourth edition of *Antitrust Law, Policy and Procedure* continues the basic approach of preceding editions. The central focus is on judicial decisions, supplemented by analytic, historical, and economic notes and questions. Principal decisions and note cases have been updated in all areas, as well as references to secondary sources, and we have added new problems. The edition also adjusts the coverage to include somewhat less in relatively quiet areas, such as vertical and conglomerate mergers, and more in areas of greater activity, such as technology and intellectual property. A few older decisions have been pruned, but we have tried not to change the book's general pitch any more than necessary to reflect new developments.

E. Thomas Sullivan
Herbert Hovenkamp
Minneapolis, Minnesota
Iowa City, Iowa
March, 1999

Preface to the Third Edition

This edition continues the same approach followed in earlier editions of heavy focus on the case law, together with simple economic analysis and notes representing a variety of ideological viewpoints. In the matter of antitrust ideology, the Supreme Court is as divided and undirected as it has ever been — witness the chasm between the 1992 *Kodak* decision and the 1993 *Spectrum Sports* and *Brooke* decisions.

The increase in the volume of Supreme Court opinions over the last five years has necessitated some pruning and editing of earlier opinions, but we have tried to leave all important concurrences and dissents as intact as possible. This edition also adds several new problems, expanded bibliographies, and all Supreme Court decisions through the October, 1992 term.

We thank Professor Richard D. Friedman of the University of Michigan Law School for numerous invaluable comments. We are also grateful to our research assistants Craig Marquiz, Hrayr A. Sayadian, and Ellen Szarleta for a variety of significant contributions.

E. Thomas Sullivan
Herbert Hovenkamp
Tucson, Arizona
Iowa City, Iowa
September, 1993

Preface to the Second Edition

We continue to believe that the best approach toward antitrust in the law school curriculum is through the cases. For that reason, this casebook emphasizes judicial opinions and contains relatively more of each one, including dissents, than other books in the field.

We also believe that antitrust should be taught with the "best" legal precedents available, and that sometimes a recent circuit court opinion is better than an outdated Supreme Court opinion. For this reason, some antitrust decisions that were important in the 1960's and earlier have been given very brief treatment or omitted as principal cases in this edition.

Finally, we believe that a casebook designed for a student's first or second antitrust course should not overwhelm the student with one particular ideology. Antitrust ideologies have come and gone, and they will continue to do so. The notes in this book are designed to take seriously the competing ideologies of left, right, and center, to confront their defects, and to present their strengths. Professors who are strongly committed to a particular ideology should find plenty of material to criticize or, alternatively, to illustrate their views.

This edition encompasses antitrust developments through the summer of 1988 and includes all Supreme Court decisions of the October, 1987 Term.

As a new feature in this edition, we offer a series of problems for class discussion or individual assignment. The problems are analyzed in detail in a Teacher's Problem Manual to be published as a companion to this volume.

E. Thomas Sullivan
Herbert Hovenkamp
St. Louis, Missouri
Iowa City, Iowa
January, 1989

Preface to the First Edition

We believe this book on federal antitrust law is a unique and valuable contribution to its genre. Although it covers the same general law as its peers, its perspective is different in several ways that make it particularly useful for teachers hoping to offer a sophisticated but litigation-oriented antitrust course.

First, this book is shorter than most others in the field. Many antitrust books have grown fat with overruled Supreme Court opinions, with opinions whose historical value far exceeds their usefulness as credible statements of current law, and long footnotes of string citations that do little for students facing their first experience in antitrust analysis and problem solving.

To be sure, brevity imposes certain costs. This book contains no separate sections on antitrust and the patent system, and no detailed discussion of the extraterritorial applications of antitrust law. It has only brief sections on antitrust in the regulated and so-called "exempt" industries. Although all these things are useful and can be profitably taught, it is our experience that few instructors emphasize them in the basic three-unit or four-unit antitrust class.

At the same time, this book offers a broader coverage than most on procedural issues, particularly on the law of private enforcement. Since more than ninety percent of all federal antitrust cases are now brought by private plaintiffs, the law of private enforcement has developed a rich and complex "substance" all its own. That law is more appropriate to a basic antitrust course than is the extensive discussion of patents or extraterritorial application. Likewise this book focuses more than most on the process of antitrust litigation — on evidentiary standards, burden of proof requirements, and standards for judgment. These emphases seem appropriate because concepts such as "market power," "agreement," or "intent" are not merely abstractions of the substantive law: They are facts that must be established in court.

An additional, important difference between this book and many others in the field is ideological. This book attempts to strike a balanced, diversified approach in presenting a wide spectrum of ideas regarding the goals and economic underpinnings of antitrust law. The authors of this book disagree with each other about many questions that are central to antitrust policy making today, such as whether increased allocative efficiency should be the exclusive or only one of many antitrust enforcement goals. As a result this book both entertains and takes seriously alternative viewpoints and permits the students (or the teacher) a larger perspective for individual choice.

Ideological narrowness is nowhere more evident than in the editing of opinions. Antitrust casebooks have become notorious for "ideological editing" that either supports the view of the editor or else makes the court's position appear far less rational than it really was. Antitrust opinions are particularly conducive to such editing because they are so long — in many cases a fifty-page opinion must be reduced to five or six.

Neither of the authors has permitted an editorial atrocity that reflects too favorably on the ideology of the other. Although nonideological editing does not exist, nothing succeeds like competition in bringing differences of ideology into the light of day. The result in most instances is that the edited opinions contained here are longer than those in other antitrust casebooks. Furthermore, this book prints excerpts from many more concurring and dissenting opinions, particularly when the secondary opinion foreshadowed a position later taken by the Supreme Court.

The book also employs the positive use of economic theories as an analytical device. As to the level of economic sophistication and difficulty, this book must be classified as "medium." Today no one can ask *whether* an antitrust casebook should develop price theory and industrial organization; the only question is how much. This book is addressed to students, however, who are assumed to have no prior experience in economics. Its approach centers on the fundamentals. It offers an introductory chapter and then builds in succeeding chapters on the models created. Unlike casebooks in which economic analysis can be found only in an opening chapter or appendix, the economic analysis in this book is integrated into the notes and discussions following each case selection. Economics in antitrust is valuable only to the extent that it enhances our ability to analyze disputes and make useful policy judgments. For that, a few comments about price theory hidden in an appendix are simply inadequate. Famous and influential opinions such as *Alcoa*, *du Pont* and *Brown Shoe* have an imposing if dubious economics content, but most students will not discern that content unless they are given at least minimal guidance. We attempt to do that.

In sum, this offering attempts to integrate into the traditional antitrust casebook an appreciation for the rich historical, socio-political, and economic development of the antitrust laws and policies. How the law has evolved and the implications for future development are central to this book's format. In addition to the doctrinal development, this book attempts to focus the attention of students on the evidentiary and procedural context within which the "substantive" material may be utilized. We hope these objectives will be successful.

E. Thomas Sullivan
Herbert Hovenkamp
Columbia, Missouri
San Francisco, California
February, 1984

Summary Table of Contents

Table of Contents

Chapter 1
INTRODUCTION TO THE COMPETITION MODEL

SECTION I. OVERVIEW: THE POLICIES AND GOALS OF ANTITRUST REGULATION

Throughout history, antitrust law has been concerned with governmental control of business concentration and economic power. Since 1890 the antitrust laws have had varying interpretations so as to promote certain policies and goals perceived to underlie the original statutes. Antitrust analysis, like much of antitrust conduct, however, is cyclical in nature. Sullivan, *The Economic Jurisprudence of the Burger Court's Antitrust Policy: The First Thirteen Years,* 58 Notre Dame L. Rev. 1 (1982). As the decisional law indicates, at various times Congress and the courts have defined and refined the values sought to be advanced by enforcement of the antitrust laws. Current antitrust analysis suggests that courts interpret the law so as to promote the maximization of consumer welfare. Such an approach, however, deemphasizes certain prior precedents and displaces other analytical approaches toward antitrust. To put antitrust in perspective and to understand the analysis today, one must consider the interdisciplinary nature of the subject and the historical debates and enforcement trends that encircle the law's development.

Probably the single most important factor affecting antitrust analysis has been the introduction and application of economics into antitrust law. But the positive use or misuse of economics in antitrust decision-making is only of relatively recent origin. As the judicial debate began concerning how "competition" as the goal of antitrust should be defined, economic models were introduced into the definitional analysis. If the challenged conduct was foreseen as unreasonably anticompetitive then it was to be condemned under the antitrust laws. Economics was offered, then, as an analytical measure to inform the content and rationale of the antitrust laws. But because economists differ markedly on the assumptions that underlie their economic modeling, no solid consensus has emerged as to which models better inform and facilitate antitrust analysis and policy. This is so largely because economics is based, among other things, upon many assumptions concerning behavior. Some of the assumptions draw on social and political values as well as experience. Moreover, it is difficult to quantify or isolate with precision an economic model that measures all the relevant antitrust concerns. Consequently, many antitrust observers believe that there is a wide gap between economic theory and actual market conduct. With these limitations noted, the identified policies and goals of antitrust regulation will be explored.

Historically, two central themes have been recognized at one time or another as the underpinnings for antitrust policy. One supported the noneconomic approach that enforcement was to be carried out so as to control the economic concentration of industrial power. "Competition" was defined as the promotion of equality among businesses through the dispersion of economic power. Free access to markets was an objective. Economic power was the evil sought to be condemned. Freedom of individual choice, distributive justice, and pluralism were core values. The small entrepreneur was favored and protected against the encroaching economic leverage of the larger concentrated entity, even if the result was increased costs to the consumer.

The other theme viewed antitrust as a body of law designed to promote the goal of enhancing economic efficiency, without regard to the sociopolitical imbalance that such a goal might create between the large concentrated business and small struggling competitor. Under this approach, the antitrust laws were intended to protect competition rather than competitors. "The whole task of antitrust can be summed up as the effort to improve allocative efficiency without impairing productive efficiency so greatly as to produce either no gain or a net loss in consumer welfare." R. Bork, *The Antitrust Paradox* 91 (1978). Efficiency is frequently viewed in terms of whether the challenged conduct creates a restraint or limitation on output. Absent a finding of output limitation, the conduct is deemed efficient and beyond the condemnation of the antitrust laws. In practice, these goals often diverged, creating analytical and policy tensions, though few at first accepted the apparent inconsistencies. *Compare* Fox, *The Modernization of Antitrust: A New Equilibrium,* 66 Cornell L. Rev. 1140 (1981), *with* Posner, *The Chicago School of Antitrust Analysis,* 127 U. Pa. L. Rev. 925 (1979). *See* Hovenkamp, *Antitrust Policy After Chicago,* 84 Mich. L. Rev. 213 (1985).

Central to the debate underlying the values inherent in antitrust policy is the issue of how "competition" ought to be defined. *See Papers Presented at the Airlie House Conference on the Antitrust Alternative,* 62 N.Y.U. L. Rev. 931-1171 (1987); 76 Geo. L.J. 237-346 (1987); *Symposium on Antitrust Law and Economics,* 127 U. Pa. L. Rev. 918-1140 (1979). In one of the Supreme Court's first opinions on the subject, the Court suggested that one goal of the law was to protect small business units from reduced prices brought about by larger concerns. In *United States v. Trans-Missouri Freight Ass'n,* 166 U.S. 290, 322-23 (1897), Justice Peckham reasoned:

> Manufacturing or trading companies may also affect prices by joining together in forming a trust or other combination, and by making agreements in restraint of trade and commerce, which, when carried out, affect the interests of the public.... It is true the results of trusts, or combinations of that nature, may be different in different kinds of corporations, and yet they all have an essential similarity, and have been induced by motives of individual or corporate aggrandizement as against the public interest. In business or trading combinations they may even temporarily, or perhaps permanently, reduce the price of the article traded in or manufactured, by reducing the expense inseparable from the running of many different companies for the same purpose. Trade or commerce under those circumstances may nevertheless be

INTRODUCTION TO THE COMPETITION MODEL

SECTION I. OVERVIEW: THE POLICIES AND GOALS OF ANTITRUST REGULATION

Throughout history, antitrust law has been concerned with governmental control of business concentration and economic power. Since 1890 the antitrust laws have had varying interpretations so as to promote certain policies and goals perceived to underlie the original statutes. Antitrust analysis, like much of antitrust conduct, however, is cyclical in nature. Sullivan, *The Economic Jurisprudence of the Burger Court's Antitrust Policy: The First Thirteen Years,* 58 Notre Dame L. Rev. 1 (1982). As the decisional law indicates, at various times Congress and the courts have defined and refined the values sought to be advanced by enforcement of the antitrust laws. Current antitrust analysis suggests that courts interpret the law so as to promote the maximization of consumer welfare. Such an approach, however, deemphasizes certain prior precedents and displaces other analytical approaches toward antitrust. To put antitrust in perspective and to understand the analysis today, one must consider the interdisciplinary nature of the subject and the historical debates and enforcement trends that encircle the law's development.

Probably the single most important factor affecting antitrust analysis has been the introduction and application of economics into antitrust law. But the positive use or misuse of economics in antitrust decision-making is only of relatively recent origin. As the judicial debate began concerning how "competition" as the goal of antitrust should be defined, economic models were introduced into the definitional analysis. If the challenged conduct was foreseen as unreasonably anticompetitive then it was to be condemned under the antitrust laws. Economics was offered, then, as an analytical measure to inform the content and rationale of the antitrust laws. But because economists differ markedly on the assumptions that underlie their economic modeling, no solid consensus has emerged as to which models better inform and facilitate antitrust analysis and policy. This is so largely because economics is based, among other things, upon many assumptions concerning behavior. Some of the assumptions draw on social and political values as well as experience. Moreover, it is difficult to quantify or isolate with precision an economic model that measures all the relevant antitrust concerns. Consequently, many antitrust observers believe that there is a wide gap between economic theory and actual market conduct. With these limitations noted, the identified policies and goals of antitrust regulation will be explored.

Historically, two central themes have been recognized at one time or another as the underpinnings for antitrust policy. One supported the noneconomic approach that enforcement was to be carried out so as to control the economic concentration of industrial power. "Competition" was defined as the promotion of equality among businesses through the dispersion of economic power. Free access to markets was an objective. Economic power was the evil sought to be condemned. Freedom of individual choice, distributive justice, and pluralism were core values. The small entrepreneur was favored and protected against the encroaching economic leverage of the larger concentrated entity, even if the result was increased costs to the consumer.

The other theme viewed antitrust as a body of law designed to promote the goal of enhancing economic efficiency, without regard to the sociopolitical imbalance that such a goal might create between the large concentrated business and small struggling competitor. Under this approach, the antitrust laws were intended to protect competition rather than competitors. "The whole task of antitrust can be summed up as the effort to improve allocative efficiency without impairing productive efficiency so greatly as to produce either no gain or a net loss in consumer welfare." R. Bork, *The Antitrust Paradox* 91 (1978). Efficiency is frequently viewed in terms of whether the challenged conduct creates a restraint or limitation on output. Absent a finding of output limitation, the conduct is deemed efficient and beyond the condemnation of the antitrust laws. In practice, these goals often diverged, creating analytical and policy tensions, though few at first accepted the apparent inconsistencies. *Compare* Fox, *The Modernization of Antitrust: A New Equilibrium,* 66 Cornell L. Rev. 1140 (1981), *with* Posner, *The Chicago School of Antitrust Analysis,* 127 U. Pa. L. Rev. 925 (1979). *See* Hovenkamp, *Antitrust Policy After Chicago,* 84 Mich. L. Rev. 213 (1985).

Central to the debate underlying the values inherent in antitrust policy is the issue of how "competition" ought to be defined. *See Papers Presented at the Airlie House Conference on the Antitrust Alternative,* 62 N.Y.U. L. Rev. 931-1171 (1987); 76 Geo. L.J. 237-346 (1987); *Symposium on Antitrust Law and Economics,* 127 U. Pa. L. Rev. 918-1140 (1979). In one of the Supreme Court's first opinions on the subject, the Court suggested that one goal of the law was to protect small business units from reduced prices brought about by larger concerns. In *United States v. Trans-Missouri Freight Ass'n,* 166 U.S. 290, 322-23 (1897), Justice Peckham reasoned:

> Manufacturing or trading companies may also affect prices by joining together in forming a trust or other combination, and by making agreements in restraint of trade and commerce, which, when carried out, affect the interests of the public.... It is true the results of trusts, or combinations of that nature, may be different in different kinds of corporations, and yet they all have an essential similarity, and have been induced by motives of individual or corporate aggrandizement as against the public interest. In business or trading combinations they may even temporarily, or perhaps permanently, reduce the price of the article traded in or manufactured, by reducing the expense inseparable from the running of many different companies for the same purpose. Trade or commerce under those circumstances may nevertheless be

badly and unfortunately restrained by driving out of business the small dealers and worthy men whose lives have been spent therein, and who might be
unable to readjust themselves to their altered surroundings. Mere reduction
in the price of the commodity dealt in might be dearly paid for by the ruin of
such a class and the absorption of control over one commodity by an all-
powerful combination of capital.

This theme found expression, though not consistently, in many other Supreme
Court opinions, particularly during the Warren Court era. An example can be
found in *Northern Pac. Ry. v. United States*, 356 U.S. 1, 4 (1958) where the
Court observed that:

> The Sherman Act was designed to be a comprehensive charter of eco-
> nomic liberty aimed at preserving free and unfettered competition as the rule
> of trade. It rests on the premise that the unrestrained interaction of competi-
> tive forces will yield the best allocation of our economic resources, the low-
> est prices, the highest quality and the greatest material progress, while at the
> same time providing an environment conducive to the preservation of our
> democratic, political and social institutions.

Citations to this Supreme Court statement have been frequently made in support
of the argument that the antitrust laws have as their foundational goal the noneconomic objectives of preserving democratic institutions and industrial organization
in the form of small units, and the encouragement of equal competitive opportunity. *See, e.g., United States v. Von's Grocery Co.*, 384 U.S. 270, 274-75 (1966);
Brown Shoe Co. v. United States, 370 U.S. 294, 344 (1962); *United States v.
Aluminum Co. of Am.*, 148 F.2d 416, 427 (2d Cir. 1945). *See also* 21 Cong. Rec.
2457, 2459-60 (1890).

The most forceful articulation of this antitrust policy can be found in the Warren Court's *Brown Shoe* decision. Although the context was section 7 of the
Clayton Act, Chief Justice Warren stated in *Brown Shoe* that the Court had struck
the balance in favor of competition "equity" rather than efficiency:

> [W]e cannot fail to recognize Congress' desire to promote competition
> through the protection of viable, small, locally owned businesses. Congress
> appreciated that occasional higher costs and prices might result from the
> maintenance of fragmented industries and markets. It resolved these com-
> peting considerations in favor of decentralization.

370 U.S. 294, 344 (1961). *See also FTC v. Procter & Gamble Co.*, 386 U.S. 568,
580 (1967). Certain lower court opinions embraced the same values for antitrust.
See United States v. Aluminum Co. of Am., 148 F.2d 416 (2d Cir. 1945)
("Throughout the history of [antitrust] statutes it has been constantly assumed
that one of their purposes was to perpetuate and preserve, for its own sake and in
spite of possible costs, an organization of industry in small units which can effectively compete with each other.").

The above quoted statement from *Northern Pacific* could perhaps be interpreted to yield an antitrust policy concerned predominantly with economic efficiency. Evidence that the Supreme Court has gradually accepted the economic objectives of efficiency and increased consumer welfare as the underlying policies of antitrust is emerging from recent decisions. This is particularly true since 1974. For example, relying on earlier pronouncements by Justice Brandeis in *Chicago Board of Trade v. United States,* 246 U.S. 231 (1918), the Court in 1978 held that the trial court's responsibility is limited to determining the "competitive effect" of the challenged restraint. *National Soc'y of Prof. Eng'rs v. United States,* 435 U.S. 679, 691-95 (1978). Such an economic approach explores only "the facts peculiar to the business, the history of the restraint, and the reasons why it was imposed."

Thus, the analytical framework requires an economic inquiry that weighs the competitive harms and the economic benefits. The factual and economic issues are reduced to whether the challenged conduct promotes or suppresses competition in the final analysis. The weighing of economic and noneconomic goals was rejected, Justice Stevens concluded for the Court, because the underlying assumption of the Sherman Act implicitly dictates that "competition will produce not only lower prices, but also better goods and services." And, "the statutory policy precludes inquiry into the question whether competition is good or bad." Social benefits are not to be weighed against competition factors. The Court reasoned that a weighing of the public interest against the anticompetitive restraint would be beyond the judicial prerogative and "would be tantamount to a repeal of the statute."

Other recent decisions seem to conclude that the antitrust laws should be read as advancing only a consumer welfare prescription. Implicit in the Court's reasoning has been a call for performance efficiency criteria as the standard upon which competition ought to be judged. *See, e.g., Reiter v. Sonotone Corp.,* 442 U.S. 330 (1979); *Broadcast Music, Inc. v. Columbia Broadcasting Sys.,* 441 U.S. 1 (1979); *Continental T.V., Inc. v. GTE Sylvania, Inc.,* 433 U.S. 36 (1977); *Brunswick Corp. v. Pueblo Bowl-O-Mat, Inc.,* 429 U.S. 477 (1977). This theme continues with the Rehnquist Court. *Business Elec. Corp. v. Sharp Elec. Corp.,* 485 U.S. 717 (1988), reprinted in Chapter 5, *infra*; and *Brooke Group Ltd. v. Brown & Williamson Tobacco Corp.,* 113 S. Ct. 2578 (1993), reprinted in Chapter 6.

As the study of antitrust reveals, the Supreme Court's interpretation of the policies and goals of the antitrust laws has not been static nor even consistent. The debate continues not only among the Court's members but, as the following suggests, also among the antitrust academic community.

PITOFSKY, THE POLITICAL CONTENT OF ANTITRUST, 127 University of Pennsylvania Law Review 1051 (1979)*

Although the political forces that produced the major antitrust statutes — in 1890, 1914, 1936, and 1950 — varied widely, those statutes once enacted have

---

* Reprinted by permission.

almost always been enforced and interpreted so that economic considerations were paramount. The issue among most serious people has never been whether non-economic considerations should outweigh significant long-term economics of scale, but rather whether they had any role to play at all, and if so, how they should be defined and measured.

There probably has never been a period comparable to the last decade, however, when antitrust economists and lawyers have had such success in persuading the courts to adopt an *exclusively* economic approach to antitrust questions.... [This approach however] is bad history, bad policy, and bad law to exclude certain political values in interpreting the antitrust laws. By "political values," I mean, first, a fear that excessive concentration of economic power will breed antidemocratic political pressures, and second, a desire to enhance individual and business freedom by reducing the range within which private discretion by a few in the economic sphere controls the welfare of all. A third and overriding political concern is that if the free-market sector of the economy is allowed to develop under antitrust rules that are blind to all but economic concerns, the likely result will be an economy so dominated by a few corporate giants that it will be impossible for the state not to play a more intrusive role in economic affairs.

This view is not at odds with the central beliefs of both the "Chicago" and "Harvard" schools that the major goals of antitrust relate to economic efficiency — to avoid the allocative inefficiencies of monopoly power, encourage efficiency and progressiveness in the use of resources, and perhaps, on fairness grounds, to maintain price close to cost in order to minimize unnecessary and undesirable accumulations of private wealth. Because interpretations that exclude all but economic concerns have lately become so influential, ... it is important to explain why economic concerns, although properly of paramount importance, should not control exclusively.

It can be argued that the political considerations discussed here are ill-defined and incapable of exact or even meaningful definition. Also, it will be difficult to balance vague concepts such as a fear of economic conditions conducive to totalitarianism against the efficiency loss of an industry structure that is disassembled or a series of business transactions that are disallowed. Finally, it may be that when such vague and controversial factors are introduced into antitrust considerations, some enforcement officials and judges will lose sight of the secondary role of these political factors and will distort and misinterpret antitrust policy. There is merit to each of these concerns. But despite the inconvenience, lack of predictability, and general mess introduced into the economists' allegedly cohesive and tidy world of exclusively micro-economic analysis, an antitrust policy that failed to take political concerns into account would be unresponsive to the will of Congress and out of touch with the rough political consensus that has supported antitrust enforcement for almost a century.

....

If the choice were posed solely between monopoly power achieved individually, solely as a result of efficiencies, and government intervention to prevent concentration, the legislative history of the Sherman Act and the overwhelming weight of subsequent judicial interpretation would opt for monopoly power. The most famous judicial statement of the case for a political dimension to antitrust — Judge Learned Hand's explanation in *United States v. Aluminum Co. of America* [*Alcoa*] that "great industrial consolidations are inherently undesirable" for political as well as economic reasons — granted as much by accepting as an absolute defense the explanation that such a market position was brought about solely through superior skill, foresight, and industry.

The issue is rarely posed that way, however. Instead, there is characteristically a legal challenge to business behavior that produced or maintained monopoly power, or to mergers or cartel arrangements that tend to concentrate or coordinate market power, and a defense that the behavior or arrangements are efficient and therefore tend to contribute to consumer welfare.

....

Factors other than strictly economic concerns should be taken into account because the legislative history of the antitrust statutes, in its own right and as interpreted authoritatively in the courts, so requires, because an exclusively economic approach reflects an unrealistically optimistic view of the certainty introduced by that kind of analysis, and because the introduction of non-economic factors does not result in an undue interference with effective enforcement.

....

The Sherman Act and most of its amendments do not address specific issues of antitrust enforcement. The key terms "restraint of trade" in section 1 of the Sherman Act and "monopolize" in section 2 were not defined, and the legislative history does not reflect consideration of the possibility that unrelieved pursuit of a free-market competitive system might lead to adverse non-economic effects.

This failure to address the efficiency/political-effects trade-off is not hard to understand. Comprehensive antitrust regulation was a new concept to all legislators, and the most authoritative and exhaustive reviews of the legislative history have detected a series of vague and not always consistent strands of legislative intent. As many have observed, Congress elected generally to leave specific enforcement decisions to the judiciary.

But putting aside the Sherman Act and its admittedly obscure legislative history, can we discern anything with respect to legislative intent from subsequent antitrust statutes? If we can, it seems clear that those subsequent statutes must be interpreted to incorporate political concerns, and it appears arguable that these subsequent expressions define Congress' vague intentions in earlier enactments.

....

To some extent, preservation of a competitive *process* would achieve the goals that were of concern ...; hence it is arguable that the statute is responsibly enforced if exclusively economic considerations, including the dispersal of monopoly power achieved other than by patents or economies of scale, are applied.

Legislative history focusing on the protection of competition, not competitors, supports that view.

....

Even if economic theory were clear and consistent, economics provides no system for reliably determining economic effect. We know that a market served by fifteen or twenty firms that is converted by merger to a monopoly or duopoly will produce a different level of price and perhaps efficiency. In contrast, a merger in a ten-firm market between the sixth and eighth firms reduces the total number to nine but allows the combined enterprise to challenge the leaders more effectively. There is no reliable way to determine either the pro- or anti-competitive effect of that merger with anything approaching scientific reliability. As a result, antitrust enforcement along economic lines already incorporates large doses of hunch, faith, and intuition.

....

Vigorous antitrust enforcement usually serves both economic and political goals, at least as political goals have been defined here. Elimination or containment of monopoly and elimination of unnecessary barriers to entry and unreasonable business practices not only promote economic efficiency but tend to avoid undue concentrations of economic power, to reduce the range of private discretion in the business field, and to minimize the risks of state interference. But unavoidable inconsistencies occasionally do arise, and the question at that point is whether inclusion of political values, reasonably defined and weighted, leads to unacceptable administrative or anti-efficiency costs. That depends on how political values are introduced into the antitrust equation.

....

[T]he Supreme Court in the 1950's and 1960's believed that Congress preferred less concentrated market structures, including situations in which there could be an efficiency loss and the likelihood of cartelizing tendencies was remote. Even if a narrow exception for evidence of efficiencies were permitted — when the likelihood of competitive injuries was slight, the predicted efficiencies were capable of clear demonstration in court, and there was some likelihood that the efficiencies would be converted into significant competitive effects — that would still reflect an essentially "political" determination to pay an economic price to serve non-economic goals. That position seems to be a valid interpretation of Congress' will.

....

[T]he trend toward use of an exclusively economic approach to antitrust analysis excludes important political considerations that have in the past been seen as relevant by Congress and the courts. Such considerations as the fear that excessive concentration of economic power will foster antidemocratic political pressures, the desire to reduce the range of private discretion by a few in order to enhance individual freedom, and the fear that increased governmental intrusion will become necessary if the economy is dominated by the few, can and should be feasibly incorporated into the antitrust equation. Although economic concerns would remain paramount, to ignore these non-economic factors would be to ignore the bases of antitrust legislation and the political consensus by which antitrust has been supported.

R. BORK, THE ANTITRUST PARADOX: A POLICY AT WAR WITH ITSELF 6-11 (REV. ED. 1992)*

Antitrust presents itself as a body of developed knowledge and principle worked out over years of investigation, thought, and litigation. That image is misleading. Antitrust is not all of a piece.

Because antitrust's basic premises are mutually incompatible, and because some of them are incorrect, the law has been producing increasingly bizarre results. Certain of its doctrines preserve competition, while others suppress it, resulting in a policy at war with itself. During the past twenty years or so, the protectionist, anticompetitive strain in the law has undergone a spectacular acceleration, bringing to pass ... the "crisis in antitrust." The resolution of this crisis will determine antitrust's future. The law must either undergo a difficult process of reform, based upon a correct understanding of fundamental legal and economic concepts, or resume its descent to the status of an internal tariff against domestic competition and free trade.

Given the pace and direction of its development, the overriding need of antitrust today is a general theory of its possibilities and limitations as a tool of rational social policy. Yet there exists among those professionally concerned with antitrust a surprising lack of agreement concerning the most basic questions. The disagreement, though variously phrased, is finally two issues: (1) the goals or values the law may legitimately and profitably implement; and (2) the validity of the law's vision of economic reality.... A consideration of the virtues appropriate to law as law demonstrates that the only legitimate goal of antitrust is the maximization of consumer welfare. Current law lacks these virtues precisely because the Supreme Court has introduced conflicting goals, the primary one being the survival or comfort of small business.

A consumer-oriented law must employ economic theory to judge which market structures and practices are harmful and which beneficial. Modern antitrust has performed this task very poorly. Its version of economics is a melange of valid insights and obviously incorrect — sometimes fantastic — assumptions about the motivations and effects of business behavior. There are many problems here, but perhaps the core of the difficulty is that the courts, and particularly the Supreme Court, have failed to understand and give proper weight to the crucial concept of business efficiency. Since productive efficiency is one of the two opposing forces that determine the degree of consumer well-being (the other being resource misallocation due to monopoly power), this failure has skewed legal doctrine

---

disastrously. Business efficiency necessarily benefits consumers by lowering the costs of goods and services or by increasing the value of the product or service offered; this is true whether the business unit is a competitor or a monopolist. When efficiency is not counted, or when it is seen as a positive evil, it appears that no business structure or behavior has any potential for social good, and there is consequently no reason to uphold its legality if any remote danger can be imagined. The results could not have been worse, and would probably have been better, if the Court had made the opposite mistake and refused to recognize any harm in cartels and monopolies. Yet neither mistake need have been made. The hopeful development in the current Supreme Court's approach to antitrust ... is a single case weighing in favor of a business practice its capacity to create efficiency. That approach seems obvious, but against the background of the jurisprudence of the last two decades it appears revolutionary. Applied generally, it could save antitrust as useful and respectable policy. It is too soon to tell whether the Court will follow up its new beginning.

....

Antitrust is, first and most obviously, law, and law made primarily by judges. We are right to be concerned about the integrity and legitimacy of that lawmaking process, both for its own sake and because ideas about the power and discretion proper to courts in one field of law will inevitably affect their performance elsewhere. At issue is the question central to democratic society: Who governs?

Antitrust is also a set of continually evolving theories about the economics of industrial organization. These theories affect the thought of laymen about business and its behavior, of course, but it is nothing short of extraordinary to see how powerfully the enshrinement of an economic theory in a Supreme Court opinion affects the thought even of economists. For this and other reasons the political fate of the competitive, free-market ideal is heavily involved with developments in antitrust. The capture of the field by anti-free-market theories will have impact far beyond the confines of antitrust itself.

The struggle between economic freedom and regulation also reflects and reacts upon the tension in our society between the ideals of liberty and equality. Neither of these can be an absolute, of course, but the balance between them and the movement of that balance are crucial.

Within the limited frame for observation provided by antitrust, therefore, it is worth noting that the general movement has been away from legislative decision by Congress and toward political choice by courts, away from the ideal of competition and toward the older idea of protected status for each producer, away from concern for general welfare and toward concern for interest groups, and away from the ideal of liberty toward the ideal of enforced equality. No one can know how far these trends may go, but if, as I believe, they have already gone much too far in antitrust as elsewhere in our polity, they should be recognized and reversed, for they are ultimately incompatible with the preservation of a liberal capitalist social order. Antitrust should not be permitted to remain an unknown policy.

....

LANDE, WEALTH TRANSFERS AS THE ORIGINAL AND PRIMARY CONCERN OF ANTITRUST: THE EFFICIENCY INTERPRETATION CHALLENGED, 34 Hastings Law Journal 67-106 (1982)*

Considerable dispute over the goals of the antitrust laws has surfaced in scholarly commentary on the subject. While it is unanimously agreed that Congress enacted these laws to encourage competition, disagreement continues over Congress' ultimate goals....

The prevailing view is that Congress intended the antitrust laws only to increase economic efficiency. Others, however, contend that Congress was largely motivated by a number of social, moral, and political concerns. This Article presents a third view, one suggested by the antitrust laws' legislative histories. This Article will argue that Congress passed the antitrust laws to further economic objectives, but primarily objectives of a distributive rather than of an efficiency nature. In other words, Congress was concerned principally with preventing "unfair" transfers of wealth from consumers to firms with market power. This Article ... also demonstrate[s] that Congress intended to subordinate all other concerns to the basic purpose of preventing firms with market power from directly harming consumers....

[T]he antitrust laws were passed primarily to further what may be called a distributive goal, the goal of preventing unfair acquisitions of consumers' wealth by firms with market power. It should be stressed, however, that Congress did not pass the antitrust laws to secure the "fair" overall distribution of wealth in our economy or even to help the poor. Congress merely wanted to prevent one transfer of wealth that it considered inequitable, and to promote the distribution of wealth that competitive markets would bring. In other words, Congress implicitly declared that "consumers' surplus"[18] was the rightful entitlement of consumers; consumers were given the right to purchase competitively priced goods. Firms with market power were condemned because they acquired this property right

---

[18] Consumers' surplus is the difference between the maximum amount that a consumer would pay and the price that he or she actually pays. Suppose that widgets are priced at $2.00, the competitive price. Marginal consumers of widgets would be willing to pay only this amount. Some consumers, however, would particularly desire widgets and willingly pay more — as much as $3.00. These consumers receive $1.00 in consumers' surplus when they purchase competitively priced widgets. If a monopolist gained control of the widget market and raised the price of widgets to $3.00, marginal consumers would no longer purchase widgets, and nonmarginal consumers would lose their surplus. The widget monopoly would acquire $1.00 of monopoly profits at the expense of widget consumers. For a more detailed definition, see E. MANSFIELD, MICROECONOMICS: THEORY AND APPLICATIONS 15 (4th ed. 1982); G. STIGLER, THE THEORY OF PRICE 78-81 (1966).

without compensation to consumers.... [T]he antitrust laws embody a strong preference for consumers over firms with market power.[19]

....

Economic Effects of Monopoly Power: A Brief Overview

The observation that monopolies cause increased prices and reduced output is hardly new. This conclusion finds expression in early English common law and in classical economic theory....

Modern economists have, of course, made many important advances in the theory of monopoly. The most important development may be the modern analysis of the implications of monopoly self-interest, long recognized as including higher prices and restricted output. These effects can be divided into three categories. The first, allocative inefficiency, describes the misallocation of resources, which diminishes the total wealth of society. A second effect is a transfer of wealth from consumers to monopolists. The third involves the effect of monopolies, and antimonopoly statutes, on firms' productive efficiency....

Allocative Inefficiency

Monopoly pricing reduces the total amount of wealth in society. Because a monopolist produces less than would be produced under competitive conditions, some resources that would otherwise have been used to make the monopoly product will instead be used for other purposes, ones that consumers value demonstrably less. This misallocation of resources results in diminished satisfaction of society's wants, and thus, in terms of what society values, a reduction of society's total wealth. This effect is termed "allocative inefficiency." Elimination of monopoly pricing would, *ceteris paribus*, increase society's total wealth and, therefore, increase consumer satisfaction.

Transfer of "Consumers' Surplus" from Consumers to Monopolists

The most visible and obvious result of monopoly pricing is a transfer of wealth from purchasers to the monopolist; consumers become poorer while the monopolist becomes richer. The relative size of the transferred wealth and the allocative inefficiency will vary considerably from case to case depending upon a number of factors. Under market conditions most likely to be encountered, however, the transferred wealth usually will be between two and forty times as great as the accompanying allocative inefficiency. Thus, the redistributive effects of market power generally exceed the allocative inefficiency effects by a substantial amount.

---

[19] Thus, although Congress was strongly interested in increasing the size of the economic "pie" when it passed the antitrust laws, it was even more interested in ensuring its "fair" ownership. It should also be observed that all purchasers were to be protected, whether they were resellers, farmers or ultimate consumers.

The two principal effects of monopolistic pricing, the transfer of wealth from consumers to monopolists and the decrease in allocative efficiency, are different in one fundamental manner: the latter represents a decrease in society's absolute wealth, while the former merely redistributes that wealth. As Professor Williamson has observed, "[t]his [redistributive] transformation of benefits from one form (consumers' surplus) to another (profit) is treated as a wash under the conventional welfare economics model."[40]

Nevertheless, this transfer of wealth raises a very controversial question: is the transfer of "good," "bad," or neutral result of monopoly pricing? The value-laden answer in large part is determined by whether anyone is thought to be entitled to the economic benefit of the "consumer's surplus." Under monopoly pricing, some consumers' surplus is acquired by the monopolist. Depending on one's perspective, one can be entirely indifferent to the result, or one can conclude either that the monopoly is "unfairly taking" property from consumers, or that the monopoly is only reaping its just reward.

The redistributive effects of monopoly power are clearly good or bad only with respect to the assumptions and welfare criteria that are used to evaluate them. Condemnation of the direct consumer impact of monopoly power is therefore normally and properly termed "subjective" or a "value judgment," because it is based upon a preference for consumers over monopolists....

Congress decided that consumers were entitled to the benefits of a competitive economic system. Consumers were deemed entitled to the "consumer's surplus" because Congress regarded the competitive scenario as the normal one. Monopoly pricing represented a change from the norm which Congress condemned as an "unfair" taking of consumers' property.

....

In summary, considerable controversy exists over the proper treatment of monopolistic transfers of wealth.... Congress believed consumers were entitled to products priced at competitive levels and to the opportunity to buy the quantity of products a competitive market would offer.... When Congress passed the antitrust laws it condemned the use of market power to interfere with these property rights or entitlements out of an explicit antimonopolistic, proconsumer bias.

....

Congressional Goals

It is axiomatic that when the words of a statute are clear and unambiguous, courts need go no further in their interpretation of that law. Ambiguous, doubtful, or undefined words or phrases require interpretation, however, by reference to the statute's legislative history. Examination of a legislative history generally seeks determination of legislative intent regarding particular applications of the statute. The analysis often goes one step further in an attempt to determine what

---

[40] Williamson, *Economies as an Antitrust Defense Revisited*, 125 U. Pa. L. Rev. 699, 711 (1977).

legislative intent "would have been" had Congress considered situations never actually contemplated.

The antitrust laws are among the least precise statutes enacted by Congress. The central terms, including "competition," "unfair methods of competition," "conspiracy in restraint of trade," and "monopolize," are inherently vague and not self-defining. One commentator has observed that antitrust legislation has, perhaps more than any other field, stimulated the courts to consider, as an interpretative aid, the history of the era that gave rise to the legislation.

It is not possible to ascertain with certainty the original goals of the antitrust laws. Not only are there conflicting statements of legislative purpose, but it is often difficult to decide whether certain statements represent isolated, unimportant views or infrequently mentioned but nevertheless significant motivating factors....

The Sherman Act

From the language of the Sherman Act, its legislative history, and the history of late nineteenth century America, it is clear Congress was concerned about those activities of trusts and monopolies that unduly restrained trade or caused a monopolization of interstate commerce. It is equally clear that with the Sherman Act "'Congress was dealing with competition, which it sought to protect, and monopoly, which it sought to prevent.'" These truisms do not, however, reveal why Congress passed the Sherman Act, or what goals it attempted to implement. If the goals of the antitrust laws are to be understood, the crucial issue is the explanation behind Congress' effort to protect competition....

[T]he legislative history of the Sherman Act reveals a total lack of concern for allocative inefficiency. Trusts and monopolies were condemned principally because they "unfairly" extracted wealth from consumers. Productive efficiency also was an aim of the Act. Congress wanted the economy to function efficiently primarily to provide consumers the benefits of free competition.... [I]n balancing the competing considerations, Congress condemned firms with monopoly power despite their acknowledged efficiencies, and with the knowledge that this condemnation might not maximize society's economic efficiency. Indeed, the evidence suggests that Congress was unwilling to subordinate its distributive-based distaste for trusts and monopolists to the goal of corporate efficiency when the efficiency gains would be retained by the monopolists.... Congress passed the Sherman Act because it believed that trusts and monopolies possess excessive social and political power, and reduce entrepreneurial liberty and opportunity.

....

Protecting Consumers from Unfair Transfers of Wealth

In the legislative debates over the Sherman Act, Congress clearly condemned the use of market power to raise prices and restrict output. This condemnation, however, did not arise from concern with allocative efficiency. The debates strongly suggest that Congress condemned trusts and monopolies because they had enough market power to raise prices and "unfairly" extract wealth from consumers, turning it into monopoly profits.

In the legislative debates, Congress discussed at length price increases by trusts and the resulting higher consumer prices. For example, Senator Sherman, defending the bill's constitutionality, asked that Congress protect the public from trusts that "restrain commerce, turn it from its natural course, increase the price of articles, and therefore diminish the amount of commerce." From this and other similar evidence Judge Bork correctly concluded, "The touchstone of illegality is raising prices to consumers. There were no exceptions."

The debates strongly suggest that higher prices to consumers were condemned because they unfairly extracted wealth from consumers and turned it into monopoly profit. For example, during the debates Senator Sherman termed monopolistic overcharges "extortion which makes the people poor," and "extorted wealth." Congressman Coke referred to the overcharges as "robbery." Representative Heard declared that the trusts, "without rendering the slightest equivalent," have "stolen untold millions from the people." Congressman Wilson complained that the beef trust "robs the farmer on the one hand and the consumer on the other." Representative Fithian declared that the trusts were "impoverishing" the people through "robbery." Senator Hoar declared that monopolistic pricing was "a transaction the direct purpose of which is to extort from the community ... wealth which ought to be generally diffused over the whole community." Senator George complained that "They aggregate to themselves great enormous wealth by extortion which makes the people poor."

Congress condemned monopolistic overcharges in strong moral terms, rather than because of their efficiency effects. Purchasers, whether resellers or ultimate consumers, were entitled to purchase competitively priced products. Members of Congress also condemned the unequal distribution of wealth resulting from mono-polistic overcharges. The legislators decided that competitive prices were "fair" whereas monopoly prices were not; therefore, consumers were entitled to own that quantity of wealth known today as "consumer surplus." The unfair prices, in effect, robbed consumers of that wealth. As a result, Congress was willing to risk some immediate efficiency losses in order to benefit consumers ultimately. Congress was willing to pass the Sherman Act in large part in an attempt to prevent such "unfair" transfers of wealth from consumers to monopolies.

Other Goals

Curbing the Social and Political Power of Trusts and Monopolies

Evidence also suggests that more than economic considerations motivated Congress to curb the power of trusts and monopolies. Although the concerns discussed thus far relate to the economic power of monopolies and trusts, Congress was also motivated by a desire to curb the social and political power of large businesses. This additional purpose is demonstrated by analyzing the history of the Sherman Act in light of the economic, social, and political context in which the law was passed.

The legislative history demonstrates that Congress condemned monopolies in part because they increased the cost of goods to consumers. Logic would seem to indicate that pressure from consumers burdened by higher prices contributed to the passage of the Sherman Act. This cannot be the complete explanation, however, because just prior to the passage of the Act, price levels in the United States were stable or slowly decreasing. In 1890, American consumers paid less for goods than at almost any time since the end of the Civil War.

Despite the then-recent rise of trusts, this phenomenon of falling prices is easily explained. The first trusts of any significance probably did not achieve their full power until a few years before passage of the Act. Although some trusts did raise prices in the years immediately before 1890, overall consumer prices decreased dramatically from the end of the Civil War until approximately 1884, when they leveled off. In addition, the last half of the nineteenth century witnessed a great industrial revolution; large-scale production, new technology, and increased production speed resulted in tremendous efficiencies. The industries that spawned some of the most notorious trusts also benefitted most from the new efficiencies. As a consequence, prices often fell despite the existence of the trusts.

Falling prices during this period in fact contributed to the formation of the trusts. Viewing falling prices and increased production with alarm, producers sought to arrest this trend by combining or entering agreements to stabilize or raise prices, restrict output, and suppress competition. This trend was only beginning, however, by 1890. Most large and significant trusts were formed or achieved full power after and in spite of the passage of the Sherman Act.

While prices might have fallen more rapidly had the trusts not attempted to halt their decline, it seems unlikely that consumers would strongly condemn the trusts only because prices were not dropping as rapidly as they should have been. It is possible that even though overall prices were stable or decreasing, Congress or the public could have focused their attention on those prices that were rising and concluded that trusts were, on the whole, causing higher prices. It is more likely that other factors were at work. Consumers probably were angered less by the reduction in their wealth than by the way in which the wealth was extracted.

The legislative history reveals that a major factor leading to the passage of the Sherman Act was a congressional desire to curb the power of trusts. While Congress was concerned about the uses of this power to raise prices and restrict output, it also desired, as an end in itself, the prevention of accumulation of power by large corporations and the men who controlled them. Alarm over corporate aggrandizement of economic, social, and political power pervaded the debate. The legislators feared not only the economic consequences of monopoly power, but potential social disruptions as well. Moreover, this apprehension has been recognized repeatedly by courts interpreting the legislative history of the Act.

A review of the social history of the period illuminates the reasons underlying Congress' alarm. The post-Civil War period saw a rural agricultural nation transformed into an increasingly urban and industrial society. Work patterns changed. By the end of the Civil War individual yeoman farmers had all but vanished. In their places stood entrepreneurs and commercial farmers who shipped their goods to markets and then used the resulting cash to purchase goods from small businesses. Thus, traditional independence gradually changed into interdependence.

With the rise of trusts, interdependence became impotence. Decision making was transferred from traditional power centers to the great industrialists. Self-reliant farmers, business owners, and local leaders became dependant on the discretionary power of a few very rich men. Local control of society ended as numerous small power centers were swept away by the new class, one perceived as greedy and evil. This transfer of power generated hostility towards the trusts and resulted in political pressure on Congress to pass antitrust legislation.

The political and social evils of accumulated power, recited in the legislative debates and reiterated by the cases and historians, probably engendered more public resentment toward the trusts than did an isolated rise in prices during an era of stable and declining prices. The congressional complaint, therefore, was directed not solely at the effects of monopoly power — higher prices and poorer consumers — but also at the process that produced them. The Sherman Act was intended not only to achieve competitive prices but also to restructure the economy in ways insuring a "fair" process for economic, social, and political decision making by reducing the unfairly accumulated power of the trusts.

Protecting Small Businesses

Congress also expressed concern for preserving business opportunities for small firms. The opportunity to compete has been viewed as particularly important for small entrepreneurs, perhaps because of their vulnerability to predatory activities....

Judicial statements of congressional intention to assist small businesses have been frequent. Courts have even occasionally viewed congressional interest in protecting small businesses as overriding its consumer-oriented goals.

Despite clear judicial recognition, close examination reveals relatively little support in the legislative history, beyond the few references above, for the "small producer" rationale. Although there are a few statements suggesting that the protection of the opportunity of small business to compete was one motivating factor for the legislators, these statements do not imply that protection of small businesses was meant to override other goals. Congress probably did not intend to go further than establishment of an economic system providing free opportunities for entry and enough producers to ensure vigorous competition, a system in which no company became large enough to dominate.

Additionally, the congressional intent to assist small businesses can be interpreted as promoting distributive, rather than efficiency, considerations. Passage of the Sherman Act may have been intended, in part, to transfer wealth to small businesses. The legislative history does not indicate, however, that Congress intended to help small businesses as a means of improving the overall efficiency of the economy. The debate suggests only a possible intent to assist small businesses as an end in itself, not as a means of increasing total economic output.

Sympathetic to the plight of small businesses harmed by trusts, Congress expressed a desire to create an environment in which small businesses could effectively compete. It can fairly be said that one of Congress' goals was to assist small businesses; although consumers' interests were meant to be paramount, and conflicts between the welfare of consumers and small businesses were generally to be resolved in favor of consumers, Congress' desire to help small businesses certainly extended to those circumstances in which small businesses would be helped but consumers would not significantly suffer.... [T]his expression of sympathy did not amount to a congressional directive to assist small businesses in ways conflicting with the essential purpose of the Act, the protection of consumers.

Summary

Congress passed the Sherman Act to further a number of goals. Its main concern was with firms acquiring or possessing enough market power to raise prices artificially and to restrict output. Congress' primary aim was to enable consumers to purchase products at competitive prices. Artificially high prices were condemned not for causing allocative inefficiency but for "unfairly" transforming consumers' wealth into monopoly profits. All purchasers, whether consumers or businesses, were given the right to purchase competitively priced goods. All sellers were given the right to face rivals selling at competitive prices.

Concurrently, Congress was interested in encouraging efficient behavior in firms. Congress wanted a competitive economy to encourage the greater efficiencies resulting from competition. Efficiency gains were particularly desired when benefits passed through directly to consumers. A concern with productive efficiency could not, however, explain why Congress passed the Sherman Act. Congress condemned the relatively efficient trusts and monopolies for redistributive reasons. With the unlikely possibility of an exception for the "efficient monopolist," monopolizing conduct was not permitted merely because it produced efficiency gains for the monopolist.

The Act also involved efforts to decentralize economic, social, and political decision making to ensure that narrow private interests would be unable to override the public good flowing from free competition. The corporate power that the free market inadequately curbed was the target of the Act. Thus, the Act was also aimed at curbing the social and political power of large corporations and at encouraging opportunities for small entrepreneurs to compete, both thought to flow from the desired economic order as expressed in the Act.

The Sherman Act, the first antitrust law, set the tone for future antitrust legislation. Subsequent antitrust laws represented either extensions of the same ideas to different economic arenas, or attempts to better implement the same fundamental principles.

....

SECTION II. COMMON LAW LEGACIES

A. ENGLISH FOUNDATIONS

Many of the framers of the Sherman Act believed they were merely enacting and federalizing the common law of trade restraints. 21 Cong. Rec. 2456, 3146, 3151-52 (1890). But as the rich literature of today indicates, the common law had numerous branches, English and American, which included statutory as well as judge-made doctrines. H. Thorelli, *The Federal Antitrust Policy* 10 (1954). Because of the diversity of the sources and versions of the common law up to the 1890's, no single integrated common law existed. No single standard governed the concept of restraint of competition. H. Hovenkamp, *Enterprise and American Law, 1836-1937*, ch. 21 (1991); Dewey, *The Common-Law Background of Antitrust Policy*, 41 Va. L. Rev. 759, 761 (1955); L. Sullivan, *Handbook of the Law of Antitrust* 155 (1977). Of course, the framers of the Sherman Act believed that there was a single "general" common law. Consider *Swift v. Tyson*, 41 U.S. (16 Pet.) 1 (1842), which was not overruled until *Erie R.R. v. Tompkins*, 304 U.S. 64 (1938), decided almost fifty years after the Sherman Act was enacted. Certain developments in the common law are helpful for a general understanding of the status of the law on restraints of trade at the time of the passage of the first federal statute in 1890. *See generally* May, *Antitrust Practice and Procedure in the Formative Era: The Constitutional and Conceptual Reach of State Antitrust Law, 1980-1988*, 135 U. Pa. L. Rev. 495 (1987).

It seems clear that the common law developed and changed direction during the eighteenth and nineteenth centuries depending upon the economic policies being espoused at a particular time. That common-law development regarding monopolies has been described as follows.

W. LETWIN, LAW AND ECONOMIC POLICY IN AMERICA 18-32 (1965)*

Monopoly at Common Law

The Sherman Act was founded on the common law, the body of judicial decisions that the United States inherited from England. The common law, it has been widely believed, always favored freedom of trade. When English and

---

* Reprinted by permission.

American judges during the eighteenth and nineteenth centuries decided cases against monopolists, engrossers, or restrainers of trade, they thought they were continuing a tradition that reached back into "time of which no man hath memory." The congressmen who drafted and passed the Sherman Antitrust Law thought they were merely declaring the illegality of offenses that the common law had always prohibited. Those judges and legislators, like other lawyers, must have known, or at least would not have doubted, that the common law rules on these subjects had changed in the course of time, for it is taken as axiomatic that the common law "grows." But it is not always recognized that the common law can change its direction, and without much warning begin to prohibit practices it had formerly endorsed, or to protect arrangements it had earlier condemned. Lawyers do not so readily see that the common law at any given time reflects the economic theories and policies then favored by the community, and may change as radically as those theories and policies. As a result they have too easily accepted the mistaken view that the attitude of the common law toward freedom of trade was essentially the same throughout its history.

The common law did not always defend freedom of trade and abhor monopoly. For a long time it did quite the opposite: it supported an economic order in which the individual's getting and spending were closely controlled by kings, parliaments, and mayors, statutes, and customs, and his opportunities limited by the exclusive powers of guilds, chartered companies, and patentees. The common law first began to oppose this system of regulation and privilege at the end of the sixteenth century; it did not do so wholeheartedly until the eighteenth century; and by the middle of the nineteenth century, it had again lost its enthusiasm for the task. It would have been surprising if the pattern of development had been different. Changes in the common law are changes in the attitudes of judges and lawyers; it would have been remarkable if they had persistently opposed monopoly when the rest of the community did not know the word and considered the phenomenon natural or desirable. It would have been strange if lawyers had upheld *laissez faire* policies centuries before any statesman or economist had advocated or stated them, and had continued following them long after they had been abandoned or denied by the rest of the community. In fact, English laws governing monopoly and English policies for the economic organization of society changed together, except for minor differences in timing. The English law of monopoly traditionally includes four branches: the law on monopoly proper, whether by patent, charter, or custom; on forestalling, engrossing, and regrating; on contracts in restraint of trade; and on combinations in restraint of trade. These branches, distinct in form and based on more or less independent bodies of precedent, nevertheless show the same development from an active support of monopolies in the earliest period, through active opposition during an interlude of less than two centuries, to leniency and indifference which characterized them in 1890.

....

The idea that the common law opposed monopolies from the earliest time on-ward was invented largely by Sir Edward Coke, who argued that monopoly was forbidden by the Civil Law, and implicitly by Magna Carta as well as by certain statutes of Edward III's reign. The earliest common-law precedent he could mention was a case that arose during the fourteenth century, and the modern law-yers and historians who follow his authority continue to cite that case as evidence of the ancient antagonism of common law to monopolies. Yet the case gives at least equally good evidence to the contrary.

....

The great movement against the granting of monopolies by letter-patent began only at the end of the sixteenth century, although it was [so] strongly supported that within less than a hundred years the principle had been established that Par-liament alone could grant a monopoly, and that generally even it could not, as the King had regularly done, sell a patent or award it on a whim or as a friendly ges-ture. By the end of the seventeenth century the royal letter-patent had been con-verted into a more or less modern version of the patent, justifiable only by a solid contribution to economic development. The process was not, however, moved by coherent opposition to monopoly; it was brought about mainly by disturbances within the monopolistic system administered largely by the guilds, and by objec-tions not to the broad economic effect of monopolies but to the political power which the crown exercised in granting them.

The first recorded case on monopolies was *Davenant v. Hurdis*, or *The Mer-chant Tailors'* case decided in 1599, which shows not only the extent of monopo-listic control that the guilds exercised, but also the ends that such controls were supposed to serve, and the collisions that were taking place between several guilds as each tried to maintain intact its power over a trade. The case arose un-der a by-law passed by the London tailors' guild in 1571.... [The ordinance re-quired guild members who had clothes finished by others to have at least half the finishing done by a guild member. Plaintiff, a member of the tailors' guild, brought an action of trespass. Sir Edward Coke argued for Davenant that the by-law was unreasonable and illegal because it created a monopoly, although no clear basis in common law could be cited for the proposition. Judgment was unanimous that such a by-law that brought "all trade on traffic into the hands of one company, or one person, and to exclude all others, is illegal."]

....

The decision represented an innovation in the law as much as in economic policy. There is no reported common-law case on monopoly prior to *Davenant v. Hurdis*; Coke later mentioned in Parliament some unreported cases, but their pre-cise content is unknown.... A number of prior cases are known, but these were heard in the Star Chamber, Privy Council, and other prerogative courts, which generally defended such monopolies as proper exercises of the King's power. The law was still so divided on the validity of monopolies as late as 1624 that Parliament felt it necessary to include in the Statute of Monopolies a provision that "all monopolies ... and the force and validity of them and of every of them, ought to be and shall be forever hereafter examined, heard, tried and determined by and according to the common laws of this Realm and not otherwise."

The next step, and perhaps the greatest single one, in creating the modern common law on monopolies was *Darcy v. Allen*, or *The Case of Monopolies*, decided in 1603. Where *Davenant v. Hurdis* established that a corporate by-law was invalid if it created a monopoly, *Darcy v. Allen* went further, laying down the principle that even a royal grant [by Queen Elizabeth] by patent would be invalid if it did so.... In short, Darcy's patent was held void on the argument that it violated the right of others to carry on their trade.

....

There is no doubt that the series of cases at the turn of the seventeenth century radically changed the attitude of the common law toward monopolies.

....

The first important law contributing to that result was the Statute of Monopolies of 1624, which, however, has a deceptive ring. For though it was certainly directed against monopolies, it was based not on a preference for competition, but on constitutional objections to the power which the Crown presumed in granting monopolies and to the arbitrary reasons for which it had granted them. Parliament did not at this period oppose monopolies in themselves. As Bacon told the House of Commons in 1601, its attitude was inconsistent and suspect: "If her Majesty make a patent or a monopoly unto any of her servants, that we must go and cry out against: but if she grant it to a number of burgesses or a corporation, that must stand, and that forsooth is no monopoly."

This inconsistency the House of Commons carried over into the Statute of Monopolies. The first section declared void "all monopolies and all commissions, grants, licenses, charters, and letter patents heretofore made or granted, or hereafter to be made or granted to any person or persons, bodies politic or corporate whatsoever, of or for the sole buying, selling, making, working, or using of anything, or of any other monopolies." The ninth section nevertheless provides that the Act shall not apply to any cities or towns, or any of their privileges, "or unto any corporations, companies, or fellowships of any trade, occupation, or mystery, or to any companies or societies of merchants within this Realm, erected for the maintenance, enlargement, or ordering of any trade of merchandise...." And this inconsistency, which symbolized Parliament's willingness to have monopolies, provided Parliament alone granted them, was not merely a matter of words in statute. It justified the final irony in the case of *Darcy v. Allen*: only a few years after Darcy's monopoly of playing cards was judged void at common law, the same monopoly was given, under authority of the Statute of Monopolies, to the Company of Card Makers.

The Statute of Monopolies soon put an end to the arbitrary granting of private monopolies, but it was not intended to abolish customary monopoly privileges of corporations. Cities and boroughs, guilds, and chartered trading companies continued to exercise their monopoly powers to exclude strangers from various trades. The common law continued to protect them, though with lessening fervor as the influence of economic liberalism grew, and some of these monopolistic controls were finally abolished only by legislation in the nineteenth century.

The related offenses of forestalling (buying the product before it was sold to general market), engrossing (buying in bulk to increase the price) and regrating (buying to resell) were also denounced at common law. These practices concerned conduct in the marketing and distribution of a product, particularly the wholesale distribution process. It was thought that during the trade process the merchant tended to raise the price of the good. Statutes were enacted against such conduct in the commodities, grain, and food markets beginning in the thirteenth century. The theory behind the common-law proscription was twofold: "middlemen ... served no useful purpose" in the market and the "common law favored 'low' prices rather than free prices." W. Letwin, *supra*, at 32-38; H. Thorelli, *supra*, at 15-17. But as markets grew into national ones and as the *laissez faire*, economic movement of free trade prospered in England, the statutes were repealed in 1772, though the English decisional law seemed to retain the statutory proscriptions until 1844, when another statute specifically barred suits challenging these practices. As a result, the free trade movement was on the ascendancy in England.

1. CONTRACTS IN RESTRAINT OF TRADE

At common law a contract in restraint of trade included agreements restricting a party from engaging in a particular trade or occupation or restricting the time, place, or manner in which that trade or occupation could be engaged. The earliest reported case was decided in 1414. In the *Case of John Dyer*, Y.B. 2 Hen. V, 5f. 5 (1414), the defendant was restricted from engaging in the trade of dyeing in a certain location for a prescribed period of time. The court condemned the restriction.

The most famous case of a common law restraint was *Mitchel v. Reynolds*, 24 Eng. Rep. 347 (K.B. 1711). The plaintiff had entered a contract to lease a bakehouse for a period of years on the condition that the lessor, also a baker, would refrain from engaging in the bakery business for the term of the lease. Contrary to the decision in the *Dyer* case, the court held that a contract not to compete in a particular trade or occupation was valid and enforceable, as long as certain conditions were met. The first requirement was that the covenant not to compete was supported by valid consideration. Second, the covenant had to be voluntary. Third, a determination was to be made whether the contract was reasonable in limitations of time and place. Finally, the restraint could only be lawful if it were ancillary, that is secondary to an otherwise lawful main purpose. *See generally* W. Letwin, *supra*, at 42-44. *Mitchel v. Reynolds* thus established the "ancillary restraint" doctrine at common law: a contract not to compete which is ancillary to an otherwise lawful main purpose, such as the sale of a business or employment contract, is lawful when specifically limited in scope, time and geographic area. To the extent that the court in *Mitchel v. Reynolds* required an inquiry into the purpose behind the restraint and the effects of the restraint, it established a "reasonableness" test, which later came to be known as the "rule of reason" standard.

During the nineteenth century the English courts also considered whether the lawful purpose of the restraint could be obtained through less restrictive means. In *Horner v. Graves* Chief Justice Tindal cautioned that the issue is:

> whether the restraint is such only as to afford a fair protection to the interests of the party in favour of whom it is given, and not so large as to interfere with the interests of the public. Whatever restraint is larger than the necessary protection of the party, can be of no benefit to either, it can only be oppressive; and if oppressive, it is, in the eye of the law, unreasonable.

7 Bing. 735, 743, 131 Eng. Rep. 284, 287 (1831).

Not until some time later, however, did English courts consider whether the interest of the public was to be considered as well in determining the "reasonableness" of the restraint. The House of Lords settled the issue in 1894.

> The public have an interest in every person's carrying on his trade freely: so has the individual. All interference with individual liberty of action in trading, and all restraints of trade of themselves, if there is nothing more, are contrary to public policy, and therefore void. That is the general rule. But there are exceptions: restraints of trade and interference with individual liberty of action may be justified by the special circumstances of a particular case. It is a sufficient justification, and indeed it is the only justification, if the restriction is reasonable — reasonable, that is, in reference to the interests of the parties concerned and reasonable in reference to the interests of the public, so framed and so guarded as to afford adequate protection to the party in whose favour it is imposed, while at the same time it is in no way injurious to the public.

Nordenfelt v. Maxim Nordenfelt Guns & Ammunition Co., [1894] App. Cas. 535, 565.

Letwin makes the point that by 1894:

> English law on contracts in restraint of trade was not in any important respect an instrument for the maintenance of a competitive economic order. If ever, then only for a very short period after *Mitchel v. Reynolds* did the courts give the public policy of promoting competition an important part in deciding cases on contracts in restraint of trade.... [It seemed] that competition was no longer public policy, or at least that freedom of contract had become a more important end than freedom of trade.

W. Letwin, *supra*, at 45-46.

2. COMBINATIONS IN RESTRAINT OF TRADE

The labor union movement in England during the nineteenth century had an effect on the development of the law on combinations in restraint of trade.

> The common law, influenced by a feeling that employers should not be denied rights granted to workers, matched the new legal power of the latter with a solicitous concern for employers' combinations; in the end it came to put a higher value on the freedom of entrepreneurs to use any means short of violence to outstrip competitors than on the right of the public to enjoy the advantages of competition.
>
> [A]fter the beginning of the nineteenth century, the common law came to regard an agreement between competitors to combine as analogous to a contract in restraint of trade, and judged such agreements by whether they left the parties reasonably free to act as they desired. All along less attention was paid to whether the agreement seriously interfered with competition.

W. Letwin, *supra*, at 46, 48-49. For the American developments, see Hovenkamp, *Labor Conspiracies in American Law, 1880-1930*, 66 Tex. L. Rev. 919 (1988).

After a series of cases beginning in 1815 and continuing through the nineteenth century, it became rather clear that combinations or agreements in restraint of trade would be unenforceable as against public policy, but they were not deemed illegal in the sense that affirmative relief was available unless it became a conspiracy that sought unlawful means or ends. In the early 1800's conspiracy was still considered a tort rather than a crime. H. Thorelli, *supra*, at 29. *But see* Dewey, *supra*, at 766-71. The doctrine of conspiracy in restraint of trade began to develop first as a means to control the organization of labor unions. Statutes in England were also adopted to make union combinations criminal offenses. W. Letwin, *supra*, at 46-48. By the middle of the nineteenth century, the courts were beginning to apply the law of combination in restraint of trade against manufacturers and merchants as well as labor unions, and refused to enforce agreements between competitors that set wages of employees. *Hilton v. Eckersly*, 6 El. & Bl. 47 (1855). The law also condemned production reductions and price-fixing agreements among competitors as unenforceable combinations. *Mogul Steamship Co. v. McGregor, Gow & Co.*, 23 Q.B.D. 598 (1889), *aff'd*, A.C. 25 (1892).

But in England the challenges to restraints of trade during the 1800's were in the context of private party litigation; public litigation at this time was out of the question.

> By 1890, what little there had ever been of English common law against monopolies had become quite weak. The common law against monopoly proper had been superseded by the Statute of Monopolies. The common law against forestalling had been abolished by the statute of 1844. The common law against combinations of workmen and of masters had been overruled by the Trade Union Acts. The common law against contracts and combinations

> in restraint of trade alone remained in force, but it was governed by principles that condoned more than they prohibited. If monopolies were to be restrained, the common law would have to change its direction again, or legislation would have to remedy its weakness.

W. Letwin, *supra*, at 51. And as Letwin noted, English common law at the time of the adoption of the Sherman Act hardly could be considered coherent, integrated, or consistent in light of the interaction of the *laissez faire* movement with the law's development. For a good comparative study of British and American competition policy since the late nineteenth century, *see* T. Freyer, *Regulating Big Business: Antitrust in Great Britain and America, 1880-1990* (1992).

B. AMERICAN COMMON LAW TRADITION

The common law in the United States during the nineteenth century developed independently though similarly to the English common law on restraint of trade. That which did develop prior to 1890 was accomplished largely through state judge-made decisions. There was no significant integrated federal common law on restraint of trade. H. Thorelli, *supra*, at 36, 51-52. The exceptions to this were the English common-law restrictions of forestalling, engrossing and regrating. Except in a few states these crimes were never recognized as they were in England up to the end of the eighteenth century. On the other hand, the doctrine of restraint of trade did have a significant history in the American common law with regard to monopolies, combinations, and conspiracies.

The American common law against monopolies was particularly strong. To be sure, evidence exists that restrictions on monopoly were enforced even more rigorously in the American colonies than in England. The reasons for this vary, but critical to this development were the grants of monopoly to the English trading companies that were given charters in the colonies. Such monopolies ran counter to the individualistic character of liberty as espoused in the American colonies. Unless the monopoly was, by reason of a patent, for the purpose of invention, it was contrary to the American common law. Although there are few reported cases concerning monopoly prior to 1890, the antimonopoly sentiment was expressed for the most part in state constitutions and statutes. *Compare Norwich Gas Light Co. v. Norwich City Gas Co.*, 25 Conn. 19 (1856), *with Citizens' Water Co. v. Hydraulic Co.*, 55 Conn. 1 (1887); *Chicago v. Rumpff*, 45 Ill. 906 (1867). On the relationship between politics and the law of monopolies in nineteenth century America, *see* M. Horwitz, *The Transformation of American Law, 1780-1860*, 109-39 (1977); H. Hovenkamp, *Enterprise, supra*, chs. 2, 10, & 11. *See also* Jones, *Historical Development of the Law of Business Competition*, 36 Yale L.J. 207 (1926); Miller, *The Case of Monopolies — Some of Its Results and Suggestions 1*, 15-24 (1907); May, *Antitrust Practice and Procedure in the Formative Era: The Constitutional and Conceptual Reach of State Antitrust Law*, 1880-1918, 135 U. Pa. L. Rev. 495 (1987).

The common law regarding contracts and combinations in restraint of trade was the most developed in the United States prior to adoption of the Sherman Act. Contracts "in restraint of trade" originally included only covenants or restraints not to compete in a trade or occupation, whether restricted generally or within a stated place and time. The American common law was influenced significantly by the seminal English decision of *Mitchel v. Reynolds*, 24 Eng. Rep. 347 (K.B. 1711), discussed *supra*, which established the "ancillary restraint" doctrine. This doctrine distinguished between general (non-ancillary) restraints, which were purposefully designed to eliminate competition, and a partial (ancillary) restraint, which was secondary to the otherwise lawful main purpose of the contract. The former was held void, while the ancillary restraint was considered lawful if reasonably limited as to time, place, and scope. In 1874, the United States Supreme Court recognized this common-law precedent by noting that it was a "well settled rule of law that an agreement in general restraint of trade is illegal and void; but an agreement which operates merely in partial restraint of trade is good, providing it be not unreasonable." *Oregon Steam Nav. Co. v. Winsor*, 87 U.S. (20 Wall.) 64, 66-67 (1874). The celebrated decision by Judge Taft in *United States v. Addyston Pipe & Steel Co.*, 85 F. 271 (6th Cir. 1898), *modified and aff'd*, 175 U.S. 211 (1899), is cited as the definitive authority for the acceptance of the ancillary restraint doctrine in the United States, although his analytical recapitulation of the common-law tradition regarding general (non-ancillary) restraints has been questioned. *See, e.g., United States v. Trenton Potteries Co.*, 273 U.S. 392 (1927); *Standard Oil Co. v. United States*, 221 U.S. 1 (1911).

In *Addyston Pipe & Steel*, Judge Taft surveyed the common law as it evolved from *Mitchel v. Reynolds* and suggested that partial or ancillary restraints were lawful if they were reasonably necessary to serve legitimate ends of the business arrangement, such as an employment contract or a contract to sell a business or trade. But this balancing approach, which turned on the "reasonableness" of the restraint was, according to Judge Taft's reading of the common law, applicable only in determining the legality of a restraint classified as "ancillary." If the restraint were determined to be of a "general" nature then it was illegal as contrary to public policy, and the reviewing court would not be permitted to engage in "rule of reason" analysis to determine whether the challenged restraint was reasonable. 85 F. at 282-84. *But see Wickens v. Evans*, 3 Y. & J. 318, 148 Eng. Rep. 1202 (Ex. 1829); *Jones v. North*, 19 Eq. 426 (1875); *Collins v. Locks*, 4 App. Cas. 674 (P.C. 1879). *See generally* Arthur, *Farewell to the Sea of Doubt: Jettisoning the Constitutional Sherman Act*, 74 Calif. L. Rev. 266 (1986). Thus, according to Judge Taft, restraints on trade were automatically (per se) illegal unless they were merely ancillary to one's business and reasonable. Others did not share Judge Taft's reading of the common law. Chief Justice White, in the 1911 *Standard Oil* case, 221 U.S. 1, concluded that the rule of reason analysis should be applied regardless of whether the restraint was general or ancillary; under this standard only "unreasonable" restraints were to be declared illegal. And in 1927 Justice (later Chief Justice) Stone, in *Trenton Potteries*, *supra*, stated further that restraints are illegal only if they affect price or prevent competition. 273 U.S. at 397. *See also* Dewey, *supra*, at 772-73. For a critique of Judge Taft's use of common-law sources, *see* H. Hovenkamp, *Enterprise, supra*, 285-87.

By the late 1800's "restraint of trade" came to be used more generally than the law of covenants not to compete in a trade or occupation. It covered a broader array of restraints on trade, including monopolistic practices and combinations. At first in England and later in the United States, the term became part of the doctrines of conspiracy or combinations to restrain or monopolize trade. H. Thorelli, *supra*, at 53, 155. Only in the last half of the 1800's, however, were corporate trusts and pooling arrangements (e.g., agreements by competitors to "pool" and divide "all or part of the production, markets, sales, profits or patents") in the United States challenged, mainly on the theory that the corporations involved had acted beyond the power created in their charters. H. Hovenkamp, *Enterprise, supra*, chs. 6, 20. *See generally American Biscuit & Mfg. Co. v. Klotz*, 44 F. 721 (E.D. La. 1891); *Cummings v. Union Bluestone Co.*, 58 N.E. 525 (N.Y. App. 1900); *Central Ohio Salt Co. v. Guthrie*, 35 Ohio St. 666 (1880); *Anderson v. Jett*, 12 S.W. 670 (Ky. App. 1889); *Krainka v. Scharringhausen*, 8 Mo. App. 522 (1880); *Kellog v. Larkin*, 56 Am. Dec. 164 (Wis. 1851). The rise of the corporate association, pooling arrangement, or trust, whereby competing businesses attempted to control prices and preserve profits by mutual agreement, came about largely as a result of the industrial development and expansion following the Civil War. The trust or pooling arrangement was an attempt to undermine the increased competition brought about by the post-war industrialization.

The state common-law precedents and statutes were not necessarily uniform and no strong federal common law of restraint of trade existed. Enforcement against restraints was weak, particularly since the trusts were multistate, and a state's jurisdictional reach was limited at this time to property and persons located within its territorial boundaries. The perceived jurisdictional limitation on state power, together with the commerce clause limitations on the federal government, necessitated new federal legislation. *See generally* Hovenkamp, *State Antitrust in the Federal Scheme*, 57 Ind. L.J. (1983).

C. DEVELOPMENT OF LEGISLATION

The sociopolitical and economic background of the period between 1865 and 1890 set the stage for the adoption of the Sherman Act in 1890. Public antagonism towards corporate trusts and pooling arrangements, which permitted competitors to form combinations, to set prices, and divide markets, grew during this period. *See* W. Letwin, *supra*, at 54-70, 77-85. The growth of the trusts (e.g., tight combinations between competitors) occurred generally between the time of the Civil War and 1890. *See generally* H. Thorelli, *supra*, at 72-106. At first the trusts were regional in nature. Only later did they become national in scope and control. In the 1880's and 1890's the public focused on the large, national trusts, which were often the villains in popular literature. The Standard Oil Trust (1882), the American Cotton Trust (1884), the National Linseed Oil Trust (1885), the Sugar Trust (1887), the Whiskey Trust (1887), and the National Lead Trust (1887-1889) were all challenged legally, either on the theory that they acted *ultra vires* by entering into trust arrangements or that their trust practices were unreasonable restraints of trading tending to create a monopoly.

The period from 1865 to 1890 also witnessed the dramatic growth of the railroads. As the railroads became larger, unscrupulous, anticompetitive practices developed. People believed that charges for local traffic where monopolies existed were artificially inflated to subsidize rates for more competitive routes. This cross subsidization was thought to lead to monopoly pricing in many regions and ultimately developed into pooling agreements for the purpose of fixing rail rates. The economic probability of this, however, has been questioned. *See* Hovenkamp, *Regulatory Conflict in the Gilded Age: Federalism and the Railroad Problem*, 97 Yale L.J. 1017 (1988).

Granges and farmers felt the burden of these practices. In the mid 1870's state Granger laws were enacted in an attempt to regulate the railroads. But the legality of these state statutes was quickly challenged on the ground such statutes were (1) not within the regulating authority of the state, (2) an unconstitutional interference with interstate commerce, and (3) a violation of the due process clause and obligation of contract clause. In a series of cases from 1876 to 1890, the Supreme Court changed course in several decisions and ultimately held that a state could not regulate rail rates and schedules even within its own territory when interstate commerce was involved. In addition, because of territorial jurisdictional limits on state common law against monopolies (or monopolistic practice) and combinations, the common law was considered ineffective as a device to control increased use of trusts and monopolies. Moreover, most suits against trust and monopolies in the last half of the 1800's were brought by private parties; only a small number of suits were initiated by public officials on behalf of their constituents, although by 1890 many states had constitutional and statutory provisions prohibiting monopolies. H. Thorelli, *supra*, at 155. Thus, it became clear that federal regulation was necessary. In 1887, Congress passed the Interstate Commerce Act to regulate the railroads; it was Congress' first attempt to enact a comprehensive economic regulatory measure. The Sherman Act in 1890 was the second.

A reading of the history, origins, and objectives of the Sherman Act indicates that there were differing views leading up to the legislation, as there had been with regard to the common-law development against restraint of trade.

The legislation was originally introduced in the Senate in 1888 by Senator John Sherman of Ohio. He argued initially that Congress could regulate trusts only through its taxing power, but later shifted his argument to include the power of Congress to regulate commerce through the commerce clause. W. Letwin, *supra*, at 87-90. During the two years that the legislation was debated in Congress, Senator Sherman opined that the legislation was intended "to destroy combina-

tions, not all combinations, but all those which the common law had always condemned as unlawful." After floor debate, the bill was referred to the Senate Judiciary Committee, where it was redrafted. A lengthy conference committee between the Senate and House followed, with the Senate Judiciary Committee
version finally prevailing. It was signed into law July 2, 1890. No doubt public
hostility toward trusts, monopolies and concentrations of power, however diffuse,
played a role as did the "norm of free competition" in the enactment of the first
federal antitrust law. *See* H. Thorelli, *supra*, at 162-63; W. Letwin, *supra*, at 53-
85; A. Neale & D. Goyder, *The Antitrust Laws of the U.S.A.* 16-21 (3d ed. 1980).

Although the underlying economic theories of the Sherman Act were not seriously debated by its framers, many students of antitrust law have read the legislative history as promoting a particular economic ideology, such as consumer
welfare. Bork, *Legislative Intent and the Policy of the Sherman Act*, 9 J. L. &
Econ. 7 (1966). According to them, the purpose of the antitrust laws is to promote a market that improves (1) available productive forces and materials in accordance with consumer demands (allocative efficiency) and (2) effective use of
resources by firms responding to consumer demands (productive efficiency).
Other commentators have presented more broadly based interpretations of the
legislative history.

H. THORELLI, THE FEDERAL ANTITRUST POLICY 226-27 (1954)*

There can be no doubt that Sherman's views were typical in the sense that the
vast majority of congressmen were sincere proponents of a private enterprise
system founded on the principle of "full and free competition." Most of the legislators sponsoring bills or participating in debates with speeches relating to the
principal issues involved made vigorous statements to this effect. But, generally
speaking, little need was felt to attempt penetrating analyses of the underlying
economic theory or to support the prevalent belief by extended argument — the
members of Congress proclaimed "the norm of a free competition too self-
evident to be debated, too obvious to be asserted." The two or three odd attacks
that were made on competition as the mainspring of American progress and
prosperity were given no attention, and those who launched the attacks in the end
voted for the passage of the Sherman Act.

Congress believed in competition. It believed, moreover, that competition was
the normal way of life in business. Competition was the "life of trade" in spite of
the challenging trust and combination movement. As a general rule, business operated best when left alone. The government's natural role in the system of free
private enterprise was that of a patrolman policing the highways of commerce. It
is the duty of the modern patrolman to keep the road open for all and everyone
and to prevent highway robbery, speeding, the running of red lights and other
violations that will endanger and hence, in the end, slow down the overall

---

* Reprinted by permission.

movement of the traffic. Translated into the terms of commerce this means that occupations were to be kept open to all who wished to try their luck, that the individual was to be protected in his "common right" to choose his calling and that hindrances to equal opportunity were to be eliminated. Government intervention should remove obstacles to the free flow of commerce, not itself become an additional obstacle.

There can be no doubt that the Congress felt that the ultimate beneficiary in this whole process was the consumer, enjoying a continuous increase in production and commodity quality at progressively lowered prices. The immediate beneficiary legislators had in mind, however, was in all probability the small business proprietor or tradesman whose opportunities were to be safeguarded from the dangers emanating from those recently-evolving elements of business that seemed so strange, gigantic, ruthless and awe-inspiring. This is one reason why it was natural to adopt the old doctrines of the common-law, doctrines whose meaning had been established largely in cases brought by business or professional people dissatisfied with the behavior of competitors. Perhaps we are even justified in saying that the Sherman Act is not to be viewed exclusively as an expression of economic policy. In safeguarding rights of the "common man" in business "equal" to those of evolving more "ruthless" and impersonal forms of enterprise the Sherman Act embodies what is to be characterized as an eminently "social" purpose. A moderate limitation of the freedom of contract was expected to yield a maximization of the freedom of enterprise. Sherman himself, furthermore, expressed the idea probably in the minds of many of his colleagues that the legislation contemplated constituted an important means of achieving freedom from corruption and maintaining freedom of independent thinking in political life, a treasured cornerstone of democratic government.

Not much time was wasted in Congress on the display of the merits of competition. For purposes of legislation it was more important to get a clear picture of the evil to be remedied, the obstacles to free trade that were to be eliminated. Bills and debates present a kaleidoscopic picture of definitions of trusts, monopolies and combinations in restraint of trade, as well as attacks on those institutions and the elements of society that had been responsible for their recent growth and multiplication. However great variation there was as to details, we find in its midst a general idea of the problem to be coped with, which, while vague, probably was not more dimly conceived than in many other instances in which legislation has since become imperative. The aim of Congress, to rid commerce of monopolies and restraints of trade, was explicitly set forth in the Sherman Act. It had been set forth in substantially the same terms in numerous bills and a multitude of speeches.

What was the relationship between the ideology of Congress and the intent manifested in the Sherman Act? Most congressmen, indeed most Americans, would say in 1890 that antitrust legislation was but the projection of the philosophy of competition on the plane of policy. According to this line of thinking there was a direct and reversible relationship between competition on the one hand and monopoly on the other. If you removed the monopolistic elements in any industry full and free competition would ensue automatically, or even *ex definitione*. Not until the antitrust policy had been confronted with stark realities did it dawn upon the public mind that to legislate against monopolies and restraints of trade may not necessarily be the same as to enforce, or maintain, free competition.

However one reads the legislative history, the provisions of the Sherman Act made clear that it was designed to set forth only general principles so that the courts would be able to determine the legality of challenged practices on a case-by-case basis within the context of the common-law principles and precedents. The result, of course, is that such a general document becomes subject to diverse interpretation and expansion. Indeed, that has been the history of the Sherman Act, as a study of this material indicates. To be sure the general nature of the debates and statutes has encouraged different schools of thought in advancing different values for antitrust policy.

While the drafters of the Sherman Act intended to incorporate the common-law approach to restraints of trade, the Act is, however, more expansive. It gave the federal courts new subject-matter jurisdiction. It created public offenses against restraints of trade and monopolization. It permitted enforcement on two levels: governmental and private. At common law, both in England and the United States, restraints found unreasonable were considered void and hence unenforceable. But under the Sherman Act, criminal penalties, including fine and/or imprisonment, are within the court's jurisdiction. In addition, civil injunctions may be sought by the United States. Most important, the statute, unlike the common law, was designed to create a uniform federal antitrust policy. Whether this goal of the Sherman Act has been achieved is an issue to be discussed throughout this text. But as Section A of this chapter suggests, the goals and policies of the antitrust laws have changed throughout time to meet pressing economic concerns of the time. Perhaps this is the strength of the law's development.

D. EARLY INTERPRETATIONS

Not until 1895 did the Supreme Court decide its first case under the Act. That holding bespoke of the enforcement difficulties that lay ahead in challenging trusts and monopolies. In *United States v. E.C. Knight Co.*, 156 U.S. 1 (1895), the Supreme Court, narrowly interpreting the Act's jurisdictional reach, held that the government failed to demonstrate that the sugar trust's monopoly of refining was a *direct* restraint on interstate commerce on the theory that the Sherman Act did not reach restraints affecting merely the manufacture of commodities. Under this reading, manufacturing did not come within the regulatory framework of the Sherman Act. Such a narrow holding as to what constitutes "commerce" threatened to derail the effective enforcement of the statute. *See* McCurdy, *The Knight*

Sugar Decision of 1895 and the Modernization of American Corporation Law, 1869-1903, 53 Bus. Hist. Rev. 304 (1979).

Two years later the Court considered *United States v. Trans-Missouri Freight Ass'n*, 166 U.S. 290 (1897). A cartel was created by eighteen railroads which provided rail service west of the Mississippi River for the purpose of setting freight schedules and rates for all railroads. The Department of Justice charged that the cartel was a restraint of trade in violation of section 1 of the Sherman Act. The defense urged that such a commercial arrangement was not unlawful at common law since the fixed rates were reasonable, and therefore the cartel was not unlawful under the Sherman Act. Justice Peckham, writing for the Court, declined to consider whether the challenged practice violated the common law. Instead, the Court interpreted section 1 literally as condemning "every" restraint without exception as unlawful.

UNITED STATES v. TRANS-MISSOURI FREIGHT ASS'N

166 U.S. 290 (1897)

[After deciding that the Sherman Act covers railroad common carriers, the Court turned to the question of whether the railroad cartel violated any provision of the Sherman Act.]

JUSTICE PECKHAM delivered the opinion of the Court.

....

The next question to be discussed ... is the true construction of the statute.... Is it confined to a contract or combination which is only in unreasonable restraint of trade or commerce, or does it include what the language of the act plainly and in terms covers, all contracts of that nature?

We are asked to regard the title of this act as indicative of its purpose to include only those contracts which were unlawful at common law, but which require the sanction of a Federal statute in order to be dealt with in a Federal court. It is said that when terms which are known to the common law are used in a Federal statute those terms are to be given the same meaning that they received at common law, and that when the language of the title is "to protect trade and commerce against unlawful restraints and monopolies," it means those restraints and monopolies which the common law regarded as unlawful, and which were to be prohibited by the Federal statute. We are of opinion that the language used in the title refers to and includes and was intended to include those restraints and monopolies which are made unlawful in the body of the statute. It is to the statute itself that resort must be had to learn the meaning thereof, though a resort to the title here creates no doubt about the meaning of and does not alter the plain language contained in its text.

It is now with much amplification of argument urged that the statute, in declaring illegal every combination in the form of trust or otherwise, or conspiracy in restraint of trade or commerce, does not mean what the language used therein plainly imports, but that it only means to declare illegal any such contract which is in *unreasonable* restraint of trade, while leaving all others unaffected by the provisions of the act; that the common-law meaning of the term "contract in restraint of trade" includes only such contracts as are in *unreasonable* restraint of trade, and when that term is used in the Federal statute it is not intended to include all contracts in restraint of trade, but only those which are in unreasonable restraint thereof.

The term is not of such limited signification. Contracts in restraint of trade have been known and spoken of for hundreds of years both in England and in this country, and the term includes all kinds of those contracts which in fact restrain or may restrain trade. Some of such contracts have been held void and unenforceable in the courts by reason of their restraint being unreasonable, while others have been held valid because they were not of that nature. A contract may be in restraint of trade and still be valid at common law. Although valid, it is nevertheless a contract in restraint of trade, and would be so described either at common law or elsewhere. By the simple use of the term "contract in restraint of trade," all contracts of that nature, whether valid or otherwise, would be included, and not alone that kind of contract which was invalid and unenforceable as being in unreasonable restraint of trade. When, therefore, the body of an act pronounces as illegal every contract or combination in restraint of trade or commerce among the several States, etc., the plain and ordinary meaning of such language is not limited to that kind of contract alone which is in unreasonable restraint of trade, but all contracts are included in such language, and no exception or limitation can be added without placing in the act that which has been omitted by Congress....

A contract which is the mere accompaniment of the sale of property, and thus entered into for the purpose of enhancing the price at which the vendor sells it, which in effect is collateral to such sale, and where the main purpose of the whole contract is accomplished by such sale, might not be included, within the letter or spirit of the statute in question. But we cannot see how the statute can be limited, as it has been by the courts below, without reading into its text an exception which alters the natural meaning of the language used, and that, too, upon a most material point, and where no sufficient reason is shown for believing that such alteration would make the statute more in accord with the intent of the law-making body that enacted it.

The great stress of the argument for the defendants on this branch of the case has been to show, if possible, some reason in the attendant circumstances, or some fact existing in the nature of railroad property and business upon which to found the claim, that although by the language of the statute agreements or combinations in restraint of trade or commerce are included, the statute really means to declare illegal only those contracts, etc., which are in unreasonable restraint of trade....

The plaintiffs are, however, under no obligation in order to maintain this action to show that by the common law all agreements among competing railroad companies to keep up rates to such as are reasonable were void as in restraint of trade or commerce. There are many cases which look in that direction if they do not precisely decide that point.... But assuming that agreements of this nature are not void at common law and that the various cases cited by the learned courts below show it, the answer to the statement of their validity now is to be found in the terms of the statute under consideration....

The claim that the company has the right to charge reasonable rates, and that, therefore, it has the right to enter into a combination with competing roads to maintain such rates, cannot be admitted. The conclusion does not follow from an admission of the premise. What one company may do in the way of charging reasonable rates is radically different from entering into an agreement with other and competing roads to keep up the rates to that point. If there be any competition the extent of the charge for the service will be seriously affected by that fact. Competition will itself bring charges down to what may be reasonable, while in the case of an agreement to keep prices up, competition is allowed no play; it is shut out, and the rate is practically fixed by the companies themselves by virtue of the agreement, so long as they abide by it....

In the view we have taken of the question, the intent alleged by the Government is not necessary to be proved. The question is one of law in regard to the meaning and effect of the agreement itself, namely: Does the agreement restrain trade or commerce in any way so as to be a violation of the act? We have no doubt that it does. The agreement on its face recites that it is entered into "for the purpose of mutual protection by establishing and maintaining reasonable rates, rules and regulations on all freight traffic, both through and local." To that end the association is formed and a body created which is to adopt rates, which, when agreed to, are to be the governing rates for all the companies, and a violation of which subjects the defaulting company to the payment of a penalty, and although the parties have a right to withdraw from the agreement on giving thirty days' notice of a desire so to do, yet while in force and assuming it to be lived up to, there can be no doubt that its direct, immediate and necessary effect is to put a restraint upon trade or commerce as described in the act.

For these reasons the suit of the Government can be maintained without proof of the allegation that the agreement was entered into for the purpose of restraining trade or commerce or for maintaining rates above what was reasonable. The necessary effect of the agreement is to restrain trade or commerce, no matter what the intent was on the part of those who signed it....

[In dissent, JUSTICE WHITE urged that the Sherman Act only condemned unreasonable restraints.]

NOTES AND QUESTIONS

1. The following year the Court reconsidered its reasoning and concluded that its interpretation of section 1 was overinclusive. In *United States v. Joint Traffic Ass'n*, 171 U.S. 505 (1898), Justice Peckham, for the Court, observed:

We are not aware that it has ever been claimed that a lease or purchase by a farmer, manufacturer, or merchant of an additional farm, manufactory, or shop, or the withdrawal from business of any farmer, merchant, or manufacturer, restrained commerce or trade within any legal definition of that term; and the sale of a goodwill of a business with an accompanying agreement not to engage in a similar business was instanced in the *Trans-Missouri* case as a contract not within the meaning of the act; and it was said that such a contract was collateral to the main contract of sale, and was entered into for the purpose of enhancing the price at which the vendor sells his business. ... [T]he statute applies only to those contracts whose direct and immediate effect is a restraint upon interstate commerce, and that to treat the act as condemning all agreements under which, as a result, the cost of conducting an interstate commercial business may be increased, would enlarge the application of the act far beyond the fair meaning of the language used.... An agreement entered into for the purpose of promoting the legitimate business of an individual or corporation, with no purpose to thereby affect or restrain interstate commerce, and which does not directly restrain such commerce, is not, as we think, covered by the act, although the agreement indirectly and remotely affects that commerce.... To suppose, as is assumed by counsel, that the effect of the decision in the *Trans-Missouri* case is to render illegal most business contracts or combinations, however indispensable and necessary they may be, because, as they assert, they all restrain trade in some remote and indirect degree, is to make a most violent assumption, and one not called for or justified by the decision mentioned, or by any other decision of this court.

2. Does Justice Peckham's opinion indicate that an arrangement that had only an incidental effect on competition would be lawful under the Sherman Act? Would it matter whether the purpose of the agreement was to lessen competition? Could the restraint be saved if its terms were reasonable in light of market conditions? What remains of *Trans-Missouri* after *Joint Traffic*? Does the Sherman Act extend beyond conduct condemned under the common law?

Implicit in Justice Peckham's opinion is a standard of competition under which subsequent cases have been judged. The decision suggests that concerted market practices, like price fixing, that affect competition directly are illegal and no inquiry as to the reasonableness of the price will be considered. *Joint Traffic* did indicate, however, that there may be market arrangements that do not directly or significantly affect competition and for which the Court should evaluate the reasonableness of the practice. The Court also alluded to the common-law "ancillary restraint" doctrine and in dicta suggested that such incidental restraints are not condemned under section 1.

Consider also Justice Peckham's statement in *Trans-Missouri* that business agreements

... may even temporarily, or perhaps permanently, reduce the price of the article traded in or manufactured, by reducing the expense inseparable from the running of many different companies for the same purpose. Trade or commerce under those circumstances may nevertheless be badly and unfortunately restrained by driving out of business the small dealers and worthy men whose lives have been spent therein, and who might be unable to readjust themselves to their altered surroundings. Mere reduction in the price of the commodity dealt in might be dearly paid for by the ruin of such a class....

166 U.S. at 323.

Does Justice Peckham's "small dealers and worthy men" phrase indicate that the Sherman Action is designed to protect small competitors and producers? If so, would this interpretation be compatible with the goal of protecting consumers? *See* R. Bork, *The Antitrust Paradox* 25 (1978).

The analysis introduced in *Joint Traffic* had been considered the same year by Judge Taft, later Chief Justice, in the famous case that established the American rule governing ancillary restraints and the standard employed in analyzing price-fixing cases.

UNITED STATES v. ADDYSTON PIPE & STEEL CO.

85 F. 271 (6th Cir. 1898), *aff'd*, 175 U.S. 211 (1899)

[Defendants were six corporations manufacturing cast iron pipe. They were charged with engaging in a cartel to divide competitive territories and to fix the price within the territories. Markets were divided in many of the southern and western states. Collusive bid practices were part of the scheme. The evidence tended to show that the cartel set the price of the iron pipe low enough to foreclose competition from east coast manufacturers, but high enough to deter competition among the defendants and that prices would have been lower had the local manufacturers competed. The questions presented were: (1) "was the association of the defendants a contract, combination, or conspiracy in restraint of trade ... (2) was the trade thus restrained trade between the states?"]

CIRCUIT JUDGE TAFT delivered the opinion of the Court.

The contention on behalf of defendants is that the association would have been valid at common law, and that the federal anti-trust law was not intended to reach any agreements that were not void and unenforceable at common law. It might be a sufficient answer to this contention to point to the decision of the Supreme Court of the United States in *United States v. Trans-Missouri Freight Ass'n*, 166 U.S. 290, in which it was held that contracts in restraint of interstate transportation were within the statute, whether the restraints would be regarded as reasonable at common law or not. It is suggested, however, that the case related to a quasi public employment necessarily under public control, and affecting public interests, and that a less stringent rule of construction applies to contracts restricting parties in sales of merchandise, which is purely a private business, having in it no element of a public or quasi public character. Whether or not there is substance in such a distinction, — a question we do not decide, — it is certain that, if the contract of association which bound the defendants was void and unenforceable at the common law because of restraint of trade, it is within the inhibition of the statute if the trade it restrained was interstate. Contracts that were in unreasonable restraint of trade at common law were not unlawful in the sense of being criminal, or giving rise to a civil action for damages in favor of one prejudicially affected thereby, but were simply void, and were not enforced by the courts.... The effect of the act of 1890 is to render such contracts unlawful in an affirmative or positive sense, and punishable as a misdemeanor, and to create a right of civil action for damages in favor of those injured thereby, and a civil remedy by injunction in favor of both private persons and the public against the execution of such contracts and the maintenance of such trade restraints.

The argument for defendants is that their contract of association was not, and could not be, a monopoly, because their aggregate tonnage capacity did not exceed 30 per cent of the total tonnage capacity of the country; that the restraints upon the members of the association, if restraints they could be called, did not embrace all the states, and were not unlimited in space; that such partial restraints were justified and upheld at common law if reasonable, and only proportioned to the necessary protection of the parties; that in this case the partial restraints were reasonable, because without them each member would be subjected to ruinous competition by the other, and did not exceed in degree of stringency or scope what was necessary to protect the parties in securing prices for their product that were fair and reasonable to themselves and the public; that competition was not stifled by the association because the prices fixed by it had to be fixed with reference to the very active competition of pipe companies which were not members of the association, and which had more than double the defendants' capacity; that in this way the association only modified and restrained the evils of ruinous competition, while the public had all the benefit from competition which public policy demanded.

From early times it was the policy of Englishmen to encourage trade in England, and to discourage those voluntary restraints which tradesmen were often induced to impose on themselves by contract. Courts recognized this public policy by refusing to enforce stipulations of this character. The objections to such restraints were mainly two. One was that by such contracts a man disabled himself from earning a livelihood with the risk of becoming a public charge, and deprived the community of the benefit of his labor. The other was that such restraints tended to give to the covenantee, the beneficiary of such restraints, a monopoly of the trade, from which he had thus excluded one competitor, and by the same means might exclude others.

....

The inhibition against restraints of trade at common law seems at first to have had no exception.... After a time it became apparent to the people and the courts that it was in the interest of trade that certain covenants in restraint of trade should be enforced.... [A]fter a man had built up a business with an extensive good will, he should be able to sell his business and good will to the best advantage, and he could not do so unless he could bind himself by an enforceable contract not to engage in the same business in such a way as to prevent injury to that which he was about to sell. It was equally for the good of the public and trade, when partners dissolved, and one took the business, or they divided the business, that each partner might bind himself not to do anything in trade thereafter which would derogate from his grant of the interest conveyed to his former partner. [T]his effect was only an incident to the main purpose of a union of their capital, enterprise, and energy to carry on a successful business, and one useful to the community....

[C]ovenants in partial restraint of trade are generally upheld as valid when they are agreements (1) by the seller of property or business not to compete with the buyer in such a way as to derogate from the value of the property or business sold; (2) by a retiring partner not to compete with the firm; (3) by a partner pending the partnership not to do anything to interfere, by competition or otherwise, with the business of the firm; (4) by the buyer of property not to use the same in competition with the business retained by the seller; and (5) by an assistant, servant, or agent not to compete with his master or employer after the expiration of his time of service. Before such agreements are upheld, however, the court must find that the restraints attempted thereby are reasonably necessary (1, 2, and 3) to the enjoyment by the buyer of the property, good will, or interest in the partnership bought; or (4) to the legitimate ends of the existing partnership; or (5) to the prevention of possible injury to the business of the seller from use by the buyer of the thing sold; or (6) to protection from the danger of loss to the employer's business caused by the unjust use on the part of the employee of the confidential knowledge acquired in such business....

It would be stating it too strongly to say that these five classes of covenants in restraint of trade include all of those upheld as valid at the common law; but it would certainly seem to follow from the tests laid down for determining the validity of such an agreement that no conventional restraint of trade can be enforced unless the covenant embodying it is merely ancillary to the main purpose of a lawful contract, and necessary to protect the covenantee in the enjoyment of the legitimate fruits of the contract, or to protect him from the dangers of an unjust use of those fruits by the other party....

[T]he rule implies that the contract must be one in which there is a main purpose, to which the covenant in restraint of trade is merely ancillary. The covenant is inserted only to protect one of the parties from the injury which, in the execution of the contract or enjoyment of its fruits, he may suffer from the unrestrained competition of the other. The main purpose of the contract suggests the measure of protection needed, and furnishes a sufficiently uniform standard by which the validity of such restraints may be judicially determined. In such a case, if the restraint exceeds the necessity presented by the main purpose of the contract, it is void for two reasons: First, because it oppresses the covenantor, without any corresponding benefit to the covenantee; and, second, because it tends to a monopoly. But where the sole object of both parties in making the contract as expressed therein is merely to restrain competition, and enhance or maintain prices, it would seem that there was nothing to justify or excuse the restraint, that it would necessarily have a tendency to monopoly, and therefore would be void. In such a case there is no measure of what is necessary to the protection of either party, except the vague and varying opinion of judges as to how much, on principles of political economy, men ought to be allowed to restrain competition. There is in such contracts no main lawful purpose, to subserve which partial restraint is permitted, and by which its reasonableness is measured, but the sole object is to restrain trade in order to avoid the competition which it has always been the policy of the common law to foster.

Much has been said in regard to the relaxing of the original strictness of the common law in declaring contracts in restraint of trade void as conditions of civilization and public policy have changed, and the argument drawn therefrom is that the law now recognizes that competition may be so ruinous as to injure the public, and, therefore, that contracts made with a view to check such ruinous competition and regulate prices, though in restraint of trade, and having no other purpose, will be upheld. We think this conclusion is unwarranted by the authorities when all of them are considered. It is true that certain rules for determining whether a covenant in restraint of trade ancillary to the main purpose of a contract was reasonably adapted and limited to the necessary protection of a party in the carrying out of such purpose have been somewhat modified by modern authorities.... But these cases all involved contracts in which the covenant in restraint of trade was ancillary to the main and lawful purpose of the contract, and was necessary to the protection of the covenantee in the carrying out of that main purpose. They do not manifest any general disposition on the part of the courts to be more liberal in supporting contracts having for their sole object the restraint of trade than did the courts of an earlier time. It is true that there are some cases in which the courts, mistaking, as we conceive, the proper limits of the relaxation of the rules for determining the unreasonableness of restraints of trade, have set sail on a sea of doubt, and have assumed the power to say, in respect to contracts which have no other purpose and no other consideration on either side than the mutual restraint of the parties, how much restraint of competition is in the public interest, and how much is not.

The manifest danger in the administration of justice according to so shifting, vague, and indeterminate a standard would seem to be a strong reason against adopting it....

Upon this review of the law and the authorities, we can have no doubt that the association of the defendants, however reasonable the prices they fixed, however great the competition they had to encounter, and however great the necessity for curbing themselves by joint agreement from committing financial suicide by ill-advised competition, was void at common law, because in restraint of trade, and tending to a monopoly. But the facts of the case do not require us to go so far as this, for they show that the attempted justification of this association on the grounds stated is without foundation.

....

It has been earnestly pressed upon us that the prices at which the cast-iron pipe was sold in pay territory were reasonable.... We do not think the issue an important one, because, as already stated, we do not think that at common law there is any question of reasonableness open to the courts with reference to such a contract. Its tendency was certainly to give defendants the power to charge unreasonable prices, had they chosen to do so. But, if it were important, we should unhesitatingly find that the prices charged in the instances which were in evidence were unreasonable....

Reversed.

[The case was affirmed the next year by the Supreme Court in an opinion by JUSTICE PECKHAM.]

NOTES AND QUESTIONS

1. On what ground did the Court find the challenged agreement to be illegal? Did the Court rely on the analysis of *Trans-Missouri* in finding a Sherman Act violation? What relevance did Judge Taft's discussion of ancillary restraints have on the cartel price-fixing agreement? Under what circumstances does the "ancillary restraint" doctrine protect a covenant not to compete?

Judge Taft's opinion on the ancillary restraint doctrine set the standard for the distinction between lawful and unlawful restraints. Moreover, he opined that if prices were set by means other than competition in the market, they were illegal regardless of their reasonableness. Thus a two-prong approach to antitrust jurisprudence emerged from Judge Taft's opinion. For Taft the "reasonableness" test (later called the "rule of reason") was applied at common law only to ancillary restraints, but not to such direct restraints as price fixing, which he characterized as "naked restraints." According to Taft, this same standard was to be incorporated into the Sherman Act, as well. This approach was challenged by Chief Justice White, however, in *Standard Oil* (1911). He had dissented in *Trans-Missouri*. The opinion charts the so-called "rule of reason" approach to antitrust.

2. In *Standard Oil Co. v. United States*, 221 U.S. 1 (1911), a combination of thirty-seven oil companies was managed through a holding company. The companies were brought together and joined through a series of devices and mergers. The combination was charged with predatory conduct and anti-competitive abuses, including price cutting and discriminatory pricing. Defendants were charged with violating sections 1 and 2 of the Sherman Act. The Court found for the government and ordered dissolution of the combinations.

Chief Justice White delivered the opinion of the Court, holding that the standard of reason which had been applied at the common law and in this country in dealing with subjects of the character embraced by the statute was intended to be the measure used for the purpose of determining whether in a given case a particular act had or had not brought about the wrong against which the statute provided....

> [C]onsidering the contracts or agreements, their necessary effect and the character of the parties by whom they were made, they were clearly restraints of trade within the purview of the statute, they could not be taken out of that category by indulging in general reasoning as to the expediency or non-expediency of having made the contracts or the wisdom or want of wisdom of the statute which prohibited their being made. [T]he nature and character of the contracts, creating as they did a conclusive presumption which brought them within the statute, such result was not to be disregarded by the substitution of a judicial appreciation of what the law ought to be for the plain judicial duty of enforcing the law as it was made.

For a good historical discussion of the development of antitrust case law from the turn of the century through *Standard Oil, see* IX A. Bickel & B. Schmidt, *Holmes Devise History of the Supreme Court*, 86-199 (1984).

3. In *United States v. American Tobacco Co.*, 221 U.S. 106, 179 (1911), decided fourteen days after *Standard Oil*, Chief Justice White observed further:

> Applying the rule of reason to the construction of the statute, it was held in the *Standard Oil Case*, that as the words "restraint of trade" at common law ... only embraced acts or contracts or agreements or combinations which operated to the prejudice of the public interests by unduly restricting competition or unduly obstructing the due course of trade or which, either because of their inherent nature or effect or because of the evident purpose of the acts, etc., injuriously restrained trade....

4. After *Standard Oil*, is the term "restraint of trade" restricted to its common-law meaning? How did Chief Justice White's Sherman Act analysis differ from Judge Taft's? Under Chief Justice White's approach, could direct and purposeful restraints ever be considered valid under section 1? *See, e.g., Chicago Board of Trade v. United States*, 246 U.S. 231 (1918); *Appalachian Coals, Inc. v. United States*, 283 U.S. 344 (1933); *National Soc'y of Prof. Eng'rs v. United States*, 435 U.S. 679 (1978); *Broadcast Music, Inc. v. CBS*, 442 U.S. 1 (1979). What probative value would evidence of the "purpose" or "effect" of the combination have in determining the reasonableness of the restraint? Do we know from Chief Justice White's "standard of reason" whether harmful effects can be inferred from the purpose of the arrangement? Does the "reasonableness" standard permit defense counsel to argue that the challenged practice will promote the public interest better than market forces?

Chief Justice White's reasoning suggests that Judge Taft's line-drawing regarding the limits of judicial discretion in section 1 cases was too narrow. Taft would have limited the judicial inquiry into reasonableness of the restraint only as to restraints classified as incidental or ancillary. If the restraint was not ancillary it was automatically illegal. In *Addyston Pipe*, Taft made it clear that those defending deliberate restraints of trade as being within the public interest were setting "sail on a sea of doubt." White, however, would apply the rule of reason analysis to direct, as well as ancillary, restraints in determining whether they were reasonable. Only "unreasonable" or "undue" restraints of trade were illegal under the later view. The standard seemed to be whether there has been a significant interference with or impact on *competition*, although competition was never defined.

White's observation in *American Tobacco* sets forth the critical inquiry for determining this standard: an illegal restraint is one that includes a contract, agreement, or combination, which either by its inherent nature or anticompetitive purpose or effect unduly restricts competition. Consider *Standard Oil*'s admonition that rate fixing between competitors is by its "nature, character and necessary effect" anticompetitive and hence subject to a "conclusive presumption" of invalidity. Thus, if the restraint is not by its nature or character inherently anticompetitive, then the purpose or effect of the contract, combination or agreement must be considered. In sum, Chief Justice White focused the analysis on whether the nature, purpose, or effect of the restraint was unreasonably anticompetitive. Evidence or reasonable inferences therefrom could support a finding of unreasonableness. The rule of reason standard was thus created as a model of analysis and construction for decision-making.

5. *Clayton Act and FTC Act*. Applying his newly articulated rule of reason, Chief Justice White found that the defendants in *Standard Oil* did in fact engage in unreasonable restraints of trade and ordered dissolution of Standard Oil. But the rule of reason approach announced by White caused critics to fear that the broader analysis set forth by White might weaken the statute, given its vagueness. Bills were introduced in Congress to amend the Sherman Act so that reasonable as well as unreasonable restraints of trade would come within its ambit. Because no consensus emerged on the proposed amendments, it was not until after the presidential elections of 1912 that new antitrust laws became a reality.

In 1914 President Wilson proposed that the Sherman Act not be amended, but that supplementary legislation be enacted which would be more explicit in condemning specific conduct. He advocated also the establishment of an independent trade commission, which was to be an expert body that would investigate trade practices and be involved in the remedial stage of antitrust suits. W. Letwin, *supra*, at 270-73.

As a result of Wilson's proposals, the Clayton Act and the Federal Trade Commission Act were adopted in 1914. These statutes were designed to reach trade practices in their "incipiency," before they reached monopoly status. The Clayton Act specifically targeted interlocking directors (section 8), exclusive dealing and tying arrangements (section 3), price discriminations (section 2), and acquisitions or mergers (section 7). The operative language qualifying the conduct was whether the effects of the challenged practice "may be to substantially lessen competition or tend to create a monopoly in any line of commerce."

The open-endedness of these standards defied specificity and clarity. The Conference Committee Report amplified why Congress was unable to be more precise regarding the prohibitive conducts:

> It is now generally recognized that the only effective means of establishing and maintaining monopoly, where there is no control of a natural resource as of transportation, is the use of unfair competition. The most certain way to stop monopoly at the threshold is to prevent unfair competition.
>
> ....
>
> It is impossible to frame definitions which embrace all unfair practices. There is no limit to human inventiveness in this field.... If Congress were to adopt the method of definition, it would undertake an endless task.

63rd Cong. 2d Sess., H.R. Rep. 1142, 18-29 (1914).

But subsequent interpretations have included within its scope practices found unlawful under the Sherman and Clayton Act, incipient conduct bordering on Sherman and Clayton Act violations, and there is indication that it might also include merely "unfair" conduct.

The Federal Trade Commission, also established in 1914, was designed to operate separately from the Antitrust Division of the Department of Justice. Originally its authority was limited to issuing cease and desist orders. No private right of action or criminal jurisdiction was provided. Its principal substantive provision declared illegal unfair methods of competition and unfair or deceptive acts or practices in or affecting commerce. Section 5 of the Act originally proscribed only "unfair or deceptive acts or practices." The Wheeler-Lee Act of 1938 amended the statute to prohibit "unfair or deceptive acts or practices." In general the Commission and the Department of Justice have concurrent jurisdiction over enforcement of the Clayton Act, while the Department of Justice has primary responsibility over enforcement of the Sherman Act. The Department has no jurisdiction over the FTC Act.

BIBLIOGRAPHY AND COLLATERAL READINGS

Books

G. Amato, Antitrust and the Bounds of Power: The Dilemma of Liberal Democracy in the History of the Market (1997).

D. Dewey, The Antitrust Experiment in America (1990).

M. Eisner, Antitrust and the Triumph of Economics: Institutions, Expertise, and Policy Change (1991).

H. First, E. Fox, & R. Pitofsky, eds., Revitalizing Antitrust in Its Second Century (1991).

E. Gellhorn & W. Kovacic, Antitrust Law and Economics 1-14 (4th ed. 1994).

H. Hovenkamp, Federal Antitrust Policy (2d ed. 1994).

H. Hovenkamp, Enterprise and American Law 1836-1837 (1991).

R. Peritz, Competition Policy in America, 1888-1992 (1996).

M. Porter, The Competitive Advantage of Nations (1990).

S. Ross, Principles of Antitrust Law 1-20 (1993).

E.T. Sullivan, ed., The Political Economy of the Sherman Act (1991).

E.T. Sullivan & J. Harrison, Understanding Antitrust and Its Economic Implications 1-7 (3d ed. 1998).

R. Willis, J. Caswell, & J. Culberston, Issues After a Century of Federal Competition Policy (1987).

Articles

Adams and Brock, Antitrust, Ideology, and the Arabesques of Economic Theory, 66 U. Colo. L. Rev. 257 (1995).

Arthur, Workable Antitrust Law: The Statutory Approach to Antitrust, 62 Tulane L. Rev. 1163 (1988).

Bork, Legislative Intent and the Policy of the Sherman Act, 9 J. Law & Econ. 7 (1966).

Easterbrook, The Limits of Antitrust, 63 Tex. L. Rev. 1 (1984).

Fox, The Modernization of Antitrust: A New Equilibrium, 66 Cornell L. Rev. 1140 (1981).

Gerhart, The Supreme Court and Antitrust Analysis: The (Near) Triumph of the Chicago School, 1982 Sup. Ct. Rev. 319.

Gerla, A Micro-Microeconomic Approach to Antitrust Law: Games Managers Play, 86 Mich. L. Rev. 892 (1988).

Hovenkamp, Antitrust Policy After Chicago, 84 Mich. L. Rev. 213 (1985).

Jacobs, An Essay on the Normative Foundations of Antitrust Economics, 74 N.C. L. Rev. 219 (1995).

Lande, Wealth Transfers as the Original and Primary Concern of Antitrust: The Efficiency Interpretation Challenged, 34 Hastings L.J. 65 (1982).

May, Historical Analysis in Antitrust Law, 35 N.Y.L. Sch. L. Rev. 857 (1990).

May, The Role of the States in the First Century of the Sherman Act and the Larger Picture of Antitrust History, 59 Antitrust L.J. 93 (1990).

Millon, The Sherman Act and the Balance of Power, 61 S. Cal. L. Rev. 1219 (1988).

Page, Ideological Conflict and the Origins of Antitrust Policy, 66 Tul. L. Rev. 1 (1991).

Papers Presented at the Airlie House Conference on The Antitrust Alternative, 62 N.Y.U. L. Rev. 931 (1987); 76 Geo. L.J. 237 (1987).

Rowe, The Decline of Antitrust and the Delusions of Models: The Faustian Pact of Law and Economics, 72 Geo. L.J. 1511 (1984).

Sullivan, Antitrust, Microeconomics, and Politics: Reflections on Some Recent Relationships, 68 Calif. L. Rev. 1 (1980).

Sullivan, The Economic Jurisprudence of the Burger Court's Antitrust Policy: The First Thirteen Years, 58 Notre Dame L. Rev. 1 (1982).

Symposium, Antitrust Law and Economics, 127 U. Pa. L. Rev. 918-1140 (1979).

Symposium, On the 100th Anniversary of the Sherman Act and Upon the 75th Anniversary of the Clayton Act, 35 Antitrust Bull. 1-1036 (1990).

Symposium, The Future of Antitrust, 31 Antitrust Bull. 383 (1986).

Symposium, The Goals of Antitrust: A Dialogue on Policy, 65 Colum. L. Rev. 33 (1965).

Symposium, The Sherman Act's First Century: A Historical Perspective, 74 Iowa L. Rev. 987 (1989).

Symposium, Observing the Sherman Act Centennial: The Past and Future of Antitrust as Public Interest Law, 35 N.Y.L. Sch. L. Rev. 767 (1990).

Chapter 2

FRAMEWORK FOR ANALYSIS

SECTION I. THE ECONOMIC PROBLEM

A. INTRODUCTION

The economic theory of antitrust law is based on two parts of microeconomics called price theory and industrial organization. Together, these are concerned with the behavior and structure of firms under various competitive conditions.

Every society must make decisions regarding what products are to be produced, in what quantities, and to whom the products are to be distributed. Societies over the ages and those of contemporary times have found but three types of systems that separately or in combinations enable us to solve economic problems. These systems are economies run by tradition, economies run by command of the sovereign, and economies run by the market.

Although economies based on tradition or command may pre-date market economies, market economies today dominate the world. In the United States, notwithstanding a large government, most resources are still allocated through some type of market exchange.

Several important factors distinguish a market economy from any other form of economic organization. In a market economy no central authority decides what to produce, how much of each product to produce, and what prices to charge. How then are these decisions made? They are made by individuals, both producers and consumers, seeking not the good of the community but only their own self-interest. Central to the economist's model of predicting behavior is the underlying assumption that each person in society strives to maximize his or her own personal wealth and by doing so maximizes the wealth of the entire community. For instance, the behavioral model predicts that consumers will make purchase decisions in order to maximize their own desires, given their income and the price. On the other side, producers will strive to satisfy consumer demands by producing products at output levels that maximize their profits. The force that channels the avarice of individuals, whether consumers or producers, into socially productive ends is competition. Without competition the "free enterprise" system falls apart: resources are used in a socially inefficient manner and income is redistributed from those who compete to those who do not.

B. LAW OF DEMAND

The law of demand refers to a phenomenon each of us observes every day: more of a given product is purchased if its price is lowered, providing nothing else changes. Graphically, this corresponds to a downward sloping curve as pictured in Figure 1. At price P_1, only Q_1 units of the commodity are demanded while at the lower price, P_2, Q_2 units are demanded. As the price moves from P_1 to P_2 the quantity demanded increases from Q_1 to Q_2. The demand curve in this figure is a straight line, implying that demand changes and price changes occur at exactly the same rate. In the real world this is never the case. The linear demand curve oversimplifies the real-world dynamics but often makes market behavior easier to understand.

Figure 1

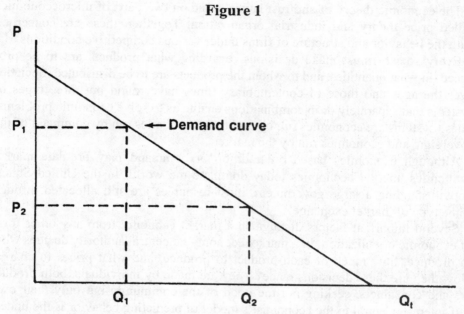

Of special importance are the determinants of the shape and slope (steepness) of the demand curve. Consider the two diagrams in Figure 2.

Panel (a) depicts a situation where the product in question is indispensable in some invariable amount. Therefore a predetermined quantity of Q_1 will be demanded no matter what price is charged. We sometimes say that such a product has no substitutes. For example, only polio vaccine will prevent the disease of polio; no other will do. A product of this kind is said to be perfectly price-*inelastic*. But such products are extremely rare, and very likely not even polio vaccine qualifies. Some people who will choose not to be vaccinated if the price goes too high. Thus, even this demand curve will probably have a slightly horizontal slope. In fact, few, if any, scarce resources have a perfectly vertical demand curve.

Panel (b) depicts the polar extreme. This product is so similar to others that a slight increase in its price will result in an immediate shift to the other products by consumers and leave zero demand for this product. For example, if farmer A attempts to market his wheat at prices higher than prevailing, then consumers will shift to farmer B's wheat, a perfect substitute. From the farmer's point of view, the demand for wheat is said to be perfectly elastic.

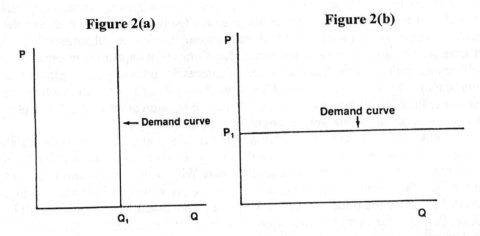

Figure 2(a)   Figure 2(b)

Consider the difference between a demand curve faced by an entire industry versus the demand curve faced by each of several firms within the industry. Figure 3 depicts the demand curve for the entire market for some product. Suppose that from the consumer's viewpoint all firms in the industry produce identical products. Then any one firm in the industry will face a demand structure as pictured in Figure 2(b), above. A single firm acting alone cannot charge a price higher than P_1 without losing all sales and will not charge a price lower than P_1 because all output can be sold at price P_1. If a large number of firms produce identical products each firm faces a perfectly elastic demand curve. This concept is crucial to understanding the respective performances of competitive and monopoly market structures.

Figure 3

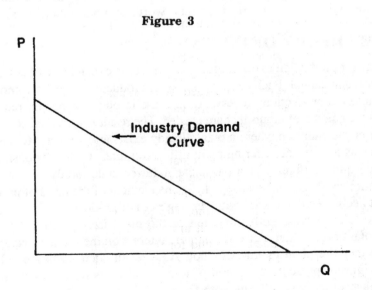

A final word on elasticities. The elasticity of demand facing a particular individual firm is a function not only of the price it attempts to charge but also of the ability of other firms to offer products that consumers view as substitutes. If firm A attempts to raise the price of product X, two things will happen: first, customers will try to switch away from X; second, competing producers will attempt to manufacture something that resembles X, or if they are already manufacturing a close substitute, to increase their production. The measurement of this latter phenomenon is called the market "elasticity of supply."

Elasticity of supply can be a function of many things: the closeness with which consumers view one product as a substitute for another one, excess capacity in the hands of competing producers, and the ease with which competing firms can enter firm A's market. At the limit, elasticity of supply will be infinite and if firm A attempts to raise the price of product X by even a small amount, A will lose all its sales. Perhaps, for example, customers view product Y as a good substitute for X, and the firms manufacturing Y have unused capacity in their factories. These firms will respond to A's price increase by producing more of Y. Likewise, if entry into manufacture of X is very easy, new firms will enter the market when the price of X rises. In an extreme case, A might have 100% of the market for X at the current price, but be absolutely unable to raise the price of X without losing all sales. Although economists commonly refer to this phenomenon as "elasticity of supply," courts have given it a number of names — such as "production substitutability" or "exchangeability."

In evaluating elasticity of supply a court must consider not only the likelihood that new firms will enter the market, but also the amount of time that new entry will require. If entry into a market is relatively easy, but construction of a plant and creation of a distribution network takes five years, an existing monopolist in that market will be able to earn five years' worth of monopoly profits.

C. THE THEORY OF COSTS

In order for production to occur there must be some expenditure of land, raw materials, labor, and capital. Each of these factors of production requires compensation to bring it into the production process. An increase in output generally requires an increase in the amount of inputs that are needed. The result is increased costs.

Consider the situation where a plant already exists and we want to describe how costs vary as a result of differing plant utilization rates. Cost relationships may, of course, be quite different for a particular industry under study. We will describe this situation as short run because at least one element of the costs of production — the plant itself — will not vary with varying rates of production.

The costs associated with provision of the plant itself do not depend on the level of plant production. For example, the interest on the plant mortgage must be paid whether the plant operates or not. As a result such costs are called "fixed costs." Figure 4 presents the graph of total fixed costs to the plant output level. By contrast, other costs change with the rate of output — the higher the output, the higher these costs become. Raw materials, utilities, and most kinds of labor are included in this category of "variable costs."

Figure 4

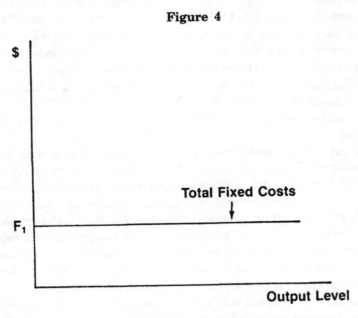

the higher these costs become. Raw materials, utilities, and most kinds of labor

Figure 5, panel (a) presents the relationship of "total variable costs" to the plant output level. The graph is drawn to reflect phenomena observed in many production processes. At low levels of output (say below A) variable costs rise rather rapidly but at a decreasing rate. In the middle range of utilization,

Figure 5

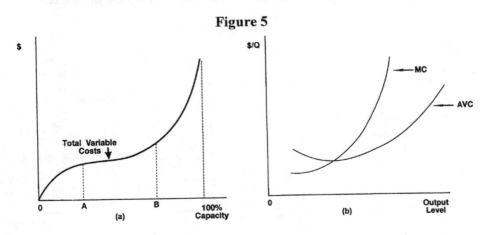

between points A and B, variable costs rise more slowly with increased output. At high levels of utilization, above point B, variable costs rise at an increasing rate. The shape of the total variable cost curve indicates that a plant operates most efficiently in certain ranges of output. If the plant is operated outside of these ranges a substantial penalty is incurred in terms of higher per unit costs. Notice that panel (b) of Figure 5 presents the graph of variable costs per unit of output against the output level. These average variable costs are obtained by dividing total variable costs by the output level. In many industries a plant's costs are fairly constant over a wide output range. In that case the average variable cost (AVC) curve will have a flatter bottom than the curve in Figure 5(b).

Combining Figures 4 and 5, we obtain a total short run cost function illustrated in Figure 6, panel (a). Consider that its shape is identical to that of the total variable cost function, with the only difference being the addition of F_1 (fixed cost) at every output level.

Panel (b) of Figure 6 presents the average total cost curve and the marginal cost curve. Average total costs are calculated by dividing total cost at any given output level by the quantity produced. Marginal cost, on the other hand, refers to the cost associated with producing an additional unit of output or the value of resources that must be sacrificed to get an additional unit of output. Notice the relationship of the marginal to the average costs in Figure 6. When marginal cost is below average cost the latter falls. When marginal cost is above average cost the average value rises. Most students are quite aware of marginal-average relationships. If a student's grade average is 80 and the student receives a 70 in Torts (the marginal exam), then the average must fall. If she receives a 90 in Antitrust, it will rise.

Over the long run nearly all costs must be counted as variable. For example, even the plant itself must eventually be replaced. Previously we assumed that a plant of a given size already existed and the rate of utilization was the only variable of interest. But how was the size of the plant determined initially? This question is answered by considering the relationship of costs to variation in plant size.

Figure 6

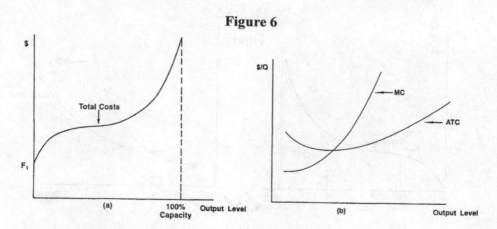

The plant cost structure shown in Figure 6(b) represents the minimum costs possible for a plant of that size. But suppose the plant size is doubled and the two cost structures are pictured as in Figure 7, where ATC_1 is the average total cost curve for the plant in Figure 6 and ATC_2 is the curve for a plant twice as big. The larger plant has the capability of producing the product at lower per unit costs if enough is produced. The production of this product in the range from A to B is said to be subject to economies of scale — that is, within that range the larger the plant, the lower the price.

Figure 7

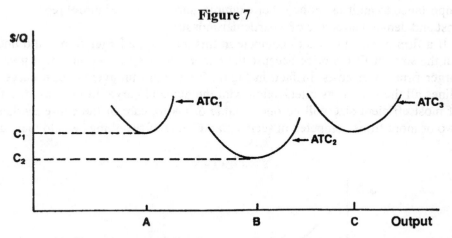

Suppose ATC_3 is the average total cost curve for a plant three times the size of the original plant. The minimum per unit costs associated with plant 3 are higher than those associated with plant 2. Consequently in the range B to C the production of the product is said to be subject to diseconomies of scale because costs per unit rise with increased plant size in that range. By considering a variety of plant sizes and the cost curves associated with each it is possible to derive a new curve that relates the minimum achievable cost for each plant to the output level. This curve is called the long run average cost curve and is illustrated in Figure 8.

Figure 8

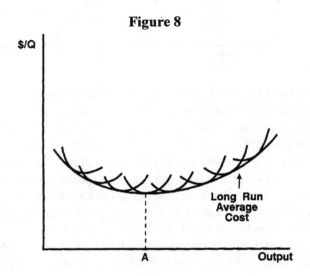

In the region to the left of point A, production is subject to economies of scale and in the region to the right of point A to diseconomies of scale. The plant associated with point A is said to be the optimally scaled plant since it is the one in which per unit costs are at an irreducible minimum.

The shape of the long run average cost curve of a given industry is of extreme importance to antitrust policy. For example, suppose that Figure 9 represents the cost and demand structure of a particular industry.

If a firm of size q_1 tries to compete in this industry, a larger firm could undercut the smaller firm's price because the larger scale of production would give the larger firm lower costs. In fact, in Figure 9 the long run average cost curve declines all the way to its intersection with the demand curve. In this case the firm of most efficient size will be one capable of taking care of the entire market. If two or more firms competed in such a market, one of two things would inevitably

Figure 9

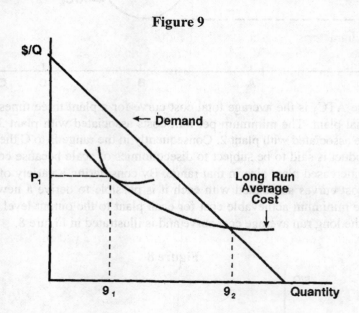

happen: one of the firms would eventually obtain a larger market share and a cost advantage over the other firm and drive it out of business. Otherwise, if the two firms continued to operate in the market, total market output would be lower than optimal and price would be higher than optimal. Such a market is called a natural monopoly. Examples of natural monopoly may include electric and gas distribution systems, many delivery routes (such as newspaper routes) and perhaps railroads and bridges. What characterizes many (although not all) such markets is either price regulation by the state or else outright public ownership. See discussion of natural monopoly and regulation in Chapter 9, *infra*.

Compare the natural monopoly market with the situation depicted in Figure 10. At price P_1 the market could support about five optimally sized plants (of size A).

Figure 10

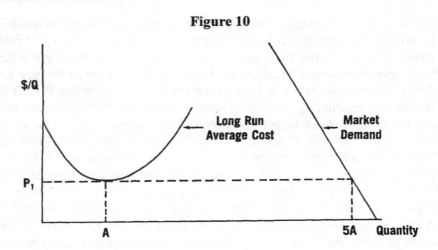

The cost characteristics of a particular industry, which are determined primarily by technological considerations and transaction costs, are a major factor in determining the maximum number of firms the industry will support. Industries with small scale requirements relative to market demand, such as agriculture, will be able to support a large number of firms, while industries with large scale requirements, such as automobile production, may have only a few firms. The technology of an industry is therefore of major importance in determining the level of industrial concentration and the parameters of competition, as those terms are defined under sections one and two of the Sherman Act.

For more on industry cost characteristics, scale economies, and their effect on industrial structure, *see* F.M. Scherer & D. Ross, *Industrial Market Structure and Economic Performance* (3d ed. 1990); W. K. Viscusi, J. M. Vernon, & J. E. Harrington, Jr., *Economics of Regulation and Antitrust*, ch. 3 (2d ed. 1995).

SECTION II. THE MARKET IN MOVEMENT

A. PERFECT COMPETITION

Given these basic ideas about demand and costs, we can understand how the perfectly competitive market adjusts to achieve a socially optimal mix of products. The driving force in a market system is the behavior of the competitive firm.

Within the competitive model the perfectly competitive firm has the following characteristics:

1. It is only one among many firms producing identical products,
2. No individual firm is large enough to affect the market price by its individual actions, and
3. There are no significant inhibitions on entry into and exit from the industry.

Given these environmental assumptions, how does the profit maximizing firm determine the quantity to be produced? Referring to Figure 11, suppose the market price which the firm takes as quoted is P_1. Since there are a large number of firms producing identical products the demand curve for any individual firm is perfectly elastic and is represented by the dashed line P_1A. If this firm decided to produce q_0 units of output it would not be making as much profit as it could. This can be seen by noting that at output level q_0 the cost to produce an additional unit of output is C_0 while it can be sold for P_1. Therefore by producing the additional unit profit is increased by the quantity P_1-C_0. Now consider output level q_2. By producing this much the firm has incurred a marginal loss of C_2 on the last unit of output but can sell it for only P_1. Therefore by not producing this last unit the firm avoids a loss of C_2-P_1 on this unit and profits rise. Without belaboring the point, it can be shown that the profit maximizing output level for this firm is q_1, the point that price equals marginal cost. Thus, the competitive firm attempts to maximize profits by setting output levels at the place where the firm's marginal costs equal the obtainable price. This market condition is the point of equilibrium.

Figure 11

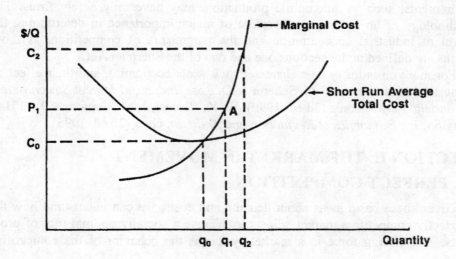

If each of the firms in the competitive industry follows this decision rule, then we can obtain a market supply curve by adding up the quantities produced by each firm at any given price. For example if there were one hundred identical firms in the industry and a price P_1 prevailed as in Figure 11, then the market supply of this product at price P_1 would be 100 q_1. If price rose to C_2 then market supply would rise to 100 q_2. The industry supply curve is traced out in Figure 12.

Figure 12

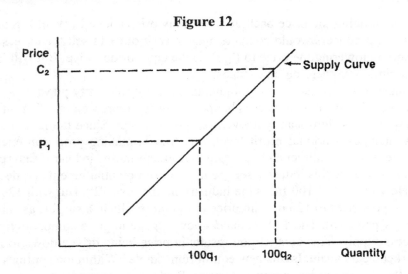

We are now ready to explain the adjustment process of a competitive market. As discussed above, consumers express their desires for goods and services in the marketplace by their willingness and ability to pay for items. This information is summarized in the schedule of quantities demanded at various price levels — the demand curve. Producers express their willingness to provide products at various prices by adjusting output in order to maximize their profits. This information is expressed in the supply curve. By combining these two curves an equilibrium price and quantity can be ascertained.

Figure 13 contains two diagrams. Panel (a) is a reproduction of Figure 11 which presents the cost curves for a representative firm in the industry. Panel (b)

Figure 13

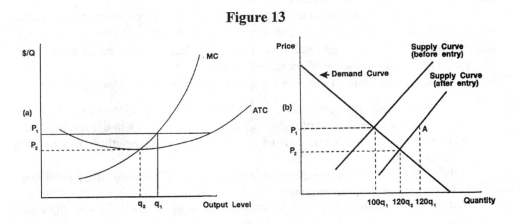

is a reproduction of Figure 12 with the addition of a market demand curve. Referring to panel (b) it is seen that price P_1 is the price that initially "clears the market." That is, any price below P_1 would result in a shortage of the product and consumers bidding the price back up to P_1. Any price above P_1 would result in a surplus and producers would compete against each other to sell the excess products, thereby lowering the price to P_1. P_1 is the equilibrium price. But will P_1 prevail indefinitely in these circumstances?

The answer to this question highlights the integral role entry plays in a market system. At price P_1, notice what is happening to the representative firm in panel (a). First, price is significantly above average total cost. Since the latter quantity already includes a normal profit level, this firm is making profits in excess of what is necessary to attract and maintain investment in this industry. Enterprising individuals outside this industry see the high profit potential herein and decide to enter. Now instead of 100 firms the industry might have 120. But with 120 firms market supply rises to 120 q_1 with price at P_1 and results in a surplus as shown at point A of panel (b). The 120 producers now engage in price competition to sell the excess supply. This competition results in price being driven down to P_2 and the market clears again. Is this new equilibrium stable? Within the confines of the model the answer is yes because at price P_2 the representative firm no longer makes extraordinary profits. Thus the inducement for further entry is gone and price will stay at P_2 so long as the demand and cost structures remain steady. In the real world, however, no market remains in equilibrium for long. Markets are subject to almost daily shocks — new technology and new uses for products, seasonal changes, wars, famines, and the weather can upset the market's balance and force it to seek a new equilibrium.

If demand conditions change, resulting in a shift to the left of the market demand curve, price would fall. This in turn would result in economic losses to the firm and ultimately cause some firms to exit the market or reduce their output. In turn the reduction in total market output shifts the supply curve leftward and moves price up. Exit ceases when price reaches P_2.

P_2 is the stable equilibrium price because it is the only price where there are no economic profits or losses. Note further that price P_2 causes the firm to operate at the minimum of the average total cost curve. This has positive performance implications that will be discussed more fully below.

To summarize the market mechanism briefly consider the following outline:

1. Consumers choose goods that satisfy their personal preferences.
2. Consumers reveal these preference by making purchases in the marketplace.
3. Producers choose a quantity of output that maximizes their profits at a given price.
4. If profits are above necessary levels in a given industry other producers are attracted into the industry.
5. The excess supply at the high price forces producers to compete for sales; the result is that price is reduced so as to eliminate above normal profits.
6. The resulting equilibrium point is where marginal costs equal price.
7. The outcome is that products are supplied at prices which reflect minimum costs.

B. MONOPOLY

Consider next a monopoly. By definition there is only one firm producing the product in question and, for purposes of analysis, assume that there is no possibility of competitive entry. Even the monopolist faces a certain kind of "competition" — that is, it is unable to charge an infinite price for its product. However, the monopolist may be able to charge more than the competitive price without losing so many sales that the price increase is unprofitable. Assume that the monopolist desires to maximize profits and that it must charge all customers the same price. Since the monopolist is the only firm in the industry the market demand curve is also the firm demand curve. The monopolist must choose how much to produce and also what price to charge. Figure 14 illustrates this point.

First, some explanation of the curve labeled "marginal revenue" is in order. Marginal revenue is the amount a seller receives by selling an additional unit, as opposed to marginal costs, which is the additional cost that the producer incurs in making one additional unit. Because the monopolist is unable to charge higher prices to those people willing to pay them and at the same time lower prices to others, each reduction in price loses some revenue that could have been earned from people willing to pay the higher price. Thus for a one dollar reduction in selling price the change in revenue is the difference between the new price times the new quantity and the old quantity times the old price.

What quantity of output will the monopolist choose so as to maximize profits? Consider the output level Q_0. If one more unit of output is produced at this point it would have to be sold at a loss since marginal cost exceeds marginal revenue just to the right of point Q_0. If one less unit were produced the monopolist would be missing an opportunity to increase profit because just to the left of point Q_0 marginal revenue exceeds marginal cost. Therefore the point Q_0 must be the profit maximizing output; the point where marginal revenue equals marginal cost.

The monopolist's profits are represented by the shaded box in Figure 14.

Figure 14

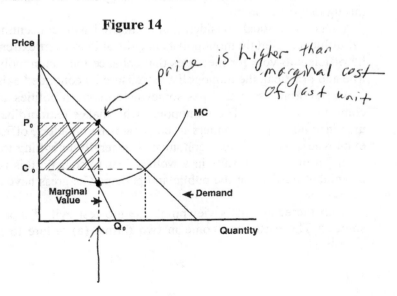

price is higher than marginal cost of last unit

Those profits will continue because there is no competitive entry.

The monopoly price-output decision can be summarized as follows:

1. Consumers choose goods that satisfy their personal preferences.
2. These preferences are revealed by actual purchases of products.
3. The monopolist's downward sloping demand curve indicates that it can charge more by reducing output.
4. The monopolist maximizes its profits by choosing an output level that equates marginal cost to marginal revenue.
5. Profits can remain at supracompetitive levels because competitive entry is foreclosed.
6. The outcome is that products are supplied at prices higher than costs, and higher than prices in competitive markets, and market output is lower than it would be in a competitive market.

These same effects occur when competitors form a cartel and set the price or output by agreement.

C. RELATIVE PERFORMANCES OF COMPETITION AND MONOPOLY

What is wrong with monopoly? Why are "competitive" markets generally preferred to monopoly? The answers to these questions involve both economic and noneconomic considerations and values. The latter will be discussed first.

Monopoly industrial structure results in a concentration of power unknown to most competitive markets. The structure of a competitive market decentralizes and disperses power because competitive markets contain many firms each acting in its own self-interest. On the other hand a monopoly capitalist social structure places a great deal of reliance on the decisions of a single firm and its managers. If these individuals make errors in judgment the consequences reverberate throughout the economy.

A second political consideration associated with concentrated power is political influence. Certain monopolists may be able to exert extreme pressure on public officials to vote for measures that enhance their monopoly position. If this is true and practical, the monopolist can ensure its continued existence.

An important issue that lies somewhere between politics and economics is income redistribution. The monopolist who makes extraordinary profits redistributes income from consumers to corporate shareholders, officers, and perhaps to employees. Although the economist is generally unwilling to say that this redistribution of wealth results in a welfare loss to society, this is probably the most prominent reason that the public and perhaps Congress have condemned monopoly power.

From the economist's viewpoint, the greatest evil of monopoly is wasted resources. The waste can come in two forms: (a) failure to produce the "right" quantity of goods at minimum price and (b) the wasted resources the monopolist spends creating or preserving its monopoly position.

A competitive market is said to be allocatively efficient because in equilibrium the market price equals the marginal cost of production. This means that in an economy where consumers dictate the mix of goods to be produced, by comparing their preferences for additional units of each good to the costs of additional units, it is imperative that accurate information regarding costs be communicated to the public. In most circumstances, the only piece of information that is available about the costs of production is the product price. Therefore, product price must reflect the cost of additional production. In short, price must equal marginal cost. If price is held above marginal cost then the consumer is receiving inaccurate signals and will make suboptimal choices. There will be less of the product produced than is socially desirable and more of some less desirable product will be produced. Figure 15 illustrates the point. For purposes of this comparison, assume that the firm has the same costs per unit of output, no matter how much it produces. This assumption will be discussed at length below.

The monopoly output in this case is q_m and the price charged is P_m. Society is being told that the cost to produce an additional unit of output is P_m when in fact it is P_c. The competitive solution results in price stabilizing at the minimum of the average total cost curve. At this price a quantity of q_c is produced. Thus the monopolist restricts output relative to the competitive market and charges a higher price. Resources are wasted in the sense that they are diverted to less socially desirable ends.

Figure 15

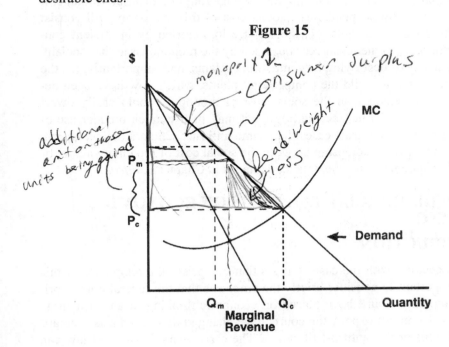

The other form of wasted resources is a result not of monopoly pricing, but of monopoly conduct. In the model it was assumed that entry by potential competitors into the market controlled by the monopolist is impossible. As a general rule that is not the case in real markets. In fact, the monopolist's high profits will be more attractive to people with capital to invest than the available profits in competitive markets. All things being equal, the investor would like to put her money where profits are the highest. The monopolist, by contrast, would prefer that the investor look somewhere else.

If a monopoly is worth $1,000,000 per year in monopoly profits to a particular firm, that firm will be willing to spend any amount up to $1,000,000 to exclude potential rivals from the market. In short, at the outer limit, the shaded box in Figure 14 does not represent monopoly profits at all, but money spent by the monopolist in order to exclude potential rivals. Some of this money might be spent in socially useful ways, such as cost-justified research and investment. Much of it may be spent in harmful ways, however: predatory pricing, false advertising, espionage or sabotage, or perhaps bribery or lobbying. It is possible that the social waste caused by these entry deterring practices is far larger than the social waste caused by monopoly pricing itself.

A third important social cost of monopoly that is often overlooked, because the economic model we have described does not account for it, is the social cost that results from the injuries that monopolistic exclusionary practices impose on others — most frequently the monopolist's competitors. To take an extreme example, suppose that a firm creates a monopoly by engaging in industrial sabotage: it dynamites its competitors' plants. The social cost of this monopoly will consist of three quite distinct elements: (1) the welfare loss caused by inefficient consumer substitutions; (2) the resources consumed by the monopolist in the (socially inefficient) activity of destroying its competitors' plants; and, importantly, (3) the social resources used to build the competitors' plants, which now have been destroyed. This third element in the social cost of monopoly could easily dwarf elements (1) and (2). Further, accounting for it may justify much broader use of competitor lawsuits in antitrust cases than some antitrust scholars believe appropriate. For more on the relationship between the social cost of monopoly and optimal rules of enforcement, see the note on damages in Chapter 3, *infra.*

SECTION III. JUDICIAL EMPHASIS ON ECONOMIC REASONING

A. INTRODUCTION

Before proceeding with the case analysis that comprises the remainder of this book, it is important to consider briefly the emphasis that the federal courts, primarily the Supreme Court, have placed on economic thinking in antitrust jurisprudence. As one might expect, the courts have changed their emphasis dramatically over the history of antitrust litigation. The early years of antitrust law can be characterized as years of socio-political concern. The emphasis of antitrust analysis was on fairness and equality in business dealings. The populist political tenor of the times condemned large enterprises because they threatened the fabric of a free society — the small business. The idea is ably presented by Judge Hand's oft-quoted passage from *United States v. Aluminum Co. of Am.*, 148 F.2d 416, 428-29 (2d Cir. 1945).

> We have been speaking only of the economic reasons which forbid mono-poly; but, as we have already implied, there are others, based upon the belief that great industrial consolidations are inherently undesirable, regardless of their economic results. In the debates in Congress Senator Sherman himself ... showed that among the purposes of Congress in 1890 was a desire to put an end to great aggregations of capital because of the helplessness of the individual before them.... Throughout the history of these statutes it has been constantly assumed that one of their purposes was to perpetuate and pre-serve, for its own sake and in spite of possible cost, an organization of in-dustry in small units which can effectively compete with each other.

B. STRUCTURALIST ANALYSIS

Historically, federal antitrust policy has been dominated by an industrial organi-zation theory called "structuralism." The premise of the structuralist approach is that the structure of the industry (basically the number and size distribution of the firms in the industry) *determines* the conduct and behavior of firms. The conduct in turn determines the economic performance of the industry in terms of prices, product quality, and output levels. For example, the majority opinion in *United States v. Container Corp. of Am.*, 393 U.S. 333 (1969), places great emphasis on the competitive consequences of markets dominated by a few sellers in the con-text of price information exchanges:

> Price information exchanged in some markets may have no effect on a truly competitive price. But the corrugated containers industry is dominated by relatively few sellers.... The inferences are irresistible that the exchange of price information has had an anticompetitive effect in the industry, chilling the vigor of price competition.

393 U.S. at 337. There was no finding of a formal agreement to fix prices. The Court reasoned, nevertheless, that the oligopolistic structure of the industry made price fixing likely. Thus any conduct that had the effect of facilitating the fixing of prices within a highly concentrated industry structure was said to be repugnant to public policy.

Structuralism in antitrust has been severely qualified by our knowledge that markets can vary greatly in their details but that the fact finding abilities of an antitrust tribunal, such as a court, are severely limited. For example, general prin-ciples of economic theory tell us that when a substantial portion of the market is shared by a few firms these firms will recognize their interdependence and act

accordingly. But how many firms are a few? Are all actions by oligopolists pernicious? Does every firm in a concentrated market actually act as the model predicts? The most famous economic expression of structuralism is the "Structure-
Conduct-Performance Paradigm," which holds that highly concentrated market
structures necessarily lead to anticompetitive conduct, which in turn leads to poor
economic performance. The merits of the Structure-Conduct-Performance Paradigm are discussed more fully in Chapter 6 on monopolization and Chapter 7
on merger policy, *infra. See also* H. Hovenkamp, *Federal Antitrust Policy* § 1.7
(2d ed. 1994).

Most significantly, the implications of forced changes in industry structure are
usually unclear. If firms are subject to significant economies of scale, judicial
intervention breaking up large firms may make the firms *behave* more competitively, by pricing closer to marginal costs. But their marginal costs could be significantly higher, given their smaller size.

C. EFFICIENCY ANALYSIS

At odds with the structuralist theory is the efficiency or Chicago school theory
of industrial organization. The framework of this economic analysis is price theory as described in the first sections of this chapter. The underlying assumption is
that the interaction of supply and demand will determine a set of prices that
maximize society's economic welfare. The profit-maximizing firm will seek
cost-reducing production techniques in order to enhance its own market position
and in so doing inadvertently improve economic welfare by charging lower
prices. Monopoly power is limited, even for the firm with a high market share, by
a vanguard of potential entrants ready, willing, and able to enter the industry if
profit levels are attractive. Thus, under this view of the market an economy
dominated by a few large firms could indeed be socially optimal because (a) the
large firms achieve production efficiency through economies of scale, and (b) the
problems of allocative efficiency are eliminated by potential entry, because each
firm knows that it will face additional competition if it charges too high a price.
This view thus rejects the Structure-Conduct-Performance Paradigm, arguing
instead that performance causes concentration, rather than vice-versa. Firms become big because they are innovative and do better than their competitors. As a
result, high concentration in a market may be as much a sign of vigorous, innovative behavior as of anticompetitiveness. *See* James W. Meehan, Jr. & Robert J.
Larner, "The Structural School, Its Critics, and Its Progeny: An Assessment," in
Economics and Antitrust Policy (Robert J. Larner & James W. Meehan, Jr., eds.
New York: Quorum, 1989), at 182.

Recall the previous discussion of monopoly output and pricing decisions. In
the absence of potential entry the monopolist will set prices above marginal cost
and thereby produce less of the product than socially desirable. This condition
was referred to as allocative inefficiency. If it is assumed, however, that potential
entry is easy, and can be accomplished in a short time, then the allocative effi-

ciency problem is no longer pressing because entrants limit the monopolist's pricing prerogatives. This is to say that the potential entry causes the monopolist's demand curve to become more elastic and closer to that of a competitive firm. The implications of easy entry, as well as problems of measurement, are discussed in both Chapter 7 on mergers and Chapter 9 on deregulation and its antitrust implications, *infra*.

The policy prescription of those who endorse the efficiency theory is as follows. If the conduct under scrutiny leads to lower potential costs and thus to lower prices to consumers then the conduct should not be found unlawful. This analysis has received considerable but not unanimous acceptance in the courts. See especially the cases discussed in Chapter 6, *infra*. For example, in *Telex Corp. v. IBM Corp.*, 510 F.2d 894 (10th Cir.), *cert. dismissed*, 423 U.S. 802 (1975), the court of appeals reversed a finding of the district court that IBM had engaged in predatory behavior by lowering prices on its peripheral equipment. The court adopted the efficiency theory, stating, "The record shows, during the period under consideration, that the parties and others in the market produced more advanced products better suited to the needs of customers at lower prices." 510 F.2d at 926. Under the efficiency methodology better products at lower prices is the *sine qua non* of legality.

The differences between the structuralist and efficiency schools of thought are more profound than is apparent from reading the material above. The efficiency school has a deeply held belief that competition will work even though only a few firms dominate the industry. Structuralists are much more suspicious, believing that a monopolist can do nothing other than act as a monopolist. Likewise, a group of oligopolists can do nothing other than act like a shared monopoly.

The debate continues both in the literature and the process of federal judicial appointments. As a consequence, analytical inconsistencies emerge in the case law and must ultimately be rationalized. For example, the Supreme Court decision in *Eastman Kodak Co. v. Image Technical Servs., Inc.*, 504 U.S. 451 (1992), reprinted in Chapter 5, reflects a deep-seated suspicion about dominant firms in product differentiated markets — largely the consequence of a structuralist approach. By contrast, the Supreme Court's decision only a year later in *Brooke Group Ltd. v. Brown & Williamson Tobacco Corp.*, 509 U.S. 209 (1993), reprinted in Chapter 6, reflects the Chicago School view that even highly concentrated markets are likely to reflect substantial amounts of competition.

D. STRATEGIC BEHAVIOR ANALYSIS

A third approach that attempts to assimilate aspects of the other two is called the strategic behavior approach. It recognizes that structuralists probably err in placing too little emphasis on technological efficiencies and that the efficiency school ignores the dangers of increased market concentration, strategic creation of barriers to entry, and strategic raising of rivals' costs. This approach attempts to balance the conflicting aspects of a given business practice in order to assess the net competitive effect of any challenged conduct. The Federal Trade Commission case, *In re E.I. du Pont*, 96 F.T.C. 650 (1980), is a good example of this approach. The Commission concluded that it was essential to the analysis that it "weigh the relative competitive virtues and evils of dominant firm behavior even in the monopoly context." Note that this approach allows not only the efficiency defenses but also evidence of exclusionary effects of strategic planning. Perhaps most importantly, the approach attempts to incorporate the insights of game theory, which are just beginning to make their way into antitrust analysis.

Insofar as policy is concerned, the strategic approach to antitrust adjudication places a great deal of faith in the ability of courts to weigh competing economic models and make enlightened decisions that effectively determine the future structure of the United States economy. Increased emphasis is placed on expert economic testimony in trying to ascertain the viability of potential competition, the scale required for efficient production, the concentration of industry, the most likely responses of profit-maximizing firms, and other matters relevant to a full economic inquiry into strategic possibilities. Increasingly, courts focus on the economics of opportunistic behavior, the costs of consumer switching, and information costs. Whether these are fruitful avenues of inquiry remains to be seen, but for the time being at least they cannot be ignored.

BIBLIOGRAPHY AND COLLATERAL READINGS

Books

ABA (E.T. Sullivan, ed.), Nonprice Predation Under Section 2 of the Sherman Act (A.B.A. 1991).

R. Blair & D. Kaserman, Antitrust Economics (1985).

M. Eisner, Antitrust and the Triumph of Economics (1991).

E. Gellhorn & W. Kovacic, Antitrust Law and Economics 45-78 (4th ed. 1994).

A. Hirschman, Rival Views of Market Society (1988).

J. Hirshleifer, Price Theory and Applications (3d ed. 1984).

H. Hovenkamp, Federal Antitrust Policy, chs. 1-2 (2d ed. 1994).

A. Jacquemin, The New Industrial Organization: Market Forces and Strategic Behavior (1987).

E. Mansfield, Microeconomics: Theory & Applications (8th ed. 1995).

S. Ross, Principles of Antitrust Law (1993).

R. Schmallensee & R. Willig, eds., Handbook of Industrial Organization (1989).

F.M. Sherer & D. Ross, Industrial Market Structure and Economic Performance (3d ed. 1990).

E.T. Sullivan & J. Harrison, Understanding Antitrust and Its Economic Implications (3d ed. 1998).

W. K. Viscusi, J. M. Vernon, & J. E. Harrington, Jr., Economics of Regulation and Antitrust (2d ed. 1995).

Articles

Carstensen, Antitrust Law and the Paradigm of Industrial Organization, 16 U.C. Davis L. Rev. 487 (1983).

Fox, The Politics of Law and Economics in Judicial Decision Making: Antitrust as a Window, 61 N.Y.U. L. Rev. 554 (1986).

Gellhorn, An Introduction to Antitrust Economics, 1975 Duke L.J. 1.

Gerla, A Micro-Microeconomic Approach to Antitrust Law: Games Managers Play, 86 Mich. L. Rev. 892 (1988).

Harrison, Egoism, Altruism, and Market Illusions: The Limits of Law and Economics, 33 UCLA L. Rev. 1309 (1986).

Krattenmaker & Salop, Anticompetitive Exclusion: Raising Rivals' Costs to Achieve Power Over Price, 96 Yale L.J. 209 (1986).

McCloskey, The Rhetoric of Law and Economics, 86 Mich. L. Rev. 752 (1988).

Posner, Some Uses and Abuses of Economics in Law, 46 U. Chi. L. Rev. 281 (1979).

White, Countervailing Power: Different Rules for Different Markets?, 41 Duke L.J. 1045 (1992).

Chapter 3

SPECIAL PROBLEMS OF ANTITRUST ENFORCEMENT

SECTION I. ENFORCEMENT

A. TRIPARTITE APPROACH

The antitrust and trade regulation laws are enforced by the United States Department of Justice, the Federal Trade Commission (FTC), and private individuals or entities. In addition, state attorneys general have authority under section 4C of the Clayton Act to bring federal antitrust suits as *parens patriae* on behalf of natural persons residing within the state. Most states also have enacted statutes patterned after the federal antitrust and trade regulation laws.

The responsibility for enforcement of antitrust by the two federal agencies has been divided. The Antitrust Division of the Department of Justice is charged with enforcing the Sherman, Clayton, and Robinson-Patman Acts, through either civil or criminal prosecution. The FTC is the sole enforcer of the Federal Trade Commission Act with the exception of section 12, and has concurrent jurisdiction with the Antitrust Division over sections 2, 3, 7, and 8 of the Clayton Act. Since both agencies have jurisdiction over the Clayton Act, they have adopted informal clearance procedures which are to be invoked before an investigation begins. *See* Trade Reg. Rep. (CCH) ¶9565.05.

1. DEPARTMENT OF JUSTICE

The Antitrust Division of the Department of Justice, together with the offices of the United States Attorneys, is delegated the authority to enforce the antitrust laws. The enforcement can be through either civil or criminal means. Sections 1, 2, and 3 of the Sherman Act, section 3 of the Robinson-Patman Act, and section 14 of the Clayton Act all contain criminal penalties. Only the Department of Justice can seek criminal sanctions under any of these statutes. A violation of section 12 of the FTC Act may also be a criminal violation; therefore, it is enforced by the Department. In addition, the Department may bring civil suits under sections 1, 2, and 3 of the Sherman Act. Sections 2, 3, 7, and 8 of the Clayton Act, as amended by the Robinson-Patman Act, provide only for civil suits with enforcement either by the Antitrust Division or the FTC.

a. Civil Action

In investigating a civil charge, the Antitrust Division may discover and examine records of a business under investigation by issuing a civil investigative demand

(CID) before a formal complaint has been filed. This means of compulsory process was first permitted in 1962 under the Antitrust Civil Process Act. 15 U.S.C. §§ 1311-1314. The original Act required that there be reason to believe that a "company" was in control or possession of documents relevant to the investigation. Section 3 of the Act required that before a CID could be enforced the company to which it was directed must have been "under investigation" and the material sought to be discovered must have been relevant to the ongoing investigation. An individual's records were not subject to scrutiny under the original revision of the Act. Under the Hart-Scott-Rodino Antitrust Improvements Act of 1976, however, the Department may use a CID to discover information from individuals and third parties.

The enforcement of a CID is analogous to that of a subpoena duces tecum issued by a grand jury. Moreover, its scope is similar to that permitted under the Federal Rules of Civil Procedure. The information obtained through the CID cannot be turned over to the FTC, but it can be used by the Department in any related civil or criminal proceeding, including use before a grand jury. A CID enforcement suit must be brought in the federal district court where the target company is found or transacts business, or if it transacts business in more than one district, where its principal place of business is located.

After a civil suit has been filed, the Department can use the Federal Rules of Civil Procedure to acquire discoverable material. The civil action can be initiated for either injunctive relief under section 4 of the Sherman Act and section 15 of the Clayton Act, or damages under section 4A of the Clayton Act if the United States government itself was injured by the violation. If the Department files a civil suit to recover damages, it is entitled to claim the same as that allowable to private parties when injured by reason of a price-fixing scheme.

Under section 4B of the Clayton Act, the statute of limitation for a civil antitrust action for damages is four years from the time the claim for relief "accrues." Since suits for injunctive relief are equitable in nature, no statute of limitation governs the commencement of the suit. The equitable argument of laches does apply to an action for injunctive or other equitable relief brought by private parties but not generally to equitable suits brought by the government.

b. Criminal Prosecutions

A criminal proceeding is generally commenced by the Antitrust Division through use of a grand jury to investigate allegations of antitrust violations. The grand jury has authority to investigate alleged violations of sections 1 and 2 of the Sherman Act, and section 3 of the Robinson-Patman Act. If conviction for a Sherman Act violation is obtained after grand jury indictment, it is considered a felony, and fines up to $350,000 for an individual and up to $10 million dollars for a corporation may be imposed, as well as prison terms for individuals up to three years. 15 U.S.C. §§ 1 and 2. Violation of the criminal provision of section 3 of the Robinson-Patman Act can yield a fine up to $5,000 and a prison term up to one year. 15 U.S.C. § 21e. This provision has seldom been enforced. Indeed, the Department of Justice has not enforced any part of the Robinson-Patman Act in nearly two decades.

The United States Sentencing Commission has had an increasingly important role to play in establishing antitrust sentencing guidelines. The new guidelines apply to market allocations, bid rigging, and cartel price fixing schemes. Although the sentencing guidelines are complicated to apply and contain quantitative calculations, they do provide qualitative benchmarks. For example, in a price fixing case, the sentencing judge will consider, among other issues, two factors: (1) the amount of the increase of the artificially inflated price and (2) the injury to the consumer who did not buy the product at the inflated, higher price. *See generally* 56 Fed. Reg. 22762 (1991).

The federal sentencing guidelines, which guide federal judges in sentencing convicted violators of federal criminal statutes, distinguish between price fixing and bid rigging. Before the sentencing guidelines were enacted, "bid rigging" did not constitute a distinct offense but was "merely a descriptive term for a subset of price fixing cases." Many cases used the terms "bid rigging," "bid rotation," and "noncompetitive bidding" interchangeably. In *United States v. Heffernan*, 43 F.3d 1144, 1146 (7th Cir. 1994), the Seventh Circuit held that since the purchasers were private firms, not public entities, and since sealed bidding was not used in the conduct at issue, it was indistinguishable from price fixing and thus not entitled to the enhanced sentence contemplated by the sentencing guidelines for bid rigging. Bid rigging is given a higher sentence than price fixing because bid rigging disproportionately affects government agencies due to the frequent use of sealed bids, particularly when the bidding is on a fixed quantity of products.

Do you see why bid rigging is more dangerous than the general run of price fixes? When firms rig a bid and the winning bid is opened, all the cartel members know immediately whether one of their number "cheated" by supplying a lower bid than previously agreed. As a result, cartels in bidding markets where the winning bid is publicly announced are particularly susceptible to collusion. Since the government often purchases in this manner, it is a particularly vulnerable victim. In the more general run of price fixes, particularly where prices are discretely negotiated between buyer and seller, a firm could cheat on the cartel for a long period without getting caught. This makes cartels in such markets less stable.

United States v. Nippon Paper Indus. Co., 109 F.3d 1 (1st Cir. 1997), *cert. denied*, 118 S. Ct. 685 (1998), held that price fixing that had occurred entirely in Japan could be the subject of a United States criminal indictment. Nippon and unnamed co-conspirators were accused of fixing the price of facsimile paper sold in North America, including the United States. The relevant meetings culminating in the challenged agreement all occurred in Japan. The alleged agreement was apparently facilitated with resale price maintenance agreements under which firms purchasing the paper in Japan promised to resell it at specified minimum prices in North America. Nippon then allegedly monitored resale prices within the United States in order to ensure that the maintained price was the one actually charged.

In concluding that the criminal jurisdiction of the federal antitrust laws could reach conduct abroad just as the civil jurisdiction could, the court stated that "one datum sticks out like a sore thumb" — namely, "in both criminal and civil cases, the claim that Section One applies extraterritorially is based on the same language in the same section of the same statute..." and

> common sense suggests that courts should interpret the same language in the same section of the same statute uniformly, regardless of whether the impetus for interpretation is criminal or civil....

The court rejected the defendant's argument that the lack of any precedent made the assertion of criminal liability improper — that is, the case law failed to give the foreign actor fair notice that its wholly extraterritorial act might subject it to criminal antitrust prosecution. But as the court noted, while there is little in the way of *antitrust* precedent for applying a United States criminal statute to extraterritorial conduct, there was ample precedent from other statutes. For example, the manufacturing and sale of addictive drugs abroad targeting United States markets has frequently been condemned under criminal statutes notwithstanding that the defendants performed no acts within the United States.

Perhaps the most important rationale for expansive reach and even criminal punishment in such cases is that the sovereign representing purchasers has a significantly greater interest at stake than the sovereign representing sellers. As a general matter, a cartel in one country fixing the price of its goods elsewhere transfers wealth away from the territory containing the buyers and toward the territory containing the sellers. As a result, sovereigns including the United States itself have typically been less concerned with condemning restraints on export trade where all the buyers are foreign, than with restraints on imports.

Venue Rule 18 of the Federal Rules of Criminal Procedure provides that suit is to be brought in the district where the offense is committed. Service of the summons or warrant may be nationwide. Removal of the suit under Rule 21 from the district where the offense was committed is possible if the district presents "so great a prejudice against the defendant" that a fair trial is not possible.

The statute of limitation governing a criminal antitrust violation requires that suit must be commenced within five years from the date of the offense. 18 U.S.C. § 3282. Whatever act triggers the substantive violation will also start the statute of limitation running. For a conspiracy which is continuing in nature, the statute commences to run from the last act in furtherance of the conspiracy.

The Department has frequently announced that criminal prosecution will be directed only at per se violations, such as price fixing, where the legality of the challenged conduct is unquestioned, and to cases where the defendant has willfully violated the law. This standard of prosecution has become problematic in recent years, however, as the per se classification has undergone reevaluation and reformulation. The Department has announced that the following special circumstances: "in which criminal sanctions might not be used even in *per se* cases are: 1) confusion of law; 2) truly novel issues of law or fact; 3) confusion caused by past prosecutorial decisions; or 4) clear evidence that defendants did not appreciate the consequences of their actions." Remarks by John H. Shenefeld, "Antitrust Division Enforcement Policy," to the Federal Bar Association, Cleveland (April 18, 1979).

2. FEDERAL TRADE COMMISSION

The FTC, together with the Antitrust Division, has authority to enforce the Clayton Act's civil provisions. It also has primary authority over the FTC Act, section 5 of which prohibits unfair methods of competition and unfair or deceptive acts or practices. The agency mission is divided between antitrust enforcement (Bureau of Competition) and consumer protection (Bureau of Consumer Protection). It carries out its enforcement role through case-by-case adjudication or industry-wide rulemaking. Traditionally the FTC, composed of five Commissioners appointed by the President, functions through its power to issue cease and desist orders, which are enforced through civil penalties and court injunctions. The Commission's authority is exercised through administrative proceedings. Under section 13(a), the Commission can also initiate civil actions in federal district courts to obtain injunctive relief for the maintenance of the status quo pending the outcome of an administrative hearing.

The FTC has broad power to conduct investigations under section 6 of the FTC Act. *See* 16 C.F.R. § 2.1 et seq. (1988). Pursuant to its investigative powers, the Commission can issue subpoenas under section 9 for allegations of unfair methods of competition during the precomplaint investigation stage. Moreover, since 1980 its precomplaint investigation of competition issues under section 5(a) of the Act is governed by procedures akin to the Department of Justice's CID process. For example, a CID is the only "form of compulsory process issued in investigations with respect to unfair or deceptive acts." 16 C.F.R. § 2.7, 15 U.S.C. § 576-1 (1988 Supp.). It also can require the attendance and testimony of a witness at a precomplaint investigative hearing conducted by a Commission staff member authorized to administer oaths. Failure to comply with a FTC subpoena can lead to fines up to $5,000, or up to one year's imprisonment, or both.

Acting through its Commissioners, the FTC commences administrative adjudicative proceedings by issuing a complaint, setting forth a factual statement of the acts or practices alleged to be in violation of the law together with the legal authority for the action. 16 C.F.R. § 3.11 (1988). After completion of discovery, and if summary judgment has not been granted, an adjudicative hearing is held before an administrative law judge appointed by the Commission. The Commission is represented by staff counsel, called complaint counsel. After the hearing, the administrative law judge is required to file an "initial decision" within ninety days. On filing the initial decision, the jurisdiction of the administrative law judge is terminated. Under section 5(b) of the Act, an appeal of the initial decision comes before the five Commissioners. A respondent, but not complaint counsel, may appeal a decision by the Commission to the United States Court of Appeals. The standard of review is whether the findings and conclusions are supported by substantial evidence in the record.

If the Commission's final cease and desist order is upheld or not appealed, the FTC has authority to seek enforcement and civil penalties in federal district court for "knowing violations." The penalties for each violation may be up to $10,000, with a provision that a continuing failure to comply is considered to be a separate violation for each day of noncompliance.

As of 1975, the FTC also has authority to represent itself, either by commencing or defending an action in court, rather than having the Department of Justice as its counsel. Cases in which such authority exists include: (1) injunctions in false advertising cases, (2) judicial review of a rule promulgated by the FTC, (3) judicial review of a cease and desist order, (4) subpoena enforcement, (5) consumer redress cases (section 19), and (6) cases involving collection of civil penalties.

The Commission, in addition to its adjudicative power, has adopted formal rulemaking procedures for the promulgation of industry-wide trade regulation rules. The authority to make rules and regulations is under section 6(g) of the FTC Act. *See* 16 C.F.R. §§ 1.7 and 1.22 (1988). Notice of proposed rules is given in the Federal Register and interested parties are permitted participation in the rulemaking through submission of written and/or oral argument. 16 C.F.R. § 1.11. The Commission, in connection with its rulemaking, may conduct investigations, studies, conferences, and hearings. 16 C.F.R. §§ 1.13 and 1.26.

Rulemaking, other than of rules of practice and procedure, generally has been reserved for consumer protection issues rather than antitrust competition issues. But nothing in the rulemaking authority explicitly limits the FTC's power in this regard. *See National Petr. Refs. Ass'n v. FTC*, 482 F.2d 671 (D.C. Cir. 1973), *cert. denied*, 415 U.S. 951 (1974); 120 Cong. Rec. 41407 (1974) (remarks of Rep. Broyhill, Conference Manager of the Magnuson-Moss Warranty FTC Improvement Act); 15 U.S.C. § 57a(a)(2) (1976).

3. PRIVATE SUITS

Section 4 of the Clayton Act provides that any person, whether an individual, business entity, or government, who has been injured in its "business or property" by reason of an antitrust violation may sue to recover treble damages, costs of the suit, and attorney's fees. 15 U.S.C. § 15. *See generally* Lande, *Are Antitrust "Treble" Damages Really Single Damages?*, 54 Ohio St. L.J. 115 (1993) (arguing that, as a result of numerous limitations, antitrust treble damages are really only "single" damages — only equal to or even less than the actual damages caused by antitrust violations). *See generally* D. Floyd and E. Thomas Sullivan, *Private Antitrust Actions* § 6 (1996).

Once a violation, causation, and injury have been found, the award of attorney's fees, costs, and treble damages is mandatory. The trial judge or jury have no discretion to modify it. Indeed, the jury is not even informed of the trebling procedure. The trial judge automatically multiplies the damage award by three. *Pollock & Riley, Inc. v. Pearl Brewing Co.*, 498 F.2d 1240 (5th Cir. 1974), *cert. denied sub nom. Gulf Oil Corp. v. Wood*, 420 U.S. 992 (1975). This provision was designed to create deterrence from violations, monetary incentives to sue for violations, and compensation to victims. Since 1914 and the adoption of section 16 of the Clayton Act, injunctive relief is also available for threatened loss or damage. 15 U.S.C. § 26 (1988 Supp.). Section 16 also gives attorney's fees to a prevailing plaintiff. *See Blue Cross and Blue Shield of Wis. v. Marshfield Clinic*, ___ F.3d ___ (7th Cir. 1998) (plaintiff who could not prove damages had an "inadequate remedy at law" and could thus still obtain an injunction).

One study demonstrates dramatically the influence of private antitrust actions in the development of the law. The 1985 Georgetown Study of Private Antitrust Litigation found that the filing of private cases outnumbered government cases twenty-to-one from the mid 1960s until the late 1970s. Until 1965, the ratio was six-to-one. In the 1980s the ratio was ten-to-one.

The Georgetown Study surveyed filed cases in 1973-1983 in five district courts — Manhattan, Chicago, San Francisco, Kansas City, and Atlanta. The Sherman Act was the most frequently cited statute. Less than one-fifth involved Robinson-Patman actions. Only six percent implicated mergers under section 7 of the Clayton Act. The most frequent allegations were horizontal price fixing and refusals to deal. Tying arrangements or exclusive dealing were next, followed by price discrimination. The largest category of plaintiffs was downstream entities — dealers, franchises, and licensees. Competitors were the next largest group to sue. Predictably, "dealers are overwhelmingly the parties who allege illegal dealer terminations; competitors are the main parties who allege predatory pricing; dealers are the main parties who allege vertical price fixing." In addition, "competitors challenged mergers two to one over suppliers, dealers or customers".

The study found that "the average case lasted slightly over two years; the median case lasted less than a year and a half." Typically antitrust cases are longer than other federal cases, but three-quarters of the cases settled. In those cases achieving final judgment, plaintiffs prevailed in less than 30%. The authors of the Study, Professor Salop of Georgetown University and Professor White of New York University, concluded that the "current total annual costs of private antitrust litigation are probably in the range of $250 million." *See* Salop & White, *Economic Analysis of Private Antitrust Litigation*, 74 Geo. L.J. 201 (1986).

In order to maintain a private antitrust action, a plaintiff must demonstrate a causal connection among the following: (1) injury suffered, (2) to business or property, by (3) the violation of an antitrust law. *Brunswick Corp. v. Pueblo Bowl-O-Mat, Inc.*, 429 U.S. 477 (1977). The "antitrust" laws included within the meaning of section 4 of the Clayton Act are: (1) sections 1, 2, and 3 of the

Sherman Act, (2) section 2(a)-(f) of the Clayton Act (price discrimination), (3) section 3 of the Clayton Act (exclusive dealing and tying arrangements), (4) section 7 of the Clayton Act (merger), and (5) section 8 of the Clayton Act (interlocking directorates). The FTC Act and section 3 of the Robinson-Patman Act, amending the Clayton Act, are not considered "antitrust" laws; therefore, a private right of action for treble damages or injunctive relief does not exist under section 4 of the Clayton Act for conduct within these statutes.

The pleading requirements for a private suit vary depending on which statute the conduct allegedly violated. Consider these recent pronouncements from the Supreme Court regarding the burden of pleading and proving an antitrust violation under section 4.

> Section 4 ... is in essence a remedial provision.... [T]reble damages ... play an important role in penalizing wrongdoers and deterring wrongdoing...
>
> [T]o recover damages ... [plaintiff] must prove more than injury causally linked to an illegal [course of conduct]. Plaintiffs must prove *antitrust* injury, which is to say injury of the type the antitrust laws were intended to prevent and that flows from that which makes defendants' acts unlawful. The injury should reflect the anticompetitive effect either of the violation or of anticompetitive acts made possible by the violation. It should, in short, be "the type of loss that the claimed violations ... would be likely to cause."

Brunswick Corp. v. Pueblo Bowl-O-Mat, Inc., 429 U.S. 477, 485-89 (1977).

> [In interpreting section 4 of the Clayton Act] we look (1) to the physical and economic nexus between the alleged violation and the harm to the plaintiff, and, (2) more particularly, to the relationship of the injury alleged with those forms of injury about which Congress was likely to have been concerned in making defendant's conduct unlawful and in providing a private remedy under § 4.

Blue Shield of Va. v. McCready, 457 U.S. 465, 477-78 (1982). The individual issues presented by these requirements are addressed next.

a. Jurisdiction, Venue, and Service

Sections 4 and 16 of the Clayton Act are jurisdiction-creating statutes. They require no minimum "amount in controversy." The jurisdiction is exclusive within the federal district courts, but it has been held that a prior state decision may operate as a bar to a subsequent federal antitrust claim, and that the subsequent federal antitrust court should consider the preclusive effect of the prior state judgment with regard to preclusion law of the state court. *Marrese v. American Academy of Orthopaedic Surgeons*, 47 U.S. 373 (1985), see discussion this chapter, Section I.F, *infra*.

Section 4 of the Clayton Act permits venue to be located where the defendant, including an individual, partnership, or unincorporated association, "resides, or is found, or has an agent." Section 12 of the Clayton Act provides that when the defendant is a corporation, venue is also appropriate "not only in the judicial district [where the corporate defendant] is an inhabitant, but also in any district wherein [defendant] may be found or transacts business." This special antitrust venue provision is supplemented by a general venue statute permitting venue in the district where the "defendant resides, if all defendants reside in the same state ... or [where] a substantial part of the events or omissions giving rise to the claim occurred, or [where] a substantial part of property that is the subject of the action is situated, or [where] the defendant may be found [if there is no other district where the action may be brought]," or in the district where the corporate defendant is "subject to personal jurisdiction." 28 U.S.C. § 1391(b), (c).

These venue provisions have been construed liberally so as to interpret the requirements of identifying the district where the suit should be brought in a "practical, everyday business or commercial" context. The decisional law suggests that in interpreting the statutes the "transacting business" test is broader than the "doing business" or "claim-arising" tests. As these statutes indicate, the law of venue is directed to an inquiry concerning the physical presence of the defendant so that the litigation can be located in a fair forum. *See* Hovenkamp, *Personal Jurisdiction and Venue in Private Antitrust Actions in the Federal Courts: A Policy Analysis*, 67 Iowa L. Rev. 485 (1982). When the Department of Justice sues for damages for its own injury, it is subject to these same venue provisions. 15 U.S.C. § 15a.

The question of venue becomes problematic in a multiple defendant antitrust case. Generally, venue requirements must be met separately for each defendant. *See* Hovenkamp, *supra*, at 518. While substantively the co-conspiracy doctrine creates an agency relationship, this vicarious litigation strategy has not found acceptance in the interpretation of section 4 of the Clayton Act or the supplementary provisions of the general revenue statute. The Supreme Court in *Bankers Life & Cas. Co. v. Holland*, 346 U.S. 379, 384 (1953), held that in government antitrust suits venue is proper "where the conspiracy was formed or in part carried on or where an overt act was committed in furtherance thereof," but that in private suits under section 4 for treble damages, Congress "placed definite limits on venue." *See also Piedmont Label Co. v. Sun Garden Packing Co.*, 598 F.2d 491, 495 (9th Cir. 1979). *Contra Giusti v. Pyrotechnic Indus.*, 156 F.2d 351 (9th Cir. 1946).

Venue may be changed, for the convenience of parties and witnesses and in the interest of justice, to any other district where the action "might have been brought" originally. 28 U.S.C. § 1404(a). This general venue transfer provision requires that before transfer is appropriate under section 1404(a) three prerequisites are required: (1) that the venue is proper in the transferor forum court, (2) that the venue is proper in the transferee court, and (3) that the personal jurisdiction can be obtained over defendant in the transferee court. *Hoffman v. Blaski*, 363 U.S. 335 (1960). *See also Piper Aircraft Co. v. Reyno*, 454 U.S. 235 (1981). In addition, section 1406(a) permits transfer to a district where the action could have been brought when in fact it was brought in a district where venue was improper. In order to invoke section 1406(a), the transferor court must have the appropriate subject matter jurisdiction, but apparently it need not have personal jurisdiction over the defendant. *See Goldlawr, Inc. v. Heiman*, 369 U.S. 463 (1962).

Finally, 28 U.S.C. § 1407 permits the transfer of the case for pretrial discovery purposes to a single district when there are numerous related cases in several districts that involve common questions of fact. The transfer is accomplished by a petition to transfer, which is filed with the Judicial Panel on Multidistrict Litigation. The purpose underlying the multidistrict transfer provision is to achieve economies by avoiding duplication of effort in resolving common questions. Moreover, transfer is designed for the convenience of the parties and witnesses and should facilitate the promotion of the efficient conduct of the multidistrict actions. After the pretrial matters have been decided, the transferee court must remand the case back to the original transferor court. *See Lexecon Inc. v. Milberg Weiss Bershad Hynes & Lerach*, 118 S. Ct. 956 (1998).

Section 12 of the Clayton Act provides for service of process wherever the corporate defendant is an inhabitant or may be found. 15 U.S.C. § 22. This language has been interpreted to mean that service outside the forum district is proper "only when the action is brought in the district where the defendant resides, is found, or transacts business." Hovenkamp, *supra*, at 509. The extraterritorial service under section 12 applies only to corporations, not to individuals, partnerships, or unincorporated associations. If there is an attempt to serve process outside the limits of section 12, such as when the defendant is not a corporation, plaintiff must rely on the forum state's long arm statute. Otherwise, service is restricted to the judicial district where the suit is filed or, under Rule 4(f) of the Federal Rules of Civil Procedure, service may be made anywhere within the state where the forum court sits.

In *Go-Video v. Akai Elec. Co.*, 885 F.2d 1406 (9th Cir. 1989), the Ninth Circuit approved the use of worldwide service of process against an alien defendant even though venue was established under the Alien Venue Statute, which permits an alien to be sued in any district. Consider whether under that combination a foreign defendant doing business only in Iowa could be sued in Arizona.

b. Statute of Limitation

Section 4B of the Clayton Act requires that a private treble damages suit be brought within four years after the claim for relief accrues. Under certain circumstances, the statute of limitation may be suspended, thus extending the time within which an action can be brought.

As discussed *infra*, in order to allege a claim for relief plaintiff must plead injury to business or property by reason of a violation of an antitrust law. Once damage or injury has been sustained, the statute of limitation commences to run. The question of when injury is sustained depends on the nature of the antitrust violation alleged. The Court in *Zenith Radio Corp. v. Hazeltine Research, Inc.*,

401 U.S. 321, 338-39 (1971), where the alleged damage occurred more than four years before suit was filed, held that

> a cause of action accrues and the statute begins to run when a defendant commits an act that injures a plaintiff's business.... In the context of a continuing conspiracy to violate the antitrust laws, ... this has usually been understood to mean that each time a plaintiff is injured by an act of the defendants a cause of action accrues to him to recover the damages caused by that act and that, as to those damages, the statute of limitation runs from the commission of the act.... [E]ach separate cause of action that so accrues entitles a plaintiff to recover not only those damages which he has suffered at the date of accrual, but also those which he will suffer in the future from the particular invasion....

The Court concluded that if damages are too speculative no claim for relief has yet accrued, and the statute of limitation will not commence until the damages have been suffered.

The statute of limitation can be tolled or suspended under certain circumstances. Fraudulent concealment of the claim for relief can suspend the running of the statute of limitation. When the fraud is discovered, or should have been discovered, the statute will begin to run. Likewise, evidence of duress may be grounds for tolling the statute of limitation, although the degree of duress required to toll the statute may be so substantial as to render the application of this exception very narrow. At least one court has held that the duress must result from a threat to do an unlawful act. *Philco Corp. v. Radio Corp. of Am.*, 186 F. Supp. 155 (E.D. Pa. 1960). *See* D. Floyd and E. Thomas Sullivan, *Private Antitrust Actions* §5.4.1 (1998).

Some antitrust violations, such as naked price-fixing conspiracies, are "concealed" from victims by their very nature — i.e., the defendants knew that what they were doing was illegal and so hid it from the public. This has inspired some courts to develop the notion of a "self-concealing" conspiracy. If a plaintiff can prove such a conspiracy, the statute of limitation will not be tolled. *See Bethlehem Steel Corp. v. Fischbach & Moore*, 641 F. Supp. 271, 274 (E.D. Pa. 1986), holding that "[i]f the conspiracy conceals itself, it would be anomalous to require plaintiff to allege affirmative acts by defendants to conceal the conspiracy because such acts would be unnecessary and therefore never performed."

In addition to equitable justifications for tolling the statute of limitation, section 5(i) of the Clayton Act provides that if a "civil or criminal proceeding is instituted by the United States" for violations of antitrust laws, a subsequent private action "based in whole or in part on any matter complained of" in the government suit is not barred until one year after the completion of the government suit. *See, e.g., Leh v. General Petr. Corp.*, 382 U.S. 54 (1965). While the statute is unclear whether the reference to the United States includes the FTC, the Supreme Court has held that actions by the FTC, at least when enforcing the Clayton Act, toll the statute for the one-year period. *Minnesota Mining & Mfg. Co. v. New Jersey Wood Fin. Co.*, 381 U.S. 311, 320-21 (1965). Whether FTC actions brought under statutes other than the Clayton Act (e.g. section 5 of FTC Act) come within section 5(i)'s tolling provision is unclear. *Compare Rader v. Balfour*, 440 F.2d 469, 473 (7th Cir.), *cert. denied*, 404 U.S. 983 (1971) (section 5 of FTC Act included) *with Laitram Corp. v. Deepsouth Packing Co.*, 279 F. Supp. 883, 891 (E.D. La. 1968) (section 5 of FTC Act not included since not an antitrust law). *See also Greyhound Corp. v. Mt. Hood Stages, Inc.*, 437 U.S. 322 (1978). It is clear, however, from the language of section 5(i) that its tolling provision does not apply to government damage actions under section 4A of the Clayton Act unless the government also seeks injunctive relief. *See, e.g., Chipanno v. Champion Int'l Corp.*, 702 F.2d 827 (9th Cir. 1983); 15 U.S.C. § 15a. The Seventh Circuit has held that the statute of limitation was not tolled during a patent-interference proceeding before the Patent Office since a patent validity claim is not within the Patent Office's primary jurisdiction. *Brunswick Corp. v. Riegel Textile Corp.*, 752 F.2d 261 (7th Cir. 1984), *cert. denied*, 472 U.S. 1018 (1985). This suggests that the one-year extension under section 5(i) may have a narrower application than earlier thought.

The "identity of the issues" requirement under section 5(i) is determined, regardless of the outcome of the first suit, by comparing the government and private complaints. *Leh v. General Petr. Corp.*, 382 U.S. 54 (1965). It does not matter whether the party defendants in the private suit are identical with defendants in the government suit in order for the statute of limitation to be suspended during the pendency of the government suit. *Zenith Radio Corp. v. Hazeltine Research, Inc.*, 401 U.S. 321 (1971).

Finally, it has been held that the one-year period begins to run when a final judgment as to all defendants in the government action has been resolved on appeal or when the time for filing the appeal has expired. *Russ Togs, Inc. v. Grinnell Corp.*, 426 F.2d 850 (2d Cir. 1970); *New Jersey v. Morton Salt Co.*, 387 F.2d 94 (3d Cir. 1967), *cert. denied*, 391 U.S. 967 (1968).

c. Interstate and Foreign Commerce Requirement

Congress' authority to regulate commercial transactions under the antitrust laws derives from its constitutional power to regulate interstate and foreign trade or commerce. Since the jurisdictional base of the antitrust laws rests on the commerce clause of the Constitution, a plaintiff must initially plead a statement invoking commerce clause jurisdiction for an alleged antitrust violation.

It is often said that, in passing the Sherman Act, Congress exerted its full power to regulate commerce. Initially the Supreme Court took the view, however, that the Commerce Clause permitted the national government to regulate only those activities "in the flow" of commerce. In *United States v. E.C. Knight Co.*, 156 U.S. 1, 12 (1895) the Court held that "[c]ommerce succeeds to manufacture, [but] is not a part of it." Under the *E.C. Knight* theory the Sherman Act would not even reach a manufacturer who manufactured goods in several states and shipped them to other states if the restraint was in the goods, not in the commerce. Consistent with that rule the Court had no problem finding jurisdiction two years later in *United States v. Trans-Missouri Freight Ass'n*, 166 U.S. 290 (1897), where the alleged price fixing involved interstate rail transportation.

E.C. Knight was overruled by *Mandeville Island Farms, Inc. v. American Crystal Sugar Co.*, 334 U.S. 219 (1948), where the Supreme Court held that the Sherman Act reaches restraints of trade which are either "in" interstate commerce, or which have a substantial "effect" on interstate commerce. As Justice Jackson once put it, "[i]f it is interstate commerce that feels the pinch, it does not matter how local the operation which applies the squeeze." *United States v. Women's Sportswear Mfrs. Ass'n*, 336 U.S. 460 (1949). Under this rule the Sherman Act has been held to reach activities that are quite local in nature, if a substantial effect on interstate commerce is perceived. For example, in *McLain v. Real Estate Bd. of New Orleans*, 444 U.S. 232 (1980), the Supreme Court held that the Sherman Act would reach price fixing among real estate brokers in a single city, because many of the purchasers and sellers of those homes were either moving from or going to a different state, and because out-of-state lending institutions participated in the financing.

If the challenged restraint affects an "appreciable" amount of interstate commerce, defined qualitatively, the quantitative volume of commerce is not ordinarily measured. This is particularly true for per se violations where it has been held that the amount of commerce affected is immaterial. *United States v. Columbia Steel Co.*, 334 U.S. 495 (1948). This commerce requirement can initially be satisfied at the pleading stage through the filing of affidavits. *McLain, supra.*

Traditionally the key to commerce clause jurisdiction has been whether there is a causal connection between the restraint and a demonstrated consequence on interstate commerce. In this regard, consider the following case.

SUMMIT HEALTH, LTD. V. PINHAS

500 U.S. 322 (1991)

JUSTICE STEVENS delivered the opinion of the Court.

The question presented is whether the interstate commerce requirement of antitrust jurisdiction is satisfied by allegations that petitioners conspired to exclude respondent, a duly licensed and practicing physician and surgeon, from the market for ophthalmological services in Los Angeles because he refused to follow an unnecessarily costly surgical procedure. In 1987, respondent Dr. Simon J. Pinhas filed a complaint in District Court alleging that petitioners Summit Health, Ltd. (Summit), Midway Hospital Medical Center (Midway), its medical staff, and others, had entered into a conspiracy to drive him out of business "so that other ophthalmologists and eye physicians [including four of the petitioners] will have a greater share of the eye care and ophthalmic surgery in Los Angeles." Among his allegations was a claim that the conspiracy violated § 1 of the Sherman Act. The District Court granted defendants' (now petitioners') motion to dismiss the First Amended Complaint (complaint) without leave to amend, but the United States Court of Appeals for the Ninth Circuit reinstated the antitrust claim. 894 F.2d 1024 (1989).

....

I

Because this case comes before us from the granting of a motion to dismiss on the pleadings, we must assume the truth of the material facts as alleged in the complaint. Respondent, a diplomate of the American Board of Ophthalmology, has earned a national and international reputation as a specialist in corneal eye problems. Since October 1981, he has been a member of the staff of Midway in Los Angeles, and because of his special skills, has performed more eye surgical procedures, including cornea transplants and cataract removals, than any other surgeon at the hospital. Prior to 1986, most eye surgeries in Los Angeles were performed by a primary surgeon with the assistance of a second surgeon. This practice significantly increased the cost of eye surgery. In February of that year, the administrators of the Medicare program announced that they would no longer reimburse physicians for the services of assistants, and most hospitals in southern California abolished the assistant surgeon requirement. Respondent, and certain other ophthalmologists, asked Midway to abandon the requirement, but the medical staff refused to do so. Respondent explained that because Medicare reimbursement was no longer available, the requirement would cost him about $60,000 per year in payments to competing surgeons for assistance that he did not need. Although respondent expressed a desire to maintain the preponderance of his practice at Midway, he nevertheless advised the hospital that he would leave if the assistant surgeon requirement were not eliminated.

Petitioners responded to respondent's request to forgo an assistant in two ways. First, Midway and its corporate parent offered the respondent a "sham" contract that provided for payments of $36,000 per year (later increased by oral offer to $60,000) for services that he would not be asked to perform. Second, when respondent refused to sign or return the "sham" contract, petitioners initiated peer-review proceedings against him and summarily suspended, and subsequently terminated, his medical staff privileges. The proceedings were conducted in an unfair manner by biased decision makers, and ultimately resulted in an order upholding one of the seven charges against respondent, and imposing severe restrictions on his practice. When this action was commenced, petitioners were preparing to distribute an adverse report about respondent that would "preclude him from continued competition in the market place, not only at defendant Midway Hospital [but also] ... in California, if not the United States." The defendants allegedly planned to disseminate the report "to all hospitals which Dr. Pinhas is a member, and to all hospitals to which he may apply so as to secure similar actions by those hospitals, thus effectuating a boycott of Dr. Pinhas." The complaint alleges that petitioner Summit owns and operates 19 hospitals, including Midway, and 49 other health care facilities in California, six other States, and Saudi Arabia. Summit, Midway, and each of the four ophthalmic surgeons named as individual defendants, as well as respondent, are all allegedly engaged in interstate commerce. The provision of ophthalmological services affects interstate commerce because both physicians and hospitals serve nonresident patients and receive reimbursement through Medicare payments. Reports concerning peer-review proceedings are routinely distributed across state lines and affect doctors' employment opportunities throughout the Nation.

....

II

Congress enacted the Sherman Act in 1890. During the past century, as the dimensions and complexity of our economy have grown, the federal power over commerce, and the concomitant coverage of the Sherman Act, have experienced similar expansion. This history has been recounted before, and we need not reiterate it today.[10] We therefore begin by noting certain propositions that are undisputed in this case. Petitioner Summit, the parent of Midway as well as several other general hospitals, is unquestionably engaged in interstate commerce. Moreover, although Midway's primary activity is the provision of health care services in a local market, it also engages in interstate commerce. A conspiracy to prevent Midway from expanding would be covered by the Sherman Act, even though any actual impact on interstate commerce would be "indirect" and "fortuitous." *Hospital Bldg. Co. v. Rex Hospital Trustees*, 425 U.S. 738, 744 (1976). No specific purpose to restrain interstate commerce is required. As a "matter of practical economics," the effect of such a conspiracy on the hospital's "purchases of out-of-state medicines and supplies as well as its revenues from out-of-state insurance companies," would establish the necessary interstate nexus.

This case does not involve the full range of activities conducted at a general hospital. Rather, this case involves the provision of ophthalmological services. It seems clear, however, that these services are regularly performed for out-of-state patients and generate revenues from out-of-state sources; their importance as part of the entire operation of the hospital is evident from the allegations of the complaint. A conspiracy to eliminate the entire ophthalmological department of the hospital, like a conspiracy to destroy the hospital itself, would unquestionably affect interstate commerce.

Petitioners contend, however, that a boycott of a single surgeon has no such obvious effect because the complaint does not deny the existence of an adequate supply of other surgeons to perform all of the services that respondent's current

---

[10] It is firmly settled that when Congress passed the Sherman Act, it "left no area of its constitutional power [over commerce] unoccupied." United States v. Frankfort Distilleries, Inc., 324 U.S. 293, 298 (1945)....

and future patients may ever require. Petitioners argue that respondent's complaint is insufficient because there is no factual nexus between the restraint on this one surgeon's practice and interstate commerce.

There are two flaws in petitioners' argument. First, because the essence of any violation of § 1 is the illegal agreement itself — rather than the overt acts performed in furtherance of it — proper analysis focuses, not upon actual consequences, but rather upon the potential harm that would ensue if the conspiracy were successful. As we explained in *McLain v. Real Estate Bd. of New Orleans, Inc.*, 444 U.S. 232 (1980): "If establishing jurisdiction required a showing that the unlawful conduct itself had an effect on interstate commerce, jurisdiction would be defeated by a demonstration that the alleged restraint failed to have its intended anticompetitive effect. A violation may still be found in such circumstances because in a civil action under the Sherman Act, liability may be established by proof of either an unlawful purpose or an anticompetitive effect. Thus, respondent need not allege, or prove, an actual effect on interstate commerce to support federal jurisdiction. Second, if the conspiracy alleged in the complaint is successful, "as a matter of practical economics" there will be a reduction in the provision of ophthalmological services in the Los Angeles market. In cases involving horizontal agreements to fix prices or allocate territories within a single State, we have based jurisdiction on a general conclusion that the defendants' agreement "almost surely" had a market-wide impact and therefore an effect on interstate commerce, *Burke v. Ford*, 389 U.S. 320, 322 (1967) (per curiam), or that the agreement "necessarily affect[ed]" the volume of residential sales and therefore the demand for financing and title insurance provided by out-of-state concerns. *McLain*, 444 U.S., at 246. In the latter, we explained: "To establish the jurisdictional element of a Sherman Act violation it would be sufficient for petitioners to demonstrate a substantial effect on interstate commerce generated by respondents' brokerage activity. Petitioners need not make the more particularized showing of an effect on interstate commerce caused by the alleged conspiracy to fix commission rates, or by those other aspects of respondents' activity that are alleged to be unlawful." Although plaintiffs in *McLain* were consumers of the conspirators' real estate brokerage services, and plaintiff in this case is a competing surgeon whose complaint identifies only himself as the victim of the alleged boycott, the same analysis applies. The case involves an alleged restraint on the practice of ophthalmological services.... The restraint was accomplished by an alleged misuse of a congressionally regulated peer-review process,[12] which respondent characterizes as the gateway that controls access to the market for his services. The gateway was closed to respondent, both at Midway and at

---

[12] See Health Care Quality Improvement Act of 1986, 100 Stat. 3784, 42 U.S.C. § 11101 et seq. The statute provides for immunity from antitrust, and other, actions if the peer-review process proceeds in accordance with § 11112. Respondent alleges that the process did not conform with the requirements set forth in § 11112, such as adequate notice, representation by an attorney, access to a transcript of the proceedings, and the right to cross-examine witnesses....

other hospitals, because petitioners insisted upon adhering to an unnecessarily costly procedure.

The competitive significance of respondent's exclusion from the market must be measured, not just by a particularized evaluation of his own practice, but rather, by a general evaluation of the impact of the restraint on other participants and potential participants in the market from which he has been excluded. We have no doubt concerning the power of Congress to regulate a peer-review process controlling access to the market for ophthalmological surgery in Los Angeles. Thus respondent's claim that members of the peer-review committee conspired with others to abuse that process and thereby deny respondent access to the market for ophthalmological services provided by general hospitals in Los Angeles has a sufficient nexus with interstate commerce to support federal jurisdiction. The judgment of the Court of Appeals is affirmed.

It is so ordered.

JUSTICE SCALIA, with whom JUSTICE O'CONNOR, JUSTICE KENNEDY, and JUSTICE SOUTER join, dissenting.

[T]he question before us is not whether Congress could reach the activity before us here if it wanted to, but whether it has done so via the Sherman Act. That enactment does not prohibit all conspiracies using instrumentalities of commerce that Congress could regulate. Nor does it prohibit all conspiracies that have sufficient constitutional "nexus" to interstate commerce to be regulated. It prohibits only those conspiracies that are "in restraint of trade or commerce among the several States." This language commands a judicial inquiry into the nature and potential effect of each particular restraint. "The jurisdictional inquiry under general prohibitions ... like § 1 of the Sherman Act, turning as it does on the circumstances presented in each case and requiring a particularized judicial determination, differs significantly from that required when Congress itself has defined the specific persons and activities that affect commerce and therefore require federal regulation." *Gulf Oil Corp. v. Copp Paving Co.*, 419 U.S. 186, 197, n.12 (1974).

Until 1980, the nature of this jurisdictional inquiry with respect to alleged restraints not targeted at the very flow of interstate commerce was clear: the question was whether the restraint at issue, if successful, would have a substantial effect on interstate commercial activity.... Unfortunately, in 1980, the Court seemed to abandon this approach. *McLain v. Real Estate Bd. of New Orleans, Inc.*, 444 U.S. 232 (1980), appeared to shift the inquiry away from the effects of the restraint itself, asking instead whether the "[defendants'] activities which allegedly have been infected by a price-fixing conspiracy ... have a not insubstantial effect on the interstate commerce involved."

....

With respect to a restraint like the one at issue here, for example, how does one decide which "activities of the defendants" are "infected"? Are they all the activities of the hospital? Only the activities of the eye surgery department? The entire practice of eye surgeons who use the hospital? Or, as the Ninth Circuit apparently found in this case, the peer review process itself? Today the Court could have cleared up the confusion created by *McLain*, refocused the inquiry along the lines marked out by our previous cases (and still adhered to by most circuits), and reversed the judgment below. Instead, it compounds the confusion by rejecting the two competing interpretations of *McLain* and adding yet a third candidate to the field, one that no court or commentator has ever suggested, let alone endorsed. To determine Sherman Act jurisdiction it looks neither to the effect on commerce of the restraint, nor to the effect on commerce of the defendants' infected activity, but rather, it seems, to the effect on commerce of the activity from which the plaintiff has been excluded. As I understand the Court's opinion, the test of Sherman Act jurisdiction is whether the entire line of commerce from which Dr. Pinhas has been excluded affects interstate commerce. Since excluding him from eye surgery at Midway Hospital effectively excluded him from the entire Los Angeles market for eye surgery (because no other Los Angeles hospital would accord him practice privileges after Midway rejected him), the jurisdictional question is simply whether that market affects interstate commerce, which of course it does. This analysis tells us nothing about the substantiality of the impact on interstate commerce generated by the particular conduct at issue here. Determining the "market" for a product or service, meaning the scope of other products or services against which it must compete, is of course necessary for many purposes of antitrust analysis. But today's opinion does not identify a relevant "market" in that sense. It declares Los Angeles to be the pertinent "market" only because that is the entire scope of Dr. Pinhas's exclusion from practice. If the scope of his exclusion had been national, it would have declared the entire United States to be the "market," though it is quite unlikely that all eye surgeons in the United States are in competition.

I cannot understand why "market" in the Court's peculiar sense has any bearing upon this restraint's impact on interstate commerce, and hence upon Sherman Act jurisdiction. The Court does not even attempt to provide an explanation. The Court's focus on the Los Angeles market would make some sense if Midway was attempting to monopolize that market, or conspiring with all (or even most) of the hospitals in Los Angeles to fix prices there, cf. *McLain v. Real Estate Bd. of New Orleans, Inc.*, 444 U.S. 232 (1980). But the complaint does not mention Section 2 of the Sherman Act, and Dr. Pinhas does not allege a conspiracy to affect eye surgery in the Los Angeles market. He merely alleges a conspiracy to exclude him from that market by a sort of group boycott. Since group boycotts are per se violations (not because they necessarily affect competition in the relevant market, but because they deprive at least some consumers of a preferred supplier, see R. Bork, The Antitrust Paradox 331-32 (1978)), Dr. Pinhas need not prove an effect on competition in the Los Angeles area to prevail, if the Sherman Act applies. But the question before us today is whether the Act does apply, and that must be answered by determining whether in its practical economic consequences, the boycott substantially affects interstate commerce by restricting competition or, as in *Klor's Inc. v. Broadway-Hale Stores, Inc.*, 359 U.S. 207, 213 (1959), interrupts the flow of interstate commerce.

NOTES AND QUESTIONS

1. Suppose a restraint covers an entire, properly defined relevant market but the market itself is located within a single state. Does *Summit* permit jurisdiction? For example, suppose the only three gasoline stations in a rural community fix their prices, and the court found the community to be a relevant geographic market. Would it matter where the stations purchased the gasoline? Where the gasoline was refined or the crude oil produced? Would it matter whether all or nearly all of the stations' customers were from within the state? How would you balance all of these factors?

2. If a defendant wishes to challenge the "commerce" requirement after *Summit*, should she use a motion to dismiss under Fed. Rule 12(b)(1) (subject matter jurisdiction) or under Fed. Rule 12(b)(6) (failure to state a claim for relief)? *See* Calkins, *The 1990-91 Supreme Court Term and Antitrust*, 60 Antitrust L.J. 603, 631-34 (1991).

Following *Summit* the Seventh Circuit reinstated a § 1 complaint, noting that the commerce clause requirements are met if the plaintiff alleges that the defendants' conduct restrained interstate commerce. *Hammes v. AAMCO Transmissions, Inc.*, 33 F.3d 774 (7th Cir. 1994). Judge Posner noted that it is "enough for the plaintiff to have alleged, without further particulars, that the defendants' conduct in excluding it from [the market] restrained (impeded, impaired, diminished — there is no magic word) interstate commerce." He offered that "[t]hough some cases state otherwise, the complaint would not have had to add that the restraint was substantial. No such limitations are stated in the Act." Although he admits that there is "a deep tension in commerce cases," he opts for "simplification" in holding that "[i]t is quite enough, probably more than enough, if the complaint alleges that the plaintiff was engaged in interstate commerce and was injured by the alleged antitrust violation." *Id.* at 779-82. Hence, no factual connection between commerce and the restraint needs to be alleged, at least in the Seventh Circuit. There is still some ambiguity about whether antitrust commerce clause jurisdiction is measured by the defendants' activities in or affecting interstate commerce or by the alleged restraint's effect on interstate commerce.

In *Hamilton Chapter of Alpha Delta Phi, Inc. v. Hamilton College*, 128 F.3d 59 (2d Cir. 1997), the Second Circuit reversed the dismissal of plaintiff's Sherman Act claim. At issue was the defendant college's requirement that all its students live in college-owned housing facilities and buy meal plans sponsored by the college. The parties disagreed on whether the plan had a commercial purpose, with the defendant claiming that it had the noncommercial purpose of making the college experience more pleasant for female students. The court admitted that, "[i]n the context of higher education, certain activities have been held to be so central to the educational mission, and so far removed from the 'business competition' regulated by the Sherman Act, that they are not 'trade or commerce.'" *Id.* at 64. The court also disagreed with the plaintiff's claim that *any* activity undertaken by a college or university to enhance its reputation is commercial and thus subject to antitrust scrutiny. *Id.* at 65. Nonetheless, the court found that the plaintiff had offered sufficient facts suggesting a nexus between the allegedly illegal behavior and interstate commerce, including the fact that the college solicited applicants from all over the globe and that plaintiff and other providers of off-campus housing stood to lose around $1 million per year if the new policy was upheld. Thus, the defendant's conduct had "a substantial effect on interstate commerce." *Id.* at 66.

3. In *United States v. Lopez*, 514 U.S. 549 (1995), a 5-4 decision in a nonantitrust criminal case, the Supreme Court struck down a federal statute that forbad the possession of a firearm in a school zone. In this case (a) Congress, in passing the statute, made no fact findings at all concerning the impact that possession of a firearm in a school zone might have on interstate commerce; (b) the statute itself condemned the mere possession of the firearm — buying it, selling it, or using it in some other kind of criminal activity were unnecessary; and (c) the indictment alleged no effects on interstate commerce. Does *Lopez* place the Sherman or Clayton Acts in any danger of being struck down or limited in its coverage? Probably not. First, as a matter of substantive interpretation the antitrust laws apply only to "commerce." Second, an antitrust complaint is generally required to allege that the defendant's activities had the requisite effect on interstate commerce.

4. The 1990s have seen increased interest in the application of antitrust principles in the global marketplace. In 1991 the United States entered into a bilateral agreement with the Commission of the European Communities (the EC) that provides for notification and consultation on antitrust issues where there are important mutual interests. Similar agreements had been entered earlier with Germany, Australia, and Canada. But the agreement with the EC contemplates coordinated investigations, as well as requests ("positive comity") within the home country to invoke its own domestic antitrust laws against domestic defendants who engage in anticompetitive conduct.

The Sherman Act applies to restraints of trade with foreign nations, including the import or export of goods to or from the United States. The application of United States antitrust laws to transnational business operations goes back to at least 1906, when the Department of Justice started to bring suits, the challenged conduct of which allegedly had substantial adverse "effects" on the United States economy. In incorporating the "effects" doctrine within the interpretation of the jurisdictional reach of the Sherman Act, courts have held that the following conduct comes within the Sherman Act: (1) activities of foreign firms in the United States with an effect in this country, (2) activities of foreign firms outside the United States which have an effect on the United States economy, and (3) activities of United States firms outside the United States which have effects on the

United States economy. Conversely, the antitrust laws generally have not been applied to overseas conduct by United States firms or foreign firms, the result of which does not affect United States markets, consumers or export opportunities.

As a supplement to the Sherman Act, Congress in 1894 enacted the Wilson Tariff Act. 15 U.S.C. § 8. The act was designed explicitly to cover restraints of trade involved in the importation of goods into the United States.

Since 1976 the courts have also started to apply the doctrine of "comity" when the United States antitrust laws are applied extraterritorially. *See Mannington Mills, Inc. v. Congoleum Corp.*, 595 F.2d 1287 (3d Cir. 1979); *Timberlane Lumber Co. v. Bank of Am. (Timberlane I)*, 549 F.2d 597 (9th Cir. 1976); *Timberlane II*, 574 F. Supp. 1453 (N.D. Cal. 1983). This approach is essentially a balancing of interests test, which seeks to evaluate the propriety of applying United States law as a matter of good relations with foreign countries. *See Laker Airways v. Sabena, Belgian World Airlines*, 731 F.2d 909, 937 (D.C. Cir. 1984) ("when possible, the decisions of foreign tribunals should be given effect in domestic courts, since recognition fosters international cooperation and encourages reciprocity, thereby promoting predictability and stability"); Restatement of Foreign Relations Law (Revised) §§ 402, 403, 415 (Tentative Draft No. 6 1985). *See also* Justice Department and Federal Trade Commission, *Antitrust Enforcement Guidelines for International Operations* (1995) (reprinted as Appendix B in P. Areeda & H. Hovenkamp, *Antitrust Law* (supp.)).

Courts have issued injunctions to parties, under principles of concurrent jurisdiction and comity, that bar actions in foreign courts that would interfere with a United States court's jurisdiction over a pending antitrust suit. *Laker Airways Ltd. v. Sabena, Belgian World Airlines*, 731 F.2d 909 (D.C. Cir. 1984). Recently, the issue of antitrust jurisdiction over extraterritorial conduct has turned on whether the comity analysis is part of the jurisdictional inquiry. *Compare Timberlane III*, 749 F.2d 1378 (9th Cir. 1984) (incorporating comity into jurisdictional analysis), *with Laker Airways* (comity not a part of jurisdiction). *See also* Note, *The Laker Antitrust Legislation: The Jurisdictional Rule of Reason Applied to Transnational Injunctive Relief*, 71 Cornell L. Rev. 645 (1986).

The Supreme Court most recently considered the scope of international comity in *Hartford Fire Ins. Co. v. California*, 509 U.S. 764 (1993). Nineteen states and various private plaintiffs alleged that the defendants, both domestic and foreign insurance carriers, conspired to restrict the terms of coverage for commercial general liability (CGL) insurance within the United States. In their complaint, the plaintiffs alleged that the purpose behind the conspiracy was to force certain primary insurers (those insurers who sell insurance directly to consumers) to change the terms of their standard CGL insurance policies to conform with the policies the defendant insurers wanted to sell.

The foreign defendants argued that the principle of international comity precluded extraterritorial application of the Sherman Act to the alleged conduct. With respect to the foreign defendants' claims, the district court granted their motions to dismiss based upon the Ninth Circuit's holding in *Timberlane*. On appeal, however, the Court of Appeals for the Ninth Circuit reversed. Commenting that "the foreign insurers were beyond the regulatory jurisdiction of the States" under the McCarran-Ferguson Act, the court concluded that "the principle of international comity was no bar to exercising Sherman Act jurisdiction."

The Supreme Court affirmed the extraterritorial application of the Sherman Act to this anticompetitive conduct abroad, noting that it adversely affected commerce within the United States. The Court, commenting that "the Sherman Act applies to foreign conduct that was meant to produce and did in fact produce some substantial effect in the United States," held that the alleged conduct was within the purview of the Sherman Act and, therefore, was subject to federal jurisdiction. In reaching its decision, the Court relied on the Restatement (Third) Foreign Relations Law of the United States which provides "the fact that conduct is lawful in the state in which it took place will not, of itself, bar application of the United States antitrust laws." This standard applies even if the foreign state has a strong policy to permit or encourage such conduct. In this particular case, however, the only policy that the foreign state (Great Britain) cited was one of permitting its insurers to regulate themselves. The specific acts complained of were neither mandated nor prevented by British law.

In addition to considerations of comity, the extraterritorial reach of the United States antitrust laws has been limited by the substantive defense of the "act of state" doctrine. This doctrine holds that a United States court cannot review or question the validity of a "sovereign" act by a foreign government or instrumentality of a foreign government when the act is consummated within the boundaries of the foreign country. In addition, the law's reach has been limited by the doctrine of "foreign governmental compulsion," which may excuse otherwise illegal acts that were compelled by a foreign sovereign. *See, e.g., American Banana Co. v. United Fruit Co.*, 213 U.S. 347 (1909); *Interamerican Ref. Corp. v. Texaco Maracaibo, Inc.*, 307 F. Supp. 1291 (D. Del. 1970).

In *W.S. Kirkpatrick & Co. v. Environmental Tectonics Corp.*, 493 U.S. 400 (1990), the Supreme Court held that the act of state doctrine does not apply to a cause of action that does not rest upon the asserted invalidity of an official act of a foreign sovereign. The action was filed against a successful bidder on a foreign government contract by an unsuccessful bidder, on the theory that the successful bidder had violated federal racketeering and other statutes by paying bribes to foreign government officials in the Republic of Nigeria. The parties agreed "that Nigerian law prohibits both the payment and receipt of bribes in connection with the award of a government contract." In this case, the allegation was that Kirkpatrick paid a "commission" equal to 20% of the contract price as a bribe to officials of the Nigerian Government.

Defendants moved that the action be dismissed under Rule 12(b)(6) on the ground that the act of state doctrine barred the suit. The legal advisor to the United States Department of State filed a letter with the district court stating that the United States court's "judicial inquiry into the purpose behind the act of a foreign sovereign would not produce the 'unique embarrassment, and the particular interference with the conduct of foreign affairs, that may result from the judicial determination that a foreign sovereign's acts are invalid.'"

The Supreme Court determined that the factual predicate for application of the act of state doctrine did not exist in this case. "Neither the claim nor any asserted defense requires a determination that Nigeria's contract with Kirkpatrick was, or was not, effective." The Court observed that in each prior instance where it held the act of state doctrine applicable, the claim for relief or the defense required the Court to declare invalid the official act of a foreign sovereign performed within its own territory. But here the Court did not accept the invitation to apply the doctrine. "Act of state issues only arise when a court *must decide* — that is, when the outcome of the case turns upon — the effect of official action by a foreign sovereign. When that question is not in the case, neither is the act of state doctrine." The Court held that the legality of the Nigerian contract — a prerequisite for the application of the act of state doctrine — "is simply not a question to be decided." Rather, the Court seemed persuaded by the State Department's logic that the act of state doctrine is not applicable nor dispositive when the inquiry "involves only the 'motivation' for, rather than the 'validity' of, a foreign sovereign act." The Court did not suggest, given the factual record, that the award of the contract by the foreign government in this case qualified for the commercial activity exception to the act of state doctrine.

The act of state doctrine does not bar, according to *Kirkpatrick*, judicial inquiry into the motivation of a foreign sovereign act. Since the claim for relief did not ask the Court to invalidate the contract entered into by the Nigerian Government — the official act of the sovereign performed within its own territory — the mere challenge to the motivation of the contract was insufficient to trigger the act of state doctrine. Thus, the suit could proceed to resolution of the American RICO and Robinson-Patman Act claims by the private parties.

In addition, the *Kirkpatrick* decision opens the way for the Justice Department and the FTC to challenge conduct by private companies in foreign countries as long as the challenge does not directly seek to invalidate an official act of the sovereign. To be sure, the Justice Department has announced recently it will investigate conduct by foreign-owned companies if there is an anticompetitive effect on United States consumers in domestic or export markets. The fact that the conspiracy or conduct took place overseas will not prevent the United States from exercising jurisdiction, the Department has declared. *Kirkpatrick* seems to reduce a litigation barrier for these kinds of government enforcement actions. An example might be that, if the Japanese auto makers entered a conspiracy to restrict the markets for American cars or parts in Japan, the Justice Department could sue the American subsidiaries of the Japanese companies under the "effects doctrine." *See generally United States v. Aluminum Co. of Am.*, 148 F.2d 416 (2d Cir. 1945).

Related to, but distinct from, Act of State is the doctrine of foreign sovereign immunity, which gives foreign governments and their instrumentalities a limited immunity from suit. The immunity applies when the sovereign is acting in a "sovereign" capacity, but not when it is merely pursuing "proprietary" or "commercial" interests. *Alfred Dunhill of London v. Republic of Cuba*, 425 U.S. 682 (1976). The Foreign Sovereign Immunities Act of 1976, 28 U.S.C. § 1330 and §§ 1602-1611 (1976), regulates personal jurisdiction and many elements of subject-matter jurisdiction in all actions against foreign sovereigns and their agents, including actions brought under the federal antitrust laws. *See International Ass'n of Machinists v. Organization of Petr. Exporting Countries*, 649 F.2d 1354 (9th Cir. 1981), *cert. denied*, 454 U.S. 1163 (1982); Hovenkamp, *Sovereign Immunities Act Jurisdiction and Antitrust Policy*, 14 U.C. Davis L. Rev. 839 (1982); Hovenkamp, *Can a Foreign Sovereign Be an Antitrust Defendant?*, 32 Syracuse L. Rev. 879 (1981).

Moreover, the Webb-Pomerene Export Trade Act of 1918, 15 U.S.C. §§ 61-65, permits a limited antitrust immunity for exporting associations for joint marketing activities as long as such exporting activities do not hinder competition by other United States exporters or affect the United States economy through a resultant restraint. *See generally Pfizer, Inc. v. Government of India*, 434 U.S. 308 (1978). Section 4 of the Act explicitly gives the FTC transnational jurisdiction over export practices, whether in or outside the United States, that amount to "unfair methods of competition."

The Foreign Trade Antitrust Improvements Act of 1982 added section 7 to the Act *prohibiting* the application of the Sherman Act to export or nonimport foreign commerce unless the alleged practice has a "direct, substantial and reasonably foreseeable effect" on commerce. This is the approach essentially taken under the revised Antitrust Enforcement Guidelines for International Operations, *supra*.

Extraterritorial application of the antitrust laws is limited by the requirement of personal jurisdiction and the ability of parties to invoke discovery procedures in foreign countries.

The original Clayton Act and the Robinson-Patman Act have a jurisdictional reach narrower than the Sherman Act. These statutes apply only to persons or entities "in" interstate commerce. In 1980, Congress amended section 7 of the Clayton Act to require that jurisdiction over mergers meet only the "effect" test on commerce similar to that governing the Sherman Act.

In light of the more onerous jurisdictional test of the Clayton and Robinson-Patman Acts, conduct which also violates the Sherman Act could be brought under the easier subject matter jurisdictional requirements of the Sherman Act, though the substantive provisions of Sherman generally carry a heavier burden of proof.

Since 1975, the FTC's authority extends to conduct which affects interstate commerce, similar to jurisdiction under the Sherman Act. This broader jurisdictional reach is applicable, even though the Commission may apply the Clayton or Robinson-Patman Acts under section 5 of the Act for "unfair methods of competition or unfair acts or practices." As "commerce" is defined within section 4 of the FTC Act, it also includes the regulation of "commerce with foreign nations," similar to that discussed above regarding the Sherman Act, including the limitations and defenses. The Foreign Trade Antitrust Improvements Act of 1982, discussed *supra*, also amended section 5(a) of the FTC Act to redefine "effects" on foreign commerce, as it did under section 7 of the Sherman Act, to require a direct, foreseeable, and substantial effect on commerce before jurisdiction is present.

In 1992 the Department of Justice announced a new interpretation of the Sherman Act's application to foreign business conduct. The import of the change is to prevent foreign companies from conspiring to avoid purchase of exports from the United States. The new interpretation is designed to protect American exporters without regard to harm to American consumers, as long as the challenged conduct would violate the antitrust law of the United States if the conduct had occurred within United States boundaries. The language of the international guidelines cautioned that "the Department is concerned only with adverse effects on competition that would harm U.S. consumers by reducing output or raising prices." This restrictive interpretation now has been removed. The Department's new interpretation broadens the sweep of the Sherman Act to cover cases of direct, substantial, and reasonably foreseeable harm to export commerce. The Clinton Administration has signaled its support of 1992 Department policy change.

For example, under the Department's new interpretations, a foreign cartel aimed at limiting purchases of American exports, depressing the price of those exports, or boycotting American goods or services abroad would be subject to the Sherman Act.

Although the Department announced that its new interpretation was "one of general application and is not aimed at any particular foreign country," many American firms have complained that the Japanese *Keiretsu* system of interlocking companies and suppliers discriminates against American exports. Importantly, the new interpretation by the Department might encourage private, treble damage suits against import cartels in foreign countries that harm U.S. exports, without the support of the Department, thus causing increased friction on trade issues between the United States and the country of the foreign importer. Consider the new interpretation within the following problem.

NOTE: INTERNATIONAL ANTITRUST GUIDELINES

Nearly twenty-five percent of domestic output from the United States is directly related in some way to international trade. In 1995 the Federal Trade Commission and the Department of Justice issued joint guidelines designed to complement Congress' enactment of the International Antitrust Enforcement Assistance Act of 1994.

The International Antitrust Enforcement Assistance Act allows the United States to enter into mutual legal assistance treaties with foreign governments and foreign agencies, to share antitrust evidence, and to assist each other in determining whether a person has violated or is about to violate any foreign antitrust law. Reciprocal assistance between foreign countries and enforcement officials from the United States is sanctioned. The intent of the Act, in substantial part, is to internationalize antitrust enforcement, and to promote free competition in global markets.

In announcing the Guidelines, Ann Bingaman, the Assistant Attorney General for the Antitrust Division, noted that the antitrust laws would be enforced "against anticompetitive [foreign] practices that harm U.S. commerce." Specifically, the Guidelines 1) recognize the broader antitrust jurisdiction involving imports, recognized by the Supreme Court in *Hartford Fire Ins. Co. v. California*, 509 U.S. 764 (1993); 2) protect exports of the United States from anticompetitive foreign restraints; and 3) establish practices and policies for the Department to obtain evidence in foreign countries.

Hartford stated that "the Sherman Act applies to foreign conduct that was meant to produce and did in fact produce some substantial effect in the United States." 509 U.S. at 795. The Guidelines state that imports coming into the United States "by definition affect the U.S. market directly, and will, therefore, almost invariably satisfy the intent part of the *Hartford* test." Whether *Hartford's* "substantial effects" test is met, however, will depend on a fact-specific analysis in each case. Generally, the present enforcement standard is that United States jurisdiction exists when the challenged conduct has "a direct, substantial, and reasonably foreseeable effect" on domestic, import, or export commerce of the United States. Interestingly, the Guidelines opine that if the substantial effects test is not met jurisdiction might still be found if the United States acts: (1) as a commercial purchaser or (2) in a financial role to finance the purchase for consumption or use in a foreign country.

The Guidelines take the position that a merger between two foreign firms with no United States subsidiaries is reachable under the antitrust laws if one or both firms have substantial United States sales. If such a merger is anticompetitive, the Guidelines reason, substantial effects in the United States are foreseeable, given the United States sales. To be sure, the Guidelines acknowledge that relief may be difficult to obtain. However, "positive comity" allows our government to request the sovereign where the corporations are domiciled to intervene. *International Guidelines, supra,* § 3.12.

Suppose (a) that Mercedes and BMW are both German automobile manufactures; (b) neither produces anything in the United States; but (c) both sell a significant volume of automobiles to the United States. Mercedes now proposes to acquire BMW and the United States decides to challenge the merger. How should the Germans respond to an attempt by an American agency applying American law to restructure German industry? Should it matter that if Mercedes/BMW was able to obtain a monopoly of a market for luxury cars, that Germans as sellers would be the principal beneficiaries of the merger, while people in the United States as buyers would be the principal victims? Compare *Oerlikon-buhrle Holding AG*, 5 Trade Reg. Rep. ¶ 23697 (F.T.C. 1994) (consent decree requiring collateral divestitures and then approving Swiss scientific equipment manufacturer's acquisition of German competitor).

The International Guidelines also claim jurisdiction over a foreign cartel that makes no sales into the United States directly, but that sells to an intermediary with the knowledge that the latter intends to resell into the United States. *Guidelines, id.* at § 3.13. Suppose a cartel in the country of Erehwon is completely legal under Erehwon law; should that cartel's members be forbidden from selling to a firm located in, say, France, simply because they know that the French firm intends to resell the product in the United States?

American antitrust courts generally hesitate to condemn a defendant for conduct compelled by a foreign sovereign with appropriate jurisdiction. But permission or approval is not compulsion; the foreign law must mandate an act that is inconsistent with American law. *Hartford, supra,* 509 U.S. at 797-99. The sovereign compulsion defense is thus considerably narrower than the "state action" doctrine in domestic antitrust law. That doctrine grants immunity not only to conduct that is compelled by a domestic sovereign such as a state or municipality, but also to private conduct that is merely "authorized," provided that the conduct is also supervised by a public agency or official.

Traditionally, the foreign sovereign compulsion doctrine applied only to actions performed within the territory of the foreign sovereign, but that limitation seems unduly narrow when numerous sovereigns including the United States assert jurisdiction over business and activities outside their territory. The Guidelines insist that the key is not strict territoriality but the legitimate power of the foreign sovereign to force its law upon the firm in question. Still, the Guidelines disallow any foreign compulsion for conduct within the United States itself: No foreign sovereign has the power to force a firm or person claimed to be under its jurisdiction to commit a United States antitrust violation within United States territory. *Guidelines,* § 3.332

Academic commentary on the *Hartford Insurance* case has been mixed. *See, e.g.,* James P. Rhatican, Hartford Fire Ins. Co. v. California: *A Mixed Blessing for Insurance Antitrust Defendants,* 47 Rutgers L. Rev. 905, 955 (1995) (criticizing *Hartford* and observing that increased antitrust enforcement against foreign competitors after *Hartford* could negatively impact the international trading status of the United States); Varun Gupta, Note, *After* Hartford Fire: *Antitrust & Comity,* 84 Geo. L.J. 2287, 2315-17 (1996) (praising the holding of *Hartford* as consistent with the modern notion of the global marketplace and remarking that the United States already fulfills the principle of international comity through courts' "intended effects" and "minimum contacts" tests).

PROBLEM 3.1

Ten Japanese companies were members of a fish import association. Within the import association, the members exchanged market information about demand, supply and prices paid for imported fish. During an 18-month period, all of the Alaska tanner crab that was purchased within Japan was purchased at the same price, regardless of demand or supply. The ten Japanese import (buying) companies that regularly exchanged the commercial data controlled 80% of the crab import (buying) market. The Alaska tanner crab exporters believe that the Japanese fish import association was used to fix and coordinate at depressed levels the price paid for the processed crab imported into Japan. If you were the district court judge faced with a motion to dismiss a suit under the Sherman Act brought by the Alaska exporters against the ten Japanese importers in federal district court in Alaska, how would you rule on the jurisdictional issue presented?

d. The Direct Purchaser Requirement and the Problem of Passing On

The "direct purchaser" and "antitrust injury" rules, which are discussed in this section and the next, are analytically distinct doctrines but often are confused or merged together with the standing requirement, which is discussed in the following section. Each of the three doctrines limits the domain of those who can recover for an antitrust violation.

ILLINOIS BRICK CO. V. ILLINOIS
431 U.S. 720 (1977)

JUSTICE WHITE delivered the opinion of the Court.

In *Hanover Shoe* this Court rejected as a matter of law the defense that indirect rather than direct purchasers were the parties injured by the antitrust violation. The Court held that except in certain limited circumstances,[2] a direct purchaser suing for treble damages under § 4 of the Clayton Act is injured within the meaning of § 4 by the full amount of the overcharge paid by it and that the antitrust defendant is not permitted to introduce evidence that indirect purchasers were in fact injured by the illegal overcharge. The first reason for the Court's rejection of this offer of proof was an unwillingness to complicate treble-damages actions with attempts to trace the effects of the overcharge on the purchaser's prices, sales, costs, and profits, and of showing that these variables would have behaved differently without the overcharge.[3]

---

[2] The Court cited, as an example of when a pass-on defense might be permitted, the situation where "an overcharged buyer has a pre-existing 'cost-plus' contract, thus making it easy to prove that he has not been damaged...."

[3] The Court explained the economic uncertainties and complexities involved in proving pass-on as follows:

> A wide range of factors influence a company's pricing policies. Normally the impact of a single change in the relevant conditions cannot be measured after the fact; indeed a businessman may be unable to state whether, had one fact been different (a single supply less expensive, general economic conditions more buoyant, or the labor market tighter, for example), he would have chosen a different price. Equally difficult to determine, in the real economic world rather than an economist's hypothetical model, is what effect a change in a

A second reason for barring the pass-on defense was the Court's concern that unless direct purchasers were allowed to sue for the portion of the overcharge arguably passed on to indirect purchasers, antitrust violators "would retain the fruits of their illegality" because indirect purchasers "would have only a tiny stake in the lawsuit" and hence little incentive to sue.

In this case we once again confront the question whether the overcharged direct purchaser should be deemed for purposes of § 4 to have suffered the full injury from the overcharge; but the issue is presented in the context of a suit in which the plaintiff, an indirect purchaser, seeks to show its injury by establishing pass-on by the direct purchaser and in which the antitrust defendants rely on *Hanover Shoe*'s rejection of the pass-on theory. Having decided that in general a pass-on theory may not be used defensively by an antitrust violator against a direct purchaser plaintiff, we must now decide whether that theory may be used offensively by an indirect purchaser plaintiff against an alleged violator.

I

Petitioners manufacture and distribute concrete block in the Greater Chicago area. They sell the block primarily to masonry contractors, who submit bids to general contractors for the masonry portions of construction projects. The general contractors in turn submit bids for these projects to customers such as the respondents in this case, the State of Illinois and 700 local governmental entities in the Greater Chicago area, including counties, municipalities, housing authorities, and school districts. Respondents are thus indirect purchasers of concrete block, which passes through two separate levels in the chain of distribution before reaching respondents. The block is purchased directly from petitioners by masonry contractors and used by them to build masonry structures; those structures are incorporated into entire buildings by general contractors and sold to respondents.

Respondent State of Illinois, on behalf of itself and respondent local governmental entities, brought this antitrust treble-damages action under § 4 of the Clayton Act, alleging that petitioners had engaged in a combination and conspir-

---

company's price will have on its total sales. Finally, costs per unit for a different volume of total sales are hard to estimate. Even if it could be shown that the buyer raised his price in response to, and in the amount of, the overcharge and that his margin of profit and total sales had not thereafter declined, there would remain the nearly insuperable difficulty of demonstrating that the particular plaintiff could not or would not have raised his prices absent the overcharge or maintained the higher price had the overcharge been discontinued. Since establishing the applicability of the passing-on defense would require a convincing showing of each of these virtually unascertainable figures, the task would normally prove insurmountable. On the other hand, it is not unlikely that if the existence of the defense is generally confirmed, antitrust defendants will frequently seek to establish its applicability. Treble-damage actions would often require additional long and complicated proceedings involving massive evidence and complicated theories.

392 U.S., at 492-493, 88 S. Ct., at 2231. (Footnote omitted.)

acy to fix the prices of concrete block in violation of § 1 of the Sherman Act. The complaint alleged that the amounts paid by respondents for concrete block were more than $3 million higher by reason of this price-fixing conspiracy. The only way in which the antitrust violation alleged could have injured respondents is if all or part of the overcharge was passed on by the masonry and general contractors to respondents, rather than being absorbed at the first two levels of distribution.

Petitioner manufacturers moved for partial summary judgment against all plaintiffs that were indirect purchasers of concrete block from petitioners, contending that as a matter of law only direct purchasers could sue for the alleged overcharge....

We granted certiorari, to resolve a conflict among the Courts of Appeals on the question whether the offensive use of pass-on authorized by the decision below is consistent with *Hanover Shoe*'s restrictions on the defensive use of pass-on. We hold that it is not, and we reverse. We reach this result in two steps. First, we conclude that whatever rule is to be adopted regarding pass-on in antitrust damages actions, it must apply equally to plaintiffs and defendants. Because *Hanover Shoe* would bar petitioners from using respondents' pass-on theory as a defense to a treble-damages suit by the direct purchasers (the masonry contractors), we are faced with the choice of overruling (or narrowly limiting) *Hanover Shoe* or of applying it to bar respondents' attempt to use this pass-on theory offensively. Second, we decline to abandon the construction given § 4 in *Hanover Shoe* — that the overcharged direct purchaser, and not others in the chain of manufacture or distribution, is the party "injured in his business or property" within the meaning of the section — in the absence of a convincing demonstration that the Court was wrong in *Hanover Shoe* to think that the effectiveness of the antitrust treble-damages action would be substantially reduced by adopting a rule that any party in the chain may sue to recover the fraction of the overcharge allegedly absorbed by it.

II

....

First, allowing offensive but not defensive use of pass-on would create a serious risk of multiple liability for defendants. Even though an indirect purchaser had already recovered for all or part of an overcharge passed on to it, the direct purchaser would still recover automatically the full amount of the overcharge that the indirect purchaser had shown to be passed on; similarly, following an automatic recovery of the full overcharge by the direct purchaser, the indirect purchaser could sue to recover the same amount. The risk of duplicative recoveries created by unequal application of the *Hanover Shoe* rule is much more substantial than in the more usual situation where the defendant is sued in two different lawsuits by plaintiffs asserting conflicting claims to the same fund. A one-sided application of *Hanover Shoe* substantially increases the possibility of inconsistent adjudications — and therefore of unwarranted multiple liability for the defendant

— by *presuming* that one plaintiff (the direct purchaser) is entitled to full recovery while preventing the defendant from using that presumption against the other plaintiff; overlapping recoveries are certain to result from the two lawsuits unless the indirect purchaser is unable to establish any pass-on whatsoever....

Second, the reasoning of *Hanover Shoe* cannot justify unequal treatment of plaintiffs and defendants with respect to the permissibility of pass-on arguments. The principal basis for the decision in *Hanover Shoe* was the Court's perception of the uncertainties and difficulties in analyzing price and output decisions "in the real economic world rather than an economist's hypothetical model," and of the costs to the judicial system and the efficient enforcement of the antitrust laws of attempting to reconstruct those decisions in the courtroom. This perception that the attempt to trace the complex economic adjustments to a change in the cost of a particular factor of production would greatly complicate and reduce the effectiveness of already protracted treble-damages proceedings applies with no less force to the assertion of pass-on theories by plaintiffs than it does to the assertion by defendants. However "long and complicated" the proceedings would be when defendants sought to prove pass-on, *ibid.*, they would be equally so when the same evidence was introduced by plaintiffs. Indeed, the evidentiary complexities and uncertainties involved in the defensive use of pass-on against a direct purchaser are multiplied in the offensive use of pass-on by a plaintiff several steps removed from the defendant in the chain of distribution. The demonstration of how much of the overcharge was passed on by the first purchaser must be repeated at each point at which the price-fixed goods changed hands before they reached the plaintiff.

It is argued, however, that *Hanover Shoe* rests on a policy of ensuring that a treble-damages plaintiff is available to deprive antitrust violators of "the fruits of their illegality."... [14]

---

[14] ....

Congress made clear, however, that this legislation [Hart-Scott-Rodino Act] did not alter the definition of which overcharged persons were injured within the meaning of § 4. It simply created a new procedural device — *parens patriae* actions by States on behalf of their citizens — to enforce existing rights of recovery under § 4. The House Report quoted above stated that the parens patriae provision "creates no new substantive liability"; the relevant language of the newly enacted § 4C(a) of the Clayton Act tracks that of existing § 4, showing that it was intended only as "an alternative means ... for the vindication of existing substantive claims." H.R. Rep. No. 94-499, *supra*, at 9, 1976 U.S. Code Cong. & Admin. News, p. 2578. "The establishment of an alternative remedy does not increase any defendant's liability." *Ibid.* Representative Rodino himself acknowledged in the remarks cited above that this legislation did not create a right of recovery for consumers where one did not already exist.

We thus cannot agree with the dissenters that the legislative history of the 1976 Antitrust Improvements Act is dispositive as to the interpretation of § 4 of the Clayton Act, enacted in 1914, or the predecessor section of the Sherman Act, enacted in 1890. *Post*, at 2080-2081....

While we do not lightly disagree with the reading of *Hanover Shoe* urged by these legislators [who regard *Hanover Shoe* as applying only to defendants], we think the construction of § 4 adopted in that decision cannot be applied for the exclusive benefit of plaintiffs. Should Congress

We thus decline to construe § 4 to permit offensive use of a pass-on theory against an alleged violator that could not use the same theory as a defense in an action by direct purchasers. In this case, respondents seek to demonstrate that masonry contractors, who incorporated petitioners' block into walls and other masonry structures, passed on the alleged overcharge on the block to general contractors, who incorporated the masonry structures into entire buildings, and that the general contractors in turn passed on the overcharge to respondents in the bids submitted for those buildings. We think it clear that under a fair reading of *Hanover Shoe* petitioners would be barred from asserting this theory in a suit by the masonry contractors.

In *Hanover Shoe* this Court did not endorse the broad exception that had been recognized in that case by the courts below — permitting the pass-on defense against middlemen who did not alter the goods they purchased before reselling them. The masonry contractors here could not be included under this exception in any event, because they transform the concrete block purchased from defendants into the masonry portions of buildings. But this Court in *Hanover Shoe* indicated the narrow scope it intended for any exception to its rule barring pass-on defenses by citing, as the only example of a situation where the defense might be permitted, a pre-existing cost-plus contract. In such a situation, the purchaser is insulated from any decrease in its sales as a result of attempting to pass on the overcharge, because its customer is committed to buying a fixed quantity regardless of price. The effect of the overcharge is essentially determined in advance, without reference to the interaction of supply and demand that complicates the determination in the general case. The competitive bidding process by which the concrete block involved in this case was incorporated into masonry structures and then into entire buildings can hardly be said to circumvent complex market interactions as would a cost-plus contract.[16]

We are left, then, with two alternatives: either we must overrule *Hanover Shoe* (or at least narrowly confine it to its facts), or we must preclude respondents from seeking to recover on their pass-on theory. We choose the latter course.

III

In considering whether to cut back or abandon the *Hanover Shoe* rule, we must bear in mind that considerations of *stare decisis* weigh heavily in the area of statutory construction, where Congress is free to change this Court's interpretation of its legislation.... This presumption of adherence to our prior decisions construing legislative enactments would support our reaffirmance of the *Hanover Shoe* construction of § 4, joined by eight Justices without dissent only a few years ago, even if the Court were persuaded that the use of pass-on theories by

---

disagree with this result, it may, of course, amend the section to change it. But it has not done so in the recent *parens patriae* legislation.

[16] Another situation in which market forces have been superseded and the pass-on defense might be permitted is where the direct purchaser is owned or controlled by its customer....

plaintiffs and defendants in treble-damages actions is more consistent with the policies underlying the treble-damages action than is the *Hanover Shoe* rule. But we are not so persuaded.

Permitting the use of pass-on theories under § 4 essentially would transform treble-damages actions into massive efforts to apportion the recovery among all potential plaintiffs that could have absorbed part of the overcharge — from direct purchasers to middlemen to ultimate consumers. However appealing this attempt to allocate the overcharge might seem in theory, it would add whole new dimensions of complexity to treble-damages suits and seriously undermine their effectiveness.

As we have indicated, potential plaintiffs at each level in the distribution chain are in a position to assert conflicting claims to a common fund — the amount of the alleged overcharge — by contending that the entire overcharge was absorbed at that particular level in the chain.[18] A treble-damages action brought by one of these potential plaintiffs (or one class of potential plaintiffs) to recover the overcharge implicates all three of the interests that have traditionally been thought to support compulsory joinder of absent and potentially adverse claimants; the interest of the defendant in avoiding multiple liability for the fund; the interest of the absent potential plaintiffs in protecting their right to recover for the portion of the fund allocable to them; and the social interest in the efficient administration of justice and the avoidance of multiple litigation....

It is unlikely, of course, that all potential plaintiffs could or would be joined. Some may not wish to assert claims to the overcharge; others may be unmanageable as a class; and still others may be beyond the personal jurisdiction of the court. We can assume that ordinarily the action would still proceed, the absent parties not being deemed "indispensable" under Fed. Rule Civ. Proc. 19(b). But allowing indirect purchasers to recover using pass-on theories, even under the optimistic assumption that joinder of potential plaintiffs will deal satisfactorily with problems of multiple litigation and liability, would transform treble-damages actions into massive multiparty litigations involving many levels of distribution and including large classes of ultimate consumers remote from the defendant. In treble-damages actions by ultimate consumers, the overcharge would have to be apportioned among the relevant wholesalers, retailers, and other middlemen, whose representatives presumably should be joined. And in suits by direct purchasers or middlemen, the interests of ultimate consumers are similarly implicated.

---

[18] In this Part, we assume that use of pass-on will be permitted symmetrically, if at all. This assumption, of course, reduces the substantial risk of multiple liability for defendants that is posed by allowing indirect purchasers to recover for the overcharge passed on to them while at the same time allowing direct purchasers automatically to collect the entire overcharge. *See supra*, at 2067-2068. But the possibility of inconsistent judgments obtained by conflicting claimants remains nonetheless. Even this residual possibility justifies bringing potential and actual claimants together in one action if possible.

There is thus a strong possibility that indirect purchasers remote from the defendant would be parties to virtually every treble-damages action (apart from those brought against defendants at the retail level). The Court's concern in *Hanover Shoe* to avoid weighing down treble-damages actions with the "massive evidence and complicated theories," involved in attempting to establish a pass-on defense against a direct purchaser applies *a fortiori* to the attempt to trace the effect of the overcharge through each step in the distribution chain from the direct purchaser to the ultimate consumer. We are no more inclined than we were in *Hanover Shoe* to ignore the burdens that such an attempt would impose on the effective enforcement of the antitrust laws.

....

More important, as the *Hanover Shoe* Court observed, "in the real economic world rather than an economist's hypothetical model," the latter's drastic simplifications generally must be abandoned. Overcharged direct purchasers often sell in imperfectly competitive markets. They often compete with other sellers that have not been subject to the overcharge; and their pricing policies often cannot be explained solely by the convenient assumption of profit maximization. As we concluded in *Hanover Shoe*, attention to "sound laws of economics" can only heighten the awareness of the difficulties and uncertainties involved in determining how the relevant market variables would have behaved had there been no overcharge.

....

We reject these attempts to carve out exceptions to the *Hanover Shoe* rule for particular types of markets. An exception allowing evidence of pass-on by middlemen that resell the goods they purchase of course would be of no avail to respondents, because the contractors that allegedly passed on the overcharge on the block incorporated it into buildings. An exception for the contractors here on the ground that they purport to charge a fixed percentage above their costs would substantially erode the *Hanover Shoe* rule without justification. Firms in many sectors of the economy rely to an extent on cost-based rules of thumb in setting prices. See F. Scherer, Industrial Market Structure and Economic Performance 173-179 (1970). These rules are not adhered to rigidly, however; the extent of the markup (or the allocation of costs) is varied to reflect demand conditions. The intricacies of tracing the effect of an overcharge on the purchaser's prices, costs, sales, and profits thus are not spared the litigants.

More generally, the process of classifying various market situations according to the amount of pass-on likely to be involved and its susceptibility of proof in a judicial forum would entail the very problems that the *Hanover Shoe* rule was meant to avoid. The litigation over where the line should be drawn in a particular class of cases would inject the same "massive evidence and complicated theories" into treble-damages proceedings, albeit at a somewhat higher level of generality. As we have noted, ... *Hanover Shoe* itself implicitly discouraged the creation of exceptions to its rule barring pass-on defenses, and we adhere to the narrow scope of exemption indicated by our decision there.

The concern in *Hanover Shoe* for the complexity that would be introduced into treble-damages suits if pass-on theories were permitted was closely related to the Court's concern for the reduction in the effectiveness of those suits if brought by indirect purchasers with a smaller stake in the outcome than that of direct purchasers suing for the full amount of the overcharge. The apportionment of the recovery throughout the distribution chain would increase the overall costs of recovery by injecting extremely complex issues into the case; at the same time such an apportionment would reduce the benefits to each plaintiff by dividing the potential recovery among a much larger group. Added to the uncertainty of how much of an overcharge could be established at trial would be the uncertainty of how that overcharge would be apportioned among the various plaintiffs. This additional uncertainty would further reduce the incentive to sue. The combination of increasing the costs and diffusing the benefits of bringing a treble-damages action could seriously impair this important weapon of antitrust enforcement.

We think the longstanding policy of encouraging vigorous private enforcement of the antitrust laws, supports our adherence to the *Hanover Shoe* rule, under which direct purchasers are not only spared the burden of litigating the intricacies of pass-on but also are permitted to recover the full amount of the overcharge. We recognize that direct purchasers sometimes may refrain from bringing a treble-damages suit for fear of disrupting relations with their suppliers. But on balance, and until there are clear directions from Congress to the contrary, we conclude that the legislative purpose in creating a group of "'private attorneys general'" to enforce the antitrust laws under § 4, is better served by holding direct purchasers to be injured to the full extent of the overcharge paid by them than by attempting to apportion the overcharge among all that may have absorbed a part of it.

It is true that, in elevating direct purchasers to a preferred position as private attorneys general, the *Hanover Shoe* rule denies recovery to those indirect purchasers who may have been actually injured by antitrust violations. Of course, as Mr. Justice Brennan points out in dissent, "from the deterrence standpoint, it is irrelevant to whom damages are paid, so long as some one redresses the violation." But § 4 has another purpose in addition to deterring violators and depriving them of "the fruits of their illegality," it is also designed to compensate victims of antitrust violations for their injuries. *Hanover Shoe* does further the goal of compensation to the extent that the direct purchaser absorbs at least some and often most of the overcharge. In view of the considerations supporting the *Hanover Shoe* rule, we are unwilling to carry the compensation principle to its logical extreme by attempting to allocate damages among all "those within the defendant's chain of distribution," especially because we question the extent to which such an attempt would make individual victims whole for actual injuries suffered rather than simply depleting the overall recovery in litigation over pass-on issues. Many of the indirect purchasers barred from asserting pass-on claims under the *Hanover Shoe* rule have such a small stake in the lawsuit that even if they were to recover as part of a class, only a small fraction would be likely to come forward to collect their damages. And given the difficulty of ascertaining the amount absorbed by any particular indirect purchaser, there is little basis for believing that the amount of the recovery would reflect the actual injury suffered.

Reversed.

[JUSTICES BRENNAN, MARSHALL and BLACKMUN dissented.]

NOTES AND QUESTIONS

1. The Court made clear that a plaintiff did not state a claim for *damages* under section 4 of the Clayton Act unless it alleged it was a "direct purchaser" from an antitrust violator. The issue was not "standing" as such. In light of this rule, which procedural option, a Rule 12(b)(6) motion to dismiss, a Rule 12(c) motion for judgment on the pleadings, or a Rule 56 summary judgment motion, would be preferred in challenging a claim by an indirect purchaser?

2. Consider the Court's stated reasons for rejecting claims of indirect purchasers through the "pass-on" theory: (1) litigation complexity and uncertainty due to tracing problems and (2) exposure to multiple liability or duplicative recovery. Would these same concerns be present should a plaintiff other than a direct purchaser seek *injunctive* relief rather than monetary damages? The courts have generally answered in the negative and permitted injunction suits. *E.g., Mid-West Paper Prods. Co. v. Continental Group*, 596 F.2d 573, 590 (3d Cir. 1979).

The Court's approach represents a balancing of interests: in its view, antitrust policies are better served by permitting the direct purchaser to recover the full amount of the overcharge paid by the direct purchaser than apportionment of damages by all parties in the distribution process. Do you agree with the Court that the deterrent effect of the antitrust laws will increase by permitting only the direct purchaser to recover? Consider whether deterrence is enhanced by the risk of increased magnitude of the loss compared to increased detection of the violation by a larger class of potential plaintiffs?

3. The *Illinois Brick* opinion discussed the Court's earlier decision in *Hanover Shoe, Inc. v. United Shoe Mach. Corp.*, 392 U.S. 481 (1968), where the Court held that an antitrust defendant could not defeat a private damages action by arguing that the plaintiff had suffered no financial injury, because the entire overcharge was "passed on" to consumers. Read together, *Hanover Shoe* and *Illinois Brick* prohibit both "defensive" and "offensive" use of passing on. Exceptions to this prohibition were noted by the Court. Presumably the exceptions apply to both offensive and defensive uses of passing on. Under the articulated exceptions indirect purchasers may state a claim for relief and demonstrate that overcharges were passed on when (1) a preexisting (from before the cartel was formed) cost-plus contract existed between the first purchaser from the price fixer and the indirect purchaser (plaintiff), and (2) the first purchaser is "controlled or owned" by either the price fixer or the indirect purchaser. Under either exception, problems of tracing and duplicative recovery were considered manageable.

The rationale for the first exception is that the existing cost-plus contract, which automatically passes on the overcharge, determines in advance the effect of the overcharge because the indirect purchaser (the customer of the first purchaser) "is committed to buying a fixed quantity regardless of price." Without the additional contractual requirement of fixed quantities, however, this exception may not be applicable, for a purchaser under a fixed-cost contract would reduce the amount of its purchases in response to a cartel's price increase. In that instance the decrease in volume would create passing-on problems similar to those in *Illinois Brick. See generally* Hovenkamp, *The Indirect Purchaser Rule and Cost-Plus Sales*, 103 Harv. L. Rev. 1717 (1990). *Compare Mid-West Paper Prods. Co. v. Continental Group, Inc.*, 596 F.2d 573 (3d Cir. 1979), *with In re Beef Indus. Antitrust Litig.*, 600 F.2d 1148 (5th Cir. 1979).

The second exception (ownership *or* control) was not defined by the Court in *Illinois Brick*, although the latter term would seem easier to establish than ownership. The factual inquiry is directed towards answering whether the application of the exception will create multiple liability for the defendants and whether in reality one transaction has occurred.

Subsequent lower courts have also created an additional exception to the direct purchaser rule where a vertical agreement (resale price maintenance) is alleged between the price fixer and the middleman direct purchaser. In this instance, the plaintiff consumer becomes the direct purchaser from a co-conspirator; price tracing thus is not problematic. *See, e.g., Arizona v. Shamrock Foods Co.*, 729 F.2d 1208 (9th Cir. 1984); *Jewish Hosp. Ass'n v. Stewart Mech. Enters.*, 628 F.2d 971, 975 (6th Cir. 1980). Some courts have indicated, however, that the vertical price fixing conspiracy will not be applicable unless the alleged co-conspirator middleman is a party to the suit. This requirement would foreclose the possibility of multiple liability. *See, e.g., In re Beef Indus. Antitrust Litig.*, 600 F.2d 1148, 1161-63 (5th Cir. 1979).

4. Consider whether an indirect supplier can sue buyers for agreeing to set prices artificially low. *Illinois Brick* has been applied to deny recovery to an indirect seller for undercharges caused by the indirect buyer's illegal activities. In *Zinser v. Continental Grain Co.*, 660 F.2d 754 (10th Cir. 1981), defendant grain exporters allegedly conspired to suppress information regarding impending wheat sales to the Soviet Union. The result was a depressed market in which plaintiffs sold wheat to middlemen at reduced prices who, in turn, sold wheat to defendants. In rejecting plaintiffs' "inverted" chain of distribution theory, the Tenth Circuit said "in an antitrust treble damage case involving price-fixing the plaintiff must have dealt directly with the alleged violator." *Id.* at 760. *See also In re Beef Indus. Antitrust Litig.*, 600 F.2d 1148 (5th Cir. 1979) (where the court held that cattle feeders failed to establish that retail grocers engaged in a conspiracy to set wholesale beef prices; the cattle feeders did not sell directly to retailers but to beef packers).

5. In sum, four exceptions have been articulated to the *Illinois Brick* direct purchaser limitation: (1) preexisting, fixed quantity, cost-plus contract, (2) ownership or control over the first purchaser, (3) a vertical price fixing conspiracy, and (4) injunctive relief.

6. To what extent does the *Illinois Brick* rule amount to a windfall for direct purchasers? At one extreme — where the direct purchaser is able to "pass on" the full overcharge and suffers no reduction in output — the direct purchaser suffers no injury but is given an action for three times the amount of the overcharge. At the other extreme the direct purchaser must bear the full overcharge itself.

Neither of these extremes is likely to occur in the real world. Even a monopolist as direct purchaser would not be able to pass on the entire monopoly overcharge: although the monopolist's profit-maximizing price generally rises as its costs rise, it does not rise enough to offset the higher costs. The monopolist will make the highest profit if it can buy in a competitive market. It is possible to calculate the percentage of overcharge that a given direct purchaser will pass on to its customers. However, the formula requires knowledge of the elasticities of supply and demand, and these figures are very difficult if not impossible to measure, particularly in litigation. *See* Landes & Posner, *Should Indirect Purchasers Have a Standing to Sue Under the Antitrust Laws? An Economic Analysis of the Rule of Illinois Brick*, 46 U. Chi. L. Rev. 602 (1979); *but see* Harris & Sullivan, *Passing On the Monopoly Overcharge: A Comprehensive Policy Analysis*, 128 U. Pa. L. Rev. 269 (1979), where the authors argue that the relevant elasticities can in fact be measured in litigation, and thus measurement of damages in actions by indirect purchasers is feasible. For a reply, *see* Landes & Posner, *The Economics of Passing On: A Reply to Harris and Sullivan*, 128 U. Pa. L. Rev. 1274 (1980).

7. Consider also whether the direct purchaser who passes on the complete overcharge has a claim for relief for lost customers (or potential customers) by reason of the increased price.

8. In *California v. ARC America Corp.*, 490 U.S. 93 (1989), the Supreme Court held that state antitrust laws permitting indirect purchasers to sue to recover illegal overcharges were not preempted by the federal statute. Sixteen states had enacted such laws in response to the Court's decision in *Illinois Brick*.

Under *ARC America*, downstream antitrust victims retain a remedy in those states that have enacted such statutes even though the damage recovery is not available in federal court. Consider whether these two approaches are complementary or inconsistent. How serious is the threat under *ARC America* to antitrust defendants of multiple liability from both indirect purchasers (in state court) and direct purchasers (in federal court)? Will this dual enforcement approach unfairly favor plaintiffs in settlement negotiations? Does it create over-deterrence from a public policy perspective? Or, does the Court's decision in both cases strike an appropriate balance for federalism?

9. Suppose that the direct purchaser is a price-regulated utility, forced to pay a cartel price for natural gas. Should *Illinois Brick* bar a damage action by the utility's customers? Suppose it could be shown that price-regulated utilities operate under rules that *always* permit them to pass their costs plus a "fair rate of return" on to their customers. Furthermore, customer use is very insensitive to price (that is, price elasticity of demand is low); as a result, the utility loses very little volume. Should *Illinois Brick* apply anyway? The Court answered yes in *Kansas and Missouri v. Utilicorp United, Inc.*, 497 U.S. 199 (1990). *See* 2 P. Areeda & H. Hovenkamp, *Antitrust Law* ¶ 371 (rev. ed. 1994).

Utilities, unlike firms in competitive markets, generally do not price at marginal cost. Rather, the regulatory agency grants them a rate predicated on direct costs (such as the price of natural gas), operating expenses, plus a "fair rate of return" on invested capital. This pricing formula suggests that some departures from *Illinois Brick* are in order. First, the utility, unlike the competitive firm, will probably be permitted to pass through its gas costs precisely. Second, in the short run the utility may receive the same "fair rate of return" on its plant even if the plant is not operating at capacity. Thus, the utility suffers *neither* lost profits *nor* an overcharge when it is subjected to short-term price fixing. The overcharge is passed on directly; the rate of return is based on previous investment in plant and equipment, not on volume of sales. Over the long run, however, the reduced demand caused by a monopoly overcharge will make the construction of additional plants less likely. In that case, the utility will be denied a fair rate of return on these additional plants.

In addition, many studies suggest that the demand for electricity and natural gas is quite inelastic in the short run. As a result, the reduction in volume that follows a cartel's price increase may not be all that large. In that case, the utility's lost profits are not significant.

However, as the Supreme Court noted in *Utilicorp*, different regulatory agencies use different formulas for computing allowable rate increases, and some might permit increases even though "costs" have not gone up. But the formula itself is public information, much easier to parse out than is the pricing decision of the competitive firm. For example, the regulatory agency might decide (1) to raise the rate of return on invested capital from 7% to 7.3%; (2) to give a specified increase reflecting increased labor costs; and (3) to permit the utility to pass on a particular price increase in the cost of gas. But each of these three elements in the increase would usually be stated in the agency's decision, or in the regulated firm's application. Should that not make pass-on far easier to compute in the case of the regulated public utility?

Suppose a group of utility customers, who are indirect purchasers of natural gas, believe that the gas suppliers are fixing prices. They petition their utility to sue, but the utility refuses, saying (a) the suit will be expensive, and (b) suing is not in the best interest of the utility's shareholders, for any damage award would have to be reimbursed to the customers. What alternatives do the customers now have?

Suppose further that it could be shown that a public utility company was always permitted by the regulatory agency to pass on gas price increases to consumers dollar for dollar. In that case the utility would not be injured by an "overcharge" at all, for the entire overcharge is passed on. Rather, its injury comes from any loss in volume that results when its customers respond to the price increase by consuming less gas. Should not the utility's recovery be based on lost profits rather than a monopoly overcharge? *See* Hovenkamp, *The Indirect Purchaser Rule and Cost-Plus Sales*, 103 Harv. L. Rev. 1717 (1990).

10. In *McCarthy v. Recordex Service, Inc.*, 80 F.3d 842 (3d Cir. 1996), plaintiffs from medical malpractice suits attacked the validity of photocopying charges for providing medical records. The Third Circuit held that the plaintiffs' attorneys were the direct purchasers of the copies, not the plaintiffs themselves, based on retainer agreements that the plaintiffs were not required to reimburse the law firm for photocopying expenses unless the firm obtained a monetary recovery for the client. The majority rejected the plaintiffs' contention that the attorneys passed on the overcharges, stating that the *Illinois Brick* direct purchaser requirement was fashioned to dismiss claims such as the present one that involved complex damages apportionment and duplicative recoveries. The court also rejected the plaintiffs' argument that the Supreme Court had receded from the rule of *Illinois Brick* by instituting the five-part standing analysis of *Associated General Contractors v. California State Council of Carpenters*, 459 U.S. 519 (1983). According to the Third Circuit, the *Associated General* Court merely incorporated the *Illinois Brick* doctrine in two of its five factors.

11. *Campos v. Ticketmaster*, 140 F.3d 1166 (8th Cir. 1998), *cert. denied*, ___ S. Ct. ___ (Jan. 19, 1999), held that *Illinois Brick* barred a damages class action brought by those who purchased event tickets from Ticketmaster. Ticketmaster was alleged to be a monopoly supplier "of ticket distribution or ticket delivery services to large-scale popular music shows." It was alleged to have a long-term exclusive contract with "almost every promoter of concerts in the United States" giving it the sole right to sell tickets to customers over the telephone, through numerous outlets including some retail stores, and in some cases at the concert venue itself. The crux of the plaintiffs' complaint was that Ticketmaster charged very high processing and handling fees, sometimes as much as $20 per ticket.

The court followed the plaintiffs' complaint in presenting the concert promoters as purchasers of distribution services, the costs of which were then added to the price of the tickets. However, an important difference between this case and the typical *Illinois Brick* case involving a "passed-on" good or service is that Ticketmaster itself dealt directly with customers and set the price for its distribution services.

In this case, high commission rates would certainly injure the concert promoter by reducing the demand for its tickets. But the issue was whether the promoter's injury was an "overcharge" injury, part of which was then "passed on" to the plaintiffs. Significantly, the contracts were long term, which meant that concert promoters could take distribution costs into account in computing ticket prices. Thus it is plausible that high distribution costs forced the promoters to set lower ticket prices in order to keep up demand. In that case, they absorbed at least some of the injury of the high promotional price, and presumably passed some of it on to the plaintiffs. If so, the plaintiffs were properly the victims of passed-on damages and *Illinois Brick* would bar the damages action.

The court rejected the plaintiffs' argument that they should be treated as direct purchasers because Ticketmaster set the price for its distribution fees and charged the plaintiffs directly. Presumably, it makes no difference whether in the final accounting the fee appears to be paid by the seller or the buyer. For example, suppose that real estate brokers who represent sellers are unlawfully fixing commission rates at eight percent. They offer two types of contracts. Under one, the commission comes out of the agreed-upon price, which effectively means that it is "paid by" the seller. Under the other, the commission is added to the agreed upon price, which means that it is "paid by" the buyer. With well-informed buyers and sellers the form of the contract will make no difference. The price will be adjusted to reflect the existence of the price-fixed commission, no matter how payment shows up for accounting purposes. Presumably, the seller, who engaged the broker, is the direct purchaser of the broker's services; the home buyer is an indirect purchaser, and we presume that part of the commission was passed on in the form of a higher sale price, but the buyer would lack a damage action under *Illinois Brick*.

A dissenter complained that the majority had gotten the distribution chain upside-down, and presented a rather different view of the facts:

> The monopoly product at issue in this case is ticket distribution services, not tickets. Ticketmaster supplies the product directly to concert-goers; it does not supply it first to venue operators who in turn supply it to concert-goers. It is immaterial that Ticketmaster would not be supplying the service but for its antecedent agreement with the venues. But it is quite relevant that the antecedent agreement was not one in which the venues bought some product from Ticketmaster in order to resell it to concert-goers. More important, and more telling, is the fact that the entirety of the monopoly overcharge, if any, is borne by concert-goers. In contrast to the situations described in *Illinois Brick* and the literature that the court cites, the venues do not pay any portion of the alleged monopoly overcharge — in fact, they receive a portion of that overcharge from Ticketmaster.

12. The Seventh Circuit considered the indirect purchaser doctrine in the *Brand Name Prescription Drugs Litigation*, 123 F.3d 599 (7th Cir. 1997). The court consolidated hundreds of section 1 claims brought by pharmacies against drug manufacturers and wholesalers. At issue was the defendant's practice of giving large discounts to so-called "favored customers." This was accomplished through a "charge back system," where the manufacturer and customer contractually agreed to a discount price, which the wholesalers then charged. The manufacturers would then reimburse the wholesalers for any difference between the discounted and regular prices. The manufacturers and wholesalers had agreed not to offer the discount plan to pharmacies, which, according to the plaintiffs, amounted to price discrimination. The court found that, had the wholesalers rightfully been excluded as defendants, the federal antitrust claims by the pharmacies would have to be barred under the direct purchaser rule. *Id.* at 607.

> The plaintiffs are the disfavored customers. They did not have contracts with the manufacturers, they did not receive discounts, and the wholesalers did not receive chargebacks on sales to them. The plaintiffs' complaint is that they were over-charged because the wholesalers passed on to them the over-charge that the wholesalers had to pay the manufacturers by virtue of the price-fixing conspiracy. This is just the kind of complaint that *Illinois Brick* bars. The only entities permitted to complain about the manufacturers' over-charging the wholesalers are the wholesalers themselves, the direct purchasers, even if every cent of the overcharge was promptly and fully passed on to the pharmacies in the form of a higher wholesale price.

Id. at 606. However, in determining whether to uphold the dismissal of the wholesalers as defendants, the Seventh Circuit rejected the contention that it made no economic sense for the wholesalers to participate in the conspiracy. *Id.* at 614-5.

> The pharmacies were trying to get into the act by forming buying groups. Buying groups frequently act as their members' wholesaler, buying directly from the manufacturer and thus cutting out independent wholesalers. Desiring a piece of the action with the favored customers, who were proliferating, the wholesalers agreed to implement a chargeback system that would shore up the manufacturers' system of price discrimination, an integral component of the price-fixing conspiracy. And desiring to discourage buying groups they joined with the manufacturers to hold the line against granting any discounts to such groups and so discourage their formation by reducing the advantages of membership.

Id. at 614. "Wafer-thin profit margins," past examples of arbitrage activity, and discounts previously given to pharmacies only constituted evidence to be "weighed in the balance by the trier of fact," and did not constitute conclusive evidence of not joining a conspiracy so as to uphold a grant of summary judgment. *Id.* at 615. As such, the direct purchaser rule did not bar the pharmacies' antitrust claims.

PROBLEM 3.2

Zedco manufactures plywood bird houses and sells them to independent regional distributors, one of which is Quarty. Quarty in turn sells the bird houses to retail stores. On January 1 Retailer A entered into a contract with Quarty to supply it with 1,000 plywood bird houses yearly at Quarty's cost plus 10%. Later that year, Retailer A purchased an additional 400 bird houses from Quarty at the same price. At the same time Retailer B contracted with Quarty to supply as many bird houses as Retailer B could sell at Quarty's cost plus 10%. Retailer B ended up purchasing 500 bird houses from Quarty. Quarty purchased all the bird houses from Zedco in March or later.

The following year Zedco and two other plywood bird house manufacturers were indicted for price fixing. The court found that the cartel came into existence on January 15, and that the competitive manufacturer's price for the bird houses should have been $8.00, but the cartel price was in fact $10.00.

Claiming offensive collateral estoppel (see the discussion *infra*), Quarty, Retailer A, and Retailer B all sought damages with respect to the above sales. Quarty claimed damages for the cartel overcharge on sales of 1,900 bird houses. Retailer A claimed damages for the cartel overcharge on sales of 1,400 bird houses. Retailer B claimed damages for the cartel overcharge on sales of 500 bird houses. To what extent will the court recognize each plaintiff's claim? How much will each receive?

e. "Business or Property" Requirement

In order for a plaintiff to bring a private treble damages suit under section 4 of the Clayton Act, plaintiff's complaint must allege injuries to its "business or property." Frequently the issue has been whether this requires that the plaintiff have an injury to a "commercial interest." *Hawaii v. Standard Oil Co. of Cal.*, 405 U.S. 251, 264 (1972) (denying standing to states for injury to general economy). In 1979 the Supreme Court decided whether a consumer had standing to sue for damages by reason of injury to business or property caused by a price fixing agreement. The Court distinguished between "business" and "property" injuries, and held that personal injuries alone would not suffice under section 4.

REITER V. SONOTONE CORP.

442 U.S. 330 (1979)

CHIEF JUSTICE BURGER delivered the opinion of the Court.

Petitioner brought a class action on behalf of herself and all persons in the United States who purchased hearing aids manufactured by five corporations, respondents here. Her complaint alleges that respondents have committed a variety of antitrust violations, including vertical and horizontal price fixing.[1]

---

[1] She claims respondents restricted the territories, customers, and brands of hearing aids offered by their retail dealers, used the customer lists of their retail dealers for their own purposes, prohibited unauthorized retailers from dealing in or repairing their hearing aids, and conspired among themselves and with their retail dealers to fix the retail prices of the hearing aids.

Because of these violations, the complaint alleges, petitioner and the class of persons she seeks to represent have been forced to pay illegally fixed higher prices for the hearing aids and related services they purchased from respondents' retail dealers....

Respondents moved for dismissal of the complaint or summary judgment in the District Court. Among other things, respondents argued that Reiter, as a retail purchaser of hearing aids for personal use, lacked standing to sue for treble damages under § 4 of the Clayton Act because she had not been injured in her "business or property" within the meaning of the Act.

....

[T]he word "property" has a naturally broad and inclusive meaning. In its dictionary definitions and in common usage "property" comprehends anything of material value owned or possessed. Money, of course, is a form of property....

Respondents protest that, if the reference to "property" in § 4 means "money," the term "business" then becomes superfluous, for every injury in one's business necessarily involves a pecuniary injury. They argue that if Congress wished to permit one who lost only money to bring suit under § 4, it would not have used the restrictive phrase "business or property"; rather, it would have employed more generic language akin to that of § 16, for example, which provides for injunctive relief against any "threatened loss or damage." 15 U.S.C. § 26. Congress plainly intended to exclude *some* category of injury in choosing the phrase "business or property" for § 4. Only a "commercial interest" gloss, they argue, both gives the phrase the restrictive significance intended for it and at the same time gives independent significance to the word "business" and the word "property." The argument of respondents is straightforward: the phrase "business or property" means "business activity or property related to one's business."

That strained construction would have us ignore the disjunctive "or" and rob the term "property" of its independent and ordinary significance; moreover, it would convert the noun "business" into an adjective. In construing a statute we are obliged to give effect, if possible, to every word Congress used. Canons of construction ordinarily suggest that terms connected by a disjunctive be given separate meanings, unless the context dictates otherwise; here it does not. Congress' use of the word "or" makes plain that "business" was not intended to modify "property," nor was "property" intended to modify "business."

When a commercial enterprise suffers a loss of money it suffers an injury in both its "business" and its "property." But neither term is rendered redundant by recognizing that a consumer not engaged in a "business" enterprise, but rather acquiring goods or services for personal use, is injured in "property" when the price of those goods or services is artificially inflated by reason of the anticompetitive conduct complained of. The phrase "business or property" also retains restrictive significance. It would, for example, exclude personal injuries suffered. Congress must have intended to exclude some class of injuries by the phrase "business or property." But it taxes the ordinary meaning of common terms to argue, as respondents do, that a consumer's monetary injury arising directly out of a retail purchase is not comprehended by the natural and usual meaning of the phrase "business or property." We simply give the word "property" the independent significance to which it is entitled in this context. A consumer whose money has been diminished by reason of an antitrust violation has been injured "in his ... property" within the meaning of § 4.

....

Nor does her status as a "consumer" change the nature of the injury she suffered or the intrinsic meaning of "property" in § 4. That consumers of retail goods and services have standing to sue under § 4 is implicit in our decision in *Goldfarb v. Virginia State Bar*, 421 U.S. 773 (1975). There we held that a bar association was subject to a treble-damages suit brought under § 4 by persons who sought legal services in connection with the purchase of a residence. Furthermore, we have often referred to "consumers" as parties entitled to seek damages under § 4 without intimating that consumers of goods and services purchased for personal rather than commercial use were in any way foreclosed by the statutory language from asserting an injury in their "property." [Citing cases.]

Hawaii v. Standard Oil Co., is not to the contrary. There we held that injury to a state's total economy, for which the state sought redress in its *parens patriae* capacity, was not cognizable under § 4. It is true we noted that the words "business or property" refer to "commercial interests or enterprises," and reasoned that Hawaii could not recover on its claim for damage done to its "general economy" because such injury did not harm Hawaii's "commercial interests."

However, the language of an opinion is not always to be parsed as though we were dealing with language of a statute. Use of the phrase "commercial interests or enterprises," read in context, in no sense suggests that only injuries to a business entity are within the ambit of § 4.... The phrase "commercial interests" was used there as a generic reference to the interests of the State of Hawaii as a party to a commercial transaction....

Nothing in the legislative history of § 4 conflicts with our holding today....

Respondents also argue that allowing class actions to be brought by retail consumers like the petitioner here will add a significant burden to the already crowded dockets of the federal courts. That may well be true but cannot be a controlling consideration here. We must take the statute as we find it. Congress created the treble-damages remedy of § 4 precisely for the purpose of encouraging *private* challenges to antitrust violations. These private suits provide a significant supplement to the limited resources available to the Department of Justice for enforcing the antitrust laws and deterring violations. Indeed, nearly 20 times as many private antitrust actions are currently pending in the federal courts as actions filed by the Department of Justice.... To be sure, these private suits impose a heavy litigation burden on the federal courts; it is the clear responsibility of Congress to provide the judicial resources necessary to execute its mandates.

Finally, respondents argue that the cost of defending consumer class actions will have a potentially ruinous effect on small businesses in particular and will ultimately be paid by consumers in any event. These are not unimportant considerations, but they are policy considerations more properly addressed to Congress than to this Court. However accurate respondents' arguments may prove to be — and they are not without substance — they cannot govern our reading of the plain language in § 4.

District courts must be especially alert to identify frivolous claims brought to extort nuisance settlements; they have broad power and discretion vested in them by Fed. Rule Civ. Proc. 23 with respect to matters involving the certification and management of potentially cumbersome or frivolous class actions. ... Recognition of the plain meaning of the statutory language "business or property" need not result in administrative chaos, class-action harassment, or "windfall" settlements if the district courts exercise sound discretion and use the tools available.

....

Reversed.

NOTES AND QUESTIONS

1. Section 4 of the Clayton Act states that a private treble damages action may be maintained by "any person ... injured in ... business or property." It does not, however, define the class of individuals or entities that comes within the statutory language of "any person." That is partially done by section 1 of the Clayton Act, which speaks in terms of foreign and domestic corporations and associations. 15 U.S.C. § 12 (1988 Supp.). Others have been included in the definition through decisional and statutory developments.

A state alleging a proprietary or commercial injury is a "person" for purposes of section 4. A state also has authority to sue as *parens patriae* on behalf of its citizens who have been injured. Likewise, a city is a "person" within the statute. *Chattanooga Foundry & Pipe Works v. Atlanta*, 203 U.S. 390 (1906). The Court has even permitted foreign governments to sue for treble damages. *Pfizer, Inc. v. Government of India*, 434 U.S. 308 (1978). But the *Pfizer* rule permitting treble damages to foreign governments was modified in 1982 when Congress amended section 4 of the Clayton Act limiting the right of foreign governments to recover only *actual* damages. Foreign Sovereign Antitrust Recoveries Act, P.L. 97-393. An amendment to section 4A of the Clayton Act permits the United States Government to recover treble damages, the same as that allowable to private parties, when it is injured by an antitrust violation.

2. While the Supreme Court has been liberal in interpreting the definition of "any person," the term is not without limitations. Indeed, the Court's definitional approach has generally included only consumers and competitors within the statutory term.

f. Antitrust Injury

Prior to the Supreme Court decision in *Klor's, Inc. v. Broadway-Hale Stores*, 359 U.S. 207 (1959), an antitrust plaintiff was required to plead and prove injury to the general public as well as specific injury to herself. In *Klor's* the Supreme Court concluded that Congress had "determined its own criteria of public harm" and therefore it was unnecessary for the plaintiff to plead such harm, thus implying that public injury is inherent in antitrust violations. But *Klor's* and the subsequent case *Radiant Burners, Inc. v. Peoples Gas Light & Coke Co.*, 364 U.S. 656 (1961), dealt only with per se violations of sections 1 and 2 of the Sherman Act. Other courts in rule of reason cases under the Sherman Act have suggested that where the offense is not per se unlawful evidence that competition has been affected is the equivalent of a showing of public injury. The private plaintiff must also still prove injury to himself.

Another judicially created exception to treble damage liability is the "antitrust injury" requirement. It focuses on the "by reason of" language of section 4.

BRUNSWICK CORP. V. PUEBLO BOWL-O-MAT, INC.

429 U.S. 477 (1977)

JUSTICE MARSHALL delivered the opinion of the Court.

I

Petitioner is one of the two largest manufacturers of bowling equipment in the United States. Respondents are three of the 10 bowling centers owned by Treadway Companies, Inc. Since 1965, petitioner has acquired and operated a large number of bowling centers, including six in the markets in which respondents operate. Respondents instituted this action contending that these acquisitions violated various provisions of the antitrust laws.

In the late 1950's, the bowling industry expanded rapidly, and petitioner's sales of lanes, automatic pinsetters, and ancillary equipment rose accordingly....

In the early 1960's, the bowling industry went into a sharp decline. Petitioner's sales quickly dropped to preboom levels....

To meet this difficulty, petitioner began acquiring and operating defaulting bowling centers when their equipment could not be resold and a positive cash flow could be expected from operating the centers. During the seven years preceding the trial in this case, petitioner acquired 222 centers, 54 of which it either disposed of or closed. These acquisitions made petitioner by far the largest operator of bowling centers, with over five times as many centers as its next largest competitor....

At issue here are acquisitions by petitioner in the three markets in which respondents are located: Pueblo, Colo., Poughkeepsie, N. Y., and Paramus, N. J. In 1965, petitioner acquired one defaulting center in Pueblo, one in Poughkeepsie, and two in the Paramus area. In 1969, petitioner acquired a third defaulting center in the Paramus market, and in 1970 petitioner acquired a fourth. Petitioner closed its Poughkeepsie center in 1969 after three years of unsuccessful operation; the Paramus center acquired in 1970 also proved unsuccessful, and in

March 1973 petitioner gave notice that it would cease operating the center when its lease expired. The other four centers were operational at the time of trial.

....

II

The issue for decision is a narrow one. Petitioner does not presently contest the Court of Appeals' conclusion that a properly instructed jury could have found the acquisitions unlawful. Nor does petitioner challenge the Court of Appeals' determination that the evidence would support a finding that had petitioner not acquired these centers, they would have gone out of business and respondents' income would have increased. Petitioner questions only whether antitrust damages are available where the sole injury alleged is that competitors were continued in business, thereby denying respondents an anticipated increase in market shares.

To answer that question it is necessary to examine the antimerger and treble-damages provisions of the Clayton Act. Section 7 of the Act proscribes mergers whose effect *"may be* substantially to lessen competition, or *to tend to* create a monopoly." (Emphasis added.) It is, as we have observed many times, a prophylactic measure, intended "primarily to arrest apprehended consequences of intercorporate relationships before those relationships could work their evil ...." [Citing cases.]

Section 4, in contrast, is in essence a remedial provision. It provides treble damages to "[a]ny person who shall be injured in his business or property by reason of anything forbidden in the antitrust laws ...." Of course, treble damages also play an important role in penalizing wrongdoers and deterring wrongdoing, as we also have frequently observed.... It nevertheless is true that the treble-damages provision, which makes awards available only to injured parties, and measures the awards by a multiple of the injury actually proved, is designed primarily as a remedy.

Intermeshing a statutory prohibition against acts that have a potential to cause certain harms with a damages action intended to remedy those harms is not without difficulty. Plainly, to recover damages respondents must prove more than that petitioner violated § 7, since such proof establishes only that injury may result. Respondents contend that the only additional element they need demonstrate is that they are in a worse position than they would have been had petitioner not committed those acts. The Court of Appeals agreed, holding compensable any loss "causally linked" to "the mere presence of the violator in the market." Because this holding divorces antitrust recovery from the purposes of the antitrust laws without a clear statutory command to do so, we cannot agree with it.

Every merger of two existing entities into one, whether lawful or unlawful, has the potential for producing economic readjustments that adversely affect some persons. But Congress has not condemned mergers on that account; it has condemned them only when they may produce anticompetitive effects. Yet under the

Court of Appeals' holding, once a merger is found to violate § 7, all dislocations caused by the merger are actionable, regardless of whether those dislocations have anything to do with the reason the merger was condemned. This holding would make § 4 recovery entirely fortuitous, and would authorize damages for losses which are of no concern to the antitrust laws.

Both of these consequences are well illustrated by the facts of this case. If the acquisitions here were unlawful, it is because they brought a "deep pocket" parent into a market of "pygmies." Yet respondents' injury — the loss of income that would have accrued had the acquired centers gone bankrupt — bears no relationship to the size of either the acquiring company or its competitors. Respondents would have suffered the identical "loss" — but no compensable injury — had the acquired centers instead obtained refinancing or been purchased by "shallow pocket" parents as the Court of Appeals itself acknowledged. Thus, respondents' injury was not of "the type that the statute was intended to forestall," *Wyandotte Co. v. United States*, 389 U.S. 191.

But the antitrust laws are not merely indifferent to the injury claimed here. At base, respondents complain that by acquiring the failing centers petitioner preserved competition, thereby depriving respondents of the benefits of increased concentration. The damages respondents obtained are designed to provide them with the profits they would have realized had competition been reduced. The antitrust laws, however, were enacted for "the protection of *competition* not *competitors*," *Brown Shoe Co. v. United States*. It is inimical to the purposes of these laws to award damages for the type of injury claimed here.

Of course, Congress is free, if it desires, to mandate damages awards for all dislocations caused by unlawful mergers despite the peculiar consequences of so doing. But because of these consequences, "we should insist upon a clear expression of a congressional purpose," before attributing such an intent to Congress. We can find no such expression in either the language or the legislative history of § 4. To the contrary, it is far from clear that the loss of windfall profits that would have accrued had the acquired centers failed even constitutes "injury" within the meaning of § 4. And it is quite clear that if respondents were injured, it was not "by reason of anything forbidden in the antitrust laws": while respondents' loss occurred "by reason of" the unlawful acquisitions, it did not occur "by reason of" that which made the acquisitions unlawful.

We therefore hold that for the plaintiffs to recover treble damages on account of § 7 violations, they must prove more than injury causally linked to an illegal presence in the market. Plaintiffs must prove *antitrust* injury, which is to say injury of the type the antitrust laws were intended to prevent and that flows from that which makes defendants' acts unlawful. The injury should reflect the anticompetitive effect either of the violation or of anticompetitive acts made possible by the violation. It should, in short, be "the type of loss that the claimed violations ... would be likely to cause." *Zenith Radio Corp. v. Hazeltine Research*, 395 U.S., at 125.

III

We come, then, to the question of appropriate disposition of this case. At the very least, petitioner is entitled to a new trial, not only because of the instructional errors noted by the Court of Appeals that are not at issue here but also because the District Court's instruction as to the basis for damages was inconsistent with our holding as outlined above. Our review of the record, however, persuades us that a new trial on the damages claim is unwarranted. Respondents based their case solely on their novel damages theory which we have rejected. While they produced some conclusory testimony suggesting that in operating the acquired centers petitioner had abused its deep pocket by engaging in anticompetitive conduct, they made no attempt to prove that they had lost any income as a result of such predation. Rather, their entire proof of damages was based on their claim to profits that would have been earned had the acquired centers closed. Since respondents did not prove any cognizable damages and have not offered any justification for allowing respondents, after two trials and over 10 years of litigation, yet a third opportunity to do so, it follows that, petitioner is entitled, in accord with its motion made pursuant to Rule 50(b), to judgment on the damages claim notwithstanding the verdict....

Respondents' complaint also prayed for equitable relief, and the Court of Appeals held that if respondents established a § 7 violation, they might be entitled to an injunction against "those practices by which a deep pocket market entrant harms competition." Because petitioner has not contested this holding, respondents remain free, on remand, to seek such a decree.

NOTES AND QUESTIONS

1. Following its *Brunswick* decision, the Court in *J. Truett Payne Co. v. Chrysler Motors Corp.*, 451 U.S. 557 (1981), held that the "antitrust injury" limitation had application beyond section 7, including price discrimination violations alleged under section 2 of the Clayton Act, as amended by the Robinson-Patman Act. The Court in *Payne* reaffirmed that in order to meet the "antitrust injury" requirement plaintiff must plead and demonstrate an actual diminution of competition.

2. In light of *Brunswick* consider the accuracy of this rule: In order for plaintiff to recover for "antitrust injury" within the meaning of section 4, it must plead, and ultimately establish, that the injury flowed from an antitrust violation which produced a decrease in competition. Is it accurate to state that the focus of *Brunswick*'s inquiry is on the "nature" of plaintiff's injury? Evaluate whether the "antitrust injury" test is discernibly different from the "standing" requirement. Is the latter limitation concerned only with the directness or remoteness of the injury from the antitrust violation? *See generally* Page, *Antitrust Damages and Economic Efficiency: An Approach to Antitrust Injury*, 47 U. Chi. L. Rev. 467 (1980).

3. In *Brunswick* the plaintiff alleged that its competitor would have gone out of business but for the fact that it was acquired by the defendant. Why couldn't the defendant successfully assert the "failing company" defense, which permits mergers under certain circumstances when one of the parties is in danger of business failure? For an argument that the merger at issue in *Brunswick* was really legal because the defendant could have successfully raised the "failing company" defense, see Areeda, *Antitrust Violations Without Damage Recoveries*, 89 Harv. L. Rev. 1127 (1976). For more on the "failing company" defense, see Chapter 7, *infra.*

4. *Brunswick* left open the question whether the "antitrust injury" standard was a requirement in injunctive suits under section 16 of the Clayton Act, where the statute speaks in terms of "threatened conduct that will cause loss or damages." The next case answers this issue.

CARGILL, INC. V. MONFORT OF COLORADO, INC.

479 U.S. 104 (1986)

JUSTICE BRENNAN delivered the opinion of the Court.

Under § 16 of the Clayton Act private parties "threatened [with] loss or damage by a violation of the antitrust laws" may seek injunctive relief. This case presents two questions: whether a plaintiff seeking relief under § 16 must prove a threat of antitrust injury, and, if so, whether loss or damage due to increased competition constitutes such injury.

I

Respondent Monfort of Colorado, Inc. (Monfort), the plaintiff below, owns and operates three integrated beef-packing plants, that is, plants for both the slaughter of cattle and the fabrication of beef. Monfort operates in both the market for fed cattle (the input market) and the market for fabricated beef (the output market). These markets are highly competitive, and the profit margins of the major beef packers are low. The current markets are a product of two decades of intense competition, during which time packers with modern integrated plants have gradually displaced packers with separate slaughter and fabrication plants.

Monfort is the country's fifth-largest beef packer. Petitioner Excel Corporation (Excel), one of the two defendants below, is the second-largest packer. Excel operates five integrated plants and one fabrication plant. It is a wholly owned subsidiary of Cargill, Inc., the other defendant below, a large privately owned corporation with more than 150 subsidiaries in at least 35 countries.

On June 17, 1983, Excel signed an agreement to acquire the third-largest packer in the market, Spencer Beef, a division of the Land O'Lakes agricultural cooperative. Spencer Beef owned two integrated plants and one slaughtering plant. After the acquisition, Excel would still be the second-largest packer, but would command a market share almost equal to that of the largest packer, IBP, Inc. (IBP).[2]

---

[2] The District Court relied on the testimony of one of Monfort's witnesses in determining market share. 591 F. Supp. at 706-707. According to this testimony, Monfort's share of the cattle

Monfort brought an action under § 16 of the Clayton Act, 15 U.S.C. § 26, to enjoin the prospective merger. Its complaint alleged that the acquisition would "violat[e] Section 7 of the Clayton Act because the effect of the proposed acquisition may be substantially to lessen competition or tend to create a monopoly in several different ways...." Monfort described the injury that it allegedly would suffer in this way:

> "(f) *Impairment of plaintiff's ability to compete.* The proposed acquisition will result in a concentration of economic power in the relevant markets which threatens Monfort's supply of fed cattle and its ability to compete in the boxed beef market."

II

This case requires us to decide, at the outset, a question we have not previously addressed: whether a private plaintiff seeking an injunction under § 16 of the Clayton Act must show a threat of antitrust injury. To decide the question, we must look first to the source of the antitrust injury requirement, which lies in a related provision of the Clayton Act, § 4, 15 U.S.C. § 15.

Like § 16, § 4 provides a vehicle for private enforcement of the antitrust laws. Under § 4, "any person who shall be injured in his business or property by reason of anything forbidden in the antitrust laws may sue therefor in any district court of the United States ..., and shall recover threefold the damages by him sustained, and the cost of suit, including a reasonable attorney's fee." 15 U.S.C. § 15. In *Brunswick Corp. v. Pueblo Bowl-O-Mat, Inc.* we held that plaintiffs seeking treble damages under § 4 must show more than simply an "injury causally linked" to a particular merger; instead, "plaintiffs must prove *antitrust* injury, which is to say injury of the type the antitrust laws were intended to prevent and that flows from that which makes the defendants' acts unlawful." 429 U.S., at 489 (emphasis in original)....

Section 16 of the Clayton Act provides in part that "[a]ny person, firm, corporation, or association shall be entitled to sue for and have injunctive relief ... against threatened loss or damage by a violation of the antitrust laws...." 15 U.S.C. § 26. It is plain that § 16 and § 4 do differ in various ways. For example, § 4 requires a plaintiff to show actual injury, but § 16 requires a showing only of "threatened" loss or damage; similarly, § 4 requires a showing of injury to "business or property," while § 16 contains no such limitation.[6]

---

slaughter market was 5.5%, Excel's share was 13.3%, and IBP's was 24.4%. Monfort's share of the production market was 5.7%, Excel's share was 14.1%, and IBP's share was 27.3%. After the merger, Excel's share of each market would increase to 20.4%. *Id.* at 64, 69; 761 F.2d 570, 577 (10 Cir. 1985).

[6] Standing analysis under § 16 will not always be identical to standing analysis under § 4. For example, the difference in the remedy each section provides means that certain considerations relevant to a determination of standing under § 4 are not relevant under § 16. The treble-damage remedy, if afforded to "every person tangentially affected by an antitrust

Although these differences do affect the nature of the injury cognizable under each section, the lower courts, including the courts below, have found that under both § 16 and § 4 the plaintiff must still allege an injury of the type the antitrust laws were designed to prevent. We agree.

The wording concerning the relationship of the injury to the violation of the antitrust laws in each section is comparable. Section 4 requires proof of injury "by reason of anything forbidden in the antitrust laws"; § 16 requires proof of "threatened loss or damage by a violation of the antitrust laws." It would be anomalous, we think, to read the Clayton Act to authorize a private plaintiff to secure an injunction against a threatened injury for which he would not be entitled to compensation if the injury actually occurred.

There is no indication that Congress intended such a result. Indeed, the legislative history of § 16 is consistent with the view that § 16 affords private plaintiffs injunction relief only for those injuries cognizable under § 4. According to the House Report,

> "Under section 7 of the act of July 2, 1890 [revised and incorporated into Clayton Act as § 4], a person injured in his business and property by corporations or combinations acting in violation of the Sherman antitrust law, may recover loss and damage for such wrongful act. There is, however, no provision in the existing law authorizing a person, firm, corporation, or association to enjoin threatened loss or damage to his business or property by the commission of *such unlawful acts, and the purpose of this section is to remedy such defect in the law.*" H.R. Rep. No. 627, Pt. 1, 63d Cong., 2d Sess. 21 (1914) (emphasis added).

Sections 4 and 16 are thus best understood as providing complementary remedies for a single set of injuries. Accordingly, we conclude that in order to seek injunctive relief under § 16, a private plaintiff must allege threatened loss or damage "of the type the antitrust laws were designed to prevent and that flows from that which makes defendants' acts unlawful." *Brunswick*, 429 U.S., at 489. We therefore turn to the question of whether the proposed merger in this case threatened respondent with antitrust injury.

---

violation," or for "all injuries that might conceivably be traced to an antitrust violation," would "open the door to duplicative recoveries," and to multiple lawsuits. In order to protect against multiple lawsuits and duplicative recoveries, courts should examine other factors in addition to antitrust injury, such as the potential for duplicative recovery, the complexity of apportioning damages, and the existence of other parties that have been more directly harmed, to determine whether a party is a proper plaintiff under § 4. Conversely, under § 16, the only remedy available is equitable in nature, and, as we recognized in *Hawaii v. Standard Oil Co.*, "the fact is that one injunction is as effective as 100, and, concomitantly, that 100 injunctions are no more effective than one." 405 U.S., at 261. Thus, because standing under § 16 raises no threat of multiple lawsuits or duplicative recoveries, some of the factors other than antitrust injury that are appropriate to a determination of standing under § 4 are not relevant under § 16.

III

Initially, we confront the problem of determining what Monfort alleged the source of its injury to be. Monfort's complaint is of little assistance in this regard, since the injury alleged therein — "an impairment of plaintiff's ability to compete" — is alleged to result from "a concentration of economic power." The pretrial order largely restates these general allegations. At trial, however, Monfort did present testimony and other evidence that helped define the threatened loss. Monfort alleged that after the merger, Excel would attempt to increase its market share at the expense of smaller rivals, such as Monfort. To that end, Monfort claimed, Excel would bid up the price it would pay for cattle, and reduce the price at which it sold boxed beef. Although such a strategy, which Monfort labeled a "cost-price squeeze," would reduce Excel's profits, Excel's parent corporation had the financial reserves to enable Excel to pursue such a strategy. Eventually, according to Monfort, smaller competitors lacking significant reserves and unable to match Excel's prices would be driven from the market; at this point Excel would raise the price of its boxed beef to supracompetitive levels, and would more than recoup the profits it lost during the initial phase.

From this scenario two theories of injury to Monfort emerge: (1) a threat of a loss of profits stemming from the possibility that Excel, after the merger, would lower its prices to a level at or only slightly above its costs; (2) a threat of being driven out of business by the possibility that Excel, after the merger, would lower its prices to a level below its costs.[9] We discuss each theory in turn.

A

Monfort's first claim is that after the merger, Excel would lower its prices to some level at or slightly above its costs in order to compete with other packers for market share. Excel would be in a position to do this because of the multi-plant efficiencies its acquisition of Spencer would provide. To remain competitive, Monfort would have to lower its prices; as a result, Monfort would suffer a loss in profitability, but would not be driven out of business.[10] The question is whether Monfort's loss of profits in such circumstances constitutes antitrust injury.

To resolve the question, we look again to *Brunswick v. Pueblo Bowl-O-Mat*, *supra*. In *Brunswick*, we evaluated the antitrust significance of several competitors' loss of profits resulting from the entry of a large firm into its market. We concluded:

---

[9] In its brief, Monfort also argues that it would be injured by "the trend toward oligopoly pricing" that could conceivably follow the merger. Brief for Respondent 18-20. There is no indication in the record that this claim was raised below, however, and so we do not address it here.

[10] In this case, Monfort has conceded that its viability would not be threatened by Excel's decision to lower prices: "Because Monfort's operations were as efficient as those of Excel, only below-cost pricing could remove Monfort as an obstacle." ("Monfort proved it was just as efficient as Excel"); ("Monfort would only be harmed by sustained predatory pricing").

"[T]he antitrust laws are not merely indifferent to the injury claimed here. At base, respondents complain that by acquiring the failing centers petitioner preserved competition, thereby depriving respondents of the benefits of increased concentration. The damages respondents obtained are designed to provide them with the profits they would have realized had competition been reduced. The antitrust laws, however, were enacted for 'the protection of *competition,* not *competitors.' Brown Shoe Co. v. United States,* 370 U.S., at 320. It is inimical to the purposes of these laws to award damages for the type of injury claimed here." 429 U.S., at 488.

The loss of profits to the competitors in *Brunswick* was not of concern under the antitrust laws, since it resulted only from continued competition. Respondent argues that the losses in *Brunswick* can be distinguished from the losses alleged here, since the latter will result from an increase, rather than from a mere continuation, of competition. The range of actions unlawful under § 7 of the Clayton Act is broad enough, respondent claims, to support a finding of antitrust injury whenever a competitor is faced with a threat of losses from increased competition.[11] We find respondent's proposed construction of § 7 too broad, for reasons that *Brunswick* illustrates. *Brunswick* holds that the antitrust laws do not require the courts to protect small businesses from the loss of profits due to continued competition, but only against the loss of profits from practices forbidden by the antitrust laws. The kind of competition that Monfort alleges here, competition for increased market share, is not activity forbidden by the antitrust laws. It is simply, as petitioners claim, vigorous competition. To hold that the antitrust laws protect competitors from the loss of profits due to such price competition would, in effect, render illegal any decision by a firm to cut prices in order to increase market share. The antitrust laws require no such perverse result, for "[i]t is in the interest of competition to permit dominant firms to engage in vigorous competition, including price competition." *Arthur S. Langenderfer, Inc. v. S.E. Johnson Co.,* 729 F.2d 1050, 1057 (6th Cir.), cert. denied, 469 U.S. 1036 (1984). The logic of *Brunswick* compels the conclusion that the threat of loss of profits due to possible price competition following a merger does not constitute a threat of antitrust injury.

---

[11] Respondent finds support in the legislative history of the Hart-Scott Antitrust Improvements Act of 1976 for the view that Congress intends the courts to apply § 7 so as to protect the viability of small competitors. The Senate Report, for example, cites with approval this Court's statement in *United States v. Von's Grocery Co.,* 384 U.S. 270, 275 (1966) that "the basic purpose of the 1950 Celler-Kefauver Act [amending § 7 of the Clayton Act] was to prevent economic concentration in the American economy by keeping a large number of small competitors in business." S. Rep. No. 94-803, 63 (1976). Even if respondent is correct that Congress intended the courts to apply § 7 so as to keep small competitors in business at the expense of efficiency, a proposition about which there is considerable disagreement, such congressional intent is of no use to Monfort, which has conceded that it will suffer only a loss of profits, and not be driven from the market, should Excel engage in a cost-price squeeze.

B

The second theory of injury argued here is that after the merger Excel would attempt to drive Monfort out of business by engaging in sustained predatory pricing. Predatory pricing may be defined as pricing below an appropriate measure of cost for the purpose of eliminating competitors in the short run and reducing competition in the long run. It is a practice that harms both competitors *and* competition. In contrast to price cutting aimed simply at increasing market share, predatory pricing has as its aim the elimination of competition. Predatory pricing is thus a practice "inimical to the purposes of [the antitrust] laws," *Brunswick*, 429 U.S., at 488, and one capable of inflicting antitrust injury.[13]

The Court of Appeals held that Monfort had alleged "what we consider to be a form of predatory pricing...." 761 F.2d, at 575. The Court also found that Monfort "could only be harmed by sustained predatory pricing," and that "it is impossible to tell in advance of the acquisition" whether Excel would in fact engage in such a course of conduct; because it could not rule out the possibility that Excel would engage in predatory pricing, it found that Monfort was threatened with antitrust injury.

Although the Court of Appeals did not explicitly define what it meant by predatory pricing, two interpretations are plausible. First, the court can be understood to mean that Monfort's allegation of losses from the above-cost "cost-price squeeze" was equivalent to an allegation of injury from predatory conduct. If this is the proper interpretation, then the court's judgment is clearly erroneous because (a) Monfort made no allegation that Excel would act with predatory intent after the merger, and (b) price competition is not predatory activity, for the reason discussed in Part III-A, *supra*.

Second, the Court of Appeals can be understood to mean that Monfort had shown a credible threat of injury from below-cost pricing. To the extent the judgment rests on this ground, however, it must also be reversed, because Monfort did not allege injury from below-cost pricing before the District Court. The District Court twice noted that Monfort had made no assertion that Excel would engage in predatory pricing. See 591 F. Supp., at 691 ("Plaintiff does not contend that predatory practices would be engaged in by Excel or IBP."); *Id.*, at 710 ("Monfort does not allege that IBP and Excel will in fact engage in predatory activities as part of the cost-price squeeze").[14]

... We conclude that Monfort neither raised nor proved any claim of predatory pricing before the District Court.[15]

---

[13]   See also *Brunswick*, 429 U.S., at 489, n. 14 ("The short-term effect of certain anticompetitive behavior — predatory below-cost pricing, for example — may be to stimulate price competition. But competitors may be able to prove antitrust injury before they actually are driven from the market and competition is thereby lessened.").

[14]   The Court of Appeals may have relied on the District Court's speculation that the merger raised "a distinct possibility ... of predatory pricing." 591 F. Supp., at 710. This statement directly followed the District Court's second observation that Monfort did not raise such a claim, however, and thus was clearly dicta.

[15]   Even had Monfort actually advanced a claim of predatory pricing, we doubt whether the

IV

In its *amicus* brief, the United States argues that the "danger of allowing a competitor to challenge an acquisition on the basis of necessarily speculative claims of post-acquisition predatory pricing far outweighs the danger that any anticompetitive merger will go unchallenged." On this basis, the United States invites the Court to adopt in effect a *per se* rule "denying competitors standing to challenge acquisitions on the basis of predatory pricing theories."

We decline the invitation. As the foregoing discussion makes plain, predatory pricing is an anticompetitive practice forbidden by the antitrust laws. While firms may engage in the practice only infrequently, there is ample evidence suggesting that the practice does occur.[16] It would be novel indeed for a court to deny standing to a party seeking an injunction against threatened injury merely because such injuries rarely occur.[17] In any case, nothing in the language or legislative history of the Clayton Act suggests that Congress intended this Court to ignore injuries caused by such anticompetitive practices as predatory pricing.

V

We hold that a plaintiff seeking injunctive relief under § 16 of the Clayton Act must show a threat of antitrust injury, and that a showing of loss or damage due merely to increased competition does not constitute such injury. The record below does not support a finding of antitrust injury, but only of threatened loss from increased competition. Because respondent has therefore failed to make the showing § 16 requires, we need not reach the question of whether the proposed

---

facts as found by the District Court would have supported it. Although Excel may have had the financial resources to absorb losses over an extended period, other factors, such as Excel's share of market capacity and the barriers to entry after competitors have been driven from the market, must also be considered.

[16] See Koller, *The Myth of Predatory Pricing: An Empirical Study*, 4 Antitrust Law & Econ. Rev. 105 (1971); Miller, *Comments on Baumol and Ordover*, 28 J. Law & Econ. 267 (1985).

[17] Claims of threatened injury from predatory pricing must, of course, be evaluated with care. As we discussed in *Matsushita Electric Industrial Co. v. Zenith Radio Corp.*, the likelihood that predatory pricing will benefit the predator is "inherently uncertain: the short run loss [from pricing below cost] is definite, but the long-run gain depends on successfully neutralizing the competition.... [and] on maintaining monopoly power for long enough both to recoup the predator's losses and to harvest some additional gain." 475 U.S. 574, 588. Although the commentators disagree as to whether it is ever rational for a firm to engage in such conduct, it is plain that the obstacles to the successful execution of a strategy of predation are manifold, and that the disincentives to engage in such a strategy are accordingly numerous. As we stated in *Matsushita*, "predatory pricing schemes are rarely tried, and even more rarely successful." Moreover, the mechanism by which a firm engages in predatory pricing — lowering prices — is the same mechanism by which a firm stimulates competition; because "cutting prices in order to increase business often is the very essence of competition ... mistaken inferences ... are especially costly, because they chill the very conduct the antitrust laws are designed to protect."

merger violates § 7. The judgment of the Court of Appeals is reversed and the case is remanded for further proceedings consistent with this opinion.

NOTES AND QUESTIONS

1. Does *Cargill* also answer the issue of whether a target company suffers an antitrust injury by reason of a tender offer takeover? Is a target able to allege any diminution in competition? Consider the following problem: Company *A* seeks to "take over" Company *B* by means of a tender offer for *B*'s outstanding stock. *B* objects to the takeover. Its directors sue *A*, claiming that the proposed takeover would be an illegal merger. If the merger is illegal, however, it is because the post-merger firm, *AB*, will have more market power than the two firms did before the merger. *B* will therefore be the beneficiary, not the victim, of any illegal merger. Has *B* suffered antitrust injury? *See Anago, Inc. v. Tecnol Medical Products, Inc.*, 976 F.2d 248 (5th Cir. 1992). The court found that tender offer targets lack antitrust injury. *See* Easterbrook & Fischel, *Antitrust Suits by Targets of Tender Offers*, 80 Mich. L. Rev. 1155 (1982).

2. For further discussion of the "antitrust injury" in the context of section 7 of the Clayton Act (mergers), see Chapter 7, *infra*.

3. It seems clear after a review of the antitrust injury and direct purchaser limitations on section 4 that the Supreme Court is concerned with litigation problems that implicate speculative injury claims, complex damage tracing problems, duplicative recoveries, and questionable causal connection theories.

ATLANTIC RICHFIELD CO. V. USA PETROLEUM CO.

495 U.S. 328 (1990)

BRENNAN, J., delivered the opinion of the Court.

This case presents the question whether a firm incurs an "injury" within the meaning of the antitrust laws when it loses sales to a competitor charging non-predatory prices pursuant to a vertical, maximum price-fixing scheme. We hold that such a firm does not suffer an "antitrust injury" and that it therefore cannot bring suit under § 4 of the Clayton Act.

I

Respondent USA Petroleum Company (USA) sued petitioner Atlantic Richfield Company (ARCO) in the United States District Court for the Central District of California, alleging the existence of a vertical, maximum price-fixing agreement prohibited by § 1 of the Sherman Act, and an attempt to monopolize the local retail gasoline sales market in violation of § 2 of the Sherman Act, and other misconduct not relevant here. Petitioner ARCO is an integrated oil company that, inter alia, markets gasoline in the western United States. It sells gasoline to consumers both directly through its own stations and indirectly through ARCO-brand dealers. Respondent USA is an independent retail marketer of gasoline which, like other independents, buys gasoline from major petroleum companies for resale under its own brand name. Respondent competes directly with ARCO dealers at the retail level. Respondent's outlets typically are low-overhead, high-volume "discount" stations that charge less than stations selling equivalent quality gasoline under major brand names.

In early 1982, petitioner ARCO adopted a new marketing strategy in order to compete more effectively with discount independents such as respondent.[2] Petitioner encouraged its dealers to match the retail gasoline prices offered by independents in various ways; petitioner made available to its dealers and distributors such short-term discounts as "temporary competitive allowances" and "temporary volume allowances," and it reduced its dealers' costs by, for example, eliminating credit card sales. ARCO's strategy increased its sales and market share.

In its amended complaint, respondent USA charged that ARCO engaged in "direct head-to-head competition with discounters" and "drastically lowered its prices and in other ways sought to appeal to price-conscious consumers." Respondent asserted that petitioner conspired with retail service stations selling ARCO brand gasoline to fix prices at below-market levels: "ARCO and its co-conspirators have organized a resale price maintenance scheme, as a direct result of which competition that would otherwise exist among ARCO-branded gasoline had been fixed, stabilized and maintained at artificially low and uncompetitive levels." Respondent alleged that petitioner "has solicited its dealers and distributors to participate or acquiesce in the conspiracy and has used threats, intimidation and coercion to secure compliance with its terms." According to respondent, this conspiracy drove many independent gasoline dealers in California out of business. Count one of the amended complaint charged that petitioner's vertical, maximum price-fixing scheme constituted an agreement in restraint of trade and thus violated § 1 of the Sherman Act. Count two, later withdrawn with prejudice by respondent, asserted that petitioner had engaged in an attempt to monopolize the retail gasoline market through predatory pricing in violation of § 2 of the Sherman Act.

The District Court granted summary judgment for ARCO on the § 1 claim. The court stated that "[e]ven assuming that [respondent USA] can establish a vertical conspiracy to maintain low prices, [respondent] cannot satisfy the 'antitrust injury' requirement of Clayton Act § 4, without showing such prices to be predatory." The court then concluded that respondent could make no such showing of predatory pricing because, given petitioner's market share and the ease of entry into the market, petitioner was in no position to exercise market power.

A divided panel of the Court of Appeals for the Ninth Circuit reversed, holding that injuries resulting from vertical, nonpredatory, maximum price-fixing agree-

---

[2]   Because the case comes to us on review of summary judgment, "inferences to be drawn from the underlying facts ... must be viewed in the light most favorable to the party opposing the motion." *Matsushita Electric Industrial Co. v. Zenith Radio Corp.*, 475 U.S. 574, 587 (1986) (quoting *United States v. Diebold, Inc.*, 369 U.S. 654, 655 (1962)).

ments could constitute "antitrust injury" for purposes of a private suit under § 4 of the Clayton Act....

II

A private plaintiff may not recover damages under § 4 of the Clayton Act merely by showing "injury causally linked to an illegal presence in the market." *Brunswick Corp. v. Pueblo Bowl-O-Mat, Inc.*, 429 U.S. 477, 489 (1977). Instead, a plaintiff must prove the existence of "*Antitrust* injury, which is to say injury of the type the antitrust laws were intended to prevent and that flows from that which makes defendants' acts unlawful." (emphasis in original). In *Cargill, Inc. v. Monfort of Colorado, Inc.*, 479 U.S. 104 (1986), we reaffirmed that injury, although causally related to an antitrust violation, nevertheless will not qualify as "antitrust injury" unless it is attributable to an anticompetitive aspect of the practice under scrutiny, "since '[i]t is inimical to [the antitrust] laws to award damages' for losses stemming from continued competition."

Respondent argues that, as a competitor, it can show antitrust injury from a vertical conspiracy to fix maximum prices that is unlawful under § 1 of the Sherman Act, even if the prices were set above predatory levels. In addition, respondent maintains that any loss flowing from a per se violation of § 1 automatically satisfies the antitrust injury requirement. We reject both contentions and hold that respondent has failed to meet the antitrust injury test in this case. We therefore reverse the judgment of the Court of Appeals.

A

In *Albrecht v. Herald Co.*, 390 U.S. 145 (1968), we found that a vertical, maximum price-fixing scheme was unlawful per se under § 1 of the Sherman Act because it threatened to inhibit vigorous competition by the dealers bound by it and because it threatened to become a minimum price-fixing scheme.[5]

....

Respondent alleges that it has suffered losses as a result of competition with firms following a vertical, maximum price-fixing agreement. But in *Albrecht* we held such an agreement per se unlawful because of its potential effects on dealers and consumers, not because of its effects on competitors. Respondent's asserted injury as a competitor does not resemble any of the potential dangers described in *Albrecht*.[6] For example, if a vertical agreement fixes "[m]aximum prices ... too

---

[5]   We assume, arguendo, that *Albrecht* correctly held that vertical, maximum price-fixing is subject to the per se rule. [In 1997 the Court reversed *Albrecht*, holding that vertical, maximum price fixing is not subject to the per se rule, but should be analyzed under the reasonableness test. *State Oil v. Kahn* 118 S. Ct. 275 (1997).]

[6] *Albrecht* is the only case in which the Court has confronted an unadulterated vertical, maximum price-fixing arrangement. In *Kiefer-Stewart Co. v. Joseph E. Seagram & Sons, Inc.*, 340 U.S. 211, 213 (1951), we also suggested that such an arrangement was illegal because it restricted vigorous competition among dealers. The restraint in *Kiefer-Stewart* had an additional horizontal

low for the dealer to furnish services" desired by consumers, or in such a way as to channel business to large distributors, then a firm dealing in a competing brand would not be harmed. Respondent was benefitted rather than harmed if petitioner's pricing policies restricted ARCO sales to a few large dealers or prevented petitioner's dealers from offering services desired by consumers, such as credit card sales. Even if the maximum price agreement ultimately had acquired all of the attributes of a minimum price-fixing scheme, respondent still would not have suffered antitrust injury because higher ARCO prices would have worked to USA's advantage. A competitor "may not complain of conspiracies that ... set minimum prices at any level." *Matsushita Electric Industrial Corp. v. Zenith Radio Corp.*, 475 U.S. 574, 585, n. 8 (1986); see also *id.*, at 582-83 ("respondents [cannot] recover damages for any conspiracy by petitioners to charge higher than competitive prices in the ... market. Such conduct would indeed violate the Sherman Act, but it could not injure respondents: as petitioners' competitors, respondents stand to gain from any conspiracy to raise the market price ..."). Indeed, the gravamen of respondent's complaint — that the price-fixing scheme between petitioner and its dealers enabled those dealers to increase their sales — amounts to an assertion that the dangers with which we were concerned in *Albrecht* have not materialized in the instant case. In sum, respondent has not suffered "antitrust injury," since its losses do not flow from the aspects of vertical, maximum price-fixing that render it illegal. Respondent argues that even if it was not harmed by any of the anticompetitive effects identified in *Albrecht*, it nonetheless suffered antitrust injury because of the low prices produced by the vertical restraint. We disagree. When a firm, or even a group of firms adhering to a vertical agreement, lowers prices but maintains them above predatory levels, the business lost by rivals cannot be viewed as an "anticompetitive" consequence of the claimed violation.[7] A firm complaining about the harm it suffers from nonpredatory price competition "is really claiming that it [is] unable to raise prices." Blair & Harrison, Rethinking Antitrust Injury, 42 Vand. L. Rev. 1539, 1554 (1989). This is not antitrust injury; indeed, "cutting prices in order to increase business often is the very essence of competition." The antitrust laws were enacted for "the protection of *competition*, not competitors." *Brown Shoe Co. v.*

---

component, however, see *Arizona v. Maricopa County Medical Society*, 457 U.S. 332, 348, n. 18 (1982), since the agreement was between two suppliers that had agreed to sell liquor only to wholesalers adhering to "maximum prices above which the wholesalers could not resell." *Kiefer-Stewart, supra*, 340 U.S., at 212.

[7] The Court of Appeals implied that the antitrust injury requirement could be satisfied by a showing that the "long-term" effect of the maximum price agreements could be to eliminate retailers and ultimately reduce competition. 859 F.2d, at 694, 696. We disagree. Rivals cannot be excluded in the long run by a nonpredatory maximum price scheme unless they are relatively inefficient. Even if that were false, however, a firm cannot claim antitrust injury from nonpredatory price competition on the asserted ground that it is "ruinous." Cf. *United States v. Topco Associates, Inc.*, 405 U.S. 596, 610-12 (1972); *United States v. Socony-Vacuum Oil Co.*, 310 U.S. 150, 220-21 (1940). "[T]he statutory policy precludes inquiry into the question whether competition is good or

United States, 370 U.S. 294, 320 (1962) (emphasis in original). "To hold that the antitrust laws protect competitors from the loss of profits due to [nonpredatory] price competition would, in effect, render illegal any decision by a firm to cut prices in order to increase market share." *Cargill*, 479 U.S., at 116.

Respondent further argues that it is inappropriate to require a showing of predatory pricing before antitrust injury can be established when the asserted antitrust violation is an agreement in restraint of trade illegal under § 1 of the Sherman Act, rather than an attempt to monopolize prohibited by § 2. Respondent notes that the two sections of the Act are quite different. Price fixing violates § 1, for example, even if a single firm's decision to price at the same level would not create § 2 liability. See generally *Copperweld Corp. v. Independence Tube Corp.*, 467 U.S. 752, 767-69 (1984). In a § 1 case, the price agreement itself is illegal, and respondent contends that all losses flowing from such an agreement must by definition constitute "antitrust injuries." Respondent observes that § 1 in general and the per se rule in particular are grounded "on faith in price competition as a market force [and not] on a policy of low selling prices at the price of eliminating competition." *Arizona v. Maricopa County Medical Society*, 457 U.S. 332, 348 (1982). In sum, respondent maintains that it has suffered antitrust injury even if petitioner's pricing was not predatory under § 2 of the Sherman Act.

We reject respondent's argument. Although a vertical, maximum price-fixing agreement is unlawful under § 1 of the Sherman Act, it does not cause a competitor antitrust injury unless it results in predatory pricing. Antitrust injury does not arise for purposes of § 4 of the Clayton Act, until a private party is adversely affected by an anticompetitive aspect of the defendant's conduct, see *Brunswick*, 429 U.S., at 487; in the context of pricing practices, only predatory pricing has the requisite anticompetitive effect.[9] See Areeda & Turner, *Predatory Pricing and Related Practices Under Section 2 of the Sherman Act*, 88 Harv. L. Rev. 697, 697-99 (1975); McGee, *Predatory Pricing Revisited*, 23 J. Law & Econ. 289, 292-94 (1980). Low prices benefit consumers regardless of how those prices are set, and so long as they are above predatory levels, they do not threaten competition. Hence, they cannot give rise to antitrust injury. We have adhered to this principle regardless of the type of antitrust claim involved....

Similarly, we determined that antitrust injury was absent in *Brunswick Corp. v. Pueblo Bowl-O-Mat, Inc.*, even though the plaintiffs alleged that an illegal acquisition threatened to bring a "deep pocket 'parent into a market of' pygmies," *Id.*, at 487, a scenario that would cause the plaintiffs economic harm. We opined nevertheless that "if [the plaintiffs] were injured, it was not 'by reason of any-

---

bad." *National Society of Professional Engineers v. United States*, 435 U.S. 679, 695 (1978).

[9] This is not to deny that a vertical price-fixing scheme may facilitate predatory pricing. A supplier, for example, can reduce its prices to its own downstream dealers and share the losses with them, while forcing competing dealers to bear by themselves the full loss imposed by the lower prices. Cf. *FTC v. Sun Oil Co.*, 371 U.S. 505, 522 (1963). But because a firm always is able to challenge directly a rival's pricing as predatory, there is no reason to dispense with the antitrust injury requirement in an action by a competitor against a vertical agreement.

thing forbidden in the antitrust laws': while [the plaintiffs'] loss occurred 'by reason of' the unlawful acquisitions, it did not occur 'by reason of' that which made the acquisitions unlawful." To be sure, the source of the price competition in the instant case was an agreement allegedly unlawful under § 1 of the Sherman Act rather than a merger in violation of § 7 of the Clayton Act. But that difference is not salient.

When prices are not predatory, any losses flowing from them cannot be said to stem from an anticompetitive aspect of the defendant's conduct. "It is in the interest of competition to permit dominant firms to engage in vigorous competition, including price competition." *Cargill*, 479 U.S., at 116 (quoting *Arthur S. Langenderfer, Inc. v. S.E. Johnson Co.*, 729 F.2d 1050, 1057 (6th Cir.), *cert. denied* 469 U.S. 1036 (1984)).

B

We also reject respondent's suggestion that no antitrust injury need be shown where a per se violation is involved. The per se rule is a method of determining whether § 1 of the Sherman Act has been violated, but it does not indicate whether a private plaintiff has suffered antitrust injury and thus whether he may recover damages under § 4 of the Clayton Act. Per se and rule-of-reason analysis are but two methods of determining whether a restraint is "unreasonable," i.e., whether its anticompetitive effects outweigh its procompetitive effects. The per se rule is a presumption of unreasonableness based on "business certainty and litigation efficiency." *Arizona v. Maricopa County Medical Society*, 457 U.S., at 344. It represents a "long-standing judgment that the prohibited practices 'by their nature have' a substantial potential for impact on competition." *FTC v. Superior Court Trial Lawyers Assn.*, 493 U.S. 411, 432 (1990) (quoting *Jefferson Parish Hospital Dist. No. 2 v. Hyde*, 466 U.S. 2, 16 (1984)). "Once experience with a particular kind of restraint enables the Court to predict with confidence that the rule of reason will condemn it, it has applied a conclusive presumption that the restraint is unreasonable." *Maricopa County Medical Society, supra*, at 344.

The purpose of the antitrust injury requirement is different. It ensures that the harm claimed by the plaintiff corresponds to the rationale for finding a violation of the antitrust laws in the first place, and it prevents losses that stem from competition from supporting suits by private plaintiffs for either damages or equitable relief. Actions per se unlawful under the antitrust laws may nonetheless have some procompetitive effects, and private parties might suffer losses therefrom.[13]

---

[13] When a manufacturer provides a dealer an exclusive area within which to distribute a product, the manufacturer's decision to fix a maximum resale price may actually protect consumers against exploitation by the dealer acting as a local monopolist. The manufacturer acts not out of altruism, of course, but out of a desire to increase its own sales, whereas the dealer's incentive, like that of any monopolist, is to reduce output and increase price. If an exclusive dealership is the most efficient means of distribution, the public is not served by forcing the manufacturer to abandon this method and resort to self-distribution or competing distributors.

Conduct in violation of the antitrust laws may have three effects, often inter-woven: in some respects the conduct may reduce competition, in other respects it may increase competition, and in still other respects effects may be neutral as to competition. The antitrust injury requirement ensures that a plaintiff can recover only if the loss stems from a competition-*reducing* aspect or effect of the defen-dant's behavior. The need for this showing is at least as great under the per se rule as under the rule of reason. Indeed, in so far as the per se rule permits the prohibition of efficient practices in the name of simplicity, the need for the anti-trust injury requirement is underscored. "[P]rocompetitive or efficiency-enhancing aspects of practices that nominally violate the antitrust laws may cause serious harm to individuals, but this kind of harm is the essence of competition and should play no role in the definition of antitrust damages." Page, *The Scope of Liability for Antitrust Violations*, 37 Stan. L. Rev. 1445, 1460 (1985). Thus, "proof of a per se violation and of antitrust injury are distinct matters that must be shown independently." P. Areeda & H. Hovenkamp, *Antitrust Law* ¶ 334.2c, at 330 (1989 Supp.).

For this reason, we have previously recognized that even in cases involving per se violations, the right of action under § 4 of the Clayton Act is available only to those private plaintiffs who have suffered antitrust injury. For example, in a case involving horizontal price-fixing, "perhaps the paradigm of an unrea-sonable restraint of trade," we observed that the plaintiffs were still required to "show that the conspiracy caused *them* an injury for which the antitrust laws provide relief."...

Vertical, minimum price-fixing thus may have procompetitive interbrand effects even if it is per se illegal because of its potential effects on dealers and consumers. See *Albrecht v. Herald Co.*, 390 U.S. 145, 159 (1968) (Harlan, J., dissenting) (maximum price ceilings "do not lessen horizontal competition," but instead "drive prices toward the level that would be set by intense competition," by "prevent[ing] retailers or wholesalers from reaping monopoly or supercompetitive profits"). Indeed, we acknowledged in *Albrecht* that "[m]aximum and minimum price fixing may have different consequences in many situations." *Id.*, at 152. The procompetitive potential of a vertical maximum price restraint is more evident now than it was when *Albrecht* was decided, because exclusive territorial arrangements and other nonprice restrictions were unlawful per se in 1968. See *id.*, at 154; *United States v. Arnold, Schwinn & Co.*, 388 U.S. 365, 375-76 (1967). These agreements are currently subject only to rule-of-reason scrutiny, making monopolistic behavior by dealers more likely. See *Monsanto Co. v. Spray-Rite Service Corp.*, 465 U.S. 752, 761 (1984); *Continental T.V., Inc. v. GTE Sylvania Inc.*, 433 U.S. 36, 47-59 (1977). Many commentators have identified procompetitive effects of vertical, maximum price-fixing. See, e.g., P. Areeda & H. Hovenkamp, Antitrust Law ¶ 340.3b, at 378, n. 24 (1988 Supp.); Blair & Harrison, *Rethinking Antitrust Injury*, 42 Vand. L. Rev. 1539, 1553 (1989); Blair & Schafer, *Evolutionary Models of Legal Change and the Albrecht Rule*, 32 Antitrust Bull. 989, 995-1000 (1987); Bork, *The Rule of Reason and the Per Se Concept: Price Fixing and Market Division, Part 2*, 75 Yale L.J. 373, 464 (1966); Easterbrook, *Maximum Price Fixing*, 48 U. Chi. L. Rev. 886, 887-90 (1981); Hovenkamp, *Vertical Integration by the Newspaper Monopolist*, 69 Iowa L. Rev. 451, 452-56 (1984); Polden, *Antitrust Standing and the Rule Against Resale Price Maintenance*, 37 Clev. St. L. Rev. 179, 216-17 (1989); Turner, *The Durability, Relevance, and Future of American Antitrust Policy*, 75 Cal. L. Rev. 797, 803-04 (1987).

C

We decline to dilute the antitrust injury requirement here because we find that there is no need to encourage private enforcement by competitors of the rule against vertical, maximum price-fixing. If such a scheme causes the anticompetitive consequences detailed in *Albrecht*, consumers and the manufacturers' own dealers may bring suit. The "existence of an identifiable class of persons whose self-interest would normally motivate them to vindicate the public interest in antitrust enforcement diminishes the justification for allowing a more remote party ... to perform the office of a private attorney general." *Associated General Contractors*, 459 U.S., at 542.

Respondent's injury, moreover, is not "inextricably intertwined" with the antitrust injury that a dealer would suffer, and thus does not militate in favor of permitting respondent to sue on behalf of petitioner's dealers. A competitor is not injured by the anticompetitive effects of vertical, maximum price-fixing, and does not have any incentive to vindicate the legitimate interests of a rival's dealer. See Easterbrook, *The Limits of Antitrust*, 63 Texas L. Rev. 1, 33-39 (1984). A competitor will not bring suit to protect the dealer against the maximum price that is set too low, in as much as the competitor would benefit from such a situation. Instead, a competitor will be motivated to bring suit only when the vertical restraint promotes interbrand competition between the competitor and the dealer subject to the restraint. In short, a competitor will be injured and hence motivated to sue only when a vertical, maximum price-fixing arrangement has a procompetitive impact on the market. Therefore, providing the competitor a cause of action would not protect the rights of dealers and consumers under the antitrust laws.

III

Respondent has failed to demonstrate that it has suffered any antitrust injury. The allegation of a per se violation does not obviate the need to satisfy this test. The judgment of the Court of Appeals is reversed, and the case is remanded for proceedings consistent with this opinion. It is so ordered.

[JUSTICE STEVENS and JUSTICE WHITE dissented.]

....

NOTES AND QUESTIONS

1. On remand, 972 F.2d 1070 (9th Cir. 1992), the Ninth Circuit held that the Supreme Court's conclusion that the independent gasoline marketers lacked standing to challenge the alleged vertical maximum resale price maintenance scheme applied only in the absence of predatory pricing. But the plaintiffs might still have standing to prove that the maintained prices were predatory. Is this consistent with the Supreme Court's decision?

2. Does the majority opinion in *Atlantic Richfield* suggest that competitors lack antitrust injury in all pricing cases under section 1, or only vertical, maximum price fixing cases? What outcome if the Court's logic in *Atlantic Richfield* is applied to a vertical, minimum price fixing agreement? If the per se rule of *Albrecht* is still good law, what kind of plaintiff can meet the antitrust injury test?

3. Is it clear after the decision that even in per se cases under section 1 of the Sherman Act all plaintiffs must first demonstrate "antitrust injury"? Will antitrust injury be inferred in some cases? How about direct purchaser lawsuits against cartels? *See Rebel Oil Co. v. Atlantic Richfield Co.*, 51 F.3d 1421 (9th Cir. 1994), *cert. denied*, 516 U.S. 987 (1995):

> Rebel argues that market power is not a prerequisite to antitrust injury if the claim is premised on Sherman Act § 1 ... because vertical price fixing is per se illegal.... Rebel confuses proof of liability with proof of antitrust injury.... The "mere presence" of a per se violation under the Sherman Act § 1 "does not by itself bestow on any plaintiff a private right of action for damages." A plaintiff must prove that his injury flows from the anti-competitive aspect of the defendant's conduct. For example, in *USA Petroleum*, the plaintiff did not suffer antitrust injury from defendant's conspiracy to fix low prices. Although per se illegal, maximum price fixing cannot cause antitrust injury because low prices are the "very essence of competition." (Citing *Atlantic Richfield*, quoting *Matsushita*.)

4. *Caribe BMW, Inc. v. Bayerische Motoren Werke Aktiengesellschaft*, 19 F.3d 745 (1st Cir. 1994), considered whether a dealer's lost profits resulting from a maximum resale price fixing agreement constitutes antitrust injury. The court distinguished *Atlantic Richfield*, noting that the plaintiffs in that case were not dealers but *competitors* of the dealers. The court held that the district court erred in dismissing the antitrust claims because Caribe was the very firm that the alleged price maintenance agreement forced to keep its prices below the level that some customers — those seeking greater service, for example — presumably were willing to pay.

5. *See also SAS of Puerto Rico v. Puerto Rico Tel. Co.*, 48 F.3d 39 (1st Cir. 1995), which denied standing to a pay telephone company claiming that the defendant telephone company excluded its product, which would have increased competition among long distance carriers serving pay telephone companies. The telephone company thereafter entered into a contract with a long distance carrier, whose provisions included preferred access for that carrier to pay telephones. In denying standing the court noted that any reduction in competition for access to pay telephones injured (a) customers using pay telephones for long distance calls, who would find access to alternative long distance carriers more difficult and perhaps pay higher prices to the preferred carrier; (b) alternative long distance carriers who did not enjoy the status of "default" carrier at pay telephones; and (c) the plaintiff, who lost the profits from installing its equipment that would have facilitated competition among long distance carriers. The court concluded that both the customers and the competing long distance carriers were probably victims of antitrust injury, but that the plaintiff was a mere supplier, and in this case a "second best" plaintiff. The court stated:

> The most obvious reason for conferring standing on a second-best plaintiff is that, in some general category of cases, there may be no first best with the incentive or ability to sue.... That is hardly likely here: those threatened by the market injury alleged by SAS include various potential plaintiffs, above all, long distance carriers, who should have ample incentive and ability to challenge violations that foreclose their access to customers.

Compare G.K.A. Beverage Corp. v. Honickman, 55 F.3d 762 (2d Cir.), *cert. denied*, 516 U.S. 944 (1995) (soft drink distributors lacked standing to challenge alleged soft drink company's anticompetitive acts directed at a bottler whose output plaintiffs distributed; the injury belonged to the bottler. The alleged purpose of the predation was to drive the bottler into bankruptcy, thus terminating its distribution agreements.

6. Lack of antitrust injury also has prevented plaintiffs from bringing antitrust claims in the health care arena. In *Ambroze v. Aetna Health Plans of New York Inc.*, No. 95 CIV. 6631, 1996 WL 282069 (S.D.N.Y. May 28, 1996), individual anesthesiologists and group providers of anesthesiology services asserted that Aetna, the health care provider that employed them, used threats to terminate existing managed care agreements with hospitals to force the anesthesiologists to enter into employment agreements. The plaintiffs argued that they suffered antitrust injury because the threats of termination reduced competition among the Aetna anesthesiologists, in turn undermining their independent judgment about the services they offered patients. The district court relied on *Kartell v. Blue Shield of Massachusetts Inc.*, 749 F.2d 922 (1st Cir. 1984), and *Westchester Radiological Assocs. P.C. v. Empire Blue Cross & Blue Shield Inc.*, 707 F. Supp. 708 (S.D.N.Y. 1989), in holding that Aetna, the buyer of the anesthesiology services, could set the terms of its agreement with the plaintiffs without creating "antitrust injury." The court stated that the employment agreement, not another party, restrained the anesthesiologists' provision of services.

7. In *State Oil v. Kahn*, 118 S. Ct. 275 (1997), the court overruled *Albrecht* (discussed in the *Atlantic Richfield* decision) and held that vertical maximum price fixing is not per se unlawful. See Chapter 5, *infra*.

PROBLEM 3.3

Arlen, Inc. and Spectro, Inc., are the country's only two manufacturers of cardiac transponders, high tech electronic devices for monitoring heart activity. Both the devices and the process by which they are manufactured are covered by several patents. Arlen is a large manufacturer, well established in the cardiac transponder business. Spectro is a small upstart that is not yet as well established and has a much smaller output, but it has patented some new transponder designs that have the potential to make its transponders superior to those of Arlen.

In 1987 Arlen made Spectro an offer it could not refuse: $10,000,000 for its plant and exclusive licenses on its patents, plus 10% of gross sales on all the transponders which were made in the acquired plant or which employed the acquired patents. Spectro sold both its plant and its patents to Arlen and went out of business.

A year later Arlen closed down the Spectro plant, announced to Spectro that it would continue to manufacture cardiac transponders under the old technology, and claimed that it thus owed Spectro no money under the "10% of gross sales" part of the sale agreement.

Spectro sued Arlen, alleging monopolization of the cardiac transponder market and that the Spectro-Arlen acquisition was an illegal merger. Does Spectro have standing? Does the Supreme Court's *Brunswick* decision apply? Would it make a difference if Spectro had owned two plants and Arlen had purchased only one of them? *See McDonald v. Johnson & Johnson*, 722 F.2d 1370 (8th Cir. 1983), *cert. denied*, 469 U.S. 870 (1984).

PROBLEM 3.4

The National Collegiate Athletic Association restricts member-school institutions in the amount of compensation student athletes may be paid while on an athletic scholarship. The NCAA rules provide sanctions against member schools, including suspension and expulsion, for violations of the compensation rule.

The Oxford Institute of Intelligence is a major football power and a member of the All-Academic Conference. In order to recruit football players, it made side payments in excess of the NCAA compensation rules. Each of its 30 football players received $200 per month more than the NCAA rules permit.

Upon investigation of the violations, the NCAA suspended Oxford Institute from NCAA-sponsored competitions for the 1990 season. Other penalties were imposed as well. A group of Oxford Institute alumni, students, football players, and cheerleaders challenged the NCAA suspensions, contending that the NCAA violated section 1 of the Sherman Act by promulgating and enforcing rules restricting benefits that may be awarded student athletes.

1. Consider whether each category of plaintiff (loyal students, alumni, football players, and cheerleaders) has:

    (a) been injured in a "business or property";
    (b) standing to bring suit;
    (c) alleged an "antitrust injury."

2. Would Oxford Institute meet these section 4 requirements were it to bring an antitrust action against the NCAA? *See McCormack v. NCAA*, 845 F.2d 1338 (5th Cir. 1988).

PROBLEM 3.5

Plaintiff is a disabled person needing frequent medical care. Plaintiff's community contains two clinics, Clinic A and Clinic B. After obtaining services at Clinic A for several years, plaintiff has a bad experience there and files a malpractice action against one of Clinic A's physicians. Plaintiff then transfers his business to Clinic B. Thereafter Clinic A and Clinic B merge. The management of the post-merger firm, Clinic AB, then informs plaintiff that he can no longer use the services of the clinic. Plaintiff sues, alleging that the merger of Clinic A and B has ended competition in the delivery of health care services in the community, that Clinic AB is restricting output after a merger giving it monopoly, and that plaintiff is therefore a victim of antitrust injury. What outcome? *See Nelson v. Monroe Regional Med. Center*, 925 F.2d 1555 (7th Cir. 1991). Query: When a monopolist reduces its output, does it arbitrarily divide its customer base into two classes and refuse to serve one class, or does it simply increase its price? Suppose Clinic AB can show that plaintiff was willing to pay the price that the clinic was charging following the merger. In that case, is plaintiff a victim of antitrust injury?

PROBLEM 3.6

Fuelco is the only company at a marina selling fuel to cruise ships. The owners of the ships believe that Fuelco is charging monopoly prices. They attempt to get another company, Gasco, to open a facility at the marina, but Gasco will not do so unless the ship owners agree to purchase half of the gasoline from Gasco. After speaking with one another the ship owners agree that each will purchase one-half of its fuel needs from Gasco, and Gasco enters the market. Fuelco now sues, alleging that it has been the victim of an unlawful conspiracy. What outcome? *See Belcher Oil Co. v. Florida Fuels*, 749 F. Supp. 1104 (S.D. Fla. 1990).

PROBLEM 3.7

Yellow Pages Cost Consultants (YPCC) provides consulting advice to advertisers in yellow page directories. GTE, the publisher of a yellow page directory, decides to end its long-standing practice of allowing consultants like YPCC to order, place, and process advertisements on behalf of client advertisers. As soon as GTE refuses to deal with YPCC and other advertising consultants, YPCC sues GTE, claiming an illegal attempt to monopolize and a refusal to deal under sections 1 and 2 of the Sherman Act. How should the court rule on YPCC's antitrust injury and standing?

g. Standing to Sue

Standing is a judicially created concept which has the effect of limiting the class of persons who can sue for injuries. The analysis of the federal courts focuses on the "directness" of the injury to the plaintiff, or stated differently, the remoteness of the plaintiff's injury from the antitrust violation.

BLUE SHIELD OF VIRGINIA V. McCREADY

457 U.S. 465 (1982)

JUSTICE BRENNAN delivered the opinion of the Court.

The antitrust complaint at issue in this case alleges that a group health plan's practice of refusing to reimburse subscribers for psychotherapy performed by psychologists, while providing reimbursement for comparable treatment by psychiatrists, was in furtherance of an unlawful conspiracy to restrain competition in the psychotherapy market. The question presented is whether a subscriber who employed the services of a psychologist has standing to maintain an action under § 4 of the Clayton Act based upon the plan's failure to provide reimbursement for the costs of that treatment.

I

From September 1975 until January 1978, respondent Carol McCready was an employee of Prince William County, Virginia. As part of her compensation, the county provided her with coverage under a prepaid group health plan purchased from petitioner Blue Shield of Virginia (Blue Shield). The plan specifically provided reimbursement for a portion of the cost incurred by subscribers with respect to outpatient treatment for mental and nervous disorders, including psychotherapy. Pursuant to this provision, Blue Shield reimbursed subscribers for psychotherapy provided by *psychiatrists*. But Blue Shield did not provide reimbursement for the services of *psychologists* unless the treatment was supervised by and billed through a physician. While a subscriber to the plan, McCready was treated by a clinical psychologist. She submitted claims to Blue Shield for the costs of that treatment, but those claims were routinely denied because they had not been billed through a physician.

In 1978, McCready brought this class action ... on behalf of all Blue Shield subscribers who had incurred costs for psychological services since 1973 but who had not been reimbursed. The complaint alleged that Blue Shield and petitioner Neuropsychiatric Society of Virginia, Inc., had engaged in an unlawful conspiracy in violation of § 1 of the Sherman Act, "to exclude and boycott clinical psychologists from receiving compensation under" the Blue Shield plans. McCready further alleged that Blue Shield's failure to reimburse had been in furtherance of the alleged conspiracy, and had caused injury to her business or property for which she was entitled to treble damages and attorney's fees under § 4 of the Clayton Act....

B

Analytically distinct from the restrictions on the § 4 remedy recognized in *Hawaii* and *Illinois Brick*, there is the conceptually more difficult question "of which persons have sustained injuries *too remote* [from an antitrust violation] to give them standing to sue for damages under § 4." An antitrust violation may be expected to cause ripples of harm to flow through the Nation's economy; but "despite the broad wording of § 4 there is a point beyond which the wrongdoer should not be held liable." It is reasonable to assume that Congress did not intend to allow every person tangentially affected by an antitrust violation to maintain an action to recover threefold damages for the injury to his business or property.... In applying that elusive concept to this statutory action, we look (1) to the physical and economic nexus between the alleged violation and the harm to the plaintiff, and, (2) more particularly, to the relationship of the injury alleged with those forms of injury about which Congress was likely to have been concerned in making defendant's conduct unlawful and in providing a private remedy under § 4.

(1)

It is petitioners' position that McCready's injury is too "fortuitous," "incidental," and "remote" from the alleged violation to provide the basis for a § 14 action. At the outset, petitioners argue that because the alleged conspiracy was directed by its protagonists at psychologists, and not at subscribers to group health plans, only psychologists might maintain suit. This argument may be quickly disposed of.

We do not think that because the goal of the conspirators was to halt encroachment by psychologists into a market that physicians and psychiatrists sought to preserve for themselves, McCready's injury is rendered "remote." The availability of the § 4 remedy to some person who claims its benefit is not a question of the specific intent of the conspirators. Here the remedy cannot reasonably be restricted to those competitors whom the conspirators hoped to eliminate from the market. McCready claims that she has been the victim of a concerted refusal to pay on the part of Blue Shield, motivated by a desire to deprive psychologists of the patronage of Blue Shield subscribers. Denying reimbursement to subscribers for the cost of treatment was the very means by which it is alleged that Blue Shield sought to achieve its illegal ends. The harm to McCready and her class was clearly foreseeable; indeed, it was a necessary step in effecting the ends of the illegal conspiracy. Where the injury alleged is so integral an aspect of the conspiracy alleged, there can be no question but that the loss was precisely "'the type of loss that the claimed violations ... would be likely to cause.'" *Brunswick Corp. v. Pueblo Bowl-O-Mat, Inc.*, 429 U.S., at 489....

Petitioners next argue that even if the § 4 remedy might be available to persons other than the competitors of the conspirators, it is not available to McCready because she was not an economic actor in the market that had been restrained. In petitioners' view, the proximate range of the violation is limited to the sector of the economy in which a violation of the type alleged would have its most direct anticompetitive effects. Here, petitioner contends that that market, for purposes of the alleged conspiracy, is the market in group health care plans. Thus, in petitioners' view, standing to redress the violation alleged in this case is limited to participants in that market — that is, to entities, such as McCready's employer, who were purchasers of group health plans, but not to McCready as a beneficiary of the Blue Shield plan.[16]

Petitioners misconstrue McCready's complaint. McCready does not allege a restraint in the market for group health plans. Her claim of injury is premised on a concerted refusal to reimburse under a plan that was, in fact, purchased and retained by her employer for her benefit, and that as a matter of contract construction and state law permitted reimbursement for the services of psychologists without any significant variation in the structure of the contractual relationship between her employer and Blue Shield. See n. 2, *supra*. As a consumer of psychotherapy services entitled to financial benefits under the Blue Shield plan, we think it clear that McCready was "within that area of the economy ... endangered by [that] breakdown of competitive conditions" resulting from Blue Shield's selective refusal to reimburse. *Multidistrict Vehicle Air Pollution M.D.L. No. 31*, 481 F.2d 122, 129 (9th Cir. 1973).

(2)

We turn finally to the manner in which the injury alleged reflects Congress' core concerns in prohibiting the antitrust defendants' course of conduct. Petitioners phrase their argument on this point in a manner that concedes McCready's participation in the market for psychotherapy services and rests instead on the notion that McCready's injury does not reflect the "anti-competitive" effect of the alleged boycott. They stress that McCready did not visit a psychiatrist whose fees were artificially inflated as a result of the competitive advantage he gained by Blue Shield's refusal to reimburse for the services of psychologists; she did not pay additional sums for the services of a physician to supervise and bill for the psychotherapy provided by her psychologist; and that there is no "claim that her psychologist's bills are higher than they would have been had the conspiracy not existed.".…

[W]hile an increase in price resulting from a dampening of competitive market forces is assuredly one type of injury for which § 4 potentially offers redress that is not the only form of injury remediable under § 4. We think it plain that McCready's injury was of a type that Congress sought to redress in providing a private remedy for violations of the antitrust laws.

McCready charges Blue Shield with a purposefully *anticompetitive scheme*. She seeks to recover as damages the sums lost to her as the consequence of Blue Shield's attempt to pursue that scheme.[19] She alleges that Blue Shield sought to

---

[16] Petitioners borrow selectively from *Brunswick Corp. v. Pueblo Bowl-O-Mat, Inc.*, 429 U.S. 477 (1979), in arguing that McCready's § 4 claim is "unrelated to any reduction in competition caused by the alleged boycott," because the injury she alleges "is the result of the terms of her insurance contract, and not the result of a reduction in competition." Extracting additional language from Brunswick, they argue that "McCready would have suffered the identical 'loss' — but no compensable 'injury' — as long as her employer, which acted independently in an unrestrained market, continued to purchase a group insurance contract that did not cover the services of clinical psychologists." *Id.*, at 16-17.

[19] ... Most obviously, McCready's claim is quite unlike the claim asserted by the plaintiff in Brunswick for she does not seek to label increased competition as a harm to her. Nevertheless, we

induce its subscribers into selecting psychiatrists over psychologists for the psychotherapeutic services they required, and that the heart of its scheme was the offer of a Hobson's choice to its subscribers. Those subscribers were compelled to choose between visiting a psychologist and forfeiting reimbursement, or receiving reimbursement by forgoing treatment by the practitioner of their choice. In the latter case, the antitrust injury would have been borne in the first instance by the competitors of the conspirators, and inevitably — though indirectly — by the customers of the competitors in the form of suppressed competition in the psychotherapy market; in the former case, as it happened, the injury was borne directly by the customers of the competitors. McCready did not yield to Blue Shield's coercive pressure, and bore Blue Shield's sanction in the form of an increase in the net cost of her psychologist's services. Although McCready was not a competitor of the conspirators, the injury she suffered was inextricably intertwined with the injury the conspirators sought to inflict on psychologists and the psychotherapy market. In light of the conspiracy here alleged we think that McCready's injury "flows from that which makes defendants' acts unlawful" within the meaning of *Brunswick*, and falls squarely within the area of congressional concern.

IV

Section 4 of the Clayton Act provides a remedy to "any person" injured "by reason of" anything prohibited in the antitrust laws. We are asked in this case to infer a limitation on the rule of recovery suggested by the plain language of § 4. But having reviewed our precedents and, more importantly, the policies of the antitrust laws, we are unable to identify any persuasive rationale upon which McCready might be denied redress under § 4 for the injury she claims. The judgment of the Court of Appeals is

Affirmed.

[JUSTICES REHNQUIST, O'CONNOR and STEVENS and CHIEF JUSTICE BURGER dissented.]

ASSOCIATED GENERAL CONTRACTORS V. CALIFORNIA STATE COUNCIL OF CARPENTERS

459 U.S. 519 (1983)

JUSTICE STEVENS delivered the opinion of the Court.

....

This case arises out of a dispute between parties to a multiemployer collective bargaining agreement. The plaintiff unions allege that, in violation of the antitrust

---

agree with petitioners that the relationship between the claimed injury and that which is unlawful in the defendant's conduct, as analyzed in Brunswick, is one factor to be considered in determining the redressability of a particular form of injury under § 4.

laws, the multiemployer association and its members coerced certain third parties, as well as some of the association's members, to enter into business relationships with nonunion firms. This coercion, according to the complaint, adversely affected the trade of certain unionized firms and thereby restrained the business activities of the unions. The question presented is whether the complaint sufficiently alleges that the unions have been "injured in [their] business or property by reason of anything forbidden in the antitrust laws" and may therefore recover treble damages under § 4 of the Clayton Act. 15 U.S.C. § 15....

I

The two named plaintiffs (the "Union") — the California State Council of Carpenters and the Carpenters 46 Northern Counties Conference Board — are affiliated with the United Brotherhood of Carpenters and Joiners of America, AFL-CIO. The plaintiffs represent more than 50,000 individuals employed by the defendants in the carpentry, drywall, piledriving, and related industries throughout the state of California. The Union's complaint is filed as a class action on behalf of numerous affiliated local unions and district councils. The defendants are Associated General Contractors of California, Inc. ("Associated"), a membership corporation composed of various building and construction contractors, approximately 250 members of Associated who are identified by name in an exhibit attached to the complaint, and 1,000 unidentified co-conspirators.

The Union and Associated, and their respective predecessors, have been parties to collective bargaining agreements governing the terms and conditions of employment in construction-related industries in California for over 25 years. The wages and other benefits paid pursuant to these agreements amount to more than $750,000,000 per year. In addition, approximately 3,000 contractors who are not members of Associated have entered into separate "memorandum agreements" with the Union, which bind them to the terms of the master collective bargaining agreements between the Union and Associated. The amended complaint does not state the number of nonsignatory employers or the number of nonunion employees who are active in the relevant market.

... Paragraph 23 [of the amended complaint] alleges generally that the defendants conspired to abrogate and weaken the collective bargaining relationship between the Union and the signatory employers.... The most specific allegations relate to the labor relations between the parties. The complaint's description of actions affecting nonparties is both brief and vague. It is alleged that defendants:

> ....
> (3) Advocated, encouraged, induced, and aided nonmembers of defendant Associated General Contractors of California, Inc. to refuse to enter into collective bargaining relationships with plaintiffs and each of them;
> (4) Advocated, encouraged, induced, *coerced*, aided and encouraged owners of land and other letters of construction contracts to hire contractors and

subcontractors who are not signatories to collective bargaining agreements with plaintiffs and each of them;

(5) Advocated, induced, *coerced*, encouraged, and aided members of Associated General Contractors of California, Inc., non-members of Associated General Contractors of California, Inc., and "memorandum contractors" to enter into subcontracting agreements with subcontractors who are not signatories to any collective bargaining agreements with plaintiffs and each of them; (emphasis added).

....

II

....

We first note that the Union's most specific claims of injury involve matters that are not subject to review under the antitrust laws. The amended complaint alleges that the defendants have breached their collective bargaining agreements in various ways, and that they have manipulated their corporate names and corporate status in order to divert business to nonunion divisions or firms that they actually control. Such deceptive diversion of business to the nonunion portion of a so-called "double-breasted" operation might constitute a breach of contract, an unfair labor practice, or perhaps even a common-law fraud or deceit, but in the context of the bargaining relationship between the parties to this litigation, such activities are plainly not subject to review under the federal antitrust laws. Similarly, the charge that the defendants "advocated, encouraged, induced, and aided nonmembers ... to refuse to enter into collective bargaining relationships" with the Union (23(3)) does not describe an antitrust violation.

The Union's antitrust claims arise from alleged restraints caused by defendants in the market for construction contracting and subcontracting. The complaint alleges that defendants "coerced" two classes of persons: (1) landowners and others who let construction contracts, i.e. the defendants' customers and potential customers; and (2) general contractors, i.e. defendants' competitors and defendants themselves. Coercion against the members of both classes was designed to induce them to give some of their business — but not necessarily all of it — to nonunion firms. Although the pleading does not allege that the coercive conduct increased the aggregate share of nonunion firms in the market, it does allege that defendants' activities weakened and restrained the trade "of certain contractors."... Thus, particular victims of coercion may have diverted particular contracts to nonunion firms and thereby caused certain unionized subcontractors to lose some business....

III

... A literal reading of the statute is broad enough to encompass every harm that can be attributed directly or indirectly to the consequences of an antitrust violation. Some of our prior cases have paraphrased the statute in an equally expansive way. But before we hold that the statute is as broad as its words suggest, we must consider whether Congress intended such an open-ended meaning....

As this Court has observed, the lower federal courts have been "virtually unanimous in concluding that Congress did not intend the antitrust laws to provide a remedy in damages for all injuries that might conceivably be traced to an antitrust violation."...

It is plain, therefore, that the question whether the Union may recover for the injury it allegedly suffered by reason of the defendants' coercion against certain third parties cannot be answered simply by reference to the broad language of § 4. Instead, as was required in common-law damages litigation in 1890, the question requires us to evaluate the plaintiff's harm, the alleged wrongdoing by the defendants, and the relationship between them. [31]

IV

....

The factors that favor judicial recognition of the Union's antitrust claim are easily stated. The complaint does allege a causal connection between an antitrust violation and harm to the Union and further alleges that the defendants intended to cause that harm. As we have indicated, however, the mere fact that the claim is literally encompassed by the Clayton Act does not end the inquiry. We are also satisfied that an allegation of improper motive, although it may support a plaintiff's damages claim under § 4, is not a panacea that will enable any complaint to withstand a motion to dismiss. Indeed, in *McCready*, we specifically held: "The availability of the § 4 remedy to some person who claims its benefit is not a question of the specific intent of the conspirators."

A number of other factors may be controlling. In this case it is appropriate to focus on the nature of the plaintiff's alleged injury. As the legislative history shows, the Sherman Act was enacted to assure customers the benefits of price competition, and our prior cases have emphasized the central interest in protecting the economic freedom of participants in the relevant market. Last Term in *Blue Shield of Virginia v. McCready*, we identified the relevance of this central policy to a determination of the plaintiff's right to maintain an action under § 4. McCready alleged that she was a consumer of psychotherapeutic services and that she had been injured by the defendants' conspiracy to restrain competition in the market for such services. The Court stressed the fact that "McCready's injury was of a type that Congress sought to redress in providing a private remedy for violations of the antitrust laws."... After noting that her injury "was inextricably

---

[31] The label "antitrust standing" has traditionally been applied to some of the elements of this inquiry. As commentators have observed, the focus of the doctrine of "antitrust standing" is somewhat different from that of standing as a constitutional doctrine. Harm to the antitrust plaintiff is sufficient to satisfy the constitutional standing requirement of injury in fact, but the court must make a further determination whether the plaintiff is a proper party to bring a private antitrust action.

intertwined with the injury the conspirators sought to inflict on psychologists and the psychotherapy market," ... the Court concluded that such an injury "falls squarely within the area of congressional concern."

In this case, however, the Union was neither a consumer nor a competitor in the market in which trade was restrained.[40] It is not clear whether the Union's interests would be served or disserved by enhanced competition in the market. As a general matter, a union's primary goal is to enhance the earnings and improve the working conditions of its membership; that goal is not necessarily served, and indeed may actually be harmed, by uninhibited competition among employers striving to reduce costs in order to obtain a competitive advantage over their rivals. At common law — as well as in the early days of administration of the federal antitrust laws — the collective activities of labor unions were regarded as a form of conspiracy in restraint of trade. Federal policy has since developed not only a broad labor exemption from the antitrust laws, but also a separate body of labor law specifically designed to protect and encourage the organizational and representational activities of labor unions. Set against this background, a union, in its capacity as bargaining representative, will frequently not be part of the class the Sherman Act was designed to protect, especially in disputes with employers with whom it bargains. In each case its alleged injury must be analyzed to determine whether it is of the type that the antitrust statute was intended to forestall.... In this case, particularly in light of the longstanding collective bargaining relationship between the parties, the Union's labor-market interests seem to predominate, and the *Brunswick* test is not satisfied.

An additional factor is the directness or indirectness of the asserted injury. In this case, the chain of causation between the Union's injury and the alleged restraint in the market for construction subcontracts contains several somewhat vaguely defined links. According to the complaint, defendants applied coercion against certain landowners and other contracting parties in order to cause them to divert business from certain union contractors to nonunion contractors. As a result, the Union's complaint alleges, the Union suffered unspecified injuries in its "business activities." It is obvious that any such injuries were only an indirect result of whatever harm may have been suffered by "certain" construction contractors and subcontractors.

If either these firms, or the immediate victims of coercion by defendants, have been injured by an antitrust violation, their injuries would be direct and, as we held in *McCready, supra,* they would have a right to maintain their own treble damages actions against the defendants. An action on their behalf would encounter none of the conceptual difficulties that encumber the Union's claim. The existence of an identifiable class of persons whose self-interest would normally motivate them to vindicate the public interest in antitrust enforcement diminishes

---

[40] Moreover, it has not even alleged any marketwide restraint of trade. The allegedly unlawful conduct involves predatory behavior directed at "certain" parties, rather than a claim that output has been curtailed or prices enhanced throughout an entire competitive market.

the justification for allowing a more remote party such as the Union to perform the office of a private attorney general. Denying the Union a remedy on the basis of its allegations in this case is not likely to leave a significant antitrust violation undetected or unremedied.

Partly because it is indirect, and partly because the alleged effects on the Union may have been produced by independent factors, the Union's damages claim is also highly speculative. There is, for example, no allegation that any collective bargaining agreement was terminated as a result of the coercion, no allegation that the aggregate share of the contracting market controlled by union firms has diminished, no allegation that the number of employed union members has declined, and no allegation that the Union's revenues in the form of dues or initiation fees have decreased. Moreover, although coercion against certain firms is alleged, there is no assertion that any such firm was prevented from doing business with any union firms or that any firm or group of firms was subjected to a complete boycott. Other than the alleged injuries flowing from breaches of the collective bargaining agreements — injuries that would be remediable under other laws — nothing but speculation informs the Union's claim of injury by reason of the alleged unlawful coercion. Yet, as we have recently reiterated, it is appropriate for § 4 purposes "to consider whether a claim rests at bottom on some abstract conception or speculative measure of harm."

The indirectness of the alleged injury also implicates the strong interest, identified in our prior cases, in keeping the scope of complex antitrust trials within judicially manageable limits. These cases have stressed the importance of avoiding either the risk of duplicate recoveries on the one hand, or the danger of complex apportionment of damages on the other....

The same concerns should guide us in determining whether the Union is a proper plaintiff under § 4 of the Clayton Act.... In this case, if the Union's complaint asserts a claim for damages under § 4, the District Court would face problems of identifying damages and apportioning them among directly victimized contractors and subcontractors and indirectly affected employees and union entities. It would be necessary to determine to what extent the coerced firms diverted business away from union subcontractors, and then to what extent those subcontractors absorbed the damage to their businesses or passed it on to employees by reducing the workforce or cutting hours or wages. In turn it would be necessary to ascertain the extent to which the affected employees absorbed their losses and continued to pay union dues.

We conclude, therefore, that the Union's allegations of consequential harm resulting from a violation of the antitrust laws, although buttressed by an allegation of intent to harm the Union, are insufficient as a matter of law. Other relevant factors — the nature of the Union's injury, the tenuous and speculative character of the relationship between the alleged antitrust violation and the Union's alleged injury, the potential for duplicative recovery or complex apportionment of damages, and the existence of more direct victims of the alleged conspiracy — weigh heavily against judicial enforcement of the Union's antitrust claim. Accordingly, we hold that, based on the allegations of this complaint, the District Court was correct in concluding that the Union is not a person injured by reason of a violation of the antitrust laws within the meaning of § 4 of the Clayton Act. The judgment of the Court of Appeals is

Reversed.

[Only JUSTICE MARSHALL dissented.]

NOTES AND QUESTIONS

1. On the issue of standing, should courts distinguish between actions alleging violations of section 1 of the Sherman Act and those alleging violations of section 7 of the Clayton Act? What are the important differences?

Does Justice Stevens' opinion in *Associated General Contractors* further limit the scope of standing beyond the two-pronged "remoteness" inquiry articulated in *McCready*: (1) the physical and economic nexus between the antitrust violation and injury and (2) the relationship of the injury and the intended scope of the statutes' coverage? Is the answer that *Associated General Contractors* limits section 4 standing to consumers or competitors?

2. Does an employee who was discharged or disciplined because he refused to join in an antitrust violation have standing to sue his employer under section 4? The courts of appeal are divided. While the Supreme Court has not explicitly decided this issue, *Associated General Contractors* may have signaled implicitly its resolution of this question. Subsequently the Court denied review of the Seventh Circuit's opinion in *Bichan v. Chemetron Corp.*, 681 F.2d 514 (1982) (where the Seventh Circuit held that a discharged executive who refused to comply with his employer's illegal anticompetitive activities did not suffer "antitrust injury" and lacked standing under section 4). On the same day the Court vacated the judgment of the Ninth Circuit in *Ostrofe v. H.S. Crocker Co.*, 670 F.2d 1378 (9th Cir. 1982) (where the Ninth Circuit had held that discharged employee had standing).

On remand after the Supreme Court decision in *Associated General*, the Ninth Circuit held that the discharged employee in *Ostrofe v. H.S. Crocker Co.* had standing to bring a treble damage claim against the employer under section 4. Because the discharged employee was the victim of an intentional boycott, which resulted in the elimination of competition in a specific market, the court reasoned that the discharge was an "integral and inextricable" means of achieving the illegal scheme. 740 F.2d 739 (9th Cir. 1984).

Other circuits have been less generous in granting standing. *Province v. Cleveland Press Pub'g Co.*, 787 F.2d 1047 (6th Cir. 1986) (no standing under sections 1 and 2 of Sherman Act for former employees who lost jobs when newspaper closed); *Gregory Mktg. Corp. v. Wakefern Food Corp.*, 787 F.2d 92 (3d Cir. 1986) (terminated broker lacks standing on price discrimination claim).

The Ninth Circuit later reconsidered its *Ostrofe* decision. In *Vinci v. Waste Management, Inc.*, 80 F.3d 1372 (9th Cir. 1996), the court was asked by a former employee of Waste Management to approve the employee's standing to allege that he was terminated for his refusal to participate in his employer's anticompetitive behavior. This time the Ninth Circuit denied standing, and indicated that *Ostrofe* recognized a limited exception to a general rule precluding employees from standing, and that such an exception was limited to instances in which the dismissed employee is an "essential participant in an antitrust scheme, the dismissal is a 'necessary means' to accomplish the scheme, and the employee has the greatest incentive to challenge the antitrust violation." Because Vinci had not alleged facts indicating that he was an essential part of the antitrust scheme, or that his termination was necessary to continue or accomplish the scheme, he did not fall within the *Ostrofe* exception.

The Seventh Circuit dismissed the antitrust claim in *O'Regan v. Arbitration Forums, Inc.*, 121 F.3d 1060 (7th Cir. 1997), where a terminated employee who filed a claim against her former employer had been fired for refusing to sign a noncompete agreement that was overbroad in geographic scope. However, the court found that, by refusing to sign the agreement, the employee merely refused to engage in the proposed anticompetitive activity. This did not give her standing to sue based on an antitrust violation, as her injuries were not a direct result of it. In order for a federal antitrust violation to occur in such a case, the defendant must have attempted to enforce the agreement against the plaintiff employee.

For negative academic commentary on the *Vinci* decision, *see* Sean P. Gates, *California Antitrust: Standing Room for the Wrongfully Discharged Employee?*, 47 Hastings L.J. 509, 544-48 (1996) (arguing that the federal definition of antitrust injury did not mandate the holding of *Vinci* and that the *Vinci* court failed to take advantage of the effective antitrust enforcement opportunity presented by the discharged employee in the case).

3. In *McCready*, the Supreme Court treated the exclusion in Blue Shield's insurance policy as a concerted refusal to deal aimed at psychologists. For that reason the standing of insured McCready, who was not the intended "target" of the conspiracy, gave the Court some pause. But why didn't the Court simply treat this as a price fixing case? Hadn't the defendants agreed to reduce output — the amount of coverage to be provided by the policy — and wasn't Ms. McCready (or her employer) a direct purchaser of the policy? Direct purchasers of a cartelized product have virtually undisputed standing under the antitrust laws.

The answer is probably that the codefendants — Blue Shield and the Neuropsychiatric Society of Virginia — were not competitors. Suppose, however, that the Neuropsychiatric Society's motive in entering the agreement was to weaken the competitive position of psychologists; Blue Shield, on the other hand, was not particularly interested in competition between psychologists and psychiatrists but rather wanted to reduce the amount of coverage under its insurance policy. Is it clear that the case should be treated as a concerted refusal, and not as price fixing?

4. In *McCready* the Court reiterated two types of limitations on treble damages: the denial of standing to prevent duplicative recovery and denial of standing because injuries are too remote from an antitrust violation. The distinction

between these two section 4 inquiries is evident when you compare *McCready* with *Illinois Brick, supra.*

5. On the question of whether an owner/lessor has standing to complain about the antitrust conduct of lessees of the property, which results in a loss of rent and royalties to the owner/lessor, *see R.C. Dick Geothermal Corp. v. Thermogenics, Inc.*, 890 F.2d 139 (9th Cir. 1989). An en banc court for the Ninth Circuit held no, employing a five-factor test: (1) intent, (2) the directness of the injury, (3) the character of damages, (4) the existence of other, more appropriate plaintiffs, and (5) the nature of the injury.

Suppose a landlord and commercial tenant agree to a rental of 20% of the tenant's gross sales. The tenant then enters into a price-fixing agreement that requires it to reduce its output in order to clear the market at the higher price. If the cartel is successful, the landlord has not been injured, has he? Total revenue at the cartel price would ordinarily be higher than the total revenue at the competitive price. Suppose the agreed rental was $1 for each unit sold rather than a percentage of sales, and the tenant then enters a cartel requiring it to reduce its output. Now the landlord, a supplier of an input, has been injured even though the monopoly price shows up in the output market. Should the landlord have standing?

Is the landlord in the example any different from other suppliers of inputs? Suppose a group of paper box manufacturers forms a cartel and reduces its output, thereby reducing its purchases of wood pulp as well. Should the wood pulp manufacturers have standing? Can you think of any principled difference between the injury that accrues to the manufacturers of the wood pulp and that which accrues to buyers of the finished boxes?

6. As a basic proposition shareholders in a company lack standing to enforce the antitrust laws with respect to violations for which their company is a victim. But suppose the company is about to be taken over, and several possible acquiring firms agree not to bid competitively against each other. Such competitive bidding would of course raise the price of the acquired firm's shares. Does the shareholder now have standing? Why? *See Finnegan v. Campeau Corp.*, 915 F.2d 824 (2d Cir. 1990).

7. The Seventh Circuit recently addressed the issue of associational standing under section 4 of the Clayton Act. A farmers association, along with a number of named soybean farmers, brought an action against the Chicago Board of Trade alleging that an emergency resolution adopted by the Board violated the Sherman Act. The resolution required all holders of long positions in soybean futures to liquidate their positions by at least 20% daily until the end of the trading period for the futures. Plaintiffs claimed that the resolution led to a price decline, resulting in a proportionate decline in the cash market for soybeans which harmed farmers who were cash market sellers of soybeans.

The court held that the association lacked standing to represent the farmers. Importantly, the association was requesting damages on behalf of its members, and the only way damages could be computed was if each individual member participated. Thus the court applied the generally accepted rule that an association has standing to bring an action on behalf of its members only if it is seeking an injunction or some other kind of relief that is common to the individual members. The court then went on to conclude that the farmers themselves had standing. *Sanner v. Chicago Board of Trade*, 62 F.3d 918 (7th Cir. 1995).

B. PARENS PATRIAE

In *Hawaii v. Standard Oil Co. of Cal.*, 405 U.S. 251 (1972), the Supreme Court denied states the right to sue in their sovereign capacity as "parens patriae" for treble damages for injuries to their general economy under section 4 of the Clayton Act. The Court concluded that the states could sue for injunctive relief as parens patriae, but that they did not have a cause of action in that capacity for treble damages. *See also Georgia v. Pennsylvania R.R.*, 324 U.S. 439 (1945).

In 1976, Congress passed the Hart-Scott-Rodino Antitrust Improvement Act, P.L. 94-435 (Sept. 30, 1976), which permits states, through their attorneys general, to sue in their parens patriae capacity for treble damages for "any violation of the Sherman Act." With this addition, parens patriae is an alternative to class action in situations where there are many individual victims, each of whom has sustained only modest monetary injury.

The monetary relief under parens patriae is threefold actual damages, excluding any damages that duplicate "amounts which have been awarded for the same injury." This provision is designed to prevent multiple liability. In addition, any state citizen who wishes to exclude her claim from the suit may opt out under section 4 C(b)(2), as is the case under a Rule 23(b)(3) class action.

Further limitations permit states to sue only on behalf of injured consumers, not businesses. Section 4 G(3) specifically excludes partnerships and proprietorships from the "natural persons" definition.

In the first interpretation of the Hart-Scott-Rodino Amendments to come before the Court, the Supreme Court held in *Illinois Brick* that the parens patriae amendments did not create a new claim for relief. Therefore, if the consumer lacked an actionable claim under section 4 because it was not a "direct purchaser," then the state attorney general also failed to state a claim when suing on behalf of the indirect consumer. In drawing the distinction between standing to sue and an actionable claim, the Court concluded that:

> Congress made clear, however, that this legislation did not alter the definition of which overcharged persons were injured within the meaning of § 4. It simply created a new procedural device — *parens patriae* actions by States on behalf of their citizens — to enforce existing rights of recovery under § 4. The House Report quoted above states that the *parens patriae* provision "creates no new substantive liability"; the relevant language of the newly enacted § 4C (a) of the Clayton Act tracks that of existing § 4, showing that it was intended only as "an alternative means ... for the vindication

of existing substantive claims." H. R. Rep. No. 94-499, *supra*, at 9. "The establishment of an alternative remedy does not increase any defendant's liability." *Ibid*. Representative Rodino himself acknowledged in the remarks cited above that this legislation did not create a right of recovery for consumers where one did not already exist.

431 U.S. 720, 734 n.14 (1977).

C. ADVISORY OPINIONS AND CLEARANCES PROCEDURE

Upon request both the Department of Justice and the FTC will review business conduct and give their opinions as to the legality of specific practices. The opinions are given in the form of statements regarding present enforcement intentions. The Federal Trade Commission will issue an "advisory opinion," while the Department of Justice will review the conduct through a "business review letter." Technically, the Department has no authority to give an advisory opinion. The submission of hypothetical questions will not result in a review by either agency.

Neither agency is legally bound by the issued opinion, since both lack general authority to immunize antitrust conduct. Generally, the agencies reserve the option to commence enforcement proceedings at any time. If either agency decides to proceed against the firm that relied upon the advisory opinion or clearance, generally the firm, in the agency's discretion, will be given the opportunity to discontinue its practice before a proceeding will be instituted. *See* 16 C.F.R. § 1.3 (1993); 28 C.F.R. § 50.6 (1992). However, "[a]s to a stated present intention not to bring an action ... the Division has never exercised its right to bring a criminal action where there has been full and true disclosure at the time of presenting the request." 28 C.F.R. § 50.6(9) (1992).

Both agencies' procedures require the submission of accurate and full information before the advisory opinion or business review letter will issue and before there can be reliance on the government's enforcement intentions. Supplemental data may also be required.

Until 1979 the FTC's advisory opinion program was limited to issuance of opinions on a firm's "proposed" course of action. The rules were amended in 1979 to include opinions concerning a firm's ongoing practices. The Department's business review clearance procedure is limited to reviewing "proposed business conduct." 28 C.F.R. § 50.6 (1992). The Commission rules state that the Commission "will not proceed against the requesting party with respect to any action taken in good faith reliance upon the Commission's advice ... where all the relevant facts were fully, completely, and accurately presented ... and where such action was promptly discontinued upon notification of rescission." 16 C.F.R. § 1.3 (1993). The Department's procedures are not as specific. 28 C.F.R. § 50.6(8) (1992). The FTC advisory opinions are published on a regular basis. 16 C.F.R. § 1.4 (1993).

It should be noted that the approval or clearance of a firm's conduct by one agency does not preclude enforcement action by the other. Nor does it prohibit suit by a private party challenging the conduct. Courts, likewise, are not bound by agencies' procedure or rulings, though weight may be given to the agencies' interpretations.

From time to time both agencies issue specific enforcement guidelines, such as the recent merger guidelines discussed in Chapter 7. In addition, the FTC issues industry guidelines (sometimes referred to as trade practice rules) to regulate the practice of certain industries; noncompliance may result in the Commission bringing "corrective action." 16 C.F.R. § 1.5 (1993).

D. SANCTIONS AND RULE 11

Because antitrust cases generally are long and complex, they can be the subject of abuse during the pretrial litigation stage. The 1993 amendments to Rule 11 of the Federal Rules of Civil Procedure state that a signature of an attorney or client constitutes a certificate that the individual has read the paper filed with the court and warrants that individual statements, after a reasonable inquiry, (1) are not being presented for any improper purpose or needless increase in cost of litigation, (2) are warranted by existing law or by a nonfrivolous argument for the extension, modification, or reversal of existing law, and (3) contain factual allegations that have evidentiary support or are likely to after a reasonable opportunity for discovery. If a violation of Rule 11 is found, the court may impose sanctions within the court's discretion. Sanctions are to be directed "to deter repetition."

The purpose behind Rule 11 is deterrence. Baseless claims and arguments are the target of the provision. The rule requires that the attorney make a reasonable inquiry under the circumstances.

The new changes to Rule 11 include removing discovery disputes from the purview of Rule 11. The discovery provisions of the rules have their own sanction provisions. Moreover, a "safe-harbor" of 21 days after receiving notice of an alleged violation to withdraw the offending pleading before a request for sanctions may be filed has been added.

E. SETTLEMENT

As would be expected, a large percentage (70% to 88%) of antitrust cases are settled. *See* S. Salop and L. White, "Private Antitrust Litigation: An Introduction and Framework," in *Private Antitrust Litigation* 10-11 (L. White ed. 1988). Both the Antitrust Division and the FTC have established procedures for settlement of cases. The Antitrust Division's procedure permits entry of a consent decree following a settlement, while the FTC has authority to enter into a consent order. *See, e.g.,* 16 C.F.R. § 2.31 (1993). These procedures often represent an efficient means for management of limited litigation resources and the termination of the lawsuit.

Questions have been raised whether interested third parties can intervene under Rule 24 of the Federal Rules of Civil Procedure when a government suit is in the process of settlement. Unless the intervenor can demonstrate inadequate representation, bad faith, or malfeasance by government counsel, courts have generally not been inclined to permit intervention during the consent process. *Sam Fox Pub'g Co. v. United States*, 366 U.S. 683 (1961). The exception came in 1967 when the Supreme Court in *Cascade Nat. Gas Corp. v. El Paso Natural Gas Co.*, 386 U.S. 129 (1967), permitted intervention at the settlement stage after the case had been litigated and won by the government. In *Cascade Gas*, the Department settled for less than all the relief claimed and the Court apparently concluded that by settling for less than that demonstrated by the record, the Department "knuckled under to El Paso and [fell] far short of representing" the interest of the intervenor. Subsequent cases have narrowly interpreted *Cascade Gas* and generally have followed the rule established in *Sam Fox*, with the result that intervention is denied to third parties.

The issue of intervention has been less problematic since 1974. In that year Congress amended the Clayton Act to require the Department to give public notice of proposed settlements 60 days prior to the entry of the consent decree. Antitrust Procedure and Penalties Act of 1974, 15 U.S.C. § 16(b)-(h) (1988) (the Tunney Act). *See also* 28 C.F.R. § 50.13 (1992). During the sixty-day public comment period, interested persons are invited to submit comments. The Department is required also to file a "competitive impact statement" with the court. This statement, found at 15 U.S.C. § 16(b) (1988), is to set forth:

(1) the nature and purpose of the proceeding;

(2) a description of the practices or events giving rise to the alleged violation of the antitrust laws;

(3) an explanation of the proposal for a consent judgment, including an explanation of any unusual circumstances giving rise to such proposal or any provision contained therein, relief to be obtained thereby, and the anticipated effects on competition of such relief;

(4) the remedies available to potential private plaintiffs damaged by the alleged violation in the event that such proposal for the consent judgment is entered in such proceeding;

(5) a description of the procedures available for modification of such proposal; and

(6) a description and evaluation of alternatives to such proposal actually considered by the United States.

The defendant may also file a statement.

The 1974 amendments permit the reviewing court to enter the consent decree as a judgment only if the court finds that the decree is in the "public interest." This determination may require a hearing and testimony. In considering whether a consent judgment should enter, based on a finding of public interest the court may consider — 1) the competitive impact of such judgment, including termination of alleged violations, provisions for enforcement and modification, duration of relief sought, anticipated effects of alternative remedies actually considered, and any other considerations bearing upon the adequacy of such judgment; 2) the impact of such entry of such judgment upon the public generally and individuals alleging specific injury from the violations set forth in the complaint, including consideration of the public benefit, if any, to be derived from a determination of the issues at trial.

Section 5(e) of Clayton Act, 15 U.S.C. § 16(e).

In most instances the court's determination that a proposed consent decree is in the public interest is routine, and the court's judgment reaches that conclusion in a single sentence. Occasionally, however, where the case is complex and many interests are likely to be affected by the proposed consent decree, the public interest analysis is complex and extensive. For example, in examining the consent decree under which American Telephone and Telegraph Co. divested itself of many of its subsidiaries, the district court concluded that "Congress wanted the courts to act as an independent check on the terms of decrees negotiated by the Department of Justice." *United States v. AT&T*, 552 F. Supp. 131, 149 (D.D.C. 1982), *aff'd sub nom. Maryland v. United States*, 460 U.S. 1001 (1983). For that reason, the court concluded, it must analyze the effects on competition of each element in the proposed consent decree. The court noted, however, that it would approve a proposed decree "even if it falls short of the remedy the court would impose on its own, so long as it falls within the range of acceptability or is 'within the reaches of the public interest.'" *Id.* at 51. Having said that, the court went on to identify ten modifications that must be made in the decree before it would win judicial approval.

More recently, District Court Judge Stanley Sporkin rejected the government-Microsoft consent decree in 1995 as not in the public interest. But the United States Court of Appeals for the District of Columbia reversed the decision as straying too far outside the boundaries of review set forth in the Tunney Act. In reversing, the court said:

> At the heart of this case, then, is the proper scope of the district court's inquiry into the "public interest." Is the district judge entitled to seize hold of the matter — the investigation into the putative defendant's business practices — and decide for himself the appropriate combined response of the executive and judicial branches to those practices? With respect to the specific allegations in the government's complaint, may the court interpose its own views of the appropriate remedy over those the government seeks as a part of its overall settlement? To be sure, Congress, in passing the Tunney Act, intended to prevent "judicial rubber stamping" of the Justice Department's proposed consent decree.... The Court was to "make an independent determination as to whether or not entry of a proposed consent decree [was] in the public interest."
>
> ...

Although the language of section 16(e) is not precise, we think the government is correct in contending that section 16(e)(1)'s reference to the alleged violations suggests that Congress did not mean for a district judge to construct his own hypothetical case and then evaluate the decree against that case. Moreover, in section 16(e)(2), the court is authorized to consider "the public benefit ... of the determination of the issues at trial." Putting aside the perplexing question of how the district judge could insure a trial if the government did not wish one, "the issues" referred to must be those formulated in the complaint. Congress surely did not contemplate that the district judge would, by reformulating the issues, effectively redraft the complaint himself. We therefore dismiss the claim that the last line in section 16(e)(1), the catchall clause allowing the district court to entertain "any other considerations bearing upon the adequacy of such judgment," authorizes the wide-ranging inquiry the district court wished to conduct in this case. That language recognizes, inter alia, that a consent decree might well do unexpected harm to persons other than those "alleging specific injury from the violations set forth in the complaint." 15 U.S.C. S 16(e)(2). And the district court might ponder those sort of concerns in determining whether to enter the judgment.

To be sure, the Act also authorizes the district judge to "take testimony of Government officials ... as the court may deem appropriate." 15 U.S.C. S 16(f)(1) (1988). We do not read this language, however, to authorize the district judge to seek the kind of information concerning the government's investigation and settlement negotiations that he wished to obtain here. Even when a court is explicitly authorized to review government action under the Administrative Procedure Act, "there must be a strong showing of bad faith or improper behavior" before the court may "inquir[e] into the mental processes of administrative decisionmakers." Citizens to Preserve Overton Park, Inc. v. Volpe, 401 U.S. 402, 420, (1971). Here, the district court is not empowered to review the actions or behavior of the Department of Justice; the court is only authorized to review the decree itself. It is unnecessary to consider whether the district court might have broader authority to inquire into the Department's deliberations, even though not authorized to "review" the Department's action, if there were a credible showing of bad faith.... There is no such claim here.

The district court was troubled that if its review were limited to the market and practices within that market against which the complaint was directed, the government could, by narrow drafting, artificially limit the court's review under the Tunney Act.... We think, with all due respect, that the district court put the cart before the horse. The court's authority to review the decree depends entirely on the government's exercising its prosecutorial discretion by bringing a case in the first place.

United States v. Microsoft, 56 F.3d 1448, 1458-60 (D.C. Cir. 1995).

The Court of Appeals also reversed the district court's finding of an inadequate remedy and an inadequate compliance mechanism in the consent decree. The Court of Appeals held that short of making a "mockery of judicial power," a decree should be respected as an aspect of prosecutorial discretion.

> [W]hen the government is challenged for not bringing as extensive an action as it might, a district judge must be careful not to exceed his or her constitutional role. A decree, even entered as a pretrial settlement, is a judicial act, and therefore the district judge is not obliged to accept one that, on its face and even after government explanation, appears to make a mockery of judicial power. Short of that eventuality, the Tunney Act cannot be interpreted as an authorization for a district judge to assume the role of Attorney General.
>
> Accordingly, the case is remanded with instructions to enter the proposed decree.

56 F.3d 1448, 1462.

Either party to the consent decree may seek modification of the consent decree once entered. The party seeking a change must make a "clear showing of grievous wrong evoked by new and unforeseen conditions." *United States v. Swift & Co.*, 286 U.S. 106, 119 (1932). Whether the burden is less on the government when seeking a modification is unclear. *Chrysler Corp. v. United States*, 316 U.S. 556 (1942); *Ford Motor Co. v. United States*, 335 U.S. 303 (1948). Generally, third parties not bound by the consent decree cannot seek to enforce the decree or seek damages under it even though they are beneficiaries of the decree. *See Data Processing Fin. & Gen. Corp. v. IBM*, 403 F.2d 1277 (8th Cir. 1970). *Contra* Sullivan, *Enforcement of Government Antitrust Decrees by Private Parties: Third Party Beneficiary Rights and Intervenor Status*, 123 U. Pa. L. Rev. 822 (1975).

In the *AT&T* divestiture litigation discussed above, the question was raised whether the Tunney Act's "public interest determination" and other procedural provisions applied to voluntary dismissals signed by all the parties under Rule 41(a)(1)(ii) of the Federal Rules of Civil Procedure, or whether the statute was limited to the entering of consent judgments. The district court ruled that "when the dismissal of a major antitrust action has substantive aspects or is so closely tied to a 'modification' of another [antitrust] decree as is the case here, Tunney Act procedures apply." The court went on to hold that the procedural provisions of the Tunney Act apply whether the consent judgment "is regarded as 'new' or as a modification" of an earlier decree. *United States v. AT&T*, 552 F. Supp. 131, 144 n.52 & 147-48 n.67 (D.D.C. 1982), *aff'd sub nom. Maryland v. United States*, 460 U.S. 1001 (1983). *But see* 460 U.S., at 1002 (Rehnquist, J., dissenting). On the issue whether a trial court can invoke the Tunney Act or disapprove a voluntary dismissal stipulated between the parties under Rule 41(a)(1)(ii), *see In re IBM Corp.*, 687 F.2d 591 (2d Cir. 1982) (court issued a writ of mandamus to the district court judge, holding that judicial supervision or Tunney Act review does not apply to voluntary dismissals between parties).

The FTC rules permit a party being investigated to submit prior to the issuance of a formal complaint a proposed consent order agreement. 16 C.F.R. § 2.31 (1993). The Commission may accept or reject the proposed consent order or take other appropriate action. If accepted, the consent order is to be published in the Federal Register for a period of sixty days for the purpose of receiving comments. The comments may cause the Commission to either withdraw the order, modify it, or issue a complaint. 16 C.F.R. § 2.34. If the consent order is finalized it may contain a provision that the entered agreement "does not constitute an admission by any party that the law has been violated." 16 C.F.R. § 2.32. The legal effect of such statement is to undercut the application of the doctrines of res judicata and collateral estoppel in any related subsequent litigation.

If a party wishes to propose a consent agreement *after* a complaint has issued, "a motion to withdraw the matter from adjudication" should be filed with the Commission. The Administrative Law Judge (ALJ) is required to stay the adjudication if FTC counsel (complaint counsel) agrees pending Commission determination. 16 C.F.R. § 3.25(b), (c). Otherwise, upon the filing of the motion the ALJ may certify the matter to the Commission, which has the authority to act on the motion to withdraw the matter from the adjudication docket. *Id.* at § 3.25(c), (d). Once the matter is withdrawn from adjudication, the Commission may accept, reject, or modify the consent agreement. *Id.* at § 3.25(f).

F. PRECLUSION EFFECTS OF A PRIOR JUDGMENT ON SUBSEQUENT PRIVATE SUITS

Under certain circumstances, a final consent judgment or decree entered in a suit brought by the government can be used as prima facie evidence of a violation in a subsequent suit. Section 5(a) of the Clayton Act states:

> (a) A final judgment or decree ... rendered in any civil or criminal proceeding brought by or on behalf of the United States under the antitrust laws to the effect that a defendant has violated said laws shall be prima facie evidence against such defendant in any action or proceeding brought by any other party against such defendant under said laws as to all matters respecting which said judgment or decree would be an estoppel as between the parties thereto: *Provided*, that this section shall not apply to consent judgments or decrees entered before any testimony has been taken. Nothing contained in this section shall be construed to impose any limitation on the application of collateral estoppel, except that, in any action or proceeding brought under the antitrust laws, collateral estoppel effect shall not be given to any finding made by the Federal Trade Commission under the antitrust laws or under section 5 of the Federal Trade Commission Act which could give rise to a claim for relief under the antitrust laws.

15 U.S.C. § 16(a) (1988). The statute was designed to ease a private plaintiff's burden of proof and to encourage the use of consent judgments or decrees in the disposition of government suits. In light of this provision, precise language in a judgment is necessary so that it can be accurately determined what issues were adjudged in the prior government suit. The problem of ambiguity is frequently present when the jury returns a general verdict.

Section 5(a) specifically states that the prima facie rule does *not* apply if the consent judgment or decree was entered before testimony was taken. This is designed to encourage settlement. In this regard the entry of a consent decree prior to testimony has the same subsequent effect as a nolo contendere plea in a prior criminal case. *See* Fed. R. Crim. P. 11(b); *Burbank v. General Elec. Co.*, 329 F.2d 825, 834-36 (9th Cir. 1964). In neither situation is the earlier determination prima facie evidence in the subsequent private suit.

The case law has addressed several issues regarding the application of section 5(a). First, does a consent order or agreement entered by the FTC come within section 5(a)? The difficulty is presented because section 5(a) speaks in terms of a proceeding "brought by … the United States under the antitrust laws." Frequently courts have held that the FTC Act (§ 5) is not an "antitrust law." *See, e.g., Wendkos v. ABC Consol. Corp.*, 379 F. Supp. 15, 20 (E.D. Pa. 1974). But what if the FTC is proceeding to enforce the Clayton Act? *Purex Corp. v. Procter & Gamble Co.*, 453 F.2d 288 (9th Cir. 1971), *cert. denied*, 405 U.S. 1065 (1972) (holding that an order regarding § 7 of the Clayton Act came within section 5(a)).

Second, although section 5(a) is rather clear that a consent judgment shall not be prima facie evidence in a second suit if entered before testimony, this provision has not been uniformly applied to consent decrees entered after testimony has commenced. *See* 2 P. Areeda & H. Hovenkamp, *Antitrust Law* ¶ 337 (rev. ed. 1994).

As originally written, section 5(a)'s prima facie rule, from an evidence standpoint, meant that once plaintiff in the second suit introduced the prior consent judgment the first judgment was not considered conclusive but rather could be rebutted by the record evidence. This presumption, usable in the second suit, is available, however, "only on the basis of a judgment 'to the effect that a defendant has violated [the antitrust] laws.'" *United States v. AT&T*, 552 F. Supp. 131, 211 (D.D.C. 1982). Thus, the consent judgment must include a finding or admission that defendant violated the antitrust laws before the prima facie rule is applicable.

Today the value of section 5(a) has been considerably mitigated by the doctrine of nonmutual, or offensive, collateral estoppel. In *Parklane Hosiery Co. v. Shore*, 439 U.S. 322 (1979), the Supreme Court held that a plaintiff, not a party to the first suit, could offensively use collateral estoppel to bar the defendant from relitigating issues in the second suit that were decided against the defendant in the first suit. In 1980 Congress amended section 5(a) to clarify the use of the collateral estoppel doctrine in subsequently related antitrust suits. The section now provides that the "prima facie" language of section 5(a) is not a limitation on the application of collateral estoppel. *See also Aluminum Co. of Am. v. United States*, 302 U.S. 230 (1937); *Cromwell v. County of Sac*, 94 U.S. 351 (1876);

United States v. AT&T, 524 F. Supp. 1336, 1353 n.70 (D.D.C. 1981). Does the 1980 amendment imply that collateral estoppel effect can be given to a consent judgment or decree entered before testimony begins? The answer is probably no since *Parklane* requires both "final" and "actual" litigation of an issue before offensive collateral estoppel will apply.

On the subject of the preclusion effects of a prior judgment, consider whether a prior action based on a state antitrust claim, which results in a judgment in favor of the defendant, can be refiled under the federal antitrust statute. Should the doctrine of res judicata be invoked? Does it matter to the outcome that jurisdiction over federal antitrust claims is exclusively within the federal courts?

In *Marrese v. American Academy of Orthopedic Surgeons*, 470 U.S. 373 (1985), the Supreme Court held that it was error to fail to consider the state law's interpretation of the preclusive effect of the state judgment before foreclosing suit in federal court. On remand, the district court held that the federal antitrust claim is not precluded by the prior Illinois judgment. The court reasoned that the Sherman Act claim was exclusively within the jurisdiction of the federal court, that it could not have been decided by the state court, that Illinois had adopted the Restatement (Second) of Judgments and "would seemingly accept the rule of inapplicability of *res judicata* to exclusively federal suits."

Consider whether a class member who opts out of a class action may invoke a favorable decision to the class by claiming issue preclusion under *Parklane Hosiery* in a subsequent suit against the common defendant. *See Premier Elec. Constr. Co. v. National Elec. Contrs. Ass'n*, 814 F.2d 358 (7th Cir. 1987) (holding that class member who opts out of class may not benefit from favorable decision to class by invoking offensive collateral estoppel). Judge Easterbrook, writing for the Seventh Circuit in *Premier Electrical*, held that the issue of whether class members should be entitled to benefit from a favorable judgment, despite not being bound by an unfavorable judgment, was considered when Rule 23 was amended in 1966. "Under the revised rule, a class member must cast his lot at the beginning of the suit and all parties are bound, for good or ill, by the results. Someone who opted out could take his chances separately, but the separate suit would proceed as if the class action had never been filed." *Id.*

Judge Easterbrook opined that:

> An approach that asks how to hold down the costs of litigation given the existence of multiple suits is an ex post perspective on judicial economy. It is the wrong perspective when inquiring about the consequences of a legal rule. A decision to make preclusion available to those who opt out of a class influences *whether* there will be multiple suits. The more class members who opt out may benefit from preclusion, the more class members will opt out. Preclusion thus may increase the number of suits, undermining the economy the district court hoped to achieve. The effect of the legal rule may be the opposite of the effect of applying preclusion to a given case. To

determine whether a rule is beneficial, a court must examine how that rule influences future behavior. The influence of a rule of preclusion cannot be known for sure, but we are not confident that there would be net benefits.

G. ANTITRUST COUNTERCLAIMS

When a claim and a counterclaim raise common issues of law and fact, involve largely the same evidence, are logically related, and would implicate the principle of res judicata if pursued separately, the counterclaim is deemed "compulsory." Fed. R. Civ. P. 13(a). Defendants are barred from bringing compulsory counterclaims in subsequent actions if they fail to bring them in the original suit, unless they are protected under a recognized exception to the rule.

One such exception involves antitrust counterclaims in patent infringement litigation. In *Mercoid Corp. v. Mid-Continent Investment Co.*, 320 U.S. 661, 671 (1944), the Supreme Court stated that although the antitrust claim in question could have been asserted as a counterclaim in the original patent infringement proceeding, res judicata did not bar the original defendant from bringing it in a subsequent action. Thus, the Court held that the antitrust counterclaim in a patent infringement action was "permissive" under Rule 13(b) of the Federal Rules of Civil Procedure.

The Fifth Circuit recently revisited the issue in *Tank Insulation International, Inc. v. Insultherm, Inc.*, 104 F.3d 83 (5th Cir. 1997), where the court held that the *Mercoid* exception to Rule 13(a) still applies to antitrust claims that otherwise would fall within the category of compulsory counterclaims. The court could not distinguish *Mercoid* on its facts, following the Ninth Circuit's decision to apply the exception in *Hydranautics v. Filmtec Corp.*, 70 F.3d 533, 536-37 (9th Cir. 1995). In so doing, the court refused to limit *Mercoid* to cases involving identical facts, as suggested by commentators and other courts. *See, e.g., United States Philips Corp. v. Sears Roebuck & Co.*, 55 F.3d 592, 595-97 (Fed. Cir. 1995); *United States v. Eastport Steamship Corp.*, 255 F.2d 795, 805 (2d Cir. 1958); *Rohm & Haas Co. v. Brotech Corp.*, 770 F. Supp. 928, 932-33 (D. Del. 1991) (all refusing to apply the *Mercoid* exception). *See also* Laurence I. Wood, *The Tangle of* Mercoid *Case Implications*, 13 Geo. Wash. L. Rev. 61, 81-83 (1944) (criticizing the *Mercoid* court for considering the financial interests of the parties rather than legitimate public policy reasons in finding the antitrust counterclaims permissive, not compulsory).

SECTION II. ADDITIONAL ANTITRUST DEFENSES
A. FIRST AMENDMENT PROTECTIONS

1. *NOERR-PENNINGTON* DOCTRINE

The Supreme Court, in a series of decisions beginning in 1961, has recognized a first amendment freedom of expression defense, regardless of anticompetitive intent, when competitors combine to influence governmental action. The defense is known as the *Noerr-Pennington* doctrine, named after the Court's two leading cases which developed the doctrine. The doctrine has received substantial attention and is used frequently as an antitrust defense. It is discussed further in Chapter 9, *infra*.

2. ECONOMIC/POLITICAL BOYCOTTS

In some cases, economic boycotts (concerted refusals to deal) which are motivated by political purposes have been immunized from antitrust scrutiny on the basis of the first amendment right to petition government even when the boycott results in a commercial injury. See Chapter 4, Section I.E5, *infra*, where the leading cases are discussed. *NAACP v. Claiborne Hdwe. Co.*, 458 U.S. 886 (1982); *Missouri v. National Org. for Women*, 620 F.2d 1301 (8th Cir. 1980). *But cf. Allied Tube & Conduit Corp. v. Indian Head, Inc.*, 486 U.S. 492 (1988); *FTC v. Superior Ct. Trial Lawyers Ass'n*, 493 U.S. 411 (1991), discussed in Chapter 9.

3. OVERBROAD REMEDIAL ORDERS

A large part of the antitrust enforcement effort results in the issuance of judicial or FTC orders designed to regulate business behavior. The first amendment is a relevant restraint on overbroad orders that invade constitutionally protected economic activity.

That the activity sought to be regulated is purely economic or commercial in nature does not mean that it is constitutionally insignificant or unprotected. Since 1975 the Supreme Court has signaled that overbroad governmental regulations could be challenged even if the activities sought to be regulated are commercial or economic in nature. *Virginia State Bd. of Pharmacy v. Virginia Citizens Consumer Council, Inc.*, 425 U.S. 748 (1976) (striking down state statute which declared it unprofessional conduct for a pharmacist to advertise prescription drug prices); *Bigelow v. Virginia*, 421 U.S. 809 (1975) (abortion advertising held constitutionally protected). Even in the absence of political content, first amendment defenses are available to protect commercial speech because of its importance to the free market exchange of ideas in the allocation of resources. The Court has recognized that business speech has a marketplace focus and concern for both purchaser-oriented and seller-motivated profit interests. 425 U.S. 748, 761; *Bates v. State Bar*, 433 U.S. 350, 374-75 (1977) (where the Court held that a state could not prohibit price advertising for routine legal services).

When economically motivated communications are given first amendment protection, tensions develop between the proper government regulation of that business and the values which underlie the first amendment. It does seem evident, however, that the commercial speech component of the first amendment is inapplicable if the speech sought to be protected is part of an illegal activity. *Pittsburgh Press Co. v. Pittsburgh Comm'n on Human Rels.*, 413 U.S. 376, 389 (1973) (where the Court held that an ordinance prohibiting gender-designated captions in advertising did not violate the first amendment. The advertisement could have facilitated the illegal activity of employment discrimination).

In light of this developing defense, it is important for antitrust counsel to consider (1) whether and under what circumstances a remedial order can restrict economic conduct which arguably comes within the commercial speech doctrine, (2) whether any principles delimit the "illegal conduct" exception to the commercial speech defense, and (3) whether traditional standards of overbreadth analysis and vagueness are applicable.

Consider the Supreme Court's broad statement in *FTC v. National Lead Co.*, 352 U.S. 419, 429 (1957), that the government is not confined to blocking "the narrow lane the transgressor has traveled; it must be allowed effectively to close all roads to the prohibited goal." There the Court approved an FTC order prohibiting the quoting of prices calculated on a territorial zone price system. How can the parameters of such an order be defined? In Chapter 4, parallel conduct among competitors and the competitive consequences of such conduct are discussed. There it is noted that one enforcement theory is based on the price theory of interdependence: sellers in an oligopoly recognize that their own price and production decisions are dictated, given the industry structure, in large part by what the reactions of other sellers will be to price moves. Anticipating those reactions, competitors adopt parallel pricing. *See* Turner, *The Definition of Agreement Under the Sherman Act: Conscious Parallelism and Refusal to Deal*, 75 Harv. L. Rev. 655 (1962). Would a remedial order, which prohibits public price announcements by competitors in an oligopolistic market, violate the first amendment by reducing the amount of useful information in the marketplace?

On several occasions, the Supreme Court has implied that if the commercial speech is used to further or facilitate an illegal scheme, the speech (or conduct) is not protected. *See, e.g., Bigelow v. Virginia*, 421 U.S. 809, 828 (1975). Thus, if the public price announcement was a facilitating device in an antitrust price fixing scheme, the speech arguably would not be protected. Accordingly, an order could be drawn to fence in this otherwise protected conduct. The central inquiry is probably the remoteness of the challenged conduct to the demonstrated illegality. In short, the protection afforded economic speech may depend on the illegality of the interest served by the speech and the closeness of the connection between the speech and the illegal conduct. *See* Sullivan, *First Amendment Defenses in Antitrust Litigation*, 46 Mo. L. Rev. 517 (1981).

The most definitive statement on constitutional protection from overbroad regulatory orders came in *Central Hudson Gas & Elec. Corp. v. Public Serv. Comm'n*, 447 U.S. 557 (1980). The New York Public Service Commission issued an order prohibiting the promotional advertising of the use of electricity. The state interest underlying the ban centered on energy conservation. After the energy shortage ended, the promotional ban continued, but the regulations permitted informational advertising designed to encourage time shifts in energy consumption. Central Hudson, a public utility, challenged the promotional ban, arguing that it violated the commercial speech doctrine. The New York Court of Appeals upheld the ban on the theory that there was "little value to advertising in 'the noncompetitive market in which electric corporations operate.'" *Id.* at 561. The Supreme Court reversed, holding that the ban violated Central Hudson's commercial speech rights.

The Court established a four-tiered analysis for scrutinizing regulations and orders which restrict commercial speech. The first question is whether the speech is protected, i.e., whether it is commercial speech that is accurate and unrelated to illegal conduct. If it is inaccurate or related to illegal conduct, then it is entitled to no constitutional protection. If it is not deceptive and does not encourage illegal activity, the speech is then protected and the second inquiry is whether the regulating authority has a substantial interest to be served by the regulation. Next, the restriction on the speech must advance directly the stated governmental interest. Finally, the restriction cannot be more extensive than necessary to serve that interest. *Id.* at 566.

The requirement that an order be no broader than necessary to achieve a governmental interest is one of the most litigated requirements in trade regulation. It mandates that the order can "extend only as far as the interest it serves." *Id.* at 565. If a less restrictive order will suffice to protect that interest, the order must be tailored to protect only the substantial governmental interest promoted. In other words, to support an order the government must demonstrate that alternative means which would burden or impair the defendant less are unavailable.

In *Florida Bar v. Went For It, Inc.*, 115 S. Ct. 2371 (1995), the Supreme Court reversed a Court of Appeals decision finding a violation of the *Central Hudson* test. The Eleventh Circuit had found that Florida Bar rules that prohibited lawyers from using direct mail to solicit injured clients until 30 days after the injury violated the First Amendment. But Justice O'Connor, applying the *Central Hudson* test, accepted the protection of potential clients' privacy and the preservation of the "integrity of the legal profession" as substantial Bar interests and found the rule "reasonably well-tailored to its stated objective of eliminating targeted mailings whose type and timing are a source of distress to Floridians, distress that has caused many of them to lose respect for the legal profession." 115 S. Ct. at 2380.

In sum, the Supreme Court's opinions teach that economic conduct which is an essential, substantial, or facilitating part of an antitrust violation can be proscribed through a remedial order without violating the commercial speech protection. But care must be taken so that a conduct-oriented order does not sweep so broadly as to deter other conduct that may be competitive. *See Edenfield v. Fane*, 507 U.S. 761 (1993); *Virginia State Bd. of Pharmacy v. Virginia Citizens Consumer Council, Inc.*, 425 U.S. 748 (1976).

B. *IN PARI DELICTO* AND THE UNCLEAN HANDS DOCTRINE

In pari delicto is a common law defense raised when the plaintiff is a party to the alleged illegality. The term means "of equal fault." From its early application in *Eastman Kodak Co. v. Blackmore*, 277 F. 694 (2d Cir. 1921), the Supreme Court has narrowly restricted the use of the doctrine as an airtight defense to an antitrust charge. The following case discusses antitrust violations as a defense.

PERMA LIFE MUFFLERS, INC. V. INTERNATIONAL PARTS CORP.

392 U.S. 134 (1968)

JUSTICE BLACK delivered the opinion of the Court.

The principal question presented is whether the plaintiffs in this private antitrust action were barred from recovery by a doctrine known by the Latin phrase *in pari delicto*, which literally means "of equal fault." The plaintiffs, petitioners here, were all dealers who had operated "Midas Muffler Shops" under sales agreements granted by respondent Midas, Inc. Their complaint charged that Midas had entered into a conspiracy with the other named defendants — its parent corporation International Parts Corp., two other subsidiaries, and six individual defendants who were officers or agents of the corporations — to restrain and substantially lessen competition in violation of § 1 of the Sherman Act and § 3 of the Clayton Act.... In 1955 the owners of International initiated a detailed plan for promoting the sale of mufflers by extensively advertising the "Midas" trade name and establishing a nationwide chain of dealers who would specialize in selling exhaust system equipment. Each prospective dealer was offered a sales agreement prepared by Midas, Inc., a wholly owned subsidiary of International. The agreement obligated the dealer to purchase all his mufflers from Midas, to honor the Midas guarantee on mufflers sold by any dealer, and to sell the mufflers at resale prices fixed by Midas and at locations specified in the agreement. The dealers were also obligated to purchase all their exhaust system parts from Midas, to carry the complete line of Midas products, and in general to refrain from dealing with any of Midas' competitors. In return Midas promised to underwrite the cost of the muffler guarantee and gave the dealer permission to use the registered trademark "Midas" and the service mark "Midas Muffler Shops." The dealer was also granted the exclusive right to sell "Midas" products within his defined territory. He was not required to pay a franchise fee or to purchase or lease substantial capital equipment from Midas, and the agreement was cancelable by either party on 30 days' notice.

Petitioners' complaint challenged as illegal restraints of trade numerous provisions of the agreements, such as the terms barring them from purchasing from other sources of supply, preventing them from selling outside the designated territory, tying the sale of mufflers to the sale of other products in the Midas line, and requiring them to sell at fixed retail prices. Petitioners alleged that they had often requested Midas to eliminate these restrictions but that Midas had refused and had threatened to terminate their agreements if they failed to comply. Finally they alleged that one of the plaintiffs had his agreement canceled by Midas for purchasing exhaust parts from a Midas competitor, and that the other plaintiff dealers had themselves canceled their agreements. All the plaintiffs claimed treble damages for the monetary loss they had suffered from having to abide by the restrictive provisions.

The Court of Appeals ... held the suit barred because petitioners were *in pari delicto*. The court noted that each of the petitioners had enthusiastically sought to acquire a Midas franchise with full knowledge of these provisions and had "solemnly subscribed" to the agreement containing the restrictive terms. Petitioners had all made enormous profits as Midas dealers, had eagerly sought to acquire additional franchises, and had voluntarily entered into additional franchise agreements, all while fully aware of the restrictions they now challenge....

We find ourselves in complete disagreement with the Court of Appeals. There is nothing in the language of the antitrust acts which indicates that Congress wanted to make the common-law *in pari delicto* doctrine a defense to treble-damage actions, and the facts of this case suggest no basis for applying such a doctrine even if it did exist. Although *in pari delicto* literally means "of equal fault," the doctrine has been applied, correctly or incorrectly, in a wide variety of situations in which a plaintiff seeking damages or equitable relief is himself involved in some of the same sort of wrongdoing. We have often indicated the inappropriateness of invoking broad common-law barriers to relief where a private suit serves important public purposes. It was for this reason that we held in *Kiefer-Stewart Co. v. Joseph E. Seagram & Sons*, 340 U.S. 211 (1951), that a plaintiff in an antitrust suit could not be barred from recovery by proof that he had engaged in an unrelated conspiracy to commit some other antitrust violation. Similarly, in *Simpson v. Union Oil Co.*, 377 U.S. 13 (1964), we held that a dealer whose consignment agreement was canceled for failure to adhere to a fixed resale price could bring suit under the antitrust laws even though by signing the agreement he had to that extent become a participant in the illegal, competition-destroying scheme. Both *Simpson* and *Kiefer-Stewart* were premised on a recognition that the purposes of the antitrust laws are best served by insuring that the private action will be an ever-present threat to deter anyone contemplating business behavior in violation of the antitrust laws. The plaintiff who reaps the reward of treble damages may be no less morally reprehensible than the defendant, but the law encourages his suit to further the overriding public policy in favor of competition. A more fastidious regard for the relative moral worth of the parties would only result in seriously undermining the usefulness of the private action as a bulwark of antitrust enforcement. And permitting the plaintiff to recover a windfall gain does not encourage continued violations by those in his position since they remain fully subject to civil and criminal penalties for their own illegal conduct.

... Although petitioners may be subject to some criticism for having taken any part in respondents' allegedly illegal scheme and for eagerly seeking more franchises and more profits, their participation was not voluntary in any meaningful sense. They sought the franchises enthusiastically but they did not actively seek each and every clause of the agreement. Rather, many of the clauses were quite clearly detrimental to their interests, and they alleged that they had continually objected to them. Petitioners apparently accepted many of these restraints solely because their acquiescence was necessary to obtain an otherwise attractive business opportunity.... Moreover, even if petitioners actually favored and supported some of the other restrictions, they cannot be blamed for seeking to minimize the disadvantages of the agreement once they had been forced to accept its more onerous terms as a condition of doing business. The possible beneficial byproducts of a restriction from a plaintiff's point of view can of course be taken into consideration in computing damages, but once it is shown that the plaintiff did not aggressively support and further the monopolistic scheme as a necessary part and parcel of it, his understandable attempts to make the best of a bad situation should not be a ground for completely denying him the right to recover which the antitrust acts give him. We therefore hold that the doctrine of *in pari delicto*, with its complex scope, contents, and effects, is not to be recognized as a defense to an antitrust action.

Respondents, however, seek to support the judgment below on a considerably narrower ground. They picture petitioners as actively supporting the entire restrictive program as such, participating in its formulation and encouraging its continuation. We need not decide, however, whether such truly complete involvement and participation in a monopolistic scheme could ever be a basis, wholly apart from the idea of *in pari delicto*, for barring a plaintiff's cause of action, for in the present case the factual picture respondents attempt to paint is utterly refuted by the record....

Reversed.

NOTES AND QUESTIONS

1. Justices White and Fortas suggested in their concurring opinions that if a plaintiff's participation in the antitrust violation is equal to or greater than the defendant's, the plaintiff may have difficulty proving causation of the injury, with the result that recovery would be denied.

2. In *Perma Life* the Court was confronted with the determination of how best to maintain an effective deterrent policy for antitrust enforcement. Noting the "inappropriateness of invoking broad common law barriers," the Supreme Court weighed the relative degrees of fault among alleged antitrust violators and held that the law's deterrent policies would be better served (maximized) if courts do not recognize the common rule of *in pari delicto* as a defense, even though the plaintiff had knowingly participated in the illegal scheme and could stand to recover a windfall. *See also Bangor Punta Opers., Inc. v. Bangor & A.R.R.*, 417 U.S. 703, 719 (1974) (Marshall, J., dissenting).

3. In evaluating the application of the defense to the facts, the Court apparently concluded that the antitrust violators were not of equal fault. Note the Court's conclusion that because of Perma Life's relative lack of bargaining power and unequal economic leverage, its participation in the illegal scheme "was not voluntary in any meaningful sense." Since the Court found that the wrongdoers were not of equal fault, perhaps the Court's language implied that the *in pari delicto* defense is available if the plaintiff's degree of fault was relatively equal with that of defendants. Consider Justice Black's statement that

> We need not decide, however, whether such truly complete involvement and participation in a monopolistic scheme could ever be a basis, wholly apart from the idea of *in pari delicto*, for barring a plaintiff's cause of action, for in the present case the factual picture respondents attempt to paint is utterly refuted by the record.

392 U.S. at 141. The four concurring opinions supported the continuing availability of the defense where the violators are of equal fault. The lower courts are in apparent agreement. *See, e.g., Bernstein v. Universal Pictures, Inc.*, 517 F.2d 976 (2d Cir. 1975); *THI-Hawaii, Inc. v. First Commerce Fin. Corp.*, 627 F.2d 991 (9th Cir. 1980).

4. Consider the separate question whether the jury should be instructed to consider the plaintiff's own antitrust conduct when determining the defendant's liability. *See* 2 P. Areeda & H. Hovenkamp, *Antitrust Laws* ¶ 390 (rev. ed. 1994). In *Eichler v. Berner*, 472 U.S. 299, 310-11 (1985), the Supreme Court observed that:

> a private action for damages ... may be barred on the grounds of the plaintiff's own culpability only where: 1) as a direct result of his own actions, the plaintiff bears at least substantially equal responsibility for the violations he seeks to redress, and 2) preclusion of suit would not significantly interfere with the effective enforcement of the ... laws....

Is the *Eichler* test an easier standard for the defense to meet than that announced in *Perma Life*? At what time in the pretrial or trial stage is the defense assertable? Consider the two-part test. Is the first a jury question and the second a legal issue only the judge can determine? Could a summary judgment motion raise the defense? Consider how the Court has characterized its test in *Eichler*:

> The first prong of this test captures the essential elements of the classic *in pari delicto* doctrine. The second prong, which embodies the doctrine's traditional requirement that public policy implications be carefully considered before the defense is allowed, ensures that the broad judge-made law does not undermine the congressional policy favoring private suits as an important mode of enforcing federal ... statutes.

Pinter v. Dahl, 486 U.S. 622, 633 (1988).

For a case where the Seventh Circuit affirmed a jury's special verdict finding that plaintiff "bore substantially equal responsibility" for a territorial restriction and rendered damages in the amount of "zero" dollars, *see General Leaseways, Inc. v. National Truck Leasing Ass'n*, 830 F.2d 717 (7th Cir. 1987). Subsequently, the Seventh Circuit, in a case between lawyers and former law partners, applied the equal responsibility defense announced in *Perma Life* and denied treble damages. In *Blackburn v. Sweeney*, 53 F.3d 825 (7th Cir. 1995), former partners in a law firm sued other former partners, alleging that the "withdrawal from partnership agreement" which they each entered was a horizontal market division agreement unlawful under the Sherman Act. Although agreeing that the agreement was unlawful, the court held that the former partners could not recover damages because the parties had relatively equal bargaining power and freely entered the restrictive agreement. The court also concluded that the plaintiff had not suffered antitrust injury since, as one of the two colluding competitors, he did not suffer from the effects of the collusion on competition.

However, the court declared the agreement illegal, and thus unenforceable. The result thus suggests this outcome: when A and B enter into a per se unlawful cartel or territorial division conspiracy, neither A nor B can later claim that the agreement is unlawful and obtain damages or an injunction (plus attorneys fees) against the other; however, neither can the agreement be enforced, and one party could presumably bring a Declaratory Judgment action to that effect. The ordinary rules of antitrust standing, injury, and probably *pari delicto* do not apply to the Declaratory Judgment Act — where, in any event, relief would ordinarily be limited to a declaration that the provision at issue is unlawful and unenforceable.

See subsection F, Chapter 3, *supra*. Note that in the state of New York, such a "no compete" restriction in a partnership agreement would be unethical. *Cohen v. Lord, Day & Lord*, 550 N.E. 2d 410 (N.Y. 1989), but not in the state of California, *Howard v. Babcock*, 863 P. 2d 150 (Cal. 1993). *See* Robert W. Hillman, *The Law Firm As Jurassic Park: Comments on Howard v. Babcock*, 27 U.C. Davis L. Rev. 533 (1994).

5. Generally, the equitable doctrine of unclean hands has been interpreted to have broader application than the *in pari delicto* defense. It has found expression when the plaintiff may have violated some other antitrust provision or related statute in a separate illegality. Its application, however, has been upheld rather infrequently. *See Kiefer-Stewart Co. v. Joseph E. Seagram & Sons*, 340 U.S. 211 (1951); Handler & Sacks, *The Continued Vitality of In Pari Delicto as an Antitrust Defense*, 70 Geo. L.J. 1123 (1982).

6. Chrysler Corp. challenged the 1983-1984 joint venture between General Motors and Toyota to build subcompact cars. The defendants argued that the joint venture was legal, and also that Chrysler had unclean hands because it had anticompetitive motives in bringing the antitrust action against its two competitors. After deciding that Chrysler had standing to challenge the joint venture and noting that the "lower courts have almost uniformly declined to permit the unclean hands defense in antitrust suits where injunctive relief is sought," the district court ruled that defendants could not raise unclean hands as an affirmative defense to block Chrysler's suit. Citing the "overriding public interest in preventing anticompetitive injury," the district court struck the unclean hands defense. *Chrysler Corp. v. General Motors Corp.*, 596 F. Supp. 416 (D.D.C. 1984).

SECTION III. REMEDIES

A. DAMAGES

Section 4 of the Clayton Act, 15 U.S.C. § 15, provides that "[a]ny person who shall be injured in his business or property by reason of anything forbidden in the antitrust laws may sue therefor ... and shall recover threefold the damages by him sustained." Both the legislative history and judicial interpretations suggest that this statute has two central, but not always consistent, purposes. One is to deter potential antitrust violators; the other is to encourage private litigants to bring suit.

An antitrust plaintiff seeking damages must first show the "fact" of antitrust injury. This includes (1) the existence of an antitrust violation; (2) causation, or cause-in-fact; that is, the plaintiff cannot recover unless it can show that the violation was responsible for the injury; and (3) that the injury is of the type the antitrust laws were intended to prevent; that is, the plaintiff must make out the "antitrust injury" requirements of *Brunswick Corp. v. Pueblo Bowl-O-Mat, Inc.*, 429 U.S. 477 (1977), reprinted *supra*. After fact of injury has been established the plaintiff must prove the amount of its injury. Most courts hold that the fact of injury has to be established with some rigor, but that proof standards respecting the amount of damages are far more relaxed. *See Bigelow v. RKO Radio Pictures*, 327 U.S. 251, 265 (1946). Plaintiffs who can establish the fact of injury, but who cannot establish the amount with sufficient precision, may be awarded nominal damages. *E.g., Rosebrough Monument Co. v. Memorial Park Cem. Ass'n*, 736 F.2d 441 (8th Cir. 1984).

Today courts recognize two types of damage measurement. If the plaintiffs are purchasers of a monopolized or cartelized product, their damages will generally be the "overcharge" — or the amount by which the illegal activity enhanced the price. The Supreme Court approved damage measurement based on "the difference between the price paid and the market or fair price" in *Chattanooga Foundry & Pipe Works v. Atlanta*, 203 U.S. 390, 396 (1906). If the plaintiffs are competitors or terminated dealers, damages are generally based on lost profits. *See Eastman Kodak Co. v. Southern Photo Materials Co.*, 273 U.S. 359, 379 (1927). Of course, under section 4 of the Clayton Act, all damages are trebled. As a general rule, the jury is not instructed in advance that its damage award will be multiplied by three.

Today damages are most commonly proved by the "before-and-after" method and the "yardstick" method. Under the "before-and-after" method a plaintiff tries to show what was happening in the market both before and after the violation occurred and argues that its damages should be based on these numbers. For example, if a purchaser from a cartel can show that widgets cost $1.00 before a cartel came into existence and $1.00 after it fell apart, but $1.25 during the cartel period, one can presume that the cartel raised prices by 25 cents. As you might suspect, a good deal of adjustment, guesswork, and even some speculation goes into such estimates. Under the "yardstick" method, the plaintiff looks at some other firm or some other market presumed to be similar to the market in which the antitrust violation occurred, except for the violation. Damages are then based on the difference between prices or profits in the "yardstick" market and the market at issue. For example, if the price of widgets was $1.35 in Boston during the operation of a local cartel, but only $1.00 in Chicago at the same time, where the market was presumably competitive, then the difference may approximate the amount of the cartel overcharge. These prices will have to be adjusted to account for differences in costs, taxes, etc. For more on the mechanics of damage measurement under these two methods, *see* H. Hovenkamp, *Federal Antitrust Policy*, ch. 17 (2d ed. 1994).

Damage measurement becomes more difficult, and correspondingly more speculative, when the plaintiff was actually forced to exit the market as a result of a violation. The prevailing rules permit the plaintiff to show damages as a function of the business' value as a "going concern" — or its market value in a hypothetical market in which the antitrust violation had not occurred. Even more problematic is the plight of the "precluded entrant" — the plaintiff who was prohibited from ever entering a market as a result of an antitrust violation. Should such a plaintiff be entitled to show the "going concern" value of a business that never went anywhere? Or to show lost profits from a business that never made any sales? Courts generally permit such showings in principle, but few precluded plaintiffs have made substantial damage recoveries. Courts require that the plaintiff show both an "intention" to enter a market, and sufficient "preparedness" to do so to make the award of damages reasonable. *See Neumann v. Reinforced Earth Co.*, 786 F.2d 424 (9th Cir. 1986), which held that the plaintiff had not been sufficiently "prepared" to enter the market when all his applications for financing had been rejected. The sad irony of the precluded entrant cases is that people who have not yet entered a market may be uniquely vulnerable to certain kinds of antitrust violations. As a general rule, the less unrecoverable investment a firm has made in a market, the more easily it can be driven out. For example, predatory pricing strategies designed to deter firms thinking about entering a market might be much more successful than predatory pricing against established rivals. O. Williamson, *Predatory Pricing: A Strategic and Welfare Analysis*, 87 Yale L.J. 284 (1977).

In sum, injured competitors may be awarded damages for: 1) recovery for increased costs; 2) recovery for lost profits of a continuing business; 3) recovery for lost profits of a terminated business; and 4) recovery for reduction in business value. *See* D. Floyd & E. Thomas Sullivan, *Private Antitrust Actions*, ch. 9 (1996).

1. OPTIMAL ANTITRUST DAMAGES

The language of section 4 of the Clayton Act permitting a private plaintiff to recover three times the damages "by him sustained" suggests rather strongly that compensation of victims, rather than deterrence of violators, is the principal goal of private damage actions under the antitrust laws.

Nevertheless, the Supreme Court has suggested that deterrence is an important goal of private antitrust enforcement. *Illinois Brick Co. v. Illinois*, 431 U.S. 720, 746 (1977); *Brunswick Corp. v. Pueblo Bowl-O-Mat, Inc.*, 429 U.S. 477, 485-86 (1977). Recent scholarship, which relies on an influential article by economist Gary Becker, *Crime and Punishment: An Economic Approach*, 76 J. Pol. Econ. 169 (1968), argues that deterrence should be the *only* goal of private damage actions. This Optimal Deterrence Model begins with the premise that many of the things the antitrust laws condemn are efficient, largely because courts are unable to distinguish precisely between efficient and inefficient practices. An optimal damages rule should deter inefficient conduct, while permitting efficient conduct.

There is little correlation between the size of this optimal fine and the losses experienced by potential plaintiffs, particularly when the plaintiff is a competitor of the defendant rather than a seller or purchaser. Thus the model often yields results inconsistent with section 4's mandate that the victim of an antitrust violation recover an award based on losses "by him sustained."

Within the neoclassical model, you may recall (see Chapter 2, *supra*), monopoly produces both a wealth transfer, caused by consumers forced to pay monopoly prices, and a "deadweight" loss, caused by those consumers who choose not to purchase the product at the higher price, but rather make inefficient substitutions to something else. In evaluating the social consequences of monopoly, the neoclassical economist views the wealth transfer as relatively unimportant. She is concerned principally with the overall size of the pie, not with how big the individual pieces are. However, the deadweight loss is a matter of great concern, for it represents lost social value. This has led some people to suppose that if the goal of private antitrust enforcement is efficiency, the optimal sanction must be a function of the deadweight loss. *E.g.*, Schwartz, *An Overview of the Economics of Antitrust Enforcement*, 68 Geo. L.J. 1075, 1081-85 (1980).

But often a fine equal to the deadweight loss is too small to deter inefficient conduct. For example, in a market with a perfectly linear demand curve price fixing that produces $1,000 in excess profits to the violators will generate consumer overcharges of $1,000 and a deadweight loss of $500. A fine equal to the deadweight loss would be too small. The fine would have to be marginally greater than $1,000 in order to make the price fixing unprofitable.

The Optimal Deterrence Model identifies optimal damages as the *sum* of the wealth transfer and the deadweight loss. Requiring the violator to pay damages that include the deadweight loss will induce him to refrain from violating the antitrust laws only if his conduct is socially harmful. For example, an efficiency-producing merger or joint venture, or even some exclusionary practices by monopolists, may simultaneously increase firms' market power and reduce their production or distribution costs. In such cases the size of the deadweight loss becomes theoretically relevant. Suppose that conduct which permits the defendant to charge monopoly prices produces a wealth transfer of $1,000 and a deadweight loss of $400. However, it also reduces the defendant's production costs. The conduct is efficient on balance if the production cost savings are greater than $400, but inefficient if the savings are less than $400. Under the Optimal Deterrence Model the perfect penalty would be the *sum* of the monopoly overcharge and the deadweight loss, or $1,400. If the production cost savings are greater than $400, it will be worth more than $1,400 and the defendant will engage in it, the threat of a penalty notwithstanding. If the production cost savings are less than $400, and the activity inefficient, then it will be worth less to the defendant than the anticipated fine, and the defendant will not engage in the conduct. Thus the optimal fine will deter inefficient conduct but permit efficient conduct. *See* W. Breit & K. Elzinga, *Antitrust Penalty Reform: An Economic Analysis* (1986); Easterbrook, *Detrebling Antitrust Damages*, 28 J. L. & Econ. 445 (1985); Landes, *Optimal Sanctions for Antitrust Violations*, 50 U. Chi. L. Rev. 652 (1983). For a critique, *see* H. Hovenkamp, *Federal Antitrust Policy*, ch. 17 (2d ed. 1994).

One conceptual problem with the Optimal Deterrence Model is that it fails to account for the full social cost of monopoly in dynamic markets — i.e., markets where firms behave strategically. The incipient monopolist may consume many of its own resources or those of others in order to create or maintain its monopoly position. As a result, the social cost of *de facto* monopoly consists of three things:

(1) the deadweight loss triangle, which measures inefficient consumer substitutions away from the monopolized goods;

(2) that part of the wealth "transfer," as the neoclassical model identifies it, that the *de facto* monopolist or monopolist-to-be spends in socially harmful ways in order to retain or obtain monopoly power (see Chapter 2, *infra* on the social cost of monopoly); and importantly,

(3) the socially harmful losses that the monopolist or incipient monopolist imposes on competitors or others in the same effort.

The Optimal Deterrence Model expressly takes cost element (1) into account by including the deadweight loss triangle as part of the basis for damages. It also takes cost element (2) into account because the cost to the monopolist of its exclusionary practices reduces the anticipated profitability of monopoly. But the Model completely ignores the social cost of any injury that the monopolist's exclusionary practices may impose on others. For example, if Chrysler should bomb all the plants owned by General Motors, Ford, and its other competitors and murder their executives, it might attain a monopoly. But the social cost of that monopoly caused by inefficient consumer substitutions would be trivial in comparison to the social cost of the means by which Chrysler created it. Chrysler presumably will not spend more on arsonists and assassins than the value of the expected monopoly. But the social cost of the losses it imposes on its competitors could be far larger. The largest social cost of many forms of monopolizing conduct is the inefficient losses imposed on competitors or other nonconsumers.

By failing to consider this element of social cost, the "Optimal" Deterrence Model frequently yields suboptimal damages. For example, suppose a monopolist uses a combination of predatory pricing, exclusive contracts, and patent fraud to lengthen the duration of its monopoly. The activity permits the firm to earn $1,000 in additional monopoly profits, costs the firm $100, and produces a deadweight loss of $400. As a result of scale economies, the activity also generates cost savings. The Optimal Deterrence Model would assess a penalty of $1,400. In this case the monopolist would pursue the activity only if the cost savings exceeded $500.

But suppose that the monopolistic activity additionally imposes $700 in inefficient losses on competitors whose plants must be dismantled, research discarded, opportunities lost, and contracts broken. In that case the Optimal Deterrence Model might end up approving socially costly activity simply because injuries to other firms, rather than injuries that accrue to consumers, are not calculated into the social cost of monopoly. An optimal model for antitrust damages would try to predicate damages on the sum of the monopoly overcharge plus the *entire* social cost of monopoly, and the deadweight loss alone reflects only part — sometimes a very small part — of the social cost of monopoly.

One important difference between that part of the social cost of monopoly that falls upon competitors and the social cost described by the traditional deadweight loss triangle is that society may have to pay the first cost whether or not the scheme succeeds. That is, some attempts to create monopolies fail, but they are costly to competitors and to society nonetheless. It has been argued that such failed attempts should not be actionable, for they are self-deterring and the incipient monopolist bears the full social cost of its failures. Landes, *Optimal Sanctions, id.* at 668-72.

The resources spent by the incipient monopolist in the monopolistic scheme are costs borne by itself, and if the scheme fails there will be no monopoly overcharge or deadweight loss. Once again, however, this perspective ignores the social cost that might be borne by competitors, whether or not the scheme fails. For example, suppose that a putative predator calculates that predatory pricing (discussed in Chapter 6) will cost $300 and generate monopoly returns of $2,000. It will also produce a deadweight loss of $800. Under the Optimal Deterrence Model the penalty is $2,800 if the scheme succeeds, but zero if the scheme fails, for there will be neither a monopoly overcharge nor a deadweight loss. But suppose that the predation forces inefficient plant closings, bankruptcies, loss of contracts and jobs, and other social injuries that equal $2,000. Many of these inefficiencies may result whether or not the predation scheme succeeds.

This critique of the Optimal Deterrence Model suggests much more room for competitor lawsuits than its advocates would allow. For example, many failed attempts to monopolize impose socially harmful losses on competitors even though they never yield a monopoly overcharge and deadweight loss. But to deny that the inefficient losses imposed by failed attempts are social costs of "monopoly" is quite wrong. They are social costs of the *prospect* of monopoly, which tempts some people, and which the antitrust laws are designed to discourage. Competitors — who must be driven out of a market before a monopoly can be created — may be in a unique position to detect the *first* social costs of monopoly to be incurred, the money inefficiently spent and the injuries inefficiently imposed by the monopolist or incipient monopolist in establishing its position. The social cost of waiting until the monopolist spends more of its own resources, inflicts more injuries on competitors, and begins charging monopoly prices could be enormous. Further, the chances of prosecution are less if we rely on consumers, for they are less likely to detect monopoly than are the immediate victims of exclusionary practices. *See* Hovenkamp, *Antitrust Policy and the Social Cost of Monopoly*, 78 Iowa L. Rev. 371 (1993).

2. THE OPTIMAL DETERRENCE MODEL AND TREBLE DAMAGES

Section 4 of the Clayton Act also provides that the successful antitrust plaintiff is entitled to *three times* its losses. The requirement that antitrust damages be trebled is very old, going back at least as far as the English Statute of Monopolies, passed in 1623.

The Optimal Deterrence Model presents an economic argument for a damages multiplier — although the correct multiplier may not be three. Damages are trebled because there is a less than 100% likelihood that the violation will be detected and prosecuted, and the damages paid. Treble damages are appropriate on the assumption of a 0.33 probability that the fine will ever be paid. In short, an antitrust regime in which damages are based on three times the anticipated monopoly profits from a violation will deter such conduct if we can assume that such violators will have to pay the fine one time for every three such violations. As a general rule, the sanction should equal the sum of the monopoly overcharge plus the deadweight loss, multiplied by the reciprocal of the probability that the violation will be detected and prosecuted and the penalty paid.

But this economic rationale for treble damages meets substantial problems of both computation and strategy. First, coming up with the relevant data is well-nigh impossible. How many undetected cartels are there? Finding out would be difficult without detecting them.

More importantly, there is no single probability of detection for antitrust violations generally. At one extreme is naked bid rigging in which the conspirators know they are doing something criminal and take elaborate precautions to conceal it. Here the probability of detection is clearly less than 100%, or there would be no such conspiracies. At the other extreme are actions like airline or automobile company mergers which are announced to the Department of Justice before they occur and are described in public newspapers such as the *Wall Street Journal*. Here the probability of detection is so close to 100% that no firm could hope to escape antitrust liability by avoiding it. Rather, the firm must rely on its ability to convince an agency or court that its merger is legal. In between are explicit agreements that incorporate resale price maintenance and exclusive dealing or tying arrangements, and that are known to the parties to the agreement but perhaps not to the public generally. In many such cases the eventual plaintiff is a party to the agreement, so the probability of "detection" is very high, although the likelihood of successful prosecution is much lower. Likewise ambiguous is monopolization where certain acts, such as an express refusal to deal or controlling an essential facility, are quite public, while other acts, such as patent fraud or predatory pricing, are concealed.

Perhaps the damage multiplier should consider the average of all of these. If we could identify the probability of detection of price fixing, resale price maintenance (RPM), exclusive dealing, monopolization and attempt, mergers, etc., weigh the numbers to account for the relative occurrence of each, and then average them, we might discover that, on the whole, one of every three antitrust violations is detected. As a result, treble damages is the optimal sanction.

But the immediate effect of our rule would be that firms bent on violating the antitrust laws would behave strategically. There would be relatively more of those violations where the probability of detection was less than one-third, and relatively fewer of those violations where the probability of detection was greater. Over time the average probability of detection would decrease and our treble damage rule would prove underdeterrent.

Even if we segregated those antitrust offenses for which the probability of detection was relatively small and developed multiple damages rules for them, the problem would be the same. For example, suppose we decided that the probability that a cartel will be detected is one-third, and assigned a treble damage rule to naked price fixing. Were we omniscient we would soon discover that, although the *average* probability that a cartel might be detected is one-third, not all cartels are alike. The probability that a cartel will be detected varies with the number of competitors, the extent of otherwise lawful communication among them, the presence or absence of nonparticipating competitors, the amount of detail with which price and output agreements have to be drawn, the nature of sales in the market, etc. Assuming an average probability of 0.33 that cartels will be detected, for some particular cartels that probability is far greater than 0.33 and for others it is far less. A treble damages rule will discourage cartels in the former category, where the rule will be overdeterrent, and encourage those in the latter category, where it is underdeterrent. Within a few years the average probability of detection will no longer be one-third, and the number will have to be adjusted.

In short, there is no equilibrium in which a damage multiplier will work. As soon as one is established it will become underdeterrent, as firms choose those antitrust violations that are, on balance, more profitable. *See* Hovenkamp, *Antitrust Damages Reform*, 33 Antitrust Bull. 233 (1988).

B. AWARD OF ATTORNEY'S FEES

In addition to treble damages, costs and interest, a successful plaintiff, whether an individual, entity or state attorney general, in an antitrust action is entitled to receive a "reasonable attorney's fee." Under section 4 of the Clayton Act, the court is without discretion to decide whether the plaintiff who recovers damages is entitled to an attorney fee; the award is mandatory. Under section 16 of the Clayton Act (15 U.S.C. § 26) the same rule applies to suits requesting injunctive relief. But the court does have discretion on how the fee is computed. *See* Floyd and Sullivan, *Private Antitrust Actions*, 1047-1115 (1996).

Under section 4C(d)(2) of the Hart-Scott-Rodino amendments of 1976 the district court has discretion to award a successful *defendant* attorney's fees, but only if a *parens patriae* suit has been brought by a state attorney general in "bad faith, vexatiously, wantonly or for oppressive reasons."

After experimenting with a formula based on a percentage of the recovery, courts have adopted through the years several methods of calculating the attorney fee based on the statutory requirement that the fee be "reasonable." While the methods vary, the outcome seems clear that attorney fees under section 4 are to be awarded and calculated without regard to a preexisting contingent fee agreement between the plaintiff and counsel. *Farmington Dowel Prods. Co. v. Forster Mfg. Co.*, 421 F.2d 61 (1st Cir. 1970).

In permitting attorney's fees to the prevailing plaintiff under section 16 of the Clayton Act for equitable relief, the Ninth Circuit has ruled that the standard is 42 U.S.C. § 1988, which requires "a causal relationship between the litigation brought and the practical outcome realized." *Southwest Marine, Inc. v. Campbell Indus.*, 732 F.2d 744 (9th Cir. 1984). This standard suggests that a reasonable fee under section 1988 reflects the attorney time reasonably spent on the law suit. *See generally Blum v. Stenson*, 465 U.S. 886 n.16 (1984).

The trend in calculating the award has been towards establishing objective benchmarks rather than an evaluation based purely on subjective factors. The prevailing criteria today is known as the "lodestar" approach. In *Lindy Bros. Bldrs. v. American Radiator & Std. San. Corp.*, 487 F.2d 161 (3d Cir. 1973) (*Lindy I*), the Third Circuit stated that the computation should include the multiplication of the numbers of hours utilized by the normal billing rate for antitrust litigation, including the attorney's reputation and status, together with adjustments made for more subjective factors such as the likelihood of success or risk involved and quality of the professional service rendered. *See also* 540 F.2d 102 (3d Cir. 1976) (*Lindy II*). *Accord Grunin v. International House of Pancakes*, 513 F.2d 114 (8th Cir.), *cert. denied*, 423 U.S. 864 (1975); *City of Detroit v. Grinnell Corp.*, 495 F.2d 448 (2d Cir. 1974). *See generally Pennsylvania v. Delaware Valley Citizens' Council for Clean Air*, 483 U.S. 711 (1987) (where a majority of the Court agreed that federal fee-shifting statutes permit an upward adjustment of the lodestar for the risk of nonrecovery); Note, *Attorney's Fee Contingency Enhancements*, 63 Wash. L. Rev. 469 (1988).

The major criticism of the lodestar approach is that it creates a disincentive to settle, since the attorney fee is largely based on the number of hours worked. Recently, the courts have seemed more willing to scrutinize the attorney's work in order to curtail the abuse of working excessive hours and prolonging the case so as to increase the award. *See, e.g., City of Detroit v. Grinnell Corp.*, 495 F.2d 448 (2d Cir. 1974); Hornstein, *Legal Therapeutics: The "Salvage" Factor in Counsel Fee Awards*, 69 Harv. L. Rev. 658 (1956).

Several courts have held that the fee award must reflect the amount of damages won by the plaintiff, as well as other relief obtained. *Rosebrough Monument Co. v. Memorial Park Cem. Ass'n*, 572 F. Supp. 92, 94-95 (E.D. Mo. 1983), *citing Hensley v. Eckerhart*, 461 U.S. 424 (1983) (an award of attorney's fees should be based on "degree of success obtained"). But the Supreme Court in *City of Riverside v. Rivera*, 477 U.S. 561 (1986), by a divided majority, ruled against a general "requirement of proportionality between damages recovered and fees awardable." Rowe, *The Supreme Court on Attorney Fee Awards, 1985 and 1986 Terms: Economics, Ethics, and Ex Ante Analysis*, 1 Geo. J. Leg. Ethics 621, 623 (1988).

Is an award of attorney's fees permitted when the action is settled? The issue has been addressed most frequently in the settlement of antitrust class action suits. The Clayton Act does not specifically provide for the award of attorney fees when actions are settled. *Decorative Stone Co. v. Building Trades Council*, 23 F.2d 426, 428 (2d Cir. 1928). But the inherent equitable powers of the antitrust court have given rise to an "equitable fund doctrine," which has been used to permit the payment of attorney fees for an action resulting in settlement. *Compare Lindy I*, 487 F.2d 161, 165 (3d Cir. 1973), *with City of Detroit v. Grinnell Corp.*, 495 F.2d 448, 459 (2d Cir. 1974).

The first exception to the "American Rule" requiring parties to pay their own attorney fees, absent a statutory authorization, came in *Trustees v. Greenough*, 105 U.S. 527 (1882). The Supreme Court held that a "common fund" is established for the payment of attorney's fees when a suit is brought that results in an economic benefit or increase of a fund, the interest in which is shared by many. This "common fund" doctrine provides an incentive to sue and prevents, at the time, unjust enrichment so that persons who obtain benefits of a lawsuit without contributing to its costs are not unjustly enriched at the successful litigants' expense. *See, e.g., Boeing Co. v. Van Gemert*, 444 U.S. 472, 478-82 (1980) (attorney's fees may be "assessed against the unclaimed portion" of the class action "fund created by the judgment"); *Mills v. Electric Auto Lite Co.*, 396 U.S. 375, 389-97 (1970).

In *United States Football League v. National Football League*, 887 F.2d 408 (2d Cir. 1989), the Second Circuit held that an attorney fee award of over $5.5 million was appropriate, even though a professional football league won only $1 in actual damages on its monopolization claim against the NFL. The court reasoned that the fact of injury, not the amount of damages, triggers the mandatory grant of fees under the Clayton Act. Although minimal damages may be relevant in determining the amount of fees allowed, it does not affect the entitlement, the court observed, because the policy behind fee awards is to encourage the detection and cessation of anticompetitive behavior. The court also held that in this case it was not necessary to apply the "prevailing party" standard to determine the fee entitlement because section 4 requires only that there be injury, and once the jury makes a finding of injury, an award of attorney's fees will follow. The court proceeded to uphold a lodestar computation by the trial court.

One decision has required plaintiffs' attorneys to submit sealed bids to handle an antitrust case on a contingent-fee basis. *In re Oracle Securities Litig.*, 131 F.R.D. 688 (N.D. Cal. 1990).

Section 4 of the Clayton Act also permits the award of costs to the prevailing party. Recoverable costs have been defined as reimbursements for court filing fees, court reporter fees, transcript costs, witnesses' expenses, document copy expenses, etc. *See* Fed. R. Civ. P. 54(d). Other expenses, however, such as expert witness fees, are not included within the recoverable costs section of the Clayton Act, except by specific authorization.

C. INJUNCTIVE RELIEF AND STRUCTURAL REMEDIES

Section 16 of the Clayton Act permits private suits for injunctive relief. Similarly, section 4 of the Sherman Act and section 15 of the Clayton Act grant jurisdiction to the district court to entertain actions brought by the government "in equity to prevent and restrain violations of these Acts." Injunctions sought by either private or government enforcement action generally focus on restraining anticompetitive conduct or behavior. Under certain circumstances, injunctive relief may also be brought to alter the structure of the corporation or industry under review.

Conduct-oriented injunctions are most generally in the form of "cease and desist" orders. Defendants are restrained from engaging in future violations of the statutes, or in addition, may be required to refrain from conduct not specifically forbidden by the statute. They have no effect on prior conduct, although the law may have been violated and anticompetitive profits obtained, unless the injunction is complementary to a damage award. If the injunction is violated, a "show cause" order may issue to determine whether defendant should be held in contempt of court, in addition to other sanctions.

In recent years, antitrust litigants have been bringing an increased number of appeals regarding the standards for the issuance of preliminary injunctions. The Seventh Circuit has been particularly active in articulating the prerequisites in antitrust cases:

(1) The plaintiff has no adequate remedy at law and will suffer irreparable harm if the preliminary injunction is not granted.

(2) The award of damages to the plaintiff would be inadequate.

(3) The court must consider any irreparable harm that the defendant might suffer from the injunction.

(4) The plaintiff must show some likelihood of success on the merits.

(5) The court must determine how likely the success of the plaintiff is because "[t]he more likely the plaintiff is to win, the less heavily need the balance of harms weigh in his favor."

(6) The public interest must be considered.

Roland Mach. Co. v. Dresser Indus., 749 F.2d 380 (7th Cir. 1984); *General Leaseways, Inc. v. National Leasing Ass'n*, 744 F.2d 588 (7th Cir. 1984). Appellate review is based on an "abuse of discretion."

Subsequent to *Roland*, Judge Posner on the Seventh Circuit attempted to express the standard for preliminary injunction in terms of a mathematical formula. The district court judge has discretion to grant a preliminary injunction if $P \times H_p > (1-P) \times H_d$, where:

> P = probability that the denial would be an error; ((1-P), in that case, refers to the possibility that granting of the injunction would be an error);
>
> H_p = harm to the plaintiff;
>
> H_d = harm to the defendant.

In other words, "only if harm to the plaintiff if the injunction is denied, multiplied by the probability that the denial would be an error, exceeds the harm to the defendant if the injunction is granted, multiplied by the probability that granting the injunction would be an error," should the injunction issue. *American Hosp. Supply Corp. v. Hospital Prods. Ltd.*, 780 F.2d 589 (7th Cir. 1986) (supplier terminated a distributor, who sued for breach of contract). The formula is designed to minimize the costs associated with a mistaken issuance of an injunction. Do you think this quantitative expression is merely a distillation of the six prerequisites set out above? If so, as the dissent in *American Hospital* opines, "why bother?" Specifically, does the formula include the equitable factors of irreparable injury, the balance of equities, the likelihood of success, and the public interest? Does it suggest a more rigid standard for issuance of a preliminary injunction? *See also Lawson Prods., Inc. v. Avnet, Inc.*, 782 F.2d 1429 (7th Cir. 1986). Remember that the standard of review on appeal is generally whether the district court abused its discretion in either granting or denying the injunction. This is in contrast to the Second Circuit's new standard which mandates that the court of appeal should engage in a *de novo* review of the factual findings. *Nortlin Corp. v. Rooney, Pace, Inc.*, 744 F.2d 255 (2d Cir. 1985). Leubsdorf, *The Standard for Preliminary Injunctions*, 91 Harv. L. Rev. 525 (1978).

In contrast to conduct-directed injunctions, equitable relief may be fashioned so as to alter the structure of defendant's corporation, either through dissolution, divestiture, or divorcement. Litigation has addressed the question whether section 16 of the Clayton Act limits a private plaintiff's options, in seeking equitable relief, to conduct-oriented injunctions, or whether structural remedies are available as well.

CALIFORNIA V. AMERICAN STORES CO.

495 U.S. 271 (1990)

STEVENS, J., delivered the opinion for a unanimous Court.

By merging with a major competitor, American Stores Co. (American) more than doubled the number of supermarkets that it owns in California. The State sued claiming that the merger violates the federal antitrust laws and will harm consumers in 62 California cities. The complaint prayed for a preliminary injunction requiring American to operate the acquired stores separately until the case is decided, and then to divest itself of all of the acquired assets located in California. ... We conclude that [divesture] is [possible].

I

....

On its face, the simple grant of authority in § 16 to "have injunctive relief" would seem to encompass divestiture just as plainly as the comparable language in § 15. Certainly § 16's reference to "injunctive relief ... against threatened loss or damage" differs from § 15's grant of jurisdiction to "prevent and restrain violations," but it obviously does not follow that one grant encompasses remedies excluded from the other.[7] Indeed, we think it could plausibly be argued that § 16's terms are the more expansive. In any event, ... § 16 "states no restrictions or exceptions to the forms of injunctive relief a private plaintiff may seek, or that a court may order.... Rather, the statutory language indicates Congress' intention that traditional principles of equity govern the grant of injunctive relief." We agree that the plain text of § 16 authorizes divestiture decrees to remedy § 7 violations.

American rests its contrary argument upon two phrases in § 16 that arguably narrow its scope. The entitlement "to sue for and have injunctive relief" affords relief "against threatened loss or damage by a violation of the antitrust laws." Moreover, the right to such relief exists "when and under the same conditions and principles as injunctive relief against threatened conduct that will cause loss or damage is granted by courts of equity." ... In this case, however, the requirement of "threatened loss or damage" is unquestionably satisfied. The allegations of the complaint, the findings of the District Court and the opinion of the Court of Appeals all assume that even if the merger is a completed violation of law, the threatened harm to California consumers exists. If divestiture is an appropriate means of preventing that harm, the statutory reference to "threatened loss or damage" surely does not negate the Court's power to grant such relief.

The second phrase, which refers to "threatened conduct that will cause loss or damage," is not drafted as a limitation on the power to grant relief, but rather is a part of the general reference to the standards that should be applied in fashioning injunctive relief. It is surely not the equivalent of a directive stating that unlawful conduct may be prohibited but structural relief may not be mandated. Indeed, as the Ninth Circuit's analysis of the issue demonstrates, the distinction between conduct and structure — or between prohibitory and mandatory relief — is illu-

---

[7] That the two provisions do differ is not surprising at all, since § 15 was largely copied from § 4 of the Sherman Act while § 16, which had to incorporate standing limits appropriate to private actions — see *Cargill, Inc. v. Monfort of Colorado, Inc.*, 479 U.S. 104 (1986) — had no counterpart in the Sherman Act.

sory in a case of this kind. Thus, in the *IT&T* case, the Court recognized that an injunction prohibiting a parent company from voting the stock of the subsidiary should not be treated differently from a mandatory order of divestiture. And in this case the court treated the "Hold Separate Agreement" as a form of "indirect divestiture." In both cases the injunctive relief would unquestionably prohibit "conduct" by the defendants. American's textual arguments — which rely on a distinction between mandatory and prohibited relief — do not explain why such remedies would not be appropriate.

If we assume that the merger violated the antitrust laws, and if we agree with the District Court's finding that the conduct of the merged enterprise threatens economic harm to California consumers, the literal text of § 16 is plainly sufficient to authorize injunctive relief, including an order of divestiture, that will prohibit that conduct from causing that harm. This interpretation is consistent with our precedents, which have upheld injunctions issued pursuant to § 16 regardless of whether they were mandatory or prohibitory in character. *See Zenith Radio Corp. v. Hazeltine Research, Inc.*, 395 U.S. 100, 129-33 (1969) (reinstating injunction that required defendants to withdraw from patent pools); *see also Silver v. New York Stock Exchange*, 373 U.S. 341, 345, 365 (1963) (reinstating judgment for defendants in suit to compel installation of wire services). We have recognized when construing § 16 that it was enacted "not merely to provide private relief, but ... to serve as well the high purpose of enforcing the antitrust laws." *Zenith Radio Corp. v. Hazeltine Research, Inc.*, 395 U.S., at 130-31....

Finally, by construing § 16 to encompass divestiture decrees we are better able than American to harmonize the section with its statutory context. The Act's other provisions manifest a clear intent to encourage vigorous private litigation against anticompetitive mergers. Section 7 itself creates a relatively expansive definition of antitrust liability: to show that a merger is unlawful, a plaintiff need only prove that its effect "*may* be substantially to lessen competition." *See Brown Shoe Co. v. United States*, 370 U.S. 294, 323 (1962). In addition, § 5 of the Act provided that during the pendency of a government action, the statute of limitations for private actions would be tolled. The section also permitted plaintiffs to use the final judgment in a government antitrust suit as a prima facie evidence of liability in a later civil suit. Private enforcement of the Act was in no sense an afterthought; it was an integral part of the congressional plan for protecting competition. *See Minnesota Mining & Mfg. Co. v. New Jersey Wood Finishing Co.*, 381 U.S. 311, 318 (1965). Congress also made express its view that divestiture was the most suitable remedy in a suit for relief from a § 7 violation: in § 11 of the Act, Congress directed the Federal Trade Commission to issue [an] order requiring that a violator of § 7 "cease and desist from the violation," and, specifically, that the violator "divest itself of the stock held" in violation of the Act. Section 16, construed to authorize a private divestiture remedy when appropriate in light of equitable principles, fits well in a statutory scheme that favors private

enforcement, subjects mergers to searching scrutiny, and regards divestiture as the remedy best suited to redress the ills of anticompetitive merger.
....

IV

Our conclusion that a district court has the power to order divestiture in appropriate cases brought under § 16 of the Clayton Act does not, of course, mean that such power should be exercised in every situation in which the Government would be entitled to such relief under § 15. In a Government case the proof of a violation of law may itself establish sufficient public injury to warrant relief.... A private litigant, however, must have standing — in the words of § 16, he must prove "threatened loss or damage" to his own interests in order to obtain relief. See Cargill, Inc. v. Monfort of Colorado, Inc., 479 U.S. 104 (1986). Moreover, equitable defenses such as laches, or perhaps "unclean hands," may protect consummated transactions from belated attacks by private parties when it would not be too late for the Government to vindicate the public interest.

Such questions, however, are not presented in this case. We are merely confronted with the naked question whether the District Court had the power to divest American of any part of its ownership interests in the acquired Lucky Stores either by forbidding the exercise of the owner's normal right to integrate the operations of the two previously separate companies, or by requiring it to sell certain assets located in California. We hold that such a remedy is a form of "injunctive relief" within the meaning of § 16 of the Clayton Act. Accordingly, the judgment of the Court of Appeals is reversed and the case is remanded for further proceedings consistent with this opinion. It is so ordered.

NOTES AND QUESTIONS

1. Should it matter whether the private plaintiff seeking divestiture is a state suing as parens patriae, as in the *American Stores* decision, rather than a private competitor? What would a private competitor have to show in order to obtain divestiture of an admittedly illegal merger? When the state sues as parens patriae, whose interest is it protecting? Consumers'? Competitors'? Are state enforcement agencies ever "captured" by special interest groups? If so, should this be relevant in an antitrust case? Suppose it was widely known that the state attorney general's office was heavily lobbied to challenge a merger by a group of competitors who would be injured by the post-merger firm's increased efficiency. Would the state have standing? Could it obtain divestiture?

2. What importance should a court attach to the fact that one of the enforcement agencies (FTC or Department of Justice Antitrust Division) had already reviewed and approved a merger that is now being challenged by a private party? As a basic premise, the agency decision is not binding on any private litigant. Suppose the agency decides that, although a merger may have some short-run anticompetitive effects within the United States, in the long run it will improve

America's competitive position in world markets. Should a private plaintiff be able to "restructure" an industry by obtaining a divestiture decree in a way that conflicts with basic American economic policy? Could this problem be solved by any means other than new legislation?

3. At one time there was a question whether the FTC, in addition to the Justice Department, had the authority to seek divestiture. In *FTC v. Eastman Kodak Co.*, 274 U.S. 619 (1926), the Supreme Court held that the FTC lacked authority to order divestiture of some of Kodak's laboratories. Later the Court changed its mind, however, and today the power of the FTC to order divestiture in appropriate circumstances is clearly established. *See FTC v. Procter & Gamble Co.*, 386 U.S. 566 (1967), reprinted in Chapter 7, *infra*.

4. The use of structural relief, in conjunction with conduct-directed injunction, might be particularly appropriate in remedying monopolization violations under section 2 of the Sherman Act or illegal mergers under section 7 of the Clayton Act. Violators of section 1 of the Sherman Act might also be candidates, though to a lesser extent. Structural remedies might include an order to divest assets, stock or securities, or to "spin off" a firm so that it can become an independent competitor in the market. *See* Sullivan, *The Antitrust Division as a Regulatory Agency: An Enforcement Policy in Transition*, 64 Wash. U.L.Q. 997 (1986). Consider whether a "spin off" divestiture which results in a dissolution of the firm might not create diseconomies of scale. Is a court equipped to determine the minimum output level below which a firm cannot survive? *See White House Task Force [Report] on Antitrust Policy* 311-12 (1968).

D. CONTRIBUTION AND CLAIM REDUCTION

Under present law, a plaintiff has a right to sue and attempt to recover all its damages against a single defendant, although other, perhaps more culpable, defendants exist. This is so because each defendant is liable for all of the treble damages caused by the antitrust violation — that is, liability is "joint and several." In the absence of a rule permitting contribution, a sued defendant may pay damages far in excess of its responsibility, while others escape liability. *See generally* Sullivan, *New Perspectives in Antitrust Litigation: Toward a Right of Comparative Contribution*, 1980 U. Ill. L.F. 389.

Reacting to the unfairness caused by the no-contribution rule, and the effect that it might have on the deterrent effect of the antitrust laws, the Eighth Circuit Court of Appeals in *Professional Beauty Supply, Inc. v. National Beauty Supply, Inc.*, 594 F.2d 1179 (8th Cir. 1979), adopted a discretionary rule permitting contribution among joint tortfeasors in an antitrust action. Defendants in *Professional Beauty* filed a third-party complaint asking for contribution. The third-party complaint was dismissed for failure to state a claim. In rejecting the district court's dismissal, the Eighth Circuit reasoned that both deterrence and fairness dictated the adoption of a pro-contribution rule.

Deterrence would be increased, the court concluded, because it would be less likely that an antitrust violator would escape liability if a defendant could sue absent defendants for contribution. The misallocation of damages caused by the no-contribution rule would also be alleviated as the damages could be apportioned among all the defendants. The decision whether contribution should be invoked was left to the trier of fact, with discretion to be exercised in light of the relative bargaining power of the wrongdoers and the extent of their participation in the illegal conduct.

The contribution rule adopted by the court in *Professional Beauty* was rejected by other courts which considered the issue. The Supreme Court, speaking on the issue, in *Texas Indus., Inc. v. Radcliff Materials, Inc.*, 451 U.S. 630 (1981), held that Congress did not intend to create contribution rights when it adopted the Sherman and Clayton Acts. Thus the federal courts were without power to fashion common-law rules sanctioning contribution in antitrust litigation. The Court, although not signaling its own view on how the competing interests involved should be weighed, did invite Congress to consider the policies and values at issue.

On a related issue, the Fourth Circuit, subsequent to *Texas Industries*, held in *Burlington Indus. v. Milliken & Co.*, 690 F.2d 380, 390-95 (4th Cir. 1980) that *Texas Industries'* logic should extend to claim reductions. In *Burlington Industries* the plaintiff had settled with one defendant before suit. The district court found for plaintiff, but reduced its damage judgment by treble the settlement figure. The Fourth Circuit overturned the district court when it reaffirmed the prevailing rule that any amount received in settlement should be deducted from plaintiff's damages after trebling, not before. Reasoning that claim reduction was analogous to contribution, the court held that the district court lacked the authority to implement claim reduction.

Since the *Texas Industries* decision, Congress has considered a number of contribution and claim reduction bills. None has passed both houses of the Congress, although substantial support for some variation of a pro-contribution/claim reduction rule does exist. *See* Cavanagh, *Contribution, Claim Reduction and Individual Treble Damage Responsibility: Which Path to Reform of Antitrust Remedies*, 40 Vand. L. Rev. 1278 (1987); Polden & Sullivan, *Contribution and Claim Reduction in Antitrust Litigation: A Legislative Analysis*, 20 Harv. J. Leg. 397 (1983).

BIBLIOGRAPHY AND COLLATERAL READINGS

Books

2 P. Areeda & H. Hovenkamp, Antitrust Law (rev. ed. 1995).
H. Hovenkamp, Federal Antitrust Policy, chs. 15-17 (2d ed. 1994).
S. Ross, Principles of Antitrust Law (1993).

E.T. Sullivan & J. Harrison, Understanding Antitrust and Its Economic Implications, 39-70 (3d ed. 1998).

D. Floyd & E. Thomas Sullivan, Private Antitrust Actions (1996).

Articles

Benston, Indirect Purchasers Standing to Claim Damage in Price Fixing Antitrust Actions, 55 Antitrust L.J. 213 (1986).

Blair & Harrison, Rethinking Antitrust Injury, 42 Vand. L. Rev. 1539 (1989).

Block, Nold, & Sidak, The Deterrent Effect of Antitrust Enforcement, 89 J. Pol. Econ. 429 (1981).

Cavanagh, Contribution, Claim Reduction and Individual Treble Damage Responsibility: Which Path to Reform of Antitrust Remedies?, 40 Vand. L. Rev. 1278 (1987).

Cavanagh, Detrebling Antitrust Damages: An Idea Whose Time Has Come?, 61 Tulane L. Rev. 777 (1987).

Easterbrook, Detrebling Antitrust Damages, 28 J.L. Econ. 445 (1985).

Floyd, Antitrust Victims Without Antitrust Remedies: The Narrowing of Standing in Private Antitrust Actions, 82 Minn. L. Rev. 1 (1997).

Flynn, Which Past Is Prolog? The Future of Private Antitrust Enforcement, 35 Antitrust Bull. 879 (1990).

Fox, Extraterritoriality, Antitrust and the New Restatement: Is Reasonableness the Answer?, 19 N.Y.U. J. Int'l. L. & Pol. 565 (1987).

Hovenkamp, Antitrust's Protected Classes, 88 Mich. L. Rev. 1 (1989).

Lande, Are Antitrust "Treble Damages" Really Single Damages?, 54 Ohio St. L.J. 117 (1993).

Landes, Optimal Sanctions for Antitrust Violations, 50 Chi. L. Rev. 652 (1983).

Lenich, The Collateral Estoppel Effect of State Court Judgments in Federal Antitrust Actions, 38 Rutgers L. Rev. 241 (1986).

Note, Divestiture as a Remedy in Private Actions Brought Under Section 16 of the Clayton Act, 84 Mich. L. Rev. 1579 (1986).

Page, The Chicago School and the Evolution of Antitrust: Characterization, Antitrust Injury, and Evidentiary Sufficiency, 75 Va. L. Rev. 1221 (1989).

Page, The Scope of Liability for Antitrust Violations, 37 Stan. L. Rev. 1445 (1985).

Pokempner, The Scope of Noerr Immunity for Direct Action Protestors: Antitrust Meets the Anti-abortionists, 89 Colum. L. Rev. 662 (1989).

Salop & White, Economic Analysis of Private Antitrust Litigation, 74 Geo. L.J. 1001 (1986).

Schwartz, An Overview of the Economics of Antitrust Enforcement, 68 Geo. L.J. 1075 (1980).

Snyder & Kauper, Misuse of the Antitrust Laws: The Competitor Plaintiff, 90 Mich. L. Rev. 551 (1991).

Stern & Getzendanner, Gauging the Impact of Associated General Contractors on Antitrust Standing Under Section 4 of the Clayton Act, 20 U.C. Davis L. Rev. 159 (1986).

Waller, The Internationalization of Antitrust Enforcement, 77 B.U. L. Rev. 343 (1997).

Chapter 4

CARTELS AND OTHER JOINT CONDUCT BY COMPETITORS

SECTION I. HORIZONTAL RESTRAINTS

A. THE DEVELOPMENT OF ANALYTICAL AND EVIDENTIARY RULES

1. INTRODUCTION: THE PROBLEMS OF HORIZONTAL ARRANGEMENTS

Section 1 of the Sherman Act is directed toward conduct which significantly interferes with trade and is the product of an "agreement" among two or more independent actors. When the agreement is among competitors, the conduct is classified as horizontal. Horizontal arrangements include, inter alia, price fixing, and bid rigging market divisions or allocations, bid rigging, group boycotts and other concerted activities that restrict output or exclude competition. In contrast to section 2 of the Sherman Act, which is concerned with single firm activity, section 1 requires concerted conduct by more than one entity. However not all agreements — not even all agreements of competitors — are illegal. The problem is to characterize the conduct and understand how it affects competition.

The protection of competition is the central policy of the Sherman Act. In a competitive market, individual firms attempt to maximize profits within the context of consumer desires and limited available resources. Each firm takes costs and prices as given and sets output at a level maximizing returns at the given prices. But if the firms can agree on price and output, they will behave much more like a monopolist. Industry output will be lower and prices higher. Such an agreement is called a cartel.

The success of a cartel may depend upon the structure of industry in which it operates. Cooperation among cartel members is essential. The larger the number of firms in the cartel, the more likely that cartelization will be impracticable. Hay & Kelley, *An Empirical Survey of Price Fixing Conspiracies*, 17 J. L. & Econ. 13, 14, 27 (1974). *See also* McGee, *Ocean Freight Rate Conferences and The American Merchant Marine*, 27 U. Chi. L. Rev. 191, 200 (1960). For a cartel to work effectively, there must be an agreement on output and price. Production quotas may be assigned to cartel members "to minimize the total cost of producing whatever output is decided upon."

Moreover, if the sellers have different costs, they will have different profit maximizing prices. As a result it may be difficult for them to agree about either the resale price or the output quota for each member. Any agreement that they reach will necessarily be a compromise, and some firms are likely to feel cheated. For this reason many cartels are inherently unstable. R. Posner, *Antitrust Law: An Economic Perspective* 52-54 (1976); *Business Elec. Corp. v. Sharp Elec. Corp.*, 485 U.S. 717 (1988) ("Cartels are neither easy to form nor easy to maintain. Uncertainty over the terms of the cartel, particularly the prices to be charged in the future, obstructs both formation and adherence by making cheating easier.").

In addition to administrative difficulties and costs of the cartel, which may increase the overall cartel price of the product, the cartel faces enforcement problems. First, if the cartel sets the price of the product too high, it may encourage new firms to enter the market, which will increase market output and reduce prices. Second, the cartel may be subject to cheating by cartel members. Individual competitors may wish to drop prices and undercut competitors in order to capture a larger share of the market. Under these conditions, the cartel will not survive unless artificial entry barriers are erected against the new entrant or unless the discounter is detected and persuaded to comply. Otherwise the other cartel members will individually increase output and reduce price in order to meet the new competition. Interdependence of conduct which was a prerequisite under the cartel arrangement will disappear. *See* H. Hovenkamp, *Federal Antitrust Policy* § 4.1 (2d ed. 1994). Section 1 of the Sherman Act addresses these types of cartel practices and interdependent conduct.

2. RULES OF REASON AND PER SE ILLEGALITY

As discussed in Chapter 1, the rule of reason developed as a rule of construction under the Sherman Act from Judge Taft's decision in *United States v. Addyston Pipe*, 85 F. 271 (6th Cir. 1898), *aff'd*, 175 U.S. 211 (1899), and Chief Justice White's opinions in *Standard Oil Co. v. United States*, 221 U.S. 1 (1911), and *United States v. American Tobacco Co.*, 221 U.S. 106 (1911). Unlike the ancillary-direct restraint dichotomy adopted in *Addyston Pipe*, Chief Justice White applied the rule of reason analysis to all trade restraints, whether ancillary or direct. The result was that only *unreasonable* restraints of trade were deemed illegal. But how was a court to determine the "reasonableness" of the restraint?

Chief Justice White set out a three-prong test for weighing the reasonableness of the restraint. He was particularly concerned with the competitive effects that an agreement between competing firms would have in the market. He expressed the belief that any analysis of section 1 of the Sherman Act had to examine the effects of the challenged conduct. He implicitly recognized, however, that certain conduct is by its nature or character unreasonable because it is inherently anticompetitive. In the earlier Supreme Court case of *United States v. Joint Traffic Ass'n*, 171 U.S. 505, 568 (1898), the Court noted that price fixing arrangements which have a "direct and immediate effect" are illegal.

From Chief Justice White's early reasoning, several methods of analyzing antitrust conduct emerge. Initially, the court must find that a contract, combination, or agreement existed. The court must further inquire whether, because of the inherent nature of the practice, trade is restrained. If the conduct (such as a cartel arrangement) is likely to have no beneficial effect and if it significantly impairs competition, it is classified as "per se" illegal. From an evidentiary standpoint, the inquiry is over once the Court has determined that the conduct is, by its nature, inherently anticompetitive. No further inquiry is needed to determine the reasonableness of the restraint or actual competitive effect. Neither purpose nor market power to accomplish the anticompetitive effect will be examined. The per se analysis thus is a conclusive presumption of illegality. In application it is the functional equivalent of a rule of evidence. Once the restrictive conduct is found to come within a category defined as per se illegal, evidentiary matters that might be relevant in a rule of reason case become irrelevant.

Not all restrictive conduct is inherently anticompetitive, however. If the court has not previously classified the challenged practice as per se illegal, or if the court has not had substantial experience with the practice, it will decide anew whether the practice has an unlawful purpose *or* anticompetitive effect. The rule of reason analysis will be applied in this situation by a detailed factual inquiry which will scrutinize the purpose and the effect of the practice and reasonable inferences derived therefrom.

As the cases in this chapter indicate, distinctions between the per se rule of illegality and the rule of reason analysis are often finely drawn. The judicial function is to examine the challenged conduct within a limited range of judicial discretion. That discretion is guided by the rules of construction and rules of evidence discussed herein. The line drawing is not always clear; subtle distinctions are made and significant overlap exists between the various analyses.

Over the years judges have drawn distinctions and established classifications which decide questions of fact and policy. By definition and practice, the process of decision-making is flexible and multifaceted. This is not only its strength but its weakness as well. Clear judicial guidelines are not always forthcoming. Ultimately, however, the question is whether the courts' approach to antitrust analysis is faithful to the legislative policy and intent.

B. PRICE FIXING

1. THE FOUNDATION CASES

CHICAGO BOARD OF TRADE V. UNITED STATES

246 U.S. 231 (1918)

[The Board of Trade, which operated a commodity grain exchange, enacted rules which governed the regulation of grain sales. The first rule governed "spot sales," or the sale of grain which was located in Chicago and ready for delivery. The second concerned "future sales," or contracts which required the purchase of grain for future delivery. The third rule regulated "to arrive sales," or sales of grain which had not yet arrived in Chicago, but were enroute and would be ready for delivery upon arrival. During the regular hours of the Board, traders would buy and sell "spot and future sales." After the close of the regular hours, "call" sessions were held for the purpose of permitting traders to make sales for the "to arrive" grain. In addition, members of the Board were individually permitted to buy and sell "to arrive" grain during the nonregular hours.

In 1906 the Board established a "call" rule which precluded members of the Board from buying or selling "to arrive" grain during a period after the "call" session and before the exchange opened the next day at a price other than the one established as the closing price at the end of each call session. The Department of Justice challenged the "call" rule and sought an injunction to prohibit its enforcement. The Government argued that the rule amounted to an agreement to fix the price of the "to arrive" grain in violation of section 1 of the Sherman Act, though the "call" did not purport to set the price level. The defendant maintained that the rule had neither an unlawful purpose or effect; that, in fact, the purpose was to restrict the hours of trading for the convenience of the exchange members; to reduce the monopoly held by a certain, though small, group of grain traders who bought and sold during the nonregular hours; and to promote more competition during the regular hours. The lower court, on a motion from the Government, struck the defense allegations concerning the purpose of the rule. The rule was found to be a restraint of trade and the Board was enjoined from acting on it.]

JUSTICE BRANDEIS delivered the opinion of the Court.

... The Government proved the existence of the rule and described its application and the change in business practice involved. It made no attempt to show that the rule was designed to or that it had the effect of limiting the amount of grain shipped to Chicago; or of retarding or accelerating shipment; or of raising or depressing prices; or of discriminating against any part of the public; or that it resulted in hardship to anyone. The case was rested upon the bald proposition, that a rule or agreement by which men occupying positions of strength in any branch of trade, fixed prices at which they would buy or sell during an important part of the business day, is an illegal restraint of trade under the Anti-Trust Law. But the legality of an agreement or regulation cannot be determined by so simple a test, as whether it restrains competition. Every agreement concerning trade, every regulation of trade, restrains. To bind, to restrain, is of their very essence. The true test of legality is whether the restraint imposed is such as merely regulates and perhaps thereby promotes competition or whether it is such as may suppress or even destroy competition. To determine that question the court must ordinarily consider the facts peculiar to the business to which the restraint is applied; its condition before and after the restraint was imposed; the nature of the restraint and its effect, actual or probable. The history of the restraint, the evil believed to exist, the reason for adopting the particular remedy, the purpose or end sought to be attained, are all relevant facts. This is not because a good intention will save an otherwise objectionable regulation or the reverse; but because knowledge of intent may help the court to interpret facts and to predict consequences. The District Court erred, therefore, in striking from the answer allegations concerning the history and purpose of the Call rule and in later excluding evidence on that subject. But the evidence admitted makes it clear that the rule was a reasonable regulation of business consistent with the provisions of the Anti-Trust Law.

First: The nature of the rule: The restriction was upon the period of price-making. It required members to desist from further price-making after the close of the Call until 9:30 A. M. the next business day: but there was no restriction upon the sending out of bids after close of the Call. Thus it required members who desired to buy grain "to arrive" to make up their minds before the close of the Call how much they were willing to pay during the interval before the next session of the Board. The rule made it to their interest to attend the Call; and if they did not fill their wants by purchases there, to make the final bid high enough to enable them to purchase from country dealers.

Second: The scope of the rule: It is restricted in operation to grain "to arrive." It applies only to a small part of the grain shipped from day to day to Chicago, and to an even smaller part of the day's sales: members were left free to purchase grain already in Chicago from anyone at any price throughout the day. It applies only during a small part of the business day; members were left free to purchase during the sessions of the Board grain "to arrive," at any price, from members anywhere and from non-members anywhere except on the premises of the Board. It applied only to grain shipped to Chicago: members were left free to purchase at any price throughout the day from either members or non-members, grain "to arrive" at any other market....

Third: The effects of the rule: As it applies to only a small part of the grain shipped to Chicago and to that only during a part of the business day and does not apply at all to grain shipped to other markets, the rule had no appreciable effect on general market prices; nor did it materially affect the total volume of grain coming to Chicago. But within the narrow limits of its operation the rule helped to improve market conditions thus:

> *(a)* It created a public market for grain "to arrive." Before its adoption, bids were made privately. Men had to buy and sell without adequate knowledge of actual market conditions. This was disadvantageous to all concerned, but particularly so to country dealers and farmers.
>
> *(b)* It brought into the regular market hours of the Board sessions more of the trading in grain "to arrive."
>
> *(c)* It brought buyers and sellers into more direct relations; because on the Call they gathered together for a free and open interchange of bids and offers.
>
> *(d)* It distributed the business in grain "to arrive" among a far larger number of Chicago receivers and commission merchants than had been the case there before.

(e) It increased the number of country dealers engaging in this branch of the business; supplied them more regularly with bids from Chicago; and also increased the number of bids received by them from competing markets.

(f) It eliminated risks necessarily incident to a private market, and thus enabled country dealers to do business on a smaller margin. In that way the rule made it possible for them to pay more to farmers without raising the price to consumers.

(g) It enabled country dealers to sell some grain to arrive which they would otherwise have been obliged either to ship to Chicago commission merchants or to sell for "future delivery."

(h) It enables those grain merchants of Chicago who sell to millers and exporters to trade on a smaller margin and, by paying more for grain or selling it for less, to make the Chicago market more attractive for both shippers and buyers of grain.

(i) Incidentally it facilitated trading "to arrive" by enabling those engaged in these transactions to fulfil their contracts by tendering grain arriving at Chicago on any railroad, whereas formerly shipments had to be made over the particular railroad designated by the buyer.

… Every board of trade and nearly every trade organization imposes some restraint upon the conduct of business by its members. Those relating to the hours in which business may be done are common; and they make a special appeal where, as here, they tend to shorten the working day or, at least, limit the period of most exacting activity. The decree of the District Court is reversed with directions to dismiss the bill.

Reversed.

NOTES AND QUESTIONS

1. At the time the call rule was adopted, the members of the Board of Trade also had fixed commission rates for executing sales. Should not Justice Brandeis have analyzed this fact? The Board members probably adopted the call rule to prevent members from "cheating" on the commission rates. For example, suppose that a commodity closed at the end of a trading session at a price of $10 per unit, and that the commission on ten units was $10. An agent who negotiated a sale of 10 units at $10 would charge the buyer $110 and pay the seller $100. The agent would keep the $10 commission. On the floor, the commissions were fixed by agreement and all transactions had to take place at the posted price. The combination of these two rules effectively eliminated all price competition between agents. Before the call rule was adopted, however, an agent could "cheat" in order to obtain a particular transaction: although he still had to charge the $10 commission, he could shave $5 off the price to the buyer, effectively collecting $105 from the buyer and paying $100 to the seller. The call rule made price competition among the agents impossible both during the trading session and after it was over.

2. While the restraint in *Chicago Board of Trade* was deemed reasonable because it protected a socially desirable class of grain traders, Professor Carstensen posits that an alternative justification exists: the restraint controlled the risks of opportunistic behavior and was ancillary to a joint venture. *See* Carstensen, "The Content of the Hollow Core of Antitrust: The Chicago Board of Trade Case and the Meaning of the 'Rule of Reason' in Restraint of Trade Analysis," in *Research in Law and Economics* 1-88 (1992).

3. Justice Brandeis' opinion in *Chicago Board of Trade* should be compared with the next case, *Trenton Potteries*, where the Court rejected a rule of reason analysis for price fixing. What factors did Justice Brandeis say should be evaluated in determining the legality of the restraint? Does the Court's language indicate that in a price fixing case it will consider the reasonableness of the price? Were other alternatives available to the Board that would have countered the monopoly enjoyed by the traders who conducted business during the nonregular hours?

UNITED STATES V. TRENTON POTTERIES CO.

273 U.S. 392 (1927)

[Twenty-three corporations and twenty individuals were indicted and charged with fixing the price of pottery for bathrooms. Defendants, members of a pottery trade association, controlled 82 percent of the sanitary pottery fixtures in the United States. Defendants were convicted in the district court, but the court of appeals reversed on the ground that the jury had been erroneously instructed on the law. The trial court charged that if the jury found "the agreements or combination complained of, it might return a verdict of guilty without regard to the reasonableness of the price fixed, or the good intentions of the combining units, whether prices were actually lowered or raised ... since [such] agreements ... were unreasonable restraints." Defendant argued that the challenged conduct was lawful because the established prices were reasonable and noninjurious to the public. The Supreme Court reversed the court of appeals, the effect of which was to reinstate the convictions.]

JUSTICE STONE delivered the opinion of the Court.

... Reasonableness is not a concept of definite and unchanging content. Its meaning necessarily varies in the different fields of the law, because it is used as a convenient summary of the dominant considerations which control in the application of legal doctrines. Our view of what is a reasonable restraint of commerce is controlled by the recognized purpose of the Sherman Law itself. Whether this type of restraint is reasonable or not must be judged in part at least in the light of its effect on competition, for whatever difference of opinion there may be among economists as to the social and economic desirability of an unrestrained competitive system, it cannot be doubted that the Sherman Law and the judicial decisions interpreting it are based upon the assumption that the public interest is best protected from the evils of monopoly and price control by the maintenance of competition.

The aim and result of every price-fixing agreement, if effective, is the elimination of one form of competition. The power to fix prices, whether reasonably exercised or not, involves power to control the market and to fix arbitrary and unreasonable prices. The reasonable price fixed today may through economic and business changes become the unreasonable price of tomorrow. Once established, it may be maintained unchanged because of the absence of competition secured by the agreement for a price reasonable when fixed. Agreements which create such potential power may well be held to be in themselves unreasonable or unlawful restraints, without the necessity of minute inquiry whether a particular price is reasonable or unreasonable as fixed and without placing on the government in enforcing the Sherman Law the burden of ascertaining from day to day whether it has become unreasonable through the mere variation of economic conditions. Moreover, in the absence of express legislation requiring it, we should hesitate to adopt a construction making the difference between legal and illegal conduct in the field of business relations depend upon so uncertain a test as whether prices are reasonable — a determination which can be satisfactorily made only after a complete survey of our economic organization and a choice between rival philosophies.... Thus viewed, the Sherman law is not only a prohibition against the infliction of a particular type of public injury. It is a limitation of rights, ... which may be pushed to evil consequences and therefore restrained.

That such was the view of this Court in deciding the *Standard Oil* and *Tobacco* cases, and that such is the effect of its decisions both before and after those cases, does not seem fairly open to question. Beginning with *Trans-Missouri* [and] *Joint Traffic Association*, where agreements for establishing reasonable and uniform freight rates by competing lines of railroad were held unlawful, it has since often been decided and always assumed that uniform price-fixing by those controlling in any substantial manner a trade or business in interstate commerce is prohibited by the Sherman Law, despite the reasonableness of the particular prices agreed upon. In *Addyston Pipe & Steel Co. v. United States*, 175 U.S. 211, 237, a case involving a scheme for fixing prices, this Court quoted with approval the following passage from the lower court's opinion: "... the affiants say that, in their opinion, the prices at which pipe has been sold by defendants have been reasonable. We do not think the issue an important one, because, as already stated, we do not think that at common law there is any question of reasonableness open to the courts with reference to such a contract."

....

That the opinions in the *Standard Oil* and *Tobacco* cases were not intended to affect this view of the illegality of price-fixing agreements affirmatively appears from the opinion in the *Standard Oil* case where ... the court said:

That as considering the contracts or agreements, their necessary effect and the character of the parties by whom they were made, they were clearly restraints of trade within the purview of the statute, they could not be taken out of that category by indulging in general reasoning as to the expediency or non-expediency of having made the contracts or the wisdom or want of wisdom of the statute which prohibited their being made. That is to say, the cases but decided that the nature and character of the contracts, creating as they did a conclusive presumption which brought them within the statute, such result was not to be disregarded by the substitution of a judicial appreciation of what the law ought to be for the plain judicial duty of enforcing the law as it was made.

....

Cases in both the federal and state courts have generally proceeded on a like assumption, and in the second circuit the view maintained below that the reasonableness or unreasonableness of the prices fixed must be submitted to the jury has apparently been abandoned. *See Poultry Dealers' Association v. United States*, 4 Fed. (2d) 840. While not necessarily controlling, the decisions of this Court denying the validity of resale price agreements, regardless of the reasonableness of the price, are persuasive....

Respondents rely upon *Chicago Board of Trade* in which an agreement by members of the Chicago Board of Trade controlling prices during certain hours of the day in a special class of grain contracts and affecting only a small proportion of the commerce in question was upheld. The purpose and effect of the agreement there was to maintain for a part of each business day the price which had been that day determined by open competition on the floor of the Exchange. That decision, dealing as it did with a regulation of a board of trade, does not sanction a price agreement among competitors in an open market such as is presented here.

The charge of the trial court, viewed as a whole, fairly submitted to the jury the question whether a price-fixing agreement as described in the first count was entered into by the respondents. Whether the prices actually agreed upon were reasonable or unreasonable was immaterial in the circumstances charged in the indictment and necessarily found by the verdict.

....

It follows that the judgment of the circuit court of appeals must be reversed and the judgment of the district court reinstated.

Reversed.

[JUSTICE BRANDEIS, the author of the *Chicago Board of Trade* decision, took no part in the consideration of the decision.]

NOTES AND QUESTIONS

1. Did Justice Stone distinguish *Chicago Board of Trade* adequately? Or did *Trenton Potteries* implicitly overrule *Chicago Board of Trade*? Recall that in

Chicago Board of Trade the concerted arrangement established the price at which grain could be sold during nonregular hours. What if the arrangement merely fixed the hours that trading was permissible? Is that a restraint of competition? Consider whether the degree of the restraint is relevant in determining legality. *See Detroit Auto Dealers v. FTC*, 1992-1 Trade Cas. (CCH) ¶ 69696 (6th Cir. 1992) (condemning an agreement among automobile dealers to restrict showroom hours, after applying the rule of reason). How would you distinguish *Chicago Board*?

2. Was it relevant to the Court that defendants controlled over 80% of the national production of sanitary pottery? Does it matter under a price fixing charge whether the defendant has the ability (i.e. market power) actually to affect the price? Can market power be inferred from the fact that the defendants entered into the agreement? Can one infer market power from market share?

3. The Court in *Trenton Potteries* implied that the range of judicial discretion is narrow in a price fixing case. The limited inquiry is whether an agreement to fix the price can be established. From the agreement, illegal purpose can be inferred. And from the nature of the conduct (i.e. price fixing) the inherent anticompetitive effects are obvious. Thus, the Court suggested that price fixing is illegal per se. Evidence demonstrating the reasonableness of the price and the circumstances surrounding the practice are, from an evidentiary standpoint, irrelevant.

A more careful reading of *Trenton Potteries* reveals, however, that Justice Stone assumed that the challenged price fix was effective, that is that defendants had the market power to affect price. Defendants' control of over 80% of the market would support this conclusion. Perhaps, then, the per se approach to price fixing is applicable only where the price fixing arrangement is effective because of the defendant's market power. But what if defendants lacked market power to affect price? Would the establishment of the illegal agreement be sufficient for the submission of a prima facie case on a per se theory?

4. A part of the opinion not reprinted details a second agreement by the defendants to destroy all "seconds" — i.e. imperfect products — or else to sell them abroad. What was the purpose of that agreement? Suppose that the defendants agreed that each would reduce its output by 30%, but the agreement contained no provision concerning "seconds." If the price for seconds was higher than the cost of producing them, it would be profitable for a cartel member to continue producing at full capacity but designate 30% of its output as "seconds" and sell them at a price lower than the cartel price, but a profitable price nevertheless. The manufacturer could achieve this either by designating perfect products as "seconds," or else by grading its output using extraordinarily high standards. If every manufacturer did this, the output restriction agreement would be undermined. The only way the cartel could effectively detect such cheating would be to prohibit the selling of seconds in the cartelized market.

In *Standard Mfg. Co. v. United States*, 226 U.S. 20 (1912), the Supreme Court held that a licensing agreement by manufacturers of sanitary enameled iron ware, such as bath tubs, violated section 1 of the Sherman Act when it restricted the production and distribution of "seconds." Such licensing restriction, the Court reasoned, amounted to an output limitation and was not necessary to protect the use of the patent of the lawful monopoly conferred by the grant of the patent. The Court concluded that the agreement on "seconds" was for "the purpose and accomplished a restraint on trade," in that it affected price. *Id.* at 48.

APPALACHIAN COALS, INC. V. UNITED STATES

288 U.S. 344 (1933)

[Given the economic conditions caused, at least in part, by the Great Depression, 137 producers of bituminous coal in the Appalachian area entered into an arrangement to establish an exclusive selling agent. The agent, Appalachian Coals, Inc. was to sell, at the highest prices, the entire bituminous production for all 137 producers. The stock of the company was owned by the producers in proportion to their production percentages. Price of the coal was set by the selling agent. The 137 producers accounted for 12% of the bituminous production east of the Mississippi, but 74% of the Appalachian territory, including Tennessee, Kentucky, Virginia, and West Virginia.

[Prior to implementation of the plan, Department of Justice approval was sought. Upon reviewing the exclusive selling arrangement, the Department sought and obtained an injunction against the plan, which had not yet gone into effect, on the theory that the concerted arrangement actually established a cartel which would eliminate competition between the member producers.]

CHIEF JUSTICE HUGHES delivered the opinion of the Court.

....

Defendants insist that the primary purpose of the formation of the selling agency was to increase the sale, and thus the production, of Appalachian coal through better methods of distribution, intensive advertising and research; to achieve economies in marketing, and to eliminate abnormal, deceptive and destructive trade practices. They disclaim any intent to restrain or monopolize interstate commerce; and in justification of their design they point to the statement of the District Court that "it is but due to defendants to say that the evidence in the case clearly shows that they have been acting fairly and openly, in an attempt to organize the coal industry and to relieve the deplorable conditions resulting from over-expansion, destructive competition, wasteful trade practices, and the inroads of competing industries." ... Defendants contend that the evidence establishes that the selling agency will not have the power to dominate or fix the price of coal in any consuming market; that the price of coal will continue to be set in an open competitive market; and that their plan by increasing the sale of bituminous coal from Appalachian territory will promote, rather than restrain, interstate commerce.

There is no question as to the test to be applied in determining the legality of the defendants' conduct. The purpose of the Sherman Anti-Trust Act is to pre-

vent undue restraints of interstate commerce, to maintain its appropriate freedom
in the public interest, to afford protection from the subversive or coercive influences of monopolistic endeavor. As a charter of freedom, the Act has a generality and adaptability comparable to that found to be desirable in constitutional
provisions. It does not go into detailed definitions which might either work injury to legitimate enterprise or through particularization defeat its purposes by
providing loopholes for escape. The restrictions the Act imposes are not mechanical or artificial. Its general phrases, interpreted to attain its fundamental
objects, set up the essential standard of reasonableness. They call for vigilance in
the detection and frustration of all efforts unduly to restrain the free course of
interstate commerce, but they do not seek to establish a mere delusive liberty
either by making impossible the normal and fair expansion of that commerce or
the adoption of reasonable measures to protect it from injurious and destructive
practices and to promote competition upon a sound basis....

In applying this test, a close and objective scrutiny of particular conditions and
purposes is necessary in each case. Realities must dominate the judgment. The
mere fact that the parties to an agreement eliminate competition between themselves is not enough to condemn it. "The legality of an agreement or regulation
cannot be determined by so simple a test, as whether it restrains competition.
Every agreement concerning trade, every regulation of trade, restrains." *Chicago
Board of Trade v. United States, supra.* The familiar illustrations of partnerships,
and enterprises fairly integrated in the interest of the promotion of commerce, at
once occur. The question of the application of the statute is one of intent and
effect, and is not to be determined by arbitrary assumptions. It is therefore necessary in this instance to consider the economic conditions peculiar to the coal industry, the practices which have obtained, the nature of defendant's plan of
making sales, the reasons which led to its adoption, and the probable consequences of the carrying out of that plan in relation to market prices and other
matters affecting the public interest in interstate commerce in bituminous coal.

....

With respect to defendant's purposes, we find no warrant for determining that
they were other than those they declared. Good intentions will not save a plan
otherwise objectionable, but knowledge of actual intent is an aid in the interpretation of facts and prediction of consequences. *Chicago Board of Trade v.
United States, supra.* The evidence leaves no doubt of the existence of the evils
at which defendants' plan was aimed. The industry was in distress. It suffered
from over-expansion and from a serious relative decline through the growing use
of substitute fuels. It was afflicted by injurious practices within itself, — practices which demanded correction. If evil conditions could not be entirely cured,
they at least might be alleviated. The unfortunate state of the industry would not
justify any attempt unduly to restrain competition or to monopolize, but the existing situation prompted defendants to make, and the statute did not preclude
them from making, an honest effort to remove abuses, to make competition
fairer, and thus to promote the essential interests of commerce. The interests of

producers and consumers are interlinked. When industry is grievously hurt, when producing concerns fail, when unemployment mounts and communities dependent upon profitable production are prostrated, the wells of commerce go dry. So far as actual purposes are concerned, the conclusion of the court below was amply supported that defendants were engaged in a fair and open endeavor to aid the industry in a measurable recovery from its plight. The inquiry, then, must be whether despite this objective the inherent nature of their plan was such as to create an undue restraint upon interstate commerce.

The question thus presented chiefly concerns the effect upon prices. The evidence as to the conditions of the production and distribution of bituminous coal, the available facilities for its transportation, the extent of developed mining capacity, and the vast potential undeveloped capacity, makes it impossible to conclude that defendants through the operation of their plan will be able to fix the price of coal in the consuming markets. The ultimate finding of the District Court is that the defendants "will not have monopoly control of any market, nor the power to fix monopoly prices"; and in its opinion the court stated that "the selling agency will not be able, we think, to fix the market price of coal." Defendants' coal will continue to be subject to active competition. In addition to the coal actually produced and seeking markets in competition with defendants' coal, enormous additional quantities will be within reach and can readily be turned into the channels of trade if an advance of price invites that course. While conditions are more favorable to the position of defendants' group in some markets than in others, we think that the proof clearly shows that, wherever their selling agency operates, it will find itself confronted by effective competition backed by virtually inexhaustible sources of supply, and will also be compelled to cope with the organized buying power of large consumers. The plan cannot be said either to contemplate or to involve the fixing of market prices.

The contention is, and the court below found, that while defendants could not fix market prices, the concerted action would "affect" them, that is, that it would have a tendency to stabilize market prices and to raise them to a higher level than would otherwise obtain. But the facts found do not establish, and the evidence fails to show, that any effect will be produced which in the circumstances of this industry will be detrimental to fair competition. A cooperative enterprise, otherwise free from objection, which carries with it no monopolistic menace, is not to be condemned as an undue restraint merely because it may effect a change in market conditions, where the change would be in mitigation of recognized evils [distressed, over-expanded market] and would not impair, but rather foster, fair competitive opportunities. Voluntary action to rescue and preserve these opportunities, and thus to aid in relieving a depressed industry and in reviving commerce by placing competition upon a sounder basis, may be more efficacious than an attempt to provide remedies through legal processes. The fact that the correction of abuses may tend to stabilize a business, or to produce fairer price levels, does not mean that the abuses should go uncorrected or that cooperative endeavor to correct them necessarily constitutes an unreasonable restraint of trade. The intelligent conduct of commerce through the acquisition of full information of all relevant facts may properly be sought by the cooperation of those engaged in trade, although stabilization of trade and more reasonable prices may be the result. Putting an end to injurious practices, and the consequent improvement of the competitive position of a group of producers, is not a less worthy aim and may be entirely consonant with the public interest, where the group must still meet effective competition in a fair market and neither seeks nor is able to effect a domination of prices.

... Defendants insist that on the evidence adduced as to their competitive position in the consuming markets, and in the absence of proof of actual operations showing an injurious effect upon competition, either through possession or abuse of power, no valid objection could have been interposed under the Sherman Act if the defendants had eliminated competition between themselves by a complete integration of their mining properties in a single ownership. We agree that there is no ground for holding defendants' plan illegal merely because they have not integrated their properties and have chosen to maintain their independent plants, seeking not to limit but rather to facilitate production.... The question in either case is whether there is an unreasonable restraint of trade or an attempt to monopolize. If there is, the combination cannot escape because it has chosen corporate form; and, if there is not, it is not to be condemned because of the absence of corporate integration. As we stated at the outset, the question under the Act is not simply whether the parties have restrained competition between themselves but as to the nature and effect of that restraint.

The fact that the suit is brought under the Sherman Act does not change the principles which govern the granting of equitable relief. There must be "a definite factual showing of illegality." We think that the Government has failed to show adequate grounds for an injunction in this case. We recognize, however, that the case has been tried in advance of the operation of defendants' plan, and that it has been necessary to test that plan with reference to purposes and anticipated consequences without the advantage of the demonstrations of experience. If in actual operation it should prove to be an undue restraint upon interstate commerce, if it should appear that the plan is used to the impairment of fair competitive opportunities, the decision upon the present record should not preclude the Government from seeking the remedy which would be suited to such a state of facts.

....

Reversed and remanded.

NOTES AND QUESTIONS

1. Can the Court's decision be reconciled with the earlier per se approach of *Trenton Potteries*? If permitted, would this plan have had the effect of reducing price competition among the cartel members? Would it not also have had the effect of reducing the supply of distress or spot coal, with the result that prices would have been raised or stabilized? Would this have had a direct price effect on consumers purchasing coal? From Justice Hughes' opinion, how is a price fixing arrangement to be defined? How direct must the effect be on prices before it is considered a price fixing agreement? Should any practice that may affect price be viewed as price fixing within the category of conduct deemed per se illegal?

2. Like *Chicago Board of Trade* before it, *Appalachian Coals* sanctioned a rule of reason analysis in determining the legality of a scheme that on its face had characteristics of a price fixing agreement. The Court in *Appalachian Coals* stated that its reasoning was justified because of the realities of "deplorable economic conditions in the industry." Moreover, after accepting the defendants' argument that their intent was benign, the Court implied that they lacked market power to affect price, having only a 12% market share nationally. The implication was that in order to establish a price fixing arrangement, something more than the agreement itself was necessary. But what of the fact that the sales agent controlled 74% of the market in the Appalachian area? Isn't that market power within a definable market?

3. Hadn't the Supreme Court established in the *Trans-Missouri* and *Joint Traffic* cases, thirty years before *Trenton Potteries*, that price fixing agreements were unlawful without regard to the "reasonableness" of the price that was fixed? (See Chapter 1, *supra*.) Why did the Supreme Court bother to entertain the question again? Perhaps it was because in 1897 Associate Justice White dissented in *Trans-Missouri* (a 5-4 decision), arguing that all restraints on trade ought to be governed by a rule of reason. White's dissent appeared to leave open the possibility that in a price fixing case he would accept the defense that the prices fixed were reasonable. In 1911, White, then Chief Justice, wrote the majority opinion adopting the "rule of reason" in *Standard Oil Co. v. United States*, 221 U.S. 1 (1911). Many people, reading the two opinions together, believed that *Standard Oil* effectively overruled older cases like *Trans-Missouri*, and adopted a rule of reason for all alleged antitrust violations, including price fixing agreements. Whether Chief Justice White intended this in the *Standard Oil* opinion is unclear; however, the *Trenton Potteries* case made it plain that the pre-*Standard Oil* law of price fixing survived. Incidentally, three justices in *Trenton Potteries* dissented without opinion — Van Devanter, Sutherland, and Butler — probably the three most conservative judges on the Court.

2. SUPPLY OR OUTPUT RESTRICTIONS

UNITED STATES V. SOCONY-VACUUM OIL CO.

310 U.S. 150 (1940)

JUSTICE DOUGLAS delivered the opinion of the Court.

Respondents [major oil companies in the Midwest] were convicted by a jury ... under an indictment charging violations of § 1 of the Sherman Anti-Trust Act.... The Circuit Court of Appeals reversed and remanded for a new trial....

I. *The Indictment*

[The indictment charged that defendants] from February 1935 to December 1936 "have knowingly and unlawfully engaged and participated in two concerted gasoline buying programs" for the purchase "from independent refiners in spot transactions of large quantities of gasoline in the East Texas and Mid-Continent fields at uniform, high, and at times progressively increased prices." ... The Mid-Continent buying program is alleged to have included "large and increased purchases of gasoline" by defendants from independent refiners located in the Mid-Continent fields pursuant to allotments among themselves.

....

The methods of marketing and selling gasoline in the Mid-Western area are set forth in the indictment in some detail.... Each defendant major oil company owns, operates or leases retail service stations in this area. It supplies those stations, as well as independent retail stations, with gasoline from its bulk storage plants. All but one sell large quantities of gasoline to jobbers in tank car lots under term contracts. In this area these jobbers exceed 4,000 in number and distribute about 50% of all gasoline distributed to retail service stations therein, the bulk of the jobbers' purchases being made from the defendant companies. The price to the jobbers under those contracts with defendant companies is made dependent on the spot market price, pursuant to a formula hereinafter discussed. And the spot market tank car prices of gasoline directly and substantially influence the retail prices in the area. In sum, it is alleged that defendants by raising and fixing the tank car prices of gasoline in these spot markets could and did increase the tank car prices and the retail prices of gasoline sold in the Mid-Western area.

....

III. *The Alleged Conspiracy*

[During February, 1935, the coconspirators met] ... and decided that certain major companies (including the corporate respondents) would purchase gasoline from these refiners.... Each of the major companies was to select one (or more) of the independent refiners having distress gasoline as its "dancing partner," and would assume responsibility for purchasing its distress supply. In this manner buying power would be coordinated, purchases would be effectively placed, and the results would be much superior to the previous haphazard purchasing. There were to be no formal contractual commitments to purchase this gasoline, either between the major companies or between the majors and the independents. Rather it was an informal gentlemen's agreement or understanding whereby each undertook to perform his share of the joint undertaking. Purchases were to be made at the "fair going market price."

....

As a result of these buying programs it was hoped and intended that both the tank car and the retail markets would improve. The conclusion is irresistible that defendants' purpose was not merely to raise the spot market prices but, as the real and ultimate end, to raise the price of gasoline in their sales to jobbers and consumers in the Mid-Western area. Their agreement or plan embraced not only buying on the spot markets but also, at least by clear implication, an understanding to maintain such improvements in Mid-Western prices as would result from those purchases of distress gasoline.... In essence the raising and maintenance of the spot market prices were but the means adopted for raising and maintaining prices to jobbers and consumers.

....

The defendant companies sold about 83% of all gasoline sold in the Mid-Western area during 1935.... During the greater part of the indictment period the defendant companies owned and operated many retail service stations through which they sold about 20% of their Mid-Western gasoline in 1935 and about 12% during the first seven months of 1936.

....

V. *Application of the Sherman Act*

The court charged the jury that it was a violation of the Sherman Act for a group of individuals or corporations to act together to raise the prices to be charged for the commodity which they manufactured where they controlled a substantial part of the interstate trade and commerce in that commodity. The court stated that where the members of a combination had the power to raise prices and acted together for that purpose, the combination was illegal; and that it was immaterial how reasonable or unreasonable those prices were or to what extent they had been affected by the combination. It further charged that if such illegal combination existed, it did not matter that there may also have been other factors which contributed to the raising of the prices.... The court then charged that, unless the jury found beyond a reasonable doubt that the price rise and its continuance were "caused" by the combination and not caused by those other factors, verdicts of "not guilty" should be returned....

The Circuit Court of Appeals held this charge to be reversible error, since it was based upon the theory that such a combination was illegal *per se*. In its view respondents' activities were not unlawful unless they constituted an unreasonable restraint of trade....

In *United States v. Trenton Potteries Co.*, 273 U.S. 392, this Court sustained a conviction under the Sherman Act where the jury was charged that an agreement on the part of the members of a combination, controlling a substantial part of an industry, upon the prices which the members are to charge for their commodity is in itself an unreasonable restraint of trade without regard to the reasonableness of the prices or the good intentions of the combining units.

....

But respondents claim that other decisions of this Court afford them adequate defenses to the indictment. Among those on which they place reliance are

Appalachian Coals, Inc. v. United States, 288 U.S. 344; *Chicago Board of Trade v. United States*, 246 U.S. 231; and the *American Tobacco* and *Standard Oil* cases, *supra*.

But we do not think that line of cases is apposite. As clearly indicated in the *Trenton Potteries* case, the *American Tobacco* and *Standard Oil* cases have no application to combinations operating directly on prices or price structures.

And we are of the opinion that *Appalachian Coals, Inc. v. United States*, is not in point.

... This Court concluded that so far as actual purpose was concerned, the defendant producers were engaged in a "fair and open endeavor to aid the industry in a measurable recovery from its plight." And it observed that the plan did not either contemplate or involve "the fixing of market prices"; that defendants would not be able to fix the price of coal in the consuming markets; that their coal would continue to be subject to "active competition."...

Thus in reality the only essential thing in common between the instant case and the *Appalachian Coals* case is the presence in each of so-called demoralizing or injurious practices. The methods of dealing with them were quite divergent. In the instant case there were buying programs of distress gasoline which had as their direct purpose and aim the raising and maintenance of spot market prices and of prices to jobbers and consumers in the Mid-Western area, by the elimination of distress gasoline as a market factor. The increase in the spot market prices was to be accomplished by a well organized buying program on that market: regular ascertainment of the amounts of surplus gasoline; assignment of sellers among the buyers; regular purchases at prices which would place and keep a floor under the market. Unlike the plan in the instant case, the plan in the *Appalachian Coals* case was not designed to operate *vis-à-vis* the general consuming market and to fix the prices on that market. Furthermore, the effect, if any, of that plan on prices was not only wholly incidental but also highly conjectural. For the plan had not then been put into operation. Hence this Court expressly reserved jurisdiction in the District Court to take further proceedings if, *inter alia*, in "actual operation" the plan proved to be "an undue restraint upon interstate commerce." And as we have seen it would *per se* constitute such a restraint if price-fixing were involved.

....

Nor can respondents find sanction in *Chicago Board of Trade* for the buying programs here under attack. That case involved a prohibition on the members of the Chicago Board of Trade from purchasing or offering to purchase between the closing of the session and its opening the next day grains (under a special class of contracts) at a price other than the closing bid. The rule was somewhat akin to rules of an exchange limiting the period of trading, for as stated by this Court the "restriction was upon the period of price-making." No attempt was made to show that the purpose or effect of the rule was to raise or depress prices. The rule affected only a small proportion of the commerce in question. And among its effects was the creation of a public market for grains under that special contract class, where prices were determined competitively and openly. Since it was not aimed at price manipulation or the control of the market prices and since it had "no appreciable effect on general market prices," the rule survived as a reasonable restraint of trade.

....

Thus for over forty years this Court has consistently and without deviation adhered to the principle that price-fixing agreements are unlawful *per se* under the Sherman Act and that no showing of so-called competitive abuses or evils which those agreements were designed to eliminate or alleviate may be interposed as a defense....

Therefore the sole remaining question on this phase of the case is the applicability of the rule of the *Trenton Potteries* case to these facts.

....

In the first place, there was abundant evidence that the combination had the purpose to raise prices. And likewise, there was ample evidence that the buying programs at least contributed to the price rise and the stability of the spot markets, and to increases in the price of gasoline sold in the Mid-Western area during the indictment period. That other factors also may have contributed to that rise and stability of the markets is immaterial. For in any such market movement, forces other than the purchasing power of the buyers normally would contribute to the price rise and the market stability. So far as cause and effect are concerned it is sufficient in this type of case if the buying programs of the combination resulted in a price rise and market stability which but for them would not have happened. For this reason the charge to the jury that the buying programs must have "caused" the price rise and its continuance was more favorable to respondents than they could have required. Proof that there was a conspiracy, that its purpose was to raise prices, and that it caused or contributed to a price rise is proof of the actual consummation or execution of a conspiracy under § 1 of the Sherman Act.

Secondly, the fact that sales on the spot markets were still governed by some competition is of no consequence. For it is indisputable that competition was restricted through the removal by respondents of a part of the supply which but for the buying programs would have been a factor in determining the going prices on those markets. But the vice of the conspiracy was not merely the restriction of supply of gasoline by removal of a surplus....

The elimination of so-called competitive evils is no legal justification for such buying programs. The elimination of such conditions was sought primarily for its effect on the price structures. Fairer competitive prices, it is claimed, resulted when distress gasoline was removed from the market. But such defense is typical of the protestations usually made in price-fixing cases. Ruinous competition, financial disaster, evils of price cutting and the like appear throughout our history as ostensible justifications for price-fixing. If the so-called competitive abuses were to be appraised here, the reasonableness of prices would necessarily become an issue in every price-fixing case. In that event the Sherman Act would soon be emasculated; its philosophy would be supplanted by one which is wholly alien to a system of free competition; it would not be the charter of freedom which its framers intended.

The reasonableness of prices has no constancy due to the dynamic quality of business facts underlying price structures. Those who fixed reasonable prices today would perpetuate unreasonable prices tomorrow, since those prices would not be subject to continuous administrative supervision and readjustment in light of changed conditions. Those who controlled the prices would control or effectively dominate the market. And those who were in that strategic position would have it in their power to destroy or drastically impair the competitive system. But the thrust of the rule is deeper and reaches more than monopoly power. Any combination which tampers with price structures is engaged in an unlawful activity. Even though the members of the price-fixing group were in no position to control the market, to the extent that they raised, lowered, or stabilized prices they would be directly interfering with the free play of market forces. The Act places all such schemes beyond the pale and protects that vital part of our economy against any degree of interference. Congress has not left with us the determination of whether or not particular price-fixing schemes are wise or unwise, healthy or destructive. It has not permitted the age-old cry of ruinous competition and competitive evils to be a defense to price-fixing conspiracies. It has no more allowed genuine or fancied competitive abuses as a legal justification for such schemes than it has the good intentions of the members of the combination. If such a shift is to be made, it must be done by the Congress. Certainly Congress has not left us with any such choice.... There was accordingly no error in the refusal to charge that in order to convict the jury must find that the resultant prices were raised and maintained at "high, arbitrary and noncompetitive levels." The charge in the indictment to that effect was surplusage.

Nor is it important that the prices paid by the combination were not fixed in the sense that they were uniform and inflexible. Price-fixing as used in the *Trenton Potteries* case has no such limited meaning. An agreement to pay or charge rigid, uniform prices would be an illegal agreement under the Sherman Act. But so would agreements to raise or lower prices whatever machinery for price-fixing was used. That price-fixing includes more than the mere establishment of uniform prices is clearly evident from the *Trenton Potteries* case itself .... Hence, prices are fixed within the meaning of the *Trenton Potteries* case if the range within which purchases or sales will be made is agreed upon, if the prices paid or charged are to be at a certain level or on ascending or descending scales, if they are to be uniform, or if by various formulae they are related to the market prices. They are fixed because they are agreed upon. And the fact that, as here, they are fixed at the fair going market price is immaterial. For purchases at or under the market are one species of price-fixing. In this case, the result was to place a floor under the market — a floor which served the function of increasing the stability and firmness of market prices. That was repeatedly characterized in this case as stabilization. But in terms of market operations stabilization is but one form of manipulation. And market manipulation in its various manifestations is implicitly an artificial stimulus applied to (or at times a brake on) market prices, a force which distorts those prices, a factor which prevents the determination of those prices by free competition alone....

As we have indicated, the machinery employed by a combination for price-fixing is immaterial.

Under the Sherman Act a combination formed for the purpose and with the effect of raising, depressing, fixing, pegging, or stabilizing the price of a commodity in interstate or foreign commerce is illegal *per se.* Where the machinery for price-fixing is an agreement on the prices to be charged or paid for the commodity in the interstate or foreign channels of trade, the power to fix prices exists if the combination has control of a substantial part of the commerce in that commodity. Where the means for price-fixing are purchases or sales of the commodity in a market operation or, as here, purchases of a part of the supply of the commodity for the purpose of keeping it from having a depressive effect on the markets, such power may be found to exist though the combination does not control a substantial part of the commodity. In such a case that power may be established if as a result of market conditions, the resources available to the combinations, the timing and the strategic placement of orders and the like, effective means are at hand to accomplish the desired objective. But there may be effective influence over the market though the group in question does not control it. Price-fixing agreements may have utility to members of the group though the power possessed or exerted falls far short of domination and control. Monopoly power (*United States v. Patten*, 226 U.S. 525) is not the only power which the Act strikes down, as we have said. Proof that a combination was formed for the purpose of fixing prices and that it caused them to be fixed or contributed to that result is proof of the completion of a price-fixing conspiracy under § 1 of the Act.[59] The indictment in this case charged that this combination had that pur-

---

[59] Under this indictment proof that prices in the Mid-Western area were raised as a result of the activities of the combination was essential, since sales of gasoline by respondents at the increased prices in that area were necessary in order to establish jurisdiction in the Western District of Wisconsin. Hence we have necessarily treated the case as one where exertion of the power to fix prices (i.e., the actual fixing of prices) was an ingredient of the offense. But that does not mean that both a purpose and a power to fix prices are necessary for the establishment of a conspiracy under § 1 of the Sherman Act. That would be true if power or ability to commit an offense was necessary in order to convict a person of conspiring to commit it. But it is well established that a person "may be guilty of conspiring although incapable of committing the objective offense."

... And it is likewise well settled that conspiracies under the Sherman Act are not dependent on any overt act other than the act of conspiring. It is the "contract, combination ... or conspiracy in restraint of trade or commerce" which § 1 of the Act strikes down, whether the concerted activity be wholly nascent or abortive on the one hand, or successful on the other. See *United States v. Trenton Potteries Co.*, 273 U.S. 392, 402. And the amount of interstate or foreign trade involved is not material since § 1 of the Act brands as illegal the character of the restraint not the amount of

pose and effect. And there was abundant evidence to support it. Hence the existence of power on the part of members of the combination to fix prices was but a conclusion from the finding that the buying programs caused or contributed to the rise and stability of prices.

....

Accordingly we conclude that the Circuit Court of Appeals erred in reversing the judgments on this ground. *A fortiori* the position taken by respondents in their cross petition that they were entitled to directed verdicts of acquittal is untenable.

Reversed.

NOTES AND QUESTIONS

1. Does Justice Douglas' opinion leave any doubt that price fixing cartels are illegal per se? Are the distinctions drawn by Justice Douglas between *Appalachian Coals* and *Socony-Vacuum* persuasive? Would Justice Douglas' conclusion, that "any combination which tampers with price structure," regardless of whether the defendant was in a "position to control the market," is unlawful, apply to a cartel scheme which introduced efficiencies into the market, as in *Chicago Board of Trade* and *Appalachian Coals*?

2. Does footnote 59 of the *Socony* opinion suggest that the prosecution need not introduce evidence of market power to effectuate the agreement — that the agreement to tamper with a component of price is itself illegal? Can one infer

---

commerce affected. In view of these considerations a conspiracy to fix prices violates § 1 of the Act though no overt act is shown, though it is not established that the conspirators had the means available for accomplishment of their objective, and though the conspiracy embraced but a part of the interstate or foreign commerce in the commodity. Whatever may have been the status of price-fixing agreements at common law the Sherman Act has a broader application to them than the common law prohibitions or sanctions. See *United States v. Trans-Missouri Freight Assn.,* 166 U.S. 290, 328. Price-fixing agreements may or may not be aimed at complete elimination of price competition. The group making those agreements may or may not have power to control the market. But the fact that the group cannot control the market prices does not necessarily mean that the agreement as to prices has no utility to the members of the combination. The effectiveness of price-fixing agreements is dependent on many factors, such as competitive tactics, position in the industry, the formula underlying price policies. Whatever economic justification particular price-fixing agreements may be thought to have, the law does not permit an inquiry into their reasonableness. They are all banned because of their actual or potential threat to the central nervous system of the economy.

The existence or exertion of power to accomplish the desired objective ... becomes important only in cases where the offense charged is the actual monopolizing of any part of trade or commerce in violation of § 2 of the Act. An intent and a power to produce the result which the law condemns are then necessary.... But the crime under § 1 is legally distinct from that under § 2 ... though the two sections overlap in the sense that a monopoly under § 2 is a species of restraint of trade under § 1.... Only a confusion between the nature of the offenses under those two sections ... would lead to the conclusion that power to fix prices was necessary for proof of a price-fixing conspiracy under § 1.

from such an agreement that the parties have the requisite market power? *See, e.g., United States v. General Motors Corp.*, 384 U.S. 127 (1966); *United States v. McKesson & Robbins, Inc.*, 351 U.S. 305 (1956). Consider whether an agreement between two sellers which together hold a three percent market share should be challenged as an illegal price fix under the Sherman Act.

3. Justice Douglas' statement in *Socony-Vacuum* that "[a]ny combination which tampers with price structure ... is unlawful" stands as a classic definition of a price fixing agreement. Its clearly articulated per se rule established firmly that price fixing, as a classification of conduct, was per se illegal. It drew this conclusion from the earlier pronouncements in *Joint Traffic, Standard Oil* and *Trenton Potteries.* Although not an explicit price fixing agreement, the scheme in *Socony-Vacuum* to affect the flow of output and surplus in the market is the most basic method of affecting price. And it does not matter whether that market is depressed or the price reasonable. Under the per se evidentiary analysis, the judicial inquiry is limited to whether the challenged conduct, once established, comes within the price fixing category.

The policy justification for the per se approach was described by the Supreme Court in *Northern Pac. Ry. v. United States*, 356 U.S. 1, 5 (1958):

> [T]here are certain agreements or practices which because of their pernicious effect on competition and lack of any redeeming virtue are conclusively presumed to be unreasonable and therefore illegal without elaborate inquiry as to the precise harm they have caused or the business excuse for their use. This principle of *per se* unreasonableness not only makes the type of restraints which are proscribed by the Sherman Act more certain to the benefit of everyone concerned, but it also avoids the necessity for an incredibly complicated and prolonged economic investigation into the entire history of the industry involved, as well as related industries, in an effort to determine at large whether a particular restraint has been unreasonable — an inquiry so often wholly fruitless when undertaken.

The per se rule of illegality, therefore, furthers the goals of clarifying the law for business certainty and promoting judicial economy.

3. AGREEMENTS LIMITING PRICE COMPETITION

a. Introduction: Fee Schedules

If one of the central goals of antitrust policy is the welfare of the consumer, is the setting of a maximum price, above which a seller cannot go, in violation of the Sherman Act? In *Kiefer-Stewart Co. v. Joseph E. Seagram & Sons*, 340 U.S. 211 (1951), the Court was presented with the issue whether it was a violation of section 1 for two distillers to agree on the maximum resale prices that they would permit their distributors to charge. The jury had returned a verdict for plaintiff. The Court of Appeals for the Seventh Circuit reversed, holding as a matter of law "that an agreement among respondents to fix maximum resale prices did not violate the Sherman Act because such prices promoted rather than restrained competition." *Id.* at 212.

Justice Black, writing for the Court, said:

> The Court of Appeals erred in holding that an agreement among competitors to fix maximum resale prices of their products does not violate the Sherman Act. For such agreements, no less than those to fix minimum prices, cripple the freedom of traders and thereby restrain their ability to sell in accordance with their own judgment. We reaffirm what we said in *United States v. Socony-Vacuum Oil Co.*, 310 U.S. 150, 223: "Under the Sherman Act a combination formed for the purpose and with the effect of raising, depressing, fixing, pegging, or stabilizing the price of a commodity in interstate or foreign commerce is illegal *per se.*"
>
> The Court of Appeals also erred in holding the evidence insufficient to support a finding by the jury that respondents had conspired to fix maximum resale prices. The jury was authorized by the evidence to accept the following as facts: Seagram refused to sell to petitioner and others unless the purchasers agreed to the maximum resale price fixed by Seagram. Calvert was at first willing to sell without this restrictive condition and arrangements were made for petitioner to buy large quantities of Calvert liquor. Petitioner subsequently was informed by Calvert, however, that the arrangements would not be carried out because Calvert had "to go along with Seagram." Moreover, about this time conferences were held by officials of the respondents concerning sales of liquor to petitioner. Thereafter, on identical terms as to the fixing of retail prices, both Seagram and Calvert resumed sales to other Indiana wholesalers who agreed to abide by such conditions, but no shipments had been made to petitioner.
>
> The foregoing is sufficient to justify the challenged jury finding that respondents had a unity of purpose or a common design and understanding when they forbade their purchasers to exceed the fixed ceilings. Thus, there is support for the conclusion that a conspiracy existed, *American Tobacco Co. v. United States*, 328 U.S. 781, 809-810, even though, as respondents point out, there is other testimony in the record indicating that the price policies of Seagram and Calvert were arrived at independently.

For what reasons would sellers agree to fix a maximum price with the effect of holding prices down? It has been suggested that under certain conditions such a practice does serve the self-interest of the seller. First, higher prices which result in greater profit could encourage entry of more competition into the market; thus the price fixed may be an entry-deterring price. Is this theory plausible? Second, the maximum price fix may be an indirect method of achieving a minimum price; the price will rise to the level of the fixed price and not go below it. Third, by fixing the level of the price, above which the price will not rise, demand for the product may be increased. Fourth, it may be a means to establish price leadership. Fifth, it may have the result of inhibiting product innovation which might result in higher prices and greater competition. L. Sullivan, *Handbook of the Law of Antitrust* 211 (1977); *but see* Easterbrook, *Maximum Price Fixing*, 48 U. Chi. L. Rev. 886 (1981), arguing that in markets with poorly informed buyers advance announcement of maximum prices may enable customers to locate the most competitive sellers.

The Court reaffirmed its holding in *Keifer-Stewart*: agreements that establish maximum prices are illegal per se without further inquiry. In *Arizona v. Maricopa Cty. Med. Soc'y*, 457 U.S. 332 (1982), the Court examined the legality of an arrangement entered into by a medical foundation which set the maximum fee schedules that any member doctor could charge "for services performed for patients insured under [insurance] plans approved by the foundation." The arrangement included an agreement by insurance firms, "including self-insured employers," to pay the doctors' charges up to the scheduled amounts, and in exchange the doctors agreed to accept those amounts as payment in full for their services. The Court, in a 4-3 opinion, found the arrangement to be a per se illegal price fixing agreement. The Court's analysis will be explored more fully in Subsection B6 of this section.

It would seem that *Trenton Potteries* and *Socony-Vacuum* would have settled the issue whether the fixing of a minimum price would constitute a per se violation. The question was presented to the Court again in 1975, however, in the context of a professional fee schedule. In *Goldfarb v. Virginia State Bar*, 421 U.S. 773 (1975), the Court considered whether a minimum fee schedule for lawyers, which was enforced by the state bar association, violated section 1 of the Sherman Act. In holding that sellers of professional services come within the Sherman Act, Chief Justice Burger found that the minimum fee schedule came within the "price fixing" classification.

A purely advisory fee schedule issued to provide guidelines, or an exchange of price information without a showing of an actual restraint on trade, would present us with a different question .... The record here, however, reveals a situation quite different from what would occur under a purely advisory fee schedule. Here a fixed, rigid price floor arose from respondents' activities: every lawyer who responded to petitioners' inquiries adhered to the fee schedule, and no lawyer asked for additional information in order to set an individualized fee. The price information disseminated did not concern past standards, ... but rather minimum fees to be charged in future transactions, and those minimum rates were increased over time. The fee schedule was enforced through the prospective professional discipline from the State Bar, and the desire of attorneys to comply with announced professional norms ...; the motivation to conform was reinforced by the assurance that other lawyers would not compete by underbidding. This is not merely a case of an agreement that may be inferred from an exchange of price information, *United States v. Container Corp.*, 393 U.S. 333, 337

(1969), for here a naked agreement was clearly shown, and the effect on prices is plain.

....

> ... Indeed, our cases have specifically included the sale of services within § 1.... Whatever else it may be, the examination of a land title is a service; the exchange of such a service for money is "commerce" in the most common usage of that word. It is no disparagement of the practice of law as a profession to acknowledge that it has this business aspect,[60] .... In the modern world it cannot be denied that the activities of lawyers plays an important part in commercial intercourse, and that anticompetitive activities by lawyers may exert a restraint on commerce.

The Court's opinion suggested greater toleration of a restraint imposed by a professional organization. It even suggested that the Court would adopt, at least for professions, a broader decisional analysis which would balance and perhaps accommodate noneconomic interests and policies. E.T. Sullivan & J. Harrison, *Understanding Antitrust and Its Economic Implications*, ch. 4 (3d ed. 1998).

Nevertheless Chief Justice Burger also described the minimum fee schedule as a "naked agreement," language generally used to connote per se illegality. In any event, the "professional organization" exemption to the per se approach soon came under increased attack, and was eventually at least partially repudiated. *See, e.g., Virginia State Bd. of Pharmacy v. Virginia Citizens Consumer Council*, 425 U.S. 749 (1976); *Bates v. State Bar of Ariz.*, 433 U.S. 350 (1977). In both cases, the Court struck down state enforced disciplinary rules restricting advertising by professions on the ground that the restrictions violated commercial speech rights protected under the first amendment. Because of the significant state involvement in the adoption and enforcement of the regulation, the Court held that the restrictions were immune from antitrust scrutiny, under the state action doctrine (see Chapter 9, *infra*).

Commercial cooperation and coordination among competitors can take many forms. *See generally* Sullivan, *On Nonprice Competition: An Economic and Marketing Analysis*, 45 U. Pitt. L. Rev. 771 (1984); Easterbrook, *The Limits of Antitrust*, 63 Tex. L. Rev. 1 (1984). As *Socony-Vacuum* indicated, agreements may affect price without being an explicit price-fix. One of the keys to the analysis is measuring how attenuated the agreement at issue is from an explicit price fixing arrangement. Courts generally agree that an agreement on a term or condition that is inseparable or related to a commercial component of the price or

---

[60] [The Court noted that] the fact that a restraint operates upon a profession as distinguished from a business is, of course, relevant in determining whether that particular restraint violates the Sherman Act. It would be unrealistic to view the practice of professions as interchangeable with other business activities, and automatically to apply to the professions antitrust concepts which originated in other areas. The public service aspect, and other features of the professions, may require that a particular practice, which could properly be viewed as a violation of the Sherman Act in another context, be treated differently. We intimate no view on any other situation than the one with which we are confronted today.

sale should be classified as a price fixing arrangement. While the conclusion may be that the challenged arrangement is price fixing, the reasoning employed is not always clear. The cases that follow in this chapter explore the decisional process as it has developed to the present. First, some examples of industry cooperation may be helpful.

Suppose that a group of competitors got together and, because of limited resources, joined in a cooperative advertising program. If the advertising mentioned specific prices, must one infer that the competitors agreed upon price if the product were sold at the advertised price? Could the defense of efficiency be interposed on the ground that cooperative advertising programs enable smaller retailers to compete against larger competitors by permitting the former to share advertising costs? In the alternative, could sellers, in agreeing to joint advertising programs, agree not to advertise price?

In some industries it is customary for sellers to include in the purchase contract "price protection" clauses, in which sellers agree to sell to customers at the lowest price offered by any competitor; or, "most favored nation" clauses, where sellers agree to give the lower price retroactively to a customer, if the seller, after the first purchase, sells to another customer at a lower price. Assume that such practices are industry-wide. What arguments would you advance that they are anticompetitive? Procompetitive? Do such practices inure to the benefit of the customer? Do they encourage customer fraud? Or do they make price cutting by the seller more expensive? *See* Hay, *Oligopoly, Shared Monopoly, and Antitrust Law*, 67 Cornell L. Rev. 455 (1982). In weighing the competitive harms and benefits, does it matter whether customer fraud is present?

Other commercial arrangements, such as standard check cashing policies, transportation fees, and seasonal pricing changes all implicate section 1 of the Sherman Act because they may be "price affecting" conduct. On the issue of agreements which have effects on credit terms or conditions of sale, the Supreme Court in *Catalano, Inc. v. Target Sales, Inc.*, 446 U.S. 643 (1980), reprinted in Subsection B6 of this section, recently returned to the narrow *Socony-Vacuum* per se analysis.

It may be helpful to examine several related price-affecting practices in understanding the analytic progression achieved by the Court. The first issue presented is the effect that price or data disclosures among competitors have in the market and the role the structure of the industry might play in determining the legality of certain industry cooperative practices.

4. DATA DISSEMINATION AND INFORMATION EXCHANGES

As the previous cases and discussions reveal, antitrust analysis, at least in part, centers on factual and economic distinctions between certain kinds of behavior. The nature, character, purpose or effect of the conduct will be determinative of the conduct's classification and legality. How the conduct is to be characterized or classified is not, however, always easy to determine. The decisional process often involves borderline questions of fact which may alter the characterization of the conduct and, accordingly, its legality. Because not all agreements between competitors are inherently anticompetitive, courts must sometimes examine the competitive effect of the arrangement rather than engage only in a summary per se analysis.

A case in point is the exchange of information by competitors, often by means of a trade association, where competitors come together to share mutual industry interests and objectives and to collect and share industry data. *See generally* G. Lamb & C. Shields, *Trade Association Law and Practice* (1971). The data exchanged between competitors include such things as statistics about production, inventory, sales, shipments, price, or plant capacity. Competitors may also engage in standardization programs for the industry, which attempt to set terms and guidelines for products, contracts, credit, freight charges, etc. Among the questions presented by such arrangements is whether the cooperative commercial arrangement has the effect of limiting competition by facilitating price coordination. The competitive effects of an exchange will vary, according to the following cases, depending on what data are exchanged, how firms react to the information, and the structure of the industry where the exchange takes place. Section 1 of the Sherman Act is implicated because trade associations constitute a "combination" within the meaning of the statute. Moreover, the "agreement" to exchange commercial information may come within the "contract" language of the statute. The following cases explore the antitrust limits of exchange agreements among competitors. In each case, you should compare the challenged conduct, market power, and the purpose and effect of the cooperative programs.

In *American Column & Lumber Co. v. United States*, 257 U.S. 377 (1921), the Supreme Court struck down a trade association program which mandated compliance with several restrictive requirements, including immediate reporting of price changes and the filing of daily reports on sales, production, and purchases. The dangers of overproduction were stressed in speeches and memoranda. Restrictions on output and price maintenance were discussed. Monthly meetings were held and members were encouraged to set high prices. The association's membership accounted for 33% of the industry production, but there was some evidence of increases in prices. Said the Court:

> Genuine competitors do not make daily, weekly and monthly reports of the minutest details of their business to their rivals, as the defendants did; they do not contract, as was done here, to submit their books to the discretionary audit and their stocks to the discretionary inspection of their rivals for the purpose of successfully competing with them; and they do not submit the details of their business to the analysis of an expert, jointly employed, and obtain from him a "harmonized" estimate of the market as it is and as, in his specially and confidentially informed judgment, it promises to be. This is not the conduct of competitors but is so clearly that of men united in an agreement, express or implied, to act together and pursue a common purpose

under a common guide that, if it did not stand confessed a combination to restrict production and increase prices in interstate commerce and as, therefore, a direct restraint upon that commerce, as we have seen that it is, that conclusion must inevitably have been inferred from the facts which were proved. To pronounce such abnormal conduct on the part of 365 natural competitors, controlling one-third of the trade of the country in an article of prime necessity, a "new form of competition" and not an old form of combination in restraint of trade, as it so plainly is, would be for this court to confess itself blinded by words and forms to realities which men in general very plainly see and understand and condemn, as an old evil in a new dress and with a new name.

The "Plan" is, essentially, simply an expansion of the gentlemen's agreement of former days, skillfully devised to evade the law. To call it open competition because the meetings were nominally open to the public, or because some voluminous reports were transmitted to the Department of Justice, or because no specific agreement to restrict trade or fix prices is proved, cannot conceal the fact that the fundamental purpose of the "Plan" was to procure "harmonious" individual action among a large number of naturally competing dealers with respect to the volume of production and prices, without having any specific agreement with respect to them, and to rely for maintenance of concerted action in both respects, not upon fines and forfeitures as in earlier days, but upon what experience has shown to be the more potent and dependable restraints, of business honor and social penalties, — cautiously reinforced by many and elaborate reports, which would promptly expose to his associates any disposition in any member to deviate from the tacit understanding that all were to act together under the subtle direction of a single interpreter of their common purposes, as evidenced in the minute reports of what they had done and in their expressed purposes as to what they intended to do.

In the presence of this record it is futile to argue that the purpose of the "Plan" was simply to furnish those engaged in this industry, with widely scattered units, the equivalent of such information as is contained in the newspaper and government publications with respect to the market for commodities sold on boards of trade or stock exchanges. One distinguishing and sufficient difference is that the published reports go to both seller and buyer, but these reports go to the seller only; and another is that there is no skilled interpreter of the published reports, such as we have in this case, to insistently recommend harmony of action likely to prove profitable in proportion as it is unitedly pursued.

Convinced, as we are, that the purpose and effect of the activities of the "Open Competition Plan," here under discussion, were to restrict competition and thereby restrain interstate commerce in the manufacture and sale of hardwood lumber by concerted action in curtailing production and in in-

creasing prices, we agree with the District Court that it constituted a combination and conspiracy in restraint of interstate commerce within the meaning
of the Anti-Trust Act of 1890 and the decree of that court must be affirmed.

Justice Brandeis dissented, pointing out that the hardwood industry was
populated by small, isolated manufacturers who had very poor access to information about market conditions and who might be taken advantage of by large
buyers. The market would run more efficiently, Brandeis argued, if everyone in
the market had access to the same reliable information about price and output
conditions.

Two years after *American Column & Lumber*, the Supreme Court in *United
States v. American Linseed Oil Co.*, 262 U.S. 371 (1923), followed the standard
used in the earlier case and held that an association of twelve corporations,
which manufactured linseed products and which exchanged detailed current
price and production data through regular meetings and a coercive enforcement
plan, was an illegal combination because the plan resulted in higher prices.

As the next case indicates, however, the legality of a cooperative plan may
depend on the content of the exchange and the enforcement mechanism.

MAPLE FLOORING MANUFACTURERS ASS'N V. UNITED STATES

268 U.S. 563 (1925)

JUSTICE STONE delivered the opinion of the Court.

The defendants are the Maple Flooring Manufacturers Association, an unincorporated "trade association"; twenty-two corporate defendants, members of the
Association, engaged in the business of selling and shipping maple, beech and
birch flooring in interstate commerce, all but two of them having their principal
places of business in Michigan, Minnesota or Wisconsin (one defendant being
located in Illinois and one in New York) .... Estimates submitted in behalf of the
Government indicate that in the year 1922 the defendants produced 70% of the
total production of these types of flooring....

... The defendants have engaged in many activities to which no exception is
taken by the Government and which are admittedly beneficial to the industry and
to consumers; such as co-operative advertising and the standardization and improvement of the product. The activities, however, of the present Association of
which the Government complains may be summarized as follows:

(1) The computation and distribution among the members of the association of the average cost to association members of all dimensions and grades
of flooring.

(2) The compilation and distribution among members of a booklet showing freight rates on flooring from Cadillac, Michigan, to between five and
six thousand points of shipment in the United States.

(3) The gathering of statistics which at frequent intervals are supplied by
each member of the Association to the Secretary of the Association giving

complete information as to the quantity and kind of flooring sold and prices received by the reporting members, and the amount of stock on hand, which information is summarized by the Secretary and transmitted to members without, however, revealing the identity of the members in connection with any specific information thus transmitted.

(4) Meetings at which the representatives of members congregate and discuss the industry and exchange views as to its problems.

Before considering these phases of the activities of the Association, it should be pointed out that it is neither alleged nor proved that there was any agreement among the members of the Association either affecting production, fixing prices or for price maintenance. Both by the articles of association and in actual practice, members have been left free to sell their product at any price they choose and to conduct their business as they please. Although the bill alleges that the activities of the defendants hereinbefore referred to resulted in the maintenance of practical uniformity of net delivered prices as between the several corporate defendants, the evidence fails to establish such uniformity and it was not seriously urged before this Court that any substantial uniformity in price had in fact resulted from the activities of the Association, although it was conceded by defendants that the dissemination of information as to cost of the product and as to production and prices would tend to bring about uniformity in prices through the operation of economic law. Nor was there any direct proof that the activities of the Association had affected prices adversely to consumers. On the contrary, the defendants offered a great volume of evidence tending to show that the trend of prices of the product of the defendants corresponded to the law of supply and demand and that it evidenced no abnormality when compared with the price of commodities generally. There is undisputed evidence that the prices of members were fair and reasonable and that they were usually lower than the prices of nonmembers and there is no claim that defendants were guilty of unfair or arbitrary trade practices.

. . . .

Computation and distribution, among the members, of information
as to the average cost of their product.

. . . .

In order to determine the cost of a given type or grade of flooring, it was necessary to distribute the total cost of the aggregate of the different types and grades of finished flooring produced from a given amount of rough lumber among the several types and grades thus produced. This distribution was made by the officials of the Association and the estimated cost thus determined was tabulated and distributed among the members of the Association. There is no substantial claim made on the part of the Government that the preparation of these estimates of cost was not made with all practicable accuracy or that they were in any respect not what they purported to be, an estimate of the actual cost of commercial grades of finished flooring fairly ascertained from the actual experience of members of the Association, except that the point is made by the Government that the distribution of cost among the several types and grades of finished flooring produced from a given amount of rough lumber was necessarily arbitrary and that it might be or become a cover for price fixing. Suffice it to say that neither the Government nor the defendants seem to have found it necessary to prove upon what principle of cost accounting this distribution of cost was made and there are no data from which any inference can be drawn as to whether or not it conformed to accepted practices of cost accounting applied to the manufacture of a diversified product from a single type of raw material.

The compilation and distribution among members of information as to freight rates.

Through the agency of the Secretary of the Association a booklet was compiled and distributed to members of the Association showing freight rates from Cadillac, Michigan, to numerous points throughout the United States to which the finished flooring is shipped by members of the Association. It appears from the evidence to have been the usual practice in the maple flooring trade, to quote flooring at a delivered price and that purchasers of flooring usually will not buy on any other basis. The evidence, however, is undisputed that the defendants quote and sell on an f. o. b. mill basis whenever a purchaser so requests. It also appears that the mills of most of the members of the Association are located in small towns in Michigan and Wisconsin and that the average freight rates from these principal producing points in Michigan and Wisconsin to the principal centers of consumption in the United States are approximately the same as the freight rate from Cadillac, Michigan, to the same centers of consumption. There is abundant evidence that there were delays in securing quotations of freight rates from the local agents of carriers in towns in which the factories of defendants are located, which seriously interfered with prompt quotations of delivered prices to customers; that the actual aggregate difference between local freight rates for most of defendants' mills and the rate appearing in defendant's freight-rate book based on rates at Cadillac, Michigan, were so small as to be only nominal, and that the freight-rate book served a useful and legitimate purpose in enabling members to quote promptly a delivered price on their product by adding to their mill price a previously calculated freight rate which approximated closely to the actual rate from their own mill towns.

The Government bases its criticism of the use of the freight-rate book upon the fact that antecedent associations, maintained by defendants, incorporated in the freight-rate book a delivered price which was made up by adding the calculated freight rate from Cadillac, Michigan, to a minimum price under the so-called "minimum price plan" of previous associations, whereby the price was fixed at cost plus ten per cent of profit. It is conceded that the present Association does not include a delivered price in the freight-rate book, but it is urged by the Government that the circulation of the tables of estimated cost of flooring, together with a freight-rate book, enables members of the Association to fix a delivered price by adding to the estimated cost circulated among members, the calculated freight rate published in the freight-rate book, and that the freight-rate book used in conjunction with the published material as to estimated cost is merely a device whereby the defendants have continued the so-called minimum price plan formerly maintained by predecessor associations, which was a plan whereby the members co-operated in the maintenance of a fixed minimum price. Defendants maintain that the minimum price plan was never actually carried out by any predecessor association and that it was formally abandoned in February or March, 1920, after the failure to secure the approval of the plan by the Federal Trade Commission, and was never revived or continued.

... [D]ata as to the average cost of flooring circulated among the members of the Association when combined with a calculated freight rate which is either exactly or approximately the freight rate from the point of shipment, plus an arbitrary percentage of profit, could be made the basis for fixing prices or for an agreement for price maintenance, which, if found to exist, would under the decisions of this Court, constitute a violation of the Sherman Act. But, as we have already said, the record is barren of evidence that the published list of costs and the freight-rate book have been so used by the present Association. Consequently, the question which this Court must decide is whether the use of this material by members of the Association will necessarily have that effect so as to produce that unreasonable restraint of interstate commerce which is condemned by the Sherman Act.

The gathering and distributing among members of trade statistics.

... [M]embers reported weekly to the Secretary of the Association on forms showing dates of sales made by the reporting member, the quantity, the thickness and face, the grade, the kind of wood, the delivery, the prices at which sold, the average freight rate to destination and the rate of commission paid, if any. Members also reported monthly the amount of flooring on hand of each dimension and grade and the amount of unfilled orders. Monthly reports were also required showing the amount of production for each period and the new orders booked for each variety of flooring. The Association promptly reported back to the members statistics compiled from the reports of members including the identifying numbers of the mills making the reports, and information as to quantities, grades, prices, freight rates, etc., with respect to each sale. The names of purchasers were not reported and from and after July 19, 1923, the identifying number of the mill making the report was omitted. All reports of sales and prices dealt exclusively with past and closed transactions. The statistics gathered by the defendant Association are given wide publicity. They are published in trade journals which are read by from 90 to 95% of the persons who purchase the products of

Association members. They are sent to the Department of Commerce which publishes a monthly survey of current business. They are forwarded to the Federal Reserve and other banks and are available to anyone at any time desiring to use them. It is to be noted that the statistics gathered and disseminated do not include current price quotations; information as to employment conditions; geographical distribution of shipments; the names of customers or distribution by classes of purchasers; the details with respect to new orders booked, such as names of customers, geographical origin of orders; or details with respect to unfilled orders, such as names of customers, their geographical location; the names of members having surplus stocks on hand; the amount of rough lumber on hand; or information as to cancellation of orders. Nor do they differ in any essential respect from trade or business statistics which are freely gathered and publicly disseminated in numerous branches of industry producing a standardized product such as grain, cotton, coal oil, and involving interstate commerce, whose statistics disclose volume and material elements affecting costs of production, sales price and stock on hand.

Association meetings.

... [T]here was no discussion of prices in meetings. There was no occasion to discuss past prices, as those were fully detailed in the statistical reports, and the Association was advised by counsel that future prices were not a proper subject of discussion. It was admitted by several witnesses, however, that upon occasion the trend of prices and future prices became the subject of discussion outside the meeting among individual representatives of the defendants attending the meeting. The Government, however, does not charge, nor is it contended, that there was any understanding or agreement, either express or implied, at the meetings or elsewhere, with respect to prices.

Upon this state of the record, the District Court ... held that the plan or system operated by the defendants had a direct and necessary tendency to destroy competition ....

In *American Column & Lumber Co. v. United States*, [the] record disclosed a systematic effort, participated in by the members of the Association and led and directed by the secretary of the Association, to cut down production and increase prices. The court not only held that this concerted effort was in itself unlawful, but that it resulted in an actual excessive increase of price to which the court found the "united action of this large and influential membership of dealers contributed greatly." The opinion of the court in that case rests squarely on the ground that there was a combination on the part of the members to secure concerted action in curtailment of production and increase of price, which actually resulted in a restraint of commerce, producing increase of price.

In *United States v. American Linseed Oil Co.*, ... [it] was held that the agreement for price maintenance accompanied by free exchange of information between competitors as to current prices of the product offered for sale; full details as to purchasers, actual and prospective; and the exchange of information as to buyers and those to whom offerings were made by sellers and of the terms of such offerings, could necessarily have only one purpose and effect, namely to restrain competition among sellers.

....

It is not, we think, open to question that the dissemination of pertinent information concerning any trade or business tends to stabilize that trade or business and to produce uniformity of price and trade practice. Exchange of price quotations of market commodities tends to produce uniformity of prices in the markets of the world. Knowledge of the supplies of available merchandise tends to prevent over-production and to avoid the economic disturbances produced by business crises resulting from over-production. But the natural effect of the acquisition of wider and more scientific knowledge of business conditions, on the minds of the individuals engaged in commerce, and its consequent effect in stabilizing production and price, can hardly be deemed a restraint of commerce or if so it cannot, we think, be said to be an unreasonable restraint, or in any respect unlawful.

....

We do not conceive that the members of trade associations become such conspirators merely because they gather and disseminate information, such as is here complained of, bearing on the business in which they are engaged and make use of it in the management and control of their individual businesses; nor do we think that the proper application of the principles of decision of *American Column & Lumber Co. v. United States* ... leads to any such result....

We decide only that trade associations or combinations of persons or corporations which openly and fairly gather and disseminate information as to the cost of their product, the volume of production, the actual price which the product has brought in past transactions, stocks of merchandise on hand, approximate cost of transportation from the principal point of shipment to the points of consumption, as did these defendants, and who, as they did, meet and discuss such information and statistics without however reaching or attempting to reach any agreement or any concerted action with respect to prices or production or restraining competition, do not thereby engage in unlawful restraint of commerce.

Reversed.

[JUSTICES TAFT, SANFORD and MCREYNOLDS dissented.]

NOTES AND QUESTIONS

1. In *Cement Mfrs. Protective Ass'n v. United States*, 268 U.S. 588 (1925), handed down the same day, the Court found no section 1 violation where the government had challenged the statistical and credit activities of the association, but no charge had been made that the association had restricted production or prices. The evidence showed that the price of cement changed frequently though uniformly. The Court also found that inferences of any agreement or uniformity of trade practices could not be drawn from the exchange of statistics on production, shipments, stocks, or credit terms. Moreover, the Court opined that the exchange of information was necessary to inhibit customer fraud and misrepresentation.

2. Did the relatively small number of members (22) in the Maple Flooring Manufacturer's Association make it more or less likely that the information exchange would have an impact on price?

3. Why did the defendants compile and distribute to themselves a book showing freight rates from Cadillac, Michigan? One possibility is that Cadillac, Michigan was a point central to all of them, from which freight rates could easily be computed. Another possibility, however, is that they were engaged in basepoint pricing. See the discussion of base-point pricing in Subsection C3 of this section.

4. The next data exchange case to reach the Court was *Sugar Inst. v. United States*, 297 U.S. 553 (1936), where the Court decided whether a "code of ethics" which required sugar refiners not to deviate from announced prices violated section 1. Intense competition characterized the sugar industry at this time. Because sugar was a homogenous product, competition focused on price. The agreement prohibited secret price concessions and discriminatory rebates. Refiners were free to set price and announce price changes; once announced, however, the code prevented price changes and discrimination unless openly announced in advance.

The Court held that it was a violation of section 1 for the trade association members to agree to refrain from changing an announced price through a secret price concession. In delivering the opinion for the Court, Chief Justice Hughes reasoned as follows:

> We have said that the Sherman Act, as a charter of freedom, has a generality and adaptability comparable to that found to be desirable in constitutional provisions. It does not go into detailed definitions. Thus in applying its broad prohibitions, each case demands a close scrutiny of its own facts. Questions of reasonableness are necessarily questions of relation and degree. In the instant case, a fact of outstanding importance is the relative position of defendants in the sugar industry. We have noted that the fifteen refiners, represented in the Institute, refine practically all the imported raw sugar processed in this country. They supply from 70 to 80 per cent of the sugar consumed. Their refineries are in the East, South, and West, and their agreements and concerted action have a direct effect upon the entire sugar trade. While their product competes with beet sugar and "offshore" sugar, the maintenance of fair competition between the defendants themselves in the sale of domestic refined sugar is manifestly of serious public concern. Another outstanding fact is that defendants' product is a thoroughly standardized commodity. In their competition, price, rather than brand, is generally the vital consideration. The question of unreasonable restraint of competition thus relates in the main to competition in prices, terms and conditions of sales. The fact that, because sugar is a standardized commodity,

there is a strong tendency to uniformity of price, makes it the more important that such opportunities as may exist for fair competition should not be impaired.

Defendants point to the abuses which existed before they formed the Institute, and to their remedial efforts. But the controversy that emerges is not as to the abuses which admittedly existed, but whether defendants' agreement and requirements went too far and imposed unreasonable restraints. After a hearing of extraordinary length, in which no pertinent fact was permitted to escape consideration, the trial court subjected the evidence to a thorough and acute analysis which has left but slight room for debate over matters of fact. Our examination of the record discloses no reason for overruling the court's findings in any matter essential to our decision.

In determining the relief to be afforded, appropriate regard should be had to the special and historic practice of the sugar industry. The restraints, found to be unreasonable, were the offspring of the basic agreement. The vice in that agreement was not in the mere open announcement of prices and terms in accordance with the custom of the trade. That practice which had grown out of the special character of the industry did not restrain competition. The trial court did not hold that practice to be illegal and we see no reason for condemning it. The unreasonable restraints which defendants imposed lay not in advance announcements, but in the steps taken to secure adherence, without deviation, to prices and terms thus announced. It was that concerted undertaking which cut off opportunities for variation in the course of competition however fair and appropriate they might be.

On the question of the proper remedy, *Sugar Institute* struck down as too expansive the injunction issued by the district court. The order entered by the trial court forbade conduct:

> Effectuating any system for ... reporting ... among ... competitors or to a common agency, information as to current or future prices, terms, conditions.... 4. Relaying by or through The Sugar Institute ... information as to current or future prices, terms, conditions.... 5. Giving any prior notice of any change or contemplated change in prices, terms, conditions... or relaying, reporting or announcing any such change in advance there thereof.

297 U.S. at 603. In reviewing this decree, the Court said:

> The trial court left defendants free to provide for immediate publicity as to prices and terms in all closed transactions. We think that a limitation to that sort of publicity fails to take proper account of the practice of the trade in selling on "moves" [a condition of the industry which permitted a customer a grace period in which to purchase at the old price]. That custom involves advance announcements, and it does not appear that arrangements merely to circulate or relay such announcements threaten competitive opportunities.

On the other hand, such provision for publicity may be helpful in promoting fair competition. If the requirement that there must be adherence to prices and terms openly announced in advance is abrogated and the restraints which followed that requirement are removed, the just interests of competition will be safeguarded and the trade will still be left with whatever advantage may be incidental to its established practice.

Id. at 601-02.

Thus the Court approved the advance announcement of price information, although the *agreement* not to deviate from the announced prices, which had the effect of eliminating price concessions and reductions, was found unlawful. *See* Sullivan, *First Amendment Defenses in Antitrust Litigation*, 46 Mo. L. Rev. 517, 554 (1981). The Court's analysis suggests that before an order can enjoin the exchange of price information, there must be an inquiry into how closely the disclosure is related to an agreement that might affect prices and the role the price announcement or exchange played in the trade practice. *Cf. Broadcast Music, Inc. v. CBS, Inc.*, 441 U.S. 1 (1979) (Court examined market purpose of a blanket licensing agreement to determine whether it was a per se illegal price fixing arrangement).

Did the Court in the preceding cases articulate why it applies a rule of reason approach in data dissemination cases rather than a per se analysis? Consider whether the 1940 *Socony-Vacuum* decision implicitly overruled *Maple Flooring*. In comparing *Maple Flooring* to *Socony-Vacuum*, can you define what constitutes price fixing? Does it matter whether there is an agreement concerning the use of the disclosed prices? What advice can you give a trade association client in establishing guidelines for a lawful statistical exchange program?

Sugar Institute, and to a lesser extent the earlier cases, suggested that the structure of the industry might play a role in determining the legality of a cooperative exchange program. The Court noted that "[q]uestions of reasonableness are necessarily questions of relation and degree.... [A] fact of outstanding importance is the relative position of defendants in the ... industry." 297 U.S. at 600. This comment foreshadowed the market structure analysis and economic theory that achieved acceptance in the next case. While *Sugar Institute* considered how the communication was affected by market conditions and trade practices, the following case focused on how market structure may be determinative of the legality of the communication.

UNITED STATES V. CONTAINER CORP. OF AMERICA

393 U.S. 333 (1969)

JUSTICE DOUGLAS delivered the opinion of the Court.

This is a civil antitrust action charging a price-fixing agreement in violation of § 1, of the Sherman Act.... The District Court dismissed the complaint....

The case as proved is unlike any of other price decisions we have rendered. There was here an exchange of price information but no agreement to adhere to a price schedule .... There was here an exchange of information concerning specific sales to identified customers, not a statistical report on the average cost to all members, without identifying the parties to specific transactions .... While there was present here ... an exchange of prices to specific customers, there was absent the controlling circumstance, [found in *Cement*] that cement manufacturers, to protect themselves from delivering to contractors more cement than was needed for a specific job and thus receiving a lower price, exchanged price information as a means of protecting their legal rights from fraudulent inducements to deliver more cement than needed for a specific job.

Here all that was present was a request by each defendant of its competitor for information as to the most recent price changed or quoted, whenever it needed such information and whenever it was not available from another source. Each defendant on receiving that request usually furnished the data with the expectation that it would be furnished reciprocal information when it wanted it. That concerted action is of course sufficient to establish the combination or conspiracy, the initial ingredient of a violation of § 1 of the Sherman Act.

There was of course freedom to withdraw from the agreement. But the fact remains that when a defendant requested and received price information, it was affirming its willingness to furnish such information in return.

There was to be sure an infrequency and irregularity of price exchanges between the defendants; and often the data were available from the records of the defendants or from the customers themselves. Yet the essence of the agreement was to furnish price information whenever requested.

Moreover, although the most recent price charged or quoted was sometimes fragmentary, each defendant had the manuals with which it could compute the price charged by a competitor on a specific order to a specific customer.

Further, the price quoted was the current price which a customer would need to pay in order to obtain products from the defendant furnishing the data.

The defendants account for about 90% of the shipment of corrugated containers from plants in the Southeastern United States. While containers vary as to dimensions, weight, color, and so on, they are substantially identical, no matter who produces them, when made to particular specifications. The prices paid depend on price alternatives. Suppliers when seeking new or additional business or keeping old customers, do not exceed a competitor's price. It is common for purchasers to buy from two or more suppliers concurrently. A defendant supplying a customer with containers would usually quote the same price on additional orders, unless costs had changed. Yet where a competitor was charging a particular price, a defendant would normally quote the same price or even a lower price.

The exchange of price information seemed to have the effect of keeping prices within a fairly narrow ambit. Capacity has exceeded the demand from 1955 to 1963, the period covered by the complaint, and the trend of corrugated container prices has been downward. Yet despite this excess capacity and the downward trend of prices, the industry has expanded in the Southeast from 30 manufacturers with 49 plants to 51 manufacturers with 98 plants. An abundance of raw materials and machinery makes entry into the industry easy with an investment of $50,000 to $75,000.

The result of this reciprocal exchange of prices was to stabilize prices though at a downward level. Knowledge of a competitor's price usually meant matching that price. The continuation of some price competition is not fatal to the Government's case. The limitation or reduction of price competition brings the case within the ban, for as we held in *United States v. Socony-Vacuum Oil Co.*, interference with the setting of price by free market forces is unlawful *per se*. Price information exchanged in some markets may have no effect on a truly competitive price. But the corrugated container industry is dominated by relatively few sellers. The product is fungible and the competition for sales is price. The demand is inelastic, as buyers place orders only for immediate, short-run needs. The exchange of price data tends toward price uniformity. For a lower price does not mean a larger share of the available business but a sharing of the existing business at a lower return. Stabilizing prices as well as raising them is within the ban of § 1 of the Sherman Act. As we said in *United States v. Socony-Vacuum Oil Co.*, "in terms of market operations stabilization is but one form of manipulation." The inferences are irresistible that the exchange of price information has had an anticompetitive effect in the industry, chilling the vigor of price competition....

Price is too critical, too sensitive a control to allow it to be used even in an informal manner to restrain competition.

Reversed.

JUSTICE FORTAS, concurring.

I join in the judgment and opinion of the Court. I do not understand the Court's opinion to hold that the exchange of specific information among sellers as to prices charged to individual customers, pursuant to mutual arrangement, is a *per se* violation of the Sherman Act.

Absent *per se* violation, proof is essential that the practice resulted in an unreasonable restraint of trade. There is no single test to determine when the record adequately shows an "unreasonable restraint of trade"; but a practice such as that here involved, which is adopted for the purpose of arriving at a determination of prices to be quoted to individual customers, inevitably suggests the probability that it so materially interfered with the operation of the price mechanism of the marketplace as to bring it within the condemnation of this Court's decisions.

Theoretical probability, however, is not enough unless we are to regard mere exchange of current price information as so akin to price-fixing by combination or conspiracy as to deserve the *per se* classification. I am not prepared to do this, nor is it necessary here. In this case, the probability that the exchange of specific price information led to an unlawful effect upon prices is adequately buttressed by evidence in the record. This evidence, although not overwhelming, is sufficient in the special circumstances of this case to show an actual effect on pricing and to compel us to hold that the court below erred in dismissing the Government's complaint.

In summary, the record shows that the defendants sought and obtained from competitors who were part of the arrangement information about the competitors' prices to specific customers. "[I]n the majority of instances," the District Court found, 273 F. Supp. 18, 27, that once a defendant had this information he quoted substantially the same price as the competitor, although a higher or lower price would "occasionally" be quoted. Thus the exchange of prices made it possible for individual defendants confidently to name a price equal to that which their competitors were asking. The obvious effect was to "stabilize" prices by joint arrangement — at least to limit any price cuts to the minimum necessary to meet competition. In addition, there was evidence that, in some instances, during periods when various defendants ceased exchanging prices exceptionally sharp and vigorous price reductions resulted.

On this record, taking into account the specially sensitive function of the price term in the antitrust equation, I cannot see that we would be justified in reaching any conclusion other than that defendants' tacit agreement to exchange information about current prices to specific customers did in fact substantially limit the amount of price competition in the industry. That being so, there is no need to consider the possibility of a *per se* violation.

JUSTICE MARSHALL, with whom JUSTICE HARLAN and JUSTICE STEWART join, dissenting.

I agree with the Court's holding that there existed an agreement among the defendants to exchange price information whenever requested. However, I cannot agree that that agreement should be condemned, either as illegal *per se*, or as having had the purpose or effect of restricting price competition in the corrugated container industry in the Southeastern United States.

....

Per se rules always contain a degree of arbitrariness. They are justified on the assumption that the gains from imposition of the rule will far outweigh the losses and that significant administrative advantages will result. In other words, the potential competitive harm plus the administrative costs of determining in what particular situations the practice may be harmful must far outweigh the benefits that may result. If the potential benefits in the aggregate are outweighed to this degree, then they are simply not worth identifying in individual cases.

I do not believe that the agreement in the present case is so devoid of potential benefit or so inherently harmful that we are justified in condemning it without proof that it was entered into for the purpose of restraining price competition or that it actually had that effect....

Complete market knowledge is certainly not an evil in perfectly competitive markets. This is not, however, such a market, and there is admittedly some danger that price information will be used for anticompetitive purposes, particularly the maintenance of prices at a high level. If the danger that price information will be so used is particularly high in a given situation, then perhaps exchange of information should be condemned.

I do not think the danger is sufficiently high in the present case. Defendants are only 18 of the 51 producers of corrugated containers in the Southeastern United States. Together, they do make up 90% of the market and the six largest defendants do control 60% of the market. But entry is easy; an investment of $50,000 to $75,000 is ordinarily all that is necessary. In fact, the number of sellers has increased from 30 to the present 51 in the eight-year period covered by the complaint. The size of the market has almost doubled because of increased demand for corrugated containers. Nevertheless, some excess capacity is present. The products produced by defendants are undifferentiated. Industry demand is inelastic, so that price changes will not, up to a certain point, affect the total amount purchased. The only effect of price changes will be to reallocate market shares among sellers.

In a competitive situation, each seller will cut his price in order to increase his share of the market, and prices will ultimately stabilize at a competitive level — i.e., price will equal cost, including a reasonable return on capital. Obviously, it would be to a seller's benefit to avoid such price competition and maintain prices at a higher level, with a corresponding increase in profit. In a market with very few sellers, and detailed knowledge of each other's price, such action is possible. However, I do not think it can be concluded that this particular market is sufficiently oligopolistic, especially in light of the ease of entry, to justify the inference that price information will necessarily be used to stabilize prices. Nor do I think that the danger of such a result is sufficiently high to justify imposing a *per se* rule without actual proof.

In this market, we have a few sellers presently controlling a substantial share of the market. We have a large number competing for the remainder of the market, also quite substantial. And total demand is increasing. In such a case, I think it just as logical to assume that the sellers, especially the smaller and newer ones will desire to capture a larger market share by cutting prices as it is that they will acquiesce in oligopolistic behavior. The likelihood that prices will be cut and that those lower prices will have to be met acts as a deterrent to setting prices at an artificially high level in the first place. Given the uncertainty about the probable effect of an exchange of price information in this context, I would require that the Government prove that the exchange was entered into for the purpose of, or that it had the effect of, restraining price competition.

NOTES AND QUESTIONS

1. Did Justice Douglas' opinion hold that price exchanges are illegal per se? Did the Court find that the exchange of price information was inherently anticompetitive? Or did the Court find anticompetitive purpose or effect?

2. Did Justice Douglas find an "agreement" to exchange price information? If so, how did he reach this conclusion? Consider the fact that the exchanges were infrequent; does this bode against an inference of agreement? What if it were an exchange of past sale transactions? Is an agreement to exchange price information the equivalent of an agreement to fix prices? If there was no "agreement" to exchange the information, could the defendants have violated section 1?

3. Under the economic analysis employed by Justice Douglas, how concentrated must the market be before a price exchange will be considered illegal? What relevance should excess capacity, the collective market power of the defendants and ease of entry into the market have on determining the legality of a price exchange? Do falling prices and increased costs indicate evidence of market power? If these economic conditions were present in the market, is it likely that the prices exceeded a competitive level? Under what structural conditions would you expect that exchange of prices would lead to more, rather than less, competition?

The *Container* decision was the first explicit indication that the Supreme Court would expand its analysis to consider the relationship between market structure and the effect of price exchanges. Previously, the Court had concentrated its analysis on conduct or behavior of the defendant. *Container* also raised the question as to the proper standard of analysis for price-affecting conduct, such as exchanges of price information. Although ambiguous, *Container* suggested a per se rule: it is not necessary to establish evidence of either unlawful purpose or actual anticompetitive effect in order to find a violation in an oligopolistic market. As an evidentiary and substantive law concern, the standard employed is obviously important. But as Justices Fortas and Marshall pointed out in their separate opinions in *Container*, there was uncertainty as to the actual approach utilized in the majority opinion.

The issue was clarified six years later when the Court, in *United States v. Citizens & S. Nat'l Bank*, 422 U.S. 86, 113 (1975), stated unequivocally that the disclosure or exchange of price information is not a per se violation. Interestingly, the Court cited Justice Fortas' concurring opinion in *Container* for his statement of the law, rather than Justice Douglas' majority opinion. For the antitrust lawyer the message seemed clear: actual proof "that the practice resulted in an unreasonable restraint of trade" (Fortas, J., concurring) was necessary in a price or data exchange case. 394 U.S. at 339.

In the next case, the standard was applied in a criminal case where the issue was whether an interseller price verification plan among competitors, for the purpose of defending a price discrimination charge under the Robinson-Patman Act, was exempt from the Sherman Act's coverage. In addition to clarifying its analytic approach, the Court articulated distinctions between civil and criminal violations.

UNITED STATES V. UNITED STATES GYPSUM CO.

438 U.S. 422 (1978)

CHIEF JUSTICE BURGER delivered the opinion of the Court.

This case presents the following questions: (a) whether intent is an element of a criminal antitrust offense; (b) whether an exchange of price information for purposes of compliance with the Robinson-Patman Act is exempt from Sherman Act scrutiny ....

I

Gypsum board, a laminated type of wall board composed of paper, vinyl or other specially treated coverings over a gypsum core, has in the last 30 years substantially replaced wet plaster as the primary component of interior walls and ceilings in residential and commercial construction. The product is essentially fungible; differences in price, credit terms and delivery services largely dictate the purchasers' choice between competing suppliers. Overall demand, however, is governed by the level of construction activity and is only marginally affected by price fluctuations.

The gypsum board industry is highly concentrated with the number of producers ranging from nine to 15 in the period 1960-1973. The eight largest companies accounted for some 94% of the national sales with the seven "single plant producers" accounting for the remaining 6%. Most of the major producers and a large number of the single plant producers are members of the Gypsum Association which since 1930 has served as a trade association of gypsum board manufacturers.

....

B

The focus of the Government's price fixing case at trial was interseller price verification — that is, the practice allegedly followed by the gypsum board manufacturers of telephoning a competing producer to determine the price currently being offered on gypsum board to a specific customer. The Government contended that these price exchanges were part of an agreement among the defendants, had the effect of stabilizing prices, and policing agreed upon price increases, and were undertaken on a frequent basis until sometime in 1973. Defendants disputed both the scope and duration of the verification activities, and further maintained that those exchanges of price information which did occur were for the purposes of complying with the Robinson-Patman Act and preventing customer fraud. These purposes, in defendants' view, brought the disputed communications among competitors within a "controlling circumstance" exception to Sherman Act liability — at the extreme, precluding, as a matter of law, consideration of verification by the jury in determining defendants' guilt on the price fixing charge, and at the minimum, making the defendants' purposes in engaging in such communications a threshold factual question.

The instructions on the verification issue given by the trial judge provided that if the exchanges of price information were deemed by the jury to have been undertaken "in a good faith effort to comply with the Robinson-Patman Act," verification standing alone would not be sufficient to establish an illegal price fixing agreement. The paragraphs immediately following, however, provided that the purpose was essentially irrelevant if the jury found that the effect of verification was to raise, fix, maintain or stabilize prices. The instructions on verification closed with the observation:

> The law presumes that a person intends the necessary and natural consequences of his acts. Therefore, if the effect of the exchanges of pricing information was to raise, fix, maintain and stabilize prices, then the parties to them are presumed, as a matter of law, to have intended that result.

....

D

The Court of Appeals for the Third Circuit reversed the convictions.

....

II

....

We agree with the Court of Appeals that an effect on prices, without more, will not support a criminal conviction under the Sherman Act, but we do not base that conclusion on the existence of any conflict between the requirements of the Robinson-Patman and the Sherman Acts. Rather, we hold that a defendant's state of mind or intent is an element of a criminal antitrust offense which must be established by evidence and inferences drawn therefrom and cannot be taken from the trier of fact through reliance on a legal presumption of wrongful intent from proof of an effect on prices. Cf. *Morissette v. United States*, 342 U.S. 246, 274-275. Since the challenged instruction, as we read it, had this prohibited effect, it is disapproved. We are unwilling to construe the Sherman Act as mandating a regime of strict liability criminal offenses.[13]

A

We start with the familiar proposition that "[t]he existence of a *mens rea* is the rule of, rather than the exception to, the principles of Anglo-American criminal jurisprudence."... Although Blackstone's requisite "vicious will" has been re-

---

[13] Our analysis focuses solely on the elements of a criminal offense under the antitrust laws, and leaves unchanged the general rule that a civil violation can be established by proof of either an unlawful purpose or an anticompetitive effect. See *United States v. Container Corp.*, 393 U.S. 333 (1969); (Marshall, J., dissenting). Of course, consideration of intent may play an important role in divining the actual nature and effect of the alleged anticompetitive conduct. See *Chicago Board of Trade v. United States*, 246 U.S. 231, 238.

placed by more sophisticated and less colorful characterizations of the mental state required to support criminality, see ALI Model Penal Code § 2.02 (Prop. Official Draft 1962), intent generally remains an indispensable element of a criminal offense. This is as true in a sophisticated criminal antitrust case as in one involving any other criminal offense....

While strict liability offenses are not unknown to the criminal law and do not invariably offend constitutional requirements, ... the limited circumstances in which Congress has created and this Court has recognized such offenses, ... attest to their generally disfavored status. Certainly far more than the simple omission of the appropriate phrase from the statutory definition is necessary to justify dispensing with an intent requirement. In the context of the Sherman Act, this generally inhospitable attitude to non- *mens rea* offenses is reinforced by an array of considerations arguing against treating antitrust violations as strict liability crimes.

B

The Sherman Act, unlike most traditional criminal statutes, does not, in clear and categorical terms, precisely identify the conduct which it proscribes. Both civil remedies and criminal sanctions are authorized with regard to the same generalized definitions of the conduct proscribed — restraints of trade or commerce and illegal monopolization — without reference to or mention of intent or state of mind. Nor has judicial elaboration of the Act always yielded the clear and definitive rules of conduct, which the statute omits; instead open-ended and fact-specific standards like the "rule of reason" have been applied to broad classes of conduct falling within the purview of the Act's general provisions.... Simply put the Act has not been interpreted as if it were primarily a criminal statute; it has been construed to have a "generality and adaptability comparable to that found desirable in constitutional provisions."...

....

... With certain exceptions for conduct regarded as *per se* illegal because of its unquestionably anticompetitive effects, ... the behavior proscribed by the Act is often difficult to distinguish from the gray zone of socially acceptable and economically justifiable business conduct. Indeed, the type of conduct charged in the indictment in this case — the exchange of price information among competitors — is illustrative in this regard.[16] The imposition of criminal liability on

---

[16] The exchange of price data and other information among competitors does not invariably have anticompetitive effects; indeed such practices can in certain circumstances increase economic efficiency and render markets more, rather than less, competitive. For this reason, we have held that such exchanges of information do not constitute a *per se* violation of the Sherman Act. See, e.g., *United States v. Citizens & S. Nat. Bank*, 422 U.S. 86, 113 (1975); *United States v. Container Corp.*, 393 U.S., at 338 (Fortas, J., concurring). A number of factors including most prominently the structure of the industry involved and the nature of the information exchanged are generally considered in divining the procompetitive or anticompetitive effects of this type of interseller communication. See *United States v. Container Corp.* See generally L. Sullivan, Law of Antitrust 265-74 (1977). Exchanges of

a corporate official, or for that matter on a corporation directly, for engaging in such conduct which only after the fact is determined to violate the statute because of anticompetitive effects, without inquiring into the intent with which it was undertaken, holds out the distinct possibility of overdeterrence; salutary and procompetitive conduct lying close to the borderline of impermissible conduct might be shunned by businessmen who chose to be excessively cautious in the face of uncertainty regarding possible exposure to criminal punishment for even a good-faith error of judgment.... Further, the use of criminal sanctions in such circumstances would be difficult to square with the generally accepted functions of the criminal law.... The criminal sanctions would be used not to punish conscious and calculated wrongdoing at odds with statutory proscriptions, but instead simply to *regulate* business practices regardless of the intent with which they were undertaken....

For these reasons, we conclude that the criminal offenses defined by the Sherman Act should be construed as including intent as an element.

C

....

... Our question ... is whether a criminal violation of the antitrust laws requires, in addition to proof of anticompetitive effects, a demonstration that the disputed conduct was undertaken with the "conscious object" of producing such effects or whether it is sufficient that the conduct is shown to have been undertaken with knowledge that the proscribed effects would most likely follow.... [W]e conclude that action undertaken with knowledge of its probable consequences and having the requisite anticompetitive effects can be a sufficient predicate for a finding of criminal liability under the antitrust laws.[21]

Nothing in our analysis of the Sherman Act persuades us that this general understanding of intent should not be applied to criminal antitrust violations such as charged here. The business behavior which is likely to give rise to criminal antitrust charges is conscious behavior normally undertaken only after a full consideration of the desired results and a weighing of the costs, benefits and risks. A requirement of proof not only of this knowledge of likely effects, but also of a conscious desire to bring them to fruition or to violate the law would seem,

---

current price information, of course, have the greatest potential for generating anticompetitive effects and although not *per se* unlawful have consistently been held to violate the Sherman Act. See *American Column & Lumber Co. v. United States*, 257 U.S. 377 (1921); *United States v. American Linseed Oil Co.*, 262 U.S. 371 (1923); *United States v. Container Corp.*

[21] In so holding, we do not mean to suggest that conduct undertaken with the purpose of producing anticompetitive effects would not also support criminal liability, even if such effects did not come to pass. Cf. *United States v. Griffith*, 334 U.S. 100, 105 (1948). We hold only that this elevated standard of intent need not be established in cases where anticompetitive effects have been demonstrated; instead, proof that the defendant's conduct was undertaken with knowledge of its probable consequences will satisfy the Government's burden.

particularly in such a context, both unnecessarily cumulative and unduly burdensome. Where carefully planned and calculated conduct is being scrutinized in the context of a criminal prosecution, the perpetrator's knowledge of the anticipated consequences is a sufficient predicate for a finding of criminal intent.

D

When viewed in terms of this standard, the jury instructions on the price fixing charge cannot be sustained. "A conclusive presumption [of intent], which testimony could not overthrow would effectively eliminate intent as an ingredient of the offense." The challenged jury instruction, as we read it, had precisely this effect; the jury was told that the requisite intent followed, *as a matter of law*, from a finding that the exchange of price information had an impact on prices. Although an effect on prices may well support an inference that the defendant had knowledge of the probability of such a consequence at the time he acted, the jury must remain free to consider additional evidence before accepting or rejecting the inference. Therefore, although it would be correct to instruct the jury that it may infer intent from an effect on prices, ultimately the decision on the issue of intent must be left to the trier of fact alone. The instruction given invaded this fact finding function.[22]

Affirmed.

---

[22] Respondents contend that "prior to the trial of this case, no court had ever held that a mere exchange of information which had a stabilizing effect on prices violated the Sherman Act, regardless of the purposes of the exchange." Retroactive application of "this judicially expanded definition of the crime" would, the argument continues, "contravene the principles of fair notice in the Due Process Clause." While we have rejected on other grounds the "effects only" test in the context of criminal proceedings, we do not agree with respondents that the prior case law dealing with the exchange of price information required proof of a purpose to restrain competition in order to make out a Sherman Act violation.

Certainly our decision in *United States v. Container Corp.*, 393 U.S. 333 (1969), is fairly read as indicating that proof of an anticompetitive effect is a sufficient predicate for liability. In that case, liability followed from proof that "the exchange of price information had an anticompetitive effect in the industry," *Id.*, at 337, and no suggestion was made that proof of a purpose to restrain trade or competition was also required. Thus, at least in the post-*Container* period, which comprises almost the entire period at issue here, respondent's claimed lack of notice cannot be credited.

Nor are the prior cases treating exchanges of information among competitors more favorable to respondent's position. See *American Column Co. v. United States*, 257 U.S. 377, 400 (1921) ("any concerted action ... to cause, or which in fact does cause ... restraint of competition is unlawful"); *United States v. American Linseed Oil Co.*, 262 U.S. 371, 389 (1923) ("necessary tendency ... to suppress competition is unlawful"); *Maple Flooring Mfrs. Ass'n v. United States*, 268 U.S. 563, 585 (1925) (purpose to restrain trade or conduct which "had resulted or would necessarily result in tendency to less production or increased prices" sufficient for liability). While in *Cement Mfrs. [Protective] Ass'n v. United States*, 268 U.S. 588 (1925), an exception from Sherman Act liability was recognized for conduct intended to prevent fraud, we do not read that case as repudiating the rule set out in prior cases; instead *Cement* highlighted a narrow limitation on the application of the general rule that either purpose or effect will support liability.

NOTES AND QUESTIONS

1. Reflect on the distinctions drawn in *Gypsum* between a civil and criminal violation for an exchange of price information. What evidentiary factors are relevant, under *Gypsum*, for determining the legality of the price exchange? In defining a price fixing agreement, does it matter that there is no agreement concerning the use of the prices exchanged? Does *Gypsum* stand for the proposition that an agreement that may affect price, though not a direct price fixing arrangement, should be analyzed under the rule of reason? Did the *Gypsum* Court disavow *Container*'s pronouncement that a concentrated industry is predisposed towards cartelization?

2. How would you write a jury instruction in a criminal case on the intent element of a section 1 charge? Is the standard specific intent or general intent? Consider whether intent can be presumed if the indictment charges only a per se violation, thus negating the *Gypsum* requirement that the issue be submitted to the jury. Can the requisite criminal intent be inferred if the agreement is established? *See generally United States v. Continental Group, Inc.*, 603 F.2d 444 (3d Cir. 1978); *Phillips v. Crown Cent. Petr. Corp.*, 602 F.2d 616 (4th Cir. 1979); *United States v. Brighton Bldg. & Main. Co.*, 598 F.2d 1101 (7th Cir. 1979); *United States v. Gillen*, 599 F.2d 541 (3d Cir. 1979), for a discussion of whether there is a distinction between an agreement to exchange prices (*Gypsum*) and an agreement to fix prices, and whether the prosecution in a criminal case must prove intent with respect to any anticompetitive effect beyond the existence of a price fixing agreement. Do you agree that "conduct that clearly constitutes a per se offense carries with it its own intent"? If price information exchanges are analyzed under the rule of reason, can they ever be a criminal violation?

3. In a civil case after *Gypsum*, are unlawful purpose and anticompetitive consequences prerequisites of a section 1 violation? Can unlawful purpose be inferred from evidence of an effect on price? In either civil or criminal cases, what factors should the prosecutor or plaintiff's counsel consider in attempting to establish anticompetitive effect?

After *Gypsum* Professor Handler wrote that he was unaware "of any case in which a court has found that a defendant was civilly liable under section 1 because he had a bad intent where his actions did not rise to the level of an unreasonable restraint of trade." He opined that "many cases have looked at the defendant's intent in determining the legality of challenged conduct. But these cases, while mouthing the ... 'purpose and effect' test, in reality apply the ... approach of considering intent merely as a means of determining the actual effect of an alleged restraint of trade." Handler, *Antitrust — 1978*, 78 Colum. L. Rev. 1363, 1401-02 (1978). The same standard was expressed before *Gypsum* by the Fifth Circuit in *Northwest Power Prods. v. Omark Indus.*, 576 F.2d 83, 90 (5th Cir. 1978), where the court said that "[a]n evil intent alone is insufficient to establish a violation under the rule of reason, although proof of intent may help a court assess the market impact of the defendants' conduct." Do you agree that in a civil case intent evidence should be used only in determining the actual effect of the challenged action? Is this contradicted by *Gypsum?*

4. How workable is a rule that a price information exchange is illegal where the exchange has an "effect" on price? Prices in most markets change daily, and there are literally thousands of variables that determine them. How does one go about deciding whether a particular exchange of information has an "impact" on the price that a party to the exchange actually charges? One answer, of course, is that the parties also agree to be bound by the price information they obtain from a competitor. If this is true, however, they can be charged with price fixing, not merely with the exchange of price information.

5. THE MEANING AND SCOPE OF THE RULE OF REASON

The distinction between per se conduct and conduct analyzed under the rule of reason standard has not always been clear. The problem of selecting the correct analysis arguably seems dependent upon the directness of the "agreement" to an effect on price. As recent Supreme Court opinions indicate, however, confusion still exists on how that standard is measured and when the per se rules of analysis will be employed. One conclusion is that not all concerted action that affects price is "price fixing."

NATIONAL SOCIETY OF PROFESSIONAL ENGINEERS
V. UNITED STATES

435 U.S. 679 (1978)

JUSTICE STEVENS delivered the opinion of the Court.

This is a civil antitrust case brought by the United States to nullify an association's canon of ethics prohibiting competitive bidding by its members. The question is whether the canon may be justified under the Sherman Act, ... because it was adopted by members of a learned profession for the purpose of minimizing the risk that competition would produce inferior engineering work endangering the public safety.... Because we are satisfied that the asserted defense rests on a fundamental misunderstanding of the Rule of Reason frequently applied in antitrust litigation, we affirm.

I

Engineering is an important and learned profession. There are over 750,000 graduate engineers in the United States, of whom about 325,000 are registered as professional engineers. Registration requirements vary from State to State, but usually require the applicant to be a graduate engineer with at least four years of practical experience and to pass a written examination. About half of those who are registered engage in consulting engineering on a fee basis.... Engineering fees, amounting to well over $2 billion each year, constitute about 5% of total construction costs. In any given facility, approximately 50% to 80% of the cost of construction is the direct result of work performed by an engineer concerning the systems and equipment to be incorporated in the structure.

The National Society of Professional Engineers (Society) was organized in 1935 to deal with the nontechnical aspects of engineering practice, including the promotion of the professional, social, and economic interests of its members. Its present membership of 69,000 resides throughout the United States and in some foreign countries. Approximately 12,000 members are consulting engineers who offer their services to governmental, industrial, and private clients....

The charges of a consulting engineer may be computed in different ways. He may charge the client a percentage of the cost of the project, may set his fee at his actual cost plus overhead plus a reasonable profit, may charge fixed rates per hour for different types of work, may perform an assignment for a specific sum, or he may combine one or more of these approaches. Suggested fee schedules for particular types of services in certain areas have been promulgated from time to time by various local societies. This case does not, however, involve any claim that the National Society has tried to fix specific fees, or even a specific method of calculating fees. It involves a charge that the members of the Society have unlawfully agreed to refuse to negotiate or even to discuss the question of fees until after a prospective client has selected the engineer for a particular project....

... The Society's Code of Ethics thus "prohibits engineers from both soliciting and submitting such price information," and seeks to preserve the profession's "traditional" method of selecting professional engineers. Under the traditional method, the client initially selects an engineer on the basis of background and reputation, not price.

....

In its answer the Society admitted the essential facts alleged by the Government and pleaded a series of affirmative defenses, only one of which remains in issue. In that defense, the Society averred that the standard set out in the Code of Ethics was reasonable because competition among professional engineers was contrary to the public interest. It was averred that it would be cheaper and easier for an engineer "to design and specify inefficient and unnecessarily expensive structures and methods of construction." Accordingly, competitive pressure to offer engineering services at the lowest possible price would adversely affect the quality of engineering. Moreover, the practice of awarding engineering contracts to the lowest bidder, regardless of quality, would be dangerous to the public health, safety, and welfare. For these reasons, the Society claimed that its Code of Ethics was not an "unreasonable restraint of interstate trade or commerce."

....

II

In *Goldfarb v. Virginia State Bar*, 421 U.S. 773, the Court held that a bar association's rule prescribing minimum fees for legal services violated § 1 of the Sherman Act. In that opinion the Court noted that certain practices by members of a learned profession might survive scrutiny under the Rule of Reason even though they would be viewed as a violation of the Sherman Act in another context....

....

A. *The Rule of Reason*

One problem presented by the language of § 1 of the Sherman Act is that it cannot mean what it says. The statute says that "every" contract that restrains trade is unlawful. But, as Mr. Justice Brandeis perceptively noted, restraint is the very essence of every contract; read literally, § 1 would outlaw the entire body of private contract law. Yet it is that body of law that establishes the enforceability of commercial agreements and enables competitive markets — indeed, a competitive economy — to function effectively.

Congress, however, did not intend the text of the Sherman Act to delineate the full meaning of the statute or its application in concrete situations. The legislative history makes it perfectly clear that it expected the courts to give shape to the statute's broad mandate by drawing on common-law tradition. The Rule of Reason, with its origins in common-law precedents long antedating the Sherman Act, has served that purpose. It has been used to give the Act both flexibility and definition, and its central principle of antitrust analysis has remained constant. Contrary to its name, the Rule does not open the field of antitrust inquiry to any argument in favor of a challenged restraint that may fall within the realm of reason. Instead, it focuses directly on the challenged restraint's impact on competitive conditions.

This principle is apparent in even the earliest of cases applying the Rule of Reason, *Mitchel v. Reynolds, supra. Mitchel* involved the enforceability of a promise by the seller of a bakery that he would not compete with the purchaser of his business. The covenant was for a limited time and applied only to the area in which the bakery had operated. It was therefore upheld as reasonable, even though it deprived the public of the benefit of potential competition. The long-run benefit of enhancing the marketability of the business itself — and thereby providing incentives to develop such an enterprise — outweighed the temporary and limited loss of competition.

The Rule of Reason suggested by *Mitchel v. Reynolds* has been regarded as a standard for testing the enforceability of covenants in restraint of trade which are ancillary to a legitimate transaction, such as an employment contract or the sale of a going business. Judge (later Mr. Chief Justice) Taft so interpreted the Rule in his classic rejection of the argument that competitors may lawfully agree to sell their goods at the same price as long as the agreed-upon price is reasonable. *United States v. Addyston Pipe & Steel Co.*, 85 F. 271, 282-283 (6th Cir. 1898), aff'd, 175 U.S. 211. That case, and subsequent decisions by this Court, unequivocally foreclose an interpretation of the Rule as permitting an inquiry into the reasonableness of the prices set by private agreement.

The early cases also foreclose the argument that because of the special characteristics of a particular industry, monopolistic arrangements will better promote trade and commerce than competition.... That kind of argument is properly addressed to Congress and may justify an exemption from the statute for specific industries, but it is not permitted by the Rule of Reason. As the Court observed in *Standard Oil Co. v. United States*, 221 U.S., at 65, "restraints of trade within the purview of the statute ... [can]not be taken out of that category by indulging in general reasoning as to the expediency or nonexpediency of having made the contracts or the wisdom or want of wisdom of the statute which prohibited their being made."

The test prescribed in *Standard Oil* is whether the challenged contracts or acts "were unreasonably restrictive of competitive conditions." Unreasonableness under that test could be based either (1) on the nature or character of the contracts, or (2) on surrounding circumstances giving rise to the inference or presumption that they were intended to restrain trade and enhance prices. Under either branch of the test, the inquiry is confined to a consideration of impact on competitive conditions.

In this respect the Rule of Reason has remained faithful to its origins. From Mr. Justice Brandeis' opinion for the Court in *Chicago Board of Trade* to the Court opinion written by Justice Powell in *Continental T.V., Inc.*, the Court has adhered to the position that the inquiry mandated by the Rule of Reason is whether the challenged agreement is one that promotes competition or one that suppresses competition. "The true test of legality is whether the restraint imposed is such as merely regulates and perhaps thereby promotes competition or whether it is such as may suppress or even destroy competition."

There are, thus, two complementary categories of antitrust analysis. In the first category are agreements whose nature and necessary effect are so plainly anticompetitive that no elaborate study of the industry is needed to establish their illegality — they are "illegal *per se*." In the second category are agreements whose competitive effect can only be evaluated by analyzing the facts peculiar to the business, the history of the restraint, and the reasons why it was imposed. In either event, the purpose of the analysis is to form a judgment about the competitive significance of the restraint; it is not to decide whether a policy favoring competition is in the public interest, or in the interest of the members of an industry. Subject to exceptions defined by statute, that policy decision has been made by the Congress.

B. *The Ban on Competitive Bidding*

Price is the "central nervous system of the economy," *United States v. Socony-Vacuum Oil Co.*, 310 U.S. 150, and an agreement that "interfere[s] with the setting of price by free market forces" is illegal on its face. *United States v. Container Corp.*, 393 U.S. 333, 337. In this case we are presented with an agreement among competitors to refuse to discuss prices with potential customers until after negotiations have resulted in the initial selection of an engineer. While this is not price fixing as such, no elaborate industry analysis is required to demonstrate the anticompetitive character of such an agreement. It operates as an absolute ban on competitive bidding, applying with equal force to both complicated and simple projects and to both inexperienced and sophisticated customers. As the District Court found, the ban "impedes the ordinary give and take of the market place," and substantially deprives the customer of "the ability to utilize and compare prices in selecting engineering services." On its face, this agreement restrains trade within the meaning of § 1 of the Sherman Act.

The Society's affirmative defense confirms rather than refutes the anticompetitive purpose and effect of its agreement. The Society argues that the restraint is justified because bidding on engineering services is inherently imprecise, would lead to deceptively low bids, and would thereby tempt individual engineers to do inferior work with consequent risk to public safety and health. The logic of this argument rests on the assumption that the agreement will tend to maintain the price level; if it had no such effect, it would not serve its intended purpose. The Society nonetheless invokes the Rule of Reason, arguing that its restraint on price competition ultimately inures to the public benefit by preventing the production of inferior work and by insuring ethical behavior. As the preceding discussion of the Rule of Reason reveals, this Court has never accepted such an argument.

It may be, as petitioner argues, that competition tends to force prices down and that an inexpensive item may be inferior to one that is more costly. There is some risk, therefore, that competition will cause some suppliers to market a defective product. Similarly, competitive bidding for engineering projects may be inherently imprecise and incapable of taking into account all the variables which will be involved in the actual performance of the project. Based on these considerations, a purchaser might conclude that his interest in quality — which may embrace the safety of the end product — outweighs the advantages of achieving cost savings by pitting one competitor against another. Or an individual vendor might independently refrain from price negotiation until he has satisfied himself that he fully understands the scope of his customers' needs. These decisions might be reasonable; indeed, petitioner has provided ample documentation for that thesis. But these are not reasons that satisfy the Rule; nor are such individual decisions subject to antitrust attack.

The Sherman Act does not require competitive bidding; it prohibits unreasonable restraints on competition. Petitioner's ban on competitive bidding prevents all customers from making price comparisons in the initial selection of an engineer, and imposes the Society's views of the costs and benefits of competition on the entire marketplace. It is this restraint that must be justified under the Rule of Reason, and petitioner's attempt to do so on the basis of the potential threat that competition poses to the public safety and the ethics of its profession is nothing less than a frontal assault on the basic policy of the Sherman Act.

The Sherman Act reflects a legislative judgment that ultimately competition will produce not only lower prices, but also better goods and services. "The heart of our national economic policy long has been faith in the value of competition." *Standard Oil Co. v. FTC*, 340 U.S. 231, 248. The assumption that competition is the best method of allocating resources in a free market recognizes that all elements of a bargain — quality, service, safety, and durability — and not just the immediate cost, are favorably affected by the free opportunity to select among alternative offers. Even assuming occasional exceptions to the presumed consequences of competition, the statutory policy precludes inquiry into the question whether competition is good or bad.

The fact that engineers are often involved in large-scale projects significantly affecting the public safety does not alter our analysis. Exceptions to the Sherman Act for potentially dangerous goods and services would be tantamount to a repeal of the statute. In our complex economy the number of items that may cause serious harm is almost endless — automobiles, drugs, foods, aircraft components, heavy equipment, and countless others, cause serious harm to individuals or to the public at large if defectively made. The judiciary cannot indirectly protect the public against this harm by conferring monopoly privileges on the manufacturers.

By the same token, the cautionary footnote in *Goldfarb*, 421 U.S., at 788-789, n. 17, cannot be read as fashioning a broad exemption under the Rule of Reason for learned professions. We adhere to the view expressed in *Goldfarb* that, by their nature, professional services may differ significantly from other business services, and, accordingly, the nature of the competition in such services may vary. Ethical norms may serve to regulate and promote this competition, and thus fall within the Rule of Reason.[22] But the Society's argument in this case is a far cry from such a position. We are faced with a contention that a total ban on competitive bidding is necessary because otherwise engineers will be tempted to submit deceptively low bids. Certainly, the problem of professional deception is a proper subject of an ethical canon. But, once again, the equation of competition with deception, like the similar equation with safety hazards, is simply too broad; we may assume that competition is not entirely conducive to ethical behavior, but that is not a reason, cognizable under the Sherman Act, for doing away with competition.

In sum, the Rule of Reason does not support a defense based on the assumption that competition itself is unreasonable. Such a view of the Rule would create the "sea of doubt" on which Judge Taft refused to embark in *Addyston*, 85 F., at 284, and which this Court has firmly avoided ever since.

---

[22] Courts have, for instance, upheld marketing restraints related to the safety of a product, provided that they have no anticompetitive effect and that they are reasonably ancillary to the seller's main purpose of protecting the public from harm or itself from product liability. *See, e.g., Tripoli Co. v. Wella Corp.*, 425 F.2d 932 (3d Cir. 1970) (en banc); *cf. Continental T.V.*, 433 U.S., at 55 n. 23. [In *Tripoli* the Third Circuit held that the restraint on wholesale distributors' reselling products to nonprofessionals was not a per se violation because some of the products could cause dangerous adverse effects, and the motivation for the restriction was to protect the public from harm or to protect defendant manufacturer from potential product liability. 425 F.2d, at 932, 936-37.]

III

The judgment entered by the District Court, as modified by the Court of Appeals, prohibits the Society from adopting any official opinion, policy statement, or guideline stating or implying that competitive bidding is unethical. Petitioner argues that this judgment abridges its First Amendment rights. We find no merit in this contention.

Affirmed.

NOTE

The Court's analysis in *Professional Engineers* raised two questions: first, whether the Court would apply the rule of reason to commercial conduct outside a profession and, second, whether the defenses would be limited to economic justifications. In light of the broad per se rule announced in *Socony-Vacuum*, the resolution of these issues seemed critical, because after *Socony-Vacuum* the continued vitality of *Chicago Board of Trade* and *Appalachian Coals* was questionable. But after *Professional Engineers*, the rule of reason analysis was ascendant and *Socony-Vacuum* seemed less important. A partial answer was forthcoming the next year.

BROADCAST MUSIC, INC. V. COLUMBIA BROADCASTING SYSTEM

441 U.S. 1 (1979)

JUSTICE WHITE delivered the opinion of the Court.

This case involves an action under the antitrust and copyright laws brought by respondent Columbia Broadcasting System, Inc. (CBS), against petitioners, American Society of Composers, Authors and Publishers (ASCAP) and Broadcast Music, Inc. (BMI), and their members and affiliates. The basic question presented is whether the issuance by ASCAP and BMI to CBS of blanket licenses to copyrighted musical compositions at fees negotiated by them is price fixing *per se* unlawful under the antitrust laws.

I

CBS operates one of three national commercial television networks, supplying programs to approximately 200 affiliated stations and telecasting approximately 7,500 network programs per year. Many, but not all, of these programs make use of copyrighted music recorded on the soundtrack. CBS also owns television and radio stations in various cities....

Since 1897, the copyright laws have vested in the owner of a copyrighted musical composition the exclusive right to perform the work publicly for profit, but the legal right is not self-enforcing. In 1914, Victor Herbert and a handful of other composers organized ASCAP because those who performed copyrighted music for profit were so numerous and widespread, and most performances so fleeting, that as a practical matter it was impossible for the many individual copyright owners to negotiate with and license the users and to detect unauthorized uses. "ASCAP was organized as a 'clearing-house' for copyright owners and users to solve these problems" associated with the licensing of music. As ASCAP operates today, its 22,000 members grant it nonexclusive rights to license nondramatic performances of their works, and ASCAP issues licenses and distributes royalties to copyright owners in accordance with a schedule reflecting the nature and amount of the use of their music and other factors.

BMI, a nonprofit corporation owned by members of the broadcasting industry, was organized in 1939, is affiliated with or represents some 10,000 publishing companies and 20,000 authors and composers, and operates in much the same manner as ASCAP. Almost every domestic copyrighted composition is in the repertory either of ASCAP, with a total of three million compositions, or of BMI, with one million.

Both organizations operate primarily through blanket licenses, which give the licensees the right to perform any and all of the compositions owned by the members or affiliates as often as the licensees desire for a stated term. Fees for blanket licenses are ordinarily a percentage of total revenues or a flat dollar amount, and do not directly depend on the amount or type of music used. Radio and television broadcasters are the largest users of music, and almost all of them hold blanket licenses from both ASCAP and BMI. Until this litigation, CBS held blanket licenses from both organizations for its television network on a continuous basis since the late 1940's and had never attempted to secure any other form of license from either ASCAP or any of its members.

The complaint filed by CBS charged various violations of the Sherman Act and the copyright laws. CBS argued that ASCAP and BMI are unlawful monopolies and that the blanket license is illegal price fixing, an unlawful tying arrangement, a concerted refusal to deal, and a misuse of copyrights. The District Court, though denying summary judgment to certain defendants, ruled that the practice did not fall within the *per se* rule. After an 8-week trial, limited to the issue of liability, the court dismissed the complaint, rejecting again the claim that the blanket license was price fixing and a *per se* violation of § 1 of the Sherman Act, and holding that since direct negotiation with individual copyright owners is available and feasible there is no undue restraint of trade, illegal tying, misuse of copyrights, or monopolization.

Though agreeing with the District Court's factfinding and not disturbing its legal conclusions on the other antitrust theories of liability, the Court of Appeals held that the blanket license issued to television networks was a form of price fixing illegal *per se* under the Sherman Act. This conclusion, without more, settled the issue of liability under the Sherman Act, established copyright misuse, and required reversal of the District Court's judgment, as well as a remand to consider the appropriate remedy.[10]

---

[10] The Court of Appeals went on to suggest some guidelines as to remedy, indicating that despite its conclusion on liability the blanket license was not totally forbidden. The Court of Appeals said:

... Because we disagree with the Court of Appeals' conclusions with respect to the *per se* illegality of the blanket license, we reverse its judgment and remand the cause for appropriate proceedings.

II

In construing and applying the Sherman Act's ban against contracts, conspiracies, and combinations in restraint of trade, the Court has held that certain agreements or practices are so "plainly anticompetitive," ... and so often "lack ... any redeeming virtue," ... that they are conclusively presumed illegal without further examination under the rule of reason generally applied in Sherman Act cases. This *per se* rule is a valid and useful tool of antitrust policy and enforcement.[11] And agreements among competitors to fix prices on their individual goods or services are among those concerted activities that the Court has held to be within the *per se* category. But easy labels do not always supply ready answers.

A

To the Court of Appeals and CBS, the blanket license involves "price fixing" in the literal sense: the composers and publishing houses have joined together into an organization that sets its price for the blanket license it sells. But this is not a question simply of determining whether two or more potential competitors have literally "fixed" a "price." As generally used in the antitrust field, "price fixing" is a shorthand way of describing certain categories of business behavior to which the *per se* rule has been held applicable. The Court of Appeals' literal

---

Normally, after a finding of price-fixing, the remedy is an injunction against the price-fixing — in this case, the blanket license. We think, however, that if on remand a remedy can be fashioned which will ensure that the blanket license will not affect the price or negotiations for direct licenses, the blanket license need not be prohibited in all circumstances. The blanket license is not simply a "naked restraint" ineluctably doomed to extinction. There is not enough evidence in the present record to compel a finding that the blanket license does not serve a market need for those who wish full protection against infringement suits or who, for some other business reason, deem the blanket license desirable. The blanket license includes a practical covenant not to sue for infringement of any ASCAP copyright as well as an indemnification against suits by others.

Our objection to the blanket license is that it reduces price competition among the members and provides a disinclination to compete. We think that these objections may be removed if ASCAP itself is required to provide some form of per use licensing which will ensure competition among the individual members with respect to those networks which wish to engage in per use licensing. *Id.*, at 140 (footnotes omitted).

[11] "This principle of *per se* unreasonableness not only makes the type of restraints which are proscribed by the Sherman Act more certain to the benefit of everyone concerned, but it also avoids the necessity for an incredibly complicated and prolonged economic investigation into the entire history of the industry involved, as well as related industries, in an effort to determine at large whether a particular restraint has been unreasonable — an inquiry so often wholly fruitless when undertaken." *Northern Pac. Ry. Co. v. United States*, 356 U.S. 1, 5 (1958).

approach does not alone establish that this particular practice is one of those types or that it is "plainly anticompetitive" and very likely without "redeeming virtue." Literalness is overly simplistic and often overbroad. When two partners set the price of their goods or services they are literally "price fixing," but they are not *per se* in violation of the Sherman Act. See *United States v. Addyston Pipe & Steel Co.*, 85 F. 271, 280 (6th Cir. 1898), aff'd, 175 U.S. 211 (1899). Thus, it is necessary to characterize the challenged conduct as falling within or without that category of behavior to which we apply the label "*per se* price fixing." That will often, but not always, be a simple matter.

Consequently, as we recognized in *United States v. Topco Associates, Inc.*, 405 U.S. 596, 607-608 (1972), "[i]t is only after considerable experience with certain business relationships that courts classify them as *per se* violations ...." We have never examined a practice like this one before; indeed, the Court of Appeals recognized that "[i]n dealing with performing rights in the music industry we confront conditions both in copyright law and in antitrust law which are *sui generis*." And though there has been rather intensive antitrust scrutiny of ASCAP and its blanket licenses, that experience hardly counsels that we should outlaw the blanket license as a *per se* restraint of trade.

B

....

The 1950 decree [which resulted from a consent decree entered by ASCAP and the Department of Justice "that imposed tight restrictions on ASCAP's operations," including giving ASCAP "only nonexclusive rights to license" works], as amended from time to time, continues in effect, and the blanket license continues to be the primary instrument through which ASCAP conducts its business under the decree. The courts have twice construed the decree not to require ASCAP to issue licenses for selected portions of its repertory. It also remains true that the decree guarantees the legal availability of direct licensing of performance rights by ASCAP members; and the District Court found, and in this respect the Court of Appeals agreed, that there are no practical impediments preventing direct dealing by the television networks if they so desire. Historically, they have not done so. Since 1946, CBS and other television networks have taken blanket licenses from ASCAP and BMI. It was not until this suit arose that the CBS network demanded any other kind of license.

Of course, a consent judgment, even one entered at the behest of the Antitrust Division, does not immunize the defendant from liability for actions, including those contemplated by the decree, that violate the rights of nonparties. But it cannot be ignored that the Federal Executive and Judiciary have carefully scrutinized ASCAP and the challenged conduct, have imposed restrictions on various of ASCAP's practices, and, by the terms of the decree, stand ready to provide further consideration, supervision, and perhaps invalidation of asserted anticompetitive practices. In these circumstances, we have a unique indicator that the challenged practice may have redeeming competitive virtues and that the search for those values is not almost sure to be in vain. Thus, although CBS is not bound by the Antitrust Division's actions, the decree is a fact of economic and legal life in this industry, and the Court of Appeals should not have ignored it completely in analyzing the practice. That fact alone might not remove a naked price-fixing scheme from the ambit of the *per se* rule, but, as discussed *infra*, Part III, here we are uncertain whether the practice on its face has the effect, or could have been spurred by the purpose, of restraining competition among the individual composers.

....

III

Finally, we note that Congress itself, in the new Copyright Act, has chosen to employ the blanket license and similar practices. Congress created a compulsory blanket license for secondary transmissions by cable television systems and provided that "[n]otwithstanding any provisions of the antitrust laws, ... any claimants may agree among themselves as to the proportionate division of compulsory licensing fees among them, may lump their claims together and file them jointly or as a single claim, or may designate a common agent to receive payment on their behalf." 17 U.S.C. App. § 111 (d) (5) (A). And the newly created compulsory license for the use of copyrighted compositions in jukeboxes is also a blanket license, which is payable to the performing-rights societies such as ASCAP unless an individual copyright holder can prove his entitlement to a share. § 116 (c) (4). Moreover, in requiring noncommercial broadcasters to pay for their use of copyrighted music, Congress again provided that "[n]otwithstanding any provision of the antitrust laws" copyright owners "may designate common agents to negotiate, agree to, pay, or receive payments." § 118 (b). Though these provisions are not directly controlling, they do reflect an opinion that the blanket license, and ASCAP, are economically beneficial in at least some circumstances.

....

As a preliminary matter, we are mindful that the Court of Appeals' holding would appear to be quite difficult to contain. If, as the court held, there is a *per se* antitrust violation whenever ASCAP issues a blanket license to a television network for a single fee, why would it not also be automatically illegal for ASCAP to negotiate and issue blanket licenses to individual radio or television stations or to other users who perform copyrighted music for profit? Likewise, if the present network licenses issued through ASCAP on behalf of its members are *per se* violations, why would it not be equally illegal for the members to authorize ASCAP to issue licenses establishing various categories of uses that a network might have for copyrighted music and setting a standard fee for each described use?

Although the Court of Appeals apparently thought the blanket license could be saved in some or even many applications, it seems to us that the *per se* rule does not accommodate itself to such flexibility and that the observations of the Court of Appeals with respect to remedy tend to impeach the *per se* basis for the holding of liability.[27]

CBS would prefer that ASCAP be authorized, indeed directed, to make all its compositions available at standard per-use rates within negotiated categories of use.... But if this in itself or in conjunction with blanket licensing constitutes illegal price fixing by copyright owners, CBS urges that an injunction issue forbidding ASCAP to issue any blanket license or to negotiate any fee except on behalf of an individual member for the use of his own copyrighted work or works. Thus, we are called upon to determine that blanket licensing is unlawful across the board. We are quite sure, however, that the *per se* rule does not require any such holding.

B

... Although the copyright laws confer no rights on copyright owners to fix prices among themselves or otherwise to violate the antitrust laws, we would not expect that any market arrangements reasonably necessary to effectuate the rights that are granted would be deemed a *per se* violation of the Sherman Act. Otherwise, the commerce anticipated by the Copyright Act and protected against restraint by the Sherman Act would not exist at all or would exist only as a pale reminder of what Congress envisioned.

C

More generally, in characterizing this conduct under the *per se* rule, our inquiry must focus on whether the effect and, here because it tends to show effect, the purpose of the practice are to threaten the proper operation of our predominantly free-market economy — that is, whether the practice facially appears to be one that would always or almost always tend to restrict competition and decrease output, and in what portion of the market, or instead one designed to "increase economic efficiency and render markets more, rather than less, competitive."...

---

[27] The Court of Appeals would apparently not outlaw the blanket license across the board but would permit it in various circumstances where it is deemed necessary or sufficiently desirable. It did not even enjoin blanket licensing with the television networks, the relief it realized would normally follow a finding of *per se* illegality of the license in that context. Instead, as requested by CBS, it remanded to the District Court to require ASCAP to offer in addition to blanket licensing some competitive form or per-use licensing. But per-use licensing by ASCAP, as recognized in the consent decrees, might be even more susceptible to the *per se* rule than blanket licensing.

The rationale for this unusual relief in a *per se* case was that "[t]he blanket license is not simply a 'naked restraint' ineluctably doomed to extinction." 562 F.2d, at 140. To the contrary, the Court of Appeals found that the blanket license might well "serve a market need" for some. *Ibid.* This, it seems to us, is not the *per se* approach, which does not yield so readily to circumstances, but in effect is a rather bobtailed application of the rule of reason, bobtailed in the sense that it is unaccompanied by the necessary analysis demonstrating why the particular licensing system is an undue competitive restraint.

The blanket license, as we see it, is not a "naked restrain[t] of trade with no purpose except stifling of competition," but rather accompanies the integration of sales, monitoring, and enforcement against unauthorized copyright use. As we have already indicated, ASCAP and the blanket license developed together out of the practical situation in the marketplace: thousands of users, thousands of copyright owners, and millions of compositions. Most users want unplanned, rapid, and indemnified access to any and all of the repertory of compositions, and the owners want a reliable method of collecting for the use of their copyrights. Individual sales transactions in this industry are quite expensive, as would be individual monitoring and enforcement, especially in light of the resources of single composers. Indeed, as both the Court of Appeals and CBS recognize, the costs are prohibitive for licenses with individual radio stations, nightclubs, and restaurants, and it was in that milieu that the blanket license arose.

A middleman with a blanket license was an obvious necessity if the thousands of individual negotiations, a virtual impossibility, were to be avoided. Also, individual fees for the use of individual compositions would presuppose an intricate schedule of fees and uses, as well as a difficult and expensive reporting problem for the user and policing task for the copyright owner. Historically, the market for public-performance rights organized itself largely around the single-fee blanket license, which gave unlimited access to the repertory and reliable protection against infringement. When ASCAP's major and user-created competitor, BMI, came on the scene, it also turned to the blanket license.

With the advent of radio and television networks, market conditions changed, and the necessity for and advantages of a blanket license for those users may be far less obvious than is the case when the potential users are individual television or radio stations, or the thousands of other individuals and organizations performing copyrighted compositions in public. But even for television network licenses, ASCAP reduces costs absolutely by creating a blanket license that is sold only a few, instead of thousands, of times, and that obviates the need for closely monitoring the networks to see that they do not use more than they pay for. ASCAP also provides the necessary resources for blanket sales and enforcement, resources unavailable to the vast majority of composers and publishing houses. Moreover, a bulk license of some type is a necessary consequence of the integration necessary to achieve these efficiencies, and a necessary consequence of an aggregate license is that its price must be established.

D

This substantial lowering of costs, which is of course potentially beneficial to both sellers and buyers, differentiates the blanket license from individual use licenses. The blanket license is composed of the individual compositions plus the aggregating service. Here, the whole is truly greater than the sum of its parts; it is, to some extent, a different product. The blanket license has certain unique characteristics: It allows the licensee immediate use of covered compositions, without the delay of prior individual negotiations, and great flexibility in the choice of musical material. Many consumers clearly prefer the characteristics and cost advantages of this marketable package, and even small performing-rights societies that have occasionally arisen to compete with ASCAP and BMI have offered blanket licenses. Thus, to the extent the blanket license is a different product, ASCAP is not really a joint sales agency offering the individual goods of many sellers, but is a separate seller offering its blanket license, of which the individual compositions are raw material. ASCAP, in short, made a market in which individual composers are inherently unable to compete fully effectively.

E

Finally, we have some doubt — enough to counsel against application of the *per se* rule — about the extent to which this practice threatens the "central nervous system of the economy," *United States v. Socony-Vacuum Oil Co.*, 310 U.S. 150, 226 n. 59 (1940), that is, competitive pricing as the free market's means of allocating resources. Not all arrangements among actual or potential competitors that have an impact on price are *per se* violations of the Sherman Act or even unreasonable restraints. Mergers among competitors eliminate competition, including price competition, but they are not *per se* illegal, and many of them withstand attack under any existing antitrust standard. Joint ventures and other cooperative arrangements are also not usually unlawful, at least not as price-fixing schemes, where the agreement on price is necessary to market the product at all.

Here, the blanket-license fee is not set by competition among individual copyright owners, and it is a fee for the use of any of the compositions covered by the license. But the blanket license cannot be wholly equated with a simple horizontal arrangement among competitors. ASCAP does set the price for its blanket license, but that license is quite different from anything any individual owner could issue. The individual composers and authors have neither agreed not to sell individually in any other market nor use the blanket license to mask price fixing in such other markets. Moreover, the substantial restraints placed on ASCAP and its members by the consent decree must not be ignored. The District Court found that there was no legal, practical, or conspiratorial impediment to CBS's obtaining individual licenses; CBS, in short, had a real choice.

With this background in mind, which plainly enough indicates that over the years, and in the face of available alternatives, the blanket license has provided an acceptable mechanism for at least a large part of the market for the performing rights to copyrighted musical compositions, we cannot agree that it should automatically be declared illegal in all of its many manifestations. Rather, when attacked, it should be subjected to a more discriminating examination under the rule of reason. It may not ultimately survive that attack, but that is not the issue before us today.

IV

... We reverse that judgment [of the Court of Appeals] and the copyright misuse judgment dependent upon it, and remand for further proceedings to consider any unresolved issues that CBS may have properly brought to the Court of Appeals.

[The dissenting opinion of Justice Stevens is omitted. On remand, the Second Circuit held that under the efficiency standard employed by the Court, the blanket licensing did not create an unreasonable restraint because the individual transaction costs were too high for individual licensing to work competitively. *CBS, Inc. v. ASCAP*, 620 F.2d 930 (1st Cir. 1980). The Second Circuit also found that since the blanket license did not prohibit the freedom of individual composers from direct licensing, price competition was not eliminated by the arrangement.]

NOTES AND QUESTIONS

1. Did *Professional Engineers* and *Broadcast Music* indicate a shift away from a broad reading of the "tamper with price structure" standard of *Socony-Vacuum*? Can these cases be reconciled with *Socony-Vacuum*? Did the Court in each apply a rule of reason analysis? How does Justice Stevens define the boundaries of the decisional analysis after *Professional Engineers*? Under this standard, why did the engineers' defense fail? Are there any conditions under which the Court might accept the "quality/safety" defense? Might the ancillary restraint doctrine have application under this defense? Do you accept Justice Stevens' Sherman Act assumption that "competition will produce not only lower prices, but also better goods and services"? Might noneconomic values be important as well?

2. Does *Professional Engineers* articulate how a trial judge is to measure the net competitive effect of a restraint? In measuring the competitive benefits versus the costs of the restraint might the outcome differ depending whether the restraint is engaged in by a professional organization rather than a commercial venture?

3. After *Professional Engineers* and *Broadcast Music*, how should you define the scope of the per se rule's application? Is a competitive benefit/harm analysis permitted before the per se label is attached? How direct must the effect on price be before a per se classification will result?

4. What justification did the Court give in *Broadcast Music* for approving one kind of analysis for the market facilitating scheme in *Socony-Vacuum* and another in *Broadcast Music*? Consider whether the distinction can be based on economic efficiency and the reduction of transaction costs and whether output is limited.

5. CBS asked the lower court to force ASCAP to "make all its compositions available at standard per-use rates within negotiated categories of use." Wouldn't this be just as illegal under the Sherman Act as the blanket licensing scheme? Artists would still be "agreeing" on a uniform fee within a particular category of music, and ASCAP would obtain the fee for them.

The lower court actually found rather few alternatives to blanket licensing that would avoid all price agreements. One would be to require each radio station or network to purchase individually each right to play a composition from the owner of the performance right. A radio station that played 100 different songs would engage in 100 separate transactions. In this case transaction costs alone (that is, the costs of negotiating the individual contracts) would have been far greater than the total price that many stations were paying for the right to play a particular composition. An alternative would have been for the purchaser to go to each composer and obtain performance rights for everything that composer owned. The district court expressly found that many artists would have been willing to negotiate with CBS for such rights. CBS represented thousands of affiliated radio stations, and could negotiate for all of them together. How about the small, unaffiliated radio station that would also have to negotiate with each artist individually?

Professor Richard Friedman posits this solution: What if the blanket license agreement were eliminated in favor of allowing ASCAP and BMI to license each artist's product at a rate posted by the artists, thus obviating the need for users to negotiate with each artist. Would his solution avoid the anticompetitive effect of the blanket license? Would it increase the costs to the user? Should the absence of a less restrictive alternative incline the court to condemn the current arrangement?

6. The marginal cost to a performance right holder of having his composition played is virtually zero. Furthermore, capacity in the industry is infinite. Once a song is composed it can be played 1,000,000 times as easily as 10 times. In a competitive market, wouldn't you therefore expect the performance rights to compositions to be sold for almost nothing? That would certainly be true if the product were fungible. For example, if one hundred different people owned performance rights to "Born in the U.S.A.," and competed with each other in the sale of those rights, we would expect the price of the right to perform "Born in the U.S.A." to be extremely small. In fact, however, listeners differentiate substantially between songs. If one person owns the performance rights to "Born in the U.S.A.," another to "Graceland," a third to "Sergeant Pepper's Lonely Hearts Club Band," etc., we would expect each to sell performance rights at substantially above marginal cost. The different owners of the performance rights to different compositions are monopolists, some of whom have substantial market power, which is the power to set a profit-maximizing price above marginal cost. But if they are all monopolists, then the rights that each of them offers is a distinct "product."

Is it a price fixing agreement when a manufacturer of wheelbarrows and a manufacturer of bicycles get together and agree that each will charge $100 for its product? What can they hope to accomplish? This analysis suggests that the most likely explanation for the blanket licensing program was the reduction of transaction costs, and these would have been substantial under alternative arrangements.

7. One reading of the opinions in *Professional Engineers* and *Broadcast Music* is that the Burger Court was more inclined to avoid initially a rigid per se analysis so that it could explore the business justification for the conduct and whether it promotes market integration and economic efficiency without sacrificing output. Implicitly, *Socony* seemed to be on the decline. The next term of the Court, however, signaled the continued validity of the summary per se analysis, though a subsequent opinion indicates that the Court continues to vacillate on where the line should be drawn in defining price fixing agreements.

8. In *All-Care Nursing Service v. High Tech Staffing Services*, 135 F.3d 740 (11th Cir. 1998), the court applied the rule of reason and then upheld an agreement by hospitals to create a PPP, or preferred provider program. Under the program the hospitals jointly took competitive bids for providers of nursing services, and then used the services provided by winning bidders to the full extent of their capacity before turning to other nursing services. The plaintiff was one of the losing bidders. The court wrote:

> Plaintiffs-appellants claim that the PPP's arrangement is per se illegal as both price fixing and as a group boycott. Thus, plaintiffs-appellants have the burden to make a threshold showing that the PPP falls into one of these forbidden categories. In this case, plaintiffs-appellants allege that, because price bids were a consideration in determining which temporary nurse agencies would become preferred providers, this conduct falls into the forbidden category of price fixing. They also claim that the exclusion of the non-preferred agencies from the PPP amounts to a group boycott....
>
> But, the PPP, arranged by the SFHA and the Palm Beach County hospitals, is not inherently an anticompetitive practice. No temporary nursing agency was precluded from competing to become a preferred agency. Also, all agencies are still able to provide nurses to medical facilities other than hospitals and even to hospitals should the need for nurses not be met by the preferred agencies. Although the PPP may stabilize prices to some degree, it is not the kind of "stabilization" that can be viewed as price fixing, especially when the escape clauses in the contracts are taken into account. These escape clauses allow the market and not the SFHA to be the ultimate decisionmaker for each hospital and each agency on the issues of price, demand, supply, and terms of dealing.

On the refusal to deal claim, the court noted:

> In this case, no refusal to deal has been shown. All agencies were able to participate in the bidding to become preferred providers, and generally a hospital will still deal with any nursing agency when the preferred agencies with which the hospital has contracted for nursing services fail to meet its needs. The record shows, in fact, that more than a trifling portion of hospital nursing business in Palm Beach County continued to go to nonpreferred agencies after the PPP was in operation. Also, due to the rise in HMOs, home care, and similar trends in the medical world, facilities other than hos-

pitals provide the market, the supply, and the facilities necessary for non-preferred agencies to compete with each other and with preferred agencies in the marketplace.

Per se treatment has been given to those practices which history has shown have only anticompetitive effects. "[A]nalyzing this case under the per se rubric would remain inappropriate absent some demonstration that the practice at issue historically leads to anticompetitive effects in the market." No history of this kind seems to exist for health-care preferred-provider programs materially similar to what we have before us now.

We conclude, based upon undisputed facts, that the practice of this PPP is not deserving of per se treatment and was properly evaluated under the rule of reason.

The court then dismissed the complaint for lack of a market power showing.

CATALANO, INC. V. TARGET SALES, INC.

446 U.S. 643 (1980)

PER CURIAM.

Petitioners, a conditionally certified class of brewer retailers in the Fresno, Cal. area, brought suit against respondent wholesalers alleging that they had conspired to eliminate short term trade credit formerly granted on beer purchases in violation of § 1 of the Sherman Act. The District Court entered an interlocutory order, which among other things, denied petitioners' "motion to declare this a case of *per se* illegality," and then certified to the United States Court of Appeals for the Ninth Circuit, pursuant to 28 U.S.C. § 1292(b), the question whether the alleged agreement among competitors fixing credit terms, if proven, was unlawful on its face. The Court of Appeals granted permission to appeal, and, with one judge dissenting, agreed with the District Court that a horizontal agreement among competitors to fix credit terms does not necessarily contravene the antitrust laws....

For purposes of decision we assume the following facts alleged in the amended complaint to be true. Petitioners allege that, beginning in early 1967, respondent wholesalers secretly agreed, in order to eliminate competition among themselves, that as of December 1967 they would sell to retailers only if payment were made in advance or upon delivery. Prior to the agreement, the wholesalers had extended credit without interest up to the 30 and 42 day limits permitted by state law. According to the Petition, prior to the agreement wholesalers had competed with each other with respect to trade credit, and the credit terms for individual retailers had varied substantially. After entering into the agreement, respondents uniformly refused to extend any credit at all.

The Court of Appeals decided that the credit fixing agreement should not be characterized as a form of price fixing. The court suggested that such an agreement might actually enhance competition in two ways: (1) "by removing a barrier perceived by some sellers to entry," and (2) "by the increased visibility of prices made possible by the agreement to eliminate credit."

In dissent, Judge Blumenfeld expressed the opinion that an agreement to eliminate credit was a form of price fixing. He reasoned that the extension of interest-free credit is an indirect price reduction and that the elimination of such credit is therefore a method of raising prices:

> The purchase of goods creates an obligation to pay for them. Credit is one component of the overall price paid for a product. The cost to a retailer of purchasing goods consists of (1) the amount he has to pay to obtain the goods, and (2) the date on which he has to make that payment. If there is a differential between a purchase for cash and one on time, that difference is not interest but part of the price. Allowing a retailer interest-free short-term credit on beer purchases effectively reduces the price of beer, when compared to a requirement that the retailer pay the same amount immediately in cash; and conversely, the elimination of free credit is the equivalent of price increase.

It followed, in his view, that the agreement was just as plainly anticompetitive as a direct agreement to raise prices. Consequently, no further inquiry under the rule of reason, see *National Society of Professional Engineers v. United States*, 435 U.S. 679 (1978), was required in order to establish the agreement's unlawfulness.

Our cases fully support Judge Blumenfeld's analysis and foreclose both of the possible justifications on which the majority relied.[8] In *Broadcast Music*, we said:

> In construing and applying the Sherman Act's ban against contracts, conspiracies, and combinations in restraint of trade, the Court has held that certain agreements or practices are so "plainly anticompetitive,"... and so often "lack ... any redeeming virtue," that they are conclusively presumed illegal without further examination under the rule of reason generally applied in Sherman Act cases."

A horizontal agreement to fix prices is the archetypal example of such a practice. It has long been settled that an agreement to fix prices is unlawful *per se*. It is no excuse that the prices fixed are themselves reasonable.... [In *Socony-Vacuum*] we held that an agreement among competitors to engage in a program of buying surplus gasoline on the spot market in order to prevent prices from falling sharply to be unlawful without any inquiry into the reasonableness of the program, even though there was no direct agreement on the actual prices to be maintained. In the course of the opinion, the Court made clear that the machinery employed by a combination for price-fixing is immaterial.

---

[8] Respondents nowhere suggest a procompetitive justification for a horizontal agreement to fix credit. Their argument is confined to disputing that settled case law establishes that such an agreement is unlawful on its face.

Under the Sherman Act a combination formed for the purpose and with the effect of raising, depressing, fixing, pegging, or stabilizing the price of a commodity in interstate or foreign commerce is illegal *per se.*

Thus, we have held agreements to be unlawful *per se* that had substantially less direct impact on price than the agreement alleged in this case. For example, in *Sugar Institute v. United States*, 297 U.S. 533, 601-602 (1933), the Court held unlawful an agreement to adhere to previously announced prices and terms of sale, even though advance price announcements are perfectly lawful and even though the particular prices and terms were not themselves fixed by private agreement. Similarly, an agreement among competing firms of professional engineers to refuse to discuss prices with potential customers until after negotiations have resulted in the initial selection of an engineer was held unlawful without requiring further inquiry. *National Society of Professional Engineers v. United States.* Indeed, a horizontal agreement among competitors to use a specific method of quoting prices [multiple basing point pricing system] may be unlawful. *Cf. Federal Trade Commission v. Cement Institute.*

It is virtually self evident that extending interest-free credit for a period of time is equivalent to giving a discount equal to the value of the use of the purchase price for that period of time. Thus, credit terms must be characterized as an inseparable part of the price. An agreement to terminate the practice of giving credit is thus tantamount to an agreement to eliminate discounts, and thus falls squarely within the traditional *per se* rule against price fixing. While it may be that the elimination of a practice of giving variable discounts will ultimately lead in a competitive market to corresponding decreases in the invoice price, that is surely not necessarily to be anticipated. It is more realistic to view an agreement to eliminate credit sales as extinguishing one form of competition among the sellers. In any event, when a particular concerted activity entails an obvious risk of anticompetitive impact with no apparent potentially redeeming value, the fact that a practice may turn out to be harmless in a particular set of circumstances will not prevent its being declared unlawful *per se.*

The majority of the panel of the Court of Appeals suggested, however, that a horizontal agreement to eliminate credit sales may remove a barrier to other sellers who may wish to enter the market. But in any case in which competitors are able to increase the price level or to curtail production by agreement, it could be argued that the agreement has the effect of making the market more attractive to potential new entrants. If that potential justifies horizontal agreements among competitors imposing one kind of voluntary restraint or another on their competitive freedom, it would seem to follow that the more successful an agreement is in raising the price level, the safer it is from antitrust attack. Nothing could be more inconsistent with our cases.

Nor can the informing function of the agreement, the increased price visibility, justify its restraint on the individual wholesaler's freedom to select his own prices and terms of sale. For, again, it is obvious that any industry wide agreement on prices will result in a more accurate understanding of the terms offered by all parties to the agreement. As the *Sugar Institute* case demonstrates, however, there is a plain distinction between the lawful right to publish prices and terms of sale, on the one hand, and an agreement among competitors limiting action with respect to the published prices, on the other.

Thus, under the reasoning of our cases, an agreement among competing wholesaler to refuse to sell unless the retailer makes payment in cash either in advance or upon delivery is "plainly anticompetitive." Since it is merely one form of price fixing, and since price-fixing agreements have been adjudged to lack any "redeeming virtue," it is conclusively presumed illegal without further examination under the rule of reason.

Accordingly, the judgment of the Court of Appeals is reversed, and the case is remanded for further proceedings consistent with this opinion.

ARIZONA V. MARICOPA COUNTY MEDICAL SOCIETY

457 U.S. 332 (1982)

JUSTICE STEVENS delivered the opinion of the Court.

The question presented is whether § 1 of the Sherman Act, 15 U.S.C. § 1, has been violated by an agreement among competing physicians setting, by majority vote, the maximum fees that they may claim in full payment for health services provided to policyholders of specified insurance plans. The United States Court of Appeals for the Ninth Circuit held that the question could not be answered without evaluating the actual purpose and effect of the agreement at a full trial.... Because the undisputed facts disclose a violation of the statute, we granted certiorari, and now reverse.

....

II

The Maricopa Foundation for Medical Care is a non-profit Arizona corporation composed of licensed doctors of medicine, osteopathy, and podiatry engaged in private practice. Approximately 1,750 doctors, representing about 70% of the practitioners in Maricopa County, are members.

... The foundation performs three primary activities. It establishes the schedule of maximum fees that participating doctors agree to accept as payment in full for services performed for patients insured under plans approved by the foundation. It reviews the medical necessity and appropriateness of treatment provided by its members to such insured persons. It is authorized to draw checks on insurance company accounts to pay doctors for services performed for covered patients. In performing these functions, the foundation is considered an "insurance administrator" by the Director of the Arizona Department of Insurance. Its participating doctors, however, have no financial interest in the operation of the foundation. [A similar foundation, the Pima Foundation for Medical Care, had 400 member doctors.]

At the time this lawsuit was filed, each foundation made use of "relative values" and "conversion factors" in compiling its fee schedule.

The fee schedules limit the amount that the member doctors may recover for services performed for patients insured under plans approved by the foundations. To obtain this approval the insurers — including self-insured employers as well as insurance companies — agree to pay the doctors' charges up to the scheduled amounts, and in exchange the doctors agree to accept those amounts as payment in full for their services. The doctors are free to charge higher fees to uninsured patients and they also may charge any patient less than the scheduled maxima. A patient who is insured by a foundation-endorsed plan is guaranteed complete coverage for the full amount of his medical bills only if he is treated by a foundation member. He is free to go to a nonmember physician and is still covered for charges that do not exceed the maximum fee schedule, but he must pay any excess that the nonmember physician may charge.

The impact of the foundation fee schedules on medical fees and on insurance premiums is a matter of dispute. The State of Arizona contends that the periodic upward revisions of the maximum fee schedules have the effect of stabilizing and enhancing the level of actual charges by physicians, and that the increasing level of their fees in turn increases insurance premiums. The foundations, on the other hand, argue that the schedules impose a meaningful limit on physicians' charges, and that the advance agreement by the doctors to accept the maxima enables the insurance carriers to limit and to calculate more efficiently the risks they underwrite and therefore serves as an effective cost containment mechanism that has saved patients and insurers millions of dollars....

III

The respondents recognize that our decisions establish that price fixing agreements are unlawful on their face. But they argue that the *per se* rule does not govern this case because the agreements at issue are horizontal and fix maximum prices, are among members of a profession, are in an industry with which the judiciary has little antitrust experience, and are alleged to have procompetitive justifications....

A

....

The application of the *per se* rule to maximum price fixing agreements in *Kiefer-Stewart Co. v. Seagram & Sons*, 340 U.S. 211 (1951), followed ineluctably from *Socony-Vacuum*:

> For such agreements, no less than those to fix minimum prices, cripple the freedom of traders and thereby restrain their ability to sell in accordance with their own judgment. We reaffirm what we said in *United States v. Socony-Vacuum Oil Co.*, 310 U.S. 150, 223: "Under the Sherman Act a com-

bination formed for the purpose and with the effect of raising, depressing, fixing, pegging, or stabilizing the price of a commodity in interstate or foreign commerce is illegal *per se.*" *Id.*, at 213.

Over the objection that maximum price fixing agreements were not the "economic equivalent" of minimum price fixing agreements, *Kiefer-Stewart* was reaffirmed in *Albrecht v. Herald Co.*, 390 U.S. 145 (1968):

> Maximum and minimum price fixing may have different consequences in many situations. But schemes to fix maximum prices, by substituting the perhaps erroneous judgment of a seller for the forces of the competitive market, may severely intrude upon the ability of buyers to compete and survive in that market. Competition, even in a single product, is not cast in a single mold. Maximum prices may be fixed too low for the dealer to furnish services essential to the value which goods have for the consumer or to furnish services and conveniences which consumers desire and for which they are willing to pay. Maximum price fixing may channel distribution through a few large or specifically advantaged dealers who otherwise would be subject to significant nonprice competition. Moreover, if the actual price charged under a maximum price scheme is nearly always the fixed maximum price, which is increasingly likely as the maximum price approaches the actual cost of the dealer, the scheme tends to acquire all the attributes of an arrangement fixing minimum prices. *Id.*, at 152-153.

We have not wavered in our enforcement of the *per se* rule against price fixing. Indeed, in our most recent price fixing case we summarily reversed the decision of another Ninth Circuit panel that a horizontal agreement among competitors to fix credit terms does not necessarily contravene the antitrust laws. *Catalano, Inc. v. Target Sales, Inc.*

B

Our decisions foreclose the argument that the agreements at issue escape *per se* condemnation because they are horizontal and fix maximum prices. *Kiefer-Stewart* and *Albrecht* place horizontal agreements to fix maximum prices on the same legal — even if not economic — footing as agreements to fix minimum or uniform prices. The *per se* rule "is grounded on faith in price competition as a market force [and not] on a policy of low selling prices at the price of eliminating competition." In this case the rule is violated by a price restraint that tends to provide the same economic rewards to all practitioners regardless of their skill, their experience, their training, or their willingness to employ innovative and difficult procedures in individual cases. Such a restraint also may discourage entry into the market and may deter experimentation and new developments by individual entrepreneurs. It may be a masquerade for an agreement to fix uniform prices, or it may in the future take on that character.

Nor does the fact that doctors — rather than nonprofessionals — are the parties to the price fixing agreements support the respondents' position…. The price fixing agreements in this case … are not premised on public service or ethical norms. The respondents do not argue, … that the quality of the professional service that their members provide is enhanced by the price restraint. The respondents' claim for relief from the *per se* rule is simply that the doctors' agreement not to charge certain insureds more than a fixed price facilitates the successful marketing of an attractive insurance plan. But the claim that the price restraint will make it easier for customers to pay does not distinguish the medical profession from any other provider of goods or services.

We are equally unpersuaded by the argument that we should not apply the *per se* rule in this case because the judiciary has little antitrust experience in the health care industry.[19] The argument quite obviously is inconsistent with *Socony-Vacuum*. In unequivocal terms, we stated that, "[w]hatever may be its peculiar problems and characteristics, the Sherman Act, so far as price-fixing agreements are concerned, establishes one uniform rule applicable to all industries alike." We also stated that "[t]he elimination of so-called competitive evils [in an industry] is no legal justification" for price fixing agreements, yet the Court of Appeals refused to apply the *per se* rule in this case in part because the health care industry was so far removed from the competitive model…. Finally, the argument that the *per se* rule must be rejustified for every industry that has not been subject to significant antitrust litigation ignores the rationale for *per se* rules, which in part is to avoid "the necessity for an incredibly complicated and prolonged economic investigation into the entire history of the industry involved, as well as related industries, in an effort to determine at large whether a particular restraint has been unreasonable — an inquiry so often wholly fruitless when undertaken."

The respondents' principal argument is that the *per se* rule is inapplicable because their agreements are alleged to have procompetitive justifications. The argument indicates a misunderstanding of the *per se* concept. The anticompetitive potential inherent in all price fixing agreements justifies their facial invalidation even if procompetitive justifications are offered for some. Those claims of enhanced competition are so unlikely to prove significant in any particular case that we adhere to the rule of law that is justified in its general application. Even when the respondents are given every benefit of the doubt, the limited record in this case is not inconsistent with the presumption that the respondents' agreements will not significantly enhance competition.

The respondents contend that their fee schedules are procompetitive because they make it possible to provide consumers of health care with a uniquely de-

---

[19] The argument should not be confused with the established position that a *new per se* rule is not justified until the judiciary obtains considerable rule of reason experience with the particular type of restraint challenged.

sirable form of insurance coverage that could not otherwise exist. The features of the foundation-endorsed insurance plans that they stress are a choice of doctors, complete insurance coverage, and lower premiums. The first two characteristics, however, are hardly unique to these plans. Since only about 70% of the doctors in the relevant market are members of either foundation, the guarantee of complete coverage only applies when an insured chooses a physician in that 70%. If he elects to go to a non-foundation doctor, he may be required to pay a portion of the doctor's fee. It is fair to presume, however, that at least 70% of the doctors in other markets charge no more than the "usual, customary, and reasonable" fee that typical insurers are willing to reimburse in full. Thus, in Maricopa and Pima Counties as well as in most parts of the country, if an insured asks his doctor if the insurance coverage is complete, presumably in about 70% of the cases the doctor will say yes and in about 30% of the cases he will say no.

It is true that a binding assurance of complete insurance coverage — as well as most of the respondents' potential for lower insurance premiums — can be obtained only if the insurer and the doctor agree in advance on the maximum fee that the doctor will accept as full payment for a particular service. Even if a fee schedule is therefore desirable, it is not necessary that the doctors do the price fixing. The record indicates that the Arizona Comprehensive Medical Dental Program for Foster Children is administered by the Maricopa foundation pursuant to a contract under which the maximum fee schedule is prescribed by a state agency rather than by the doctors....

Having declined the respondents' invitation to cut back on the *per se* rule against price fixing, we are left with the respondents' argument that their fee schedules involve price fixing in only a literal sense. For this argument, the respondents rely upon *Broadcast Music, Inc. v. Columbia Broadcasting System, Inc.*, 441 U.S. 1 (1979).

In *Broadcast Music* we were confronted with an antitrust challenge to the marketing of the right to use copyrighted compositions derived from the entire membership of ASCAP. The so-called "blanket license" was entirely different from the product that any one composer was able to sell by himself.[31] Although there was little competition among individual composers for their separate compositions, the blanket license arrangement did not place any restraint on the right of any individual copyright owner to sell his own compositions separately to any buyer at any price. But a "necessary consequence" of the creation of the blanket license was that its price had to be established. We held that the delegation by the composers to ASCAP of the power to fix the price for the blanket license was not a species of the price fixing agreements categorically forbidden by the Sherman Act. The record disclosed price fixing only in a "literal sense."

---

[31] "Thus, to the extent the blanket license is a different product, ASCAP is not really a joint sales agency offering the individual goods of many sellers, but is a separate seller offering its blanket license, of which the individual compositions are raw material." 441 U.S. 1, 22 (1979).

This case is fundamentally different. Each of the foundations is composed of individual practitioners who compete with one another for patients. Neither the foundations nor the doctors sell insurance, and they derive no profits from the sale of health insurance policies. The members of the foundations sell medical services. Their combination in the form of the foundation does not permit them to sell any different product. Their combination has merely permitted them to sell their services to certain customers at fixed prices and arguably to affect the prevailing market price of medical care.

The foundations are not analogous to partnerships or other joint arrangements in which persons who would otherwise be competitors pool their capital and share the risks of loss as well as the opportunities for profit. In such joint ventures the partnership is regarded as a single firm competing with other sellers in the market. The agreement under attack is an agreement among hundreds of competing doctors concerning the price at which each will offer his own services to a substantial number of consumers. It is true that some are surgeons, some anesthesiologists, and some psychiatrists, but the doctors do not sell a package of three kinds of services. If a clinic offered complete medical coverage for a flat fee, the cooperating doctors would have the type of partnership arrangement in which a price fixing agreement among the doctors would be perfectly proper. But the fee agreements disclosed by the record in this case are among independent competing entrepreneurs. They fit squarely into the horizontal price fixing mold.

The judgment of the Court of Appeals is reversed.

JUSTICE POWELL dissenting, with whom the CHIEF JUSTICE and JUSTICE REHNQUIST join.

I do not think today's decision on an incomplete record is consistent with proper judicial resolution of an issue of this complexity, novelty, and importance to the public. I therefore dissent.

.....

II

This case comes to us on a plaintiff's motion for summary judgment after only limited discovery. Therefore, as noted above, the inferences to be drawn from the record must be viewed in the light most favorable to the respondents. This requires, as the Court acknowledges, that we consider the foundation arrangement as one that "impose[s] a meaningful limit on physicians' charges," that "enables the insurance carriers to limit and to calculate more efficiently the risks they underwrite," and that "therefore serves as an effective cost containment mechanism that has saved patients and insurers millions of dollars." The question is whether we should condemn this arrangement forthwith under the Sherman Act, a law designed to *benefit* consumers.

Several other aspects of the record are of key significance but are not stressed by the Court. First, the foundation arrangement forecloses *no* competition. Unlike the classic cartel agreement, the foundation plan does not instruct potential competitors: "Deal with consumers on the following terms and no others." Rather, physicians who participate in the foundation plan are free both to associate with other medical insurance plans — at any fee level, high or low — and directly to serve uninsured patients — at any fee level, high or low. Similarly, insurers that participate in the foundation plan also remain at liberty to do business outside the plan with any physician — foundation member or not — at any fee level. Nor are physicians locked into a plan for more than one year's membership. Thus freedom to compete as well as freedom to withdraw, is preserved. The Court cites no case in which a remotely comparable plan or agreement is condemned on a *per se* basis.

Second, on this record we must find that insurers represent consumer interests. Normally consumers search for high quality at low prices. But once a consumer is insured — i.e. has chosen a medical insurance plan — he is largely indifferent to the amount that his physician charges if the coverage is full, as under the foundation-sponsored plan.

The insurer, however, is *not* indifferent. To keep insurance premiums at a competitive level and to remain profitable, insurers — including those who have contracts with the foundations — step into the consumer's shoes with his incentive to contain medical costs. Indeed, insurers may be the only parties who have the effective power to restrain medical costs, given the difficulty that patients experience in comparing price and quality for a professional service such as medical care.

....

III

It is settled law that once an arrangement has been labeled as "price fixing" it is to be condemned *per se*. But it is equally well settled that this characterization is not to be applied as a talisman to every arrangement that involves a literal fixing of prices. Many lawful contracts, mergers, and partnerships fix prices. But our cases require a more discerning approach. The inquiry in an antitrust case is not simply one of "determining whether two or more potential competitors have literally 'fixed' a 'price.'... [Rather], it is necessary to characterize the challenged conduct as falling within or without that category of behavior to which we apply the label '*per se* price fixing.' That will often, but not always, be a simple matter."

Before characterizing an arrangement as a *per se* price fixing agreement meriting condemnation, a court should determine whether it is a "naked restrain[t] of trade with no purpose except stifling of competition." Such a determination is necessary because "departure from the rule-of-reason standard must be based upon demonstrable economic effect rather than ... upon formalistic line drawing." As part of this inquiry, a court must determine whether the procompetitive economies that the arrangement purportedly makes possible are substantial and realizable in the absence of such an agreement.

For example, in *National Society of Professional Engineers v. United States*, 435 U.S. 679 (1978), we held unlawful as a *per se* violation an engineering association's canon of ethics that prohibited competitive bidding by its members. After the parties had "compiled a voluminous discovery and trial record," we carefully considered — rather than rejected out of hand — the engineers' "affirmative defense" of their agreement: that competitive bidding would tempt engineers to do inferior work that would threaten public health and safety. We refused to accept this defense because its merits "confirm[ed] rather than refut[ed] the anticompetitive purpose and effect of [the] agreement." The analysis incident to the "price fixing" characterization found no substantial procompetitive efficiencies. See also *Catalano, Inc. v. Target Sales, Inc.*, 446 U.S. 643, 646 n. 8 & 649-650 (1980) (challenged arrangement condemned because it lacked "a procompetitive justification" and had "no apparent potentially redeeming value").

In *Broadcast Music, Inc.* there *was* minimum price fixing in the most "literal sense." We nevertheless agreed, unanimously, that an arrangement by which copyright clearinghouses sold performance rights to their entire libraries on a blanket rather than individual basis did not warrant condemnation on a *per se* basis. Individual licensing would have allowed competition between copyright owners. But we reasoned that licensing on a blanket basis yielded substantial efficiencies that otherwise could not be realized. Indeed, the blanket license was itself "to some extent a different product."

In sum, the fact that a foundation sponsored health insurance plan *literally* involves the setting of ceiling prices among competing physicians does not, of itself, justify condemning the plan as *per se* illegal. Only if it is clear from the record that the agreement among physicians is "so plainly anticompetitive that no elaborate study of [its effects] is needed to establish [its] illegality" may a court properly make a *per se* judgment. *National Society of Professional Engineers v. United States, supra*, 435 U.S., at 692. And, as our cases demonstrate, the *per se* label should not be assigned without carefully considering substantial benefits and procompetitive justifications. This is especially true when the agreement under attack is novel, as in this case.

IV

The Court acknowledges that the *per se* ban against price fixing is not to be invoked every time potential competitors *literally* fix prices. One also would have expected it to acknowledge that *per se* characterization is inappropriate if the challenged agreement or plan achieves for the public procompetitive benefits that otherwise are not attainable. The Court does not do this. And neither does it provide alternative criteria by which the *per se* characterization is to be determined. It is content simply to brand this type of plan as "price fixing" and describe the agreement in *Broadcast Music* — which also literally involved the fixing of prices — as "fundamentally different."

In fact, however, the two agreements are similar in important respects. Each involved competitors and resulted in cooperative pricing. Each arrangement also was prompted by the need for better service to the consumers. And each arrangement apparently makes possible a new product by reaping otherwise unattainable efficiencies. The Court's effort to distinguish *Broadcast Music* thus is unconvincing.

....

V

I believe the Court's action today loses sight of the basic purposes of the Sherman Act. As we have noted, the antitrust laws are a "consumer welfare prescription." *Reiter v. Sonotone*, 442 U.S. 330, 343 (1979). In its rush to condemn a novel plan about which it knows very little, the Court suggests that this end is achieved only by invalidating activities that *may* have some potential for harm. But the little that the record does show about the effect of the plan suggests that it is a means of providing medical services that in fact benefits rather than injures persons who need them.

In a complex economy, complex economic arrangements are commonplace. It is unwise for the Court, in a case as novel and important as this one, to make a final judgment in the absence of a complete record and where mandatory inferences create critical issues of fact.

NOTES AND QUESTIONS

1. Do you agree with the *Catalano* Court's characterization that *Professional Engineers* and *Sugar Institute* utilized per se approaches? Does the Court's analysis in *Catalano* and *Maricopa County* seem consistent with *Professional Engineers* and *Broadcast Music*? Did the Court in *Catalano* even attempt to reconcile these two earlier opinions? Perhaps the reason for the lack of a clear statement justifying the distinctions between the cases is the fact that *Catalano* was decided by summary reversal on a petition for certiorari that did not allow the parties to file briefs on the merits or argue the case orally.

2. After *Maricopa County*, what, if anything, is left of *Goldfarb's and Professional Engineers'* special protection for professionals? Did the Court, at least implicitly, draw an analytical distinction between ethical and commercial objectives?

3. The Court in *Maricopa* suggested that the "maximum" price fixing at issue may have been nothing more than disguised "minimum" price fixing, if all doctors actually charged the agreed-upon price. In that case why would the insurance companies participate in the scheme? The insurers and the doctors stand in a vertical relationship. Does it strike you as plausible that automobile insurers would participate in a price fixing agreement among auto body repair shops?

Isn't an insurer generally best off when the costs of the risk that it is insuring are minimized?

4. Do *Catalano* and *Maricopa County* give the lower courts a clear standard for subsequent litigation? Has business certainty been advanced by the Court's most recent cases? Can any systematic criteria for reviewing horizontal price-affecting conduct be stated after these decisions? *See* Gerhart, *The Supreme Court and Antitrust Analysis: The (Near) Triumph of the Chicago School*, 1982 Sup. Ct. Rev. 319.

Consider whether *Maricopa County* can be distinguished from *Broadcast Music* in that the price fixing agreement in the former was not central to the attainment of the procompetitive objective, while in *Broadcast Music* the license agreement was found indispensable to increasing integration and efficiency in the market. Was it necessary in *Maricopa County* that the physicians be a party to the agreement for it to be effective?

The Court made clear in *Maricopa County* that weighing the competitive benefits and harms, which was the centerpiece of the analysis in *Professional Engineers* and *Broadcast Music*, has no place once inferences are drawn that the challenged conduct amounts to a price-fixing agreement. At that point in the analysis, "[t]he anticompetitive potential inherent in all price fixing agreements justifies their facial invalidation even if procompetitive justifications are offered." Is this approach consistent with other recent Supreme Court opinions, discussed herein, which indicate that the goals of antitrust laws are efficiency and consumer welfare? *See, e.g., Reiter v. Sonotone Corp.*, 442 U.S. 330 (1979); *Brunswick Corp. v. Pueblo Bowl-O-Mat, Inc.*, 429 U.S. 477 (1977); *Continental T.V., Inc. v. GTE Sylvania, Inc.*, 433 U.S. 36 (1977).

5. After *Maricopa County*, would it be illegal for a health insurer, such as Blue Shield, to pay physicians for treating patients only on the condition that each doctor not charge the patient-subscriber an additional charge not covered under the policy? The First Circuit has held that such a "ban on balance billing" practices does not violate either section 1 or 2 of the Sherman Act. *Kartell v. Blue Shield of Mass., Inc.*, 749 F.2d 922 (1st Cir. 1984) (see discussion in Chapter 6, *infra*). Is Blue Shield in essence the buyer of medical services for others? Is the holding consistent with *Maricopa County*? Is the difference that this arrangement is vertical (between buyer and seller) rather than horizontal as in *Maricopa County*?

NATIONAL COLLEGIATE ATHLETIC ASS'N V. BOARD OF REGENTS

468 U.S. 85 (1984)

JUSTICE STEVENS delivered the opinion of the Court.

The University of Oklahoma and the University of Georgia contend that the National Collegiate Athletic Association has unreasonably restrained trade in the televising of college football games. After an extended trial, the District Court found that the NCAA had violated § 1 of the Sherman Act and granted injunctive relief.... The Court of Appeals agreed that the statute had been violated but modified the remedy in some respects....

We granted certiorari, ... and now affirm.

I.

The NCAA

Since its inception in 1905, the NCAA has played an important role in the regulation of amateur collegiate sports. It has adopted and promulgated playing rules, standards of amateurism, standards for academic eligibility, regulations concerning recruitment of athletes, and rules governing the size of athletic squads and coaching staffs.... With the exception of football, the NCAA has not undertaken any regulation of the televising of athletic events.

The NCAA has approximately 850 voting members. The regular members are classified into separate divisions to reflect differences in size and scope of their athletic programs. Division I includes 276 colleges with major athletic programs; in this group only 187 play intercollegiate football. Divisions II and III include approximately 500 colleges with less extensive athletic programs. Division I has been subdivided into Divisions I-A and I-AA for football.

....

The Current Plan

The plan adopted in 1981 for the 1982-1985 seasons is at issue in this case. This plan, like each of its predecessors, recites that it is intended to reduce, insofar as possible, the adverse effects of live television upon football game attendance.[6] It provides that "all forms of television of the football games of NCAA member institutions during the Plan control periods shall be in accordance with this Plan."...

In separate agreements with each of the carrying networks, ABC and the Columbia Broadcasting System (CBS), the NCAA granted each the right to telecast the 14 live "exposures" described in the plan, in accordance with the "ground rules" set forth therein. Each of the networks agreed to pay a specified "minimum aggregate compensation to the participating NCAA member institutions" during the 4-year period in an amount that totaled $131,750,000. In

---

[6] "The purposes of this Plan shall be to reduce, insofar as possible, the adverse effects of live television upon football game attendance and, in turn, upon the athletic and related educational programs dependent upon the proceeds therefrom; to spread football television participation among as many colleges as practicable; to reflect properly the image of universities as educational institutions; to promote college football through the use of television, to advance the overall interests of intercollegiate athletics, and to provide college football television to the public to the extent compatible with these other objectives." *Id.*, at 35 (parenthetical omitted).

essence the agreement authorized each network to negotiate directly with member schools for the right to televise their games. The agreement itself does not describe the method of computing the compensation for each game, but the practice that has developed over the years and that the District Court found would be followed under the current agreement involved the setting of a recommended fee by a representative of the NCAA for different types of telecasts, with national telecasts being the most valuable, regional telecasts being less valuable, and Division II or Division III games commanding a still lower price. The aggregate of all these payments presumably equals the total minimum aggregate compensation set forth in the basic agreement. Except for differences in payment between national and regional telecasts, and with respect to Division II and Division III games, the amount that any team receives does not change with the size of the viewing audience, the number of markets in which the game is telecast, or the particular characteristic of the game or the participating teams. Instead, the "ground rules" provide that the carrying networks make alternate selections of those games they wish to televise, and thereby obtain the exclusive right to submit a bid at an essentially fixed price to the institutions involved.[11]

The plan also contains "appearance requirements" and "appearance limitations" which pertain to each of the 2-year periods that the plan is in effect. The basic requirement imposed on each of the two networks is that it must schedule appearances for at least 82 different member institutions during each 2-year period. Under the appearance limitations no member institution is eligible to appear on television more than a total of six times and more than four times nationally, with the appearances to be divided equally between the two carrying networks.... The number of exposures specified in the contracts also sets an absolute maximum on the number of games that can be broadcast.

Thus, although the current plan is more elaborate than any of its predecessors, it retains the essential features of each of them. It limits the total amount of televised intercollegiate football and the number of games that any one team may televise. No member is permitted to make any sale of television rights except in accordance with the basic plan.

---

[11] The District Court explained how the agreement eliminates competition for broadcasting rights: "First, the networks have no intention to engage in bidding. Second, once the network holding first choice for any given date has made its choice and agreed to a rights fee for that game with the two teams involved, the other network is then in a monopsony position. The schools cannot threaten to sell the broadcast rights to any other network. They cannot sell to NBC without committing a violation of NCAA rules. They cannot sell to the network which had first choice over that particular date because, again, they would be in violation of NCAA rules, and the network would be in violation of its agreement with NCAA. Thus, NCAA creates a single eligible buyer for the product of all but the two schools selected by the network having first choice. Free market competition is thus destroyed under the new plan." 546 F. Supp. at 1292-1293.

II

There can be no doubt that the challenged practices of the NCAA constitute a "restraint of trade" in the sense that they limit members' freedom to negotiate and enter into their own television contracts. In that sense, however, every contract is a restraint of trade, and as we have repeatedly recognized, the Sherman Act was intended to prohibit only unreasonable restraints of trade.

It is also undeniable that these practices share characteristics of restraints we have previously held unreasonable. The NCAA is an association of schools which compete against each other to attract television revenues, not to mention fans and athletes. As the District Court found, the policies of the NCAA with respect to television rights are ultimately controlled by the vote of member institutions. By participating in an association which prevents member institutions from competing against each other on the basis of price or kind of television rights that can be offered to broadcasters, the NCAA member institutions have created a horizontal restraint — an agreement among competitors on the way in which they will compete with one another. A restraint of this type has often been held to be unreasonable as a matter of law. Because it places a ceiling on the number of games member institutions may televise, the horizontal agreement places an artificial limit on the quantity of televised football that is available to broadcasters and consumers. By restraining the quantity of television rights available for sale, the challenged practices create a limitation on output; our cases have held that such limitations are unreasonable restraints of trade. Moreover, the District Court found that the minimum aggregate price in fact operates to preclude any price negotiation between broadcasters and institutions, thereby constituting horizontal price fixing, perhaps the paradigm of an unreasonable restraint of trade.

Horizontal price-fixing and output limitation are ordinarily condemned as a matter of law under an "illegal per se" approach because the probability that these practices are anticompetitive is so high; a *per se* rule is applied when "the practice facially appears to be one that would always or almost always tend to restrain competition and decrease output." *Broadcast Music, Inc. v. CBS*, 441 U.S. 1, 19-20 (1979). In such circumstances a restraint is presumed unreasonable without inquiry into the particular market context in which it is found. Nevertheless, we have decided that it would be inappropriate to apply a *per se* rule to this case. This decision is not based on a lack of judicial experience with this type of arrangement,[21] on the fact that the NCAA is organized as a nonprivate entity, or on our respect for the NCAA's historic role in the preservation and encouragement of intercollegiate amateur athletics. Rather, what is critical is that this case involves an industry in which horizontal restraints on competition are essential if the product is to be available at all.

---

[21] While judicial inexperience with a particular arrangement counsels against extending the reach of *per se* rules ... the likelihood that horizontal price and output restrictions are anticompetitive is generally sufficient to justify application of the per se rule without inquiry into the special characteristics of a particular industry....

As Judge Bork has noted: "[S]ome activities can only be carried out jointly. Perhaps the leading example is league sports. When a league of professional lacrosse teams is formed, it would be pointless to declare their cooperation illegal on the ground that there are no other professional lacrosse teams." R. Bork, The Antitrust Paradox 278 (1978). What the NCAA and its member institutions market in this case is competition itself — contests between competing institutions. Of course, this would be completely ineffective if there were no rules on which the competitors agreed to create and define the competition to be marketed. A myriad of rules affecting such matters as the size of the field, the number of players on a team, and the extent to which physical violence is to be encouraged or proscribed, all must be agreed upon, and all restrain the manner in which institutions compete. Moreover, the NCAA seeks to market a particular brand of football — college football. The identification of this "product" with an academic tradition differentiates college football from and makes it more popular than professional sports to which it might otherwise be comparable, such as, for example, minor league baseball. In order to preserve the character and quality of the "product," athletes must not be paid, must be required to attend class, and the like. And the integrity of the "product" cannot be preserved except by mutual agreement; if an institution adopted such restrictions unilaterally, its effectiveness as a competitor on the playing field might soon be destroyed. Thus, the NCAA plays a vital role in enabling college football to preserve its character, and as a result enables the product to be marketed which might otherwise be unavailable. In performing this role, its actions widen consumer choice — not only the choices available to sports fans but also those available to athletes — and hence can be viewed as procompetitive.

Broadcast Music squarely holds that a joint selling arrangement may be so efficient that it will increase sellers' aggregate output and thus be procompetitive.... Similarly, as we indicated in *Continental T.V., Inc. v. GTE Sylvania Inc.*, 433 U.S. 36, 51-57 (1977), a restraint in a limited aspect of a market may actually enhance market-wide competition. Respondents concede that the great majority of the NCAA's regulations enhance competition among member institutions. Thus, despite the fact that this case involves restraints on the ability of member institutions to compete in terms of price and output, a fair evaluation of their competitive character requires consideration of the NCAA's justifications for the restraints.

Our analysis of this case under the Rule of Reason, of course, does not change the ultimate focus of our inquiry. Both per se rules and the Rule of Reason are employed "to form a judgment about the competitive significance of the restraint." *National Society of Professional Engineers v. United States*, 435 U.S. 679, 692 (1978)....

Per se rules are invoked when surrounding circumstances make the likelihood of anticompetitive conduct so great as to render unjustified further examination of the challenged conduct. But whether the ultimate finding is the product of a presumption or actual market analysis, the essential inquiry remains the same —

whether or not the challenged restraint enhances competition.[26] Under the
Sherman Act the criterion to be used in judging the validity of a restraint on
trade is its impact on competition.

III

Because it restrains price and output, the NCAA's television plan has a significant potential for anticompetitive effects.[28] The findings of the District
Court indicate that this potential has been realized. The District Court found that
if member institutions were free to sell television rights, many more games
would be shown on television, and that the NCAA's output restriction has the
effect of raising the price the networks pay for television rights. Moreover, the
court found that by fixing a price for television rights to all games, the NCAA
creates a price structure that is unresponsive to viewer demand and unrelated to
the prices that would prevail in a competitive market. And, of course, since as a
practical matter all member institutions need NCAA approval, members have no
real choice but to adhere to the NCAA's television controls.

The anticompetitive consequences of this arrangement are apparent. Individual
competitors lose their freedom to compete. Price is higher and output lower than
they would otherwise be, and both are unresponsive to consumer preference.
This latter point is perhaps the most significant, since "Congress designed the
Sherman Act as a 'consumer welfare prescription.'"... A restraint that has the
effect of reducing the importance of consumer preference in setting price and
output is not consistent with this fundamental goal of antitrust law. Restrictions
on price and output are the paradigmatic examples of restraints of trade that the
Sherman Act was intended to prohibit.... At the same time, the television plan
eliminates competitors from the market, since only those broadcasters able to bid
on television rights covering the entire NCAA can compete. Thus, as the District
Court found, many telecasts that would occur in a competitive market are foreclosed by the NCAA's plan.

---

[26] Indeed, there is often no bright line separating *per se* from Rule of Reason analysis. *Per se*
rules may require considerable inquiry into market conditions before the evidence justifies a presumption of anticompetitive conduct. For example, while the Court has spoken of a "per se" rule
against tying arrangements, it has also recognized that tying may have procompetitive justifications
that make it inappropriate to condemn without considerable market analysis. See *Jefferson Parish
Hosp. Dist. No. 2 v. Hyde*, 466 U.S. 2 (1984).

[28] In this connection, it is not without significance that Congress felt the need to grant professional sports an exemption from the antitrust laws for joint marketing of television rights. See 15
U.S.C. §§ 1291-1295. The legislative history of this exemption demonstrates Congress' recognition
that agreements among league members to sell television rights in a cooperative fashion could run
afoul of the Sherman Act, and in particular reflects its awareness of the decision in *United States v.
National Football League*, 116 F. Supp. 319 (E.D. Pa. 1953), which held that an agreement between the teams of the National Football League that each team would not permit stations within
75 miles of the home city of another team to telecast its games on a day when that team was playing
at home violated § 1 of the Sherman Act....

Petitioner argues, however, that its television plan can have no significant anticompetitive effect since the record indicates that it has no market power — no ability to alter the interaction of supply and demand in the market. We must reject this argument for two reasons, one legal, one factual.

As a matter of law, the absence of proof of market power does not justify a naked restriction on price or output. To the contrary, when there is an agreement not to compete in terms of price or output, "no elaborate industry analysis is required to demonstrate the anticompetitive character of such an agreement." *Professional Engineers*, 435 U.S. at 692. Petitioner does not quarrel with the District Court's finding that price and output are not responsive to demand. Thus the plan is inconsistent with the Sherman Act's command that price and supply be responsive to consumer preference. We have never required proof of market power in such a case. This naked restraint on price and output requires some competitive justification even in the absence of a detailed market analysis.[42]

As a factual matter, it is evident that petitioner does possess market power. The District Court employed the correct test for determining whether college football broadcasts constitute a separate market — whether there are other products that are reasonably substitutable for televised NCAA football games. Petitioner's argument that it cannot obtain supracompetitive prices from broadcasters since advertisers, and hence broadcasters, can switch from college football to other types of programming simply ignores the findings of the District Court. It found that intercollegiate football telecasts generate an audience uniquely attractive to advertisers and that competitors are unable to offer programming that can attract a similar audience. These findings amply support its conclusion that the NCAA possesses market power. Indeed, the District Court's subsidiary finding that advertisers will pay a premium price per viewer to reach audiences watching college football because of their demographic characteristics is vivid evidence of the uniqueness of this product.... Thus, respondents have demonstrated that there is a separate market for telecasts of college football which "rest[s] on generic qualities differentiating" viewers.... It inexorably follows that if college football broadcasts be defined as a separate market — and we are convinced they

---

[42] The Solicitor General correctly observes: "There was no need for the respondents to establish monopoly power in any precisely defined market for television programming in order to prove the restraint unreasonable. Both lower courts found not only that NCAA has power over the market for intercollegiate sports, but also that in the market for television programming — no matter how broadly or narrowly the market is defined — the NCAA television restrictions have reduced output, subverted viewer choice, and distorted pricing. Consequently, unless the controls have some countervailing procompetitive justification, they should be deemed unlawful regardless of whether petitioner has substantial market power over advertising dollars. While the 'reasonableness' of a particular alleged restraint often depends on the market power of the parties involved, because a judgment about market power is the means by which the effects of the conduct on the market place can be assessed, market power is only one test of 'reasonableness.' And where the anticompetitive effects of conduct can be ascertained through means short of extensive market analysis, and where no countervailing competitive virtues are evident, a lengthy analysis of market power is not necessary."...

are — then the NCAA's complete control over those broadcasts provides a solid basis for the District Court's conclusion that the NCAA possesses market power with respect to those broadcasts....

Thus, the NCAA television plan on its face constitutes a restraint upon the operation of a free market, and the findings of the District Court establish that it has operated to raise price and reduce output. Under the Rule of Reason, these hallmarks of anticompetitive behavior place upon petitioner a heavy burden of establishing an affirmative defense which competitively justifies this apparent deviation from the operations of a free market.... We turn now to the NCAA's proffered justifications.

IV

Relying on *Broadcast Music*, petitioner argues that its television plan constitutes a cooperative "joint venture" which assists in the marketing of broadcast rights and hence is procompetitive. While joint ventures have no immunity from the antitrust laws, as *Broadcast Music* indicates, a joint selling arrangement may "mak[e] possible a new product by reaping otherwise unattainable efficiencies."... The essential contribution made by the NCAA's arrangement is to define the number of games that may be televised, to establish the price for each exposure, and to define the basic terms of each contract between the network and a home team. The NCAA does not, however, act as a selling agent for any school or for any conference of schools. The selection of individual games, and the negotiation of particular agreements, is a matter left to the networks and the individual schools. Thus, the effect of the network plan is not to eliminate individual sales of broadcasts, since these still occur albeit subject to fixed prices and output limitations. Unlike *Broadcast Music*'s blanket license covering broadcast rights to a large number of individual compositions, here the same rights are still sold on an individual basis, only in a non-competitive market.

The District Court did not find that the NCAA's television plan produced any procompetitive efficiencies which enhanced the competitiveness of college football television rights; to the contrary it concluded that NCAA football could be marketed just as effectively without the television plan. There is therefore no predicate in the findings for petitioner's efficiency justification. Indeed, petitioner's argument is refuted by the District Court's finding concerning price and output. If the NCAA's television plan produced procompetitive efficiencies, the plan would increase output and reduce the price of televised games. The District Court's contrary findings accordingly undermine petitioner's position. In light of these findings, it cannot be said that "the agreement on price is necessary to market the product at all."... In *Broadcast Music* the availability of a package product that no individual could offer enhanced the total volume of music that was sold. Unlike this case, there was no limit of any kind placed on the volume that might be sold in the entire market and each individual remained free to sell his own music without restraint. Here production has been limited, not enhanced.

No individual school is free to televise its own games without restraint. The NCAA's efficiency justification is not supported by the record.

....

V

Throughout the history of its regulation of intercollegiate football telecasts, the NCAA has indicated its concern with protecting live attendance. This concern, it should be noted, it not with protecting live attendance at games which *are* shown on television; that type of interest is not at issue in this case. Rather, the concern is that fan interest in a televised game may adversely affect ticket sales for games that will not appear on television.

... Under the current plan, games are shown on television during all hours that college football games are played. The plan simply does not protect live attendance by ensuring that games will not be shown on television at the same time as live events.

There is, however, a more fundamental reason for rejecting this defense. The NCAA's argument that its television plan is necessary to protect live attendance is not based on a desire to maintain the integrity of college football as a distinct and attractive product, but rather on a fear that the product will not prove sufficiently attractive to draw live attendance when faced with competition from televised games. At bottom the NCAA's position is that ticket sales for most college games are unable to compete in a free market. The television plan protects ticket sales by limiting output — just as any monopolist increases revenues by reducing output. By seeking to insulate live ticket sales from the full spectrum of competition because of its assumption that the product itself is insufficiently attractive to consumers, petitioner forwards a justification that is inconsistent with the basic policy of the Sherman Act. "[T]he Rule of Reason does not support a defense based on the assumption that competition itself is unreasonable."...

VI

Petitioner argues that the interest in maintaining a competitive balance among amateur athletic teams is legitimate and important and that it justifies the regulations challenged in this case. We agree with the first part of the argument but not the second.

Our decision not to apply a *per se* rule to this case rests in large part on our recognition that a certain degree of cooperation is necessary if the type of competition that petitioner and its member institutions seek to market is to be preserved. It is reasonable to assume that most of the regulatory controls of the NCAA are justifiable means of fostering competition among amateur athletic teams and therefore procompetitive because they enhance public interest in intercollegiate athletics. The specific restraints on football telecasts, that are challenged in this case do not, however, fit into the same mold as do rules defining the conditions of the contest, the eligibility of participants, or the manner in which members of a joint enterprise shall share the responsibilities and the benefits of the total venture.

....

The television plan is not even arguably tailored to serve such an interest. It does not regulate the amount of money that any college may spend on its football program, nor the way in which the colleges may use the revenues that are generated by their football programs, whether derived from the sale of television rights, the sale of tickets, or the sale of concessions or program advertising. The plan simply imposes a restriction on one source of revenue that is more important to some colleges than to others. There is no evidence that this restriction produces any greater measure of equality throughout the NCAA than would a restriction on alumni donations, tuition rates, or any other revenue producing activity. At the same time, as the District Court found, the NCAA imposes a variety of other restrictions designed to preserve amateurism which are much better tailored to the goal of competitive balance than is the television plan, and which are "clearly sufficient" to preserve competitive balance to the extent it is within the NCAA's power to do so. And much more than speculation supported the District Court's findings on this score. No other NCAA sport employs a similar plan, and in particular the court found that in the most closely analogous sport, college basketball, competitive balance has been maintained without resort to a restrictive television plan.

Perhaps the most important reason for rejecting the argument that the interest in competitive balance is served by the television plan is the District Court's unambiguous and well supported finding that many more games would be televised in a free market than under the NCAA plan. The hypothesis that legitimates the maintenance of competitive balance as a procompetitive justification under the Rule of Reason is that equal competition will maximize consumer demand for the product. The finding that consumption will materially increase if the controls are removed is a compelling demonstration that they do not in fact serve any such legitimate purpose.

VII

The NCAA plays a critical role in the maintenance of a revered tradition of amateurism in college sports. There can be no question but that it needs ample latitude to play that role, or that the preservation of the student-athlete in higher education adds richness and diversity to intercollegiate athletics and is entirely consistent with the goals of the Sherman Act. But consistent with the Sherman Act, the role of the NCAA must be to *preserve* a tradition that might otherwise die; rules that restrict output are hardly consistent with this role. Today we hold only that the record supports the District Court's conclusion that by curtailing output and blunting the ability of member institutions to respond to consumer preference, the NCAA has restricted rather than enhanced the place of intercollegiate athletics in the Nation's life. Accordingly, the judgment of the Court of Appeals is

Affirmed.

[JUSTICES WHITE and REHNQUIST dissented. They argued that the challenged limitations were necessary to promote amateur competition, that the definition of "output" should be based on total viewers, not games telecast, and that the NCAA lacked market power.]

NOTES AND QUESTIONS

1. After *NCAA*, what is the plaintiff's burden in proving a per se violation? If an agreement to fix price and output is not analyzed as per se unlawful, is any conduct hereafter? What remains of *Socony*'s per se test: "any combination which tampers with price structure"?

2. The Court in *NCAA* used the associational nature of defendant and the need for economic interdependence among competitors in this market as justification for applying a rule of reason approach. Did the Court give any guidance when cooperation among competitors and the resulting restraint will be deemed legal? Does the nature and purpose of the joint undertaking indicate the result? Or is it determined by whether the challenged practice produces countervailing procompetitive benefits? Is that the difference between the results in *Broadcast Music* and *NCAA*? Or is the difference the fact that in *Broadcast Music*, unlike *NCAA*, there was no output limitation? If the latter argument is determinative, why then is there no per se standard in *NCAA*?

3. *NCAA* focused on an output-restriction analysis more than previous cases. Does it necessarily follow that an agreement on price will lead to a decrease in output and in turn an increase in price? Consider whether a decrease in price competition might result in an increase in nonprice competition, such as increased product quality and service. Is it possible that nonprice competition could increase output, and hence be procompetitive? Does *NCAA* suggest that the link between the variables of price and nonprice competition is output, with output-expanding agreements deemed competitive? *See also* Sullivan, *On Nonprice Competition: An Economic and Marketing Analysis*, 45 U. Pitt. L. Rev. 771 (1984).

4. *NCAA* held that output-restricting agreements are anticompetitive. Was the Court's market power analysis essential to the finding that output was reduced? Does the Court imply that market power is a prerequisite for finding a section 1 violation? Have any other section 1 cases used this standard? Consider the Court's reasoning: If the market indicates that price and supply, by reason of the agreement, are not responsive to consumer preferences, a market power analysis is not required. Is an output restriction enough to condemn the practice regardless of market power?

5. Does the *NCAA* decision foreclose the NCAA or a conference from limiting the number of times a school might have its games shown on television, or enforcing

a television blackout rule to avoid competition between gate attendance and television audiences? *See generally* McKenzie & Sullivan, *Does the NCAA Exploit College Athletes? An Economics and Legal Reinterpretation*, 32 Antitrust Bull. 373 (1987).

6. Consider whether a television viewer would have standing to bring an action to challenge the NCAA plan or whether a consumer had suffered "antitrust injury." Does *NCAA* turn on a finding that viewers were adversely affected by the NCAA plan? Would an advertiser have standing?

7. In evaluating the Court's economic theory in *NCAA*, consider the 1984 college football television revenue compared to the year before the Court's decision: In 1983, a total of 89 TV games produced revenues of $69 million. And in 1984, 195 games produced only $45 million (including regional and local syndication). By 1986, 99 games on TV (excluding regional and local telecasts) produced $53 million.

8. On a request for a permanent injunction, consider whether a district court needs to define the relevant market under section 1 when there is an output restriction shown and the defendant fails to offer a pro-consumer justification for the challenged output restriction. In *Chicago Prof. Sport, Ltd. Pt'ship v. National Basketball Ass'n*, 961 F.2d 667 (7th Cir. 1992), Judge Easterbrook, writing for the court, held that the issuance of a permanent injunction barring the NBA from enforcing a rule reducing the number of games from 25 to 20, broadcast over certain superstations, was proper because plaintiff demonstrated that an agreement to reduce the number of games shown was an output restriction without an offsetting efficiency justification. Since defendant failed to show some explanation connecting the restriction to consumers' benefits, there was no need to define the relevant market, as it was clear that the output restriction was enough to condemn the practice under a "quick look" analysis under the rule of reason.

9. More recently, the NCAA was condemned for further antitrust violations, this time stemming from its salary cap for entry-level basketball coaches. In *Law v. National Collegiate Athletic Association*, 134 F.3d 1010 (10th Cir.), *cert. denied*, 119 S. Ct. 65 (1998), the Tenth Circuit applied a quick look rule of reason analysis to uphold the NCAA's section 1 liability. The court decided that evidence suggested an anticompetitive effect, since the NCAA used the rule to reduce part-time coaches' salaries from up to $60,000 annually to $16,000 per year. None of the justifications offered by the NCAA was found sufficient to overcome this presumption of anticompetitive effect.

PROBLEM 4.1

Consider restrictions on price advertising by a professional dental association. The rules prohibit "false and misleading" advertising. For example, the rules permit a dentist to advertise the dollar amount of his "regular" fee and a percentage discount, but do not permit him to make statements to the affect that his fees are "reasonable" or "affordable." The association recommends discipline for dentists who advertise "reasonable fees quoted in advance" and "major savings." The regulations on advertising of discounts require the provision of so much supporting information that one member acknowledged that advertising in compliance would probably occupy two pages in a telephone directory, thus operating as a significant deterrent to advertising discounts at all. This was so because the rules generally required dentists advertising discounts to list every single service they performed and the undiscounted and discounted fees for each. If a dentist is denied membership because she merely advertised "20% off for new patients" but did not list every service provided, the "base" price, and the discounted price, does this arrangement violate the antitrust laws?

See California Dental Association, 5 CCH Trade Reg. Rep. ¶ 24007 (FTC 1996), *aff'd*, 128 F.3d 720 (9th Cir. 1997).

PROBLEM 4.2

Bank credit cards, such as VISA and MasterCard, are issued by individual banks, and each bank ordinarily sets the terms of its own card: user annual fees, interest rates, and merchant fees. Suppose that all the banks that issue VISA cards agree with each other that (1) they will charge their individual card holders a $15.00 annual fee for card membership; (2) they will charge individual card holders an interest rate of 18% annually on unpaid charges; (3) they will charge merchants who accept the VISA card a fee of 1.5% of each transaction in which the card is used; (4) they will exchange with each other the names of people who are in substantial default on their VISA payments; and (5) they will not issue a VISA card to someone who has lost a VISA card issued by another bank because of nonpayment.

Which of these agreements would receive per se treatment? Which would be analyzed under the rule of reason? What would be the consequences of each bank's determining for itself what merchant transaction fee to charge? Suppose that a merchant were willing to accept VISA if the transaction fee were 1.5%, but not if it were higher. It would then have to call the issuing bank each time a potential customer presented a VISA card to see what its transaction fee was. Should this fact be sufficient to justify rule of reason treatment for agreement (3)? Should it matter that VISA transactions collectively account for 55% of all bank credit card transactions? That VISA transactions account for only .05% of all transactions, including cash and check transactions?

On agreement (3), *see National Bancard Corp. v. VISA U.S.A., Inc.*, 779 F.2d 592 (11th Cir. 1986); Baxter, *Bank Interchange of Transactional Paper: Legal and Economic Perspectives*, 26 J.L. & Econ. 541, 572-82 (1983).

PROBLEM 4.3

Each year the top ten most elite and selective colleges get together through their financial aid officers to determine financial aid awards for those applicants who have been accepted by more than one of the schools in this elite group. Each year the schools agree to offer the same financial aid package to each applicant who had applied and was accepted.

Does the agreement violate section 1? Would the answer change if at this yearly meeting the colleges also set, either explicitly or implicitly, the tuition at the respective schools? *See United States v. Brown Univ.*, 5 F.3d 658 (3d Cir. 1993).

Consider also whether it violates section 1 if these same schools decide not to disclose to Barrons or any other publisher of college guidebooks the yearly admission data on each school which could result in changes in the ranking of the individual schools. Does it matter to the antitrust conclusion if all the elite schools that entered into these agreements are not-for-profit corporations? *Compare Hospital Corp. of Am. v. FTC*, in Chapter 7, *infra, and United States v. Carilion Health Sys.*, 707 F. Supp. 840 (W.D. Va. 1989), *aff'd*, 892 F.2d 1042 (4th Cir. 1989).

PROBLEM 4.4

Troubled by escalating costs of recruiting law students for law firm positions, several law firms in San Francisco, Atlanta, Chicago, New York, and Los Angeles get together yearly to establish guidelines and rules that limit the amount of money law students can spend during recruiting trips to the participating law firms. Such guidelines include the requirements that students can only fly economy-class on airlines and that they take shuttle buses instead of taxis to and from the airports. Does the agreement that sets these guidelines and requirements violate section 1? Who would have standing and antitrust injury to bring the antitrust suit? What if these same law firms arrange for all the airline tickets and hotel rooms for interviewing students through a travel agent shared by the firms?

PROBLEM 4.5

The City of Cosmos contains nine physicians practicing in the field of internal medicine (internists); they all have independent practices. Recently a new machine called the Diagnition was invented, which scans the bodies of people with certain symptoms and greatly aids internists in diagnosing what is wrong. Several of the Cosmos internists would like to own a Diagnition, but they are extremely expensive to purchase and to operate, since they require a specialized technician, and a single internist would probably only use it three or four times a month. One day six of the internists happen to meet at a local athletic club and decide to invest jointly in a Diagnition, share the cost of the technician's salary, and share the rent for an office where it can be located. In reaching their decision, the six physicians agree that they will (1) split the initial cost of the technician's salary on a per use basis; (2) allocate the operating costs and the technician's salary on a per use basis, with each internist initially paying $500 into a central pool each time a patient of that particular internist uses the Diagnition;

(3) charge patients $700 for one use of the Diagnition; and (4) permit other internists in Cosmos to prescribe the Diagnition for their patients, but only if they pay $1000 per use. Discuss likely antitrust consequences of each of the four agreements; assume there is adequate federal jurisdiction under the commerce clause.

C. PROOF OF AGREEMENT

1. INTRODUCTION

Section 1 of the Sherman Act requires a "contract, combination or conspiracy" in restraint of trade before a violation can be found. Although the principal basis for a monopolization charge under section 2 of the Sherman Act is single firm conduct, it is not covered by section 1. Two or more parties must be engaged in the restraint. The "agreement" requirement raises problems in litigation because the requisite agreement is often difficult to establish. The cases and discussion that follow are concerned with how one proves "agreement."

The antitrust lawyer confronts this problem in both a procedural and evidentiary sense. There must be sufficient evidence of an "agreement" to survive a directed verdict motion and post-trial motions on the sufficiency of the evidence. A motion for a directed verdict will generally only be granted when "a review of the evidence demonstrates conclusively that reasonable minds could not differ about the controlling issue of fact." Fed. R. Civ. P. 50(a). Under this rule, courts will construe the proof in a manner most favorable to the party against whom the motion is made. Generally, this part of the antitrust case will be demonstrated through circumstantial evidence.

Inferences can usually be drawn from conduct evidence about the existence of a common understanding, agreement, or conspiracy. Suffice it to say that the agreement requirement under section 1 does not require proof of explicit collusion. The agreement can be tacit (silent, unspoken, implied) and still be illegal. Evidence showing that there has been a "meeting of the minds," concerted action, or mutual understanding is sufficient to support an inference of agreement. More than one antitrust lawyer has argued to a jury that "*but for* an agreement this type of joint conduct would not have occurred." Thus the inquiry is largely fact-oriented: from specific behavior indicating a common course of action, an agreement can be drawn inferentially.

Several courts have considered whether evidence of coercion precludes a finding of conspiracy — for example, when one or more co-conspirators act unwillingly, reluctantly, or under duress. The Seventh Circuit recently said that the combination or conspiracy element of section 1 is not negated by coercion or reluctance. *MCM Partners, Inc. v. Andrews-Bartlett & Assoc.*, 62 F.3d 967 (7th Cir. 1995). Defendants urged the court to vary the remedy for anticompetitive conduct when coerced defendants are involved, but the court declined, though acknowledging that there was some support for this approach. Said the Seventh

Circuit: "[S]o long as defendants knew that they were acquiescing in conduct that was in all likelihood unlawful, we have no difficulty concluding that they thereby joined a combination or conspiracy for which they can be held accountable under [Section] 1."

The cases that follow discuss the standard of proof that is required to establish an "agreement" under section 1. Concepts such as conscious parallelism, oligopoly pricing, and facilitating devices have emerged as theories under which the "agreement" requirement can be satisfied. These theories attempt to explain the nature of agreements in the context of market structure. The first issue is whether parallel conduct engaged in by competitors with knowledge of each other's actions constitutes an "agreement" in restraint of trade within section 1.

2. CONSCIOUS PARALLELISM AND THE *INTERSTATE CIRCUIT* DOCTRINE

INTERSTATE CIRCUIT V. UNITED STATES

306 U.S. 208 (1939)

JUSTICE STONE delivered the opinion of the Court.

[The case is] now before us on findings of the District Court specifically stating that appellants did in fact agree with each other to enter into and carry out the contracts, which the court found to result in unreasonable and therefore unlawful restraints of interstate commerce.

Appellants comprise the two groups of defendants in the District Court.... The distributor appellants are engaged in the business of distributing in interstate commerce motion picture films, copyrights on which they own or control, for exhibition in theatres throughout the United States. They distribute about 75 per cent of all first-class feature films exhibited in the United States. They solicit from motion picture theatre owners and managers in Texas and other states applications for licenses to exhibit films, and forward the applications, when received from such exhibitors, to their respective New York offices, where they are accepted or rejected. If the applications are accepted, the distributors ship the films from points outside the states of exhibition to their exchanges within those states, from which, pursuant to the license agreements, the films are delivered to the local theatres for exhibition. After exhibition the films are reshipped to the distributors at points outside the state.

The exhibitor group of appellants consists of Interstate Circuit, Inc., and Texas Consolidated Theatres, Inc., and Hoblitzelle and O'Donnell, who are respectively president and general manager of both and in active charge of their business operations. The two corporations are affiliated with each other and with Paramount Pictures Distributing Co., Inc., one of the distributor appellants.

Interstate operates forty-three first-run and second-run motion picture theatres, located in six Texas cities. It has a complete monopoly of first-run theatres in these cities, except for one in Houston operated by one distributor's Texas agent. In most of these theatres the admission price for adults for the better seats at night is 40 cents or more. Interstate also operates several subsequent-run theatres in each of these cities, twenty-two in all, but in all but Galveston there are other subsequent-run theatres which compete with both its first- and subsequent-run theatres in those cities.

Texas Consolidated operates sixty-six theatres, some first- and some subsequent-run houses, in various cities and towns in the Rio Grande Valley and elsewhere in Texas and in New Mexico. In some of these cities there are no competing theatres, and in six leading cities there are no competing first-run theatres. It has no theatres in the six Texas cities in which Interstate operates. That Interstate and Texas Consolidated dominate the motion picture business in the cities where their theatres are located is indicated by the fact that at the time of the contracts in question Interstate and Consolidated each contributed more than 74 per cent of all the license fees paid by the motion picture theatres in their respective territories to the distributor appellants.

On July 11, 1934, following a previous communication on the subject to the eight branch managers of the distributor appellants, O'Donnell, the manager of Interstate and Consolidated, sent to each of them a letter on the letterhead of Interstate, each letter naming all of them as addressees, in which he asked compliance with two demands as a condition of Interstate's continued exhibition of the distributors' films in its "A" or first-run theatres at a night admission of 40 cents or more. One demand was that the distributors "agree that in selling their product to subsequent runs, that this "A" product will never be exhibited at any time or in any theatre at a smaller admission price than 2 for adults in the evening." The other was that "on 'A' pictures which are exhibited at a night admission of 4 or more — they shall never be exhibited in conjunction with another feature picture under the so-called policy of double features." The letter added that with respect to the "Rio Grande Valley situation," with which Consolidated alone was concerned, "We must insist that all pictures exhibited in our 'A' theatres at a maximum night admission price of 3 must also be restricted to subsequent runs in the Valley at 2."

The admission price customarily charged for preferred seats at night in independently operated subsequent-run theatres in Texas at the time of these letters was less than 25 cents. In seventeen of the eighteen independent theatres of this kind whose operations were described by witnesses the admission price was less than 25 cents. In one only was it 25 cents. In most of them the admission was 15 cents or less. It was also the general practice in those theatres to provide double bills either on certain days of the week or with any feature picture which was weak in drawing power. The distributor appellants had generally provided in their license contracts for a minimum admission price of 10 or 15 cents, and three of them had included provisions restricting double billing. But none was at any time previously subject to contractual compulsion to continue the restrictions. The trial court found that the proposed restrictions constituted an important departure from prior practice.

The local representatives of the distributors, having no authority to enter into the proposed agreements, communicated the proposal to their home offices. Conferences followed between Hoblitzelle and O'Donnell, acting for Interstate and Consolidated, and the representatives of the various distributors. In these conferences each distributor was represented by its local branch manager and by one or more superior officials from outside the state of Texas. In the course of them each distributor agreed with Interstate for the 1934-35 season to impose both the demanded restrictions upon their subsequent-run licensees in the six Texas cities served by Interstate, except Austin and Galveston. While only two of the distributors incorporated the agreement to impose the restrictions in their license contracts with Interstate, the evidence establishes, and it is not denied, that all joined in the agreement, four of them after some delay in negotiating terms other than the restrictions and not now material. These agreements for the restrictions ... were carried into effect by each of the distributors' imposing them on their subsequent-run licensees in the four Texas cities during the 1934-35 season. One agreement, that of Metro-Goldwyn-Mayer Distributing Corporation, was for three years. The others were renewed in the two following seasons and all were in force when the present suit was begun.

None of the distributors yielded to the demand that subsequent runs in towns in the Rio Grande Valley served by Consolidated should be restricted. One distributor, Paramount, which was affiliated with Consolidated, agreed to impose the restrictions in certain other Texas and New Mexico cities.

....

Although the films were copyrighted, appellants do not deny that the conspiracy charge is established if the distributors agreed among themselves to impose the restrictions upon subsequent-run exhibitors. As is usual in cases of alleged unlawful agreements to restrain commerce, the Government is without the aid of direct testimony that the distributors entered into any agreement with each other to impose the restrictions upon subsequent-run exhibitors. In order to establish agreement it is compelled to rely on inferences drawn from the course of conduct of the alleged conspirators.

The trial court drew the inference of agreement from the nature of the proposals made on behalf of Interstate and Consolidated; from the manner in which they were made; from the substantial unanimity of action taken upon them by the distributors; and from the fact that appellants did not call as witnesses any of the superior officials who negotiated the contracts with Interstate or any official who, in the normal course of business, would have had knowledge of the existence or non-existence of such an agreement among the distributors. This conclusion is challenged by appellants because not supported by subsidiary findings or by the evidence. We think this inference of the trial court was rightly drawn from the evidence. In the view we take of the legal effect of the cooperative action of the distributor appellants in carrying into effect the restrictions imposed upon subsequent-run theatres in the four Texas cities and of the legal effect of the separate agreements for the imposition of those restrictions entered into between

Interstate and each of the distributors, it is unnecessary to discuss in great detail the evidence concerning this aspect of the case.

The O'Donnell letter named on its face as addressees the eight local representatives of the distributors, and so from the beginning each of the distributors knew that the proposals were under consideration by the others. Each was aware that all were in active competition and that without substantially unanimous action with respect to the restrictions for any given territory there was risk of a substantial loss of the business and good will of the subsequent-run and independent exhibitors, but that with it there was the prospect of increased profits. There was, therefore, strong motive for concerted action, full advantage of which was taken by Interstate and Consolidated in presenting their demands to all in a single document.

There was risk, too, that without agreement diversity of action would follow. Compliance with the proposals involved a radical departure from the previous business practices of the industry and a drastic increase in admission prices of most of the subsequent-run theatres. Acceptance of the proposals was discouraged by at least three of the distributors' local managers. Independent exhibitors met and organized a futile protest which they presented to the representatives of Interstate and Consolidated....

....

... Taken together, the circumstances of the case which we have mentioned, when uncontradicted and with no more explanation than the record affords, justify the inference that the distributors acted in concert and in common agreement in imposing the restrictions upon their licensees in the four Texas cities.

This inference was supported and strengthened when the distributors, with like unanimity, failed to tender the testimony, at their command, of any officer or agent of a distributor who knew, or was in a position to know, whether in fact an agreement had been reached among them for concerted action. When the proof supported, as we think it did, the inference of such concert, the burden rested on appellants of going forward with the evidence to explain away or contradict it. They undertook to carry that burden by calling upon local managers of the distributors to testify that they had acted independently of the other distributors, and that they did not have conferences with or reach agreements with the other distributors or their representatives. The failure under the circumstances to call as witnesses those officers who did have authority to act for the distributors and who were in a position to know whether they had acted in pursuance of agreement is itself persuasive that their testimony, if given, would have been unfavorable to appellants. The production of weak evidence when strong is available can lead only to the conclusion that the strong would have been adverse. [Cases cited.]

While the District Court's finding of an agreement of the distributors among themselves is supported by the evidence, we think that in the circumstances of this case such agreement for the imposition of the restrictions upon subsequent-run exhibitors was not a prerequisite to an unlawful conspiracy. It was enough that, knowing that concerted action was contemplated and invited, the distributors gave their adherence to the scheme and participated in it. Each distributor was advised that the others were asked to participate; each knew that cooperation was essential to successful operation of the plan. They knew that the plan, if carried out, would result in a restraint of commerce, which, we will presently point out, was unreasonable within the meaning of the Sherman Act, and knowing it, all participated in the plan. The evidence is persuasive that each distributor early became aware that the others had joined. With that knowledge they renewed the arrangement and carried it into effect for the two successive years.

It is elementary that an unlawful conspiracy may be and often is formed without simultaneous action or agreement on the part of the conspirators. Acceptance by competitors, without previous agreement, of an invitation to participate in a plan, the necessary consequence of which, if carried out, is restraint of interstate commerce, is sufficient to establish an unlawful conspiracy under the Sherman Act....

....

We think the conclusion is unavoidable that the conspiracy and each contract between Interstate and the distributors by which those consequences were effected are violations of the Sherman Act and that the District Court rightly enjoined enforcement and renewal of these agreements, as well as of the conspiracy among the distributors.

Affirmed.

[JUSTICES ROBERTS, MCREYNOLDS and BUTLER dissented, arguing that the Court should not have found a conspiracy under the stipulated facts and that these kinds of agreements were not contemplated by earlier courts as conspiracies under the Sherman Act. JUSTICE FRANKFURTER did not participate.]

NOTES AND QUESTIONS

1. *American Tobacco Co. v. United States*, 328 U.S. 781 (1946), held that firms which engaged in monopolization under section 2 could be enjoined without any proof of an agreement to monopolize. The Court indicated:

> No formal agreement is necessary to constitute an unlawful conspiracy. Often crimes are a matter of inference deduced from the acts of the person accused and done in pursuance of a criminal purpose.... The essential combination or conspiracy in violation of the Sherman Act may be found in a course of dealing or other circumstances as well as in an exchange of words .... Where the circumstances are such as to warrant a jury in finding that the conspirators had a unity of purpose or a common design and understanding or a meeting of minds in an unlawful arrangement, the conclusion that a conspiracy is established is justified.

Id. at 809-10.

In *United States v. Masonite Corp.*, 316 U.S. 265 (1942), the Court said "[i]t was enough that, knowing that concerted action was contemplated and invited, the distributors gave their adherence to the scheme and participated in it .... The fixing of prices by one member of a group pursuant to express delegation, acquiescence, or understanding is just as illegal as the fixing of prices by direct, joint action." Further, in *United States v. Paramount Pictures, Inc.*, 334 U.S. 131 (1948), the Court concluded that "it is not necessary to find an express agreement in order to find a conspiracy. It is enough that a concert of action is contemplated and that defendants conformed to the arrangement." *See also United States v. United States Gypsum Co.*, 333 U.S. 364, 394 (1948), where the Court said that "when a group of competitors enters into a series of separate but similar agreements with competitors or others, a strong inference arises that such agreements are the result of concerted action. That inference is strengthened when contemporaneous declarations indicate that supposedly separate actions are part of a common plan."

2. Did the Court in *Interstate Circuit* and its subsequent opinions hold that an agreement is not a prerequisite to a conspiracy charge under section 1 where there is evidence of conscious parallelism? In other words, will mere evidence of parallel conduct by competitors with knowledge of each other's actions establish a prima facie case in support of an unlawful agreement?

3. Proof of withdrawal from a conspiracy is an effective affirmative defense to a section 1 claim. To withdraw effectively, one must either report the conspiracy to the proper authorities or clearly communicate an intent to withdraw. *In re Brand Name Prescription Drugs Antitrust Litigation*, 123 F.3d 599, 616 (7th Cir. 1997). However, withdrawal does not protect the once-conspiring party from liability under other theories or causes of action, such as section 2 of the Sherman Act. For example, the Seventh Circuit in *In re Brand Name Prescription Drugs Antitrust Litigation* held that the withdrawal of a particular drug manufacturer defendant from a price fixing activity in the form of specialized discounts to preferred customers did not prevent subsequent liability under section 2. *Id.*

THEATRE ENTERPRISES, INC. V. PARAMOUNT FILM DISTRIBUTING CORP.

346 U.S. 537 (1954)

JUSTICE CLARK delivered the opinion of the Court.

Petitioner brought this suit for treble damages and an injunction under §§ 4 and 16 of the Clayton Act, alleging that respondent motion picture producers and distributors had violated the antitrust laws by conspiring to restrict "first-run" pictures to downtown Baltimore theatres, thus confining its suburban theatre to subsequent runs and unreasonable "clearances." After hearing the evidence a jury returned a general verdict for respondents. The Court of Appeals for the Fourth Circuit affirmed the judgment based on the verdict. We granted certiorari.

Petitioner now urges, as it did in the Court of Appeals, that the trial judge should have directed a verdict in its favor and submitted to the jury only the question of the amount of damages. Alternatively, petitioner claims that the trial judge erred by inadequately instructing the jury as to the scope and effect of the decrees in *United States v. Paramount Pictures, Inc.*, the Government's prior equity suit against respondents. We think both contentions are untenable.

... Petitioner owns and operates the Crest Theatre, located in a neighborhood shopping district some six miles from the downtown shopping center in Baltimore, Maryland. The Crest, possessing the most modern improvements and appointments, opened on February 26, 1949. Before and after the opening, petitioner, through its president, repeatedly sought to obtain first-run features for the theatre. Petitioner approached each respondent separately, initially requesting exclusive first-runs, later asking for first-runs on a "day and date" basis. But respondents uniformly rebuffed petitioner's efforts and adhered to an established policy of restricting first-runs in Baltimore to the eight downtown theatres. Admittedly there is no direct evidence of illegal agreement between the respondents and no conspiracy is charged as to the independent exhibitors in Baltimore, who account for 63% of first-run exhibitions. The various respondents advanced much the same reasons for denying petitioner's offers. Among other reasons, they asserted that day-and-date first-runs are normally granted only to noncompeting theatres. Since the Crest is in "substantial competition" with the downtown theatres, a day-and-date arrangement would be economically unfeasible. And even if respondents wished to grant petitioner such a license, no downtown exhibitor would waive his clearance rights over the Crest and agree to a simultaneous showing. As a result, if petitioner were to receive first-runs, the license would have to be an exclusive one. However, an exclusive license would be economically unsound because the Crest is a suburban theatre, located in a small shopping center, and served by limited public transportation facilities; and, with a drawing area of less than one-tenth that of a downtown theatre, it cannot compare with those easily accessible theatres in the power to draw patrons. Hence the downtown theatres offer far greater opportunities for the widespread advertisement and exploitation of newly released features, which is thought necessary to maximize the over-all return from subsequent runs as well as first-runs. The respondents, in the light of these conditions, attacked the guaranteed offers of petitioner, one of which occurred during the trial, as not being made in good faith. Respondents Loew's and Warner refused petitioner an exclusive license because they owned the three downtown theatres receiving their first-run product.

The crucial question is whether respondents' conduct toward petitioner stemmed from independent decision or from an agreement, tacit or express. To be sure, business behavior is admissible circumstantial evidence from which the fact finder may infer agreement. *Interstate Circuit, Inc. v. United States*, 306

U.S. 208 (1939).... But this Court has never held that proof of parallel business behavior conclusively establishes agreement or, phrased differently, that such behavior itself constitutes a Sherman Act offense. Circumstantial evidence of consciously parallel behavior may have made heavy inroads into the traditional judicial attitude toward conspiracy; but "conscious parallelism" has not yet read conspiracy out of the Sherman Act entirely. Realizing this, petitioner attempts to bolster its argument for a directed verdict by urging that the conscious unanimity of action by respondents should be "measured against the background and findings in the *Paramount* case." In other words, since the same respondents had conspired in the *Paramount* case to impose a uniform system of runs and clearances without adequate explanation to sustain them as reasonable restraints of trade, use of the same device in the present case should be legally equated to conspiracy. But the *Paramount* decrees, even if admissible, were only prima facie evidence of a conspiracy covering the area and existing during the period there involved. Alone or in conjunction with the other proof of the petitioner, they would form no basis for a directed verdict. Here each of the respondents had denied the existence of any collaboration and in addition had introduced evidence of the local conditions surrounding the Crest operation which, they contended, precluded it from being a successful first-run house. They also attacked the good faith of the guaranteed offers of the petitioner for first-run pictures and attributed uniform action to individual business judgment motivated by the desire for maximum revenue. This evidence, together with other testimony of an explanatory nature, raised fact issues requiring the trial judge to submit the issue of conspiracy to the jury.

*Affirmed.**

NOTES AND QUESTIONS

1. What probative evidence supports the inference of agreement in *Interstate Circuit*? Note that the Court inferred collusion from defendants' failure to present evidence. Who has the burden of proof on the issue of an "agreement"? What evidence might defendant introduce to rebut plaintiff's evidence, for example, of common price? When might that burden shift? Can the burden of proving noncollusion be placed on the defendant in a criminal case? *See Patterson v. New York*, 432 U.S. 197 (1977); *Mullaney v. Wilbur*, 421 U.S. 684 (1975); *Barnes v. United States*, 412 U.S. 837 (1973).

2. Do the different procedural issues addressed by the Court in *Interstate Circuit* and *Theatre Enterprises* account for the different results? Does the Court apply one standard when the issue is whether a directed verdict should have been granted in defendant's favor, and another when the issue is whether there was sufficient evidence to sustain a jury finding of conspiracy?

---

* Justice Black dissented on other grounds. Justice Douglas took no part in the decision.

PROBLEM 4.6

Recently, major medical research has discovered that aspirin can prevent heart attacks. (In a study, more than 11,000 physicians over age 40 took one aspirin every other day, while another group of physicians took placebos. At the end of 57 months, the study showed that those taking aspirin had 47% fewer heart attacks.) Upon news of this discovery, the five major pharmaceutical companies that produce aspirin, with a total market share of 86% of the over-the-counter (OTC) pain-reliever market, each began advertising separately its aspirin product with a spectacular campaign of claims about the link of its product to heart attack avoidance.

After each companies' ads had run for three weeks, representatives of the five majors met to discuss the impact of the ads and whether they should be withdrawn. There were statements at this meeting that the Food and Drug Administration was opposed to the ads because they may be misleading to the public, given the nature of the medical information. But most of the representatives at the meeting were not concerned with the FDA's warning; they were concerned that each ad was conveying essentially the same message but pitched to the particular brand of the product.

When the majors could not agree on the form of the future ads, they discussed withdrawing the ads. The week following the meeting all ads regarding the aspirin-heart attack avoidance link were canceled.

Discuss what, if any, antitrust issues are presented by these facts, and how they would be decided by a court.

3. DELIVERED PRICING AND BASE-POINT PRICING

After the decision in *Interstate Circuit*, courts began to consider whether the "agreement" requirement of section 1 also applied to an unfair method of competition charge under section 5 of the Federal Trade Commission Act. The next cases in this section discuss this issue in the context of a "delivered pricing" program. *See generally* Kaysen, *Basing Point Pricing and Public Policy*, 63 Q.J. Econ. 289 (1948); G. Stigler, *The Organization of Industry* 147-70 (1968); Haddock, *Basing Point Pricing: Competitive Versus Collusive Theories*, 72 Am. Econ. Rev. 289 (1982). Generally, a "delivered price" is a price to the buyer which includes a charge for delivery. "[I]f the seller fixes a price at which [it] undertakes to deliver goods to the purchaser where they are to be used, the cost to the purchaser is the 'delivered price.'" *FTC v. Cement Inst.*, 333 U.S. 683, 687 (1948). If a buyer purchases "f.o.b.," the cost is generally set at the seller's location and the buyer will bear its own transportation cost. Obviously, varying transportation costs will affect price and hence competition. The related concept of base-point pricing sets the "delivered price" at a figure which includes transportation costs from a standard reference point, but not necessarily from where the product is shipped. The important question here is whether an industry-wide delivered pricing system can give rise to an inference of collusion under section

5 of the FTC Act. The cases also illustrate the relationship between the Sherman Act and the FTC Act.

FEDERAL TRADE COMMISSION V. CEMENT INSTITUTE

333 U.S. 683 (1948).

JUSTICE BLACK delivered the opinion of the Court.

... The Cement Institute, an unincorporated trade association composed of 74 corporations which manufacture, sell and distribute cement; the 74 corporate members of the Institute; and 21 individuals who are associated with the Institute ....

The proceedings were begun by a [Federal Trade] Commission complaint of two counts. The first charged that certain alleged conduct set out at length constituted an unfair method of competition in violation of § 5 of the Federal Trade Commission Act. The core of the charge was that the respondents had restrained and hindered competition in the sale and distribution of cement by means of a combination among themselves made effective through mutual understanding or agreement to employ a multiple basing point system of pricing. It was alleged that this system resulted in the quotation of identical terms of sale and identical prices for cement by the respondents at any given point in the United States. This system had worked so successfully, it was further charged, that for many years prior to the filing of the complaint, all cement buyers throughout the nation, with rare exceptions, had been unable to purchase cement for delivery in any given locality from any one of the respondents at a lower price or on more favorable terms than from any of the other respondents. [The complaint also charged price discrimination among buyers in violation of § 2 of the Clayton Act. *See* Chapter 8 *infra*.]...

As early as 1920 this Court considered it an "unfair method of competition" to engage in practices "against public policy because of their dangerous tendency unduly to hinder competition or create monopoly."... Again in 1926 this Court sustained a Commission unfair-method-of-competition order against defendants who had engaged in a price-fixing combination, a plain violation of § 1 of the Sherman Act. *Federal Trade Comm'n v. Pacific States Paper Trade Assn.*, 273 U.S. 52. In 1941 we reiterated that certain conduct of a combination found to conflict with the policy of the Sherman Act could be suppressed by the Commission as an unfair method of competition. *Fashion Originators Guild v. Federal Trade Comm'n*, 312 U.S. 457, 465. The Commission's order was sustained in the *Fashion Originators* case not only because the prohibited conduct violated the Clayton Act but also because the Commission's findings brought the "combination in its entirety well within the inhibition of the policies declared by the Sherman Act itself." In other cases this Court has pointed out many reasons which support interpretation of the language "unfair methods of competition" in § 5 of the Federal Trade Commission Act as including violations of the Sherman

Act. Thus it appears that soon after its creation the Commission began to interpret the prohibitions of § 5 as including those restraints of trade which also were outlawed by the Sherman Act, and that this Court has consistently approved that interpretation of the Act.

[O]n the whole the Act's legislative history shows a strong congressional purpose not only to continue enforcement of the Sherman Act by the Department of Justice and the federal district courts but also to supplement that enforcement through the administrative process of the new Trade Commission. Far from being regarded as a rival of the Justice Department and the district courts in dissolving combinations in restraint of trade, the new Commission was envisioned as an aid to them and was specifically authorized to assist them in the drafting of appropriate decrees in antitrust litigation....

We adhere to our former rulings. The Commission has jurisdiction to declare that conduct tending to restrain trade is an unfair method of competition even though the selfsame conduct may also violate the Sherman Act.

....

[A]lthough all conduct violative of the Sherman Act may likewise come within the unfair trade practice prohibitions of the Trade Commission Act, the converse is not necessarily true. It has long been recognized that there are many unfair methods of competition that do not assume the proportions of Sherman Act violations.... Hence a conclusion that respondents' conduct constituted an unfair method of competition does not necessarily mean that their same activities would also be found to violate § 1 of the Sherman Act. In the second place, the fact that the same conduct may constitute a violation of both acts in nowise requires us to dismiss this Commission proceeding. Just as the Sherman Act itself permits the Attorney General to bring simultaneous civil and criminal suits against a defendant based on the same misconduct, so the Sherman Act and the Trade Commission Act provide the Government with cumulative remedies against activity detrimental to competition. Both the legislative history of the Trade Commission Act and its specific language indicate a congressional purpose, not to confine each of these proceedings within narrow, mutually exclusive limits, but rather to permit the simultaneous use of both types of proceedings. Marquette's objections to the Commission's jurisdiction are overruled.

....

The Multiple Basing Point Delivered Price System. — Since the multiple basing point delivered price system of fixing prices and terms of cement sales is the nub of this controversy, it will be helpful at this preliminary stage to point out in general what it is and how it works. A brief reference to the distinctive characteristics of "factory" or "mill prices" and "delivered prices" is of importance to an understanding of the basing point delivered price system here involved.

Goods may be sold and delivered to customers at the seller's mill or warehouse door or may be sold free on board (f. o. b.) trucks or railroad cars immediately adjacent to the seller's mill or warehouse. In either event the actual cost of the goods to the purchaser is, broadly speaking, the seller's "mill price" plus the purchaser's cost of transportation. However, if the seller fixes a price at which he undertakes to deliver goods to the purchaser where they are to be used, the cost to the purchaser is the "delivered price." A seller who makes the "mill price" identical for all purchasers of like amount and quality simply delivers his goods at the same place (his mill) and for the same price (price at the mill). He thus receives for all f. o. b. mill sales an identical net amount of money for like goods from all customers. But a "delivered price" system creates complications which may result in a seller's receiving different net returns from the sale of like goods. The cost of transporting 500 miles is almost always more than the cost of transporting 100 miles. Consequently if customers 100 and 500 miles away pay the same "delivered price," the seller's net return is less from the more distant customer. This difference in the producer's net return from sales to customers in different localities under a "delivered price" system is an important element in the charge under Count I of the complaint....

The best known early example of a basing point price system was called "Pittsburgh plus." It related to the price of steel. The Pittsburgh price was the base price, Pittsburgh being therefore called a price basing point. In order for the system to work, sales had to be made only at delivered prices. Under this system the delivered price of steel from anywhere in the United States to a point of delivery anywhere in the United States was in general the Pittsburgh price plus the railroad freight rate from Pittsburgh to the point of delivery. Take Chicago, Illinois, as an illustration of the operation and consequences of the system. A Chicago steel producer was not free to sell his steel at cost plus a reasonable profit. He must sell it at the Pittsburgh price plus the railroad freight rate from Pittsburgh to the point of delivery. Chicago steel customers were by this pricing plan thus arbitrarily required to pay for Chicago produced steel the Pittsburgh base price plus what it would have cost to ship the steel by rail from Pittsburgh to Chicago had it been shipped. The theoretical cost of this fictitious shipment became known as "phantom freight." But had it been economically possible under this plan for a Chicago producer to ship his steel to Pittsburgh, his "delivered price" would have been merely the Pittsburgh price, although he actually would have been required to pay the freight from Chicago to Pittsburgh. Thus the "delivered price" under these latter circumstances required a Chicago (non-basing point) producer to "absorb" freight costs. That is, such a seller's net returns became smaller and smaller as his deliveries approached closer and closer to the basing point.

Several results obviously flow from use of a single basing point system such as "Pittsburgh plus" originally was. One is that the "delivered prices" of all producers in every locality where deliveries are made are always the same regardless of the producers' different freight costs. Another is that sales made by a non-base mill for delivery at different localities result in net receipts to the seller which vary in amounts equivalent to the "phantom freight" included in, or the "freight absorption" taken from the "delivered price."

As commonly employed by respondents, the basing point system is not single but multiple. That is, instead of one basing point, like that in "Pittsburgh plus," a number of basing point localities are used. In the multiple basing point system, just as in the single basing point system, freight absorption or phantom freight is an element of the delivered price on all sales not governed by a basing point actually located at the seller's mill. And all sellers quote identical delivered prices in any given locality regardless of their different costs of production and their different freight expenses. Thus the multiple and single systems function in the same general manner and produce the same consequences — identity of prices and diversity of net returns. Such differences as there are in matters here pertinent are therefore differences of degree only....

That basic problem is whether the Commission made findings of concerted action, whether those findings are supported by evidence, and if so whether the findings are adequate as a matter of law to sustain the Commission's conclusion that the multiple basing point system as practiced constitutes an "unfair method of competition," because it either restrains free competition or is an incipient menace to it.

Findings and Evidence. — ... The Commission found that many of these activities were carried on by the Cement Institute, the industry's unincorporated trade association, and that in other instances the activities were under the immediate control of groups of respondents. Among the collective methods used to accomplish these purposes, according to the findings, were boycotts; discharge of uncooperative employees; organized opposition to the erection of new cement plants; selling cement in a recalcitrant price cutter's sales territory at a price so low that the recalcitrant was forced to adhere to the established basing point prices; discouraging the shipment of cement by truck or barge; and preparing and distributing freight rate books which provided respondents with similar figures to use as actual or "phantom" freight factors, thus guaranteeing that their delivered prices would be identical on all sales whether made to individual purchasers under open bids or to governmental agencies under sealed bids....

Although there is much more evidence to which reference could be made, we think that the following facts shown by evidence in the record, some of which are in dispute, are sufficient to warrant the Commission's finding of concerted action.

When the Commission rendered its decision there were about 80 cement manufacturing companies in the United States operating about 150 mills. Ten companies controlled more than half of the mills and there were substantial corporate affiliations among many of the others. This concentration of productive capacity made concerted action far less difficult than it would otherwise have been. The belief is prevalent in the industry that because of the standardized nature of cement, among other reasons, price competition is wholly unsuited to it. That belief is historic. It has resulted in concerted activities to devise means and measures to do away with competition in the industry. Out of those activities came the multiple basing point delivered price system. Evidence shows it to be a handy instrument to bring about elimination of any kind of price competition. The use of the multiple basing point delivered price system by the cement producers has been coincident with a situation whereby for many years, with rare exceptions, cement has been offered for sale in every given locality at identical prices and terms by all producers. Thousands of secret sealed bids have been received by public agencies which corresponded in prices of cement down to a fractional part of a penny.[15]

Occasionally foreign cement has been imported, and cement dealers have sold it below the delivered price of the domestic product. Dealers who persisted in selling foreign cement were boycotted by the domestic producers. Officers of the Institute took the lead in securing pledges by producers not to permit sales f. o. b. mill to purchasers who furnished their own trucks, a practice regarded as seriously disruptive of the entire delivered price structure of the industry.

During the depression in the 1930's, slow business prompted some producers to deviate from the prices fixed by the delivered price system. Meetings were held by other producers; an effective plan was devised to punish the recalcitrants and bring them into line. The plan was simple but successful. Other producers made the recalcitrant's plant an involuntary base point. The base price was driven down with relatively insignificant losses to the producers who imposed the punitive basing point, but with heavy losses to the recalcitrant who had to make all its sales on this basis. In one instance, where a producer had made a low public bid, a punitive base point price was put on its plant and cement was reduced 1 per barrel; further reductions quickly followed until the base price at which this recalcitrant had to sell its cement dropped to 7 per barrel, scarcely one-half of its former base price of $1.45. Within six weeks after the base price hit 7 capitulation occurred and the recalcitrant joined a portland cement association. Cement in that locality then bounced back to $1.15, later to $1.35, and finally to $1.75.

The foregoing are but illustrations of the practices shown to have been utilized to maintain the basing point price system. Respondents offered testimony that

---

[15] The following is one among many of the Commission's findings as to the identity of sealed bids:

An abstract of the bids for 6,000 barrels of cement to the United States Engineer Office at Tucumcari, New Mexico, opened April 23, 1936, shows the following:

Name of Bidder	Price per Bbl.	Name of Bidder	Price per Bbl.
Monarch	$3.286854	Oklahoma	$3.286854
Ash Grove	3.286854	Consolidated	3.286854
Lehigh	3.286854	Trinity	3.286854
Southwestern	3.286854	Lone Star	3.286854
U. S. Portland		Universal	3.286854
Cement Co.	3.286854	Colorado	3.286854

All bids subject to 1 per barrel discount for payment in 15 days. (Com. Ex. 175-A.) *See* 157 F.2d at 576.

cement is a standardized product, that "cement is cement," that no differences existed in quality or usefulness, and that purchasers demanded delivered price quotations because of the high cost of transportation from mill to dealer. There was evidence, however, that the Institute and its members had, in the interest of eliminating competition, suppressed information as to the variations in quality that sometimes exist in different cements. Respondents introduced the testimony of economists to the effect that competition alone could lead to the evolution of a multiple basing point system of uniform delivered prices and terms of sale for an industry with a standardized product and with relatively high freight costs. These economists testified that for the above reasons no inferences of collusion, agreement, or understanding could be drawn from the admitted fact that cement prices of all United States producers had for many years almost invariably been the same in every given locality in the country. There was also considerable testimony by other economic experts that the multiple basing point system of delivered prices as employed by respondents contravened accepted economic principles and could only have been maintained through collusion.

The Commission did not adopt the views of the economists produced by the respondents. It decided that even though competition might tend to drive the price of standardized products to a uniform level, such a tendency alone could not account for the almost perfect identity in prices, discounts, and cement containers which had prevailed for so long a time in the cement industry. The Commission held that the uniformity and absence of competition in the industry were the results of understandings or agreements entered into or carried out by concert of the Institute and the other respondents. It may possibly be true, as respondents' economists testified, that cement producers will, without agreement express or implied and without understanding explicit or tacit, always and at all times (for such has been substantially the case here) charge for their cement precisely, to the fractional part of a penny, the price their competitors charge. Certainly it runs counter to what many people have believed, namely, that without agreement, prices will vary — that the desire to sell will sometimes be so strong that a seller will be willing to lower his prices and take his chances. We therefore hold that the Commission was not compelled to accept the views of respondents' economist-witnesses that active competition was bound to produce uniform cement prices. The Commission was authorized to find understanding, express or implied, from evidence that the industry's Institute actively worked, in cooperation with various of its members, to maintain the multiple basing point delivered price system; that this pricing system is calculated to produce, and has produced, uniform prices and terms of sale throughout the country; and that all of the respondents have sold their cement substantially in accord with the pattern required by the multiple basing point system.

....

Unfair Methods of Competition. — We sustain the Commission's holding that concerted maintenance of the basing point delivered price system is an unfair method of competition prohibited by the Federal Trade Commission Act....

We cannot say that the Commission is wrong in concluding that the delivered-price system as here used provides an effective instrument which, if left free for use of the respondents, would result in complete destruction of competition and the establishment of monopoly in the cement industry.... We uphold the Commission's conclusion that the basing point delivered price system employed by respondents is an unfair trade practice which the Trade Commission may suppress.[19]

The Commission's order should not have been set aside by the Circuit Court of Appeals. Its judgment is reversed and the cause is remanded to that court with directions to enforce the order.

[JUSTICE BURTON dissented, urging that the lower court's judgment setting aside the FTC order should have been affirmed because of insufficient evidence to support the finding of a "combination." JUSTICES DOUGLAS and JACKSON took no part in the consideration of the opinion.]

NOTES AND QUESTIONS

1. Following *Cement Institute*, the Seventh Circuit in *Triangle Conduit & Cable Co. v. FTC*, 168 F.2d 175 (7th Cir. 1948), *aff'd by an equally divided court*, 336 U.S. 956 (1949), affirmed an FTC cease and desist order, holding that individual use of base-point delivery pricing, with knowledge that parallel competitive conduct would yield identical delivered price quotations, was an unfair method of competition. Reasoned the court:

> [P]rice uniformity especially if accompanied by an artificial price level not related to the supply and demand of a given commodity may be evidence from which an agreement or understanding, or some concerted action of sellers operating to restrain commerce, may be inferred.

Id. at 179, *citing Cement Mfrs. Protective Ass'n v. United States*, 268 U.S. 588, 606 (1925).

2. If a defendant were successful in defending an "unfair method of competition" charge under section 5, could it be charged by the Department of Justice under section 1 of the Sherman Act on the same theory of parallel conduct and same facts? What defenses could be raised? Do the opinions in either decision define the meaning of "unfair method of competition"? How would you advise a client as to what is proscribed under section 5?

3. Does basing-point pricing ever make sense absent an agreement between the competing sellers to engage in the practice? Assume that there are three cement manufacturers located in Dallas, Chicago, and Pittsburgh. They are equally effi-

---

[19] While we hold that the Commission's findings of combination were supported by evidence, that does not mean that existence of a "combination" is an indispensable ingredient of an "unfair method of competition" under the Trade Commission Act. *See Federal Trade Comm'n v. Beech-Nut Packing Co.*, 257 U.S. 441, 455 (1922).

cient. All three are asked to bid on a construction project in Houston. In this case the Dallas cement manufacturer, which is much closer, has a substantial cost advantage over its two competitors. Would it engage in "Pittsburgh plus" computation of the price — thereby risking loss of the sale — unless it had an "understanding" that the Chicago and Pittsburgh manufacturers would later do the same thing when the bid was for a project in a city for which the Dallas manufacturer was disadvantaged, such as Cleveland?

In some cases, basing-point pricing may actually be unilateral, and it may be competitive. Suppose, for example, that sellers in a particular industry are spatially dispersed and have high transportation costs. As a result, each firm has "captive" customers located near its own plant, but there are "competitive" territories consisting of customers who are more-or-less equidistant from two or more sellers. Sellers would like to retain monopoly profits from the captive customers, but they would like to compete for the customers in the competitive territories. One way they can do this is by identifying a city in the competitive territory as a "base point" and charging customers in the competitive territories freight from that city instead of from the actual shipping point. The result is that customers in the competitive territory pay a lower effective price, even though the nominal price (without transportation costs) charged to competitive and captive customers is the same. See D. Haddock, *Basing Point Pricing: Competitive versus Collusive Theories*, 72 Am. Econ. Rev. 289 (1982).

In such a case, one could not infer the existence of a cartel from the fact that many firms in the same market used base-point pricing. What does it tell you that base-point pricing most often occurs in industries such as cement (*Cement Institute*), steel products (*Triangle Conduit*), and unfinished wood products (*Maple Flooring*) — products for which transportation costs are a high percentage of the delivered price?

4. What are the effects of base-point pricing on efficiency and consumer welfare? The competitive market gives a natural cost advantage to the supplier who is closest to the purchaser. All other things being equal, we would expect the Dallas cement supplier in the above example to win the bid, for it can manufacture and transport cement to Houston at the lowest cost. Base-point pricing, however, may make it equally likely that the purchaser will choose to buy its cement from Chicago or Pittsburgh. In that case the extra transportation costs necessary to ship the cement a longer distance is pure social loss.

5. Notwithstanding *Cement Institute*'s dictum that individual conduct not including the agreement required of the Sherman Act may be an unfair method of competition under section 5, the FTC later decided that it would prosecute under section 5 only if there was evidence of conspiracy. *FTC v. Cement Inst.*, 333 U.S. 683, 721 n. 19 (1948); *FTC v. Beechnut Packing Co.*, 257 U.S. 441, 455 (1922). *See Interim Report on the Study of the Federal Trade Commission Pricing Policies*, S. Doc. No. 27, 81st Cong., 1st Sess. 62-63 (1949). *Accord Crouse-Hinds Co.*, 46 F.T.C. 1114 (1950). Indeed, commentators urged that *Triangle Conduit*'s influence as precedent for an independent violation under section 5 for conscious parallel action was suspect because "a conspiracy had been properly established ... and the second charge was essentially directed to preventing its revival." A. Neale & D. Goyder, *The Antitrust Laws of the U.S.A.* 88 (3d ed. 1980).

In addition, in 1955 the Attorney General's National Commission to study the antitrust laws concluded that

[c]onscious parallelism is not a blanket equivalent of conspiracy. Its probative value in establishing the ultimate fact of conspiracy will vary case by case. Proof of agreement, express or implied, is still indispensable to the establishment of a conspiracy under the antitrust laws.

The significance of uniform action may depend, in any one instance, on a variety of factors. How persuasive is the uniformity? Does it extend to price alone or to all other terms and conditions of sale? How nearly identical is the uniformity? How long has the uniformity continued? What is the time lag, if any between a change by one competitor and that of the other or others? Is the product involved homogeneous or differentiated? In the case of price uniformity have the defendants raised as well as lowered prices in parallel fashion? Can the conduct no matter how uniform, be adequately explained by independent business justifications? Upon the answers to questions like these depends the weight to be accorded parallel action in any given case.

In short, evidence of uniformity will have varying probative significance depending on the particular business setting in which it occurs. Proof of independent business justification for the allegedly concerted conduct is, of course, always important to rebut agreement. No hard and fast rule can be formulated for all possible combinations of evidentiary features.

Report of Attorney General's National Committee to Study the Antitrust Laws 39-40 (1955).

In interpreting the Supreme Court's opinions, subsequent lower court cases indicate that the agreement requirement can be met if there is evidence of consciously parallel conduct (i.e., common plan) in addition to so-called "plus factors." *See, e.g., First Nat'l Bank v. Cities Serv. Co.*, 391 U.S. 253 (1968); *Michelman v. Clark-Schwebel Fiber Glass Corp.*, 534 F.2d 1036 (2d Cir.), *cert. denied*, 429 U.S. 885 (1976); *see generally* R. Bork, *The Antitrust Paradox* 178-97 (2d ed. 1993); 1 M. Handler, *Twenty-Five Years of Antitrust* 531 (1973); C. Kaysen & D. Turner, *Antitrust Policy* 106-09 (1959); Nye, *Can Conduct Oriented Enforcement Inhibit Conscious Parallelism?*, 44 Antitrust L.J. 206, 222 (1975). As the cases reveal, this latter requirement is conduct evidence from which inferences can be drawn demonstrating that competitors had agreed, either explicitly or implicitly, to a common design and course of action. Evidence indicating that competitors were involved in "a proposal for joint action, a complex yet identical set of responses, direct communication or an opportunity for it, a failure to deny agreement, [or] a set of circumstances which made each participant aware that it was in its interest to participate if all did, but adverse to its interest to participate if others did not" has been identified as "plus factors" from which concerted action can be inferred. L. Sullivan, *Handbook of the Law of Antitrust* 317 (1977). Evidence that the common action was contrary to defendants' own economic self interests is critical to the inquiry.

As this chapter has indicated, courts have difficulty identifying and characterizing cartel conduct. This portion of the chapter has addressed the problem of parallel conduct by competitors when evidence of explicit agreement is lacking. When the issues presented here are considered in light of the previous discussion concerning the relationship between market structure and price-affecting conduct, one can see how certain economic theories have shaped the law's development and enforcement approaches. The problem essentially is one of price coordination in concentrated markets, where only a few sellers dictate market terms. Oligopoly pricing and the use of facilitating devices to effectuate price coordination are considered next.

4. OLIGOPOLY PRICING AND FACILITATING DEVICES

Economic theory has informed antitrust enforcement from numerous directions. From economists we know that structure is one variable that affects market competition. In a perfectly competitive market, any one competitor cannot have an effect on price or output. The number of buyers or sellers is too large. But rarely do we observe a perfectly competitive market. Rather, a market may have only a few sellers, as in an oligopoly. In such a market each seller may take into account the pricing and output decisions of the other competitors. This "interdependence" may lead sellers into foregoing price cuts for fear that if one seller were to drop the price each would follow with a retaliatory price, the result of which would nullify a gain achieved by reason of the initial price decrease. Knowing that this response will follow, the original seller will not reduce prices in order to increase sales or market share. This theory posits that in a highly concentrated industry interdependent pricing and production decisions will be the norm. Consequently, price competition is avoided. *See generally* Turner, *The Definition of Agreement Under the Sherman Act: Conscious Parallelism and Refusals to Deal*, 75 Harv. L. Rev. 655 (1962); R. Posner, *Oligopoly and the Antitrust Laws: A Suggested Approach*, 21 Stan. L. Rev. 1562 (1969).

Conventional economic theory predicts that an exchange or disclosure of price information among competitors in a highly concentrated market will increase further the already present structural phenomenon of "interdependence," thereby facilitating anticompetitive performance through coordinated behavior. This theory was accepted by the Court in *Container* where anticompetitive conduct was inferred from market structure. The analysis of market structure was deemed critical to predicting anticompetitive market behavior. Justice Douglas observed that while "[p]rice information exchanged in some markets may have no effect on a truly competitive price ... [t]he exchange of price data tends toward price uniformity" in oligopolistic markets. 393 U.S. at 337. The structure of an industry, then, may indicate that it is predisposed toward collusive stabilization of prices. The more oligopolistic the market, the more likely an exchange will encourage price collusion.

As the cases in the preceding section indicate, antitrust enforcers have used the economic theory of interdependence as a means of challenging parallel pricing conduct in oligopoly markets. The argument is that sellers in an oligopoly recognize that their own price and production decisions are dictated, given the industry structure, in large part by the predicted reactions of other sellers to price moves. Anticipating those reactions, competitors adopt parallel pricing.

These economic theories, together with *Theatre Enterprise*, have, to be sure, spawned intense debate in the antitrust community. There is a continuous antitrust concern whether the Sherman Act is sufficiently inclusive to encompass oligopoly behavior. The issue of agreement and the role conscious parallelism places in setting the limits of that requirement continue to be central to the discussion.

For example, Professor Turner urged that it is rational for an oligopolist to price its product and determine its output by anticipating the reaction of its competitors in exactly the same way we would expect a seller to react in a competitive market. No agreement is necessarily involved, he argues, but rather merely a prudential judgment about probable reactions. Rational and lawful in one market but not another, he asks? Under his theory, if conscious parallelism is the only evidence before the court, then the "agreement" requirement has not been fulfilled and interdependent pricing should not be illegal. Anticipating a rival's market reaction is thus inherent in competition and the structure of the market. Therefore, injunctive relief would be inadequate because it would condemn rational market behavior.

For Turner, the solution was to change the structure of the oligopoly market. But, because section 1 was aimed at conduct or behavior and not structure, the structural remedy would have to be accomplished either under section 2, which traditionally challenged single-firm monopolization, or under new legislation. The concept known as "shared monopoly" is often used interchangeably with oligopoly pricing. They both have been referred to in describing interdependent concerted conduct by oligopolists that employ facilitating devices to create noncompetitive coordinated behavior in the market. *See generally Antitrust Division Memorandum on Identification and Challenge of Parallel Pricing Practices in Concentrated Industries*, 874 Antitrust & Trade Reg. Rep. (BNA) F-6 (1978). The Turner article began a continuing discussion on the subject.

From the antitrust litigator's perspective, the issue is largely one of the standard of proof in determining whether collusion can be inferred from parallel pricing in a concentrated market, so that the challenged conduct can be brought within section 1's requirement that there be a "contract, combination or conspiracy" in restraint of trade. In 1969 Professor Turner, after serving a term in the Department of Justice, wrote another article in which he reaffirmed that consciously parallel pricing in an oligopoly does not meet the definition of agreement under section 1. He opined, however, that unjustified exclusionary conduct by an oligopolist could be challenged under an attempt to monopolize theory under section 2. And where the "exclusionary practices are interdependent, where one would not have carried on the practices unless the others had gone along," he advocated they be charged with a conspiracy or combination to monopolize. *See* Turner, *The Scope of Antitrust and Other Economic Regulatory Policies*, 82 Harv. L. Rev. 1207 (1969).

Professor (now Judge) Posner challenged the Turner article seven years later. He argued that while noncompetitive pricing by oligopolists may be facilitated by market structure, it was not inevitably compelled. Posner, *Oligopoly and the Antitrust Laws: A Suggested Approach*, 21 Stan. L. Rev. 1562 (1969). He urged that such conduct required voluntary and coordinated action among sellers, similar to that found in the traditional cartel. Because of the market structure, however, no explicit agreement was necessary to accomplish the objective. Thus, from a combination of voluntary price moves such as price signaling and acceptances, and market structure, the agreement requirement could be proven by an inference of tacit collusion. Posner would not, however, prove evidence of a "meeting of the minds" solely through traditional conduct evidence such as a price exchange or announcement. The burden of proof would also be carried by the introduction of economic evidence.

The following economic factors and conduct evidence could be used, Posner argues, to infer tacit collusion resulting in noncompetitive pricing: systematic price discrimination, prolonged excess capacity over demand, infrequent price changes, price leadership, abnormally high profits, market shares fixed over time, filing of identical sealed bids on nonstandard items, refusal to offer discounts where there is substantial excess capacity, price increase announcements far in advance, and public discussions of prices. While Posner does recognize the evidentiary difficulty of using this type of evidence to convince the fact finder of tacit collusion, he offers an explanation of how such an inference can be drawn.

> When a seller has substantial excess capacity, the pressure to cut prices is strong, because the cost of utilizing idle capacity will be only a fraction of the usual cost of production. For sellers in these circumstances to refuse to reduce price suggests collusion. The practices of announcing prices increased long in advance, and of discussing publicly what is the right price for the industry (not the individual firm) are methods of indirect communication by which sellers iron out possible differences among them and arrive at the mutually agreeable price. Evidence relating to public discussion or announcements of price increases will usually not be sufficient by itself, but together with evidence of the actual pricing of the industry members could provide convincing support for an inference of tacit collusion.

Id. at 1582-83. Because voluntary conduct, rather than market structure, is the centerpiece of Posner's oligopoly pricing explanation, he concludes that injunctive relief such as broad behavioral remedies or conduct-oriented orders are workable and preferable. The literature since the Turner and Posner articles is voluminous. *See, e.g.,* H. Hovenkamp, *Federal Antitrust Policy*, ch. 4 (2d ed. 1994);

R. Schmalensee & R. Willig, *Handbook of Industrial Organization*, ch. 6 (1989); R. Bork, *The Antitrust Paradox* 174-82 (1978); Kauper, *New Approaches to the Old Problem*, 46 Antitrust L.J. 435 (1977); Scherer, Book Review, 86 Yale L.J. 974 (1977); L. Sullivan, *Handbook of the Law of Antitrust* 321-22 (1977); Markovits, *Oligopolistic Pricing Suits, the Sherman Act, and Economic Welfare*, 28 Stan. L. Rev. 45 (1975); 26 Stan. L. Rev. 717 (1975); 26 Stan. L. Rev. 493 (1974).

From an evidentiary standpoint, how difficult would it be to litigate a section 1 case under the suggested theory of Posner? Could a jury or even the judge be expected to understand and evaluate the intricacies of the economic evidence? Consider whether the costs of litigating the "big case" justify the remedy achieved. If collusion were inferred, how would a conduct-oriented injunction be written so as not to stifle competitive performance or run afoul of first amendment commercial speech rights? *See generally* Sullivan, *First Amendment Defenses in Antitrust Litigation*, 46 Mo. L. Rev. 517 (1981).

The economic theories advanced by Turner, Posner, and others have been utilized in various enforcement actions since the early 1970's. The target has been concentrated industries which are characterized by inflated prices and reduced output, conduct similar to that of a monopolist but engaged in by individual firms. At first, enforcement by the FTC was structurally oriented. Thereafter the enforcement approach has been directed "at the concerted adoption by firms in a concentrated industry of mechanisms that facilitate the achievement of industry pricing or output consensus." Present actions generally challenge the legality of the "facilitating devices" rather than merely targeting the oligopoly status.

The first enforcement efforts challenging oligopoly pricing (or shared monopoly) were brought by the Federal Trade Commission. In *In re Kellogg Co.*, No. 8883 (F.T.C. April 26, 1972) (complaint) and *In re Exxon Corp.*, No. 8934 (F.T.C. July 17, 1973) (complaint), defendants were charged with collective use of monopoly-like power under the theory of "shared monopoly" similar to the approach advocated in the Turner articles. The actions sought structural relief, such as divestiture of individual firms. They also challenged specific conduct such as expensive advertising and product differentiation as exclusionary and anticompetitive. The industries were characterized as having noncompetitive prices, excess profits and high entry barriers. Each action charged "unfair methods of competition" under section 5 of the FTC Act. The *Kellogg* case was dismissed by the Commission after an administrative law judge found no violation. See the discussion of shared monopoly, *infra*. The *Exxon* case was dismissed at the investigative discovery stage by the Commission after it had issued a complaint.

In 1978, after the FTC's unpromising start under its shared monopoly theory of enforcement, the Department of Justice announced its enforcement drive under section 1.

The enforcement centered on the economic theory of challenging the use of "facilitating devices" as means of price signaling and price coordination among oligopolistic firms. It attempted to reach under section 1 joint action by individual firms which had the same market effect, increased prices and reduced output, as a monopoly by a single firm governed under section 2.

The Justice Department identified two prerequisites for the shared monopoly (oligopolistic pricing) to exist: (1) noncompetitive price structure, and (2) low probability that firms acting independently of the consensus price structure will be successful in achieving increased profits. A violation of section 1 was alleged to have occurred if firms adopted mechanisms or practices that facilitated the achievement of these conditions. Certain objectionable facilitating devices were identified: price information exchanges, useful for monitoring prices; price and product standardization systems, useful in detecting noncompliance (examples include delivered pricing system, price books, bidding system, etc.); and price protection clauses, useful in punishing deviations from established price levels.

In order to find oligopoly pricing and the facilitating devices used to effectuate it unlawful under section 1, the government's prosecution theory required the challenged practices to have been adopted by agreement. In this regard, it was influenced, at least implicitly, by Posner's tacit agreement theory of prosecution. Its legal theory rested on (1) the market structure analysis adopted in *Container*, (2) inferences drawn from parallel behavior, as sanctioned in *Interstate Circuit* and *American Tobacco*, and (3) the broad language in *Socony-Vacuum* regarding tampering with price structures. In essence, the government's section 1 "shared monopoly" theory was directed against facilitating devices which required an agreement to be inferred from: (1) parallel conduct by firms in concentrated industry, (2) awareness by each firm that rivals are following a parallel course, (3) anticompetitive benefits, and (4) actions contradictory to the independent self-interest of each firm.

The government's theory was tested in a suit brought against General Electric and Westinghouse, which were the largest manufacturers of large turbine generators. The government alleged that there had been an elimination of price competition by the "conscious adoption and publication of identical pricing." *United States v. GE Co.*, 1977-2 Trade Cas. (CCH) ¶¶ 61,659, 72,715. The challenged scheme allegedly utilized a book detailing prices regarding all aspects of the complex machinery in question, formulas for computing prices, and examples of how the formulas were to be used. The price books allegedly enabled each defendant to predict the price and type of machine on which each competitor would bid. A price protection plan was also utilized. It was coupled with a public announcement of all outstanding orders and prices. If the price paid by any customer was discounted, all buyers in the previous six months would receive retroactively the same discount.

The government concluded that the price book, with its published multiplier, and the protection plan resulted in identical pricing in the turbine generator industry. The Justice Department asserted from these facts that an inference of agreement could be made. To establish the inference, the government was prepared to argue that internal documents of defendants would demonstrate that

G.E., through public signals, was inviting Westinghouse to accept its offer to stabilize prices, and that Westinghouse perceived G.E.'s actions as invitations to join. Thus the action was commenced on the theory that circumstantial evidence would establish that there was a conspiracy between defendants to fix prices.

Rather than engage in a protracted suit, defendants in *GE/Westinghouse, supra*, agreed to a modification of an earlier order. Defendants denied the theory of the case. Conceding that equal price levels existed between the two competitors, they argued that the result was due to either price leadership by GE or conscious parallelism between the two competitors. While admitting interdependent pricing, defendants argued that the duopoly structure of the industry dictated that each consider the other's pricing decisions. The consent decree prohibited defendants from engaging in a broad range of communications relevant to pricing. It prohibited, inter alia, the publication or distribution of so-called price-signaling information, certain conduct that acted as an enforcement device on the agreed-on-price; and dissemination of price-related commercial data from which competitors could track each other's pricing policies.

The conduct-oriented order in *GE/Westinghouse*, which fenced in and proscribed all forms of price signaling resulting in a pattern of identical pricing, was heralded as the government's new approach in attacking oligopoly parallel pricing. The government was prepared to argue that its new "signaling" theory went beyond mere conscious parallelism and that, from the evidence, a conspiracy to restrain trade could be inferred.

In an action brought by the FTC, the United States Court of Appeals for the Ninth Circuit held that "in the absence of evidence of overt agreement to utilize a pricing system to avoid price competition, the Commission must demonstrate that the challenged pricing system actually had the effect of fixing or stabilizing prices. Without such effect, a mere showing of parallel action will not establish a section 5 violation." *Boise Cascade Corp. v. FTC*, 637 F.2d 573 (9th Cir. 1980).

In *Boise*, the Ninth Circuit refused to enforce the Commission's order prohibiting a delivered pricing system where the FTC's theory rested on conscious parallel conduct as an unfair method of competition in the absence of an agreement. In declining to accept the Commission's theory "that industry-wide adoption of an artificial method of price-quoting" should be deemed a per se violation of section 5, the court observed that the debate comes down to "whether it is ever appropriate for evidence of anticompetitive effect of certain types of parallel conduct to serve as a substitute for the Sherman Act requirement of agreement." The court did not reach the broader issue because it found that the FTC failed to prove anticompetitive effect.

After the *Boise Cascade* decision a private class action based on the same facts ended in a jury verdict for the plaintiffs. The Fifth Circuit, in part, affirmed. The jury awarded the plaintiffs the difference between the "phantom freight" they had been charged and the actual freight costs that the seller paid. Was this the proper measure of damages? If a group of competitors agreed (explicitly or implicitly) to fix their freight rates, would their basic sale price remain unchanged, or would they continue to compete by discounting the price? Review was granted. *In re Plywood Antitrust Litig.*, 655 F.2d 627 (5th Cir. 1981), *cert. granted sub nom. Weyerhaeuser Co. v. Lyman Lamb Co.*, 456 U.S. 971 (1982). The parties settled their suit before the Court had an opportunity to decide the issues.

The FTC also advanced the price signaling theory in an action under section 5 of the FTC Act charging unfair methods of competition in a complaint against manufacturers of gasoline "antiknock" additives. In *In re Ethyl Corp.*, 101 F.T.C. 425 (1983), the FTC sought to test the constitutional sweep of a proposed conduct-oriented order which was designed to prohibit price signaling, together with other facilitating practices. Initially, the Commission staff attempted to establish its charge of "unfairness" in the absence of evidence of a conspiracy, agreement, or improper intent. The case, like *GE/Westinghouse*, was directed at oligopoly parallel pricing. The FTC approach was an apparent rejection of its 1949 pronouncement that it would not prosecute under section 5 in absence of evidence of conspiracy or at least tacit collusion.

On appeal, the Second Circuit in *Ethyl* reversed the FTC decision, holding that there was insufficient evidence to support the decision. The opinion follows. In reading the decision, consider whether an attack on oligopoly pricing under section 5 is dead after the Second Circuit's reversal in *Ethyl*.

E.I. DU PONT DE NEMOURS & CO. V. FTC

729 F.2d 128 (2d Cir. 1984)

JUDGE MANSFIELD: E.I. Du Pont De Nemours and Company ("Du Pont") and Ethyl Corporation ("Ethyl"), the nation's two largest manufacturers of lead antiknock gasoline additives, petition this court pursuant to § 5(c) of the Federal Trade Commission Act, 15 U.S.C. § 45(c), to review and set aside a final order of the Federal Trade Commission ("FTC") entered with an accompanying opinion on April 1, 1983. The FTC held that Du Pont, Ethyl and two other antiknock compound manufacturers, PPG Industries, Inc. ("PPG") and Nalco Chemical Company ("Nalco"), had engaged in unfair methods of competition in violation of § 5(a)(1) when each firm independently and unilaterally adopted at different times some or all of three business practices that were neither restrictive, predatory, nor adopted for the purpose of restraining competition. These challenged practices were: (1) the sale of the product by all four firms at a delivered price which included transportation costs, (2) the giving by Du Pont and Ethyl of extra advance notice of price increases, over and above the 30 days provided by contract, and (3) the use by Du Pont and Ethyl (and infrequently by PPG) of a "most favored nation" clause under which the seller promised that no customer would be charged a higher price than other customers. The Commission reasoned that, although the petitioner's adoption of these practices was non-collusive, they collectively had the effect, by removing some of the uncertainties about price determination, of substantially lessening competition by facilitating price parallelism at non-competitive levels higher than might have otherwise existed. The order is set aside.

Lead-based antiknock compounds have been used in the refining of gasoline since the 1920's. The compounds are essentially homogeneous .... They are now usually sold as mixtures, sometimes with additives. The compounds are added to gasoline to prevent "knock," i.e., premature detonation in a gasoline engine's cylinders. Resistance to knock is measured by octane ratings; for a gasoline refiner use of lead-based antiknock mixtures is the most economical way to raise the octane rating of gasoline for vehicles that take leaded gas....

....

The only purchasers of lead antiknocks are the gasoline refining companies which are large, aggressive and sophisticated buyers. Indeed, several are among the largest industrial corporations in the world. If prospective profits from the sale of antiknock compounds were sufficiently attractive, nothing would prevent them from integrating backwards into the antiknock industry. Of the 154 refiners who purchase the product, the ten largest buy about 30% of the total amount produced in this country.

....

[C]haracteristics of the industry — high concentration, small likelihood of new entries because of a sharply declining market, inelastic demand, and homogeneity of product — led to a natural oligopoly with a high degree of pricing interdependence in which there was far less incentive to engage in price competition than if there had been many sellers in an expanding market. Although a manufacturer in an inelastic market can temporarily capture an increased market share by price reductions or secret discounts, the reductions or discounts are usually discovered and met sooner or later by some form of competition by the other producers without increasing the volume of total sales in the market. The sole effect of a price reduction in a declining, inelastic market, therefore, is to reduce the industry's total profits. For these reasons Du Pont and Ethyl (as distinguished from PPG and Nalco) each independently chose not to offer price discounts, which they believed would be unprofitable. Du Pont instead decided to raise its prices by an amount that would offset its increasing costs and in addition yield a 20% pre-tax return on investment. As a result, during the 1970's, profits in the industry — particularly Du Pont's and Ethyl's — were substantially greater than what is described as the benchmark in the chemical industry, which in this case is 150% of the average rate of return in that industry....

....

Each of the challenged practices was initiated by Ethyl during the period prior to 1948 when it was the sole producer in the industry. There is no suggestion that the practices constituted unfair methods of competition at that time. For example, Ethyl began quoting prices on a delivered basis in 1937 in response to customer demand. Each of the three subsequent manufacturers, upon entry into the market, followed that practice. There is no evidence that the practice was adopted by any of the respondents for other than legitimate business reasons, the principal of which were tradition and customer demand. Customers demanded a delivered price because it would require the manufacturers to retain title to and responsibility for the dangerously volatile compounds during transit to the refiner's plant and in at least some cases would result in savings on state transportation and inventory taxes which the customer would pay if title passed prior to delivery. It is undisputed that, as the ALJ found, the delivery charge is a very small factor in relation to the sales price of the compounds. In 1979, for instance, average delivery costs to respondents' customers amounted to $1.53 cents per pound or less than 2% of list price, hardly a substantial competitive factor.

....

Similarly, Ethyl adopted the "most favored nation" contractual clause more than fifty years ago when it was the sole producer of antiknocks as a guarantee against price discrimination between its own customers who competed against each other in the sale of gasoline containing antiknock compounds. The clause assured the smaller refiners that they would not be placed at a competitive disadvantage on account of price discounts to giants such as Standard Oil, Texaco and Gulf. For the same legitimate business reason Du Pont adopted the same contractual clause when it later entered the industry. Even though such clauses arguably reduce price discounting, they comport with the requirements of the Robinson-Patman Act, 15 U.S.C. § 13, which prohibits price discrimination between customers. There is no evidence that Ethyl or Du Pont adopted or continued to use the most favored nation clause for the purpose of influencing the price discounting policies of other producers or of facilitating their adoption of or adherence to uniform prices. Indeed, PPG did not include the clause in its standard contract with customers and the complaint did not charge it with engaging in this practice. Nalco made only limited use of the clause.

Finally, the issuance of advance notice of price increases both to buyers and to the press, a common practice in the chemical industry, was initiated by Ethyl, well before the entry of Du Pont or the other two manufacturers into the market, as a means of aiding buyers in their financial and purchase planning. The contract clause used by two producers (Ethyl and Nalco) required them to give 30 days notice to the customer of price changes, while the clause used by the others (Du Pont and PPG) was limited to price increases. Du Pont and Ethyl gave customers a few days additional notice of their price increases (sometimes called a "grace period") but Nalco did not do so and PPG did not do so in any price increase that it initiated. Although the advance noticing had the indirect effect of informing competitors as to the producer's price increases, the record, not surprisingly, contains considerable proof that in such a small industry manufacturers quickly learn of competitors' price changes, usually within hours, regardless of the advance public notice. Typically, when one producer changed its price and communicated that change to its buyers, those buyers would immediately call the other producers to secure the best price. Moreover, the giving of 30 or more days advance notice of a price increase did not preclude the initiator, upon finding that competitors did not follow, from rescinding or modifying the increase or extending its effective date at any time prior to the end of the 30-day period.

....

The Commission concluded from its examination of the record that the structure of the antiknock industry — high concentration, high barriers to entry, a homogeneous product, and inelastic demand — rendered it susceptible to unilateral but interdependent conduct which lessened competition. The Commission further decided that the record contained substantial evidence of noncompetitive performance in the industry: highly uniform prices and price changes, limited price discounting, stable market shares, relatively high profits, prices in excess of marginal cost, and rising prices despite excess capacity and sluggish demand. On such a record, the FTC held that unilateral but interdependent practices engaged in by the petitioners constituted an unfair method of competition in violation of § 5. Conceding that the challenged practices each had a legitimate business purpose, the Commission concluded nevertheless that the anticompetitive effect of those practices rendered them unlawful.

....

The FTC issued a cease and desist order only against Ethyl and Du Pont, prohibiting them from announcing price changes prior to the 30-day contractual period and from using "most favored nation" clauses in their sales contracts. The order also required Ethyl and Du Pont to afford their customers the option of purchasing antiknocks additives at a "point of origin" price. The Commission did not prohibit the use of press releases or the 30-day advance notice of price increases. No order was entered against PPG because that company has withdrawn from the industry and no order was entered against Nalco because of the Commission's conclusion that Nalco was unlikely to be an initiator of price increases.

The essential question is whether, given the characteristics of the antiknock industry, the Commission erred in holding that the challenged business practices constitute "unfair methods of competition" in violation of § 5 simply because they "facilitate" consciously parallel pricing at identical levels....

....

The Commission here asks us to ... hold that the "unfair methods of competition" provision of § 5 can be violated by non-collusive, non-predatory and independent conduct of a non-artificial nature, at least when it results in a substantial lessening of competition. We recognize that § 5 invests the Commission with broad powers designed to enable it to cope with new threats to competition as they arise.... However, ... appropriate standards must be adopted and applied to protect a respondent against abuse of power. As the Commission moves away from attacking conduct that is either a violation of the antitrust laws or collusive, coercive, predatory, restrictive or deceitful, and seeks to break new ground by enjoining otherwise legitimate practices, the closer must be our scrutiny upon judicial review. A test based solely upon restraint of competition, even if qualified by the requirement that the conduct be "analogous" to an antitrust violation, is so vague as to permit arbitrary or undue government interference with the reasonable freedom of action that has marked our country's competitive system....

When a business practice is challenged by the Commission, even though, as here, it does not violate the antitrust or other laws and is not collusive, coercive, predatory or exclusionary in character, standards for determining whether it is "unfair" within the meaning of § 5 must be formulated to discriminate between normally acceptable business behavior and conduct that is unreasonable or unacceptable. Otherwise the door would be open to arbitrary or capricious administration of § 5; the FTC could, whenever it believed that an industry was not achieving its maximum competitive potential, ban certain practices in the hope that its action would increase competition. The mere existence of an oligopolistic market structure in which a small group of manufacturers engages in consciously parallel pricing of an identical product does not violate the antitrust laws. It represents a condition not a "method"; indeed it could be consistent with intense competition. Labelling one producer's price change in such a market as a "signal," parallel price changes as "lock-step," or prices as "supercompetitive," hardly converts its pricing into an "unfair" method of competition. To so hold would be to condemn any such price increase or moves, however independent; yet the FTC has not suggested that § 5 authorizes it to ban all price increases in an oligopolistic market. On the contrary, it states that "Section 5 should not prohibit oligopolistic pricing *alone*, even supercompetitive parallel prices, in the absence of specific conduct which promotes such a result." This fine distinction creates doubt as to the types of otherwise legitimate conduct that are lawful and those that are not. The doubt is increased by the Commission's concession that price uniformity is normal in a market with few sellers and homogeneous products, such as that in the antiknock compound industry.

In view of this patent uncertainty the Commission owes a duty to define the conditions under which conduct claimed to facilitate price uniformity would be unfair so that businesses will have an inkling as to what they can lawfully do rather than be left in a state of complete unpredictability. The Commission's decision in the present case does not provide any guidelines, it would require each producer not only to assess the general conduct of the antiknock business but also that of each of its competitors and the reaction of each to the other, which would be virtually impossible....

In our view, before business conduct in an oligopolistic industry may be labelled "unfair" within the meaning of § 5 a minimum standard demands that, absent a tacit agreement, at least some indicia of oppressiveness must exist such as (1) evidence of anticompetitive intent or purpose on the part of the producer charged, or (2) the absence of an independent legitimate business reason for its conduct. If, for instance, a seller's conduct, even absent identical behavior on the part of its competitors, is contrary to its independent self-interest, that circumstance would indicate that the business practice is "unfair" within the meaning of § 5. In short, in the absence of proof of a violation of the antitrust laws or evidence of collusive, coercive, predatory, or exclusionary conduct, business practices are not "unfair" in violation of § 5 unless those practices either have an anticompetitive purpose or cannot be supported by an independent legitimate reason. To suggest, as does the Commission in its opinion, that the defendant can escape violating § 5 only by showing that there are "countervailing procompetitive justifications" for the challenged business practices goes too far.

In the present case the FTC concedes that the petitioners did not engage in the challenged practices by agreement or collusively. Each acted independently and unilaterally. There is no evidence of coercive or predatory conduct. If the petitioners nevertheless were unable to come forward with some independent legitimate reason for their adoption of these practices, the Commission's argument that they must be barred as "unfair" when they have the effect of facilitating conscious price parallelism and interdependence might have some merit. But the evidence is overwhelming and undisputed, as the ALJ found, that each petitioner independently adopted its practices for legitimate business reasons.

The Commission contends that although the business practices at issue here might not be unfair under other market conditions, they assume that unlawful character when adopted in a concentrated or oligopolistic market in which a few producers sell a homogenous product, demand is inelastic, prices are "supracompetitive," and barriers to entry are high. It is argued that in such a milieu the practices assist the producers in independently maintaining prices at higher levels than would otherwise be the case. Perhaps this argument would be acceptable if the market were clearly as so described and a causal connection could be shown between the practices and the level of prices. Indeed the Commission majority concedes that "facilitating practices will be found to violate § 5 as unfair methods of competition only if the weight of the evidence shows that competition has been substantially lessened" and that it was required to "establish a *clear nexus* between the challenged conduct and adverse competitive effects before invoking our authority in this regard." But the record does not contain substantial evidence supporting many of the Commission's conclusions or showing a causal connection between the challenged practices and market prices. Indeed, it appears to be riddled with deficiencies and inconsistencies, many of which are noted by Chairman Miller in his dissent.

In the first place, price uniformity and parallelism was much more limited than the FTC would have it. During the relevant period (1974-1979) Nalco extended price discounts on more than 80% of its sales and PPG on more than one-third of its sales, the latter increasing to 58% of its sales in 1979 as the sellers competed for fewer buyers in a diminishing market. Although there was for the most part price parallelism on the part of Du Pont and Ethyl, they effectively met the price discounts of the other two producers by providing competition in the form of extensive services which had the effect of retaining old customers or luring away new ones. Thus the total package, including free valuable services and discounts, presents a picture of a competitive market in which large, sophisticated and aggressive buyers were making demands and were satisfied with the results. To the extent that there was price uniformity, that condition is as consistent with competitive as with anticompetitive behavior.

The problems faced by anyone thinking of entering the market were not "barriers" in the usual sense used by economists, such as requirements for high capital investment or advanced technological know-how. The main problem has been that market demand, due to factors uncontrolled by petitioners, is sharply declining. A dying market, which will soon dry up altogether, does not attract new entries. Absent some reasonable prospect that a price reduction would increase demand — and there is none — it is not surprising that existing producers have not engaged in as much price competition as might exist under other conditions. To suggest that industry-wide use of delivered instead of f.o.b. pricing restrained price competition in such a market ignores the de minimis part freight charges played in the price paid by customers. It also overlooks the fact that f.o.b. pricing is not necessarily more competitive than delivered pricing.

In short, we do not find substantial evidence in this record as a whole that the challenged practices significantly lessened competition in the antiknock industry or that the elimination of those practices would improve competition.

The Federal Trade Commission's order is

Vacated.

5. INTRA-ENTERPRISE CONSPIRACY

As the previous cases in this chapter have pointed out, section 1 of the Sherman Act requires a contract, combination, or conspiracy between two or more legal persons. In defining the requirement of plurality, the question arises whether concerted conduct by persons within a single legal entity comes within the statutory proscription of an agreement in restraint of trade. Literally, of course, conduct entered between two or more persons would come within the definition. Since a corporation can act only through its officers and employees, however, it would be impossible for it to conduct its affairs if its every conduct comes within the agreement requirement. *See Report of the Attorney General's National Committee to Study the Antitrust Laws* 30-36 (1955). The decisional law has created exceptions to section 1's application where there is concerted action on the corporations' behalf by officers of a single corporation. The rule is generally that a single corporation cannot conspire with itself under section 1. Related questions are raised regarding conduct by subsidiary corporations and by unincorporated divisions on behalf of a parent corporation. Central to the inquiry is whether concerted action has been engaged in by separate economic entities. Still other questions raised under the plurality requirement concern the coverage of conduct by agents. The following cases set forth the standards that have been applied to these categories under the doctrine of intra-enterprise (intracorporate) conspiracy.

On the issue of affiliated corporate status where there is concerted action, the Supreme Court said in *United States v. Yellow Cab Co.*, 332 U.S. 218, 227

(1947), that the legality may depend on whether the actual creation of the affiliation was illegal. The Court said "a conspiracy among those who are affiliated or integrated under common ownership" may violate section 1 as if it were a conspiracy between independent firms. In *Yellow Cab* the Court was addressing a potential restraint, where a cab manufacturer acquired several cab operating companies which were joined as a single entity. The restraint concerned cab purchasing contracts which allegedly foreclosed competitors of the manufacturer from selling cabs to the operating companies. The Court found that, notwithstanding the resulting single business entity, an illegal "combination" may have been formed during the creation of the enterprise, and if so, section 1 would be violated if a restraint were found. While the language of the Court was broader than the ultimate holding, subsequent opinions are in agreement. *See* 338 U.S. 338 (1949) where the Court eventually affirmed the district court's finding that the cab operating companies had been obtained lawfully.

COPPERWELD CORP. V. INDEPENDENCE TUBE CORP.

467 U.S. 752 (1984)

CHIEF JUSTICE BURGER delivered the opinion of the Court.

We granted certiorari to determine whether a parent corporation and its wholly owned subsidiary are legally capable of conspiring with each other under § 1 of the Sherman Act.

I

A

The predecessor to petitioner Regal Tube Co. was established in Chicago in 1955 to manufacture structural steel tubing used in heavy equipment, cargo vehicles, and construction. From 1955 to 1968 it remained a wholly owned subsidiary of C. E. Robinson Co. In 1968 Lear Siegler, Inc., purchased Regal Tube Co. and operated it as an unincorporated division. David Grohne, who had previously served as vice president and general manager of Regal, became president of the division after the acquisition.

In 1972 petitioner Copperweld Corp. purchased the Regal division from Lear Siegler; the sale agreement bound Lear Siegler and its subsidiaries not to compete with Regal in the United States for five years. Copperweld then transferred Regal's assets to a newly formed, wholly owned Pennsylvania corporation, petitioner Regal Tube Co. The new subsidiary continued to conduct its manufacturing operations in Chicago but shared Copperweld's corporate headquarters in Pittsburgh.

Shortly before Copperweld acquired Regal, David Grohne accepted a job as a corporate officer of Lear Siegler. After the acquisition, while continuing to work for Lear Siegler, Grohne set out to establish his own steel tubing business to compete in the same market as Regal. In May 1972 he formed respondent Independence Tube Corp., which soon secured an offer from the Yoder Co. to supply a tubing mill. In December 1972 respondent gave Yoder a purchase order to have a mill ready by the end of December 1973.

When executives at Regal and Copperweld learned of Grohne's plans, they initially hoped that Lear Siegler's noncompetition agreement would thwart the new competitor. Although their lawyer advised them that Grohne was not bound by the agreement, he did suggest that petitioners might obtain an injunction against Grohne's activities if he made use of any technical information or trade secrets belonging to Regal. The legal opinion was given to Regal and Copperweld along with a letter to be sent to anyone with whom Grohne attempted to deal. The letter warned that Copperweld would be "greatly concerned if [Grohne] contemplates entering the structural tube market ... in competition with Regal Tube" and promised to take "any and all steps which are necessary to protect our rights under the terms of our purchase agreement and to protect the know-how, trade secrets, etc., which we purchased from Lear Siegler." Petitioners later asserted that the letter was intended only to prevent third parties from developing reliance interests that might later make a court reluctant to enjoin Grohne's operations.

When Yoder accepted respondent's order for a tubing mill on February 19, 1973, Copperweld sent Yoder one of these letters; two days later Yoder voided its acceptance. After respondent's efforts to resurrect the deal failed, respondent arranged to have a mill supplied by another company, which performed its agreement even though it too received a warning letter from Copperweld. Respondent began operations on September 13, 1974, nine months later than it could have if Yoder had supplied the mill when originally agreed.

Although the letter to Yoder was petitioners' most successful effort to discourage those contemplating doing business with respondent, it was not their only one. Copperweld repeatedly contacted banks that were considering financing respondent's operations. One or both petitioners also approached real estate firms that were considering providing plant space to respondent and contacted prospective suppliers and customers of the new company.

B

In 1976 respondent filed this action in the District Court against petitioners and Yoder. The jury found that Copperweld and Regal had conspired to violate § 1 of the Sherman Act ... but that Yoder was not part of the conspiracy....

... The jury then awarded $2,499,009 against petitioners on the antitrust claim, which was trebled to $7,497,027....

C

The United States Court of Appeals for the Seventh Circuit affirmed.... It noted that the exoneration of Yoder from antitrust liability left a parent corporation and its wholly owned subsidiary as the only parties to the § 1 conspiracy. The court questioned the wisdom of subjecting an "intra-enterprise" conspiracy to antitrust liability, when the same conduct by a corporation and an unincorporated division would escape liability for lack of the requisite two legal persons. However, relying on its decision in *Photovest Corp. v. Fotomat Corp.*, 606 F.2d 704 (1979), *cert. denied*, 445 U.S. 917 (1980), the Court of Appeals held that liability was appropriate "when there is enough separation between the two entities to make treating them as two independent actors sensible." ...

We granted certiorari to reexamine the intra-enterprise conspiracy doctrine ... and we reverse.

II

Review of this case calls directly into question whether the coordinated acts of a parent and its wholly owned subsidiary can, in the legal sense contemplated by § 1 of the Sherman Act, constitute a combination or conspiracy. The so-called "intra-enterprise conspiracy" doctrine provides that § 1 liability is not foreclosed merely because a parent and its subsidiary are subject to common ownership. The doctrine derives from declarations in several of this Court's opinions.

In no case has the Court considered the merits of the intra-enterprise conspiracy doctrine in depth. Indeed, the concept arose from a far narrower rule. Although the Court has expressed approval of the doctrine on a number of occasions, a finding of intra-enterprise conspiracy was in all but perhaps one instance unnecessary to the result.

The problem began with *United States v. Yellow Cab Co.*, 332 U.S. 218 (1947). The controlling shareholder of the Checker Cab Manufacturing Corp., Morris Markin, also controlled numerous companies operating taxicabs in four cities. With few exceptions, the operating companies had once been independent and had come under Markin's control by acquisition or merger. The complaint alleged conspiracies under §§ 1 and 2 of the Sherman Act among Markin, Checker, and five corporations in the operating system. The Court stated that even restraints in a vertically integrated enterprise were not "necessarily" outside of the Sherman Act, observing that an unreasonable restraint

> "may result as readily from a conspiracy among those who are affiliated or integrated under common ownership as from a conspiracy among those who are otherwise independent. Similarly, any affiliation or integration flowing from an illegal conspiracy cannot insulate the conspirators from the sanctions which Congress has imposed. The corporate interrelationships of the conspirators, in other words, are not determinative of the applicability of the Sherman Act. That statute is aimed at substance rather than form....
>
> "And so in this case, the common ownership and control of the various corporate appellees are impotent to liberate the alleged combination and conspiracy from the impact of the Act. The complaint charges that the restraint

of interstate trade was not only effected by the combination of the appellees but was the primary object of the combination. The theory of the complaint ... is that 'dominating power' over the cab operating companies 'was not obtained by normal expansion ... but by deliberate, calculated purchase for control.'" ...

It is the underscored language that later breathed life into the intra-enterprise conspiracy doctrine. The passage as a whole, however, more accurately stands for a quite different proposition. It has long been clear that a pattern of acquisitions may itself create a combination illegal under § 1, especially when an original anticompetitive purpose is evident from the affiliated corporations' subsequent conduct. The *Yellow Cab* passage is most fairly read in light of this settled rule. In *Yellow Cab*, the affiliation of the defendants was irrelevant because the original acquisitions were *themselves* illegal.[5] An affiliation "flowing from an illegal conspiracy" would not avert sanctions. Common ownership and control are irrelevant because restraint of trade was "the primary object of the combination," which was created in a "'deliberate, calculated'" manner....

The ambiguity of the *Yellow Cab* holding yielded the one case giving support to the intra-enterprise conspiracy doctrine. In *Kiefer-Stewart Co. v. Joseph E. Seagram & Sons, Inc.*, 340 U.S. 211 (1951), the Court held that two wholly owned subsidiaries of a liquor distiller were guilty under § 1 of the Sherman Act for jointly refusing to supply a wholesaler who declined to abide by a maximum resale pricing scheme. The Court off-handedly dismissed the defendants' argument that "their status as 'mere instrumentalities of a single manufacturing-merchandizing unit' makes it impossible for them to have conspired in a manner forbidden by the Sherman Act." ... With only a citation to *Yellow Cab* and no further analysis, the Court stated that the

"suggestion runs counter to our past decisions that common ownership and control does not liberate corporations from the impact of the antitrust laws"

and stated that this rule was "especially applicable" when defendants "hold themselves out as competitors." ...

Unlike the *Yellow Cab* passage, this language does not pertain to corporations whose initial affiliation was itself unlawful. In straying beyond *Yellow Cab*, the *Kiefer-Stewart* Court failed to confront the anomalies an intra-enterprise doctrine entails. It is relevant nonetheless that, were the case decided today, the same result probably could be justified on the ground that the subsidiaries conspired with wholesalers other than the plaintiff.[9] An intra-enterprise conspiracy doc-

---

[5] Contrary to the dissent's suggestion ... our point is not that *Yellow Cab* found only the initial acquisition illegal; our point is that the illegality of the initial acquisition was a predicate for its holding that any post-acquisition conduct violated the Act.

[9] Although the plaintiff apparently never acquiesced in the resale price maintenance scheme, *Kiefer-Stewart Co. v. Joseph E. Seagram & Sons, Inc.*, 182 F.2d 228, 231 (7th Cir. 1950), *rev'd,*

trine thus would no longer be necessary to a finding of liability on the facts of *Kiefer-Stewart*. ...

In short, while this Court has previously seemed to acquiesce in the intra-enterprise conspiracy doctrine, it has never explored or analyzed in detail the justifications for such a rule; the doctrine has played only a relatively minor role in the Court's Sherman Act holdings.

III

Petitioners, joined by the United States as *amicus curiae*, urge us to repudiate the intra-enterprise conspiracy doctrine. The central criticism is that the doctrine gives undue significance to the fact that a subsidiary is separately incorporated and thereby treats as the concerted activity of two entities what is really unilateral behavior flowing from decisions of a single enterprise.

We limit our inquiry to the narrow issue squarely presented: whether a parent and its wholly owned subsidiary are capable of conspiring in violation of § 1 of the Sherman Act. We do not consider under what circumstances, if any, a parent may be liable for conspiring with an affiliated corporation it does not completely own.

A

The Sherman Act contains a "basic distinction between concerted and independent action.".... The conduct of a single firm is governed by § 2 alone and is unlawful only when it threatens actual monopolization. It is not enough that a single firm appears to "restrain trade" unreasonably, for even a vigorous competitor may leave that impression....

Section 1 of the Sherman Act, in contrast, reaches unreasonable restraints of trade effected by a "contract, combination ... or conspiracy" between *separate* entities. It does not reach conduct that is "wholly unilateral." ... Concerted activity subject to § 1 is judged more sternly than unilateral activity under § 2....

The reason Congress treated concerted behavior more strictly than unilateral behavior is readily appreciated. Concerted activity inherently is fraught with anticompetitive risk. It deprives the marketplace of the independent centers of decision making that competition assumes and demands. In any conspiracy, two or more entities that previously pursued their own interests separately are combining to act as one for their common benefit. This not only reduces the diverse directions in which economic power is aimed but suddenly increases the economic power moving in one particular direction....

---

340 U.S. 211 (1951), one of the subsidiaries did gain the compliance of other wholesalers after once terminating them for refusing to abide by the pricing scheme.... A theory of combination between the subsidiaries and the wholesalers could now support § 1 relief, whether or not it could have when *Kiefer-Stewart* was decided....

B

The distinction between unilateral and concerted conduct is necessary for a proper understanding of the terms "contract, combination ... or conspiracy" in § 1. Nothing in the literal meaning of those terms excludes coordinated conduct among officers or employees of the *same* company. But it is perfectly plain that an internal "agreement" to implement a single, unitary firm's policies does not raise the antitrust dangers that § 1 was designed to police. The officers of a single firm are not separate economic actors pursuing separate economic interests, so agreements among them do not suddenly bring together economic power that was previously pursuing divergent goals. Coordination within a firm is as likely to result from an effort to compete as from an effort to stifle competition. In the marketplace, such coordination may be necessary if a business enterprise is to compete effectively. For these reasons, officers or employees of the same firm do not provide the plurality of actors imperative for a § 1 conspiracy.

There is also general agreement that § 1 is not violated by the internally coordinated conduct of a corporation and one of its unincorporated divisions. Although this Court has not previously addressed the question, there can be little doubt that the operations of a corporate enterprise organized into divisions must be judged as the conduct of a single actor. The existence of an unincorporated division reflects no more than a firm's decision to adopt an organizational division of labor. A division within a corporate structure pursues the common interests of the whole rather than interests separate from those of the corporation itself; a business enterprise establishes divisions to further its own interests in the most efficient manner. Because coordination between a corporation and its division does not represent a sudden joining of two independent sources of economic power previously pursuing separate interests, it is not an activity that warrants § 1 scrutiny.

Indeed, a rule that punished coordinated conduct simply because a corporation delegated certain responsibilities to autonomous units might well discourage corporations from creating divisions with their presumed benefits. This would serve no useful antitrust purpose but could well deprive consumers of the efficiencies that decentralized management may bring.

C

For similar reasons, the coordinated activity of a parent and its wholly owned subsidiary must be viewed as that of a single enterprise for purposes of § 1 of the Sherman Act. A parent and its wholly owned subsidiary have a complete unity of interest. Their objectives are common, not disparate; their general corporate actions are guided or determined not by two separate corporate consciousnesses, but one. They are not unlike a multiple team of horses drawing a vehicle under the control of a single driver. With or without a formal "agreement," the subsidiary acts for the benefit of the parent, its sole shareholder. If a parent and a wholly owned subsidiary do "agree" to a course of action, there is no sudden joining of economic resources that had previously served different interests, and there is no justification for § 1 scrutiny.

Indeed, the very notion of an "agreement" in Sherman Act terms between a parent and a wholly owned subsidiary lacks meaning. A § 1 agreement may be found when "the conspirators had a unity of purpose or a common design and understanding, or a meeting of minds in an unlawful arrangement." *American Tobacco Co. v. United States*, 328 U.S. 781, 810 (1946). But in reality a parent and a wholly owned subsidiary *always* have a "unity of purpose or a common design." They share a common purpose whether or not the parent keeps a tight rein over the subsidiary; the parent may assert full control at any moment if the subsidiary fails to act in the parent's best interests.

The intra-enterprise conspiracy doctrine looks to the form of an enterprise's structure and ignores the reality. Antitrust liability should not depend on whether a corporate sub-unit is organized as an unincorporated division or a wholly owned subsidiary. A corporation has complete power to maintain a wholly owned subsidiary in either form. The economic, legal, or other considerations that lead corporate management to choose one structure over the other are not relevant to whether the enterprise's conduct seriously threatens competition. Rather, a corporation may adopt the subsidiary form of organization for valid management and related purposes. Separate incorporation may improve management, avoid special tax problems arising from multistate operations, or serve other legitimate interests. Especially in view of the increasing complexity of corporate operations, a business enterprise should be free to structure itself in ways that serve efficiency of control, economy of operations, and other factors dictated by business judgment without increasing its exposure to antitrust liability. Because there is nothing inherently anticompetitive about a corporation's decision to create a subsidiary, the intra-enterprise conspiracy doctrine "impose[s] grave legal consequences upon organizational distinctions that are of *de minimis* meaning and effect."...

If antitrust liability turned on the garb in which a corporate subunit was clothed, parent corporations would be encouraged to convert subsidiaries into unincorporated divisions. Indeed, this is precisely what the Seagram company did after this Court's decision in *Kiefer-Stewart Co. v. Joseph E. Seagram & Sons, Inc.*, 340 U.S. 211 (1951). Such an incentive serves no valid antitrust goals but merely deprives consumers and producers of the benefits that the subsidiary form may yield.

The error of treating a corporate division differently from a wholly owned subsidiary is readily seen from the facts of this case. Regal was operated as an unincorporated division of Lear Siegler for four years before it became a wholly owned subsidiary of Copperweld. Nothing in this record indicates any meaningful difference between Regal's operations as a division and its later operations as a separate corporation. Certainly nothing suggests that Regal was a greater threat to competition as a subsidiary of Copperweld than as a division of Lear Siegler.

Under either arrangement, Regal might have acted to bar a new competitor from entering the market. In one case it could have relied on economic power from other quarters of the Lear Siegler corporation; instead it drew on the strength of its separately incorporated parent, Copperweld. From the standpoint of the anti-trust laws, there is no reason to treat one more harshly than the other....

D

Any reading of the Sherman Act that remains true to the Act's distinction between unilateral and concerted conduct will necessarily disappoint those who find that distinction arbitrary. It cannot be denied that § 1's focus on concerted behavior leaves a "gap" in the Act's proscription against unreasonable restraints of trade.... An unreasonable restraint of trade may be effected not only by two independent firms acting in concert; a single firm may restrain trade to precisely the same extent if it alone possesses the combined market power of those same two firms. Because the Sherman Act does not prohibit unreasonable restraints of trade as such — but only restraints effected by a contract, combination, or conspiracy — it leaves untouched a single firm's anticompetitive conduct (short of threatened monopolization) that may be indistinguishable in economic effect from the conduct of two firms subject to § 1 liability.

We have already noted that Congress left this "gap" for eminently sound reasons. Subjecting a single firm's every action to judicial scrutiny for reasonableness would threaten to discourage the competitive enthusiasm that the antitrust laws seek to promote.... Moreover, whatever the wisdom of the distinction, the Act's plain language leaves no doubt that Congress made a purposeful choice to accord different treatment to unilateral and concerted conduct. Had Congress intended to outlaw unreasonable restraints of trade as such, § 1's requirement of a contract, combination, or conspiracy would be superfluous, as would the entirety of § 2. Indeed, this Court has recognized that § 1 is limited to concerted conduct at least since the days of *United States v. Colgate & Co.*, 250 U.S. 300 (1919)....

Although we recognize that any "gap" the Sherman Act leaves is the sensible result of a purposeful policy decision by Congress, we also note that the size of any such gap is open to serious question. Any anticompetitive activities of corporations and their wholly owned subsidiaries meriting antitrust remedies may be policed adequately without resort to an intra-enterprise conspiracy doctrine. A corporation's initial acquisition of control will always be subject to scrutiny under § 1 of the Sherman Act and § 7 of the Clayton Act .... Thereafter, the enterprise is fully subject to § 2 of the Sherman Act and § 5 of the Federal Trade Commission Act .... That these statutes are adequate to control dangerous anti-competitive conduct is suggested by the fact that not a single holding of antitrust liability by this Court would today be different in the absence of an intra-enterprise conspiracy doctrine. It is further suggested by the fact that the Federal Government, in its administration of the antitrust laws, no longer accepts the concept that a corporation and its wholly owned subsidiaries can "combine" or "conspire" under § 1. Elimination of the intra-enterprise conspiracy doctrine with respect to corporations and their wholly owned subsidiaries will therefore not cripple antitrust enforcement. It will simply eliminate treble damages from private state tort suits masquerading as antitrust actions.

IV

We hold that Copperweld and its wholly owned subsidiary Regal are incapable of conspiring with each other for purposes of § 1 of the Sherman Act. To the extent that prior decisions of this Court are to the contrary, they are disapproved and overruled. Accordingly, the judgment of the Court of Appeals is reversed.

NOTES AND QUESTIONS

1. In its amicus curiae brief to the Court, the Department of Justice stated, "the [intra-enterprise conspiracy] doctrine has played a relatively minor role in government enforcement actions, and the government has not relied on the doctrine in recent years." Thus, the Court's rejection of the intra-enterprise conspiracy doctrine would not affect public enforcement. But recall that about only 10% of antitrust enforcement is brought by the federal government.

2. The Court in *Copperweld* held that a corporation and its wholly owned subsidiary are a single enterprise and thus are incapable of conspiring under section 1. In so doing, a rule of per se legality under section 1 was created for the corporation and its wholly owned subsidiary. In light of the Court's rationale, is a corporation legally capable of conspiring with a firm it controls through a 60 percent ownership interest? *See Fishman v. Estate of Wirtz*, 807 F.2d 520 (7th Cir. 1986) (requiring a complete unity of interests). What in the Court's economic reasoning would support the same result announced in *Copperweld*? Consider whether the Court's functional "unity of interest" test is determinative. Or, is the severity of the restraint a factor in determining whether there is a single enterprise? The First and Third Circuits have suggested that *Copperweld* does not shield a parent corporation from the legal ability to enter a conspiracy with a less than wholly owned subsidiary. *Tunis Bros. v. Ford Motor Co.*, 763 F.2d 1482 (3d Cir. 1985) (defendant owned 100% of voting stock and 79% of equity stock); *Computer Identics Corp. v. Southern Pac. Co.*, 756 F.2d 200 (1st Cir. 1985) (defendant owned 80% of subsidiary). The *Computer Identics* court approved a jury instruction which avoids a direct numerical analysis in favor of a functional test:

> "If the defendants were so closely related that they were in fact one entity, there can be no conspiracy .... You are to decide whether the defendant corporations acted as a single entity sharing common management .... If they operated separately, then they are capable of conspiracy. If they acted as one common entity, then they could not enter into a conspiracy."

Id. at 204-05. In practice, it may not be critical to focus on the relationship between the parent and partially owned subsidiary because the plurality requirement might be satisfied by the conduct of the other owner; partial ownership of the subsidiary means that the subsidiary has at least two owners.

3. After *Copperweld*, is it likely that the Court will consider efficiency as a valid defense to the corporate structure? Consider the Court's language: "a business enterprise should be free to structure itself in ways that serve efficiency of control, economy of operations, and other factors dictated by business judgment without increasing its exposure to antitrust liability." Are there reasons for distinguishing between a parent and subsidiary and vertical integration if both are designed to achieve competitive efficiencies?

4. Justices Stevens, Brennan and Marshall dissented in *Copperweld*. They argued that a rule of reason approach should be used to determine whether the cooperative activity restrained competition, regardless of the form of the arrangement. In challenging the majority's repudiation of this antitrust doctrine, the dissent argued that the legislative history of Congress in 1890 was contrary to the Court's decision. The Congress considered, the dissent urged, that subsidiaries were being used as means to eliminate competition: "The anomaly in [the majority] holding is that corporate devices most similar to the original 'trusts' are now those which free an enterprise from antitrust scrutiny." Does the majority opinion turn on an economic theory or legislative history?

5. In 1986, the Supreme Court in *Fisher v. City of Berkeley*, 475 U.S. 260 (1986), held that a municipality could not conspire with itself or its officials within the meaning of section 1 in adopting a rent control ordinance where there was no private influence alleged. The *Fisher* decision is reprinted *infra* Chapter 9.

6. The Fourth Circuit has held in *Advanced Health-Care Servs. v. Radford Community Hosp.*, 910 F.2d 139 (4th Cir. 1990), that two subsidiaries wholly owned by the same parent corporation are not legally capable of conspiring with one another for purposes of the Sherman Act. *Accord Hood v. Tenneco Tex. Life Ins. Co.*, 739 F.2d 1012 (5th Cir. 1984); *Greenwood Utils. Comm'n v. Mississippi Power Co.*, 751 F.2d 1484, 1496-97, n.8 (5th Cir. 1985); *Weiss v. York Hosp.*, 745 F.2d 786 (3d Cir. 1984). *Contra Ray Dobbins Lincoln-Mercury v. Ford Motor Co.*, 604 F. Supp. 203, 205 (W.D. Va. 1984) (action under Virginia conspiracy statute).

7. The Sixth Circuit held that *Copperweld* precludes a finding of conspiracy between a hospital and its medical staff but that the requisite agreement might be found among individual obstetricians who agreed to block medical care by midwives. *Nurse Midwifery Ass'n v. Hibbett*, 918 F.2d 2342 (6th Cir. 1990). The difference, the court observed, is that the medical staff, when making staff-privilege decisions, only act as officers of the hospital who cannot compete with the hospital. But when the medical staff employee has a personal stake in the outcome, as when a competitor is denied staff privileges by a hospital board composed of physicians with independent practices, the board members may not be immune from antitrust suit under the intracorporate conspiracy doctrine. The court also suggested that concerns about competition emerged only when the doctors on the staff were in competition with those excluded:

> When the staff as a group makes decisions or recommendations for the hospital in areas that do not affect the market in which they compete as individuals, there is no reason not to treat them as agents of the hospital. However, when competing physicians are making privilege recommendations concerning another competitor, sufficient anticompetitive concerns are raised to warrant a conclusion that the members of the medical staff are not acting as agents of the hospital for purposes of applying the intracorporate conspiracy doctrine....

Under the court's reasoning, an obstetrician on a hospital board who had an independent practice might be suable for voting to deny hospital staff privileges to a competing obstetrician; however, an anesthesiologist would not be suable, since anesthesiologists do not compete directly with obstetricians as a general matter. Query: suppose that the obstetricians agreed to defer to the opinion of the anesthesiologists when an anesthesiologist's application for staff privileges was being considered, and vice-versa? The Supreme Court, over the objection of Justice White, refused to grant certiorari from the Sixth Circuit's decision in *Nurse Midwifery.* See also *Weiss v. York Hosp.,* 745 F.2d 786, 813-17 (3d Cir. 1984).

8. In *Chicago Professional Sports Ltd. Partnership v. NBA*, 95 F.3d 593 (7th Cir. 1996), the Seventh Circuit decided that, notwithstanding superficial similarities to the NCAA (where the Supreme Court had assumed multiple actors) the NBA was more like a single entity than a cartel of independent teams. The district court had held that the NBA could not be a single entity unless there was a "complete unity of interest," which the individual teams did not have since each was a separately owned, profit-making entity. The NBA argued that it was an incorporated entity and that it should be treated as a corporate board, with the teams treated as the corporation's subsidiaries. Of course this relationship is not the same as the parent-subsidiary relationship, for the teams are not commonly owned by their "parent." Nevertheless, it does produce a single product, namely, NBA basketball.

The court concluded:

> *Copperweld* ... asks why the antitrust laws distinguish between unilateral and concerted action, and then assigns a parent-subsidiary group to the "unilateral" side in light of those functions. Like a single firm, the parent-subsidiary combination cooperates internally to increase efficiency. Conduct that "deprives the marketplace of the independent centers of decision-making that competition assumes," [*Copperweld,*] 467 U.S. at 769, without the efficiencies that come with integration inside a firm, go on the "concerted" side of the line. And there are entities in the middle: "mergers, joint ventures, and various vertical agreements" (*id.* at 768) that reduce the number of independent decisionmakers yet may improve efficiency. These are assessed under the Rule of Reason. We see no reason why a sports league

cannot be treated as a single firm in this typology. It produces a single product; cooperation is essential (a league with one team would be like one hand clapping); and a league need not deprive the market of independent centers of decisionmaking.

While all of this would seem to apply equally to the *NCAA* case, where the court found an agreement of separate colleges and their football teams, the Seventh Circuit made this important distinction:

> [T]he NBA has no existence independent of sports. It makes professional basketball; only it can make "NBA Basketball" games; and unlike the NCAA the NBA also "makes" teams. .... [T]he NBA created new teams in Toronto and Vancouver, stocked with players from the 27 existing teams plus an extra helping of draft choices. All of this makes the league look like a single firm. Yet the 29 clubs, unlike GM's plants, have the right to secede .... and rearrange into two or three leagues. Professional sports leagues have been assembled from clubs that formerly belonged to other leagues.... Moreover, the league looks more or less like a firm depending on which facet of the business one examines. From the perspective of fans and advertisers (who use sports telecasts to reach fans), "NBA Basketball" is one product from a single source..., just as General Motors is a single firm even though a Corvette differs from a Chevrolet. But from the perspective of college basketball players who seek to sell their skills, the teams are distinct....

The Seventh Circuit would thus extend *Copperweld* to situations where a second corporation is separately owned but was created by the first corporation — at least for some purposes. The colleges in *NCAA* were unquestionably separate entities with significant functions "outside of the NCAA," thus justifying their treatment as distinct. By contrast, a professional sports team typically has no other function than the provision of professional sports and, as the court pointed out, the creation of many of the separate teams is actually instigated by the parent organization.

But suppose that at some later time, and after relaxation of NBA rules limiting collateral activities, two or more of these NBA teams individually entered the manufacture of sporting goods such as basketballs. The Seventh Circuit's rationale would not protect a subsequent price fixing agreement in basketballs, since the teams were not created for that purpose and, would thus have to be regarded as distinct entities. Further, basketball production differs from basketball game production in that the former does not require an ongoing network joint venture.

The court also suggested that in considering the NBA's output limitation rule, the *Copperweld* doctrine determining whether the NBA teams are a joint venture or a single entity may not be all that important. *Copperweld*'s real bite, the court concluded, occurs when the relevant question is whether the per se rule or the rule of reason is to be applied. Once the tribunal has settled on the rule of reason, the additional decision whether the venture is to be treated as a single entity or a group of distinct entities may not be all that important.

But doesn't that conclusion understate the separate importance of concerted activity *within* a rule of reason case? For example, the *NCAA* decision applied the rule of reason to the NCAA football teams' joint rule limiting the televising of college football games. But even under the rule of reason, the Supreme Court ultimately condemned the NCAA's television restrictions, finding that on balance they reduced output and increased the price of television advertising without a compelling, offsetting justification.

This treatment stands in sharp contrast to the "rule of reason" treatment that would be accorded a similar output restriction undertaken by a single firm. Suppose, for example, that General Motors should instruct its wholly owned subsidiaries — Chevrolet, Pontiac, Oldsmobile, and Buick — each to reduce their output of automobiles by twenty-five percent. A complaint making this allegation would be dismissed on the pleadings, without any inquiry into power or market effects. That is to say, the output restriction decision of a true single entity, not accompanied by any exclusionary practice, is legal per se. This is a necessary corollary of the proposition that an "innocent" monopolist is free to charge its monopoly price. In the process of settling on its profit-maximizing price, the single monopolist necessarily must also settle on its profit-maximizing rate of output.

PROBLEM 4.7

Samaritan Hospital is a corporation operated by a Board of Directors composed entirely of physicians. Four of the seven members of the Board are currently pediatricians, each of whom has an extensive private practice. The Board members are not paid for being on the Board. Dr. Smith is the proprietor of the "Pediatric Health Clinic," an outpatient pediatric clinic offering cut-rate health care services. Over the past years all four of the pediatricians on the Board have complained to Dr. Smith about his fees.

Dr. Smith would like to have staff privileges at Samaritan Hospital so he can better serve his patients who need hospital care. He applies, but the Board declines his application by a vote of 4-3, the four pediatricians voting against him. Smith sues, alleging that the hospital conspired with members of its Board of Directors to exclude Smith from the market. Should *Copperweld* preclude his suit? Suppose that at the same meeting the Board voted 4-3 to raise the price of hospital rooms by $10.00 per day. The hospital is sued for engaging in price fixing with its Board. Should *Copperweld* preclude the second suit? *See Bahn v. NME Hosps.*, 669 F. Supp. 998 (E.D. Cal. 1987); *Smith v. Underwood Mem. Hosp.*, 1987-1 Trade Cas. ¶ 67538 at 60,275 (D.N.J.).

PROBLEM 4.8

1. A group of rural electric corporations, which are separately incorporated and owned companies, comprises a part of a rural electric cooperative. The cooperative is organized on three functional levels. It is a three-tier organization made up of one corporation which owns nearly all of the cooperative's electric generating capacity and the power lines. The next level is six generation/transmission companies responsible for transporting and selling wholesale power. The third group consists of 43 local retail/distribution cooperatives, which are owned by 425,000 consumer-members. These retail cooperatives buy electric power wholesale and, in turn, sell it to their consumer-members in certain service areas.

The cooperative management flows from the top to the bottom, but ownership runs from the bottom up. For example, the 425,000 consumer-members own the 43 local retail distribution cooperatives. Members join the cooperative that sells them retail electricity, and each distribution cooperative is managed by a board of directors elected by its members. Each local cooperative owns part of one or more of the six wholesale companies that transmit and sell the power, and the wholesale company boards of directors are elected by the cooperative members. Moreover, the six wholesale generation transmission companies, in turn, are common owners of the company that owns the generating capacity and power lines.

Although each cooperative is autonomous, setting its own rates for the power it sells and managing its own profits and losses, the organization is "linked" by long-term requirements contracts. The owner of the power capacity and power lines supplies the wholesalers, which in turn sell to the retail cooperatives. They then sell to the cooperative members.

2. The City of Mount Pleasant, a non-member of the cooperative, entered a contract to buy a certain amount of energy from a cooperative. Thereafter the city, believing that it had been economically injured by reason of the cooperative's pricing schedule, sued numerous members of the cooperative, including the corporation that owned nearly all of the electric generating capacity and power lines and the companies responsible for the transmission and wholesale distribution of the power.

3. Counsel for the plaintiff city alleges that defendant members of the cooperative have: (1) participated in a "price-squeeze" conspiracy; (2) monopolized the relevant markets for wholesale electricity and for transporting electricity; and (3) charged the city a higher price for wholesale electricity than that charged retail cooperative members.

4. As counsel for defendants, what arguments would you make under *Copperweld*? Should your arguments be directed to the court as a question of law in a motion for a summary judgment, or is the *Copperweld* defense a question of fact which must be presented to a jury? *See City of Mt. Pleasant v. Associated Elec. Coop.*, 838 F.2d 268 (8th Cir. 1988).

PROBLEM 4.9

Jim and Tammy own 100% of the shares of Alpha Corporation, which manufactures and distributes leather gloves. Jim, Tammy, and Francis own 100% of

Beta Corporation, which manufactures similar gloves. Together, Jim and Tammy's shares of Beta constitute 53% of the whole, and they have effective control. Alpha and Beta agree with each other to set the same price for gloves. Do the two firms have conspiratorial capacity under the Sherman Act? *See American Vision Centers v. Cohen*, 711 F. Supp. 721 (E.D.N.Y. 1989).

PROBLEM 4.10

Consider whether a patent holder can conspire with a sublicensee under the intra-enterprise conspiracy doctrine.

Larry Shea holds a patent on air conditioning ductwork. In order to market and exploit the patent, he incorporates ATS Products and conveys to ATS an exclusive license to use the patent. Later Shea and ATS enter a contract to give a non-exclusive license for use of the patent to Levi Co. to manufacture ductwork. Thereafter, ATS and Levi Co. agree that ATS would not give a similar license to Levi's chief competitor, Case Systems. Case sues ATS and Levi on a refusal to deal theory under section 1 of the Sherman Act. Does the intra-enterprise conspiracy doctrine apply? What outcome?

6. BURDENS OF PROOF AND SUMMARY JUDGMENT PROBLEMS

MATSUSHITA ELECTRIC INDUSTRIAL CO. V. ZENITH RADIO CORP.

475 U.S. 574 (1986)

JUSTICE POWELL delivered the opinion of the Court.

This case requires that we again consider the standard district courts must apply when deciding whether to grant summary judgment in an antitrust conspiracy case.

I

....

... Since we review only the standard applied by the Court of Appeals in deciding this case, and not the weight assigned to particular pieces of evidence, we find it unnecessary to state the facts in great detail. What follows is a summary of this case's long history.

A

Petitioners, defendants below, are 21 corporations that manufacture or sell "consumer electronic products" (CEPs) — for the most part, television sets. Petitioners include both Japanese manufacturers of CEPs and American firms, controlled by Japanese parents, that sell the Japanese-manufactured products. Respondents, plaintiffs below, are Zenith Radio Corporation (Zenith) and National Union Electric Corporation (NUE). Zenith is an American firm that manufactures and sells television sets. NUE is the corporate successor to Emerson Radio Company, an American firm that manufactured and sold television sets until 1970, when it withdrew from the market after sustaining substantial losses. Zenith and NUE began this lawsuit in 1974, claiming that petitioners had illegally conspired to drive American firms from the American CEP market. According to respondents, the gist of this conspiracy was a "'scheme to raise, fix and maintain artificially *high* prices for television receivers sold by [petitioners] in Japan and, at the same time, to fix and maintain *low* prices for television receivers exported to and sold in the United States.'" 723 F.2d at 251. These "low prices" were allegedly at levels that produced substantial losses for petitioners. 513 F. Supp., at 1125. The conspiracy allegedly began as early as 1953, and according to respondents was in full operation by sometime in the late 1960's. Respondents claimed that various portions of this scheme violated §§ 1 and 2 of the Sherman Act, § 2(a) of the Robinson-Patman Act, § 73 of the Wilson Tariff Act, and the Antidumping Act of 1916.

After several years of detailed discovery, petitioners filed motions for summary judgment on all claims against them....

... In an opinion spanning 217 pages, the court found that the admissible evidence did not raise a genuine issue of material fact as to the existence of the alleged conspiracy. At bottom, the court found, respondents' claims rested on the inferences that could be drawn from petitioners' parallel conduct in the Japanese and American markets, and from the effects of that conduct on petitioners' American competitors. 513 F. Supp., at 1125-1127. After reviewing the evidence both by category and *in toto*, the court found that any inference of conspiracy was unreasonable, because (i) some portions of the evidence suggested that petitioners conspired in ways that did not injure respondents, and (ii) the evidence that bore directly on the alleged price-cutting conspiracy did not rebut the more plausible inference that petitioners were cutting prices to compete in the American market and not to monopolize it. Summary judgment therefore was granted on respondents' claims under § 1 of the Sherman Act and the Wilson Tariff Act. Because the Sherman Act § 2 claims, which alleged that petitioners had combined to monopolize the American CEP market, were functionally indistinguishable from the § 1 claims, the court dismissed them also. Finally, the court found that the Robinson-Patman Act claims depended on the same supposed conspiracy as the Sherman Act claims. Since the court had found no genuine issue of fact as to the conspiracy, it entered judgment in petitioners' favor on those claims as well.

B

The Court of Appeals for the Third Circuit reversed.[4]...

On the merits, and based on the newly enlarged record, the court found that the District Court's summary judgment decision was improper. The court acknowl-

---

[4] As to three of the 24 defendants, the Court of Appeals affirmed the entry of summary judgment. Petitioners are the 21 defendants who remain in the case.

edged that "there are legal limitations upon the inferences which may be drawn from circumstantial evidence," 723 F.2d, at 304, but it found that "the legal problem ... is different" when "there is direct evidence of concert of action." *Ibid.* Here, the court concluded, "there is both direct evidence of certain kinds of concert of action and circumstantial evidence having some tendency to suggest that other kinds of concert of action may have occurred." *Id.*, at 304-305. Thus, the court reasoned, cases concerning the limitations on inferring conspiracy from ambiguous evidence were not dispositive. *Id.*, at 305. Turning to the evidence, the court determined that a fact finder reasonably could draw the following conclusions:

1. The Japanese market for CEPs was characterized by oligopolistic behavior, with a small number of producers meeting regularly and exchanging information on price and other matters. *Id.*, at 307. This created the opportunity for a stable combination to raise both prices and profits in Japan. American firms could not attack such a combination because the Japanese government imposed significant barriers to entry. *Ibid.*

2. Petitioners had relatively higher fixed costs than their American counterparts, and therefore needed to operate at something approaching full capacity in order to make a profit. *Ibid.*

3. Petitioners' plant capacity exceeded the needs of the Japanese market. *Ibid.*

4. By formal agreements arranged in cooperation with Japan's Ministry of International Trade and Industry (MITI), petitioners fixed minimum prices for CEPs exported to the American market. *Id.*, at 310. The parties refer to these prices as the "check prices," and to the agreements that require them as the "check price agreements."

5. Petitioners agreed to distribute their products in the United States according to a "five-company rule": each Japanese producer was permitted to sell only to five American distributors. *Ibid.*

6. Petitioners undercut their own check prices by a variety of rebate schemes. *Id.*, at 311. Petitioners sought to conceal these rebate schemes both from the United States Customs Service and from MITI, the former to avoid various customs regulations as well as action under the antidumping laws, and the latter to cover up petitioners' violations of the check price agreements.

Based on inferences from the foregoing conclusions,[5] the Court of Appeals concluded that a reasonable fact finder could find a conspiracy to depress prices in the American market in order to drive out American competitors, which conspiracy was funded by excess profits obtained in the Japanese market. The court

---

[5] In addition to these inferences, the court noted that there was expert opinion evidence that petitioners' export sales "generally were at prices which produced losses, often as high as twenty-five percent on sales." 723 F.2d, at 311. The court did not identify any direct evidence of below-cost pricing; nor did it place particularly heavy reliance on this aspect of the expert evidence.

apparently did not consider whether it was as plausible to conclude that petitioners' price-cutting behavior was independent and not conspiratorial.

The court found it unnecessary to address petitioners' claim that they could not be held liable under the antitrust laws for conduct that was compelled by a foreign sovereign. The claim, in essence, was that because MITI required petitioners to enter into the check price agreements, liability could not be premised on those agreements. The court concluded that this case did not present any issue of sovereign compulsion, because the check price agreements were being used as "evidence of a low export price conspiracy" and not as an independent basis for finding antitrust liability. The court also believed it was unclear that the check prices in fact were mandated by the Japanese government, notwithstanding a statement to that effect by MITI itself. *Id.*, at 315.

We granted certiorari to determine (i) whether the Court of Appeals applied the proper standards in evaluating the District Court's decision to grant petitioners' motion for summary judgment, and (ii) whether petitioners could be held liable under the antitrust laws for a conspiracy in part compelled by a foreign sovereign. We reverse on the first issue, but do not reach the second.

II

We begin by emphasizing what respondents' claim is *not*. Respondents cannot recover antitrust damages based solely on an alleged cartelization of the Japanese market, because American antitrust laws do not regulate the competitive conditions of other nations' economies. *United States v. Aluminum Company of America*, 148 F.2d 416, 443 (2d. Cir. 1945) (L. Hand, J.); 1 P. Areeda & D. Turner, *Antitrust Law* ¶ 236d (1978).[6] Nor can respondents recover damages for any conspiracy by petitioners to charge higher than competitive prices in the American market. Such conduct would indeed violate the Sherman Act, but it could not injure respondents: as petitioners' competitors, respondents stand to gain from any conspiracy to raise the market price in CEPs. Cf. *Brunswick Corp. v. Pueblo Bowl-O-Mat, Inc.*, 429 U.S. 477, 488-489 (1977). Finally, for the same

---

[6] The Sherman Act does reach conduct outside our borders, but only when the conduct has an effect on American commerce. *Continental Ore Co. v. Union Carbide & Carbon Corp.*, 370 U.S. 690, 704 (1962) ("A conspiracy to monopolize or restrain the domestic or foreign commerce of the United States is not outside the reach of the Sherman Act just because part of the conduct complained of occurs in foreign countries"). The effect on which respondents rely is the artificially depressed level of prices for CEPs in the United States.

Petitioners' alleged cartelization of the Japanese market could not have caused that effect over a period of some two decades. Once petitioners decided, as respondents allege, to reduce output and raise prices in the Japanese market, they had the option of either producing fewer goods or selling more goods in other markets. The most plausible conclusion is that petitioners chose the latter option because it would be more profitable than the former. That choice does not flow from the cartelization of the Japanese market. On the contrary, were the Japanese market perfectly competitive petitioners would still have to choose whether to sell goods overseas, and would still presumably make that choice based on their profit expectations. For this reason, respondents' theory of recovery depends on proof of the asserted price-cutting conspiracy in this country.

reason, respondents cannot recover for a conspiracy to impose nonprice restraints that have the effect of either raising market price or limiting output. Such restrictions, though harmful to competition, actually *benefit* competitors by making supracompetitive pricing more attractive. Thus, neither petitioners' alleged supracompetitive pricing in Japan, nor the five-company rule that limited distribution in this country, nor the check prices insofar as they established minimum prices in this country, can by themselves give respondents a cognizable claim against petitioners for antitrust damages. The Court of Appeals therefore erred to the extent that it found evidence of these alleged conspiracies to be "direct evidence" of a conspiracy that injured respondents.

Respondents nevertheless argue that these supposed conspiracies, if not themselves grounds for recovery of antitrust damages, are circumstantial evidence of another conspiracy that *is* cognizable: a conspiracy to monopolize the American market by means of pricing below the market level.[7] The thrust of respondents' argument is that petitioners used their monopoly profits from the Japanese market to fund a concerted campaign to price predatorily and thereby drive respondents and other American manufacturers of CEPs out of business. Once successful, according to respondents, petitioners would cartelize the American CEP market, restricting output and raising prices above the level that fair competition would produce. The resulting monopoly profits, respondents contend, would more than compensate petitioners for the losses they incurred through years of pricing below market level.

The Court of Appeals found that respondents' allegation of a horizontal conspiracy to engage in predatory pricing,[8] if proved,[9] would be a *per se* violation of § 1

---

[7] Respondents also argue that the check prices, the five-company rule, and the price-fixing in Japan are all part of one large conspiracy that includes monopolization of the American market through predatory pricing. The argument is mistaken. However one decides to describe the contours of the asserted conspiracy — whether there is one conspiracy or several — respondents must show that the conspiracy caused them an injury for which the antitrust laws provide relief. *Associated General Contractors v. California State Council of Carpenters*, 459 U.S. 519, 538-540 (1983); *Brunswick Corp. v. Pueblo Bowl-O-Mat, Inc.*, 429 U.S. 477, 488-489 (1977). That showing depends in turn on proof that petitioners conspired to price predatorily in the American market, since the other conduct involved in the alleged conspiracy cannot have caused such an injury.

[8] Throughout this opinion, we refer to the asserted conspiracy as one to price "predatorily." This term has been used chiefly in cases in which a single firm, having a dominant share of the relevant market, cuts its prices in order to force competitors out of the market, or perhaps to deter potential entrants from coming in. *E.g., Southern Pacific Communications Co. v. American Telephone & Telegraph Co.*, 238 U.S. App. D.C. 309, 331-336, 740 F.2d 980, 1002-1007 (1984), cert. denied, 470 U.S. 1005 (1985). In such cases, "predatory pricing" means pricing below some appropriate measure of cost. *E.g., Barry Wright Corp. v. ITT Grinnell Corp.*, 724 F.2d 227, 232-235 (1st Cir. 1983); see *Utah Pie Co. v. Continental Baking Co.*, 386 U.S. 685, 698, 701, 702, n. 14 (1967).

There is a good deal of debate, both in the cases and in the law reviews, about what "cost" is relevant in such cases. We need not resolve this debate here, because unlike the cases cited above, this is a Sherman Act § 1 case. For purposes of this case, it is enough to note that respondents have not suffered an antitrust injury unless petitioners conspired to drive respondents out of the relevant of the Sherman Act. 723 F.2d, at 306. Petitioners did not appeal from that conclusion. The issue in this case thus becomes whether respondents adduced sufficient evidence in support of their theory to survive summary judgment. We therefore examine the principles that govern the summary judgment determination.

III

To survive petitioners' motion for summary judgment, respondents must establish that there is a genuine issue of material fact as to whether petitioners entered into an illegal conspiracy that caused respondents to suffer a cognizable injury. Fed. Rule Civ. Proc. 56(e); *First National Bank of Arizona v. Cities Service Co.*, 391 U.S. 253, 288-289 (1968). This showing has two components. First, respondents must show more than a conspiracy in violation of the antitrust laws; they must show an injury to them resulting from the illegal conduct. Respondents charge petitioners with a whole host of conspiracies in restraint of trade. Except for the alleged conspiracy to monopolize the American market through predatory pricing, these alleged conspiracies could not have caused respondents to suffer an "antitrust injury," *Brunswick Corp. v. Pueblo Bowl-O-Mat*, 429 U.S., at 489, because they actually tended to benefit respondents. Therefore, unless, in context, evidence of these "other" conspiracies raises a genuine issue concerning the existence of a predatory pricing conspiracy, that evidence cannot defeat petitioners' summary judgment motion.

Second, the issue of fact must be "genuine." When the moving party has carried its burden under Rule 56(c), its opponent must do more than simply show that there is some metaphysical doubt as to the material facts. In the language of the Rule, the non-moving party must come forward with "specific facts showing that there is a *genuine issue for trial*." Where the record taken as a whole could not lead a rational trier of fact to find for the non-moving party, there is no "genuine issue for trial."

It follows from these settled principles that if the factual context renders respondents' claim implausible — if the claim is one that simply makes no economic sense — respondents must come forward with more persuasive evidence to support their claim than would otherwise be necessary....

---

markets by (i) pricing below the level necessary to sell their products, or (ii) pricing below some appropriate measure of cost. An agreement without these features would either leave respondents in the same position as would market forces or would actually benefit respondents by raising market prices. Respondents therefore may not complain of conspiracies that, for example, set maximum prices above market levels, or that set minimum prices at *any* level.

[9] We do not consider whether recovery should ever be available on a theory such as respondents' when the pricing in question is above some measure of incremental cost. See generally Areeda & Turner, *Predatory Pricing and Related Practices Under Section 2 of the Sherman Act*, 88 Harv. L. Rev. 697, 709-718 (1975) (discussing cost-based test for use in § 2 cases). As a practical matter, it may be that only direct evidence of below-cost pricing is sufficient to overcome the strong inference that rational businesses would not enter into conspiracies such as this one. See Part IV-A, *infra*.

Respondents correctly note that "[o]n summary judgment the inferences to be drawn from the underlying facts ... must be viewed in the light most favorable to the party opposing the motion." But antitrust law limits the range of permissible inferences from ambiguous evidence in a § 1 case. Thus, in *Monsanto Co. v. Spray-Rite Service Corp.*, 465 U.S. 752 (1984), we held that conduct as consistent with permissible competition as with illegal conspiracy does not, standing alone, support an inference of antitrust conspiracy. To survive a motion for summary judgment or for a directed verdict, a plaintiff seeking damages for a violation of § 1 must present evidence "that tends to exclude the possibility" that the alleged conspirators acted independently. 465 U.S., at 764. Respondents in this case, in other words, must show that the inference of conspiracy is reasonable in light of the competing inferences of independent action or collusive action that could not have harmed respondents.

Petitioners argue that these principles apply fully to this case. According to petitioners, the alleged conspiracy is one that is economically irrational and practically infeasible. Consequently, petitioners contend, they had no motive to engage in the alleged predatory pricing conspiracy; indeed, they had a strong motive *not* to conspire in the manner respondents allege. Petitioners argue that, in light of the absence of any apparent motive and the ambiguous nature of the evidence of conspiracy, no trier of fact reasonably could find that the conspiracy with which petitioners are charged actually existed. This argument requires us to consider the nature of the alleged conspiracy and the practical obstacles to its implementation.

IV

A

A predatory pricing conspiracy is by nature speculative. Any agreement to price below the competitive level requires the conspirators to forego profits that free competition would offer them. The foregone profits may be considered an investment in the future. For the investment to be rational, the conspirators must have a reasonable expectation of recovering, in the form of later monopoly profits, more than the losses suffered. As then-Professor Bork, discussing predatory pricing by a single firm, explained:

> "Any realistic theory of predation recognizes that the predator as well as his victims will incur losses during the fighting, but such a theory supposes it may be a rational calculation for the predator to view the losses as an investment in future monopoly profits (where rivals are to be killed) or in future undisturbed profits (where rivals are to be disciplined). The future flow of profits, appropriately discounted, must then exceed the present size of the losses." R. Bork, *The Antitrust Paradox* 145 (1978).

See also McGee, *Predatory Pricing Revisited*, 23 J. Law & Econ. 289, 295-297 (1980). As this explanation shows, the success of such schemes is inherently uncertain: the short-run loss is definite, but the long-run gain depends on successfully neutralizing the competition. Moreover, it is not enough simply to achieve monopoly power, as monopoly pricing may breed quick entry by new competitors eager to share in the excess profits. The success of any predatory scheme depends on *maintaining* monopoly power for long enough both to recoup the predator's losses and to harvest some additional gain. Absent some assurance that the hoped-for monopoly will materialize, *and* that it can be sustained for a significant period of time, "[t]he predator must make a substantial investment with no assurance that it will pay off." Easterbrook, *Predatory Strategies and Counter-strategies*, 48 U. Chi. L. Rev. 263, 268 (1981). For this reason, there is a consensus among commentators that predatory pricing schemes are rarely tried, and even more rarely successful.

These observations apply even to predatory pricing by a *single firm* seeking monopoly power. In this case, respondents allege that a large number of firms have conspired over a period of many years to charge below-market prices in order to stifle competition. Such a conspiracy is incalculably more difficult to execute than an analogous plan undertaken by a single predator. The conspirators must allocate the losses to be sustained during the conspiracy's operation, and must also allocate any gains to be realized from its success. Precisely because success is speculative and depends on a willingness to endure losses for an indefinite period, each conspirator has a strong incentive to cheat, letting its partners suffer the losses necessary to destroy the competition while sharing in any gains if the conspiracy succeeds. The necessary allocation is therefore difficult to accomplish. Yet if conspirators cheat to any substantial extent, the conspiracy must fail, because its success depends on depressing the market price for *all* buyers of CEPs. If there are too few goods at the artificially low price to satisfy demand, the would-be victims of the conspiracy can continue to sell at the "real" market price, and the conspirators suffer losses to little purpose.

Finally, if predatory pricing conspiracies are generally unlikely to occur, they are especially so where, as here, the prospects of attaining monopoly power seem slight. In order to recoup their losses, petitioners must obtain enough market power to set higher than competitive prices, and then must sustain those prices long enough to earn in excess profits what they earlier gave up in below-cost prices. Two decades after their conspiracy is alleged to have commenced, petitioners appear to be far from achieving this goal: the two largest shares of the retail market in television sets are held by RCA and respondent Zenith, not by any of the petitioners. Moreover, those shares, which together approximate 40% of sales, did not decline appreciably during the 1970's. *Ibid.* Petitioners' collective share rose rapidly during this period, from one-fifth or less of the relevant markets to close to 50%.[14] Neither the District Court nor the Court of Appeals

---

[14] During the same period, the number of American firms manufacturing television sets declined from 19 to 13. 5 App. to Brief for Appellant in No. 81-2331 (3d Cir.), p. 1961a. This decline

found, however, that petitioners' share presently allows them to charge monopoly prices; to the contrary, respondents contend that the conspiracy is ongoing — that petitioners are still artificially *depressing* the market price in order to drive Zenith out of the market. The data in the record strongly suggests that that goal is yet far distant.[15]

The alleged conspiracy's failure to achieve its ends in the two decades of its asserted operation is strong evidence that the conspiracy does not in fact exist. Since the losses in such a conspiracy accrue before the gains, they must be "repaid" with interest. And because the alleged losses have accrued over the course of two decades, the conspirators could well require a correspondingly long time to recoup. Maintaining supracompetitive prices in turn depends on the continued cooperation of the conspirators, on the inability of other would-be competitors to enter the market, and (not incidentally) on the conspirators' ability to escape antitrust liability for their *minimum* price-fixing cartel.[16] Each of these factors weighs more heavily as the time needed to recoup losses grows. If the losses have been substantial — as would likely be necessary in order to drive out the

---

continued a trend that began at least by 1960, when petitioners' sales in the United States market were negligible. *Ibid.* See Zenith Complaint ¶¶ 35, 37.

[15] Respondents offer no reason to suppose that entry into the relevant market is especially difficult, yet without barriers to entry it would presumably be impossible to maintain supracompetitive prices for an extended time. Judge Easterbrook, commenting on this case in a law review article, offers the following sensible assessment:

> "The plaintiffs [in this case] maintain that for the last fifteen years or more at least ten Japanese manufacturers have sold TV sets at less than cost in order to drive United States firms out of business. Such conduct cannot possibly produce profits by harming competition, however. If the Japanese firms drive some United States firms out of business, they could not recoup. Fifteen years of losses could be made up only by very high prices for the indefinite future. (The losses are like investments, which must be recovered with compound interest.) If the defendants should try to raise prices to such a level, they would attract new competition. There are no barriers to entry into electronics, as the proliferation of computer and audio firms shows. The competition would come from resurgent United States firms, from other foreign firms (Korea and many other nations make TV sets), and from defendants themselves. In order to recoup, the Japanese firms would need to suppress competition among themselves. On plaintiffs' theory, the cartel would need to last at least thirty years, far longer than any in history, even when cartels were not illegal. None should be sanguine about the prospects of such a cartel, given each firm's incentive to shave price and expand its share of sales. The predation-recoupment story therefore does not make sense, and we are left with the more plausible inference that the Japanese firms did not sell below cost in the first place. They were just engaged in hard competition." Easterbrook, *The Limits of Antitrust*, 63 Texas L. Rev. 1, 26-27 (1984) (footnotes omitted).

[16] The alleged predatory scheme makes sense only if petitioners can recoup their losses. In light of the large number of firms involved here, petitioners can achieve this only by engaging in some form of price-fixing after they have succeeded in driving competitors from the market. Such price-fixing would, of course, be an independent violation of § 1 of the Sherman Act. *United States v. Socony-Vacuum Oil Co.*, 310 U.S. 150 (1940).

competition[17] — petitioners would most likely have to sustain their cartel for years simply to break even.

Nor does the possibility that petitioners have obtained supracompetitive profits in the Japanese market change this calculation. Whether or not petitioners have the *means* to sustain substantial losses in this country over a long period of time, they have no *motive* to sustain such losses absent some strong likelihood that the alleged conspiracy in this country will eventually pay off. The courts below found no evidence of any such success, and — as indicated above — the facts actually are to the contrary: RCA and Zenith, not any of the petitioners, continue to hold the largest share of the American retail market in color television sets. More important, there is nothing to suggest any relationship between petitioners' profits in Japan and the amount petitioners could expect to gain from a conspiracy to monopolize the American market. In the absence of any such evidence, the possible existence of supracompetitive profits in Japan simply cannot overcome the economic obstacles to the ultimate success of this alleged predatory conspiracy. [18]

V

... The Court of Appeals did not take account of the absence of a plausible motive to enter into the alleged predatory pricing conspiracy. It focused instead on whether there was "direct evidence of concert of action." 723 F.2d, at 304. The Court of Appeals erred in two respects: (i) the "direct evidence" on which the court relied had little, if any, relevance to the alleged predatory pricing conspiracy; and (ii) the court failed to consider the absence of a plausible motive to engage in predatory pricing.

The "direct evidence" on which the court relied was evidence of *other* combinations, not of a predatory pricing conspiracy. Evidence that petitioners conspired to raise prices in Japan provides little, if any, support for respondents' claims: a conspiracy to increase profits in one market does not tend to show a conspiracy to sustain losses in another. Evidence that petitioners agreed to fix *minimum* prices (through the "check price" agreements) for the American market actually works in petitioners' favor, because it suggests that petitioners were seeking to place a floor under prices rather than to lower them. The same is true of evidence that petitioners agreed to limit the number of distributors of their products in the American market — the so-called "Five Company Rule." That

---

[17] The predators' losses must actually increase as the conspiracy nears its objective: the greater the predators' market share, the more products the predators sell; but since every sale brings with it a loss, an increase in market share also means an increase in predatory losses.

[18] The same is true of any supposed excess production capacity that petitioners may have possessed. The existence of plant capacity that exceeds domestic demand does tend to establish the ability to sell products abroad. It does not, however, provide a motive for selling at prices lower than necessary to obtain sales; nor does it explain why petitioners would be willing to *lose* money in the United States market without some reasonable prospect of recouping their investment.

practice may have facilitated a horizonal territorial allocation, see *United States v. Topco Associates, Inc.*, 405 U.S. 596 (1972), but its natural effect would be to raise market prices rather than reduce them. Evidence that tends to support any of these collateral conspiracies thus says little, if anything, about the existence of a conspiracy to charge below-market prices in the American market over a period of two decades.

That being the case, the absence of any plausible motive to engage in the conduct charged is highly relevant to whether a "genuine issue for trial" exists within the meaning of Rule 56(e). Lack of motive bears on the range of permissible conclusions that might be drawn from ambiguous evidence: if petitioners had no rational economic motive to conspire, and if their conduct is consistent with other, equally plausible explanations, the conduct does not give rise to an inference of conspiracy. Here, the conduct in question consists largely of (i) pricing at levels that succeeded in taking business away from respondents, and (ii) arrangements that may have limited petitioners' ability to compete with each other (and thus kept prices from going even lower). This conduct suggests either that petitioners behaved competitively, or that petitioners conspired to *raise* prices. Neither possibility is consistent with an agreement among 21 companies to price below market levels. Moreover, the predatory pricing scheme that this conduct is said to prove is one that makes no practical sense: it calls for petitioners to destroy companies larger and better established than themselves, a goal that remains far distant more than two decades after the conspiracy's birth. Even had they succeeded in obtaining their monopoly, there is nothing in the record to suggest that they could recover the losses they would need to sustain along the way. In sum, in light of the absence of any rational motive to conspire, neither petitioners' pricing practices, nor their conduct in the Japanese market, nor their agreements respecting prices and distribution in the American market, suffice to create a "genuine issue for trial." Fed. Rule Civ. Proc. 56(e).[21]

On remand, the Court of Appeals is free to consider whether there is other evidence that is sufficiently unambiguous to permit a trier of fact to find that petitioners conspired to price predatorily for two decades despite the absence of any apparent motive to do so. The evidence must "tend[] to exclude the possibility" that petitioners underpriced respondents to compete for business rather than to implement an economically senseless conspiracy. In the absence of such evidence, there is no "genuine issue for trial" under Rule 56(e), and petitioners are entitled to have summary judgment reinstated.

---

[21] We do not imply that, if petitioners had a plausible reason to conspire, ambiguous conduct could suffice to create a triable issue of conspiracy. Our decision in *Monsanto Co. v. Spray-Rite Service Corp.*, 465 U.S. 752 (1984), establishes that conduct that is as consistent with permissible competition as with illegal conspiracy does not, without more, support even an inference of conspiracy. *Id.*, at 763-764.

VI

Our decision makes it unnecessary to reach the sovereign compulsion issue. The heart of petitioners' argument on that issue is that MITI, an agency of the Government of Japan, required petitioners to fix minimum prices for export to the United States, and that petitioners are therefore immune from antitrust liability for any scheme of which those minimum prices were an integral part. As we discussed in part II, *supra*, respondents could not have suffered a cognizable injury from any action that *raised* prices in the American CEP market. If liable at all, petitioners are liable for conduct that is distinct from the check price agreements. The sovereign compulsion question that both petitioners and the Solicitor General urge us to decide thus is not presented here.

The decision of the Court of Appeals is reversed, and the case is remanded for further proceedings consistent with this opinion.

It is so ordered.

JUSTICE WHITE, with whom JUSTICE BRENNAN, JUSTICE BLACKMUN, and JUSTICE STEVENS join, dissenting.

It is indeed remarkable that the Court, in the face of the long and careful opinion of the Court of Appeals, reaches the result it does. The Court of Appeals faithfully followed the relevant precedents, and it kept firmly in mind the principle that proof of a conspiracy should not be fragmented. After surveying the massive record, including very significant evidence that the District Court erroneously had excluded, the Court of Appeals concluded that the evidence taken as a whole creates a genuine issue of fact whether petitioners engaged in a conspiracy in violation of §§ 1 and 2 of the Sherman Act, and § 2(a) of the Robinson-Patman Act. In my view, the Court of Appeals' opinion more than adequately supports this judgment.

The Court's opinion today, far from identifying reversible error, only muddies the waters. In the first place, the Court makes confusing and inconsistent statements about the appropriate standard for granting summary judgment. Second, the Court makes a number of assumptions that invade the factfinder's province. Third, the Court faults the Third Circuit for nonexistent errors and remands the case although it is plain that respondents' evidence raises genuine issues of material fact.

I

... [T]he Court summarizes *Monsanto v. Spray-Rite Corp.* as holding that "courts should not permit factfinders to infer conspiracies when such inferences are implausible...." Such language suggests that a judge hearing a defendant's motion for summary judgment in an antitrust case should go beyond the traditional summary judgment inquiry and decide for himself whether the weight of the evidence favors the plaintiff. *Cities Service* and *Monsanto* do not stand for any such proposition. Each of those cases simply held that a particular piece of evidence standing alone was insufficiently probative to justify sending a case to the jury. These holdings in no way undermine the doctrine that all evidence must be construed in the light most favorable to the party opposing summary judgment.

If the Court intends to give every judge hearing a motion for summary judgment in an antitrust case the job of determining if the evidence makes the inference of conspiracy more probable than not, it is overturning settled law. If the Court does not intend such a pronouncement, it should refrain from using unnecessarily broad and confusing language.

II

In defining what respondents must show in order to recover, the Court makes assumptions that invade the factfinder's province. The Court states with very little discussion that respondents can recover under § 1 of the Sherman Act only if they prove that "petitioners conspired to drive respondents out of the relevant markets by (i) pricing below the level necessary to sell their products, or (ii) pricing below some appropriate measure of cost." This statement is premised on the assumption that "[a]n agreement without these features would either leave respondents in the same position as would market forces or would actually benefit respondents by raising market prices." *Ibid.* In making this assumption, the Court ignores the contrary conclusions of respondents' expert DePodwin, whose report in very relevant part was erroneously excluded by the District Court.

The DePodwin Report, on which the Court of Appeals relied along with other material, indicates that respondents were harmed in two ways that are independent of whether petitioners priced their products below "the level necessary to sell their products or ... some appropriate measure of cost." First, the Report explains that the price-raising scheme in Japan resulted in lower consumption of petitioners' goods in that country and the exporting of more of petitioners' goods to this country than would have occurred had prices in Japan been at the competitive level. Increasing exports to this country resulted in depressed prices here, which harmed respondents. Second, the DePodwin Report indicates that petitioners exchanged confidential proprietary information and entered into agreements such as the five-company rule with the goal of avoiding intragroup competition in the United States market. The Report explains that petitioners' restrictions on intragroup competition caused respondents to lose business that they would not have lost had petitioners competed with one another.[3]

---

[3] The DePodwin Report has this, among other things, to say in summarizing the harm to respondents caused by the five-company rule, exchange of production data, price coordination, and other allegedly anti-competitive practices of petitioners:

"The impact of Japanese anti-competitive practices on United States manufacturers is evident when one considers the nature of competition. When a market is fully competitive, firms pit their resources against one another in an attempt to secure the business of individual customers. However, when firms collude, they violate a basic tenet of competitive behavior, i.e., that they act independently. United States firms were confronted with Japanese competitors who collu-

The DePodwin Report alone creates a genuine factual issue regarding the harm to respondents caused by Japanese cartelization and by agreements restricting competition among petitioners in this country. No doubt the Court prefers its own economic theorizing to Dr. DePodwin's, but that is not a reason to deny the fact finder an opportunity to consider Dr. DePodwin's views on how petitioners' alleged collusion harmed respondents.[4]

The Court, in discussing the unlikelihood of a predatory conspiracy, also consistently assumes that petitioners valued profit-maximization over growth. In light of the evidence that petitioners sold their goods in this country at substantial losses over a long period of time, I believe that this is an assumption that should be argued to the factfinder, not decided by the Court.

III

In reversing the Third Circuit's judgment, the Court identifies two alleged errors: "(i) [T]he direct evidence on which the [Court of Appeals] relied had little, if any, relevance to the alleged predatory pricing conspiracy, and (ii) the court failed to consider the absence of a plausible motive to engage in predatory pricing." The Court's position is without substance.

---

sively were seeking to destroy their established customer relationships. Each Japanese company had targeted customers which it could service with reasonable assurance that its fellow Japanese cartel members would not become involved. But just as importantly, each Japanese firm would be assured that what was already a low price level for Japanese television receivers in the United States market would not be further depressed by the actions of its Japanese associates.

"The result was a phenomenal growth in exports, particularly to the United States. Concurrently, Japanese manufacturers, and the defendants in particular, made large investments in new plant and equipment and expanded production capacity. It is obvious, therefore, that the effect of the Japanese cartel's concerted actions was to generate a larger volume of investment in the Japanese television industry than would otherwise have been the case. This added capacity both enabled and encouraged the Japanese to penetrate the United States market more deeply than they would have had they competed lawfully." 5 App. to Brief for Appellant in No. 81-2331 (3d Cir.), pp. 1628a-1629a....

[4] In holding that Parts IV and V of the Report had been improperly excluded, the Court of Appeals said:

"The trial court found that DePodwin did not use economic expertise in reaching the opinion that the defendants participated in a Japanese television cartel. 505 F. Supp. at 1342-46. We have examined the excluded portions of Parts IV and V in light of the admitted portions, and we conclude that this finding is clearly erroneous. As a result, the court also held the opinions to be unhelpful to the factfinder. What the court in effect did was to eliminate all parts of the report in which the expert economist, after describing the conditions in the respective markets, the opportunities for collusion, the evidence pointing to collusion, the terms of certain undisputed agreements, and the market behavior, expressed the opinion that there was concert of action consistent with plaintiffs' conspiracy theory. Considering the complexity of the economic issues involved, it simply cannot be said that such an opinion would not help the trier of fact to understand the evidence or determine that fact in issue." *In re Japanese Electronics Products Antitrust Litigation*, 723 F.2d 238, 280 (3d Cir. 1983).

The Court of Appeals had similar views about Parts VI and VII.

A

The first claim of error is that the Third Circuit treated evidence regarding price-fixing in Japan and the so-called five-company rule and check prices as "'direct evidence' of a conspiracy that injured respondents." The passage from the Third Circuit's opinion in which the Court locates this alleged error makes what I consider to be a quite simple and correct observation, namely, that this case is distinguishable from traditional "conscious parallelism" cases, in that there is direct evidence of concert of action among petitioners. The Third Circuit did not, as the Court implies, jump unthinkingly from this observation to the conclusion that evidence regarding the five-company rule could support a finding of antitrust injury to respondents. The Third Circuit twice specifically noted that horizontal agreements allocating customers, though illegal, do not ordinarily injure competitors of the agreeing parties. However, after reviewing evidence of cartel activity in Japan, collusive establishment of dumping prices in this country, and long-term, below-cost sales, the Third Circuit held that a factfinder could reasonably conclude that the five-company rule was not a simple price-raising device:

"[A] factfinder might reasonably infer that the allocation of customers in the United States, combined with price-fixing in Japan, was intended to permit concentration of the effects of dumping upon American competitors while eliminating competition among the Japanese manufacturers in either market." *Id.*, at 311.

I see nothing erroneous in this reasoning.

B

The Court's second charge of error is that the Third Circuit was not sufficiently skeptical of respondents' allegation that petitioners engaged in predatory pricing conspiracy. But the Third Circuit is not required to engage in academic discussions about predation; it is required to decide whether respondents' evidence creates a genuine issue of material fact. The Third Circuit did its job, and remanding the case so that it can do the same job again is simply pointless.

The Third Circuit indicated that it considers respondents' evidence sufficient to create a genuine factual issue regarding long-term, below-cost sales by petitioners. The Court tries to whittle away at this conclusion by suggesting that the "expert opinion evidence of below-cost pricing has little probative value in comparison with the economic factors ... that suggest that such conduct is irrational." But the question is not whether the Court finds respondents' experts persuasive, or prefers the District Court's analysis; it is whether, viewing the evidence in the light most favorable to respondents, a jury or other factfinder could reasonably conclude that petitioners engaged in long-term below-cost sales. I agree with the Third Circuit that the answer to this question is yes.

. . . .

IV

Because I believe that the Third Circuit was correct in holding that respondents have demonstrated the existence of genuine issues of material fact, I would affirm the judgment below and remand this case for trial.

NOTES AND QUESTIONS

1. As a matter of procedure, the Court holds that when a defendant files a motion for summary judgment the burden shifts to the plaintiff to demonstrate that there exists a dispute as to a material fact, and that the burden is increased when the court in the first instance determines that plaintiff's underlying theory is implausible. This burden of persuasion, the Court opines, requires more evidence than is normally required under a summary judgment motion. This burden includes the requirement that plaintiff produce evidence, in rebuttal to the motion, showing that under a section one theory defendants acted in concert and not independently.

Consider whether the Court's approach in *Matsushita* now sanctions the use of summary judgment as a means of disposing of complex antitrust cases. Has the Court amended Rule 56, giving the trial judge broader discretion in granting summary judgment?

In another antitrust context, the Court has said that summary judgment "should be used sparingly in complex antitrust litigation where motive and intent play leading roles." *Poller v. Columbia Broadcasting Sys.*, 368 U.S. 464 (1962). Are not motive and intent central elements of predatory pricing where a defendant[s] is charged with selling at artificially low prices? *See Utah Pie Co. v. Continental Baking Co.*, 386 U.S. 685 (1967) ("existence of predatory intent might bear on the likelihood of injury to competition"). One commentator, after reviewing all the cases and *Matsushita*, has concluded that summary judgments in antitrust cases are as frequent as in other cases — a finding which substantially undercuts the continuing validity of *Poller*. Calkins, *Summary Judgment, Motions to Dismiss, and Other Examples of Equilibrating Tendencies in the Antitrust System*, 74 Geo. L.J. 1065, 1137 (1986).

Do you agree with the Court that a plaintiff has the burden on a defendant's summary judgment motion to establish that there is a genuine issue of material fact as to the existence of a conspiracy and that injury flowed from the conspiratorial conduct? Or, is the majority opinion a reformulation of the traditional summary judgment standard?

2. Throughout its opinion, the *Matsushita* Court refers, as it does in its remand order to the Third Circuit, to the plaintiffs' obligation to produce "unambiguous" evidence of predatory pricing. Doesn't the fact that the evidence is or may be ambiguous suggest the presence of a genuine fact issue?

In *Corner Pocket of Sioux Falls, Inc. v. Video Lottery Technologies*, 123 F.3d 1107 (8th Cir. 1997), the court applied *Matsushita* to ambiguous evidence concerning an alleged conspiracy between the owners of stores featuring video lottery machines and a trade association of video lottery distributors. The plaintiffs, own-ers of lottery machines other than Video Lottery Technologies (VLT) machines, claimed that the section one conspiracy was enforced by VLT, the most popular producer of the machines, in an attempt to assist distributors in allocating territo-ries and fixing prices. The theory was that VLT had agreed to engage in the con-spiracy as a favor to the trade association, the Music & Vending Association (MVA), and as repayment for the lobbying activities of MVA, which helped to legalize video gambling in South Dakota.

VLT argued that its policy was not to sell directly to retail establishments, but, instead, to distributors. This prevented VLT or bar/restaurant owners from being charged with maintaining the machines, making them better serviced through the distributors. This also made VLT machines more popular and profitable.

The Eighth Circuit found that, given the defendant's description of the mar-ketplace, the district court acted properly in inferring lawful conduct on the part of VLT. Because the evidence was ambiguous, the court, following *Matsushita*, had to weigh the evidence presented by each side to determine whether the non-movant's evidence "tend[ed] to exclude the possibility that the alleged con-spirators acted independently." *Id.* at 1112. The Eighth Circuit sided with VLT's assertions of unilateral action without conspiracy.

3. In discussing the summary judgment standard, the *Matsushita* Court rea-soned that plaintiffs' underlying claim was implausible — that in this factual context there was no conspiracy to predatorily price. "The alleged conspiracy's failure to achieve its ends in the two decades of its asserted operation is strong evidence that the conspiracy does not in fact exist." The Court chided the Third Circuit for "relying on 'direct evidence' that had little, if any, relevance to the alleged conspiracy and in failing to consider the lack of a plausible motive to engage in predatory pricing."

The "direct evidence" the Court referred to was evidence that defendants con-spired to raise prices in Japan as a means of cross-subsidizing the losses in the United States market. Does the Court explain how it concluded that this evidence was not related to the domestic predatory pricing conspiracy? The Court states "a conspiracy to increase profits in one market does not tend to show a conspir-acy to sustain losses in another." Is any reasoned explanation given for this con-clusion? Is this the type of fact issue that juries traditionally decide? Is it plausi-ble that a predator might use profits from one market to fund a scheme in another market that would produce losses? *See generally United States v. AT&T*, 524 F. Supp. 1336 (D.D.C. 1981), 552 F. Supp. 131, *aff'd*, 460 U.S. 1001 (1983) (AT&T charged with cross-subsidization from one market to another).

On the issue of "motive," is it not possible that defendants miscalculated the length of time needed to complete successfully the predation and raise the price to recoup lost profits? Does the fact that the scheme continued to last into its twentieth year necessarily mean, through hindsight, that predatory pricing could not possibly have been intended? Again, does the Court's use of a motive and intent standard suggest the resolution of fact questions? Can motive and intent be determined through objective criteria?

4. Does the Court's opinion hold that as a matter of law the threat of predatory pricing is an implausible basis for relief? Does *Matsushita*, at least, make it very difficult for a plaintiff who asserts injury due to predatory pricing to ever survive a motion to dismiss or a motion for summary judgment?

In *Cargill*, reprinted *supra* Chapter 3, the Supreme Court declined to reject predatory pricing as a cognizable claim for relief. Said the Court, "It would be novel indeed for a court to deny standing to a party seeking an injunction against threatened injury merely because such injuries rarely occur. In any case, nothing in the language or legislative history of the Clayton Act suggests that Congress intended this Court to ignore injuries caused by such anticompetitive practices as predatory pricing." Does this language suggest a substantive change from *Matsushita*, or merely the different burdens placed on litigants depending on the statute invoked (i.e., section 4 or section 16) or the procedure employed (i.e., motion to dismiss or motion for summary judgment)?

Even before *Matsushita* only a few plaintiffs were successful in winning on predatory pricing theories, at least since the Areeda-Turner test for predatory pricing was adopted in 1975.

5. In attempting to harmonize the Supreme Court's *Matsushita* holding with the Constitution's right to a jury trial, the Ninth Circuit said:

> We do not [interpret *Matsushita* to hold] that a district court may grant summary judgment to antitrust defendants whenever the court concludes that inferences of conspiracy and inferences of innocent conduct are equally plausible. Allowing the district court to make that decision would lead to a dramatic judicial encroachment on the province of the jury. To read *Matsushita* as requiring judges to ask whether the circumstantial evidence is more "consistent" with the defendants' theory than with the plaintiff's theory would imply that the jury should be permitted to chose an inference of conspiracy *only* if the judge has first decided that he would himself draw that inference. This approach would essentially convert the judge into a thirteenth juror, who must be persuaded before an antitrust violation may be found.

Petroleum Prods. Antitrust Litig., 906 F.2d 432, 438 (9th Cir. 1990).

6. Clearly, the *Matsushita* summary judgment standard was designed for plaintiffs who must prove an agreement on the basis of circumstantial evidence. What if there is explicit evidence of a written agreement? See discussion of *Palmer v. BRG of Georgia, Inc.*, 498 U.S. 46 (1990), *infra*.

7. *Expert Testimony. Matsushita* has strong implications for the use of expert witness affidavits in antitrust cases. Suppose a plaintiff seeking to prove predatory pricing, which requires a showing of high entry barriers, finds an economist whose affidavit says, "I have a Ph.D. in economics from one prestigious university and a professorship at another. I have written three books and twelve articles on this subject and I believe entry barriers in the relevant market are very high."

The expert cites no empirical evaluations of the particular market at issue and cites no facts explaining why entry barriers are high. Does the affidavit create a fact issue that satisfies the *Matsushita* test? Or must the affidavit contain specific factual information showing *why* entry barriers in this particular market are high? In *Orthopedic & Sports Injury Clinic v. Wang Labs.*, 922 F.2d at 220, 224 (5th Cir. 1991), a non-antitrust case, the court said:

> [T]here is a level of conclusoriness below which an affidavit must not sink if it is to provide the basis for a genuine issue of material fact. We have held that the district court may inquire into the reliability and foundation of any expert's opinion to determine its admissibility.... When the "source upon which an expert's opinion relies" is of little weight, we have held "that the jury should not be permitted to receive that opinion."... Indeed, "unsupported ... affidavits setting forth 'ultimate or conclusory facts and conclusions of law' are insufficient to either support or defeat a motion for summary judgment."... "Without more than credentials and a subjective opinion, an expert's testimony that 'it is so' is not admissible...."

Accord Town Sound & Custom Tops v. Chrysler Motors, 959 F.2d 468 (3d Cir. 1991), *rehearing en banc granted* (expert affidavit in antitrust case that does nothing more than state conclusions will not raise fact issue for summary judgment purposes); *City of Chanute v. Williams Nat. Gas Co.*, 743 F. Supp. 1437, 1445-46 (D. Kan. 1990), *aff'd*, 955 F.2d 641 (10th Cir. 1992) (expert's affidavit in antitrust case that does not contain a "firm foundation" in facts would be insufficient for summary judgment purposes).

In *Daubert v. Merrell Dow Pharmaceutical*, 509 U.S. 579 (1993), a nonantitrust decision, the Supreme Court held that before expert testimony is admissible it must be "reliable." Further, assessing reliability

> does not require, although it does permit, explicit identification of a relevant scientific community and an express determination of a particular degree of acceptance within that community. Widespread acceptance can be an important factor in ruling particular evidence admissible, and "a known technique that has been able to attract only minimal support within the community," ... may properly be viewed with skepticism.

The factors to be used in assessing reliability include:

> 1) Whether the offered theory or technique can be and has been tested;
> 2) Whether the theory or technique has been subjected to peer review and publication;
> 3) The known or potential rate of error or the existence of standards; and
> 4) Whether the theory or technique used has been generally accepted.

Applying these criteria, several antitrust decisions have held that the testimony of an economic expert did not create a fact issue precluding summary judgment.

For example, in *City of Tuscaloosa v. Hacros Chemicals*, 877 F. Supp. 1504 (N.D. Ala. 1995), the plaintiffs' expert offered his opinion that the defendants were engaged in collusion by noting that (a) there were few defendants with similar cost structures and standardized products, thus making collusion easier; (b) the market was subject to frequent, predictable sales by means of sealed bids with announced winners, thus making bid rigging more plausible; and (c) price-cost margins suggested prices above the competitive level. In addition, there was some evidence that the defendant's employees were instructed not to deviate from published list prices and that one firm had used a price change as a "signal to get prices up." From such evidence the expert opined that the market was subject to tacit collusion by "signalling." He testified that "[d]efendants were using explicit price signals through bids not intended to win contracts in order to reach an agreement to bid (and quote) higher prices, while always honoring one another's incumbencies." *Id.* at 1516.

On appeal, the Eleventh Circuit reversed, holding first that the economist had used methods that were acceptable within the discipline of economics, and thus admissable. Second, the court held that the testimony, once admitted, was sufficient to entitle the plaintiffs to go to trial. *Tuscaloosa*, 158 F.3d. 548 (11th Cir. 1998).

8. Some circuits have adopted a slightly stronger version of *Matsushita*, but most continue to profess that they are merely following the standard set out by the Supreme Court. For example, the Second Circuit, in *Apex Oil Co. v. Dimauro*, 822 F.2d 246, 253 (2d Cir. 1987), stated that the evidence necessary to properly infer a conscious commitment to an unlawful conspiracy must be *strong* direct or circumstantial evidence. Similarly, the Fourth Circuit, in *Laurel Sand & Gravel, Inc. v. CSX Transp., Inc.*, 924 F.2d 539, 543 (4th Cir. 1991), claimed that the plaintiff, in order to succeed in a summary judgment motion, must bring evidence that does not just "tend to" exclude the possibility of independent conduct, but *actually excludes* such an inference. For further examples of stricter applications of *Matsushita*, *see Dimidowich v. Bell & Howell*, 803 F.2d 1473 (9th Cir. 1986) and *Flegel v. Christian Hosp., Northeast-Northwest*, 4 F.3d 682 (8th Cir. 1993).

On the other hand, the Third Circuit has adopted a more liberal version of the *Matsushita* standard. It has been more willing to deduce that evidence excludes all possibility of independent action than other circuits. *Id.* This suggests a propensity to side with plaintiffs in antitrust summary judgment issues. Many Third Circuit cases have contained vigorous dissents, however, often faulting the majority for confusing evidence showing an *opportunity* to conspire with evidence excluding the possibility that the defendant did anything other than conspire. The Third Circuit has accepted business necessity defenses to summary judgment motions, however. *See Hauser v. Fox Theatres Management Corp.*, 845 F.2d 1225 (3d Cir. 1986). *See generally* O'Connor Murphy, *Survey of the Circuits: Standard of Review for Summary Judgment in Sherman Act § 1 Conspiracy Cases—Third Circuit*, 27 Antitrust Litigator 2, 6 (Sept. 1997).

The rest of the circuits strike a middle ground, with some adopting *Matsushita*'s exact wording and some varying the standard by applying step-by-step tests to summary judgment motions in antitrust cases. The First Circuit follows the language of *Matsushita* without variance, requiring the plaintiff to present "evidence reasonably tending to show a conscious commitment by [the alleged conspirators] to a common scheme designed to achieve an unlawful objective." *Moffat v. Lane Co.*, 595 F. Supp. 43 (D. Mass. 1984). The Fifth Circuit uses this language, as well. *See e.g.*, *Johnson v. Hosp. Corp. of Am.*, 95 F.3d 383 (5th Cir. 1996). The Sixth, Seventh, Tenth, and Eleventh Circuits undertake an initial consideration of the plausibility of the plaintiff's evidence, then apply *Matsushita*'s "tending to exclude" language should any ambiguity exist. Sometimes these circuits weigh business justifications into the initial balance. *See Riverview Investments, Inc. v. Ottawa Community Improvement Corp.*, 899 F.2d 474 (6th Cir. 1990); *Gibson v. Greater Park City Co.*, 818 F.2d 722 (10th Cir. 1987). The Sixth and Seventh Circuits also employ "plus factors," or supplementary evidence, in deciding whether a violation has occurred.

D. MARKET ALLOCATION

1. JOINT VENTURES AND COOPERATIVE RESEARCH VENTURES

Before proceeding into the cases that evaluate the evidence and standards relevant to market allocation agreements, it may be helpful to discuss briefly other kinds of market-sharing arrangements. One such arrangement is the joint venture, which is an agreement between firms to carry on a business or activity of some nature in a cooperative fashion. See also Chapter 7, where joint ventures are discussed as mergers which may violate section 7 of the Clayton Act. As one antitrust commentator has observed, "[t]he very definition of a joint venture is unclear. More than a simple contract yet less than a merger ... the key element is continuity ... [of the] association of two or more to carry on as co-owners an enterprise for one or a series of transactions." Brodley, *The Legal Status of Joint Ventures Under the Antitrust Laws: A Summary Assessment*, 21 Antitrust Bull. 453, 454 (1976).

When firms engage in joint activities, there is a potential for anticompetitive conduct that can violate section 1 of the Sherman Act. Specifically, the anticompetitive risks involved are collusion, loss of competition, and market exclusion. Brodley, *Joint Ventures and Antitrust Policy*, 95 Harv. L. Rev. 1521, 1530 (1982). With regard to cartel behavior, "the joint venture has been used as a means of restraining competition between the participants, typically by fixing prices and dividing markets, thus depriving the public of the benefits of competition." Though the joint venture may have a legitimate purpose, the Sherman Act is concerned with measuring the competitive consequences of the restraint that may result.

Chicago Board of Trade, Appalachian Coals, Broadcast Music, and *NCAA* all involved joint ventures. In those cases the legality of the arrangement and its consequence were examined under section 1. *See also United States v. Penn-Olin Chem. Co.*, 378 U.S. 158 (1964), reprinted *infra*, where the Court began examining joint ventures under section 7 of the Clayton Act. In all the cases the Supreme Court was reluctant to apply a per se rule. Instead, it employed a balancing analysis, even where the defendants had significant market power, so that the benefits of the venture could be weighed against the resulting restraint. In each of the cases, the Court, using rule of reason analysis, balanced the economic efficiencies achieved by the joint venture against the social costs and potential harms.

In essence, the analysis centered on whether the joint venture (generally a joint sales agency) was formed to accomplish a competitively beneficial purpose; if so, the Court applied a rule of reason. *See also United States v. Morgan*, 118 F. Supp. 621 (S.D.N.Y. 1953). *But see Citizen Pub'g Co. v. United States*, 394 U.S. 131 (1969), where the Court held that horizontal joint ventures may be inherently unlawful. However, as the cases which follow in this subsection imply, the directness of the effect of the joint venture on price, and whether markets are actually divided, significantly alters the standards of analysis under section 1.

Cooperation among businesses often involves research. Joint ventures may facilitate business research given the risks and costs involved. Furthermore, research activities often generate external benefits that can give rise to substantial "free rider" problems. Once a firm has put the results of expensive research to profitable use — for example, by marketing a product incorporating the new innovations — they become public information. If the innovations cannot easily be patented, or if a copyist can "invent around" the patents, the second and subsequent firms will be able to take advantage of the first firm's research at a far lower cost. These free rider problems can become a substantial disincentive to research and development — particularly where research costs are relatively high and the protection afforded by the patent laws is relatively low. The well constructed research joint venture can help solve this free rider problem by ensuring that all the firms in a position to profit from a particular innovation will also share in its costs. Joint research among competitors can maximize resources but it can also affect competition, giving rise to antitrust concerns. Pure research joint ventures are not problematic from an antitrust standpoint. They become so, however, when they are accompanied by restrictive agreements among the parties to the joint project or with outsiders.

In 1980 the Department of Justice issued guidelines for businesses engaged in or contemplating research joint ventures. The antitrust scrutiny of research joint ventures centers on the activities' effect on competition between existing competitors, whether the joint venture imposes specific restrictions on participants or outsiders that retain trade, and whether other parties will have access to the benefits of the project. Consider the Department's approach:

> The legality of a research joint venture depends on the nature of the proposed research, the joint venturers, the industry and the restraints on con-

duct imposed in connection with the project. In general, the closer the joint activity is to the basic research end of the research spectrum — i.e. the farther removed it is from substantial market effects and developmental issues — the more likely it is to be acceptable under the antitrust laws. Also, the greater the number of actual and potential competitors in an industry, the more likely that a joint research project will not unreasonably restrain competition. And, the narrower the field of joint activity and the more limited the collateral restraints involved, the greater the chances that the project will not offend the antitrust laws.

In evaluating the legality of a particular joint research project, it is useful to distinguish between three different kinds of effects on competition. The first is the effect that the essential elements of the joint research project would have in lessening existing and potential competition between the participating firms. If the joint activity has some probable and significant (non *de minimis*) anticompetitive effect, the question becomes whether the venture is, on balance, pro-competitive, taking into account all aspects economically and technically necessary for its success. Second, the project agreement, or other related agreements between the participants, may contain specific restrictions that restrain competition. If these restrictions are not reasonably ancillary to the essential elements of the project or are of undue scope or duration, they, too, will present major antitrust concerns. Finally, limitations on access to participation in joint research or to the fruits of that research may present antitrust problems if the effect of those limitations is to create or abuse market power in the hands of the joint venturers....

Antitrust Guide Concerning Research Joint Ventures, U.S. Dep't of Justice (Nov. 1980).

In 1984 Congress passed the National Cooperative Research Act of 1984. The purpose of the legislation was to encourage procompetitive joint research and development ventures and to decrease antitrust liability over such activity. The legislative history reveals that Congress believed that the perceived antitrust risk and the uncertainty of the law's application may have prevented procompetitive research and development.

Among other provisions, the statute detrebles antitrust liability to actual damages through a notification procedure, excludes per se liability, and allows the prevailing defendants to recover attorney's fees and costs attributable to frivolous claims or conduct. In order to come within the Act, defendants must give notification to the Department of Justice and FTC of the intended venture and identify the parties involved and the nature and goals of the undertaking. If the notification procedures are satisfied, an antitrust claimant under either federal or state law is limited to single (actual) damages. The Act does not cover (1) commercial data exchanges among competitors relating to costs, prices, marketing, or distribution unless reasonably required to carry out the venture,

(2) marketing or distribution agreements which are restrictive, other than proprietary information (patents and trade secrets) that develop from the joint venture, and (3) unrelated conduct not reasonably required for the success of the venture.

In 1993, the Clinton Administration signed its first antitrust legislation: The National Cooperative Production Amendments Act 1993. As an extension of the 1984 Act, it applies to *production* joint ventures. It accomplishes several objectives: (1) it permits parties participating in joint research and development ventures to limit their antitrust damage exposure to actual, rather than treble, damages for qualifying ventures; (2) it requires a voluntary notification procedure in order for its provisions to apply; (3) it employs a rule of reason analysis to assess the alleged restraint; and (4) it provides special attorneys' fees in any antitrust case where the joint venture is challenged.

However, contrary to the 1984 Act, the new statute limits the actual damage recovery only in cases where the principal facilities for production are located in the United States or its territories, and then only to United States companies that control such ventures or companies from foreign countries whose law accords antitrust treatment "no less favorable to United States persons than to such country's domestic persons regarding participation in joint ventures for production." Further, except for the product manufactured by the joint venture, marketing and distribution agreements are excluded from the antitrust immunity.

In the last several years, a large literature on joint ventures and innovation has developed. Much of the attention has been on collaborative high technology industries, with criticism that traditional antitrust interpretation inhibits the creation of cooperative, procompetitive ventures and dynamic innovation. In substantial part, the new 1993 joint venture statute is in response to the contemporary literature. *See generally* T. Jorde & D. Teece, *Antitrust, Innovation and Competitiveness* (1992); Katten, *Antitrust Analysis of Technology Joint Ventures: Allocative Efficiency and the Rewards of Innovation*, 61 Antitrust L.J. 937 (1993); Jorde & Teece, *Rule of Reason Analysis of Horizontal Arrangements: Agreements Designed to Advance Innovation and Commercialize Technology*, 61 Antitrust L.J. 579 (1993); Jorde & Teece, *Acceptable Cooperation Among Competitors in the Face of Growing International Competition*, 58 Antitrust L.J. 2 (1989); P. Stoneman, *The Economic Analysis of Technological Change* (1993); Ordover & Willig, *Antitrust for High Technology Industries: Assessing Research Joint Ventures and Mergers*, 28 J.L. & Econ. 311 (1985).

The cases that follow establish the analytical process by which the courts have evaluated objectionable exclusionary agreements such as market divisions and concerted refusals to deal. Such agreements can arise from joint ventures in the form of restrictions on the venture members or outsiders regarding exclusion of access to markets. They can be created, in addition, through a more traditional cartel agreement which lacks any lawful purpose.

2. JOINT VENTURES AND PATENT LICENSING UNDER INTELLECTUAL PROPERTY GUIDELINES

Recent Guidelines concerning the licensing of patents and other intellectual property rights take a generally benign attitude toward joint ventures that involve patent or copyright licensing. *Antitrust Guidelines for the Licensing and Acquisition of Intellectual Property* (1994), reprinted in P. Areeda & H. Hovenkamp, *Antitrust Law*, Appendix C (Supp.). Under these Guidelines "the licensor and the licensee [of an intellectual property right] are deemed to be horizontal competitors only if they own or control technologies that are economic substitutes for each other or if they are competitors in a goods market other than through the use by the licensee of the licensed technology." Further, "[h]orizontal restraints in licensing arrangements that constitute price fixing, allocation of markets or customers, agreements to reduce output, and certain group boycotts may merit per se treatment." Beyond that, however, the rule of reason will be applied. The Guidelines then create a "safety zone" of reasonableness when the licensor and licensees collectively account for less than twenty percent of any market affected by the restraint. *Id.* at § 4.1.

If a joint activity does not fall within the safety zone, the Antitrust Division will first inquire whether the restraint has an anticompetitive effect. If so, it then asks whether "the restraint is reasonably necessary to achieve procompetitive benefits that outweigh those anticompetitive effects." *Id.* at § 4.2. Possible anticompetitive effects will be assessed by a structural inquiry similar to that described in the government's *1992 Horizontal Merger Guidelines*, at least if two or more of the parties are deemed to be competitors. (The *1992 Horizontal Merger Guidelines* are reprinted as Appendix A in this casebook.) By contrast, if the relationship between the licensor and licensee is vertical, "harm to competition from a restraint may occur if it forecloses access to, or increases competitors' costs of obtaining, important inputs (other than as a natural consequence of the licensee acquiring a licensed technology for its own use)." *See Intellectual Property Guidelines*, § 4.3.1:

> An example is a licensing arrangement with most of the established manufacturers in an industry preventing those manufacturers from using any other technology. The risk of foreclosing access or increasing competitors' costs is related to the fraction of the markets affected by the licensing restraint and to other characteristics of the input and output markets, such as concentration, difficulty of entry, and elasticities of supply and demand.

Licensing arrangements meriting particularly close attention under the rule of reason involve exclusivity, in the sense that the licensor (1) forbids the licensee from licensing others; (2) limits the uses that the licensee may make of the licensed technology; or (3) restrains the licensee in the use of competing technologies. The Guidelines indicate that (1) and (2) raise competitive concerns only if the licensor and licensees are actual or potential competitors absent the licensing arrangement itself. § 4.3.2. In all cases, if a threat to competition is found, the rule of reason inquiry requires an examination of efficiencies (§ 4.4) and less restrictive alternatives. On the latter, the Guidelines note that:

> The existence of practical and significantly less restrictive alternatives is relevant to a determination of whether a restraint is reasonably necessary. If it is clear that the parties could have achieved similar efficiencies by means that are significantly less restrictive, then the Department will not give weight to the parties' efficiency claim. In making this assessment, however, the Department will not engage in a search for a theoretically least restrictive alternative that might be easier to construct in hindsight than in the practical prospective business situation faced by the parties.

Ibid.

The Department also identifies a category of licensing agreements that are subject to a "quick look" analysis, falling somewhere between per se and full rule of reason inquiry. *Id.* at § 4.5. "When the restraint is one that ordinarily warrants per se treatment, and a quick look at the claimed efficiencies reveals that the restraint is not reasonably necessary to achieve procompetitive efficiencies, the Department will likely challenge the restraint without further analysis."

3. HORIZONTAL MARKET DIVISIONS

A market division agreement is one in which firms agree not to compete in a designated market. Agreements between competitors to divide markets (whether territories, customers, or products), can be as anticompetitive as price fixing agreements. Indeed, such agreements can be the means by which competitors may avoid competing on price, enhance market power without an explicit price fixing agreement, and thus facilitate creation of a monopoly in a given area. Generally, such agreements serve the direct purpose of controlling market entry by new competitors who are parties to the agreement or regulating the exit from the market of old competitors. In short, the purpose or effect of a market allocation agreement is often the reduction of competition. Analysis of such agreements may raise the same evidentiary question that alleged price fixing agreements raise, such as how collusion can be established, and whether an express agreement is necessary.

In *Timken Roller Bearing Co. v. United States*, 341 U.S. 593 (1951), a corporation and its partially owned subsidiaries were parties to agreements that licensed a trademark, allocated territories for marketing purposes, and set prices within the territories. The United States firm owned 30 percent of the British firm and, with another firm, it owned all of a French firm (see discussion in *Sealy, infra*). In rejecting defendants' argument that the joint venture restrictions were ancillary and necessary to protect the trademark, the Court found that the challenged agreement was overbroad. The main purpose of the agreement, the Court held, was not trademark protection but rather market division. Moreover, the restraints affected interbrand competition as well as intraband competition. But the Court did not state with clarity whether a market division was *per se* illegal.

UNITED STATES V. SEALY

388 U.S. 350 (1967)

JUSTICE FORTAS delivered the opinion of the Court.

Appellee and its predecessors have, for more than 40 years, been engaged in the business of licensing manufacturers of mattresses and bedding products to make and sell such products under the Sealy name and trademarks. In this civil action the United States charged that appellee had violated § 1 of the Sherman Act, by conspiring with its licensees to fix the prices at which the retail customers of the licensees might resell bedding products bearing the Sealy name, and to allocate mutually exclusive territories among such manufacturer-licensees.

After trial, the District Court found that the appellee was engaged in a continuing conspiracy with its manufacturer-licensees to agree upon and fix minimum retail prices on Sealy products and to police the prices so fixed. It enjoined the appellee from such conduct ....

With respect to the charge that appellee conspired to allocate mutually exclusive territory among its manufacturers, the District Court held that the United States had not proved conduct "in unreasonable restraint of trade in violation of Section 1 of the Sherman Act."...

There is no dispute that exclusive territories were allotted to the manufacturer-licensees. Sealy agreed with each licensee not to license any other person to manufacture or sell in the designated area; and the licensee agreed not to manufacture or sell "Sealy products" outside the designated area. A manufacturer could make and sell his private label products anywhere he might choose.

Because this Court has distinguished between horizontal and vertical territorial limitations for purposes of the impact of the Sherman Act, it is first necessary to determine whether the territorial arrangements here are to be treated as the creature of the licensor, Sealy, or as the product of a horizontal arrangement among the licensees.

....

There are about 30 Sealy "licensees." They own substantially all of its stock. Sealy's bylaws provide that each director must be a stockholder or a stockholder-licensee's nominee. Sealy's business is managed and controlled by its board of directors. Between board meetings, the executive committee acts. It is composed of Sealy's president and five board members, all licensee-stockholders. Control does not reside in the licensees only as a matter of form. It is exercised by them in the day-to-day business of the company including the grant, assignment, reassignment, and termination of exclusive territorial licenses. Action of this sort is taken either by the board of directors or the executive committee of Sealy, both of which, as we have said, are manned, wholly or almost entirely, by licensee-stockholders.

Appellee argues that "there is no evidence that Sealy is a mere creature or instrumentality of its stockholders." In support of this proposition, it stoutly asserts that "the stockholders and directors wore a 'Sealy hat' when they were acting on behalf of Sealy." But the obvious and inescapable facts are that Sealy was a joint venture of, by, and for its stockholder-licensees; and the stockholder-licensees are themselves directly, without even the semblance of insulation, in charge of Sealy's operations.

....

It is true that the licensees had an interest in Sealy's effectiveness and efficiency, and, as stockholders, they welcomed its profitability — at any rate within the limits set by their willingness as licensees to pay royalties to the joint venture. But that does not determine whether they as licensees are chargeable with action in the name of Sealy.... The arrangements for exclusive territories are necessarily chargeable to the licensees of appellee whose interests such arrangements were supposed to promote and who, through select members, guaranteed or withheld and had the power to terminate licenses for inadequate performance. The territorial arrangements must be regarded as the creature of horizontal action by the licensees. It would violate reality to treat them as equivalent to territorial limitations imposed by a manufacturer upon independent dealers as incident to the sale of a trademarked product. Sealy, Inc., is an instrumentality of the licensees for purposes of the horizontal territorial allocation. It is not the principal.

....

Timken involved agreements between United States, British, and French companies for territorial division among themselves of world markets for antifriction bearings. The agreements included fixing prices on the products of one company sold in the territory of the others; restricting imports to and exports from the United States; and excluding outside competition. This Court held that the "aggregation of trade restraints such as those existing in this case are illegal under the [Sherman] Act."

In the present case, we are also faced with an "aggregation of trade restraints." Since the early days of the company in 1925 and continuously thereafter, the prices to be charged by retailers to whom the licensee-stockholders of Sealy sold their products have been fixed and policed by the licensee-stockholders directly, by Sealy itself, and by collaboration between them....

... [T]his unlawful resale price-fixing activity refutes appellee's claim that the territorial restraints were mere incidents of a lawful program of trademark licensing. Cf. *Timken Roller Bearing Co. v. United States* [341 U.S. 593 (1951)].[3]

---

[3] In *Timken*, as in the present case, it was argued that the restraints were reasonable steps incident to a valid trademark licensing system. But the Court summarily rejected the argument, as we do here. It pointed out that the restraints went far beyond the protection of the trademark and included nontrademarked items, and it concluded that: "A trademark cannot be legally used as a device for Sherman Act violation."... In *Timken*, the restraints covered nonbranded merchandise as well as the "Timken" line. In the present case the restraints were in terms of "Sealy products" only.

The territorial restraints were a part of the unlawful price-fixing and policing. As specific findings of the District Court show, they gave to each licensee an enclave in which it could and did zealously and effectively maintain resale prices, free from the danger of outside incursions. It may be true, as appellee vigorously argues, that territorial exclusivity served many other purposes. But its connection with the unlawful price-fixing is enough to require that it be condemned as an unlawful restraint and that appellee be effectively prevented from its continued or further use.

It is urged upon us that we should condone this territorial limitation among manufacturers of Sealy products because of the absence of any showing that it is unreasonable. It is argued, for example, that a number of small grocers might allocate territory among themselves on an exclusive basis as incident to the use of a common name and common advertisements, and that this sort of venture should be welcomed in the interests of competition, and should not be condemned as *per se* unlawful. But condemnation of appellee's territorial arrangements certainly does not require us to go so far as to condemn that quite different situation, whatever might be the result if it were presented to us for decision. For here, the arrangements for territorial limitations are part of "an aggregation of trade restraints" including unlawful price-fixing and policing. *Timken Roller Bearing Co. v. United States, supra*, 341 U.S., at 598. Compare *United States v. General Motors*, 384 U.S. 127, 147-148 (1966). Within settled doctrine, they are unlawful under § 1 of the Sherman Act without the necessity for an inquiry in each particular case as to their business or economic justification, their impact in the marketplace, or their reasonableness.

Accordingly, the judgment of the District Court is reversed and the case remanded for the entry of an appropriate decree.

NOTES AND QUESTIONS

1. How did the Court justify classifying the territorial restrictions as horizontal? Do you agree? Did the Court hold that once the market divisions are characterized as horizontal restraints they are necessarily per se illegal? Did the Court consider whether the *Sealy* defendants had sufficient market power to effect a price increase? Why did the *Sealy* defense, maintaining that the joint venture was reasonable because it produced economies that would enhance their competitive position against larger firms, fail?

2. In dissent, Justice Harlan argued that the market division restrictions at issue in *Sealy* should be considered vertical, thereby permitting the restraints to be

---

As to their private label products, the licensees were free to sell outside of the given territory and, so far as appears, without resale price collaboration or enforcement. But this difference in fact is not consequential in this case. A restraint such as is here involved of the resale price of a trademarked article, not otherwise permitted by law, cannot be defended as ancillary to a trademark licensing scheme.

examined under the rule of reason approach, where the business justifications could be weighed against the harms to determine net competitive effect.

> [V]ertical restraints — that is, limitations imposed by a manufacturer on his own dealers, ... or by a licensor on his licensees — may have independent and valid business justifications. The person imposing the restraint cannot necessarily be said to be acting for anticompetitive purposes. Quite to the contrary, he can be expected to be acting to enhance the competitive position of his product vis-à-vis other brands.

> With respect to vertical restrictions, it has long been recognized that in order to engage in effective *interbrand* competition, some limitations on *intraband* competition may be necessary. Restraints of this type "may be allowable protections against aggressive competitors or the only practicable means a small company has for breaking into or staying in business ... and within the 'rule of reason'." For these reasons territorial limitations imposed vertically should be tested by the rule of reason, namely, whether in the context of the particular industry, "the restraint imposed is such as merely regulates and perhaps thereby promotes competition or whether it is such as may suppress or even destroy competition." *Chicago Board of Trade v. United States*, 246 U.S. 231, 238.

388 U.S. at 359-60 (Harlan, J., dissenting). What alternatives to the territorial division exist? Did *Sealy* hold that a market allocation agreement, unaccompanied by a price fixing arrangement, is per se illegal? The Court, five years later, addressed that issue again, as well as the important distinction between horizontal and vertical agreements. In the interim, the Court in a per curiam decision in *Burke v. Ford*, 389 U.S. 320, 321 (1967), stated that "[h]orizontal territorial divisions almost invariably reduce competition among the participants."

UNITED STATES V. TOPCO ASSOCIATES
405 U.S. 596 (1972)

JUSTICE MARSHALL delivered the opinion of the Court.

The United States brought this action for injunctive relief against alleged violation by Topco Associates, Inc. (Topco), of § 1 of the Sherman Act....

I

Topco is a cooperative association of approximately 25 small and medium-sized regional supermarket chains that operate stores in some 33 States. Each of the member chains operates independently; there is no pooling of earnings, profits, capital, management, or advertising resources. No grocery business is conducted under the Topco name. Its basic function is to serve as a purchasing agent for its members. In this capacity, it procures and distributes to the members more than 1,000 different food and related nonfood items, most of which are distributed under brand names owned by Topco. The association does not itself own any manufacturing, processing, or warehousing facilities, and the items that it procures for members are usually shipped directly from the packer or manufacturer to the members. Payment is made either to Topco or directly to the manufacturer at a cost that is virtually the same for the members as for Topco itself.

All of the stock in Topco is owned by the members, with the common stock, the only stock having voting rights, being equally distributed. The board of directors, which controls the operation of the association, is drawn from the members and is normally composed of high-ranking executive officers of member chains. It is the board that elects the association's officers and appoints committee members, and it is from the board that the principal executive officers of Topco must be drawn....

Topco was founded in the 1940's by a group of small, local grocery chains, independently owned and operated, that desired to cooperate to obtain high quality merchandise under private labels in order to compete more effectively with larger national and regional chains.[3] With a line of canned, dairy, and other products, the association began.... By 1964, Topco's members had combined retail sales of more than $2 billion; by 1967, their sales totaled more than $2.3 billion, a figure exceeded by only three national grocery chains.

Members of the association vary in the degree of market share that they possess in their respective areas. The range is from 1.5% to 16%, with the average being approximately 6%. While it is difficult to compare these figures with the market shares of larger regional and national chains because of the absence in the record of accurate statistics for these chains, there is much evidence in the record that Topco members are frequently in as strong a competitive position in their respective areas as any other chain. The strength of this competitive position is due, in some measure, to the success of Topco-brand products. Although

---

[3] The founding members of Topco were having difficulty competing with larger chains. This difficulty was attributable in some degree to the fact that the larger chains were capable of developing their own private-label programs.

Private-labeled products differ from other brand-name products in that they are sold at a limited number of easily ascertainable stores. A&P, for example, was a pioneer in developing a series of products that were sold under an A&P label and that were only available in A&P stores. It is obvious that by using private-label products, a chain can achieve significant cost economies in purchasing, transportation, warehousing, promotion, and advertising. These economies may afford the chain opportunities for offering private-label products at lower prices than other brand-name products. This, in turn, provides many advantages of which some of the more important are: a store can offer national-brand products at the same price as other stores, while simultaneously offering a desirable, lower priced alternative; or, if the profit margin is sufficiently high on private-brand goods, national-brand products may be sold at reduced price. Other advantages include: enabling a chain to bargain more favorably with national-brand manufacturers by creating a broader supply base of manufacturers, thereby decreasing dependence on a few, large national-brand manufacturers; enabling a chain to create a "price-mix" whereby prices on special items can be lowered to attract customers while profits are maintained on other items; and creation of general goodwill by offering lower priced, higher quality goods.

only 10% of the total goods sold by Topco members bear the association's brand names, the profit on these goods is substantial and their very existence has improved the competitive potential of Topco members with respect to other large and powerful chains.

It is apparent that from meager beginnings approximately a quarter of a century ago, Topco has developed into a purchasing association wholly owned and operated by member chains, which possess much economic muscle, individually as well as cooperatively.

II

... The United States charged that, beginning at least as early as 1960 and continuing up to the time that the complaint was filed, Topco had combined and conspired with its members to violate § 1 in two respects. First, the Government alleged that there existed:

> a continuing agreement, understanding and concert of action among the co-conspirator member firms acting through Topco, the substantial terms of which have been and are that each co-conspirator member firm will sell Topco-controlled brands only within the marketing territory allocated to it, and will refrain from selling Topco-controlled brands outside such marketing territory.

[Second,] [m]embership must first be approved by the board of directors, and thereafter by an affirmative vote of 75% of the association's members. If, however, the member whose operations are closest to those of the applicant, or any member whose operations are located within 100 miles of the applicant, votes against approval, an affirmative vote of 85% of the members is required for approval. Bylaws, Art. I, § 5. Because, as indicated by the record, members cooperate in accommodating each other's wishes, the procedure for approval provides, in essence, that members have a veto of sorts over actual or potential competition in the territorial areas in which they are concerned.

Following approval, each new member signs an agreement with Topco designating the territory in which that member may sell Topco-brand products. No member may sell these products outside the territory in which it is licensed. Most licenses are exclusive, and even those denominated "coextensive" or "non-exclusive" prove to be *de facto* exclusive. Exclusive territorial areas are often allocated to members who do no actual business in those areas on the theory that they may wish to expand at some indefinite future time and that expansion would likely be in the direction of the allocated territory. When combined with each member's veto power over new members, provisions for exclusivity work effectively to insulate members from competition in Topco-brand goods. Should a member violate its license agreement and sell in areas other than those in which it is licensed, its membership can be terminated.... Once a territory is classified as exclusive, either formally or *de facto*, it is extremely unlikely that the classification will ever be changed....

Topco's answer to the complaint is illustrative of its posture in the District Court and before this Court:

> Private label merchandising is a way of economic life in the food retailing industry, and exclusivity is the essence of a private label program; without exclusivity, a private label would not be private. Each national and large regional chain has its own exclusive private label products in addition to the nationally advertised brands which all chains sell. Each such chain relies upon the exclusivity of its own private label line to differentiate its private label products from those of its competitors and to attract and retain the repeat business and loyalty of consumers. Smaller retail grocery stores and chains are unable to compete effectively with the national and large regional chains without also offering their own exclusive private label products.

> ....

> The only feasible method by which Topco can procure private label products and assure the exclusivity thereof is through trademark licenses specifying the territory in which each member may sell such trademarked products.

Topco essentially maintains that it needs territorial divisions to compete with larger chains; that the association could not exist if the territorial divisions were anything but exclusive; and that by restricting competition in the sale of Topco-brand goods, the association actually increases competition by enabling its members to compete successfully with larger regional and national chains.

....

III

....

It is only after considerable experience with certain business relationships that courts classify them as *per se* violations of the Sherman Act. One of the classic examples of a *per se* violation of § 1 is an agreement between competitors at the same level of the market structure to allocate territories in order to minimize competition. Such concerted action is usually termed a "horizontal" restraint, in contradistinction to combinations of persons at different levels of the market structure, *e.g.*, manufacturers and distributors, which are termed "vertical" restraints. This Court has reiterated time and time again that "[h]orizontal territorial limitations ... are naked restraints of trade with no purpose except stifling of competition." [Citing cases.]

We think that it is clear that the restraint in this case is a horizontal one, and, therefore, a *per se* violation of § 1. The District Court failed to make any determination as to whether there were *per se* horizontal territorial restraints in this case and simply applied a rule of reason in reaching its conclusions that the restraints were not illegal. In so doing, the District Court erred.

....

Whether or not we would decide this case the same way under the rule of reason used by the District Court is irrelevant to the issue before us. The fact is that courts are of limited utility in examining difficult economic problems.[10] Our inability to weigh, in any meaningful sense, destruction of competition in one sector of the economy against promotion of competition in another sector is one important reason we have formulated *per se* rules.

In applying these rigid rules, the Court has consistently rejected the notion that naked restraints of trade are to be tolerated because they are well intended or because they are allegedly developed to increase competition.

....

The District Court determined that by limiting the freedom of its individual members to compete with each other, Topco was doing a greater good by fostering competition between members and other large supermarket chains. But, the fallacy in this is that Topco has no authority under the Sherman Act to determine the respective values of competition in various sectors of the economy. On the contrary, the Sherman Act gives to each Topco member and to each prospective member the right to ascertain for itself whether or not competition with other supermarket chains is more desirable than competition in the sale of Topco-brand products. Without territorial restrictions, Topco members may indeed "[cut] each other's throats." But, we have never found this possibility sufficient to warrant condoning horizontal restraints of trade.

....

There have been tremendous departures from the notion of a free-enterprise system as it was originally conceived in this country. These departures have been the product of congressional action and the will of the people. If a decision is to be made to sacrifice competition in one portion of the economy for greater competition in another portion, this too is a decision that must be made by Congress and not by private forces or by the courts. Private forces are too keenly aware of their own interests in making such decisions and courts are ill-equipped and ill-situated for such decisionmaking. To analyze, interpret, and evaluate the myriad of competing interests and the endless data that would surely be brought to bear on such decisions, and to make the delicate judgment on the relative values to society of competitive areas of the economy, the judgment of the elected representatives of the people is required.

Just as the territorial restrictions on retailing Topco-brand products must fall, so must the territorial restrictions on wholesaling. The considerations are the same, and the Sherman Act requires identical results.

---

[10] There has been much recent commentary on the wisdom of per se rules....

Without the *per se* rules, businessmen would be left with little to aid them in predicting in any particular case what courts will find to be legal and illegal under the Sherman Act. Should Congress ultimately determine that predictability is unimportant in this area of the law, it can, of course, make per se rules inapplicable in some or all cases, and leave courts free to ramble through the wilds of economic theory in order to maintain a flexible approach.

We also strike down Topco's other restrictions on the right of its members to wholesale goods. These restrictions amount to regulation of the customers to whom members of Topco may sell Topco-brand goods. Like territorial restrictions, limitations on customers are intended to limit intra-brand competition and to promote inter-brand competition. For the reasons previously discussed, the arena in which Topco members compete must be left to their unfettered choice absent a contrary congressional determination.

We reverse the judgment of the District Court and remand the case for entry of an appropriate decree.

CHIEF JUSTICE BURGER, dissenting.

This case does not involve restraints on interbrand competition or an allocation of markets by an association with monopoly or near-monopoly control of the sources of supply of one or more varieties of staple goods. Rather, we have here an agreement among several small grocery chains to join in a cooperative endeavor that, in my view, has an unquestionably lawful principal purpose; in pursuit of that purpose they have mutually agreed to certain minimal ancillary restraints that are fully reasonable in view of the principal purpose and that have never before today been held by this Court to be *per se* violations of the Sherman Act.

In joining in this cooperative endeavor, these small chains did not agree to the restraints here at issue in order to make it possible for them to exploit an already established line of products through noncompetitive pricing. There was no such thing as a Topco line of products until this cooperative was formed. The restraints to which the cooperative's members have agreed deal only with the marketing of the products in the Topco line, and the only function of those restraints is to permit each member chain to establish, within its own geographical area and through its own local advertising and marketing efforts, a local consumer awareness of the trademarked family of products as that member's "private label" line. The goal sought was the enhancement of the individual members' abilities to compete, albeit to a modest degree, with the large national chains which had been successfully marketing private-label lines for several years. The sole reason for a cooperative endeavor was to make economically feasible such things as quality control, large quantity purchases at bulk prices, the development of attractively printed labels, and the ability to offer a number of different lines of trademarked products. All these things, of course, are feasible for the large national chains operating individually, but they are beyond the reach of the small operators proceeding alone.

After a careful review of the economic considerations bearing upon this case, the District Court determined that "the relief which the government here seeks would not increase competition in Topco private label brands"; on the contrary, such relief "would substantially diminish competition in the supermarket field."

...

I do not believe that our prior decisions justify the result reached by the majority. Nor do I believe that a new *per se* rule should be established in disposing of this case, for the judicial convenience and ready predictability that are made possible by *per se* rules are not such overriding considerations in antitrust law as to justify their promulgation without careful prior consideration of the relevant economic realities in the light of the basic policy and goals of the Sherman Act.

....

II

With all respect, I believe that there are two basic fallacies in the Court's approach here. First, while I would not characterize our role under the Sherman Act as one of "rambl[ing] through the wilds," it is indeed one that requires our "examin[ation of] difficult economic problems." We can undoubtedly ease our task, but we should not abdicate that role by formulation of *per se* rules with no justification other than the enhancement of predictability and the reduction of judicial investigation. Second, from the general proposition that *per se* rules play a necessary role in antitrust law, it does not follow that the particular *per se* rule promulgated today is an appropriate one. Although it might well be desirable in a proper case for this Court to formulate a *per se* rule dealing with horizontal territorial limitations, it would not necessarily be appropriate for such a rule to amount to a blanket prohibition against all such limitations. More specifically, it is far from clear to me why such a rule should cover those division-of-market agreements that involve no price fixing and which are concerned only with trademarked products that are not in a monopoly or near-monopoly position with respect to competing brands. The instant case presents such an agreement; I would not decide it upon the basis of a *per se* rule.

The District Court specifically found that the horizontal restraints involved here tend positively to promote competition in the supermarket field and to produce lower costs for the consumer. The Court seems implicitly to accept this determination, but says that the Sherman Act does not give Topco the authority to determine for itself "whether or not competition with other supermarket chains is more desirable than competition in the sale of Topco-brand products." But the majority overlooks a further specific determination of the District Court, namely, that the invalidation of the restraints here at issue "would not increase competition in Topco private label brands." Indeed, the District Court seemed to believe that it would, on the contrary, lead to the likely demise of those brands in time. And the evidence before the District Court would appear to justify that conclusion.

....

[After remand the Supreme Court affirmed the district court's order permitting Topco to engage in areas of "primary responsibility," thereby permitting individual members to select designated warehouse locations, to identify locations of places of business for trademark licensees, and to terminate membership of businesses not adequately promoting Topco products, unless the practices resulted in territorial exclusivity. *United States v. Topco Assocs.*, 319 F. Supp. 1031 (N.D. Ill. 1970), *aff'd*, 414 U.S. 801 (1973).]

NOTES AND QUESTIONS

1. What was the basis for the district court's refusal to apply a per se rule? Does the *per se* analysis adopted by the Supreme Court meet the previously announced test that such a standard be employed only when the conduct has a "pernicious effect on competition" and lacks "any redeeming virtue"? Does the Court in *Sealy* and *Topco* indicate that market division agreements will be considered illegal per se without regard to market power or countervailing procompetitive consequences? Do the Court's holdings in *Sealy* and *Topco* imply that any agreement among competitors that alters competition is by definition a price fixing agreement and subject to per se treatment? Was Justice Marshall characterizing the per se rule correctly when he said "whether or not we would decide this case the same way under the rule of reason ... is irrelevant"?

In light of the rule of reason approach utilized in the *Broadcast Music* decision for a joint sales agency do you consider *Topco* implicitly overruled? Consider whether a market allocation agreement between competitors is more pernicious than a price fixing agreement? Does the latter still permit room for competition on nonprice factors such as service and quality?

2. Is there any authority in *Topco* for treating joint ventures differently if the restrictions are imposed by smaller firms seeking to be more competitively efficient? Recall that the Court permitted the continuance of the independent grocers' joint purchasing agency.

3. After *Sealy* and *Topco*, what would you advise a client who is a manufacturer or trademark licensor, utilizing independent distributors, who wants to impose territorial restrictions on them? Does your analysis depend on whether the client competes with its own distributors? *Compare Williams & Co. v. Williams & Co.-East*, 542 F.2d 1053 (9th Cir. 1976), *cert. denied*, 433 U.S. 908 (1977), *with American Motor Inns, Inc. v. Holiday Inns, Inc.*, 521 F.2d 1230, 1253-54 (3d Cir. 1975), *and Hobart Bros. v. Malcolm T. Gilliland, Inc.*, 471 F.2d 894 (5th Cir.), *cert. denied*, 412 U.S. 923 (1973). Are you persuaded by Chief Justice Burger's argument that the legal distinctions should turn on whether the restraint affects *interbrand* competition rather than *intrabrand* competition? What effect would there be on competition if such a standard were adopted? Can the effect on consumers be predicted? Should the legal analysis (and outcome) be dependent upon the conduct characterization employed (horizontal vs. vertical) or whether the defendants have market power to restrict output or affect price in the interbrand market? *See* Liebeler, Book Review, 66 Calif. L. Rev. 1317, 1333-41 (1978). See also Chapter 5, where the standard for analyzing intrabrand restraints is discussed in the context of *Continental T.V., Inc. v. GTE Sylvania, Inc.*, 433 U.S. 36 (1977).

4. How could the individual members of Topco reduce output or raise prices if each controlled, on average, only 6% of the retail grocery trade in its area?

5. Consider whether *Sealy* and *Topco* leave any room for a rule of reason analysis when the agreement between the competitors does not divide the entire market, but leaves the parties a residual zone in which to compete. On this question, the Supreme Court in 1984 denied certiorari in a case in which the lower appellate court held that the per se rule of illegality is applicable only when the entire geographic market is divided. *Atkin v. Union Processing Corp.*, 453 N.E.2d 522 (N.Y. App. 1983), *cert. denied*, 465 U.S. 1038 (1984). The three dissenting Justices from the certiorari denial believed that the New York Court of Appeals decision conflicted with *Topco*, and thus presented a substantial federal question.

POLK BROS. V. FOREST CITY ENTERPRISES

776 F.2d 185 (7th Cir. 1985)

JUDGE EASTERBROOK.

In 1972 Polk Bros., which owned some land in Burbank, Illinois, discussed with Forest City Enterprises the possibility of building a store large enough for both firms. Polk sells appliances and home furnishings; Forest City sells building materials, lumber, tools, and related products. Both have substantial chains of stores. They reached an agreement. Polk built a single building on a large parcel of land. The building is partitioned internally; Polk and Forest City have separate entrances; Polk's store contains 64,000 square feet, Forest City's 68,000 square feet. One parking lot serves both businesses. Forest City became Polk's lessee in 1973. The stores opened in 1975. In 1978 Forest City exercised its option to buy, and Polk took back a mortgage for some $1.4 million.

The attraction of the arrangement was the complementary nature of the firms' products. The two stores together could offer a full line of goods for furnishing and maintaining a home. Both Polk and Forest City were concerned, however, that competition might replace cooperation. They negotiated a covenant restricting the products each could sell. Forest City promised not to sell "major appliances and furniture," although it reserved the right to sell "built-in appliances in connection with Kitchen-Build-In business." Polk Bros. promised not to "stock or sell Toro and Lawnboy products including lawn mowers, building materials, lumber and related products, tools, paints and sundries, hardware, garden supplies, automotive supplies or plumbing supplies." The parties agreed on a long list of things that both could sell, including "Gas & Electric Heaters[,] Built-In-Ranges[,] ... Snow Blowers[,] Lawn Mowers[,] ... [and] Hardware/Garden Mdse." When Forest City became an owner in 1978 the parties agreed that the restrictions in the lease would become covenants running with the land for 50 years.

Forest City's management changed in 1982. The new managers were concerned about declining profits from its three stores near Chicago. Two stores sold some major appliances; the one at Burbank did not. Forest City found it un-economical to advertise the large appliances when one of the three outlets could not sell them. Forest City asked to be relieved of its covenant at Burbank. Polk said no. In January 1983 Forest City informed Polk that it considered the covenant invalid; Polk responded with a suit in state court seeking an injunction. Forest City removed the action to the district court under 28 U.S.C. § 1441, where it could have been filed initially under the diversity jurisdiction.

....

I

The district court held the covenant invalid under § 3(1)(c) of the antitrust law of Illinois, which declares unlawful contracts "allocating or dividing customers, territories, supplies, sales or markets, functional or geographical, for any commodity." That state's antitrust law, however, refers courts to federal antitrust law as a guide to questions of interpretation. In order to find out what Illinois law forbids, we inquire what federal antitrust law forbids. Cf. *Marrese v. American Academy of Orthopaedic Surgeons*, 726 F.2d 1150, 1155 (7th Cir. 1984) (en banc), *rev'd on other grounds*, 470 U.S. 373 (1985).

Like federal law, Illinois law recognizes a difference between contracts unlawful *per se* and those that must be assessed under a Rule of Reason. Although federal law treats almost all contracts allocating products and markets as unlawful *per se*, the *per se* rule is designed for "naked" restraints rather than agreements that facilitate productive activity. Any firm involves cooperation among people who could otherwise be competitors. Polk Bros. and Forest City each comprise many stores. The managers of each store could set prices independently, competing against each other, but antitrust law does not require this.

Cooperation is the basis of productivity. It is necessary for people to cooperate n some respects before they may compete in others, and cooperation facilitates efficient production. See *Monsanto Co. v. Spray-Rite Service Corp.*, 465 U.S. 752 (1984). Joint ventures, mergers, systems of distribution — all these and more require extensive cooperation, and all are assessed under a Rule of Reason that focuses on market power and the ability of the cooperators to raise price by restricting output. The war of all against all is not a good model for any economy. Antitrust law is designed to ensure an appropriate blend of cooperation and competition, not to require all economic actors to compete full tilt at every moment. When cooperation contributes to productivity through integration of efforts, the Rule of Reason is the norm. *National Collegiate Athletic Association v. Board of Regents of University of Oklahoma*, 468 U.S. 85 (1984) (*NCAA*).

A court must distinguish between "naked" restraints, those in which the restriction on competition is unaccompanied by new production or products, and "ancillary" restraints, those that are part of a larger endeavor whose success they promote. If two people meet one day and decide not to compete, the restraint is "naked"; it does nothing but suppress competition. If A hires B as a salesman and passes customer lists to B, then B's reciprocal covenant not to compete with A is "ancillary." At the time A and B strike their bargain, the enterprise (viewed as a whole) expands output and competition by putting B to work. The covenant not to compete means that A may trust B with broader responsibilities, the better to compete against third parties. Covenants of this type are evaluated under the Rule of Reason as ancillary restraints, and unless they bring a large market share under a single firm's control they are lawful. See *United States v. Addyston Pipe & Steel Co.*, 85 F. 271, 280-83 (6th Cir. 1898) (Taft, J.), *aff'd*, 172 U.S. 211 (1899).

The evaluation of ancillary restraints under the Rule of Reason does not imply that ancillary agreements are not real horizontal restraints. They are. A covenant not to compete following employment does not operate any differently from a horizontal market division among competitors — not at the time the covenant has its bite, anyway. The difference comes at the time people enter beneficial arrangements. A legal rule that enforces covenants not to compete, even after an employee has launched his own firm, makes it easier for people to cooperate productively in the first place. Knowing that he is not cutting his own throat by doing so, the employer will train the employee, giving him skills, knowledge, and trade secrets that make the firm more productive. Once that employment ends, there is nothing left but restraint — but the aftermath is the wrong focus.

A court must ask whether an agreement promoted enterprise and productivity at the time it was adopted. If it arguably did, then the court must apply the Rule of Reason to make a more discriminating assessment. "[I]t is sometimes difficult to distinguish robust competition from conduct with long-run anti-competitive effects" (*Copperweld Corp. v. Independence Tube Corp.*, 467 U.S. 752), and so a court must be very sure that a category of acts is anti-competitive before condemning that category *per se*. Both *BMI* and *NCAA* emphasize that condemnation *per se* is an unusual step, one that depends on confidence that a whole category of restraints is so likely to be anticompetitive that there is no point in searching for a potentially beneficial instance.

A restraint is ancillary when it may contribute to the success of a cooperative venture that promises greater productivity and output. If the restraint, viewed at the time it was adopted, may promote the success of this more extensive cooperation, then the court must scrutinize things carefully under the Rule of Reason. Only when a quick look reveals that "the practice facially appears to be one that would always or almost always tend to restrict competition and decrease output" should a court cut off further inquiry.

Polk Bros. and Forest City were deciding in 1972-73 whether to embark on a new venture — the building of a joint facility — that would expand output. The endeavor not only would increase the retail selling capacity in Burbank but also would provide a convenience to consumers. Polk Bros. does about 80% of its business in large appliances. If it could bring to the same location building supplies and the other items in which Forest City specializes, shopping would be more convenient for consumers. As the district court put it, the parties "hoped to attract more customers because of the proximity of two stores, selling different but complementary items for the home."

This was productive cooperation. The covenant allocating items between the retailers played an important role in inducing the two retailers to cooperate. The district court found that Polk "would not have entered into this arrangement, however, unless it had received assurances that [Forest City] would not compete with it in the sale of products that are the 'foundation of [Polk's] business'.... The agreement not to compete was an integral part of the lease and land sale."

It is easy to see why. Polk spent substantial sums in advertising to attract customers to its stores, where it displayed and demonstrated the appliances. It might be tempting for another retailer to take a free ride on these efforts. Once Polk had persuaded a customer to purchase a color TV, its next door neighbor might try to lure the customer away by quoting a lower price. It could afford to do this if, for example, it simply kept the TV sets in boxes and let Polk bear the costs of sales personnel and demonstrations. Polk would not continue doing the work while its neighbor took the sales. It would do less demonstrating and promotion, to the detriment of consumers who valued the information. The Supreme Court has recognized that the control of free riding is a legitimate objective of a system of distribution. See *Monsanto Co. v. Spray-Rite Serv. Corp.*, 465 U.S. 752; *Continental T.V., Inc. v. GTE Sylvania, Inc.*, 433 U.S. at 55-57.

The district court nonetheless concluded that the covenant is not ancillary because it was an essential part of the arrangement. It reasoned: "The agreement not to compete was an integral part of the lease and land sale. This was not a sale with an ancillary agreement designed to protect an original owner's established business interests. The lease and land sale would not have been made by Polk Bros. absent an agreement not to compete.... Because the covenant not to compete was not merely ancillary to a sale of land or business, it constitutes a horizontal restraint of trade and a *per se* violation of the Illinois Antitrust Act...." There are two possible interpretations of this reasoning. One is that this covenant is not ancillary because it is so important. The other is that the agreement is not ancillary when it is part of the establishment of a new business, as opposed to the sale of an existing business. Neither is correct.

The reason for distinguishing between "ancillary" and "naked" restraints is to determine whether the agreement is part of a cooperative venture with prospects for increasing output. If it is, it should not be condemned *per se*. Only by exalting Webster's Third over the function of antitrust law could a court determine that a restraint is not "ancillary" because it was so important to the productive undertaking. The suggestion that the ancillary restraints doctrine does not apply to new ventures also slights the functions of the rule. The partners of a newly-formed law firm agree on fees and allocate subjects of specialty and clients among them; this "price fixing" and "market division" do not become unlawful just because the firm is new. The benefits of cooperation may be greatest when launching a new venture.

Polk Bros. and Forest City were cooperating to produce, not to curtail output; the cooperation increased the amount of retail space available and was at least potentially beneficial to consumers; the restrictive covenant made the cooperation possible. The Rule of Reason therefore applies....

....

Polk is entitled to the permanent injunction it seeks. Polk's relief may be conditioned, however, on its iron-clad undertaking to live up to its end of the bargain, and the district court should incorporate this into the injunction. Forest City also has an action for damages caused by Polk's sales, if it can establish any and if it has preserved the claim.

....

Reversed.

NOTE

In *Palmer v. BRG of Georgia, Inc.*, 498 U.S. 46 (1990), the Supreme Court reaffirmed with both clarity and brevity that horizontal market division is unlawful per se. The per curiam opinion cited *Socony-Vacuum* and *Topco* for the rule that an allocation of markets or submarkets by competitors is unlawful whether or not the competitors had previously competed between themselves in the same market.

In *Palmer*, HBJ offered on a limited basis in 1976 a bar review course in Georgia in competition with BRG. In 1980 they entered an agreement that gave BRG an exclusive license to use HBJ's written materials in Georgia, along with the trade name Bar/Bri. In return the parties agreed that HBJ would not compete in Georgia and BRG would not compete outside Georgia. In this agreement HBJ received $100 per student enrolled in Georgia by BRG and 40% of all revenues over $350. After the 1980 agreement became effective, the price of BRG's bar review course went from $150 to $400.

Said the Court: "The revenue-sharing formula in the 1980 agreement between BRG and HBJ, coupled with the price increase that took place immediately after the parties agreed to cease competing with each other in 1980, indicates that this agreement was 'formed for the purpose and with the effect of raising' the price of the bar review course." Does this language suggest that for a market division agreement to be per se unlawful it must have a direct effect on price?

Relying on *Topco*, the Court answered in the negative. "Here, HBJ and BRG had previously competed in the Georgia market; under their allocation agreement, BRG received that market, while HBJ received the remainder of the United States. Each agreed not to compete in the other's territories. Such agreements are anticompetitive regardless of whether the parties split a market within which both do business or whether they merely reserve one market for one and another for the other. Thus, the 1980 agreement between HBJ and BRG was unlawful on its face."

Palmer makes clear that market allocations between competitors are per se unlawful even (1) in the absence of an agreement on price or evidence that one party has the right to be consulted about the other's prices, and (2) when the parties had not previously competed in the same market.

Interestingly, the District Court had granted a summary judgment for the defendants under the authority of *Matsushita*, and the Court of Appeals had affirmed. Perhaps *Palmer* is the first signal from the Court to the lower courts that its expansive language in *Matsushita* in favor of granting a summary judgment is not applicable when the underlying theory of enforcement rests on a traditional per se theory. As Judge Clark observed in his dissent from the Court of Appeal decision, "it is ... doubtful whether the standards announced in *Matsushita* and *Monsanto* apply in situations, such as the instant action, where the direct evidence of concerted action is manifest in explicit written agreements between dominant firms allocating and monopolizing the market and interfering with independent price setting," 874 F.2d 1417, 1431 (11th Cir. 1989) (Clark, J., dissenting). *See also In re Coordinated Pretrial Proceedings in Petroleum Prods. Antitrust Litig.*, 915 F.2d 542 (9th Cir. 1990).

Horizontal market division can affect professionals once in practice as well. Consider the traditional partnership agreement, which may contain a "no compete" clause within a certain territory if one leaves the partnership. Is a partnership agreement that limits the geographic area in which each partner or former partner can practice and advertise an enforceable contract or illegal under the Sherman Act? Does it matter if the agreement only restricts advertising and not areas of practice? Are such restrictions ancillary to the larger agreement to form or dissolve the partnership and thus legal?

Blackburn v. Sweeny, 53 F.3d 825 (7th Cir. 1995), applied the per se rule to an agreement not to advertise in one another's territories entered by two lawyers who had previously dissolved their relationship. The court found that the agreement "sufficiently approximate[d] an agreement to allocate markets so that the per se rule of illegality" applied. The court rejected the defense that the agreement was ancillary to the larger partnership dissolution agreement, because the partnership had already been dissolved when the territorial agreement was entered.

Although the agreement was held per se illegal, treble damages and attorneys fees were denied because the parties were adjudged of equal fault or responsibility. See Chapter 3 *supra* on the defenses of *in pari delicto* and unclean hands.

Query: How anticompetitive is an agreement between two lawyers (in this case, personal injury lawyers) dividing their territory, when the market contains dozens or perhaps even hundreds of other lawyers in competition with them?

The Ninth Circuit has held that per se rule against horizontal market divisions does not apply in the international context. In *Metro Industries, Inc. v. Sammi Corp.*, 82 F.3d 839 (9th Cir.), *cert. denied*, 519 U.S. 868 (1996), a domestic importer of Korean kitchenware alleged that the Korean system of export registration constituted an illegal market division. After determining that it had jurisdiction to rule on the claim, the court granted the defendant's motion for summary judgment. According to the court, even if the defendant's conduct was so inherently suspect that it would be subject to per se analysis had it occurred domestically, "application of the per se rule is not appropriate where the conduct in question occurred in another country. Determining whether the registration system was a violation of the antitrust laws would still require an examination of the impact of the system on commerce in the United States ...." The court proceeded to award summary judgment in favor of the defendant because the plaintiff did nothing more than suggest it could produce evidence of injury to itself and its customers.

E. BOYCOTTS AND OTHER CONCERTED REFUSALS TO DEAL

Up to this point in the study of cartel-like horizontal behavior, we have seen the Court adopt per se standards of analysis for conduct characterized as price fixing or market division. Exclusionary arrangements can also take the form of collective agreements designed to limit competition either by creating barriers to entry for new competition or facilitating market exit by existing competitors. Group boycotts or concerted refusals to deal are examples. The boycott, a refusal to deal with a particular firm, can be aimed at competitors on the same level of competition or at customers or suppliers on different levels of the market. The objective of the refusal to deal and the effect on competition influence the Court's analysis. The objective and effect will also determine how the boycott will be classified for purposes of analysis. As the following cases indicate, the legality of the boycott is determined by examining how essential the design of the agreement is to a lawful objective.

1. DEVELOPMENT OF A PER SE ANALYSIS: COLLECTIVE AGREEMENTS AIMED AT COMPETITORS

EASTERN STATES RETAIL LUMBER DEALERS' ASS'N V. UNITED STATES

234 U.S. 600 (1914)

JUSTICE DAY delivered the opinion of the Court.

[Defendants were lumber trade associations composed largely of retail lumber dealers. The associations circulated among themselves the membership lists of wholesalers who also sold lumber retail directly to consumers. "The particular thing which this case concerns is the retailers' efforts ... by the circulation of the reports in question, to keep the wholesalers from selling directly to the local trade."]

... When viewed in the light of the history of these associations and the conflict in which they were engaged to keep the retail trade to themselves and to prevent wholesalers from interfering with what they regarded as their rights in such trade there can be but one purpose in giving the information in this form to the members of the retail associations of the names of all wholesalers who by their attempt to invade the exclusive territory of the retailers, as they regard it, have been guilty of unfair competitive trade. These lists were quite commonly spoken of as blacklists, and when the attention of a retailer was brought to the name of a wholesaler who had acted in this wise it was with the evident purpose that he should know of such conduct and act accordingly. True it is that there is no agreement among the retailers to refrain from dealing with listed wholesalers, nor is there any penalty annexed for the failure so to do, but he is blind indeed who does not see the purpose in the predetermined and periodical circulation of this report to put the ban upon wholesale dealers whose names appear in the list of unfair dealers trying by methods obnoxious to the retail dealers to supply the trade which they regard as their own....

[T]he circulation of such information among the hundreds of retailers as to the alleged delinquency of a wholesaler with one of their number had and was intended to have the natural effect of causing such retailers to withhold their patronage from the concern listed.

....

Here are wholesale dealers in large number engaged in interstate trade upon whom it is proposed to impose as a condition of carrying on that trade that they shall not sell in such manner that a local retail dealer may regard such sale as an infringement of his exclusive right to trade, upon pain of being reported as an unfair dealer to a large number of other retail dealers associated with the offended dealer, the purpose being to keep the wholesaler from dealing not only with the particular dealer who reports him but with all others of the class who may be informed of his delinquency.... This record abounds in instances where the offending dealer was thus reported, the hoped for effect, unless he discontinued the offending practice, realized, and his trade directly and appreciably impaired.

But it is said that in order to show a combination or conspiracy within the Sherman Act some agreement must be shown under which the concerted action is taken. It is elementary, however, that conspiracies are seldom capable of proof by direct testimony and may be inferred from the things actually done, and when in this case by concerted action the names of wholesalers who were reported as having made sales to consumers were periodically reported to the other members of the associations, the conspiracy to accomplish that which was the natural consequence of such action may be readily inferred.

The circulation of these reports not only tends to directly restrain the freedom of commerce by preventing the listed dealers from entering into competition with retailers, as was held by the District Court, but it directly tends to prevent other retailers who have no personal grievance against him and with whom he might trade from so doing, they being deterred solely because of the influence of the report circulated among the members of the associations....

A retail dealer has the unquestioned right to stop dealing with a wholesaler for reasons sufficient to himself, and may do so because he thinks such dealer is acting unfairly in trying to undermine his trade. "But," as was said ... in *Grenada Lumber Co. v. Mississippi*, 217 U.S. 433, 440, "when the plaintiffs in error combine and agree that no one of them will trade with any producer or wholesaler who shall sell to a consumer within the trade range of any of them, quite another case is presented. An act harmless when done by one may become a public wrong when done by many acting in concert, for it then takes on the form of a conspiracy, and may be prohibited or punished, if the result be hurtful to the public or to the individual against whom the concerted action is directed."

When the retailer goes beyond his personal right, and, conspiring and combining with others of like purpose, seeks to obstruct the free course of interstate trade and commerce and to unduly suppress competition by placing obnoxious wholesale dealers under the coercive influence of a condemnatory report circulated among others, actual or possible customers of the offenders, he exceeds his lawful rights, and such action brings him and those acting with him within the condemnation of the act of Congress, and the District Court was right in so holding. It follows that its decree must be

Affirmed.

NOTES AND QUESTIONS

1. Did the Court find an agreement to boycott or merely an agreement to exchange data? Does a distinction between the two matter with regard to the analysis utilized? Did the Court conclude that this boycott was per se illegal? Did it imply that competitive injury can be inferred without regard to market power?

2. Did the Court in *Eastern States* suggest that a unilateral refusal to deal is lawful? *See Lorain Journal Co. v. United States*, 342 U.S. 143 (1951). Consider the analysis adopted subsequently in *Interstate Circuit* and *Container*.

3. In *Fashion Originator's Guild of Am. ("FOGA") v. FTC*, 312 U.S. 457 (1941), the Court reached the same conclusion as in *Eastern States*. Defendant manufacturers of fashionable clothes for women in *Fashion Guild* attempted to prevent "style piracy" by agreeing to boycott retailers who purchased from the defendants' competitors that dealt in copied designs. As a result of the Guild's collective action, 12,000 retailers signed agreements to cooperate with the boycott in refusing to buy from the targeted discount manufacturers.

The Court affirmed the FTC's refusal to consider the "reasonableness" of the Guild's methods. Said the Court: "reasonableness of the methods pursued by the combination to accomplish its unlawful object is no more material than would be the reasonableness of the prices fixed by unlawful combination." The effect of this refusal to deal, the Court concluded, was to foreclose access to retail outlets and thus to reduce competition from lower-priced competitors.

KLOR'S, INC. V. BROADWAY-HALE STORES, INC.

359 U.S. 207 (1959)

JUSTICE BLACK delivered the opinion of the Court.

Klor's, Inc., operates a retail store on Mission Street, San Francisco, California; Broadway-Hale Stores, Inc., a chain of department stores, operates one of its stores next door. The two stores compete in the sale of radios, television sets, refrigerators and other household appliances. Claiming that Broadway-Hale and 10 national manufacturers and their distributors have conspired to restrain and monopolize commerce in violation of §§ 1 and 2 of the Sherman Act, Klor's brought this action for treble damages and injunction in the United States District Court.

In support of its claim Klor's made the following allegations: George Klor started an appliance store some years before 1952 and has operated it ever since either individually or as Klor's, Inc. Klor's is as well equipped as Broadway-Hale to handle all brands of appliances. Nevertheless, manufacturers and distributors of such well-known brands as General Electric, RCA, Admiral, Zenith, Emerson and others have conspired among themselves and with Broadway-Hale either not to sell to Klor's or to sell to it only at discriminatory prices and highly unfavorable terms. Broadway-Hale has used its "monopolistic" buying power to bring about this situation. The business of manufacturing, distributing and selling household appliances is in interstate commerce. The concerted refusal to deal with Klor's has seriously handicapped its ability to compete and has already caused it a great loss of profits, goodwill, reputation and prestige.

The defendants did not dispute these allegations, but sought summary judgment and dismissal of the complaint for failure to state a cause of action. They submitted unchallenged affidavits which showed that there were hundreds of other household appliance retailers, some within a few blocks of Klor's who sold many competing brands of appliances, including those the defendants refused to sell to Klor's. From the allegations of the complaint, and from the affidavits supporting the motion for summary judgment, the District Court concluded that the controversy was a "purely private quarrel" between Klor's and Broadway-Hale, which did not amount to a "public wrong proscribed by the [Sherman] Act." On this ground the complaint was dismissed and summary judgment was entered for the defendants. The Court of Appeals for the Ninth Circuit affirmed the summary judgment. It stated that "a violation of the Sherman Act requires conduct of defendants by which the public is or conceivably may be ultimately injured." It held that here the required public injury was missing since "there was no charge or proof that by any act of defendants the price, quantity, or quality offered the public was affected, nor that there was any intent or purpose to effect a change in, or an influence on, prices, quantity, or quality...." The holding, if correct, means that unless the opportunities for customers to buy in a competitive market are reduced, a group of powerful businessmen may act in concert to deprive a single merchant like Klor, of the goods he needs to compete effectively....

We think Klor's allegations clearly show one type of trade restraint and public harm the Sherman Act forbids, and that defendants' affidavits provide no defense to the charges....

Group boycotts, or concerted refusals by traders to deal with other traders, have long been held to be in the forbidden category. They have not been saved by allegations that they were reasonable in the specific circumstances, nor by a failure to show that they "fixed or regulated prices, parcelled out or limited production, or brought about a deterioration in quality."...

Plainly the allegations of this complaint disclose such a boycott. This is not a case of a single trader refusing to deal with another, nor even of a manufacturer and a dealer agreeing to an exclusive distributorship. Alleged in this complaint is a wide combination consisting of manufacturers, distributors and a retailer. This combination takes from Klor's its freedom to buy appliances in an open competitive market and drives it out of business as a dealer in the defendants' products. It deprives the manufacturers and distributors of their freedom to sell to Klor's at the same prices and conditions made available to Broadway-Hale, and in some instances forbids them from selling to it on any terms whatsoever. It interferes with the natural flow of interstate commerce. It clearly has, by its "nature" and "character," a "monopolistic tendency." As such it is not to be tolerated merely because the victim is just one merchant whose business is so small that his destruction makes little difference to the economy.[7] Monopoly can as surely thrive by the elimination of such small businessmen, one at a time, as it can by driving them out in large groups. In recognition of this fact the Sherman Act has consistently been read to forbid all contracts and combinations "which 'tend to create a monopoly,'" whether "the tendency is a creeping one" or "one that proceeds at full gallop."

The judgment of the Court of Appeals is reversed and the cause is remanded to the District Court for trial.

NOTES AND QUESTIONS

1. Since the Court reversed the grant of summary judgment for the defendant, what would the plaintiff have to prove at trial to establish a prima facie case? Will actual competitive injury have to be demonstrated? If Klor's is not required to establish actual competitive injury, why wasn't summary judgment entered for plaintiff? What levels of competition were affected in both *FOGA* and *Klor's*? Does *Klor's* require a showing of market power before a section 1 violation is found?

The complaint in *Klor's* alleged that Broadway-Hale Stores, Inc., used its "monopolistic" buying power to force General Electric, RCA, Admiral, Zenith, Emerson, and other large appliance manufacturers not to deal with Klor's. Since

---

[7] The court below relied heavily on *Apex Hosiery Co. v. Leader*, 310 U.S. 469, in reaching its conclusion. While some language in that case can be read as supporting the position that no restraint on trade is prohibited by § 1 of the Sherman Act unless it has or is intended to have an effect on market prices, such statements must be considered in the light of the fact that the defendant in that case was a labor union. The Court in *Apex* recognized that the Act is aimed primarily at combinations having commercial objectives and is applied only to a very limited extent to organizations, like labor unions, which normally have other objectives. Moreover, cases subsequent to *Apex* have made clear that an effect on prices is not essential to a Sherman Act violation. See, e.g., *Fashion Originators' Guild v. Federal Trade Comm'n*, 312 U.S. 457, 466.

the Supreme Court merely reversed a grant of summary judgment for the defendant, it never dealt with the plausibility of such a scheme. Is it likely that a small retail chain had monopsony power vis-à-vis General Electric, RCA, and such companies? Much more likely, the companies were engaged in resale price maintenance (see discussion, *infra*) and Broadway-Hale was merely reporting Klor's violation of the resale price maintenance provision.

It is also possible that Klor's was injuring Broadway-Hale, which was right next door, by taking a "free ride" on Broadway-Hale's efforts to service its customers. Customers would go to a "full service" store like Broadway-Hale to see a complex item described and to receive helpful information about purchasing — then they would go next door to Klor's and purchase it at a discount price.

Resale price maintenance is illegal per se, but under the *Colgate* exception (see discussion Chapter 5, *infra*) a simple unilateral refusal to deal with a company that charges less than the manufacturer's "suggested" retail price is legal. It became illegal once again in *Klor's*, however, if done pursuant to a conspiracy, either between a group of competing wholesalers, or between a wholesaler and a competitor of the retailer.

2. How did defendants' defense in *Klor's* differ from those posited in *FOGA* and *Eastern States*? Does the decisional analysis change accordingly?

3. The Court said that the challenged agreement in *Klor's* was something more than a vertical arrangement between customer (dealer) and supplier (manufacturer). Explain. Did the Court imply that the standard of analysis will vary according to the relationship between the parties involved? Should it matter whether the plaintiff is an excluded competitor or a consumer denied an opportunity to buy something at a lower price? What is the legal and economic rationale for such a distinction? If such an inference can be drawn from the opinion, is it unlawful per se to have an exclusive distributorship (such as an exclusive franchise) where a manufacturer agrees to sell only to a single retailer? What economic rationale supports such an arrangement? Will the boycott doctrine be applied to such a case?

4. After *Klor's*, is a plaintiff required to plead economic injury to the public at large? The rule of per se illegality set forth in *Klor's* was followed in subsequent Supreme Court cases. In *Radiant Burners, Inc. v. Peoples Gas Light & Coke Co.*, 364 U.S. 656 (1961), the Court reversed a lower court's dismissal of a complaint. The district court had dismissed a complaint charging that a trade association's standard setting "seal of approval" amounted to a concerted refusal to deal. The Seventh Circuit upheld the dismissal, stating that "no boycott, conspiracy to boycott or other form of per se violation is established by the facts alleged." In addition the Court added that "in the absence of a per se violation the Sherman Act protects the individually injured competitor and affords him relief, but only under circumstances where there is such general injury to the competitive process that the public at large suffers economic harm." The Seventh Circuit went on to hold that this element of the claim for relief was lacking since "the allegations of [the] plaintiffs' complaint fail to establish that there has been any appreciable lessening in the sale of [products involved] or that the public has been deprived of a product of overall superiority." In reversing the Seventh Circuit, the Supreme Court stated:

> We think the decision of the Court of Appeals does not accord with our recent decision in *Klor's, Inc. v. Broadway-Hale Stores*, 359 U.S. 207. The allegation in the complaint that "AGA and its Utility members, including Peoples and Northern, effectuate the plan and purpose of the unlawful combination and conspiracy ... by ... refusing to provide gas for use in the plaintiff's Radiant Burner[s]" because they "are not approved by AGA" clearly shows "one type of trade restraint and public harm the Sherman Act forbids...." It is obvious that petitioner cannot sell its gas burners, whatever may be their virtues, if, because of the alleged conspiracy, the purchasers cannot buy gas for use in those burners. The conspiratorial refusal "to provide gas for use in the plaintiff's Radiant Burner[s] [because they] are not approved by AGA" therefore falls within one of the "classes of restraints which from their 'nature or character' [are] unduly restrictive, and hence forbidden by both the common law and the statute.... As to these classes of restraints ... Congress [has] determined its own criteria of public harm and it [is] not for the courts to decide whether in an individual case injury [has] actually occurred."... The alleged conspiratorial refusal to provide gas for use in plaintiff's Radiant Burners "interferes with the natural flow of interstate commerce [and] clearly has, by its 'nature' and 'character', a 'monopolistic tendency.' As such it is not to be tolerated merely because the victim is just one [manufacturer] whose business is so small that his destruction makes little difference to the economy." *Id.*, 359 U.S. at 213.
>
> Therefore ... to state a claim upon which relief can be granted under that section, allegations adequate to show a violation and, in a private treble damage action, that plaintiff was damaged thereby are all the law requires.

But see Allied Tube & Conduit Corp. v. Indian Head, Inc., 486 U.S. 492 (1988), which calls into question *Radiant Burners*, at least suggesting a rule of reason analysis.

5. Does the language in the preceding Supreme Court cases indicate that boycotts are all alike, or that all nonunilateral commercial boycotts are per se illegal? A recent decision, together with earlier boycott cases which follow, suggests that the Court may have established certain boycott categories, which call for analytical distinctions. In *St. Paul Fire & Marine Ins. Co. v. Barry*, 438 U.S. 531 (1978), one insurer tried to reduce its malpractice policy coverage, and physicians objected. The insurer then allegedly agreed with other insurers that they would withdraw from the market, leaving the physicians to deal with a monopolist. The plaintiff physicians alleged that this was a "boycott," which, under an explicit provision of the McCarran-Ferguson Act, denied the insurers an antitrust exemption. (For more on McCarran-Ferguson and the insurance exemption, see Chapter 9.) The Court observed:

The generic concept of boycott refers to a method of pressuring a party with whom one has a dispute by withholding, or enlisting others to withhold, patronage or services from the target. The word gained currency in this country largely as a term of opprobrium to describe certain tactics employed by parties to labor disputes.... Thus it is not surprising that the term first entered the lexicon of antitrust law in decisions involving attempts by labor unions to encourage third parties to cease or suspend doing business with employers unwilling to permit unionization.

Petitioners define "boycott" as embracing only those combinations which target *competitors* of the boycotters as the ultimate objects of a concerted refusal to deal. They cite commentary that attempts to develop a test for distinguishing the types of restraints that warrant *per se* invalidation from other concerted refusals to deal that are not inherently destructive of competition. But the issue before us is whether the conduct in question involves a boycott, not whether it is *per se* unreasonable. In this regard, we have not been referred to any decision of this Court holding that petitioners' test states the necessary elements of a boycott within the purview of the Sherman Act. Indeed, the decisions reflect a marked lack of uniformity in defining the term.

Petitioners refer to cases stating that "group boycotts" are "concerted refusals by traders to deal with other traders," ... or are combinations of businessmen "to deprive others of access to merchandise which the latter wish to sell to the public." We note that neither standard in terms excludes respondents — for whom medical malpractice insurance is necessary to ply their "trade" of providing health care services, from the class of cognizable victims. But other verbal formulas also have been used. [F]or example, the Court noted that "[u]nder the Sherman Act, any agreement by a group of competitors to boycott a particular buyer or group of buyers is illegal *per se*." The Court also has stated broadly that "group boycotts or concerted refusals to deal, clearly run afoul of § 1 [of the Sherman Act]." Hence, "boycotts are not a unitary phenomenon."

As the labor-boycott cases illustrate, the boycotters and the ultimate target need not be in a competitive relationship with each other. This Court also has held unlawful concerted refusal to deal in cases where the target is a customer of some or all of the conspirators who is being denied access to a desired good or service because of a refusal to accede to particular terms set by some or all of the sellers.... As the Court put it in *Kiefer-Stewart Co. v. Seagram & Sons*, 340 U.S. 211 (1951), "the Sherman Act makes it an offense for [businessmen] to agree among themselves to stop selling to particular customers."

Whatever other characterizations are possible, petitioners' conduct fairly may be viewed as "an organized boycott" of St. Paul's policyholders. Solely for the purpose of forcing physicians and hospitals to accede to a substantial curtailment of the coverage previously available, St. Paul induced its competitors to refuse to deal on any terms with its customers. This agreement did not simply fix rates or terms of coverage; it effectively barred St. Paul's policyholders from all access to alternative sources of coverage and even from negotiating for more favorable terms elsewhere in the market. The pact served as a tactical weapon invoked by St. Paul in support of a dispute with its policyholders. The enlistment of third parties in an agreement not to trade, as a means of compelling capitulation by the boycotted group, long has been viewed as conduct supporting a finding of unlawful boycott. *Eastern States Lumber Assn. v. United States*, 234 U.S. 600, 612-613 (1914).

The Supreme Court later stated in *Hartford Fire Ins. Co. v. California*, 509 U.S. 764 (1993), that, in the context of an insurance industry boycott, conduct among insurers will not qualify for the insurance exemption if it represents a refusal to deal involving the coordinated action of multiple insurers. The refusal to deal need not be absolute in nature nor must the boycott entail unequal treatment between the targets and the insurers. Furthermore, "concerted activity," although a necessary element, is not by itself sufficient to justify a finding of boycott. The Court distinguished between cartels and boycotts. A mere agreement by insurers not to offer a certain kind of coverage is a cartel, but it is not a boycott even though the result is that the insurers collectively refuse to sell the excluded coverage. Before the cartel becomes a boycott, said the Court, the cartel members must enlist the aid of third parties or else pressure the cartel's victims by threatening to withhold goods or services other than those subject to the cartel agreement. Ordinarily, of course, the distinction between cartels and boycotts is not all that important, since both are illegal. But the McCarran-Ferguson Act exempts mere cartels of insurers, while it excepts boycotts from the exemption.

For an interesting discussion of the interaction of antitrust concerted refusal to deal law and agency principles, *see Alvord Polk, Inc. v. F. Schumacher & Co.*, 37 F.3d 996 (3d. Cir. 1994), where the Third Circuit found that antitrust liability could be attributable to a trade association "through agents whom it imbued with apparent authority." *Id.* at 1009. The allegations were that conventional retailers of wallpaper, acting through the National Decorating Products Association, conspired to pressure wallpaper manufacturers to stop selling to wallpaper dealers who sold to customers through 800 numbers, often at significant discounts below the price charged to full service dealers. *See also, Hialeah, Inc. v. Florida Horsemens' Benevolent & Protective Ass'n., Inc.* 899 F. Supp. 616 (S.D. Fla. 1995) (refusal to deal constituted the "action of a number of horsemen, taken by one association representing them").

NYNEX CORPORATION V. DISCON, INC.

119 S. Ct. 493 (1998)

JUSTICE BREYER delivered the opinion of the Court.

In this case we ask whether the antitrust rule that group boycotts are illegal per se as set forth in *Klor's, Inc. v. Broadway-Hale Stores, Inc.*, 359 U.S. 207, 212

(1959), applies to a buyer's decision to buy from one seller rather than another, when that decision cannot be justified in terms of ordinary competitive objectives. We hold that the per se group boycott rule does not apply.

I

Before 1984 American Telephone and Telegraph Company (AT&T) supplied most of the Nation's telephone service and, through wholly owned subsidiaries such as Western Electric, it also supplied much of the Nation's telephone equipment. In 1984 an antitrust consent decree took AT&T out of the *local* telephone service business and left AT&T a *long-distance* telephone service provider, competing with such firms as MCI and Sprint.... The decree transformed AT&T's formerly owned local telephone companies into independent firms. At the same time, the decree insisted that those local firms help assure competitive long-distance service by guaranteeing long-distance companies physical access to their systems and to their local customers. See *United States v. American Telephone & Telegraph Co.*, 552 F. Supp. 131, 225, 227 (DC 1982), *aff'd sub nom. Maryland v. United States*, 460 U. S 1001 (1983). To guarantee that physical access, some local telephone firms had to install new call-switching equipment; and to install new call-switching equipment, they often had to remove old call-switching equipment. This case involves the business of removing that old switching equipment (and other obsolete telephone equipment) — a business called *"removal services."*

Discon, Inc., the respondent, sold removal services used by New York Telephone Company, a firm supplying local telephone service in much of New York State and parts of Connecticut. New York Telephone is a subsidiary of NYNEX Corporation. NYNEX also owns Materiel Enterprises Company, a purchasing entity that bought removal services for New York Telephone. Discon, in a lengthy detailed complaint, alleged that the NYNEX defendants (namely, NYNEX, New York Telephone, Materiel Enterprises, and several NYNEX related individuals) engaged in unfair, improper, and anticompetitive activities in order to hurt Discon and to benefit Discon's removal services competitor, AT&T Technologies, a lineal descendant of Western Electric. The Federal District Court dismissed Discon's complaint for failure to state a claim. The Court of Appeals for the Second Circuit affirmed that dismissal with an exception, and that exception is before us for consideration.

The Second Circuit focused on one of Discon's specific claims, a claim that Materiel Enterprises had switched its purchases from Discon to Discon's competitor, AT&T Technologies, as part of an attempt to defraud local telephone service customers by hoodwinking regulators. According to Discon, Materiel Enterprises would pay AT&T Technologies more than Discon would have charged for similar removal services. It did so because it could pass the higher prices on to New York Telephone, which in turn could pass those prices on to telephone consumers in the form of higher regulatory-agency-approved telephone service charges. At the end of the year, Materiel Enterprises would receive a special rebate from AT&T Technologies, which Materiel Enterprises would share with its parent, NYNEX. Discon added that it refused to participate in this fraudulent scheme, with the result that Materiel Enterprises would not buy from Discon, and Discon went out of business.

These allegations, the Second Circuit said, state a cause of action under §1 of the Sherman Act, though under a "different legal theory" from the one articulated by Discon. 93 F.3d 1055, 1060 (1996). The Second Circuit conceded that ordinarily "the decision to discriminate in favor of one supplier over another will have a pro-competitive intent and effect." *Id.*, at 1061. But, it added, in this case, "no such pro-competitive rationale appears on the face of the complaint." *Ibid.* Rather, the complaint alleges Materiel Enterprises' decision to buy from AT&T Technologies, rather than from Discon, was intended to be, and was, "anti-competitive." *Ibid.* Hence, "Discon has alleged a cause of action under, at least, the rule of reason, and possibly under the per se rule applied to group boycotts in *Klor's*, if the restraint of trade '"has no purpose except stifling competition."'" *Ibid.* (quoting *Oreck Corp. v. Whirlpool Corp.*, 579 F.2d 126, 131 (CA2) (en banc) (in turn quoting *White Motor Co. v. United States*, 372 U.S. 253, 263 (1963)), cert. denied, 439 U.S. 946 (1978)). For somewhat similar reasons the Second Circuit believed the complaint stated a valid claim of conspiracy to monopolize under §2 of the Sherman Act. See 93 F.3d, at 1061-1062.

...

II

As this Court has made clear, the Sherman Act's prohibition of "[e]very" agreement in "restraint of trade,"... prohibits only agreements that *unreasonably* restrain trade. See *Business Electronics Corp. v. Sharp Electronics Corp.*, 485 U.S. 717, 723 (1988) (citing *National Collegiate Athletic Assn. v. Board of Regents of Univ. of Okla.*, 468 U.S. 85, 98 (1984)); *Standard Oil Co. of N. J. v. United States*, 221 U.S. 1, 59-62 (1911); 2 P. Areeda & H. Hovenkamp, Antitrust Law ¶ 320b, p. 49 (1995). Yet certain kinds of agreements will so often prove so harmful to competition and so rarely prove justified that the antitrust laws do not require proof that an agreement of that kind is, in fact, anticompetitive in the particular circumstances. See *State Oil Co. v. Khan*, 522 U.S. 3, 10 (1997); *Northwest Wholesale Stationers, Inc. v. Pacific Stationery & Printing Co.*, 472 U.S. 284, 289-290 (1985); 2 Areeda & Hovenkamp, *supra*, ¶ 320b, at 49-52. An agreement of such a kind is unlawful *per se*. See, *e.g.*, *United States v. Socony-Vacuum Oil Co.*, 310 U.S. 150, 218 (1940) (finding horizontal price-fixing agreement *per se* illegal); *Dr. Miles Medical Co. v. John D. Park & Sons Co.*, 220 U.S. 373, 408 (1911) (finding vertical price-fixing agreement *per se* illegal); *Palmer v. BRG of Ga., Inc.*, 498 U.S. 46, 49-50 (1990) (*per curiam*) (finding horizontal market division *per se* illegal).

The Court has found the *per se* rule applicable in certain group boycott cases. Thus, in *Fashion Originators' Guild of America, Inc. v. FTC*, 312 U.S. 457

(1941), this Court considered a group boycott created by an agreement among a group of clothing designers, manufacturers, suppliers, and retailers. The defendant designers, manufacturers, and suppliers had promised not to sell their clothes to retailers who bought clothes from competing manufacturers and suppliers. The defendants wanted to present evidence that would show their agreement was justified because the boycotted competitors used "pira[ted]" fashion designs. *Id.*, at 467. But the Court wrote that "it was not error to refuse to hear the evidence offered" — evidence that the agreement was reasonable and necessary to "protect ... against the devastating evils" of design pirating — for that evidence "is no more material than would be the reasonableness of the prices fixed" by a price-fixing agreement. *Id.*, at 467-468.

In *Klor's* the Court also applied the *per se* rule. The Court considered a boycott created when a retail store, Broadway-Hale, and 10 household appliance manufacturers and their distributors agreed that the distributors would not sell, or would sell only at discriminatory prices, household appliances to Broadway-Hale's small, nearby competitor, namely, Klor's. 359 U.S., at 208-209. The defendants had submitted undisputed evidence that their agreement hurt only one competitor (Klor's) and that so many other nearby appliance-selling competitors remained that competition in the marketplace continued to thrive. *Id.*, at 209-210. The Court held that this evidence was beside the point. The conspiracy was "not to be tolerated merely because the victim is just one merchant." *Id.*, at 213. The Court thereby inferred injury to the competitive process itself from the nature of the boycott agreement. And it forbade, as a matter of law, a defense based upon a claim that only one small firm, not competition itself, had suffered injury.

The case before us involves *Klor's*. The Second Circuit did not forbid the defendants to introduce evidence of "justification." To the contrary, it invited the defendants to do so, for it said that the "*per se* rule" would apply only if no "procompetitive justification" were to be found. 93 F.3d, at 1061; cf. 7 P. Areeda & H. Hovenkamp, Antitrust Law ¶ 1510, p. 416 (1986) ("Boycotts are said to be unlawful per se but justifications are routinely considered in defining the forbidden category"). Thus, the specific legal question before us is whether an antitrust court considering an agreement by a buyer to purchase goods or services from one supplier rather than another should (after examining the buyer's reasons or justifications) apply the *per se* rule if it finds no legitimate business reason for that purchasing decision. We conclude no boycott-related *per se* rule applies and that the plaintiff here must allege and prove harm, not just to a single competitor, but to the competitive process, i.e., to competition itself.

Our conclusion rests in large part upon precedent, for precedent limits the *per se* rule in the boycott context to cases involving horizontal agreements among direct competitors. The agreement in *Fashion Originators' Guild* involved what may be called a group boycott in the strongest sense: A group of competitors threatened to withhold business from third parties unless those third parties would help them injure their directly competing rivals. Although *Klor's* involved a threat made by a *single* powerful firm, it also involved a horizontal agreement among those threatened, namely, the appliance suppliers, to hurt a competitor of the retailer who made the threat. See 359 U.S., at 208-209; see also P. Areeda & L. Kaplow, Antitrust Analysis: Problems, Text, and Cases 333 (5th ed. 1997) (defining paradigmatic boycott as "collective action among a group of competitors that may inhibit the competitive vitality of rivals"); 11 H. Hovenkamp, Antitrust Law ¶ 1901e, pp. 189-190 (1998). This Court emphasized in *Klor's* that the agreement at issue was "not a case of a single trader refusing to deal with another, nor even of a manufacturer and a dealer agreeing to an exclusive distributorship. Alleged in this complaint is a wide combination consisting of manufacturers, distributors and a retailer." 359 U.S., at 212-213 (footnote omitted).

This Court subsequently pointed out specifically that *Klor's* was a case involving not simply a "vertical" agreement between supplier and customer, but a case that also involved a "horizontal" agreement among competitors. See *Business Electronics*, 485 U.S., at 734. And in doing so, the Court held that a "vertical restraint is not illegal *per se* unless it includes some agreement on price or price levels." *Id.*, at 735-736. This precedent makes the *per se* rule inapplicable, for the case before us concerns only a vertical agreement and a vertical restraint, a restraint that takes the form of depriving a supplier of a potential customer. See 11 Hovenkamp, *supra*, ¶ 1902d, at 198.

Nor have we found any special feature of this case that could distinguish it from the precedent we have just discussed. We concede Discon's claim that the petitioners' behavior hurt consumers by raising telephone service rates. But that consumer injury naturally flowed not so much from a less competitive market for removal services, as from the exercise of market power that is *lawfully* in the hands of a monopolist, namely, New York Telephone, combined with a deception worked upon the regulatory agency that prevented the agency from controlling New York Telephone's exercise of its monopoly power.

To apply the *per se* rule here — where the buyer's decision, though not made for competitive reasons, composes part of a regulatory fraud — would transform cases involving business behavior that is improper for various reasons, say, cases involving nepotism or personal pique, into treble-damages antitrust cases. And that *per se* rule would discourage firms from changing suppliers — even where the competitive process itself does not suffer harm. Cf. *Poller v. Columbia Broadcasting System, Inc.*, 368 U.S. 464, 484 (1962) (Harlan, J., dissenting) (citing *Packard Motor Car Co. v. Webster Motor Car Co.*, 243 F.2d 418, 421 (CADC 1957)).

The freedom to switch suppliers lies close to the heart of the competitive process that the antitrust laws seek to encourage. Cf. *Standard Oil*, 221 U.S., at 62 (noting "the freedom of the individual right to contract when not unduly or improperly exercised [is] the most efficient means for the prevention of monopoly"). At the same time, other laws, for example, "unfair competition" laws, business tort laws, or regulatory laws, provide remedies for various "competitive practices thought to be offensive to proper standards of business morality."

3 P. Areeda & H. Hovenkamp, Antitrust Law ¶ 651d, p. 78 (1996). Thus, this Court has refused to apply *per se* reasoning in cases involving that kind of activity. See *Brooke Group Ltd. v. Brown & Williamson Tobacco Corp.*, 509 U.S. 209, 225 (1993) ("Even an act of pure malice by one business competitor against another does not, without more, state a claim under the federal antitrust laws."); 3 Areeda & Hovenkamp, *supra*, ¶ 651d, at 80 ("[I]n the presence of substantial market power, some kinds of tortious behavior could anticompetitively create or sustain a monopoly, [but] it is wrong categorically to condemn such practices ... or categorically to excuse them").

Discon points to another special feature of its complaint, namely, its claim that Materiel Enterprises hoped to drive Discon from the market lest Discon reveal its behavior to New York Telephone or to the relevant regulatory agency. That hope, says Discon, amounts to a special anticompetitive motive.

We do not see how the presence of this special motive, however, could make a significant difference. That motive does not turn Materiel Enterprises' actions into a "boycott" within the meaning of this Court's precedents.... Nor, for that matter, do we understand how Discon believes the motive affected Materiel Enterprises' behavior. Why would Discon's demise have made Discon's employees less likely, rather than more likely, to report the overcharge/rebate scheme to telephone regulators? Regardless, a *per se* rule that would turn upon a showing that a defendant not only knew about but also hoped for a firm's demise would create a legal distinction — between corporate knowledge and corporate motive — that does not necessarily correspond to behavioral differences and which would be difficult to prove, making the resolution of already complex antitrust cases yet more difficult. We cannot find a convincing reason why the presence of this special motive should lead to the application of the *per se* rule.

Finally, we shall consider an argument that is related tangentially to Discon's *per se* claims. The complaint alleges that New York Telephone (through Materiel Enterprises) was the largest buyer of removal services in New York State ... and that only AT&T Technologies competed for New York Telephone's business.... One might ask whether these accompanying allegations are sufficient to warrant application of a *Klor's*-type presumption of consequent harm to the competitive process itself.

We believe that these allegations do not do so, for, as we have said... antitrust law does not permit the application of the *per se* rule in the boycott context in the absence of a horizontal agreement. (Though in other contexts, say, vertical price fixing, conduct may fall within the scope of a *per se* rule not at issue here. See, *e.g.*, *Dr. Miles Medical Co.*, 220 U.S., at 408.) The complaint itself explains why any such presumption would be particularly inappropriate here, for it suggests the presence of other potential or actual competitors, which fact, in the circumstances, could argue against the likelihood of anticompetitive harm. The complaint says, for example, that New York Telephone itself was a potential competitor in that New York Telephone considered removing its equipment by itself, and in fact did perform a few jobs itself.... The complaint also suggests that other nearby small local telephone companies needing removal services must have worked out some way to supply them... The complaint's description of the removal business suggests that entry was easy, perhaps to the point where other firms, employing workers who knew how to remove a switch and sell it for scrap, might have entered that business almost at will.... To that extent, the complaint suggests other actual or potential competitors might have provided roughly similar checks upon "equipment removal" prices and services with or without Discon. At the least, the complaint provides no sound basis for assuming the contrary. Its simple allegation of harm to Discon does not automatically show injury to competition.

III

The Court of Appeals also upheld the complaint's charge of a conspiracy to monopolize in violation of §2 of the Sherman Act. It did so, however, on the understanding that the conspiracy in question consisted of the very same purchasing practices that we have previously discussed. Unless those agreements harmed the competitive process, they did not amount to a conspiracy to monopolize. We do not see, on the basis of the facts alleged, how Discon could succeed on this claim without prevailing on its §1 claim. See 3 Areeda & Hovenkamp, *supra*, ¶ 651e, at 81-82. Given our conclusion that Discon has not alleged a §1 *per se* violation, we think it prudent to vacate this portion of the Court of Appeals' decision and allow the court to reconsider its finding of a §2 claim.

....

V

For these reasons, the judgment of the Court of Appeals is vacated, and the case is remanded for further proceedings consistent with this opinion.

NOTES AND QUESTIONS

1. The Court likens its decision to *Business Electronics Corp. v. Sharp Electronics Corp.*, 485 U.S. 717, 723 (1988), which involved an intrabrand restraint. But don't the facts resemble an "interbrand" restraint? Isn't *NYNEX* just a garden variety exclusive dealing claim, but for the claim of fraudulent overcharging by a price regulated utility? What if *NYNEX* had simply contracted with a single firm to perform all its removal services? How would a court have analyzed exclusive dealing? What would the likely outcome have been?

2. After *NYNEX*, can you name the kinds of boycotts that would still be illegal per se under the Sherman Act? Suppose that two equipment removal companies had agreed with each other, as well as with *NYNEX*, to participate in the fraudulent scheme and to exclude Discon for refusing to participate. What would the outcome have been? Do you agree with Justice Breyer's characterization that this decision made virtually no new law, but was driven entirely by existing precedent?

3. The only apparent purpose of the kickback scheme challenged in *NYNEX* was to defraud consumers by inflating their telephone bills. Doesn't that make this a "naked" restraint? Does the case stand for the proposition that there is no such thing as "naked" vertical exclusion — at least not for purposes of employing the *per se* rule. Consider the practice briefly described in Chapter 6 in which Alcoa, an aluminum monopolist, entered into contracts with electric utilities under which they promised not to provide electricity to any competitor of Alcoa's. Presumably, those agreements were unlawful only because Alcoa had substantial market power, but they were also "naked" in the sense that they had no redeeming virtue. Would you agree with the proposition that if NYNEX had substantial market power in the purchase of telephone removal services, then the agreement at issue should be *per se* unlawful? Given that NYNEX is a regulated monopolist in the supply of local telephone services in New York, isn't monopoly power almost a foregone conclusion?

2. TOWARD A LIMITED BALANCING APPROACH: COLLECTIVE AGREEMENTS AIMED AT CUSTOMER DEALINGS

PARAMOUNT FAMOUS LASKY CORP. V. UNITED STATES

282 U.S. 30 (1930)

JUSTICE MCREYNOLDS delivered the opinion of the Court.

[Defendants] are the Paramount Famous Lasky Corporation and nine other Corporations (Distributors), producers and distributors throughout the Union of sixty per cent of the films used for displaying motion pictures by some 25,000 theatre owners (Exhibitors); the Motion Picture Producers and Distributors of America, a corporation with class "B" membership composed of the above-mentioned Distributors; and thirty-two Film Boards of Trade, which severally function within certain defined Regions.

Each Distributor produces and then distributes films through its own exchanges maintained in thirty-two centrally located cities.... Each of these exchanges has a manager and under his supervision contracts are made for the use of his Distributor's films within the designated territory or region and thereafter placed in the hands of the Exhibitors. Other Distributors, who with [Defendants] control 98 per cent of the entire business, also have managers with like duties in the same cities. In each Region all of these managers are associated through and constitute the entire membership of the local Film Board of Trade.

Under the common practice, ... each Distributor announces its intended program of distribution for twelve months. After this announcement Exhibitors are solicited to enter into written contracts for permission to display such of the pictures as they desire. And as no Distributor can offer enough pictures to supply the average Exhibitor's full requirement, he must deal with several.

Under an agreement amongst themselves [Defendant] Distributors will only contract with Exhibitors according to the terms of the Standard Exhibition Contract, dated May 1, 1928....

....

Section 18 ... provides in substance that each party shall submit any controversy that may arise to a Board of Arbitration .... And further:

"In the event that the Exhibitor shall fail or refuse to consent to submit to arbitration any claim or controversy ... or to ... comply with any decision or award of such Board of Arbitration upon any such claim or controversy so submitted, the Distributor may, at its option, demand ... payment by the Exhibitor of an additional sum not exceeding $500 under each existing contract, such sum to be retained by the Distributor until the complete performance of all such contracts...."

The record discloses that ten competitors in interstate commerce, controlling sixty per cent of the entire film business, have agreed to restrict their liberty of action by refusing to contract for display of pictures except upon a Standard Form which provides for compulsory joint action by them in respect of dealings with one who fails to observe such a contract with any Distributor, all with the manifest purpose to coerce the Exhibitor and limit the freedom of trade.

....

The fact that the Standard Exhibition Contract and Rules of Arbitration were evolved after six years of discussion and experimentation does not show that they were either normal or reasonable regulations. That the arrangement existing between the parties cannot be classed among "those normal and usual agreements in aid of trade and commerce" spoken of in *Eastern States Lumber Ass'n v. United States*, page 612, of 234 U.S., is manifest. Certainly it is unusual and we think it necessarily and directly tends to destroy "the kind of competition to which the public has long looked for protection."

The Sherman Act seeks to protect the public against evils commonly incident to the unreasonable destruction of competition and no length of discussion or experimentation amongst parties to a combination which produces the inhibited result can give validity to their action....

It may be that arbitration is well adapted to the needs of the motion picture industry; but when under the guise of arbitration parties enter into unusual arrangements which unreasonably suppress normal competition their action becomes illegal.

In order to establish violation of the Sherman Act it is not necessary to show that the challenged arrangement suppresses all competition between the parties or that the parties themselves are discontented with the arrangement. The interest of the public in the preservation of competition is the primary consideration.

Affirmed.

NOTES AND QUESTIONS

1. A similar issue was presented in a companion case decided the same day, when the Court considered the legality of credit committees and other standard trade terms set up by the same challenged association. In *United States v. First Nat'l Pictures, Inc.*, 282 U.S. 44 (1930), the Court found that the distributors agreed not to make films available to new exhibitors who refused to assume the contractual obligations of prior owners. The Court followed its approach set forth in *Paramount Famous Lasky* and declared the concerted refusal to deal anticompetitive. In evaluating these opinions, consider whether the concerted agreements were designed to reduce competition among the defendants themselves.

In each case, the Court rejected defendant's arguments that industry-wide standardized contracts with security and arbitration clauses were required to regulate and protect the industry. But the decisional analysis used by the Court to strike down those industry self-regulation programs, which were not designed to eliminate direct competitors, was unclear. It was not clearly articulated whether the Court would employ a per se rule of illegality regardless of the reasonableness of the ends sought or regardless of whether the concerted action was aimed at denying direct competitors a market. Compare these motion picture cases with the Court's approach in *Eastern States*. What level of competition was affected in each case? Should a distinction be drawn between concerted conduct which regulates trade terms and concerted conduct affecting market entry? *See* L. Sullivan, *Handbook of the Law of Antitrust* 256-61 (1977).

2. In *Cement Mfrs. Protective Ass'n v. United States*, 268 U.S. 588 (1925), a trade association of cement manufacturers exchanged credit information on buyers (contractors) on a specific job basis. The Supreme Court held that this kind of data dissemination was not a section 1 violation.

> That a combination existed for the purpose of gathering and distributing … information is not denied. That a consequence of the gathering and dissemination of information with respect to the specific job contracts was to afford to manufacturers of cement, opportunity and grounds for refusing deliveries of cement which the contractors were not entitled to call for, — an opportunity of which manufacturers were prompt to avail themselves — is also not open to dispute. We do not see, however, in the activity of the defendants with respect to specific job contracts any basis for the contention that they constitute an unlawful restraint of commerce. The Government does not rely on any agreement or understanding among members of the Association that members would either make use of the specific job contract, or that they would refuse to deliver "excess" cement under specific job contracts. Members were left free to use this type of contract and to make such deliveries or not as they chose, and the evidence already referred to shows that in 1920 padded specific job contracts were cut down something less than two-thirds of the total amount of the padding, as a result of the system of gathering and reporting this information. It may be assumed, however, if manufacturers take the precaution to draw their sales contracts in such form that they are not to be required to deliver cement not needed for the specific jobs described in these contracts, that they would, to a considerable extent, decline to make deliveries, upon receiving information showing that the deliveries claimed were not called for by the contracts. Unless the provisions

in the contract are waived by the manufacturer, demand for and receipt of such deliveries by the contractor would be a fraud on the manufacturer; and, in our view, the gathering and dissemination of information which will enable sellers to prevent the perpetration of fraud upon them, which information they are free to act upon or not as they choose, cannot be held to be an unlawful restraint upon commerce, even though in the ordinary course of business most sellers would act on the information and refuse to make deliveries for which they were not legally bound.

... Distribution of information as to credit and responsibility of buyers undoubtedly prevents fraud and cuts down to some degree commercial transactions which would otherwise be induced by fraud. But ... we cannot regard the procuring and dissemination of information which tends to prevent the procuring of fraudulent contracts or to prevent the fraudulent securing of deliveries of merchandise on the pretense that the seller is bound to deliver it by his contract, as an unlawful restraint of trade even though such information be gathered and disseminated by those who are engaged in the trade or business principally concerned.

3. Did the Court in *Cement Manufacturers* hold that a concerted agreement which had the effect of a refusal to deal is lawful as long as it was designed to achieve a lawful end (preventing customer fraud)? Was it dispositive to the outcome that no explicit agreement to refuse to deal was established? But wasn't there an agreement to exchange information which encouraged participants not to deal? Consider whether the result should depend upon whether the refusal to deal was implicit or explicit. Can this decision be reconciled with the analysis and holdings in *Eastern States, Paramount Famous Lasky* and the more recent decision in *Container*? How does the antitrust lawyer know, from an evidentiary standpoint, when the court will infer an agreement from conduct and effect? Recall that defendants did not agree to refuse to deal with bad credit risks; apparently, the purpose of the exchange was to lead defendants (acting individually) not to deal with certain customers.

4. Consider a more recent boycott opinion in the District of Columbia Circuit. The issue was whether the National Football League's draft constituted a "group boycott" because NFL clubs concertedly refused to deal with any player before or after he has been drafted. In drawing a distinction between classic group boycotts, which are concerted attempts by competitors at one level to protect themselves from nonmembers who seek to compete at that level, and a concerted refusal to deal, which is not aimed at a competitor, the District of Columbia Circuit held that the player draft was not a per se illegal group boycott because the NFL clubs which implemented the draft are not competitors with the players, and the refusal to deal with players did not result in a decrease in competition for "providing football entertainment to the public." Second, the clubs were not in competition with each other in any economic sense. The Court reasoned that the clubs operate as a joint venture in producing an entertainment product. None-

theless, the Court found the agreement to be an unreasonable restraint of trade under the rule of reason because it was anticompetitive in purpose and effect. *Smith v. Pro Football, Inc.*, 593 F.2d 1173 (D.C. Cir. 1979).

With regard to professional regulation through codes of ethics which affect price, reconsider the analysis adopted in *National Soc'y of Prof. Eng'rs v. United States*, 435 U.S. 679, 696 (1978), and *Goldfarb v. Virginia State Bar*, 421 U.S. 773, 788-89 n.17 (1975), suggesting that the "public service aspect, and other features of professions" may require different treatment. *But cf. Arizona v. Maricopa Cty. Med. Soc'y*, 457 U.S. 332 (1982) (where the Court implied that absent a "public service" defense, professions were not to be treated differently regarding per se analysis for price-affecting conduct).

Following *Maricopa County*, the Seventh Circuit, in a case where the plaintiffs charged that certain medical organizations conspired to refuse to deal professionally with chiropractors, held that the jury should not have been given the opportunity to find a per se violation. The court concluded that since there was substantial evidence that the medical doctors acted out of a desire to promote quality treatment and patient care, the case was "inappropriate for *per se* treatment." Thus, a modified rule of reason was sanctioned for a case involving a "question of ethics for the medical profession which had the effect of denying chiropractors the use of laboratory and X-ray facilities among other services." The plaintiff's burden, the court ruled, was to show that the challenged conduct (a principle of ethics requiring the refusal to deal professionally with those who practice a method of healing without scientific basis) restricted, rather than promoted, competition. *Wilk v. AMA*, 719 F.2d 207 (7th Cir. 1983).

Finally, consider the competition issues implicated when a standard code-setting trade association refuses to certify a product. *See American Soc'y of Mech. Eng'rs v. Hydrolevel Corp.*, 456 U.S. 556 (1982). Does a denial of certification or a "seal of approval" which results in market foreclosure constitute an illegal boycott? *See Radiant Burners, Inc. v. Peoples Gas Light & Coke Co.*, 364 U.S. 656 (1961). Might the legality of the rating associations' conduct turn on whether the standards used were objective and for the purpose of protecting the public as opposed to protecting manufacturers from additional competition? Does a per se approach permit the balancing of competitive harms against benefits in the refusal to deal context? Does the per se rule apply only in the *explicit* boycott case? In answering these questions consider whether the per se analysis permits the Court to weigh the industry's regulation need against the public interest.

In *Eliason Corp. v. National San. Found.*, 614 F.2d 126 (6th Cir.), *cert. denied*, 449 U.S. 826 (1980), the court held that it was not per se illegal for a testing organization to refuse to grant plaintiff its "seal of approval," even though the seal and the testing procedures had been approved by the competitors in the market. The defendant did not force resellers not to deal in the plaintiff's product, but the plaintiff's failure to obtain the seal of approval was acknowledged to be very costly to the plaintiff. The court held that when "the alleged boycott arises from standard-making or even industry self-regulation, the plaintiff must show either that it was barred from obtaining approval of its products on a discriminatory basis from its competitors, or that the conduct as a whole was manifestly unreasonable."

3. INDUSTRY SELF-REGULATION AND DISCIPLINARY ACTIONS

In *Silver v. New York Stock Exch.*, 373 U.S. 341 (1963), the stock exchange denied access to facilities (wire service) to nonmember broker-dealers. In refusing to deal with Mr. Silver, the NYSE relied on what it thought was an implied, qualified immunity from antitrust coverage under the federal securities law. The Supreme Court found, however, that immunity from antitrust coverage under the federal securities laws is "implied only if necessary to make the Securities Exchange Act work and even then only to the minimum extent necessary."

The Court concluded by holding that the self-regulation by the NYSE was not justified here because it did not comport with basic due process; Mr. Silver was "not informed of the charges underlying the decision to invoke the Exchange rules and was not afforded an appropriate opportunity to explain or refute the charge against [him]." Before self-regulation and anticompetitive collective action will be approved under an implied exception to antitrust, procedures must be established that satisfy fundamental fairness. By failing to provide notice and opportunity for hearing, the NYSE had "plainly exceeded the scope of its authority under the SEC Act to engage in self-regulation and therefore [had] not even reached the threshold of justification under the statute for what would otherwise be an antitrust violation." In passing, the Court made clear that in an unregulated industry the challenged conduct at issue here — a refusal to deal with a competitor — would have been a per se violation.

NORTHWEST WHOLESALE STATIONERS, INC. V. PACIFIC STATIONERY & PRINTING CO.

472 U.S. 284 (1985)

JUSTICE BRENNAN delivered the opinion of the Court.

This case requires that we decide whether a *per se* violation of § 1 of the Sherman Act ... occurs when a cooperative buying agency comprising various retailers expels a member without providing any procedural means for challenging the expulsion. The case also raises broader questions as to when per se antitrust analysis is appropriately applied to joint activity that is susceptible of being characterized as a concerted refusal to deal.

I

Because the District Court ruled on cross-motions for summary judgment after only limited discovery, this case comes to us on a sparse record. Certain background facts are undisputed. Petitioner Northwest Wholesale Stationers is a purchasing cooperative made up of approximately 100 office supply retailers in the Pacific Northwest States. The cooperative acts as the primary wholesaler for the retailers. Retailers that are not members of the cooperative can purchase whole-sale supplies from Northwest at the same price as members. At the end of each year, however, Northwest distributes its profits to members in the form of a per-centage rebate on purchases. Members therefore effectively purchase supplies at a price significantly lower than do nonmembers. Northwest also provides certain warehousing facilities. The cooperative arrangement thus permits the participat-ing retailers to achieve economies of scale in purchasing and warehousing that would otherwise be unavailable to them. In fiscal 1978 Northwest had $5.8 mil-lion in sales....

Respondent Pacific Stationery, Inc., sells office supplies at both the retail and wholesale levels. Its total sales in fiscal 1978 were approximately $7.6 million; the record does not indicate what percentage of revenue is attributable to retail and what percentage is attributable to wholesale. Pacific became a member of Northwest in 1958. In 1974 Northwest amended its bylaws to prohibit members from engaging in both retail and wholesale operations.... A grandfather clause preserved Pacific's membership rights.... In 1977 ownership of a controlling share of the stock of Pacific changed hands ... and the new owners did not offi-cially bring this change to the attention of the directors of Northwest. This fail-ure to notify apparently violated another of Northwest's bylaws....

In 1978 the membership of Northwest voted to expel Pacific. Most factual mat-ters relevant to the expulsion are in dispute. No explanation for the expulsion was advanced at the time and Pacific was given neither notice, a hearing, nor any other opportunity to challenge the decision. Pacific argues that the expulsion resulted from Pacific's decision to maintain a wholesale operation.... Northwest contends that the expulsion resulted from Pacific's failure to notify the cooperative members of the change in stock ownership.... The minutes of the meeting of Northwest's directors do not definitively indicate the motive for the expulsion.... It is undis-puted that Pacific received approximately $10,000 in rebates from Northwest in 1978, Pacific's last year of membership. Beyond a possible inference of loss from this fact, however, the record is devoid of allegations indicating the nature and ex-tent of competitive injury the expulsion caused Pacific to suffer.

Pacific brought suit in 1980 in the United States District Court for the District of Oregon alleging a violation of § 1 of the Sherman Act.... Finding no anticom-petitive effect on the basis of the record as presented, the court granted summary judgment for Northwest....

The Court of Appeals for the Ninth Circuit reversed, holding "that the uncon-troverted facts of this case support a finding of *per se* liability."...

II

The decision of the cooperative members to expel Pacific was certainly a re-straint of trade in the sense that every commercial agreement restrains trade....

Whether this action violates § 1 of the Sherman Act depends on whether it is adjudged an *unreasonable* restraint.... Rule-of-reason analysis guides the inquiry, ... unless the challenged action falls into the category of "agreements or practices which because of their pernicious effect on competition and lack of any redeeming virtue are conclusively presumed to be unreasonable and therefore illegal without elaborate inquiry as to the precise harm they have caused or the business excuse for their use."...

This *per se* approach permits categorical judgments with respect to certain business practices that have proved to be predominantly anticompetitive. Courts can thereby avoid the "significant costs" in "business certainty and litigation efficiency" that a full-fledged rule-of-reason inquiry entails.... The decision to apply the *per se* rule turns on "whether the practice facially appears to be one that would always or almost always tend to restrict competition and decrease output ... or instead one designed to 'increase economic efficiency and render markets more, rather than less, competitive.'"...

This Court has long held that certain concerted refusals to deal or group boycotts are so likely to restrict competition without any offsetting efficiency gains that they should be condemned as *per se* violations of § 1 of the Sherman Act.... The question presented in this case is whether Northwest's decision to expel Pacific should fall within this category of activity that is conclusively presumed to be anticompetitive....

A

The Court of Appeals drew from *Silver v. New York Stock Exchange* a broad rule that the conduct of a cooperative venture — including a concerted refusal to deal — undertaken pursuant to a legislative mandate for self-regulation is immune from *per se* scrutiny and subject to rule of reason analysis only if adequate procedural safeguards accompany self-regulation. We disagree and conclude that the approach of the Court in *Silver* has no proper application to the present controversy.

The Court in *Silver* framed the issue as follows:

"[W]hether the New York Stock Exchange is to be held liable to a nonmember broker-dealer under the antitrust laws or regarded as impliedly immune therefrom when, pursuant to rules the Exchange has adopted under the Securities Exchange Act of 1934, it orders a number of its members to remove private direct telephone wire connections previously in operation between their offices and those of the nonmember, without giving the nonmember notice, assigning him any reason for the action, or affording him an opportunity to be heard." 373 U.S., at 343.

Because the New York Stock Exchange occupied such a dominant position in the securities trading markets that the boycott would devastate the nonmember, the Court concluded that the refusal to deal with the nonmember would amount to a *per se* violation of § 1 unless the Securities Exchange Act provided an immunity.... The question for the Court thus was whether effectuation of the policies of the Securities Exchange Act required partial repeal of the Sherman Act insofar as it proscribed this aspect of exchange self-regulation.

Finding exchange self-regulation — including the power to expel members and limit dealings with nonmembers — to be an essential policy of the Securities Exchange Act, the Court held that the Sherman Act should be construed as having been partially repealed to permit the type of exchange activity at issue. But the interpretive maxim disfavoring repeals by implication led the Court to narrow permissible self-policing to situations in which adequate procedural safeguards had been provided.

> "Congress ... cannot be thought to have sanctioned and protected self-regulative activity when carried out in a fundamentally unfair manner. The point is not that the antitrust laws impose the requirement of notice and a hearing here, but rather that, in acting without according petitioners these safeguards in response to their request, the Exchange has plainly exceeded the scope of its authority under the Securities Exchange Act to engage in self-regulation."...

Thus it was the specific need to accommodate the important national policy of promoting effective exchange self-regulation, tempered by the principle that the Sherman Act should be narrowed only to the extent necessary to effectuate that policy, that dictated the result in *Silver.*

Section 4 of the Robinson-Patman Act is not comparable to the self-policing provisions of the Securities Exchange Act. That section is no more than a narrow immunity from the price discrimination prohibitions of the Robinson-Patman Act itself. The Conference Report makes clear that the exception was intended solely to "safeguard producer and consumer cooperatives against any charge of violation of the act *based on their distribution of earnings or surplus among their members on a patronage basis.*" H.R. Conf. Rep. No. 2951, 74th Cong., 2d Sess., 9 (1936) (emphasis added). This section has never been construed as granting cooperatives a blanket exception from the Robinson-Patman Act and cannot plausibly be construed as an exemption to or repeal of any portion of the Sherman Act....

In light of this circumscribed congressional intent, there can be no argument that § 4 of the Robinson-Patman Act should be viewed as a broad mandate for industry self-regulation. No need exists, therefore, to narrow the Sherman Act in order to accommodate any competing congressional policy requiring discretionary self-policing. Indeed, Congress would appear to have taken some care to make clear that no constriction of the Sherman Act was intended. In any event, the absence of procedural safeguards can in no sense determine the antitrust analysis. If the challenged concerted activity of Northwest's members would amount to a *per se* violation of § 1 of the Sherman Act, no amount of procedural protection would save it. If the challenged action would not amount to a violation of § 1, no lack of procedural protections would convert it into a *per se* violation because the antitrust laws do not themselves impose on joint ventures a requirement of process.

B

This case therefore turns not on the lack of procedural protections but on whether the decision to expel Pacific is properly viewed as a group boycott or concerted refusal to deal mandating *per se* invalidation. "Group boycotts" are often listed among the classes of economic activity that merit *per se* invalidation under § 1.... Exactly what types of activity fall within the forbidden category is, however, far from certain. "[T]here is more confusion about the scope and operation of the *per se* rule against group boycotts than in reference to any other aspect of the *per se* doctrine." L. Sullivan, Law of Antitrust 229-230 (1977). Some care is therefore necessary in defining the category of concerted refusals to deal that mandate *per se* condemnation....

Cases to which this Court has applied the *per se* approach have generally involved joint efforts by a firm or firms to disadvantage competitors by "either directly denying or persuading or coercing suppliers or customers to deny relationships the competitors need in the competitive struggle."... In these cases, the boycott often cut off access to a supply, facility, or market necessary to enable the boycotted firm to compete, ... and frequently the boycotting firms possessed a dominant position in the relevant market.... In addition, the practices were generally not justified by plausible arguments that they were intended to enhance overall efficiency and make markets more competitive. Under such circumstances the likelihood of anticompetitive effects is clear and the possibility of countervailing procompetitive effects is remote.

Although a concerted refusal to deal need not necessarily possess all of these traits to merit *per se* treatment, not every cooperative activity involving a restraint or exclusion will share with the *per se* forbidden boycotts the likelihood of predominantly anticompetitive consequences. For example, we recognized last Term in *National Collegiate Athletic Assn. v. Board of Regents of University of Oklahoma* that *per se* treatment of the NCAA's restrictions on the marketing of televised college football was inappropriate — despite the obvious restraint on output — because the "case involves an industry in which horizontal restraints on competition are essential if the product is to be available at all."...

Wholesale purchasing cooperatives such as Northwest are not a form of concerted activity characteristically likely to result in predominantly anticompetitive effects. Rather, such cooperative arrangements would seem to be "designed to increase economic efficiency and render markets more, rather than less, competitive."... The arrangement permits the participating retailers to achieve economies of scale in both the purchase and warehousing of wholesale supplies, and also ensures ready access to a stock of goods that might otherwise be unavailable on short notice. The cost savings and order-filling guarantees enable smaller retailers to reduce prices and maintain their retail stock so as to compete more effectively with larger retailers.

Pacific, of course, does not object to the existence of the cooperative arrangement, but rather raises an antitrust challenge to Northwest's decision to bar Pacific from continued membership.[4] It is therefore the action of expulsion that must be evaluated to determine whether *per se* treatment is appropriate. The act of expulsion from a wholesale cooperative does not necessarily imply anticompetitive animus and thereby raise a probability of anticompetitive effect.... Wholesale purchasing cooperatives must establish and enforce reasonable rules in order to function effectively. Disclosure rules, such as the one on which Northwest relies, may well provide the cooperative with a needed means for monitoring the creditworthiness of its members. Nor would the expulsion characteristically be likely to result in predominantly anticompetitive effects, at least in the type of situation this case presents. Unless the cooperative possesses market power or exclusive access to an element essential to effective competition, the conclusion that expulsion is virtually always likely to have an anticompetitive effect is not warranted.... Absent such a showing with respect to a cooperative buying arrangement, courts should apply a rule-of-reason analysis. At no time has Pacific made a threshold showing that these structural characteristics are present in the case....

The District Court appears to have followed the correct path of analysis — recognizing that not all concerted refusals to deal should be accorded *per se* treatment and deciding this one should not. The foregoing discussion suggests, however, that a satisfactory threshold determination whether anticompetitive effects would be likely might require a more detailed factual picture of market structure than the District Court had before it. Nonetheless, in our judgment the District Court rejection of *per se* analysis in this case was correct. A plaintiff seeking application of the *per se* rule must present a threshold case that the challenged activity falls into a category likely to have predominantly anticompetitive effects. The mere allegation of a concerted refusal to deal does not suffice because not all concerted refusals to deal are predominantly anticompetitive. When the plaintiff challenges expulsion from a joint buying cooperative, some showing must be made that the cooperative possesses market power or unique access to a business element necessary for effective competition. Focusing on the argument that the lack of procedural safeguards required *per*

---

[4] Because Pacific has not been wholly excluded from access to Northwest's wholesale operations, there is perhaps some question whether the challenged activity is properly characterized a concerted refusal to deal. To be precise, Northwest's activity is a concerted refusal to deal with Pacific on substantially equal terms. Such activity might justify *per se* invalidation if it placed a competing firm at a severe competitive disadvantage. *See generally* Brodley, *Joint Ventures and Antitrust Policy*, 95 Harv. L. Rev. 1521, 1532 (1982) ("Even if the joint venture does deal with outside firms, it may place them at a severe competitive disadvantage by treating them less favorably than it treats the [participants in the joint venture.]").

se liability, Pacific did not allege any such facts. Because the Court of Appeals applied an erroneous *per se* analysis in this case, the court never evaluated the District Court's rule-of-reason analysis rejecting Pacific's claim. A remand is therefore appropriate for the limited purpose of permitting appellate review of that determination.

III

… In this case, the Court of Appeals failed to exercise the requisite care and applied *per se* analysis inappropriately. The judgment of the Court of Appeals is therefore reversed, and the case is remanded for further proceedings consistent with this opinion.

It is so ordered.

JUSTICE MARSHALL and JUSTICE POWELL took no part in the decision of this case.

QUESTIONS

1. Is it clear that *Northwest Stationers* has abandoned the per se rule for group boycott cases except where defendant possesses market power or where access to supply is cut off?

2. On the issue of contract integration between legally separable companies, consider the interstate system of van line moving companies. Would it violate section 1 of the Sherman Act if a national van line company such as Atlas agreed with its agents to adopt a policy of terminating ("boycotting") independent, local agents who pursued their own accounts or competed against the national van line, or who dealt with another national carrier as their local agent while using the Atlas name? Does the language in *BMI, NCAA,* and *Northwest Stationers* suggest that the Supreme Court has implicitly overruled *Sealy* and *Topco* as they apply to the horizontal restraints of this problem? *See Rothery Storage & Van Co. v. Atlas Van Lines,* 792 F.2d 210 (D.C. Cir. 1986) (where Judge Bork ruled that horizontal restraints such as boycotts that reduce free-rider problems and promote efficiency are legal, absent market power, even when the shipping rates are established by the national van line). The Court in *Rothery* stated:

> If *Topco* and *Sealy,* rather than *Addyston Pipe,* state the law of horizontal restraints, the restraints imposed by Atlas would appear to be a per se violation of the Sherman Act. An examination of more recent Supreme Court decisions [*BMI, NCAA* and *Northwest*], however, demonstrates that, to the extent that *Topco* and *Sealy* stand for the proposition that all horizontal restraints are illegal per se, they must be regarded as effectively overruled. *Id.* at 226, 229.

Petition for certiorari was denied without dissent.

FTC V. INDIANA FEDERATION OF DENTISTS

476 U.S. 447 (1986)

JUSTICE WHITE delivered the opinion of the Court.

This case concerns commercial relations among certain Indiana dentists, their patients, and the patients' dental health care insurers. The question presented is whether the Federal Trade Commission correctly concluded that a conspiracy among dentists to refuse to submit x rays to dental insurers for use in benefits determinations constituted an "unfair method of competition" in violation of § 5 of the Federal Trade Commission Act.

I

Since the 1970's, dental health insurers, responding to the demands of their policyholders, have attempted to contain the cost of dental treatment by, among other devices, limiting payment of benefits to the cost of the "least expensive yet adequate treatment" suitable to the needs of individual patients. Implementation of such cost-containment measures, known as "alternative benefits" plans, requires evaluation by the insurer of the diagnosis and recommendation of the treating dentist, either in advance of or following the provision of care. In order to carry out such evaluation, insurers frequently request dentists to submit, along with insurance claim forms requesting payment of benefits, any dental x rays that have been used by the dentist in examining the patient as well as other information concerning their diagnoses and treatment recommendations. Typically, claim forms and accompanying x rays are reviewed by lay claims examiners, who either approve payment of claims or, if the materials submitted raise a question whether the recommended course of treatment is in fact necessary, refer claims to dental consultants, who are licensed dentists, for further review. On the basis of the materials available, supplemented where appropriate by further diagnostic aids, the dental consultant may recommend that the insurer approve a claim, deny it, or pay only for a less expensive course of treatment.

Such review of diagnostic and treatment decisions has been viewed by some dentists as a threat to their professional independence and economic well-being. In the early 1970's, the Indiana Dental Association, a professional organization comprising some 85% of practicing dentists in the State of Indiana, initiated an aggressive effort to hinder insurers' efforts to implement alternative benefits plans by enlisting member dentists to pledge not to submit x rays in conjunction with claim forms. The Association's efforts met considerable success: large numbers of dentists signed the pledge, and insurers operating in Indiana found it difficult to obtain compliance with their requests for x rays and accordingly had to choose either to employ more expensive means of making alternative benefits determinations (for example, visiting the office of the treating dentist or conducting an independent oral examination) or to abandon such efforts altogether.

By the mid-1970's, fears of possible antitrust liability had dampened the Association's enthusiasm for opposing the submission of x rays to insurers. In 1979, the Association and a number of its constituent societies consented to a Federal Trade Commission order requiring them to cease and desist from further efforts to prevent member dentists from submitting x rays. *In re Indiana Dental Assn.*, 93 F.T.C. 392 (1979). Not all Indiana dentists were content to leave the matter of submitting x rays to the individual dentist. In 1976, a group of such dentists formed the Indiana Federation of Dentists, respondent in this case, in order to continue to pursue the Association's policy of resisting insurers' requests for x rays. The Federation, which styled itself a "union" in the belief that this label would stave off antitrust liability,[2] immediately promulgated a "work rule" forbidding its members to submit x rays to dental insurers in conjunction with claim forms. Although the Federation's membership was small, numbering less than 100, its members were highly concentrated in and around three Indiana communities: Anderson, Lafayette, and Fort Wayne. The Federation succeeded in enlisting nearly 100% of the dental specialists in the Anderson area, and approximately 67% of the dentists in and around Lafayette. In the areas of its strength, the Federation was successful in continuing to enforce the Association's prior policy of refusal to submit x rays to dental insurers.

In 1978, the Federal Trade Commission issued a complaint against the Federation, alleging in substance that its efforts to prevent its members from complying with insurers' requests for x rays constituted an unfair method of competition in violation of § 5 of the Federal Trade Commission Act....

The Commission found that the Federation had conspired both with the Indiana Dental Association and with its own members to withhold cooperation with dental insurers' requests for x rays; that absent such a restraint, competition among dentists for patients would have tended to lead dentists to compete with respect to their policies in dealing with patients' insurers; and that in those areas where the Federation's membership was strong, the Federation's policy had had the actual effect of eliminating such competition among dentists and preventing insurers from obtaining access to x rays in the desired manner. These findings of anticompetitive effect, the Commission concluded, were sufficient to establish that the restraint was unreasonable even absent proof that the Federation's policy had resulted in higher costs to the insurers and patients than would have occurred had the x rays been provided. Further, the Commission rejected the Federation's argument that its policy of withholding x rays was reasonable because the provision of x rays might lead the insurers to make inaccurate determinations of the proper level of care and thus injure the health of the insured patients: the Commission found no evidence that use of x rays by insurance companies in evaluating claims would result in inadequate dental care. Finally, the Commission rejected the Federation's contention that its actions were exempt from anti-

---

[2] Respondent no longer makes any pretense of arguing that it is immune from antitrust liability as a labor organization.

trust scrutiny because the withholding of x rays was consistent with the law and policy of the State of Indiana against the use of x rays in benefit determination by insurance companies. The Commission concluded that no such policy existed, and that in any event the existence of such a policy would not have justified the dentists' private and unsupervised conspiracy in restraint of trade.

....

II

The issue is whether the Commission erred in holding that the Federation's policy of refusal to submit x rays to dental insurers for use in benefits determinations constituted an "unfair method of competition," unlawful under § 5 of the Federal Trade Commission Act. The question involves review of both factual and legal determinations. As to the former, our review is governed by 15 U.S.C. § 45(c), which provides that "[t]he findings of the Commission as to the facts, if supported by evidence, shall be conclusive." The statute forbids a court to "make its own appraisal of the testimony, picking and choosing for itself among uncertain and conflicting inferences." Rather, as under the essentially identical "substantial evidence" standard for review of agency factfinding, the court must accept the Commission's findings of fact if they are supported by "such relevant evidence as a reasonable mind might accept as adequate to support a conclusion."

... The standard of "unfairness" under the FTC Act is, by necessity, an elusive one, encompassing not only practices that violate the Sherman Act and the other antitrust laws, but also practices that the Commission determines are against public policy for other reasons. In the case now before us, the sole basis of the FTC's finding of an unfair method of competition was the Commission's conclusion that the Federation's collective decision to withhold x rays from insurers was an unreasonable and conspiratorial restraint of trade in violation of § 1 of the Sherman Act. Accordingly, the legal question before us is whether the Commission's factual findings, if supported by evidence, make out a violation of Sherman Act § 1.

III

The relevant factual findings are that the members of the Federation conspired among themselves to withhold x rays requested by dental insurers for use in evaluating claims for benefits, and that this conspiracy had the effect of suppressing competition among dentists with respect to cooperation with the requests of the insurance companies. As to the first of these findings there can be no serious dispute; abundant evidence in the record reveals that one of the primary reasons — if not *the* primary reason — for the Federation's existence was the promulgation and enforcement of the so-called "work rule" against submission of x rays in conjunction with insurance claim forms.

... The Commission's finding that "[i]n the absence of ... concerted behavior, individual dentists would have been subject to market forces of competition, creating incentives for them to ... comply with the requests of patients' third-party insurers," finds support not only in common sense and economic theory, upon both of which the FTC may reasonably rely, but also in record documents, including newsletters circulated among Indiana dentists, revealing that Indiana dentists themselves perceived that unrestrained competition tended to lead their colleagues to comply with insurers' requests for x rays. Moreover, there was evidence that outside of Indiana, in States where dentists had not collectively refused to submit x rays, insurance companies found little difficulty in obtaining compliance by dentists with their requests. A "reasonable mind" could conclude on the basis of this evidence that competition for patients, who have obvious incentives for seeking dentists who will cooperate with their insurers, would tend to lead dentists in Indiana (and elsewhere) to cooperate with requests for information by their patients' insurers.

The Commission's finding that such competition was actually diminished where the Federation held sway also finds adequate support in the record. The Commission found that in the areas where Federation membership among dentists was most significant (that is, in the vicinity of Anderson and Lafayette) insurance companies were unable to obtain compliance with their requests for submission of x rays in conjunction with claim forms and were forced to resort to other, more costly, means of reviewing diagnoses for the purpose of benefit determination... The Federation's collective activities resulted in the denial of the information the customers requested in the form that they requested it, and forced them to choose between acquiring that information in a more costly manner or foregoing it altogether. To this extent, at least, competition among dentists with respect to cooperation with the requests of insurers was restrained.

IV

The question remains whether these findings are legally sufficient to establish a violation of § 1 of the Sherman Act — that is, whether the Federation's collective refusal to cooperate with insurers' requests for x rays constitutes an "unreasonable" restraint of trade. Under our precedents, a restraint may be adjudged unreasonable either because it fits within a class of restraints that has been held to be "*per se*" unreasonable, or because it violates what has come to be known as the "Rule of Reason," under which the "test of legality is whether the restraint imposed is such as merely regulates and perhaps thereby promotes competition or whether it is such as may suppress or even destroy competition." *Chicago Board of Trade v. United States*, 246 U.S., at 238.

The policy of the Federation with respect to its members' dealings with third-party insurers resembles practices that have been labeled "group boycotts": the policy constitutes a concerted refusal to deal on particular terms with patients covered by group dental insurance. Although this Court has in the past stated that group boycotts are unlawful *per se*, see *United States v. General Motors Corp.*, 384 U.S. 127 (1966); *Klor's, Inc. v. Broadway-Hale Stores, Inc.*, 359 U.S.

207 (1959), we decline to resolve this case by forcing the Federation's policy into the "boycott" pigeonhole and invoking the *per se* rule. As we observed last Term in *Northwest Wholesale Stationers, Inc. v. Pacific Stationery and Printing Co.*, 472 U.S. 284 (1985), the category of restraints classed as group boycotts is not to be expanded indiscriminately, and the *per se* approach has generally been limited to cases in which firms with market power boycott suppliers or customers in order to discourage them from doing business with a competitor — a situation obviously not present here. Moreover, we have been slow to condemn rules adopted by professional associations as unreasonable *per se*, see *National Society of Professional Engineers v. United States*, 435 U.S. 679 (1978), and, in general, to extend *per se* analysis to restraints imposed in the context of business relationships where the economic impact of certain practices is not immediately obvious, see *Broadcast Music, Inc. v. CBS*, 441 U.S. 1 (1979). Thus, as did the FTC, we evaluate the restraint at issue in this case under the Rule of Reason rather than a rule of *per se* illegality.

Application of the Rule of Reason to these facts is not a matter of any great difficulty. The Federation's policy takes the form of a horizontal agreement among the participating dentists to withhold from their customers a particular service that they desire — the forwarding of x rays to insurance companies along with claim forms. "While this is not price fixing as such, no elaborate industry analysis is required to demonstrate the anticompetitive character of such an agreement." *Society of Professional Engineers, supra*, at 692. A refusal to compete with respect to the package of services offered to customers, no less than a refusal to compete with respect to the price term of an agreement, impairs the ability of the market to advance social welfare by ensuring the provision of desired goods and services to consumers at a price approximating the marginal cost of providing them. Absent some countervailing procompetitive virtue — such as, for example, the creation of efficiencies in the operation of a market or the provision of goods and services, see *Broadcast Music, Inc. v. CBS, supra; Chicago Board of Trade, supra*; cf. *NCAA v. Board of Regents of Univ. of Okla.*, 468 U.S. 85 (1984) — such an agreement limiting consumer choice by impeding the "ordinary give and take of the market place," *Society of Professional Engineers, supra*, at 692, cannot be sustained under the Rule of Reason. No credible argument has been advanced for the proposition that making it more costly for the insurers and patients who are the dentists' customers to obtain information needed for evaluating the dentists' diagnoses has any such procompetitive effect.

The Federation advances three principal arguments for the proposition that, notwithstanding its lack of competitive virtue, the Federation's policy of withholding x rays should not be deemed an unreasonable restraint of trade. First… the Federation suggests that in the absence of specific findings by the Commission concerning the definition of the market in which the Federation allegedly restrained trade and the power of the Federation's members in that market, the conclusion that the Federation unreasonably restrained trade is erroneous as a matter of law, regardless of whether the challenged practices might be impermissibly anticompetitive if engaged in by persons who together possessed power in a specifically defined market. This contention, however, runs counter to the Court's holding in *NCAA v. Board of Regents, supra,* that "[a]s a matter of law, the absence of proof of market power does not justify a naked restriction on price or output," and that such a restriction "requires some competitive justification even in the absence of a detailed market analysis." 468 U.S., at 109-110. Moreover, even if the restriction imposed by the Federation is not sufficiently "naked" to call this principle into play, the Commission's failure to engage in detailed market analysis is not fatal to its finding of a violation of the Rule of Reason. The Commission found that in two localities in the State of Indiana (the Anderson and Lafayette areas), Federation dentists constituted heavy majorities of the practicing dentists and that as a result of the efforts of the Federation, insurers in those areas were, over a period of years, actually unable to obtain compliance with their requests for submission of x rays. Since the purpose of the inquiries into market definition and market power is to determine whether an arrangement has the potential for genuine adverse effects on competition, "proof of actual detrimental effects, such as a reduction of output" can obviate the need for an inquiry into market power, which is but a "surrogate for detrimental effects." 7 P. Areeda, Antitrust Law ¶ 1511, p. 429 (1986). In this case, we conclude that the finding of actual, sustained adverse effects on competition in those areas where IFD dentists predominated, viewed in light of the reality that markets for dental services tend to be relatively localized, is legally sufficient to support a finding that the challenged restraint was unreasonable even in the absence of elaborate market analysis.[3]

Second, the Federation ... argues that a holding that its policy of withholding x rays constituted an unreasonable restraint of trade is precluded by the Commission's failure to make any finding that the policy resulted in the provision of dental services that were more costly than those that the patients and their insurers would have chosen were they able to evaluate x rays in conjunction with claim forms. This argument, too, is unpersuasive. Although it is true that the goal of the insurers in seeking submission of x rays for use in their review of benefits claims was to minimize costs by choosing the least expensive adequate course of dental treatment, a showing that this goal was actually achieved through the means chosen is not an essential step in establishing that the dentists' attempt to thwart its achievement by collectively refusing to supply the requested information was an unreasonable restraint of trade. A concerted and effective effort to withhold (or make more costly) information desired by consumers for the purpose of determining whether a particular purchase is cost-justified is likely

---

[3] Because we find that the Commission's findings can be sustained on this basis, we do not address the Commission's contention that the Federation's activities can be condemned regardless of market power or actual effect merely because they constitute a continuation of the restraints formerly imposed by the Indiana Dental Association, which allegedly had market power throughout the State of Indiana.

enough to disrupt the proper functioning of the price-setting mechanism of the market that it may be condemned even absent proof that it resulted in higher prices or, as here, the purchase of higher-priced services, than would occur in its absence. *Society of Professional Engineers, supra.* Moreover, even if the desired information were in fact completely useless to the insurers and their patients in making an informed choice regarding the least costly adequate course of treatment — or, to put it another way, if the costs of evaluating the information were far greater than the cost savings resulting from its use — the Federation would still not be justified in deciding on behalf of its members' customers that they did not need the information: presumably, if that were the case, the discipline of the market would itself soon result in the insurers' abandoning their requests for x rays. The Federation is not entitled to pre-empt the working of the market by deciding for itself that its customers do not need that which they demand.

Third, the Federation complains that the Commission erred in failing to consider, as relevant to its Rule of Reason analysis, noncompetitive "quality of care" justifications for the prohibition on provision of x rays to insurers in conjunction with claim forms.... The gist of the claim is that x rays, standing alone, are not adequate bases for diagnosis of dental problems or for the formulation of an acceptable course of treatment. Accordingly, if insurance companies are permitted to determine whether they will pay a claim for dental treatment on the basis of x rays as opposed to a full examination of all the diagnostic aids available to the examining dentist, there is a danger that they will erroneously decline to pay for treatment that is in fact in the interest of the patient, and that the patient will as a result be deprived of fully adequate care.

The Federation's argument is flawed both legally and factually. The premise of the argument is that, far from having no effect on the cost of dental services chosen by patients and their insurers, the provision of x rays will have too great an impact: it will lead to the reduction of costs through the selection of inadequate treatment. Precisely such a justification for withholding information from customers was rejected as illegitimate in the *Society of Professional Engineers* case. The argument is, in essence, that an unrestrained market in which consumers are given access to the information they believe to be relevant to their choices will lead them to make unwise and even dangerous choices. Such an argument amounts to "nothing less than a frontal assault on the basic policy of the Sherman Act." *Society of Professional Engineers, supra,* at 695. Moreover, there is no particular reason to believe that the provision of information will be more harmful to consumers in the market for dental services than in other markets. Insurers deciding what level of care to pay for are not themselves the recipients of those services, but it is by no means clear that they lack incentives to consider the welfare of the patient as well as the minimization of costs. They are themselves in competition for the patronage of the patients — or, in most cases, the unions or businesses that contract on their behalf for group insurance coverage — and must satisfy their potential customers not only that they will provide coverage at a reasonable cost, but also that coverage will be adequate to meet their customers' dental needs. There is thus no more reason to expect dental insurance companies to sacrifice quality in return for cost savings than to believe this of consumers in, say, the market for engineering services. Accordingly, if noncompetitive quality-of-service justifications are inadmissible to justify the denial of information to consumers in the latter market, there is little reason to credit such justifications here.

In any event, the Commission did not, as the Federation suggests, refuse even to consider the quality of care justification for the withholding of x rays. Rather, the Commission held that the Federation had failed to introduce sufficient evidence to establish such a justification: "IFD has not pointed to any evidence — or even argued — that any consumers have in fact been harmed by alternative benefits determinations, or that actual determinations have been medically erroneous." 101 F.T.C., at 177. The evidence before the Administrative Law Judge on this issue appears to have consisted entirely of expert opinion testimony, with the Federation's experts arguing that x rays generally provide an insufficient basis, standing alone, for dental diagnosis, and the Commission's experts testifying that x rays may be useful in assessing diagnosis of and appropriate treatment for a variety of dental complaints. The Commission was amply justified in concluding on the basis of this conflicting evidence that even if concern for the quality of patient care could under some circumstances serve as a justification for a restraint of the sort imposed here, the evidence did not support a finding that the careful use of x rays as a basis for evaluating insurance claims is in fact destructive of proper standards of dental care.

In addition to arguing that its conspiracy did not effect an unreasonable restraint of trade, the Federation appears to renew its argument ... that the conspiracy to withhold x rays is immunized from antitrust scrutiny by virtue of a supposed policy of the State of Indiana against the evaluation of dental x rays by lay employees of insurance companies. Allegedly, such use of x rays by insurance companies — even where no claim was actually denied without examination of an x ray by a licensed dentist — would constitute unauthorized practice of dentistry by the insurance company and its employees. The Commission found that this claim had no basis in any authoritative source of Indiana law and the Federation has not identified any adequate reason for rejecting the Commission's conclusion. Even if the Commission were incorrect in its reading of the law, however, the Federation's claim of immunity would fail. That a particular practice may be unlawful is not, in itself, a sufficient justification for collusion among competitors to prevent it. See *Fashion Originators' Guild of America, Inc. v. FTC*, 312 U.S. 457, 468 (1941). Anticompetitive collusion among private actors, even when its goal is consistent with state policy, acquires antitrust immunity only when it is actively supervised by the State. See *Southern Motor Carriers Rate Conference, Inc. v. United States*, 471 U.S. 48, 57 (1985). There is no suggestion of any such active supervision here; accordingly, whether or not the policy that Federation has taken upon itself to advance is consistent with the policy of the State of Indiana, the Federation's activities are subject to Sherman Act condemnation.

V

The factual findings of the Commission regarding the effect of the Federation's policy of withholding x rays are supported by substantial evidence, and those findings are sufficient as a matter of law to establish a violation of § 1 of the Sherman Act, and, hence, § 5 of the Federal Trade Commission Act.... The judgment of the Court of Appeals is accordingly

Reversed.

NOTES AND QUESTIONS

1. Did the Court explain why it did not apply a per se analysis to this boycott? Is it because the dentists were professionals or because they lacked market power, or both? Is a boycott per se unlawful only when the concerted action is horizontal, supported with market power, without business justification, and aimed at a competitor?

2. Consider whether the legal and economic arguments in *Indiana Federation* are the same as those in *Professional Engineers.* Was the purpose behind the insurance requirement of submitting X-rays to reduce the marginal costs of providing insurance in the dental services market? If so, does *Professional Engineers* permit this evidence to be weighed against noneconomic patient care objectives (e.g., preventing the illegal practice of dentistry)? Does the Court make clear that only economic factors that promote competition would be acceptable business justifications for trade restraints?

If the X-ray submission requirement reduced the costs of insurance, was the Federation's refusal to submit X-rays the equivalent of an overcharge to the patient-consumer? If so, does the Court require evidence of a price increase before finding a violation? Did the Court conclude that the boycott was illegal because it interfered with the normal market forces of cost containment, which resulted in increased costs to the consumer (patients and insurers)?

3. Do you think the burden of establishing a violation under section 5 of the Federal Trade Act is less than under section 1 of the Sherman Act?

4. In a 6-3 decision, the Supreme Court ruled in *FTC v. Superior Court Trial Lawyers Ass'n,* 493 U.S. 411 (1990) (reprinted in Chapter 9, *infra*), that private attorneys who represent indigent criminal defendants may not agree to withhold professional services in order to pressure the local government to increase professional fees under the Criminal Justice Act. Because of the effectiveness of the lawyers' boycott, the city raised the attorneys' fees to $35 an hour from the previous $20 an hour. But the Court found that the concerted refusal to take more indigent cases was a "classic restraint of trade." The means employed (the boycott) to obtain favorable legislation was commercial, not political, in nature, and was designed to increase the price that the lawyers would be paid for services. Unlike *Claiborne Hardware* (*infra* this chapter) where the boycott was designed to achieve "equality and freedom," the boycott in *Superior Court Trial Lawyers Ass'n* was characterized as purely commercial, although there was a political impact. Moreover, the Court reasoned that such boycotts were not entitled to first amendment protection. Said the Court, "Every concerted refusal to do business with a potential customer or supplier has an expressive component." To recognize an exception to section 1 "whenever an economic boycott has an expressive component, would create a gaping hole in the fabric of [the law]." Finally, the Court seemed to invoke a per se test of illegality for this commercial boycott. It rebuked the appellate court for implying that per se rules were designed only for "administrative convenience and efficiency." "The per se rules are, of course, the product of judicial interpretations of the Sherman Act, but the rules nevertheless have the same force and effect as any other statutory commands." Rather, the per se characterization is applied, the Court noted, when the conduct under challenge is inherently dangerous, regardless whether actual harm results. Furthermore, market power is not necessarily a precondition to finding liability. "Conspirators need not achieve the dimensions of a monopoly, or even a degree of market power any greater than that already disclosed by this record [the boycott achieved a crisis in the administration of criminal justice in the District of Columbia and it achieved its economic goal of higher salaries], to warrant condemnation under the antitrust laws."

4. NAKED AND ANCILLARY CONCERTED REFUSALS TO DEAL

ASSOCIATED PRESS V. UNITED STATES

326 U.S. 1 (1945)

JUSTICE BLACK delivered the opinion of the Court.

The publishers of more than 1,200 newspapers are members of the Associated Press (AP), a cooperative association incorporated under the Membership Corporation Law of the State of New York. Its business is the collection, assembly and distribution of news. The news it distributes is originally obtained by direct employees of the Association, employees of the member newspapers, and the employees of foreign independent news agencies with which AP has contractual relations, such as the Canadian Press. Distribution of the news is made through interstate channels of communication to the various newspaper members of the Association, who pay for it under an assessment plan which contemplates no profit to AP.

....

The heart of the government's charge was that appellants had by concerted action set up a system of By-Laws which prohibited all AP members from selling news to non-members, and which granted each member powers to block its non-member competitors from membership. These By-Laws, to which all AP members had assented, were, in the context of the admitted facts, charged to be in violation of the Sherman Act....

These By-Laws, for a violation of which members may be thus fined, suspended, or expelled, require that each newspaper member publish the AP news
regularly in whole or in part, and that each shall "promptly furnish to the corporation, through its agents or employees, all the news of such member's district,
the area of which shall be determined by the Board of Directors." All members
are prohibited from selling or furnishing their spontaneous news to any agency
or publisher except to AP. Other By-Laws require each newspaper member to
conduct his or its business in such manner that the news furnished by the corporation shall not be made available to any non-member in advance of publication.
The joint effect of these By-Laws is to block all newspaper non-members from
any opportunity to buy news from AP or any of its publisher members. Admission to membership in AP thereby becomes a prerequisite to obtaining AP news
or buying news from any one of its more than twelve hundred publishers. The
erection of obstacles to the acquisition of membership consequently can make it
difficult, if not impossible, for non-members to get any of the news furnished by
AP or any of the individual members of this combination of American newspaper publishers.

....

The District Court found that the By-Laws in and of themselves were contracts
in restraint of commerce in that they contained provisions designed to stifle
competition in the newspaper publishing field. The court also found that AP's
restrictive By-Laws had hindered and impeded the growth of competing newspapers. This latter finding, as to the *past* effect of the restrictions, is challenged.
We are inclined to think that it is supported by undisputed evidence, but we do
not stop to labor the point. For the court below found, and we think correctly,
that the By-Laws on their face, and without regard to their past effect, constitute
restraints of trade. Combinations are no less unlawful because they have not as
yet resulted in restraint. An agreement or combination to follow a course of conduct which will necessarily restrain or monopolize a part of trade or commerce
may violate the Sherman Act, whether it be "wholly nascent or abortive on the
one hand, or successful on the other." For these reasons the argument, repeated
here in various forms, that AP had not yet achieved a complete monopoly is
wholly irrelevant. Undisputed evidence did show, however, that its By-Laws had
tied the hands of all of its numerous publishers, to the extent that they could not
and did not sell any part of their news so that it could reach any of their nonmember competitors. In this respect the court did find, and that finding cannot
possibly be challenged, that AP's By-Laws had hindered and restrained the sale
of interstate news to non-members who competed with members.

Inability to buy news from the largest news agency, or any one of its multitude
of members, can have most serious effects on the publication of competitive
newspapers, both those presently published and those which, but for these restrictions, might be published in the future.... The net effect is seriously to limit
the opportunity of any new paper to enter these cities. Trade restraints of this

character, aimed at the destruction of competition, tend to block the initiative which brings newcomers into a field of business and to frustrate the free enterprise system which it was the purpose of the Sherman Act to protect.

....

It has been argued that the restrictive By-Laws should be treated as beyond the prohibitions of the Sherman Act, since the owner of the property can choose his associates and can, as to that which he has produced by his own enterprise and sagacity, efforts or ingenuity, decide for himself whether and to whom to sell or not to sell. While it is true in a very general sense that one can dispose of his property as he pleases, he cannot "go beyond the exercise of this right, and by contracts or combinations, express or implied, unduly hinder or obstruct the free and natural flow of commerce in the channels of interstate trade." The Sherman Act was specifically intended to prohibit independent businesses from becoming "associates" in a common plan which is bound to reduce their competitor's opportunity to buy or sell the things in which the groups compete. Victory of a member of such a combination over its business rivals achieved by such collective means cannot consistently with the Sherman Act or with practical, everyday knowledge be attributed to *individual* "enterprise and sagacity"; such hampering of business rivals can only be attributed to that which really makes it possible — the collective power of an unlawful combination. That the object of sale is the creation or product of a man's ingenuity does not alter this principle. *Fashion Originators' Guild v. Federal Trade Commission*, 312 U.S. 457. It is obviously fallacious to view the By-Laws here in issue as instituting a program to encourage and permit full freedom of sale and disposal of property by its owners. Rather, these publishers have, by concerted arrangements, pooled their power to acquire, to purchase, and to dispose of news reports through the channels of commerce. They have also pooled their economic and news control power and, in exerting that power, have entered into agreements which the District Court found to be "plainly designed in the interest of preventing competition."

It is further contended that since there are other news agencies which sell news, it is not a violation of the Act for an overwhelming majority of American publishers to combine to decline to sell their news to the minority. But the fact that an agreement to restrain trade does not inhibit competition in all of the objects of that trade cannot save it from the condemnation of the Sherman Act. It is apparent that the exclusive right to publish news in a given field, furnished by AP and all of its members, gives many newspapers a competitive advantage over their rivals. Conversely, a newspaper without AP service is more than likely to be at a competitive disadvantage. The District Court stated that it was to secure this advantage over rivals that the By-Laws existed. It is true that the record shows that some competing papers have gotten along without AP news, but morning newspapers, which control 96% of the total circulation in the United States, have AP news service. And the District Court's unchallenged finding was that "AP is a vast, intricately reticulated organization, the largest of its kind, gathering news from all over the world, the chief single source of news for the American press, universally agreed to be of great consequence."

....

Here as in *Fashion Originators' Guild* ... "the combination is in reality an extra-governmental agency, which prescribes rules for the regulation and restraint of interstate commerce, and provides extra-judicial tribunals for determination and punishment of violations, and thus 'trenches upon the power of the national legislature and violates the statute.'" By the restrictive By-Laws each of the publishers in the combination has, in effect, "surrendered himself completely to the control of the association," in respect to the disposition of news in interstate commerce. Therefore this contractual restraint of interstate trade, "designed in the interest of preventing competition," cannot be one of the "normal and usual agreements in aid of trade and commerce which may be found not to be within the [Sherman] Act...." *Eastern States Lumber Dealers' Assn. v. United States*. It is further said that we reach our conclusion by application of the "public utility" concept to the newspaper business. This is not correct. We merely hold that arrangements or combinations designed to stifle competition cannot be immunized by adopting a membership device accomplishing that purpose.

Affirmed.

[JUSTICES DOUGLAS and FRANKFURTER concurred. CHIEF JUSTICE STONE and JUSTICES ROBERTS and MURPHY dissented. JUSTICE JACKSON did not participate.]

NOTES AND QUESTIONS

1. Were the by-laws held illegal per se? In determining this, consider whether the Court weighed the economies achieved by the integration against the anti-competitive harm. How did the Court measure the legality of the restraint? Was market power a factor? Was the concerted refusal to deal merely ancillary to an otherwise lawful purpose (attainment of economies of scale) and, if so, would such a defense be entertained? Consider whether the Court's analysis of the joint venture boycott issue is consistent with those cases discussed *supra* concerning price fixing or market division by joint ventures. Indeed, does the Court's analysis survive *Klor's* and *Silver's* per se prescription against boycotts aimed at competitors?

The Court in *Associated Press* ordered AP to make its membership available to nonmembers on a reasonable basis and, although admission could be restricted, it prohibited members from imposing discriminatory conditions that took into account possible competitive consequences of the new entrant into a member's geographical market. 326 U.S. at 21.

2. Isn't news simply a form of property? *See International News Serv. v. Associated Press*, 248 U.S. 215 (1918); Reich, *The New Property*, 73 Yale L.J. 733 (1964). Wasn't the holding in *Associated Press* simply a requirement that the members of Associated Press sell their property to others?

If three firms join in a research venture and develop a new invention, should they be required to share the invention with all other competitors? The "competitive advantage" that AP obtained over its rivals was merely an advantage that accrued from the fact that they produced better news than anyone else. Should anyone who develops a better device or scheme than someone else be required to sell it? Should it make a difference that two or more people developed it jointly?

In short, is *Associated Press* really a "boycott" case at all? The members of AP developed a product jointly and used it among themselves. No outsiders were excluded from having something that they had before AP was created. "Associated Press News" did not exist until Associated Press came into existence.

3. Consider the following refusal to deal within a credit card joint venture. Visa is a joint venture of some 5000 firms (mostly banks and other financial institutions) that issue VISA credit cards. Visa USA provides technology to process credit card transactions and coordinates individual credit card programs through rules and by-laws proposed by management and adopted by its Board of Directors. The Visa Board adopts an amendment that states that Visa "shall not accept for membership any applicant which is issuing, directly or indirectly, Discover cards or American Express cards, or any other cards deemed competitive by the Board of Directors; an applicant shall be deemed to be issuing such cards if its parent, subsidiary or affiliate issues such cards." Sears, which issues the Discover card, is denied membership in Visa USA pursuant to this regulation. What results if Sears sues?

See SCFC ILC, Inc. v. Visa USA, Inc. 36 F.3d 958 (10th Cir. 1994), *cert. denied*, 515 U.S. 1152 (1995), where the issue presented was whether the refusal to admit Sears (the Discover Card) to this joint venture violated section 1 of the Sherman Act. The district court found in favor of Sears, after a jury verdict rejected Visa's legal and factual arguments. The Tenth Circuit reversed, rejecting per se treatment, and observing that the "[r]ule of reason analysis first asks whether the offending competitor, here Visa USA, possesses market power in the relevant market where the alleged anti-competitive activity occurs."

The parties had agreed that the relevant market was the "general purpose charge card market in the United States," of which there were six market participants, including Visa and Discover. The court found, however, that the relevant market was the "issuing" market, as opposed to the "systems" market. Although only six issuers participated at the "systems" level (Visa, MasterCard, American Express, Diners Club and Carte Blanche, and Discover), there were some 19,000 "participating members" offering cards. The court concluded that this atomistic market precluded a finding of power as a matter of law.

But query: when exclusion is undertaken by means of an explicit and enforced by-law, does the number of members matter to the exercise of market power? *Cf. American Society of Mechanical Engineers, Inc. v. Hydrolevel*, 456 U.S. 556 (1982) (association of 90,000 members held liable when members of one of its Committees conspired with each other to withhold approval of plaintiff's production innovation; no price fixing); *National Society of Professional Engineers v.*

United States, 435 U.S. 679 (1978) (69,000 members; condemning canon against competitive bidding); *Associated Press v. United States*, 326 U.S. 1, 3 (1945) (condemning joint-venture rule excluding competitors as members; approximately 1200 members at time of litigation); *Indiana Federation of Dentists*, 476 U.S. 447 (1986) (condemning collective refusal to provide X-rays by federation of some 2500 dentists, 84 of whom participated in the agreement); *National Collegiate Athletic Ass'n (NCAA) v. Board of Regents of the Univ. of Oklahoma*, 468 U.S. 85, 89 (1984) (striking down output limitation agreement among collegiate athletic association with 850 members); *Arizona v. Maricopa County Medical Society*, 457 U.S. 332 (1982) (condemning maximum price fixing agreement involving 1750 physicians).

The Tenth Circuit then considered the efficiency justification offered by Visa USA. The court found that the by-law that prohibited Sears from joining the network was ancillary to effectuate Visa's business and was no broader than necessary to achieve its business purpose. The court cited "free-rider" problems associated with Visa's competitors and concluded that the by-law was "reasonably necessary to ensure the effective operation of its credit card services." The court concluded:

> Bylaw 2.06 did not alter the character of the general purpose credit card market or change any present pattern of distribution. Nor did it bar Sears from access to this market. There was no evidence that Sears could only introduce a ... card with Visa USA's help or that Visa USA's exclusion from its joint venture disabled Sears from developing its new card under the Discover mantle. More importantly, there was no evidence that the by-law harms consumers, the focus of the alleged violation. [Both authors of the Casebook jointly filed an amicus brief in this case.]

36 F.3d at 97-91.

5. NONCOMMERCIAL BOYCOTTS

In addressing the legality of boycotts, one needs to inquire to what extent a "noneconomic" political or social boycott is covered under section 1 of the Sherman Act. First it should be noted that the District of Columbia Circuit in *Smith v. Pro Football, Inc.*, 593 F.2d 1173, 1178 (D.C. Cir. 1978), distinguished a boycott of competitors at one level of competition by competitors on the same level (horizontal boycott) from other refusals to deal where the target is on a different level of competition (vertical boycott). The former was characterized as a classic per se illegal boycott. The latter was evaluated under a rule of reason.

Are consumers liable for treble damages under the antitrust laws for economic injury caused by a consumer boycott? Should the fact that the consumer might have an economic interest in the result affect the standard of analysis? Suppose the boycott is directed at a merchant that is forced, by reason of the boycott, to offer substantial loss. Is there a distinction between this and a politically motivated boycott? Should legality turn on whether economic means (such as a boycott) are used to achieve a political result or whether political means are used to achieve an economic result? See Chapter 3, Section II.A. *See also* Comment, *Protest Boycotts Under the Sherman Act*, 128 U. Pa. L. Rev. 1131 (1980); Note, *Concerted Refusals to Deal by Non-Business Groups: A Critique of* Missouri v. NOW, 49 Geo. Wash. L. Rev. 143 (1980); Note, *Political Boycott Activity and the First Amendment*, 91 Harv. L. Rev. 659 (1978).

Should the commercial or business interest of the participant in the boycott play a role in the decisional analysis? Recall the Supreme Court's earlier cautions in *Apex Hosiery* and *Klor's* that the Sherman Act is directed at commercial transactions or combinations having commercial objectives. 320 U.S. at 492-93; 359 U.S. at 213 n. 7. The Ninth Circuit has ruled that lobbying activities with anticompetitive effects do not lose their first amendment protection merely because the government entity is involved in a commercial enterprise. The court distinguished the first amendment protection from the state-action doctrine (see Chapter 3) where the commercial nature of the government's conduct becomes relevant. *In re Airport Car Rental Antitrust Litig.*, 693 F.2d 84 (9th Cir. 1982). Finally, if the protest boycott is not outside the scope of the Sherman Act, should its legality be tested by the per se rule or by an open-end Sherman Act balancing analysis that considers reasonableness in the context of purpose and effects? While few cases have addressed these issues, two recent decisions are worth noting.

In the following case, the Eighth Circuit considered whether a concerted convention boycott directed at several states that failed to ratify the Equal Rights Amendment violated section 1 of the Sherman Act. The defendant (NOW) was a nonprofit organization established for the purpose of furthering the legal rights of women. The convention boycott was designed to influence the Missouri legislature, but the economic victims were Missouri motels, restaurants, and convention centers. The conduct challenged by Missouri was characterized by the court as "an economic boycott, politically motivated, to achieve a legislative goal." 620 F.2d at 1309.

MISSOURI V. NATIONAL ORGANIZATION FOR WOMEN

620 F.2d 1301 (8th Cir.), *cert. denied*, 449 U.S. 842 (1980)

JUDGE STEPHENSON.

[Finding the concerted boycott protected by the first amendment, Judge Stephenson reasoned that the] ERA is not a "financial," "economic," or "commercial" piece of legislation. It is a social or political piece of legislation. While it is obviously perceived by the members of NOW as beneficial, the record indicates, and it seems apparent, that the orientation of both parties, NOW and Missouri, to the ERA is not one of profit motivation. The only financial, economic or commercial matter involved here is Missouri's concern about the financial repercussion of the boycott.

Keeping in mind that what we are discussing is the applicability of the Sherman Act to the facts, and the intent of the Congress to cover such situations, the difference in the content of the legislation — if anything — makes it more clear that NOW's efforts to influence the legislature's action on the ERA are beyond the scope and intent of the Sherman Act. A social piece of legislation and the efforts involved in influencing the legislature's actions on such legislation is further afield from the central focus of the Sherman Act than a commercial piece of legislation and the petitioning efforts associated therewith.

....

Here, NOW's concerted activities and publicity campaign were initiated to show that in not ratifying the ERA, Missouri was denying rights to women, and in order to show displeasure with Missouri and to show support for the ERA, organizations were urged by NOW not to hold their conventions in Missouri. The ultimate goal was to have the ERA ratified and the hope was that by boycotting the state for as long as the ERA remained unratified in that state, it would result in a favorable legislative vote.

It is true that there were active solicitations by NOW followed by a boycott decision by the recipients of the solicitation. And yet, borrowing from the Supreme Court's language in *Noerr*, the finding by the district court in the instant case that NOW's campaign was intended to and did in fact injure Missouri in its relationship with its convention customers can mean no more than that Missouri sustained a *direct injury* as an incidental effect of NOW's campaign to influence governmental action.

> It is inevitable, whenever an attempt is made to influence legislation by a campaign of publicity, that an incidental effect of that campaign may be the infliction of some direct injury upon the interests of the party against whom the campaign is directed.... To hold that the knowing infliction of such injury renders the campaign itself illegal would thus be tantamount to outlawing all such campaigns.

NOW appears to have utilized its political power to bring about the ratification of the ERA by the State of Missouri. The tool it chose was a boycott, a device economic by nature. However, using a boycott in a non-competitive political arena for the purpose of influencing legislation is not proscribed by the Sherman Act.

....

There resulted a restraint of trade in the *Noerr* case just as has occurred in this case. In *Noerr* it was accomplished by means of a publicity campaign with the ultimate goal of obtaining legislation that commercially or competitively affected the competitor-campaigners and competitor-target. In the instant case, it was accomplished by means of a publicity-boycott campaign with the ultimate goal of obtaining socially or politically-oriented legislation that had no effect upon the campaigners or target, at least in a commercial or business sense. These distinctions are not where our focus should be.

....

[M]any of the cases do focus on the *Noerr* Court's reliance on the right of petition and the important constitutional questions that would be raised should the Court impute to Congress via the Sherman Act an intent to cover the *Noerr* activities. [Citing cases.]

Of those cases that emphasize the *Noerr* Court's reference to the constitutional concerns involved in *Noerr, California Motor Transport Co. v. Trucking Unlimited* was the one that dealt with it in the most expanded manner. In *Motor Transport*, Justice Douglas stated that the *Noerr* decision rested upon two grounds: (1) that there was no basis in the Sherman Act's legislative history by which to impute a purpose to regulate political activity and (2) that "[t]he right of petition is one of the freedoms protected by the Bill of Rights, and we cannot, of course, lightly impute to Congress an intent to invade these freedoms." *Id.*, 404 U.S. at 510. After stating this, the Court then extended the *Noerr* philosophy to the use of the channels and procedures of state and federal agencies and courts on the basis that not to do so would be destructive of the rights of association and of petition. *Id.*, 404 U.S. at 510. More importantly, in the course of invoking the sham exception to the *Noerr* case, the Court's focus is on the First Amendment rights. "First Amendment rights may not be used as the means or the pretext for achieving 'substantive evils' … which the legislature has the power to control." *Id.* at 515.

The parties do not even argue that there is a sham in this case; indeed, Missouri specifically argues that even those residents of Missouri who support the ERA must suffer as a result of this boycott. Thus the central point in *California Motor* and the other cases citing *Noerr* is the shift in focus from the *Noerr* holding that the railroads' activities are beyond the intent of Congress, insofar as the Sherman Act is concerned, to the *Noerr* statement that there are serious constitutional questions involved also.

The Court continued its mention of the constitutional issue presented in *Noerr* in *Lafayette v. Louisiana Power & Light Co., supra*, 435 U.S. at 399 and in *First National Bank v. Bellotti, supra*, 435 U.S. at 792 n.31.

In *Lafayette*, the Court stated that only two policies have been held to be "sufficiently weighty to override the presumption against implied exclusions from coverage of the antitrust laws" — one of which was the *Noerr* doctrine. (The other was the *Parker* state action exemption.) "[A] contrary construction [in *Noerr*] would impede the open communication between the polity and its lawmakers which is vital to the functioning of a representative democracy.... '[A]nd of at least equal significance,' is the threat to the constitutionally protected right of petition which a contrary construction would entail."

Thus, we feel that the Supreme Court's treatment of its *Noerr* doctrine requires recognition of the constitutional ramifications inherent in prohibiting, or considering as improper, activities such as NOW's boycott.... We hold that Missouri has no common law tort claim against NOW.

We hold today that the Sherman Act does not cover NOW's boycott activities on the basis of the legislative history of the Act and of the Supreme Court's considerations of the legislative history. We hold the same reasoning is applicable to Missouri's Antitrust Act. We hold that NOW's boycott activities are privileged on the basis of the First Amendment right to petition and the Supreme Court's recognition of that important right when it collides with commercial effects of trade restraints....

In 1982 the Supreme Court decided whether a civil rights boycott by members of the National Association for the Advancement of Colored People (NAACP) against local merchants in Mississippi was protected under the first amendment. *NAACP v. Claiborne Hardware Co.*, 458 U.S. 886 (1982). The purpose of the boycott was to secure compliance with a list of demands for social and racial justice. The state trial court found the NAACP members guilty of, inter alia, the tort of malicious interference with plaintiffs' business, a secondary boycott, and the state antitrust statute. The Mississippi Supreme Court held that the secondary boycott statute was inapplicable and the court "declined to rely on the restraint of trade statute, noting that the 'United States Supreme Court has seen fit to hold boycotts to achieve political ends are not a violation of the Sherman Act.'" The trial court's liability finding was upheld by the Mississippi Supreme Court, however, on a common law tort theory which outlawed boycotts. In reversing on first amendment grounds, Justice Stevens, writing for the Court, concluded that:

> The boycott of white merchants at issue in this case took many forms. The boycott was launched at a meeting of a local branch of the NAACP attended by several hundred persons. Its acknowledged purpose was to secure compliance by both civic and business leaders with a lengthy list of demands for equality and racial justice. The boycott was supported by speeches and nonviolent picketing. Participants repeatedly encouraged others to join in its cause.
>
> Each of these elements of the boycott is a form of speech or conduct that is ordinarily entitled to protection under the First and Fourteenth Amendments. The black citizens named as defendants in this action banded together and collectively expressed their dissatisfaction with a social structure that had denied them rights to equal treatment and respect. As we so recently acknowledged, ... "the practice of persons sharing common views banding together to achieve a common end is deeply embedded in the American political process." We recognized that "by collective effort individuals can make their views known, when, individually, their voices would be faint or lost.... There are, of course, some activities, legal if engaged in by one, yet illegal if performed in concert with others, but political expression is not one of them."
>
> ....
>
> Speech itself also was used to further the aims of the boycott. Nonparticipants repeatedly were urged to join the common cause, both through public

address and through personal solicitation. These elements of the boycott involve speech in its most direct form. In addition, names of boycott violators were read aloud at meetings at the First Baptist Church and published in a local black newspaper. Petitioners admittedly sought to persuade others to join the boycott through social pressure and the "threat" of social ostracism. Speech does not lose its protected character, however, simply because it may embarrass others or coerce them into action....

In sum, the boycott clearly involved constitutionally protected activity. The established elements of speech, assembly, association and petition, "though not identical, are inseparable." Through exercise of these First Amendment rights, petitioners sought to bring about political, social, and economic change. Through speech, assembly, and petition — rather than through riot or revolution — petitioners sought to change a social order that had consistently treated them as second-class citizens.

The presence of protected activity, however, does not end the relevant constitutional inquiry....

While States have broad power to regulate economic activity, we do not find a comparable right to prohibit peaceful political activity such as that found in the boycott in this case. This Court has recognized that expression on public issues "has always rested on the highest rung of the hierarchy of First Amendment values." "[S]peech concerning public affairs is more than self-expression; it is the essence of self-government." There is a "profound national commitment" to the principle that "debate on public issues should be uninhibited, robust, and wide-open."

....

It is not disputed that a major purpose of the boycott in this case was to influence governmental action. [T]he petitioners certainly foresaw — and directly intended — that the merchants would sustain economic injury as a result of their campaign. [T]he purpose of petitioners' campaign was not to destroy legitimate competition. Petitioners sought to vindicate rights of equality and of freedom that lie at the heart of the Fourteenth Amendment itself. The right of the States to regulate economic activity could not justify a complete prohibition against a nonviolent, politically-motivated boycott designed to force governmental and economic change and to effectuate rights guaranteed by the Constitution itself.

... We hold that the nonviolent elements of petitioners' activities are entitled to the protection of the First Amendment.

458 U.S. at 907-15.

NOTES AND QUESTIONS

1. *The Sherman Act and Nonprofit Organizations.* Do the antitrust laws reach the activities of nonprofit organizations, such as church-sponsored hospitals? Does *NOW* speak to that proposition? To be sure, nonprofit institutions do not necessarily "maximize profits" in the sense of equating marginal cost and marginal revenue. But nonprofits may seek monopoly profits and cause competitive injury even when acting for purely charitable purposes. For example, the Sisters of Mercy may own a nonprofit hospital and a soup kitchen and conclude that, while all patrons of the soup kitchen are needy, not all patients at the hospital are. As a result, they may use monopoly profits from the hospital to subsidize the activities of the soup kitchen. If this completely charitable set of intentions is accompanied by power and exclusionary practices in the hospital, its patients have suffered competitive injury notwithstanding the Sisters' good motives. *See* W. Lynk, *Property Rights and the Presumptions of Merger Analysis*, 39 Antitrust Bull. 363, 377 (1994).

Two things seem fairly well settled. *First*, nonprofit organizations do not enjoy any general exemption from the Sherman or Clayton Acts, and the antitrust laws presumptively apply to them. *Second*, although *NOW* and other cases declare an exemption for noncommercial activities, the exemption question responds to the nature of the *activity being challenged*, not to the nature of the organization engaging in it. Thus if a nonprofit organization such as *NOW* engages in a purely economic boycott, the Sherman Act applies. By contrast, if Campbell's Soup Company gave free soup to a local charitable organization on the condition that they not charge more than twenty-five cents a bowl, the conduct would presumably be exempt.

Did the *NOW* and *NAACP* opinions express an unqualified immunity from the antitrust laws for noncommercial concerted refusals to deal? Even though these cases were decided under the first amendment, at least in part, could such refusals to deal be found lawful under the prior boycott decisional law? If so, by what analysis, per se or rule of reason, would you reach your decision? Consider the analytical themes expressed throughout the prior decisions studied: (1) whether the boycott had a commercial objective; (2) whether the boycott was explicitly formed, or merely an incidental effect of some other agreement; (3) whether it had an otherwise lawful self-regulatory purpose; (4) whether it was a horizontal agreement entered between competitors; (5) whether its aim was horizontal, that is, in the direction of a competitor; (6) whether it was directed vertically to a supplier or customer; and (7) whether there were elements of coercion.

Determining whether the boycott is commercial in purpose or effect is sometimes problematic. Compare the language in *NOW* and *NAACP* with the results in *Allied Tube & Conduit Corp. v. Indian Head, Inc.*, 486 U.S. 492 (1988); *Superior Court Trial Lawyers Ass'n v. FTC*, 856 F.2d 226 (D.C. Cir. 1988). *See* Calkins, *Developments in Antitrust and the First Amendment: The Disaggregation of* Noerr, 57 Antitrust L.J. 327 (1988).

For an extended discussion of the *Noerr* doctrine, see Chapter 9, *infra.*

———————

BIBLIOGRAPHY AND COLLATERAL READINGS

Books

R. Blair & D. Kaserman, Antitrust Economics 132-225 (1985).

E. Gellhorn & W. Kovacic, Antitrust Law and Economics 156-285 (4th ed. 1994).

H. Hovenkamp, Federal Antitrust Policy, chs. 4-5 (2d ed. 1994).

T. Jorde & D. Teece, Antitrust Innovation and Competitiveness (1992).

S. Ross, Principles of Antitrust (1993).

E.T. Sullivan & J. Harrison, Understanding Antitrust and Its Economic Implications 71-144 (3d ed. 1998).

Articles

Ayres, How Cartels Punish: A Structural Theory of Self-Enforcing Collusion, 87 Colum. L. Rev. 295 (1987).

Blair & Fesmine, Maximum Price Fixing and the Goals of Antitrust, 37 Syracuse L. Rev. 43 (1986).

Brodley, Joint Ventures and Antitrust Policy, 95 Harv. L. Rev. 1523 (1982).

Calkins, Copperweld in the Courts: The Road to *Caribe*, 63 Antitrust L. J. 345 (1995).

Carstensen, "The Content of the Hollow Core of Antitrust: The Chicago Board of Trade Case and the Meaning of the 'Rule of Reason' in Restraint of Trade Analysis," Research in Law and Economics 1-88 (1992).

Clark, Antitrust Comes Full Circle: The Return to a Cartelization Standard, 38 Vand. L. Rev. 1125 (1985).

Easterbrook, Maximum Price Fixing, 48 U. Chi. L. Rev. 88 (1981).

Easterbrook, The Limits of Antitrust, 63 Tex. L. Rev. 1 (1984).

Gerhart, The Supreme Court and Antitrust Analysis: The (Near) Triumph of the Chicago School, 1982 S. Ct. Rev. 319.

Harrison, Price Fixing, the Professions and Ancillary Restraint: Coping with *Maricopa County*, 1982 U. Ill. L. Rev. 925.

Heidt, A Redrafted Section 1 of the Sherman Act, 66 Notre Dame L. Rev. 603 (1991).

Heidt, Industry Self-Regulation and the Useless Concept of "Group Boycott," 39 Vand. L. Rev. 1507 (1986).

Hovenkamp, Exclusive Joint Ventures and Antitrust Policy, 1995 Colum. Bus. L. Rev. 1.

Jones, Concerted Refusals to Deal and the Producer Interest in Antitrust, 50 Ohio St. L.J. 73 (1989).

Jorde & Teece, Innovation and Cooperation: Implications for Competition and Antitrust, 4 J. Econ. Persp. 75 (1990).

Liebeler, 1984 Economic Review of Antitrust Development: Horizontal Restrictions, Efficiency and Per Se Rules, 33 UCLA L. Rev. 1019 (1986).

Louis, Restraints Ancillary to Joint Ventures Licensing Agreements, 66 Va. L. Rev. 879 (1980).

Note, Conscious Parallelism and Price Fixing: Defining the Boundary, 52 U. Chi. L. Rev. 508 (1905).

Piraino, Beyond Per Se, Rule of Reason or Merger Analysis: A New Antitrust Standard for Joint Ventures, 76 Minn. L. Rev. 1 (1991).

Piraino, Reconciling the Per Se and Rule of Reason Approaches to Antitrust Analysis, 64 S. Cal. L. Rev. 685 (1991).

Pitofsky, Joint Ventures Under the Antitrust Laws: Some Reflections on *Penn-Olin*, 82 Harv. L. Rev. 1007 (1969).

Posner, Oligopoly and the Antitrust Laws: A Suggested Approach, 21 Stan. L. Rev. 1562 (1969).

Sullivan, On Nonprice Competition: An Economic and Marketing Analysis, 45 U. Pitt. L. Rev. 401 (1984).

Turner, The Definition of Agreement Under the Sherman Act: Conscious Parallelism and Refusal to Deal, 75 Harv. L. Rev. 655 (1962).

Wood-Hutchinson, Antitrust 1984: Five Decisions in Search of a Theory, 1984 S. Ct. Rev. 69.

Chapter 5

VERTICAL RESTRICTIONS

SECTION I. INTRABRAND DISTRIBUTIONAL RESTRAINTS

The preceding chapter considered agreements between competitors, or firms operating at the same level of activity in the same market. The antitrust concern there centered mainly on conduct which facilitated collusion between competitors. Restraints on trade may also develop between firms at different levels in the production and distribution network. Agreements between a manufacturer and distributor, or between a wholesaler and retailer, or between any two sequential parties in a production-distribution chain, are characterized as vertical.

Contractual arrangements between participants in the production-distribution chain may be similar to those discussed in the chapter on horizontal agreements. For example, a manufacturer may set the price at which the product will be distributed, or limit distributors to an exclusive territory, or allocate customers to distributors, thereby precluding the distributors from selling outside their designated area or to customers of another distributor. Still other vertical agreements may require distributors, wholesalers or retailers to deal only in the products of a certain manufacturer, or may require those customers to take additional products if they want to purchase a particular product from the manufacturer. The first type of conduct is known as resale price maintenance (RPM), while the second is a market division. The third and fourth examples are exclusive dealing and tying arrangements. Generally, the restraints discussed in this chapter can be classified as restrictions on production or distribution and restrictions foreclosing competition. Vertical agreements may take many forms, but different objectives and consequences may result, requiring distinctions to be drawn between vertical and horizontal restraints. The problems discussed in this chapter often come up in the context of franchise agreements, where the manufacturer desires to control the distribution of its products downstream.

A. ECONOMIC IMPLICATIONS

The questions addressed in this chapter are whether vertical restraints should be condemned under the Sherman and Clayton Acts and, if so, under what standard they should be judged. The law of vertical restraints has been subject to significant reconsideration over the last several years. Like horizontal agreements, vertical restraints may be used to facilitate collusion at the horizontal level. The instigation for such a restraint might come from either a dealer cartel or manufacturer cartel. The vertical restraint may be used to promote price fixing or create barriers to entry that foreclose competition. Such consequences or objectives do not necessarily follow from a vertical agreement, however. If the effect or intent of a vertical agreement is to improve horizontal cooperation, or to foreclose competitors from the market, or to promote price discrimination, a restraint of trade can be demonstrated. But the vertical restraint may be designed instead to increase distributional efficiency and welfare in the intrabrand market so as to promote competition in the larger interbrand market. The welfare trade-off arguably is between decreased intrabrand rivalry in favor of increased interbrand competition, which by virtue of the vertical restraint results in increased welfare to the ultimate consumer. A decrease in intrabrand price rivalry may result in stronger interbrand competition. A related concern is whether vertical restraints promote increased collusion among competitors at the manufacturing level. The decisional law is only beginning to address these issues.

One of the primary justifications advanced for the use of vertical restraints is to permit manufacturers and dealers to avoid "free-rider" problems. Depending on the nature of the product, incentives may be necessary to encourage retail dealers to represent effectively the manufacturer's product. Restraints may be designed to encourage maintenance of product quality and promotion of the product at the vertical level. If distributional restraints are not enforced uniformly, distributors that adhere to restraints will incur costs associated with the restraints, while those that do not will have lower costs. With lower costs, the maverick distributor will be able to sell the product at a price below that of the cooperating distributor by taking a "free ride" on the promotion of the product by the cooperative distributor, thus reducing the incentive to adhere to the vertical restraint. The presence of the successful free-rider will cause the cooperative distributor to lose sales. The result may be that in the absence of an enforceable vertical restraint, the manufacturer will be unable to control the manner in which the product is marketed, sold or serviced. This in turn may affect the image of the manufacturer's product and ultimately the effectiveness of the product. *See* Posner, *The Next Step in the Antitrust Treatment of Restricted Distribution: Per Se Legality*, 48 U. Chi. L. Rev. 6 (1981); Telser, *Why Should Manufacturers Want Fair Trade?*, 3 J.L. & Econ. 86 (1960).

The free rider problem suggests that the economic incentives of manufacturer and dealer are not always similar. While promotion of the product should benefit both manufacturer and dealer, how the product is promoted and serviced and the price at which it is sold are considerations over which the parties may have divergent viewpoints. Vertical restraints play a role in reconciling marketing techniques, with the result that distribution efficiencies may increase for the manufacturer while at the same time they may reduce intrabrand competition. In order to reconcile increased distributional efficiency with the risk of reduced competition, as the following cases indicate, courts have begun to apply a broader balancing analysis in determining the legality of certain vertical restraints, while maintaining per se rules for others.

As you explore the diverse approaches utilized by the courts, consider whether legal and economic policies support the distinctions drawn between vertical price and nonprice restraints. Consider the role that evidence of industry structure might play in determining the legality of the vertical restraint. Might the structure of the industry dictate whether the vertical restraint facilitates cartelization (collusion among competitors) at either the dealer or manufacturing level? Should the legality of the restraint vary depending on whether the restraint imposed is due to pressure from dealers who are interested in price coordination, or whether it is a genuine device designed to increase the manufacturer's distribution efficiency? Should it matter whether any resulting anticompetitive effects occur at the manufacturer level or retail level? Consider also what evidentiary relevancy there is to a market characterized by vertical restraints and substantial barriers to entry at the manufacturing level.

B. RESALE PRICE MAINTENANCE

1. SETTING VERTICAL MINIMUM PRICES

DR. MILES MEDICAL CO. V. JOHN D. PARK & SONS CO.

220 U.S. 373 (1911)

JUSTICE HUGHES delivered the opinion of the Court.

The complainant, a manufacturer of proprietary medicines which are prepared in accordance with secret formulas ... seeks to maintain certain prices fixed by it for all the sales of its products both at wholesale and retail. Its purpose is to establish minimum prices at which sales shall be made by its vendees and by all subsequent purchasers who traffic in its remedies. Its plan is thus to govern directly the entire trade in the medicines it manufactures, embracing interstate commerce as well as commerce within the States respectively. To accomplish this result it has adopted two forms of restrictive agreements limiting trade in the articles to those who become parties to one or the other. The one sort of contract known as "*Consignment Contract — Wholesale*," has been made with over four hundred jobbers and wholesale dealers, and the other, described as "*Retail Agency Contract*," with twenty-five thousand retail dealers in the United States.

The defendant is a wholesale drug concern which has refused to enter into the required contract, and is charged with procuring medicines for sale at "cut prices" by inducing those who have made the contracts to violate the restrictions. The complainant invokes the established doctrine that an actionable wrong is committed by one who maliciously interferes with a contract between two parties and induces one of them to break that contract to the injury of the other and that, in the absence of an adequate remedy at law, equitable relief will be granted....

The principal question is as to the validity of the restrictive agreements.

....

Turning to the agreement itself, we find that it purports to appoint the party with whom it is made one of the complainant's "Wholesale Distributing Agents," and it is agreed that the complainant, as proprietor, shall consign to the agent "for sale for the account of said Proprietor" such goods as it may deem necessary, "the title thereto and property therein to be and remain in the Proprietor absolutely until sold under and in accordance with the provisions hereof, and all unsold goods to be immediately returned to said Proprietor on demand and the cancellation of this agreement." The goods are to be invoiced to the consignee at stated prices, which are the same as the minimum prices at which the consignee is allowed to sell. It is also agreed that the consignee shall "faithfully and promptly account and pay to the Proprietor the proceeds of all sales, after deducting as full compensation ... a commission of ten per cent of the invoice value, and a further commission of five per cent on the net amount of each consignment, after deducting the said ten per cent commission, on all advances on account remitted within ten days from the date of any consignment," such advances, however, not to affect the title to the goods and to be repaid should the agreement be terminated and unsold goods, on which advances had been made, be returned. The consignee guarantees payment for all goods sold and promises "to render a full account and remit the net proceeds on the first day of each month of and for the sales of the month preceding."

The consignee agrees "to sell only to the designated Retail Agents of said Proprietor as specified in lists of such Retail Agents furnished by said Proprietor and alterable at the will of said Proprietor." A further provision permits sales "only to the said Retail or Wholesale Agents of said Proprietor, as per list furnished." No time is fixed for the duration of the agreement.

....

The other form of contract, adopted by the complainant, while described as a "retail agency contract," is clearly an agreement looking to sale and not to agency. The so-called "retail agents" are not agents at all, either of the complainant or of its consignees, but are contemplated purchasers who buy to sell again, that is, retail dealers. It is agreed that they may purchase the medicines manufactured by the complainant at stated prices. There follows this stipulation:

> In consideration whereof said Retail Agent agrees in no case to sell or furnish the said Proprietary Medicines to any person, firm or corporation whatsoever, at less than the full retail price as printed on the packages, without reduction for quantity; and said Retail Agent further agrees not to sell the said Proprietary Medicines at any price to Wholesale or Retail dealers not accredited agents of the Dr. Miles Medical Company.

It will be noticed that the "retail agents" are not forbidden to sell either to wholesale or retail dealers if these are "accredited agents" of the complainant, that is if the dealers have signed either of the two contracts the complainant requires. But the restriction is intended to apply whether the retail dealers have bought the goods from those who held under consignment or from other dealers, wholesale or retail, who had purchased them. And the way in which the "retail agents" who supplied the medicines to the defendant had bought them is not shown.

The bill asserts complainant's "right to maintain and preserve the aforesaid system and method of contracts and sales adopted and established by it." It is, as we have seen, a system of interlocking restrictions by which the complainant seeks to control not merely the prices at which its agents may sell its products, but the prices for all sales by all dealers at wholesale or retail, whether purchasers or subpurchasers, and thus to fix the amount which the consumer shall pay, eliminating all competition....

That these agreements restrain trade is obvious. That, having been made, ... with "most of the jobbers and wholesale druggists and a majority of the retail druggists of the country" and having for their purpose the control of the entire trade, they relate directly to interstate as well as intrastate trade, and operate to restrain trade or commerce among the several States, is also clear....

But it is insisted that the restrictions are not invalid either at common law or under [the antitrust laws] upon the following grounds, which may be taken to embrace the fundamental contentions for the complainant: (1) That the restrictions are valid because they relate to proprietary medicines manufactured under a secret process; and (2) that, apart from this, a manufacturer is entitled to control the prices on all sales of his own products.

....

But whatever rights the patentee may enjoy are derived from statutory grant under the authority conferred by the Constitution. This grant is based upon public considerations. The purpose of the patent law is to stimulate invention by protecting inventors for a fixed time in the advantages that may be derived from exclusive manufacture, use and sale.... "The great object and intention of the act is to secure to the public the advantages to be derived from the discoveries of individuals, and the means it employs are the compensation made to those individuals for the time and labor devoted to these discoveries, by the exclusive right to make, use and sell, the things discovered for a limited time."

The complainant has no statutory grant. So far as appears, there are no letters patent relating to the remedies in question. The complainant has not seen fit to make the disclosure required by the statute and thus to secure the privileges it confers. Its case lies outside the policy of the patent law, and the extent of the right which that law secures is not here involved or determined.

....

Second. We come, then, to the second question, whether the complainant, irrespective of the secrecy of its process, is entitled to maintain the restrictions by virtue of the fact that they relate to products of its own manufacture.

The basis of the argument appears to be that, as the manufacturer may make and sell, or not, as he chooses, he may affix conditions as to the use of the article or as to the prices at which purchasers may dispose of it. The propriety of the restraint is sought to be derived from the liberty of the producer.

But because a manufacturer is not bound to make or sell, it does not follow that in case of sales actually made he may impose upon purchasers every sort of restriction. Thus a general restraint upon alienation is ordinarily invalid. "The right of alienation is one of the essential incidents of a right of general property in movables, and restraints upon alienation have been generally regarded as obnoxious to public policy, which is best subserved by great freedom of traffic in such things as pass from hand to hand. General restraint in the alienation of articles, things, chattels, except when a very special kind of property is involved, such as a slave or an heirloom, have been generally held void...."

With respect to contracts in restraint of trade, the earlier doctrine of the common law has been substantially modified in adaptation to modern conditions. But the public interest is still the first consideration. To sustain the restraint, it must be found to be reasonable both with respect to the public and to the parties and that it is limited to what is fairly necessary, in the circumstances of the particular case, for the protection of the covenantee....

The present case is not analogous to that of a sale of good will, or of an interest in a business, or of the grant of a right to use a process of manufacture. The complainant has not parted with any interest in its business or instrumentalities of production. It has conferred no right by virtue of which purchasers of its products may compete with it. It retains complete control over the business in which it is engaged, manufacturing what it pleases and fixing such prices for its own sales as it may desire. Nor are we dealing with a single transaction, conceivably unrelated to the public interest. The agreements are designed to maintain prices, after the complainant has parted with the title to the articles, and to prevent competition among those who trade in them.

The bill asserts the importance of a standard retail price and alleges generally that confusion and damage have resulted from sales at less than the prices fixed. But the advantage of established retail prices primarily concerns the dealers. The enlarged profits which would result from adherence to the established rates would go to them and not to the complainant. It is through the inability of the favored dealers to realize these profits, on account of the described competition, that the complainant works out its alleged injury. If there be an advantage to a manufacturer in the maintenance of fixed retail prices, the question remains whether it is one which he is entitled to secure by agreements restricting the freedom of trade on the part of dealers who own what they sell. As to this, the complainant can fare no better with its plan of identical contracts than could the dealers themselves if they formed a combination and endeavored to establish the same restrictions, and thus to achieve the same result, by agreement with each other. If the immediate advantage they would thus obtain would not be sufficient to sustain such a direct agreement, the asserted ulterior benefit to the complainant cannot be regarded as sufficient to support its system.

But agreements or combinations between dealers, having for their sole purpose the destruction of competition and the fixing of prices, are injurious to the public interest and void. They are not saved by the advantages which the participants expect to derive from the enhanced price to the consumer. [Citing cases.]

The complainant's plan falls within the principle which condemns contracts of this class. It, in effect, creates a combination for the prohibited purposes. No distinction can properly be made by reason of the particular character of the commodity in question.... Nor does the fact that the margin of freedom is reduced by the control of production make the protection of what remains, in such a case, a negligible matter. And where commodities have passed into the channels of trade and are owned by dealers, the validity of agreements to prevent competition and to maintain prices is not to be determined by the circumstance whether they were produced by several manufacturers or by one, or whether they were previously owned by one or by many. The complainant having sold its product at prices satisfactory to itself, the public is entitled to whatever advantage may be derived from competition in the subsequent traffic.

....

Affirmed.

JUSTICE HOLMES, dissenting.
The second contract is that of the retail agents, so called, being really the first purchasers, fixing the price below which they will not sell to the public.... The sale to the retailers is made by the plaintiff, and the only question is whether the law forbids a purchaser to contract with his vendor that he will not sell below a certain price. This is the important question in this case. I suppose that in the case of a single object such as a painting or a statue the right of the artist to make such a stipulation hardly would be denied. In other words, I suppose that the reason why the contract is held bad is that it is part of a scheme embracing other similar contracts each of which applies to a number of similar things, with the object of fixing a general market price. This reason seems to me inadequate in the case before the court. In the first place by a slight change in the form of the contract the plaintiff can accomplish the result in a way that would be beyond successful attack. If it should make the retail dealers also agents in law as well as in name and retain the title until the goods left their hands I cannot conceive that even the present enthusiasm for regulating the prices to be charged by other people would deny that the owner was acting within his rights. It seems to me that this consideration by itself ought to give us pause.

There is no statute covering the case; there is no body of precedent that by ineluctable logic requires the conclusion to which the court has come. The conclusion is reached by extending a certain conception of public policy to a new sphere. On such matters we are in perilous country. I think that, at least, it is safe to say that the most enlightened judicial policy is to let people manage their own business in their own way, unless the ground for interference is very clear. What then is the ground upon which we interfere in the present case? Of course, it is not the interest of the producer. No one, I judge, cares for that. It hardly can be the interest of subordinate vendors, as there seems to be no particular reason for preferring them to the originator and first vendor of the product. Perhaps it may be assumed to be the interest of the consumers and the public. On that point I confess that I am in a minority as to larger issues than are concerned here. I think that we greatly exaggerate the value and importance to the public of competition in the production or distribution of an article (here it is only distribution), as fixing a fair price. What really fixes that is the competition of conflicting desires. We, none of us, can have as much as we want of all the things that we want. Therefore, we have to choose. As soon as the price of something that we want goes above the point at which we are willing to give up other things to have that, we cease to buy it and buy something else. Of course, I am speaking of things that we can get along without. There may be necessaries that sooner or later must be dealt with like short rations in a shipwreck, but they are not Dr. Miles's medicines. With regard to things like the latter it seems to me that the point of most profitable returns marks the equilibrium of social desires and determines the fair price in the only sense in which I can find meaning in those words. The Dr. Miles Medical Company knows better than we do what will enable it to do the best business. We must assume its retail price to be reasonable, for it is so alleged and the case is here on demurrer; so I see nothing to warrant my assuming that the public will not be served best by the company being allowed to carry out its plan. I cannot believe that in the long run the public will profit by this court permitting knaves to cut reasonable prices for some ulterior purpose of their own and thus to impair, if not to destroy, the production and sale of articles which it is assumed to be desirable that the public should be able to get.

....

NOTES AND QUESTIONS

1. Does *Dr. Miles* hold that it is a per se violation under the Sherman Act for a manufacturer to set the price at which the product will be sold at retail? In finding a Sherman Act violation, what reasoning did the Court advance in support of its conclusion? What arguments are available that counter the common-law approach used by the Court? How central to the Court's ultimate conclusion was the restraint on alienation doctrine? To what argument of Dr. Miles was it directed?

2. Did the Court consider whether a resale price maintenance agreement might produce procompetitive effects? Did it indicate whether any business justification might save an RPM agreement? Did it matter to the Court's reasoning whether the price restraint was initiated by the wholesalers or the manufacturer?

Consider the economic consequences of *Dr. Miles*. Does RPM imposed by a manufacturer have the same competitive effects as RPM instituted at the behest of a dealer cartel? In terms of antitrust policy, should the law draw distinctions between RPM imposed by the manufacturer as a means of increasing distribution efficiency and RPM which has the effect of facilitating either a manufacturers' or dealers' cartel? If a per se decisional process is utilized, could courts draw such a distinction? Can it necessarily be inferred from RPM supported by dealers that dealer collusion is present? Did Justice Hughes cite evidence *in his opinion* that would support a finding of dealer cartelization?

When *Dr. Miles* was decided, the drug industry was plagued by collusion. Trade associations of drug wholesalers and retailers had entered into agreements for the purpose of maintaining retail prices of patent and proprietary medicines. These price agreements were communicated to the manufacturers with the admonition that they "desist from selling to "aggressive cutters, or suppliers of cutters, when solicited to do so by the respective local [trade] associations." *Joyne v. Loder*, 149 F. 21, 25 (3d Cir. 1906). *See* H. Hovenkamp, *Enterprise and American Law 1836-1937*, ch. 25 (1991). If this evidence was a part of the record in *Dr. Miles*, could it be argued that the imposed RPM was a vertical substitute for and manifestation of a horizontal cartel, and therefore illegal?

But for the availability of RPM, how can a manufacturer encourage its dealers to invest in product marketing, service, and sales? Assuming that the free-rider condition exists, if a manufacturer was not able to enforce RPM wouldn't retail prices to the consumer be reduced, at least in the short run? What would you anticipate would be the long run effects of such a practice? Consider the effects on incentives that such market conduct might have.

3. Congress' reaction to *Dr. Miles* was critical. For a discussion of the congressional efforts to override it, see *Schwegmann Bros. v. Calvert Distillers Corp.*, 341 U.S. 384 (1951). In 1937 Congress passed the Miller-Tydings Fair Trade Amendment, ch. 690, 50 Stat. 693 (1937), which permitted states to authorize resale price maintenance agreements for branded commodities. State legislation thereafter was designed to insulate small businesses from price and marketing practices of large concerns that might be in a position, due to marketing economies, to offer products at discount. *See generally Old Dearborn Distrib. Co. v. Seagram-Distillers Corp.*, 299 U.S. 183 (1936) (upholding constitutionality of state fair trade laws). Minimum retail prices were approved under certain state "fair trade" laws so that small retail establishments might not face lower prices from larger, more efficient competitors. In those forty-six states that adopted fair trade laws under the Miller-Tydings Act, the effect of *Dr. Miles* was suspended.

The Supreme Court at first applied a strict interpretation to the Miller-Tydings exemptions. *See Schwegmann Bros. v. Calvert Distillers Corp.*, 341 U.S. 384 (1951). In reaction to this decision, Congress enacted through the McGuire Act of 1952, ch. 745 (66 Stat. 632), broader language permitting states to allow manufacturers to control retail pricing more pervasively. But the "fair trade" amendments never excluded horizontal price collusion from antitrust enforcement, nor did they exempt vertical price restrictions imposed by a manufacturer that was competing on the same level as the distributor or retailer against whom the RPM was in force. This "dual distribution" restraint was discussed by the Court in *United States v. McKesson & Robbins, Inc.*, 351 U.S. 305 (1956). The Court concluded that the issue was "whether the contracting parties compete with each other. If they do, the Miller-Tydings and McGuire Acts do not permit them to fix resale prices.... Since

[McKesson] competes 'at the same functional level' with each of the ... wholesalers with whom it has price-fixing agreements, the proviso prevents these agreements from falling within the statutory exemption." *Id.* at 313.

The suspension lasted almost forty years. In 1975, Congress, dissatisfied with the competitive effects of the state fair trade laws, repealed its 1937 approval of the fair trade legislation. Consumer Goods Pricing Act, Pub. L. No. 94-145, 89 Stat. 801 (codified at 15 U.S.C. § 45 (amending 15 U.S.C. §§ 1, 45)). As a result, vertical price restrictions again came within the reach of *Dr. Miles.*

4. In *California Retail Liquor Dealers Ass'n v. Midcal Aluminum, Inc.*, 445 U.S. 97 (1980), the Court reaffirmed "that resale price maintenance illegally restrains trade," but the Court continued to discuss vertical restraints in terms of "control." Justice Powell, writing for the Court and citing *Dr. Miles*, restated that "vertical control destroys horizontal competition as effectively as if wholesalers 'formed a combination and endeavored to establish the same restrictions by ... agreement with each other.'" Are you satisfied that this is the correct approach? By applying the per se decisionmaking style to vertical price restrictions, the Court withdraws discretion from the trial court to inquire into the particular utility of the commercial practice. What procompetitive results might be achieved by placing restrictions on retail price? What of the idea that price restraints will promote nonprice competition, such as service and/or product differentiation? Without an economic analysis of the particular restraint and market circumstances under which it is employed, it will be difficult for a court to predict whether a particular vertical price restraint is as pernicious as horizontal price agreements. Are you confident that a court will be able to weigh the divergent competitive consequences?

5. It has been suggested by many legal commentators that as an alternative to a broad prophylactic rule banning all RPM, the Court should weigh the competitive features of the vertical arrangement to determine its net competitive effect. This argument is based on the theory that vertical restraints such as RPM can be efficiency-enhancing as a means of promoting resaler services and avoiding free rider problems. The judicial inquiry should be flexible enough, this argument urges, to go beyond a mere investigation of who initiated the vertical restraint. In determining whether the restraint facilitated or had the potential to facilitate horizontal collusion, the Court could consider certain preconditions, such as the structure and conduct of the market, to determine whether there was significant concentration at the manufacturing level and whether substantial numbers of manufacturers were using RPM as a means to control resale prices. These preconditions are necessary, absent direct evidence of collusion, to demonstrate that the vertical restraint facilitated collusion. The same structural and conduct inquiry could be used at the distributor level to determine the horizontal effect.

The direction of the inquiry in each instance is aimed at determining the actual competitive conditions which existed before the restraint was imposed and the consequences of the restraint. In economic terms, the marketing objectives of the manufacturer and resaler may be quite different; thus, arguably, RPM should be viewed within each commercial context where it is employed. If the evidence demonstrates that the RPM facilitates or has the potential to facilitate cartelization because of specific structural characteristics and conduct, the practice should be characterized as unlawful, but only after a careful weighing of the market conditions. On the other hand, if the RPM is used to offset free riding by dealers, a per se analysis should not be applied. E.T. Sullivan & J. Harrison, *Understanding Antitrust and Its Economic Implications*, ch. 5 (3d ed. 1998); H. Hovenkamp, *Federal Antitrust Policy*, ch. 11 (1994); *see also* Posner, *The Rule of Reason and the Economic Approach: Reflections on the* Sylvania *Decision*, 45 U. Chi. L. Rev. 1 (1977).

6. Recent studies suggest both that RPM is not a very reliable way to facilitate collusion and that only a very small percentage of RPM prosecutions have involved collusion at either the dealer or supplier level. *See* Ornstein, *Resale Price Maintenance and Cartels*, 30 Antitrust Bull. 401 (1985). But for a strongly stated contrary opinion, *see* 8 P. Areeda, *Antitrust Law*, ch. 16, especially ¶ 1604 and specifically ¶ 1604a (1989).

The most widely accepted "efficiency" explanation for resale price maintenance is that it is used by suppliers of products that require point-of-sale services in order to prevent "free riding." Free riding occurs when a "cut-rate" dealer underprices a high service dealer by reducing point of sale services, such as trained personnel to demonstrate a product, working displays, consultation about the customer's needs, and so on. The presence of the cut-rate dealers encourages customers to go to the high service dealers to obtain their "education," and then to the cut-rate dealers to make their purchase at a lower price. The high service dealers will be able to stay in business only by cutting services themselves so that they can match the cut-rate dealers' prices. Soon none of the dealers of the product will be offering the efficient amount of point-of-sale services, and the total number of sales will decline.

Figure 1

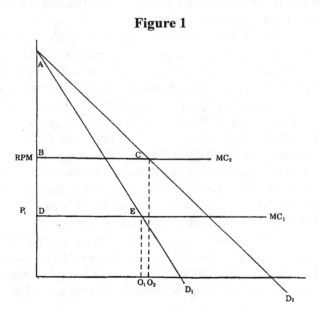

RPM forces *all* dealers to charge the same price. The (former) cut-rate dealer will no longer have a price advantage over the high service dealer, and will have to increase the number of services it provides if it is to continue making sales. As a result, the dealers will compete with each other, not by cutting price, but rather by offering increased point-of-sale services until the amount of these services rises to the optimal level. As a result, the number of sales can actually *increase*, even though the prevailing price is higher. *See* Telser, *Why Should Manufacturers Want Fair Trade?*, 3 J.L. & Econ. 86 (1960). Does this mean that RPM is in the best interest of consumers? Not necessarily. *See* Scherer, *The Economics of Vertical Restraints*, 52 Antitrust L.J. 687 (1983); Comanor, *Vertical Price-Fixing, Vertical Market Restrictions, and the New Antitrust Policy*, 98 Harv. L. Rev. 983 (1985). Consider the illustration. P_1, which is equal to MC_1, is the dealers' marginal cost and the resale price when dealers' prices are unregulated and few point-of-sale services are offered. D_1 is the demand curve for the product at that price. Suppose now that the supplier imposes RPM at level "RPM" on the figure. The dealers will now all charge price RPM. They will compete for sales by increasing the number of point-of-sale services, education, more expensive showrooms, etc., until their costs rise to MC_2, at which point they will once again be earning competitive returns. At the same time, however, the demand curve for the product will shift outward from D_1 to D_2, as demand increases in response to the increased number of point-of-sale services and other forms of dealer investment. Although MC_2 is higher than MC_1, output under RPM is actually higher than it was before RPM was in place, for the demand curve has shifted more than enough to make up the difference. Before RPM the manufacturer sold O_1 of the product; now it sells O_2.

As a general rule, an output increase is a good sign that a practice is efficient. In fact, some writers virtually equate output increases with efficiency. *E.g.*, Easterbrook, *Vertical Arrangements and the Rule of Reason*, 53 Antitrust L.J. 135 (1984). But the efficiency of a practice is generally equal to the amount of economic surplus that it creates — i.e., the sum of consumers' surplus and producers' surplus. In Figure 1, although output has increased under RPM, it appears that consumers' surplus has actually been reduced. Before RPM was in place consumers' surplus (or the difference between the collective value that consumers place on a product and the amount they must pay for it; for a review, see Chapter 2) equalled triangle A-D-E. Under RPM consumers' surplus is triangle A-B-C, which in this particular illustration is smaller than triangle A-D-E. Assuming the manufacturer is earning monopoly profits, its surplus is larger by the distance from O_1 to O_2 times the monopoly profits it is earning, but this may not be enough to offset the reduction in consumers' surplus. The dealers, which are in fierce competition with each other, are not earning a surplus, for they are competing away the higher retail price in increased point-of-sale services. As a result, RPM may be inefficient, *even* though it is being used to combat free riding, and even though supplier output is higher under RPM than it had been before.

Ever since Telser's seminal 1960 article cited above, advocates of the free-rider argument for RPM have generally assumed that demand curves D_1 (before RPM) and D_2 (under RPM) are parallel. This assumes that all customers place precisely the same value on the increased point-of-sale services that RPM produces. If demand curves D_1 and D_2 are parallel, RPM that increases output will also increase consumers' surplus. But as an empirical matter that assumption seems questionable.

Consider the market for personal computers, for example. Some "marginal" consumers will have to be educated about why they need a computer, what kind of computer they need, how to operate it, and so on. Other people — perhaps business firms that already own half a dozen personal computers and want to purchase some more — already know exactly what they need, and for them the point-of-sale services are a waste of money. Figure 1 is drawn on the more realistic assumption that different consumers value point-of-sale services by different amounts, and that "marginal" consumers (those who place the lowest value on the product) are those whose surplus will increase the most from the point-of-sale services. That is, marginal consumers are those most in need of the educational and other services supplied by the dealer. Once this assumption is made, it can no longer be shown that any particular instance of RPM is efficient, even if it increases output. Some are and some are not.

Finally, note that consumers who do not place a high value on point-of-sale services can be forced to pay for them only if there are no lower priced alternatives to which they can turn. This would be true if (1) the manufacturer imposing RPM had substantial market power; or (2) all (or nearly all) manufacturers in the market were using RPM. These assumptions suggest that as a matter of economic efficiency RPM ought to be evaluated under the rule of reason, instead of the current per se rule, and that a showing of market power would be important.

7. Other commentators have argued that the Court should retain the conclusive presumption of illegality in RPM cases without engaging in a detailed, sweeping economic and factual analysis. The argument is based on two theories of cartelization. First, as the Court reasoned in *Dr. Miles*, the disadvantage of RPM is the same whether initiated by a dealer cartel or a manufacturer: intrabrand competition is restrained. Moreover, a dealer cartel has an effect at the manufacturing level because once the cartel is in place with the effect of inhibiting a pass-on of a price cut, there is no advantage to the manufacturer to cut price, and therefore profits could be shared. The dealer cartel is thus a facilitating device for a resulting manufacturing cartel. Second, the vertical restraint can be used initially by manufacturers to facilitate collusion among themselves by controlling prices at the retail level rather than at a selling point upstream. Thus, RPM can also be used to advance a manufacturer's cartel. In short, these theories suggest that vertical price setting is often used as a substitute for a horizontal cartel. *See generally* Pitofsky, *In Defense of Discounters: The No-Frills Case for a Per Se Rule Against Vertical Price Fixing*, 71 Geo. L.J. 1487 (1983); Comanor, *Vertical*

Price-Fixing, Vertical Market Restrictions and the New Antitrust Policy, 95 Harv. L. Rev. 983 (1985). *Compare* Flynn, *The "Is" and "Ought" of Vertical Restraints After Monsanto Co. v. Spray-Rite Service Corp.*, 71 Cornell L. Rev. 1095 (1986), *with* Goldberg, *The Free Rider Problem, Imperfect Pricing and Economics of Retailing Services*, 79 Nw. L. Rev. 736 (1984).

2. CONSIGNMENT CONTRACTS AS A MEANS TO CONTROL VERTICAL PRICE

Cases after *Dr. Miles* seem not to make the legality of RPM depend on whether the product was patented, trademarked, copyrighted, or semi-finished. *See, e.g., United States v. Univis Lens Co.*, 316 U.S. 241 (1942) (patented); *United States v. Sealy, Inc.*, 388 U.S. 350, 356 n.3 (1967) (trademark); *and see Bobbs-Merrill Co. v. Straus*, 210 U.S. 339 (1908) (copyright). But the question left open by *Dr. Miles* — whether the rule applied to a manufacturer that transferred the product through a consignment or agency relationship rather than an outright sale — was addressed in 1926 in *United States v. General Elec. Co.*, 272 U.S. 476 (1926). General Electric distributed lamps to wholesalers and dealers, which acted as agents for the company. Under the theory that these company agents were the first sellers of the product, General Electric attempted to control the price of the lamps as they were sold to customers. The Department of Justice challenged this arrangement as a contrived scheme to avoid *Dr. Miles*. The Supreme Court, speaking through Chief Justice Taft, disagreed.

> We are of opinion, therefore, that there is nothing as a matter of principle, or in the authorities, which requires us to hold that genuine contracts of agency like those before us, however comprehensive as a mass or whole in their effect, are violations of the Anti-Trust Act. The owner of an article, patented or otherwise, is not violating the common law or the Anti-Trust law, by seeking to dispose of his article directly to the consumer and fixing the price by which his agents transfer the title from him directly to such consumer.

272 U.S. at 488. As one would expect, after *General Electric* the consignment contract became a favored method by which suppliers could control the product price through distribution to the retail seller. Under the consignment arrangement, dealers were considered agents of the manufacturer (consignor), who would retain title to the products until sold at retail. Not until 1964 did the Supreme Court reevaluate *General Electric* in light of the pervasive use of consignment contracts as a means to avoid the *Dr. Miles* proscription against RPM.

SIMPSON V. UNION OIL CO.

377 U.S. 13 (1964)

JUSTICE DOUGLAS delivered the opinion of the Court.

This is a suit for damages under § 4 of the Clayton Act, for violation of §§ 1 and 2 of the Sherman Act. The complaint grows out of a so-called retail dealer "consignment" agreement which, it is alleged, Union Oil requires lessees of its retail outlets to sign, of which Simpson was one. The "consignment" agreement is for one year and thereafter until canceled, is terminable by either party at the end of any year and, by its terms, ceases upon any termination of the lease. The lease is also for one year; and it is alleged that it is used to police the retail prices charged by the consignees, renewals not being made if the conditions prescribed by the company are not met. The company, pursuant to the "consignment" agreement, sets the prices at which the retailer sells the gasoline. While "title" to the consigned gasoline "shall remain in Consignor until sold by Consignee," and while the company pays all property taxes on all gasoline in possession of Simpson, he must carry personal liability and property damage insurance by reason of the "consigned" gasoline and is responsible for all losses of the "consigned" gasoline in his possession, save for specified acts of God. Simpson is compensated by a minimum commission and pays all the costs of operation in the familiar manner.

The retail price fixed by the company for the gasoline during the period in question was 29.9 cents per gallon; and Simpson, despite the company's demand that he adhere to the authorized price, sold it at 27.9 cents, allegedly to meet a competitive price. Solely because Simpson sold gasoline below the fixed price, Union Oil refused to renew the lease; termination of the "consignment" agreement ensued; and this suit was filed. The terms of the lease and "consignment" agreement are not in dispute nor the method of their application in this case. The interstate character of Union Oil's business is conceded, as is the extensive use by it of the lease-consignment agreement in eight western States.[1]

After two pretrial hearings, the company moved for a summary judgment. Simpson moved for a partial summary judgment — that the consignment lease program is in violation of §§ 1 and 2 of the Sherman Act. The District Court, concluding that "all the factual disputes" had been eliminated from the case, entertained the motions. The District Court granted the company's motion and denied Simpson's, holding as to the latter that he had not established a violation of the Sherman Act and, even assuming such a violation, that he had not suffered any actionable damage. The Court of Appeals affirmed. While it assumed that there were triable issues of law, it concluded that Simpson suffered no actionable wrong or damage, 311 F.2d 764....

We disagree with the Court of Appeals that there is no actionable wrong or damage if a Sherman Act violation is assumed. If the "consignment" agreement achieves resale price maintenance in violation of the Sherman Act, it and the

---

[1] As of December 31, 1957, Union Oil supplied gasoline to 4,133 retail stations in the eight western States of California, Washington, Oregon, Nevada, Arizona, Montana, Utah and Idaho. Of that figure, 2,003 stations were owned or leased by Union Oil and, in turn, leased or subleased to an independent retailer; 14 were company-operated training stations; and the remaining 2,116 stations were owned by the retailer or leased by him from third persons. Union Oil had "consignment" agreements as of that date with 1,978 (99%) of the lessee-retailers and with 1,327 (63%) of the nonlessee-retailers.

lease are being used to injure interstate commerce by depriving independent dealers of the exercise of free judgment whether to become consignees at all, or remain consignees, and, in any event, to sell at competitive prices. The fact that a retailer can refuse to deal does not give the supplier immunity if the arrangement is one of those schemes condemned by the antitrust laws.

....

We made clear in *United States v. Parke, Davis & Co.*, 362 U.S. 29, that a supplier may not use coercion on its retail outlets to achieve resale price maintenance. We reiterate that view, adding that it matters not what the coercive device is. *United States v. Colgate*, 250 U.S. 300, as explained in *Parke, Davis*, 362 U.S., at 37, was a case where there was assumed to be no agreement to maintain retail prices. Here we have such an agreement; it is used coercively, and, it promises to be equally if not more effective in maintaining gasoline prices than were the *Parke, Davis* techniques in fixing monopoly prices on drugs.

Consignments perform an important function in trade and commerce, and their integrity has been recognized by many courts, including this one. Yet consignments, though useful in allocating risks between the parties and determining their rights *inter se*, do not necessarily control the rights of others, whether they be creditors or sovereigns. Thus the device has been extensively regulated by the States....

....

We are enlightened on present-day marketing methods by recent congressional investigations. In the automobile field the price is "the manufacturer's suggested retail price," not a price coercively exacted; nor do automobiles go on consignment; they are sold. Resale price maintenance of gasoline through the "consignment" device is increasing. The "consignment" device in the gasoline field is used for resale price maintenance. The theory and practice of gasoline price fixing in vogue under the "consignment" agreement has been well exposed by Congress. A Union Oil official in recent testimony before a House Committee on Small Business explained the price mechanism:

> Mr. Roosevelt. Who sets the price in your consignment station, dealer consignment station?
> Mr. Rath. We do.
> Mr. Roosevelt. You do?
> Mr. Rath. Yes. We do it on this basis: You see, he is paid a commission to sell these products for us. Now, we go out into the market area and find out what the competitive major price is, what that level is, and we set our house-brand price at that.

Dealers, like Simpson, are independent businessmen; and they have all or most of the indicia of entrepreneurs, except for price fixing. The risk of loss of the gasoline is on them, apart from acts of God. Their return is affected by the rise and fall in the market price, their commissions declining as retail prices drop. Practically the only power they have to be wholly independent businessmen, whose service depends on their own initiative and enterprise, is taken from them by the proviso that they must sell their gasoline at prices fixed by Union Oil. By reason of the lease and "consignment" agreement dealers are coercively laced into an arrangement under which their supplier is able to impose noncompetitive prices on thousands of persons whose prices otherwise might be competitive. The evil of this resale price maintenance program, like that of the requirements contracts held illegal ... is its inexorable potentiality for and even certainty in destroying competition in retail sales of gasoline by these nominal "consignees" who are in reality small struggling competitors seeking retail gas customers.

As we have said, an owner of an article may send it to a dealer who may in turn undertake to sell it only at a price determined by the owner. There is nothing illegal about that arrangement. When, however, a "consignment" device is used to cover a vast gasoline distribution system, fixing prices through many retail outlets, the antitrust laws prevent calling the "consignment" an agency, for then the end result of *United States v. Socony-Vacuum Oil Co.*, would be avoided merely by clever manipulation of words, not by differences in substance. The present, coercive "consignment" device, if successful against challenge under the antitrust laws, furnishes a wooden formula for administering prices on a vast scale.

....

The Court in the *General Electric* case did not restrict its ruling to patented articles; it indeed said that the use of the consignment device was available to the owners of articles "patented or otherwise."... But whatever may be said of the *General Electric* case on its special facts, involving patents, it is not apposite to the special facts here.

To allow Union Oil to achieve price fixing in this vast distribution system through this "consignment" device would be to make legality for antitrust purposes turn on clever draftsmanship. We refuse to let a matter so vital to a competitive system rest on such easy manipulation.

Hence on the issue of resale price maintenance under the Sherman Act there is nothing left to try, for there was an agreement for resale price maintenance, coercively employed.

The case must be remanded for a hearing on all the other issues in the case, including those raised under the McGuire Act, 66 Stat. 631, 15 U. S. C. § 45, and the damages, if any, suffered. We intimate no views on any other issue; we hold only that resale price maintenance through the present, coercive type of "consignment" agreement is illegal under the antitrust laws, and that petitioner suffered actionable wrong or damage....

Reversed and remanded.

[JUSTICE HARLAN took no part in the decision; JUSTICES BRENNAN, GOLDBERG, and STEWART dissented, concluding that the case should not have been decided on motion for summary judgment. JUSTICE STEWART also was unconvinced that the majority opinion adequately distinguished *General Electric*: "Instead of expressly overruling *General Electric*, however, the Court seeks to distinguish that case upon the specious ground that its underpinnings rest on patent law."]

NOTES AND QUESTIONS

1. After *Simpson*, what remains of the *General Electric* holding? Is the Court's condemnation of RPM in *Simpson* consistent with the economic rationale against RPM set forth in *Dr. Miles*?

Identify the source of Justice Douglas' discontent with the consignment/agency relationship. It seems to center on whether a supplier has economic leverage over its dealers. Is there authority in prior case law for the protection of small businesses where there is an inequitable bargaining power with suppliers? Under Justice Douglas' approach how should the "independence" of the dealer be defined so as to come within the protection of the law afforded by *Simpson*?

From the manufacturer's viewpoint, what distributional options remain after *Simpson* if the manufacturer desires to control dealer price cutting that may injure the product image? If *Simpson* forces manufacturers to buy or build their own retail outlets, has the independence of the local retailer been preserved? Finally, consider how much integration will be required by a manufacturer under *Simpson* before the sale to the consumer will be considered the first sale, and thus free of RPM limitations.

2. *Simpson* discussed limitations on consignment agreements with dealers as a means to circumvent the per se rule of illegality for RPM arrangements. Consider whether a supplier can dictate the retail price to a broker who merely takes orders from the retailer, forwards them to the supplier, and has the supplier ship the order directly to the retailer. Does this brokerage arrangement constitute under *Simpson* a vertical price fixing agreement between the supplier and broker? The Seventh Circuit has answered in the negative. *Morrison v. Murray Biscuit Co.*, 797 F.2d 1430 (7th Cir. 1986). Judge Posner reasoned that the broker, described above, is merely an "order taker," whose costs are a trivial fraction of the product's total cost "so that to make him determine the final price to charge the consumer would be telling the tail to wag its dog." The supplier can dictate to the sale agent (broker) what price to charge. Judge Posner opined that:

> Efficiency would not be promoted by a rule that forbade principals to tell their agents at what price to sell the principal's product unless the agent was an employee. Principals would either convert their sales agents from independent contractors to employees or give their sales agents a discretion over price that the agents, for lack of information and expertise, would not be in a position to exercise intelligently. Neither result would further the goals of antitrust law; nor can it seriously be argued that the ancient and ubiquitous practice of principals' telling their agents what price to charge the consumer is just some massive evasion of the rule against price fixing. Brokerage is no more a device for evading the Sherman Act than is telling one's sales clerk what price to mark on a bag of sugar rather than letting him decide for himself.

Id. at 1437. Thus the characterization of the middleperson as having the capacity and incentive to set resale prices, as opposed to being a mere order taker, is critical to the antitrust conclusion.

3. The term "agency" has a somewhat different meaning for the law of RPM than it does in other contexts, such as determining whether a person and a firm have conspiratorial capacity under the Supreme Court's *Copperweld* decision (see Chapter 4, Section I.C5, *supra*). For example, the independent travel agency that sells tickets for an airline is an "agent" of the airline rather than an independent reseller, and thus the airline can legally dictate the price at which the tickets are to be sold. *See Illinois Corporate Travel v. American Airlines*, 806 F.2d 722 (7th Cir. 1986). But the travel agency and the airline would not become a single entity for all purposes, would they?

This is simply another way of noting that the "agency" question in resale price maintenance cases looks at a particular transaction, while *Copperweld* looks at the structural relationship between the two entities. For example, if a supplier sold milk to an independent grocery store for resale, but gave it bread on consignment, a claim of resale price maintenance with respect to the bread would be defeated by the defense that the store was merely acting as "agent" for the supplier. But with respect to sales of the milk, the store and its supplier would continue to have the capacity to conspire, whether for the law of resale price maintenance or some other purpose. For example, *see Hardwick v. Nu-Way Oil Co.*, 589 F.2d 806, 809-10 (5th Cir.), *cert. denied*, 444 U.S. 836 (1979), holding that a convenience store operator was an "agent" when making gasoline sales but an independent businesswoman when making grocery sales.

3. UNILATERAL REFUSAL TO DEAL AS A MEANS TO ENFORCE VERTICAL PRICE MAINTENANCE: THE *COLGATE* DOCTRINE

Do the cases studied to this point permit a manufacturer to *recommend* resale prices? Can the price recommendations be followed up with sanctions against the dealer who fails to comply? In terms of relevancy, what role might evidence of coercive effect on a dealer, either directly or indirectly, have in establishing a Sherman Act violation? These issues are considered by the following cases in this subsection, concerning the legality of a manufacturer's refusal to deal because a dealer failed to comply with a RPM.

UNITED STATES V. COLGATE & CO.

250 U.S. 300 (1919)

JUSTICE McREYNOLDS delivered the opinion of the Court.

The indictment runs only against Colgate & Company, a corporation engaged in manufacturing soap and toilet articles and selling them throughout the Union. It makes no reference to monopoly, and proceeds solely upon the theory of an unlawful combination.... [The indictment charges that]

During the aforesaid period of time, within the said eastern district of Virginia and throughout the United States, the defendant knowingly and unlawfully created and engaged in a combination with said wholesale and retail dealers, in the eastern district of Virginia and throughout the United States, for the purpose and with the effect of procuring adherence on the part of such dealers (in reselling such products sold to them as aforesaid) to resale prices fixed by the defendant, and of preventing such dealers from reselling such products at lower prices, thus suppressing competition amongst such wholesale dealers, and amongst such retail dealers, in restraint of the aforesaid trade and commerce among the several States, in violation of the act entitled "An Act to protect trade and commerce against unlawful restraints and monopolies," approved July 2, 1890.

Following this is a summary of things done to carry out the purposes of the combination: Distribution among dealers of letters, telegrams, circulars and lists showing uniform prices to be charged; urging them to adhere to such prices and notices, stating that no sales would be made to those who did not; requests, often complied with, for information concerning dealers who had departed from specified prices; investigation and discovery of those not adhering thereto and placing their names upon "suspended lists"; requests to offending dealers for assurances and promises of future adherence to prices, which were often given; uniform refusals to sell to any who failed to give the same; sales to those who did; similar assurances and promises required of, and given by, other dealers followed by sales to them; unrestricted sales to dealers with established accounts who had observed specified prices, etc.

. . . .

Our problem is to ascertain, as accurately as may be, what interpretation the trial court placed upon the indictment — not to interpret it ourselves; and then to determine whether, so construed, it fairly charges violation of the Sherman Act. Counsel for the Government maintain, in effect, that, as so interpreted, the indictment adequately charges an unlawful combination (within the doctrine of *Dr. Miles Medical Co. v. Park & Sons Co.*, 220 U.S. 373) resulting from restrictive agreements between defendant and sundry dealers whereby the latter obligated themselves not to resell except at agreed prices....

Considering all said in the opinion (notwithstanding some serious doubts) we are unable to accept the construction placed upon it by the Government. We cannot, *e.g.*, wholly disregard the statement that "The retailer, after buying, could, if he chose, give away his purchase, or sell it at any price he saw fit, or not sell it at all; his course in these respects being affected only by the fact that he might by his action incur the displeasure of the manufacturer, who could refuse to make further sales to him, as he had the undoubted right to do." And we must conclude that, as interpreted below, the indictment does not charge Colgate & Company with selling its products to dealers under agreements which obligated the latter not to resell except at prices fixed by the company.

....

The purpose of the Sherman Act is to prohibit monopolies, contracts and combinations which probably would unduly interfere with the free exercise of their rights by those engaged, or who wish to engage, in trade and commerce — in a word to preserve the right of freedom to trade. In the absence of any purpose to create or maintain a monopoly, the act does not restrict the long recognized right of trader or manufacturer engaged in an entirely private business, freely to exercise his own independent discretion as to parties with whom he will deal. And, of course, he may announce in advance the circumstances under which he will refuse to sell....

Affirmed.

NOTES AND QUESTIONS

1. Did the indictment charge an agreement? What role did this omission play in the decision? Consider whether the Court could have inferred a tacit agreement from the price announcement and acquiescence. Recall the *Interstate Circuit* theory of prosecution discussed in Chapter 4. *See generally FTC v. Beechnut Packing Co.*, 257 U.S. 441 (1922). What limitations did the Court place on its holding? Under what circumstances might this same conduct be considered a violation of the Sherman Act? Is the *Colgate* doctrine logically consistent with *Dr. Miles*?

2. Consider what class of plaintiffs could bring a suit under the theory of an illegal RPM when there had been a vertical refusal to deal. Could a retailer who was terminated after refusing to adhere to the RPM bring suit? What about a retailer who initially consented to the RPM but who later ceased adhering to the RPM? Could a customer of a retailer who adhered to the RPM sue? *See generally Albrecht v. Herald Co.*, 390 U.S. 145 (1968).

3. The *Colgate* doctrine implied that a manufacturer (or franchisor) could avoid the limitations of *Dr. Miles* by not entering into contracts to maintain vertical prices. As long as no maintenance agreement existed, the manufacturer could merely, though unilaterally, refuse to deal with a dealer who declined to adhere to the suggested price. In this limited manner, the manufacturer could attempt to influence pricing behavior of its dealers or franchisees. The line drawing seems finely tuned. Interestingly, Charles Evans Hughes, who wrote the majority opinion in *Dr. Miles*, was counsel for Colgate.

4. In *United States v. Parke, Davis & Co.*, 362 U.S. 29 (1960), a manufacturer informed wholesalers that their supply would be terminated if they sold for less than the announced wholesale price or if they dealt with retailers who resold for less than the manufacturer's suggested retail price. The Court declared that conduct to be outside *Colgate's* protection. The Court reasoned that "an unlawful combination is not just as arises from a price maintenance agreement, express or implied, such a combination is also organized if the producer secures adherence to his prices by means which go beyond his mere declination to a customer who will not observe his announced policy."

Parke, Davis narrowed the channel through which a supplier could recommend vertical prices. How much affirmative action, in addition to an announcement of a price and a unilateral refusal to deal, is necessary to trigger a finding of per se illegality?

4. VERTICAL MAXIMUM PRICE FIXING

In *Albrecht v. Herald Co.*, 390 U.S. 145 (1968), a newspaper publisher attempted to set the *maximum* price at which independent carriers sold at retail. The Court held that a combination in restraint of trade existed when the newspaper combined with a subscription solicitor and route carrier to *coerce* the independent carrier into following the newspaper's suggested RPM. The Court reasoned as follows:

> If a combination arose when Parke Davis threatened its wholesalers with termination unless they put pressure on their retail customers, then there can be no doubt that a combination arose between [the newspaper and subscription solicitor and route carrier] to force petitioner to conform to the advertised retail price. When respondent learned that petitioner was overcharging, it hired Milne to solicit customers away from petitioner in order to get petitioner to reduce his price. It was through the efforts of Milne, as well as because of respondent's letter to petitioner's customers, that about 300 customers were obtained for Kroner. Milne's purpose was undoubtedly to earn its fee, but it was aware that the aim of the solicitation campaign was to force petitioner to lower his price. Kroner knew that respondent was giving him the customer list as part of a program to get petitioner to conform to the advertised price, and he knew that he might have to return the customers if petitioner ultimately complied with respondent's demands. He undertook to deliver papers at the suggested price and materially aided in the accomplishment of respondent's plan. Given the uncontradicted facts recited by the Court of Appeals, there was a combination within the meaning of § 1 between respondent, Milne, and Kroner, and the Court of Appeals erred in holding to the contrary.

Why would a manufacturer impose maximum resale price maintenance on its retail outlets? Actually, the explanation for that is far simpler than is the explanation for minimum RPM. If a retailer has any market power at all, it will be able to maximize its profits by reducing output below the competitive level. This monopoly pricing will generate a monopoly profit — but the profit will go to the retailer, not to the manufacturer. Any firm, even a monopolist, is best off if all other firms in the distribution chain are behaving competitively. This is easy to see intuitively if you look at backward integration. If a monopolist manufacturing aluminum must purchase its bauxite, a necessary ingredient, from another monopolist at $2.00 per pound, the monopolist will make less money than if it can purchase bauxite competitively at $1.50 per pound. Even the monopolist wants to deal on the market with people who behave like competitors. The same concept applies to forward integration: if the retail store is making a 25% monopoly profit, that is money that could be going into the hands of the manufacturer. *See* 3A P. Areeda & H. Hovenkamp, *Antitrust Law*, Ch. 7D-1 (rev. ed. 1996).

The extreme case is where the retailers are natural monopolists, as they were in *Albrecht.* A newspaper delivery route is a natural monopoly — it is far cheaper for one person to travel the route than it is for two to travel it and split the deliveries. The carriers in *Albrecht* had exclusive territories. 390 U.S. at 147. This gave the carriers an incentive to sell newspaper subscriptions at a monopoly price, with the result that circulation along the routes declined. The newspaper lost money from the carriers' exercise of monopoly power in two different ways: first, they lost money from reduced circulation; second, and much more significantly, they lost advertising revenues, because advertising rates are based on circulation. *See* Hovenkamp, *Vertical Integration by the Newspaper Monopolist*, 69 Iowa L. Rev. 45 (1984).

In 1997 the Supreme Court overruled *Albrecht*, holding that vertical price fixing should be evaluated under the rule of reason.

STATE OIL COMPANY V. KHAN

118 S. Ct. 275 (1997)

JUSTICE O'CONNOR delivered the opinion of the Court.

Under § 1 of the Sherman Act, "[e]very contract, combination ..., or conspiracy, in restraint of trade" is illegal. In *Albrecht v. Herald Co.*, 390 U.S. 145, (1968), this Court held that vertical maximum price fixing is a per se violation of that statute. In this case, we are asked to reconsider that decision in light of subsequent decisions of this Court. We conclude that *Albrecht* should be overruled.

I

Respondents, Barkat U. Khan and his corporation, entered into an agreement with petitioner, State Oil Company, to lease and operate a gas station and convenience store owned by State Oil. The agreement provided that respondents would obtain the station's gasoline supply from State Oil at a price equal to a suggested retail price set by State Oil, less a margin of 3.25 cents per gallon. Under the agreement, respondents could charge any amount for gasoline sold to the station's customers, but if the price charged was higher than State Oil's suggested retail price, the excess was to be rebated to State Oil. Respondents could sell gasoline for less than State Oil's suggested retail price, but any such decrease would reduce their 3.25 cents-per-gallon margin.

About a year after respondents began operating the gas station, they fell behind in lease payments. State Oil then gave notice of its intent to terminate the agreement and commenced a state court proceeding to evict respondents. At State Oil's request, the state court appointed a receiver to operate the gas station. The receiver operated the station for several months without being subject to the price restraints in respondents' agreement with State Oil. According to respondents, the receiver obtained an overall profit margin in excess of 3.25 cents per gallon by lowering the price of regular-grade gasoline and raising the price of premium grades.

Respondents sued State Oil ... alleging in part that State Oil had engaged in price fixing in violation of § 1 of the Sherman Act by preventing respondents from raising or lowering retail gas prices. According to the complaint, but for the agreement with State Oil, respondents could have charged different prices based on the grades of gasoline, in the same way that the receiver had, thereby achieving increased sales and profits. State Oil responded that the agreement did not actually prevent respondents from setting gasoline prices, and that, in substance, respondents did not allege a violation of antitrust laws by their claim that State Oil's suggested retail price was not optimal.

The District Court found that the allegations in the complaint did not state a per se violation of the Sherman Act because they did not establish the sort of "manifestly anticompetitive implications or pernicious effect on competition" that would justify per se prohibition of State Oil's conduct. Subsequently, in ruling on cross-motions for summary judgment, the District Court concluded that respondents had failed to demonstrate antitrust injury or harm to competition. The District Court held that respondents had not shown that a difference in gasoline pricing would have increased the station's sales; nor had they shown that State Oil had market power or that its pricing provisions affected competition in a relevant market. Accordingly, the District Court entered summary judgment for State Oil on respondents' Sherman Act claim.

The Court of Appeals for the Seventh Circuit reversed. 93 F.3d 1358 (1996). The court first noted that the agreement between respondents and State Oil did indeed fix maximum gasoline prices by making it "worthless" for respondents to exceed the suggested retail prices. *Id.* at 1360. After reviewing legal and economic aspects of price fixing, the court concluded that State Oil's pricing scheme was a per se antitrust violation under *Albrecht v. Herald Co.* Although the Court of Appeals characterized *Albrecht* as "unsound when decided" and "inconsistent with later decisions" of this Court, it felt constrained to follow that decision. 93 F.3d, at 1363. In light of *Albrecht* and *Atlantic Richfield Co. v. USA Petroleum Co.*, 495 U.S. 328 (1990) (ARCO), the court found that respondents could have suffered antitrust injury from not being able to adjust gasoline prices.

We granted certiorari to consider two questions, whether State Oil's conduct constitutes a per se violation of the Sherman Act and whether respondents are entitled to recover damages based on that conduct.

II

A

Although the Sherman Act, by its terms, prohibits every agreement "in restraint of trade," this Court has long recognized that Congress intended to outlaw only unreasonable restraints.... As a consequence, most antitrust claims are analyzed under a "rule of reason," according to which the finder of fact must decide whether the questioned practice imposes an unreasonable restraint on competition, taking into account a variety of factors, including specific information about the relevant business, its condition before and after the restraint was imposed, and the restraint's history, nature, and effect....

Some types of restraints, however, have such predictable and pernicious anti-competitive effect, and such limited potential for procompetitive benefit, that they are deemed unlawful per se.... Per se treatment is appropriate "[o]nce experience with a particular kind of restraint enables the Court to predict with confidence that the rule of reason will condemn it...." Thus, we have expressed reluctance to adopt per se rules with regard to "restraints imposed in the context of business relationships where the economic impact of certain practices is not immediately obvious...."

A review of this Court's decisions leading up to and beyond *Albrecht* is relevant to our assessment of the continuing validity of the per se rule established in *Albrecht*. Beginning with *Dr. Miles Medical Co. v. John D. Park & Sons Co.*, 220 U.S. 373 (1911), the Court recognized the illegality of agreements under which manufacturers or suppliers set the minimum resale prices to be charged by their distributors. By 1940, the Court broadly declared all business combinations "formed for the purpose and with the effect of raising, depressing, fixing, pegging, or stabilizing the price of a commodity in interstate or foreign commerce" illegal per se. *United States v. Socony-Vacuum Oil Co.*, 310 U.S. 150 (1940). Accordingly, the Court condemned an agreement between two affiliated liquor distillers to limit the maximum price charged by retailers in *Kiefer-Stewart Co. v. Joseph E. Seagram & Sons, Inc.*, 340 U.S. 211 (1951), noting that agreements to fix maximum prices, "no less than those to fix minimum prices, cripple the freedom of traders and thereby restrain their ability to sell in accordance with their own judgment." Id. at 213.

In subsequent cases, the Court's attention turned to arrangements through which suppliers imposed restrictions on dealers with respect to matters other than resale price. In *White Motor Co. v. United States*, 372 U.S. 253 (1963), the Court considered the validity of a manufacturer's assignment of exclusive territories to its distributors and dealers. The Court determined that too little was known about the competitive impact of such vertical limitations to warrant treating them as per se unlawful. Four years later, in *United States v. Arnold, Schwinn & Co.*, 388 U.S. 365 (1967), the Court reconsidered the status of exclusive dealer territories and held that, upon the transfer of title to goods to a distributor, a supplier's imposition of territorial restrictions on the distributor was "so obviously destructive of competition" as to constitute a per se violation of the Sherman Act. In *Schwinn*, the Court acknowledged that some vertical restrictions, such as the conferral of territorial rights or franchises, could have procompetitive benefits by allowing smaller enterprises to compete, and that such restrictions might avert vertical integration in the distribution process. The Court drew the line, however, at permitting manufacturers to control product marketing once dominion over the goods had passed to dealers.

Albrecht, decided the following Term, involved a newspaper publisher who had granted exclusive territories to independent carriers subject to their adherence to a maximum price on resale of the newspapers to the public. Influenced by its decisions in *Socony-Vacuum*, *Kiefer-Stewart*, and *Schwinn*, the Court concluded that it was per se unlawful for the publisher to fix the maximum resale price of its newspapers. The Court acknowledged that "[m]aximum and minimum price fixing may have different consequences in many situations," but nonetheless condemned maximum price fixing for "substituting the perhaps erroneous judgment of a seller for the forces of the competitive market." Id. at 152.

Albrecht was animated in part by the fear that vertical maximum price fixing could allow suppliers to discriminate against certain dealers, restrict the services that dealers could afford to offer customers, or disguise minimum price fixing schemes. The Court rejected the notion (both on the record of that case and in the abstract) that, because the newspaper publisher "granted exclusive territories, a price ceiling was necessary to protect the public from price gouging by dealers who had monopoly power in their own territories." Id. at 153.

In a vigorous dissent, Justice Harlan asserted that the majority had erred in equating the effects of maximum and minimum price fixing. Justice Harlan pointed out that, because the majority was establishing a per se rule, the proper inquiry was "not whether dictation of maximum prices is ever illegal, but whether it is always illegal." Id. at 165-166. He also faulted the majority for conclusively listing "certain unfortunate consequences that maximum price dictation might have in other cases," even as it rejected evidence that the publisher's practice of fixing maximum prices counteracted potentially anticompetitive actions by its distributors. Justice Stewart also dissented, asserting that the publisher's maximum price fixing scheme should be properly viewed as promoting competition, because it protected consumers from dealers such as Albrecht, who, as "the only person who could sell for home delivery the city's only daily morning newspaper," was "a monopolist within his own territory." Id. at 168.

Nine years later, in *Continental T.V., Inc. v. GTE Sylvania Inc.*, 433 U.S. 36 (1977), the Court overruled *Schwinn*, thereby rejecting application of a per se rule in the context of vertical nonprice restrictions. The Court acknowledged the principle of stare decisis, but explained that the need for clarification in the law justified reconsideration of *Schwinn*:

Since its announcement, *Schwinn* has been the subject of continuing controversy and confusion, both in the scholarly journals and in the federal courts. The great weight of scholarly opinion has been critical of the decision, and a number of the federal courts confronted with analogous vertical restrictions have sought to limit its reach. In our view, the experience of the past 10 years should be brought to bear on this subject of considerable commercial importance. 433 U.S., at 47-49 (footnotes omitted).

In *GTE Sylvania*, the Court declined to comment on *Albrecht*'s per se treatment of vertical maximum price restrictions, noting that the issue "involve[d] significantly different questions of analysis and policy." 433 U.S., at 51, n. 18. Subsequent decisions of the Court, however, have hinted that the analytical underpinnings of *Albrecht* were substantially weakened by *GTE Sylvania*. We noted in Maricopa County that vertical restraints are generally more defensible than horizontal restraints. See 457 U.S., at 348, n. 18. And we explained in *324 Liquor Corp. v. Duffy*, 479 U.S. 335 (1987), that decisions such as *GTE Sylvania* "recognize the possibility that a vertical restraint imposed by a single manufacturer or wholesaler may stimulate interbrand competition even as it reduces intrabrand competition."

Most recently, in *ARCO*, 495 U.S. 328 (1990), although *Albrecht*'s continuing validity was not squarely before the Court, some disfavor with that decision was signaled by our statement that we would "assume, arguendo, that *Albrecht* correctly held that vertical, maximum price fixing is subject to the per se rule." 495 U.S., at 335, n. 5. More significantly, we specifically acknowledged that vertical maximum price fixing "may have procompetitive interbrand effects," and pointed out that, in the wake of *GTE Sylvania*, "[t]he procompetitive potential of a vertical maximum price restraint is more evident … than it was when *Albrecht* was decided, because exclusive territorial arrangements and other nonprice restrictions were unlawful per se in 1968." 495 U.S., at 344, n. 13 (citing several commentators identifying procompetitive effects of vertical maximum price fixing, including, e.g., P. Areeda & H. Hovenkamp, *Antitrust Law* ¶ 340.30b, p. 378, n. 24 (1988 Supp.); Blair & Harrison, *Rethinking Antitrust Injury*, 42 Vand. L. Rev. 1539, 1553 (1989); Easterbrook, *Maximum Price Fixing*, 48 U. Chi. L. Rev. 886, 887-890 (1981)).

B

Thus, our reconsideration of *Albrecht*'s continuing validity is informed by several of our decisions, as well as a considerable body of scholarship discussing the effects of vertical restraints. Our analysis is also guided by our general view that the primary purpose of the antitrust laws is to protect interbrand competition.... "Low prices," we have explained, "benefit consumers regardless of how those prices are set, and so long as they are above predatory levels, they do not threaten competition." *ARCO*, supra, at 340. Our interpretation of the Sherman Act also incorporates the notion that condemnation of practices resulting in lower prices to consumers is "especially costly" because "cutting prices in order to increase business often is the very essence of competition...."

So informed, we find it difficult to maintain that vertically-imposed maximum prices could harm consumers or competition to the extent necessary to justify their per se invalidation. As Chief Judge Posner wrote for the Court of Appeals in this case:

> As for maximum resale price fixing, unless the supplier is a monopsonist he cannot squeeze his dealers' margins below a competitive level; the attempt to do so would just drive the dealers into the arms of a competing supplier. A supplier might, however, fix a maximum resale price in order to prevent his dealers from exploiting a monopoly position..... [S]uppose that State Oil, perhaps to encourage ... dealer services ... has spaced its dealers sufficiently far apart to limit competition among them (or even given each of them an exclusive territory); and suppose further that Union 76 is a sufficiently distinctive and popular brand to give the dealers in it at least a modicum of monopoly power. Then State Oil might want to place a ceiling on the dealers' resale prices in order to prevent them from exploiting that monopoly power fully. It would do this not out of disinterested malice, but in its commercial self-interest. The higher the price at which gasoline is resold, the smaller the volume sold, and so the lower the profit to the supplier if the higher profit per gallon at the higher price is being snared by the dealer. 93 F.3d, at 1362.

We recognize that the *Albrecht* decision presented a number of theoretical justifications for a per se rule against vertical maximum price fixing. But criticism of those premises abounds. The *Albrecht* decision was grounded in the fear that maximum price fixing by suppliers could interfere with dealer freedom. In response, as one commentator has pointed out, "the ban on maximum resale price limitations declared in *Albrecht* in the name of 'dealer freedom' has actually prompted many suppliers to integrate forward into distribution, thus eliminating the very independent trader for whom *Albrecht* professed solicitude." 7 P. Areeda, *Antitrust Law*, ¶ 1635, p. 395 (1989). For example, integration in the newspaper industry since *Albrecht* has given rise to litigation between independent distributors and publishers. See P. Areeda & H. Hovenkamp, *Antitrust Law* ¶ 729.7, pp. 599-614 (1996 Supp.).

The *Albrecht* Court also expressed the concern that maximum prices may be set too low for dealers to offer consumers essential or desired services. But such conduct, by driving away customers, would seem likely to harm manufacturers as well as dealers and consumers, making it unlikely that a supplier would set such a price as a matter of business judgment. In addition, *Albrecht* noted that vertical maximum price fixing could effectively channel distribution through large or specially-advantaged dealers. It is unclear, however, that a supplier would profit from limiting its market by excluding potential dealers. Further, although vertical maximum price fixing might limit the viability of inefficient dealers, that consequence is not necessarily harmful to competition and consumers.

Finally, *Albrecht* reflected the Court's fear that maximum price fixing could be used to disguise arrangements to fix minimum prices, 390 U.S., at 153, which remain illegal per se. Although we have acknowledged the possibility that maximum pricing might mask minimum pricing … we believe that such conduct as with the other concerns articulated in *Albrecht* can be appropriately recognized and punished under the rule of reason.

Not only are the potential injuries cited in *Albrecht* less serious than the Court imagined, the per se rule established therein could in fact exacerbate problems related to the unrestrained exercise of market power by monopolist-dealers. Indeed, both courts and antitrust scholars have noted that *Albrecht*'s rule may actually harm consumers and manufacturers.… Other commentators have also explained that *Albrecht*'s per se rule has even more potential for deleterious effect on competition after our decision in *GTE Sylvania*, because, now that vertical nonprice restrictions are not unlawful per se, the likelihood of dealer monopoly power is increased.… We do not intend to suggest that dealers generally possess sufficient market power to exploit a monopoly situation. Such retail market power may in fact be uncommon.… Nor do we hold that a ban on vertical maximum price fixing inevitably has anticompetitive consequences in the exclusive dealer context.

After reconsidering *Albrecht*'s rationale and the substantial criticism the decision has received, however, we conclude that there is insufficient economic justification for per se invalidation of vertical maximum price fixing. That is so not only because it is difficult to accept the assumptions underlying *Albrecht*, but also because *Albrecht* has little or no relevance to ongoing enforcement of the Sherman Act.… Moreover, neither the parties nor any of the amici curiae have called our attention to any cases in which enforcement efforts have been directed solely against the conduct encompassed by *Albrecht*'s per se rule.

***

C

Despite what Chief Judge Posner aptly described as *Albrecht*'s "infirmities, [and] its increasingly wobbly, moth-eaten foundations," 93 F.3d, at 1363, there remains the question whether *Albrecht* deserves continuing respect under the doctrine of stare decisis. The Court of Appeals was correct in applying that principle despite disagreement with *Albrecht*, for it is this Court's prerogative alone to overrule one of its precedents.

We approach the reconsideration of decisions of this Court with the utmost caution. Stare decisis reflects "a policy judgment that 'in most matters it is more important that the applicable rule of law be settled than that it be settled right.'" *Agostini v. Felton*, 117 S. Ct. 1997, 2016 (1997) (quoting *Burnet v. Coronado Oil*

& Gas Co., 285 U.S. 393 (1932) (Brandeis, J., dissenting)). It "is the preferred course because it promotes the evenhanded, predictable, and consistent development of legal principles, fosters reliance on judicial decisions, and contributes to the actual and perceived integrity of the judicial process." *Payne v. Tennessee*, 501 U.S. 808 (1991). This Court has expressed its reluctance to overrule decisions involving statutory interpretation ... and has acknowledged that stare decisis concerns are at their acme in cases involving property and contract rights. Both of those concerns are arguably relevant in this case.

But "[s]tare decisis is not an inexorable command." In the area of antitrust law, there is a competing interest, well-represented in this Court's decisions, in recognizing and adapting to changed circumstances and the lessons of accumulated experience. Thus, the general presumption that legislative changes should be left to Congress has less force with respect to the Sherman Act in light of the accepted view that Congress "expected the courts to give shape to the statute's broad mandate by drawing on common-law tradition." *National Soc. of Professional Engineers v. United States*, 435 U.S. 679 (1978). As we have explained, the term "restraint of trade," as used in § 1, also "invokes the common law itself, and not merely the static content that the common law had assigned to the term in 1890." Accordingly, this Court has reconsidered its decisions construing the Sherman Act when the theoretical underpinnings of those decisions are called into serious question.

Although we do not "lightly assume that the economic realities underlying earlier decisions have changed, or that earlier judicial perceptions of those realities were in error," we have noted that "different sorts of agreements" may amount to restraints of trade "in varying times and circumstances," and "[i]t would make no sense to create out of the single term 'restraint of trade' a chronologically schizoid statute, in which a 'rule of reason' evolves with new circumstances and new wisdom, but a line of per se illegality remains forever fixed where it was." *Business Electronics, supra*, at 731-732. Just as *Schwinn* was "the subject of continuing controversy and confusion" under the "great weight" of scholarly criticism, *Albrecht* has been widely criticized since its inception. With the views underlying *Albrecht* eroded by this Court's precedent, there is not much of that decision to salvage....

Although the rule of *Albrecht* has been in effect for some time, the inquiry we must undertake requires considering "'the effect of the antitrust laws upon vertical distributional restraints in the American economy today.'" As the Court noted in *ARCO*, there has not been another case since *Albrecht* in which this Court has "confronted an unadulterated vertical, maximum-price-fixing arrangement." Now that we confront *Albrecht* directly, we find its conceptual foundations gravely weakened.

In overruling *Albrecht*, we of course do not hold that all vertical maximum price fixing is per se lawful. Instead, vertical maximum price fixing, like the majority of commercial arrangements subject to the antitrust laws, should be evaluated under the rule of reason. In our view, rule-of-reason analysis will effectively identify those situations in which vertical maximum price fixing amounts to anticompetitive conduct.

NOTES AND QUESTIONS

1. What will it take to show per se unlawful resale price maintenance under the rule of reason? On remand Khan did not pursue the question whether the maximum price-fixing was unlawful under the rule of reason and thus the Seventh Circuit ruled the claim was waived. 143 F.3d 362, 363 (7th Cir. 1998). Kahn changed its theory to one of minimum resale price maintenance. The court found this argument to have no merit. *Id.* at 364. Judge Posner noted: "A supplier is free to charge any price he wants to his retailers. The fact that the higher that price is, the higher the retailer's price will have to be unless he is willing to sell below his cost has never been thought to be price-fixing." *Id.*

5. DEALER TERMINATION

Vertical restraint issues typically are litigated after a dealer has been terminated, allegedly for noncompliance with the restraint. The antitrust litigation dockets are filled with complaints filed by dealers and distributors alleging wrongful termination or nonrenewal. While claims are brought frequently under tort or contract law, they often implicate antitrust laws as well. The terminated dealer generally asserts that the termination was caused by its failure to adhere to vertical restraints imposed by the manufacturer or supplier. The typical dealer termination case raises the same "characterization" issues discussed in this chapter, specifically whether the requisite "agreement" can be established, whether the agreement is horizontal or vertical in nature, and whether the agreement was for a "price" or "nonprice" reason. *See generally* Piraino, *Distributor Terminations Pursuant to Conspiracies Among a Supplier and Complaining Distributors: A Suggested Antitrust Analysis*, 67 Cornell L. Rev. 297 (1982); Bohling, *Franchise Terminations Under the Sherman Act: Populism and Relational Power*, 53 Tex. L. Rev. 1180 (1975).

The *Colgate* doctrine is sometimes interposed as a defense to the dealer's charge that the termination amounts to a refusal to deal. The defense is available as long as the refusal to deal is unilateral and not in furtherance of conduct from which an "agreement" could be inferred or motivated by monopolistic purpose. When the decision to terminate is imposed by the supplier through an inducement or pressure from other dealers or franchisees, however, it will be scrutinized carefully in order to determine whether the termination was in fact unilateral.

Read together, *Colgate* and *Sylvania* appear to require that a terminated dealer must show (1) that there was a qualifying "agreement" and (2) that this was a price, rather than nonprice, agreement. If the plaintiff fails to show (1), the termination is legal. If the plaintiff fails to show (2), the termination will be analyzed under the rule of reason, and the defendant will probably win.

Ever since the Supreme Court's *Colgate* decision the lower courts have struggled with the issue of how to determine when manufacturer-imposed resale price maintenance (RPM) is "unilateral" conduct, unreachable under section 1, or concerted behavior, which is illegal per se. The distinction has been faulted countless times, largely for being so artificial. Why should an announcement of future intent not to deal with price cutters be legal, while a mere telephone call to a dealer telling it that it will be terminated if it continues to cut price becomes illegal per se?

In recent years commentators and some courts have begun to argue that *Colgate* or something like it can have a very important economic function after all. The agreement requirement can serve to distinguish situations in which RPM is consistent with the manufacturer's independent best interests from those when it is undertaken principally at the behest of dealers.

For example, suppose that a manufacturer is concerned about "free-riding" by some of its dealers, who might take advantage of the point-of-sale services or fixed-cost investments made by other dealers. Controlling free-riding is in the manufacturer's independent best interest, and it does not need a contract with Dealer A in order to have a motive to control the free-riding of Dealer B. In such a case the supplier's motive for imposing RPM may be quite "unilateral." To be sure, Dealer A would also be concerned about Dealer B's free-riding — *both* the manufacturer and Dealer A lose as a result. But if Dealer A complains about Dealer B's price-cutting and Dealer B is engaged in free-riding, then the complaint may serve the function of simply informing the manufacturer what Dealer B is doing. One could not infer from the fact of the complaint and the termination in response that there was an "agreement" between Dealer A and the manufacturer that Dealer A's prices would be maintained at a certain level.

What would you think of a rule that persistent free-riding by the terminated dealer (presumably the plaintiff) creates a presumption that the manufacturer was acting unilaterally? *See Lomar Whsle. Grocery, Inc. v. Dieter's Gourmet Foods, Inc.*, 824 F.2d 582 (8th Cir. 1987), *cert. denied*, 484 U.S. 1010 (1988), *and Valley Liquors, Inc. v. Renfield Importers, Ltd.*, 678 F.2d 742 (7th Cir. 1982), both suggesting that a desire to eliminate free-riders gives a supplier acting unilaterally a motive to terminate price cutters.

By contrast, RPM may be the product of dealer cartels or the influence of individual dealers who have a great deal of power in their respective retail markets. If Clancy's Department Store is the most prestigious store in Lansing, Michigan, and Clancy's tells the supplier that it will carry the supplier's product only if other Lansing dealers keep the price up, the supplier may be forced to impose RPM rather than risk losing Clancy's business. When Clancy's later complains about Dealer B's prices and the manufacturer terminates Dealer B, the inference is much stronger that there was a quid-pro-quo: that the manufacturer terminated Dealer B *in exchange for* Clancy's promise to continue selling the manufacturer's product. What would you think of a rule that if the complaining dealer is powerful and the defendant cannot show specific instances of free-riding, a presumption is created that the termination was the product of an agreement? *See McCabe's Furn. v. La-Z-Boy Chair Co.*, 798 F.2d 323 (8th Cir. 1986).

The *Monsanto* decision, reprinted below, formulates a test for determining whether an agreement can be inferred from dealer complaints followed by a termination.

MONSANTO CO. V. SPRAY-RITE SERVICE CORP.

465 U.S. 752 (1984)

JUSTICE POWELL delivered the opinion of the Court.

This case presents a question as to the standard of proof required to find a vertical price-fixing conspiracy in violation of Section 1 of the Sherman Act.

Petitioner Monsanto Company manufactures chemical products, including agricultural herbicides. By the late 1960's, the time at issue in this case, its sales accounted for approximately 15% of the corn herbicide market and 3% of the soybean herbicide market. In the corn herbicide market, the market leader commanded a 70% share. In the soybean herbicide market, two other competitors each had between 30% and 40% of the market. Respondent Spray-Rite Service Corporation was engaged in the wholesale distribution of agricultural chemicals from 1955 to 1972. Spray-Rite was essentially a family business, whose owner and president, Donald Yapp, was also its sole salaried salesman. Spray-Rite was a discount operation, buying in large quantities and selling at a low margin.

In October 1968 Monsanto declined to renew Spray-Rite's distributorship. At that time, Spray-Rite was the tenth largest out of approximately 100 distributors of Monsanto's primary corn herbicide. Ninety percent of Spray-Rite's sales volume was devoted to herbicide sales, and 16% of its sales were of Monsanto products. After Monsanto's termination, Spray-Rite continued as a herbicide dealer until 1972. It was able to purchase some of Monsanto's products from other distributors, but not as much as it desired or as early in the season as it needed....

Spray-Rite brought this action under Section 1 of the Sherman Act, 15 U.S.C. § 1. It alleged that Monsanto and some of its distributors conspired to fix the resale prices of Monsanto herbicides. Its complaint further alleged that Monsanto terminated Spray-Rite's distributorship, adopted compensation programs and shipping policies, and encouraged distributors to boycott Spray-Rite in furtherance of this conspiracy. Monsanto denied the allegations of conspiracy, and asserted that Spray-Rite's distributorship had been terminated because of its failure to hire trained salesmen and promote sales to dealers adequately.

The case was tried to a jury. The District Court instructed the jury that Monsanto's conduct was *per se* unlawful if it was in furtherance of a conspiracy to fix prices. In answers to special interrogatories, the jury found that the termination of Spray-Rite was pursuant to a conspiracy between Monsanto and one or more of its distributors to set resale prices....

The Court of Appeals for the Seventh Circuit affirmed. 684 F.2d 1226 (1982). It held that there was sufficient evidence to satisfy Spray-Rite's burden of proving a conspiracy to set resale prices. The court stated that "proof of termination following competitor complaints is sufficient to support an inference of concerted action." Canvassing the testimony and exhibits that were before the jury, the court found evidence of numerous complaints from competing Monsanto distributors about Spray-Rite's price-cutting practices. It also noted that there was testimony that a Monsanto official had said that Spray-Rite was terminated because of the price complaints.

In substance, the Court of Appeals held that an antitrust plaintiff can survive a motion for a directed verdict if it shows that a manufacturer terminated a price-cutting distributor in response to or following complaints by other distributors. This view brought the Seventh Circuit into direct conflict with a number of other Courts of Appeals. We reject the statement by the Court of Appeals for the Seventh Circuit of the standard of proof required to submit a case to the jury in distributor-termination litigation, but affirm the judgment under the standard we announce today.

....

Monsanto does not dispute Spray-Rite's view that if the nonprice practices were proven to have been instituted as part of a price-fixing conspiracy, they would be subject to *per se* treatment. Instead, Monsanto argues that there was insufficient evidence to support the jury's finding that the nonprice practices were "created by Monsanto pursuant to" a price-fixing conspiracy....

In view of Monsanto's concession that a proper finding that nonprice practices were part of a price-fixing conspiracy would suffice to subject the entire conspiracy to *per se* treatment, *Sylvania* is not applicable to this case. In that case only a nonprice restriction was challenged. *See* 433 U.S., at 51, n.18. Nothing in our decision today undercuts the holding of *Sylvania* that nonprice restrictions are to be judged under the rule of reason. In fact, the need to ensure the viability of *Sylvania* is an important consideration in our rejection of the Court of Appeal's standard of sufficiency of the evidence.

This Court has drawn two important distinctions that are at the center of this and any other distributor-termination case. First, there is the basic distinction between concerted and independent action — a distinction not always clearly drawn by parties and courts. Section 1 of the Sherman Act requires that there be a "contract, combination ... or conspiracy" between the manufacturer and other distributors in order to establish a violation. 15 U.S.C. § 1. Independent action is not proscribed. A manufacturer of course generally has a right to deal, or refuse to deal, with whomever it likes, as long as it does so independently. *United States v. Colgate & Co.*, 250 U.S. 300, 307 (1919); *cf. United States v. Parke, Davis & Co.*, 362 U.S. 29 (1960). Under *Colgate*, the manufacturer can announce its resale prices in advance and refuse to deal with those who fail to comply. And a distributor is free to acquiesce in the manufacturer's demand in order to avoid termination.

The second important distinction in distributor-termination cases is that between concerted action to set prices and concerted action on nonprice restrictions. The former have been *per se* illegal since the early years of national antitrust enforcement. *See Dr. Miles Medical Co. v. John D. Park & Sons Co.*, 220 U.S. 373, 404-409 (1911). The latter are judged under the rule of reason, which requires a weighing of the relevant circumstances of a case to decide whether a restrictive practice constitutes an unreasonable restraint on competition. *See Continental T.V., Inc. v. GTE Sylvania Inc.*, 433 U.S. 36 (1977).[7]

While these distinctions in theory are reasonably clear, often they are difficult to apply in practice. In *Sylvania* we emphasized that the legality of arguably anticompetitive conduct should be judged primarily by its "market impact." *See, e.g., id.*, at 51. But the economic effect of all of the conduct described above — unilateral and concerted vertical price-setting, agreements on price and nonprice restrictions — is in many, but not all, cases similar or identical. *See, e.g., Parke, Davis, supra*, at 43; note 7 *supra*. And judged from a distance, the conduct of the parties in the various situations can be indistinguishable. For example, the fact that a manufacturer and its distributors are in constant communication about prices and marketing strategy does not alone show that the distributors are not making independent pricing decisions. A manufacturer and its distributors have legitimate reasons to exchange information about the prices and the reception of their products in the market. Moreover, it is precisely in cases in which the manufacturer attempts to further a particular marketing strategy by means of agreements on often costly nonprice restrictions that it will have the most interest in the distributors' resale prices. The manufacturer often will want to ensure that its distributors earn sufficient profit to pay for programs such as hiring and training additional salesmen or demonstrating the technical features of the product, and will want to see that "free-riders" do not interfere. *See Sylvania, supra*, at 55. Thus, the manufacturer's strongly felt concern about resale prices does not necessarily mean that it has done more than the *Colgate* doctrine allows.

---

[7] The Solicitor General (by brief only) and several other amici suggest that we take this opportunity to reconsider whether "contract[s], combination[s] ... or conspirac[ies]" to fix resale prices should always be unlawful. They argue that the economic effect of resale price maintenance is little different from agreements on nonprice restrictions. *See generally Continental T.V., Inc. v. GTE Sylvania Inc.*, 433 U.S. 36, 69-70 (1977) (WHITE, J., concurring in the judgment) (citing sources); Baker, *Interconnected Problems of Doctrine and Economics in the Section One Labyrinth: Is Sylvania a Way Out?*, 67 Va. L. Rev. 1457, 1465-1466 (1981). They say that the economic objections to resale price maintenance that we discussed in *Sylvania* — such as that it facilitates horizontal cartels — can be met easily in the context of rule-of-reason analysis.

Certainly in this case we have no occasion to consider the merits of this argument. This case was tried on *per se* instructions to the jury. Neither party argued in the District Court that the rule of reason should apply to a vertical price-fixing conspiracy, nor raised the point on appeal. In fact, neither party before this Court presses the argument advanced by amici. We therefore decline to reach the question, and we decide the case in the context in which it was decided below and argued here.

Nevertheless, it is of considerable importance that independent action by the manufacturer, and concerted action on nonprice restrictions, be distinguished from price-fixing agreements, since under present law the latter are subject to *per se* treatment and treble damages. On a claim of concerted price-fixing, the antitrust plaintiff must present evidence sufficient to carry its burden of proving that there was such an agreement. If an inference of such an agreement may be drawn from highly ambiguous evidence, there is a considerable danger that the doctrines enunciated in *Sylvania* and *Colgate* will be seriously eroded.

The flaw in the evidentiary standard adopted by the Court of Appeals in this case is that it disregards this danger. Permitting an agreement to be inferred merely from the existence of complaints, or even from the fact that termination came about "in response to" complaints, could deter or penalize perfectly legitimate conduct. As Monsanto points out, complaints about price-cutters "are natural — and from the manufacturer's perspective, unavoidable — reactions by distributors to the activities of their rivals." Such complaints, particularly where the manufacturer has imposed a costly set of nonprice restrictions, "arise in the normal course of business and do not indicate illegal concerted action." Moreover, distributors are an important source of information for manufacturers. In order to assure an efficient distribution system, manufacturers and distributors constantly must coordinate their activities to assure that their product will reach the consumer persuasively and efficiently. To bar a manufacturer from acting solely because the information upon which it acts originated as a price complaint would create an irrational dislocation in the market. *See* F. Warren-Boulton, Vertical Control of Markets 13, 164 (1978). In sum, "[t]o permit the inference of concerted action on the basis of receiving complaints alone and thus to expose the defendant to treble damage liability would both inhibit management's exercise of independent business judgment and emasculate the terms of the statute." *Edward J. Sweeney & Sons, Inc. v. Texaco, Inc.*, 637 F.2d 105, 111, n.2 (3d Cir. 1980), *cert. denied*, 451 U.S. 911 (1981).

Thus, something more than evidence of complaints is needed. There must be evidence that tends to exclude the possibility that the manufacturer and nonterminated distributors were acting independently. As Judge Aldisert has written, the antitrust plaintiff should present direct or circumstantial evidence that reasonably tends to prove that the manufacturer and others "had a conscious commitment to a common scheme designed to achieve an unlawful objective." *Edward J. Sweeney & Sons, supra*, at 111.

Applying this standard to the facts of this case, we believe there was sufficient evidence for the jury reasonably to have concluded that Monsanto and some of its distributors were parties to an "agreement" or "conspiracy" to maintain resale prices and terminate price-cutters. In fact there was substantial direct evidence of agreements to maintain prices. There was testimony from a Monsanto direct manager, for example, that Monsanto on at least two occasions in early 1969, about five months after Spray-Rite was terminated, approached price-cutting distributors and advised that if they did not maintain the suggested resale price, they would not receive adequate supplies of Monsanto's new corn herbicide. When one of the distributors did not assent, this information was referred to the Monsanto regional office, and it complained to the distributor's parent company. There was evidence that the parent instructed the subsidiary to comply, and the distributor informed Monsanto that it would charge the suggested price. Evidence of this kind plainly is relevant and persuasive as to a meeting of minds.

....

If, as the courts below reasonably could have found, there was evidence of an agreement with one or more distributors to maintain prices, the remaining question is whether the termination of Spray-Rite was part of or pursuant to that agreement. It would be reasonable to find that it was, since it is necessary for competing distributors contemplating compliance with suggested prices to know that those who do not comply will be terminated. Moreover, there is some circumstantial evidence of such a link. Following the termination, there was a meeting between Spray-Rite's president and a Monsanto official. There was testimony that the first thing the official mentioned was the many complaints Monsanto had received about Spray-Rite's prices. In addition, there was reliable testimony that Monsanto never discussed with Spray-Rite prior to the termination the distributorship criteria that were the alleged basis for the action. By contrast, a former Monsanto salesman for Spray-Rite's area testified that Monsanto representatives on several occasions in 1965-1966 approached Spray-Rite, informed the distributor of complaints from other distributors — including one major and influential one — and requested that prices be maintained. Later that same year, Spray-Rite's president testified, Monsanto officials made explicit threats to terminate Spray-Rite unless it raised its prices.

We conclude that the Court of Appeals applied an incorrect standard to the evidence in this case. The correct standard is that there must be evidence that tends to exclude the possibility of independent action by the manufacturer and distributor. That is, there must be direct or circumstantial evidence that reasonably tends to prove that the manufacturer and others had a conscious commitment to a common scheme designed to achieve an unlawful objective. Under this standard, the evidence in this case created a jury issue as to whether Spray-Rite was terminated pursuant to a price-fixing conspiracy between Monsanto and its distributors. The judgment of the court below is

Affirmed.

JUSTICE WHITE took no part in the consideration or decision of this case.

JUSTICE BRENNAN, concurring.

As the Court notes, the Solicitor General has filed a brief in this Court as *amicus curiae* urging us to overrule the Court's decision in *Dr. Miles Medical Co. v. John D. Park & Sons Co.*, 220 U.S. 373 (1911). That decision has stood for 73 years, and Congress has certainly been aware of its existence throughout that time. Yet Congress has never enacted legislation to overrule the interpretation of the Sherman Act adopted in that case. Under these circumstances, I see no reason for us to depart from our longstanding interpretation of the Act. Because the Court adheres to that rule and, in my view, properly applies *Dr. Miles* to this case, I join the opinion and judgment of the Court.

NOTES AND QUESTIONS

1. Is it clear that Monsanto was imposing "price" rather than "nonprice" restraints? Under the rule established by the Supreme Court in *Continental T.V., Inc. v. GTE Sylvania, Inc.*, 433 U.S. 36 (1977), reprinted *infra*, Subsection C of this section, nonprice restraints receive rule of reason treatment even if they are the product of an "agreement" between the supplier and the dealer. However, does the fact that Dealer *A* was terminated by a supplier as a result of complaints from Dealer *B* about *A*'s price cutting imply that the supplier was imposing price restraints? How does a dealer violate vertical nonprice restraints — more often than not, by price cutting. The following argument comes from Hovenkamp, *Vertical Restrictions and Monopoly Power*, 64 B.U. L. Rev. 521 (1984):

> The Supreme Court's characterization notwithstanding, the facts of *Monsanto Co. v. Spray-Rite Service Corp.* suggest that the defendant had been imposing nonprice rather than price restraints. Spray-Rite was a wholesale distributor of Monsanto's products for eleven years, until Monsanto terminated Spray-Rite's distributorship. Spray-Rite argued that it was terminated because it was a price cutter and other dealers complained about the price cutting. Monsanto argued in return that Spray-Rite was terminated, not because it was a price cutter, but because it "fail[ed] to hire trained salesmen and adequately promote sales to dealers." The posture of this argument put the Court and the jury in the position of deciding that Spray-Rite was terminated for either a price reason or a nonprice reason, and both chose the former.

> Actually, Spray Rite was a price cutter *because* it lacked adequately trained employees. It was able to charge less because it took advantage of information provided by the specialists hired by its competitors. When competing dealers complained, naturally they complained about the phenomenon that appeared to cause their injury: the price cutting, not the absence of skilled personnel.

> Suppose that a manufacturer plagued with dealer free riding imposes a vertical territorial division. It gives Dealer A Massachusetts as an exclusive territory and Dealer B New Hampshire. Dealer B, however, persists in cheating by making unauthorized sales in Massachusetts. Dealer B probably can make these illicit sales in Massachusetts at a lower price than Dealer A because, unlike B, A bears the burden of promotional and post-sale service expenses in Massachusetts. Dealer B is likely to steal customers in Dealer A's territory only by underselling Dealer A there; customers in A's territory will not ordinarily buy from remote Dealer B, unless B offers them a lower price.

Although everything about this illustrated distribution practice suggests that it involves "nonprice" restraints, a court is likely to characterize the restrictions as pertaining to price. When Dealer A complains to the supplier that Dealer B has been violating the restrictions, A will complain about the territorial invasion and the price-cutting in the same sentence. Even though the supplier has said nothing about what price Dealer B may charge in B's own territory and would never discipline B for price cutting in B's territory, it will discipline B for invading A's territory and cutting prices there.

Most vertical restraints, whether characterized as "price" or "nonprice," are designed to combat free rider problems. A free rider, however, invariably *cuts price* by taking advantage of services provided by other dealers of the same product. In short, violations of *both* resale price maintenance and of nonprice restraints are evidenced by price cutting, and it is generally the price cutting that results in the competitor's complaint.

But cf. Note, *A Functional Rule of Reason Analysis for the Law of Resale Price Maintenance and Its Application to* Spray-Rite, 1984 Wis. L. Rev. 1205.

2. Consider the following: RPM can be used to: (1) facilitate horizontal price-fixing with other suppliers or manufacturers, (2) facilitate a dealer cartel, insulating retail dealers from price competition, or (3) provide higher dealer margins to support pre- and post-sale services to consumers, avoid free-riding, and maintain quality control over the product. In the first two categories, consumers are injured because output restrictions will increase price above competitive levels. In the third, consumers benefit through greater product services and stronger competition in the interbrand market. Thus an RPM can be either service-enhancing or collusive and restrictive in nature.

In a recent study of 203 reported private and government cases alleging RPM between 1976 and 1982, the FTC found that the collusion theory (either at the manufacturer or retail level) accounted for only 15 percent of the RPM cases filed, while the proefficiency, service-enhancing theories potentially explained a substantial percentage of the cases. Moreover, in 30 percent of the filed cases, the supplier was charged with maximum price fixing, the arrangement which attempts to put a ceiling on the price that can be charged at retail. And in 53 percent of the cases that reached a judicial decision (109/203), judgment was entered for the defendant. *See FTC Bureau of Economics Staff Report, Resale Price Maintenance* (Apr. 1, 1988).

PROBLEM 5.1

Spree, Inc., is a manufacturer of clothing for teenagers, a very competitive market in which the key to success is convincing fashionable department stores to give the product display space. Products that do not receive prominent, glitzy displays do not sell, no matter how high their quality. Spree sells to several stores in Boston, one of which is Mack's Department Store, a high quality, eminently fashionable, high priced store that is all the rage among teens. A block away is Feline's Bargains Galore, an offprice retailer. Spree also sells to Feline's, which resells Spree clothing at about one-half the price that Mack's charges.

Mack's suddenly announces a policy to all its suppliers. It will give prominent floor space only to suppliers who either limit the distribution of their product in Boston to Mack's, or else who promise to pressure other stores to "keep their prices up." If the supplier fails to do this Mack's will either (1) stop dealing in that supplier's product or (2) move the product downstairs into "Mack's Bargain Basement," where clothing is piled indiscriminately on large tables and sold at substantial discounts. Two weeks after issuing this communication, Mack's writes Spree a letter, stating that henceforth it will sell Spree clothing only in its bargain basement. A week after that Spree informs Feline's that it will no longer sell it Spree clothing.

Has there been an agreement under *Monsanto*? Is it a price agreement? *See Burlington Coat Factory Whse. v. Esprit de Corp.*, 769 F.2d 919 (2d Cir. 1985); *McCabe's Furn. v. La-Z-Boy Chair Co.*, 798 F.2d 323 (8th Cir. 1986).

PROBLEM 5.2

Zedco, Inc., manufactures small radios, which it places in boxes that are marked with suggested retail prices. Often the markings are prominent, saying such things as "Only $19.99," or "Manufacturer's Suggested Retail Price, $19.99." Zedco does not say anything to retailers about the prices they must charge for its radios. However, Zedco's warranty and some instructions are printed on the back of the box; as a result, if retailers take the product out of the box it becomes much less attractive to consumers.

Blast, Inc., is a retailer of consumer electronics located in an area where rent is high and demand for consumer electronics is strong. Blast would like to sell Zedco's radios for more than the suggested retail price printed on Zedco's boxes. When it has tried that, however, it has encountered great consumer resistance and even outrage. Even relatively affluent customers feel "cheated" if they are asked to pay more than the preprinted price marked on the box.

Blast sues Zedco, claiming illegal maximum resale price maintenance, forbidden by section 1 of the Sherman Act. Outcome? *See* 8 P. Areeda, *Antitrust Law* ¶ 1639d (1989).

BUSINESS ELECTRONICS V. SHARP ELECTRONICS

485 U.S. 717 (1988)

JUSTICE SCALIA delivered the opinion of the Court.

Petitioner Business Electronics Corporation seeks review of a decision of the United States Court of Appeals for the Fifth Circuit holding that a vertical restraint is *per se* illegal under § 1 of the Sherman Act, only if there is an express or implied agreement to set resale prices at some level. 780 F.2d 1212, 1215-1218 (1986)....

I

In 1968, petitioner became the exclusive retailer in the Houston, Texas area of electronic calculators manufactured by respondent Sharp Electronics Corporation. In 1972, respondent appointed Gilbert Hartwell as a second retailer in the Houston area. During the relevant period, electronic calculators were primarily sold to business customers for prices up to $1000. While much of the evidence in this case was conflicting — in particular, concerning whether petitioner was "free riding" on Hartwell's provision of presale educational and promotional services by providing inadequate services itself — a few facts are undisputed. Respondent published a list of suggested minimum retail prices, but its written dealership agreements with petitioner and Hartwell did not obligate either to observe them, or to charge any other specific price. Petitioner's retail prices were often below respondent's suggested retail prices and generally below Hartwell's retail prices, even though Hartwell too sometimes priced below respondent's suggested retail prices. Hartwell complained to respondent on a number of occasions about petitioner's prices. In June 1973, Hartwell gave respondent the ultimatum that Hartwell would terminate his dealership unless respondent ended its relationship with petitioner within 30 days. Respondent terminated petitioner's dealership in July 1973.

Petitioner brought suit ... alleging that respondent and Hartwell had conspired to terminate petitioner and that such conspiracy was illegal *per se* under § 1 of the Sherman Act. The case was tried to a jury. The District Court submitted a liability interrogatory to the jury that asked whether "there was an agreement or understanding between Sharp Electronics Corporation and Hartwell to terminate Business Electronics as a Sharp dealer because of Business Electronics' price cutting."... The District Court instructed the jury at length about this question:

> The Sherman Act is violated when a seller enters into an agreement or understanding with one of its dealers to terminate another dealer because of the other dealer's price cutting. Plaintiff contends that Sharp terminated Business Electronics in furtherance of Hartwell's desire to eliminate Business Electronics as a price-cutting rival.
>
> If you find that there was an agreement between Sharp and Hartwell to terminate Business Electronics because of Business Electronics' price cutting, you should answer yes to Question Number 1.
>
> ....
>
> A combination, agreement or understanding to terminate a dealer because of his price cutting unreasonably restrains trade and cannot be justified for any reason. Therefore, even though the combination, agreement or understanding may have been formed or engaged in ... to eliminate any alleged evils of price cutting, it is still unlawful....
>
> If a dealer demands that a manufacturer terminate a price cutting dealer, and the manufacturer agrees to do so, the agreement is illegal if the manufacturer's purpose is to eliminate the price cutting.

The jury answered Question 1 affirmatively and awarded $600,000 in damages....

The Fifth Circuit reversed, holding ... that, to render illegal *per se* a vertical agreement between a manufacturer and a dealer to terminate a second dealer, the first dealer "must expressly or impliedly agree to set its prices at some level, though not a specific one. The distributor cannot retain complete freedom to set whatever price it chooses." 780 F.2d, at 1218.

....

II

A

....

Although vertical agreements on resale prices have been illegal *per se* since *Dr. Miles Medical Co. v. John D. Park & Sons Co.*, 220 U.S. 373 (1911), we have recognized that the scope of *per se* illegality should be narrow in the context of vertical restraints. In *GTE Sylvania*, we refused to extend *per se* illegality to vertical nonprice restraints, specifically to a manufacturer's termination of one dealer pursuant to an exclusive territory agreement with another. We noted that especially in the vertical restraint context "departure from the rule-of-reason standard must be based on demonstrable economic effect rather than ... upon formalistic line drawing." *Id.*, 433 U.S., at 58-59. We concluded that vertical nonprice restraints had not been shown to have such a "'pernicious effect on competition'" and to be so "'lack[ing] [in] ... redeeming value'" as to justify *per se* illegality. *Id.*, at 58, quoting *Northern Pacific R. Co. v. United States*, 356 U.S. 1, 5 (1958). Rather, we found, they had real potential to stimulate interbrand competition, "the primary concern of antitrust law," 433 U.S., at 52, n. 19.

> [N]ew manufacturers and manufacturers entering new markets can use the restrictions in order to induce competent and aggressive retailers to make the kind of investment of capital and labor that is often required in the distribution of products unknown to the consumer. Established manufacturers can use them to induce retailers to engage in promotional activities or to provide service and repair facilities necessary to the efficient marketing of their products. Service and repair are vital for many products.... The availability and quality of such services affect a manufacturer's goodwill and the competitiveness of his product. Because of market imperfections such as the so-called 'free-rider' effect, these services might not be provided by retailers in a purely competitive situation, despite the fact that each retailer's benefit would be greater if all provided the services than if none did. *Id.*, at 55.

Moreover, we observed that a rule of *per se* illegality for vertical nonprice restraints was not needed or effective to protect *intra* brand competition. First, so long as interbrand competition existed, that would provide a "significant check" on any attempt to exploit intrabrand market power. *Id.*, at 52, n. 19. In fact, in order to meet that interbrand competition, a manufacturer's dominant incentive is to lower resale prices. *Id.*, at 56, and n. 24. Second, the *per se* illegality of vertical restraints would create a perverse incentive for manufacturers to integrate vertically into distribution, an outcome hardly conductive to fostering the creation and maintenance of small businesses. *Id.*, at 57, n. 26.

Finally, our opinion in *GTE Sylvania* noted a significant distinction between vertical nonprice and vertical price restraints. That is, there was support for the proposition that vertical price restraints reduce *inter* brand price competition because they "'facilitate cartelizing.'" *Id.*, at 51, n. 18, quoting Posner, Antitrust Policy and the Supreme Court: An Analysis of the Restricted Distribution, Horizontal Merger and Potential Competition Decisions, 75 Colum. L. Rev. 282, 294 (1975). The authorities cited by the Court suggested how vertical price agreements might assist horizontal price fixing at the manufacturer level (by reducing the manufacturer's incentive to cheat on a cartel, since its retailers could not pass on lower prices to consumers) or might be used to organize cartels at the retailer level.... Similar support for the cartel-facilitating effect of vertical nonprice restraints was and remains lacking.

We have been solicitous to assure that the market-freeing effect of our decision in *GTE Sylvania* is not frustrated by related legal rules. In *Monsanto Co. v. Spray-Rite Service Corp.*, 465 U.S. 752, 763 (1984), which addressed the evidentiary showing necessary to establish vertical concerted action, we expressed concern that "[i]f an inference of such an agreement may be drawn from highly ambiguous evidence, there is considerable danger that the doctrin[e] enunciated in *Sylvania...* will be seriously eroded." See also *id.*, at 761, n. 6. We eschewed adoption of an evidentiary standard that "could deter or penalize perfectly legitimate conduct" or "would create an irrational dislocation in the market" by preventing legitimate communication between a manufacturer and its distributors. *Id.*, at 763, 764.

Our approach to the question presented in the present case is guided by the premises of *GTE Sylvania* and *Monsanto:* that there is a presumption in favor of a rule-of-reason standard; that departure from that standard must be justified by demonstrable economic effect, such as the facilitation of cartelizing, rather than formalistic distinctions; that interbrand competition is the primary concern of the antitrust laws; and that rules in this area should be formulated with a view towards protecting the doctrine of *GTE Sylvania.* These premises lead us to conclude that the line drawn by the Fifth Circuit is the most appropriate one.

There has been no showing here that an agreement between a manufacturer and a dealer to terminate a "price cutter," without a further agreement on the price or price levels to be charged by the remaining dealer, almost always tends to restrict competition and reduce output. Any assistance to cartelizing that such an agreement might provide cannot be distinguished from the sort of minimal assistance that might be provided by vertical nonprice agreements like the exclusive territory agreement in *GTE Sylvania*, and is insufficient to justify a *per se* rule. Cartels are neither easy to form nor easy to maintain. Uncertainty over the terms of the cartel, particularly the prices to be charged in the future, obstructs both formation and adherence by making cheating easier.... Without an agreement with the remaining dealer on price, the manufacturer both retains its incentive to cheat on any manufacturer-level cartel (since lower prices can still be passed on to consumers) and cannot as easily be used to organize and hold together a retailer-level cartel.[2]

The District Court's rule on the scope of *per se* illegality for vertical restraints would threaten to dismantle the doctrine of *GTE Sylvania*. Any agreement between a manufacturer and a dealer to terminate another dealer who happens to have charged lower prices can be alleged to have been directed against the terminated dealer's "price cutting." In the vast majority of cases, it will be extremely difficult for the manufacturer to convince a jury that its motivation was to ensure adequate services, since price cutting and some measure of service cutting usually go hand in hand. Accordingly, a manufacturer that agrees to give one dealer an exclusive territory and terminates another dealer pursuant to that agreement, or even a manufacturer that agrees with one dealer to terminate another for failure to provide contractually-obligated services, exposes itself to the highly plausible claim that its real motivation was to terminate a price cutter. Moreover, even vertical restraints that do not result in dealer termination, such as the initial granting of an exclusive territory or the requirement that certain services be provided, can be attacked as designed to allow existing dealers to charge higher prices. Manufacturers would be likely to forgo legitimate and competitively useful conduct rather than risk treble damages and perhaps even criminal penalties.

We cannot avoid this difficulty by invalidating as illegal *per se* only those agreements imposing vertical restraints that contain the word "price," or that affect the "prices" charged by dealers. Such formalism was explicitly rejected in *GTE Sylvania*. As the above discussion indicates, all vertical restraints, including the exclusive territory agreement held not to be *per se* illegal in *GTE Sylvania*, have the potential to allow dealers to increase "prices" and can be characterized as intended to achieve just that. In fact, vertical nonprice restraints only accomplish the benefits identified in *GTE Sylvania* because they reduce intrabrand price competition to the point where the dealer's profit margin permits provision of the desired services. As we described it in *Monsanto:* "The manufacturer often will want to ensure that its distributors earn sufficient profit to pay for programs such as hiring and training additional salesmen or demonstrating the technical features of the product, and will want to see that 'free-riders' do not interfere." 465 U.S., at 762-763.

---

[2] The dissent's principal fear appears to be not cartelization at either level, but Hartwell's assertion of dominant retail power. This fear does not possibly justify adopting a rule of *per se* illegality. Retail market power is rare, because of the usual presence of interbrand competition and other dealers, see *Continental T.V., Inc. v. GTE Sylvania Inc.*, 433 U.S. 36, 54, 97 S. Ct. 2549, 2559-60, 53 L. Ed. 2d 568 (1977), and it should therefore not be assumed but rather must be proved. Cf. Baxter, *The Viability of Vertical Restraints Doctrine*, 75 Cal. L. Rev. 933, 948-949 (1987). Of course this case was not prosecuted on the theory, and therefore the jury was not asked to find, that Hartwell possessed such market power.

The dissent erects a much more complex analytic structure, which ultimately rests, however, upon the same discredited premise that the only function this nonprice vertical restriction can serve is restraint of dealer-level competition. Specifically, the dissent's reasoning hinges upon its perception that the agreement between Sharp and Hartwell was a "naked" restraint — that is, it was not "ancillary" to any other agreement between Sharp and Hartwell. But that is not true, unless one assumes, contrary to *GTE Sylvania* and *Monsanto*, and contrary to our earlier discussion, that it is not a quite plausible purpose of the restriction to enable Hartwell to provide better services under the sales franchise agreement.[3] From its faulty conclusion that what we have before us is a "naked" restraint, the dissent proceeds, by reasoning we do not entirely follow, to the further conclusion that it is therefore a horizontal rather than a vertical restraint. We pause over this only to note that in addition to producing what we think the wrong result in the present case, it introduces needless confusion into antitrust terminology. Restraints imposed by agreement between competitors have traditionally been denominated as horizontal restraints, and those imposed by agreement between firms at different levels of distribution as vertical restraints.[4]

---

[3] The conclusion of "naked" restraint could also be sustained on another assumption, namely that an agreement is not "ancillary" unless it is designed to enforce a contractual obligation of one of the parties to the contract. The dissent appears to accept this assumption. It is plainly wrong. The classic "ancillary" restraint is an agreement by the seller of a business not to compete within the market.... That is not ancillary to any other contractual obligation, but, like the restraint here, merely enhances the value of the contract, or permits the "enjoyment of [its] fruits." ...

More important than the erroneousness of the dissent's common-law analysis of "naked" and "ancillary" restraints are the perverse economic consequences of permitting nonprice vertical restraints to avoid *per se* invalidity only through attachment to an express contractual obligation. Such an approach is contrary to the express views of the principal scholar on whom the dissent relies. See 7 P. Areeda, Antitrust Law § 1457c, p. 170 (1986) (hereinafter Areeda) (legality of terminating price cutter should not depend upon formal adoption of service obligations that termination is assertedly designed to protect). In the precise case of a vertical agreement to terminate other dealers, for example, there is no conceivable reason why the existence of an exclusivity commitment by the manufacturer to the one remaining dealer would render anticompetitive effects less likely, or the procompetitive effects on services more likely — so that the dissent's line for *per se* illegality fails to meet the requirement of *Continental T.V., Inc. v. GTE Sylvania Inc., supra,* that it be based on "demonstrable economic effect." If anything, the economic effect of the dissent's approach is perverse, encouraging manufacturers to agree to otherwise inefficient contractual provisions for the sole purpose of attaching to them efficient nonprice vertical restraints which, only by reason of such attachment, can avoid *per se* invalidity as "naked" restraints. The dissent's approach would therefore create precisely the kind of "irrational dislocation in the market" that legal rules in this area should be designed to avoid. *Monsanto Co. v. Spray-Rite Service Corp.,* 465 U.S. 752, 764 (1984).

[4] The dissent apparently believes that whether a restraint is horizontal depends upon whether its anticompetitive *effects* are horizontal, and not upon whether it is the product of a horizontal agreement. That is of course a conceivable way of talking, but if it were the language of antitrust analysis there would be no such thing as an unlawful vertical restraint, since all anticompetitive effects are by definition horizontal effects.... [We believe] that a restraint is horizontal not because it has horizontal effects, but because it is the product of a horizontal agreement.

Finally, we do not agree with petitioner's contention that an agreement on the remaining dealer's price or price levels will so often follow from terminating another dealer "because of [its] price cutting" that prophylaxis against resale price maintenance warrants the District Court's *per se* rule. Petitioner has provided no support for the proposition that vertical price agreements generally underlie agreements to terminate a price cutter. That proposition is simply incompatible with the conclusion of *GTE Sylvania* and *Monsanto* that manufacturers are often motivated by a legitimate desire to have dealers provide services, combined with the reality that price cutting is frequently made possible by "free riding" on the services provided by other dealers. The District Court's *per se* rule would therefore discourage conduct recognized by *GTE Sylvania* and *Monsanto* as beneficial to consumers.

B

In resting our decision upon the foregoing economic analysis, we do not ignore common-law precedent concerning what constituted "restraint of trade" at the time the Sherman Act was adopted. But neither do we give that pre-1890 precedent the dispositive effect some would. The term "restraint of trade" in the statute, like the term at common law, refers not to a particular list of agreements, but to a particular economic consequence, which may be produced by quite different sorts of agreements in varying times and circumstances....

The Sherman Act adopted the term "restraint of trade" along with its dynamic potential. It invokes the common law itself, and not merely the static content that the common law had assigned to the term in 1890.... If it were otherwise, not only would the line of *per se* illegality have to be drawn today precisely where it was in 1890, but also case-by-case evaluation of legality (conducted where *per se* rules do not apply) would have to be governed by 19th-century notions of reasonableness. It would make no sense to create out of the single term "restraint of trade" a chronologically schizoid statute, in which a "rule of reason" evolves with new circumstances and new wisdom, but a line of *per se* illegality remains forever fixed where it was.

Of course the common law, both in general and as embodied in the Sherman Act, does not lightly assume that the economic realities underlying earlier decisions have changed, or that earlier judicial perceptions of those realities were in error. It is relevant, therefore, whether the common law of restraint of trade ever prohibited as illegal *per se* an agreement of the sort made here, and whether our decisions under § 1 of the Sherman Act have ever expressed or necessarily implied such a prohibition.

With respect to this Court's understanding of pre-Sherman Act common law, petitioner refers to our decision in *Dr. Miles Medical Co. v. John D. Park & Sons Co.* Though that was an early Sherman Act case, its holding that a resale price maintenance agreement was *per se* illegal was based largely on the perception that such an agreement was categorically impermissible at common law. As the opinion made plain, however, the basis for that common-law judgment was that the resale restriction was an unlawful restraint on alienation.... *"Dr. Miles* ... decided that under the general law the owner of movables ... could not sell the movables and lawfully by contract fix a price at which the product should afterwards be sold, because to do so would be at one and the same time to sell and retain, to part with and yet to hold, to project the will of the seller so as to cause it to control the movable parted with when it was not subject to his will because owned by another." In the present case, of course, no agreement on resale price or price level, and hence no restraint on alienation, was found by the jury, so the common-law rationale of *Dr. Miles* does not apply. Cf. *United States v. General Electric Co.*, 272 U.S. 476, 486-488 (1926) (*Dr. Miles* does not apply to restrictions on price to be charged by one who is in reality an agent of, not a buyer from, the manufacturer).

Petitioner's principal contention has been that the District Court's rule on *per se* illegality is compelled not by the old common law, but by our more recent Sherman Act precedents. First, petitioner contends that since certain horizontal agreements have been held to constitute price fixing (and thus to be *per se* illegal) though they did not set prices or price levels, see, e.g., *Catalano, Inc. v. Target Sales, Inc.*, 446 U.S. 643, 647-650 (1980) (*per curiam*), it is improper to require that a vertical agreement set prices or price levels before it can suffer the same fate. This notion of equivalence between the scope of horizontal *per se* illegality and that of vertical *per se* illegality was explicitly rejected in *GTE Sylvania*, as it had to be, since a horizontal agreement to divide territories is *per se* illegal, see *United States v. Topco Assocs.*, 405 U.S. 596, 608 (1972), while *GTE Sylvania* held that a vertical agreement to do so is not....

Second, petitioner contends that *per se* illegality here follows from our two cases holding *per se* illegal a group boycott of a dealer because of its price cutting. See *United States v. General Motors Corp.*, 384 U.S. 127 (1966); *Klor's, Inc. v. Broadway-Hale Stores, Inc.*, 359 U.S. 207 (1959). This second contention is merely a restatement of the first, since both cases involved horizontal combinations....

Third, petitioner contends, relying on *Albrecht v. Herald Co.*, 390 U.S. 145 (1968), and *United States v. Parke, Davis & Co.*, 362 U.S. 29 (1960), that our vertical price-fixing cases have already rejected the proposition that *per se* illegality requires setting a price or a price level. We disagree. In *Albrecht*, the maker of the product formed a combination to force a retailer to charge the maker's advertised retail price. This combination had two aspects. Initially, the maker hired a third party to solicit customers away from the noncomplying retailer. This solicitor "was aware that the aim of the solicitation campaign was to force [the noncomplying retailer] to lower his price" to the suggested retail price. Next, that maker engaged another retailer who "undertook to deliver [products] at the suggested price" to the noncomplying retailer's customers obtained by the solicitor. *Ibid.* This combination of maker, solicitor, and new retailer was held to be *per se* illegal. It is plain that the combination involved both an explicit agreement on resale price and an agreement to force another to adhere to the specified price.

In *Parke, Davis*, a manufacturer combined first with wholesalers and then with retailers in order to gain "the retailers' adherence to its suggested minimum retail prices." The manufacturer also brokered an agreement among its retailers not to advertise prices below its suggested retail prices, which agreement was held to be part of the *per se* illegal combination. This holding also does not support a rule that an agreement on price or price level is not required for a vertical restraint to be *per se* illegal — first, because the agreement not to advertise prices was part and parcel of the combination that contained the price agreement, and second because the agreement among retailers that the manufacturer organized was a *horizontal* conspiracy among competitors.

....

In sum, economic analysis supports the view, and no precedent opposes it, that a vertical restraint is not illegal *per se* unless it includes some agreement on price or price levels. Accordingly, the judgment of the Fifth Circuit is *Affirmed*.

JUSTICE STEVENS, with whom JUSTICE WHITE joins, dissenting.
....

II

It may be helpful to begin by explaining why the agreement in this case does not fit into certain categories of agreement that are frequently found in antitrust litigation. First, despite the contrary implications in the majority opinion, this is not a case in which the manufacturer is alleged to have imposed any vertical nonprice restraints on any of its dealers. The term "vertical nonprice restraint," as used in *Continental T.V., Inc. v. GTE Sylvania Inc.*, 433 U.S. 36 (1977), and similar cases, refers to a contractual term that a dealer must accept in order to qualify for a franchise. Typically, the dealer must agree to meet certain standards in its advertising, promotion, product display, and provision of repair and maintenance services in order to protect the goodwill of the manufacturer's product. Sometimes a dealer must agree to sell only to certain classes of customers — for example, wholesalers generally may only sell to retailers and may be required not to sell directly to consumers. In *Sylvania*, to take another example, we examined agreements between a manufacturer and its dealers that included "provisions barring the retailers from selling franchised products from locations other than those specified in agreements." *Id.*, 433 U.S., at 37. Restrictions of that kind, which are a part of, or ancillary to, the basic franchise agreement, are perfectly lawful unless the "rule of reason" is violated. Although vertical nonprice restraints may have some adverse effect on competition, as long as they serve the main purpose of a procompetitive distribution agreement, the ancillary restraints may be defended under the rule of reason. And, of course, a dealer who violates such a restraint may properly be terminated by the manufacturer.

In this case, it does not appear that respondent imposed any vertical nonprice restraints upon either petitioner or Hartwell. Specifically, respondent did not enter into any "exclusive" agreement, as did the defendant in *Sylvania*. It is true that before Hartwell was appointed and after petitioner was terminated, the manufacturer was represented by only one retailer in the Houston market, but there is no evidence that respondent ever made any contractual commitment to give either of them any exclusive rights. This therefore is not a case in which a manufacturer's right to grant exclusive territories, or to change the identity of the dealer in an established exclusive territory, is implicated. The case is one in which one of two competing dealers entered into an agreement with the manufacturer to terminate a particular competitor without making any promise to provide better or more efficient services and without receiving any guarantee of exclusivity in the future. The contractual relationship between respondent and Hartwell was exactly the same after petitioner's termination as it had been before that termination.

Second, this case does not involve a typical vertical price restraint. As the Court of Appeals noted, there is some evidence in the record that may support the conclusion that respondent and Hartwell implicitly agreed that Hartwell's prices would be maintained at a level somewhat higher than petitioner had been charging before petitioner was terminated. 780 F.2d 1212, 1219 (5th Cir. 1986). The illegality of the agreement found by the jury does not, however, depend on such evidence. For purposes of analysis, we should assume that no such agreement existed and that respondent was perfectly willing to allow its dealers to set prices at levels that would maximize their profits. That seems to have been the situation during the period when petitioner was the only dealer in Houston. Moreover, after respondent appointed Hartwell as its second dealer, it was Hartwell, rather than respondent, who objected to petitioner's pricing policies.

Third, this is not a case in which the manufacturer acted independently. Indeed, given the jury's verdict, it is not even a case in which the termination can be explained as having been based on the violation of any distribution policy adopted by respondent. The termination was motivated by the ultimatum that respondent received from Hartwell and that ultimatum, in turn, was the culmination of Hartwell's complaints about petitioner's competitive price cutting. The termination was plainly the product of coercion by the stronger of two dealers rather than an attempt to maintain an orderly and efficient system of distribution.[4]

---

[4] "When a manufacturer acts on its own, in pursuing its own market strategy, it is seeking to compete with other manufacturers by imposing what may be defended as reasonable vertical restraints. This would appear to be the rationale of the *GTE Sylvania* decision. However, if the action of a manufacturer or other supplier is taken at the direction of its customer, the restraint becomes primarily horizontal in nature in that one customer is seeking to suppress its competition by utilizing the power of a common supplier. Therefore, although the termination in such a situation is, itself, a vertical restraint, the desired impact is horizontal and on the dealer, not the manufacturer, level." *Cernuto, Inc. v. United Cabinet Corp.*, 595 F.2d 164, 168 (3d Cir. 1979).

In sum, this case does not involve the reasonableness of any vertical restraint imposed on one or more dealers by a manufacturer in its basic franchise agreement. What the jury found was a simple and naked "'agreement between Sharp and Hartwell to terminate Business Electronics because of Business Electronics' price cutting.'"

....

IV

What is most troubling about the majority's opinion is its failure to attach any weight to the value of intrabrand competition. In *Continental T.V., Inc. v. GTE Sylvania Inc.*, 433 U.S. 36 (1977), we correctly held that a demonstrable benefit to interbrand competition will outweigh the harm to intrabrand competition that is caused by the imposition of vertical nonprice restrictions on dealers. But we also expressly reaffirmed earlier cases in which the illegal conspiracy affected only intrabrand competition. Not a word in the *Sylvania* opinion implied that the elimination of intrabrand competition could be justified as reasonable without any evidence of a purpose to improve interbrand competition.

In the case before us today, the relevant economic market was the sale at retail in the Houston area of calculators manufactured by respondent. There is no dispute that an agreement to fix prices in that market, either horizontally between petitioner and Hartwell or vertically between respondent and either or both of the two dealers, would violate the Sherman Act. The "quite plausible" assumption that such an agreement might enable the retailers to provide better services to their customers would not have avoided the strict rule against price fixing that this Court has consistently enforced in the past.

Under petitioner's theory of the case, an agreement between respondent and Hartwell to terminate petitioner because of its price cutting was just as indefensible as any of those price-fixing agreements. At trial the jury found the existence of such an agreement to eliminate petitioner's price competition. Respondent had denied that any agreement had been made and asked the jury to find that it had independently decided to terminate petitioner because of its poor sales performance, but after hearing several days of testimony, the jury concluded that this defense was pretextual.

Neither the Court of Appeals nor the majority questions the accuracy of the jury's resolution of the factual issues in this case. Nevertheless, the rule the majority fashions today is based largely on its concern that in other cases juries will be unable to tell the difference between truthful and pretextual defenses. Thus, it opines that "even a manufacturer that agrees with one dealer to terminate another for failure to provide contractually-obligated services, exposes itself to the highly plausible claim that its real motivation was to terminate a price cutter." But such a "plausible" concern in a hypothetical case that is so different from this one should not be given greater weight than facts that can be established by hard evidence. If a dealer has, in fact, failed to provide contractually obligated services, and if the manufacturer has, in fact, terminated the dealer for that reason, both of those objective facts should be provable by admissible evidence. Both in its disposition of this case and in its attempt to justify a new approach to agreements to eliminate price competition, the majority exhibits little confidence in the judicial process as a means of ascertaining the truth.

The majority fails to consider that manufacturers such as respondent will only be held liable in the rare case in which the following can be proved: First, the terminated dealer must overcome the high hurdle of *Monsanto Co. v. Spray-Rite Service Corp.*, 465 U.S. 752 (1984). A terminated dealer must introduce "evidence that tends to exclude the possibility that the manufacturer and nonterminated distributors were acting independently." *Id.*, at 764. Requiring judges to adhere to the strict test for agreement laid down in *Monsanto*, in their jury instructions or own findings of fact, goes a long way toward ensuring that the many legitimate dealer termination decisions do not succumb improperly to antitrust liability.

Second, the terminated dealer must prove that the agreement was based on a purpose to terminate it because of its price cutting. Proof of motivation is another commonplace in antitrust litigation of which the majority appears apprehensive, but as we have explained or demonstrated many times, ... in antitrust, as in many other areas of the law, motivation matters and factfinders are able to distinguish bad from good intent.

Third, the manufacturer may rebut the evidence tending to prove that the sole purpose of the agreement was to eliminate a price cutter by offering evidence that it entered the agreement for legitimate, nonprice-related reasons.

Although in this case the jury found a naked agreement to terminate a dealer because of its price cutting, the majority boldly characterizes the same agreement as "this nonprice vertical restriction." That characterization is surely an oxymoron when applied to the agreement the jury actually found. Nevertheless, the majority proceeds to justify it as "ancillary" to a "quite plausible purpose ... to enable Hartwell to provide better services under the sales franchise agreement." There are two significant reasons why that justification is unacceptable.

First, it is not supported by the jury's verdict. Although it did not do so with precision, the District Court did instruct the jury that in order to hold respondent liable it had to find that the agreement's purpose was to eliminate petitioner because of its price cutting and that no valid vertical nonprice restriction existed to which the motivation to eliminate price competition at the dealership level was merely ancillary.

Second, the "quite plausible purpose" the majority hypothesizes as salvation for the otherwise anticompetitive elimination of price competition — "to enable Hartwell to provide better services under the sales franchise agreement" — is simply not the type of concern we sought to protect in *Continental T.V., Inc. v. GTE Sylvania Inc.*, 433 U.S. 36 (1977). I have emphasized in this dissent the difference between restrictions imposed in pursuit of a manufacturer's structuring of its product distribution, and those imposed at the behest of retailers who care less about the general efficiency of a product's promotion than their own profit margins. *Sylvania* stressed the importance of the former, not the latter; we referred to the use that *manufacturers* can make of vertical nonprice restraints, and nowhere did we discuss the benefits of permitting dealers to structure intrabrand competition at the retail level by coercing manufacturers into essentially anticompetitive agreements. Thus, while Hartwell may indeed be able to provide better services under the sales franchise agreement with petitioner out of the way, one would not have thought, until today, that the mere possibility of such a result — at the expense of the elimination of price competition and absent the salutary overlay of a manufacturer's distribution decision with the entire product line in mind — would be sufficient to legitimate an otherwise purely anticompetitive restraint. In fact, given the majority's total reliance on "economic analysis," it is hard to understand why, if such a purpose were sufficient to avoid the application of a *per se* rule in this context, the same purpose should not also be sufficient to trump the *per se* rule in all other price-fixing cases that arguably permit cartel members to "provide better services."

. . . .

The "plausible purpose" posited by the majority as its sole justification for this mischaracterized "nonprice vertical restriction" is inconsistent with the legislative judgment that underlies the Sherman Act itself. Under the facts as found by the jury in this case, the agreement before us is one whose "sole object is to restrain trade in order to avoid the competition which it has always been the policy of the common law to foster." *United States v. Addyston Pipe & Steel Co.*, 85 F., at 283, *aff'd*, 175 U.S. 211 (1899).

V

In sum, this simply is not a case in which procompetitive vertical nonprice restraints have been imposed; in fact, it is not a case in which *any* procompetitive agreement is at issue. The sole purpose of the agreement between respondent and Hartwell was to eliminate price competition at Hartwell's level. As Judge Bork has aptly explained: "Since the naked boycott is a form of predatory behavior, there is little doubt that it should be a per se violation of the Sherman Act." Bork, The Antitrust Paradox, at 334.

I respectfully dissent.

NOTES AND QUESTIONS

1. What was the error in the district court's jury instruction? After *Business Electronics*, how would you draft the instruction setting forth the proper standard for a per se violation? For a violation under the rule of reason?

2. Notice the Court's rejection of the traditional antitrust "characterization" process which, at times, has resulted in formalistic line drawing. The Court emphasizes that a plaintiff must, instead, show a demonstrable economic (negative) effect, such as an output restriction or evidence of cartelization. How does this standard differ from that required under the rule of reason? Didn't *Sylvania* hold that a nonprice vertical restraint that results in a net anticompetitive consequence in the interbrand market violates the Sherman Act even under the rule of reason? If so, is there anything left, after *Business Electronics*, of the per se standard?

3. *Monsanto* and *Business Electronics* substantially increase the burden of proof required of a plaintiff, thus decreasing the possibility that a terminated dealer will succeed in a case against a manufacturer. Given *Business Electronics'* holding that for a per se instruction the plaintiff must present evidence from which a jury could find that the agreement to terminate was part of a scheme to fix an actual resale price, how successful would a plaintiff be if she could demonstrate that after the defendant manufacturer had made a *Colgate* announcement, specifying the resale price to be charged, she was terminated because competing dealers, all of whom adhered to the suggested resale price, complained to the manufacturer about the discount pricing of the plaintiff? Could the *Colgate*-announced price be the actual retail price or price level that the Court in *Business Electronics* required?

4. *Business Electronics* is an important case in many respects, including its admonition that horizontal per se cases are not analytical equivalents or precedents for vertical per se cases. In other words, the per se conclusion (or, as in this case, a per se jury instruction) will be substantially harder to justify than in a case where there is a proven agreement between competitors. For example, the Court makes clear that a vertical agreement that ultimately affects price is not to be condemned as per se illegal, absent an *actual* agreement to fix a specific price or price level. This is true, the Court holds, even though it concedes that the "free-rider" defense is designed to permit a termination of a discounter so that the remaining dealers can maintain higher prices and dealer margins that will support retail services.

The Court thus rejects the idea that a vertical agreement having the purpose or effect of eliminating price competition is a naked restraint that is per se illegal. The "free-rider" argument, at least in the vertical context, is accepted by a majority of the Court as a bona fide defense within the common law doctrine of ancillary restraints. According to the majority, if the restraint (the termination of a price discounter) "enhances the value of the contract or permits the 'enjoyment of [its] fruits,'" it comes within the ancillary restraint doctrine.

5. Did Justice Scalia's opinion cite any specific evidence in the trial record to support the free-rider defense — that is, that the defendant manufacturer was motivated in its termination by a desire to ensure adequate retail services that would require higher retail prices? Consider the dissent on the point. It notes that there were no contractual provisions that imposed the typical nonprice restraints that are designed to avoid free-rider problems. 108 U.S., at 1528. Hence, is the majority's free-rider justification based on a theoretical possibility or conjecture, or on an ex-post rationalization?

If the dissent is correct that the dealer was not terminated for failure to provide contractually-obligated services, what could have motivated the manufacturer, other than to suppress intrabrand price competition? Could it be possible that although there were no contractual obligations for pre- and post-sale service, the manufacturer nevertheless desired its retailers to provide such service on their own and thus was motivated by the lack of service provided by the plaintiff?

6. Does *Business Electronics*, together with *Monsanto*, leave the *per se* status of vertical price fixing only nominally intact? Has the Court gradually moved away from its pronouncements in *Dr. Miles* on per se illegality for vertical price fixing agreements? Do you agree that the *Colgate* doctrine has been strengthened by *Business Electronics* at the expense of *Dr. Miles*? Or is it more accurate to say that *Business Electronics* merely narrows the definition of RPM? *See* E.T. Sullivan & J. Harrison, *Understanding Antitrust and Its Economic Implications* 157-58 (2d ed. 1994).

7. Importantly, *Business Electronics* has articulated a clear benchmark by which to judge future vertical cases:

> [T]here is a presumption in favor of a rule-of-reason standard; that departure from that standard must be justified by demonstrable economic effect, such as the facilitation of cartelizing, rather than formalistic distinctions; that interbrand competition is the primary concern of the antitrust laws; and that the rules in this area should be formulated with a view towards protecting the doctrine of *GTE Sylvania*.

485 U.S. at 726.

PROBLEM 5.3

Parkway Gallery is an independent dealer of furniture. It sells its furniture at "deep discounts" in full-service retail stores in High Point and Boone, North Carolina. Along with other suppliers, it purchases a substantial amount of its furniture stock from Kittinger/Pennsylvania House Group. Pennsylvania House Group requires that the independent retailers dedicate a certain amount of floor space to display Pennsylvania House furniture and that each dealer participate in Pennsylvania House promotional programs and invest in local tabloids to advertise Pennsylvania House lines. Parkway receives about 100 customers a day, plus about 150 telephone inquiries and sales per day.

Other independent dealers complained to Pennsylvania House that they were losing sales to Parkway because of its deep discounts. Customers would visit stores of other dealers, but then buy at a discount from Parkway. Pennsylvania House responded by revising its retail marketing policy to prohibit dealers from soliciting or selling its furniture by mail or telephone order to consumers residing outside specified sales areas.

Before establishing the new policy, Pennsylvania House discussed its proposal with the complaining dealers, made a pledge to its dealer network that it would enforce the new policy against Parkway, found that a large number of its dealers were in agreement with the "aims and purpose of the policy," and obtained assurances from dealers that they would comply with the new policy. Several dealers even said that they would report Parkway violations to Pennsylvania House. After Parkway continued its practice of selling to customers outside its specified area through mail and telephone orders, it was terminated as a dealer by Pennsylvania House. Parkway seeks your advice. What result under *Monsanto*? Do these facts support the "something more" evidentiary standard established by *Monsanto*? See *Parkway Gallery Furn. v. Kittinger/Pennsylvania House*, 878 F.2d 801 (4th Cir. 1989).

PROBLEM 5.4

Sedgwick, Inc. produces consumer electronics and has three dealers in Kansas City. Dealers A and B are full service dealers who generally charge Sedgwick's suggested retail prices, subject to some downward deviation. C is a discounter. Independently of each other, A and B complain to Sedgwick about C's pricing, and each says words to this effect: "Make C raise its prices to the same level I am charging or else I am going to stop selling Sedgwick products." Soon thereafter Sedgwick terminates C. Have the antitrust laws been violated? See *Ben Elfman & Sons v. Criterion Mills*, 774 F. Supp. 683, 684-85 (D. Mass. 1991).

C. TERRITORIAL AND CUSTOMER RESTRAINTS: FROM *WHITE MOTOR* TO *SYLVANIA*

The law of vertical nonprice restraints has changed substantially since 1963. The impact of economic analysis on antitrust law has been great in this area. The decisionmaking process itself has undergone change as a result of economic analysis. In less than two decades the Court swung from a rule of reason evidentiary approach to a strict per se conclusive presumption and back to a rule of reason analysis. As a result, the decisional process has not been free of tension. The members of the Court have debated their ability to evaluate competitive conditions in light of economic factors. Justice Marshall, in *United States v. Topco Assocs.*, 405 U.S. 596, 611-12 (1972), cautioned that:

> If a decision is to be made to sacrifice competition in one portion of the economy for greater competition in another portion, this too is a decision that must be made by Congress and not by private forces or by the courts.... To analyze, interpret, and evaluate the myriad of competing interests and the endless data that would surely be brought to bear on such decisions, and to make the delicate judgment on the relative values to society of competitive areas of the economy, the judgment of the elected representatives of the people is required.

Others on the Court have observed that the cursory analysis endorsed by the per se rule does not take into account "the relevant economic realities in the light of the basic policy and goals of the Sherman Act." *Id.* at 615 (Burger, C.J., dissenting). Economics, it was urged, should inform antitrust law's content and purpose.

As the following cases indicate, changing analysis of nonprice vertical restraints gave rise to a limited rule of reason which initially considered whether the challenged conduct lacked any redeeming merit. If the inquiry discovered that the practice had some degree of competitive merit, courts were to decide whether cost-saving efficiencies were achieved by the challenged practice and, if so, weigh those against the severity of the restraint. The result was the erosion of the per se rule of illegality, which had been established for "judicial convenience and ready predictability." *Id.* at 614-15.

The territorial and customer restraints considered in this section arise when a dealer and/or distributor of a manufacturer's product is given freedom from intrabrand competition within a particular geographic area or for trading with certain customers. Arguably, the restriction indicates that the manufacturer preferred to insulate its dealer from *intrabrand* competition so that the dealer could promote the manufacturer's product more competitively against the brand products of other manufacturers in the *interbrand* market. Such restrictions are usually contractual; the manufacturer agrees not to authorize other dealers in a given area and, in turn, the dealers agree not to compete outside the designated area. Customer restrictions are similarly drafted, restricting selling to certain customers. The dealer then is restricted from competing with other dealers (or the manufacturer) in that brand, according to territories or customers. These contractual arrangements are often associated with or found in a franchise arrangement. Because of the possible restrictions on competition, section 1 of the Sherman Act is implicated.

As you study the following cases, consider the analysis used by the Court in the horizontal market division cases studied in Chapter 4, especially the *Sealy* and *Topco* decisions. In attempting to reconcile the varying approaches, consider the analysis by which courts characterize the relationship among the parties: whether they are in a seller/buyer, supplier/competitor, or franchisor/franchisee relationship; and how courts have evaluated those relationships within legal and economic standards.

The legal status of nonprice vertical restrictions was unclear up to 1963. The Department of Justice had long taken the position that vertical restraints were per se unlawful. The issue was addressed by the Supreme Court in *White Motor Co. v. United States*, 372 U.S. 253 (1963). The defendant, White Motor, manufactured trucks and truck components and contractually agreed with its dealers that the dealers would sell White Motor trucks only in certain designated areas, and then only to certain customers within the exclusive territory. These territorial and customer restrictions were challenged by the government as per se illegal. In reversing the trial court's summary judgment finding that the restrictions were unlawful, the Court stated:

> We are asked to extend the holding in *Timken Roller Bearing Co. v. United States* (which banned *horizontal* arrangements among competitors to

divide territory) to a *vertical* arrangement by one manufacturer restricting the territory of his distributors or dealers. We intimate no view one way or the other on the legality of such an arrangement, for we believe that the applicable rule of law should be designed after a trial.

This is the first case involving a territorial restriction in a *vertical* arrangement; and we know too little of the actual impact of both that restriction and the one respecting customers to reach a conclusion on the bare bones of the documentary evidence before us.

. . . .

Horizontal territorial limitations, like "[g]roup boycotts, or concerted refusals by traders to deal with other traders" are naked restraints of trade with no purpose except stifling of competition. A vertical territorial limitation may or may not have that purpose or effect. We do not know enough of the economic and business stuff out of which these arrangements emerge to be certain. They may be too dangerous to sanction or they may be allowable protections against aggressive competitors or the only practicable means a small company has for breaking into or staying in business and within the "rule of reason." We need to know more than we do about the actual impact of these arrangements on competition to decide whether they have such a "pernicious effect on competition and lack ... any redeeming virtue" and therefore should be classified as *per se* violations of the Sherman Act.

. . . .

We conclude that the summary judgment, apart from the price-fixing phase of the case, was improperly employed in this suit. Apart from price fixing, we do not intimate any view on the merits. We only hold that the legality of the territorial and customer limitations should be determined only after a trial.

After remand, the parties entered into a consent decree, settling the suit, a part of which enjoined White Motor from engaging in the challenged restrictions.

Four years later the Court was again confronted with the question of what legal standard to apply to vertical nonprice restraints. In *United States v. Arnold, Schwinn & Co.*, 388 U.S. 365 (1967), the Court, speaking through Justice Fortas, held that vertical (territory and dealer) restrictions by manufacturers require a different analysis "between the situation where the manufacturer parts with title, dominion, or risk with respect to the article, and where he completely retains ownership and risk of loss." *Id.* at 378-79. The Court concluded that "where a manufacturer *sells* products to his distributor subject to territorial [and customer] restrictions upon resale, a per se violation of the Sherman Act results." *Id.* at 379. Ten years later, the Court, in response to criticism of *Schwinn*, reviewed its per se rule for vertical restraints.

CONTINENTAL T.V., INC. V. GTE SYLVANIA, INC.

433 U.S. 36 (1977)

JUSTICE POWELL delivered the opinion of the Court.

Franchise agreements between manufacturers and retailers frequently include provisions barring the retailers from selling franchised products from locations other than those specified in the agreements. This case presents important questions concerning the appropriate antitrust analysis of these restrictions....

I

Respondent GTE Sylvania Inc. (Sylvania) manufactures and sells television sets through its Home Entertainment Products Division. Prior to 1962, like most other television manufacturers, Sylvania sold its televisions to independent or company-owned distributors who in turn resold to a large and diverse group of retailers. Prompted by a decline in its market share to a relatively insignificant 1% to 2% of national television sales,[1] Sylvania conducted an intensive reassessment of its marketing strategy, and in 1962 adopted the franchise plan challenged here. Sylvania phased out its wholesale distributors and began to sell its televisions directly to a smaller and more select group of franchised retailers. An acknowledged purpose of the change was to decrease the number of competing Sylvania retailers in the hope of attracting the more aggressive and competent retailers thought necessary to the improvement of the company's market position.[2] To this end, Sylvania limited the number of franchises granted for any given area and required each franchisee to sell his Sylvania products only from the location or locations at which he was franchised.[3] A franchise did not constitute an exclusive territory, and Sylvania retained sole discretion to increase the number of retailers in an area in light of the success or failure of existing retailers in developing their market. The revised marketing strategy appears to have been successful during the period at issue here, for by 1965 Sylvania's share of national television sales had increased to approximately 5%, and the company ranked as the Nation's eighth largest manufacturer of color television sets.

This suit is the result of the rupture of a franchisor-franchisee relationship that had previously prospered under the revised Sylvania plan. Dissatisfied with its sales in the city of San Francisco, Sylvania decided in the spring of 1965 to franchise Young Brothers, an established San Francisco retailer of televisions, as an additional San Francisco retailer. The proposed location of the new franchise was

---

[1] RCA at that time was the dominant firm with as much as 60% to 70% of national television sales in an industry with more than 100 manufacturers.

[2] The number of retailers selling Sylvania products declined significantly as a result of the change, but in 1965 there were at least two franchised Sylvania retailers in each metropolitan center of more than 100,000 population.

[3] Sylvania imposed no restrictions on the right of the franchisee to sell the products of competing manufacturers.

approximately a mile from a retail outlet operated by petitioner Continental T.V., Inc. (Continental), one of the most successful Sylvania franchisees. Continental protested that the location of the new franchise violated Sylvania's marketing policy, but Sylvania persisted in its plans. Continental then canceled a large Sylvania order and placed a large order with Phillips, one of Sylvania's competitors.

During this same period, Continental expressed a desire to open a store in Sacramento, Cal., a desire Sylvania attributed at least in part to Continental's displeasure over the Young Brothers decision. Sylvania believed that the Sacramento market was adequately served by the existing Sylvania retailers and denied the request.[6] In the face of this denial, Continental advised Sylvania in early September 1965, that it was in the process of moving Sylvania merchandise from its San Jose, Cal., warehouse to a new retail location that it had leased in Sacramento. Two weeks later, allegedly for unrelated reasons, Sylvania's credit department reduced Continental's credit line from $300,000 to $50,000. In response to the reduction in credit and the generally deteriorating relations with Sylvania, Continental withheld all payments owed to John P. Maguire & Co., Inc. (Maguire), the finance company that handled the credit arrangements between Sylvania and its retailers. Shortly thereafter, Sylvania terminated Continental's franchises, and Maguire filed this diversity action in the United States District Court for the Northern District of California seeking recovery of money owed and of secured merchandise held by Continental.

The antitrust issues before us originated in cross-claims brought by Continental against Sylvania and Maguire. Most important for our purposes was the claim that Sylvania had violated § 1 of the Sherman Act by entering into and enforcing franchise agreements that prohibited the sale of Sylvania products other than from specified locations.[8] At the close of evidence in the jury trial of Continental's claims, Sylvania requested the District Court to instruct the jury that its location restriction was illegal only if it unreasonably restrained or suppressed competition. Relying on this Court's decision in *Schwinn* the District Court rejected the proffered instruction in favor of the following one:

> Therefore, if you find by a preponderance of the evidence that Sylvania entered into a contract, combination or conspiracy with one or more of its dealers pursuant to which Sylvania exercised dominion or control over the products sold to the dealer, after having parted with title and risk to the products, you must find any effort thereafter to restrict outlets or store locations from which its dealers resold the merchandise which they had purchased from Sylvania to be a violation of Section 1 of the Sherman Act, regardless of the reasonableness of the location restrictions.

---

[6] Sylvania had achieved exceptional results in Sacramento, where its market share exceeded 15% in 1965.

[8] Although Sylvania contended in the District Court that its policy was unilaterally enforced, it now concedes that its location restriction involved understandings or agreements with the retailers.

In answers to special interrogatories, the jury found that Sylvania had engaged "in a contract, combination or conspiracy in restraint of trade in violation of the antitrust laws with respect to location restrictions alone," and assessed Continental's damages at $591,505, which was trebled pursuant to 15 U.S.C. § 15 to produce an award of $1,774,515.

On appeal, the Court of Appeals for the Ninth Circuit, sitting en banc, reversed by a divided vote. 537 F.2d 980 (1976). The court acknowledged that there is language in *Schwinn* that could be read to support the District Court's instruction but concluded that *Schwinn* was distinguishable on several grounds. Contrasting the nature of the restrictions, their competitive impact, and the market shares of the franchisers in the two cases, the court concluded that Sylvania's location restriction had less potential for competitive harm than the restrictions invalidated in *Schwinn* and thus should be judged under the "rule of reason" rather than the *per se* rule stated in *Schwinn.* The court found support for its position in the policies of the Sherman Act and in the decisions of other federal courts involving nonprice vertical restrictions.[10]

....

II

A

We turn first to Continental's contention that Sylvania's restriction on retail locations is a *per se* violation of § 1 of the Sherman Act as interpreted in *Schwinn....*

B

In the present case, it is undisputed that title to the television sets passed from Sylvania to Continental. Thus, the *Schwinn per se* rule applies unless Sylvania's restriction on locations falls outside *Schwinn*'s prohibition against a manufacturer's attempting to restrict a "retailer's freedom as to where and to whom it will resell the products." *Id.,* at 378. As the Court of Appeals conceded, the language of *Schwinn* is clearly broad enough to apply to the present case. Unlike the Court of Appeals, however, we are unable to find a principled basis for distinguishing *Schwinn* from the case now before us.

Both Schwinn and Sylvania sought to reduce but not to eliminate competition among their respective retailers through the adoption of a franchise system. Although it was not one of the issues addressed by the District Court or presented on appeal by the Government, the Schwinn franchise plan included a location

---

[10] There were two major dissenting opinions. Judge Kilkenny argued that the present case is indistinguishable from *Schwinn* and that the jury had been correctly instructed. Agreeing with Judge Kilkenny's interpretation of *Schwinn*, Judge Browning stated that he found the interpretation responsive to and justified by the need to protect "'individual traders from unnecessary restrictions upon their freedom of action.'" 537 F.2d, at 1021. See n. 21, *infra.*

restriction similar to the one challenged here. These restrictions allowed Schwinn and Sylvania to regulate the amount of competition among their retailers by preventing a franchisee from selling franchised products from outlets other than the one covered by the franchise agreement. To exactly the same end, the Schwinn franchise plan included a companion restriction, apparently not found in the Sylvania plan, that prohibited franchised retailers from selling Schwinn products to nonfranchised retailers. In *Schwinn* the Court expressly held that this restriction was impermissible under the broad principle stated there. In intent and competitive impact, the retail-customer restriction in *Schwinn* is indistinguishable from the location restriction in the present case. In both cases the restrictions limited the freedom of the retailer to dispose of the purchased products as he desired. The fact that one restriction was addressed to territory and the other to customers is irrelevant to functional antitrust analysis and, indeed, to the language and broad thrust of the opinion in *Schwinn*.[12] As Mr. Chief Justice Hughes stated in *Appalachian Coals, Inc. v. United States*, 288 U.S. 344, 360, 377 (1933): "Realities must dominate the judgment.... The Anti-Trust Act aims at substance."

III

Sylvania argues that if *Schwinn* cannot be distinguished, it should be reconsidered. Although *Schwinn* is supported by the principle of *stare decisis*, ... we are convinced that the need for clarification of the law in this area justifies reconsideration. *Schwinn* itself was an abrupt and largely unexplained departure from *White Motor Co. v. United States*, 372 U.S. 253 (1963), where only four years earlier the Court had refused to endorse a *per se* rule for vertical restrictions. Since its announcement, *Schwinn* has been the subject of continuing controversy and confusion, both in the scholarly journals and in the federal courts. The great weight of scholarly opinion has been critical of the decision, and a number of the federal courts confronted with analogous vertical restrictions have sought to limit

---

[12] The distinctions drawn by the Court of Appeals and endorsed in Mr. Justice White's separate opinion have no basis in *Schwinn*. The intrabrand competitive impact of the restrictions at issue in *Schwinn* ranged from complete elimination to mere reduction; yet, the Court did not even hint at any distinction on this ground. Similarly, there is no suggestion that the *per se* rule was applied because of Schwinn's prominent position in its industry. That position was the same whether the bicycles were sold or consigned, but the Court's analysis was quite different. In light of Mr. Justice White's emphasis on the "superior consumer acceptance" enjoyed by the Schwinn brand name, we note that the Court rejected precisely that premise in *Schwinn*. Applying the rule of reason to the restrictions imposed in nonsale transactions, the Court stressed that there was "no showing that [competitive bicycles were] not in all respects reasonably interchangeable as articles of competitive commerce with the Schwinn product" and that it did "not regard Schwinn's claim of product excellence as establishing the contrary." 388 U.S., at 381, and n. 7. Although *Schwinn* did hint at preferential treatment for new entrants and failing firms, the District Court below did not even submit Sylvania's claim that it was failing to the jury. Accordingly, Mr. Justice White's position appears to reflect an extension of *Schwinn* in this regard. Having crossed the "failing firm" line, Mr. Justice White attempts neither to draw a new one nor to explain why one should be drawn at all.

its reach. In our view, the experience of the past 10 years should be brought to bear on this subject of considerable commercial importance.

The traditional framework of analysis under § 1 of the Sherman Act is familiar and does not require extended discussion. Section 1 prohibits "[e]very contract, combination ..., or conspiracy, in restraint of trade or commerce." Since the early years of this century a judicial gloss on the statutory language has established the "rule of reason" as the prevailing standard of analysis. *Standard Oil Co. v. United States*, 221 U.S. 1 (1911). Under this rule, the factfinder weighs all of the circumstances of a case in deciding whether a restrictive practice should be prohibited as imposing an unreasonable restraint on competition.[15] *Per se* rules of illegality are appropriate only when they relate to conduct that is manifestly anticompetitive. As the Court explained in *Northern Pac. R. Co. v. United States*, 356 U.S. 1, 5 (1958), "there are certain agreements or practices which because of their pernicious effect on competition and lack of any redeeming virtue are conclusively presumed to be unreasonable and therefore illegal without elaborate inquiry as to the precise harm they have caused or the business excuse for their use."[16]

In essence, the issue before us is whether *Schwinn's per se* rule can be justified under the demanding standards of *Northern Pac. R. Co.* The Court's refusal to endorse a *per se* rule in *White Motor Co.* was based on its uncertainty as to whether vertical restrictions satisfied those standards. Addressing this question for the first time, the Court stated:

> We need to know more than we do about the actual impact of these arrangements on competition to decide whether they have such a "pernicious

---

[15] One of the most frequently cited statements of the rule of reason is that of Justice Brandeis in *Chicago Bd. of Trade v. United States*, 246 U.S. 231, 238 (1918):

> The true test of legality is whether the restraint imposed is such as merely regulates and perhaps thereby promotes competition or whether it is such as may suppress or even destroy competition. To determine that question the court must ordinarily consider the facts peculiar to the business to which the restraint is applied; its condition before and after the restraint was imposed; the nature of the restraint and its effect, actual or probable. The history of the restraint, the evil believed to exist, the reason for adopting the particular remedy, the purpose or end sought to be attained, are all relevant facts. This is not because a good intention will save an otherwise objectionable regulation or the reverse; but because knowledge of intent may help the court to interpret facts and to predict consequences.

[16] *Per se* rules thus require the Court to make broad generalizations about the social utility of particular commercial practices. The probability that anticompetitive consequences will result from a practice and the severity of those consequences must be balanced against its procompetitive consequences. Cases that do not fit the generalization may arise, but a *per se* rule reflects the judgment that such cases are not sufficiently common or important to justify the time and expense necessary to identify them. Once established, *per se* rules tend to provide guidance to the business community and to minimize the burdens on litigants and the judicial system of the more complex rule-of-reason trials, ... but those advantages are not sufficient in themselves to justify the creation of *per se* rules. If it were otherwise, all of antitrust law would be reduced to *per se* rules, thus introducing an unintended and undesirable rigidity in the law.

effect on competition and lack ... any redeeming virtue" and therefore should be classified as *per se* violations of the Sherman Act.

372 U.S., at 263. Only four years later the Court in *Schwinn* announced its sweeping *per se* rule without even a reference to *Northern Pac. R. Co.* and with no explanation of its sudden change in position. We turn now to consider *Schwinn* in light of *Northern Pac. R. Co.*

The market impact of vertical restrictions[18] is complex because of their potential for a simultaneous reduction of intrabrand competition and stimulation of interbrand competition.[19] Significantly, the Court in *Schwinn* did not distinguish among the challenged restrictions on the basis of their individual potential for intrabrand harm or interbrand benefit. Restrictions that completely eliminated intrabrand competition among Schwinn distributors were analyzed no differently from those that merely moderated intrabrand competition among retailers. The pivotal factor was the passage of title: All restrictions were held to be *per se* illegal where title had passed, and all were evaluated and sustained under the rule of reason where it had not. The location restriction at issue here would be subject to the same pattern of analysis under *Schwinn.*

It appears that this distinction between sale and nonsale transactions resulted from the Court's effort to accommodate the perceived intrabrand harm and inter-

---

[18] As in *Schwinn*, we are concerned here only with nonprice vertical restrictions. The *per se* illegality of price restrictions has been established firmly for many years and involves significantly different questions of analysis and policy. As Mr. Justice White notes, some commentators have argued that the manufacturer's motivation for imposing vertical price restrictions may be the same as for nonprice restrictions. There are, however, significant differences that could easily justify different treatment. In his concurring opinion in *White Motor Co. v. United States*, Mr. Justice Brennan noted that, unlike nonprice restrictions, "[r]esale price maintenance is not only designed to, but almost invariably does in fact, reduce price competition not only *among* sellers of the affected product, but quite as much *between* that product and competing brands." 372 U.S., at 268.... Furthermore, Congress recently has expressed its approval of a *per se* analysis of vertical price restrictions by repealing those provisions of the Miller-Tydings and McGuire Acts allowing fair-trade pricing at the option of the individual States. Consumer Goods Pricing Act of 1975, 89 Stat. 801, amending 15 U.S.C. §§ 1, 45 (a). No similar expression of congressional intent exists for nonprice restrictions.

[19] Interbrand competition is the competition among the manufacturers of the same generic product — television sets in this case — and is the primary concern of antitrust law. The extreme example of a deficiency of interbrand competition is monopoly, where there is only one manufacturer. In contrast, intrabrand competition is the competition between the distributors — wholesale or retail — of the product of a particular manufacturer.

The degree of intrabrand competition is wholly independent of the level of interbrand competition confronting the manufacturer. Thus, there may be fierce intrabrand competition among the distributors of a product produced by a monopolist and no intrabrand competition among the distributors of a product produced by a firm in a highly competitive industry. But when interbrand competition exists, as it does among television manufacturers, it provides a significant check on the exploitation of intrabrand market power because of the ability of consumers to substitute a different brand of the same product.

brand benefit of vertical restrictions. The *per se* rule for sale transactions reflected the view that vertical restrictions are "so obviously destructive" of intrabrand competition that their use would "open the door to exclusivity of outlets and limitations of territory further than prudence permits." 388 U.S., at 379-380.[21] Conversely, the continued adherence to the traditional rule of reason for nonsale transactions reflected the view that the restrictions have too great a potential for the promotion of interbrand competition to justify complete prohibition. The Court's opinion provides no analytical support for these contrasting positions. Nor is there even an assertion in the opinion that the competitive impact of vertical restrictions is significantly affected by the form of the transaction. Nonsale transactions appear to be excluded from the *per se* rule, not because of a greater danger of intrabrand harm or a greater promise of interbrand benefit, but rather because of the Court's unexplained belief that a complete *per se* prohibition would be too "inflexibl[e]." *Id.*, at 379.

Vertical restrictions reduce intrabrand competition by limiting the number of sellers of a particular product competing for the business of a given group of buyers. Location restrictions have this effect because of practical constraints on the effective marketing area of retail outlets. Although intrabrand competition may be reduced, the ability of retailers to exploit the resulting market may be limited both by the ability of consumers to travel to other franchised locations and, perhaps more importantly, to purchase the competing products of other manufacturers. None of these key variables, however, is affected by the form of the transaction by which a manufacturer conveys his products to the retailers.

Vertical restrictions promote interbrand competition by allowing the manufacturer to achieve certain efficiencies in the distribution of his products. These "redeeming virtues" are implicit in every decision sustaining vertical restrictions under the rule of reason. Economists have identified a number of ways in which manufacturers can use such restrictions to compete more effectively against other manufacturers....[23] For example, new manufacturers and manufacturers entering

---

[21] ... We are similarly unable to accept Judge Browning's interpretation of *Schwinn*. In his dissent below he argued that the decision reflects the view that the Sherman Act was intended to prohibit restrictions on the autonomy of independent businessmen even though they have no impact on "price, quality, and quantity of goods and services," 537 F.2d, at 1019. This view is certainly not explicit in *Schwinn*, which purports to be based on an examination of the "impact [of the restrictions] upon the marketplace." 388 U.S., at 374. Competitive economies have social and political as well as economic advantages, see *e.g., Northern Pac. R. Co. v. United States*, 356 U.S., at 4, but an antitrust policy divorced from market considerations would lack any objective benchmarks. As Justice Brandeis reminded us: "Every agreement concerning trade, every regulation of trade, restrains. To bind, to restrain, is of their very essence." *Chicago Bd. of Trade v. United States*, 246 U.S., at 238.

[23] Marketing efficiency is not the only legitimate reason for a manufacturer's desire to exert control over the manner in which his products are sold and serviced. As a result of statutory and common-law developments, society increasingly demands that manufacturers assume direct responsibility for the safety and quality of their products. For example, at the federal level, apart from more specialized requirements, manufacturers of consumer products have safety responsibilities

new markets can use the restrictions in order to induce competent and aggressive retailers to make the kind of investment of capital and labor that is often required in the distribution of products unknown to the consumer. Established manufacturers can use them to induce retailers to engage in promotional activities or to provide service and repair facilities necessary to the efficient marketing of their products. Service and repair are vital for many products, such as automobiles and major household appliances. The availability and quality of such services affect a manufacturer's goodwill and the competitiveness of his product. Because of market imperfections such as the so-called "free rider" effect, these services might not be provided by retailers in a purely competitive situation, despite the fact that each retailer's benefit would be greater if all provided the services than if none did....

Economists also have argued that manufacturers have an economic interest in maintaining as much intrabrand competition as is consistent with the efficient distribution of their products. Although the view that the manufacturer's interest necessarily corresponds with that of the public is not universally shared, even the leading critic of vertical restrictions concedes that *Schwinn's* distinction between sale and nonsale transactions is essentially unrelated to any relevant economic impact. Indeed, to the extent that the form of the transaction is related to interbrand benefits, the Court's distinction is inconsistent with its articulated concern for the ability of smaller firms to compete effectively with larger ones. Capital requirements and administrative expenses may prevent smaller firms from using the exception for nonsale transactions....[26]

We conclude that the distinction drawn in *Schwinn* between sale and nonsale transactions is not sufficient to justify the application of a *per se* rule in one situation and a rule of reason in the other. The question remains whether the *per se* rule stated in *Schwinn* should be expanded to include nonsale transactions or abandoned in favor of a return to the rule of reason. We have found no persuasive support for expanding the *per se* rule. As noted above, the *Schwinn* Court recognized the undesirability of "prohibit[ing] all vertical restrictions of territory and all franchising ...." 388 U.S., at 379-380. And even Continental does not urge us to hold that all such restrictions are *per se* illegal.

We revert to the standard articulated in *Northern Pac. R. Co.*, and reiterated in *White Motor*, for determining whether vertical restrictions must be "conclusively

---

under the Consumer Product Safety Act, 15 U.S.C. § 2051 *et seq.* (1970 ed., Supp. V), and obligations for warranties under the Consumer Product Warranties Act, 15 U.S.C. § 2301 *et seq.* (1970 ed., Supp. V). Similar obligations are imposed by state law. See, *e.g.*, Cal. Civ. Code Ann. § 1790 *et seq.* (West 1973). The legitimacy of these concerns has been recognized in cases involving vertical restrictions. See, *e.g.*, *Tripoli Co. v. Wella Corp.*, 425 F.2d 932 (3d Cir. 1970).

[26] We also note that *per se* rules in this area may work to the ultimate detriment of the small businessmen who operate as franchisees. To the extent that a *per se* rule prevents a firm from using the franchise system to achieve efficiencies that it perceives as important to its successful operation, the rule creates an incentive for vertical integration into the distribution system, thereby eliminating to that extent the role of independent businessmen.

presumed to be unreasonable and therefore illegal without elaborate inquiry as to the precise harm they have caused or the business excuse for their use." 356 U.S., at 5. Such restrictions, in varying forms, are widely used in our free market economy. As indicated above, there is substantial scholarly and judicial authority supporting the economic utility. There is relatively little authority to the contrary.[28] Certainly, there has been no showing in this case, either generally or with respect to Sylvania's agreements, that vertical restrictions have or are likely to have a "pernicious effect on competition" or that they "lack ... any redeeming virtue."[29] Accordingly, we conclude that the *per se* rule stated in *Schwinn* must be overruled. In so holding we do not foreclose the possibility that particular applications of vertical restrictions might justify *per se* prohibition under *Northern Pac. R.. Co.* But we do make clear that departure from the rule-of-reason standard must be based upon demonstrable economic effect rather than — as in *Schwinn* — upon formalistic line drawing.

In sum, we conclude that the appropriate decision is to return to the rule of reason that governed vertical restrictions prior to *Schwinn.* When anticompetitive effects are shown to result from particular vertical restrictions they can be adequately policed under the rule of reason, the standard traditionally applied for the majority of anticompetitive practices challenged under § 1 of the Act. Accordingly, the decision of the Court of Appeals is *Affirmed.*

JUSTICE WHITE, concurring.

Although I agree with the majority that the location clause at issue in this case is not a *per se* violation of the Sherman Act and should be judged under the rule of reason, I cannot agree that this result requires the overruling of *United States v. Arnold, Schwinn & Co.,* 388 U.S. 365 (1967). In my view this case is distinguishable from *Schwinn* because there is less potential for restraint of intrabrand competition and more potential for stimulating interbrand competition. As to intrabrand competition, Sylvania, unlike Schwinn, did not restrict the customers to whom or the territories where its purchasers could sell. As to interbrand competition, Sylvania, unlike Schwinn, had an insignificant market share at the time it

---

[28] There may be occasional problems in differentiating vertical restrictions from horizontal restrictions originating in agreements among the retailers. There is no doubt that restrictions in the latter category would be illegal *per se,* see, *e.g., United States v. General Motors Corp.,* 384 U.S. 127 (1966); *United States v. Topco Associates, Inc., supra,* but we do not regard the problems of proof as sufficiently great to justify a *per se* rule.

[29] The location restriction used by Sylvania was neither the least nor the most restrictive provision that it could have used. But we agree with the implicit judgment in *Schwinn* that a *per se* rule based on the nature of the restriction is, in general, undesirable. Although distinctions can be drawn among the frequently used restrictions, we are inclined to view them as differences of degree and form.... We are unable to perceive significant social gain from channeling transactions into one form or another. Finally, we agree with the Court in *Schwinn* that the advantages of vertical restrictions should not be limited to the categories of new entrants and failing firms. Sylvania was faltering, if not failing, and we think it would be unduly artificial to deny it the use of valuable competitive tools.

adopted its challenged distribution practice and enjoyed no consumer preference that would allow its retailers to charge a premium over other brands....

One element of the system of interrelated vertical restraints invalidated in *Schwinn* was a retail-customer restriction prohibiting franchised retailers from selling Schwinn products to nonfranchised retailers. The Court rests its inability to distinguish *Schwinn* entirely on this retail-customer restriction, finding it "[i]n intent and competitive impact ... indistinguishable from the location restriction in the present case," because "[i]n both cases the restrictions limited the freedom of the retailer to dispose of the purchased products as he desired." The customer restriction may well have, however, a very different "intent and competitive impact" than the location restriction: It prevents discount stores from getting the manufacturer's product and thus prevents intrabrand price competition. Suppose, for example, that interbrand competition is sufficiently weak that the franchised retailers are able to charge a price substantially above wholesale. Under a location restriction, these franchisers are free to sell to discount stores seeking to exploit the potential for sales at prices below the prevailing retail level. One of the franchised retailers may be tempted to lower its price and act in effect as a wholesaler for the discount house in order to share in the profits to be had from lowering prices and expanding volume.

Under a retail customer restriction, on the other hand, the franchised dealers cannot sell to discounters, who are cut off altogether from the manufacturer's product and the opportunity for intrabrand price competition. This was precisely the theory on which the Government successfully challenged Schwinn's customer restrictions in this Court....

Just as there are significant differences between *Schwinn* and this case with respect to intrabrand competition, there are also significant differences with respect to interbrand competition. Unlike Schwinn, Sylvania clearly had no economic power in the generic product market. At the time they instituted their respective distribution policies, Schwinn was "the leading bicycle producer in the Nation," with a national market share of 22.5%, 388 U.S., at 368, 374, whereas Sylvania was a "faltering, if not failing" producer of television sets, with "a relatively insignificant 1% to 2%" share of the national market in which the dominant manufacturer had a 60% to 70% share. Moreover, the Schwinn brand name enjoyed superior consumer acceptance and commanded a premium price as, in the District Court's words, "the Cadillac of the bicycle industry." This premium gave Schwinn dealers a margin of protection from interbrand competition and created the possibilities for price cutting by discounters that the Government argued were forestalled by Schwinn's customer restrictions. Thus, judged by the criteria economists use to measure market power — product differentiation and market share — Schwinn enjoyed a substantially stronger position in the bicycle market than did Sylvania in the television market. This Court relied on Schwinn's market position as one reason not to apply the rule of reason to the vertical restraints challenged there. "Schwinn was not a newcomer, seeking to break into or stay in the bicycle business. It was not a 'failing company.' On the contrary, at the initiation of these practices, it was the leading bicycle producer in the Nation." 388 U.S., at 374. And the Court of Appeals below found "another significant distinction between our case and *Schwinn*" in Sylvania's "precarious market share," which "was so small when it adopted its locations practice that it was threatened with expulsion from the television market." 537 F.2d, at 991.

In my view there are at least two considerations, both relied upon by the majority to justify overruling *Schwinn*, that would provide a "principled basis" for instead refusing to extend *Schwinn* to a vertical restraint that is imposed by a "faltering" manufacturer with a "precarious" position in a generic product market dominated by another firm. The first is that, as the majority puts it, "when interbrand competition exists, as it does among television manufacturers, it provides a significant check on the exploitation of intrabrand market power because of the ability of consumers to substitute a different brand of the same product." Second is the view, argued forcefully in the economic literature cited by the majority, that the potential benefits of vertical restraints in promoting interbrand competition are particularly strong where the manufacturer imposing the restraints is seeking to enter a new market or to expand a small market share. The majority even recognizes that *Schwinn* "hinted" at an exception for new entrants and failing firms from its *per se* rule.

....

After summarily rejecting this concern, reflected in our interpretations of the Sherman Act, for "the autonomy of independent businessmen," the majority not surprisingly finds "no justification" for *Schwinn*'s distinction between sale and nonsale transactions because the distinction is "essentially unrelated to any relevant economic impact." But while according some weight to the businessman's interest in controlling the terms on which he trades in his own goods may be anathema to those who view the Sherman Act as directed solely to economic efficiency, this principle is without question more deeply embedded in our cases than the notions of "free rider" effects and distributional efficiencies borrowed by the majority from the "new economics of vertical relationships." Perhaps the Court is right in partially abandoning this principle and in judging the instant nonprice vertical restraints solely by their "relevant economic impact"; but the precedents which reflect this principle should not be so lightly rejected by the Court. The rationale of *Schwinn* is no doubt difficult to discern from the opinion, and it may be wrong; it is not, however, the aberration the majority makes it out to be here.

....

NOTES AND QUESTIONS

1. The majority opinion in *Sylvania* held that the ancient rule against restraints on alienation did not justify the per se approach in the nonprice vertical restraint case. Was this conclusion a result of the *Schwinn* failure to identify an economic basis for its distinction between sale and consignment transactions? Does an economic rationale exist for the *Schwinn* distinction? Consider Justice White's concurring opinion on this point. Consider whether there are societal values in protecting the exercise of discretion by independent businesses. Wasn't one of the goals of the Sherman Act the protection of unfettered decisionmaking by independent business persons? What role under *Sylvania* does dealer independence play in defining competition standards and in determining legality? If dealer independence does have a value to society apart from the effect on competition, can this noneconomic value be considered under the *Sylvania* analysis?

In considering whether *Sylvania* is hostile to the interest of small business, evaluate how *Sylvania* might protect the small business franchise. Consider the argument that but for the ability of a manufacturer to impose vertical restraints in promoting distributional efficiency, the manufacturer might be forced to integrate vertically, thereby eliminating the independent business entity. *See* Justice Douglas' opinions in *Simpson v. Union Oil Co.*, 377 U.S. 13 (1964), and *Standard Oil Co. v. United States (Standard Stations)*, 337 U.S. 293 (1949) (dissenting).

2. In rejecting the restraint on alienation doctrine as an adequate justification for treating sale and nonsale transactions differently, did the *Sylvania* Court undercut the rationale for the *Dr. Miles* per se analysis of RPM? Are you satisfied with the Court's expressed economic distinction between the two forms of vertical restraints?

In comparing *Dr. Miles* to *Sylvania*, is there an argument that vertical restrictions on territories are more pernicious than price restrictions? An exclusive territory arrangement would insulate the dealer from *all* intrabrand competition, while RPM would only restrict price competition and may, in fact, promote nonprice competition in the intrabrand market. If this is economically sound, is it legally prudent to maintain a per se proscription against RPM, while employing a "reasonableness" test for nonprice vertical restraints?

In light of the new economic analysis sanctioned in *Sylvania*, is the Court's citation to an "implied" approval of the per se approach for price restraints by Congress, when it repealed its authority for state fair trade laws, an adequate substitute for economic analysis? *See* footnote 18 of *Sylvania*.

3. Do you agree that *Sylvania* values economic efficiency as the principal goal of antitrust law? If so, how is efficiency defined? Is it limited to distribution economies? *Sylvania* indicates that courts are to weigh economic interests, policies and factual variables in determining whether the "[v]ertical restriction [will] promote interbrand competition by allowing the manufacturer to achieve certain efficiencies." Consider what "objective benchmarks" the courts are to use in this analysis. Are the acceptable benchmarks limited to economic factors? Is the inquiry simply whether the benefits outweigh the adverse effects? Is there a suggestion in *Sylvania* that the balancing analysis inherent in the approved rule of reason standard is broader than that articulated in *Broadcast Music* and *NCAA* for horizontal restraints?

By citing *Tripoli Co. v. Wella Corp.*, 425 F.2d 932 (3d Cir.), *cert. denied*, 400 U.S. 831 (1970), in note 23 of its opinion, did the Supreme Court mean to suggest that noneconomic factors should continue to be relevant in nonprice restraint cases? In *Tripoli*, the Third Circuit upheld summary judgment for a manufacturer that had imposed vertical customer restraints to protect against serious physical injury to customers and to insulate the manufacturer from product liability suits. Does a thorough reading of *Sylvania* indicate that the Court sanctioned a weighing of factors such as these? Are the *Tripoli* factors "economic" or noneconomic?

4. Some commentators have questioned whether the judiciary is capable of balancing the consequences to intrabrand competition against the competitive effects on interbrand competition. Which party carries the burden of proof in demonstrating the net competitive effect? Consider whether the rule of reason approach sanctioned in *Sylvania* contains a presumption of illegality which remains until disproved by the defendant. Need the plaintiff only show the existence of the vertical restraint before the burden shifts to the defendant to establish its reasonableness? Are the increased transaction costs of enforcement and litigation and the reduced deterrence, which arguably are associated with the rule of reason decisional analysis, less important in terms of antitrust law than is promotion of interbrand competition?

5. Does *Sylvania*'s rule of reason require a structural analysis? If so, one may have to decide what amount of market power or level of market concentration is necessary to trigger illegality. Should it matter to the analysis whether a healthy interbrand market exists or whether the market is characterized by a monopoly or oligopoly? Perhaps the Court would apply a different approach if the vertical distributional restraint were imposed by a monopolist or an oligopolist. Moreover, the economic effect would vary depending on how many competitors engaged in the same vertical restraint or if the industry was characterized by other industry-wide vertical restraints.

What does the Court mean by harm to "intrabrand" competition? Does it mean that, as a result of the territorial division, Sylvania retailers might begin charging a higher retail price for Sylvania televisions? They could not do this unless Sylvania had market power in Sylvania televisions, could they? Should courts adopt a rule that vertical territorial restrictions are per se *legal* unless the defendant imposing the restraints has monopoly power? Several circuits now seem to be of this opinion. *JBL Enters. v. Jhirmack Enters.*, 698 F.2d 1011, 1017 (9th Cir. 1983); *Graphic Prods. Distribs. v. Itek Corp.*, 717 F.2d 1560, 1568 (11th Cir. 1983); *Valley Liquors, Inc. v. Renfield Importers, Ltd.*, 678 F.2d 742 (7th Cir. 1982); *Muenster Butane, Inc. v. Stewart Co.*, 651 F.2d 292, 298 (5th Cir. 1981).

6. In sum, *Sylvania* implied that the rule of reason is the preferred analysis for nonprice vertical restraints, including territorial, customer, and location clause restrictions, because such restraints might be dictated for economic reasons such as economies of scale, distribution efficiency, dealer goodwill, and "free rider" problems. This is so, moreover, regardless of whether the restriction involved a sale or nonsale (consignment) transaction. *See also Monsanto Co. v. Spray-Rite Serv. Corp.*, 465 U.S. 752 (1984).

7. Five years after the Supreme Court handed down the opinion in *Sylvania* and seventeen years after the litigation began, the Ninth Circuit Court of Appeals, on remand from the Supreme Court, concluded that "Sylvania's location clause was not an unreasonable restraint on trade." *Continental T.V., Inc. v. GTE Sylvania, Inc.*, 694 F.2d 1132, 1139-40 (9th Cir. 1982). The court rejected Continental's argument that once it established a vertical restraint the burden shifted to defendant to prove "reasonableness" of the restriction. Ruling that the burden of proof was on the plaintiff to demonstrate that the location clause was an unreasonable restraint of trade, the Ninth Circuit held that while Sylvania's location restrictions "harmed intrabrand competition to some extent, the restraint was neither overly restrictive nor adopted to prevent price-discounting." *Id.* at 1138.

In weighing the competitive effects in the interbrand market, the court adopted a market-structure analysis which considered the industry at the inception of the restrictive practice and at the time the challenged practice was enforced against Continental. In addition, the court examined other industry-wide restraints, and whether the imposition of the Sylvania location clause was encouraged by the retailers for the purpose of insulating them from price competition. The court concluded:

> We consider the television manufacturing industry at the time Sylvania adopted the location clause in question [1962] and at the time Sylvania enforced the restraint [1965] to prevent Continental from entering the Sacramento market to sell Sylvania television sets. In both 1962 and 1965 there were other viable television manufacturers available to sell to any retailers, who wished to enter the Sacramento market, and their products were interchangeable with Sylvania's.
>
> The precise restraints imposed by Sylvania and other manufacturers in the industry are also relevant to a determination of the effect Sylvania's location clause had on interbrand competition.... Sylvania did not prevent its retailers from handling competitor's products, and there is no evidence that any other manufacturer imposed such a restraint. A final consideration is that Sylvania did not adopt its distributorship arrangement at the request of other retailers. Rather, it independently determined that the restraint was necessary for Sylvania to remain competitive in the television industry.

694 F.2d at 1139. *See Red Diamond Supply, Inc. v. Liquid Carbonic Corp.*, 639 F.2d 1001, 1005 (5th Cir. 1981); *Eiberger v. Sony Corp.*, 622 F.2d 1068, 1072-73, 1077 (2d Cir. 1980); Pitofsky, *The Sylvania Case: Antitrust Analysis of Non-Price Vertical Restrictions*, 78 Colum. L. Rev. 1 (1978); *see also* Posner, *The Next Step in the Antitrust Treatment of Restricted Distribution: Per Se Legality*, 48 U. Chi. L. Rev. 6 (1981).

8. Since the *Sylvania* decision, the rule of reason has become, for all practical purposes, a rule of per se legality. Only two circuits have held a nonprice vertical

restraint unlawful. *See Graphic Prods. Distribs. v. Itek Corp.*, 717 F.2d 1560 (11th Cir. 1983); *Eiberger v. Sony Corp.*, 622 F.2d 1068 (2d Cir. 1980).

9. As Chapter 4 indicates, nonprice horizontal restraints, such as territorial and customer limitations between competitors, are illegal per se. Thus it is important in evaluating the evidence to determine whether the vertical restraint, though ostensibly imposed by the supplier, is in fact controlled or agreed upon by the dealers or franchisees, as a disguised horizontal combination.

1. DUAL DISTRIBUTION SYSTEMS

A dual distributing system is one in which a manufacturer (supplier) functions at the same level in the market as its dealers at the same time it acts as a supplier. The manufacturer thus operates on two separate levels of competition, facing two separate competitive forces — one interbrand (on the manufacturing level) and the other intrabrand (on the distribution level). An example is when a franchisor-owned outlet competes with a franchisee-owned outlet in the same market. In analyzing such situations, courts have often considered whether the relationship between the franchisor and the independently owned franchisee should be characterized as horizontal, thus invoking a per se condemnation, or vertical, with the implication that *Sylvania*'s rule of reason ought to control.

The issue has not been firmly decided by the Supreme Court. In *White Motor* and *Schwinn*, the Court implied that a dual distribution arrangement was vertical in nature. But in *Sylvania* the Court observed that "[t]here may be occasional problems in differentiating vertical restrictions from horizontal restrictions .... There is no doubt that restrictions in the latter category would be illegal per se...." 433 U.S. at 58 n.28.

Compare further the Court's analysis in two cases. The manufacturer in *Schwinn* competed with its wholesale distributors for sales to retailers. The Court looked to the *source* of the restraints, and finding that they were imposed by the manufacturer held that the restrictions were vertical. In *Sealy* and *Topco* (discussed in Chapter 4) the Court pierced the vertical veneer to find horizontal underpinnings. The resolution of the issue, to date, has been left to the lower federal courts. The Supreme Court has not spoken on the issue since its dictum in *Sylvania.* For a discussion of the analytical problems associated with this issue, *see* Liebeler, *Intrabrand "Cartels" Under GTE Sylvania*, 30 UCLA L. Rev. 1 (1982).

Due to the lack of guidance from the Court, the lower federal courts have adopted a variety of tests in determining whether a restraint is horizontal or vertical in the dual distributorship context. Once the court is able to characterize the conduct as either horizontal or vertical, the legal standard, whether per se or rule of reason, seems to follow automatically.

Several approaches have been employed by the lower courts during the characterization process. One approach could be labeled "the source of the restraint" rule. This analysis attempts to determine whether the restraint was initiated by competitors on the same level of the distribution chain or whether it was initiated primarily by the manufacturer for the purpose of achieving an efficient distribution system. *H & B Equip. Co. v. International Harvester Co.*, 577 F.2d 239 (5th Cir. 1978).

A second approach taken by the lower courts "focuses not on whether the vertical or horizontal aspects of the system predominate, but rather, on the actual competitive impact of the dual distribution system." *Krehl v. Baskin-Robbins Ice Cream Co.*, 664 F.2d 1348, 1356 (9th Cir. 1982). This functional economic analysis weighs the intrabrand restriction against the potential for enhancing interbrand competition, regardless of horizontal features.

In *International Logistics Group, Ltd. v. Chrysler Corp.*, 824 F.2d 904 (6th Cir. 1989), the Sixth Circuit held that a rule of reason analysis should apply to an automobile manufacturer's distribution practices regarding independent distributors and dealers. A division of Chrysler sold a Power Master engine at lower prices for the international export market than the domestic market. Plaintiffs purchased these engines "at overseas prices ostensibly for export and overseas resale." However, they did not export the engines but rather sold them for distribution in the domestic market at prices "substantially below Chrysler's prices to domestic dealers."

After Chrysler warned plaintiffs, who were independent distributors of Chrysler parts, not to resell in the domestic market parts purchased for the export market, Chrysler terminated plaintiffs for failure to comply.

The court held that Chrysler acted independently in establishing its marketing policies (pricing for particular markets), and that Chrysler announced that it "would reject all purchase orders from distributors who refused to comply with the marketing conditions." Thus, the court concluded that Chrysler's termination action was unilateral. Quoting Professor Areeda, the court reasoned that "there can be no conspiracy 'where the actor imposing the alleged restraint does not ... need the acquiescence of the other party or any quid pro quo.'" *See also Cheatham's Furn. Co. v. La-Z-Boy Chair Co.*, 1990-91 Trade Cases at ¶ 68937 (E.D. Mo.) (termination of a dealer for failure to honor an explicit resale price maintenance scheme was lawful since there was no "agreement"). The court also concluded that Chrysler's marketing practices were directed at vertically related firms, notwithstanding that Chrysler was also a distributor. Do you agree with the court that Chrysler's marketing and distribution policies were vertical and non-price in nature, thus warranting a rule of reason analysis? What argument could you advance to show horizontal competitive effects?

D. EXCLUSIVE DEALERSHIPS

One of the principal ways in which a dealer termination may occur is if the supplier decides to have its product marketed by only one dealer in the area. By definition, an "exclusive dealership" is a contractual arrangement whereby all but one dealer "in the same product of the same manufacturer are eliminated." *Packard*

Motor Car Co. v. Webster Motor Car Co., 243 F.2d 419 (D.C. Cir.), *cert. denied*, 355 U.S. 822 (1957). If the supplier unilaterally decides to sell to only one dealer in an area, there is no qualifying agreement and thus no Sherman section 1 violation. But assuming that the supplier and designated dealer "agree" to an exclusive arrangement, is there any reason for thinking it illegal?

Consider the observation in *Schwinn* that "a manufacturer of a product ... which [is] readily available in the market may select his customers, and for this purpose he may 'franchise' certain dealers to whom, alone, he will sell his goods.... If the restraint stops at that point — if nothing more is involved than vertical 'confinement' of the manufacturer's own sales of the merchandise to selected dealers, and if competitive products are readily available to others, the restriction, on these facts alone, would not violate the Sherman Act." 388 U.S. at 376. Does this language indicate an approval of the exclusive dealership, or does it merely restate the *Colgate* doctrine? *See* L. Sullivan, *Handbook of the Law of Antitrust* 425 (1977).

In evaluating this vertical arrangement, weigh the competitive effects of such a distribution system. Is the exclusive arrangement as anticompetitive as a territorial restriction on a dealer? Does the restriction in fact run against the exclusive dealer, or is it simply a restriction on the supplier's right to deal with other distributors? If this is true, could not the exclusive dealer market the product in another area outside its own? The result would be that intrabrand competition would not be as restricted as the result under a territorial limitation. What incentives are there for a manufacturer to enter into such an exclusive dealership?

A manufacturer may desire to bring a new product on the market but fear that because of competition the product will not be successful absent a vigorous promotion. If the manufacturer is permitted to extend an exclusive dealership in this product, the dealer, being free from intrabrand competition and free rider problems, will have the incentive to market aggressively the new product. If this argument is economically sound with regard to a new product, it also has application to the product where a substantial capital investment or other expenses must be incurred. The efficiency incentives for both the manufacturer and dealer seem clear, though intrabrand competition in the brand product is diminished.

In terms of antitrust analysis, should it matter whether the manufacturer has to terminate existing dealers or merely promise not to license new dealers in establishing an exclusive dealership (franchise)? Do competitive effects differ between foreclosure of potential and existing competition? Is the presence of a horizontal restraint more likely in one situation than it is in the other? *See* L. Sullivan, *supra*, at 427-29.

The courts that have confronted these issues have often used a structural approach to inform their economic analysis of the competitive impact of the exclusive distribution system. The structure of the market and the market power of the individual firm that imposes the sole outlet arrangement have been considered relevant. The focus has been on whether a dominant firm with substantial market power ought to be permitted to establish an exclusive distribution system with the purpose and perhaps effect of further increasing its dominance in the manufacturing market. A related question is whether the market power of the exclusive dealer is relevant in evaluating the economic consequence of the exclusive dealership.

In an early but significant case, the District of Columbia Court of Appeals in *Packard Motor Car Co. v. Webster Motor Car Co.*, 243 F.2d 418 (D.C. Cir. 1957), held that an agreement between the Packard Motor Company and a Baltimore dealer to give it an exclusive contract to sell Packards in Baltimore and to terminate two other Packard dealers in the area was not a violation of the Sherman Act, either under section 1 or section 2. First, with regard to the monopolization charge under section 2, the court said that since there were other cars "reasonably interchangeable by consumers," an exclusive franchise contract "for marketing Packards does not create a monopoly." Second, "[w]hen an exclusive dealership 'is not part and parcel of a scheme to monopolize and effective competition exists at both the seller and buyer levels, the arrangement has invariably been upheld as a reasonable restraint of trade ... [and] virtually one of *per se* legality [under section 1].'"

Packard, of course, was a small manufacturer attempting to compete with large manufacturers. The court opined that "[t]o penalize the small manufacturer for competing in this way not only fails to promote the policy of the antitrust laws but defeats it." Moreover, the fact that one dealer requests the exclusive dealership with the consequence that others are eliminated does not make it illegal. "Since the immediate object of an exclusive dealership is to protect the dealer from competition in the manufacturer's product, it is likely to be the dealer who asks for it."

Note that the restraint in *Packard* was on the seller rather than the buyer. When the restraint is on the seller ("exclusive selling"), section 3 of the Clayton Act does not apply. If the restraint is on the buyer, section 3 of the Clayton Act applies, as well as section 1 of the Sherman Act. Those restraints are discussed in Section II of this chapter after the *Valley Liquors* case.

What are the competitive consequences of an exclusive dealership? If the purpose behind such a commercial transaction is to improve distribution efficiencies in the intrabrand market so as to promote interbrand competition, what competitive consequence would be expected if the surviving exclusive dealer was also the sole outlet for all other suppliers in that area? Consider the effect this would have on the interbrand market. Might the dealer's pressure on the manufacturer to grant it an exclusive franchise in this context amount to monopolization or an attempt to monopolize under section 2 of the Sherman Act? See Chapter 6, *infra*. Should the *Packard Motor* rationale not apply whenever the manufacturer and/or the exclusive dealer possess market power in their respective markets?

VALLEY LIQUORS, INC. V. RENFIELD IMPORTERS, LTD.

678 F.2d 742 (7th Cir. 1982)

JUDGE POSNER.

Valley Liquors, Inc., is a wholesale wine and liquor distributor in northern Illinois, and Renfield Importers, Ltd., is one of its suppliers. Effective November 1, 1981, Renfield terminated Valley as a distributor of Renfield products (which includes such popular brands as Gordon's and Martini & Rossi) in two counties, McHenry and Du Page. Valley sued, charging that Renfield had violated section 1 of the Sherman Act, which forbids conspiracies or other agreements in restraint of trade. The case is before us on Valley's appeal under 28 U.S.C. § 1292(a)(1) from the denial by the district court of a motion for a preliminary injunction under section 16 of the Clayton Act, 15 U.S.C. § 26.

Until November 1, Renfield generally sold its products to several wholesalers in the same county. But its sales had not been growing as rapidly in Illinois as in the rest of the country, and it decided to adopt a system of restricted distribution whereby it would sell to one, or at the most two, wholesalers in each county. (In some instances, however, the plan resulted in an increase in the number of wholesalers from one to two.) Although Valley was Renfield's largest wholesaler in McHenry and Du Page Counties, accounting for some 50 percent of Renfield's total sales there, the new plan terminated Valley and all of Renfield's other distributors in the two counties except Continental and Romano; they were, however, terminated in some other areas. There is unrebutted evidence that Valley had been selling Renfield products at prices five percent below those charged by Renfield's other distributors in McHenry and Du Page Counties and that Valley's termination followed discussions between Renfield and Continental and between Renfield and Romano in which Continental and Romano had expressed unhappiness at Renfield's terminating them in other areas. There is virtually no evidence concerning Renfield's motivation for the adoption of a more restricted distribution system and the concomitant realignment of wholesaler territories, except that it was a reaction to Renfield's disappointing sales in Illinois.

Valley contends that two distinct restraints of trade can be inferred from these facts. The first is a conspiracy among Renfield, Continental, and Romano to increase the wholesale prices of Renfield products in McHenry and Du Page Counties by cutting off Valley — Valley's termination being a concession demanded by Continental and Romano in exchange for consenting to the proposed realignment, under which they lost some of their territories. This is alleged to be a "horizontal" conspiracy, unlawful without more ("per se") under section 1 of the Sherman Act. The second alleged restraint of trade is the exclusion of Valley, pursuant to its distribution agreement with Renfield, from McHenry and Du Page Counties. Valley argues that this "vertical" restriction is unreasonable and hence unlawful under section 1's "Rule of Reason."

The district judge denied a preliminary injunction against Renfield's termination of Valley because he did not think that Valley had demonstrated that it was likely to win the case if tried in full. If the judge was right in his estimation of Valley's chances of success, he was right to deny a preliminary injunction, regardless of other considerations relevant to the exercise of his equitable powers.

If Continental and Romano had agreed to raise the prices of Renfield products in McHenry and Du Page Counties and to that end had persuaded Renfield (perhaps by threatening to discontinue carrying its products if it did not cooperate with them) to terminate Valley, their pesky low-price competitor, then they and their cat's paw Renfield would be guilty of a per se unlawful restraint of trade. Although there was no direct evidence of such a chain of events — in particular no evidence that Continental and Romano ever communicated with each other about Valley — we are asked to infer from the fact that Continental and Romano (separately) expressed unhappiness at being terminated in some of their sales areas that they demanded and received, as a quid pro quo, the termination of their major competitor in the two counties, Valley. However, this hypothesis is too speculative to compel a trier of fact to infer conspiracy, at least if Renfield may have had independent reasons for wanting to terminate Valley. We are asked to exclude that possibility because Valley was Renfield's largest and lowest-priced wholesaler in McHenry and Du Page Counties, and therefore its best.... If Renfield had been content with a policy of maximizing wholesaler price competition, it would not have changed to a system of exclusive and dual wholesalers; it would have thought that the more competing wholesalers it had the better off it was. The adoption of a restricted distribution system implies a decision to emphasize nonprice competition over price competition, which such a system tends to suppress. This does not make restricted distribution good, or even lawful; we shall get to that question in a moment. Right now we are just concerned with whether Renfield may have had reasons for terminating Valley that were independent of the desires of Continental and Romano to be rid of the competition of a price cutter. It may have. That possibility is enough to rebut an inference of collusion with those distributors based solely on the termination of Valley.

We are mindful that *Cernuto, Inc. v. United Cabinet Corp.*, 595 F.2d 164 (3d Cir. 1979), held that it is unlawful per se for a manufacturer to terminate a distributor at the behest of a competing distributor who wants to reduce price competition. Valley's allegation of a horizontal conspiracy is an effort to invoke *Cernuto*. It is a clumsy effort, since *Cernuto* is not a horizontal case: a horizontal conspiracy is one between two or more competing sellers; a conspiracy between a supplier and a wholesaler is one between firms in different stages of distribution. Perhaps, though, this is a pedantic distinction, and the important point is that *Cernuto* condemns the vertical expression of a horizontal desire. But it is not enough that the distributor, that is Continental or Romano, have this desire; the supplier must have it too. *See Alloy Int'l Co. v. Hoover-NSK Bearing Co.*, 635 F.2d 1222, 1226 n.6 (7th Cir. 1980); *Edward J. Sweeney & Sons, Inc. v. Texaco, Inc.*, 637 F.2d 105, 111 (3d Cir. 1980). If Renfield wanted to restrict the distribution of its products in order to be a more effective competitor, the antitrust laws would not forbid it to do so merely because its distributors went along so that they would have less price competition. It is therefore not enough to show that Continental and Romano, acting separately (for if they acted together that would be horizontal action), wanted to get rid of a competitor; there must also be evidence that in terminating Valley Renfield was acceding to their desire rather than acting to promote an independent conception of its self-interest. There was no such direct evidence and the circumstantial evidence was as we have pointed out too tenuous to require the trier of fact to draw the inference that Valley asked him to draw.

There is, we admit, a certain unreality in the careful parsing of motives that *Cernuto* seems to require. If a supplier wants his distributors to emphasize nonprice rather than price competition, which as we said is the usual reason why he would restrict his distribution, he will be hostile to price cutters because they will make it harder for his other distributors to recoup the expenditures that he wants them to make on presale services to consumers and on other forms of nonprice competition, and of course the undersold distributors will be equally or more hostile. The motive of supplier and distributors alike could thus be described as wanting to eliminate price cutters yet there would be no per se illegality so long as the supplier was not just knuckling under to the distributors' desire for less competition. It is difficult to see how a court could distinguish empirically between such a case and the pure antipathy to price competition envisaged by *Cernuto*. But the unraveling of this skein can be left for another occasion. It is enough that in this case the plaintiff did not prove an improper motive by its supplier.

We turn to the vertical aspect of the case. If we accept, as on the state of the record we must, that Valley sold at lower prices than the other distributors in McHenry and Du Page Counties, then the territorial restriction pursuant to which it was terminated in those two counties has reduced price competition among wholesalers of the brands supplied by Renfield ("intrabrand price competition"). Valley contends that this reduction establishes a prima facie case of unreasonable restraint of trade which shifts to Renfield the burden of showing an offsetting increase in competition between brands supplied by Renfield on the one hand and brands supplied by other importers or national distributors of alcoholic beverages on the other hand ("interbrand competition").

We reject the casual equation of interbrand price competition with intrabrand competition. The elimination of a price cutter who is taking a free ride on the promotional efforts of competing distributors will tend to stimulate nonprice competition among the distributors at the same time that it dampens price competition among them, so that the net effect on intrabrand competition need not be negative. In any event, the suggestion that proof of a reduction in intrabrand competition creates a presumption of illegality is inconsistent with the test that the courts apply in restricted distribution cases. Building from a suggestive footnote in *Continental T.V., Inc. v. GTE Sylvania Inc.*, 433 U.S. 36, 57 n.27 (1976), the courts have held that the effects on intrabrand and on interbrand competition must be balanced in deciding whether a challenged restriction on distribution is unreasonable. *See, e.g., Muenster Butane, Inc. v. Stewart Co.*, 651 F.2d 292, 296 (5th Cir. 1981); *Eiberger v.*

Sony Corp. of America, 622 F.2d 1068, 1076 (2d Cir. 1980). And it is not generally true of balancing tests that the plaintiff, in order to make out a prima facie case, has only to show that if you put something on his side of the empty balance the balance will tilt his way. The plaintiff in a restricted distribution case must show that the restriction he is complaining of was unreasonable because, weighing effects on both intrabrand and interbrand competition, it made consumers worse off.

Admittedly, this test of illegality is easier to state than to apply, the effects to be weighed being so difficult to measure or even estimate by the methods of litigation. The courts have therefore looked for shortcuts. A popular one is to say that the balance tips in the defendant's favor if the plaintiff fails to show that the defendant has significant market power (that is, power to raise prices significantly above the competitive level without losing all of one's business). That is the approach of the Fifth and Ninth Circuits. *See, e.g., Muenster Butane, supra*, 651 F.2d at 298; *Cowley v. Braden Indus., Inc.*, 613 F.2d 751, 755 (9th Cir. 1980). The Second Circuit seems divided on the question. *Compare Oreck Corp. v. Whirlpool Corp.*, 579 F.2d 126, 130 n.5 (2d Cir. 1978) (*en banc*), *with Eiberger, supra*, 622 F.2d at 1081. We agree with the Fifth and Ninth Circuits. A firm that has no market power is unlikely to adopt policies that disserve its consumers; it cannot afford to. And if it blunders and does adopt such a policy, market retribution will be swift. Thus its mistakes do not seriously threaten consumer welfare, which is the objective that we are told should guide us in interpreting the Sherman Act. *See, e.g., Reiter v. Sonotone Corp.*, 442 U.S. 330, 343 (1979). Even if there is some possibility that the distribution practices of a powerless firm will have a substantial anticompetitive effect, it is too small a possibility to warrant trundling out the great machinery of antitrust enforcement.

Since market power can rarely be measured directly by the methods of litigation, it is normally inferred from possession of a substantial percentage of the sales in a market carefully defined in terms of both product and geography. *See, e.g., Red Diamond Supply, Inc. v. Liquid Carbonic Corp.*, 637 F.2d 1001, 1005 (5th Cir. 1981). In this case no evidence of market share was presented. In fact, no market was defined, either in product or in geographical terms, so that we do not have even a rough idea whether Renfield was a big firm in its market or a small firm. Nor did Valley seek to establish Renfield's market power by some alternative route, not involving proof of relevant market and market share.

On this as on all the other issues in this case our comments on the weight of the evidence have reference only to the evidence introduced in support of and in opposition to Valley's motion for a preliminary injunction. We are not prejudging Valley's right to a permanent injunction at the end of the trial. That right depends on the evidence introduced at trial, which for all we know may cure the deficiencies in Valley's proof that require us to order that the denial of its motion for a preliminary injunction be, and it hereby is,

Affirmed.

NOTES AND QUESTIONS

1. Does *Valley Liquors* hold that the per se rule applies only if the supplier is the "enforcement agent" for the distributors' desire for less price competition and accordingly when the supplier has no independent commercial reason for establishing the restricted distribution agreement? For a discussion of *Valley Liquors* in the context of the intrabrand "cartel" competition trade-off, *see* Liebeler, *Intraband "Cartels" Under* GTE Sylvania, 30 UCLA L. Rev. 1, 10-13 (1982).

2. What evidence does Judge Posner cite for the conclusion that the supplier "may have had reasons for terminating Valley that were independent of the desires of [the distributors] to be rid of the competition of a price cutter"? Doesn't Judge Posner concede that "[t]here is virtually no evidence concerning Renfield's motivation for the adoption of a more restricted distribution system?" If so, how can it be said that if the supplier "*wanted* to restrict the distribution of its products in order to be a more effective competitor, the antitrust laws would not forbid it to do so merely because its distributors went along so that they would have less price competition"? (Emphasis added.)

If the inference of collusion between the distributors can be raised, is the mere "possibility" of an independent commercial reason for the termination enough to rebut the inference of collusion? Does the defendant have the burden to go forward with rebuttal evidence once the inference is raised? Consider whether the answer depends on the standard of review for a preliminary injunction as opposed to a permanent injunction. *See generally Dos Santos v. Columbus-Cuneo-Cabrini Med. Center*, 684 F.2d 1346, 1352-55 (7th Cir. 1982). *Contra Earley Ford Tractor, Inc. v. Hesston Corp.*, 556 F. Supp. 544, 548 (W.D. Mo. 1983).

3. Judge Posner suggested that "[t]he elimination of a price cutter who is taking a free ride on the promotional efforts of competing distributors will tend to stimulate nonprice competition among the distributors at the same time that it dampens price competition among them, so that the net effect on intrabrand competition need not be negative." On what authority, economic or legal, does he make the assertion that intrabrand price restraints will promote nonprice competition? Was there evidence that the supplier wanted its "distributors to emphasize nonprice rather than price competition"? What evidence was cited to establish that Valley was "taking a free ride on the promotional efforts of competing distributors"?

4. On remand from the appeal, the district court granted summary judgment for defendant Renfield. On the second appeal, the Seventh Circuit affirmed the district court. The court of appeals held that plaintiff failed to rebut the defendant's summary judgment motion by failing to show a genuine factual issue on (1) whether there was a conspiracy between the importer and competing distributors to fix price and (2) whether the importer had sufficient market power to restrain trade. 822 F.2d 656 (7th Cir. 1987). The district court had found that Renfield's market share in metropolitan Chicago was less than 2% and in the state of Illinois or the rest of the county only 2-3%. *Id.* at 667.

5. In *Paddock v. Chicago Tribune*, 103 F.3d 42 (7th Cir. 1996), *cert. denied*, 117 S. Ct. 2435 (1997), the Seventh Circuit upheld a series of contracts under which various sellers of news and other services supplied exclusively one newspaper in a given area. For example, the New York Times News Service agreement gave the Chicago *Tribune* the exclusive right to New York Times News stores in the Chicago metropolitan area, thus denying that service to the *Tribune*'s competitors, such as the Chicago *Sun-Times* or the plaintiff Chicago *Daily Herald*. The court noted that "[e]xclusivity is one valuable feature the service offers, for a paper with exclusive rights to a service or feature is both more attractive to readers and more distinctive from its rivals."

The court also noted that the market for news services contained numerous providers and seemed to be quite competitive. Further, the contracts were of relatively short duration, and any newspaper could win an exclusive contract by offering the best deal:

> Competition-for-the-contract is a form of competition that antitrust laws protect rather than proscribe, and it is common. Every year or two, General Motors, Ford, and Chrysler invite tire manufacturers to bid for exclusive rights to have their tires used in the manufacturers' cars. Exclusive contracts make the market hard to enter in mid-year but cannot stifle competition over the longer run, and competition of this kind drives down the price of tires, to the ultimate benefit of consumers. Just so in the news business — if smaller newspapers are willing to bid with cash rather than legal talent. In the meantime, exclusive stories and features help the newspapers differentiate themselves, the better to compete with one another. A market in which every newspaper carried the same stories, columns, and cartoons would be a less vigorous market than the existing one. And a market in which the creators of intellectual property (such as the New York Times) could not decide how best to market it for maximum profit would be a market with less (or less interesting) intellectual property created in the first place.

While exclusivity might sometimes facilitate collusion, there was no allegation of any kind of forbearance by rivals. Further, while the local market for newspapers was reasonably concentrated, the national market for news services and other inputs seemed to be robustly competitive. This fact was particularly important because the allegation was of exclusive distributorships, not of exclusive dealing. The court continued:

> Despite the similarity in nomenclature, there is a difference.... An exclusive dealing contract obliges a firm to obtain its inputs from a single source. Each of the theaters [in *FTC v. Motion Picture Advertising Service Co.*, 344 U.S. 392 (1953)] was committed to one distributor for all of its ads. This was the genesis of the concern about foreclosure. A new advertising distributor could not find outlets. An exclusive distributorship, by contrast, does not restrict entry at

either level. None of the newspapers in Chicago (or anywhere else) has promised by contract to obtain all of its news from a single source — and the
sources have not locked all of their output together (unlike the "block booking" involved in Loew's). A new entrant to the supplemental news service
business could sell to every newspaper in the United States, if it chose to do so.
Existing features syndicates sell to multiple firms in the same market (although
most features go to one paper per city; this is the exclusive distribution aspect
of the contracts). So vendors can and do sell news and features to multiple
customers, and customers can and do buy news and features from multiple
vendors. "Foreclosure" of the kind about which *Motion Picture Advertising
Service* was concerned does not occur under exclusive distribution contracts.

PROBLEM 5.5

Hope Hospital had a policy of assisting patients at the hospital who were
nearing discharge and who needed home health care by using independent nurses
to assist and counsel patients in selecting an equipment supplier for their home
needs. Vendors could not solicit in the hospital. Thereafter, Hope Hospital entered into a joint venture with a medical equipment vendor to supply this service.
The previous hospital policy was changed when the hospital appointed an employee of the vendor, who had no health care training, as the patient equipment
coordinator. This employee was named the exclusive agent to assist patients and
to arrange equipment rentals. The coordinator referred patients to the joint venture medical equipment firm.

The self-employed nurses who previously served this function complained and
in response the hospital policy was changed to permit the nurses to aid in making
the patient assessment. But the nurses were encouraged to recommend the joint
venture firm. As a result, 85% of the hospital's patients who needed home
equipment received it from the joint venture firm.

If you were counsel for a competing vendor, what antitrust arguments would
you make? What counter-arguments are available for Hope Hospital? Does a
competing vendor suffer antitrust injury under the joint venture arrangement?
Does a patient suffer antitrust injury? *See Key Enters. of Del., Inc. v. Venice
Hosp.*, 919 F.2d 1550 (11th Cir. 1991).

SECTION II. INTERBRAND VERTICAL FORECLOSURE

In addition to *intrabrand* distributional restraints on dealers, suppliers may attempt to foreclose interbrand competition through vertical restrictions on distributors and dealers. Competitors allegedly may be foreclosed from competing
in a market through a supplier's exclusionary practices which restrict the buyer's
ability to deal in the goods of the competitor of the supplier. It is alleged that the
exclusionary practice might foreclose competition by means of a requirements
contract between supplier and buyer.

The two exclusionary practices discussed in this section are exclusive dealing arrangements and tie-in sales. Both of these commercial arrangements have an effect on interbrand competition because the supplier's buyer is precluded by contract, either directly or indirectly, from purchasing from the supplier's competitors. In the first category, the exclusive dealing contract, the buyer explicitly or implicitly agrees to buy exclusively the products of the contracting supplier. In the second, the same result occurs because the buyer is forced to take all its requirements or a second product if it desires to buy the principal product, thereby precluding the buyer from purchasing the second product from a competitor of the seller. The competitive process and consumer welfare arguably are compromised because outlets for the supplier's competitors are denied and the consumer is limited in the range of choices.

The exclusive dealing contract discussed here differs from an exclusive dealership described previously in Subchapter D of this chapter in that the exclusive dealership contract is an output contract rather than a requirements contract. It restricts the ability of the *supplier* to supply competitors of the dealer. In contrast, exclusive dealing is a form of a requirements contract in that it places restrictions on the *dealer* as to with whom it can deal. A traditional requirements contract forced the buyer for a certain time period to purchase some or all of its product needs from the contracting supplier. An exclusive dealing contract would require the buyer to deal only in the goods of that supplier. The distinction between an output contract and requirements contract is not without legal significance.

The Clayton Act, adopted in 1914, places restrictions on requirements contracts but not output contracts. Consider section 3 of the Act.

> It shall be unlawful for any person engaged in commerce, in the course of such commerce, to lease or make a sale or contract for sale of goods, wares, merchandise, machinery, supplies, or other commodities, whether patented or unpatented, for use, consumption, or resale within the United States or any Territory thereof or the District of Columbia or any insular possession or other place under the jurisdiction of the United States, or fix a price charged therefor, or discount from, or rebate upon, such price, on the condition, agreement, or understanding that the lessee or purchaser thereof shall not use or deal in the goods, wares, merchandise, machinery, supplies, or other commodities of a competitor or competitors of the lessor or seller, where the effect of such lease, sale, or contract for sale or such condition, agreement, or understanding may be to substantially lessen competition or tend to create a monopoly in any line of commerce.

15 U.S.C. § 14 (1976). The statute condemns limitations on lessees or purchasers, but not on suppliers, sellers, or lessors. Thus, while the exclusive dealership will be scrutinized under section 1 of the Sherman Act, the exclusive dealing contract or the buying arrangement will come within both the Sherman and the Clayton Acts if jurisdictional requirements are met. In light of the legislative history and interpre-

tation of section 3, the burden of proof is easier for the plaintiff to meet than under section 1 of the Sherman Act. Note that section 3 has a built-in standard of analysis: the conduct is unlawful if its effect "may be to substantially lessen competition or tend to create a monopoly in any line of commerce." The burden of proof under the statute is not the mere "possibility" of competitive injury, but one of "probability" that competition will be lessened. A further limitation on the application of these statutes to vertical arrangements that foreclose competition is that the Clayton Act does not apply to contracts for service, but only arrangements, including leases or sales, of "goods." The Sherman Act covers the vertical arrangement whether it involves goods or services.

A. EXCLUSIVE DEALING UNDER THE RULE OF REASON

Efficiency considerations support a rule of reason analysis of exclusive dealing contracts, since they are a form of partial vertical integration. Suppliers may be eager to enter exclusive dealing contracts as a means of obtaining assured outlets or markets for their products, as they attempt to recoup their investment with a reasonable profit. The predictability created by such a contract can enhance production and distribution efficiency, leading to increased competition. Moreover, by tying closely the buyer and supplier, the buyer's promotional efforts will center on the supplier's products, thereby creating increased dealer loyalty. This relationship may facilitate greater competitive assertiveness by the dealer on behalf of the supplier's product. Without this close contractual relationship, the supplier may be unwilling to risk investment in capital, innovation, and new products.

Conversely, buyers will be interested in obtaining a reliable source of supply to insulate themselves from market fluctuations which can be achieved through an agreement with the supplier to furnish all or substantial portions of the buyer's needs. The exclusive dealing contract thus can minimize the transaction costs and diseconomies of both suppliers and buyers. The result may be that these parties are drawn through economic objectives toward long term requirements contracts as an alternative to complete vertical integration — a single integrated entity occupying multiple levels in the distribution chain. *See* Williamson, *Transaction-Cost Economics: The Governance of Contractual Relations*, 22 J.L. & Econ. 233 (1979); MacNeil, *Contracts: Adjustment of Long-Term Economic Relations Under Classical, Neoclassical, and Relational Contract Law*, 72 Nw. U. L. Rev. 854 (1978); Carlton, *Vertical Integration in Competitive Markets Under Uncertainty*, 27 J. Indus. Econ. 189 (1979). But even if one accepts the efficiency underpinning as a basis for antitrust analysis, the exclusive dealing contract may be broader than necessary to achieve the planned economies and reasonable business practices, to the extent that it includes terms in excess of the time or conditions necessary to recoup the investment or enhance its distribution.

A growing body of economic literature argues that most exclusive dealing arrangements are efficient, and that exclusive dealing may be used to combat free rider problems, much the same way that vertical price and other nonprice restraints are used. For example, a manufacturer might use exclusive dealing to protect itself from "interbrand" free riding. Interbrand free riding occurs when a retailer is able to take advantage of amenities supplied by one manufacturer and apply them to products which originate from another manufacturer. Suppose, for example, that Exxon is a "full service" franchisor of gasoline stations, and supplies its independent franchisees (gasoline station operators) with a variety of things that make the station more attractive to the customer — "free" road maps, information services, and the big "Exxon" sign which the customer interprets as Exxon's guarantee of the quality of the products sold at that station.

Suppose, however, that the gasoline retailer also buys discounted off-brand gasoline and sells it at a substantially lower price from pumps adjacent to the Exxon gasoline pumps. Quite naturally, many of the amenities provided by Exxon will spill over to these pumps as well. Customers will drive into the station because it is a quality certified "Exxon" station, help themselves to a free road map, and buy the discount gasoline instead of Exxon's own brand. Exxon can protect itself from this problem by exclusive dealing — that is, by insisting that the dealer who owns an Exxon franchise and holds itself out as an Exxon station operator sell nothing but Exxon gasoline. In such circumstances an exclusive dealing contract might also protect customers from fraud. For more on the recent literature concerning the economics of exclusive dealing, *see* H. Hovenkamp, *Federal Antitrust Policy* § 10.8 (2d ed. 1994).

Counterarguments to the efficiency objectives suggest that exclusive dealing arrangements tend to foreclose from markets competitors and potential competitors of the supplier. If effective, these contracts will deny existing competitors the opportunity to compete for business of the contracting buyer. The anticompetitive consequences would be increased if this contractual conduct occurred in a concentrated market, as opposed to the ideal market of unlimited demand. The exclusionary effect allegedly may create barriers to entry for new firms at the supplier's level. Moreover, if effective, the supplier allegedly may be able to use the exclusive dealing agreement as a means either to achieve a monopoly or maintain a monopoly position. Authority exists that even if the use of supply contracts and exclusive arrangements have economic justifications, they may nevertheless "be undertaken with unlawful intent and in the desire to achieve [a monopoly]." *United States v. Dairymen, Inc.*, 660 F.2d 192, 195 (6th Cir. 1981).

In any event, the conventional analysis suggests that exclusive dealing implicates the use of market power and leverage of that power at one level of competition (supplier level) to affect another level (buyer level) with the result that interbrand competition is diminished. *But see* R. Posner, *Antitrust Law: An Economic Perspective* 196-206 (1976). Thus, the exclusionary effects of exclusive dealings arguably must be weighed against the economies achieved through the contract's efficiency features. Because individual exclusive dealing contracts may have procompetitive aspects, and indeed may be in the buyer's best interest, courts, as the following section indicates, have been unwilling to apply the rule of per se illegality. *See generally* Steuer, *Exclusive Dealing in Distribution*, 69 Cornell L. Rev. 101 (1983).

In *Omega Environmental, Inc. v. Gilbarco, Inc.*, 127 F.3d 1157 (9th Cir. 1997), the Ninth Circuit reversed a lower court order finding a Clayton Act section 3 violation and directing the defendant to pay $27 million in treble damages. The defendant was the market leader in manufacturing petroleum dispensing equipment and had enforced an exclusive dealing policy against two of its distributors that had been acquired by a competitor, leading to their termination. The court found that any anticompetitive effect Gilbarco's actions may have had was mitigated by the fact that competitors had the opportunity to sell their goods to end users directly or develop new distributors with which to work. The court admitted that such exclusive dealing arrangements aimed towards distributors are generally of less concern than ones designed for end users, since alternative sources and channels of distribution usually exist. Additionally, the plaintiffs failed to produce sufficient evidence that Gilbarco's behavior effectively deterred market entry, which is a necessary step in succeeding in such a claim. In fact, the court cited evidence of increased market share for some manufacturers. Finally, the short duration of the distributions agreements between the defendant and its distributors and the ease with which they could be terminated further reduced the threat of market competition foreclosure.

Although the Antitrust Division of the Department of Justice has not set out a definite description of its approach toward enforcement against exclusive dealing, insight can be gained from some of the cases the Division has brought in the last few years. Arrangements of short or moderate duration are no longer protected from antitrust scrutiny, especially when imposed by companies with "significant market power." *Id.* at 26. Moreover, the Division is more willing now to look beyond the mere terms of the contract in deciding the scope of its exclusivity. *Id. See United States v. Microsoft*, 56 F.3d 1448 (D.C. Cir. 1995). *See also* Mary Lou Steptoe & Donna L. Wilson, *Developments in Exclusive Dealing*, 20 Antitrust 25 (Summer 1997) (reviewing the increased enforcement efforts of the Clinton administration with respect to exclusive dealing and analyzing the possible effects of the *Omega* verdict); Wanda Jane Rogers, Note, *Beyond Economic Theory: A Model for Analyzing the Antitrust Implications of Exclusive Dealing Arrangements*, 45 Duke L.J. 1009, 1018-25 (1996) (discussing the procompetitive and anticompetitive effects of exclusive dealing and commenting that courts today do not generally follow a strict "Chicago-school" efficiency approach but rather look to the actual marketplace effects of exclusive dealing arrangements).

Recall that as a prerequisite for Clayton Act coverage, a plaintiff must demonstrate that the challenged exclusive dealing arrangement arose from "a condition, agreement, or understanding" which has the effect of "substantially lessen[ing] competition or tend[ing] to create a monopoly in any line of commerce." This "concert of action" requirement under section 3 of the Clayton Act, as under the Sherman Act, may not be established if the evidence demonstrates that the supplier merely, and unilaterally, refused to deal when the buyer would not consent to the exclusive dealing terms. On this element of the burden of proof, the *Colgate* doctrine arguably has continuing vitality. *See, e.g., Nelson Radio & Supply Co. v. Motorola, Inc.,* 200 F.2d 911 (5th Cir. 1952), *cert. denied,* 345 U.S. 925 (1953). In addition, the exceptions to the doctrine apply particularly when the evidence is susceptible to an inference of coercion or tacit understanding, leading to the conclusion that there has been a "meeting of the minds." Authority exists that even if the contract did not explicitly contain an exclusive dealing clause it can be inferred from the "course of dealing" between the buyer and the seller. *Barnosky Oils, Inc. v. Union Oil Co.,* 665 F.2d 74, 86-87 (6th Cir. 1981). Finally, it should be noted that the allegations in the complaint must be drawn so that the court can at least infer a claim for relief from articulated anticompetitive effects in a defined market; otherwise dismissal may be appropriate. *See Gilbuilt Homes, Inc. v. Continental Homes,* 667 F.2d 209, 212 (1st Cir. 1981); *Perington Whsle., Inc. v. Burger King Corp.,* 631 F.2d 1369 (10th Cir. 1979).

In the leading case rejecting the per se characterization for exclusive dealing contracts, *Standard Oil Co. v. United States (Standard Stations),* 337 U.S. 293, 305-06 (1949), Justice Frankfurter reasoned that while the rule of reason was the appropriate analysis to employ for determining the legality of such contracts, the Clayton Act did not require the broader-based weighing analysis embraced in *Chicago Board of Trade. Id.* at 313. A more focused analysis was adopted, designed to determine whether the contract substantially foreclosed competition. In addition to establishing the standard of legality under section 3, *Standard Stations* set forth with clarity the economic rationale for the selection of the rule of reason decisional analysis. Over a decade later, the Court reaffirmed its rule of reason approach in *Tampa Elec. Co. v. Nashville Coal Co.,* 365 U.S. 320 (1961), but seemed to suggest a more wide-open analysis that placed a greater burden of proof on the plaintiff in establishing anticompetitiveness. The analysis also implied a less mechanical application of the relevant market structure factors.

Before considering *Tampa Elec.,* examine the facts and reasoning in *Standard Stations* which concerned the legality of exclusive supply contracts with independent retail dealers of gasoline.

The Standard Oil Co. was the largest seller of gasoline in the Western states. Its sales in 1946 amounted to 23%. Sales by company-owned service stations constituted 6.8% of the total, sales under exclusive dealing contracts with independent service stations amounted to 6.7% of the total, and the remainder of sales were to industrial users. Standard's six leading competitors in the retail service station market accounted for 42.5% of the market. The remaining retail sales were divided among more than 70 small competitors. Standard's major competitors all used similar exclusive dealing arrangements. In the Western states market, 5,937 independent dealers (16%) entered into exclusive supply contracts with Standard in 1947 which amounted to nearly $58 million worth of gasoline.

The Supreme Court, speaking through Justice Frankfurter, held that contracts, which affected $58 million of business, comprising 6.7% of the independent

market, were enough from which an inference could be drawn that competition
"has been or probably [would] be substantially lessened."

    The qualifying clause of § 3 is satisfied by proof that competition has been
foreclosed in a substantial share of the line of commerce affected. It cannot
be gainsaid that observance by a dealer of his requirements contract with
Standard does effectively foreclose whatever opportunity there might be for
competing suppliers to attract his patronage, and it is clear that the affected
proportion of retail sales of petroleum products is substantial. In view of the
widespread adoption of such contracts by Standard's competitors and the
availability of alternative ways of obtaining an assured market, evidence that
competitive activity has not actually declined is inconclusive. Standard's use
of the contracts creates just such a potential clog on competition as it was the
purpose of § 3 to remove wherever, were it to become actual, it would impede a substantial amount of competitive activity.

Consider Justice Douglas' dissenting opinion, however:

    The economic theories which the Court has read into the Anti-Trust Laws
have favored rather than discouraged monopoly....

    It is common knowledge that a host of filling stations in the country are
locally owned and operated. Others are owned and operated by the big oil
companies. This case involves directly only the former. It pertains to requirements contracts that the oil companies make with these independents. It
is plain that a filling station owner who is tied to an oil company for his supply of products is not an available customer for the products of other suppliers. The same is true of a filling station owner who purchases his inventory a
year in advance. His demand is withdrawn from the market for the duration
of the contract in the one case and for a year in the other. The result in each
case is to lessen competition if the standard is day-to-day purchases.
Whether it is a substantial lessening of competition within the meaning of
the Anti-Trust Laws is a question of degree and may vary from industry to
industry.

    The Court answers the question for the oil industry by a formula which
under our decisions promises to wipe out large segments of independent
filling station operators. The method of doing business under requirements
contracts at least keeps the independents alive. They survive as small business units. The situation is not ideal from either their point of view or that of
the nation. But the alternative which the Court offers is far worse from the
point of view of both.

    The elimination of these requirements contracts sets the stage for Standard
and the other oil companies to build service-station empires of their own.
The opinion of the Court does more than set the stage for that development.
It is an advisory opinion as well, stating to the oil companies how they can
with impunity build their empires. The formula suggested by the Court is

either the use of the "agency" device, which in practical effect means control of filling stations by the oil companies, ... or the outright acquisition of them by subsidiary corporations or otherwise.... Under the approved judicial doctrine either of those devices means increasing the monopoly of the oil companies over the retail field.

....

Today there is vigorous competition between the oil companies for the market. That competition has left some room for the survival of the independents. But when this inducement for their survival is taken away, we can expect that the oil companies will move in to supplant them with their own stations. There will still be competition between the oil companies. But there will be a tragic loss to the nation. The small, independent business man will be supplanted by clerks. Competition between suppliers of accessories (which is involved in this case) will diminish or cease altogether. The oil companies will command an increasingly larger share of both the wholesale and the retail markets.

That is the likely result of today's decision. The requirements contract which is displaced is relatively innocuous as compared with the virulent growth of monopoly power which the Court encourages. The Court does not act unwittingly. It consciously pushes the oil industry in that direction. The Court approves what the Anti-Trust Laws were designed to prevent. It helps remake America in the image of the cartels.

TAMPA ELECTRIC CO. V. NASHVILLE COAL CO.

365 U.S. 320 (1961)

JUSTICE CLARK delivered the opinion of the Court.

We granted certiorari to review a declaratory judgement holding illegal under § 3 of the Clayton Act a requirements contract between the parties providing for the purchase by petitioner of all the coal it would require as boiler fuel at its Gannon Station in Tampa, Florida, over a 20-year period. Both the District Court and the Court of Appeals ... agreed with respondents that the contract fell within the proscription of § 3 and therefore was illegal and unenforceable. We cannot agree that the contract suffers the claimed anti-trust illegality[2] and therefore, do not find it necessary to consider respondents' additional argument that such illegality is a defense to the action and a bar to enforceability.

The Facts

Petitioner Tampa Electric Company is a public utility located in Tampa, Florida. It produces and sells electric energy to a service area, including the city, ex-

---

[2] In addition to their claim under § 3 of the Clayton Act, respondents argue the contract is illegal under the Sherman Act.

tending from Tampa Bay eastward 60 miles to the center of the state, and some 30 miles in width. As of 1954 petitioner operated two electrical generating plants comprising a total of 11 individual generating units, all of which consumed oil in their burners. In 1955 Tampa Electric decided to expand its facilities by the construction of an additional generating plant to be comprised ultimately of six generating units, and to be known as the "Francis J. Gannon Station." Although every electrical generating plant in peninsular Florida burned oil at that time, Tampa Electric decided to try coal as boiler fuel in the first two units constructed at the Gannon Station. Accordingly, it contracted with the respondents to furnish the expected coal requirements for the units. The agreement, dated May 23, 1955, embraced Tampa Electric's "total requirements of fuel ... for the operation of its first two units to be installed at the Gannon Station ... not less than 225,000 tons of coal per unit per year," for a period of 20 years.

....

The District Court ... granted respondents' motion for summary judgment on the sole ground that the undisputed facts, recited above, showed the contract to be a violation of § 3 of the Clayton Act. The Court of Appeals agreed. Neither court found it necessary to consider the applicability of the Sherman Act.

....

Application of § 3 of the Clayton Act

In the almost half century since Congress adopted the Clayton Act, this Court has been called upon 10 times including the present, to pass upon questions arising under § 3....

In practical application, even though a contract is found to be an exclusive-dealing arrangement, it does not violate the section unless the court believes it probable that performance of the contract will foreclose competition in a substantial share of the line of commerce affected. Following the guidelines of earlier decisions, certain considerations must be taken. *First*, the line of commerce, *i.e.*, the type of goods, wares, or merchandise, etc., involved must be determined, where it is in controversy, on the basis of the facts peculiar to the case. *Second*, the area of effective competition in the known line of commerce must be charted by careful selection of the market area in which the seller operates, and to which the purchaser can practicably turn for supplies. In short, the threatened foreclosure of competition must be in relation to the market affected....

Third, and last, the competition foreclosed by the contract must be found to constitute a substantial share of the relevant market. That is to say, the opportunities for other traders to enter into or remain in that market must be significantly limited ....

To determine substantiality in a given case, it is necessary to weigh the probable effect of the contract on the relevant area of effective competition, taking into account the relative strength of the parties, the proportionate volume of commerce involved in relation to the total volume of commerce in the relevant market area, and the probable immediate and future effects which preemption of that share of the market might have on effective competition therein. It follows that a mere showing that the contract itself involves a substantial number of dollars is ordinarily of little consequence.

The Application of § 3 Here

In applying these considerations to the facts of the case before us, it appears clear that both the Court of Appeals and the District Court have not given the required effect to a controlling factor in the case — the relevant competitive market area. This omission, by itself, requires reversal, for, as we have pointed out, the relevant market is the prime factor in relation to which the ultimate question, whether the contract forecloses competition in a substantial share of the line of commerce involved, must be decided....

Relevant Market of Effective Competition

Neither the Court of Appeals nor the District Court considered in detail the question of the relevant market. They do seem, however, to have been satisfied with inquiring only as to competition within "Peninsular Florida." It was noted that the total consumption of peninsular Florida was 700,000 tons of coal per year, about equal to the estimated 1959 requirements of Tampa Electric. It was also pointed out that coal accounted for less than 6% of the fuel consumed in the entire State. The District Court concluded that though the respondents were only one of 700 coal producers who could serve the same market, peninsular Florida, the contract for a period of 20 years excluded competitors from a substantial amount of trade. Respondents contend that the coal tonnage covered by the contract must be weighed against either the total consumption of coal in peninsular Florida, or all of Florida, or the Bituminous Coal Act area comprising peninsular Florida and the Georgia "finger," or, at most, all of Florida and Georgia. If the latter area were considered the relevant market, Tampa Electric's proposed requirements would be 18% of the tonnage sold therein. Tampa Electric says that both courts and respondents are in error, because the "700 coal producers who could serve" it, as recognized by the trial court and admitted by respondents, operated in the Appalachian coal area and that its contract requirements were less than 1% of the total marketed production of these producers; that the relevant effective area of competition was the area in which these producers operated, and in which they were willing to compete for the consumer potential.

We are persuaded that on the record in this case, neither peninsular Florida, nor the entire State of Florida, nor Florida and Georgia combined constituted the relevant market of effective competition. We do not believe that the pie will slice so thinly. By far the bulk of the overwhelming tonnage marketed from the same producing area as serves Tampa is sold outside of Georgia and Florida, and the producers were "eager" to sell more coal in those States. While the relevant competitive market is not ordinarily susceptible to a "metes and bounds" definition, ... it is of course the area in which respondents and the other 700 producers effectively compete. The record shows that, like the respondents, they sold bituminous coal "suitable for [Tampa's] requirements," mined in parts of Pennsylvania, Virginia, West Virginia, Kentucky, Tennessee, Alabama, Ohio and Illinois. We take notice of the fact that the approximate total bituminous coal (and lignite) product in the year 1954 from the districts in which these 700 producers are located was 359,289,000 tons, of which some 290,567,000 tons were sold on the open market. Of the latter amount some 78,716,000 tons were sold to electric utilities. We also note that in 1954 Florida and Georgia combined consumed at least 2,304,000 tons, 1,100,000 of which were used by electric utilities, and the sources of which were mines located in no less than seven States. We take further notice that the production and marketing of bituminous coal (and lignite) from the same districts and assumedly equally available to Tampa on a commercially feasible basis, is currently on a par with prior years. In point of statistical fact, coal consumption in the combined Florida-Georgia area has increased significantly since 1954. In 1959 more than 3,775,000 tons were there consumed, 2,913,000 being used by electric utilities including, presumably, the coal used by the petitioner. The coal continued to come from at least seven States.[15]

From these statistics it clearly appears that the proportionate volume of the total relevant coal product as to which the challenged contract pre-empted competition, less than 1%, is, conservatively speaking, quite insubstantial. A more accurate figure, even assuming pre-emption to the extent of the maximum anticipated total requirements, 2,250,000 tons a year, would be .77%.

Effect on Competition in the Relevant Market

It may well be that in the context of antitrust legislation protracted requirements contracts are suspect, but they have not been declared illegal *per se*. Even though a single contract between single traders may fall within the initial broad proscription of the section, it must also suffer the qualifying disability, tendency to work a substantial — not remote — lessening of competition in the relevant competitive market. It is urged that the present contract pre-empts competition to the extent of purchases worth perhaps $128,000,000, and that this "is, of course, not insignificant or insubstantial." While $128,000,000 is a considerable sum of money, even in these days, the dollar volume, by itself, is not the test, as we have already pointed out.

The remaining determination, therefore, is whether the pre-emption of competition to the extent of the tonnage involved tends to substantially foreclose competition in the relevant coal market. We think not. That market sees an annual

---

[15] 1,787,000 tons from certain counties in West Virginia, Virginia, Kentucky, Tennessee, and North Carolina; 1,321,000 tons from counties in Alabama, Georgia and elsewhere in Tennessee; 665,000 tons from the western Kentucky fields; 2,000 tons from other counties in West Virginia and Virginia.

trade in excess of 250,000,000 tons of coal and over a billion dollars — multiplied by 20 years it runs into astronomical figures. There is here neither a seller with a dominant position ...; nor myriad outlets with substantial sales volume, coupled with an industry-wide practice of relying upon exclusive contracts, ...; nor a plainly restrictive tying arrangement .... On the contrary, we seem to have only that type of contract which "may well be of economic advantage to buyers as well as to sellers." *Standard Oil Co. v. United States*, [337 U.S. 293 (1949)], at p. 306. In the case of the buyer it "may assure supply," while on the part of the seller it "may make possible the substantial reduction of selling expenses, give protection against price fluctuations, and ... offer the possibility of a predictable market." *Id.*, at 306-307. The 20-year period of the contract is singled out as the principal vice, but at least in the case of public utilities the assurance of a steady and ample supply of fuel is necessary in the public interest. Otherwise consumers are left unprotected against service failures owing to shutdowns; and increasingly unjustified costs might result in more burdensome rate structures eventually to be reflected in the consumer's bill. The compelling validity of such considerations has been recognized fully in the natural gas public utility field. This is not to say that utilities are immunized from Clayton Act proscriptions, but merely that, in judging the term of a requirements contract in relation to the substantiality of the foreclosure of competition, particularized considerations of the parties' operations are not irrelevant. In weighing the various factors, we have decided that in the competitive bituminous coal marketing area involved here the contract sued upon does not tend to foreclose a substantial volume of competition.

We need not discuss the respondents' further contention that the contract also violates § 1 and § 2 of the Sherman Act, for if it does not fall within the broader proscription of § 3 of the Clayton Act it follows that it is not forbidden by those of the former....

Reversed.

NOTES AND QUESTIONS

1. What analytical shift, if any, can you discern in comparing *Standard Stations* with *Tampa Electric*? Did the Court in *Tampa Electric* adopt a more complex economic standard of evaluation rejected by Justice Frankfurter earlier? If so, why?

State the Court's emphasis in *Tampa Electric*. Is the Court using the same definition of "substantial foreclosure" in both opinions?

2. How is the *Tampa Electric* "qualitative substantiality" test applied to the facts of that case under section 3? Consider the Court's progression of analysis:

First, the line of commerce ... involved must be determined, where it is in controversy, on the basis of the facts peculiar to the case. *Second*, the area of effective competition in the known line of commerce must be charted ....

Third, and last, the competition foreclosed by the contract must be found to constitute a substantial share of the relevant market. That is to say, the opportunities for other traders to enter into or remain in that market must be significantly limited...

To determine substantiality in a given case, it is necessary to weigh the probable effect of the contract on the relevant area of effective competition, taking into account the relative strength of the parties, the proportionate volume of commerce involved in relation to the total volume of commerce in the relevant market area, and the probable immediate and future effects which pre-emption of that share of the market might have on effective competition therein. It follows that a mere showing that the contract itself involves a substantial number of dollars is ordinarily of little consequence.

....

There is here neither a seller with a dominant position in the market ... nor myriad outlets with substantial sales volume, coupled with an industry-wide practice of relying upon exclusive contracts ... nor a plainly restrictive tying arrangement .... On the contrary, we seem to have only that type of contract which "may well be of economic advantage to buyers as well as to sellers."...

365 U.S. at 327-29, 334. Consider whether *Tampa Electric* makes prediction of the lawfulness of exclusive dealing less certain than the rule announced in *Standard Stations*. Is the presumptive illegality test (condemning any foreclosure that is more than de minimis) raised in *Standard Stations* operative after *Tampa Electric*? In utilizing that test, was the Court inferring competitive harm from a finding that commerce had been substantially affected? Is the effect now based on market share rather than dollar volume? Is it a relative test or an absolute one? *See, e.g., Magnus Petr. Co. v. Skelly Oil Co.*, 599 F.2d 196, 201-04 (7th Cir. 1979). Finally, consider where the line of legality is drawn between the *Tampa Electric* 1% and the *Standard Stations* 6.7%.

3. In reflecting on the present standard governing the legality of exclusive dealing as set forth in *Tampa Electric*, consider whether the same analysis should be employed regardless of the status (consumer, distributor, or retailer) of the plaintiff. Authority exists for the rule that a higher standard of proof regarding the substantiality of the foreclosure should be required when distributors rather than end-use buyers are bound. The theory is that an exclusive dealing contract with a distributor does not necessarily preclude a competing supplier from distribution of its products, when other "existing or potential distributors" are available. *See, e.g., Refrigeration Eng'g Corp. v. Frick Co.*, 370 F. Supp. 702, 709 (W.D. Tex. 1974); Turner, *The Validity of Tying Arrangements Under the Antitrust Laws*, 72 Harv. L. Rev. 50, 72-73 (1958). With respect to a contract binding retailers *compare United States v. J.I. Case Co.*, 101 F. Supp. 856 (D. Minn. 1951), *with Adolph Coors Co. v. FTC*, 497 F.2d 1178 (10th Cir. 1974), *cert. denied*, 419 U.S. 1105 (1975).

4. Note Justice Douglas' dissenting opinion in *Standard Stations*, briefly excerpted above. What did he mean when he stated that oil companies not permitted to engage in exclusive dealing would "build service-station empires of their own"? Justice Douglas was enough of an economist to know that vertical integration reduces the cost of doing business. The partial vertical integration facilitated by the requirements contracts in *Standard Stations* reduced transaction costs, gave the suppliers a chain of identifiable retail outlets, even though they did not own them, and added a great deal of predictability to a very erratic market. The cost reductions that can be achieved by vertical integration will benefit both monopolists and competitors. (See the discussion of the economics of vertical integration, *infra.*)

As a general rule, any firm is best off if other firms in the distribution chain are operating as efficiently as possible. In a competitive market, however, the consequences of not vertically integrating can be severe. If Standard Oil was a competitor — and the *Standard Stations* opinion suggests that it was — then it would lose market share to any firm able to deliver petroleum products at a lower cost. If a competitor saved money, either by means of a requirements contract or else by building its own gasoline stations, Standard Oil would have little choice but to follow. The fact that the market in *Standard Stations* was probably competitive and that requirements contracts and other forms of vertical integration, such as outright ownership of retail stations, persisted is good evidence that the vertical integration was efficient.

In short, Justice Douglas put his finger on an issue that goes to the heart of antitrust policy: whom do the laws protect? Large firms in a competitive market might be "forced" by available economies to integrate vertically — with the result that independent retailers are either restrained or eliminated. The result in a competitive market will be lower prices for consumers. Thus Justice Douglas' dissent forces us to choose sides: we must pick an antitrust policy that will protect either the independent gasoline retailers or else the preferences of the consumer. There are no easy answers — and no economic answers — to that question.

5. Should vertical integration by contract be treated any differently than vertical integration by merger? (See the discussion of vertical mergers, *infra.*) What if Standard had purchased a set of independent retail stations instead of dealing with them by means of requirements contracts? The percentages of gasoline and other products "foreclosed" from the market would be the same. Some effects would be different. For example, the merger would last indefinitely, while the requirements contracts were periodic. Presumably Standard would have even more control over retail stations that it owned than it did over independently owned stations that it controlled by contract. This need not always be the case, however. Certain franchise contracts between large firms and their independently owned franchisees are incredibly detailed — including such terms as how often lavatories must be cleaned and floors scrubbed and prescribing the uniforms that attendants must wear. *See Kypta v. McDonald's Corp.,* 671 F.2d 1282 (11th Cir.), *cert. denied,* 459 U.S. 857 (1982); *Principe v. McDonald's Corp.,* 631 F.2d 303 (4th Cir. 1980), *cert. denied,* 451 U.S. 970 (1981).

Traditionally, both the law of exclusive dealing and the law of vertical mergers have been predicated on a "foreclosure" theory. In fact, the traditional tests for legality in these two different areas of antitrust law have been remarkably similar. (See the discussion of vertical integration by merger, *infra*.) In 1984 the United States Department of Justice published a set of Guidelines that state the Justice Department's position on when certain mergers ought to be illegal. These Guidelines are generally far more lenient toward vertical mergers than much of the older Supreme Court case law suggests. The Guidelines suggest that the Department of Justice is not likely to challenge a vertical merger unless the firms involved have something like 25% or more of the relevant market. It remains to be seen whether the Guidelines for vertical mergers will have any effect on the law of exclusive dealing.

6. Consider the accuracy of this statement: The exclusive dealing cases define how markets are affected by full requirements contracts. Whether the market will be affected by a substantial lessening of competition within section 3 of the Clayton Act is determined by a relative market factor analysis which weighs the "volume of commerce affected," "strength of the parties" and the "probable immediate and future effects which pre-emption of that share of the market might have on effective competition." Do you agree? *See Tampa Electric Co.; ABA Monograph, Vertical Restrictions Upon Buyers Limiting Purchases of Goods From Others* 91 (1982).

7. In applying the rule of reason analysis, lower court decisions subsequent to *Standard Stations* and *Tampa Electric* have drawn distinctions as to whether the restraint was the "least restrictive alternative" or was "fairly necessary under the circumstances," the latter being a less burdensome defense to meet. *Compare American Motor Inns, Inc. v. Holiday Inns, Inc.*, 521 F.2d 1230, 1246-49 (3d Cir. 1975), *with Siegel v. Chicken Delight, Inc.*, 448 F.2d 43 (9th Cir. 1971), *cert. denied*, 405 U.S. 955 (1972). But the mere "existence of a less restrictive alternative [practice] will not by itself [absent a showing of anticompetitive tendency] establish the unreasonableness of the practice." *Bravman v. Bassett Furn. Indus.*, 552 F.2d 90 (3d Cir. 1977).

B. TYING ARRANGEMENTS

1. INTRODUCTION: ECONOMICS OF TYING

A contractual arrangement which conditions the sale or lease of one product on the purchase or lease of another from the same seller is characterized as a tie-in sale or tying arrangement. A related commercial transaction is a package licensing contract, where the lessee is required to take more than one copyrighted product or patent under a so-called "block" or "package" license. A third variation of the tying arrangement is the requirement that the buyer purchase the seller's full line of products if any are taken, though all products may not be desired. This practice is known as "full line forcing." The desired product is called the "tying" product, while the second required product is the "tied" product.

Three statutes govern the legality of the commercial practice of tying the sales of separate products. Sections 1 and 2 of the Sherman Act, section 3 of the Clayton Act, and section 5 of the FTC Act have application under certain circumstances as discussed in this subchapter. The Clayton Act is applicable, however, only when "goods" or commodities are involved; services which are tied are thus not covered under the Act.

The standard of legality under the Sherman and Clayton Acts has been distinguished in at least one principal Supreme Court decision, *Times-Picayune Pub'g Co. v. United States*, 345 U.S. 594 (1953). But the distinctions have been blurred subsequently in lower court decisions and it is presently unclear to what extent the burden of proof varies under the two statutes. *Compare Spartan Grain & Mill Co. v. Ayers*, 581 F.2d 419 (5th Cir.), *cert. denied*, 444 U.S. 832 (1978), *with Sergeant-Welch Scientific Co. v. Ventron Corp.*, 567 F.2d 701 (7th Cir. 1977), *cert. denied*, 439 U.S. 822 (1978). Under the FTC Act, on the other hand, the standard may be less restrictive. *FTC v. Texaco, Inc.*, 393 U.S. 223 (1968).

Traditionally, tie-ins were condemned because the forced purchase of the second product allegedly denied competitors of the seller access to the tied product market and because the tying contract forced the buyer to relinquish free choice over the purchasing decision. The underlying economic theory supporting this analysis centered on avoidance of monopoly power. This theory held that in order to prevent the seller from obtaining a monopoly in the tied product, it should be prevented from using its power or dominance in the tying product as a "lever" into the tied product market.

This leverage theory, which seeks to curtail "monopolistic exploitation," found acceptance in many Supreme Court opinions, beginning as early as 1917, and many of these classified ties as illegal *per se*. If the plaintiff could demonstrate that defendant possessed "sufficient economic power" in the tying product to force the purchase of a separate tied product, and if a "not insubstantial amount" of interstate commerce was affected, the burden of proof had been met and the tying arrangement would be declared per se illegal. No actual, specific anticompetitive effect was required to be established. The leverage theory itself supplied the projected exclusionary effect. *See generally* L. Sullivan, *Handbook of the Law of Antitrust* 431-63 (1977). Kaplow, *Extension of Monopoly Power Through Leverage*, 85 Colum. L. Rev. 515 (1985).

The leverage theory as a basis for tying arrangement analysis was first challenged in the late 1950's and more recently in the late 1970's. At first the theory was attacked as being overinclusive. It did not consider whether the tying sale was the "only means of utilizing effectively a power already possessed." Moreover, it was urged that if "the tying seller is maximizing his return on the tying product and the same output of the tied product can still be produced ... no additional or new monopoly effect should be assumed." Bowman, *Tying Arrangements and the Leverage Problem*, 67 Yale L.J. 19, 20 (1957).

In general, the economic attack on the traditional "leverage" theory of tying arrangements has gone like this: profit-maximizing prices are final output prices. Assume, for example, that a firm has a monopoly in the bolt market but that the nut market is competitive. Most customers use a nut with a bolt and buy them in equal numbers. With respect to these customers the profit-maximizing price of the "package" — a nut and a bolt — is, say, 50 cents. If nuts are being sold at a competitive price of 10 cents, the monopolist in bolts will maximize his profits by selling bolts for 40 cents. But now suppose that the bolt monopolist uses a tying arrangement: he forces all purchasers of one of his bolts to take a nut from him as well. What price will he be able to charge for the nut? The answer is 10 cents, the competitive price. By charging the profit-maximizing price for the bolt, the bolt monopolist has already extracted all available monopoly profits from the bolt-nut package. If he attempts to use a tying arrangement to force customers to take their nuts from him at a price of, say, 15 cents, he will produce less, not more, monopoly profits.

Does this mean that the leverage theory of tying arrangements will never work? No, sometimes it does work — but only where there are other factors than the above facts include. For example, what if the nut market is cartelized and nuts which would have a competitive price of 10 cents are being sold by the cartel members for 20 cents. The cartel injures the bolt monopolist, because it reduces the profit-maximizing price for bolts (remember, the profit-maximizing price is 50 cents for the *package*). By manufacturing nuts himself and selling nuts and bolts as a package the bolt monopolist will be able to transfer the 10 cents in monopoly revenues away from the nut cartel and to himself. In this case the leverage theory may have some application.

Secondly, suppose that the price of bolts is regulated by the state. Suppose, for example, that the profit-maximizing price of a bolt-nut package is 50 cents, but that the bolt monopolist is required by law to charge only 20 cents for bolts. In this situation the bolt monopolist might be able to use the tying arrangement to force purchasers to take a nonprice-regulated product as a condition of taking the price-regulated product. In that case, by selling the nonregulated product at a monopoly price the seller could effectively circumvent the price regulation scheme. There is evidence that telephone companies have used such a scheme to avoid rate regulation. For example, if the lease rate for telephone lines is price-regulated, but equipment rentals are not, a telephone company might be able to "cheat" on the price regulation statute by requiring all lessees of its lines to lease their equipment from the company as well, and then charging a monopoly price for the equipment. *See Litton Sys. v. American Tel. & Tel. Co.*, 700 F.2d 785 (2d Cir. 1983), *cert. denied*, 464 U.S. 1073 (1984); *Phonetele, Inc. v. American Tel. & Tel. Co.*, 664 F.2d 716 (9th Cir. 1981), *cert. denied*, 459 U.S. 1145 (1983); Hovenkamp, *Tying Arrangements and Class Actions*, 36 Vand. L. Rev. 213, 233-34 (1983).

Undoubtedly the most common purposes of certain types of tying arrangements, however, are price discrimination or "metering." Tying arrangements come in two general kinds: fixed proportion and variable proportion. In a fixed proportion tie-in, such as the bolt-and-nut arrangement described above, a purchaser takes one bolt with each nut, and vice-versa. Although price discrimination by means of such tie-ins is possible (see the discussion of block-booking, *infra*), variable proportion tying arrangements are much more conducive to price discrimination.

In a variable proportion arrangement purchasers or lessees of the tying product use varying amounts of some tied product. For example, suppose that a lessor of mimeograph machines requires lessees to purchase all their mimeograph paper from the lessor. *See Henry v. A.B. Dick Co.*, 224 U.S. 1 (1912). People who use the mimeograph machine more will also consume more paper. By leasing the machine to all lessees at the same price and selling the paper at a supracompetitive price, the lessor might be doing one of two things. First, it might be using the paper to "meter" the more intense wear and tear and depreciation on the machine that results from high volume users. If the extra profit on a single sheet of mimeograph paper reflects precisely the costs in wear and tear on the machine that result from making a single copy, then the variable price of the "package" — the machine plus the paper — simply reflects the fact that high intensity users of the mimeograph machine impose greater costs on the lessor.

There is another possibility, however. It is likely that high intensity users of the mimeograph machine value the machine more highly than low intensity users value it. A tying arrangement can enable the lessor or seller of the machine to price discriminate — that is, to obtain a higher rate of profit from higher intensity users of the machine, who presumably are higher preference users as well. Assume for example that a lessor charges all lessees $100 per month for the mimeograph machine, which represents a rate of return on the machine of 5%. However, it requires all lessees to purchase their paper from the lessor as well, at 2 cents per sheet. This price represents a return of 25% on the paper. The overall rate of return will then be much larger from a lessee who makes 10,000 copies monthly than from a lessee who makes 500 copies monthly, even though both are paying the same basic rate for the machine. (See the discussion of the economics of price discrimination, *infra*.)

Why would a seller want to price discriminate by means of a tying arrangement in this way? First of all, in order to do it successfully the seller would need a certain amount of market power in the tying product. If the tying product were perfectly competitive, disadvantaged purchasers or lessees (those asked to pay the higher price) would go to a different seller or lessor. A seller with market power will price discriminate because by so doing it can make more money than it can by establishing a single profit-maximizing price. The best of all possible worlds for a seller is one in which it can sell a unit to each purchaser at precisely the amount that that purchaser values the unit. Price discrimination by variable proportion tying arrangements comes as close as any mechanism to approximating this kind of "perfect" price discrimination.

Second, price discrimination is often frustrated by arbitrage. For example, if a seller sells widgets to one set of customers at $1.00 and to another set of customers at 70 cents, sooner or later the favored customers will begin selling to the disfavored customers at some price between 70 cents and $1.00. Price discrimination by tying arrangements frustrates arbitrage because all sales of all products are made at the same price. Thirdly, and for the same reason, price discrimination undertaken by tie-ins avoids the Robinson-Patman Act, which is the federal antitrust statute that most commonly is used to condemn price discrimination. The Robinson-Patman Act applies only to sales in which the same or similar product is sold to two different purchasers at two different prices. When price discrimination is undertaken by tie-in, however, all sales are made at the same price per product. In the example above, all machines are leased at $100.00 per month and all sheets of paper are sold at 2 cents each. The mimeograph example would also fall outside the Robinson-Patman Act because the statute applies only to sales, not to leases.

Should tie-ins used to facilitate price discrimination be illegal? Economists and antitrust scholars are deeply divided on this question. On the one hand, variable proportion, price-discrimination tying arrangements enable a monopolist in the tying product to make even more money than it can make by charging its uniform profit-maximizing price to all purchasers. For this reason scholars who believe that wealth distribution is an important concern of antitrust policy would condemn such tying arrangements.

On the other hand, price discrimination often results in higher output, and thus less misallocation of resources, than unitary monopoly pricing does. Many people who believe that the antitrust laws should be concerned exclusively with allocative efficiency argue that price discrimination by tying arrangements ought to be legal. Courts have generally developed a unitary rule that purports to condemn all tying arrangements by the same test whether or not they are used to price discriminate.

For a discussion of these questions of tying arrangements and antitrust policy, see *IBM Corp. v. United States*, 298 U.S. 131 (1936) (goodwill defense discussed in early case); H. Hovenkamp, *Federal Antitrust Policy*, ch. 10 (2d ed. 1994); 9 P. Areeda, *Antitrust Law*, ch. 17 (1991); R. Posner, *Antitrust Law: An Economic Perspective* 171-84 (1976); R. Bork, *The Antitrust Paradox: A Policy at War With Itself* 365-81 (1978); Burstein, *A Theory of Full-Line Forcing*, 55 Nw. U. L. Rev. 62 (1960); Bowman, *Tying Arrangements and the Leverage Problem*, 67 Yale L.J. 19 (1957).

The case for an "efficiency defense" in lawsuits alleging illegal tying arrangements continues to grow. The "defense" shows up, however, not as a rebuttal to a plaintiff's prima facie case, but rather as an argument that the plaintiff has failed to show that the defendant is selling or leasing distinct tying and tied "products." No general definition of a "product" for purposes of the law of tying arrangements has yet been produced. However, courts are increasingly inclined to view two items as a single "product" (thus precluding liability) if the combination results in certain efficiencies in production or distribution.

Consider the following analysis from Judge Posner in *Jack Walters & Sons Corp. v. Morton Bldg., Inc.*, 737 F.2d 698 (7th Cir. 1984):

> The problem is that there is no obvious way of deciding whether a product is a single product or an assemblage of components. The practice has been to classify a product as a single product if there are rather obvious economies of joint provision, as in the left-shoe-right-shoe example.... Although this approach seems to take what would otherwise be a matter of defense and make its absence a threshold requirement of the offense, it does serve to screen out many silly cases.

Judge Posner then concluded that a prefabricated building and the trademark given to the building by its manufacturer were a single "product" for purposes of the law of tying arrangements. To hold that a trademark and the product manufactured by the trademark's owner were separate "products," concluded Judge Posner, would virtually impose compulsory licensing of trademarks — at least on those firms who had some market power in the tying product. In such a case it could be illegal for someone who owned a trademark and manufactured a product under it to require those wanting the trademark to take the product as well. Would consumers be better off if IBM or Baskin-Robbins were forced to sell their trademarks to anyone who wanted to manufacture computers or ice cream?

For further discussion of efficiency and the "separate product" test in the law of tying arrangements, see H. Hovenkamp, *Federal Antitrust Policy*, ch. 10 (2d ed. 1994); E.T. Sullivan & J. Harrison, *Understanding Antitrust and Its Economic Implications*, ch. 5 (3d ed. 1998).

2. DEVELOPMENT OF UNIQUE PER SE RULE FOR TYING ARRANGEMENTS

Tying arrangements were first considered restraints of trade in patent cases. The Court in *Motion Picture Patents Co. v. Universal Film Mfg. Co.*, 243 U.S. 502 (1917), refused to sanction such a restriction in a patent infringement suit because it feared that it would lead to a monopoly. The leverage/monopoly theory found acceptance under antitrust laws quickly thereafter. Initially, the Court centered its Clayton Act analysis on whether the supplier had substantial market power or a dominant market position in the desired tying product market. *United Shoe Mach. Corp. v. United States*, 258 U.S. 451 (1922) (tying patented shoe manufacturing equipment to other related machines and supplies). Later the Court, in a section 3 case involving the alleged protection of "good will" and "quality product" defense, spoke more clearly about the per se illegality of tie-in sale contracts. In *International Salt Co. v. United States*, 332 U.S. 392 (1947), the Court considered the legality of a tying arrangement which conditioned the lease of a patented salt machine on the purchase of the salt from the same lessor. Finding that these salt sale arrangements amounted to $500,000 annually, the

Court concluded that a substantial amount of competition had been foreclosed and that it need not consider International's actual position in the tying product (salt machine) market. The Court held that when a substantial amount of commerce is affected by a tie-in contract, it is per se illegal under section 3 of the Clayton Act.

> The volume of business affected by these contracts cannot be said to be insignificant or insubstantial and the tendency of the arrangement to accomplishment of monopoly seems obvious. Under the law (§ 3 of Clayton), agreements are forbidden which "tend to create a monopoly," and it is immaterial that the tendency is a creeping one rather than one that proceeds at full gallop; nor does the law await arrival of the goal before condemning the direction of the movement.

Id. at 396. On the validity of the "quality product" defense, the Court, without deciding the merits, held that International Salt failed to carry its burden that for the machine to operate properly it had to use the salt provided by the manufacturer of the machine.

Several years later the Court was called upon to apply the Sherman Act to a tying arrangement when a newspaper publisher sold advertising in the morning and afternoon papers as a single product: an advertiser could not buy advertising separately in *either* the morning or afternoon papers. In the course of its opinion, the Court drew distinctions between the burdens of proof under the Clayton and Sherman Acts.

TIMES-PICAYUNE PUBLISHING CO. V. UNITED STATES

345 U.S. 594 (1953)

JUSTICE CLARK delivered the opinion of the Court.

At issue is the legality under the Sherman Act of the Times-Picayune Publishing Company's contracts for the sale of newspaper classified and general display advertising space. The Company in New Orleans owns and publishes the morning Time-Picayune and the evening States. Buyers of space for general display and classified advertising in its publications may purchase only combined insertions appearing in both the morning and evening papers, and not in either separately.

....

[T]he District Court at the outset denied the Government's motion for partial summary judgment [and] the case went to trial and eventuated in comprehensive and detailed findings of fact.

....

On the basis of [its] findings, the District Judge held the unit contracts in violation of the Sherman Act. The contracts were viewed as tying arrangements which the Publishing Company because of the Times-Picayune's "monopoly position" could force upon advertisers. Postulating that contracts foreclosing competitors from a substantial part of the market restrain trade within the meaning of

§ 1 of the Act, and that effect on competition tests the reasonableness of a restraint, the court deemed a substantial percentage of advertising accounts in the New Orleans papers unlawfully "restrained." Further, a violation of § 2 was found: defendants by use of the unit plan "attempted to monopolize that segment of the afternoon newspaper general and classified advertising field which was represented by those advertisers who also required morning newspaper space and who could not because of budgetary limitations or financial inability purchase space in both afternoon newspapers."

....

Tying arrangements, we may readily agree, flout the Sherman Act's policy that competition rule the marts of trade.... By conditioning his sale of one commodity on the purchase of another, a seller coerces the abdication of buyers' independent judgment as to the "tied" product's merits and insulates it from the competitive stresses of the open market. But any intrinsic superiority of the "tied" product would convince freely choosing buyers to select it over others, anyway. Thus "[i]n the usual case only the prospect of reducing competition would persuade a seller to adopt such a contract and only his control of the supply of the tying device, whether conferred by patent monopoly or otherwise obtained, could induce a buyer to enter one." Conversely, the effect on competing sellers attempting to rival the "tied" product is drastic: to the extent the enforcer of the tying arrangement enjoys market control, other existing or potential sellers are foreclosed from offering up their goods to a free competitive judgment; they are effectively excluded from the marketplace.

For that reason, tying agreements fare harshly under the laws forbidding restraints of trade....

....

When the seller enjoys a monopolistic position in the market for the "tying" product, *or* if a substantial volume of commerce in the "tied" product is restrained, a tying arrangement violates the narrower standards expressed in § 3 of the Clayton Act because from either factor the requisite potential lessening of competition is inferred. And because for even a lawful monopolist it is "unreasonable, *per se*, to foreclose competitors from any substantial market," a tying arrangement is banned by § 1 of the Sherman Act whenever *both* conditions are met.

In this case, the rule of *International Salt* can apply only if both its ingredients are met. The Government at the outset elected to proceed not under the Clayton but the Sherman Act.[27]

...

---

[27] On oral argument here, the Government explanatorily referred to an early informal Federal Trade Commission opinion to the effect that advertising space was not a "commodity" within the meaning of § 2 of the Clayton Act. 81 Cong. Rec. App. 2336-2337. *Cf. Fleetway, Inc. v. Public Service Interstate Transp. Co.*, 3 Cir., 1934, 72 F.2d 761; *United States v. Investors Diversified Services*, D.C. 1951, 102 F. Supp. 645. We express no views on that statutory interpretation.

Once granted that the volume of commerce affected was not "insignificant or insubstantial," the Times-Picayune's market position becomes critical to the case. The District Court found that the Times-Picayune occupied a "dominant position" in New Orleans; the sole morning daily in the area, it led its competitors in circulation, number of pages and advertising linage. But every newspaper is a dual trader in separate though interdependent markets; it sells the paper's news and advertising content to its readers; in effect that readership is in turn sold to the buyers of advertising space. This case concerns solely one of these markets. The Publishing Company stands accused not of tying sales to its readers but only to buyers of general and classified space in its papers. For this reason, dominance in the advertising market, not in readership, must be decisive in gauging the legality of the Company's unit plan....

[T]he essence of illegality in tying agreements is the wielding of monopolistic leverage; a seller exploits his dominant position in one market to expand his empire into the next. Solely for testing the strength of that lever, the whole and not part of a relevant market must be assigned controlling weight. Cf. *United States v. Columbia Steel Co.*, [334 U.S. 495 (1948)], at 524.

We do not think that the Times-Picayune occupied a "dominant" position in the newspaper advertising market in New Orleans. Unlike other "tying" cases where patents or copyrights supplied the requisite market control, any equivalent market "dominance" in this case must rest on comparative marketing data. Excluding advertising placed through other communications media and including general and classified linage inserted in all New Orleans dailies, as we must since the record contains no evidence which could circumscribe a broader or narrower "market" defined by buyers' habits or mobility of demand, the Times-Picayune's sales of both general and classified linage over the years hovered around 40%. Obviously no magic inheres in numbers; "the relative effect of percentage command of a market varies with the setting in which that factor is placed." ... If each of the New Orleans publications shared equally in the total volume of linage, the Times-Picayune would have sold $33^1/_3$%; in the absence of patent or copyright control, the small existing increment in the circumstances here disclosed cannot confer that market "dominance" which, in conjunction with a "not insubstantial" volume of trade in the "tied" product, would result in a Sherman Act offense under the rule of *International Salt*.

... Although advertising space in the Times-Picayune, as the sole morning daily, was doubtless essential to blanket coverage of the local newspaper readership, nothing in the record suggests that advertisers viewed the city's newspaper readers, morning or evening, as other than fungible customer potential. We must assume, therefore, that the readership "bought" by advertisers in the Times-Picayune was the selfsame "product" sold by the States ....

The factual departure from the "tying" cases then becomes manifest. The common core of the adjudicated unlawful tying arrangements is the forced purchase of a second distinct commodity with the desired purchase of a dominant "tying" product, resulting in economic harm to competition in the "tied" market.

Here, however, two newspapers under single ownership at the same place, time, and terms sell indistinguishable products to advertisers; no dominant "tying" product exists (in fact, since space in neither the Times-Picayune nor the States can by bought alone, one may be viewed as "tying" as the other); no leverage in one market excludes sellers in the second, because for present purposes the products are identical and the market the same....

The Publishing Company's advertising contracts must thus be tested under the Sherman Act's general prohibition on unreasonable restraints of trade. For purposes of § 1, "[a] restraint may be unreasonable either because a restraint otherwise reasonable is accompanied with a specific intent to accomplish a forbidden restraint or because it falls within the class of restraints that are illegal *per se*." ... Since the requisite intent is inferred whenever unlawful effects are found, and the rule of *International Salt* is out of the way, the contracts may yet be banned by § 1 if unreasonable restraint was either their object or effect. [O]ur inquiry to determine reasonableness under § 1 must focus on "the percentage of business controlled, the strength of the remaining competition [and] whether the action springs from business requirements or purpose to monopolize." ...

....

To be sure, economic statistics are easily susceptible to legerdemain, and only the organized context of all relevant factors can validly translate raw data into logical cause and effect. But we must take the record as we find it, and hack through the jungle as best we can. It may well be that any enhancement of the Times-Picayune's market position during the period of the assailed arrangements resulted from better service or lower prices, or was due to superior planning initiative or managerial skills; conversely, it is equally possible that but for the adoption of the unit contracts its market position might have turned for the worse.... [This] case has not met the *per se* criteria of Sherman Act § 1 from which proscribed effect automatically must be inferred.... Under the broad general policy directed by § 1 against unreasonable trade restraints, guilt cannot rest on speculation; the Government here has proved neither actual unlawful effects nor facts which radiate a potential for future harm.

[U]ncontradicted testimony suggests that unit insertions of classified ads substantially reduce the publisher's overhead costs. Approximately thirty separate operations are necessary to translate an advertiser's order into a published line of print. A reasonable price for a classified ad is necessarily low. And the Publishing Company processed about 2,300 classified ads for publication each day. Certainly a publisher's step to rationalize that operation do not bespeak a purposive quest for monopoly or restraint of trade.

Similarly, competitive business considerations apparently actuated the adoption of the unit rate for general display linage in 1950. At that time about 180 other publishers, the vast majority of morning-evening owners, had previously instituted similar unit plans. Doubtless, long-tolerated trade arrangements acquire no vested immunity under the Sherman Act; no prescriptive rights accrue by the prosecutor's delay.... In summary, neither unlawful effects nor aims are shown by the record.

Consequently, no Sherman Act violation has occurred unless the Publishing Company's refusal to sell advertising space except *en bloc*, viewed alone, constitutes a violation of the Act. [T]his Court's decisions have recognized individual refusals to sell as a general right, though "neither absolute nor exempt from regulation." ... If accompanied by unlawful conduct or agreement, or conceived in monopolistic purpose or market control, even individual sellers' refusals to deal have transgressed the Act.

Reversed.

NORTHERN PACIFIC RAILWAY V. UNITED STATES

356 U.S. 1 (1958)

JUSTICE BLACK delivered the opinion of the Court.

In 1864 and 1870 Congress granted the predecessor of the Northern Pacific Railway Company approximately forty million acres of land in several Northwestern States and Territories to facilitate its construction of a railroad.... By 1949 the Railroad had sold about 37,000,000 acres of its holdings, but had reserved mineral rights in 6,500,000 of those acres. Most of the unsold land was leased for one purpose or another. In a large number of its sales contracts and most of its lease agreements the Railroad had inserted "preferential routing" clauses which compelled the grantee or lessee to ship over its lines all commodities produced or manufactured on the land, provided that its rates (and in some instances its service) were equal to those of competing carriers. Since many of the goods produced on the lands subject to these "preferential routing" provisions are shipped from one State to another the actual and potential amount of interstate commerce affected is substantial. Alternative means of transportation exist for a large portion of these shipments including the facilities of two other major railroad systems.

In 1949 the Government filed suit under § 4 of the Sherman Act seeking a declaration that the defendant's "preferential routing" agreements were unlawful as unreasonable restraints of trade under § 1 of that Act. After various pretrial proceedings the Government moved for summary judgment contending that on the undisputed facts it was entitled, as a matter of law, to the relief demanded. The district judge ... granted the Government's motion....

The Sherman Act was designed to be a comprehensive charter of economic liberty aimed at preserving free and unfettered competition as the rule of trade. It rests on the premise that the unrestrained interaction of competitive forces will yield the best allocation of our economic resources, the lowest prices, the highest quality and the greatest material progress, while at the same time providing an environment conducive to the preservation of our democratic political and social institutions. But even were that premise open to question, the policy unequivocally laid down by the Act is competition. And to this end it prohibits "Every contract, combination ... or conspiracy, in restraint of trade or commerce among the several States." Although this prohibition is literally all-encompassing, the courts have construed it as precluding only those contracts or combinations which "unreasonably" restrain competition....

However, there are certain agreements or practices which because of their pernicious effect on competition and lack of any redeeming virtue are conclusively presumed to be unreasonable and therefore illegal without elaborate inquiry as to the precise harm they have caused or the business excuse for their use. This principle of *per se* unreasonableness not only makes the type of restraints which are proscribed by the Sherman Act more certain to the benefit of everyone concerned, but it also avoids the necessity for an incredibly complicated and prolonged economic investigation into the entire history of the industry involved, as well as related industries, in an effort to determine at large whether a particular restraint has been unreasonable — an inquiry so often wholly fruitless when undertaken. Among the practices which the courts have heretofore deemed to be unlawful in and of themselves are price fixing, division of markets, group boycotts, and tying arrangements....

For our purposes a tying arrangement may be defined as an agreement by a party to sell one product but only on the condition that the buyer also purchases a different (or tied) product, or at least agrees that he will not purchase that product from any other supplier. Where such conditions are successfully exacted competition on the merits with respect to the tied product is inevitably curbed. Indeed "tying agreements serve hardly any purpose beyond the suppression of competition." ... They deny competitors free access to the market for the tied product, not because the party imposing the tying requirements has a better product or a lower price but because of his power or leverage in another market. At the same time buyers are forced to forego their free choice between competing products. For these reasons "tying agreements fare harshly under the laws forbidding restraints of trade." ... They are unreasonable in and of themselves whenever a party has sufficient economic power with respect to the tying product to appreciably restrain free competition in the market for the tied product and a "not insubstantial" amount of interstate commerce is affected.... Of course where the seller has no control or dominance over the tying product so that it does not represent an effectual weapon to pressure buyers into taking the tied item any restraint of trade attributable to such tying arrangements would obviously be insignificant at most. As a simple example, if one of a dozen food stores in a community were to refuse to sell flour unless the buyer also took sugar it would hardly tend to restrain competition in sugar if its competitors were ready and able to sell flour by itself.

In this case we believe the district judge was clearly correct in entering summary judgment declaring the defendant's "preferential routing" clauses unlawful restraints of trade. We wholly agree that the undisputed facts established beyond any genuine question that the defendant possessed substantial economic power by virtue of its extensive landholdings which it used as leverage to induce large numbers of purchasers and lessees to give it preference, to the exclusion of its competitors, in carrying goods or produce from the land transferred to them. Nor can there be any real doubt that a "not insubstantial" amount of interstate commerce was and is affected by these restrictive provisions.

As pointed out before, the defendant was initially granted large acreages by Congress in the several Northwestern States through which its lines now run. This land was strategically located in checkerboard fashion amid private holdings and within economic distance of transportation facilities. Not only the testimony of various witnesses but common sense makes it evident that this particular land was often prized by those who purchased or leased it and was frequently essential to their business activities. In disposing of its holdings the defendant entered into contracts of sale or lease covering at least several million acres of land which included "preferential routing" clauses. The very existence of this host of tying arrangements is itself compelling evidence of the defendant's great power, at least where, as here, no other explanation has been offered for the existence of these restraints. The "preferential routing" clauses conferred no benefit on the purchasers or lessees. While they got the land they wanted by yielding their freedom to deal with competing carriers, the defendant makes no claim that it came any cheaper than if the restrictive clauses had been omitted. In fact any such price reduction in return for rail shipments would have quite plainly constituted an unlawful rebate to the shipper. So far as the Railroad was concerned its purpose obviously was to fence out competitors, to stifle competition. While this may have been exceedingly beneficial to its business, it is the very type of thing the Sherman Act condemns. In short, we are convinced that the essential prerequisites for treating the defendant's tying arrangements as unreasonable "*per se*" were conclusively established below and that the defendant has offered to prove nothing there or here which would alter this conclusion.

In our view *International Salt Co....* is ample authority for affirming the judgment below. In that case the defendant refused to lease its salt-dispensing machines unless the lessee also agreed to purchase all the salt it used in the machines from the defendant. It was established that the defendant had made about 900 leases under such conditions and that in the year in question it had sold about $500,000 worth of salt for use in the leased machines. On that basis we affirmed unanimously a summary judgment finding the defendant guilty of violating § 1 of the Sherman Act. The Court ruled that it was "unreasonable, *per se*, to foreclose competitors from any substantial market" by tying arrangements. As we later analyzed the decision, "it was not established that equivalent machines were unobtainable, it was not indicated what proportion of the business of supplying such machines was controlled by defendant, and it was deemed irrelevant that there was no evidence as to the actual effect of the tying clauses upon competition." ...

The defendant attempts to evade the force of *International Salt* on the ground that the tying product there was patented while here it is not. But we do not believe this distinction has, or should have, any significance. In arriving at its decision in *International Salt* the Court placed no reliance on the fact that a patent was involved nor did it give the slightest intimation that the outcome would have been any different if that had not been the case. If anything, the Court held the challenged tying arrangements unlawful *despite* the fact that the tying item was patented, not because of it. "By contracting to close this market for salt against competition, International has engaged in a restraint of trade for which its patents afford no immunity from the antitrust laws." ...

While there is some language in the *Times-Picayune* opinion which speaks of "monopoly power" or "dominance" over the tying product as a necessary pre-condition for application of the rule of *per se* unreasonableness to tying arrangements, we do not construe this general language as requiring anything more than sufficient economic power to impose an appreciable restraint on free competition in the tied product (assuming all the time, of course, that a "not insubstantial" amount of interstate commerce is affected)....

The defendant contends that its "preferential routing" clauses are subject to so many exceptions and have been administered so leniently that they do not significantly restrain competition. It points out that these clauses permit the vendee or lessee to ship by competing carrier if its rates are lower (or in some instances if its service is better) than the defendant's. Of course if these restrictive provisions are merely harmless sieves with no tendency to restrain competition, as the defendant's argument seems to imply, it is hard to understand why it has expended so much effort in obtaining them in vast numbers and upholding their validity, or how they are of any benefit to anyone, even the defendant. But however that may be, the essential fact remains that these agreements are binding obligations held over the heads of vendees which deny defendant's competitors access to the fenced-off market on the same terms as the defendant....

Affirmed.

[A dissent by JUSTICE HARLAN, joined by JUSTICES FRANKFURTER and WHITTAKER, is omitted.]

NOTES AND QUESTIONS

1. *Times-Picayune* held, inter alia, that one of the essential elements of an illegal tying arrangement was that there be two separate and distinct products. Opinions concerning how to apply the "two products" requirement have varied. The courts have considered the following factors: (1) physical characteristics, (2) business justification such as cost efficiencies, (3) end-usage, (4) whether the "challenged aggregation is an essential ingredient" of the product's success, (5) industry trade practices, and (6) whether the products are ever sold in separate markets. *See, e.g., Rosebrough Monument Co. v. Memorial Park Cem. Ass'n*, 666 F.2d 1130 (8th Cir. 1981), *cert. denied*, 457 U.S. 1111 (1982); *Hamro v. Shell Oil Co.*, 674 F.2d 784 (9th Cir. 1982); *United States v. Jerrold Elec. Corp.*, 187 F. Supp. 545 (E. D. Pa. 1960), *aff'd per curiam*, 365 U.S. 567 (1961).

Can you tell which of these factors Justice Clark relied on in the *Times-Picayune* case? Clark must have been influenced by one fact that appears several times in the record: "unit" pricing (requiring identical advertisements in the morning and evening newspapers) permitted the newspaper to set type and establish the advertising layout for the two newspapers once a day instead of twice. For example, the single largest cost to the newspaper of running a classified advertisement was the cost of arranging the advertisements on a page and setting the type. Under the unit pricing plan the classified sections in the morning and evening newspapers were identical. This resulted in a very large cost savings to the newspaper, which was passed along to its customers. However, the unit pricing plan admitted no exceptions: it would work only if *all* advertisements were placed in both the morning and evening editions. *See* Record at 1127-29, *Times-Picayune Pub'g Co. v. United States*, October Term, 1952, Docket #374, 375; Hovenkamp, *Distributive Justice and the Antitrust Laws*, 51 Geo. Wash. L. Rev. 1 (1982).

2. In light of *Northern Pacific*'s seemingly clear per se rule against tying arrangements, does anything remain of the *Times-Picayune* two prong test? Under a per se standard, could a court consider and weigh the business justification for the unit pricing scheme as the Court did in *Times-Picayune*? Are the cases, in addition, inconsistent on plaintiff's burden of establishing "sufficient economic power in the tying product?" Did *Times-Picayune* hold that plaintiff must establish market dominance in the tying product before there can be a finding of a per se violation? After *Northern Pacific* can the trier of fact presume or infer such a prerequisite? If so, from what kind of evidence do the majority and dissenting opinions state this evidence can be derived?

3. From *International Salt* through *Northern Pacific*, it seems that under a per se analysis, the plaintiff would be required to establish the following:

(a) that two separate products were involved in the tie-in sale;

(b) that defendant possessed sufficient economic power in the market of the tying product; and

(c) that the amount of commerce affected in the tied product market was not insubstantial.

4. Some circuits have explicitly adopted a three-part per se test such as the one described above. For example, *see Siegel v. Chicken Delight, Inc.*, 448 F.2d 43, 47 (9th Cir. 1971), *cert. denied*, 405 U.S. 955 (1972). Other circuits have created more detailed tests. For instance, in 1980 the Second Circuit adopted the following test:

(a) There must be separate tying and tied products;

(b) There must be "evidence of actual coercion by the seller that in fact forced the buyer to accept the tied produce";

(c) The seller must possess "sufficient economic power in the tying product market to coerce purchaser acceptance of the tied product";

    (d) There must be "anticompetitive effects in the tied market";

    (e) There must be "involvement of a 'not insubstantial' amount of interstate commerce in the tied product market."

Yentsch v. Texaco, Inc., 630 F.2d 46, 56-57 (2d Cir. 1980). The Fifth Circuit currently uses a four element test. *Bob Maxfield, Inc. v. American Motors Corp.*, 637 F.2d 1033, 1037 (5th Cir. 1981).

    5. Is it clear after *Northern Pacific* that under the Clayton Act a plaintiff need prove only the presence of *either* market dominance in the tying product *or* the involvement of a substantial amount of commerce in the tied product, but not both? Circuit courts have generally ignored Justice Clark's division in *Times-Picayune* and required both elements, regardless whether the action was brought under the Sherman Act or the Clayton Act. *Spartan Grain & Mill Co. v. Ayers*, 581 F.2d 419, 428 (5th Cir. 1978); *Moore v. Jas. H. Matthews & Co.*, 550 F.2d 1207, 1214 (9th Cir. 1977).

    Does a rule that permits a plaintiff to recover without proving market power in the tying product make any sense? If the market for the tying product is perfectly competitive, then a seller would be powerless to impose an unwanted second product on the buyer, would it not? The buyer would simply purchase the tying product from a competitor who did not assess the requirement. What would explain a "tying arrangement" in a market in which the seller has no market power in the tying product? There might, of course, be a cartel, in which all the sellers of the tying product agreed to impose the tie-in — collectively, they would have market power.

    The other explanation, however, is that the tie-in creates efficiency. In fact, if a package sale is cheaper than individual sales, a competitor may be forced to make the package sales in order to compete with other sellers. For example, it is probably far cheaper to sell shoes in pairs, because the demand for single shoes is very low in relation to the additional stocking, return, and inventory costs that selling single shoes would impose. As a result shoe stores almost universally require people to take a left shoe as a condition of purchasing a right shoe, or vice-versa, even where the shoe store involved clearly has no market power. A court would be likely to analyze such a tie-in by saying that a pair of shoes is a single product — but this simply states the result of the above economic analysis. Clearly there are certain customers — such as Captain Ahab — who would prefer to purchase right shoes alone.

    For an argument that certain tie-ins in competitive markets may nevertheless be contrary to consumer welfare, *see* Craswell, *Tying Requirements in Competitive Markets: The Consumer Protection Issues*, 62 B.U.L. Rev. 661 (1982).

    Why did Northern Pacific tie the transportation requirements to its sales and leases of land? The traditional leverage argument that the Supreme Court relied on is problematic, because the tying arrangements contained "escape clauses": a lessee or purchaser of the land had to purchase his transportation requirements from Northern Pacific only if the price was no higher than the price offered by competitors. This seems inconsistent with the Supreme Court's conclusion that the railroad was using its market power in land to monopolize the shipping of freight as well.

Several explanations have been offered for the railroad's tying arrangements. One is that they were devices for avoiding price regulation of freight transportation. If the regulated price was artificially high the railroad might increase its volume by inducing land buyers to locate along the railroad by selling the land below its fair market value. By requiring these landowners to use Northern Pacific to ship their products, the railroad could increase its freight volume at the regulated price, which had a large amount of profit built into it. The increased volume of freight at the regulated price would more than compensate for the lower price at which the land was sold.

Another explanation is that the railroad was using the tie-in clauses to gather information about competing railroads that might be rate cutting. Under the arrangements any purchaser of land from Northern Pacific could be expected to ship his products by means of the Northern Pacific unless he was getting a lower price elsewhere. If a competing railroad seduced such a customer away by means of a secret rebate or other rate regulation avoidance scheme, Northern Pacific would know about it. Thus, the argument goes, the tie-ins made it easier for Northern Pacific to monitor the rate-setting practices of its competitors. For development of this argument, *see* Cummings & Ruther, *The Northern Pacific Case*, 22 J.L. & Econ. 329 (1979). The authors note that at the time there were several small railroads that were not rate regulated (the Northern Pacific was not one of them) and were not required by law to publish their rates. The tie-ins, the authors argue, made it easier for the Northern Pacific to gather information about the rate-setting practices of these small railroads. Periodically they would use this information to petition rate-making agencies for adjustments to their own rates.

Consider whether customers would have no preference between railroads, assuming that rates and service were equivalent. Would they object to a tie-in under these circumstances? The result might be that North Pacific would get all the rail business of its lessees, as long as it maintained rate and service parity, rather than a share of the business, probably determined at random.

6. The analytical tension between *Northern Pacific* and *Times-Picayune* created confusion as to what would constitute "sufficient economic power," as required under the Sherman Act test. While the early cases, particularly *Times-Picayune*, indicated that a monopoly or dominant position in the tying product market was required, *Northern Pacific* implied that something less might suffice. Some of the decisions indicated that the requisite power in the tying market could be inferred from (1) a copyrighted or patented tying product, (2) unique desirability of the tying product as to quality, (3) strategic location or use of the tying product, (4) the fact that a substantial number of buyers accepted the tie, and (5) lack of competing products due to inability of competitors.

7. In *Fortner Enters. v. United States Steel Corp.* (*Fortner I*), 394 U.S. 495 (1969), the defendant conditioned its extension of credit (the tying product) to the purchase of prefabricated homes (the tied product). The Supreme Court held first that $190,000 involved in the sale of the tied product to plaintiff was "a 'not insubstantial'" amount of power in the tied product market, thus meeting one of the two requirements of the per se test, even though the total amount of annual loans by Credit Corp. to all buyers was over $2 million. Said the Court, "the controlling consideration is simply whether a total amount of business, substantial enough in terms of dollar-volume so as not to be merely *de minimis*, is foreclosed to competitors by the tie, for ... 'it is unreasonable, *per se*, to foreclose competitors from any substantial market' by a tying arrangement." On remand, the issue was whether U.S. Steel had market power in the credit (tying) market.

3. PROOF OF TYING PRODUCT POWER

UNITED STATES STEEL CORP. V. FORTNER ENTERPRISES (FORTNER II)

429 U.S. 610 (1977)

JUSTICE STEVENS delivered the opinion of the Court.

... We held [in *Fortner I*] that the agreement affected a "not insubstantial" amount of commerce in the tied product and that Fortner was entitled to an opportunity to prove that petitioners possessed "appreciable economic power" in the market for the tying product. The question now presented is whether the record supports the conclusion that petitioners had such power in the credit market.[1]

....

II

The evidence supporting the conclusion that the [U.S. Steel] Credit Corp. had appreciable economic power in the credit market relates to four propositions: (1) petitioner Credit Corp. and the Home Division were owned by one of the Nation's largest corporations; (2) petitioners entered into tying arrangements with a significant number of customers in addition to Fortner; (3) the Home Division charged respondent a noncompetitive price for its prefabricated homes; and (4) the financing provided to Fortner was "unique," primarily because it covered 100% of Fortner's acquisition and development costs.

---

[1] ... Petitioners do not ask us to re-examine *Fortner I*, which left only the economic-power question open on the issue of whether a *per se* violation could be proved. On the other hand, Fortner has not pursued the suggestion in *Fortner I* that it might be able to prove a § 1 violation under the rule-of-reason standard.... Thus, with respect to § 1, only the economic-power issue is before us.

....

....

The finding that the credit extended to Fortner was unique was based on factors emphasized in the testimony of Fortner's expert witness, Dr. Masten, a professor with special knowledge of lending practices in the Kentucky area. Dr. Masten testified that mortgage loans equal to 100% of the acquisition and development cost of real estate were not otherwise available in the Kentucky area; that even though Fortner had a deficit of $16,000, its loan was not guaranteed by a shareholder, officer, or other person interested in its business; and that the interest rate of 6% represented a low rate under prevailing economic conditions. Moreover, he explained that the stable price levels at the time made the risk to the lender somewhat higher than would have been the case in a period of rising prices. Dr. Masten concluded that the terms granted to respondent by the Credit Corp. were so unusual that it was almost inconceivable that the funds could have been acquired from any other source. It is a fair summary of his testimony, and of the District Court's findings, to say that the loan was unique because the lender accepted such a high risk and the borrower assumed such a low cost.

....

Accordingly, the District Court concluded "that all of the required elements of an illegal tie-in agreement did exist since the tie-in itself was present, a not insubstantial amount of interstate commerce in the tied product was restrained and the Credit Corporation did possess sufficient economic power or leverage to effect such restraint."

III

Without the finding that the financing provided to Fortner was "unique," it is clear that the District Court's findings would be insufficient to support the conclusion that the Credit Corp. possessed any significant economic power in the credit market.

Although the Credit Corp. is owned by one of the Nation's largest manufacturing corporations, there is nothing in the record to indicate that this enabled it to borrow funds on terms more favorable than those available to competing lenders, or that it was able to operate more efficiently than other lending institutions. In short, the affiliation between the petitioners does not appear to have given the Credit Corp. any cost advantage over its competitors in the credit market. Instead, the affiliation was significant only because the Credit Corp. provided a source of funds to customers of the Home Division. That fact tells us nothing about the extent of petitioners' economic power in the credit market.

The same may be said about the fact that loans from the Credit Corp. were used to obtain house sales from Fortner and others. In some tying situations a disproportionately large volume of sales of the tied product resulting from only a few strategic sales of the tying product may reflect a form of economic "leverage" that is probative of power in the market for the tying product. If, as some economists have suggested, the purpose of a tie-in is often to facilitate price discrimination, such evidence would imply the existence of power that a free market would not tolerate. But in this case Fortner was only required to purchase houses for the number of lots for which it received financing. The tying product produced no commitment from Fortner to purchase varying quantities of the tied product over an extended period of time. This record, therefore, does not describe the kind of "leverage" found in some of the court's prior decisions condemning tying arrangements.

The fact that Fortner — and presumably other Home Division customers as well — paid a noncompetitive price for houses also lends insufficient support to the judgment of the lower court. Proof that Fortner paid a higher price for the tied product is consistent with the possibility that the financing was unusually inexpensive[9] and that the price for the entire package was equal to, or below, a competitive price. And this possibility is equally strong even though a number of Home Division customers made a package purchase of homes and financing.[10]

The most significant finding made by the District Court related to the unique character of the credit extended to Fortner. This finding is particularly important because the unique character of the tying product has provided critical support for the finding of illegality in prior cases. Thus, the statutory grant of a patent monopoly in *International Salt* ... and the extensive land holdings in *Northern Pacific R. Co.*, 356 U.S. 1, represented tying products that the Court regarded as sufficiently unique to give rise to a presumption of economic power.

As the Court plainly stated in its prior opinion in this case, these decisions do not require that the defendant have a monopoly or even a dominant position

---

[9] Fortner's expert witness agreed with the statement:

> The amount of the loan as a percentage of the collateral or security is only one element in determining its advantage to a borrower. The other relevant factors include the rate of interest charged, whether the lender discounts the amount loaned or charges service for [*sic*] other fees and maturity in terms of repayment.

[10] Relying on *Advance Business Systems & Supply Co. v. SCM Corp.*, 415 F.2d 55 (4th Cir. 1969), *cert. denied*, 397 U.S. 920 (1970), Fortner contends that acceptance of the package by a significant number of customers is itself sufficient to prove the seller's economic power. But this approach depends on the absence of other explanations for the willingness of buyers to purchase the package. See 415 F.2d, at 68. In the *Northern Pacific* case, for instance, the Court explained:

> The very existence of this host of tying arrangements is itself compelling evidence of the defendant's great power, at least where, as here, no other explanation has been offered for the existence of these restraints. The "preferential routing" clauses conferred no benefit on the purchasers or lessees. While they got the land they wanted by yielding their freedom to deal with competing carriers, the defendant makes no claim that it came any cheaper than if the restrictive clauses had been omitted. In fact any such price reduction in return for rail shipments would have quite plainly constituted an unlawful rebate to the shipper. So far as the Railroad was concerned its purpose obviously was to fence out competitors, to stifle competition. 356 U.S., at 7-8 (footnote omitted).

As this passage demonstrates, this case differs from *Northern Pacific* because use of the tie-in in this case can be explained as a form of price competition in the tied product, whereas that explanation was unavailable to the Northern Pacific Railway.

throughout the market for a tying product.... They do, however, focus attention on the question whether the seller has the power, within the market for the tying product, to raise prices or to require purchasers to accept burdensome terms that could not be exacted in a completely competitive market. In short, the question is whether the seller has some advantage not shared by his competitors in the market for the tying product.

Without any such advantage differentiating his product from that of his competitors, the seller's product does not have the kind of uniqueness considered relevant in prior tying-clause cases. The Court made this point explicitly when it remanded this case for trial:

> We do not mean to accept petitioner's apparent argument that market power can be inferred simply because the kind of financing terms offered by a lending company are "unique and unusual." We do mean, however, that uniquely and unusually advantageous terms can reflect a creditor's unique economic advantages over his competitors. 394 U.S., at 505.

An accompanying footnote explained:

> Uniqueness confers economic power only when other competitors are in some way prevented from offering the distinctive product themselves. Such barriers may be legal, as in the case of patented and copyrighted products, e.g., International Salt; Loew's, or physical, as when the product is land, e.g., Northern Pacific. It is true that the barriers may also be economic, as when competitors are simply unable to produce the distinctive product profitably, but the uniqueness test in such situations is somewhat confusing since the real source of economic power is not the product itself but rather the seller's cost advantage in producing it.

Quite clearly, if the evidence merely shows that credit terms are unique because the seller is willing to accept a lesser profit — or to incur greater risks — than its competitors, that kind of uniqueness will not give rise to any inference of economic power in the credit market. Yet this is, in substance, all that the record in this case indicates.

The unusual credit bargain offered to Fortner proves nothing more than a willingness to provide cheap financing in order to sell expensive houses.[15] Without any evidence that the Credit Corp. had some cost advantage over its competitors — or could offer a form of financing that was significantly differentiated from that which other lenders could offer if they so elected — the unique character of its financing does not support the conclusion that petitioners had the kind of economic power which Fortner had the burden of proving in order to prevail in this litigation.

---

[15] The opinion of the Court in *Fortner I* notes that smaller companies might not have the "financial strength to offer credit comparable to that provided by larger competitors under tying arrangements." 394 U.S., at 509. Fortner's expert witness was unaware of the financing practices of competing sellers of prefabricated homes, App. 1691-1692, but there is nothing to suggest that they were unable to offer comparable financing if they chose to do so.

The judgment of the Court of Appeals is

Reversed.

NOTES AND QUESTIONS

1. *Fortner I* and *Fortner II* address the evidentiary question of what constitutes "sufficient economic power" under the burden of establishing a per se violation. With regard to "uniqueness," is the impression after *Fortner II*, that in order to meet this "uniqueness" test, a plaintiff would have to show that other competitors were unable, not merely unwilling, to provide the product or service, and thus an appreciable number of buyers were captured and taken in by the higher prices or burdensome terms? What specific comparative "cost advantage" factors might demonstrate "uniqueness"? Note the Court's conclusion that the existence of advantageous terms does not imply "uniqueness" within the market power context; it may merely reflect a competitor's willingness to take less profit or greater risks. If this strategic marketing decision, to take less profit or greater risks, was a fact, might it not explain the existence of a substantial number of tie-in contracts? Is this inconsistent with *Northern Pacific*? *See* footnote 10. Is *Fortner II* clear on who has the burden to show that no explanation for tie-ins exists other than economic power? *See United States v. Mercedes-Benz of N. Am.*, 1981-2 Trade Cas. (CCH) ¶ 64,188 at 73,668. *Contra Grappone, Inc. v. Subaru of New England, Inc.*, 534 F. Supp. 1282 (D.N.H. 1982).

2. Do you agree with the Court that two products were involved in *Fortner*? Or, is this really the "sale of a single product with [an] individual provision of financing"? Consider Justice Fortas' dissent in *Fortner I*:

> It is hardly conceivable, except for today's opinion of the Court, that extension of such credit as a part of a general sale transaction or distribution method could be regarded as a "tying" of the seller's goods to the credit, so that where the businessman receiving the credit agrees to handle the seller-lender's product, the arrangement is *per se* unlawful merely because the amount or terms of the credit were more favorable than could be obtained from banking institutions in the area. Arrangements of this sort run throughout the economy. They frequently, and perhaps characteristically, represent an indispensable method of financing distributive and service trades, and not until today has it been held that they are tying arrangements and therefore *per se* unlawful....
>
> ....
>
> Almost all modern selling involves providing some ancillary services in connection with making the sale — delivery, installation, supplying fixtures, servicing, training of the customer's personnel in use of the material sold, furnishing display material and sales aids, extension of credit. Customarily — indeed almost invariably — the seller offers these ancillary services only

in connection with the sale of his own products, and they are often offered without cost or at bargain rates.... [T]o condemn them out-of-hand under the "tying" rubric, is, I suggest, to use the antitrust laws themselves as an instrument in restraint of competition.

Consider whether "[t]he transaction was tantamount to any credit sale — it is no more a tie that any other in which a seller says, 'if you buy my merchandise you may pay me in 90 days.'" *See* L. Sullivan, *Handbook of the Law of Antitrust* 470 (1977).

3. Consider whether *Fortner II* signaled a significant increase in the burden of proof necessary to establish a per se violation from that articulated in *Fortner I*. Is the "economic power" test harder to establish since *Fortner II*? If so, will this have the effect of narrowing the kinds of tying arrangements that may be challenged under a per se approach? After the elaborate discussion in *Fortner II* on the issue of "sufficient economic power," is it likely that this issue is one to be decided by summary judgment, or is it a question of fact for the jury to decide? *See United States v. Mercedes-Benz of N. Am.*, 1981-82 Trade Cas. (CCH) ¶ 64,188. *In re Data Gen. Corp. Antitrust Litig.*, 490 F. Supp. 1089 (N.D. Cal. 1980).

4. What was the purpose of the alleged tying arrangement in the *Fortner* cases? Could it have been a mechanism for avoiding price regulation? Suppose, for example, that the unregulated market would support interest rates of 12% for certain kinds of loans, but that a state usury law set the limit at 8%. A seller of houses might finance the houses at 8% but charge a supracompetitive price for the houses themselves, thus circumventing the usury statute. In such a case the seller would have to make the loans only to people who also purchase its houses, or people would attempt to take the cheap money without buying the house.

5. For a superb analysis of the *Fortner* dispute and the Supreme Court's first opinion, see Dam, *Fortner Enterprises v. United States Steel: "Neither a Borrower Nor a Lender Be,"* 1969 Sup. Ct. Rev. 1.

JEFFERSON PARISH HOSPITAL DISTRICT NO. 2 V. HYDE

466 U.S. 2 (1984)

JUSTICE STEVENS delivered the opinion of the Court.

At issue in this case is the validity of an exclusive contract between a hospital and a firm of anesthesiologists. We must decide whether the contract gives rise to a *per se* violation of § 1 of the Sherman Act because every patient undergoing surgery at the hospital must use the services of one firm of anesthesiologists, and, if not, whether the contract is nevertheless illegal because it unreasonably restrains competition among anesthesiologists.

In July 1977, respondent Edwin G. Hyde, a board certified anesthesiologist, applied for admission to the medical staff of East Jefferson Hospital. The credentials committee and the medical staff executive committee recommended approval, but the hospital board denied the application because the hospital was a party to a contract providing that all anesthesiological services required by the hospital's patients would be performed by Roux & Associates, a professional medical corporation. Respondent then commenced this action seeking a declaratory judgment that the contract is unlawful and an injunction ordering petitioners to appoint him to the hospital staff.[2] After trial, the District Court denied relief, finding that the anti-competitive consequences of the Roux contract were minimal and outweighed by benefits in the form of improved patient care. 513 F. Supp. 532 (E.D. La. 1981). The Court of Appeals reversed because it was persuaded that the contract was illegal *"per se."* 686 F.2d 286 (5th Cir. 1982). We granted certiorari and now reverse.

I

In February 1971, shortly before East Jefferson Hospital opened, it entered into an "Anesthesiology Agreement" with Roux & Associates ("Roux"), a firm that had recently been organized by Dr. Kermit Roux. The contract provided that any anesthesiologist designated by Roux would be admitted to the hospital's medical staff. The hospital agreed to provide the space, equipment, maintenance, and other supporting services necessary to operate the anesthesiology department. It also agreed to purchase all necessary drugs and other supplies. All nursing personnel required by the anesthesia department were to be supplied by the hospital, but Roux had the right to approve their selection and retention.[3] The hospital agreed to "restrict the use of its anesthesia department to Roux & Associates and [that] no other persons, parties or entities shall perform such services within the Hospital for the term of this contract."

The fees for anesthesiological services are billed separately to the patients by the hospital. They cover over the hospital's costs and the professional services provided by Roux. After a deduction of eight percent to provide a reserve for uncollectible accounts, the fees are divided equally between Roux and the hospital.

The 1971 contract provided for a one-year term automatically renewable for successive one-year periods unless either party elected to terminate. In 1976, a second written contract was executed containing most of the provisions of the 1971 agreement. Its term was five years and the clause excluding other anesthesiologists from the hospital was deleted; the hospital nevertheless continued to regard itself as committed to a closed anesthesiology department. Only Roux was permitted to practice anesthesiology at the hospital. At the time of trial the department included four anesthesiologists. The hospital usually employed 13 or 14 certified registered nurse anesthetists.[6]

---

[2] In addition to seeking relief under the Sherman Act, respondent's complaint alleged violations of 42 U.S.C. § 1983 and state law. The District Court rejected these claims. The Court of Appeals passed only on the Sherman Act Claim.

[3] The contract required all of the physicians employed by Roux to confine their practice of anesthesiology to East Jefferson.

[6] Approximately 875 operations are performed at the hospital each month; as many as 12 of 13 operating rooms may be in use at one time.

The exclusive contract had an impact on two different segments of the economy: consumers of medical services, and providers of anesthesiological services. Any consumer of medical services who elects to have an operation performed at East Jefferson Hospital may not employ any anesthesiologist not associated with Roux. No anesthesiologists except those employed by Roux may practice at East Jefferson.

There are at least 20 hospitals in the New Orleans metropolitan area and about 70 percent of the patients living in Jefferson Parish go to hospitals other than East Jefferson. Because it regarded the entire New Orleans metropolitan area as the relevant geographic market in which hospitals compete, this evidence convinced the District Court that East Jefferson does not possess any significant "market power"; therefore it concluded that petitioners could not use the Roux contract to anticompetitive ends.[7] The same evidence led the Court of Appeals to draw a significant conclusion. Noting that 30 percent of the residents of the Parish go to East Jefferson Hospital, and that in fact "patients tend to choose hospitals by location rather than price or quality," the Court of Appeals concluded that the relevant geographic market was the East Bank of Jefferson Parish. The conclusion that East Jefferson Hospital possessed market power in that area was buttressed by the facts that the prevalence of health insurance eliminates a patient's incentive to compare costs, that the patient is not sufficiently informed to compare quality, and that family convenience tends to magnify the importance of location.

The Court of Appeals held that the case involves a "tying arrangement" because the "users of the hospital's operating rooms (the tying product) are also compelled to purchase the hospital's chosen anesthesia service (the tied product)." Having defined the relevant geographic market for the tying product as the East Bank of Jefferson Parish, the court held that the hospital possessed "sufficient market power in the tying market to coerce purchasers of the tied product." Since the purchase of the tied product constituted a "not insubstantial amount of interstate commerce," … the tying arrangement was therefore illegal "*per se.*"

II

… It is far too late in the history of our antitrust jurisprudence to question the proposition that certain tying arrangements pose an unacceptable risk of stifling

---

[7] The District Court found:

> The impact on commerce resulting from the East Jefferson contract is minimal. The contract is restricted in effect to one hospital in an area containing at least twenty others providing the same surgical services. It would be a different situation if Dr. Roux had exclusive contracts in several hospitals in the relevant market. As pointed out by plaintiff, the majority of surgeons have privileges at more than one hospital in the area. They have the option of admitting their patients to another hospital where they can select the anesthesiologist of their choice. Similarly a patient can go to another hospital if he is not satisfied with the physicians available at East Jefferson.

513 F. Supp., at 541.

competition and therefore are unreasonable *"per se."* The rule was first enunciated in *International Salt Co. v. United States,* and has been endorsed by this Court many times since. The rule also reflects congressional policies underlying the antitrust laws. In enacting § 3 of the Clayton Act, 15 U.S.C. § 14, Congress expressed great concern about the anticompetitive character of tying arrangements. While this case does not arise under the Clayton Act, the congressional finding made therein concerning the competitive consequences of tying is illuminating, and must be respected.

It is clear, however, that every refusal to sell two products separately cannot be said to restrain competition. If each of the products may be purchased separately in a competitive market, one seller's decision to sell the two in a single package imposes no unreasonable restraint on either market, particularly if competing suppliers are free to sell either the entire package or its several parts. For example, we have written that "if one of a dozen food stores in a community were to refuse to sell flour unless the buyer also took sugar it would hardly tend to restrain competition if its competitors were ready and able to sell flour by itself." *Northern Pac. R. Co. v. United States,* 356 U.S. 1, 7 (1958). Buyers often find package sales attractive; a seller's decision to offer such packages can merely be an attempt to compete effectively — conduct that is entirely consistent with the Sherman Act.

Our cases have concluded that the essential characteristic of an invalid tying arrangement lies in the seller's exploitation of its control over the tying product to force the buyer into the purchase of a tied product that the buyer either did not want at all, or might have preferred to purchase elsewhere on different terms. When such "forcing" is present, competition on the merits in the market for the tied item is restrained and the Sherman Act is violated.

> Basic to the faith that a free economy best promotes the public weal is that goods must stand the cold test of competition; that the public, acting through the market's impersonal judgment, shall allocate the Nation's resources and thus direct the course its economic development will take.... By conditioning his sale of one commodity on the purchase of another, a seller coerces the abdication of buyers' independent judgment as to the "tied" product's merits and insulates it from the competitive stresses of the open market. But any intrinsic superiority of the "tied" product would convince freely choosing buyers to select it over others anyway.

Times-Picayune Publishing Co. v. United States, 345 U.S. 594, 605 (1953).

Accordingly, we have condemned tying arrangements when the seller has some special ability — usually called "market power" — to force a purchaser to do something that he would not do in a competitive market.[20] When "forcing" occurs, our cases have found the tying arrangement to be unlawful.

---

[20] This type of market power has sometimes been referred to as "leverage." Professors Areeda and Turner provide a definition that suits present purposes. "'Leverage' is loosely defined here as a supplier's ability to induce his customer for one product to buy a second product from him that

Thus, the law draws a distinction between the exploitation of market power by merely enhancing the price of the tying product, on the one hand, and by attempting to impose restraints on competition in the market for a tied product, on the other. When the seller's power is just used to maximize its return in the tying product market, where presumably its product enjoys some justifiable advantage over its competitors, the competitive ideal of the Sherman Act is not necessarily compromised. But if that power is used to impair competition on the merits in another market, a potentially inferior product may be insulated from competitive pressures. This impairment could either harm existing competitors or create barriers to entry of new competitors in the market for the tied product ... and can increase the social costs of market power by facilitating price discrimination, thereby increasing monopoly profits over what they would be absent the tie.[23] And from the standpoint of the consumer — whose interests the statute was especially intended to serve — the freedom to select the best bargain in the second market is impaired by his need to purchase the tying product, and perhaps by an inability to evaluate the true cost of either product when they are available only as a package.[24] In sum, to permit restraint of competition on the merits through tying arrangements would be, as we observed in *Fortner II*, to condone "the existence of power that a free market would not tolerate." 429 U.S., at 617 (footnote omitted).

Per se condemnation — condemnation without inquiry into actual market conditions — is only appropriate if the existence of forcing is probable. Thus, application of the *per se* rule focuses on the probability of anticompetitive consequences. Of course, as a threshold matter there must be a substantial potential for impact on competition in order to justify *per se* condemnation. If only a single purchaser were "forced" with respect to the purchase of a tied item, the resultant impact on competition would not be sufficient to warrant the concern of antitrust law. It is for this reason that we have refused to condemn tying arrangements unless a substantial volume of commerce is foreclosed thereby. Similarly, when a purchaser is "forced" to buy a product he would not have otherwise bought even from another seller in the tied product market, there can be no adverse impact on competition because no portion of the market which would otherwise have been available to other sellers has been foreclosed.

Once this threshold is surmounted, *per se* prohibition is appropriate if anticompetitive forcing is likely. For example, if the government has granted the seller a patent or similar monopoly over a product, it is fair to presume that the

---

would not otherwise be purchased solely on the merit of that second product." V P. Areeda & D. Turner, Antitrust Law ¶ 1134a at 202 (1980).

[23] Sales of the tied item can be used to measure demand for the tying item; purchasers with greater needs for the tied item make larger purchases and in effect must pay a higher price to obtain the tying item.

[24] Especially where market imperfections exist, purchasers may not be fully sensitive to the price or quality implications of a tying arrangement, and hence it may impede competition on the merits.

inability to buy the product elsewhere gives the seller market power. *United States v. Loew's Inc.*, 371 U.S. 38, 45-47 (1962). Any effort to enlarge the scope of the patent monopoly by using the market power it confers to restrain competition in the market for a second product will undermine competition on the merits in that second market. Thus, the sale or lease of a patented item on condition that the buyer make all his purchases of a separate tied product from the patentee is unlawful.

The same strict rule is appropriate in situations in which the existence of market power is probable. When the seller's share of the market is high, or when the seller offers a unique product that competitors are not able to offer, the Court has held that the likelihood that market power exists and is being used to restrain competition in a separate market is sufficient to make *per se* condemnation appropriate.... When, however, the seller does not have either the degree or the kind of market power that enables him to force customers to purchase a second, unwanted product in order to obtain the tying product, an antitrust violation can be established only by evidence of and unreasonable restraint on competition in the relevant market.

In sum, any inquiry into the validity of a tying arrangement must focus on the market or markets in which the two products are sold, for that is where the anticompetitive forcing has its impact. Thus, in this case our analysis of the tying issue must focus on the hospital's sale of services to its patients, rather than its contractual arrangements with the providers of anesthesiological services. In making that analysis, we must consider whether petitioners are selling two separate products that may be tied together, and, if so, whether they have used their market power to force their patients to accept the tying arrangement.

III

The hospital has provided its patients with a package that includes the range of facilities and services required for a variety of surgical operations. At East Jefferson Hospital the package includes the services of the anesthesiologist.[28] Petitioners argue that the package does not involve a tying arrangement at all — that they are merely providing a functionally integrated package of services. Therefore, petitioners contend that it is inappropriate to apply principles concerning tying arrangements to this case.

Our cases indicate, however, that the answer to the question whether one or two products are involved turns not on the functional relation between them, but

---

[28] It is essential to differentiate between the Roux contract and the legality of the contract between the hospital and its patients. The Roux contract is nothing more than an arrangement whereby Roux supplies all of the hospital's needs for anesthesiological services. That contract raises only an exclusive dealing question. The issue here is whether the hospital's insistence that its patients purchase anesthesiological services from Roux creates a tying arrangement.

rather on the character of the demand for the two items.[30] ... These cases make it clear that a tying arrangement cannot exist unless two separate product markets have been linked....

Unquestionably, the anesthesiological component of the package offered by the hospital could be provided separately and could be selected either by the individual patient or by one of the patient's doctors if the hospital did not insist on including anesthesiological services in the package it offers to its customers. As a matter of actual practice, anesthesiological services are billed separately from the hospital services petitioners provide. There was ample and uncontroverted testimony that patients or surgeons often request specific anesthesiologists to come to a hospital and provide anesthesia, and that the choice of an individual anesthesiologist separate from the choice of a hospital is particularly frequent in respondent's specialty, obstetric anesthesiology. The District Court found that "[t]he provision of anesthesia services is a medical service separate from the other services provided by the hospital." The Court of Appeals agreed with this finding, and went on to observe that "an anesthesiologist is normally selected by the surgeon, rather than the patient, based on familiarity gained through a working relationship. Obviously, the surgeons who practice at East Jefferson Hospital do not gain familiarity with any anesthesiologists other than Roux and Associates." The record amply supports the conclusion that consumers differentiate between anesthesiological services and the other hospital services provided by petitioners.[39]

Thus, the hospital's requirement that its patients obtain necessary anesthesiological services from Roux combined the purchase of two distinguishable services in a single transaction. Nevertheless, the fact that this case involves a required purchase of two services that would otherwise be purchased separately does not make the Roux contract illegal. As noted above, there is nothing inherently anticompetitive about packaged sales. Only if patients are forced to purchase Roux's services as a result of the hospital's market power would the arrangement have anticompetitive consequences. If no forcing is present, patients are free to enter a competing hospital and to use another anesthesiologist instead

---

[30] The fact that anesthesiological services are functionally linked to the other services provided by the hospital is not in itself sufficient to remove the Roux contract from the realm of tying arrangements. We have often found arrangements involving functionally linked products at least one of which is useless without the other to be prohibited tying devices. See Mercoid Corp. v. Mid-Continent Co., 320 U.S. 661 (1944) (heating system and stoker switch); Morton Salt Co. v. Suppiger Co., 314 U.S. 488 (1942) (salt machine and salt). In fact, in some situations the functional link between the two items may enable the seller to maximize its monopoly return on the tying item as a means of charging a higher rent or purchase price to a larger user of the tying item.

[39] The record here shows that other hospitals often permit anesthesiological services to be purchased separately, that anesthesiologists are not fungible in that the services provided by each are not precisely the same, that anesthesiological services are billed separately, and that the hospital required purchases from Roux even though other anesthesiologists were available and Roux had no objection to their receiving staff privileges at East Jefferson. Therefore, the ... analysis indicates that there was a tying arrangement here....

of Roux.[41] The fact that petitioner's patients are required to purchase two separate items is only the beginning of the appropriate inquiry.[42]

IV

The question remains whether this arrangement involves the use of market power to force patients to buy services they would not otherwise purchase. Respondent's only basis for invoking the *per se* rule against tying and thereby avoiding analysis of actual market conditions is by relying on the preference of persons residing in Jefferson Parish to go to East Jefferson, the closest hospital. A preference of this kind, however, is not necessarily probative of significant market power.

Seventy percent of the patients residing in Jefferson Parish enter hospitals other than East Jefferson. Thus East Jefferson's "dominance" over persons residing in Jefferson Parish is far from overwhelming.[43] The fact that a substantial majority of the parish's residents elect not to enter East Jefferson means that the geographic data does not establish the kind of dominant market position that obviates the need for further inquiry into actual competitive conditions....

---

[41] An examination of the reason or reasons why petitioners denied respondent staff privileges will not provide the answer to the question whether the package of services they offered to their patients is an illegal tying arrangement. As a matter of antitrust law, petitioners may give their anesthesiology business to Roux because he is the best doctor available, because he is willing to work long hours, or because he is the son-in-law of the hospital administrator without violating the *per se* rule against tying. Without evidence that petitioners are using market power to force Roux upon patients there is no basis to view the arrangement as unreasonably restraining competition whatever the reasons for its creation. Conversely, with such evidence, the per se rule against tying may apply. Thus, we reject the view of the District Court that the legality of an arrangement of this kind turns on whether it was adopted for the purpose of improving patient care.

[42] Petitioners argue and the District Court found that the exclusive contract had what it characterized as procompetitive justifications in that an exclusive contract ensures 24-hour anesthesiology coverage, enables flexible scheduling, and facilitates work routine, professional standards and maintenance of equipment. The Court of Appeals held these findings to be clearly erroneous since the exclusive contract was not necessary to achieve these ends. Roux was willing to provide 24-hour coverage even without an exclusive contract and the credentials committee of the hospital could impose standards for staff privileges that would ensure staff would comply with the demands of scheduling, maintenance, and professional standards. In the past, we have refused to tolerate manifestly anticompetitive conduct simply because the health care industry is involved.... Petitioners seek no special solicitude. We have also uniformly rejected similar "goodwill" defenses for tying arrangements, finding that the use of contractual quality specifications are generally sufficient to protect quality without the use of a tying arrangement. Since the District Court made no finding as to why contractual quality specifications would not protect the hospital, there is no basis for departing from our prior cases here.

[43] In fact its position in this market is not dissimilar from the market share at issue in *Times-Picayune*, which the Court found insufficient as a basis for inferring market power. *See* 345 U.S., at 611-613. Moreover, in other antitrust contexts this Court has found that market shares comparable to the present here do not create an unacceptable likelihood of anticompetitive conduct. *See United States v. Connecticut National Bank*, 418 U.S. 656 (1974); *United States v. DuPont & Co.*, 351 U.S. 377 (1956).

Tying arrangements need only be condemned if they restrain competition on the merits by forcing purchases that would not otherwise be made. A lack of price or quality competition does not create this type of forcing. If consumers lack price consciousness, that fact will not force them to take an anesthesiologist whose services they do not want — their indifference to price will have no impact on their willingness or ability to go to another hospital where they can utilize the services of the anesthesiologist of their choice. Similarly, if consumers cannot evaluate the quality of anesthesiological services, it follows that they are indifferent between certified anesthesiologists even in the absence of a tying arrangement — such an arrangement cannot be said to have foreclosed a choice that would have otherwise been made "on the merits."

Thus, neither of the "market imperfections" relied upon by the Court of Appeals forces consumers to take anesthesiological services they would not select in the absence of a tie. It is safe to assume that every patient undergoing a surgical operation needs the services of an anesthesiologist; at least this record contains no evidence that the hospital "forced" any such services on unwilling patients.[47] The record therefore does not provide a basis for applying the *per se* rule against tying to this arrangement.

V

In order to prevail in the absence of *per se* liability, respondent has the burden of proving that the Roux contract violated the Sherman Act because it unreasonably restrained competition. That burden necessarily involves an inquiry into the actual effect of the exclusive contract on competition among anesthesiologists.

---

[47] Nor is there an indication in the record that respondents' practices have increased the social costs of its market power. Since patients' anesthesiological needs are fixed by medical judgment, respondent does not argue that the tying arrangement facilitates price discrimination. Where variable-quantity purchasing is unavailable as a means to enable price discrimination, commentators have seen less justification for condemning tying. While tying arrangements like the one at issue here are unlikely to be used to facilitate price discrimination, they could have the similar effect of enabling hospitals "to evade price control in the tying product through clandestine transfer of the profit to the tied product...." *Fortner I*, 394 U.S., at 513 (WHITE, J., dissenting). Insurance companies are the principal source of price restraint in the hospital industry; they place some limitations on the ability of hospitals to exploit their market power. Through this arrangement, petitioners may be able to evade that restraint by obtaining a portion of the anesthesiologists' fees and therefore realize a greater return than they could in the absence of the arrangement. This could also have an adverse effect on the anesthesiology market since it is possible that only less able anesthesiologists would be willing to give up part of their fees in return for the security of an exclusive contract. However, there are no findings of either the District Court or the Court of Appeals which indicate that this type of exploitation of market power has occurred here. The Court of Appeals found only that Roux's use of nurse anesthetists increased its and the hospital's profits, but there was no finding that nurse anesthetists might not be used with equal frequency absent the exclusive contract. Indeed, the District Court found that nurse anesthetists are utilized in all hospitals in the area. 513 F. Supp., at 537, 543. Moreover, there is nothing in the record which details whether this arrangement has enhanced the value of East Jefferson's market power or harmed quality competition in the anesthesiology market.

This competition takes place in a market that has not been defined. The market is not necessarily the same as the market in which hospitals compete in offering services to patients; it may encompass competition among anesthesiologists for exclusive contracts such as the Roux contract and might be statewide or merely local.[48] There is, however, insufficient evidence in this record to provide a basis for finding that the Roux contract, as it actually operates in the market, has unreasonably restrained competition. The record sheds little light on how this arrangement affected consumer demand for separate arrangements with a specific anesthesiologist.[49] The evidence indicates that some surgeons and patients preferred respondent's services to those of Roux, but there is no evidence that any patient who was sophisticated enough to know the difference between two anesthesiologists was not also able to go to a hospital that would provide him with the anesthesiologist of his choice.

In sum, all that the record established is that the choice of anesthesiologists at East Jefferson has been limited to one of the four doctors who are associated with Roux and therefore have staff privileges. Even if Roux did not have an exclusive contract, the range of alternatives open to the patient would be severely limited by the nature of the transaction and the hospital's unquestioned right to exercise some control over the identity and the number of doctors to whom it accords staff privileges. If respondent is admitted to the staff of East Jefferson, the range of choice will be enlarged from four to five doctors, but the most significant restraints on the patient's freedom to select a specific anesthesiologist will nevertheless remain.[52] Without a showing of actual adverse effect on competition, respondent cannot make out a case under the antitrust laws, and no such showing has been made.

---

[48] While there was some rather impressionistic testimony that the prevalence of exclusive contracts tended to discourage young doctors from entering the market, the evidence was equivocal and neither the District Court nor the Court of Appeals made any findings concerning the contract's effect on entry barriers. Respondent does not press the point before this Court. It is possible that under some circumstances an exclusive contract could raise entry barriers since anesthesiologists could not compete for the contract without raising the capital necessary to run a hospital-wide operation. However, since the hospital has provided most of the capital for the exclusive contractor in this case, that problem does not appear to be present.

[49] While it is true that purchasers may not be fully sensitive to the price or quality implications of a tying arrangement, so that competition may be impeded, this depends on an empirical demonstration concerning the effect of the arrangement on price or quality, and the record reveals little if anything about the effect of this arrangement on the market for anesthesiological services.

[52] The record simply tells us little if anything about the effect of this arrangement on price or quality of anesthesiological services. As to price, the arrangement did not lead to an increase in the price charged to the patient. As to quality, the record indicates little more than that there have never been any complaints about the quality of Roux's services, and no contention that his services are in any respect inferior to those of respondent. Moreover, the self interest of the hospital, as well as the ethical and professional norms under which it operates, presumably protect the quality of anesthesiological services.

VI

Petitioners' closed policy may raise questions of medical ethics, and may have inconvenienced some patients who would prefer to have their anesthesia administered by someone other than a member of Roux & Associates, but it does not have the obviously unreasonable impact on purchasers that has characterized the tying arrangements that this Court has branded unlawful. There is no evidence that the price, the quality, or the supply or demand for either the "tying product" or the "tied product" involved in this case has been adversely affected by the exclusive contract between Roux and the hospital. It may well be true that the contract made it necessary for Dr. Hyde and others to practice elsewhere, rather than at East Jefferson. But there has been no showing that the market as a whole has been affected at all by the contract. Indeed, as we previously noted, the record tells us very little about the market for the services of anesthesiologists. Yet that is the market in which the exclusive contract has had its principal impact. There is simply no showing here of the kind of restraint in competition that is prohibited by the Sherman Act. Accordingly, the judgment of the Court of Appeals is reversed and the case is remanded to that court for further proceedings consistent with this opinion.

JUSTICE BRENNAN, with whom JUSTICE MARSHALL joins, concurring.

As the opinion for the Court demonstrates, we have long held that tying arrangements are subject to evaluation for *per se* illegality under § 1 of the Sherman Act. Whatever merit the policy arguments against this longstanding construction of the Act might have, Congress, presumably aware of our decisions, has never changed the rule by amending the Act. In such circumstances, our practice usually has been to stand by a settled statutory interpretation and leave the task of modifying the statute's reach to Congress. I see no reason to depart from that principle in this case and therefore join the opinion and judgment of the Court.

JUSTICE O'CONNOR, with whom CHIEF JUSTICE BURGER, JUSTICE POWELL, and JUSTICE REHNQUIST join, concurring in the judgment.

.....

I

Some of our earlier cases did indeed declare that tying arrangements serve "hardly any purpose beyond the suppression of competition." *Standard Oil Co. of California v. United States*, 337 U.S. 293, 305-306 (1949) (dictum). However, this declaration was not taken literally even by the cases that purported to rely upon it. In practice, a tie has been illegal only if the seller is shown to have "sufficient economic power with respect to the tying product to appreciably restrain free competition in the market for the tied product...." *Northern Pacific R. Co.*, [356 U.S. 1,] at 6. Without "control or dominance over the tying product," the seller could not use the tying products as "an effectual weapon to pressure buyers into taking the tied item," so that any restraint of trade would be "insignificant." The Court has never been willing to say of tying arrangements, as it has of price-fixing, division of markets and other agreements subject to *per se* analysis, that they are always illegal, without proof of market power or anticompetitive effect.

The *"per se"* doctrine in tying cases has thus always required an elaborate inquiry into the economic effects of the tying arrangement.[1] As a result, tying doctrine incurs the costs of rule of reason approach without achieving its benefits: the doctrine calls for the extensive and time-consuming economic analysis characteristic of the rule of reason, but then may be interpreted to prohibit arrangements that economic analysis would show to be beneficial. Moreover, the *per se* label in the tying context has generated more confusion than coherent law because it appears to invite lower courts to omit the analysis of economic circumstances of the tie that has always been a necessary element of tying analysis.

The time has therefore come to abandon the *"per se"* label and refocus the inquiry on the adverse economic effects, and the potential economic benefits, that the tie may have. The law of tie-ins will thus be brought into accord with the law applicable to all other allegedly anticompetitive economic arrangements, except those few horizontal or quasi-horizontal restraints that can be said to have no economic justification whatsoever. This change will rationalize rather than abandon tie-in doctrine as it is already applied.

II

Our prior opinions indicate that the purpose of tying law has been to identify and control those tie-ins that have a demonstrable exclusionary impact in the tied product market, or that abet the harmful exercise of market power that the seller possesses in the tying product market. Under the rule of reason tying arrangements should be disapproved only in such instances.

Market power in the tying product may be acquired legitimately (*e.g.*, through the grant of a patent) or illegitimately (*e.g.*, as a result of unlawful monopolization). In either event, exploitation of consumers in the market for the tying product is a possibility that exists and that may be regulated under § 2 of the Sherman Act without reference to any tying arrangements that the seller may have developed. The existence of a tied product normally does not increase the profit that the seller with market power can extract from sales of the tying product. A seller with a monopoly on flour, for example, cannot increase the profit it can extract from flour consumers simply by forcing them to buy sugar along with their flour. Counterintuitive though that assertion may seem, it is easily demonstrated and widely accepted. *See, e.g.*, R. Bork, *The Antitrust Paradox* 372-74 (1978); P. Areeda, *Antitrust Analysis* 735 (3d ed. 1981).

---

[1] This inquiry has been required in analyzing both the prima facie case and affirmative defenses....

Tying may be economically harmful primarily in the rare cases where power in the market for the tying product is used to create additional market power in the market for the tied product. The antitrust law is properly concerned with tying when, for example, the flour monopolist threatens to use its market power to acquire additional power in the sugar market, perhaps by driving out competing sellers of sugar, or by making it more difficult for new sellers to enter the sugar market. But such extension of market power is unlikely, or poses no threat of economic harm, unless the two markets in question and the nature of the two products tied satisfy three threshold criteria.

....

First, the seller must have power in the tying product market.[6] Absent such power tying cannot conceivably have any adverse impact in the tied-product market, and can be only pro-competitive in the tying product market.[7] If the seller of flour has no market power over flour, it will gain none by insisting that its buyers take some sugar as well.

Second, there must be a substantial threat that the tying seller will acquire market power in the tied-product market. No such threat exists if the tied-product market is occupied by many stable sellers who are not likely to be driven out by the tying, or if entry barriers in the tied product market are low. If, for example, there is an active and vibrant market for sugar — one with numerous sellers and buyers who do not deal in flour — the flour monopolist's tying of sugar to flour need not be declared unlawful. If, on the other hand, the tying arrangement is likely to erect significant barriers to entry into the tied-product market, the tie remains suspect.

Third, there must be a coherent economic basis for treating the tying and tied products as distinct. All but the simplest products can be broken down into two

---

[6] The Court has failed in the past to define how much market power is necessary, but in the context of this case it is inappropriate to attempt to resolve that question....

[7] A common misconception has been that a patent or copyright, a high market share, or a unique product that competitors are not able to offer suffice to demonstrate market power. While each of these three factors might help to give market power to a seller, it is also possible that a seller in these situations will have no market power: for example, a patent holder has no market power in any relevant sense if there are close substitutes for the patented product. Similarly, a high market share indicates market power only if the market is properly defined to include all reasonable substitutes for the product. See generally, Landes & Posner, Market Power in Antitrust Cases, 94 Harv. L. Rev. 937 (1981).

Nor does any presumption of market power find support in our prior cases. Although United States v. Paramount Pictures, Inc., 334 U.S. 131 (1948), considered the legality of "block booking" of motion pictures, which ties the purchase of rights to copyrighted motion pictures to purchase of other motion pictures of the same copyright holder, the Court did not analyze the arrangement with the schema of the tying cases. Rather, the Court borrowed the patent law principle of "patent misuse," which prevents the holder of a patent from using the patent to require his customers to purchase unpatented products. Id., at 156-159. See, e.g., Mercoid Corp. v. Mid-Continent Investment Co., 320 U.S. 661, 664 (1944). The "patent misuse" doctrine may have influenced the Court's willingness to strike down the arrangement at issue in International Salt as well, although the Court did not cite the doctrine in that case.

or more components that are "tied together" in the final sale. Unless it is to be illegal to sell cars with engines or cameras with lenses, this analysis must be guided by some limiting principle. For products to be treated as distinct, the tied product must, at a minimum, be one that some consumers might wish to purchase separately without also purchasing the tying product.[8] When the tied product has no use other than in conjunction with the tying product, a seller of the tying product can acquire no additional market power by selling the two products together. If sugar is useless to consumers except when used with flour, the flour seller's market power is projected into the sugar market whether or not the two products are actually sold together; the flour seller can exploit what market power it has over flour with or without the tie. The flour seller will therefore have little incentive to monopolize the sugar market unless it can produce and distribute sugar more cheaply than other sugar sellers. And in this unusual case, where flour is monopolized and sugar is useful only when used with flour, consumers will suffer no further economic injury by the monopolization of the sugar market.

Even when the tied product does have a use separate from the tying product, it makes little sense to label a package as two products without also considering the economic justifications for the sale of the package as a unit. When the economic advantages of joint packaging are substantial the package is not appropriately viewed as two products, and that should be the end of the tying inquiry....[10]

These three conditions — market power in the tying product, a substantial threat of market power in the tied product, and a coherent economic basis for treating the products as distinct — are only threshold requirements. Under the Rule of Reason a tie-in may prove acceptable even when all three are met. Tie-ins may entail economic benefits as well as economic harms, and if the threshold requirements are met these benefits should enter the Rule of Reason balance.

"Tie-ins ... may facilitate new entry into fields where established sellers have wedded their customers to them by ties of habit and custom. *Brown Shoe Co. v. United States*, 370 U.S. 294 330 (1962).... They may permit clandestine price cutting in products which otherwise would have no price competition at all because of fear of retaliation from the few other producers dealing in the market.

---

[8] Whether the tying product is one that consumers might wish to purchase without the tied product should be irrelevant. Once it is conceded that the seller has market power over the tying product it follows that the seller can sell the tying product on non-competitive terms. The injury to consumers does not depend on whether the seller chooses to charge a super-competitive price, or charges a competitive price but insists that consumers also buy a product that they do not want.

[10] The examination of the economic advantages of tying may properly be conducted as part of the Rule of Reason analysis, rather than at the threshold of the tying inquiry. This approach is consistent with this Court's occasional references to the problem. The Court has not heretofore had occasion to set forth any general criteria for determining when two apparently separate products are components of a single product for tying analysis.... [The] cases indicate that consideration of whether a buyer might prefer to purchase one component without the other is one of the factors in tying analysis and, more generally, that economic analysis rather than mere conventional separability into different markets should determine whether one or two products are involved in the alleged tie.

They may protect the reputation of the tying product if failure to use the tied product in conjunction with it may cause it to misfunction: [citing *Pick Mfg. Co. v. General Motors Corp.*, 80 F.2d 641 (7th Cir. 1935), *aff'd*, 299 U.S. 3 (1936)].... And, if the tied and tying products are functionally related, they may reduce costs through economies of joint production and distribution." *Fortner I*, 394 U.S., at 514 n. 9 (JUSTICE WHITE, dissenting).

The ultimate decision whether a tie-in is illegal under the antitrust laws should depend upon the demonstrated economic effects of the challenged agreement. It may, for example, be entirely innocuous that the seller exploits its control over the tying product to "force" the buyer to purchase the tied product. For when the seller exerts market power only in the tying product market, it makes no difference to him or his customers whether he exploits that power by raising the price of the tying product or by "forcing" customers to buy a tied product. On the other hand, tying may make the provision of packages of goods and services more efficient. A tie-in should be condemned only when its anticompetitive impact outweighs its contribution to efficiency.

III

Application of these criteria to the case at hand is straightforward.

Although the issue is in doubt, we may assume that the Hospital does have market power in the provision of hospital services in its area....

Second, in light of the Hospital's presumed market power, we may also assume that there is a substantial threat that East Jefferson will acquire market power over the provision of anesthesiological services in its market. By tying the sale of anesthesia to the sale of other hospital services the Hospital can drive out other sellers of those services who might otherwise operate in the local market. The Hospital may thus gain local market power in the provision of anesthesiology: anesthesiological services offered in the Hospital's market, narrowly defined, will be purchased only from Roux, under the Hospital's auspices.

But the third threshold condition for giving closer scrutiny to a tying arrangement is not satisfied here: there is no sound economic reason for treating surgery and anesthesia as separate services. Patients are interested in purchasing anesthesia only in conjunction with hospital services, so the Hospital can acquire no additional market power by selling the two services together. Accordingly, the link between the Hospital's services and anesthesia administered by Roux will affect neither the amount of anesthesia provided nor the combined price of anesthesia and surgery for those who choose to become the Hospital's patients. In these circumstances, anesthesia and surgical services should probably not be characterized as distinct products for tying purposes.

Even if they are, the tying should not be considered a violation of § 1 of the Sherman Act because tying here cannot increase the seller's already absolute power over the volume of production of the tied product, which is an inevitable consequence of the fact that very few patients will choose to undergo surgery without receiving anesthesia. The Hospital-Roux contract therefore has little potential to harm the patients. On the other side of the balance, the District Court found, and the Court of Appeals did not dispute, that the tie-in conferred significant benefits upon the hospital and the patients that it served.

The tie-in improves patient care and permits more efficient hospital operation in a number of ways. From the viewpoint of hospital management, the tie-in ensures 24-hour anesthesiology coverage, aids in standardization of procedures and efficient use of equipment, facilitates flexible scheduling of operations, and permits the hospital more effectively to monitor the quality of anesthesiological services. Further, the tying arrangement is advantageous to patients because, as the District Court found, the closed anesthesiology department places upon the hospital, rather than the individual patient, responsibility to select the physician who is to provide anesthesiological services. The hospital also assumes the responsibility that the anesthesiologist will be available, will be acceptable to the surgeon, and will provide suitable care to the patient. In assuming these responsibilities — responsibilities that a seriously ill patient frequently may be unable to discharge — the hospital provides a valuable service to its patients. And there is no indication that patients were dissatisfied with the quality of anesthesiology that was provided at the hospital or that patients wished to enjoy the services of anesthesiologists other than those that the hospital employed. Given this evidence of the advantages and effectiveness of the closed anesthesiology department, it is not surprising that, as the District Court found, such arrangements are accepted practice in the majority of hospitals of New Orleans and in health care industry generally. Such an arrangement, that has little anti-competitive effect and achieves substantial benefits in the provision of care to patients, is hardly one that the antitrust law should condemn. This conclusion reaffirms our threshold determination that the joint provision of hospital services and anesthesiology should not be viewed as involving a tie between distinct products, and therefore should require no additional scrutiny under the antitrust law.

IV

Whether or not the Hospital-Roux contract is characterized as a tie between distinct products, the contract unquestionably does constitute exclusive dealing. Exclusive dealing arrangements are independently subject to scrutiny under § 1 of the Sherman Act, and are also analyzed under the Rule of Reason. *Tampa Electric Co. v. Nashville Coal Co.*, 365 U.S. 32, 333-335 (1961).

The Hospital-Roux arrangement could conceivably have an adverse effect on horizontal competition among anesthesiologists, or among hospitals. Dr. Hyde, who competes with the Roux anesthesiologists, and other hospitals in the area, who compete with East Jefferson, may have grounds to complain that the exclusive contract stifles horizontal competition and therefore has an adverse, albeit indirect, impact on consumer welfare even if it is not a tie.

....

At issue here is an exclusive dealing arrangement between a firm of four anesthesiologists and one relatively small hospital. There is no suggestion that East Jefferson Hospital is likely to create a "bottleneck" in the availability of anesthesiologists that might deprive other hospitals of access to needed anesthesiological services, or that the Roux associates have unreasonably narrowed the range of choices available to other anesthesiologists in search of a hospital or patients that will buy their services. A firm of four anesthesiologists represents only a very small fraction of the total number of anesthesiologists whose services are available for hire by other hospitals, and East Jefferson is one among numerous hospitals buying such services. Even without engaging in a detailed analysis of the size of the relevant markets we may readily conclude that there is no likelihood that the exclusive dealing arrangement challenged here will either unreasonably enhance the Hospital's market position relative to other hospitals, or unreasonably permit Roux to acquire power relative to other anesthesiologists. Accordingly, this exclusive dealing arrangement must be sustained under the Rule of Reason.

V

... Since anesthesia is a service useful to consumers only when purchased in conjunction with hospital services, the arrangement is not properly characterized as a tie between distinct products. It threatens no additional economic harm to consumers beyond that already made possible by any market power that the Hospital may possess. The fact that anesthesia is used only together with other hospital services is sufficient, standing alone, to insulate from attack the Hospital's decision to tie the two types of service.

Whether or not this case involves tying of distinct products, the Hospital-Roux contract is subject to scrutiny under the Rule of Reason as an exclusive dealing arrangement. Plainly, however, the arrangement forecloses only a small fraction of the markets in which anesthesiologists may sell their services, and a still smaller fraction of the market in which hospitals may secure anesthesiological services. The contract therefore survives scrutiny under the Rule of Reason.

NOTES AND QUESTIONS

1. For many years economists and other antitrust commentators, particularly those from the Chicago School, have been urging the Supreme Court to abolish the notion that tying arrangements are governed by a per se rule. The Court refused the invitation. However, the four participants in Justice O'Connor's concurring opinion were more than ready to jettison the per se label for tying arrangements.

What sense does it make to say that tying arrangements are governed by a per se rule when courts in fact (1) require a showing of market power in the tying product; (2) more often than not require some kind of showing of an anticompetitive *effect* in the tied product market; and (3) often hold that tying arrangements are legal — in fact, in most of the cases? Do tying arrangements fall within that category of practices that are almost always harmful to consumers, and therefore can be condemned without extensive analysis of their actual economic effects?

The economic criticism of the per se rule against tying arrangements is summarized in H. Hovenkamp, *Federal Antitrust Policy*, §§ 10.2-10.4 (2d ed. 1994).

2. What does the *Hyde* decision do to the market power requirement in tie-in cases? In *Fortner I* a simple showing that the tying product was "unique" was sufficient to create a presumption of market power. In *Hyde*, however, the defendant's market share was about 30%. How many Supreme Court tie-in cases from the 1960's and earlier were in fact overruled by *Hyde*?

3. At oral argument the Supreme Court was told that the contract at issue in *Hyde* was not a tying arrangement at all, but rather an exclusive dealing arrangement. Four Justices agreed. Distinguishing tying arrangements from exclusive dealing contracts can be very difficult. Nevertheless, the two practices are governed by very different legal tests. Reconsider the arrangement at issue in the *Standard Stations* case, noted *supra*. Is it obvious that the case involved exclusive dealing rather than tying? What if Standard required individual stations to sell nothing but its gasoline as a condition of receiving the right to bear the Standard name? In *Krehl v. Baskin-Robbins Ice Cream Co.*, 664 F.2d 1348 (9th Cir. 1982), the defendant was charged with requiring all its franchisees (Baskin-Robbins ice cream stores) to sell the defendant's ice cream exclusively. The case was characterized as a tying arrangement, however, in which the tying product was the Baskin-Robbins trademark and method of doing business, and the tied product was the ice cream.

4. What do you think of Justice O'Connor's argument that only a single "product," for the purposes of the law of tie-ins, was involved in the *Hyde* case? Justice O'Connor concluded that "[f]or products to be treated as distinct, the tied product must, at a minimum, be one that some consumers might wish to purchase separately without also purchasing the tying product." Suppose that a manufacturer of stereo equipment made buyers of its phonographic turntables agree to purchase all their phonographic records from it as well. A single "product" under Justice O'Connor's test?

EASTMAN KODAK CO. V. IMAGE TECHNICAL SERVICES, INC.

504 U.S. 451 (1992)

JUSTICE BLACKMUN delivered the opinion of the Court.

This is yet another case that concerns the standard for summary judgment in an antitrust controversy. The principal issue here is whether a defendant's lack of market power in the primary equipment market precludes — as a matter of law — the possibility of market power in derivative aftermarkets.

Petitioner Eastman Kodak Company manufactures and sells photocopiers and micrographic equipment. Kodak also sells service and replacement parts for its equipment. Respondents are 18 independent service organizations (ISOs) that in the early 1980s began servicing Kodak copying and micrographic equipment. Kodak subsequently adopted policies to limit the availability of parts to ISOs and to make it more difficult for ISOs to compete with Kodak in servicing Kodak equipment.

Respondents instituted this action ... alleging that Kodak's policies were unlawful under both §§ 1 and 2 of the Sherman Act, 15 U.S.C. §§ 1 and 2. After truncated discovery, the District Court granted summary judgment for Kodak. The Court of Appeals for the Ninth Circuit reversed. The appellate court found that the respondents had presented sufficient evidence to raise a genuine issue concerning Kodak's market power in the service and parts markets....

I

A

Because this case comes to us on petitioner Kodak's motion for summary judgment, "[t]he evidence of [respondents] is to be believed, and all justifiable inferences are to be drawn in [their] favor."...

Kodak manufactures and sells complex business machines — as relevant here, high-volume photocopier and micrographics equipment. Kodak equipment is unique; micrographic software programs that operate on Kodak machines, for example, are not compatible with competitors' machines. Kodak parts are not compatible with other manufacturers' equipment, and vice versa. Kodak equipment, although expensive when new, has little resale value.

Kodak provides service and parts for its machines to its customers. It produces some of the parts itself; the rest are made to order for Kodak by independent original-equipment manufacturers (OEMs). Kodak does not sell a complete system of original equipment, lifetime service, and lifetime parts for a single price. Instead, Kodak provides service after the initial warranty period either through annual service contracts, which include all necessary parts, or on a per-call basis. It charges, through negotiations and bidding, different prices for equipment, service, and parts for different customers. Kodak provides 80% to 95% of the service for Kodak machines.

Beginning in the early 1980s, ISOs began repairing and servicing Kodak equipment. They also sold parts and reconditioned and sold used Kodak equipment. Their customers were federal, state, and local government agencies, banks, insurance companies, industrial enterprises, and providers of specialized copy and microfilming services. ISOs provide service at a price substantially lower than Kodak does. Some customers found that the ISO service was of higher quality.

Some of the ISOs' customers purchase their own parts and hire ISOs only for service. Others choose ISOs to supply both service and parts. ISOs keep an inventory of parts, purchased from Kodak or other sources, primarily the OEMs.

In 1985 and 1986, Kodak implemented a policy of selling replacement parts for micrographic and copying machines only to buyers of Kodak equipment who use Kodak service or repair their own machines.

As part of the same policy, Kodak sought to limit ISO access to other sources of Kodak parts. Kodak and the OEMs agreed that the OEMs would not sell parts that fit Kodak equipment to anyone other than Kodak. Kodak also pressured Kodak equipment owners and independent parts distributors not to sell Kodak parts to ISOs. In addition, Kodak took steps to restrict the availability of used machines.

Kodak intended, through these policies, to make it more difficult for ISOs to sell service for Kodak machines. It succeeded. ISOs were unable to obtain parts from reliable sources and many were forced out of business, while others lost substantial revenue. Customers were forced to switch to Kodak service even though they preferred ISO service.

B

In 1987, the ISOs filed the present action in the District Court alleging *inter alia*, that Kodak had unlawfully tied the sale of service for Kodak machines to the sale of parts, in violation of § 1 of the Sherman Act, and had unlawfully monopolized and attempted to monopolize the sale of service for Kodak machines, in violation of § 2 of that Act.

Kodak filed a motion for summary judgment before respondents had initiated discovery. The District Court permitted respondents to file one set of interrogatories and one set of requests for production of documents, and to take six depositions. Without a hearing, the District Court granted summary judgment in favor of Kodak.

As to the § 1 claim, the court found that respondents had provided no evidence of a tying arrangement between Kodak equipment and service or parts. The court, however, did not address respondents' § 1 claim that is at issue here. Respondents allege a tying arrangement not between Kodak *equipment* and service, but between Kodak *parts* and service. As to the § 2 claim, the District Court concluded that although Kodak had a "natural monopoly over the market for parts its sells under its name," a unilateral refusal to sell those parts to ISOs did not violate § 2.

The Court of Appeals for the Ninth Circuit, by a divided vote, reversed. 903 F.2d 612 (1990). With respect to the § 1 claim, the court first found that whether service or parts were distinct markets and whether a tying arrangement existed between them were disputed issues of fact. Having found that a tying arrangement might exist, the Court of Appeals considered a question not decided by the District Court: was there "an issue of material fact as to whether Kodak has sufficient economic power in the tying product market [parts] to restrain competition appreciably in the tied product market [service]." The court agreed with Kodak that competition in the equipment market might prevent Kodak from possessing power in the parts market, but refused to uphold the District Court's grant of summary judgment "on this theoretical basis" because "market imperfections can keep economic theories about how consumers will act from mirroring reality." Noting that the District Court had not considered the market power issue, and that the record was not fully developed through discovery, the court declined to

require respondents to conduct market analysis or to pinpoint specific imperfections in order to withstand summary judgment. "It is enough that [respondents]
have presented evidence of actual events from which a reasonable trier of fact
could conclude that ... competition in the [equipment] market does not, in reality,
curb Kodak's power in the parts market."

The court then considered the three business justifications Kodak proffered for
its restrictive parts policy: (1) to guard against inadequate service, (2) to lower
inventory costs, and (3) to prevent ISOs from free-riding on Kodak's investment
in the copier and micrographic industry. The court then concluded that the trier of
fact might find the product quality and inventory reasons to be pretextual and that
there was a less restrictive alternative for achieving Kodak's quality-related
goals. The court also found Kodak's third justification, preventing ISOs from
profiting on Kodak's investments in the equipment markets, legally insufficient.
As to the § 2 claim, the Court of Appeals concluded that sufficient evidence existed to support a finding that Kodak's implementation of its parts policy was
"anticompetitive" and "exclusionary" and "involved a specific intent to monopolize.".... It held that the ISOs had come forward with sufficient evidence, for
summary judgment purposes, to disprove Kodak's business justifications....

II

A tying arrangement is "an agreement by a party to sell one product but only
on the condition that the buyer also purchases a different (or tied) product, or at
least agrees that he will not purchase that product from any other supplier."
Northern Pacific R. Co. v. United States, 356 U.S. 1, 5-6 (1958). Such an arrangement violates § 1 of the Sherman Act if the seller has "appreciable economic power" in the tying product market and if the arrangement affects a substantial volume of commerce in the tied market. *Fortner Enterprises, Inc. v.
United States Steel Corp.*, 394 U.S. 495, 503 (1969).

Kodak did not dispute that its arrangement affects a substantial volume of interstate commerce. It, however, did challenge whether its activities constituted a
"tying arrangement" and whether Kodak exercised "appreciable economic
power" in the tying market. We consider these issues in turn.

A

For the respondents to defeat a motion for summary judgment on their claim of
a tying arrangement, a reasonable trier of fact must be able to find, first, that
service and parts are two distinct products, and, second, that Kodak has tied the
sale of the two products.

For service and parts to be considered two distinct products, there must be sufficient consumer demand so that it is efficient for a firm to provide service separately from parts. *Jefferson Parish Hospital Dist. No. 2 v. Hyde*, 466 U.S. 2, 21-22
(1984). Evidence in the record indicates that service and parts have been sold separately in the past and still are sold separately to self-service equipment owners.

Indeed, the development of the entire high-technology service industry is evidence of the efficiency of a separate market for service.

Kodak insists that because there is no demand for parts separate from service, there cannot be separate markets for service and parts. By that logic, we would be forced to conclude that there can never be separate markets, for example, for cameras and film, computers and software, or automobiles and tires. That is an assumption we are unwilling to make. "We have often found arrangements involving functionally linked products at least one of which is useless without the other to be prohibited tying devices." *Jefferson Parish,* 466 U.S., at 19, n. 20.

Kodak's assertion also appears to be incorrect as a factual matter. At least some consumers would purchase service without parts, because some service does not require parts, and some consumers, those who self-service for example, would purchase parts without service. Enough doubt is cast on Kodak's claim of a unified market that it should be resolved by the trier of fact.

Finally, respondents have presented sufficient evidence of a tie between service and parts. The record indicates that Kodak would sell parts to third parties only if they agreed not to buy service from ISOs.[8]

B

Having found sufficient evidence of a tying arrangement, we consider the other necessary feature of an illegal tying arrangement: appreciable economic power in the tying market. Market power is the power "to force a purchaser to do something that he would not do in a competitive market." *Jefferson Parish,* 466 U.S., at 14.[9] It has been defined as "the ability of a single seller to raise price and restrict output." *Fortner Inc.,* 394 U.S., at 503; *United States v. E.I. du Pont de Nemours & Co.,* 351 U.S. 377, 391 (1956). The existence of such power ordinarily is inferred from the seller's possession of a predominant share of the market. *Jefferson Parish,* 466 U.S., at 17; *United States v. Grinnell Corp.,* 384 U.S. 563, 571 (1966); *Times-Picayune Publishing Co. v. United States,* 345 U.S. 594, 611-13 (1953).

1

Respondents contend that Kodak has more than sufficient power in the parts market to force unwanted purchases of the tied market, service. Respondents

---

[8] In a footnote, Kodak contends that this practice is only a unilateral refusal to deal, which does not violate the antitrust laws. Assuming, *arguendo,* that Kodak's refusal to sell parts to any company providing service can be characterized as a unilateral refusal to deal, its alleged sale of parts to third parties on condition that they buy service from Kodak is not.

[9] "[T]he essential characteristic of an invalid tying arrangement lies in the seller's exploitation of its control over the tying product to force the buyer into the purchase of a tied product that the buyer either did not want at all, or might have preferred to purchase elsewhere on different terms. When such 'forcing' is present, competition on the merits in the market for the tied item is restrained and the Sherman Act is violated." *Jefferson Parish,* 466 U.S., at 12.

provide evidence that certain parts are available exclusively through Kodak. Respondents also assert that Kodak has control over the availability of parts it does not manufacture. According to respondents' evidence, Kodak prohibited independent manufacturers from selling Kodak parts to ISOs, pressured Kodak equipment owners and independent parts distributors to deny ISOs the purchase of Kodak parts, and taken [*sic*] steps to restrict the availability of used machines.

Respondents also allege that Kodak's control over the parts market has excluded service competition, boosted service prices, and forced unwilling consumption of Kodak service. Respondents offer evidence that consumers have switched to Kodak service even though they preferred ISO service, that Kodak service was of higher price and lower quality than the preferred ISO service, and that ISOs were driven out of business by Kodak's policies. Under our prior precedents, this evidence would be sufficient to entitle respondents to a trial on their claim of market power.

2

Kodak counters that even if it concedes monopoly *share* of the relevant parts market, it cannot actually exercise the necessary market *power* for a Sherman Act violation. This is so, according to Kodak, because competition exists in the equipment market. Kodak argues that it could not have the ability to raise prices of service and parts above the level that would be charged in a competitive market because any increase in profits from a higher price in the aftermarkets at least would be offset by a corresponding loss in profits from lower equipment sales as consumers began purchasing equipment with more attractive service costs.

Kodak does not present any actual data on the equipment, service, or parts markets. Instead, it argues the adoption of a substantive legal rule that "equipment competition precludes any finding of monopoly power in derivative aftermarkets." Kodak argues that such a rule would satisfy its burden as the moving party of showing "that there is no genuine issue as to any material fact" on the market power issue.

Legal presumptions that rest on formalistic distinctions rather than actual market realities are generally disfavored in antitrust law. This Court has preferred to resolve antitrust claims on a case-by-case basis, focusing on the "particular facts disclosed by the record." In determining the existence of market power, and specifically the "responsiveness of the sales of one product to price changes of the other," this Court has examined closely the economic reality of the market at issue.

Kodak contends that there is no need to examine the facts when the issue is market power in the aftermarkets. A legal presumption against a finding of market power is warranted in this situation, according to Kodak, because the existence of market power in the service and parts markets absent power in the equipment market "simply makes no economic sense," and the absence of a legal presumption would deter procompetitive behavior.

Kodak analogizes this case to *Matsushita* where a group of American corporations that manufactured or sold consumer electronic products alleged that their 21 Japanese counterparts were engaging in a 20-year conspiracy to price below cost in the United States in the hope of expanding their market share sometime in the future. After several years of detailed discovery, the defendants moved for summary judgment. Because the defendants had every incentive not to engage in the alleged conduct which required them to sustain losses for decades with no foreseeable profits, the Court found an "absence of any rational motive to conspire." In that context, the Court determined that the plaintiffs' theory of predatory pricing makes no practical sense, was "speculative" and was not "reasonable." Accordingly, the Court held that a reasonable jury could not return a verdict for the plaintiffs and that summary judgment would be appropriate against them unless they came forward with more persuasive evidence to support their theory.

The Court's requirement in *Matsushita* that the plaintiffs' claims make economic sense did not introduce a special burden on plaintiffs facing summary judgment in antitrust cases. The Court did not hold that if the moving party enunciates *any* economic theory supporting its behavior, regardless of its accuracy in reflecting the actual market, it is entitled to summary judgment. *Matsushita* demands only that the nonmoving party's inferences be reasonable in order to reach the jury, a requirement that was not invented, but merely articulated, in that decision. If the plaintiff's theory is economically senseless, no reasonable jury could find in its favor, and summary judgment should be granted.

Kodak, then, bears a substantial burden in showing that it is entitled to summary judgment. It must show that despite evidence of increased prices and excluded competition, an inference of market power is unreasonable. To determine whether Kodak has met that burden, we must unravel the factual assumptions underlying its proposed rule that lack of power in the equipment market necessarily precludes power in the aftermarkets.

The extent to which one market prevents exploitation of another market depends on the extent to which consumers will change their consumption of one product in response to a price change in another, *i.e.*, the "cross-elasticity of demand." See *du Pont*, 351 U.S., at 400;[15] Kodak's proposed rule rests on a factual

---

[15] What constrains the defendant's ability to raise prices in the service market is "the elasticity of demand faced by the defendant — the degree to which its sales fall ... as its price rises." P. Areeda & L. Kaplow, Antitrust Analysis ¶ 342(c) (4th ed. 1988).

Courts have considered the relationship between price in one market and demand in another in defining the relevant market. Because market power is often inferred from market share, market definition generally determines the result of the case. Pitofsky, *New Definitions of Relevant Market and the Assault on Antitrust*, 90 Colum. L. Rev. 1805, 1806-13 (1990). Kodak chose to focus on market power directly rather than arguing that the relationship between equipment and service and parts is such that the three should be included in the same market definition. Whether considered in the conceptual category of "market definition" or "market power," the ultimate inquiry is the same — whether competition in the equipment market will significantly restrain power in the service and parts markets.

assumption about the cross-elasticity of demand in the equipment and aftermarkets: "If Kodak raised its parts or service prices above competitive levels, potential customers would simply stop buying Kodak equipment. Perhaps Kodak would be able to increase short term profits through such a strategy, but at a devastating cost to its long term interests."[16] Kodak argues that the Court should accept, as a matter of law, this "basic economic realit[y]," that competition in the equipment market necessarily prevents market power in the aftermarkets.[17]

Even if Kodak could not raise the price of service and parts one cent without losing equipment sales, that fact would not disprove market power in the aftermarkets. The sales of even a monopolist are reduced when it sells goods at a monopoly price, but the higher price more than compensates for the loss in sales. Kodak's claim that charging more for service and parts would be "a short-run game," is based on the false dichotomy that there are only two prices that can be charged — a competitive price or a ruinous one. But there could easily be a middle, optimum price at which the increased revenues from the higher-priced sales of service and parts would more than compensate for the lower revenues from lost equipment sales. The fact that the equipment market imposes a restraint on prices in the aftermarkets by no means disproves the existence of power in those markets. ("[T]he existence of significant substitution in the event of *further* price increases or even at the *current* price does not tell us whether the defendant *already* exercises significant market power") (emphasis in original). Thus, contrary to Kodak's assertion, there is no immutable physical law — no "basic economic reality" — insisting that competition in the equipment market cannot coexist with market power in the aftermarkets.

We next consider the more narrowly drawn question: Does Kodak's theory describe actual market behavior so accurately that respondents' assertion of Kodak market power in the aftermarkets, if not impossible, is at least unreasonable?[18]

---

[16] The United States as *Amicus Curiae* in support of Kodak echoes this argument: "The ISOs' claims are implausible because Kodak lacks market power in the markets for its copier and micrographic equipment. Buyers of such equipment regard an increase in the price of parts or service as an increase in the price of the equipment, and sellers recognize that the revenues from its sales of parts and services are attributable to sales of the equipment. In such circumstances, it is not apparent how an equipment manufacturer such as Kodak could exercise power in the aftermarkets for parts and service." Brief for United States as *Amicus Curiae* 8.

[17] It is clearly true, as the United States claims, that Kodak "cannot set service or parts prices without regard to the impact on the market for equipment." *Id.,* at 20. The fact that the cross-elasticity of demand is not zero proves nothing; the disputed issue is how much of an impact an increase in parts and service prices has on equipment sales and on Kodak's profits.

[18] Although Kodak repeatedly relies on *Continental T.V.* as support for its factual assertion that the equipment market will prevent exploitation of the service and parts markets, the case is inapposite. In *Continental T.V.,* the Court found that a manufacturer's policy restricting the number of retailers that were permitted to sell its product could have a procompetitive effect. See 433 U.S., at 55. The Court also noted that any negative effect of exploitation of the intrabrand market (the competition between retailers of the same product) would be checked by competition in the interbrand market (competition over the same generic product) because consumers would substitute a different

To review Kodak's theory, it contends that higher service prices will lead to a disastrous drop in equipment sales. Presumably, the theory's corollary is to the effect that low service prices lead to a dramatic increase in equipment sales. According to the theory, one would have expected Kodak to take advantage of lower-priced ISO service as an opportunity to expand equipment sales. Instead, Kodak adopted a restrictive sales policy consciously designed to eliminate the lower-priced ISO service, an act that would be expected to devastate either Kodak's equipment sales or Kodak's faith in its theory. Yet, according to the record, it has done neither. Service prices have risen for Kodak customers, but there is no evidence or assertion that Kodak's equipment sales have dropped.

Kodak and the United States attempt to reconcile Kodak's theory with the contrary actual results by describing a "marketing strategy of spreading over time the total cost to the buyer of Kodak equipment." In other words, Kodak could charge subcompetitive prices for equipment and make up the difference with supracompetitive prices for service, resulting in an overall competitive price. This pricing strategy would provide an explanation for the theory's descriptive failings — if Kodak in fact had adopted it. But Kodak never has asserted that it prices its equipment or parts subcompetitively and recoups its profits through service. Instead, it claims that it prices its equipment comparably to its competitors, and intends that both its equipment sales and service divisions be profitable. Moreover, this hypothetical pricing strategy is inconsistent with Kodak's policy toward its self-service customers. If Kodak were underpricing its equipment, hoping to lock in customers and recover its losses in the service market, it could not afford to sell customers parts without service. In sum, Kodak's theory does not explain the actual market behavior revealed in the record.

Respondents offer a forceful reason why Kodak's theory, although perhaps intuitively appealing, may not accurately explain the behavior of the primary and derivative markets for complex durable goods: the existence of significant information and switching costs. These costs could create a less responsive connection between service and parts prices and equipment sales.

For the service-market price to affect equipment demand, consumers must inform themselves of the total cost of the "package" — equipment, service and parts — at the time of purchase; that is, consumers must engage in accurate lifecycle pricing. Lifecycle pricing of complex, durable equipment is difficult and costly. In order to arrive at an accurate price, a consumer must acquire a substantial amount of raw data and undertake sophisticated analysis. The necessary information would include data on price, quality, and availability of products needed to operate, up-

---

brand of the same product. Unlike *Continental T.V.*, this case does not concern vertical relationships between parties on different levels of the same distribution chain. In the relevant market, service, Kodak and the ISOs are direct competitors; their relationship is horizontal. The interbrand competition at issue here is competition over the provision of service. Despite petitioner's best effort, repeating the mantra "interbrand competition" does not transform this case into one over an agreement the manufacturer has with its dealers that would fall under the rubric of *Continental T.V.*

grade, or enhance the initial equipment, as well as service and repair costs, including estimates of breakdown frequency, nature of repairs, price of service and parts, length of "down-time" and losses incurred from down-time.

Much of this information is difficult — some of it is impossible — to acquire at the time of purchase. During the life of a product, companies may change the service and parts prices, and develop products with more advanced features, a decreased need for repair, or new warranties. In addition, the information is likely to be customer-specific; lifecycle costs will vary from customer to customer with the type of equipment, degrees of equipment use, and costs of down-time.

Kodak acknowledges the cost of information, but suggests, again without evidentiary support, that customer information needs will be satisfied by competitors in the equipment markets. It is a question of fact, however, whether competitors would provide the necessary information....

In sum, there is a question of fact whether information costs and switching costs foil the simple assumption that the equipment and service markets act as pure complements to one another.

We conclude, then, that Kodak has failed to demonstrate that respondents' inference of market power in the service and parts markets is unreasonable, and that, consequently, Kodak is entitled to summary judgment. It is clearly reasonable to infer that Kodak has market power to raise prices and drive out competition in the aftermarkets, since respondents offer direct evidence that Kodak did so. It is also plausible, as discussed above, to infer that Kodak chose to gain immediate profits by exerting that market power where locked-in customers, high information costs, and discriminatory pricing limited and perhaps eliminated any long-term loss. Viewing the evidence in the light most favorable to respondents, their allegations of market power "mak[e] ... economic sense." Cf. *Matsushita*, 475 U.S., at 587.

Nor are we persuaded by Kodak's contention that it is entitled to a legal presumption on the lack of market power because, as in *Matsushita*, there is a significant risk of deterring procompetitive conduct. Plaintiffs in *Matsushita* attempted to prove the antitrust conspiracy "through evidence of rebates and other price-cutting activities." Because cutting prices to increase business is "the very essence of competition," the Court was concerned that mistaken inferences would be "especially costly," and would "chill the very conduct the antitrust laws were designed to protect." But the facts in this case are just the opposite. The alleged conduct — higher service prices and market foreclosure — is facially anticompetitive and exactly the harm that antitrust laws aim to prevent. In this situation, *Matsushita* does not create any presumption in favor of summary judgment for the defendant....

We need not decide whether Kodak's behavior has any procompetitive effects and, if so, whether they outweigh the anticompetitive effects. We note only that Kodak's service and parts policy is simply not one that appears always or almost always to enhance competition, and therefore to warrant a legal presumption without any evidence of its actual economic impact. In this case, when we weigh the risk of deterring procompetitive behavior by proceeding to trial against the risk that illegal behavior go unpunished, the balance tips against summary judgment. Cf. *Matsushita*, 475 U.S., at 594-95.

For the foregoing reasons, we hold that Kodak has not met the requirements of Fed. Rule Civ. Proc. 56(c). We therefore affirm the denial of summary judgment on respondents' § 1 claim.

III

Respondents also claim that they have presented genuine issues for trial as to whether Kodak has monopolized or attempted to monopolize the service and parts markets in violation of § 2 of the Sherman Act. "The offense of monopoly under § 2 of the Sherman Act has two elements: (1) the possession of monopoly power in the relevant market and (2) the willful acquisition or maintenance of that power as distinguished from growth or development as a consequence of a superior product, business acumen, or historic accident." *United States v. Grinnell Corp.*, 384 U.S., at 570-71.

A

The existence of the first element, possession of monopoly power is easily resolved. As has been noted, respondents have presented a triable claim that service and parts are separate markets, and that Kodak has the "power to control prices or exclude competition" in service and parts. *Du Pont*, 351 U.S., at 391. Monopoly power under § 2 requires, of course, something greater than market power under § 1. See *Fortner*, 394 U.S., at 502. Respondents' evidence that Kodak controls nearly 100% of the parts market and 80% to 95% of the service market, with no readily available substitutes, is, however, sufficient to survive summary judgment under the more stringent monopoly standard of § 2. See *National Collegiate Athletic Assn. v. Board of Regents of Univ. of Okla.*, 468 U.S. 85, 112 (1984). Cf. *United States v. Grinnell Corp.*, 384 U.S., at 571 (87% of the market is a monopoly); *American Tobacco Co. v. United States*, 328 U.S. 781, 797 (1946) (over $^2/_3$ of the market is a monopoly).

Kodak also contends that, as a matter of law, a single brand of a product or service can never be a relevant market under the Sherman Act. We disagree. The relevant market for antitrust purposes is determined by the choices available to Kodak equipment owners. See *Jefferson Parish*, 466 U.S., at 19. Because service and parts for Kodak equipment are not interchangeable with other manufacturers' service and parts, the relevant market from the Kodak-equipment owner's perspective is composed of only those companies that service Kodak machines. See *du Pont*, 351 U.S., at 404 (the "market is composed of products that have reasonable interchangeability"). This Court's prior cases support the proposition that in some instances one brand of a product can constitute a separate market. See *National Collegiate Athletic Assn.*, 468 U.S., at 101-02, 111-12 (1984); *International Boxing Club of New York, Inc. v. United States*, 358 U.S. 242, 249-52

(1959); *International Business Machines Corp. v. United States*, 298 U.S. 131 (1936). The proper market definition in this case can be determined only after a factual inquiry into the "commercial realities" faced by consumers. *United States v. Grinnell Corp.*, 384 U.S., at 572.

B

The second element of a § 2 claim is the use of monopoly power "to foreclose competition, to gain a competitive advantage, or to destroy a competitor." *United States v. Griffith*, 334 U.S. 100, 107 (1948). If Kodak adopted its parts and service policies as part of a scheme of willful acquisition or maintenance of monopoly power, it will have violated § 2. *Grinnell Corp.*, 384 U.S., at 570-71; *United States v. Aluminum Co. of America*, 148 F.2d 416, 432 (2d Cir. 1945); *Aspen Skiing Co. v. Aspen Highlands Skiing Corp.*, 472 U.S. 585, 600-05 (1985).

As recounted at length above, respondents have presented evidence that Kodak took exclusionary action to maintain its parts monopoly and used its control over parts to strengthen its monopoly share of the Kodak service market. Liability turns, then, on whether "valid business reasons" can explain Kodak's actions. *Aspen Skiing Co.*, 472 U.S., at 605; *United States v. Aluminum Co. of America*, 148 F.2d, at 432. Kodak contends that it has three valid business justifications for its actions: "(1) to promote interbrand equipment competition by allowing Kodak to stress the quality of its service; (2) to improve asset management by reducing Kodak's inventory costs; and (3) to prevent ISOs from free riding on Kodak's capital investment in equipment, parts and service." Factual questions exist, however, about the validity and sufficiency of each claimed justification, making summary judgment inappropriate.

Kodak first asserts that by preventing customers from using ISOs "it [can] best maintain high quality service for its sophisticated equipment" and avoid being "blamed for an equipment malfunction, even if the problem is the result of improper diagnosis, maintenance or repair by an ISO." Respondents have offered evidence that ISOs provide quality service and are preferred by some Kodak equipment owners. This is sufficient to raise a genuine issue of fact. See *International Business Machines Corp. v. United States*, 298 U.S., at 139-40 (rejecting IBM's claim that it had to control the cards used in its machines to avoid "injury to the reputation of the machines and the goodwill of" IBM in the absence of proof that other companies could not make quality cards); *International Salt Co. v. United States*, 332 U.S. 392, 397-98 (1947) (rejecting International Salt's claim that it had to control the supply of salt to protect its leased machines in the absence of proof that competitors could not supply salt of equal quality).

Moreover, there are other reasons to question Kodak's proffered motive of commitment to quality service; its quality justification appears inconsistent with its thesis that consumers are knowledgeable enough to lifecycle price, and its self-service policy. Kodak claims the exclusive-service contract is warranted because customers would otherwise blame Kodak equipment for breakdowns resulting from inferior ISO service. Thus, Kodak simultaneously claims that its customers are sophisticated enough to make complex and subtle lifecycle-pricing decisions, and yet too obtuse to distinguish which breakdowns are due to bad equipment and which are due to bad service. Kodak has failed to offer any reason why informational sophistication should be present in one circumstance and absent in the other. In addition, because self-service customers are just as likely as others to blame Kodak equipment for breakdowns resulting from (their own) inferior service, Kodak's willingness to allow self-service casts doubt on its quality claim. In sum, we agree with the Court of Appeals that respondents "have presented evidence from which a reasonable trier of fact could conclude that Kodak's first reason is pretextual." 903 F.2d, at 618.

There is also a triable issue of fact on Kodak's second justification — controlling inventory costs. As respondents argue, Kodak's actions appear inconsistent with any need to control inventory costs. Presumably, the inventory of parts needed to repair Kodak machines turns only on breakdown rates, and those rates should be the same whether Kodak or ISOs perform the repair. More importantly, the justification fails to explain respondents' evidence that Kodak forced OEMs, equipment owners, and parts brokers not to sell parts to ISOs, actions that would have no effect on Kodak's inventory costs.

Nor does Kodak's final justification entitle it to summary judgment on respondents' § 2 claim. Kodak claims that its policies prevent ISOs from "exploit[ing] the investment Kodak has made in product development, manufacturing and equipment sales in order to take away Kodak's service revenues." Kodak does not dispute that respondents invest substantially in the service market, with training of repair workers and investment in parts inventory. Instead, according to Kodak, the ISOs are free-riding because they have failed to enter the equipment and parts markets. This understanding of free-riding has no support in our caselaw.[33] To the contrary, as the Court of Appeals noted, one of the evils proscribed by the antitrust laws is the creation of entry barriers to potential competitors by requiring them to enter two markets simultaneously. *Jefferson Parish*, 466 U.S., at 14; *Fortner*, 394 U.S., at 509.

None of Kodak's asserted business justifications, then, are sufficient to prove that Kodak is "entitled to a judgment as a matter of law" on respondents' § 2 claim. Fed. Rule Civ. Proc. 56(c).

---

[33] Kodak claims that both *Continental T.V.* and *Monsanto* support its free-rider argument. Neither is applicable. In both *Continental T.V.*, 433 U.S., at 55, and *Monsanto,* 465 U.S., at 762-63, the Court accepted free-riding as a justification because without restrictions a manufacturer would not be able to induce competent and aggressive retailers to make the kind of investment of capital and labor necessary to distribute the product. In *Continental T.V.* the relevant market level was retail sale of televisions and in *Monsanto* retail sale of herbicides. Some retailers were investing in those markets; others were not, relying, instead, on the investment of the other retailers. To be applicable to this case, the ISOs would have to be relying on Kodak's investment in the service market; that, however, is not Kodak's argument.

IV

In the end, of course, Kodak's arguments may prove to be correct. It may be that its parts, service, and equipment are components of one unified market, or that the equipment market does not discipline the aftermarkets so that all three are priced competitively overall, or that any anticompetitive effects of Kodak's behavior are outweighed by its competitive effects. But we cannot reach these conclusions as a matter of law on a record this sparse. Accordingly, the judgment of the Court of Appeals denying summary judgment is affirmed.

It is so ordered.

JUSTICE SCALIA, with whom JUSTICE O'CONNOR and JUSTICE THOMAS join, dissenting.

....

The Court today finds in the typical manufacturer's inherent power over its own brand of equipment — over the sale of distinctive repair parts for that equipment, for example — the sort of "monopoly power" sufficient to bring the sledgehammer of § 2 into play. And, not surprisingly in light of that insight, it readily labels single-brand power over aftermarket products "monopoly power" sufficient to permit an antitrust plaintiff to invoke the *per se* rule against tying. In my opinion, this makes no economic sense. The holding that market power can be found on the present record causes these venerable rules of selective proscription to extend well beyond the point where the reasoning that supports them leaves off. Moreover, because the sort of power condemned by the Court today is possessed by every manufacturer of durable goods with distinctive parts, the Court's opinion threatens to release a torrent of litigation and a flood of commercial intimidation that will do much more harm than good to enforcement of the antitrust laws and to genuine competition....

II

On appeal in the Ninth Circuit, respondents, having waived their "rule of reason" claim, were limited to arguing that the record, construed in the light most favorable to them, supported application of the *per se* tying prohibition to Kodak's restrictive parts and service policy. As the Court observes, in order to survive Kodak's motion for summary judgment on this claim, respondents bore the burden of proffering evidence on which a reasonable trier of fact could conclude that Kodak possesses power in the market for the alleged "tying" product....

In the absence of the interbrand power, a seller's predominant or monopoly share of its single-brand derivative markets does not connote the power to raise derivative market prices *generally* by reducing quantity. As Kodak and its principal *amicus*, the United States, point out, a rational consumer considering the purchase of Kodak equipment will inevitably factor into his purchasing decision the expected cost of aftermarket support. "[B]oth the price of the equipment and the price of parts and service over the life of the equipment are expenditures that are necessary to obtain copying and micrographic services." If Kodak set generally supracompetitive prices for either spare parts or repair services without making an offsetting reduction in the price of its machines, rational consumers would simply turn to Kodak's competitors for photocopying and micrographic systems. True, there are — as the Court notes — the occasional irrational consumers that consider only the hardware cost at the time of purchase (a category that regrettably includes the Federal Government, whose "purchasing system," we are told, assigns foremarket purchases and aftermarket purchases to different entities). But we have never before premised the application of antitrust doctrine on the lowest common denominator of consumer.

The Court attempts to counter this theoretical point with theory of its own. It says that there are "information costs" — the costs and inconvenience to the consumer of acquiring and processing life-cycle pricing data for Kodak machines — that "could create a less responsive connection between service and parts prices and equipment sales." But this truism about the functioning of markets for sophisticated equipment cannot create "market power" of concern to the antitrust laws where otherwise there is none. "Information costs," or, more accurately, gaps in the availability and quality of consumer information, pervade real-world markets; and because consumers generally make do with "rough cut" judgments about price in such circumstances, in virtually any market there are zones within which otherwise competitive suppliers may overprice their products without losing appreciable market share. We have never suggested that the principal players in a market with such commonplace informational deficiencies (and, thus, bands of apparent consumer pricing indifference) exercise market power in any sense relevant to the antitrust laws. "While [such] factors may generate 'market power' in some abstract sense, they do not generate the kind of market power that justifies condemnation of tying." *Jefferson Parish Hospital Dist. No. 2 v. Hyde*, 466 U.S., at 27....

We have never before accepted the thesis the Court today embraces: that a seller's inherent control over the unique parts for its own brand amounts to "market power" of a character sufficient to permit invocation of the *per se* rule against tying....

I would instead evaluate the aftermarket tie alleged in this case under the rule of reason, where the tie's *actual* anticompetitive effect in the tied product market, together with its potential economic benefits, can be fully captured in the analysis, see, e.g., *Jefferson Parish Hospital Dist. No. 2 v. Hyde*, 466 U.S., at 41 (O'Connor, J., concurring in judgment). Disposition of this case does not require such an examination, however, as respondents apparently waived any rule-of-reason claim they may have had in the District Court. I would thus reverse the Ninth Circuit's judgment on the tying claim outright.

III

These considerations apply equally to respondents' § 2 claims. An antitrust defendant lacking relevant "market power" sufficient to permit invocation of the *per se* prohibition against tying *a fortiori* lacks the monopoly power that warrants heightened scrutiny of his allegedly exclusionary behavior. Without even so much as asking whether the purposes of § 2 are implicated here, the Court points to Kodak's control of "100% of the parts market and 80% to 95% of the service market," markets with "no readily available substitutes," and finds that the proffer of such statistics is sufficient to fend off summary judgment. But this showing could easily be made ... with respect to virtually any manufacturer of differentiated products requiring aftermarket support. By permitting antitrust plaintiffs to invoke § 2 simply upon the unexceptional demonstration that a manufacturer controls the supplies of its single-branded merchandise, the Court transforms § 2 from a specialized mechanism for responding to extraordinary agglomerations (or threatened agglomerations) of economic power to an all-purpose remedy against run-of-the-mill business torts.

In my view, if the interbrand market is vibrant, it is simply not necessary to enlist § 2's machinery to police a seller's intrabrand restraints. In such circumstances, the interbrand market functions as an infinitely more efficient and more precise corrective to such behavior, rewarding the seller whose intrabrand restraints enhance consumer welfare while punishing the seller whose control of the aftermarkets is viewed unfavorably by interbrand consumers. See *Business Electronics Corp.*, *supra*, at 725. Because this case comes to us on the assumption that Kodak is without such interbrand power, I believe we are compelled to reverse the judgment of the Court of Appeals. I respectfully dissent.

NOTES AND QUESTIONS

1. Does *Kodak* alter the approach taken in *Matsushita* regarding the burden of pleading and proof for a motion for summary judgment? How does the Court distinguish the moving party's burden in *Kodak* from that announced in *Matsushita*? What summary judgment standard applies when there is ambiguous evidence in the pretrial record?

2. Consider *Kodak*'s discussion of the plaintiff's burden of showing a tying arrangement violation. Does it differ from that articulated in Justice Stevens' opinion in *Jefferson Parish*, or is it closer to the analysis of Justice O'Connor's concurrence? After *Kodak*, is there still a *per se* rule for tying claims? If so, why did the majority not use the *per se* language?

3. Do you agree with Justice Scalia that the determinative question is Kodak's lack of market power in the interbrand equipment market? Is the lack of market power enough to discipline Kodak's pricing conduct in the derivative aftermarkets of service and parts? Is the majority's point simply that it is a fact question to be decided at trial whether, if Kodak raises prices too high for the aftermarkets of parts and service, customers will not continue to buy Kodak machines? Or, is the factual issue at trial whether, when a defendant lacks market power in the interbrand market, its opportunistic conduct can still violate section 1 if it exercises market power over its own parts or service because certain customers are "locked-in" to the manufacturer's equipment? *See* Hovenkamp, *Market Power in Aftermarkets: Antitrust Policy and the Kodak Case*, 40 UCLA L. Rev. 1447 (1993).

4. The majority opinion in *Kodak* restricts a broad interpretation of *Matsushita*, at least where the plaintiff's economic theory of antitrust enforcement — use of dominant market power to create a tying arrangement in the intrabrand market — can be shown to have an anticompetitive, exclusionary effect. The Court seemed to return to the traditional summary judgment standard when, in the Court's opinion, the enforcement theory is not economically implausible.

5. With regard to market power, as discussed in Chapter 6, note the Court's holding: it is not economically implausible for a firm to have the use of market power in an intrabrand (parts and service) market, even when there is competition and a lack of market power in the interbrand market (equipment). Thus, *Matsushita* does not apply. Importantly, the Court holds that a single brand of a product or service can be a relevant, separate market under the Sherman Act. This, of course, is highly relevant under both sections 1 and 2 of the Sherman Act where market power is then determined within the defined market. See discussion in Chapter 6.

6. *Kodak* rests, in the main, on a controversial analysis that relates market power to the economics of switching costs and imperfect information by consumers. The costs of switching to new products and the costs of less than perfect information may make the defendants' market power more inelastic and consumers less mobile. Does *Kodak*'s switching and information costs analysis turn section 1 or 2 into a consumer protection statute that can be triggered whenever the market does not signal, nor the seller furnish, complete product information? Does it signal that false or deceptive advertising can be an antitrust violation?

7. Any suggestion that *Kodak* signalled a return to *Poller*-like hostility toward summary judgment in predation cases was undermined by the Supreme Court's decision a year later in *Brooke Group Ltd. v. Brown & Williamson Tobacco Corp.*, 509 U.S. 209 (1993). That decision, which involved a judgment notwithstanding the verdict rather than summary judgment, indicated that the plaintiff's burden in predatory pricing cases is very high. Unless the evidence is extremely strong that predation is profitable, summary disposition is apparently appropriate. The decision is reprinted in Chapter 6.

8. For a review of representative cases subsequent to *Kodak*, *see Digital Equipment Corp v. Uniq Digital Technologies, Inc.*, 73 F. 3d. 756 (7th Cir. 1996) (rejecting an expansive reading of *Kodak*; no "lock-in" when a computer and its operating system are purchased by the customer at the same time); *Lee v. Life Ins. Co. of North America*, 23 F. 3d. 14 (1st Cir. 1994) (same; distinguishing *Kodak*'s "derivative after market analysis"); *Virtual Maintenance, Inc. v. Prime Computer, Inc.* 11 F.3d 660 (6th Cir. 1993) (reviewing on remand after *Kodak* an earlier decision on a tying claim).

In *Kodak*, you will recall, the Court concluded that aftermarket power might exist even though Kodak had no power in the primary market because poorly informed customers might purchase a copier not knowing about subsequent repair costs, and thus be "locked in," since it would ordinarily be cheaper to pay a monopoly price for parts rather than discard the copier and purchase a different brand. Both the *Digital* and *Lee* cases noted the obvious fact that the lock-in theory applies only if there is a time gap between the decision to buy the copier and the need for repair parts. Thus, in *Digital* a computer purchaser could not be locked in to an operating system when both had to be purchased at the same time; and in *Lee* a student registered in a certain college could not be locked in to a certain brand of student health insurance when the decision to register and information about mandatory health insurance were given to the student simultaneously. In such cases, power in the primary market must be established by the usual criteria.

Upon remand of *Kodak* by the Supreme Court, the district court jury found for the ISOs on the attempt to monopolize theory, but not on the tying arrangement theory, which the plaintiffs had dropped. The judge entered a ten-year permanent injunction requiring Kodak to sell "all parts" to the plaintiffs. The Ninth Circuit affirmed. *Image Technical Services, Inc. v. Eastman Kodak Co.*, 125 F.3d 1195 (9th Cir. 1997), *cert. denied*, 118 S. Ct. 1560 (1998). That decision is discussed in Chapter 6.

9. The lower courts are divided on how *Kodak's* theory of aftermarket liability without market power in the primary market affects tying claims by franchisees. In *Collins v. International Dairy Queen, Inc.*, 939 F. Supp. 875 (M.D. Ga. 1996), the plaintiff alleged that the Dairy Queen franchise indeed possesses market power in the national market for ice cream franchises, given its 91.3 percent market share. Although Dairy Queen argued that the relevant market should be fast food franchises, where it has a mere 2.5 percent market share, the court held that the franchisee had at least presented evidence that "would not foreclose a rational trier of fact from finding in their favor on the question of the proper definition of the relevant tying market ...." The court also held that the franchisee stated a claim for tying under *Kodak* because it alleged that the franchisor did not disclose adequately the scope of the tying arrangement and the extent to which it would deny franchisees the right to use cheaper comparable products. The court also noted that franchisees could face dangers similar to the information and switching costs present in *Kodak*.

By contrast, in *Queen City Pizza, Inc. v. Domino's Pizza, Inc.*, 922 F. Supp. 1055 (E.D. Pa. 1996), *aff'd*, 124 F.3d 430 (3d Cir. 1997), the court held that one franchise cannot constitute a relevant market for tying purposes. Furthermore, the court stated that *Kodak* could never apply to franchises because any claims by franchisees that franchisors did not disclose adequately the terms of the franchise agreement are strictly matters of contract law. In the words of the *Queen City* court:

> The important economic distinction that must be made is between pre- and postcontract economic power. Precontract, competition among franchisors

(such as McDonald's or Kentucky Fried Chicken) to sign up franchisees prevents [a single franchisor] from exercising any economic power in setting contract terms with potential franchisees. [The franchisor], although it possesses a trademark, does not possess any economic power in the market in which it operates — the fast food franchising (or perhaps, more generally, the franchising) market. Postcontract, on the other hand, a franchisor can use the threat of termination to "hold up" a franchisee that has made a specific investment in the marketing arrangement. However, this potential economic power has nothing to do with market power, ultimate consumers' welfare, or antitrust.

The court then concluded that:

> The economic power [the defendant] possesses results not from the unique nature of the product or from its market share in the fast food franchise business, but from the franchise agreement. And as recognized above, allegations of wrongdoing in the post-contractual setting implicate principles of contract, and are not the concern of the antitrust laws.

Which of these decisions is correct? A relevant market is a grouping of sales such that customers cannot easily switch to something else in response to a price increase in that grouping. A contract, of course, has a roughly similar effect. When a contract obligates the purchaser to take a stipulated good at a certain price, the purchaser cannot readily switch away if the contract subsequently becomes unfavorable in comparison with alternative opportunities elsewhere. Switching would place the purchaser in breach of the contract.

Indeed, most long-term purchase contracts have this type of "lock-in" effect. For example, if A contracts to sell B 100 tons of coal per year for ten years at $10 per ton, both A and B are "locked in" in the sense that (1) A is obliged to continue providing the coal at $10 even if the market price moves higher; and (2) B is obliged to take the coal and pay $10 even if the market price moves lower. The more open ended the contract, or the more issues it leaves unresolved, the more harmful might be the future consequences of such lock-in. Consider this example: L and T enter into a lease agreement for a commercial building, providing for a twenty-year lease and rental rates that increase by five percent annually. Suppose that after T has established itself the rental market goes into decline and actual market rates decrease or else increase by much less than five percent per year. The unfortunate T must pay a higher-than-market rate, however, because it is "locked-in" to the lease terms. Even if T could break the contract without penalty, it would lose any investment made in that particular location; thus the contract imposes "switching costs" that may effectively force T to pay the higher lease rate rather than moving to a building with a lower cost.

But clearly any legal problems that arise from T's injury are problems of contract law and negotiation, not antitrust problems. This is true even if the unfavorable lease forces T to pay "monopoly" rental rates for an extended period. Perhaps T did not foresee that rental rates would not increase as rapidly as the lease provided; perhaps information from which to make this prediction was not available at the time. For example, perhaps an unanticipated downturn in business depressed local rental rates, leaving only T to pay the higher rates stipulated in its agreement with L.

Further, not every instance of unfavorable contract lock-in results from unforeseen changes in market circumstances. Some contract buyers may be locked in to high contract prices because of fraud or misrepresentation by the sellers. For example, the landlord in the hypothetical lease might have misrepresented the building's value, understated its cost of operation, or overstated the traffic flow. Once again, the result of such misrepresentations might well be that the tenant under such a lease ends up paying more than the market value of the lease in question. But again, any lawsuit that the tenant might bring against the misrepresenting landlord would be in contract law, the law of landlord-tenant relations, or perhaps the law of fraud or misrepresentation; it would not be antitrust law.

This conclusion rests, in part, on the fact that the contractually defined grouping of sales covered by such a contract does not become an antitrust "relevant market" simply because the contract forces the buyer to pay more than the market price. To be sure, the lease requiring the tenant to pay more than market value has characteristics that resemble those of a relevant antitrust market. *First,* any price greater than the price that would be charged under competition might be seen as a "monopoly" price. *Second,* the contract imposes significant "switching costs" on the buyer/lessee in that he cannot abandon the lease without breaching the contract or perhaps losing any investment he has made in the leased premises. Thus we might say that the single building covered by the lease is a "relevant market" that has become monopolized by the landlord's misrepresentations.

But this conclusion would be incorrect for several reasons of both principle and policy. *First,* an economic market is a grouping of sales such that *general market circumstances* make consumer substitution very difficult. Numerous things may make it difficult for any particular buyer to substitute one product for another. For example, the fact that I own a pair of shoes accommodating only 24-inch strings means that I am "locked in" to shoestrings of that length, but that hardly establishes a relevant market for 24-inch shoestrings.

Second, given the ubiquity of contractual lock-in as described above, finding a "relevant market" on such a basis would turn antitrust into an engine for resolving contract disputes generally, and perhaps even for intervening in perfectly valid contracts where circumstances turned out to be less favorable than a buyer (or seller) predicted. The contracting system encourages market participants to take rational risks at the time of contracting. Antitrust intervention providing *ex post* "fixes" for contracts that have become unfavorable to one party or the other would not only exceed antitrust's mission, it would also undermine the market for assessing risks by providing post-hoc relief for those who lost, thus reducing or destroying the incentives for those who win as well. But the entrepreneurial market depends on parties' willingness to take risks.

Finally, who is injured by the tying arrangements in these cases? For example, in *Queen City, supra*, the plaintiffs alleged a relevant market of "pizza dough sold to Domino's Pizza franchisees." But pizza dough is made of flour, salt, water, and some other common ingredients. Not even a large pizza firm like Domino's would have a significant share of the market for these ingredients. In that case, what would happen if Domino's began charging its franchisees more money for its own pizza dough? Presumably, they would have higher costs and would respond by making less pizza. But if the pizza market is competitive, other pizza makers such as Pizza Hut, Godfathers, and thousands of independents would simply make more. Consumers would not be injured at all.

Other courts have tried to limit *Kodak* in other ways. For example, *PSI Repair Services v. Honeywell*, 104 F.3d 811 (6th Cir.), *cert. denied*, 117 S. Ct. 2434 (1997), concluded that a parts/aftermarket "lock-in" did not create significant power where the defendant had refused from the first inception of sales to provide aftermarket parts to independents. By contrast, Kodak had instituted the policy after having sold parts to ISOs for some time; as a result, there was a significant group of customers who had purchased a Kodak machine at a time when ISOs had been able to obtain aftermarket parts, and continued to use this equipment after Kodak changed its policy to one of not selling the parts to ISOs. As the court later explained:

> By changing its policy after its customers were "locked in," Kodak took advantage of the fact that its customers lacked the information to anticipate this change. Therefore, it was Kodak's own actions that increased its customers' information costs. In our view, this was the evil condemned by the Court and the reason for the Court's extensive discussion of information costs.... Put another way, the Court rejected the premise that imperfect consumer information resulting from basic market imperfections [rather than the contrivance of the defendant] could be used as a basis to infer market power for purposes of the Sherman Act.... Accepting PSI's argument would expose many manufacturers of durable, expensive equipment to potential antitrust liability for having inherent power over the aftermarkets of their products, a result certainly not intended by *Kodak.*...

The Seventh Circuit came to substantially the same conclusion in *Digital Equip. Corp. v. Uniq Digital Techs.*, 73 F.3d 756, 763 (7th Cir. 1996).

For a more detailed discussion of *Kodak's* implications for tying arrangements, *see* Lawrence T. Festa, III, Comment, Eastman Kodak Co. v. Image Technical Services, Inc.: *The Decline and Fall of the Chicago Empire?*, 68 Notre Dame L. Rev. 619, 668-72 (1993).

10. Not all circuits require a plaintiff to name a third party conspirator in order to state a claim for an illegal tying arrangement. In *Systemcare Inc. v. Wang*

Laboratories Corp., 117 F.3d 1137 (10th Cir. 1997), the Tenth Circuit held that a contract between a buyer and seller satisfies the concerted action element of section 1 of the Sherman Act where the seller coerces a buyer's acquiescence in a tying arrangement imposed by the seller:

> The essence of section 1's contract, combination, or conspiracy requirement in the tying context is the *agreement*, however reluctant, of a buyer to purchase from a seller a tied product or service along with a tying product or service. To hold otherwise would be to read the words 'contract' and 'combination' out of section 1.

Id. at 1142-3. The court went on to state that such behavior denies the general market "independent centers of decisionmaking" by effectively deciding for the buyer where certain products will be purchased. *Id.* at 1143. The Seventh and Ninth Circuits also have followed this approach to tying arrangements between buyers and sellers.

11. *Sports Racing Services, Inc. v. Sports Car Club of America, Inc.*, 131 F.3d 874 (10th Cir. 1997), concerned the interplay between standing, the direct purchaser rule, and illegal tying arrangements. At issue was defendant's policy of requiring that certain race cars, namely "Spec Racer" and "Shelby Can Am" cars, and their parts be sold solely by or through its for-profit subsidiaries.

Plaintiff John Freeman was a member of the defendant association and owner of Sports Racing Services, which, up until early 1991, sold Spec Racer cars and parts to subdealers, racing teams, and drivers, including Freeman himself. Freeman and SRS brought a few antitrust claims, including one for illegal tying of racing services (the tying product) to cars and parts (the tied products). The district court had dismissed all of the plaintiffs' claims on the basis of lack of standing; thereby ignoring all substantive claims. The Tenth Circuit reversed and remanded the case for consideration of the substantive issues. SRS was a direct purchaser of cars and parts from the wholly owned subsidiary of SCCA, but Freeman, on the other hand, could only be considered an indirect purchaser of cars and parts from SCCA and a direct purchaser from SRS. However, Freeman was a direct purchaser of the tying product (racing services) from SCCA. Quoting *Eastman Kodak*, the court held that Freeman's standing as an indirect purchaser of cars and parts did not bar his claim, since "[t]he essential characteristic of an invalid tying arrangement lies in the seller's exploitation of its control over the tying product that the buyer either did not want at all, or might have preferred to purchase elsewhere on different terms." *Id.* at 887. Furthermore:

> Critical to a tying claim is the fact that the seller forced the buyer to purchase the tied product in order to get the tying product, but it is not critical that the buyer have purchased the tied product directly from the seller. An illegal tie may be found where the seller of the tying product does not itself sell the tied product but merely requires the purchaser of the tying product to buy the

tied product from a designated third party rather than from any other competitive source that the buyer might prefer.

Id. Hence, Freeman had standing to bring a tying claim, and the case was remanded to give this and the other dismissed issues in the case proper consideration.

***

Microsoft Corp. was accused in *United States v. Microsoft*, 980 F. Supp. 537 (D.C. Cir. 1997), of acting in violation of a consent decree forbidding it from tying the sales of "other products" to the sales of its hugely successful personal computers. The decree was entered in 1995, barring the company from becoming party to any license agreement that is conditioned, either expressly or impliedly, upon the licensing of any separate product. Microsoft is not prohibited, however, from developing new integrated products. The conflict deals with the company's Internet browser (the tied product) and the question of whether it is an integrated or separate product capable of being tied to sales of Windows 95 (the tying product). The Antitrust Division, and the court, feared that Microsoft was using the browser to gain an unfair advantage on Netscape, its main competition in providing internet services. The district court ordered a preliminary injunction pending discovery, and the judge appointed a special master to assist the court in assessing the technological evidence and determining whether the browser is integrated, thus avoiding the charge of an illegal tying arrangement. Both issues were appealed.

UNITED STATES V. MICROSOFT CORPORATION

147 F.3d 935 (D.C. Cir. 1998)

JUDGE WILLIAMS.

The Department [of Justice]'s 1994 complaint alleged a variety of anticompetitive practices, chiefly in Microsoft's licensing agreements with OEMs [original equipment manufacturers, which make computers, install operating systems and other software that they have licensed from vendors such as Microsoft, and sell the package to end users]. Along with it, the Department filed a proposed consent decree limiting Microsoft's behavior, the product of negotiations between Microsoft, the Department and European competition authorities. Most relevant here is §IV(E) of the decree: Microsoft shall not enter into any License Agreement in which the terms of that agreement are expressly or impliedly conditioned upon:

> (i) the licensing of any other Covered Product, Operating System Software product or other product (provided, however, that this provision in and of itself shall not be construed to prohibit Microsoft from developing integrated products); or

(ii) the OEM not licensing, purchasing, using or distributing any non-Microsoft product. The Department sees a violation of §IV(E)(i) in Microsoft's marketing of Windows 95 and its web browser, Internet Explorer ("IE").

...

Microsoft argues that the district court failed to comply with Federal Rule of Civil Procedure 65(a)(1)'s command, "No preliminary injunction shall be issued without notice to the adverse party." We agree. Obviously the Department's request for a contempt citation provided no such notice, for the governing criteria are completely different. To defeat the contempt petition, all Microsoft had to do was to show that the Department failed to meet its burden of showing that the consent decree unambiguously barred its conduct. For a preliminary injunction, by contrast, traditional equitable standards would require the government to show substantial likelihood of success on the merits (here, that the decree, properly construed, barred the conduct), plus risk of irreparable injury, lack of substantial injury to the opposing party, and consistency with the public interest. See *City-Fed Financial Corp. v. Office of Thrift Supervision*, 58 F.3d 738, 746 (D.C. Cir. 1995). The contempt petition did not alert Microsoft to contest these factors.

Nor could the Department's request for a permanent injunction serve as notice — even putting aside Microsoft's argument that the request was contingent on a situation that never arose (see section II). The request for a permanent injunction amounted to no more than a request for a clarification, and thus would require only a showing that the Department's reading of the consent decree was correct. It did not put into play the equitable factors of interim irreparable injury to the requester, harm to the party to be enjoined, and effects on the public interest. But resolution of these is essential in granting a preliminary injunction; the proponent must make a showing about the interim risks precisely in order to counterbalance the lack of any final ruling in its favor on the merits.

...

The purpose of Rule 65(a)(1)'s notice requirement is to allow the opposing party a fair opportunity to oppose the preliminary injunction ... Preliminary injunctions entered without notice to the opposing party are generally dissolved ... Appellate courts have, however, on occasion allowed a procedurally flawed injunction to remain in place pending a proper hearing on remand if the equities support such a disposition. See, e.g., *Rosen v. Siegel*, 106 F.3d 28, 33 (2d Cir. 1997).

The Department urges us to do so here. Evaluating such a request requires the court to consider the traditional equitable factors as apparent on the existing record ... We do not believe that a reviewing court must entertain such a request; if the record were so deficient as to make effective evaluation of the equities impossible, a court might do better simply to vacate the injunction as a matter of course — especially where, as here, the injunction was sought only rather obliquely ... [H]owever, the record here is enough for us at least to make a reasonable appraisal of the Department's eventual likelihood of success on the merits, and this factor proves dispositive. Silence at this stage would risk considerable waste of litigative resources. "When the district court's estimate of the probability of success depends on an incorrect or mistakenly applied legal premise, 'the appellate court furthers the interest of justice by providing a ruling on the merits to the extent that the matter is ripe, though technically the case is only at the stage of application for preliminary injunction.'" *Air Line Pilots Ass'n Int'l v. Eastern Air Lines, Inc.*, 863 F.2d 891, 895 (D.C. Cir. 1988) (quoting *Natural Resources Defense Council, Inc. v. Morton*, 458 F.2d 827, 832 (D.C. Cir. 1972). When reviewing preliminary injunctions we have generally not been hesitant to offer interpretation and guidance on the substantive legal issues ... We thus turn to the interpretation of §IV(E)(i), on which the merits of the Department's case depend. Our review of a district court's interpretation of a consent decree is de novo ...

Section IV(E) arose from a 1993 complaint filed with the Directorate General IV of the European Union ("DG IV") (the principal competition authority in Europe). Novell, a rival software vendor, alleged that Microsoft was tying its MS-DOS operating system to the graphical user interface provided by Windows 3.11. Before the introduction of Windows 95, which integrated the two, Microsoft marketed the DOS component and the Windows component of the operating system separately, and Windows 3.11 could be operated with other DOS products. But Novell, which marketed a competing DOS product, DR-DOS, complained that by means of specific marketing practices — particularly "per processor and per system licenses," J.A. 754 — Microsoft was creating economic incentives for OEMs to preinstall MS-DOS as well as Windows 3.11, thereby using its power in the market for DOS-compatible graphical user interfaces (where it commanded a near 100% market share) to affect OEM choice in the DOS market. J.A. 839-48. During June 1994 negotiations with the Department, Microsoft proposed the possibility of a joint settlement, and representatives of DG IV participated in meetings in Brussels and later in Washington, D.C. On July 15, 1994, the three sides reached agreement and Microsoft and the Department signed a stipulation agreeing to entry of the consent decree, including §IV(E). Both Microsoft and the Department characterize §IV(E) as an "antitying" provision.

...

Section IV(E)(i) represented the parties' agreed "solution" to the problem posed by the Novell complaint. The practices complained of there, coupled with the decree's explicit acceptance of Windows 95, establish the competing models that guide our resolution of the present dispute. Whatever else §IV(E)(i) does, it must forbid a tie-in between Windows 3.11 and MS-DOS, and it must permit Windows 95. Thus if the relation between Windows 95 and IE is similar to the relation between Windows 3.11 and MS-DOS, the link is presumably barred by §IV(E)(i). On the other hand, a counter-analogy is Windows 95 itself, which the decree explicitly recognizes as a single "product" (it defines it as a "Covered Product," §II(1)(v)), even though, as we have said, Windows 95 combines the functionalities of a graphical interface and an operating system. If the Windows

95/IE combination is like the MS-DOS/graphical interface combination that comprises Windows 95 itself, then it must be permissible.

...

We think it quite possible, however, to find a construction of §IV(E)(i) that is consistent with the antitrust laws and accomplishes the parties' evident desires on entering the decree. The Department and DG IV were concerned with the alleged anticompetitive effects of tie-ins. Microsoft's goal was to preserve its freedom to design products that consumers would like. Antitrust scholars have long recognized the undesirability of having courts oversee product design, and any dampening of technological innovation would be at cross purposes with antitrust law. Thus, a simple way to harmonize the parties' desires is to read the integration proviso of §IV(E)(i) as permitting any genuine technological integration, regardless of whether elements of the integrated package are marketed separately.

...

This reading requires us, of course, to give substantive content to the concept of integration. We think that an "integrated product" is most reasonably understood as a product that combines functionalities (which may also be marketed separately and operated together) in a way that offers advantages unavailable if the functionalities are bought separately and combined by the purchaser.

The point of the test is twofold and may be illustrated by its application to the paradigm case of the Novell complaint and the subsequent release of Windows 95. First, "integration" suggests a degree of unity, something beyond merely placing disks in the same box. If an OEM or end user (referred to generally as "the purchaser") could buy separate products and combine them himself to produce the "integrated product," then the integration looks like a sham. If Microsoft had simply placed the disks for Windows 3.11 and MS-DOS in one package and covered it with a single license agreement, it would have offered purchasers nothing they could not get by buying the separate products and combining them on their own.

Windows 95, by contrast, unites the two functionalities in a way that purchasers could not; it is not simply a graphical user interface running on top of MS-DOS. Windows 95 is integrated in the sense that the two functionalities — DOS and graphical interface — do not exist separately: the code that is required to produce one also produces the other. Of course one can imagine that code being sold on two different disks, one containing all the code necessary for an operating system, the other with all the code necessary for a graphical interface. But as the code in the two would largely overlap, it would be odd to speak of either containing a discrete functionality. Rather, each would represent a disabled version of Windows 95. The customer could then "repair" each by installing them both on a single computer, but in such a case it would not be meaningful to speak of the customer "combining" two products. Windows 95 is an example of what Professor Areeda calls "physical or technological interlinkage that the customer cannot perform." X P. Areeda, E. Elhauge, & H. Hovenkamp, *Antitrust Law* ¶ 1746b at 227, 228 (1996).

So the combination offered by the manufacturer must be different from what the purchaser could create from the separate products on his own. The second point is that it must also be better in some respect; there should be some technological value to integration. Manufacturers can stick products together in ways that purchasers cannot without the link serving any purpose but an anticompetitive one. The concept of integration should exclude a case where the manufacturer has done nothing more than to metaphorically "bolt" two products together ... X Areeda, *Antitrust Law* ¶ 1746 at 227 (discussing literal bolting). Thus if there is no suggestion that the product is superior to the purchaser's combination in some respect, it cannot be deemed integrated.

It might seem difficult to put the two elements discussed above together. If purchasers cannot combine the two functionalities to make Windows 95, it might seem that there is nothing to test Windows 95 against in search of the required superiority. But purchasers can combine the functionalities in their stand- alone incarnations. They can install MS-DOS and Windows 3.11. The test for the integration of Windows 95 then comes down to the question of whether its integrated design offers benefits when compared to a purchaser's combination of corresponding stand-alone functionalities. The decree's evident embrace of Windows 95 as a permissible single product can be taken as manifesting the parties' agreement that it met this test.

The short answer is thus that integration may be considered genuine if it is beneficial when compared to a purchaser combination. But we do not propose that in making this inquiry the court should embark on product design assessment. In antitrust law, from which this whole proceeding springs, the courts have recognized the limits of their institutional competence and have on that ground rejected theories of "technological tying." A court's evaluation of a claim of integration must be narrow and deferential. As the Fifth Circuit put it, "[S]uch a violation must be limited to those instances where the technological factor tying the hardware to the software has been designed for the purpose of tying the products, rather than to achieve some technologically beneficial result. Any other conclusion would enmesh the courts in a technical inquiry into the justifiability of product innovations." *Response of Carolina, Inc. v. Leasco Response, Inc.*, 537 F.2d 1307, 1330 (5th Cir. 1976).

In fact, Microsoft did, in negotiations, suggest such an understanding of "integrated." In response to the Department and DG IV's statement of concern about tying, it asserted its right to "continue to develop integrated products like [Windows 95] that provide technological benefits to end users." Microsoft later withdrew this qualifying phrase, in order, it claims, to avoid the application of "vague or subjective criteria" — though why the absence of criteria should cure a vagueness problem is unclear. But we do not think that removing the phrase can drain the word "integrated" of all meaning, and we do not accept the suggestion that the Department and DG IV bargained for an "integrated products" proviso so boundless as to swallow §IV(E)(i). Significantly, Microsoft assured the Department and DG IV that the elimination of the qualifying phrase "did not represent a substantive change."

We believe this understanding is consistent with tying law. The Court in *Eastman Kodak Co. v. Image Tech. Servs.*, 504 U.S. 451, for example, found parts and service separate products because sufficient consumer demand existed to make separate provision efficient. See *id.* at 462. But we doubt that it would have subjected a self-repairing copier to the same analysis; i.e., the separate markets for parts and service would not suggest that such an innovation was really a tie-in. (The separate opinion, we take it, makes roughly the same point by its observation about digital cameras. See Sep. Op. at 3-4.) Similarly, Professor Areeda argues that new products integrating functionalities in a useful way should be considered single products regardless of market structure. See X Areeda, *Antitrust Law* ¶ 1746b.

We emphasize that this analysis does not require a court to find that an integrated product is superior to its stand-alone rivals. See *ILC Peripherals Leasing Corp. v. International Business Machines Corp.*, 458 F. Supp. 423, 439 (N.D. Cal. 1978) ("Where there is a difference of opinion as to the advantages of two alternatives which can both be defended from an engineering standpoint, the court will not allow itself to be enmeshed 'in a technical inquiry into the justifiability of product innovations.'") (quoting *Leasco*, 537 F.2d, at 1330), *aff'd per curiam sub nom. Memorex Corp. v. IBM Corp.*, 636 F.2d 1188 (9th Cir. 1980). We do not read §IV(E)(i) to "put[ ] judges and juries in the unwelcome position of designing computers." IX Areeda, Antitrust Law ¶ 1700j at 15 (1991). The question is not whether the integration is a net plus but merely whether there is a plausible claim that it brings some advantage. Whether or not this is the appropriate test for antitrust law generally, we believe it is the only sensible reading of § IV(E)(i).

On the facts before us, Microsoft has clearly met the burden of ascribing facially plausible benefits to its integrated design as compared to an operating system combined with a stand-alone browser such as Netscape's Navigator. Incorporating browsing functionality into the operating system allows applications to avail themselves of that functionality without starting up a separate browser application. Further, components of IE 3.0 and even more IE 4 — especially the HTML [Hypertext Markup Language] reader — provide system services not directly related to Web browsing, enhancing the functionality of a wide variety of applications. Finally, IE 4 technologies are used to upgrade some aspects of the operating system unrelated to Web browsing. For example, they are used to let users customize their "Start" menus, making favored applications more readily available. They also make possible "thumbnail" previews of files on the computer's hard drive, using the HTML reader to display a richer view of the files' contents. Even the Department apparently concedes that integration of functionality into the operating system can bring benefits; responding to a comment on the proposed 1994 consent decree (which the Department published in the Federal Register as required by the Tunney Act), it stated that "a broad injunction against such behavior generally would not be consistent with the public interest." 59 Fed. Reg. 59426, 59428 (Nov. 17, 1994).

The conclusion that integration brings benefits does not end the inquiry we have traced out. It is also necessary that there be some reason Microsoft, rather than the OEMs or end users, must bring the functionalities together. See X Areeda, Elhauge & Hovenkamp, *Antitrust Law* ¶ 1746b at 227; ¶ 1747 at 229. Some more subtleties emerge at this stage, parallel to those encountered in determining the integrated status of Windows 95. Microsoft provides OEMs with IE 4 on a separate CD-ROM (a fact to which the Department attaches great significance). It might seem, superficially, that the OEM is just as capable as Microsoft of combining the browser and the operating system.

But the issue is not which firm's employees should run particular disks or CD-ROMs. A program may be provided on three disks — Windows 95 certainly could be — but it is not therefore three programs which the user combines. Software code by its nature is susceptible to division and combination in a way that physical products are not; if the feasibility of installation from multiple disks meant that the customer was doing the combination, no software product could ever count as integrated. The idea that in installing IE 4 an OEM is combining two stand-alone products is defective in the same way that it would be nonsensical to say that an OEM installing Windows 95 is itself "combining" DOS functionality and a graphical interface. As the discussion above indicates, IE 3 and IE 4 add to the operating system features that cannot be included without also including browsing functionality. Thus, as was the case with Windows 95, the products — the full functionality of the operating system when upgraded by IE 4 and the "browser functionality" of IE 4 — do not exist separately. This strikes us as an essential point. If the products have no separate existence, it is incorrect to speak of the purchaser combining them. Purchasers who end up with the Windows 95/IE package may have installed code from more than one disk; they may have taken the browser out of hiding; they may have upgraded their operating system — indeed, Netscape characterizes the installation of IE 4 as "really an OS [operating system] upgrade." But they have not combined two distinct products.

What, then, counts as the combination that brings together the two functionalities? Since neither fully exists separately, we think the only sensible answer is that the act of combination is the creation of the design that knits the two together. OEMs cannot do this: if Microsoft presented them with an operating system and a stand-alone browser application, rather than with the interpenetrating design of Windows 95 and IE 4, the OEMs could not combine them in the way in which Microsoft has integrated IE 4 into Windows 95. They could not, for example, make the operating system use the browser's HTML reader to provide a richer view of information on the computer's hard drive, J.A. 1665 — not without changing the code to create an integrated browser. This reprogramming would be absurdly inefficient. Consequently, it seems clear that there is a reason why the integration must take place at Microsoft's level. This analysis essentially replays our comparison of Windows 95 to a bundle of MS-DOS and Windows 3.11 and concludes that the Windows 95/IE package more closely resembles Windows 95 than it does the bundle. The factual conclusion is, of course, subject to reexamination on a more complete record. On the facts before us, however, we are inclined to conclude that the Windows 95/IE package is a genuine integration; consequently, §IV(E)(i) does not bar Microsoft from offering it as one product.

...

The preliminary injunction was issued without adequate notice and on an erroneous reading of §IV(E)(i) of the consent decree. We accordingly reverse and remand. The reference to the master was in effect the imposition on the parties of a surrogate judge and either a clear abuse of discretion or an exercise of wholly non-existent discretion. We grant mandamus to vacate the reference.

NOTE

One source of Microsoft's economic power is said to be network "externalities," or situations where the value of a good increases as a larger number of people use it. In the case of computer operating systems most people value not merely performance for its own sake but also compatibility with as large a number of other users as possible. The presence of network externalities may entail that the firm that initially acquires a large installed base can maintain its position even when superior products come along. People value technical superiority, but they value compatibility with everyone else even more. If that is so, Microsoft might be able continually to fold one version of its operating system into the next by gradual improvements and assurances that new versions will be fully compatible with existing versions. For an excellent discussion of the complex issues, see M. Lemley & D. McGowan, *Legal Implications of Network Economic Effects*, 86 Cal. L. Rev. 479 (1998). Network externalities may explain how a firm can have durable market power in a rapidly changing industry such as computer software. They also suggest why practices such as bundling or exclusive dealing, which may have only modest effects in other industries, can completely exclude even superior rivals in an industry subject to network externalities.

4. PACKAGE LICENSING AND BUNDLING: INTELLECTUAL PROPERTY LICENSES

Package licensing or block-booking is a marketing device in which products are bundled together and sold or leased under a single unit price. Holders of multiple patents or copyrights have used packages to license their products. The application of the antitrust law governing tying arrangements to the marketing of patent or copyright products poses special problems.

In certain important respects, the patent and copyright laws are in conflict with, and at the same time complementary of, the antitrust laws. The antitrust laws are designed to promote competition, while the patent and copyright laws are often said to grant legal monopolies. 35 U.S.C. §§ 1-293 (1988); 17 U.S.C. §§ 1-810 (1988). The reason behind the statutorily granted rights in intellectual property is to create incentives for investment in new products or ideas, and to the extent that new innovations are forthcoming because of these laws, the policy of promoting competition is advanced. *See, e.g., Study of the Subcommittee of Patents, Trademarks and Copyrights of the Senate Committee on the Judiciary, the Patent System and the Modern Economy*, S. Rep. 167, Study No. 2, 84th Cong., 2d Sess. 2 (1957).

Many of the same arguments put forth regarding other vertical, distributional restraints apply as well to package transactions. Cost efficiencies may be achieved in the licensed distribution system if patented or copyrighted products are licensed in a package. Package pricing may be more functional than individual pricing. It has been said that patent and copyright licensing practices should be judged by their ability to facilitate collusion. Remarks of A. Lipsky, Jr., "Current Antitrust Division Views on Patent Licensing Practices," before the ABA Antitrust Section 5 (Nov. 5, 1981). On the other hand, some courts believed that the leverage theory may be applicable to package licensing because of the economic power inherent in the grant of legal monopoly from the patent and copyright laws. To the extent that the patentee wishes to extend and exploit the patent rights beyond the lawful patent itself to other products, the antitrust laws are implicated. *See generally* Bauer, *A Simplified Approach to Tying Arrangements: A Legal and Economic Analysis*, 33 Vand. L. Rev. 283, 298-99 (1980); L. Sullivan, *Handbook of the Law of Antitrust* 463-66 (1977). But as noted previously, the leverage theory has been frequently criticized and its analytical force correspondingly diminished.

UNITED STATES V. LOEW'S, INC.

371 U.S. 38 (1962)

JUSTICE GOLDBERG delivered the opinion of the Court.

These consolidated appeals* present as a key question the validity under § 1 of the Sherman Act of block booking of copyrighted feature motion pictures for television exhibition. We hold that the tying agreements here are illegal and in violation of the Act.

The United States brought separate civil antitrust actions in the Southern District of New York in 1957 against six major distributors of pre-1948 copyrighted motion picture feature films for television exhibition, alleging that each defendant had engaged in block booking in violation of § 1 of the Sherman Act. The complaints asserted that the defendants had, in selling to television stations, conditioned the license or sale of one or more feature films upon the acceptance by the station of a package or block containing one or more unwanted or inferior films.... The sole claim of illegality rested on the manner in which each defendant

---

* Although the government won on the merits below, it filed a cross-appeal arguing that the scope and specificity of the decree were inadequate. Throughout the opinion, the Court, when referring to the defendants, uses the term appellants. The term is not used in the case in reference to the government. — Eds.

had marketed its product. The successful pressure applied to television station customers to accept inferior films along with desirable pictures was the gravamen of the complaint.

....

The court entered separate final judgments against the defendants, wherein each was enjoined from

> (A) Conditioning or tying, or attempting to condition or tie, the purchase or license of the right to exhibit any feature film over any television station upon the purchase or license of any other film;
> (B) Conditioning the purchase or license of the right to exhibit any feature film over any television station upon the purchase or license for exhibition over any other television station of that feature film, or any other film;
> (C) Entering into any agreement to sell or license the right to exhibit any feature film over any television station in which the differential between the price or fee for such feature film when sold or licensed alone and the price or fee for the same film when sold or licensed with one or more other film [*sic*] has the effect of conditioning the sale or license of such film upon the sale or license of one or more other films.

I

This case raises the recurring question of whether specific tying arrangements violate § 1 of the Sherman Act. This Court has recognized that "[t]ying agreements serve hardly any purpose beyond the suppression of competition".... They are an object of anti-trust concern for two reasons — they may force buyers into giving up the purchase of substitutes for the tied product, ... and they may destroy the free access of competing suppliers of the tied product to the consuming market.... A tie-in contract may have one or both of these undesirable effects when the seller, by virtue of his position in the market for the tying product, has economic leverage sufficient to induce his customers to take the tied product along with the tying item. The standard of illegality is that the seller must have "sufficient economic power with respect to the tying product to appreciably restrain free competition in the market for the tied product...." Market dominance — some power to control price and to exclude competition — is by no means the only test of whether the seller has the requisite economic power. Even absent a showing of market dominance, the crucial economic power may be inferred from the tying product's desirability to consumers or from uniqueness in its attributes.[4]

---

[4] Since the requisite economic power may be found on the basis of either uniqueness or consumer appeal, and since market dominance in the present context does not necessitate a demonstration of market power in the sense of § 2 of the Sherman Act, it should seldom be necessary in a tie-in sale case to embark upon a full-scale factual inquiry into the scope of the relevant market for the tying product and into the corollary problem of the seller's percentage share in that market. This is

The requisite economic power is presumed when the tying product is patented or copyrighted, *International Salt Co....* This principle grew out of a long line of patent cases which had eventuated in the doctrine that a patentee who utilized tying arrangements would be denied all relief against infringements of his patent.... These cases reflect a hostility to use of the statutorily granted patent monopoly to extend the patentee's economic control to unpatented products. The patentee is protected as to his invention, but may not use his patent rights to exact tribute for other articles.

Since one of the objectives of the patent laws is to reward uniqueness, the principle of these cases was carried over into antitrust law on the theory that the existence of a valid patent on the tying product, without more, establishes a distinctiveness sufficient to conclude that any tying arrangement involving the patented product would have anticompetitive consequences.... In *United States v. Paramount Pictures, Inc.*, 334 U.S. 131, 156-159, the principle of the patent cases was applied to copyrighted feature films which had been block booked into movie theaters. The Court reasoned that

> Where a high quality film greatly desired is licensed only if an inferior one is taken, the latter borrows quality from the former and strengthens its monopoly by drawing on the other. The practice tends to equalize rather than differentiate the reward for the individual copyrights. Even where all the films included in the package are of equal quality, the requirement that all be taken if one is desired increases the market for some. Each stands not on its own footing but in whole or in part on the appeal which another film may have. As the District Court said, the result is to add to the monopoly of the copyright in violation of the principle of the patent cases involving tying clauses.

Appellants attempt to distinguish the *Paramount* decision in its relation to the present facts: the block booked sale of copyrighted feature films to exhibitors in a new medium — television. Not challenging the District Court's finding that they did engage in block booking, they contend that the uniqueness attributable to a copyrighted feature film, though relevant in the movie-theater context, is lost when the film is being sold for television use. Feature films, they point out, constitute less than 8% of television programming, and they assert that films are "reasonably interchangeable" with other types of programming material and with other feature films as well.... They say that the Government's proof did not establish their "sufficient economic power" in the sense contemplated for nonpatented products.

Appellants cannot escape the applicability of *Paramount Pictures*. A copyrighted feature film does not lose its legal or economic uniqueness because it is shown on a television rather than a movie screen.

---

even more obviously true when the tying product is patented or copyrighted, in which case, as appears in greater detail below, sufficiency of economic power is presumed. Appellants' reliance on *United States v. E.I. du Pont de Nemours & Co.,* 351 U.S. 377, is therefore misplaced.

The district judge found that each copyrighted film block booked by appellants for television use "was in itself a unique product"; that feature films "varied in theme, in artistic performance, in stars, in audience appeal, etc.," and were not fungible; and that since each defendant by reason of its copyright had a "monopolistic" position as to each tying product, "sufficient economic power" to impose an appreciable restraint on free competition in the tied product was present, as demanded by the *Northern Pacific* decision.[6]

Moreover, there can be no question in this case of the adverse effects on free competition resulting from appellants' illegal block booking contracts. Television stations forced by appellants to take unwanted films were denied access to films marketed by other distributors who, in turn, were foreclosed from selling to the stations. Nor can there be any question as to the substantiality of the commerce involved. The 25 contracts found to have been illegally block booked involved payments to appellants ranging from $60,800 in the case of Screen Gems to over $2,500,000 in the case of Associated Artists. A substantial portion of the licensing fees represented the cost of the inferior films which the stations were required to accept....

There may be rare circumstances in which the doctrine we have enunciated under § 1 of the Sherman Act prohibiting tying arrangements involving patented or copyrighted tying products is inapplicable. However, we find it difficult to conceive of such a case, and the present case is clearly not one.

Vacated and remanded.

NOTES AND QUESTIONS

1. *Loew's* indicated that a supplier could make a package offer simultaneously with an offer to license the products separately, but it prohibited differentiations in price between individual prices and package prices which were not cost justified. Thus, block pricing can be less than the sum of the individual prices to the extent of "cost savings." An element of coercion or leverage is lacking if the licenses are individually available. If the prices on individual products are higher, however, one could infer coercion. What might be included as a "legitimate cost justification?" Would this be limited to sale and distribution costs? Would a broader standard, such as "commercial reality," be too costly to administer and interpret?

2. Recall *Broadcast Music*, reprinted in Chapter 4, wherein the Court held that blanket licensing by associations of artists, writers, and publishers did not constitute a per se horizontal price fixing agreement where individual copyright licenses were available.

3. Recall from the discussion above that variable proportion tying arrangements are often used to facilitate price discrimination. It has been suggested that

---

[6] To use the trial court's apt example, forcing a television station which wants "Gone With The Wind" to take "Getting Gertie's Garter" as well is taking undue advantage of the fact that to television as well as motion picture viewers there is but one "Gone With The Wind."

block-booking — a form of fixed proportion tie-in — can be used for the same purpose. Suppose, for example, that two different television stations, which cater to two different audiences, place different values on different kinds of films. Station *A* values a license to show *Casablanca* at $7000, while it values a license for *I Was a Teenage Werewolf* at only $4000. On the other hand, station *B* values the license for *Casablanca* at only $5000, while it values the license for *Werewolf* at $6000. Assuming that the licensor must charge both stations the same price, it can do one of the following three things:

> (a) It can charge $7000 for *Casablanca* and $6000 for *Werewolf.* In this case it will license *Casablanca* once (to station *A*) and *Werewolf* once (to station *B*). Total revenues will be $13,000.
> (b) It can charge $5000 for *Casablanca* and $4000 for *Werewolf.* In this case both stations will take both films and the total revenues will be $18,000.
> (c) It can "package" the two films together and sell the package at $11,000. In this case both stations will take the package and the total revenues will be $22,000.

See G. Stigler, *United States v. Loew's, Inc.: A Note on Block-Booking,* 1963 Sup. Ct. Rev. 152-54 (1963); Markovits, *Tie-Ins, Reciprocity, and the Leverage Theory,* 76 Yale L.J. 1397, 1406-08 (1967).

Whether such block-booking is "price discrimination" depends on the meaning of the term. The ratio of price to marginal cost for the *package* is the same for both stations, assuming that both stations impose the same costs on the seller, so no price discrimination exists from the seller's viewpoint. On the other hand, the ratio of marginal cost to what each station believes it is paying for each individual film is different for station *A* than station *B*. Economists have been content to call this "simulated price discrimination."

5. FULL LINE FORCING, FULL SYSTEM CONTRACTS, AND FRANCHISE ARRANGEMENTS

When a supplier requires a dealer to purchase a complete line of related products, though less is desired, the vertical arrangement is known as full line forcing. Although the dealer is not generally explicitly forbidden from stocking the products of the supplier's competitors, the practical effect of the full system contract may inhibit the dealer from carrying competing lines of merchandise. Thus the consequences of full line forcing may be to foreclose the market to competitors or potential competitors of the seller that insists on the full system contract, and to deny the dealer freedom to choose from whom it will purchase its products and parts. The competitive effect, therefore, may be similar to the typical tying arrangement and exclusive dealing restriction.

The same efficiency justifications discussed previously in this chapter have application to full line contracts. Economies may be achieved in production, distribution, and marketing of certain products jointly, rather than individually. Moreover, cost economies may enable the manufacturer and supplier to charge less for the full line of products than the sum of individually priced products. In addition, the supplier may believe that in order to maintain its brand image and "good will" reputation it is necessary that its dealers carry its full line of products, particularly its components or parts.

While full line forcing is a form of tying arrangement, a strict per se analysis has generally not been applied. Several reasons suggest this conclusion. In addition to the emerging efficiency analysis, which permits business justification for the tie-in to be explored, it is not always clear whether separate products are involved, as is required under *Times-Picayune* and *Fortner*. Products must be defined and distinguished as separate items, rather than merely the aggregation of one or a whole system or unit of components. In the franchise context the "two product" requirement was discussed in *Siegel v. Chicken Delight, Inc.*, 448 F.2d 43 (1971), *cert. denied*, 405 U.S. 955 (1972), and *Principe v. McDonald's Corp.*, 631 F.2d 303 (4th Cir. 1980), with differing results. Consider the following courts' resolution of the "two product" problem.

UNITED STATES V. JERROLD ELECTRONICS CORP.

187 F. Supp. 545 (E.D. Pa.), *aff'd per curiam*, 365 U.S. 567 (1961)

JUDGE VAN DUSEN.

[Defendant sold television antenna systems and in doing so refused to sell separately the components or individual items of the system. The complete system and components were sold only on the condition that the purchaser also enter into a service contract with Jerrold.]

The difficult question raised by the defendants is whether this should be treated as a case of tying the sale of one product to the sale of another product or merely as the sale of a single product. It is apparent that, as a general rule, a manufacturer cannot be forced to deal in the minimum product that could be sold or is usually sold. On the other hand, it is equally clear that one cannot circumvent the anti-trust laws simply by claiming that he is selling a single product. The facts must be examined to ascertain whether or not there are legitimate reasons for selling normally separate items in a combined form to dispel any inferences that it is really a disguised tie-in.

There are several facts presented in this record which tend to show that a community television antenna system cannot properly be characterized as a single product. Others who entered the community antenna field offered all of the equipment necessary for a complete system, but none of them sold their gear exclusively as a single package as did Jerrold. The record also establishes that the number of pieces in each system varied considerably so that hardly any two versions of the alleged product were the same. Furthermore, the customer was charged for each item of equipment and not a lump sum for the total system. Finally, while Jerrold had cable and antennas to sell which were manufactured by other concerns, it only required that the electronic equipment in the system be bought from it.

In rebuttal, it must first be noted that the attitude of other manufacturers, while relevant, is hardly conclusive. Equally significant is the fact that the record indicates that some customers were interested in contracting for an installed system and not in building their own. Secondly, it was the job the system was designed to accomplish which dictated that each system be "custom made" in the sense that there were variations in the type and amount of equipment in each system. This, in turn, explains determining cost on a piece by piece, rather than a lump sum, basis. Finally, while the non-electronic equipment could be ordered from other sources and the system would be useless without the antenna and connecting cable, it is generally agreed that the electronic equipment is the most vital element in the system and Jerrold was still in charge of assembling all of the equipment into a functioning system.

Balancing these considerations only, the defendants' position would seem to be highly questionable. The several deviations from the normal situation one would expect to find become particularly suspect when viewed in the context of Jerrold's market leverage resulting from its highly regarded head end equipment. There is a further factor, however, which, in the court's opinion, makes Jerrold's decision to sell only full systems reasonable. There was a sound business reason for Jerrold to adopt this policy. Jerrold's decision was intimately associated with its belief that a service contract was essential. This court has already determined that, in view of the condition of Jerrold, the equipment, and the potential customers, the defendants' policy of insisting on a service contract was reasonable at its inception. Jerrold could not render the service it promised and deemed necessary if the customer could purchase any kind of equipment he desired. The limited knowledge and instability of equipment made specifications an impractical, if not impossible, alternative. Furthermore, Jerrold's policy could not have been carried out if separate items of its equipment were made available to existing systems or any other customer because the demand was so great that this equipment would find its way to a new system. Thus, the court concludes that Jerrold's policy of full system sales was a necessary adjunct to its policy of compulsory service and was reasonably regarded as a product as long as the conditions which dictated the use of the service contract continued to exist. As the circumstances changed and the need for compulsory service contracts disappeared, the economic reasons for exclusively selling complete systems were eliminated. Absent these economic reasons, the court feels that a full system was not an appropriate sales unit. The defendants have the burden not only of establishing the initial existence of the facts necessary to support their claim but also their continuing existence in view of the fact that it is not disputed that the conditions did change. The defendants have not satisfied this latter burden. It has already been noted that on the present record it would be a matter of speculation to determine how long the conditions justifying Jerrold's policy remained in effect.

The defendants also assert a further justification for its policy insofar as it applied to systems using a large quantity of non-Jerrold equipment. Jerrold spent considerable time and effort in developing its head end equipment. As a result, its equipment was considered the best available and an asset to any system, since it affected the quality of the initial signal which would be transmitted through the rest of the system. The head-end equipment, while intricate, did not represent a large portion of the investment in a system because only a few items were involved. The real profit in a system came from the sale of the amplifiers, since a large number were involved. Jerrold felt that other companies who had not invested time and money into the development of satisfactory head-end equipment sought to take advantage of it by competing with it as to the amplifiers, but relying on Jerrold's head end equipment to make the system successful. [It] resented these other companies "picking our brains" and competing for the real source of profit. Jerrold, therefore, felt justified in recovering its substantial investment in the development of superior head end equipment by using it to preserve for itself a share of the more lucrative market for amplifiers. While the court is sympathetic with Jerrold's predicament, it does not feel that it provides sufficient justification for the use of a tying arrangement. If the demand for Jerrold's equipment was so great, it could recover its investment by raising its prices. Admittedly, the return would not be as great, but it provides sufficient protection to serve as a more reasonable and less restrictive alternative to a tying arrangement.

The court concludes that the defendants' policy of selling full systems only was lawful at its inception but constituted a violation of § 1 of the Sherman Act and § 3 of the Clayton Act during part of the time it was in effect.

PROBLEM 5.6

Sterling Electric, Inc. manufactures electric motors and replacement parts for the motors. Easy Startup, Inc. is a distributor of Sterling brand electric motors and parts.

Easy Startup has been a Sterling distributor for several years but it also carries other brands of electric motors and parts. From 1985 through 1989, Easy Startup was the largest distributor of Sterling parts but only fifth nationally in Sterling electric motors. Easy Startup purchased $100,000 of Sterling electric motors in 1985-87, $75,000 in 1987-88, and $110,000 in 1989. Its corresponding purchases of parts were larger: $300,000 for 1985-87 and $350,000 for 1987-89. During this period of time Sterling had annual sales over $10 million.

In 1987 Sterling instituted a new distribution program. It required each of its nonexclusive distributors, like Easy Startup, to buy a minimum amount of its electric motors if the distributors wanted to continue to sell the Sterling parts. Under the contract with its distributors, Sterling had the right to terminate the distributors for failure to buy the agreed minimum quantities of electric motors.

Sterling warned Easy Startup that if it did not purchase more of the Sterling electric motors, it risked termination as a Sterling distributor. Thereafter in 1989

Easy Startup, fearing the loss of access to Sterling motors, steered its customers toward the Sterling electric motors even though Easy Startup normally would have recommended other brands of motors. As a result, Sterling motor sales increased. Nevertheless, in late 1989, Sterling terminated Easy Startup as a parts and motor distributor because Easy Startup had not purchased (and sold) a sufficient number of the electric motors.

Easy Startup decides to sue Sterling for the termination. Sterling concedes that it has 100% dominance in the parts market for its own electric motors; that is, Sterling's parts cannot be used on any other brands of electric motors and no other manufacturer makes parts compatible with and usable in the Sterling electric motor. Sterling, however, has only 12% market share in the market for electric motors parts and 5% market share in the market for electric motors. Other potential evidence suggests that there are economic barriers to entry into the market for parts compatible with Sterling motors since the demand for Sterling parts will accommodate only one manufacturer. Further evidence indicates that a large number of Sterling distributors had entered into the same minimum quantities requirements contract as did Easy Startup.

1. As counsel for Easy Startup, what antitrust arguments would you advance to show that there was a per se or rule of reason violation of section 1 of the Sherman Act and section 3 of the Clayton Act?

2. As counsel for defendant Sterling, what counter-arguments would you raise that no antitrust violations are present? *See Parts & Elec. Motors, Inc. v. Sterling Elec., Inc.*, 826 F.2d 712 (7th Cir. 1987).

NOTE

1. In *Smith Mach. Co. v. Hesston Corp.*, 878 F.2d 1290 (10th Cir. 1989), the court held that a per se analysis was inappropriate for a supplier's requirement that a farm equipment retailer wanting to sell the supplier's balers and windrowers also must sell its tractors. The court characterized this requirement as a nonprice vertical restraint that was subject to a rule of reason analysis. Under the reasonableness test, the court found the full line forcing lawful because the retailer was not prohibited from carrying competing equipment lines and the effect was that the forcing actually enhanced interbrand competition by making the manufacturer's tractor available for sale. No output reduction would occur, the court concluded, and at worst there would be only a substitution of one tractor for another. For the plaintiff to establish a violation, it would have to show that the forcing restricted the marketing of the competitor's products by limiting competition in the consumer market. "[F]oreclosure of choice to an ultimate consumer appears to be the principal key to a tie that is illegal per se." *Id.* at 1297.

A recent decision likened the purchase of patty paper as a condition to purchasing patty machines by a dealer of hamburger machines and patty paper to an arrangement in which a manufacturer requires a dealer to carry one product in its line to receive another. Consequently, the court concluded that the conditional sale was more like a full-line system or exclusive dealing arrangement which, the court observed, does not threaten competition to the same extent as a tying arrangement that more directly affects consumers. *Roy B. Taylor Sales, Inc. v. Hollymatic Corp.* 28 F.3d 1379 (5th Cir. 1994). Under the arrangement that the Fifth Circuit approved, the plaintiff dealer in restaurant equipment was required to stock the defendant's hamburger patty paper as a condition of carrying its hamburger patty machines. But the same condition was not imposed upon the plaintiff's customers: *they* were free to purchase the machine with or without the paper. If the vice of the tying arrangement is foreclosure of alternate makers of patty paper, then there was no foreclosure, was there? Is there any other way such an arrangement could injure competition?

PROBLEM 5.7

Mozart is an independent auto parts distributor and manufacturer. Mercedes-Benz is an automobile and automotive parts manufacturer. Mercedes-Benz operates in the United States through 400 franchised dealerships. Each dealer must enter a franchise contract which, in part, states:

> Dealer shall neither sell or offer to sell for use in connection with Mercedes-Benz cars nor use in the repair or servicing of Mercedes-Benz passenger cars any parts other than genuine Mercedes-Benz parts or parts expressly approved by the U.S. distributor if such parts are necessary to the mechanical operation of such passenger cars.

Mozart contends that the above contract is a tying arrangement that is per se unlawful because Mercedes-Benz is tying the Mercedes parts to the passenger car and its trademark, and that Mercedes-Benz and the dealers have conspired to boycott independent replacement parts distributors.

1. (a) Consider whether a quality control and goodwill defense by Mercedes-Benz would be a valid business justification for the exclusive dealing and tying contracts with the dealers.

(b) Are less restrictive alternatives available to protect Mercedes-Benz's reputation? If there are, does this fact make the contractual arrangement a violation of the Sherman and Clayton Acts?

2. Consider also whether Mozart has standing to raise the antitrust issues. *See Mozart Co. v. Mercedes-Benz of N. Am., Inc.*, 833 F.2d 1342 (9th Cir. 1987).

6. UNFAIR METHODS OF COMPETITION: TYING OF PRODUCTS SOLD BY OTHERS WHERE THERE IS A FINANCIAL INCENTIVE

If a supplier desires that its retailer deal in the products of another supplier with whom the first supplier has a financial relationship, the question arises whether a tie-in-like arrangement is present. Franchisors may require that the franchisee purchase supplies from approved sources. The legal inquiry centers around whether the requirement has coercive features, and this in turn may depend on whether the franchisor (supplier) has a financial stake in the sale or lease. *Kentucky Fried Chicken Corp. v. Diversified Packaging Corp.*, 549 F.2d 368 (5th Cir. 1977). If there is no financial relationship between the two suppliers, the price discrimination theory would seem to be inapplicable. The problem typically has been addressed in the petroleum marketing context: whether the supplying oil company can encourage its dealers to buy automotive products such as tires, batteries, and accessories from particular suppliers. Under the FTC Act, the question has been whether these sales-commission plans are inherently coercive and therefore an unfair method of competition.

In *FTC v. Texaco, Inc.*, 393 U.S. 223 (1968), the Supreme Court held that it was a violation of section 5 of the FTC Act (unfair method of competition) for Texaco to induce its service station dealers to buy tires, batteries, and accessories from Goodrich when, in return, Goodrich paid a commission to Texaco. As a basis for its holding, the Court upheld the FTC's finding that (1) Texaco had dominant economic power over its dealers (40% of the dealers leased stations from Texaco with only a one-year lease); (2) Goodrich paid Texaco a 10% commission on all purchases by Texaco service station dealers and in return Texaco agreed to promote the Goodrich products to Texaco dealers; and (3) from 1952 through 1956 Texaco dealers bought $245 million of Goodrich products. The Court based its economic theory on leveraging: "the utilization of economic power in one market to curtail competition in another."

> Here [Goodrich] has purchased the oil company's economic power and used it as a partial substitute for competitive merit in gaining a major share of the [product] market. The nonsponsored brands do not compete on the even terms of price and quality competition; they must overcome, in addition, the influence of the dominant oil company that has been paid to induce its dealers to buy the recommended brand.

Consider whether Texaco was simply price discriminating? Suppose that Texaco "encourages" its dealers to sell only Goodrich tires. Goodrich agrees to pay Texaco a $1.00 commission for each tire that is sold by a Texaco dealer. If the dealer has a large tire business it will make many sales, and Texaco will receive many commissions. If the dealer sells no tires at all, however, it might still be a successful dealership in the primary object of the franchise, sales of gasoline.

A second possible explanation for the arrangement, however, is protection of Texaco's goodwill. Texaco presumably uses a closely controlled franchise system so that there will be a great deal of similarity among individually owned Texaco gasoline stations all across the country. A motorist from Boston who pulls into a Texaco station in Waco, Texas, has some idea about what kind of service she will receive. Perhaps part of that expected service is that the dealer offers Goodrich tires, a brand in which she has developed some confidence.

BIBLIOGRAPHY AND COLLATERAL READINGS

Books

P. Areeda & H. Hovenkamp, Antitrust Law (vols. 8, 9, 10 (with E. Elhauge), & 11).

R. Blair & D. Kaserman, Antitrust Economics 281-425 (1985).

R. Blair & D. Kaserman, Law and Economics of Vertical Integration and Control (1983).

E. Gellhorn & W. Kovacic, Antitrust Law and Economics 278-328 (4th ed. 1994).

H. Hovenkamp, Federal Antitrust Policy, chs. 9-11 (2d ed. 1994).

S. Ross, Principles of Antitrust (1993).

E.T. Sullivan & J. Harrison, Understanding Antitrust and Its Economic Implications, ch. 5 (3d ed. 1998).

F. Warren-Boulton, Vertical Control of Markets (1978).

Articles

Arquit, Market Power in Vertical Restraints Cases, 60 Antitrust L.J. 921 (1991).

Baker, The Supreme Court and the Per Se Tying Rule: Cutting the Gordian Knot, 66 Va. L. Rev. 1235 (1980).

Bauer, A Simplified Approach to Tying Arrangements: A Legal and Economic Analysis, 33 Vand. L. Rev. 283 (1980).

Blair & Kaserman, The *Albrecht* Rule and Consumer Welfare: An Economic Analysis, 33 U. Fla. L. Rev. 461 (1982).

Bork, The Rule of Reason and Per Se Concept: Price Fixing and Market Division, 75 Yale L.J. 373 (1966).

Bowman, Prerequisites and Effects of Resale Price Maintenance, 22 U. Chi. L. Rev. 825 (1955).

Bowman, Tying Arrangements and the Leverage Problem, 67 Yale L.J. 19 (1957).

Burstein, A Theory of Full-Line Forcing, 55 Nw. U. L. Rev. 62 (1960).

Buttler, Lane & Phillips, The Futility of Antitrust Attacks on Tie-in Sales: An Economic and Legal Analysis, 36 Hastings L.J. 173 (1984).

Comanor, Vertical Price-Fixing, Vertical Market Restrictions and the New Antitrust Policy, 98 Harv. L. Rev. 983 (1985).

Dam, Fortner Enterprises v. United States Steel: Neither a Borrower Nor a Lender Be, 1969 Sup. Ct. Rev. 1.

Easterbrook, Maximum Price Fixing, 48 U. Chi. L. Rev. 886 (1981).

Faruki, The Defense of Terminated Dealer Litigation: A Survey of Legal and Strategic Considerations, 46 Ohio St. L.J. 925 (1985).

Floyd, Vertical Antitrust Conspiracies After *Monsanto* and *Russell Stover*, 33 U. Kan. L. Rev. 269 (1985).

Flynn, The "Is" and "Ought" of Vertical Restraints After *Monsanto*, 71 Cornell L. Rev. 1095 (1986).

Flynn & Ponsoldt, Legal Reasoning and the Jurisprudence of Vertical Restraints: The Limitations of Neoclassical Economic Analysis in the Resolution of Antitrust Disputes, 62 N.Y.U. L. Rev. 1125 (1987).

Goldberg, Free Rider Problems, Imperfect Pricing and Economics of Retailing Services, 79 Nw. U. L. Rev. 736 (1984).

Gould & Yamey, Professor Bork on Vertical Price-Fixing, 76 Yale L.J. 722 (1967).

Grimes, The Seven Myths of Vertical Price Fixing: The Politics and Economics of a Century-Long Debate, 21 Sw. U. L. Rev. 1285 (1992).

Hay, Vertical Restraints After *Monsanto*, 70 Cornell L. Rev. 418 (1985).

Hovenkamp, Market Power in Aftermarkets: Antitrust Policy and the *Kodak* Case, 40 UCLA L. Rev. 1447 (1993).

Hovenkamp, Tying Arrangements and Class Actions, 36 Vand. L. Rev. 213 (1983).

Hovenkamp, Vertical Restrictions and Monopoly Power, 64 B.U. L. Rev. 521 (1984).

Kaplow, Extension of Monopoly Power Through Leverage, 85 Colum. L. Rev. 515 (1985).

Klein & Murphy, Vertical Restraints as Contract Enforcement Mechanisms, 31 J.L. & Econ. 265 (1988).

Kramer, The Supreme Court and Tying Arrangements: Antitrust As History, 69 Minn. L. Rev. 1013 (1985).

Liebeler, Intrabrand Cartels Under *GTE Sylvania*, 30 UCLA L. Rev. 1 (1982).

Marvel, Exclusive Dealing, 25 J.L. & Econ. 1 (1982).

Marvel & McCafferty, The Political Economy of Resale Price Maintenance, 94 J. Pol. Econ. 1074 (1986).

Meese, Tying Meets the New Institutional Economics: Farewell to the Chimera of Forcing, 146 U. Pa. L. Rev. 1 (1997).

Perry & Besanko, Resale Price Maintenance and Manufacturer Competition for Exclusive Dealerships, 39 J. Indus. Econ. 517 (1991).

Piraino, A Reformed Antitrust Approach to Distributor Terminations, 68 Notre Dame L. Rev. 271 (1992).

Pitofsky, In Defense of Discounters: The No-Frills Case for a *Per Se* Rule Against Vertical Price Fixing, 71 Geo. L.J. 1487 (1983).

Pitofsky, The *Sylvania* Case: Antitrust Analysis of Non-Price Vertical Restrictions, 78 Colum. L. Rev. 1 (1978).

Posner, The Rule of Reason and the Economic Approach: Reflections on the Sylvania Decision, 45 U. Chi. L. Rev. 1 (1977).

Robinson, Explaining Vertical Agreements: The Colgate Puzzle and Antitrust Method, 80 Va. L. Rev. 577 (1994).

Slawson, A New Concept of Competition: Reanalyzing Tie-in Doctrine After Hyde, 30 Antitrust Bull. 257 (1985).

Slawson, Excluding Competition Without Monopoly Power: The Use of Tying Arrangements to Exploit Market Failure, 36 Antitrust Bull. 457 (1991).

Soloman & Jaffe, Exclusive Distribution and Antitrust, 53 Fordham L. Rev. 491 (1984).

Strasser, Antitrust Policy for Tying Arrangements, 34 Emory L.J. 253 (1985).

Telser, Why Should Manufacturers Want Fair Trade?, 3 J.L. & Econ. 86 (1960).

Turner, The Definition of Agreement Under the Sherman Act: Conscious Parallelism and Refusals to Deal, 75 Harv. L. Rev. 655 (1962).

White, Black and White Thinking in the Grey Areas of Antitrust: The Dismantling of Vertical Restraint Regulation, 60 Geo. Wash. L. Rev. 1 (1991).

Young, The Economic Interest Requirement in the Per Se Analysis of Tying Arrangements: A Worthless Inquiry, 58 Fordham L. Rev. 1353 (1990).

MONOPOLY STRUCTURE, POWER AND CONDUCT

Chapter 6

INTRODUCTION

"Market power" is the ability of a firm to obtain higher profits by reducing output and selling at a higher price. "Monopolization," the central concern of this chapter, is illegal conduct by which a single firm seeks either to obtain or to retain market power.

SECTION I. THE PROBLEM OF MONOPOLY

UNITED STATES V. AMERICAN CAN CO.

230 F. 859 (D. Md. 1916), *appeal dismissed*, 256 U.S. 706 (1921)

JUDGE ROSE.

The United States, hereinafter called the "government," brings this proceeding under the fourth section of the Anti-Trust Act of July 2, 1890. It says that the American Can Company, a New Jersey corporation, was formed and has since been maintained in violation of the first and second sections of that statute. [The United States sought dissolution of the company.]

... The government says the defendant, by its size, its wealth, and its power, exerts a great influence upon the entire trade in cans, and that this influence, in some very important respects ... is so great that it may, without straining words, be said to dominate the market.

The defendant answers its size is not a crime. The government replies, in substance:

> True, provided such size is the result of natural and legitimate growth, but not when it is the outcome of unlawful means used for the very purpose of securing a control of the market. In the latter case, so long as the control continues, the illegal purpose is still in process of execution, and, if nothing short of dissolving the defendant into a number of smaller companies will completely emancipate the trade, the court must decree such dissolution.

....

... It is quite possible that in an industry like can making, as it was carried on in the closing years of the last century by more than 100 separate concerns, no union, however desirable from the standpoint of either the can makers or the public, could have been brought about except by the efforts of some individuals who thought they could make a quick and large profit for themselves by uniting the various plants under one management, no matter what the immediate or even the ultimate results of such union might prove to be. If that be so, those who think the result desirable will hold that promoters' profits and the extravagant sums required to induce so many independent manufacturers to sell out were a part of the inevitable price of achieving a useful purpose. Unfortunately, under such circumstances the cost of getting rid of competition sometimes proves almost as great as that of letting it alone.

To pass from the general to the particular: The men who really brought about the organization of the defendant do not appear to have been more than five in number, and only one of them, Edwin Norton, was a can maker. He did practically all the work of persuading, inducing, or coercing the can makers to sell out. He and his brothers had been for a number of years the largest and doubtless the most generally known manufacturers of cans in the country, as he was certainly one of the most active and aggressive. The factories of his firm had probably the best equipment of labor saving machinery. Certainly in this respect they were surpassed by none.... The idea of forming a can combine seems to have occurred to him more than once, although the record appears to indicate that the scheme which was actually carried through originated, not with him, but with the defendant William H. Moore and his partner and brother, the defendant J. Hobart Moore....

The record shows that in the latter part of 1899 Norton was commissioned by the Moores to get options on can-making plants, and then, or later, on plants for making can-making machinery, as well. He set about this mission promptly, and apparently had little difficulty in getting many of the desired options.

....

How were so large a proportion of the can makers induced to sell? Fear of what would happen to them, if they did not, unquestionably had more or less influence with a good many of them. There is some testimony that Norton told some of them that if they did not sell out they would be put out.

The record does not affirmatively show that such threats were frequently made. They were not required. Apart from anything he said, apprehension was quite general that the only choice was between going out or being driven out. The country was at that time familiar with stories of the fate of those who in other lines of business had refused liberal offers from combinations previously formed. The records of the so-called Anti-Trust cases have since shown that some of these tales were not without foundation in fact. What was most feared was that a can maker who did not go into the combine would have difficulty in getting tin plate, the raw material of his business. The concern to which the defendant the American Steel & Tin Plate Company succeeded, and which, together with that successor, will be called the "Tin Plate Company," had been then recently organized. Prominent among those who officiated at its birth were the Moore Bros., Reid, and Leeds. Norton and others spoke as if the relations between the proposed can company and the new Tin Plate Company would be very close....

....

It is to be borne in mind that, for reasons already stated, few of the can makers were, or could have supposed themselves to have been, even moderately equipped to carry on a competitive struggle with a rival possessed of many times their capital. Some of them who were financially stronger than most of the others were elderly men, or were in poor health, or for other reasons were loath to venture upon so perilous a warfare.

....

As a rule, the prices paid were liberal, not only to the verge of extravagance, but in cases almost beyond the limits of prodigality. If Norton sometimes showed the can makers that there was steel in his scabbard, his hands always dropped gold. The record does not disclose a single case in which the price named in the option did not exceed the value of all the tangible property transferred. The amounts paid appear to have ranged all the way from 1½ to 25 times the sum which would have sufficed to have replaced the property sold with brand new articles of the same kind. Before agreeing on the figures to be inserted in an option, Norton does not appear to have taken the trouble either to make, or to cause to be made, any inspection or appraisement of the plant to be transferred. Under such circumstances, the ratio between the real value and the price named depended more upon the nerve or the impudence of the seller, than upon any estimate of his property's probable worth to the new combination.

....

With very few exceptions, all the options contained a clause which bound the sellers, in the event that it was accepted, not to engage for 15 years in can making within 3,000 miles of Chicago. Where the seller was a corporation, its principal officers personally bound themselves by like covenants. In some few instances, can makers declined so to restrict their freedom, and still their plants were bought. Nevertheless, the promoters obviously attached considerable importance to securing such covenants. It is in evidence that the owners of one plant struck it out from the first option they signed. Afterwards, they were induced to give another with it in, but in return were allowed to raise their price from $300,000 to $700,000.

....

Much can-making machinery, more or less in use as late as 1900 had never been patented, or, if it had been, the patents on it had expired. A great many of these machines were of such simple construction that they could be made in almost any fairly equipped machine shop. To secure control of all such would have been impossible. Some of the most modern machines, those by which a large part of the work formerly done by hand was performed automatically, were, however, covered by patents. If these patents could be secured and arrangements made with the few machine shops in the country which were then equipped for turning out machinery of that class, competition in can making and can selling would be greatly hampered. Indeed, if the possibility of competitors obtaining such machinery could be cut off for a comparatively limited period, possibly even for a year or two, the can company which acquired a number of plants equipped with such machinery, and which could obtain more of it from the manufacturers, could, if its operations otherwise were wisely carried on, secure a domination of the market, which could not be seriously shaken for years to come. The record shows that the defendant did acquire such control .... It sought for six years to close to its competitors the machine shops which really counted. The largest manufacturer of automatic machinery for can-making purposes was the E. W. Bliss Company. For the sum of $25,000 a quarter, that company agreed that for six years it would not make certain can-making machinery for anybody other than the defendant.... From the Adriance Machine Company defendant agreed it would annually for six years take $75,000 worth of machinery. That amount represented the full capacity of the machine company. To the Ferracute Machine Company, in return for exclusive privileges, the defendant guaranteed a profit of $10,000 a year for six years. Defendant induced the Bliss Company to break contracts which the latter had already made to furnish such machinery, and, when the injured parties sued the Bliss Company for damages thus resulting, the defendant paid both the expense of defending the suits and the substantial judgments some of the aggrieved parties recovered.

... The record amply justifies the assertion that for a year or two after defendant's formation it was practically impossible for any competitor to obtain the most modern, up-to-date, automatic machinery, and that the difficulties in the way of getting such machinery were not altogether removed until the expiration of the six years for which the defendant had bound up the leading manufacturers of such machinery.

....

The record does not disclose whether the promoters of the defendant really had reason to believe that they would be able practically to shut off the supply of tin plate from their competitors, as Norton in 1900 and early in 1901 was at least willing that the trade should think. As already stated, none of the promoters have seen fit to tell their story under oath. As it turned out, all the Tin Plate Company was willing to do was to bind itself to sell its tin plate to defendant at a certain fixed figure, below the price at which it sold to any one else. This preferential discount or rebate amounted, when the published list price of tin plate was $3.50 a base box, to about 64 cents on the quantity of plate required to make 1,000 3-pound packers' cans. This difference, the record shows, was far from negligible. In a close competitive struggle it might well have proved a decisive factor.

The defendant began to shut up plants [as] soon as it got possession of them. It kept on shutting them up until by April 21, 1903, it was operating only 36 can factories, and 3 machine shops, and it then proposed to close 5 more of the former and 1 or 2 of the latter. There has been a good deal of profitless dispute as to the proper term to describe what was done. What the government terms "dismantling" the defendant prefers to speak of as "transferring" or "concentrating." What actually took place is clear enough, whatever one may choose to call it. Two-thirds of the plants bought were abandoned within two years of their purchase. Many of them were never operated by the defendant at all, and others were closed after a few weeks or a few months. Where they had any machinery for which use could be found at some other of defendant's plants, such machinery was transferred to the place where it could be used, which might be a few blocks away in the same city or hundreds of miles off in another state. Where it was possible that a piece of machinery might some day be of some use, although there was no immediate call for it, it was sent to some abandoned factory building to be there stored until it was wanted, or until it became clear that it never would be. Such machines, and there appear to have been many of them, as were too obsolete for economical use, were broken up and their fragments sold as junk....

....

What happened shows that prices were put up to a point which made it apparently profitable for outsiders to start making cans with any antiquated or crude machinery they could find in old lumber rooms or which they could have made for them in a hurry, or even to resume can making by hand. The evidence on these points is absolutely conclusive. Can making became attractive. Any number of people began to make cans, or, at least, began to try to make them. Perhaps in some cases the prices which had been paid for can shops made them hope that if they could get a can shop they would be able to sell out at a figure which would make them comfortable for the rest of their days. At first, the defendant seems to have thought it would try to buy them out, and it bought a few of them, as already has been mentioned; but in a few weeks, if not in a few days, it became plain that such policy was impossible. In the first place, its money was gone.... There were too many new shops to buy them all, and, as it has turned out, it was easy enough to start some more. The real remedy would have been to reduce the price of cans. If defendant had not been under the necessity of realizing large and quick profits, doubtless it would have done so. Its mere cost of operation, excluding any allowance for capital investment, must have been below that of many of its poorly equipped competitors, who then rushed into the field. But, if prices had been reduced, the idea that there was a speedy fortune to be made by defendant's stockholders would have been too speedily dispelled. Other devices were resorted to. The attempt to keep up the price of cans was persisted in. In an effort to do so, the defendant itself sent brokers into the market and bought some millions of cans from its rivals. Some of these were very badly made, as was to be expected from new shops, equipped with wretched machinery and hastily rushed into business. These cans were stored for a while, and ultimately such of them as were salable at all were sold for what they would bring. Possibly these purchases did keep up the price longer than would otherwise have been the case.

....

Thus far consideration has been chiefly given to the government's charges against the defendant. Some of these have been held not well founded. It has been said that others are made out.

Defendant has directed much of the nine volumes of testimony it has offered, to show that whatever criticisms might be made as to the way in which it was formed, and to certain of its isolated acts since, it has on the whole served the can trade well, and that its dissolution would do harm and not good. There is no room for question that since 1901 there have been many improvements, not only in can making, but in can selling and in can delivery as well, and that these improvements are greatly appreciated by all who buy cans from can makers. There is the usual difficulty, in such cases, in telling how much of these good things are because of that which defendant has done and how much would have come about if defendant had never been thought of.

By 1904, if not earlier, the defendant had definitely abandoned the policy of charging prices which to the consumer seemed unduly high. It is natural, nevertheless, to ask whether since that time prices have been lower or higher than they would have been had it never come into being. The record does not give any certain answer to this question. A great many consumers of cans testified that the price has tended downward. Up to the time of the closing of the evidence in this case, that was generally true. There were fluctuations, and the downward trend was slight; but there was such a trend. A comparison of the price of tin plate and of cans from 1897 to 1913 shows that the prices of the latter for 1911, 1912, and 1913 were just about the same as they were in 1897, 1898, and 1899, when allowance is made for the difference in the cost of the former. The margin between the cost of the tin plate and the selling price of the cans seems to have been as great when, as now, cans were made and sold at prices fixed by the defendant, as it was when they were made and sold by its numberless predecessors in the business. The cans have been better, in that they have been more uniformly well made. With the machinery now in use there is no reason to think it costs appreciably more to make good than bad cans. The manufacturing cost is now less than it was before defendant's formation. It is true that each laborer employed now receives more wages than he did then, but so great has been the improvement in machinery that the actual labor cost per thousand cans is now materially less than it was 15 years ago. Moreover, as a result of better methods of manufacture, much less solder is now used, and a net saving of some importance is thereby effected. A reduction in the price of cans does not appear to be among the benefits the defendant has conferred upon the trade.

Defendant takes some credit to itself for bringing about a standardization in packers' cans, so that a No. 1, a No. 2, or a No. 3 can, of any one of the recognized types of openings, is now precisely the same, no matter from what shop it comes. A good deal of progress in this direction had been made before defendant was organized. The first effect, not of its formation, but of the policy adopted by it in its earlier history, was probably to retard rather than to accelerate this tendency. The prices it quoted brought about, as has been seen, an opening or reopening of a number of shops poorly fitted to make good cans. The owners of such establishments probably gave little thought to standardization or to any similar problem. Subsequently, the influence and example of defendant made greatly for uniformity. It is, however, probable that, even if it had never come into being, the pressure from the canners and other sources would ... have resulted in the general establishment of the standards now in use. It is very possible that it would have taken longer than it did.

Defendant makes good cans. It has always done so, at least after the first few months of its existence. The impression produced by the testimony is that it has been more uniformly successful in so doing than perhaps any of its competitors.... It is its policy to spare no trouble nor, within reasonable limits, expense to meet its customers' wishes. It is therefore not surprising that some users of certain sorts of general line cans feel that it can be safely depended on to make what they want. Some of them have reason to believe, or to know, that not every one of its competitors can be, and, as they are not certain that any of them can, it gets the business at the same or even a little higher price....

The defendant claims, with much reason, to have been the first of the can makers systematically and scientifically to study canners' problems, with a view to discovering the causes of damage to and deterioration in canned goods. It says it has done more in that direction than any of its competitors, or all of them together. A number of years ago the defendant established a laboratory for the investigation of such matters. It has always been ready and willing to use the resources of this laboratory to aid canners, without expense to the latter and whether they bought their cans from it or not. When, some years ago, the National Canners' Association made up its mind that it would like to establish and maintain a well-equipped and efficiently managed laboratory at Washington, the defendant, and for that matter its principal competitors, furthered the project by contributing liberally, apparently in some rough proportion to the number of packers' cans sold by each.

....

... The defendant has many shops, most of its competitors but one. The probability of its delivery of cans being altogether prevented by a factory accident is therefore almost negligible. Prompt delivery at short notice cannot, however, be assured unless the can factory is near the place of consumption. If there is a long railroad journey between, accidents and mistakes on the lines may postpone the arrival of cans which have been shipped in due season. The testimony shows that for this reason users of cans often prefer to deal with a neighboring factory, whether of the defendant or one of its competitors, in preference to buying cheaper elsewhere. The defendant has always given special attention to insuring prompt deliveries, and apparently has been rather unusually successful in so doing. Moreover, it stands ready to do its best to furnish cans on the shortest notice to any one who wants a carload or many carloads, and at its published prices. The failure of prompt delivery from one of its factories, or from a factory of one of its competitors, is no longer by any means so serious a matter as such an event formerly might have been. From one or the other of its shops the defendant is usually able in brief space to place the cans where they are needed. No concern which had not a number of plants and ample resources, both in men and money, could have done what the defendant has accomplished in protecting can users against serious delays in delivery. Perhaps this has been its most valuable service to the trade.

....

One who sells only one-half of the cans that are sold does not, of course, possess a monopoly in the same sense as he would if he sold all or nearly all of them. Yet he may have more power over the industry than it is well for any one concern to possess. No one can say with any certainty that anybody would be better off if defendant had never, in any way, restrained or controlled absolutely free competition in cans. All that can be argued is that, in view of the declared policy of Congress, the legal presumption must be that which was done was against the public weal.

If it be true that size and power, apart from the way in which they were acquired, or the purpose with which they are used, do not offend against the law, it is equally true that one of the designs of the framers of the Anti-Trust Act was to prevent the concentration in a few hands of control over great industries. They preferred a social and industrial state in which there should be many independent producers. Size and power are themselves facts some of whose consequences do not depend upon the way in which they were created or in which they are used. It is easy to conceive that they might be acquired honestly and used as fairly as men who are in business for the legitimate purpose of making money for themselves and their associates could be expected to use them, human nature being what it is, and for all that constitute a public danger, or at all events give rise to difficult social, industrial and political problems....

The problem presented by size and power is one of such far-reaching difficulty that Congress has said, while it does not see how to deal with them when acquired in the legitimate expansion of a lawful business, it will prevent their illegitimate and unnatural acquirement by any attempt to restrain trade or monopolize industry. Perhaps the framers of the Anti-Trust Act believed that, if such illegitimate attempts were effectively prevented, the occasions on which it would become necessary to deal with size and power otherwise brought about would be so few and so long postponed that it might never be necessary to deal with them at all. In administering the anti-trust acts, a number of great and powerful offenders against them have been dissolved. So far as is possible to judge, the consuming public has not as yet greatly profited by their dissolution. It is perhaps not likely that any benefit could have been expected until in the slow course of time the ownership of the newly created corporations gradually drifts into different hands. In most of the cases in which dissolution has been decreed, the defendants had, not long before proceedings against them were instituted, done things which evidenced their continued intent to dominate and restrain trade by the use of methods which interfered more or less seriously with the reasonable freedom of their customers or their competitors.

As has been shown, defendant for a number of years past has done nothing of the sort. While it had its origin in unlawful acts and thereby acquired a power which may be harmful, and the acquisition of which in any event was contrary to the policy of Congress as embodied in the statute, it has for some time past used that power, on the whole, rather for weal than for woe. In this case, if a dissolution be decreed, it will have as its sole reason the carrying out of the policy of Congress that a trading or industrial corporation shall not, by an attempt to restrain or monopolize trade, become so powerful that it exerts an influence on the industry far greater than that of any of its competitors....

....

Defendant once sought to emancipate itself from restraints of competition. Its power is great, but, as has already been pointed out, is limited by a large volume of actual competition and to a still greater extent by the potential competition, from the possibility of which in the present state of the industry it cannot escape. Those in the trade are satisfied with it. They do not want it dissolved. Whether its dissolution would profit any one is doubtful. The first and immediate effect would almost certainly be the reverse, whatever larger good might in the end come from it.

I am frankly reluctant to destroy so finely adjusted an industrial machine as the record shows defendant to be. Yet the government, too, has its rights, and has thus far been properly insistent upon them....

The government recognizes that the situation which existed before defendant was formed cannot be restored. What it principally fears is that the defendant will, to the public prejudice, hereafter dangerously use the strength which it gained by its original lawbreaking. Defendant's reply, that in that event it will be time enough for the government to act, does not fully meet the case. If this petition be dismissed upon its merits and without qualification, defendant might be entitled to claim in any future proceeding that nothing here in issue may be there used against it....

Under the circumstances, would it not be better simply to retain the bill, without at present decreeing a dissolution, but reserving the right to do so whenever, if ever, it shall be made to appear to the court that the size and power of the defendant, brought about as they originally were, are being used to the injury of the public, or whenever such size and power, without being intentionally so used, have given to the defendant a dominance and control over the industry, or some portion of it, so great as to make dissolution or other restraining decree of the court expedient. It is, of course, not suggested that this court should or could undertake the regulation of defendant's business. Courts have no such power and no fitness for its exercise. What is proposed is in default of a better way of dealing with a somewhat unusual and very difficult condition. It is to be hoped that, before any occasion to act upon the power reserved shall arise, Congress will substitute some other method than dissolution for dealing with the problems which arise when a single corporation absorbs a large part of the country's productive capacity in any one line.

....

NOTES AND QUESTIONS

1. Note the acts that the American Can Company was alleged to have committed: it threatened to drive its competitors out of business (how might it accomplish this?); it threatened to prevent can makers who did not join the "combination" from obtaining needed raw materials, such as tin plate; it bought out its rivals, often paying many times the value of the purchased company, and always paying more than the company was worth; when it purchased the plants of rivals, it required the rivals to promise not to compete in the industry for fifteen years; it bought up the patents for can-making machinery; it forced the makers of can-making machinery to agree not to sell machinery to competitors. What do these practices have in common? Are all of them equally harmful?

The allegations that American Can entered contracts with vertically related firms that exclude rivals unnecessarily have reappeared many times in antitrust. Consider the following from *United States v. Microsoft*, 56 F.3d 1448, 1451 (D.C. Cir. 1995):

> The key anticompetitive practice against which the [government's antitrust] complaint is aimed is Microsoft's use of contract terms requiring original equipment manufacturers ("OEMs") to pay Microsoft a royalty for each computer the OEM sells containing a particular microprocessor ... whether or not the OEM has included a Microsoft operating system with that computer. The practical effect of such "per processor licenses," it is alleged, is to deter OEMs from using competing operating systems during the life of their contracts with Microsoft. The complaint further charges that Microsoft has exacerbated the anticompetitive effect of the per processor licenses by executing long-term contracts with major OEMs....

Thus, the government alleged, if a computer maker wanted to put a competing operating system, such as IBM's OS/2 system, on one of its computers, it would have to pay twice: once to IBM for the right to IBM's system, and a second time to Microsoft under the "per processor" license requiring the manufacturer to pay to have Miscrosoft Windows installed on every computer it made, whether or not it was actually installed.

2. How plausible is the court's reasoning that American Can could have driven some of its competitors out of business, but chose instead to buy them out, sometimes paying them as much as 25 times the value of their assets? Would it not have been much cheaper simply to drive the competitors into bankruptcy? See the discussion of predatory pricing, *infra*.

3. Notice some of American Can's defenses: after the monopoly was created cans became much cheaper and were generally of a higher quality; the new megacompany was able to engage in substantial research and development; the new company paid employees higher wages than the older, smaller companies did; because of the unified manufacturing process permitted by a single large manufacturer, can sizes and shapes were more standardized than they had been before; the defendant's size and financial security made the can market much less convulsive than it had been before the monopoly was created: buyers of the defendant's cans could generally get them when they wanted them, without having to worry about manufacturing delays or suppliers going out of business. These and other alleged advantages of the can monopoly gave the court some pause. The judge was "reluctant to destroy so finely adjusted an industrial machine." Do you suppose that these improvements in the quality and delivery of cans occurred because of, or in spite of, the existence of a monopoly? Would some of them have happened even in the absence of a dominant firm in the market? Is there any reason to believe that monopolists pay higher wages than competitors? Is that question relevant in an antitrust case? The argument that a monopolist can "standardize" the output in a market is certainly plausible, but couldn't the same result be obtained in a less offensive way?

What about the argument that the monopolized market was more predictable for canneries, because the small competitors had a tendency to go out of business? Nothing guarantees a supplier's financial stability more than an abundance of monopoly profits. Should that ever be a defense in a monopolization case?

4. Monopolists have often attempted to defend their monopolies by arguing that the monopoly undertook research and development that would not have occurred in an industry made up of smaller, competitive firms. In fact, monopolists in this position have made two, quite different arguments: (1) only a very large firm can afford to undertake research and development or exploration in certain areas in which such activities are very expensive; and (2) only monopoly profits give a firm enough money to finance such research — that is, firms in competition are forced to reduce expenses and will cut out expenditures for research. Do both arguments strike you as equally plausible? Does the fact that the monopolist has extra money mean that the monopolist will spend it on research rather than on yachts or caviar? The answer, most likely, is that the monopolist will spend the money on research if it thinks the research is a good investment — that is, if it produces a profitable return. But if that is the case, would not the competitor do it as well?

The first argument is a little more convincing. There may be circumstances when certain kinds of research or exploration require large amounts of capital, and only relatively large firms will be able to finance it. However, is this an argument for monopoly? Wouldn't a joint venture have the same social benefits but pose fewer social evils? See the discussion of research joint ventures, *supra*.

5. One of the consequences of American Can's monopoly price increase was that the market became flooded with new entrants, many of which were so inefficient that they would not have survived in a competitive market. It became profitable to make cans with "any antiquated or crude machinery [the new entrants] could find in old lumber rooms ... or even to resume can making by hand." These fringe firms are the bane of every monopolist's existence. One way to deal with them, as the opinion notes, is to reduce price to the point that production for the inefficient fringe is unprofitable; however, that costs the monopolist part of its monopoly profits. The American Can Company took a second, ill-advised route. It bought up the cans from the inefficient producers, paying them a profitable price. This strategy was calculated to invite even more firms into the market, for they would have a guaranteed outlet for their product. The third alternative is to drive the fringe firms out of business in such a way that no new firms will dare to enter the market.

NOTE: THE ECONOMICS OF MONOPOLIZATION

Monopoly is not necessarily bad. In certain industries, such as delivery of electric power to consumers, monopoly has traditionally been regarded as the most efficient way to serve the public. Once a single set of electric cables is in place, it can service an entire city. It would be very costly to have two, three, or more sets of electric wires running through a city, and to give two or more electric companies the eminent domain power to run their wires across private property. For these reasons, electric utilities are generally considered to be "natural" monopolies — that is, firms that can deliver their services optimally if they are permitted to have a monopoly within a certain market. In general, an industry is a natural monopoly if the most efficient size of a plant or installation in that industry will satisfy 100% or more of the entire profitable demand in that market. The other side of the coin, however, is that such natural monopolies are generally priced-regulated by a state, municipality, or some other governmental body.

In industries that are not natural monopolies most people in market economies believe that monopoly is bad and competition good. Antitrust lawyers and economists generally agree about this, although different groups do so for different reasons. There are both noneconomic and economic arguments against monopoly. The noneconomic arguments focus on the tendency of monopoly to concentrate large amounts of power in the hands of a few private owners, and on the fact that monopoly pricing transfers wealth away from consumers (who must pay more for monopolized products) and toward monopoly producers (who are able to charge monopoly prices). The economic arguments, by contrast, focus on the tendency of monopoly to cause inefficiency in the production and distribution of goods and services. These inefficiencies result from two aspects of monopoly: monopoly pricing and monopolistic conduct.

At this time you might find it helpful to review the discussion of monopoly in Chapter 2. Figure 1 illustrates the demand, marginal cost, and marginal revenue curves for a firm with substantial market power. A firm with no market power would take the market price as given and produce at the rate at which its marginal cost curve crosses the market demand curve. That would be price P_c and output Q_c in Figure 1. A firm with market power, however, will not take the market price as given; rather, it will reduce its output to the point at which its marginal cost and marginal revenue curves intersect. At that point, one further unit of production would generate greater expenses than income. This is the monopolist's profit-maximizing price, and it is represented on the graph by P_m. The profit-maximizing output that will generate that price is Q_m.

Figure 1

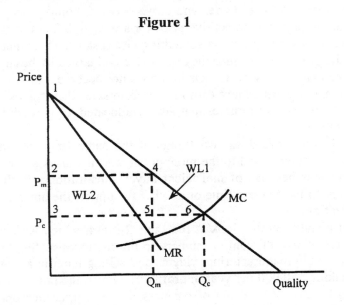

The large triangle 1-3-6 in Figure 1 represents the "consumers' surplus" generated by a competitive market. Competitive markets maximize consumers' surplus, and there is a positive correlation between consumers' surplus and consumer welfare. Consumers' surplus is the difference between the amount that a particular consumer is willing to pay for a product and the price the consumer must actually pay for it. If a consumer values a product at $1.50 but is able to purchase it at a competitive price of $1.00, the transaction generates a consumers' surplus of 50 cents. If the same consumer must pay a monopoly price of $1.20 there will still be a consumer's surplus, but it will be reduced to 30 cents. The triangle 1-3-6 illustrates the size of the consumers' surplus generated in the entire market represented by Figure 1, if the market were competitive.

Monopoly pricing at P_m with monopoly output at Q_m, reduces the size of the consumers' surplus to an area represented by triangle 1-2-4. Rectangle 2-3-5-4 represents lost consumers' surplus that the monopolist has been able to turn into "producers' surplus." Producer's surplus is the amount by which a producer's price exceeds the competitive price. If the competitive price of a widget is $1.00 (which includes a reasonable profit, sufficient to attract new capital into the industry), but a seller with market power is able to sell the widget for $1.20, the transaction has generated a producers' surplus of 20 cents. Rectangle 2-3-5-4 therefore represents, at least in part, a wealth transfer away from consumers and toward producers. However, as we shall see later, to describe rectangle 2-3-5-4 as a wealth "transfer" is an oversimplification.

What about triangle 4-5-6, which is also lost producers' surplus? Triangle 4-5-6 represents the traditional "deadweight" loss caused by monopoly. The potential purchasers located along the demand curve between points 4 and 6 would have been willing to pay the competitive price for a widget, but at the monopoly price they refuse to buy and purchase something else instead. These purchasers therefore lose the producers' surplus they would have obtained by buying widgets in a competitive market; however, their loss does not become a gain to the monopolist, for the monopolist cannot earn money from sales that it does not make. Triangle 4-5-6 represents resources that are misallocated, or wasted, because of the monopolization.

Monopoly therefore does two things at the same time: it transfers wealth away from consumers and to the monopolist, and it causes a certain amount of deadweight loss because of inefficient buyer substitutions. Both of these reasons have been used at one time or another to support the antitrust laws against monopolization.

Now let us take another look at rectangle 2-3-5-4, which we described above as a transfer of wealth from consumers to the monopolist. Suppose that a producer is currently manufacturing widgets and selling them in a competitive market and making $50,000 per year in profits. However, the producer discovers that by driving its closest rival out of business, it could price monopolistically and obtain profits of $60,000. How much is it worth to the producer to drive out the rival?

The answer, quite clearly, is $10,000. That is, the ability to obtain (or to retain) market power is valuable, and a profit-maximizing seller will therefore spend money in order to obtain or keep it. In fact, if market power is worth $10,000 a year to a seller, the seller will be willing to spend almost any amount of money less than $10,000 in order to acquire and keep the market power. *See* R. Posner, *Antitrust Law: An Economic Perspective* 10-13 (1976). This money can be spent in a variety of ways. For example, it might be spent in research and development that will make the producer more efficient than its rivals. On the other hand, the producer might spend the money sabotaging its rival's plants or making false advertisements about its own products. The first of these ways is probably socially beneficial, but the second two are almost certainly socially harmful.

In short, rectangle 2-3-5-4 does not necessarily represent a transfer of wealth from consumers to the monopolist. To the extent that the monopolist has spent extra funds in order to acquire the market power, 2-3-5-4 represents money that does not accrue to the monopolist either. Furthermore, if that money has been spent in socially inefficient ways, such as industrial sabotage or predatory pricing, much of rectangle 2-3-5-4 is also pure social, deadweight loss.

Figure 1 thus suggests that monopoly can be inefficient from a purely economic standpoint for two different reasons. Triangle 4-5-6 represents inefficiency caused by inefficient monopoly *pricing*. However, at least a part of rectangle 2-3-5-4 can represent inefficiency caused by inefficient monopoly *conduct* — i.e., resources inefficiently spent by the monopolist in attaining or retaining its position.

But there is a third social cost of monopolization that Figure 1 simply fails to illustrate: the social cost of the resources *of competitors* or others, which might be inefficiently lost by the monopolist's attempt to attain or retain a dominant position. Consider the Supreme Court's decision in *Allied Tube & Conduit Corp. v. Indian Head, Inc.*, 486 U.S. 492 (1988), reprinted in Chapter 9, as an example. Suppose that a cartel of manufacturers of steel conduit corrupts a standard-setting organization by "packing" one of its meetings and forces the passage of a rule keeping plastic conduit off the market. The result is that the steel cartel continues to make monopoly profits on its conduit. Triangle 4-5-6 in Figure 1 represents the social cost of the output reduction that results from the perpetuation of this monopoly. Part of rectangle 2-3-5-4 represents the social cost of the means by which the cartel protected its monopoly — resources inefficiently spent. But what of the social cost of the years of lost research the plaintiff spent in developing a superior product, plastic conduit, that now cannot reach the market? That loss is not even accounted for by Figure 1. It could be far larger than either triangle 4-5-6 or rectangle 2-3-5-4. Although rectangle 2-3-5-4 represents the most the putative monopolist is willing to spend in the creation or maintenance of a monopoly, there is no necessary limit to the size of the inefficient losses it might impose on competitors. Many forms of monopolization, such as predatory pricing, fraudulent petitions to the government, and patent fraud deny competitors the opportunity to use efficiently resources that are already consumed. This is a social cost of monopoly that antitrust, with its prominent concern with the socially costly processes by which monopoly is acquired, must take into account as well. *See* Hovenkamp, *Antitrust's Protected Classes*, 88 Mich. L. Rev. 1 (1989); Hovenkamp, *Antitrust Policy and the Social Cost of Monopoly*, 78 Iowa L. Rev. 371 (1993).

UNITED STATES V. ALUMINUM CO. OF AMERICA

148 F.2d 416 (2d Cir. 1945)

[In 1912 the United States had brought a monopolization action against the Aluminum Company of America (Alcoa) and obtained a consent decree. In 1937 the United States sued for additional relief, including dissolution of the company. The trial court found for the defendant. 44 F. Supp. 97 (S.D.N.Y. 1941). The Expediting Act permitted a direct appeal to the U.S. Supreme Court, but four Justices disqualified themselves. The statutory quorum is six Justices. Congress responded with a statute providing that in such cases the court of last resort should be made up of the three most senior judges of the appropriate court of appeals. As a result, the *Alcoa* case is traditionally considered to have as much authority as a Supreme Court opinion.]

JUDGE HAND.

"Alcoa" is a corporation, organized under the laws of Pennsylvania on September 18, 1888 .... It has always been engaged in the production and sale of "ingot" aluminum, and since 1895 also in the fabrication of the metal into many finished and semi-finished articles. It has proliferated into a great number of subsidiaries, created at various times between the years 1900 and 1929, as the business expanded. Aluminum is a chemical element; it is never found in a free state, being always in chemical combination with oxygen. One form of this combination is known as alumina; and for practical purposes the most available material from which alumina can be extracted is an ore, called, "bauxite."...

The extraction of aluminum from alumina requires a very large amount of electrical energy .... Beginning at least as early as 1895, "Alcoa" secured such power from several companies by contracts, containing in at least three instances, covenants binding the power companies not to sell or let power to anyone else for the manufacture of aluminum. "Alcoa" — either itself or by a subsidiary — also entered into four successive "cartels" with foreign manufacturers of aluminum by which, in exchange for certain limitations upon its import into foreign countries, it secured covenants from the foreign producers, either not to import into the United States at all, or to do so under restrictions, which in some cases involved the fixing of prices. These "cartels" and restrictive covenants and certain other practices were the subject of a suit filed by the United States against "Alcoa" on May 16, 1912, in which a decree was entered by consent on June 7, 1912, declaring several of these covenants unlawful and enjoining their performance; and also declaring invalid other restrictive covenants obtained before 1903 relating to the sale of alumina....

None of the foregoing facts are in dispute, and the most important question in the case is whether the monopoly in "Alcoa's" production of "virgin" ingot, secured by the two patents until 1909, and in part perpetuated between 1909 and 1912 by the unlawful practices, forbidden by the decree of 1912, continued for the ensuing twenty-eight years; and whether, if it did, it was unlawful under § 2 of the Sherman Act, 15 U.S.C.A. § 2. It is undisputed that throughout this period "Alcoa" continued to be the single producer of "virgin" ingot in the United States; and the plaintiff argues that this without more was enough to make it an unlawful monopoly. It also takes an alternative position: that in any event during this period "Alcoa" consistently pursued unlawful exclusionary practices, which made its dominant position certainly unlawful, even though it would not have been, had it been retained only by "natural growth." Finally, it asserts that many of these practices were of themselves unlawful, as contracts in restraint of trade under § 1 of the Act, 15 U.S.C.A. § 1. "Alcoa's" position is that the fact that it alone continued to make "virgin" ingot in this country did not, and does not, give it a monopoly of the market; that it was always subject to the competition of imported "virgin" ingot, and of what is called "secondary" ingot; and that even if it had not been, its monopoly would not have been retained by unlawful means, but would have been the result of a growth which the Act does not forbid, even when it results in a monopoly....

From 1902 onward until 1928 "Alcoa" was making ingot in Canada through a wholly owned subsidiary; so much of this as it imported into the United States it is proper to include with what it produced here. In the year 1912 the sum of these two items represented nearly ninety-one per cent of the total amount of "virgin" ingot available for sale in this country. This percentage varied year by year up to and including 1938: in 1913 it was about seventy-two per cent; in 1921 about sixty-eight per cent; in 1922 about seventy-two per cent; with these exceptions it was always over eighty per cent of the total and for the last five years 1934-1938 inclusive it averaged over ninety per cent. The effect of such a proportion of the production upon the market we reserve for the time being, for it will be necessary first to consider the nature and uses of "secondary" ingot, the name by which the industry knows ingot made from aluminum scrap. This is of two sorts, though for our purposes it is not important to distinguish between them. One of these is the clippings and trimmings of "sheet" aluminum, when patterns are cut out of it, as a suit is cut from a bolt of cloth. The chemical composition of these is obviously the same as that of the "sheet" from which they come; and, although they are likely to accumulate dust or other dirt in the factory, this may be removed by well known processes. If a record of the original composition of the "sheet" has been preserved, this scrap may be remelted into new ingot, and used again for the same purpose.... Nevertheless, there is an appreciable "sales resistance" even to this kind of scrap, and for some uses (airplanes and cables among them), fabricators absolutely insist upon "virgin": just why is not altogether clear. The other source of scrap is aluminum which has once been fabricated and the article, after being used, is discarded and sent to the junk heap ... as for example, cooking utensils, like kettles and pans, and the pistons or crank cases of motorcars. These are made with a substantial alloy and to restore the metal to its original purity costs more than it is worth. However, if the alloy is known both in quality and amount, scrap, when remelted, can be used again for the same purpose as before. In spite of this, as in the case of clippings and trimmings, the industry will ordinarily not accept ingot so salvaged upon the same terms as "virgin." There are some seventeen companies which scavenge scrap of all sorts, clean it, remelt it, test it for its composition, make it into ingots and sell it regularly to the trade. There is in all these salvage operations some inevitable waste of actual material; not only does a certain amount of aluminum escape altogether, but in the salvaging process itself some is skimmed off as scum and thrown away. The judge found that the return of fabricated products to the market as "secondary" varied from five to twenty-five years, depending upon the article; but he did not, and no doubt could not, find how many times the cycle could be repeated before the metal was finally used up.

There are various ways of computing "Alcoa's" control of the aluminum market — as distinct from its production — depending upon what one regards as competing in that market. The judge figured its share — during the years 1929-1938, inclusive — as only about thirty-three per cent; to do so he included "secondary," and excluded that part of "Alcoa's" own production which it fabricated and did not therefore sell as ingot. If, on the other hand, "Alcoa's" total production, fabricated and sold, be included, and balanced against the sum of imported "virgin" and "secondary," its share of the market was in the neighborhood of sixty-four per cent for that period. The percentage we have already mentioned — over ninety — results only if we both include all "Alcoa's" production and exclude "secondary." That percentage is enough to constitute a monopoly; it is doubtful whether sixty or sixty-four per cent would be enough; and certainly thirty-three per cent is not. Hence it is necessary to settle what he shall treat as competing in the ingot market. That part of its production which "Alcoa" itself fabricates, does not of course ever reach the market as ingot; and we recognize that it is only when a restriction of production either inevitably affects prices, or is intended to do so, that it violates § 1 of the Act. However, even though we were to assume that a monopoly is unlawful under § 2 only in case it controls prices, the ingot fabricated by "Alcoa," necessarily had a direct effect upon the ingot market. All ingot — with trifling exceptions — is used to fabricate intermediate, or end, products; and therefore all intermediate, or end, products which "Alcoa" fabricates and sells, pro tanto reduce the demand for ingot itself.... We cannot therefore agree that the computation of the percentage of "Alcoa's" control over the ingot market should not include the whole of its ingot production.

As to "secondary," as we have said, for certain purposes the industry will not accept it at all; but for those for which it will, the difference in price is ordinarily not very great; the judge found that it was between one and two cents a pound, hardly enough margin on which to base a monopoly. Indeed, there are times when all differential disappears, and "secondary" will actually sell at a higher price: i.e. when there is a supply available which contains just the alloy that a fabricator needs for the article which he proposes to make. Taking the industry as a whole, we can say nothing more definite than that, although "secondary" does not compete at all in some uses, (whether because of "sales resistance" only, or because of actual metallurgical inferiority), for most purposes it competes upon a substantial equality with "virgin." On these facts the judge found that "every pound of secondary or scrap aluminum which is sold in commerce displaces a pound of virgin aluminum which otherwise would, or might have been, sold." We agree: so far as "secondary" supplies the demand of such fabricators as will accept it, it increases the amount of "virgin" which must seek sale elsewhere; and it therefore results that the supply of that part of the demand which will accept only "virgin" becomes greater in proportion as "secondary" drives away "virgin" from the demand which will accept "secondary." (This is indeed the same argument which we used a moment ago to include in the supply that part of "virgin" which "Alcoa" fabricates; it is not apparent to us why the judge did not think it applicable to that item as well.) At any given moment therefore "secondary" competes with "virgin" in the ingot market; further, it can, and probably does, set a limit or "ceiling" beyond which the price of "virgin" cannot go, for the cost of its production will in the end depend only upon the expense of scavenging and reconditioning. It might seem for this reason that in estimating "Alcoa's" control over the ingot market, we ought to include the supply of "secondary," as the judge did. Indeed, it may be thought a paradox to say that anyone has the monopoly of a market in which at all times he must meet a competition that limits his price. We shall show that it is not.

In the case of a monopoly of any commodity which does not disappear in use and which can be salvaged, the supply seeking sale at any moment will be made up of two components: (1) the part which the putative monopolist can immediately produce and sell; and (2) the part which has been, or can be, reclaimed out of what he has produced and sold in the past. By hypothesis he presently controls the first of these components; the second he has controlled in the past, although he no longer does. During the period when he did control the second, if he was aware of his interest, he was guided, not alone by its effect at that time upon the market, but by his knowledge that some part of it was likely to be reclaimed and seek the future market. That consideration will to some extent always affect his production until he decides to abandon the business, or for some other reason ceases to be concerned with the future market. Thus, in the case at bar "Alcoa" always knew that the future supply of ingot would be made up in part of what it produced at the time, and, if it was as far-sighted as it proclaims itself, that consideration must have had its share in determining how much to produce. How accurately it could forecast the effect of present production upon the future market is another matter. Experience, no doubt, would help; but it makes no difference that it had to guess; it is enough that it had an inducement to make the best guess it could, and that it would regulate that part of the future supply, so far as it should turn out to have guessed right. The competition of "secondary" must therefore be disregarded, as soon as we consider the position of "Alcoa" over a period of years; it was as much within "Alcoa's" control as was the production of the "virgin" from which it had been derived....

We conclude therefore that "Alcoa's" control over the ingot market must be reckoned at over ninety per cent; that being the proportion which its production bears to imported "virgin" ingot. If the fraction which it did not supply were the produce of domestic manufacture there could be no doubt that this percentage gave it a monopoly — lawful or unlawful, as the case might be. The producer of so large a proportion of the supply has complete control within certain limits. It is true that, if by raising the price he reduces the amount which can be marketed — as always, or almost always, happens — he may invite the expansion of the small producers who will try to fill the place left open; nevertheless, not only is there an inevitable lag in this, but the large producer is in a strong position to check such competition; and, indeed, if he has retained his old plant and personnel, he can inevitably do so. There are indeed limits to his power; substitutes are available for almost all commodities, and to raise the price enough is to evoke them.... Moreover, it is difficult and expensive to keep idle any part of a plant or of personnel; and any drastic contraction of the market will offer increasing temptation to the small producers to expand. But these limitations also exist when a single producer occupies the whole market: even then, his hold will depend upon his moderation in exerting his immediate power.

The case at bar is however different, because, for aught that appears there may well have been a practically unlimited supply of imports as the price of ingot rose. Assuming that there was no agreement between "Alcoa" and foreign producers not to import, they sold what could bear the handicap of the tariff and the cost of transportation. For the period of eighteen years — 1920-1937 — they sold at times a little above "Alcoa's" prices, at times a little under; but there was substantially no gross difference between what they received and what they would have received, had they sold uniformly at "Alcoa's" prices. While the record is silent, we may therefore assume — the plaintiff having the burden — that, had "Alcoa" raised its prices, more ingot would have been imported. Thus there is a distinction between domestic and foreign competition: the first is limited in quantity, and can increase only by an increase in plant and personnel; the second is of producers who, we must assume, produce much more than they import, and whom a rise in price will presumably induce immediately to divert to the American market what they have been selling elsewhere. It is entirely consistent with the evidence that it was the threat of greater foreign imports which kept "Alcoa's" prices where they were, and prevented it from exploiting its advantage as sole domestic producer; indeed, it is hard to resist the conclusion that potential imports did put a "ceiling" upon those prices. Nevertheless, within the limits afforded by the tariff and the cost of transportation, "Alcoa" was free to raise its prices as it chose, since it was free from domestic competition, save as it drew other metals into the market as substitutes. Was this a monopoly within the meaning of § 2? The judge found that, over the whole half century of its existence, "Alcoa's" profits upon capital invested, after payment of income taxes, had been only about ten per cent, and, although the plaintiff puts this figure a little higher, the difference is negligible.... This assumed, it would be hard to say that "Alcoa" had made exorbitant profits on ingot, if it is proper to allocate the profit upon the whole business proportionately among all its products — ingot, and fabrications from ingot. A profit of ten per cent in such an industry, dependent, in part at any rate, upon continued tariff protection, and subject to the vicissitudes of new demands, to the obsolescence of plant and process — which can never be accurately gauged in advance — to the chance that substitutes may at any moment be discovered which will reduce the demand, and to the other hazards which attend all industry; a profit of ten per cent, so conditioned, could hardly be considered extortionate.

There are however, two answers to any such excuse; and the first is that the profit on ingot was not necessarily the same as the profit of the business as a whole, and that we have no means of allocating its proper share to ingot. It is true that the mill cost appears; but obviously it would be unfair to "Alcoa" to take, as the measure of its profit on ingot, the difference between selling price and mill cost; and yet we have nothing else. It may be retorted that it was for the plaintiff to prove what was the profit upon ingot in accordance with the general burden of proof. We think not. Having proved that "Alcoa" had a monopoly of the domestic ingot market, the plaintiff had gone far enough; if it was an excuse, that "Alcoa" had not abused its power, it lay upon "Alcoa" to prove that it had not. But the whole issue is irrelevant anyway, for it is no excuse for "monopolizing" a market that the monopoly has not been used to extract from the consumer more than a "fair" profit. The Act has wider purposes. Indeed, even though we disregarded all but economic considerations, it would by no means follow that such concentration of producing power is to be desired, when it has not been used extortionately. Many people believe that possession of unchallenged economic power deadens initiative, discourages thrift and depresses energy; that immunity from competition is a narcotic, and rivalry is a stimulant, to industrial progress; that the spur of constant stress is necessary to counteract an inevitable disposition to let well enough alone. Such people believe that competitors, versed in the craft as no consumer can be, will be quick to detect opportunities for saving and new shifts in production, and be eager to profit by them. In any event the mere fact that a producer, having command of the domestic market, has not been able to make more than a "fair" profit, is no evidence that a "fair" profit could not have been made at lower prices. *United States v. Corn Products Refining Co., supra,* 1014, 1015 (234 F. 964). True, it might have been thought adequate to condemn only those monopolies which could not show that they had exercised the highest possible ingenuity, had adopted every possible economy, had anticipated every conceivable improvement, stimulated every possible demand. No doubt, that would be one way of dealing with the matter, although it would imply constant scrutiny and constant supervision, such as courts are unable to provide. Be that as it may, that was not the way that Congress chose; it did not condone "good trusts" and condemn "bad" ones; it forbad all. Moreover, in so doing it was not necessarily actuated by economic motives alone. It is possible, because of its indirect social or moral effect, to prefer a system of small producers, each dependent for his success upon his own skill and character, to one in which the great mass of those engaged must accept the direction of a few. These considerations, which we have suggested only as possible purposes of the Act, we think the decisions prove to have been in fact its purposes.

It is settled, at least as to § 1, that there are some contracts restricting competition which are unlawful, no matter how beneficent they may be.... Starting, however, with the authoritative premise that all contracts fixing prices are unconditionally prohibited, the only possible difference between them and a monopoly is that while a monopoly necessarily involves an equal, or even greater, power to fix prices, its mere existence might be thought not to constitute an exercise of that power. That distinction is nevertheless purely formal; it would be valid only so long as the monopoly remained wholly inert; it would disappear as soon as the monopoly began to operate; for, when it did — that is, as soon as it began to sell at all — it must sell at some price and the only price at which it could sell is a price which it itself fixed. Thereafter the power and its exercise must needs coalesce. Indeed it would be absurd to condemn such contracts unconditionally, and not to extend the condemnation to monopolies; for the contracts are only steps toward that entire control which monopoly confers: they are really partial monopolies.

But we are not left to deductive reasoning. Although in many settings it may be proper to weigh the extent and effect of restrictions in a contract against its industrial or commercial advantages, this is never to be done when the contract is made with intent to set up a monopoly....

We have been speaking only of the economic reasons which forbid monopoly; but, as we have already implied, there are others, based upon the belief that great industrial consolidations are inherently undesirable, regardless of their economic results. In the debates in Congress Senator Sherman himself ... showed that among the purposes of Congress in 1890 was a desire to put an end to great aggregations of capital because of the helplessness of the individual before them.... That Congress is still of the same mind appears in the Surplus Property Act of 1944, 50 U.S.C.A. Appendix § 1611 et seq., and the Small Business Mobilization Act, 50 U.S.C.A. Appendix § 1101 et seq. Not only does § 2(d) of the first declare it to be one aim of that statute to "preserve the competitive position of small business concerns," but § 18 is given over to directions designed to "preserve and strengthen" their position.... Throughout the history of these statutes it has been constantly assumed that one of their purposes was to perpetuate and preserve, for its own sake and in spite of possible cost, an organization of industry in small units which can effectively compete with each other. We hold that "Alcoa's" monopoly of ingot was of the kind covered by § 2.

It does not follow because "Alcoa" had such a monopoly, that it "monopolized" the ingot market: it may not have achieved monopoly; monopoly may have been thrust upon it. If it had been a combination of existing smelters which united the whole industry and controlled the production of all aluminum ingot, it would certainly have "monopolized" the market. In several decisions the Supreme Court has decreed the dissolution of such combinations, although they had engaged in no unlawful trade practices.... We may start therefore with the premise that to have combined ninety per cent of the producers of ingot would have been to "monopolize" the ingot market; and, so far as concerns the public interest, it can make no difference whether an existing competition is put an end to, or whether prospective competition is prevented. The Clayton Act itself speaks in that alternative: "to injure, destroy, or prevent competition." Nevertheless, it is unquestionably true that from the very outset the courts have at least kept in reserve the possibility that the origin of a monopoly may be critical in determining its legality; and for this they had warrant in some of the congressional debates which accompanied the passage of the Act.... This notion has usually been expressed by saying that size does not determine guilt; that there must be some "exclusion" of competitors; that the growth must be something else than "natural" or "normal"; that there must be a "wrongful intent," or some other specific intent; or that some "unduly" coercive means must be used. At times there has been emphasis upon the use of the active verb, "monopolize," as the judge noted in the case at bar.... What engendered these compunctions is reasonably plain; persons may unwittingly find themselves in possession of a monopoly, automatically so to say: that is, without having intended either to put an end to existing competition, or to prevent competition from arising when none had existed; they may become monopolists by force of accident. Since the Act makes "monopolizing" a crime, as well as a civil wrong, it would be not only unfair, but presumably contrary to the intent of Congress, to include such instances. A market may, for example, be so limited that it is impossible to produce at all and meet the cost of production except by a plant large enough to supply the whole demand. Or there may be changes in taste or in cost which drive out all but one purveyor. A single producer may be the survivor out of a group of active competitors, merely by virtue of his superior skill, foresight and industry. In such cases a strong argument can be made that, although, the result may expose the public to the evils of monopoly, the Act does not mean to condemn the resultant of those very forces which it is its prime object to foster: finis opus coronat. The successful competitor, having been urged to compete, must not be turned upon when he wins.... Cardozo, J., in *United States v. Swift & Co.*, 286 U.S. 106, said, "Mere size ... is not an offense against the Sherman Act unless magnified to the point at which it amounts to a monopoly ... but size carries with it an opportunity for abuse that is not to be ignored when the opportunity is proved to have been utilized in the past." "Alcoa's" size was "magnified" to make it a "monopoly"; indeed, it has never been anything else; and its size, not only offered it an "opportunity for abuse," but it "utilized" its size for "abuse," as can easily be shown.

It would completely misconstrue "Alcoa's" position in 1940 to hold that it was the passive beneficiary of a monopoly, following upon an involuntary elimination of competitors by automatically operative economic forces. Already in 1909, when its last lawful monopoly ended, it sought to strengthen its position by unlawful practices, and these concededly continued until 1912. In that year it had two plants in New York, at which it produced less than 42 million pounds of ingot; in 1934 it had five plants (the original two, enlarged; one in Tennessee; one in North Carolina; one in Washington), and its production had risen to about 327 million pounds, an increase of almost eight-fold. Meanwhile not a pound of ingot had been produced by anyone else in the United States. This increase and this continued and undisturbed control did not fall undesigned into "Alcoa's" lap; obviously it could not have done so. It could only have resulted, as it did result, from a persistent determination to maintain the control, with which it found itself vested in 1912. There were at least one or two abortive attempts to enter the industry, but "Alcoa" effectively anticipated and forestalled all competition, and succeeded in holding the field alone. True, it stimulated demand and opened new uses for the metal, but not without making sure that it could supply what it had evoked. There is no dispute as to this; "Alcoa" avows it as evidence of the skill, energy and initiative with which it has always conducted its business; as a reason why, having won its way by fair means, it should be commended, and not dismembered. We need charge it with no moral derelictions after 1912; we may assume that all it claims for itself is true. The only question is whether it falls within the exception established in favor of those who do not seek, but cannot avoid, the control of a market. It seems to us that that question scarcely survives its statement. It was not inevitable that it should always anticipate increases in the demand for ingot and be prepared to supply them. Nothing compelled it to keep doubling and redoubling its capacity before others entered the field. It insists that it never excluded competitors; but we can think of no more effective exclusion than progressively to embrace each new opportunity as it opened, and to face every newcomer with new capacity already geared into a great organization, having the advantage of experience, trade connections and the elite of personnel. Only in case we interpret "exclusion" as limited to manoeuvres not honestly industrial, but actuated solely by a desire to prevent competition, can such a course, indefatigably pursued, be deemed not "exclusionary." So to limit it would in our judgment emasculate the Act; would permit just such consolidations as it was designed to prevent.

"Alcoa" answers that it positively assisted competitors, instead of discouraging them. That may be true as to fabricators of ingot; but what of that? They were its market for ingot, and it is charged only with a monopoly of ingot....

We disregard any question of "intent." Relatively early in the history of the Act — 1905 — Holmes, J., in *Swift & Co. v. United States*, 196 U.S. 375, explained this aspect of the Act in a passage often quoted. Although the primary evil was monopoly, the Act also covered preliminary steps, which, if continued, would lead to it. These may do no harm of themselves; but, if they are initial moves in a plan or scheme which, carried out, will result in monopoly, they are dangerous and the law will nip them in the bud. For this reason conduct falling short of monopoly, is not illegal unless it is part of a plan to monopolize, or to gain such other control of a market as is equally forbidden. To make it so, the plaintiff must prove what in the criminal law is known as a "specific intent"; an intent which goes beyond the mere intent to do the act. By far the greatest part of the fabulous record piled up in the case at bar, was concerned with proving such an intent. The plaintiff was seeking to show that many transactions, neutral on their face, were not in fact necessary to the development of "Alcoa's" business, and had no motive except to exclude others and perpetuate its hold upon the ingot market. Upon that effort success depended in case the plaintiff failed to satisfy the court that it was unnecessary under § 2 to convict "Alcoa" of practices unlawful of themselves. The plaintiff has so satisfied us, and the issue of intent ceases to have any importance; no intent is relevant except that which is relevant to any liability, criminal or civil: i.e. an intent to bring about the forbidden act.... So here, "Alcoa" meant to keep, and did keep, that complete and exclusive hold upon the ingot market with which it started. That was to "monopolize" that market, however innocently it otherwise proceeded. So far as the judgment held that it was not within § 2, it must be reversed.

As we have said, the plaintiff also sought to convict "Alcoa" of practices in which it engaged, not because they were necessary to the development of its business, but only in order to suppress competitors. Since we are holding that "Alcoa" "monopolized" the ingot market in 1940, regardless of such practices, these issues might be moot, if it inevitably followed from our holding that "Alcoa" must be dissolved. It could be argued that the new companies which would then emerge, should not be charged in retrospect with their predecessor's illegal conduct; but should be entitled to start without the handicap of injunctions, based upon its past. Possibly that would be true, except that conditions have so changed since the case was closed, that, as will appear, it by no means follows, because "Alcoa" had a monopoly in 1940, that it will have one when final judgment is entered after the war. That judgment may leave it intact as a competing unit among other competing units, and the plaintiff might argue, and undoubtedly will, that, if it was in the past guilty of practices, aimed at "monopolizing" the ingot market, it would be proper and necessary to enjoin their resumption, even though it no longer will have a monopoly. For this reason it appears to us that the issues are not altogether moot....

....

The plaintiff describes as the "Price Squeeze" a practice by which, it says, "Alcoa" intended to put out of business the manufacturers of aluminum "sheet" who were its competitors; for "Alcoa" was itself a large — in fact much the largest — maker of that product, and had been the first to introduce it many years before the period in question.... The plaintiff says that the "squeeze" had been in operation for a long time before the year 1925, and that by means of it "Alcoa" had succeeded in eliminating four out of the eight companies which competed with it.

....

The plaintiff's theory is that "Alcoa" consistently sold ingot at so high a price that the "sheet rollers," who were forced to buy from it, could not pay the expenses of "rolling" the "sheet" and make a living profit out of the price at which "Alcoa" itself sold "sheet." To establish this the plaintiff asks us to take "Alcoa's" costs of "rolling" as a fair measure of its competitors' costs, and to assume that they had to meet "Alcoa's" price for all grades of "sheet," and could not buy ingot elsewhere. It seems to us altogether reasonable, in the absence of proof to the contrary, to suppose that "Alcoa's" "rolling" costs were not higher than those of other "sheet rollers"; and, although it is true that theoretically, imported "virgin" was always available, for the reasons we have already given when we were discussing the monopoly in ingot, we think that it could at best be had at very little less than "Alcoa's" prices. As for "secondary," there were a number of uses for "sheet" for which the trade would not accept such of it as was available in the years in question. Besides, the "spread" between suitable grades of "secondary" and "virgin" was also very small.

... For all the five "gauges" of "coiled sheet" for eight years, 1925-1932, the average profit open to competing "rollers" was .84 cents a pound, as against 4.7 cents for the five succeeding years, 1933-1937. The corresponding figures for "flat sheet" were .59 cents and 4 cents; and for "Duralumin," 4.9 cents and 11.8

cents. Moreover, in 31 instances out of 112 there was no "spread" at all; that is, the cost of ingot plus the cost of "rolling" was greater than the price at which "Alcoa" was selling "sheet." Obviously, there was in the eight years little or no inducement to continue in the "sheet" business, and Baush, the only "roller" of "Duralumin," gave up in 1931, although "Alcoa" insists, and the judge found, that this was because of its inefficiency.

....

... That it was unlawful to set the price of "sheet" so low and hold the price of ingot so high, seems to us unquestionable, provided, as we have held, that on this record the price of ingot must be regarded as higher than a "fair price." True, this was only a consequence of "Alcoa's" control over the price of ingot, and perhaps it ought not to be considered as a separate wrong; moreover, we do not use it as part of the reasoning by which we conclude that the monopoly was unlawful. But it was at least an unlawful exercise of "Alcoa's" power after it had been put on notice by the "sheet rollers'" "complaints; and this is true, even though we assent to the judge's finding that it was not part of an attempt to monopolize the "sheet" market.

....

Nearly five years have passed since the evidence was closed; during that time the aluminum industry, like most other industries, has been revolutionized by the nation's efforts in a great crisis. That alone would make it impossible to dispose of the action upon the basis of the record as we have it; and so both sides agree; both appeal to us to take "judicial notice" of what has taken place meanwhile, though they differ as to what should be the result. The plaintiff wishes us to enter a judgment that "Alcoa" shall be dissolved, and that we shall direct it presently to submit a plan, whose execution, however, is to be deferred until after the war.... On the other hand, "Alcoa" argues that, when we look at the changes that have taken place — particularly the enormous capacity of plaintiff's aluminum plants — it appears that, even though we should conclude that it had "monopolized" the ingot industry up to 1941, the plaintiff now has in its hands the means to prevent any possible "monopolization" of the industry after the war, which it may use as it wills ....

[W]e refuse to take "notice" of facts relevant to the correctness of the findings; but we do take "notice" of those relevant to remedies.

After doing so, it is impossible to say what will be "Alcoa's" position in the industry after the war. The plaintiff has leased to it all its new plants and the leases do not expire until 1947 and 1948, though they may be surrendered earlier. No one can now forecast in the remotest way what will be the form of the industry after the plaintiff has disposed of these plants, upon their surrender. It may be able to transfer all of them to persons who can effectively compete with "Alcoa"; it may be able to transfer some; conceivably, it may be unable to dispose of any. The measure of its success will be at least one condition upon the propriety of dissolution, and upon the form which it should take, if there is to be any. It is as idle for the plaintiff to assume that dissolution will be proper, as it is for "Alcoa" to assume that it will not be; and it would be particularly fatuous to prepare a plan now, even if we could be sure that eventually some form of dissolution will be proper. Dissolution is not a penalty but a remedy; if the industry will not need it for its protection, it will be a disservice to break up an aggregation which has for so long demonstrated its efficiency. The need for such a remedy will be for the district court in the first instance, and there is a peculiar propriety in our saying nothing to control its decision, because the appeal from any judgment which it may enter, will perhaps be justiciable only by the Supreme Court, if there are then six justices qualified to sit.

NOTES AND QUESTIONS

1. Contrast the "bad acts" committed by Alcoa with those committed by the American Can Company. Is it just as obvious that Alcoa's bad acts were socially harmful? What about the "price squeeze," by which Alcoa allegedly monopolized the ingot market by (1) selling independent fabricators' ingot at a relatively high price and (2) pricing its own fabrications fairly low, with the result that the independent fabricators could not obtain a sufficient markup to earn a profit? Why would Alcoa bother with a "price squeeze?" Alcoa could lawfully stop selling any ingot at all to the fabricators, could it not? The alleged "price squeeze" may have been the result of nothing more than Alcoa's efficiency: its costs in fabricating its own aluminum were lower than the combined costs of selling and shipping ingot to others, plus their fabrication costs.

But there may be circumstances when a "price squeeze" is not the product of the dominant firm's efficiency. For example, suppose that the fabricators must make a very large investment in specialized fabrication plants. These costs are "sunk," in the sense that if the plants cannot be used for fabrication of aluminum, much of their value is lost. The life of a plant is twenty-five years. Suppose that after an independent fabricator had built such a plant Alcoa decided to go into fabrication for itself. Alcoa might profitably pursue a pricing strategy of high ingot prices and low fabricated prices in order to transfer to itself the returns on the fabricator's fixed cost investment. Ordinarily, a firm will not shut down as long as it earns enough to cover its variable costs, even though it is losing money because it cannot cover its fixed costs. The court in *Bonjorno v. Kaiser Alum. & Chem. Corp.*, 752 F.2d 802 (3d Cir. 1984), condemned a "price squeeze" on this theory:

> When a monopolist competes by denying a source of supply to his competitors, raises his competitor's price for raw materials without affecting his own costs, lowers his price for the finished goods, and threatens his competitors with sustained competition if they do not accede to his anticompetitive designs, then his actions have crossed the shadowy barrier of the Sherman Act.

Do you agree? *See* Hovenkamp, *Antitrust Policy After Chicago*, 84 Mich. L. Rev. 213, 268 (1985).

The "price squeeze" may also be a successful monopolistic strategy for a price-regulated utility. Utilities are generally regulated so as to earn a "fair" or "reasonable" rate of return on their investment. However, this return is almost always positive — i.e., the regulators will not permit the utility to lose money. *See* 2 A. Kahn, *The Economics of Regulation: Principles and Institutions* 49-59, 106-08 (1970). As a result, a utility has an incentive to expand its service area, even if it must drive other utility companies out of business. *See* Averch & Johnson, *Behavior of the Firm Under Regulatory Constraint*, 52 Am. Econ. Rev. 1052 (1962). A large utility that "wholesales" power to smaller utilities might try to drive the smaller utilities out by charging them high prices for electricity but setting its own rates rather low, thus competing with the smaller firm for new business or perhaps even giving the customers in the smaller firm's area an incentive to switch electric companies. *See City of Groton v. Connecticut Light & Power Co.*, 662 F.2d 921 (2d Cir. 1981); Lopatka, *The Electrical Utility Price Squeeze as an Antitrust Cause of Action*, 31 UCLA L. Rev. 640 (1984).

In *Town of Concord v. Boston Edison Co.*, 915 F.2d 17 (1st Cir. 1990), the First Circuit (Judge Breyer) refused to condemn a price "squeeze" under this theory, noting the following:

> [P]rices that squeeze a "second level" firm will benefit consumers whenever the "second-level" firm is *itself* a monopolist.... If, for example, ingot costs $40, the fabricating process costs $35, and the profit-maximizing price for sheet is $100, an ingot monopolist will charge $65 for the ingot, hoping that competition at the fabricating level will keep the total price at $100. If a different, independent monopolist dominates the fabricating level, however, that independent monopolist buying ingot at $65 will mark up the price by more than $35, because he wants to earn monopoly profits as well. The result will be a market price of more than $100.... Under these circumstances, entry by the ingot monopolist into the sheet-fabrication level — even by means of a price squeeze — will help the consumer by limiting the final price of sheet to $100....
>
> Finally, we note that it is not easy for courts to administer Judge Hand's price squeeze test. That test makes it unlawful for a monopolist to charge more than a "fair price" for the primary product while simultaneously charging so little for the secondary product that its second-level competitors cannot make a "living profit."... But how is a judge or jury to determine a "fair price"?... Is it the price that competition "would have set" were the primary level not monopolized? How can the court determine this price without examining costs and demands, indeed without acting like a rate-setting regulatory agency...?

2. The *Alcoa* opinion developed the modern two-stage definition of the offense of monopolization under section 2 of the Sherman Act. First, the court must determine whether the defendant has "monopoly power" — that is, sufficient market power to "dominate" an industry. If the answer is no, then the defendant is not guilty. If the answer is yes, however, the court must additionally determine whether the defendant is an "innocent" monopolist whose dominance was "thrust upon" it by its own skill or efficiency, or whether it engaged in anticompetitive or monopolistic acts.

3. Consider Judge Hand's notion that expanding capacity to meet anticipated demand is "exclusionary." How can this be so? In order to price monopolistically, a monopolist must limit output. One often suggested possibility is that Alcoa could build a plant larger than it actually needed to meet either current or foreseeable demand. It could then set a price higher than the competitive level but not so high as to encourage immediate entry. A firm contemplating entry would see that Alcoa had substantial excess capacity and could reduce price and enlarge output at any time. The firm would also know that its own start-up costs would be high. It would look for another industry where there was not so much excess capacity. This combination of excess capacity plus so-called "limit" pricing has frequently been alleged of monopolists who appeared not to be restricting output. See the *du Pont* (titanium dioxide) case, reprinted *infra*, where the Federal Trade Commission dismissed a case that was not all that different from *Alcoa.* One problem with the theory is that it requires the alleged monopolist to maintain a great deal of unused productive capacity. This can be very expensive. The monopoly profits generated by the scheme must be large enough to offset this cost, but not so large as to encourage a potential competitor to enter the industry.

4. Judge Hand concluded in *Alcoa* that "throughout the history of [the antitrust laws] it has been constantly assumed that one of their purposes was to perpetuate and preserve, for its own sake and in spite of possible cost, an organization of industry in small units." Assumed by whom, do you suppose? Judge Hand did not cite a single Supreme Court opinion for that proposition, although he did suggest that it is explicit in the legislative history of the Sherman Act. For an argument that Hand's interpretation of the legislative history was wrong, *see* Bork, *Legislative Intent and The Policy of The Sherman Act,* 9 J.L. & Econ. 7 (1966).

5. Judge Hand noted that Alcoa's profits were not inordinately high for a firm of its size. Would you expect a firm guilty of monopolization to have higher-than-normal rates of profit? Should the absence of high profitability be evidence that a firm is not a monopolist? It is possible that a firm engaged in illegal monopolization does not have particularly high profits, because it incurs large expenses in maintaining its monopoly power. *See* R. Posner, *Antitrust Law: An Economic Perspective* 12 (1976). In fact, measuring market power from accounting rates of return is extraordinarily difficult, and some believe that it is conceptually impossible. *See* 2A P. Areeda & H. Hovenkamp, *Antitrust Law* 520 (rev. ed. 1995).

6. *The Dilemma of the Durable Goods Monopolist.* As Judge Hand noted, Alcoa faced competition from its own aluminum — reclaimed and sold as "secondary" on the aluminum market. The monopolist of durable goods — goods that last a long time and can be re-used by people other than the original purchasers

— has one big problem. The more it sells, the more of its own product is out there in competition.

If a good is "perfectly durable" — i.e., if the demand curve for the "used" good is identical to the demand curve for the new good, because consumers are indifferent as between them — then the monopolist will simply lose its monopoly position. Can you think of such a good? Land is probably the best example. All of it is very old, none (except a little in Holland) is being manufactured, and old land is just as good as new land. Suppose that a land monopolist owned an entire island, consisting of 100 lots. As soon as it sold the first lot its market share would decline to 99%; when it had sold fifty lots, its market share would be only 50%. In short, in the very process of profiting from its monopoly, the land monopolist will have destroyed it.

To take a simple illustration of the durable goods monopolist's dilemma, suppose that a baby buggy is used by parents of a new baby for precisely one year, and that the life of a baby buggy is ten years. Assume further that customers are indifferent between new baby buggies and used baby buggies, provided they are less than ten years old. Each year, ten couples have babies and need a buggy. Finally, suppose that the cost of making a baby buggy is $100, but that the use of a baby buggy for one year is worth $50 to every customer. After one year parents place no value on the baby buggy for their own use; they either store it in the attic, where it is worthless, or sell it for the best price they can get.

What will the customers in the first year be willing to pay for the baby buggy? One would think that the buggy is worth $500 — $50 per customer multiplied by ten consecutive customers. But the first customer will not be willing to pay $500, because he knows that the second year there will be competition in the baby buggy market. There will be ten new sets of parents needing buggies and ten used baby buggies on the market. But there will also be the output of new baby buggies by the manufacturer. What will the price be the second year? The manufacturer will presumably not sell them for less than their $100 production cost. But the very first year competition may easily drive the price in this market down to the competitive level. The second year the situation will be even worse. A wise customer will probably not be willing to pay much more than $150 for the buggy — $50 for the one year's use, and $100 for a reasonable estimate of the selling price at the end of the first year. In this particular case, instead of getting the $400 in available monopoly profits from its durable good, the monopolist gets only $50.

But suppose that the durable goods monopolist rents, rather than sells, its baby buggies. Since each customer values the buggy at $50, it will charge $50 per year for nine years. The tenth year it will sell the buggy for $50 to the final customer, and then the buggy will be worn out. In this case the monopolist will be able to earn $400 in monopoly profits from each buggy. This undoubtedly explains why United Shoe Machinery, Xerox, IBM, and other durable goods monopolists who were able to do so rented, rather than sold, their products. *See also Hawaii Hous. Auth. v. Midkiff*, 467 U.S: 229 (1984), in which an apparent land cartel in Hawaii leased rather than sold its property. Once the monopolist has lost its monopoly position, of course, customer preference will dictate whether it sells or rents its output.

Alcoa sold both raw and fabricated aluminum. The transaction costs of renting aluminum kitchen utensils, aircraft and automobile parts, and building materials would be extremely high, and customers would place a much lower value on such parts if they could not purchase them. Alcoa's monopoly position was saved by the fact that aluminum is only an imperfectly durable good. Only part of it could be re-used, and many customers either found second-hand aluminum unacceptable or were willing to pay a premium for new aluminum. The monopolist of an imperfectly durable good can continue to enjoy some monopoly profits. Can you see why?

Another way that the durable goods monopolist might obtain more than the competitive price is to make a credible commitment to make less of the good than would clear the market at a competitive price. For example, what if the baby buggy manufacturer in the above illustration could make a credible promise to its customers that it was going to manufacture buggies for exactly one year and then go out of business. In that case, it should be able to obtain the full $500 for its buggies. Consider the artist who promises to make only fifty copies of a particular lithograph and then destroy the plate. Shouldn't the price be higher than if the artist made an unlimited number of copies?

See Wiley, Rasmusen & Ramseyer, *The Leasing Monopolist*, 37 UCLA L. Rev. 693 (1990); Malueg & Solow, *On Requiring the Durable Goods Monopolist to Sell*, 25 Econ. Letters 283 (1987); Coase, *Durability and Monopoly*, 15 J.L. & Econ. 143 (1972); Carlton & R. Gertner, *Market Power and Mergers in Durable-Good Industries*, 32 J.L. & Econ. S203 (1989) (arguing that mergers should be of much less concern in durable goods industries); Foreb, *Evaluating Mergers in Durable Goods Industries*, 34 Antitrust Bull. 99 (1989) (in many markets durability limits market power).

SECTION II. THE MODERN OFFENSE OF MONOPOLIZATION

Today we can state the test for illegal monopolization in a single sentence: a defendant (1) must have a large amount of market power; and (2) it must have engaged in certain monopolistic, or anticompetitive, acts.

The verbal formulation of that test has not changed for thirty years. That stability, however, belies the great deal of flux that has existed in judicial interpretation of section 2 of the Sherman Act. First, our notion of market power is much more technical today than it was at the time *Alcoa* was decided. Secondly, judges in the 1970's and 1980's have examined much more critically those practices that are alleged to be monopolistic. For example, Judge Hand believed it was illegal monopolization for a firm with market power to enlarge its plant to meet an anticipated increase in demand for its product; few courts today would agree. *See*, e.g., *Dial A Car, Inc. v. Transportation, Inc.*, 82 F.3d 484, 486 (D.C. Cir. 1996) (not unlawful for cab company to expand its service so as to compete with existing limousine companies: the expansion "would appear to be fostering competition, rather than reducing it").

One of the reasons for this shift in the definition of monopolistic or anticompetitive acts has been a major change in the fundamental ideology of the federal antitrust laws. Alcoa could expand its output of aluminum only by finding new uses for it (i.e., expanding the market) or else by lowering the price. Consumers were better off because of these activities. By expanding its plant, however, Alcoa prevented competitors from entering the market: as the market grew Alcoa was always there, ready to supply the full demand, allegedly at a low enough price that it was unprofitable for competitors to enter the market. In short, while Alcoa's expansion program benefitted consumers of aluminum, it injured competitors, or at least prevented potential competitors from entering the market. When Judge Hand looked at the "injuries" caused by the defendant's acts, he concentrated largely on injuries that accrued to competitors or potential competitors of the defendant. The same was true in the *American Can* case: most of American Can's judicially recognized "victims" were competitors. Today, on the other hand, the circuit courts are more likely to look at the effects that the alleged monopolization has on consumers rather than competitors. See the *Berkey Photo* and *California Computer Products* cases, *infra*, this chapter.

A. MARKET POWER AND THE RELEVANT MARKET

In an often-quoted passage in *Alcoa*, Judge Hand attempted to define a "monopoly" under the Sherman Act. Hand observed that Alcoa dominated over 90% of America's aluminum market. He concluded: "That percentage is enough to constitute a monopoly; it is doubtful whether sixty or sixty-four per cent would be enough; and certainly thirty-three per cent is not." Judge Hand found a very high correlation — perhaps even an identification — between the defendant's percentage of a certain market and the existence of a monopoly. This seems logical, since the historical definition of a monopoly at common law was a legal right to 100% of a certain market.

But large market share is not the evil that the Sherman Act condemns. Rather, the evil is that, perhaps *because* it has a large percentage, it is able to charge more than a competitive price for the monopolized product. "Market power" is the ability to raise price by reducing output. Today we measure market power as the ratio of the profit-maximizing price for a seller's output to the seller's marginal cost at that rate of output. A seller whose marginal cost of producing a widget is $1.00, but who can maximize its profits by selling the widget at $1.02 has a small amount of market power. A seller whose marginal cost is $1.00 but whose profit-maximizing price is $1.75 has a great deal of market power. (In perfect competition, prices are driven to marginal cost. In that case, a seller's marginal cost and its profit-maximizing price would be the same. If the seller attempted to charge more than marginal cost, and it was not more efficient than its rivals, it would lose all its sales to competitors.). The Lerner Index measures market power this way, by the expression:

$$\frac{P-MC}{P}$$

Where:

P   =   the firm's profit-maximizing price, which we generally assume is the price that the firm is charging at any given time

MC   =   the firm's marginal cost

The formula is easy to use if true marginal cost is known. For example, in a competitive market, price equals marginal cost, so the value of the Index is zero. If a firm's price is double its marginal cost, say P = 2 and MC = 1, then the index value is ½, or 0.5, suggesting significant market power.

Market power expressed as the ratio of a seller's marginal cost to its profit-maximizing price, is a function of the elasticity of demand for the seller's output. The more elastic the demand for a certain product, the more customers will opt away when the product's price goes up, and the less will be the ability of a seller to sell at a supracompetitive level.

It is easy to quantify the relationship that exists between elasticity of demand and market power.

Market power, defined as the ratio of the monopoly price (the profit-maximizing price) and the competitive price (marginal cost), varies with firm elasticity of demand by the following formula:

$$\frac{P_m}{P_c} = \frac{e}{e-1}$$

Where:

P_m = the profit-maximizing price of the product

P_c = the competitive price of the product (marginal cost)

P_e = the price elasticity of demand facing the seller

For derivation of the formula, plus analysis of some of its uses and limitations, see Landes & Posner, *Market Power in Antitrust Cases*, 94 Harv. L. Rev. 937 (1981); H. Hovenkamp, *Federal Antitrust Policy* § 3.1 (2d ed. 1994).

However, don't let the equation fool you into thinking that there are easy answers to the question of market power. The formula simply tells us that there is a fixed relationship between the amount consumers as a group are willing to pay for a particular seller's product and the amount that the seller can charge for it. That statement is a tautology. To be able to express the ability of a firm to charge a monopoly price as a function of firm elasticity of demand does us little good in the courtroom unless it is easier to determine elasticity of demand facing a firm than it is to estimate monopoly power from market share. Most often it is not. The same thing is true of the Lerner Index itself. Our ability to measure market power under the Index is no better than our ability to measure marginal cost, and direct measurement of marginal cost in antitrust cases has not yet met with much success.

As a result, market share percentages continue to dominate judicial estimates of market power. In fact, our intuition tells us that someone who has a very large market share, other things being equal, has more ability to control price than someone whose market share is very small. If someone with 1% of the market for a certain product attempts unilaterally to raise the price of the product, consumers are likely to have dozens of other places to which they can turn for the same product. The result will be that the seller will lose its customers.

By contrast, if a seller produces 90% of a certain product then it is more likely to get away with the price increase. The producers who control the remaining 10% of the market will not be able to service all the monopolist's customers, and many of those customers will have to decide either to pay the higher price or not to buy at all. In fact, the producers holding the remaining 10% of the market may find it profitable to raise their own prices to a level equal with or slightly lower than the price charged by the monopolist. The monopolist's high price will therefore provide the fringe competitors with an "umbrella" that will enable them to obtain monopoly profits as well.

This intuitive relationship between market power and market share can also be demonstrated mathematically, although the equation for market power contains more variables than market share alone. *See* Landes & Posner, *Market Power in Antitrust Cases*, 94 Harv. L. Rev. 937, 944-48 (1981). For alternative mechanisms for measuring market power, *see* 2A P. Areeda, H. Hovenkamp, & J. Solow, *Antitrust Law* ¶¶ 515-525 (rev. ed. 1995). Today the law of antitrust recognizes that market power and not market share is the evil that the antitrust laws govern, but that the correlation between market power and market share permits courts to use market share as a limited proxy or surrogate for market power.

As a general rule, therefore, courts begin their analysis in monopolization cases by determining the defendant's market share. In order to do this the court must define a certain "relevant" market. The relevant market consists of two parts, the product market and the geographic market. Clearly, a defendant who has market power does not have market power in every product, but only in the particular product that it sells. But how does one define the relevant "product"? Are Ford automobiles and Chevrolet automobiles the same product? Color televisions and black and white televisions? Secondly, it is clear that someone who has market power does not have it everywhere. The owner of the only movie theater in Ozona, Texas, may have substantial market power in Ozona — but how about twenty miles away? In Dallas? In New York City?

In determining market share the court generally does three things. First, it identifies the "product" that is alleged to be monopolized. In the *Alcoa* case Judge Hand decided that the relevant product was virgin ingot manufactured and sold in the United States and foreign-produced ingot actually sold in the United States. Second, the court determines a relevant geographic market. In *Alcoa* Judge Hand decided that the market was the entire United States. Finally, the court computes a "market share" expressed as the defendant's output of the relevant product in the relevant market, divided by the total output of the relevant product in the relevant market. Judge Hand decided that Alcoa's market share was about 90%.

As the *Alcoa* decision indicates, identifying a relevant product or geographic market can be difficult enough. However, our analysis of market power is made even more complex because market share is not a perfect expression of market power. Courts express the imperfection of the relationship in various ways — frequently by saying that a very high market share creates an "inference" of market power that can be rebutted if the defendant can show that it is not able to control output or price in the market. In fact, market power is a function of three different values: the defendant's market share, the elasticity of demand in the entire market, and the cross-elasticity of supply of competing or potentially competing firms. Can a seller with a very small percentage of the market ever control the market output or price? *See Dimmitt Agri Indus., Inc. v. CPC Int'l, Inc.*, 679 F.2d 516 (5th Cir. 1982), *cert. denied*, 460 U.S. 1082 (1983).

Suppose that Alcoa does in fact have 90% of the market share of aluminum but that consumer preferences for aluminum track the costs of producing it very closely. If the market price of aluminum rises by even a small amount, droves of customers will stop buying aluminum and substitute away. In such a case, it seems clear, Alcoa would not have power to control the price of aluminum, even though its market share is very high. In short, the more elastic the demand for the allegedly monopolized product when it is priced at marginal cost, the less market power the defendant has. For a more detailed and more technical analysis of the relationship between market power and demand elasticities, *see* Landes & Posner, *supra*, at pp. 945-48.

Secondly, suppose that Alcoa does in fact produce 90% of the virgin aluminum currently sold in the United States, but that there are dozens of underutilized steel mills that could shift over to the production of aluminum at very low cost. If the market price of aluminum rises by even a small amount, it will be profitable for these steel companies to shift to production of aluminum. Alcoa's market share will then drop and the enlarged production of aluminum in the country will force prices back down. In that case, it seems equally clear that Alcoa's control over the price of aluminum is small. The same thing would be true if Alcoa had competitors actually making aluminum, but these competitors were operating at far below their capacity. Suppose, for example, that Alcoa is currently manufacturing 7 million tons of aluminum per year and that it has competitors in the United

States who manufacture 3 million tons per year. Suppose in addition that these competitors actually have plants large enough to manufacture 7 million tons of aluminum themselves, but they have not been doing so because the price of aluminum has not been high enough. If the price goes up, however, they will have an incentive to enlarge their production. This unused productive capacity limits Alcoa's control over the price of aluminum.

The presence of unused capacity in the industry, or the existence of firms that could easily shift to production of the product, is called the elasticity of supply in the market. The greater the elasticity of supply, the less control a particular producer has over the market price. Both elasticity of demand and elasticity of supply therefore limit the ability of a producer — even a producer with a very large market share — to raise its prices to a supracompetitive level. The two elasticities are often unrelated to each other. That is, high elasticity of demand does not entail high elasticity of supply, or vice-versa. Suppose, for example, that one firm has a 90% share of the current production of tissue paper. However, the production of corrugated paper for heavy boxes is carried on by dozens of small competitors. The *demand* for tissue paper might be very inelastic. Furthermore, the cross-elasticity of demand between tissue paper and corrugated paper is probably very low; that is, the price of tissue paper would have to go very high before many customers would find corrugated paper to be an attractive substitute. But suppose additionally that at the *production* end the same plants that produce corrugated paper can, simply by making a few minor alterations, shift their equipment over to manufacturing tissue paper instead. How should we measure this? Should we say that the relevant "product" is tissue paper and corrugated paper together, or that the two are separate products? What appears clearly to be two different products on the demand side (for example, cookbooks and telephone directories) may in fact seem much more similar on the supply side (if a printer can costlessly shift over from producing cookbooks to producing telephone directories).

The concept of elasticity of supply also suggests that when we identify a defendant's percentage of a relevant market we consider the industry's production *capacity*, not merely the amount that it is actually producing. As a general matter, it is much cheaper for a competitor to increase its output in an already existing plant than it is to be build an additional plant, or for a new competitor to enter the field. Thus the existence of large amounts of excess capacity in times of slack demand can seriously distort our picture of market power, particularly if one lucky competitor is less affected by the declining demand than others are. For example, if market demand for steel drops from 90% of plant capacity to 40%, but that decrease affects certain plants much more severely than it does others, the favored plants may have a misleading percentage of output in the market which suggests that they have far more market power than they really do. Unfortunately, however, the theoretical superiority of capacity is not the only relevant consideration. Plant capacity is extraordinarily difficult to measure. Many plants can produce far more than they currently do, but only at higher costs. On the other hand, current output figures are readily available.

Virtually all courts continue to use output, rather than capacity, in measuring market share. *See* 2A P. Areeda, H. Hovenkamp & J. Solow, *Antitrust Law* ch. 5 (rev. ed. 1994).

Now let us return to one of Judge Hand's conclusions in *Alcoa*. In computing the defendant's market share, Judge Hand included foreign aluminum actually imported into the United States. However, he did not include aluminum that was manufactured and sold abroad, and he did not include excess capacity of aluminum producing foreign plants. Was Judge Hand correct?

Hand correctly noted that foreign producers operate under certain cost disadvantages; for example, they must pay transportation and tariff costs which do not have to be paid by a domestic producer. Some foreign products are at such a high cost disadvantage that none of them are imported. Sand and gravel are good examples. In such situations, we should exclude all foreign production as well as foreign capacity from the market definition. However, the fact that *some* foreign aluminum was imported into the United States indicates that it is profitable to import aluminum, cost disadvantages notwithstanding. If it is profitable to import a small amount, why would it not be profitable to import more? One answer is that there might not only be a tariff on imports, but also an absolute quota. In that case, only the maximum amount of foreign aluminum allowed to be imported under the quota ought to be included in the market. But if there is no quota, then doesn't *all* foreign aluminum actually compete with domestic aluminum? This analysis assumes that the marginal cost curve to the foreign producers is flat — that is, that it would cost them no more per unit to import additional aluminum into the United States than it is costing them to import what is already coming in. If there were only one foreign producer, it would have an upward sloping marginal cost curve, just as Alcoa does. However, in a competitive market, where plants are tending to their most efficient output level and new entry is relatively easy and common, the marginal cost for the industry as a whole remains flat. In this case, wouldn't any attempt by Alcoa to raise its prices encourage foreign producers to enlarge their American imports? *See* Landes & Posner, *Market Power, supra*, at 964-68.

One other problem of market definition that Judge Hand faced deserves attention. Alcoa sold much of its aluminum as ingot to other firms for fabrication, and it was accused of monopolizing the ingot market. But Alcoa also fabricated some aluminum itself. Should the ingot which Alcoa itself fabricated be included in the relevant market? Judge Hand was correct to include it. Ingot which is transferred from Alcoa's "ingot division" to its "fabricating division" passes through the distribution chain to consumers just as much as ingot which is sold to independent fabricators. The fact that Alcoa is vertically integrated has no impact on market definition.

In the *American Can* case, printed before *Alcoa*, the court concluded that cans made by canners who used the cans themselves ought not be included in the relevant market. The judge reasoned that a bread combination would be illegal "in spite of the fact that in that city one-half or two-thirds or even three-quarters of the bread consumed was actually baked in the kitchens of private families." *United States v. American Can Co.*, 230 F. 859, 899 (D. Md. 1916). Is that argument convincing? Apparently not, for the judge then made an observation that contradicted his conclusion: "Yet the fact that one-third of the cans used in the country are made by the people who use them is one of great significance. It shows that any considerable rise in the price of cans ... would probably lead to two things ... :" (1) self-makers would begin to sell them; and (2) other canners would begin making their own. *Id.*

The relationship between market power, market share, and supply and demand elasticities has plagued the federal courts ever since *Alcoa* was decided. The case that follows is one of the Supreme Court's most significant statements of the relationship between demand elasticities and a defendant's power over price.

Finally, one observation must be made that is a commonplace for economists but sometimes trips up noneconomist judges: the things to be grouped inside a relevant market must, to a significant degree, be *substitutes* for each other. That is, to conclude that a grouping of sales constitutes a relevant market is to conclude both (1) that the things inside the grouping do not face significant competition from the things outside the grouping; and (2) that the things inside the grouping *do* compete with each other. Consider the Ninth Circuit's *Kodak* decision, which held that a group of non-substitutable repair parts for photocopiers constituted a single relevant market:

> Consideration of the "commercial realities" in the markets for Kodak parts compels the use of an "all parts" market theory. The "commercial reality" faced by service providers and equipment owners is that a service provider must have ready access to all parts to compete in the service market. As the relevant market for service "from the Kodak equipment owner's perspective is composed of only those companies that service Kodak machines," id., the relevant market for parts from the equipment owners' and service providers' perspective is composed of "all parts" that are designed to meet Kodak photocopier and micrographics equipment specifications. The makers of these parts "if unified by a monopolist or a hypothetical cartel, would have market power in dealing with" ISOs and end users.

Image Technical Services v. Eastman Kodak Co., 125 F.3d 1195, 1203-04 (9th Cir. 1997), *cert. denied*, 118 S. Ct. 1560 (1998).

Clearly, the court has confused complements with substitutes. Granted, a photocopier needs all of its parts in order to function, just as an automobile needs both an engine and a oil filter, and computer operations require both hardware and software. But that does not mean that there is an "engine/oil filter" market or a "hardware/software" market. As the court observes, there is a "commercial reality" linking the various parts in a photocopier. But the reality in this case is precisely the opposite from the one that groups parts into a single market. When goods are substitutes for each other, and thus within the same market, their prices move up and down together. For example, if Alcoa's aluminum is a substitute for Reynold's aluminum, then the two prices will move in the same direction as the market price for aluminum rises and falls. By contrast, the prices of complementary goods move in opposite directions. For example, if the price of engines should increase dramatically, people would buy fewer cars and, as a result, demand for oil filters would fall, thus reducing their price. Combining complements into a "relevant market" undermines the entire market power inquiry because it becomes impossible to determine whether the defendant has market power in any specific parts. For example, a firm might make 70% of 100 different parts, but grouping them together deprives the fact finder of the ability to determine whether this means 70% of each of the 100 parts (which would indicate market power in all of them if other requirements were met), or whether it means 100% of some parts and lower numbers right down to zero for others.

To illustrate, consider whether four gasoline stations on the same intersection are the same relevant market for antitrust purposes. Clearly, it is not because the motorist needs to stop at all four of them. Quite the contrary, the reason they compete with each other, and thus belong in the same relevant market, is that the motorist does *not* need to stop at all four of them; as a result, they must compete with each other on price or services.

And what do you think of the Ninth Circuit's conclusion that "all parts" are a relevant market because if the makers of all these parts were unified by a monopolist or cartel, they would be able to charge monopoly prices? Suppose three firms in the aggregate make 80% of the glass plates that go on top of a photocopier and 85% of the rubber wheels that go at the bottom. If they got together, they could fix the price of both the glass plates and the wheels. But does this entail that there is a relevant "glass plate/rubber wheel" market? The court was paraphrasing (incorrectly) the government's *1992 Horizontal Merger Guidelines* §1.0 (reprinted as Appendix A); *see* 2A P. Areeda, H. Hovenkamp, & J. Solow, *Antitrust Law* ¶ 530 (rev. ed. 1995). The Ninth Circuit used the hypothetical cartel analogy correctly in *Rebel Oil Co. v. Atlantic Richfield Co.*, 51 F.3d 1421, 1436 (9th Cir.), *cert. denied*, 516 U.S. 987 (1995), when it concluded that self-service and full-service gasoline were in the same relevant market because a cartel of self-service providers could not increase price significantly without losing sales to full-service providers. That is, one asks whether the entire grouping of transactions inside the proposed market faces competition from some grouping of sales outside the proposed market. As the Merger Guidelines point out, the sine qua non for grouping things into a relevant market is "demand substitution." *Guidelines, id.* at §§ 1.0, 1.41. Faced with a merger of the above firms, the Guidelines require the government to look separately at the glass plate and rubber wheel markets, and assess the firms' respective market position in each.

PROBLEM 6.1

The intersection of Hayes Street and Rose Street has gasoline stations on three of its four corners. Beyond this, the nearest gasoline station is thirty miles away. Stations A and B have accused Station C of monopolization by predatory pricing and other exclusionary practices. The parties have stipulated that the relevant geographic market includes only these three stations. The evidence shows the following. Over the relevant time period C has sold 2000 gallons of gasoline daily. A and B have each sold 500 gallons daily. In addition, C has 8 pumps, while A and B each have 6 pumps. Each pump will generally accommodate 40 cars daily with no waiting, and a car purchases, on average, 10 gallons. What is C's market share? What is the relevant unit of output? What factors are relevant to determining C's market power?

UNITED STATES V. E.I. DU PONT DE NEMOURS & CO.

351 U.S. 377 (1956)

JUSTICE REED delivered the opinion of the Court.

The United States brought this civil action ... against E. I. du Pont de Nemours and Company. The complaint, filed December 13, 1947, ... charged du Pont with monopolizing ... interstate commerce in cellophane ... in violation of § 2 of the Sherman Act. Relief by injunction was sought against defendant and its officers, forbidding monopolizing or attempting to monopolize interstate trade in cellophane. The prayer also sought action to dissipate the effect of the monopolization by divestiture or other steps.

....

During the period that is relevant to this action, du Pont produced almost 75% of the cellophane sold in the United States, and cellophane constituted less than 20% of all "flexible packaging material" sales....

The Government contends that, by so dominating cellophane production, du Pont monopolized a "part of the trade or commerce" in violation of § 2. Respondent agrees that cellophane is a product which constitutes "a 'part' of commerce within the meaning of Section 2." But it contends that the prohibition of § 2 against monopolization is not violated because it does not have the power to control the price of cellophane or to exclude competitors from the market in which cellophane is sold. The court below found that the "relevant market for determining the extent of du Pont's market control is the market for flexible packaging materials," and that competition from those other materials prevented du Pont from possessing monopoly powers in its sales of cellophane.

The Government asserts that cellophane and other wrapping materials are neither substantially fungible nor like priced. For these reasons, it argues that the market for other wrappings is distinct from the market for cellophane and that the competition afforded cellophane by other wrappings is not strong enough to be considered in determining whether du Pont has monopoly powers. Market delimitation is necessary under du Pont's theory to determine whether an alleged monopolist violates § 2. The ultimate consideration in such a determination is whether the defendants control the price and competition in the market for such part of trade or commerce as they are charged with monopolizing. Every manufacturer is the sole producer of the particular commodity it makes but its control in the above sense of the relevant market depends upon the availability of alternative commodities for buyers: i.e., whether there is a cross-elasticity of demand between cellophane and the other wrappings. This interchangeability is largely gauged by the purchase of competing products for similar uses considering the price, characteristics and adaptability of the competing commodities. The court below found that the flexible wrappings afforded such alternatives....

... For consideration of the issue as to monopolization, a general summary of the development of cellophane is useful.

In the early 1900's, Jacques Brandenberger, a Swiss chemist, attempted to make tablecloths impervious to dirt by spraying them with liquid viscose (a cellulose solution available in quantity from wood pulp) and by coagulating this coating. His idea failed, but he noted that the coating peeled off in a transparent film. This first "cellophane" was thick, hard, and not perfectly transparent, but Brandenberger apparently foresaw commercial possibilities in his discovery. By 1908 he developed the first machine for the manufacture of transparent sheets of regenerated cellulose. The 1908 product was not satisfactory, but by 1912 Brandenberger was making a saleable thin flexible film used in gas masks. He obtained patents to cover the machinery and the essential ideas of his process....

In 1917 Brandenberger assigned his patents to La Cellophane Societe Anonyme and joined that organization....

In 1923 du Pont organized with La Cellophane an American company for the manufacture of plain cellophane.

....

An important factor in the growth of cellophane production and sales was the perfection of moistureproof cellophane, a superior product of du Pont research and patented by that company through a 1927 application. Plain cellophane has little resistance to the passage of moisture vapor. Moistureproof cellophane has a composition added which keeps moisture in and out of the packed commodity. This patented type of cellophane has had a demand with much more rapid growth than the plain.

In 1931 Sylvania began the manufacture of moistureproof cellophane under its own patents. After negotiations over patent rights, du Pont in 1933 licensed Sylvania to manufacture and sell moistureproof cellophane produced under the du Pont patents at a royalty of 2% of sales.

....

If cellophane is the "market" that du Pont is found to dominate, it may be assumed it does have monopoly power over that "market." Monopoly power is the power to control prices or exclude competition. It seems apparent that du Pont's power to set the price of cellophane has been limited only by the competition afforded by other flexible packaging materials. Moreover, it may be practically impossible for anyone to commence manufacturing cellophane without full access to du Pont's technique. However, du Pont has no power to prevent competition from other wrapping materials. The trial court consequently had to determine whether competition from the other wrappings prevented du Pont from possessing monopoly power in violation of § 2....

If a large number of buyers and sellers deal freely in a standardized product, such as salt or wheat, we have complete or pure competition. Patents, on the other hand, furnish the most familiar type of classic monopoly. As the producers of a standardized product bring about significant differentiations of quality, design, or packaging in the product that permit differences of use, competition becomes to a greater or less degree incomplete and the producer's power over price and competition greater over his article and its use, according to the differentiation he is able to create and maintain. A retail seller may have in one sense a monopoly on certain trade because of location, as an isolated country store or filling station, or because no one else makes a product of just the quality or attractiveness of his product, as for example in cigarettes. Thus one can theorize that we have monopolistic competition in every nonstandardized commodity with each manufacturer having power over the price and production of his own product. However, this power that, let us say, automobile or soft-drink manufacturers have over their trademarked products is not the power that makes an illegal monopoly. Illegal power must be appraised in terms of the competitive market for the product.

Determination of the competitive market for commodities depends on how different from one another are the offered commodities in character or use, how far buyers will go to substitute one commodity for another. For example, one can think of building materials as in commodity competition but one could hardly say that brick competed with steel or wood or cement or stone in the meaning of Sherman Act litigation; the products are too different. This is the interindustry competition emphasized by some economists. On the other hand, there are certain differences in the formulae for soft drinks but one can hardly say that each one is an illegal monopoly. Whatever the market may be, we hold that control of price or competition establishes the existence of monopoly power under § 2. Section 2 requires the application of a reasonable approach in determining the existence of monopoly power ....

... The Government argues:

> We do not here urge that in *no* circumstances may competition of substitutes negative possession of monopolistic power over trade in a product. The decisions make it clear at the least that the courts will not consider substitutes other than those which are substantially fungible with the monopolized product and sell at substantially the same price.

But where there are market alternatives that buyers may readily use for their purposes, illegal monopoly does not exist merely because the product said to be monopolized differs from others. If it were not so, only physically identical products would be a part of the market. To accept the Government's argument, we would have to conclude that the manufacturers of plain as well as moistureproof cellophane were monopolists, and so with films such as Pliofilm, foil, glassine, polyethylene, and Saran, for each of these wrapping materials is distinguishable. These were all exhibits in the case. New wrappings appear, generally similar to cellophane: is each a monopoly? What is called for is an appraisal of the "cross-elasticity" of demand in the trade.... In considering what is the relevant market for determining the control of price and competition, no more definite rule can be declared than that commodities reasonably interchangeable by consumers for the same purposes make up that "part of the trade or commerce," monopolization of which may be illegal. As respects flexible packaging materials, the market geographically is nationwide.

Industrial activities cannot be confined to trim categories. Illegal monopolies under § 2 may well exist over limited products in narrow fields where competition is eliminated. That does not settle the issue here. In determining the market under the Sherman Act, it is the use or uses to which the commodity is put that control. The selling price between commodities with similar uses and different characteristics may vary, so that the cheaper product can drive out the more expensive. Or, the superior quality of higher priced articles may make dominant the more desirable. Cellophane costs more than many competing products and less than a few. But whatever the price, there are various flexible wrapping materials that are bought by manufacturers for packaging their goods in their own plants or are sold to converters who shape and print them for use in the packaging of the commodities to be wrapped.

Cellophane differs from other flexible packaging materials. From some it differs more than from others....

It may be admitted that cellophane combines the desirable elements of transparency, strength and cheapness more definitely than any of the others. Comparative characteristics have been noted thus:

> Moistureproof cellophane is highly transparent, tears readily but has high bursting strength, is highly impervious to moisture and gases, and is resistant to grease and oils. Heat sealable, printable, and adapted to use on wrapping machines, it makes an excellent packaging material for both display and protection of commodities.

> Other flexible wrapping materials fall into four major categories: (1) opaque nonmoistureproof wrapping *paper* designed primarily for convenience and protection in handling packages; (2) moistureproof *films* of varying degrees of transparency designed primarily either to protect, or to display and protect, the products they encompass; (3) nonmoistureproof transparent *films* designed primarily to display and to some extent protect, but which obviously do a poor protecting job where exclusion or retention of moisture is important; and (4) moistureproof *materials* other than films

of varying degrees of transparency (foils and paper products) designed to protect and display.

But, despite cellophane's advantages, it has to meet competition from other materials in every one of its uses.... Food products are the chief outlet, with cigarettes next. The Government makes no challenge ... that cellophane furnishes less than 7% of wrappings for bakery products, 25% for candy, 32% for snacks, 35% for meats and poultry, 27% for crackers and biscuits, 47% for fresh produce, and 34% for frozen foods. Seventy-five to eighty percent of cigarettes are wrapped in cellophane. Thus, cellophane shares the packaging market with others. The over-all result is that cellophane accounts for 17.9% of flexible wrapping materials, measured by the wrapping surface.

Moreover a very considerable degree of functional interchangeability exists between these products .... It will be noted that except as to permeability to gases, cellophane has no qualities that are not possessed by a number of other materials. Meat will do as an example of interchangeability. Although du Pont's sales to the meat industry have reached 19,000,000 pounds annually, nearly 35%, this volume is attributed "to the rise of self-service retailing of fresh meat." In fact, since the popularity of self-service meats, du Pont has lost "a considerable proportion" of this packaging business to Pliofilm. Pliofilm is more expensive than cellophane, but its superior physical characteristics apparently offset cellophane's price advantage. While retailers shift continually between the two, the trial court found that Pliofilm is increasing its share of the business. One further example is worth noting. Before World War II, du Pont cellophane wrapped between 5 and 10% of baked and smoked meats. The peak year was 1933. Thereafter du Pont was unable to meet the competition of Sylvania and of greaseproof paper. Its sales declined and the 1933 volume was not reached again until 1947. It will be noted that greaseproof paper, glassine, waxed paper, foil and Pliofilm are used as well as cellophane. [The Court notes the competition and the] advantages that have caused the more expensive Pliofilm to increase its proportion of the business.

An element for consideration as to cross-elasticity of demand between products is the responsiveness of the sales of one product to price changes of the other. If a slight decrease in the price of cellophane causes a considerable number of customers of other flexible wrappings to switch to cellophane, it would be an indication that a high cross-elasticity of demand exists between them; that the products compete in the same market. The court below held that the "[g]reat sensitivity of customers in the flexible packaging markets to price or quality changes" prevented du Pont from possessing monopoly control over price. The record sustains these findings.

We conclude that cellophane's interchangeability with the other materials mentioned suffices to make it a part of this flexible packaging material market.

The Government stresses the fact that the variation in price between cellophane and other materials demonstrates they are noncompetitive. As these products are all flexible wrapping materials, it seems reasonable to consider, as was done at the trial, their comparative cost to the consumer in terms of square area. This can be seen in Finding 130, Appendix C. Findings as to price competition are set out in the margin.[29] Cellophane costs two or three times as much, surface measure, as its chief competitors for the flexible wrapping market, glassine and grease-proof papers. Other forms of cellulose wrappings and those from other chemical or mineral substances, with the exception of aluminum foil, are more expensive.... The wrapping is a relatively small proportion of the entire cost of the article. Different producers need different qualities in wrappings and their need may vary from time to time as their products undergo change. But the necessity for flexible wrappings is the central and unchanging demand. We cannot say that these differences in cost gave du Pont monopoly power over prices in view of the findings of fact on that subject.[31]

---

[29] "132. The price of cellophane is today an obstacle to its sales in competition with other flexible packaging materials.

"133. Cellophane has always been higher priced than the two largest selling flexible packaging materials, wax paper and glassine, and this has represented a disadvantage to sales of cellophane.

"134. Du Pont considered as a factor in the determination of its prices, the prices of waxed paper, glassine, greaseproof, vegetable parchment, and other flexible packaging materials.

"135. Du Pont, in reducing its prices, intended to narrow price differential between cellophane and packaging papers, particularly glassine and waxed paper. The objective of this effort has been to increase the use of cellophane. Each price reduction was intended to open up new uses for cellophane, and to attract new customers who had not used cellophane because of its price."

[31] "140. Some users are sensitive to the cost of flexible packaging materials; others are not. Users to whom cost is important include substantial business: for example, General Foods, Armour, Curtiss Candy Co., and smaller users in the bread industry, cracker industry, and frozen food industry. These customers are unwilling to use more cellophane because of its relatively high price, would use more if the price were reduced, and have increased their use as the price of cellophane has been reduced.

"141. The cost factor slips accounts away from cellophane. This hits at the precarious users, whose profit margins on their products are low, and has been put in motion by competitive developments in the user's trade. Examples include the losses of business to glassine in candy bar wraps in the 30's, frozen food business to waxed paper in the late 40's, and recent losses to glassine in cracker packaging.

"142. The price of cellophane was reduced to expand the market for cellophane. Du Pont did not reduce prices for cellophane with intent of monopolizing manufacture or with intent of suppressing competitors.

"143. Du Pont reduced cellophane prices to enable sales to be made for new uses from which higher prices had excluded cellophane, and to expand sales. Reductions were made as sales volume and market conditions warranted. In determining price reductions, du Pont considered relationship between its manufacturing costs and proposed prices, possible additional volume that might be gained by the price reduction, effect of price reduction upon the return du Pont would obtain on its investment. It considered the effect its lowered price might have on the manufacture by others, but this possible result of a price reduction was never a motive for the reduction.

"144. Du Pont never lowered cellophane prices below cost, and never dropped cellophane prices temporarily to gain a competitive advantage.

On the findings of the District Court, its judgment is

Affirmed.

CHIEF JUSTICE WARREN, with whom JUSTICE BLACK and JUSTICE DOUGLAS join, dissenting.

This case, like many under the Sherman Act, turns upon the proper definition of the market. In defining the market in which du Pont's economic power is to be measured, the majority virtually emasculate § 2 of the Sherman Act. They admit that "cellophane combines the desirable elements of transparency, strength and cheapness more definitely than any of "a host of other packaging materials. Yet they hold that all of those materials are so indistinguishable from cellophane as to warrant their inclusion in the market....

....

From the first, du Pont recognized that it need not concern itself with competition from other packaging materials. For example, when du Pont was contemplating entry into cellophane production, its Development Department reported that glassine "is so inferior that it belongs in an entirely different class and has hardly to be considered as a competitor of cellophane." This was still du Pont's view in 1950 when its survey of competitive prospects wholly omitted reference to glassine, waxed paper or sulphite paper and stated that "Competition for du Pont cellophane will come from competitive cellophane and from non-cellophane films made by us or by others."

....

As predicted by its 1923 market analysis, du Pont's dominance in cellophane proved enormously profitable from the outset. After only five years of production, when du Pont bought out the minority stock interests in its cellophane subsidiary, it had to pay more than fifteen times the original price of the stock. But such success was not limited to the period of innovation, limited sales and complete domestic monopoly. A confidential du Pont report shows that during the period 1937-1947, despite great expansion of sales, du Pont's "operative return" (before taxes) averaged 31%, while its average "net return" (after deduction of taxes, bonuses, and fundamental research expenditures) was 15.9%. Such profits provide a powerful incentive for the entry of competitors. Yet from 1924 to 1951 only one new firm, Sylvania, was able to begin cellophane production. And Sylvania could not have entered if La Cellophane's secret process had not been stolen. It is significant that for 15 years Olin Industries, a substantial firm, was unsuccessful in its attempt to produce cellophane, finally abandoning the project in 1944 after having spent about $1,000,000....

"145. As du Pont's manufacturing costs declined, 1924 to 1935, du Pont reduced prices for cellophane. When costs of raw materials increased subsequent to 1935, it postponed reductions until 1938 and 1939. Subsequent increases in cost of raw material and labor brought about price increases after 1947."

The trial court found that

> Du Pont has no power to set cellophane prices arbitrarily. If prices for cellophane increase in relation to prices of other flexible packaging materials it will lose business to manufacturers of such materials in varying amounts for each of du Pont cellophane's major end uses.

This further reveals its misconception of the antitrust laws. A monopolist seeking to maximize profits cannot raise prices "arbitrarily." Higher prices of course mean smaller sales, but they also mean higher per-unit profit. Lower prices will increase sales but reduce per-unit profit. Within these limits a monopolist has a considerable degree of latitude in determining which course to pursue in attempting to maximize profits. The trial judge thought that, if du Pont raised its price, the market would "penalize" it with smaller profits as well as lower sales. Du Pont proved him wrong. When 1947 operating earnings dropped below 26% for the first time in 10 years, it increased cellophane's price 7% and boosted its earnings in 1948. Du Pont's division manager then reported that "If an operative return of 31% is considered inadequate then an upward revision in prices will be necessary to improve the return." It is this latitude with respect to price, this broad power of choice, that the antitrust laws forbid. Du Pont's independent pricing policy and the great profits consistently yielded by that policy leave no room for doubt that it had power to control the price of cellophane....

NOTE: CROSS-ELASTICITY OF DEMAND

Is the concept of cross-elasticity of demand developed in the *du Pont* case an aid in defining the relevant product market? Or is it a mechanism for measuring the elasticity of demand for a given product? Or is it a hybrid? Is there any difference between saying that the relevant product is "cellophane" but the elasticity of demand for the product is very high, or saying that the relevant product is "flexible packaging materials" and the elasticity of demand is low? It makes no difference. Market share and market power vary directly with one another. Elasticity of demand and market power, however, vary inversely.

Cross-elasticity of demand is simply a way of measuring what consumers will do when a seller attempts to raise the price of something. A certain number will substitute away. Whether what they buy instead is the same "product" or a different "product" is a purely semantic question, although many courts have failed to recognize this. The fundamental question in antitrust is not how to identify the product being monopolized, but how to determine whether the defendant has the power to charge more than a competitive price.

What does the concept of cross-elasticity of demand contribute to analysis of market power? Mainly, it reminds us that when we define a seller's share of the market we must consider close substitutes as part of our product definition.

Did the court in *du Pont* apply the concept of cross-elasticity of demand correctly? Probably not. The court found that du Pont had very little power over the price of cellophane because there were many substitutes for cellophane as a packaging material, and if du Pont attempted to raise the price of cellophane many customers would buy one of these substitutes instead. In short, there was high cross-elasticity of demand. Is that analysis complete?

Suppose that there is a competitively produced product known as Widgets, which are sold at $1.00 each. Now a bright inventor develops the Flidget, which does everything a Widget can do, but which can be produced and sold for 80 cents. The inventor patents the Flidget and becomes its only producer. At what price will the inventor sell Flidgets?

The inventor will sell Flidgets at the profit maximizing price, and the profit maximizing price might very well be something like 99 cents. If Widgets and Flidgets are interchangeable in consumers' eyes, then the inventor will probably not be able to charge more than $1.00 for Flidgets, because then customers would stay with Widgets. But unless there are a large number of potential customers who will not buy Widgets at $1.00 but who would buy Flidgets at a lower price, the profit-maximizing price of Flidgets would not be substantially less than $1.00. At a price of 99 cents most former Widget customers would buy Flidgets instead, up to the capacity of the inventor to make them.

Now suppose the Flidget producer is accused of monopolization. It defends by arguing that the "cross-elasticity of demand" between Flidgets and Widgets is very high, so Widgets ought to be included in the relevant market. After all, Flidgets are currently being sold at 99 cents, and if the producer raises its price by as little as 2 cents it will lose most of its customers. Is the argument persuasive? Clearly not. The reason is simple. The profit-maximizing price of any product lies in the high elasticity region of its demand curve. When a producer with market power seeks out its profit-maximizing price, it asks "how much can I charge before too many customers will substitute away for something else?" The producer tries to get as close to this edge as possible without going over.

As a result, high cross-elasticity of demand at the current market price for a product is not persuasive evidence that the producer has no market power. It *is* evidence, however, that the producer is charging its profit-maximizing price. In order to know whether the producer has market power we need to know whether its profit-maximizing price is substantially higher than its marginal cost. But the only way we can know that is by determining the defendant's marginal cost. If we know marginal cost, there is no need to rely on market definition, for we can compute market power directly by looking at the difference between marginal cost and the price at which the product is being sold.

Du Pont's high rate of profit during the period of alleged monopolization suggests (although not very reliably) that the Supreme Court's analysis was incorrect. There was high cross-elasticity of demand between du Pont's cellophane at the current price and other packaging materials; however, the current price of cellophane was a very profitable (monopoly) price.

Today we speak of the "*Cellophane* fallacy" as concluding from observed high cross-elasticity of demand at current market prices that the defendant lacks power, while ignoring the possibility that the firm is already charging a monopoly price. Although the fallacy is well known by economists, courts continue to commit it. *See*, e.g., *Cable Holdings of Ga. v. Home Video*, 825 F.2d 1598, 1563 (11th Cir. 1987) (relevant market included not only cable television but also broadcast television and videocassette recordings)

This still does not mean du Pont was an illegal monopolist. It means only that it probably had sufficient market power to meet the first element of the monopolization test. Is there evidence in the opinion that du Pont's activities would have satisfied the conduct element as well?

TELEX CORP. V. IBM CORP.

510 F.2d 894 (10th Cir.), *cert. dismissed*, 423 U.S. 802 (1975)

PER CURIAM....

Telex has alleged in the complaint that IBM ... monopolized and attempted to monopolize the manufacture, distribution, sale, and leasing of electronic data processing equipment. The complaint was later amended to charge IBM in more specific terms with monopolization in the manufacture, distribution, sale, and leasing of plug compatible peripheral products which are attached to IBM central processing units.

....

Although IBM was recognized as [a leader in the computer industry], having more revenue from the industry than any other company, it did not, according to the finding of the trial court, have monopoly power or status in the industry as a whole.

At the outset it is necessary to distinguish between the general systems portion of the industry which encompasses the manufacture of the basic electronic data processing system, the essential equipment being a central processing unit. The number of manufacturers engaged in the manufacturing of the processing units increased dramatically, from three in 1952 to ninety-six in 1972. The court found that about eight or nine of these were considered principal manufacturers. In the segment of the industry involving the manufacture of the central processing units, IBM did not have monopoly power, although it was estimated by the court that its market share was about thirty-five per cent.

In addition to the central processing unit, a data processing system also has a number of so-called peripheral devices which are connected with the central processing unit and which perform various special functions in the data processing system. These include information storage components like magnetic tape drives, magnetic disk drives, magnetic drums and magnetic strip files; terminal devices such as printers; memory units, which are specialized storage units, and other similar types of peripheral components. Sometimes these devices are included in the central processing unit, that is, do not exist as external components. It is these peripheral components with which we are primarily concerned in this lawsuit. The importance of these can be judged from the fact that the court found that they constitute 50 to 75 per cent of the total price of an electronic data processing system. The term "plug compatible peripheral device" is the specific class of equipment that enters into this case. What is meant is that a producer of a complete electronic processing unit manufactures, as noted, the central processing unit and peripheral components which are geared to use on that central processing unit. Many manufacturers produce peripheral components primarily for attachment to central processing units of a particular manufacturer and so, therefore, the plug compatible peripheral device refers to a component which is functionally equivalent to the manufacturer's peripheral device and can be readily plugged into that central processing unit. Undoubtedly it is the wide use of the IBM central processing unit that caused Telex and others to market peripheral devices which were plug compatible with the IBM unit and which could replace IBM peripheral devices which had been made for the IBM central system.

The District Court found that there existed a definable market for all peripheral devices plug compatible with IBM processing units. The court further found that there were individual submarkets for each particular type of peripheral product.

....

The main quarrel of IBM with the court's determination of the relevant market is that it is limited mainly to peripheral products plug compatible with IBM's equipment. It encompasses only part of the peripheral equipment marketed by Telex and the other plug compatible manufacturers. It fails to include the peripheral equipment market by systems manufacturers other than IBM.[11]

....

The threshold issue is whether the court erred in its findings as to the scope and extent of the relevant product market for determination whether there existed power to control prices or to exclude competition, that is, whether there was monopoly power....

The trial court recognized that the cost of adaptation of peripherals to the CPUs [central processing units] of other systems is roughly the same with respect to every system, that is, the cost of the interface, the attachment which allows the use of peripherals manufactured by one system to be used on another central processing unit is generally about the same. But these practical interchange possibilities did not deter the court in reaching a conclusion that the products market was practically restricted. A factor which influenced the trial court was the commitment of Telex to supplying peripherals plug compatible with IBM systems.

---

[11] Over 250 companies manufacture peripheral devices for use in non-IBM computer systems, and 100 of these companies supply peripheral products for IBM systems. Because it is relatively easy to adapt peripheral equipment for installation in another system, most companies (including Telex) market their equipment for installation in more than one system. Thus, the "plug compatible" peripheral equipment marketed for use in one system is the same as that marketed for use in another system, except for a necessary change in the "interface." IBM claims that the cost of modifying an interface so that it can be used with another system amounts to less than 1% of the product's purchase price.

The court appeared to disregard the interchangeability aspect of the peripherals manufactured by companies other than IBM, giving emphasis to the fact that Telex, for example, had not chosen to manufacture such peripheral products of the kind and character manufactured by companies other than IBM. The trial court did, however, recognize the presence of interchangeability of use and the presence of cross-elasticity of demand. The court thought, however, that the presence of these factors were not sufficiently immediate....

Inasmuch as IBM's share of the data processing industry as a whole is insufficient to justify any inference or conclusion of market power in IBM, the exclusion from the defined market of those products which are not plug compatible with IBM central processing units has a significant impact on the court's decision that IBM possessed monopoly power.

....

In dealing with the issue whether peripheral products non-compatible with IBM systems ought to be considered, the court said that as a *practical* matter there is no direct competition between IBM peripherals and the peripherals of other systems manufacturers. However, this finding is out of harmony with other findings which the court made. *See*, for example, Finding 38, wherein the court said that "It cannot be gainsaid that indirectly at least and to some degree the peripheral products attached to non-IBM systems necessarily compete with and constrain IBM's power with respect to peripherals attached to IBM systems." The court also stated in Finding 38 that:

> [S]uppliers of peripherals plug compatible with non-IBM systems could in various instances shift to the production of IBM plug compatible peripherals, and vice versa, should the economic rewards in the realities of the market become sufficiently attractive and if predatory practices of others did not dissuade them. In the absence of defensive tactics on the part of manufacturers of CPU's, the cost of developing an interface for a peripheral device would generally be about the same regardless of the system to which it would be attached, and such cost has not constituted a substantial portion of the development cost of the peripheral device.

....

In essence, [a] witness said that the engineering costs of developing interfaces was minimal and that he had advocated modifying interfaces so that Telex products could be used with systems other than IBM. Another example of ease of interface design is shown by the fact that following RCA's decision to abandon the computer systems business and turn it over to Univac, Telex recognized a marketing opportunity and it began marketing its 6420 tape unit, the plug compatible equivalent of IBM's 3420 Aspen tape unit, as a plug compatible unit with RCA CPUs. The documents sought to emphasize the ease of use in the RCA system of this peripheral equipment designed for IBM equipment originally.

....

Manufacturers of peripherals were not limited to those which were plug compatible with IBM CPUs. These manufacturers were free to adapt their products through interface changes to plug into non-IBM systems. It also followed that systems manufacturers could modify interfaces so that their own peripheral products could plug into IBM CPUs. Factually, then, there existed peripheral products of other CPU manufacturers which were competitive with IBM peripherals and unquestionably other IBM peripherals were capable of having their interfaces modified so that their peripheral products would plug into non-IBM's CPU.

The fact that Telex had substantially devoted itself to the manufacture of peripheral products which were used in IBM CPUs and which competed with IBM peripheral products cannot control in determining product market since the legal standard is whether the product is reasonably interchangeable.

....

One evidence of cross-elasticity is the responsiveness of sales of one product to price changes of another. But a finding of actual fungibility is not necessary to a conclusion that products have potential substitutability....

....

It seems clear that reasonable interchangeability is proven in the case at bar and hence the market should include not only peripheral products plug compatible with IBM CPUs, but all peripheral products, those compatible not only with IBM CPUs but those compatible with non-IBM systems. This is wholly justifiable because the record shows that these products, although not fungible, are fully interchangeable and may be interchanged with minimal financial outlay, and so cross-elasticity exists ....

The court's very restrictive definition of the product market in the face of evidence which established the interchangeable quality of the products in question, together with the existence of cross-elasticity of demand, must be regarded as plain error.

....

NOTES AND QUESTIONS

1. Did the *Telex* court rely on elasticity of demand, elasticity of supply, or both, as the basis for its definition of the relevant product market?

2. Elasticity of supply has played an increasing role in circuit court determination of market power since the mid-1970's. Frequently courts use a different term, such as "supply substitutability," or "substitutability in production." For example, *see Twin City Sportservice, Inc. v. Charles O. Finley & Co.*, 512 F.2d 1264 (9th Cir. 1975), where the issue was whether the defendant monopolized the market in concession services at major league baseball stadiums. The court held that there was a "high degree of substitutability of production' "between concessions at major league baseball stadiums and concessions at other entertainment events. Therefore the market alleged to be monopolized was drawn too narrowly. *See Science Prods. Co. v. Chevron Chem. Co.*, 384 F. Supp. 793 (N.D.

Ill. 1974), where the plaintiff alleged that the defendant had monopolized the market for, inter alia, garden insecticides. The Court held that the market must be defined more broadly to include household insecticides as well:

> Household insecticides share the same chemical components and manufacturing facilities with insecticides labeled and intended for outdoor use. Once a manufacturer enters the lawn and garden chemical field, it can easily expand its product line to include household insecticides.
>
> ....
>
> Significantly, both [plaintiff and defendant] manufacture and market products falling into every category including household insecticides. Although some producers of household insecticides tend to concentrate their sales in grocery and drug stores, in general, most distributors and retailers of lawn and garden chemicals also handle household insecticides. Moreover, [the plaintiff] has been unable to point to a single manufacturer which makes any distinction in its organization or personnel based upon products sold for use inside and outside the home.
>
> [The plaintiff's] argument that household insecticides are lower in toxicity than products intended for outdoor use is equally specious. Most household insecticides are packaged in aerosol form and therefore in final diluted form. By contrast, many outdoor insecticides are packaged in concentrated form and must be diluted with water before they can safely be used....

384 F. Supp. at 800. *Contrast Fineman v. Armstrong World Indus.*, 980 F.2d 171 (3d Cir. 1992), concluding that there could be a relevant market of "video magazines" showing floor coverings. The antitrust plaintiff was in the business of making videotapes of floor covering such as linoleum for sale by subscription to dealers in floor coverings. The court relied on the plaintiff's testimony that "video magazines targeted at floor covering retailers differed from video magazines produced for other audiences." Conceding that a videotape of linoleum is not interchangeable on the demand side with a videotape of, say, the Superbowl, can you think of another question that the court should have considered?

3. Once market share has been computed, should very small shares be dispositive of the issue of market power? In *Broadway Delivery Corp. v. United Parcel Serv. of Am.*, 651 F.2d 122 (2d Cir.), *cert. denied*, 454 U.S. 968 (1981), the trial judge had instructed a jury that, "[i]f you find that the defendants possessed less than 50% of the relevant market, you don't have to go any further on a monopolization claim. Possession of less than 50% of the market fails to establish monopoly power." The Second Circuit held this instruction to be erroneous, for the jury was "entitled to assess monopoly power on the record as a whole." The Court concluded:

> The extent to which market characteristics should be explained to the jury in a particular case will vary with the nature of the underlying facts and the

expert testimony. Sometimes, but not inevitably, it will be useful to suggest that a market share below 50% is rarely evidence of monopoly power, a share between 50% and 70% can occasionally show monopoly power, and a share above 70% is usually strong evidence of monopoly power. But when the evidence presents a fair jury issue of monopoly power, the jury should not be told that it must find monopoly power lacking below a specified share or existing above a specified share. Of course, cases may arise where the parties' dispute concerning market definition creates a jury issue on monopoly power only if one side's market definition, usually the plaintiff's, is established. In such circumstances a jury can be instructed to find for the defendant if the plaintiff fails to prove its definition of the relevant market. Alternatively, a jury could be instructed to answer a special interrogatory concerning market definition, which would permit the trial judge to direct a verdict for the defendant if the plaintiff failed to prevail on its market definition. On the other hand, in some cases, there may be a genuine issue as to monopoly power in the market as defined by either party, in which event the market share under either definition would not be conclusive. However the instruction is phrased, it should not deflect the jury's attention from indicia of monopoly power other than market share.

651 F.2d at 129-30.

Under the Second Circuit's analysis, when would a defendant's motion for directed verdict or summary judgment on the basis of small market share be appropriate? What if the plaintiff had successfully defined a relevant market, but the pleadings clearly established that the defendant's market share was 25%? *See Energex Lighting Indus. v. NAPLC*, 656 F. Supp. 914 (S.D.N.Y. 1987), where the court followed *Broadway Delivery* in holding that a 25% market share could support a monopolization offense, where the number of competitors in the market had declined from eleven to four. Why should that make a difference?

The Fifth Circuit apparently disagrees with the Second. In *Dimmitt Agri Indus. v. CPC Int'l*, 679 F.2d 516 (5th Cir. 1982), *cert. denied*, 460 U.S. 1082 (1983), the record established that the defendant's market share ranged from 21% to 27% of one relevant market (starch) and 16% of another (corn syrup). The jury found that the defendant illegally monopolized. The Fifth Circuit reversed the judgment for the plaintiff, finding no case "in which monopolization was found on the basis of such meager evidence and despite undisputed proof of market shares significantly below 50 percent." However, the court found "considerable support for the proposition that low market shares, if undisputed, make monopolization an impossibility as a matter of law." It then held that market shares in the range of 16%-25% "are insufficient — at least absent other compelling structural evidence — as a matter of law to support monopolization." What kind of "structural evidence" did the court have in mind? Evidence that the market was very highly concentrated? This would suggest that the defendant was not the largest firm in the market. What if the defendant had 25% of the market, two other firms had 20% each, and smaller firms made up the balance?

4. In *Eastman Kodak Co. v. Image Tech. Servs.*, 504 U.S. 451 (1992), the Supreme Court refused to grant the defendant summary judgment against the plaintiff's claim that there could be a relevant market for Kodak brand replacement parts for Kodak photocopiers, notwithstanding the fact that the photocopier market itself was competitive. The decision is reprinted, *supra*, Chapter 4. As it turned out, however, Kodak manufactured only some 30% of "Kodak parts." On remand, the Ninth Circuit noted that courts generally require a 65 percent market share to create an inference of market power, but then found that inference met by the following facts:

> (1) [Kodak's] own manufacture of Kodak parts (30%); (2) its control of original-equipment manufacturers' sale of Kodak parts to ISOs through tooling clauses (20-25%), engineering clauses and other proprietary arrangements (exact percentage unknown); and (3) its discouragement of self-servicing and resale of parts by end users.

Image Technical Services v. Eastman Kodak Co., 125 F.3d 1195, 1203-04 (9th Cir. 1997), *cert. denied*, 118 S. Ct. 1560 (1998).

5. Does a regulated public utility with an exclusive service area have monopoly power? On the one hand, the utility is the only seller in its geographic region. On the other, it may have little or no power over price, because its rates are set by a government regulatory agency. *See Almeda Mall v. Houston Lighting & Power Co.*, 615 F.2d 343 (5th Cir. 1980), where the court concluded that a regulated public utility

> does not have the direct power to control prices or exclude competition. Monopolization cases involving such regulated industries are special in nature and require close scrutiny. The reason for this is that the regulation is considered an adequate replacement for the lack of competition that exists with a natural monopoly. In such a case controlling a predominant share of the relevant market cannot infer the traditional monopoly power associated with an entity outside the regulated field.

In *MCI Commun. Corp. v. AT&T*, 708 F.2d 1081, 1106-08 (7th Cir.), *cert. denied*, 464 U.S. 891 (1983), the court approved a jury instruction that a price-regulated monopolist would not be found to have monopoly power "if in fact regulation by regulatory agencies prevented AT&T from having the power to restrict entry or control prices." The jury found monopoly power. More recent decisions have noted that regulatory agencies frequently do not control prices effectively and often rubber stamp rate requests. Should this make a difference? *See Consolidated Gas Co. of Fla. v. City Gas Co. of Fla.*, 665 F. Supp. 1493, 1520 (S.D. Fla. 1987), finding that the defendant had monopoly power because the regulatory agency lacked adequate control over the utility's pricing.

PROBLEM 6.2

When Zyrex, a manufacturer of high technology photocopiers, refuses to sell repair parts for its photocopiers, Independent Service Organizations (ISOs) who repair these machines in competition with Zyrex allege that the defendant is attempting to use its market dominance in the photocopier market to create a secondary monopoly in the market for "servicing of Zyrex photocopy machines." The defendant disputes that servicing of its own brand of photocopiers is a relevant market. Describe how each of the following facts would be relevant to your answer: (1) customers who already own a Zyrex photocopier require a technician who is trained to service their brand; (2) the ISOs as firms actually service multiple brands of photocopiers, and the same individual technicians are typically trained to service two or more different brands; and (3) in response to a relatively high frequency of repair calls for Zyrex machines, the ISOs can retrain a technician currently servicing Alpha or Beta brand photocopiers in about three weeks. *Cf. Independent Service Organizations Antitrust Litigation*, 964 F. Supp. 1469 (D. Kansas 1997)

PROBLEM 6.3

Biffco, a manufacturer of kitchen sponges, is accused of terminating its dealers, predatory pricing, and other exclusionary practices. It appears that Biffco's market share of a nationwide market for kitchen sponges is only 20%. But the plaintiff offers an expert economist who will testify that Biffco has "power over price." The expert will testify that if Biffco wished, it could charge more than it is currently charging without losing more than a trivial number of sales. Is the testimony probative? Should the jury be permitted to consider it as "alternative" evidence of substantial market power? *See Valley Liquors, Inc. v. Renfield Importers, Ltd.*, 822 F.2d 656 (7th Cir.), *cert. denied*, 484 U.S. 977 (1987).

PROBLEM 6.4

Smalltime, Inc., a now-defunct hardware store, alleges illegal monopolization against a competitor, Bonanza Co., in a market for "the retail sale of building, plumbing, and electrical supplies for use primarily by home remodelers and do-it-yourselfers." Upon inspection, it turns out that Bonanza sells 1% of the region's building supplies, 1.5% of its electrical supplies, and 0.5% of its plumbing supplies. However, it is one of only two stores in the region that carries all three types of supplies, and it is the only one that advertises primarily to do-it-yourself home remodelers. How should the market be defined? *See Westman Commun. Co. v. Hobart Int'l*, 796 F.2d 1216 (10th Cir. 1986); *Thurman Indus. v. Pay'N'Pak Stores*, 1987-1 Trade Cas. ¶ 67,591 (W.D. Wash. 1987). *Contra JBL Enters. v. Jhirmack Enters.*, 698 F.2d 1011, 1016-17 (9th Cir.), *cert. denied*, 464 U.S. 829 (1983). *See also* Ayres, *Rationalizing Antitrust Cluster Markets*, 95 Yale L.J. 109 (1985).

PROBLEM 6.5

Lexington Power Company is an electric company charged with violating the antitrust laws in the wholesaling of electric power. Many other firms in the area also wholesale electric power, and can reach the same geographic areas that Lexington can. However, Lexington's power generation plant is very old and cost much less money to build than its competitors' new plants. When Lexington's plant wears out — perhaps in ten more years — it will have to build a more expensive plant as well. The plaintiff alleges that the antiquated, low-cost plant gives Lexington a cost advantage so substantial that Lexington's plant itself should be found to be a relevant market. In that case, of course, Lexington would have monopoly power. Should the plaintiff's argument prevail? *See Town of Concord v. Boston Edison Co.*, 915 F.2d 17 (1st Cir. 1990).

B. MEASURING THE GEOGRAPHIC MARKET

UNITED STATES V. GRINNELL CORP.

384 U.S. 563 (1966)

JUSTICE DOUGLAS delivered the opinion of the Court.

....

Grinnell manufactures plumbing supplies and fire sprinkler systems. It also owns 76% of the stock of ADT [American District Telegraph Co.], 89% of the stock of AFA [American Fire Alarm Co.], and 100% of the stock of [Holmes Electric Protective Co.]. ADT provides both burglary and fire protection services; Holmes provides burglary services alone; AFA supplies only fire protection service. Each offers a central station service under which hazard-detecting devices installed on the protected premises automatically transmit an electric signal to a central station. The central station is manned 24 hours a day. Upon receipt of a signal, the central station, where appropriate, dispatches guards to the protected premises and notifies the police or fire department direct. There are other forms of protective services. But the record shows that subscribers to accredited central station service (*i.e.*, that approved by the insurance underwriters) receive reductions in their insurance premiums that are substantially greater than the reduction received by the users of other kinds of protection service.... ADT, Holmes, and AFA are the three largest companies in the business in terms of revenue: ADT (with 121 central stations in 115 cities) has 73% of the business; Holmes (with 12 central stations in three large cities) has 12.5%; AFA (with three central stations in three large cities) has 2%. Thus the three companies that Grinnell controls have over 87% of the business.

Over the years ADT purchased the stock or assets of 27 companies engaged in the business of providing burglar or fire alarm services. Holmes acquired the stock or assets of three burglar alarm companies in New York City using a central station. Of these 30, the officials of seven agreed not to engage in the protective service business in the area for periods ranging from five years to permanently. After Grinnell acquired control of the other defendants, the latter continued in their attempts to acquire central station companies — offers being made to at least eight companies between the years 1955 and 1961, including four of the five largest nondefendant companies in the business. When the present suit was filed, each of those defendants had outstanding an offer to purchase one of the four largest nondefendant companies....

ADT over the years reduced its minimum basic rates to meet competition and renewed contracts at substantially increased rates in cities where it had a monopoly of accredited central station service. ADT threatened retaliation against firms that contemplated inaugurating central station service. And the record indicates that, in contemplating opening a new central station, ADT officials frequently stressed that such action would deter their competitors from opening a new station in that area.

....

The offense of monopoly under § 2 of the Sherman Act has two elements: (1) the possession of monopoly power in the relevant market and (2) the willful acquisition or maintenance of that power as distinguished from growth or development as a consequence of a superior product, business acumen, or historic accident. We shall see that this second ingredient presents no major problem here, as what was done in building the empire was done plainly and explicitly for a single purpose. In *United States v. du Pont & Co.*, 351 U.S. 377, 391, we defined monopoly power as "the power to control prices or exclude competition." The existence of such power ordinarily may be inferred from the predominant share of the market.... In the present case, 87% of the accredited central station service business leaves no doubt that the congeries of these defendants have monopoly power — power which, as our discussion of the record indicates, they did not hesitate to wield — if that business is the relevant market. The only remaining question therefore is, what is the relevant market?

In case of a product it may be of such a character that substitute products must also be considered, as customers may turn to them if there is a slight increase in the price of the main product. That is the teaching of the *du Pont* case, *viz.*, that commodities reasonably interchangeable make up that "part" of trade or commerce which § 2 protects against monopoly power.

The District Court treated the entire accredited central station service business as a single market and we think it was justified in so doing. Defendants argue that the different central station services offered are so diverse that they cannot under *du Pont* be lumped together to make up the relevant market. For example, burglar alarm services are not interchangeable with fire alarm services. They further urge that *du Pont* requires that protective services other than those of the central station variety be included in the market definition.

But there is here a single use, *i.e.*, the protection of property, through a central station that receives signals. It is that service, accredited, that is unique and that competes with all the other forms of property protection. We see no barrier to combining in a single market a number of different products or services where that combination reflects commercial realities. To repeat, there is here a single basic service — the protection of property through use of a central service station — that must be compared with all other forms of property protection.

... The defendants have not made out a case for fragmentizing the types of services into lesser units.

Burglar alarm service is in a sense different from fire alarm service; from waterflow alarms; and so on. But it would be unrealistic on this record to break down the market into the various kinds of central station protective services that are available. Central station companies recognize that to compete effectively, they must offer all or nearly all types of service. The different forms of accredited central station service are provided from a single office and customers utilize different services in combination....

There are, to be sure, substitutes for the accredited central station service. But none of them appears to operate on the same level as the central station service so as to meet the interchangeability test of the *du Pont* case. Nonautomatic and automatic local alarm systems appear on this record to have marked differences, not the low degree of differentiation required of substitute services as well as substitute articles.

Watchman service is far more costly and less reliable. Systems that set off an audible alarm at the site of a fire or burglary are cheaper but often less reliable....

Defendants earnestly urge that despite these differences, they face competition from these other modes of protection. They seem to us seriously to overstate the degree of competition, but we recognize that (as the District Court found) they "do not have unfettered power to control the price of their services ... due to the fringe competition of other alarm or watchmen services." What defendants overlook is that the high degree of differentiation between central station protection and the other forms means that for many customers, only central station protection will do....

We also agree with the District Court that the geographic market for the accredited central station service is national. The activities of an individual station are in a sense local as it serves, ordinarily, only that area which is within a radius of 25 miles. But the record amply supports the conclusion that the business of providing such a service is operated on a national level. There is national planning. The agreements we have discussed covered activities in many States. The inspection, certification and rate-making is largely by national insurers. The appellant ADT has a national schedule of prices, rates, and terms, though the rates may be varied to meet local conditions. It deals with multistate businesses on the basis of nationwide contracts. The manufacturing business of ADT is interstate. The fact that Holmes is more nearly local than the others does not save it, for it is part and parcel of the combine presided over and controlled by Grinnell.

As the District Court found, the relevant market for determining whether the defendants have monopoly power is not the several local areas which the individual stations serve, but the broader national market that reflects the reality of the way in which they built and conduct their business.

JUSTICE FORTAS, with whom JUSTICE STEWART joins, dissenting.

....

The geographical market is defined as nationwide. But the need and the service are intensely local .... Protection must be provided on the spot. It must be furnished by local personnel able to bring help to the scene within minutes. Even the central stations can provide service only within a 25-mile radius. Where the tenants of the premises turn to central stations for this service, they must make their contracts locally with the central station and purchase their services from it on the basis of local conditions.

But because these defendants, the trial court found, are connected by stock ownership, interlocking management and some degree of national corporate direction, and because there is some national participation in selling as well as national financing, advertising, purchasing of equipment, and the like, the court concluded that the competitive area to be considered is national. This Court now affirms that conclusion.

This is a non sequitur. It is not permissible to seize upon the nationwide scope of defendants' operation and to bootstrap a geographical definition of the market from this.... The central issue is where does a potential buyer look for potential suppliers of the service — what is the geographical area in which the buyer has, or, in the absence of monopoly, would have, a real choice as to price and alternative facilities? This depends upon the facts of the market place, taking into account such economic factors as the distance over which supplies and services may be feasibly furnished, consistently with cost and functional efficiency.

....

Here, there can be no doubt that the correct geographic market is local. The services at issue are intensely local: they can be furnished only locally. The business as it is done is local — not nationwide. If, as might well be the case on this record, defendants were found to have violated the Sherman Act in a number of these local areas, a proper decree, directed to those markets, as well as to general corporate features relevant to the condemned practices, could be fashioned. On the other hand, a gross definition of the market as nationwide leads to a gross, nationwide decree which does not address itself to the realities of the market place....

....

NOTES AND QUESTIONS

1. How do you measure the relevant geographic market when the seller is a nationwide company with retail outlets in all states, but the buyer looks for alternatives only within her own city or community? Suppose that a company owns shoe stores in fifty cities and towns across the United States. In some of these

cities it operates the only shoe store, but in others it is in intense competition. How would the company price its shoes? Clearly, absent a restraint on price discrimination it would price in each city at the profit-maximizing level. If it had a monopoly in City *A* and the profit-maximizing price there was $50, it would charge $50. On the other hand if City *B* were competitive, it might charge a competitive price of $40. If it attempted to charge $50 in *B* it would lose its sales, even though it has a monopoly elsewhere. Should the fact that the company makes all its pricing decisions at central headquarters make any difference?

Does your analysis of the relevant geographic market change if you look at elasticity of supply rather than demand? The supply of accredited central station protective service outlets was controlled by three or four large companies, each of whom did business in several states. Presumably it would be easier for one of these companies to inaugurate service into a new city than it would be for a newcomer to enter the industry.

One argument for a national rather than local markets in *Grinnell* is the doctrine of potential competition (see the discussion, *infra*). Perhaps the market for central station protective services could be structured to contain three or four national companies bidding for the business in each city. In that case, even though each city contained only one current provider of the service, there would always be other established companies available to come in should the incumbent attempt to charge monopoly prices. In other words, although on the demand side the business was entirely local, on the supply side, firms established in the business were very likely entrants. The creation of a multiplicity of national companies could increase considerably the elasticity of supply in the market.

Might there be other reasons, however, for concluding that the market ought to be nationwide rather than local? For example, since Grinnell is a national company, might it not be able to use its market power in some cities to exact a kind of monopolistic "leverage" in other cities? For example, might it use its monopoly profits from a monopoly city to subsidize predatory pricing in a different city? Even if it could do so, would that be a basis for saying that it is monopolizing the market in both cities?

2. Suppose firm *P* sells 90% of the widgets in a four-state region. The only other firm selling in the region is *Q*, which is much larger than *P* but which is located one thousand miles away from the nearest point in the four-state region. How should *P*'s market share be calculated? To say that *P* has 90% of the market would seem to overstate its share. If *P* attempted to raise prices further, *Q* could presumably divert more widgets into the four-state region. Should it make a difference if *P* is currently charging a monopoly price? *See* 2A P. Areeda, H. Hovenkamp & J. Solow, *Antitrust Law* ch. 5C-E (rev. ed. 1995). Another possibility is to include *Q*'s total production, or perhaps its productive capacity, rather than merely the amount *Q* actually imports into the four-state region. By the same token, however, that may understate *P*'s market power, since *Q* may not be able to shift all its production into the four-state region. Suppose that part of *Q*'s output is committed under long-term contracts, while the rest is not? Suppose, further, that Q's output is similar enough to P's to be included in the same product market, but the products of the two firms are quite different from each other, and there are some customers who strongly prefer P's widgets over Q's, and vice-versa? *See* Kaplow, *The Accuracy of Traditional Market Power Analysis and a Direct Adjustment Alternative*, 95 Harv. L. Rev. 1817 (1982).

3. It is important not to confuse a geographic market for antitrust purposes with a "sales area," or area in which a firm services most customers. The sales area considers the extent to which customers are willing to travel *to* the defendant in order to buy its product. The relevant geographic market, by contrast, considers the extent to which customers are willing to travel *away* from the defendant in order to avoid its product. Consider this example. Smallville is a town of 900 families located 15 miles outside Metropolis. It has a single small grocery store, frequented almost exclusively by Smallville residents. Of these residents, 400 families do their regular shopping in Smallville, while 500 families drive to Metropolis, where there are several large stores and prices are generally lower. Is Smallville a relevant market for retail groceries? Probably not. The "sales area" of Smallville Grocery is indeed Smallville. That is, if one took the address of every Smallville Grocery customer for a week, virtually all would report that they came from Smallville. But that fact is quite irrelevant to determining the relevant antitrust market. We want to know the extent to which people living in Smallville can go *elsewhere*, such as Metropolis, in order to avoid Smallville Grocery's high prices.

In *Bathke v. Casey's General Stores*, 64 F.3d 340 (8th Cir. 1995), the court followed this reasoning. It rejected the plaintiff's argument that the geographic market for retail sales of self service gasoline were equal to the defendant's "trade area," which was said to be an area from one to three miles around each store. Whether or not most of the defendant's sales were made to buyers from that area, there may have been numerous other customers within that area who purchased gasoline elsewhere. In this case, census data showed that some one-half of the employed people who lived in the proposed markets actually held jobs in other towns well outside the trade area, and could presumably have purchased gasoline where they worked.

C. MONOPOLY CONDUCT

The offense of monopolization under section 2 of the Sherman Act requires not only that the defendant have market power but also that it "exercise" that power. The exercise of monopoly power does not refer to monopolistic pricing, however, but rather to the creation or preservation of market power by means that we consider anticompetitive. It is not illegal for a firm to have a large amount of market power, and it is not illegal for a firm with market power to charge its profit-maximizing price, even if that price is far higher than the firm's costs. The more profitable the monopoly is, however, the more attractive the market becomes to other potential producers and sellers. People with money to invest look for high returns, and monopolized markets frequently provide them. The monopolist would prefer that these people invest their money somewhere else, and sometimes it will take certain actions to encourage them to do so. These "exclusionary practices" are the activities which, when combined with market power, yield the offense of monopolization.

It is impossible to edit cases in such a way as to separate issues of market power from issues of conduct. The opinions that appeared above, such as *Alcoa* and *Grinnell*, mentioned certain anticompetitive acts in the process of discussing market power. The cases that follow necessarily include analysis of market power in their discussion of conduct. Nevertheless, the following cases are particularly good examples of the kinds of conduct that courts over the years have come to regard as "exclusionary," and which, when combined with market power, will form the offense of monopolization.

1. BARRIERS TO ENTRY

UNITED STATES V. UNITED SHOE MACHINERY CORP.

110 F. Supp. 295 (D. Mass. 1953), *aff'd per curiam*, 347 U.S. 521 (1954)

JUDGE WYZANSKI.

[The United States sued to restrain violations of Section 2 of the Sherman Act.] Stripped to its essentials, the 52 page complaint charged, *first*, that since 1912 United had been "monopolizing interstate trade and commerce in the shoe machinery industry of the United States"....

....

There are 18 major processes for the manufacturing of shoes by machine. Some machine types are used only in one process, but others are used in several; and the relationship of machine types to one another may be competitive or sequential. The approximately 1460 shoe manufacturers themselves are highly competitive in many respects, including their choice of processes and other technological aspects of production. Their total demand for machine services ... constitutes an identifiable market which is a "part of the trade or commerce among the several States."

United, the largest source of supply, is a corporation lineally descended from a combination of constituent companies, adjudged lawful by the Supreme Court of the United States in 1918. It now has assets rising slightly over 100 million dollars and employment rolls of around 6,000. In recent years it has earned before federal taxes 9 to 13.5 million dollars annually.

... United at the present time is supplying over 75%, and probably 85%, of the current demand in the American shoe machinery market, as heretofore defined. This is somewhat less than the share it was supplying in 1915....

Although at the turn of the century, United's patents covered the fundamentals of shoe machinery manufacture, those fundamental patents have expired. Current patents cover for the most part only minor developments, so that it is possible to "invent around" them, to use the words of United's chief competitor. However, the aggregation of patents does to some extent block potential competition. It furnishes a trading advantage. It leads inventors to offer their ideas to United, on the general principle that new complicated machines embody numerous patents. And it serves as a hedge or insurance for United against unforeseen competitive developments.

....

In supplying its complicated machines to shoe manufacturers, United, like its more important American competitors, has followed the practice of never selling, but only leasing. Leasing has been traditional in the shoe machinery field since the Civil War. So far as this record indicates, there is virtually no expressed dissatisfaction from consumers respecting that system; and Compo, United's principal competitor, endorses and uses it. Under the system, entry into shoe manufacture has been easy. The rates charged for all customers have been uniform. The machines supplied have performed excellently. United has, without separate charge, promptly and efficiently supplied repair service and many kinds of other service useful to shoe manufacturers. These services have been particularly important, because in the shoe manufacturing industry a whole line of production can be adversely affected, and valuable time lost, if some of the important machines go out of function, and because machine breakdowns have serious labor and consumer repercussions. The cost to the average shoe manufacturer of its machines and services supplied to him has been less than 2% of the wholesale price of his shoes.

However, United's leases, in the context of the present shoe machinery market, have created barriers to the entry by competitors into the shoe machinery field.

First, the complex of obligations and rights accruing under United's leasing system in operation deter a shoe manufacturer from disposing of a United machine and acquiring a competitor's machine. He is deterred more than if he owned that same United machine, or if he held it on a short lease carrying simple rental provisions and a reasonable charge for cancellation before the end of the term. The lessee is now held closely to United by the combined effect of the 10 year term, the requirement that if he has work available he must use the machine to full capacity, and by the return charge which can in practice, through the right of deduction fund, be reduced to insignificance if he keeps this and other United machines to the end of the periods for which he leased them.

Second, when a lessee desires to replace a United machine, United gives him more favorable terms if the replacement is by another United machine than if it is by a competitive machine.

Third, United's practice of offering to repair, without separate charges, its leased machines, has had the effect that there are no independent service organizations to repair complicated machines. In turn, this has had the effect that the manufacturer of a complicated machine must either offer repair service with his machine, or must face the obstacle of marketing his machine to customers who know that repair service will be difficult to provide.

Through its success with its principal and more complicated machines, United has been able to market more successfully its other machines, whether offered only for sale, or on optional sale or lease terms. In ascending order of importance, the reasons for United's success with these simpler types are these. These other, usually more simple, machines are technologically related to the complex leased machines to which they are auxiliary or preparatory. Having business relations with, and a host of contacts with, shoe factories, United seems to many of them the most efficient, normal, and above all, convenient supplier. Finally, United has promoted the sale of these simple machine types by the sort of price discrimination between machine types, about to be stated.

Although maintaining the same nominal terms for each customer, United has followed, as between machine types, a discriminatory pricing policy. [E]xamples of this policy can be found in the wide, and relatively permanent, variations in the rates of return United secures upon its long line of machine types. United's own internal documents reveal that these sharp and relatively durable differentials are traceable, at least in large part, to United's policy of fixing a higher rate of return where competition is of minor significance, and a lower rate of return where competition is of major significance....

....

In *Aluminum* [148 F.2d 416] Judge Hand, perhaps because he was cabined by the findings of the District Court, did not rest his judgment on the corporation's coercive or immoral practices. Instead, adopting an economic approach, he defined the appropriate market, found that Alcoa supplied 90% of it, determined that this control constituted a monopoly, and ruled that since Alcoa established this monopoly by its voluntary actions, such as building new plants, though, it was assumed, not by moral derelictions, it had "monopolized" in violation of § 2. Judge Hand reserved the issue as to whether an enterprise could be said to "monopolize" if its control was purely the result of technological, production, distribution, or like objective factors, not dictated by the enterprise, but thrust upon it by the economic character of the industry; and he also reserved the question as to control achieved solely "by virtue of ... superior skill, foresight and industry." At the same time, he emphasized that an enterprise had "monopolized" if, regardless of its intent, it had achieved a monopoly by manoeuvres which, though "honestly industrial," were not economically inevitable, but were rather the result of the firm's free choice of business policies.

....

[R]ecent authorities [suggest] at least three different, but cognate, approaches. The approach which has the least sweeping implications really antedates the decision in *Aluminum*. But it deserves restatement. An enterprise has monopolized in violation of § 2 of the Sherman Act if it has acquired or maintained a power to exclude others as a result of using an unreasonable "restraint of trade" in violation of § 1 of the Sherman Act. See *United States v. Columbia Steel Co.*, 334 U.S. 495, 525; *see also United States v. Griffith*, 334 U.S. 100.

A more inclusive approach was adopted by Mr. Justice Douglas in *United States v. Griffith*, 334 U.S. 100. He stated that to prove a violation of § 2 it was not always necessary to show a violation of § 1. And he concluded that an enterprise has monopolized in violation of § 2 if it (a) has the power to exclude competition, and (b) has exercised it, or has the purpose to exercise it. The least that this conclusion means is that it is a violation of § 2 for one having effective control of the market to use, or plan to use, any exclusionary practice, even though it is not a technical restraint of trade. But the conclusion may go further.

Indeed the way in which Mr. Justice Douglas used the terms "monopoly power" and "effective market control," and cited *Aluminum* suggests that he endorses a third and broader approach, which originated with Judge Hand. It will be recalled that Judge Hand said that one who has acquired an overwhelming share of the market "monopolizes" whenever he does business, apparently even if there is no showing that his business involves any exclusionary practice. But this doctrine is softened by Judge Hand's suggestion that the defendant may escape statutory liability if it bears the burden of proving that it owes its monopoly solely to superior skill, superior products, natural advantages, (including accessibility to raw materials or markets), economic or technological efficiency, (including scientific research), low margins of profit maintained permanently and without discrimination, or licenses conferred by, and used within, the limits of law, (including patents on one's own inventions, or franchises granted directly to the enterprise by a public authority).

In the case at bar, the Government contends that the evidence satisfies each of the three approaches to § 2 of the Sherman Act, so that it does not matter which one is taken....

This Court finds it unnecessary to choose between the second and third approaches. For, taken as a whole, the evidence satisfies the tests laid down in both *Griffith* and *Aluminum*. The facts show that (1) defendant has, and exercises, such overwhelming strength in the shoe machinery market that it controls that market, (2) this strength excludes some potential, and limits some actual, competition, and (3) this strength is not attributable solely to defendant's ability, economies of scale, research, natural advantages, and adaptation to inevitable economic laws.

In estimating defendant's strength, this Court gives some weight to the 75 plus percentage of the shoe machinery market which United serves. But the Court considers other factors as well. In the relatively static shoe machinery market where there are no sudden changes in the style of machines or in the volume of demand, United has a network of long-term, complicated leases with over 90% of the shoe factories. These leases assure closer and more frequent contacts between United and its customers than would exist if United were a seller and its customers were buyers. Beyond this general quality, these leases are so drawn and so applied as to strengthen United's power to exclude competitors. Moreover, United offers a long line of machine types, while no competitor offers more than a short line. Since in some parts of its line United faces no important competition,

United has the power to discriminate, by wide differentials and over long periods of time, in the rate of return it procures from different machine types. Furthermore, being by far the largest company in the field, with by far the largest resources in dollars, in patents, in facilities, and in knowledge, United has a marked capacity to attract offers of inventions, inventors' services, and shoe machinery businesses. And, finally, there is no substantial substitute competition from a vigorous secondhand market in shoe machinery.

To combat United's market control, a competitor must be prepared with knowledge of shoemaking, engineering skill, capacity to invent around patents, and financial resources sufficient to bear the expense of long developmental and experimental processes. The competitor must be prepared for consumers' resistance founded on their long-term, satisfactory relations with United, and on the cost to them of surrendering United's leases. Also, the competitor must be prepared to give, or point to the source of, repair and other services, and to the source of supplies for machine parts, expendable parts, and the like. Indeed, perhaps a competitor who aims at any large scale success must also be prepared to lease his machines. These considerations would all affect *potential* competition, and have not been without their effect on *actual* competition.

Not only does the evidence show United has control of the market, but also the evidence does not show that the control is due entirely to excusable causes. The three principal sources of United's power have been the original constitution of the company, the superiority of United's products and services, and the leasing system. The first two of these are plainly beyond reproach. The original constitution of United in 1899 was judicially approved in *United States v. United Shoe Machinery Company of New Jersey*, 247 U.S. 32. It is no longer open to question, and must be regarded as protected by the doctrine of *res judicata*, which is the equivalent of a legal license. Likewise beyond criticism is the high quality of United's products, its understanding of the techniques of shoemaking and the needs of shoe manufacturers, its efficient design and improvement of machines, and its prompt and knowledgeable service. These have illustrated in manifold ways that "superior skill, foresight and industry" of which Judge Hand spoke in *Aluminum.*

But United's control does not rest solely on its original constitution, its ability, its research, or its economies of scale. There are other barriers to competition, and these barriers were erected by United's own business policies. Much of United's market power is traceable to the magnetic ties inherent in its system of leasing, and not selling, its more important machines. The lease-only system of distributing complicated machines has many "partnership" aspects, and it has exclusionary features such as the 10-year term, the full capacity clause, the return charges, and the failure to segregate service charges from machine charges. Moreover, the leasing system has aided United in maintaining a pricing system which discriminates between machine types....

In one sense, the leasing system and the miscellaneous activities just referred to (except United's purchases in the secondhand market) were natural and normal, for they were, in Judge Hand's words, "honestly industrial." They are the sort of activities which would be engaged in by other honorable firms. And, to a large extent, the leasing practices conform to long-standing traditions in the shoe machinery business. Yet, they are not practices which can be properly described as the inevitable consequences of ability, natural forces, or law. They represent something more than the use of accessible resources, the process of invention and innovation, and the employment of those techniques of employment, financing, production, and distribution, which a competitive society must foster. They are contracts, arrangements, and policies which, instead of encouraging competition based on pure merit, further the dominance of a particular firm. In this sense, they are unnatural barriers; they unnecessarily exclude actual and potential competition; they restrict a free market. While the law allows many enterprises to use such practices, the Sherman Act is now construed by superior courts to forbid the continuance of effective market control based in part upon such practices....

So far, nothing in this opinion has been said of defendant's *intent* in regard to its power and practices in the shoe machinery market. This point can be readily disposed of by reference once more to Aluminum. Defendant intended to engage in the leasing practices and pricing policies which maintained its market power. That is all the intent which the law requires when both the complaint and the judgment rest on a charge of "monopolizing," not merely "attempting to monopolize." Defendant having willed the means, has willed the end.

....

Where a defendant has monopolized commerce in violation of § 2, the principal objects of the decrees are to extirpate practices that have caused or may hereafter cause monopolization, and to restore workable competition in the market.

... Concentrations of power, no matter how beneficently they appear to have acted, nor what advantages they seem to possess, are inherently dangerous. Their good behavior in the past may not be continued; and if their strength were hereafter grasped by presumptuous hands, there would be no automatic check and balance from equal forces in the industrial market.... Dispersal of private economic power is thus one of the ways to preserve the system of private enterprise....

....

Judges ... do not *ex officio* have economic or political training. Their prophecies as to the economic future are not guided by unusually subtle judgment. They are not so representative as other branches of the government. The recommendations they receive from government prosecutors do not always reflect the over-all approach of even the executive branch of the government, sometimes not indeed the seasoned and fairly informed judgment of the head of the Department of Justice. Hearings in court do not usually give the remote judge as sound a feeling for the realities of a situation as other procedures do....

....

In the light of these general considerations, it is now meet to consider the principal problems respecting a proposed decree ....

The Government's proposal that the Court dissolve United into three separate manufacturing companies is unrealistic. United conducts all machine manufacture at one plant in Beverly, with one set of jigs and tools, one foundry, one laboratory for machinery problems, one managerial staff, and one labor force. It takes no Solomon to see that this organism cannot be cut into three equal and viable parts.

....

On the whole, therefore, the suggested remedy of dissolution is rejected.

From the opinion on defendant's violations it follows that some form of relief regarding defendant's leases and leasing practices is proper and necessary.

....

Although leasing should not now be abolished by judicial decree, the Court agrees with the Government that the leases should be purged of their restrictive features. In the decree filed herewith, the term of the lease is shortened, the full capacity clause is eliminated, the discriminatory commutative charges are removed, and United is required to segregate its charges for machines from its charges for repair service. For the most part, the decree speaks plainly enough upon these points. Yet, on two matters, a further word is in order.

The decree does not prohibit United from rendering service, because, in the Court's view, the rendition of service, if separately charged for, has no exclusionary effects. Moreover, the rendition of service by United will keep its research and manufacturing divisions abreast of technological problems in the shoe manufacturing industry; and this will be an economic advantage of the type fostered by the Sherman Act....

The Court also agrees with the Government that if United chooses to continue to lease any machine type, it must offer that type of machine also for sale. The principal merit of this proposal does not lie in its primary impact, that is, in its effect in widening the choices open to owners of shoe factories. For present purposes it may be assumed that the anti-trust laws are not designed, chiefly, if at all, to give a customer choice as to the selling methods by which his supplier offers that supplier's own products. The merit of the Government's proposal is in its secondary impact. Insofar as United's machines are sold rather than leased, they will ultimately, in many cases, reach a second-hand market. From that market, United will face a type of substitute competition which will gradually weaken the prohibited market power which it now exercises. Moreover, from that market, or from United itself, a competitor of United can acquire a United machine in order to study it, to copy its unpatented features, and to experiment with improvements in, or alterations of, the machine. Thus, in another and more direct way, United's market power will be diminished.

....

A ... possible objection to the decree is that it confers upon United's competitors the unearned opportunity to copy the unpatented features of United's machines. These competitors get a free ride.

In reply, it might be enough to say that there does not appear to be any federal or local, statutory or common law, principle protecting United's interest in these unpatented features. That is, the decree takes from United nothing which the policy of our law protects. A further answer is that if the creation of a sales alternative to leasing is, as this Court believes, necessary to dissipate United's monopoly power, the Court should not withhold its decree because its effect is to allow competitors to copy United's designs.

....

NOTES AND QUESTIONS

1. Judge Wyzanski identified the defendant's lease-only policy as an exclusionary practice, because the long-term leases tended to limit the ability of potential competitors to enter the market. Is this plausible? Suppose the useful life of a machine is fifteen years. The defendant could not lease a machine for longer than its lifespan, could it? A purchaser of the machine would operate it for its full lifespan, or until it became obsolete. The lessee's holding period would likely be shorter, unless the lessee was obligated to continue using the machine even after it became obsolete. In that case United would have to charge less money for the machine.

Judge Wyzanski also noted that the lease-only policy had the effect of foreclosing the market in second-hand machines, for United could always take them back when the lease expired. In this way United allegedly avoided the problem that Alcoa had faced of competing with its own "secondary" aluminum. The argument depends on several assumptions. One is that a shoe machine is still usable enough to "compete" in the market after the first owner is through with it. If it is, then why did the first owner get rid of it? Because it is obsolete? That argument won't work, unless we posit that United was afraid of competing with its own outdated machines. Perhaps if the shoe manufacturer went out of business? Isn't there a better explanation for United's wanting control over the reversions in its machines? The same reason that United leased them to begin with: so that it could maintain them itself and not have a number of machines bearing its name breaking down. Another possibility is that United Shoe Machinery's lease-only policy was designed to maximize its revenues, given the fact that shoe machinery is a durable good. See the note following the *Alcoa* decision, *supra*, on monopoly and durability.

2. *Price discrimination.* Judge Wyzanski identifies price discrimination as one of the defendant's exclusionary practices. Wyzanski found that United obtained a high rate of return from machines in which it had a monopoly, but a lower rate from machines in which it faced competition. In other words, United probably charged its profit-maximizing price for each machine. But why would that practice be exclusionary? Perhaps Judge Wyzanski believed United was using its high prices in its monopoly products to "subsidize" lower prices in the competitive products, thereby driving the competitors out of business. As we shall see in

the section on predatory pricing, *infra*, however, such an explanation is not likely. What if United were ordered by the court to obtain the same rate of return from all its machines? It could then sell or lease all of them at the monopoly price, in which case it would lose its market in the more competitive machines, and perhaps even cede a monopoly to someone else. Otherwise it could charge the competitive price in all of its markets, which would be even more "exclusionary," because then there would be no supracompetitive profits to attract new entrants.

3. Although price discrimination is not an "exclusionary" practice, it is evidence of market power. Assuming that the rate of return on the low-priced machines was profitable, the rate of return on the higher-priced machines must have been monopolistic. As the discussion of price discrimination, *infra*, suggests, only a seller with market power can engage in systematic price discrimination.

4. Judge Wyzanski took note of the fact that the case law suggested a variety of tests for illegal monopolization. The "classic" test was developed in *Standard Oil Co. v. United States*, 221 U.S. 1 (1911), and *United States v. American Tobacco Co.*, 221 U.S. 106 (1911). Under Judge Wyzanski's reading of that test, section 2 of the Sherman Act is violated if a company acquires or maintains a monopoly by means which themselves violate section 1. Cases involving mergers to monopoly would clearly fall within the definition. Section 1, however, requires a "combination" (at least initially) of two or more firms. If a firm has never merged and has never otherwise conspired with a second party to violate section 1, then the firm could not be guilty of illegal monopolization either. But Judge Wyzanski read *Standard Oil* and *American Tobacco* too narrowly. In both of them the Supreme Court made clear that section 2 of the Sherman Act was designed to supplement section 1 by reaching single-firm conduct that falls outside of section 1 because of the combination or conspiracy requirement, and which results in the creation of a monopoly.

5. Judge Wyzanski's second suggested test for monopolization has come to resemble the current formulation. It comes from the Supreme Court's decision in *United States v. Griffith*, 334 U.S. 100, 106-07 (1948), where the Court concluded:

> Section 1 [of the Sherman Act] covers contracts, combinations, or conspiracies in restraint of trade. Section 2 is not restricted to conspiracies or combinations to monopolize but also makes it a crime for any person to monopolize or to attempt to monopolize any part of ... commerce. So it is that monopoly power, whether lawfully or unlawfully acquired, may itself constitute an evil and stand condemned under § 2 even though it remains unexercised. For § 2 of the Act is aimed, *inter alia*, at the acquisition or retention of effective market control. Hence the existence of power "to exclude competition when it is desired to do so" is itself a violation of § 2, provided it is coupled with the purpose or intent to exercise that power.... It follows ... that the use of monopoly power, however lawfully acquired, to foreclose competition, to gain a competitive advantage, or to destroy a competitor, is unlawful.

6. Judge Wyzanski cited both Justice Douglas and Judge Hand for the suggestion that someone with a large amount of market power should be guilty of monopolization whenever he "does business." At various times in the history of the antitrust laws, commentators have debated so-called "no fault" or "no conduct" monopolization. Perhaps the most famous proposal was made in C. Kaysen & D. Turner, *Antitrust Policy: An Economic and Legal Analysis* 111, 265-72 (1959), which argued that "excessive" market power, without more, should be illegal. Under the Kaysen and Turner proposal, illegal market power would be conclusively presumed if for five or more years one company had 50% or more of the annual sales in the relevant market, or if four or fewer companies had 80% or more of the sales. The proposal would have permitted affirmative defenses of economies of scale, ownership and legal use of valid patents, or superior products and extraordinary efficiency. How would United Shoe Machinery have fared under the proposed statute?

Over the last two decades "no fault" monopoly statutes have been proposed to Congress several times, but there has been no legislation. *See* Brozen, *The Concentration-Collusion Doctrine*, 46 Antitrust L.J. 826 (1977); *Materials Presented to the National Commission for the Review of Antitrust Laws and Procedures*, 48 Antitrust L.J. 845 (1979). At the present time, none appears likely.

7. Compare with USM's leasing practices the government's allegations in *United States v. Microsoft* (May 18, 1998):

> Because [internet] browsers can help to overcome the incompatibility between different operating systems by allowing applications to run on a variety of other operating systems, browsers can reduce or eliminate the key barrier to entry which protects Microsoft's operating system monopoly. Microsoft's CEO Bill Gates referred in May 1995 to this possibility as the threat that Netscape's Navigator would "commoditize" the operating system....
>
> Microsoft has also recognized that Netscape's "Navigator" browser is itself a platform to which many applications were being written, and to which (if it thrives) more and more applications would be written. Since Netscape's browser can be run on virtually any PC operating system, applications written to Netscape's browser can also be used with different operating systems. Accordingly, the success of Netscape's browser created an alternative platform that, standing alone, threatened to reduce or eliminate a key barrier protecting Microsoft's operating system monopoly.
>
> In May 1995 Microsoft tried to convince Netscape to enter into an agreement not to compete and to divide the browser market. Microsoft proposed in part that Netscape provide the sole browser for non-Windows 95 operating systems and that Microsoft provide the sole browser for Windows 95 operating systems. When Netscape refused, Microsoft reacted — it began a pattern of exclusive dealing arrangements, agreements to not distribute or promote competitive browsers, tie-ins, and other exclusionary and predatory

conduct that excludes competition on the merits, robs OEMs and consumers of the opportunity to make their own choices, and deters innovation....

Since May 1995, Microsoft has substantially foreclosed non-Microsoft browsers ... by entering into agreements with Online Service Providers (including America Online and CompuServe) and other[s] that require those providers to distribute and promote Internet Explorer [IE] and *not* to distribute and promote competitive browsers. These agreements require [them] to:

- distribute and promote Internet Explorer to their subscribers exclusively or nearly exclusively;
- refrain from expressing or implying to their subscribers that a competing browser is available; and,
- limit the percentage of competing browsers they distribute, even in response to specific requests from customers.

Microsoft entered into similarly restrictive agreements with Internet Content Providers ("ICPs")....

Moreover, Microsoft tied its Internet Explorer browser to Windows 95, requiring OEMs to preinstall IE (and to agree not to remove all or part of it) as a condition of obtaining a license to Windows 95.

Microsoft's latest anticompetitive act is to tie its IE browser to Windows 98, the next version of its Windows operating system, which is being released to OEMs today and will be available to consumers on June 25, 1998. Microsoft will require OEMs as a condition of obtaining Windows 98 to agree not to remove IE or replace it with a competing browser. Microsoft's Windows 98 tie-in threatens to foreclose competing browsers from the OEM channel, the second of the two "most important channels of distribution" for browsers.

It will be a commercial necessity for OEMs to install Windows 98, so virtually every new PC shipped to end users will come with Microsoft's browser. Microsoft's tie of its Internet browser to Windows 98 is illegal under both Sherman Act Section 1 (as a restraint of trade) and Section 2 (as unlawful maintenance of Microsoft's operating system monopoly and as attempted monopolization of the Internet browser market).

NOTE: ENTRY BARRIERS IN MONOPOLIZATION AND MERGER CASES

The principal concern of the antitrust laws today is with practices that facilitate the creation or preservation of market power. Firms like to charge more than their economic costs, and the result is lower output and higher prices for consumers. But even a firm with a very large market share cannot earn monopoly returns if new firms can easily and quickly begin producing and selling the same product. Ordinarily we expect new investors to look for places where the rate of return is highest, and monopoly prices attract new investment. The new investment will result in higher output, and eventually prices will be driven back to the competitive level.

The successful monopolist must therefore be protected by "barriers to entry." *See Ball Mem. Hosp. v. Mutual Hosp. Ins. Co.*, 784 F.2d 1325, 1335 (7th Cir. 1986), concluding that even a health insurer with a very large market share could not have substantial market power, because insurers deal in money and risk — and both of these products can easily be duplicated:

> The insurance industry is not like the steel industry, in which a firm must take years to build a costly plant before having anything to sell. The "productive asset" of the insurance business is money, which may be supplied on a moment's notice, plus the ability to spread risk, which many firms possess and which has no geographic boundary....

Although economists agree that the concept of barriers to entry is important in antitrust analysis, widespread disagreement about definitions continues to divide them. Today the two most influential definitions of entry barriers are what might be called the Bainian definition that a barrier to entry is some factor in a market that permits incumbent firms to earn monopoly prices (i.e., prices above marginal cost) without attracting new entry. *See* J. Bain, *Barriers to New Competition* 3 (1956). The alternative is a much narrower definition, developed by economist George Stigler and used principally by the Chicago School, that an entry barrier is "a cost of producing (at some or every rate of output) which must be borne by firms which seek to enter an industry but is not borne by firms already in the industry." G. Stigler, *The Organization of Industry* 67 (1968). In the *United Shoe Machinery* case Judge Wyzanski identified USM's array of patents as a barrier to entry, for any potential entrant into shoe machinery manufacturing would have to invent around them or else purchase a license from USM. This would put the new entrant at a cost disadvantage. Does this qualify as a "barrier to entry" under Bain's definition? Under Stigler's definition?

The differences between these two concepts of entry barriers can be substantial. For example, under the Bainian definition economies of scale are a barrier to entry. The fact that firms with high outputs have lower costs than firms with low outputs tends to discourage entry. The new entrant will necessarily have a lower output than established firms and will therefore have higher costs. Incumbent firms should be able to charge a price slightly less than the anticipated costs of the new entrant, even though these prices are well above their own costs. Under the Stigler definition, however, there is no cost of entering the market which must be incurred by new firms that was not incurred by incumbent firms. Each of them faced the same situation at the time it entered; so there are no entry barriers.

Another important difference between the Bainian and Stiglerian approaches to entry barriers is that the Bainian approach focuses on the market as it exists and considers whether the incumbents can charge supracompetitive prices while yet discouraging entry. The Chicago School, by contrast, tends to look at the process by which firms enter the market, and finds no significant entry barriers if the process is the same for newcomers as it was for established firms.

Undoubtedly the most effective kind of barrier to entry is a monopoly restriction from the government. If a firm can persuade a state or local government to give it a monopoly, say, of all the taxicab business from Downtown Chicago to O'Hare Airport, then it will have created for itself the perfect barrier to entry, under both the Bainian and Stiglerian definitions. Antitrust controls of such barriers to entry are taken up in Chapter 9, principally under the *Noerr-Pennington* and "state action" doctrines.

Judges have been known to be careless about defining entry barriers. They have often identified high startup costs as an entry barrier — for example, the fact that it costs $100,000,000 to enter a certain market. To be sure, high startup costs may limit the number of people who are likely to enter the market, but there is little reason to think that high costs are a significant barrier to entry in today's highly efficient capital market. If the rate of return in a market requiring high startup costs appears to be significantly higher (in relation to risk) than the rate of return in other markets, people engaged in capital formation will quickly and easily find investors willing to risk the money. Standing alone, high startup costs are not a real barrier to entry under either the Bain or Stigler definitions.

In the last decade, antitrust enforcement agencies and scholars have proposed more rigor in entry barrier analysis. Most have preferred the Bainian notion of entry barriers. Although the government's 1992 Horizontal Merger Guidelines, discussed in the next chapter, are strongly influenced by the Chicago School, they adopt an essentially Bainian approach to the definition of entry barriers. Under the Guidelines, entry barriers are measured by the extent of probable entry in response to a "small but significant and nontransitory increase in price." To the extent that the case law has adopted either of these two positions the Bainian approach seems to be preferred. But see the *Waste Management* case, reprinted in Chapter 7, in which the court appeared to adopt the Stiglerian definition. The decision has been criticized for focusing too heavily on whether entry was "physically easy to accomplish," and not enough on whether incumbent firms could charge monopoly prices without encouraging new entry. Schmalensee, *Ease of Entry: Has the Concept Been Applied Too Readily?*, 56 Antitrust L.J. 41 (1987).

The Federal Trade Commission has been more receptive of the Stigler approach to entry barriers. Its *Echlin Manufacturing* merger decision defined barriers to entry as "additional long-run costs that must be incurred by an entrant relative to the long-run costs faced by incumbent firms." The Commission then continued:

> The only meaningful way to compare the risks and costs incurred by the two firms [i.e., the established firm and the prospective or new entrant] is to apply the same yardstick to each by viewing each of them at the time of its own entry.... The incumbent firm's apparently lower costs may merely reflect

compensation for the risk it incurred in entering the market. The potential entrant's apparently higher costs will decline to that of the incumbent firm if its attempted entry is successful.

Echlin Mfg., 3 Trade Reg. Rep. ¶ 22268 at 22301-02 (F.T.C. 1985). The Commission explicitly rejected the notion that the risk of failure faced by a prospective entrant was a qualifying barrier to entry, even though that risk was substantially higher than it was for an established firm.

Perhaps the most generalized "cost" that must be faced by prospective firms is risk. For the established business already earning high profits, the risk of failure is relatively small. For the prospective entrant who has not yet built a plant, the risk of failure is much, much higher. An investment of $100,000,000 "costs" much more in the presence of high risk. This probably explains why it is much easier for, say, Ford Motor Company to build a new $100,000,000 automobile plant in response to increased auto demand than it is for a new company to build the same plant and start manufacturing cars. Under the rationale of *Echlin Manufacturing*, risk should not be considered a qualifying entry barrier. Thus the firm that has already survived the risk is entitled to indefinite monopoly profits — i.e., profits sufficiently high to deter others from undergoing the same risk — assuming that the incumbent firm has market power and that there are not other entry barriers in the market. Does this analysis seem sound? Should risk be a factor when determining entry barriers? If so, how should it be quantified?

But risk alone is not really a barrier to entry even under the Bainian definition. Even if entry is expensive and the probability of failure is high, it will probably occur unless a significant amount of startup costs cannot be recovered in the event of failure. For example, suppose that you want to enter the parcel delivery business, which is extremely risky because the incumbent firms are very well established. Your chances of success are only 70%. But assume that your only investment is a fleet of trucks which will cost $100,000,000, and that if your business fails you will immediately be able to resell the entire fleet of trucks for exactly what you paid for it. In that case, you face high entry costs *and* a high risk that the business will fail — but the costs of failure are precisely zero. You get all your money back if the business goes under. This suggests that a true barrier to entry is an *unrecoverable*, or "sunk," cost that must borne by the prospective entrant.

It seems as if a barrier to entry must meet three requirements. First, there must be some relatively high cost that the prospective entrant must bear. Second, there must be a significant risk of failure. Third, a significant percentage of these costs must be "sunk," or unrecoverable, in the event of failure. In its *Echlin Manufacturing* decision, *supra*, the FTC noted that the extent of "sunk" costs in the market at issue, the assembly of carburetor repair kits from parts manufactured by others, was very small. As a result, entry barriers were not substantial.

Does this analysis tell us anything about where we might expect to find barriers to entry? It suggests that barriers to entry are most likely to exist in industries that use large amounts of durable (why durable?), expensive and specialized equipment. Once a steel mill is built, for example, it cannot easily be converted into apartment buildings or even a glass factory. If a steel mill is expensive and can be used only for manufacturing steel, then the consequences of failure in the steel industry can be rather high.

But the analysis also suggests that barriers to entry exist in some less likely places. The costs of many kinds of goods or services are "sunk" because the good or service is used up as soon as it is delivered. A good example of this is advertising. If the incumbents in a market have used advertising to produce strong customer brand loyalties, then a prospective entrant will have to match them. The new entrant may have to finance an expensive pre-production advertising campaign, as well as an expensive promotional campaign after production has started. Once the advertising has been purchased and delivered, it cannot be sold to someone else. *See* A. Jacquemin, *The New Industrial Organization: Market Forces and Strategic Behavior* 100 (1987); Mensch & Freeman, *Efficiency and Image: Advertising as an Antitrust Issue*, 1990 Duke L.J. 321.

Determining the appropriate role of barriers to entry in antitrust analysis has turned out to be a perplexing problem. The problem arises because a particularly significant "barrier to entry" is efficiency itself, particularly under the Bainian definition. Suppose, for example, that economies of scale are such that the most efficient size for a Smidget plant is one that produces 75% of the relevant market for Smidgets when they are sold at a competitive price. The firm that operates that plant might control 75% of the relevant market, or even more. Any new entrant would begin with a market share of substantially less than 75% and would thus be at a distinct cost disadvantage to the incumbent. Such economies of scale have frequently been described as a "barrier to entry." *E.g.*, J. Bain, *Barriers to New Competition*, ch. 1 (1956).

But if we are willing to recognize economies of scale as a barrier to entry, do we also want to say that the erection of barriers to entry is an anticompetitive practice which, when undertaken by a firm with substantial market power, violates the Sherman Act? Should it be illegal for a producer with market power to erect a plant of the most efficient size? The concept of "barriers to entry" is a useful part of antitrust analysis, but we must keep in mind that high entry barriers are not necessarily an antitrust violation. Mainly, they add plausibility to the plaintiff's story that a particular act was anticompetitive because it was calculated to create or maintain a monopoly. At various times a host of things have been suggested as monopolistic barriers to entry: advertising, patents, vertical integration, tying arrangements and product differentiation. All of these have in common that they may make it harder for potential competitors to enter a market. Unfortunately, that is about the only thing they have in common. What is worse, each of them can be used in socially beneficial ways that antitrust should be loathe to condemn. The antitrust tribunal has the difficult task of distinguishing the efficient from the inefficient uses.

In *United States v. Syufy Enters.*, 903 F.2d 659 (9th Cir. 1990), the Ninth Circuit dismissed the Justice Department's monopolization complaint against a movie theater owner who acquired all the movie theaters in Las Vegas, Nevada. The court found that entry was easy and by the time of suit had already reduced the defendant's market share significantly. The court rejected the government's claim that the fact that any new entrant would face a "bidding war" against the defendant was a qualifying entry barrier. This was tantamount to claiming "that Syufy's effectiveness as a competitor creates a structural barrier to entry, rendering illicit Syufy's acquisition of its competitors' screens."

For differing views of the role of entry barriers in antitrust analysis, *see* R. Bork, *The Antitrust Paradox: A Policy at War with Itself* 310-29 (1978; rev. ed. 1993); F.M. Scherer & D. Ross, *Industrial Market Structure and Economic Performance* 386-404 (3d ed. 1990). For a good but rather technical summary of the economics literature, *see* Gilbert, "Mobility Barriers and the Value of Incumbency," in *Handbook of Industrial Organization* 475 (R. Schmalensee & R. Willig, eds. 1989).

Finally, consider the relationship between barriers to entry and market definition. Suppose that Firm A produces a large share of the market for Widgets, but, in response to any price increase above the competitive level, Smidget producers, who are competitive, will begin producing Widgets as well. In such a case one might wish to define the market as Widgets but say that entry barriers are very low; or one might define the relevant market to include both Widgets and Smidgets. Which approach is correct?

Sometimes it makes little difference. A finding of low entry barriers may compensate for an excessively narrow market definition. However, a finding of high barriers will not compensate for a market definition that is too broad, for the court may determine that the broadly defined market is competitive, and then the height of entry barriers becomes irrelevant, at least in monopolization and merger cases. One important distinction must be kept in mind. Market definition encompasses only the productive assets of firms already in existence that are capable of competing with the firm under consideration. By contrast, entry barrier analysis looks both at the productive assets of firms capable of shifting into competition with the firm under consideration, and firms that are not yet in existence, but which may enter in response to higher prices. The Justice Department Merger Guidelines, which are discussed at length in the following chapter, generally include existing firms capable of switching production to the product under consideration in the same relevant market; they generally reserve the concept of entry barriers for firms that may come into existence in response to high prices.

2. THE PROBLEM OF STRATEGIC BEHAVIOR

BERKEY PHOTO, INC. V. EASTMAN KODAK CO.

603 F.2d 263 (2d Cir. 1979), *cert. denied*, 444 U.S. 1093 (1980)

JUDGE KAUFMAN.

This action, one of the largest and most significant private antitrust suits in history, was brought by Berkey Photo, Inc., a far smaller but still prominent participant in the industry. Berkey competes with Kodak in providing photofinishing services — the conversion of exposed film into finished prints, slides, or movies. Until 1978, Berkey sold cameras as well. It does not manufacture film, but it does purchase Kodak film for resale to its customers, and it also buys photofinishing equipment and supplies, including color print paper, from Kodak.

... In this action, Berkey claims that every aspect of the association has been infected by Kodak's monopoly power in the film, color print paper, and camera markets, willfully acquired, maintained, and exercised in violation of § 2 of the Sherman Act, 15 U.S.C. § 2.... Berkey alleges that these violations caused it to lose sales in the camera and photofinishing markets and to pay excessive prices to Kodak for film, color print paper, and photofinishing equipment....

....

The principal markets relevant here, each nationwide in scope, are amateur conventional still cameras, conventional photographic film, photofinishing services, photofinishing equipment, and color print paper. The numerous technological interactions among the products and services constituting these markets are manifest. To take an obvious example, not only are both camera and film required to produce a snapshot, but the two must be in compatible "formats." This means that the film must be cut to the right size and spooled in a roll or cartridge that will fit the camera mechanism....

The "amateur conventional still camera" market now consists almost entirely of the so-called 110 and 126 instant-loading cameras. These are the direct descendants of the popular "box" cameras, the best-known of which was Kodak's so-called "Brownie." Small, simple, and relatively inexpensive, cameras of this type are designed for the mass market rather than for the serious photographer.[2]

Kodak has long been the dominant firm in the market thus defined. Between 1954 and 1973 it never enjoyed less than 61% of the annual unit sales, nor less than 64% of the dollar volume, and in the peak year of 1964, Kodak cameras accounted for 90% of market revenues. Much of this success is no doubt due to the firm's history of innovation. In 1963 Kodak first marketed the 126 "Instamatic" instant-loading camera, and in 1972 it came out with the much smaller 110 "Pocket Instamatic." Not only are these cameras small and light, but they employ film packaged in cartridges that can simply be dropped in the back of the camera, thus obviating the need to load and position a roll manually. Their introduction triggered successive revolutions in the industry. Annual amateur still camera sales in the United States averaged 3.9 million units between 1954 and 1963, with little annual variation. In the first full year after Kodak's introduction of the 126, industry sales leaped 22%, and they took an even larger quantum jump when the 110 came to market. Other camera manufacturers, including Berkey,

---

[2] More complicated cameras, such as those in the 135 format ("35-millimeter") commonly used by professionals and photographic hobbyists, were found not to be part of this market. The jury also rejected Kodak's request to include in the definition "instant" cameras, pioneered by the Polaroid Corporation, which produce a finished print within minutes, or even seconds, after the shutter is snapped.

copied both these inventions but for several months after each introduction anyone desiring to purchase a camera in the new format was perforce remitted to
Kodak.

Berkey has been a camera manufacturer since its 1966 acquisition of the Keystone Camera Company, a producer of movie cameras and equipment. In 1968
Berkey began to sell amateur still cameras made by other firms, and the following year the Keystone Division commenced manufacturing such cameras itself.
From 1970 to 1977, Berkey accounted for 8.2% of the sales in the camera market
in the United States, reaching a peak of 10.2% in 1976. In 1978, Berkey sold its
camera division and thus abandoned this market.

The relevant market for photographic film comprises color print, color slide,
color movie, and black-and-white film. Kodak's grip on this market is even
stronger than its hold on cameras. Since 1952, its annual sales have always exceeded 82% of the nationwide volume on a unit basis, and 88% in revenues. Foreign competition has recently made some inroads into Kodak's monopoly, but
the Rochester firm concedes that it dominated film sales throughout the period
relevant to this case. ...

Kodak's monopoly in the film market is particularly important to this case,
because the jury accepted Berkey's contention, noted above, that it had been used
to disadvantage rivals in cameras, photofinishing, photofinishing equipment, and
other markets. Of special relevance to this finding is the color print film segment
of the industry, which Kodak has dominated since it introduced "Kodacolor," the
first amateur color print film, in 1942. In 1963, when Kodak announced the 126
Instamatic camera, it also brought out a new, faster color print film — Kodacolor X — which was initially available to amateur photographers only in the
126 format. Nine years later, Kodak repeated this pattern with the simultaneous
introduction of the 110 Pocket Instamatic and Kodacolor II film. For more than a
year, Kodacolor II was made only for 110 cameras, and Kodak has never made
any other color print film in the 110 size.

Before 1954, Kodak's Color Print and Processing Laboratories (CP&P) had a
nearly absolute monopoly of color photofinishing maintained by a variety of
practices. Accounting for over 95% of color film sales, Kodak sold every roll
with an advance charge for processing included. Consumers had little choice but
to purchase Kodak film, and in so doing they acquired the right to have that film
developed and printed by CP&P· at no further charge. Since few customers would
duplicate their costs to procure the services of a non-Kodak photofinisher, Kodak
was able to parlay its film monopoly to achieve equivalent market power in
photofinishing.

This film/processing "tie-in" attracted the attention of the Justice Department,
and in 1954 a consent decree changed the structure of the color photofinishing
market drastically. Kodak was forbidden to link photofinishing to film sales, and
it agreed to make its processing technology, chemicals, and paper available to
rivals at reasonable rates. As a result, CP&P's share of the market plummeted
from 96% in 1954 to 69% two years later, and it has declined sharply ever since.

In 1970, CP&P accounted for but 17% of the market, and by 1976 its share reached a low of 10%. There are now approximately 600 independent photofinishers in the United States.

....

Although the 1954 decree steadily loosened Kodak's grip in photofinishing, it did not immediately affect the firm's control of color paper. For more than a decade, the independent photofinishers that sprang up after the decree was entered looked only to Kodak for their paper supplies.

... Kodak's control of the film and color paper markets clearly reached the level of a monopoly. And, while the issue is a much closer one, it appears that the evidence was sufficient for the jury to find that Kodak possessed such power in the camera market as well. But our inquiry into Kodak's liability cannot end there.

[W]hile proclaiming vigorously that monopoly power is the evil at which § 2 is aimed, courts have declined to take what would have appeared to be the next logical step — declaring monopolies unlawful *per se* unless specifically authorized by law. To understand the reason for this, one must comprehend the fundamental tension — one might almost say the paradox — that is near the heart of § 2. This tension creates much of the confusion surrounding § 2. It makes the cryptic *Alcoa* opinion a litigant's wishing well, into which, it sometimes seems, one may peer and find nearly anything he wishes.

....

In *Alcoa* the crosscurrents and pulls and tugs of § 2 law were reconciled by noting that, although the firm controlled the aluminum ingot market, "it may not have achieved monopoly; monopoly may have been thrust upon it." In examining this language, which would condemn a monopolist unless it is "the passive beneficiary of a monopoly," we perceive Hand the philosopher. As an operative rule of law, however, the "thrust upon" phrase does not suffice. It has been criticized by scholars, and the Supreme Court appears to have abandoned it. *Grinnell* instructs that after possession of monopoly power is found, the second element of the § 2 offense is "the willful acquisition or maintenance of that power as distinguished from growth or development as a consequence of a superior product, business acumen, or historic accident."

This formulation appears to square with the understanding of the draftsmen of the Sherman Act that § 2 does not condemn one "who merely by superior skill and intelligence ... got the whole business because nobody could do it as well." Thus the statement in *Alcoa* that even well-behaved monopolies are forbidden by § 2 must be read carefully in context. Its rightful meaning is that, if monopoly power has been acquired or maintained through improper means, the fact that the power has not been used to extract improper benefits provides no succor to the monopolist.

But the law's hostility to monopoly power extends beyond the means of its acquisition. Even if that power has been legitimately acquired, the monopolist may not wield it to prevent or impede competition. Once a firm gains a measure of monopoly power, whether by its own superior competitive skill or because of such actions as restrictive combinations with others, it may discover that the power is capable of being maintained and augmented merely by using it. That is, a firm that has achieved dominance of a market might find its control sufficient to preserve and even extend its market share by excluding or preventing competition. A variety of techniques may be employed to achieve this end — predatory pricing, lease-only policies, and exclusive buying arrangements, to list a few.

... A firm that has lawfully acquired a monopoly position is not barred from taking advantage of scale economies by constructing, for example, a large and efficient factory. These benefits are a consequence of size and not an exercise of power over the market.[12] Nevertheless, many anticompetitive actions are possible or effective only if taken by a firm that dominates its smaller rivals....

In sum, although the principles announced by the § 2 cases often appear to conflict, this much is clear. The mere possession of monopoly power does not *ipso facto* condemn a market participant. But, to avoid the proscriptions of § 2, the firm must refrain at all times from conduct directed at smothering competition. This doctrine has two branches. Unlawfully acquired power remains anathema even when kept dormant. And it is no less true that a firm with a legitimately achieved monopoly may not wield the resulting power to tighten its hold on the market.

It is clear that a firm may not employ its market position as a lever to create — or attempt to create — a monopoly in another market. Kodak, in the period relevant to this suit, was never close to gaining control of the markets for photofinishing equipment or services and could not be held to have attempted to monopolize them. Berkey nevertheless contends that Kodak illicitly gained an advantage in these areas by leveraging its power over film and cameras. Accordingly, we must determine whether a firm violates § 2 by using its monopoly power in one market to gain a competitive advantage in another, albeit without an attempt to monopolize the second market. We hold, as did the lower court, that it does.

This conclusion appears to be an inexorable interpretation of the antitrust laws. We tolerate the existence of monopoly power, we repeat, only insofar as necessary to preserve competitive incentives and to be fair to the firm that has attained its position innocently. There is no reason to allow the exercise of such power to the detriment of competition, in either the controlled market or any other. That the competition in the leveraged market may not be destroyed but merely distorted does not make it more palatable. Social and economic effects of an extension of monopoly power militate against such conduct....

Accordingly, the use of monopoly power attained in one market to gain a competitive advantage in another is a violation of § 2, even if there has not been an

---

[12] Nor is a lawful monopolist ordinarily precluded from charging as high a price for its product as the market will accept. True, this is a use of economic power; indeed, the differential between price and marginal cost is used as an indication of the degree of monopoly power .... But high prices, far from damaging competition, invite new competitors into the monopolized market.

attempt to monopolize the second market. It is the use of economic power that creates the liability. But, as we have indicated, a large firm does not violate § 2 simply by reaping the competitive rewards attributable to its efficient size, nor does an integrated business offend the Sherman Act whenever one of its departments benefits from association with a division possessing a monopoly in its own market. So long as we allow a firm to compete in several fields, we must expect it to seek the competitive advantages of its broad-based activity — more efficient production, greater ability to develop complementary products, reduced transaction costs, and so forth. These are gains that accrue to any integrated firm, regardless of its market share, and they cannot by themselves be considered uses of monopoly power.

We turn now to the events surrounding Kodak's introduction of the 110 photographic system in 1972....

... On March 16, 1972, amid great fanfare, the system was announced. Finally, said Kodak, there was a "little camera that takes big pictures." Kodacolor II was "a remarkable new film" — indeed, the best color negative film Kodak had ever manufactured. There had long been other small cameras, Kodak explained: "But they weren't like these. Now there are films fine enough, and sharp enough, to give you big, sharp pictures from a very small negative." In accord with Kodak's 1967 plan, Kodacolor II was sold only in the 110 format for eighteen months after introduction. It remains the only 110-size color print film Kodak has ever sold.

As Kodak had hoped, the 110 system proved to be a dramatic success. In 1972 — the system's first year — the company sold 2,984,000 Pocket Instamatics, more than 50% of its sales in the amateur conventional still camera market. The new camera thus accounted in large part for a sharp increase in total market sales, from 6.2 million units in 1971 to 8.2 million in 1972. Rival manufacturers hastened to market their own 110 cameras, but Kodak stood alone until Argus made its first shipment of the "Carefree 110" around Christmas 1972. ...

Berkey's Keystone division was a late entrant in the 110 sweepstakes, joining the competition only in late 1973. Moreover, because of hasty design, the original models suffered from latent defects, and sales that year were a paltry 42,000. With interest in the 126 dwindling, Keystone thus suffered a net decline of 118,000 unit sales in 1973. The following year, however, it recovered strongly, in large part because improvements in its pocket cameras helped it sell 406,000 units, 7% of all 110s sold that year.

Berkey contends that the introduction of the 110 system was both an attempt to monopolize and actual monopolization of the camera market. It also alleges that the marketing of the new camera constituted an impermissible leveraging of Kodak's film monopoly into the two photofinishing markets, services and equipment....

It will be useful at the outset to present the arguments on which Berkey asks us to uphold its verdict:

(1) Kodak, a film and camera monopolist, was in a position to set industry standards. Rivals could not compete effectively without offering products similar to Kodak's. Moreover, Kodak persistently refused to make film available for most formats other than those in which it made cameras. Since cameras are worthless without film, this policy effectively prevented other manufacturers from introducing cameras in new formats. Because of its dominant position astride two markets, and by use of its film monopoly to distort the camera market, Kodak forfeited its own right to reap profits from such innovations without providing its rivals with sufficient advance information to enable them to enter the market with copies of the new product on the day of Kodak's introduction....

(2) The simultaneous introduction of the 110 camera and Kodacolor II film, together with a campaign advertising the two jointly, enabled Kodak to garner more camera sales than if it had merely scaled down Kodacolor X to fit the new camera. The jury could conclude that Kodacolor II was an inferior product and not technologically necessary for the success of the 110. In any event, Kodak's film monopoly prevented any other camera manufacturer from marketing such a film-camera "system" and the joint introduction was therefore anticompetitive.

(3) For eighteen months after its introduction, Kodacolor II was available only in the 110 format. Thus it followed that any consumer wishing to use Kodak's "remarkable new film" had to buy a 110 camera. Since Kodak was the leading — and at first the only — manufacturer of such devices, its camera sales were boosted at the expense of its competitors.

For the reasons explained below, we do not believe any of these contentions is sufficient on the facts of this case to justify an award of damages to Berkey....

As Judge Frankel indicated, and as Berkey concedes, a firm may normally keep its innovations secret from its rivals as long as it wishes, forcing them to catch up on the strength of their own efforts after the new product is introduced. It is the possibility of success in the marketplace, attributable to superior performance, that provides the incentives on which the proper functioning of our competitive economy rests. If a firm that has engaged in the risks and expenses of research and development were required in all circumstances to share with its rivals the benefits of those endeavors, this incentive would very likely be vitiated.

Withholding from others advance knowledge of one's new products, therefore, ordinarily constitutes valid competitive conduct. Because, as we have already indicated, a monopolist is permitted, and indeed encouraged, by § 2 to compete aggressively on the merits, any success that it may achieve through "the process of invention and innovation" is clearly tolerated by the antitrust laws.

... A significant vice of the theory propounded by Berkey lies in the uncertainty of its application. Berkey does not contend, in the colorful phrase of Judge Frankel, that "Kodak has to live in a goldfish bowl," disclosing every innovation to the world at large. However predictable in its application, such an extreme rule would be insupportable. Rather, Berkey postulates that Kodak had a duty to disclose limited types of information to certain competitors under specific circumstances. But it is difficult to comprehend how a major corporation, accustomed though it is to making business decisions with antitrust considerations in mind, could possess the omniscience to anticipate all the instances in which a jury might one day in the future retrospectively conclude that predisclosure was warranted. And it is equally difficult to discern workable guidelines that a court might set forth to aid the firm's decision. For example, how detailed must the information conveyed be? And how far must research have progressed before it is "ripe" for disclosure? These inherent uncertainties would have an inevitable chilling effect on innovation. They go far, we believe, towards explaining why no court has ever imposed the duty Berkey seeks to create here.

An antitrust plaintiff urging a predisclosure rule, therefore, bears a heavy burden in justifying his request. Berkey recognizes the weight of this burden. It contends that it has been met. Kodak is not a monolithic monopolist, acting in a single market. Rather, its camera monopoly was supported by its activity as a film manufacturer. Berkey therefore argues that by not disclosing the new format in which it was manufacturing film, Kodak unlawfully enhanced its power in the camera market. Indeed, Kodak not only participates in but monopolizes the film industry. The jury could easily have found that, when Kodak introduced a new film format, rival camera makers would be foreclosed from a substantial segment of the market until they were able to manufacture cameras in the new format. Accordingly, Berkey contended that Kodak illegitimately used its monopoly power in film to gain a competitive advantage in cameras. Thus Berkey insists that the jury was properly permitted to consider whether, on balance, the failure to predisclose the new format was exclusionary. We disagree.

We note that this aspect of Berkey's claim is in large measure independent of the fact that a new film, Kodacolor II, was introduced simultaneously with the new format. It is primarily introduction of the format itself — the size of the film and the cartridge in which it is packaged — of which Berkey complains. Indeed, at oral argument counsel for Berkey contended that predisclosure would have been required even had Kodak merely cut down Kodacolor X to fit the new 110 camera and cartridge.

We do not perceive, however, how Kodak's introduction of a new format was rendered an unlawful act of monopolization in the camera market because the firm also manufactured film to fit the cameras. The 110 system was in substantial part a camera development.... Indeed, Berkey not only argues that a new film was not necessary to introduce the new pocket cameras; it also concedes that the early models of its own 110 cameras, brought to market some eighteen months after it first learned of the new format, suffered because of the haste with which they were designed.

Clearly, then, the policy considerations militating against predisclosure requirements for monolithic monopolists are equally applicable here. The first firm, even a monopolist, to design a new camera format has a right to the lead time that follows from its success. The mere fact that Kodak manufactured film in the new format as well, so that its customers would not be offered worthless cameras, could not deprive it of that reward. Nor is this conclusion altered because Kodak not only participated in but dominated the film market. Kodak's ability to pioneer formats does not depend on it possessing a film monopoly. Had the firm possessed a much smaller share of the film market, it would nevertheless have been able to manufacture sufficient quantities of 110-size film — either Kodacolor X or Kodacolor II — to bring the new camera to market. It is apparent, therefore, that the ability to introduce the new format without predisclosure was solely a benefit of integration and not, without more, a use of Kodak's power in the film market to gain a competitive advantage in cameras....

Our analysis, however, must proceed beyond the conclusion that introduction of film to meet Kodak's new camera format was not in itself an exercise of the company's monopoly power in film. Berkey contends that Kodak in the past used its film monopoly to stifle format innovations by any other camera manufacturer. Accordingly, it argues that Kodak was barred from reaping the benefits of such developments without making predisclosure to allow its rivals to share from the beginning in the rewards.

There is, indeed, little doubt that the jury could have found that Kodak, by refusing to make film available on economical terms, obstructed sales of cameras in competing formats. Thus, Kodak has never supplied film to fit the Minox, a small camera that uses a cartridge similar to that of the Instamatics and that has been on the market since the 1930s, or similar cameras by Minolta and Mamiya that were also introduced before the Kodak 126. ...

We accept the proposition that it is improper, in the absence of a valid business policy, for a firm with monopoly power in one market to gain a competitive advantage in another by refusing to sell a rival the monopolized goods or services he needs to compete effectively in the second market.... Moreover, as indicated by our discussion of § 2 principles, such a use of power would be illegal regardless of whether the film monopoly were legally or illegally acquired. ...

But Berkey did not sue Kodak then for its refusal to sell film, and it concedes that it is not now claiming a right to damages on this basis. Rather, it contends that Kodak's past offenses created a continuing duty to disclose its new formats to competing camera manufacturers, and that its violation of that obligation supports the jury's verdict. [W]e decline to recognize such a duty....

Berkey's claims regarding the introduction of the 110 camera are not limited to its asserted right to predisclosure. The Pocket Instamatic not only initiated a new camera format, it was also promoted together with a new film. As we noted earlier, the view was expressed at Kodak that "[w]ithout a new film, the [camera] program is not a new advertisable system." Responding in large measure to this perception, Kodak hastened research and development of Kodacolor II so that it could be brought to market at the same time as the 110 system. Based on such evidence, and the earlier joint introduction of Kodacolor X and the 126 camera, the jury could readily have found that the simultaneous release of Kodacolor II and the Pocket Instamatic was part of a plan by which Kodak sought to use its combined film and camera capabilities to bolster faltering camera sales. Berkey contends that this program of selling was anticompetitive and therefore violated § 2. We disagree.

It is important to identify the precise harm Berkey claims to have suffered from this conduct. It cannot complain of a product introduction *simpliciter* for the same reason it could not demand predisclosure of the new format: any firm, even a monopolist, may generally bring its products to market whenever and however it chooses. Rather, Berkey's argument is more subtle. It claims that by marketing the Pocket Instamatics in a system with a widely advertised new film, Kodak gained camera sales at Berkey's expense. And, because Kodacolor II was not necessary to produce satisfactory 110 photographs and in fact suffered from several deficiencies, these gains were unlawful.

It may be conceded that, by advertising Kodacolor II as a "remarkable new film" capable of yielding "big, sharp pictures from a very small negative," Kodak sold more 110 cameras than it would have done had it merely marketed Kodacolor X in 110-size cartridges. The quality of the end product — a developed snapshot — is at least as dependent upon the characteristics of the film as upon those of the camera. It is perfectly plausible that some customers bought the Kodak 110 camera who would have purchased a competitor's camera in another format had Kodacolor II not been available and widely advertised as capable of producing "big, sharp pictures" from the tiny Pocket Instamatic. Moreover, there was also sufficient evidence for the jury to conclude that a new film was not necessary to bring the new cameras to market....

But necessity is a slippery concept. Indeed, the two scientists, Zwick and Groet, conceded that improvements in the quality of Kodacolor X would be "most welcome." Even if the 110 camera would produce adequate snapshots with Kodacolor X, it would be difficult to fault Kodak for attempting to design a film that could provide better results. The attempt to develop superior products is, as we have explained, an essential element of lawful competition. Kodak could not have violated § 2 merely by introducing the 110 camera with an improved film.

Accordingly, much of the evidence at trial concerned the dispute over the relative merits of Kodacolor II and Kodacolor X. There was ample evidence that for some months following the 110 introduction, Kodacolor II was inferior to its predecessor in several respects. Most notably, it degenerated more quickly than Kodacolor X, so that its shelf life was shorter. It is undisputed, however, that the grain of Kodacolor II, though not as fine as Kodak had hoped, was better than that of the older film.

In this context, therefore, the question of product quality has little meaning. A product that commends itself to many users because superior in certain respects may be rendered unsatisfactory to others by flaws they considered fatal....

It is evident, then, that in such circumstances no one can determine with any reasonable assurance whether one product is "superior" to another. Preference is a matter of individual taste. The only question that can be answered is whether there is sufficient demand for a particular product to make its production worthwhile, and the response, so long as the free choice of consumers is preserved, can only be inferred from the reaction of the market. ...

We conclude, therefore, that Kodak did not contravene the Sherman Act merely by introducing Kodacolor II simultaneously with the Pocket Instamatic and advertising the advantages of the new film for taking pictures with a small camera.

There is another aspect to Berkey's claim that introduction of Kodacolor II simultaneously with the Pocket Instamatic camera was anticompetitive. For eighteen months after the 110 system introduction, Kodacolor II was available only in the 110 format. Since Kodak was the first to have the 110s on the market, Berkey asserts it lost camera sales because consumers who wished to use the "remarkable new film" would be compelled to buy a Kodak camera. This facet of the claim, of course, is not dependent on a showing that Kodacolor II was inferior in any respect to Kodacolor X. Quite the opposite is true. The argument is that, since consumers were led to believe that Kodacolor II was superior to Kodacolor X, they were more likely to buy a Kodak 110, rather than a Berkey camera, so that the new film could be used.

... We shall assume *arguendo* that Kodak violated § 2 of the Sherman Act if its decision to restrict Kodacolor II to the 110 format was not justified by the nature of the film but was motivated by a desire to impede competition in the manufacture of cameras capable of using the new film. This might well supply the element of coercion we found lacking in the previous section. We shall assume also that there was sufficient evidence for the jury to conclude that the initial decision to market Kodacolor II exclusively in the 110 format during its introductory period was indeed taken for anticompetitive purposes.

But to prevail, Berkey must prove more, for injury is an element of a private treble damages action. Berkey must, therefore, demonstrate that some consumers who would have bought a Berkey camera were dissuaded from doing so because Kodacolor II was available only in the 110 format. This it has failed to establish. The record is totally devoid of evidence that Kodak or its retailers actually attempted to persuade customers to purchase the Pocket Instamatic because it was the only camera that could use Kodacolor II, or that, in fact, any consumers did choose the 110 in order to utilize the finer-grained film....

To summarize our conclusions on the 110 camera claims, we hold:

1. Kodak was under no obligation to predisclose information of its new film and format to its camera-making competitors.

2. It is no basis for antitrust liability that Kodacolor II, despite certain deficiencies compared to Kodacolor X, may have encouraged sales of the 110 camera.

3. Finally, although the restriction of Kodacolor II to the 110 format may have been unjustified, there was no evidence that Berkey was injured by this course of action.

CALIFORNIA COMPUTER PRODUCTS V. IBM CORP.

613 F.2d 727 (9th Cir. 1979)

JUDGE CHOY.

[The plaintiff was a manufacturer of peripheral products for computers, such as disk drives and memory units. It commonly "reverse engineered" IBM peripheral products and manufactured similar peripherals compatible with IBM mainframe computers and Central Processing Units (CPUs). Under pre-1970's technology such peripheral units were commonly connected to CPUs by cables, and it was possible to buy different units from different manufacturers, as long as they were compatible with each other. In 1971, however, IBM introduced a new line of computers which integrated disk drive and memory functions into the CPU itself. As a result, anyone who purchased such a CPU from IBM was obliged to take the IBM disk drive and memory units as well, for they were all part of the same physical unit in the new line of machines. The plaintiffs claimed that the defendant's new design was illegal monopolization in violation of section 2 of the Sherman Act.]

CalComp characterized these design changes as "technological manipulation" which did not improve performance. It also complained of the fact that the newly integrated functions were priced below their non-integrated counterparts. But as we have stated, price and performance are inseparable parts of any competitive offering; and equivalent function at lower cost certainly represents a superior product from the buyer's point of view. The evidence at trial was uncontroverted that integration was a cost-saving step, consistent with industry trends, which enabled IBM effectively to reduce prices for equivalent functions. Moreover, there was substantial evidence as well that in the case of Models 145, 158 and 168 the integration of control and memory functions also represented a performance improvement.

One of CalComp's witnesses stated: "I think in general the manufacturer will try and minimize his costs and where he integrates the control unit the assumption must be that he is achieving a lower cost solution." Other of CalComp's evidence showed that among the reasons a separate control unit is more expensive than integrated control circuitry are that the former requires its own cabinet, frames, power supply, additional cabling and electronics. According to an IBM witness, the monolithic systems technology that preceded the 145 — 2319A system required a large standalone controller, whereas the new generation technology represented by the 145 — 2319A system produced a comparable control function "which was in the area of ten times smaller .... [Y]ou could now put that into the 145 system, utilizing its frames and its covers and then passing on the advantages of that to the customer in a price reduction." CalComp's Chairman stated that as a result of integration, the customer uses less floor space which "tends to be relatively expensive in a computer room."

IBM, assuming it was a monopolist, had the right to redesign its products to make them more attractive to buyers — whether by reason of lower manufacturing cost and price or improved performance. It was under no duty to help Cal-Comp or other peripheral equipment manufacturers survive or expand.

Affirmed.

NOTES AND QUESTIONS

1. *Berkey Photo* was decided by Judge Learned Hand's court, which had decided the *Alcoa* case 35 years earlier. How much of *Alcoa* remains?

2. Should a manufacturer with substantial market power ever have a duty to predisclose a new product to competitors? One could say, for example, that if the monopolist's purpose in producing the new product was "predatory" — that is, not a function of competition on the merits, but intended merely to damage competitors — then the law requires predisclosure. However, in such cases the introduction of the new product would be illegal whether or not it was predisclosed.

Suppose that *Q*, Inc., is a very large company that manufactures two products, computers and software. It has substantial market power in its particular model of computer, but none in software. The software market contains many "pygmies" that manufacture software for *Q*'s computers. Now *Q*, without prior announcement, introduces a new model of computer and a new set of software to use with it. All other software is incompatible with the new machine. At the same time, *Q* stops manufacturing its older model of computer. The result is that for an appreciable period of time — let's say, one year — the pygmies are relegated to manufacturing software for the obsolete computer model. After a year or so, however, they will have acquired the technology to put software compatible with the new machine on the market. Courts and commentators have analyzed such behavior both as monopolization, under section 2 of the Sherman Act, and as a form of tying arrangement — sometimes known as a "physical tie-in" — under section 1 of the Sherman Act or section 3 of the Clayton Act. (See the discussion of tying arrangements in Chapter 5.) Don't such "physical tie-ins" have the same limitations as tying arrangements in general? For example, can *Q* really enlarge its monopoly profits by obtaining a monopoly in the software as well as the computer? All buyers of computers also need software. Won't they attribute a price increase in the software to the entire package? Thus wouldn't *Q* be able to extract the entire monopoly overcharge from the computer alone? Even if the physical tie-in had the effect of driving the pygmies out of business, *Q* might not be able to enlarge its monopoly profits.

It is possible, however, that software is being sold at substantially above its marginal cost by the pygmies, and *Q* would like to transfer part of this revenue to itself. As a general rule, computer software is contained on a magnetic tape or disk. It costs a great deal of money to develop a new computer program — let's say $1,000,000 — but once it has been developed it may cost only $3 to produce a single copy of the program. The $1,000,000 is sunk costs which need to be recovered, however, and such a program might sell for $200.00, even though the marginal cost of producing it is $3. Each of 10 pygmies has spent the $1,000,000 developing a certain kind of program for the older model computer. By creating the physical tie-in, however, for one year Q will be able to produce all the software for the new model, and it will undertake the large development costs for any particular program only once. Thus it might actually be more efficient for Q to be the only manufacturer of software. Whether or not it is depends a little on how much variety in software is good. If the ten pygmies offered ten different word-processing programs, all of which were substantially the same, then a great deal of development money may have been inefficiently spent. On the other hand, if the ten word-processing programs are different from one another and meet different consumer needs, then the money to develop ten different programs may have been well spent. See the discussion of *United States v. Microsoft* in Chapter 3.

3. Any new invention injures competitors of the inventor. Should a new invention ever be the basis of a monopolization claim? For an argument that sometimes technological innovation can itself be predatory, and should then be condemned, *see* Ordover & Willig, *An Economic Definition of Predation: Pricing and Product Innovation*, 91 Yale L.J. 8 (1981); for a response, *see* Sidak, *Debunking Predatory Innovation*, 83 Colum. L. Rev. 1121 (1983).

In general, we reward innovation by giving the innovator monopoly profits. That is the express policy of the patent laws. Kodak and IBM were innovators, but Berkey Photo and California Computer Products were free riders. They made money by copying the products of their competitors. Should firms have a right, protected by the law against monopolization, to copy someone else's innovations? What if the antitrust laws held that as soon as someone developed a new product everyone had a legal right of access to the new technology? What would happen to the incentive to innovate?

4. What of California Computer's allegation that IBM's new line of integrated computers, which eliminated part of the separate market for peripheral products, was nothing more than "'technological manipulation' which did not improve performance"? Suppose that the new, integrated machines were really inferior to the older, separate ones, but IBM introduced the new ones simply to destroy the independent market for peripheral devices. Why would consumers buy them? Could such a plan be profitable to IBM? Would it have to stop manufacturing its older line of computers? What if one or more other firms also manufactured computers similar to the older, superior units?

In 1969 the government also brought its own case against IBM, arguing that in the 1960's IBM introduced an entire computer line, the System/360, as "fighting machines." The Antitrust Division alleged that (1) the machines were announced long before IBM was ready to ship them, (2) their capabilities were exaggerated, and (3) they were priced at less than cost. Assuming these three allegations were true, which should be antitrust violations? For discussion of the case by authors sympathetic with the defendant, *see* F.M. Fisher, J.J. McGowan & J.E. Greenwood, *Folded, Spindled, and Mutilated: Economic Analysis and* U.S. v. IBM

(1983). For discussion from the government's perspective, *see* R.T. DeLamarter, *Big Blue: IBM's Use and Abuse of Power* (1986). The government's case was voluntarily dismissed in 1982.

5. For many years an automobile manufacturer has been manufacturing cars equipped with a particular dashboard design that accommodates a car radio. The manufacturer also makes car radios, which it sells as "factory installed" or "dealer installed." However, several small competing companies manufacture radios that will fit into the dashboard as well. These competing radios are commonly sold at a lower price than radios produced by the automobile manufacturer itself.

One year, without warning, the automobile manufacturer changes its dashboard design to make installation of radios by competitors more difficult. Worse yet, the dashboard design now changes every year with the year-end model change, and each year the competing radio manufacturers must alter the design of their radio installation kits in order to fit the new dashboard design. Since automobile models are kept secret by auto manufacturers until they are displayed for sale, the competing radio manufacturers lose sales during the lucrative period immediately after new car models are introduced, because it takes them several months to design and produce an installation kit that will fit the new models.

Suppose further that the yearly design changes are purely aesthetic; that is, there is no evidence that they improve the performance of the automobile radio. Has the automobile manufacturer violated the antitrust laws? *See Automatic Radio Mfg. Co. v. Ford Motor Co.*, 272 F. Supp. 744 (D. Mass. 1967), *aff'd*, 390 F.2d 113 (1st Cir.), *cert. denied*, 391 U.S. 914 (1968).

6. Many physical tie-ins are actually price discrimination devices. For example, if Kodak charged a monopoly price for the film in its newly developed camera-film package, a photographer who used 30 rolls of film per month (and presumably placed a high value on the camera) would yield higher profits to Kodak than a photographer who used only 3 rolls per year. For the use of tying arrangements as price discrimination devices, see Chapter 5, *supra*.

7. *Berkey Photo* breathed new life into the "leverage" theory of §2 with its statement that "the use of monopoly power attained in one market to gain a competitive advantage in another is a violation of §2, even if there has not been an attempt to monopolize the second market." The formula was developed by the Supreme Court in *United States v. Griffith*, 334 U.S. 100 (1948), which found it unlawful for theater owners to use their dominant position in one set of cities to achieve a competitive advantage in other cities, even if they did not intend to acquire monopolies in the second set of cities. One problem with the theory is that it does not seem to be covered by the language of the Sherman Act. First, the defendant is not being accused of monopolizing the towns where it already has a monopoly. Second, it is neither monopolizing nor attempting to monopolize the second set of towns.

Since *Berkey Photo*, numerous courts have considered leverage claims and, not surprisingly, have been divided on the basic issue. *See, e.g., Kerasotes Mich. Theatres v. Nat'l Amusements*, 854 F.2d 135 (6th Cir. 1988), *cert. dismissed*, 490

U.S. 1087 (1989) (defendant, who was a dominant exhibitor in many areas but not Flint, Michigan, could have used monopoly power in other areas to gain a competitive advantage in Flint, in violation of §2); *Alaska Airlines v. United Airlines*, 948 F.2d 536 (9th Cir. 1991), *cert. denied*, 506 U.S. 977 (1992) (rejecting the theory).

The Supreme Court seemed to have approved a leverage claim, at least in dicta, in its 1992 *Kodak* decision:

> The Court has held many times that power gained through some natural and legal advantage such as a patent, copyright, or business acumen can give rise to liability if "a seller exploits his dominant position in one market to expand his empire into the next."

Eastman Kodak Co. v. Image Tech. Servs., 504 U.S. 451, 479 n.29 (1992). But then the Court made a sharp about-face a year later in its *Spectrum Sports* decision, reprinted below:

> § 2 makes the conduct of a single firm unlawful only when it actually monopolizes or dangerously threatens to do so. The concern that § 2 might be applied so as to further anticompetitive ends is plainly not met by inquiring only whether the defendant has engaged in "unfair" or "predatory" tactics.

Spectrum Sports v. McQuillan, 506 U.S. 447, 448 (1993).

In *Aquatherm Indus. v. Florida Power & Light Co.*, 145 F.3d 1258, 1262 (11th Cir. 1998), an electric utility gave special concessions to contractors who installed electric swimming pool heaters rather than the plaintiff's solar heaters, but the utility itself did not sell either type of heater. It was seeking merely to increase electricity sales. The court rejected a monopoly "leveraging" claim on these facts:

> Aquatherm in effect asks this court to extend *Berkey Photo* to a situation in which a monopolist projects its power into a market it not only does not seek to monopolize, but in which it does not even seek to compete. There is no support for such an extension in either the language of §2 or the case law interpreting it.

For further discussion, *see* 3 P. Areeda & H. Hovenkamp, *Antitrust Law* ¶ 652 (rev. ed. 1995).

8. In *American Professional Testing Serv. v. Harcourt, Brace, Jovanovich*, 108 F.3d 1147 (9th Cir. 1997), the court held that the dominant offeror of bar review courses, which sent five anonymous and damaging fliers about its rival to law schools over a two month period, did not violate §2 of the Sherman Act. Ninth Circuit law required proof of a "significant and enduring adverse impact on competition," and a few instances of product disparagement, even if tortious, did not rise to that level. The court also refused to condemn the defendant's "theft" of a well known Florida law professor as a bar review lecturer, holding that stealing an employee could violate §2 only if the defendant did so merely to deprive the victim of the employee's services — but in this case, the defendant actually used the employee instead of simply paying him not to work for a rival.

ASPEN SKIING CO. V. ASPEN HIGHLANDS SKIING CORP.
472 U.S. 585 (1985)

JUSTICE STEVENS delivered the opinion for the Court.

In a private treble damages action, the jury found that petitioner Aspen Skiing Company (Ski Co.) had monopolized the market for downhill skiing services in Aspen, Colorado. The question presented is whether that finding is erroneous as a matter of law because it rests on an assumption that a firm with monopoly power has a duty to cooperate with its smaller rivals in a marketing arrangement in order to avoid violating § 2 of the Sherman Act.

I

Aspen is a destination ski resort with a reputation for "super powder," "a wide range of runs," and an "active night life," including "some of the best restaurants in North America." ... Between 1945 and 1960, private investors independently developed three major facilities for downhill skiing: Aspen Mountain (Ajax), Aspen Highlands (Highlands), and Buttermilk. A fourth mountain, Snowmass, opened in 1967....

Between 1958 and 1964, three independent companies operated Ajax, Highlands, and Buttermilk. In the early years, each company offered its own day or half-day tickets for use of its mountain.... In 1962, however, the three competitors also introduced an interchangeable ticket.... The 6-day, all-Aspen ticket provided convenience to the vast majority of skiers who visited the resort for weekly periods, but preferred to remain flexible about what mountain they might ski each day during the visit.... It also emphasized the unusual variety in ski mountains available in Aspen....

In 1964, Buttermilk was purchased by Ski Co., but the interchangeable ticket program continued.... Lift operators at Highlands monitored usage of the ticket in the 1971-1972 season by recording the ticket numbers of persons going onto the slopes of that mountain. Highlands officials periodically met with Ski Co. officials to review the figures recorded at Highlands, and to distribute revenues based on that count....

....

In the next four seasons, Ski Co. and Highlands used surveys to allocate the revenues from the 4-area, 6-day ticket. Highlands' share of the revenues from the ticket was 17.5% in 1973-1974, 18.5% in 1974-1975, 16.8% in 1975-1976, and 13.2% in 1976-1977. During these four seasons, Ski Co. did not offer its own 3-area, multi-day ticket in competition with the all-Aspen ticket.[9] By 1977, multi-

---

[9] In 1975, the Colorado Attorney General filed a complaint against Ski Co. and Highlands alleging, in part, that the negotiations over the 4-area ticket had provided them with a forum for

area tickets accounted for nearly 35% the total market.... Holders of multi-area passes also accounted for additional daily ticket sales to persons skiing with them.

... [F]or the 1977-1978 season, Ski Co. offered to continue the all-Aspen ticket only if Highlands would accept a 13.2% fixed share of the ticket's revenues.

Although that had been Highlands' share of the ticket revenues in 1976-1977, Highlands contended that that season was an inaccurate measure of its market performance since it had been marked by unfavorable weather and an unusually low number of visiting skiers. Moreover, Highlands wanted to continued to divide revenues on the basis of actual usage, as that method of distribution allowed it to compete for the daily loyalties of the skiers who had purchased the tickets.... Fearing that the alternative might be no interchangeable ticket at all, and hoping to persuade Ski Co. to reinstate the usage division of revenues, Highlands eventually accepted a fixed percentage of 15% for the 1977-1978 season.... No survey was made during that season of actual usage of the 4-area ticket at the two competitors' mountains.

In March 1978, the Ski Co. management recommended to the Board of Directors that the 4-area ticket be discontinued for the 1978-1979 season. The Board decided to offer Highlands a 4-area ticket provided that Highlands would agree to receive a 12.5% fixed percentage of the revenue — considerably below Highlands' historical average based on usage.... Later in the 1978-1979 season, a member of Ski Co.'s Board of Directors candidly informed a Highlands' official that he had advocated making Highlands "an offer that [it] could not accept." ... Ski Co. refused to consider any counterproposals, and Highlands finally rejected the offer of the fixed percentage.

As far as Ski Co. was concerned, the all-Aspen ticket was dead. In its place Ski Co. offered the 3-area, 6-day ticket featuring only its mountains. In an effort to promote this ticket, Ski Co. embarked on a national advertising campaign that strongly implied to people who were unfamiliar with Aspen that Ajax, Buttermilk, and Snowmass were the only ski mountains in the area. For example, Ski Co. had a sign changed in the Aspen Airways waiting room at Stapleton Airport in Denver. The old sign had a picture of the four mountains in Aspen touting "Four Big Mountains" whereas the new sign retained the picture but referred only to three....[12]

Ski Co. took additional actions that made it extremely difficult for Highlands to market its own multi-area package to replace the joint offering. Ski Co. dis-

---

price-fixing in violation of § 1 of the Sherman Act and that they had attempted to monopolize the market for downhill skiing services in Aspen in violation of § 2.... In 1977, the case was settled by a consent decree that permitted the parties to continue to offer the 4-area ticket provided that they set their own ticket prices unilaterally before negotiating its terms....

[12] Ski Co. circulated another advertisement to national magazines labeled "Aspen, More Mountains, More Fun."... The advertisement depicted the four mountains of Aspen, but labeled only Ajax, Buttermilk and Snowmass. Buttermilk's label is erroneously placed directly over Highlands Mountain....

continued the 3-day, 3-area pass for the 1978-1979 season, and also refused to sell Highlands any lift tickets, either at the tour operator's discount or at retail.... Highlands finally developed an alternative product, the "Adventure Pack," which consisted of a 3-day pass at Highlands and three vouchers, each equal to the price of a daily lift ticket at a Ski Co. mountain. The vouchers were guaranteed by funds on deposit in an Aspen bank, and were redeemed by Aspen merchants at full value.... Ski Co., however, refused to accept them....

Without a convenient all-Aspen ticket, Highlands basically "becomes a day ski area in a destination resort."... Highlands' share of the market for downhill skiing services in Aspen declined steadily after the 4-area ticket based on usage was abolished in 1977: from 20.5% in 1976-1977, to 15.7% in 1977-1978, to 13.1% in 1978-1979, to 12.5% in 1979-1980, to 11% in 1980-1981....

II

In 1979, Highlands filed a complaint in the United States District Court for the District of Colorado naming Ski Co. as a defendant. Among various claims, the complaint alleged that Ski Co. had monopolized the market for downhill skiing services at Aspen in violation of § 2 of the Sherman Act, and prayed for treble damages. The case was tried to a jury which rendered a verdict finding Ski Co. guilty of the § 2 violation and calculating Highlands' actual damages at $2.5 million....

In her instructions to the jury, the District Judge explained that the offense of monopolization under § 2 of the Sherman Act has two elements: (1) the possession of monopoly power in a relevant market, and (2) the willful acquisition, maintenance, or use of that power by anticompetitive or exclusionary means or for anticompetitive or exclusionary purposes.... Although the first element was vigorously disputed at the trial and in the Court of Appeals, in this Court Ski Co. does not challenge the jury's special verdict finding that it possessed monopoly power.[20] Nor does Ski Co. criticize the trial court's instructions to the jury concerning the second element of the § 2 offense.

On this element, the jury was instructed that it had to consider whether "Aspen Skiing Corporation willfully acquired, maintained, or used that power by anticompetitive or exclusionary means or for anti-competitive or exclusionary purposes."... The instructions elaborated:

> [A] firm that has lawfully acquired a monopoly position is not barred from taking advantage of scale economies by constructing a large and efficient factory. These benefits are a consequence of size and not an exercise of monopoly power. Nor is a corporation which possesses monopoly power under a

---

[20] The jury found that the relevant product market was "[d]ownhill skiing at destination ski resorts," that the "Aspen area" was a relevant geographic submarket, and that during the years 1977-1981, Ski Co. possessed monopoly power, defined as the power to control prices in the relevant market or to exclude competitors....

duty to cooperate with its business rivals. Also a company which possesses monopoly power and which refuses to enter into a joint operating agreement with a competitor or otherwise refuses to deal with a competitor in some manner does not violate Section 2 if valid business reasons exist for that refusal.

In other words, if there were legitimate business reasons for the refusal, then the defendant, even if he is found to possess monopoly power in a relevant market, has not violated the law. We are concerned with conduct which unnecessarily excludes or handicaps competitors. This is conduct which does not benefit consumers by making a better product or service available — or in other ways — and instead has the effect of impairing competition....

The jury answered a specific interrogatory finding the second element of the offense as defined in these instructions.

... The District Court ... entered a judgment awarding Highlands treble damages of $7,500,000, costs and attorney's fees....

The Court of Appeals affirmed in all respects....

....

III

In this Court, Ski Co. contends that even a firm with monopoly power has no duty to engage in joint marketing with a competitor, that a violation of § 2 cannot be established without evidence of substantial exclusionary conduct, and that none of its activities can be characterized as exclusionary. It also contends that the Court of Appeals incorrectly relied on the "essential facilities" doctrine and that an "anti-competitive intent" does not transform nonexclusionary conduct into monopolization. In response, Highlands submits that, given the evidence in the record, it is not necessary to rely on the "essential facilities" doctrine in order to affirm the judgment....

"The central message of the Sherman Act is that a business entity must find new customers and higher profits through internal expansion — that is, by competing successfully rather than by arranging treaties with its competitors." *United States v. Citizens & Southern National Bank*, 422 U.S. 86, 116 (1975). Ski Co., therefore, is surely correct in submitting that even a firm with monopoly power has no general duty to engage in a joint marketing program with a competitor. Ski Co. is quite wrong, however, in suggesting that the judgment in this case rests on any such proposition of law. For the trial court unambiguously instructed the jury that a firm possessing monopoly power has no duty to cooperate with its business rivals....

The absence of an unqualified duty to cooperate does not mean that every time a firm declines to participate in a particular cooperative venture, that decision may not have evidentiary significance, or that it may not give rise to liability in certain circumstances. The absence of a duty to transact business with another firm is, in some respects, merely the counterpart of the independent businessman's cherished right to select his customers and his associates. The high value that we have placed on the right to refuse to deal with other firms does not mean that the right is unqualified.

In *Lorain Journal v. United States*, 342 U.S. 143 (1951), we squarely held that this right was not unqualified. Between 1933 and 1948 the publisher of the Lorain Journal, a newspaper, was the only local business disseminating news and advertising in that Ohio town. In 1948, a small radio station was established in a nearby community. In an effort to destroy its small competitor, and thereby regain its "pre-1948 substantial monopoly over the mass dissemination of all news and advertising," the Journal refused to sell advertising to persons that patronized the radio station....

In holding that this conduct violated § 2 of the Sherman Act, the Court dispatched the same argument raised by the monopolist here:

> The publisher claims a right as a private business concern to select its customers and to refuse to accept advertisements from whomever it pleases. We do not dispute that general right. "But the word 'right' is one of the most deceptive of pitfalls; it is so easy to slip from a qualified meaning in the premise to an unqualified one in the conclusion. Most rights are qualified."...

The Court approved the entry of an injunction ordering the Journal to print the advertisements of the customers of its small competitor.

In *Lorain Journal*, the violation of § 2 was an "attempt to monopolize," rather than monopolization, but the question of intent is relevant to both offenses. In the former case it is necessary to prove a "specific intent" to accomplish the forbidden objective — as Judge Hand explained, "an intent which goes beyond the mere intent to do the act." *United States v. Aluminum Co. of America*, 148 F.2d 416, 432 (2d Cir. 1945). In the latter case evidence of intent is merely relevant to the question whether the challenged conduct is fairly characterized as "exclusionary" or "anticompetitive" — to use the words in the trial court's instructions — or "predatory," to use a word that scholars seem to favor. Whichever label is used, there is agreement on the proposition that "no monopolist monopolizes unconscious of what he is doing." As Judge Bork stated more recently: "Improper exclusion (exclusion not the result of superior efficiency) is always deliberately intended."[29]

The qualification on the right of a monopolist to deal with whom he pleases is not so narrow that it encompasses no more than the circumstances of *Lorain Journal*. In the actual case that we must decide, the monopolist did not merely reject a novel offer to participate in a cooperative venture that had been proposed by a competitor. Rather, the monopolist elected to make an important change in a pattern of distribution that had originated in a competitive market and had persisted for several years. The all-Aspen, 6-day ticket with revenues allocated on

---

[29] R. Bork, The Antitrust Paradox 160 (1978).

the basis of usage was first developed when three independent companies operated three different ski mountains in the Aspen area.... It continued to provide a desirable option for skiers when the market was enlarged to include four mountains, and when the character of the market was changed by Ski Co.'s acquisition of monopoly power. Moreover, since the record discloses that interchangeable tickets are used in other multi-mountain areas which apparently are competitive, it seems appropriate to infer that such tickets satisfy consumer demand in free competitive markets.

Ski Co.'s decision to terminate the all-Aspen ticket was thus a decision by a monopolist to make an important change in the character of the market.

Moreover, we must assume that the jury followed the court's instructions. The jury must, therefore, have drawn a distinction "between practices which tend to exclude or restrict competition on the one hand, and the success of a business which reflects only a superior product, a well-run business, or luck, on the other."
... Since the jury was unambiguously instructed that Ski Co.'s refusal to deal with Highlands "does not violate § 2 if valid business reasons exist for that refusal," ... we must assume that the jury concluded that there were no valid business reasons for the refusal. The question then is whether that conclusion finds support in the record.

IV

The question whether Ski Co.'s conduct may properly be characterized as exclusionary cannot be answered by simply considering its effect on Highlands. In addition, it is relevant to consider its impact on consumers and whether it has impaired competition in an unnecessarily restrictive way.[31] If a firm has been "attempting to exclude rivals on some basis other than efficiency," it is fair to characterize its behavior as predatory. It is, accordingly, appropriate to examine the effect of the challenged pattern of conduct on consumers, on Ski Co.'s smaller rival, and on Ski Co. itself.

Superior Quality of the All-Aspen Ticket

The average Aspen visitor "is a well-educated, relatively affluent, experienced skier who has skied a number of times in the past ...." ... Over 80% of the skiers visiting the resort each year have been there before — 40% of these repeat visitors have skied Aspen at least five times.... Over the years, they developed a strong demand for the 6-day, all-Aspen ticket in its various refinements. Most experienced skiers quite logically prefer to purchase their tickets at once for the whole period that they will spend at the resort; they can then spend more time on

---

[31] "Thus, 'exclusionary' comprehends at the most behavior that not only (1) tends to impair the opportunities of rivals, but also (2) either does not further competition on the merits or does so in an unnecessarily restrictive way." 3 P. Areeda & D. Turner, Antitrust Law 78 (1978).

the slopes and enjoying the amenities and less time standing in ticket lines. The 4-area attribute of the ticket allowed the skier to purchase his 6-day ticket in advance while reserving the right to decide in his own time and for his own reasons which mountain he would ski on each day. It provided convenience and flexibility, and expanded the vistas and the number of challenging runs available to him during the week's vacation.

... [T]he actual record of competition between a 3-area ticket and the all-Aspen ticket in the years after 1967 indicated that skiers demonstrably preferred four mountains to three.... Highlands' expert marketing witness testified that many of the skiers who come to Aspen want to ski the four mountains, and the abolition of the 4-area pass made it more difficult to satisfy that ambition.... A consumer survey undertaken in the 1979-1980 season indicated that 53.7% of the respondents wanted to ski Highlands, but would not; 39.9% said that they would not be skiing at the mountain of their choice because their ticket would not permit it....

Ski Co.'s Business Justification

Perhaps most significant, however, is the evidence relating to Ski Co. itself, for Ski Co. did not persuade the jury that its conduct was justified by any normal business purpose. Ski Co. was apparently willing to forgo daily ticket sales both to skiers who sought to exchange the coupons contained in Highlands' Adventure Pack, and to those who would have purchased Ski Co. daily lift tickets from Highlands if Highlands had been permitted to purchase them in bulk. The jury may well have concluded that Ski Co. elected to forgo these short run benefits because it was more interested in reducing competition in the Aspen market over the long run by harming its smaller competitor.

That conclusion is strongly supported by Ski Co.'s failure to offer any efficiency justification whatever for its pattern of conduct. In defending the decision to terminate the jointly offered ticket, Ski Co. claimed that usage could not be properly monitored. The evidence, however, established that Ski Co. itself monitored the use of the 3-area passes based on a count taken by lift operators, and distributed the revenues among its mountains on that basis. Ski Co. contended that coupons were administratively cumbersome, and that the survey takers had been disruptive and their work inaccurate. Coupons, however, were no more burdensome than the credit cards accepted at Ski Co. ticket windows.... Moreover, in other markets Ski Co. itself participated in interchangeable lift tickets using coupons.... As for the survey, its own manager testified that the problems were much overemphasized by Ski Co. officials, and were mostly resolved as they arose.... Ski Co.'s explanation for the rejection of Highlands' offer to hire — at its own expense — a reputable national accounting firm to audit usage of the 4-area tickets at Highlands' mountain, was that there was no way to "control" the audit....

In the end, Ski Co. was pressed to justify its pattern of conduct on a desire to disassociate itself from — what it considered — the inferior skiing services offered at Highlands.... The all-Aspen ticket based on usage, however, allowed consumers to make their own choice on these matters of quality. Ski Co.'s purported concern for the relative quality of Highlands' product was supported in the record by little more than vague insinuations, and was sharply contested by numerous witnesses. Moreover, Ski Co. admitted that it was willing to associate with what it considered to be inferior products in other markets....

Although Ski Co.'s pattern of conduct may not have been as "'bold, relentless, and predatory' "as the publisher's actions in *Lorain Journal*, the record in this case comfortably supports an inference that the monopolist made a deliberate effort to discourage its customers from doing business with its smaller rival. The sale of its 3-area, 6-day ticket, particularly when it was discounted below the daily ticket price, deterred the ticket holders from skiing at Highlands. The refusal to accept the Adventure Pack coupons in exchange for daily tickets was apparently motivated entirely by a decision to avoid providing any benefit to Highlands even though accepting the coupons would have entailed no cost to Ski Co. itself, would have provided it with immediate benefits, and would have satisfied its potential customers. Thus the evidence supports an inference that Ski Co. was not motivated by efficiency concerns and that it was willing to sacrifice short run benefits and consumer good will in exchange for a perceived long-run impact on its smaller rival.

Because we are satisfied that the evidence in the record,[44] construed most favorably in support of Highlands' position, is adequate to support the verdict under the instructions given by the trial court, the judgment of the Court of Appeals is

Affirmed.

JUSTICE WHITE took no part in the decision of this case.

NOTES AND QUESTIONS

1. *Raising Rivals' Costs.* The Supreme Court occasionally characterized the *Aspen* defendant's activities as "predatory." But Ski Co. almost certainly did not engage in predatory pricing — i.e., undergoing short-run losses in order to reap long-run monopoly gains. (Predatory pricing is discussed later in this chapter). Rather, Ski Co.'s activities may be an example of strategic raising of a rival's costs in order to earn higher profits. Ski Co.'s refusal to participate with Highlands in a joint ticket arrangement was "costly" to Ski Co. But it was even more

---

[44] Given our conclusion that the evidence amply supports the verdict under the instructions as given by the trial court, we find it unnecessary to consider the possible relevance of the "essential facilities" doctrine, or the somewhat hypothetical question whether nonexclusionary conduct could ever constitute an abuse of monopoly power if motivated by an anti-competitive purpose. If, as we have assumed, no monopolist monopolizes unconscious of what he is doing, that case is unlikely to arise.

costly to Highlands. To put it another way, Highlands benefitted much more from the Ski Co.-Highlands joint venture than Ski Co. did. By ceasing the venture, the costs to both Ski Co. and Highlands of filling their slopes and lodges rose, but Highlands' costs rose more. The result was that Ski Co. was able to charge a higher premium over its costs, assuming that it was a monopolist.

The dominant firm or firms in an industry may sometimes select a strategy that is calculated, not so much to exclude firms from a market, but rather to ensure that smaller firms or new entrants will have higher costs than those of the dominant firm. *See* ABA, *Non-Price Predation under Section Two of the Sherman Act* (E.T. Sullivan, ed., ABA Monograph #18, 1991); Krattenmaker & Salop, *Anticompetitive Exclusion: Raising Rivals' Cost to Achieve Power Over Price*, 96 Yale L.J. 209 (1986); Salop & Scheffman, *Raising Rivals' Costs*, 73 Am. Econ. Rev. 267 (1983); S. Salop & D. Scheffman, *Cost-Raising Strategies*, 36 J. Indus. Econ. 19 (1987).

What kinds of things might a monopoly firm do in order to raise its rivals' costs? Consider the following:

(1) The dominant firm is capital intensive, while the smaller competitors are labor intensive. The entire industry is unionized. The dominant firm agrees to a contract giving workers a considerable wage increase, and the smaller firms are forced to follow. Although the dominant firm's costs rise, the costs of the smaller firms rise even more, and the result is that the dominant firm can raise price by a greater margin over its costs. *See* O. Williamson, *Wage Rates as a Barrier to Entry: the Pennington Case in Perspective*, 82 Q.J. Econ. 85 (1968).

(2) The dominant firm litigates against its smaller rival on patent issues, whether or not the litigation is well-founded. Although the litigation costs the dominant firm and its rival the same amount, the rival has a smaller output over which the litigation costs can be distributed. Its fixed costs (why fixed?) rise by a greater amount than do those of the dominant firm. *See* Hovenkamp, *Antitrust Policy After Chicago*, 84 Mich. L. Rev. 213, 274-80 (1985).

(3) The dominant firm or firms petition a regulatory agency for rules, compliance with which is subject to substantial economies of scale. For example, a dominant firm with a plant capable of producing 100,000 units monthly has four competitors whose plants can produce 20,000 units monthly each. It successfully petitions an agency for the mandatory installation of safety devices that cost $1,000,000 per plant, regardless of size. Once again, the relative fixed costs of the smaller firms rise much more than for the dominant firm. *See* Salop, Scheffman & Schwartz, "A Bidding Analysis of Special Interest Regulation: Raising Rivals' Costs in a Rent Seeking Society," in *The Political Economy of Regulation: Private Interests in the Regulatory Process* 102 (R. Rogowsky & B. Yandle, eds. 1984).

(4) The dominant firm in an industry which uses electricity in the production process purchases from several electric utilities a promise that they will

not sell electricity to the dominant firm's rivals. *See* Rasmusen, Ramseyer, & Wiley, *Naked Exclusion*, 81 Am. Econ. Rev. 1137 (1991); Krattenmaker & Salop, *Anticompetitive Exclusion: Raising Rivals' Costs to Achieve Power Over Price*, 96 Yale L.J. 209 (1986).

What can antitrust policy do about such strategies? In some cases, such as (4), the answer is relatively easy. A "naked" agreement under which Firm A extracts a promise that a utility will not deal with Firm A's competitors is illegal per se.

The answers to (1), (2), and (3) are far more difficult. Strategies (2) and (3) in particular may involve activity protected by each person's right to petition the government. See Chapter 9. The labor contract in (1) may not be protected activity. What kind of evidence would be required to show that a dominant firm's agreement to a new wage contract was anticompetitive?

To date courts have been slow to condemn activity as monopolistic merely because it raised a rival's costs (in *Aspen* the Supreme Court condemned the activity, but did not cite the strategy of raising rivals' costs). In *Ball Mem. Hosp. v. Mutual Hosp. Ins. Co.*, 784 F.2d 1325, 1340 (7th Cir. 1986), the Seventh Circuit refused to condemn alleged monopolization by a health insurer on such a theory. The plaintiffs charged that Blue Shield's Preferred Provider Organization plan (PPO), under which Blue Shield set stringent limits on the amount it reimbursed hospitals for certain medical procedures, raised rivals' costs because it forced hospitals to shift costs to other insured patients. The theory was that the PPO actually reimbursed hospitals less than the cost of providing a particular insured medical procedure. The hospital could then break even only by increasing the price for the same procedure to other patients, who would then make claims against their insurers. As a result, the costs of other health insurers would rise as Blue Shield's costs declined.

In rejecting this argument, the court found it sufficient that Blue Shield had been found not to have substantial market power. In the absence of market power such a scheme could not succeed, for the hospitals would not tolerate it. The court refused to assess any standard that required Blue Shield to show that its low reimbursement rates were "cost-justified," particularly when it held no monopoly power. Such a requirement would force the district courts to become "little versions of the Office of Price Administration."

By contrast, *Reazin v. Blue Cross & Blue Shield of Kan.*, 899 F.2d 951 (10th Cir. 1990), found that Blue Cross violated §2 when it terminated its provider agreement with a hospital because the hospital had established an independent, competing mechanism for providing prepaid health care. Under the policy change the plaintiff hospital would not receive reimbursements directly from Blue Cross, but its patients would have to pay their bills and seek reimbursement. The result was alleged to be that patients would shift from the plaintiff hospital to other hospitals, and this would raise the plaintiff hospital's cost of doing business.

2. The *Aspen* Court made much of the fact that the defendant could not produce a satisfactory business justification for its decision to stop cooperating with the plaintiff. In *Olympia Equip. Leasing Co. v. Western Union Tel. Co.*, 797 F.2d 370 (7th Cir. 1986), the court distinguished *Aspen*, and found an adequate business justification for the defendant's actions. Western Union had sold both telex equipment and telex communications services in "bundled" packages, but decided to withdraw from the telex equipment market when deregulation led to competition there. It encouraged others, including the plaintiff, to help it liquidate its inventory of terminals, even providing sales help and customer contacts. But later Western Union decided to sell more of its own terminals, and encouraged its salesmen to sell more terminals themselves instead of referring the sales to the plaintiff. Western Union's sales of its terminals then rose dramatically, while those of the plaintiff fell to nothing and it went out of business. In declining to find monopolization, the Seventh Circuit said:

> Today it is clear that a firm with lawful monopoly power has no general duty to help its competitors, whether by holding a price umbrella over their heads or by otherwise pulling its competitive punches....
>
> If a monopolist does extend a helping hand, though not required to do so, and later withdraws it as happened in this case, does he incur antitrust liability? We think not. Conceivably he may be liable in tort or contract law, under theories of equitable or promissory estoppel or implied contract ..., or by analogy to the common law tort rule that though there is no duty to help a bystander in distress, once help is extended it may not be withdrawn.... But the controlling consideration in an antitrust case is antitrust policy rather than common law analogies. Since Western Union had no duty to encourage the entry of new firms into the equipment market, the law would be perverse if it made Western Union's encouraging gestures the fulcrum of an antitrust violation. Then no firm would dare to attempt a graceful exit from a market in which it was a major seller.... Refusing to act as your competitor's sales agent is not an unnatural practice engaged in only by firms bent on monopolization.

The court found that the defendant's decision to sell its terminals in competition with the plaintiff was quite justified by its desire to exit the market more quickly. Perhaps more to the point, as the court noted in a later opinion denying a rehearing, the offense of monopolization consists of acts calculated to create or preserve the monopolist's position in the market. Here, the defendant was trying to *exit* from the market as effectively as possible. Such conduct cannot conceivably be calculated to create or preserve a monopoly, even though, in this case, it injured a rival. In distinguishing *Aspen*, Judge Posner noted that Western Union changed a previous course of cooperation with the defendant "not because its monopoly power had grown but because it wasn't getting out [of the market] fast enough!"

3. In *Aspen* the relevant market was defined as "downhill skiing in Aspen, Colorado," and the Supreme Court approved a jury verdict forcing the defendant to continue in a marketing and sales joint venture for an "All-Aspen" skiing ticket. But suppose the plaintiff had asked for *everything* in the relevant market:

ski lodges, lifts, ski rentals — in sum, everything one needs except the labor to be set up in the business of providing skiing services. In *Image Technical Servs. v. Kodak*, 125 F.3d 1195, 1203 (9th Cir. 1997), *cert denied*, 118 S. Ct. 1560 (1998), the Ninth Circuit concluded that once a relevant market was defined for "all Kodak parts," Kodak had a duty under §2 of the Sherman Act to provide every single input in the market, including both parts that Kodak made and parts it had to buy from others, and whether or not the parts were available from alternative sources. All the plaintiffs had to supply for themselves was their labor, and presumably office space and trucks. Does anything in *Aspen* restrict its holding to things the plaintiff really needed or were capable of being monopolized? Or would the Supreme Court have forced Ski Co. to share its rental equipment and ski lodge as well?

4. *Aspen* involved a defendant who participated in a joint venture with the plaintiff and then terminated the venture without a good business reason for doing so. But should it be a §2 violation for a dominant firm never to agree to enter into a venture in the first place? In *SmileCare Dental Group v. Delta Dental Plan*, 88 F.3d 780 (9th Cir.), *cert. denied*, 117 S. Ct. 583 (1996), the plaintiff alleged that the defendant violated §2 by refusing to cooperate with it in the joint provision of a full coverage dental insurance plan under which the defendant would sell the first 80% of coverage and the plaintiff would sell the remaining, or supplemental, 20%:

> Unlike the defendant skiing company in *Aspen*, Delta Dental did not discontinue a marketing arrangement with SmileCare. Delta Dental's copayment plan pre-existed SmileCare's supplemental plan and the parties have never cooperated to supply the market with a new or better product.

5. *Submarkets in Monopolization Cases.* The *Aspen* jury found that the relevant product market was downhill skiing at destination ski resorts and that the relevant geographic market was the United States. Destination ski resorts are resorts visited principally by people who make overnight ski trips, rather than day skiers, and there was plenty of evidence that Aspen Ski Company competed with ski resorts across Colorado and the Rocky Mountains generally, and even resorts in other parts of the United States and Canada. Surely Aspen Ski Company had a minuscule share of such a market.

But the jury was also permitted to find that within these relevant markets there were relevant "submarkets," and in this case they concluded that the relevant product and geographic submarket was "downhill skiing services in the Aspen Area." A submarket is some grouping of sales *within* a relevant market that may be considered "relevant" for antitrust purposes. Once a submarket is found to exist, the defendant's share of the relevant market becomes irrelevant. Only the share of the submarket counts. As a result, the submarket is a powerful weapon for antitrust plaintiffs. If they cannot convince a court to define a small relevant market, they get a second chance: to convince the court that the relevant market contains a smaller submarket, in which the defendant's market share is very large.

The concept of submarkets received the Supreme Court's imprimatur in a merger case, *Brown Shoe Co. v. United States*, 370 U.S. 294, 325-26 (1962). Submarkets are discussed further in Chapter 7, *infra*, on mergers. But they are also used widely in monopolization cases. For example, *see SuperTurf v. Monsanto Co.*, 660 F.2d 1275 (8th Cir. 1981), where the court found a relevant market of turf for athletic fields, but a relevant submarket of artificial turf; *C.E. Servs. v. Control Data Corp.*, 759 F.2d 1241, 1246-47 (5th Cir. 1985), *cert. denied*, 474 U.S. 1037 (1985), where the court accepted "non-IBM maintenance of IBM computers" as a relevant submarket. Did the court really believe that companies other than IBM that maintained IBM computers could succeed in charging monopoly prices with IBM looking over their shoulder?

Submarket analysis generally adds nothing but confusion to antitrust. For example, consider the District Judge's instruction to the jury in the *Aspen* case:

> The basic idea of a relevant product market is that the product or services within it can be substituted for each other as a practical matter from the buyer's point of view. Two products need not be identical to be in the same market, but they must be as a matter of practical fact in the actual behavior of consumers substantially or reasonably interchangeable to fill the same consumer needs or purposes. Two products are within a single market if one item could suit buyers' needs substantially as well as the other....
>
> *Submarkets*.... Even though a group of products are sufficiently interchangeable to be grouped in one product market, there may be within that group a smaller group of products that compete so directly with each other as to constitute a submarket within the larger market; or the products or services of a particular seller may have such particular characteristics and such particular consumer appeal and are sufficiently insensitive to price variations of other products that they constitute a relevant submarket all by themselves.
>
> There can be both a relevant market and a relevant submarket or just a relevant market without any relevant submarket. Thus, if you decide that the relevant product market is downhill skiing at destination ski resorts, you must still determine whether downhill skiing services in Aspen, including multi-area, multi-day lift tickets is a submarket within the larger market.

Aspen, 738 F.2d 1509, 1528-29 (10th Cir. 1984).

What sense does it make to say that a relevant market is a grouping of sales such that "the product or services within it can be substituted for each other as a practical matter from the buyer's point of view," but that a relevant market is a subgrouping of sales that compete *more* directly with each other, or "are sufficiently insensitive to price variations of other products" that they must be grouped separately? In the process of finding a relevant market of downhill skiing in the United States, the jury in fact found that all firms in the United States offering such services competed with one another; no single one of them, assuming its share of such a market was very small, could profitably charge monopoly prices. Having found this relevant market, the jury was logically precluded from finding a smaller "relevant submarket." Nevertheless, they were permitted to do so by the judge's instructions, and they did.

The Supreme Court has not yet approved the use of "submarket" analysis in monopolization cases. In *Aspen*, the issue was not preserved for review. Since *Aspen*, some courts continue to find distinctive submarkets. *See, e.g., Ansell v. Schmid Labs.*, 757 F. Supp. 467 (D.N.J. 1991), *aff'd mem.*, 941 F.2d 1200 (3d Cir. 1991), finding a relevant submarket of branded latex condoms, excluding generic condoms distributed in plain boxes by public agencies. But other courts, without necessarily rejecting the concept, have concluded that "submarkets" are no different than "markets." *See, e.g., H.J. v. ITT Corp.*, 867 F.2d 1531, 1540 (8th Cir. 1989), concluding that "the same proof which establishes the existence of a relevant product market also shows ... the existence of a product submarket."

PROBLEM 6.6

Molar Insurance is the nation's dominant provider of dental insurance, most of which is marketed to employers for inclusion in employee benefit packages. Molar's "standard" dental protection policy includes 80% coverage for most dental procedures, requiring the patient to pick up the remaining 20% of his or her dental services out-of-pocket. Bicuspid Underwriting is a new insurance company entering the dental insurance field for the first time. It innovates and offers "complementary" dental insurance that will pick up the remaining 20% of Molar insured's costs. Thus an employer who purchases both Molar's and Bicuspid's plans can offer 100% coverage. However, Molar not only refuses to cooperate with Bicuspid in marketing the plan, but excludes from its coverage any procedures performed on a patient who is also covered by the Bicuspid complementary dental plan. Molar cites a "moral hazard" problem as its business justification: the impact of 100% coverage is that patients will use dental services more, thus increasing the costs and therefore the premiums of Molar's insureds. Under *Aspen*, has Molar violated §2? *See SmileCare Dental Group v. Delta Dental Plan*, 88 F.3d 780 (9th Cir.), *cert. denied*, 117 S. Ct. 583 (1996).

[handwritten: ↳ Valid bus. reason]

NOTE: THE ESSENTIAL FACILITY DOCTRINE

In *Aspen* the Supreme Court referred to the "essential facilities" doctrine, but did not decide the case on that basis. Several lower courts have addressed the doctrine. Briefly, the doctrine makes it illegal for the person operating a properly defined "essential facility" to deny access to someone else. The courts are hopelessly confused about what constitutes an "essential facility," and under what circumstances the controller of an essential facility has a right to deny access. The "essential facility" doctrine originated in Supreme Court decisions that really involved concerted refusals to deal, attacked principally under section 1 of the

Sherman Act. For example, in *United States v. Terminal R.R. Ass'n*, 224 U.S. 383 (1912), the Court held that toll bridges and cargo transfer facilities on the Mississippi River operated as a joint venture by several railroads had to be shared with other railroads who needed these facilities in order to move their cargo. *Associated Press v. United States*, 326 U.S. 1 (1945), then held that a news gathering agency operated as a joint venture had to be opened to nonmembers on nondiscriminatory terms. Finally, *Otter Tail Power Co. v. United States*, 410 U.S. 366 (1973), held that a public utility acting unilaterally could not refuse to transfer, or "wheel," power for the use of smaller power companies.

The more recent formulation of the "essential facility" doctrine has been left to the lower courts. In *Hecht v. Pro-Football, Inc.*, 570 F.2d 982 (D.C. Cir. 1977), *cert. denied*, 436 U.S. 956 (1978), the court characterized an "essential facility" as something which (1) is essential to the plaintiff's competitive survival; (2) cannot practically be duplicated; (3) can be used by the plaintiff without interference with the defendant's use. The court additionally suggested that in order to show a duty to share an essential facility the plaintiff must show that the defendant's denial was anticompetitively motivated, or that competition would be improved if access was granted. *Id.* at 992-93.

In *Fishman v. Estate of Wirtz*, 807 F.2d 520 (7th Cir. 1986), the Seventh Circuit applied the essential facility doctrine to a public sports stadium which had "a strategic dominance over the market for indoor team sports arenas in Chicago," and which "could charge much higher prices than the other arenas without causing its patrons to switch." The denial of the stadium lease to a group of investors constituted a per se illegal boycott and monopolization, the court found. In a strident dissent, Judge Easterbrook found that the sports arena was not even a relevant market, for there were plenty of substitutes in the Chicago area.

At the very least, it seems, an "essential facility" must constitute a relevant market. Otherwise the controller of the facility (assuming that it did not control all other sources of output as well) could not charge monopoly prices. *See Illinois Bell Tel. Co. v. Haines & Co.*, 905 F.2d 1081 (7th Cir. 1990) (alleged essential facility must dominate properly defined relevant market). Further, even the dominant firm has no *general* duty to share its production capacity or anything else with a rival. *See Olympia Equip. Leasing Co. v. Western Union Tel. Co.*, 797 F.2d 370, 376 (7th Cir. 1986): "Today it is clear that a firm with lawful monopoly power has no general duty to help its competitors, whether by holding a price umbrella over their heads or by otherwise pulling its competitive punches...."

One trend in the case law is to find essentiality under circumstances where (1) the facility is owned or somehow subsidized by the government; or (2) the controller of the essential facility is a public utility with an exclusive right created by the government. For example, the football stadium found to be an essential facility in *Hecht v. Pro-Football, supra*, was owned by the government. The duty of a regulated public utility to deal with others comes from the early common law, and the antitrust laws may do no more than carry it out. *See* Hovenkamp, *Regulatory Conflict in the Gilded Age: Federalism and the Railroad Problem*, 88 Yale

L.J. 1017 (1988). The Government lawsuit against AT&T which ended up in the divestiture of the telephone monopoly was predicated in large part on an essential facility doctrine. The theory of the case was that once competition in long distance communications became technically feasible, AT&T had a duty to share access to the local telephone networks with others. *United States v. AT&T*, 552 F. Supp. 131 (D.D.C. 1982), *aff'd mem. sub nom. Maryland v. United States*, 460 U.S. 1001 (1983).

In a case from the same period brought by a competitor, the court characterized the local telephone exchanges as an "essential facility":

> AT&T had complete control over the local distribution facilities that MCI required. The interconnections were essential for MCI to offer [long distance] service. The facilities in question met the criteria of "essential facilities" in that MCI could not duplicate Bell's local facilities. Given present technology, local telephone service is generally regarded as a natural monopoly and is regulated as such. It would not be economically feasible for MCI to duplicate Bell's local distribution facilities (involving millions of miles of cable and lines to individual homes and businesses), and regulatory authorization could not be obtained for such an uneconomical duplication.

MCI Commun. Corp. v. AT&T, 708 F.2d 1081 (7th Cir. 1983), *cert. denied*, 464 U.S. 891 (1983). *Cf. Mass. School of Law at Andover v. ABA*, 107 F.3d 1026 (3d Cir. 1997) (law school hiring and placement conferences from which the plaintiff unaccredited law school was excluded were not an essential facility where there was no showing that the conferences could not readily be duplicated).

One powerful argument against expansive use of an essential facility doctrine is that it flies in the face of antitrust principles by turning the defendant into a utility, but without appropriate agency regulation. For example, suppose the defendant owns a monopoly pipeline for which distribution costs are $5.00 per unit. Because the defendant is a monopolist, however, it charges $8.00 per unit, building the overcharge into the price of the gas delivered through the pipeline. Now the defendant is forced to share the pipeline with a rival. What price will it charge? Clearly, if $8.00 is its profit-maximizing price when it is billing consumers directly, that will also be its profit-maximizing price when it shares its space with a rival. As a result, output will be no higher and price no lower.

That is to say, forced sharing does not improve the welfare of consumers, it only makes room for another firm in the market. Further, the right to share in the defendant's pipeline undermines the rival's incentive to build its own pipeline — something that really would make the market more competitive. As a result, the essential facility doctrine probably preserves rather than destroys monopoly. Of course, the court might order the defendant to charge the competitive price of $5.00 for pipeline space, but then the court has changed from an antitrust tribunal into a regulatory agency, and someone will constantly have to monitor costs and consider what sharing price is appropriate.

Most of the secondary literature on the "essential facility" doctrine has been critical. For an argument that the basic doctrine is incoherent and should probably be abolished, *see* Werden, *The Law and Economics of the Essential Facility Doctrine*, 32 St. Louis U. L.J. 433 (1987). For an argument that it should be severely limited, *see* 3 P. Areeda & H. Hovenkamp, *Antitrust Law* ch. 7D-3 (rev. ed. 1995).

NOTE: PATENT POLICY AND SECTION 2

The federal patent laws respond to the Constitutional authorization to Congress to "promote the Progress of Science and useful Arts, by securing for limited Times to ... Inventors the exclusive Right to their ... Discoveries." U.S. Const., Art. I, § 8, cl. 8. Under the patent laws, the owner of a patent has a seventeen-year "monopoly" on the right to manufacture and sell the patented product. 35 U.S.C. § 154.

But patents can be abused, and sometimes the abuses violate §2's prohibition of monopolization and attempts to monopolize. One important caveat is in order. Both the offenses of monopolization and of attempt require a showing that the defendant has or may have monopoly power in some relevant market. Although we sometimes call the right created by a patent a "monopoly," the great majority of patents do not confer substantial market power in a relevant market. (In fact, the majority of patents are commercial failures and confer no market power whatsoever.) As a result, in a monopolization or attempt case alleging patent abuse, the plaintiff must still prove a relevant market. That market is not necessarily the product defined by any particular patent. The Supreme Court recognized this in *Walker Process* in 1965:

> To establish monopolization or attempt to monopolize a part of trade or commerce under § 2 of the Sherman Act, it would then be necessary to appraise the exclusionary power of the illegal patent claim in terms of the relevant market for the product involved. Without a definition of that market there is no way to measure [the defendant's] ability to lessen or destroy competition. It may be that the [patented] device ... does not comprise a relevant market. There may be effective substitutes for the devices which do not infringe the patent. This is a matter of proof ....

Walker Process Equip., Inc. v. Food Mach. & Chem. Corp., 382 U.S. 172, 177-78 (1965).

Assuming, then, that market power or the threat of it in a relevant market can be shown, under what circumstances might patent abuses violate section 2?

a. Improprieties in Procurement or Enforcement of an Invalid Patent. In *Walker Process, supra,* the Supreme Court held that a "knowing" and "wilful" misrepresentation to the patent office, permitting the antitrust defendant to obtain an invalid patent, could constitute illegal monopolization. A showing that the patent is valid generally undermines the plaintiff's claim. *See Brunswick*

Corp. v. Riegel Textile Corp., 752 F.2d 261 (7th Cir. 1984), *cert. denied*, 472 U.S. 1018 (1985).

The more common situation involves a firm which knows that its patent is invalid but nevertheless sues or threatens to sue rivals for infringement. Such infringement actions raise a problem: people have a constitutional right to go to court to assert their legal rights. On the other hand, "sham" litigation is not protected, and asserting a right in court that one knowingly does not have can constitute a "sham." These issues are taken up more fully in the discussion of the *Noerr-Pennington* doctrine in Chapter 9. In general, courts have addressed this problem by holding that a patent infringement lawsuit can be shown to be a sham attempt to enforce an invalid patent only if the antitrust plaintiff presents "clear and convincing" evidence that the antitrust defendant knew that its patent claim was invalid and was bringing it only to create or perpetuate a monopoly. *Handgards v. Ethicon* (*Handgards I*), 601 F.2d 986 (9th Cir. 1979), *cert. denied*, 444 U.S. 1025 (1980) ("Patentees must be permitted to test the validity of their patents in court through actions against alleged infringers .... On the other hand, infringement actions initiated and conducted in bad faith contribute nothing to the furtherance of the policies of either the patent law or the antitrust law."); *See also CVD v. Raytheon Co.*, 769 F.2d 842 (1st Cir. 1985), *cert. denied*, 475 U.S. 1016 (1986), applying a similar rule to a "sham" lawsuit to enforce a trade secret.

In *NobelPharma v. Implant Innovations*, 141 F.3d 1059 (Fed. Cir. 1998), the court decided that future decisions on "sham" patent claims would be decided under the law of the Federal Circuit rather than the court from which the appeal was taken. It then held that a patentee who had knowingly and intentionally failed to disclose important information to the Patent Office that might have undermined the patent, and knew of this fact when it later sued to enforce the patent against a rival, could be held liable under the *Walker Process* doctrine.

b. Refusal to License Valid Patent. As a basic premise, the holder of a patent has no obligation to license to competitors the right to manufacture the patented product or use the patented process. Arguments have been made that the antitrust laws should require a patent holder to license if (1) the patent holder acquired the patent from someone else rather than developing the patented innovation itself; or (2) the patent holder is not using the patent — i.e., is not producing the patented good or employing the patented process.

In *SCM Corp. v. Xerox Corp.*, 645 F.2d 1195, 1204 (2d Cir.), *cert. denied*, 455 U.S. 1016 (1982), the court held that the defendant did not have an antitrust duty to license acquired patents that were being used:

> [The plaintiff] has contended that a unilateral refusal to license a patent should be treated like any other refusal to deal by a monopolist.... Where a patent holder, however, merely exercises his "right to exclude others from making, using, or selling the invention," 35 U.S.C. § 154, by refusing unilaterally to license his patent for its seventeen-year term ... such conduct is

expressly permitted by the patent laws. "The heart of [the patentee's] legal monopoly is the right to invoke the State's power to prevent others from utilizing his discovery without his consent."

Should the outcome be any different if the antitrust defendant is not using the acquired patent? No court has held that mere non-use creates an antitrust obligation on the holder to license to others. Further, the Patent Act provides that

Every patent shall contain ... a grant to the patentee, his heirs or assigns ... the right to exclude others from making, using, or selling the invention.

35 U.S.C. §154. In 1988 Congress reaffirmed these principles in an amendment to the Patent Act:

No patent owner otherwise entitled to relief for infringement ... of a patent shall be denied relief or deemed guilty of misuse or illegal extension of the patent right by reason of ... (4) [the patent owner's] refus[al] to license or use any rights to the patent.

35 U.S.C. §271(d). In refusing to hear an interlocutory appeal from plaintiffs alleging an antitrust right that Xerox be forced to license them patented copier parts and copyrighted diagnostics software, the Federal Circuit summarized the law this way:

1. Assuming that a patent is lawfully acquired, a patent holder's unilateral refusal to sell or license its patented invention does not constitute unlawful exclusionary conduct under the antitrust laws even if the refusal impacts competition in more than one relevant antitrust market.
2. A patent holder is not required to proffer a legitimate business justification to avoid antitrust liability for exercising its right to refuse to sell or license a patented invention.
3. A patent holder is not subject to antitrust liability for exercising its right to refuse to sell or license a patented invention even if the patent holder engages in other allegedly anticompetitive conduct.
4. A patent holder is not liable for misuse or antitrust law violations for setting a "supracompetitive" sale price for a patented invention.

CSU Holdings v. Xerox, 129 F.3d 132 (Fed. Cir. 1997, unpublished). The plaintiffs' claim was that the patents in question covered Xerox's parts and software, but by refusing to license Xerox was also effectively creating a monopoly in a second market, namely photocopier servicing. By contrast, in *Image Technical Services v. Eastman Kodak Co.*, 125 F.3d 1195 (9th Cir. 1997), *cert. denied*, 118 S. Ct. 1560 (1998), the Ninth Circuit separated from other courts and accepted that argument. That court held for the first time that a firm not found to have engaged in tying, improper infringement suits, or any other patent "misuse" could nevertheless be forced under the antitrust laws to license its patents to others. The key to the duty of compulsory licensing, the court concluded, was that Kodak's reliance on intellectual property rights as a justification for refusing to license was "pretextual," or not the real motive, for its refusal.

The court noted that a patentee's motive to profit from its intellectual property must be regarded as a legitimate and lawful rationale for refusing to license. It also concluded that a motive to exclude those requesting a license from free-riding would be legitimate if proven, but could be made subject to a jury determination whether it was the real reason for the refusal. 125 F.3d at 1218-19. The court apparently believed that because Kodak was willing to permit some actual purchasers of its copying machines to repair them themselves, which required a patent license, the jury could infer that Kodak may have had some motive other than protection from free-riding in refusing to license the plaintiff independent service organizations (ISOs) who wished to repair the copying machines of others. The court also concluded that a patent or copyright gives a protected right to exclude others from a single market (in this case parts and diagnostics software), but not from a second market for service.

Referring to the previously quoted language from the Patent Act, the court noted some opinion that the statute did no more than codify existing law. 125 F.3d at 1215, citing R. Calkins, *Patent Law: The Impact of the 1988 Patent Misuse Reform Act and Noerr-Pennington Doctrine on Misuse Defenses and Antitrust Counterclaims*, 38 Drake L. Rev. 175, 197 (1989); and 5 D. Chisum, *Patents*, §19.04[1] (1992). However, existing law had never compelled licensing in the absence of misuse. The Ninth Circuit acknowledged as much. *Id.* at 1214-15, noting that "case law also supports the right of a patent or copyright holder to refuse to sell or license protected work;" citing *United States v. Westinghouse Electric Corp.*, 648 F.2d 642, 647 (9th Cir.1981) ("The right to license [a] patent, exclusively or other-wise, or to refuse to license at all, is the 'untrammeled right' of the patentee."). Indeed, the court acknowledged that it could "find no reported case in which a court has imposed antitrust liability for a unilateral refusal to sell or license a patent or copyright." Given that no court since the Sherman Act was passed had condemned a simple refusal to license a valid patent, and assuming that the 1988 amendment simply "declared" existing law, how did the court then find the duty to license?

The Ninth Circuit's holding is not easy to harmonize with the Supreme Court's 1993 decision in *Professional Real Estate Investors (PRE) v. Columbia Pictures Indus.*, 508 U.S. 49 (1993), reprinted, *infra*, Ch. 9. That decision held that the right of a copyright holder to pursue an infringement action cannot be made to depend on its anticompetitive state of mind. If the intellectual property right is objectively valid and enforceable, then the antitrust claim is forbidden altogether. The lower courts have consistently applied *PRE* to patent infringement actions as well, and in any event the scope of patent protection must be regarded as at least as broad as the scope of copyright protection.

As the Ninth Circuit would apparently interpret *PRE*, a patentee who filed an infringement action with the anticompetitive purpose of preventing a competing ISO from using a patented part would be able to pursue that action without concern for an antitrust counterclaim that the infringement plaintiff's real purpose was to create a service monopoly. But if the same patentee simply refused to license, it could be sued in antitrust and subject to inquiry into its motive. Because the Ninth Circuit neither cited nor discussed *PRE*, it did not attempt to harmonize the apparent inconsistency.

Finally, as the court managing the *Xerox* litigation observed:

> The scope of a "patent monopoly" is defined by the claims of the patent, not by the limits of what a court determines is the most analogous antitrust market.[1]...
>
> We believe that the Ninth Circuit in Kodak, in reaching its conclusion, implicitly assumed that a single patent can create at most a single "inherent" economic monopoly. The Supreme Court in Kodak certainly did not reach this issue. In Kodak, the Supreme Court stated that it "has held many times that power gained through some natural and legal advantage such as a patent, copyright, or business acumen can give rise to [antitrust] liability if 'a seller exploits his dominant position in one market to expand his empire into the next [market].'[2] The Court's statement simply is not applicable where a patent holder, exercising his unilateral right to refuse to license or use his invention, acquires a monopoly in two separate relevant antitrust markets. There is no unlawful leveraging of monopoly power when a patent holder merely exercises its rights inherent in the patent grant. In other words, to the extent Xerox gained its monopoly power in any market by unilaterally refusing to license its patents, such conduct is permissible under the antitrust laws. Xerox's legal right to exclude ISOs in the service markets from using Xerox's patented inventions arose from its patents, not from an unlawful leveraging of its monopoly power in the parts market.
>
> Patents only claim inventions. Because each use of that invention may be prevented by the patent holder, the patent may have some anticompetitive effect in each market in which it is used or not used. The patent statute expressly grants patent holders the right to exclude others from manufacturing, selling, or using their inventions. Manufacturing, retail, and service markets all fall within this statutory grant of power to patent holders. Thus, Congress, by enacting the patent statute, apparently contemplated that a single patent could implicate more than one market....
>
> The reward for a patented invention is the right to exploit the entire field of the "invention," not the right to exploit the single most analogous antitrust market.

ISO Antitrust Litigation, 989 F. Supp. 1131, 1136 (D. Kan. 1997).

---

[1] Citing, inter alia, *Dawson Chem. Co. v. Rohm & Haas*, 448 U.S. 176, 221 (1980) ("[T]he boundary of a patent monopoly is to be limited by the literal scope of the patent claims.").

[2] Quoting *Eastman Kodak Co. v. Image Tech. Servs.*, 504 U.S. 451, 479 n. 29 (1992), which was in turn quoting *Times-Picayune Pub. Co. v. United States*, 345 U.S. 594, 611 (1953).

c. Patent Accumulation. Suppose a dominant firm maintains a policy of buying up every patent that comes along in its market area. Some of these it uses; others it does not use. Its principal purpose is to make it very difficult for potential competitors to enter the same market. Suppose, for example, that the dominant firm has established patents for Process A, and is currently earning monopoly profits for goods produced under that process. A small firm now develops and patents Process B, which can do the same thing as Process A at about the same cost. As a basic proposition, Process B is worth more money to the dominant firm than it is to a competitor. If the dominant firm acquires Process B, it will maintain its monopoly. If a competitor acquires Process B, the two firms will compete away the monopoly returns. As a result, the dominant firm is likely to be the highest bidder for Process B, which it will then purchase and retire, refusing to license it to anyone else. *See* Gilbert & Newberry, *Preemptive Patenting and the Persistence of Monopoly*, 72 Am. Econ. Rev. 514 (1982); Harris & Vickers, *Patent Races and the Persistence of Monopoly*, 33 J. Indus. Econ. 461 (1985).

The Supreme Court has not been particularly helpful on the question of antitrust liability for patent accumulation. In *Transparent-Wrap Mach. Corp. v. Stokes & Smith Co.*, 329 U.S. 637, 646-47 (1947), it suggested that one

> who acquires two patents acquires a double monopoly. As patents are added to patents a whole industry may be regimented. The owner of a basic patent might thus perpetuate his control over an industry long after the basic patent expired. Competitors might be eliminated and an industrial monopoly perfected and maintained.

But only three years later the Court concluded in *Automatic Radio Mfg. Co. v. Hazeltine Res., Inc.*, 339 U.S. 827, 834 (1950), that the "mere accumulation of patents, no matter how many," is not a Sherman Act violation. In the *SCM* case, *supra*, the court echoed the latter view, holding that "where a patent has been lawfully acquired, subsequent conduct permissible under the patent laws cannot trigger any liability under the antitrust laws." 645 F.2d 1195, at 1206.

PROBLEM 6.7

Firm *A* has developed an important new process which it is about to patent. The patent, once created, will give Firm *A* an effective monopoly over the process, which is more efficient than any alternative. In the final stages of development, Firm *B* hires away a key Firm *A* employee and quickly obtains enough information to file for the patent. Firm *A* sues, claiming that the "theft" of the patent, and the attendant monopoly, is an antitrust violation. Outcome? *See Brunswick Corp. v. Riegel Textile Corp.*, 752 F.2d 261 (7th Cir. 1984), *cert. denied*, 472 U.S. 1018 (1985); *compare Fishman v. Estate of Wirtz*, 807 F.2d 520 (7th Cir. 1986), especially at 563-64 (Easterbrook, J., dissenting). Alternatively, suppose that *A* claims that the "theft" of the employee is illegal monopolization? *See Midwest Radio Co. v. Forum Pub'g Co.*, 942 F.2d 1294 (8th Cir. 1991).

3. VERTICAL INTEGRATION BY THE MONOPOLIST

When a manufacturer in competition integrates vertically — perhaps by purchasing its own distributorship or retail outlets — we generally presume that it does so to lower its costs. By obtaining its own retail outlets a manufacturer can reduce the risks, uncertainties, and transaction costs of the market, and it can control the way its product is sold. Vertical integration often enables firms to provide better products or services, at lower prices.

When the monopolist integrates vertically, however, courts have traditionally perceived substantial threats to competition. They have noted, for example, that by acquiring or building its own retail stores a monopolist in manufacturing can acquire a second monopoly at the retail level. The law of vertical mergers is concerned in large part with the problem of vertical integration when one of the firms involved has or threatens to have market power. When the monopolist integrates vertically, not by acquiring an existing company but by creating its own retail stores or distribution systems, the antimerger laws do not apply. The question then becomes whether vertical integration by a monopolist violates section 2 of the Sherman Act.

Although it is true that a monopolist can use vertical integration to create a second monopoly, it is unlikely that it will be able to enlarge its monopoly profits this way. When a retail customer purchases a product he is interested only in the total price, not in the amount of mark-up at each level in the distribution system for that product. A monopolist at any single stage in a distribution scheme should be able to extract all the monopoly profits available from a product, provided that the other stages in the distribution scheme are competitive.

That last proviso is important. Suppose that a manufacturing monopolist believes that the independent retail stores selling its product have formed a cartel. By refusing to sell to these stores and setting up its own stores instead, the manufacturing monopolist might be able to transfer the retail stores' cartel profits to itself.

In general, however, the same reasons that make vertical integration efficient for firms in competition are also likely to increase the efficiency of monopolists. The monopolist has an interest in seeing that its product is distributed as efficiently as possible, just as much as a competitive producer does. If the profit-maximizing retail price of a Widget is $1.00, it is to the monopolist's advantage to sell through retail stores that add a mark-up of 20 cents rather than stores that add a mark-up of 30 cents. Likewise, the monopolist is better off buying from low-cost sources of supply than from high-cost sources. As a general rule all producers, whether competitors or monopolists, are best off if the other links in the distribution chain for their particular product are operating at optimal efficiency.

PASCHALL V. KANSAS CITY STAR CO.

727 F.2d 692 (8th Cir.) (en banc), *cert. denied*, 469 U.S. 872 (1984)

JUDGE MCMILLIAN.

[The defendant published the only daily newspaper in the relevant geographic market. For many years it distributed its newspapers through independent carriers, each of which had an exclusive distribution area. In 1977 the defendant announced its intention to change its distribution system by replacing all the independent carriers with delivery agents who would be employees of the defendant itself. It offered to hire the independent carriers as company delivery agents, but 250 of them refused and filed suit under section 2 of the Sherman Act. A divided panel of the Eighth Circuit condemned the switch to self-distribution as illegal monopolization. A divided court sitting en banc reversed the panel with the following opinion.]

....

A. *Specific Intent or Purpose*

Generally, cases following the Supreme Court's landmark § 2 Sherman Act decisions rendered during its 1947 Term have imposed liability for unlawful monopolization upon proof of either (1) the specific intent to monopolize or (2) anticompetitive effects that result from the monopolist's actions. *See United States v. Columbia Steel Co.*, 334 U.S. 495, 531-32 (1948); *United States v. Griffith*, 334 U.S. 100, 106 (1948). One need not prove both specific intent and anticompetitive effects; either alone is a sufficient basis for the imposition of liability upon a business entity wielding monopoly power....

In the context of vertical integration, the requisite specific intent may be shown where the vertical integration was part of "a calculated scheme to gain control over an appreciable segment of the market and to restrain or suppress competition, rather than an expansion to meet legitimate business needs." *United States v. Paramount Pictures, Inc.*, 334 U.S. 131, 174 (1948). Specific intent to monopolize is also found where the monopolist, or would-be monopolist, engages in predatory tactics or "dirty tricks." The record before us discloses no evidence of Star Co. engaging in any "dirty tricks" or predatory practices against its contract carriers.

Liability based on specific intent can be negated where valid business justifications exist for the monopolist's actions. Here Star Co. has offered several legitimate business reasons for adopting the delivery agent system, including (1) the ability to set an area-wide uniform retail price to facilitate "in-paper advertising" for new subscriptions and simplify subscription collection and (2) the capability to be more responsive to customer complaints and assure more rapid starts for new subscribers. Star Co. has argued that because these points had caused Star Co., and its readers, problems under the contract carrier system, it has the unfettered business prerogative to correct these problems in the most efficient manner possible. According to Star Co., the delivery agent system is the most efficient resolution of these problems.

We readily agree with Star Co. that the existence of legitimate business reasons for its decision to integrate forward from the wholesale level (first level) to the retail or distribution level (second level) will negate any specific intent basis of liability. Proof of specific intent is necessary, however, only "where the acts fall short of the results condemned by the Act." ...

[T]he central issue of this case is whether the combination of Star Co.'s vertical integration and refusal to deal has resulted in any *unreasonable* anticompetitive effects in the market. If no unreasonable anticompetitive effects will follow from Star Co.'s implementation of its delivery agent system, its de facto acquisition of a monopoly of the retail daily metropolitan newspaper market will not be condemned by § 2 of the Sherman Act, because the Sherman Act protects the benefits of competition and not just individual competitors. Absent the specific intent to monopolize, a monopolist's legitimate business decisions will not be curtailed if those decisions promote the redeeming virtues of competition: lower prices, greater efficiency and innovation, and more responsive service.

Two contrasting theories have been advanced in this case to provide a conceptual framework for ascertaining and analyzing the impact of Star Co.'s proposed change in its method of distribution. One theory, the potential competitor theory, has been relied upon to impose liability on Star Co. The other, the optimum monopoly price theory, has been used in defense....

The potential competitor theory was first discussed in *United States v. Falstaff Brewing Corp.*, 410 U.S. 526, 532-33 (1973). In *Falstaff*, the defendant had decided to expand into the New England market by merging with an existing New England brewery. The Court held that entry through merger would violate § 7 of the Clayton Act if the entry had the effect of eliminating "a potential competitor exercising present influence on the market." It is said that a potential competitor, merely by its presence at the edge of the market, will have a retardant effect on price and will provide an incentive for better service among those already in the market. This is so because if the existing market competitors practice price gouging or provide inferior service, the potential competitor will enter the competitive fray with lower prices and better service, thereby capturing a substantial share of the market. To avoid the possibility of losing business to the potential competitor, the actual market competitors will maintain low prices and quality service. Thus, should the potential competitor merge with an existing market competitor, the market will lose the procompetitive effect of the presence of a potential competitor....

The district court grafted this potential competitor theory onto § 2 of the Sherman Act and applied it to the facts of this case.... The district court ... found that although Star Co. had not competed in the retail newspaper market to any significant degree in the past, Star Co. nonetheless existed as a powerful competitive force in the retail newspaper market because it was a potential competitor. Star Co. reserved by contract the right to sell directly to subscribers if it felt that the contract carrier was not providing proper service. As an example of this theory at work, the district court pointed to what has been referred to as the "Louisberg Square incident." In April of 1970, a contract carrier "arbitrarily" raised its retail subscription price for *The Star* to readers in an apartment complex known as Louisberg Square. Many residents of Louisberg Square complained to Star Co. about the price increase. Eventually, Star Co. delivered its newspapers at a lower price directly to those dissatisfied Louisberg Square residents who requested direct delivery from Star Co. All of the contract carriers were aware of the Louisberg Square incident, and they all knew that a similar fate possibly could befall them should they engage in price gouging or give their subscribers poor service. Thus, according to the district court, the mere presence of Star Co. as a potential competitor in the retail market produced a substantial retardant effect on the contract carriers' prices and gave the contract carriers a significant incentive to provide the best service possible. The district court went on to observe that Star Co.'s forward integration into the retail market, coupled with its refusal to deal with contract carriers, removed the beneficial influence on competitive conditions in the retail market exerted by Star Co.'s presence as a potential competitor....

The panel dissent championed the optimum monopoly price theory advanced by Star Co., the *amicus*,[8] and several leading antitrust economics scholars of the Chicago school....[9] The optimum monopoly price theory can be summarized as follows. Under any given set of cost and demand curves for a product, there is one price at which a monopolist can maximize its profits. This price is determined by computing the quantity of product that is produced at the point where the monopolist's cost in making one more item (marginal cost) equals the revenue received from selling that additional item (marginal revenue). The price at which the public will buy all of that quantity, but no more (demand curve), will be the optimum monopoly price. If the monopolist charges more than this price, its profits will decline because the lost revenues from the reduced number of sales would more than offset the added revenue from the higher price. If the monopolist charges less, the added revenue from increased sales will not compensate for the reduced revenue per sale and the added marginal costs in producing that quantity. Thus, the monopolist's profit will be less than at the optimum monopoly price.

---

[8] The United States Department of Justice.

[9] *See* R. Bork, The Antitrust Paradox (1978) (now Judge Bork of the United States Court of Appeals for the District of Columbia Circuit); R. Posner, Antitrust Law: An Economic Perspective (1976) (now Judge Posner of the United States Court of Appeals for the Seventh Circuit). *See also* P. Areeda & D. Turner, Antitrust Law (1978-80). *But cf.* Lande, *Wealth Transfers as the Original & Primary Concern of Antitrust: The Efficiency Interpretation Challenged*, 34 Hastings L.J. 65 (1982) (as the title suggests, the author agrees that Congress passed the antitrust laws to further economic objectives but argues that the economic objectives were primarily of a "distributive" rather than an "efficiency" nature, that is, to prevent unfair acquisitions of consumers' wealth by firms with market power).

If the demand for the product is at all elastic, forward vertical integration may have substantial procompetitive effects in the form of lower prices and more efficient use of resources. Further, Star Co. points out that a large portion of its revenue comes from advertising. For that revenue Star Co. must compete with many other media and, quite significantly here, advertising revenues, in turn, are dependent upon circulation. The result is that Star Co. has a greater incentive than the contract carriers have to keep the retail price as low as possible in order to increase circulation. Star Co. contends that this need to increase circulation provides a greater retardant effect on prices than any influence it exerted in the market by its mere presence as a potential competitor. Thus, even if one assumes the potential competitor theory to be true, the procompetitive effects lost through the elimination of Star Co. as a potential competitor are more than offset by the increase in procompetitive effects in the retail market generated by optimum monopoly pricing combined with Star Co.'s need to increase circulation and attract advertising.

... [W]e are mindful that the burden of proof is not on the defendant to prove the absence of anticompetitive effects. Rather, it is the plaintiff's responsibility to prove all the elements of an antitrust violation.

We recognize that on the facts of this case, elimination of Star Co. as a potential competitor will result in the elimination of some procompetitive effects in the retail market. Under the contract carrier system, two competitors existed in the distribution or retail market — one actual (the contract carrier serving the route) and one potential (Star Co.). Implementation of the delivery agent system would leave only one "competitor" in the market — Star Co. Thus, the retail market has lost the beneficial competitive interaction between business entities that the antitrust laws were enacted to preserve. However, the loss of the procompetitive effects engendered by the substitution of Star Co. for the contract carriers, that is, Star Co.'s forward integration into the retail market as a self-distributor, may be offset by the introduction into the market of the procompetitive factors under which Star Co. must function as the sole "competitor" in the retail market. The optimum monopoly price theory is useful in ascertaining whether such procompetitive effects are sufficient to counteract the anticompetitive effects of removing potential competition from the market so that in the end there are no *unreasonable* anticompetitive effects.

It may well be true, as the panel majority opinion pointed out, that in certain circumstances a first level monopolist will desire to integrate forward even if it is less efficient than the second level entity. These situations include (1) price or service discrimination, (2) increased barriers to entry at the first level, and (3) evasion of government regulation of first level monopoly profits. *See* F. Scherer, *Industrial Market Structure and Economic Performance* 302-06 (2d ed. 1980). Courts have sought to limit imposing liability upon newspapers which vertically integrate into distribution only to situations where one or more of these incentives are present. In the present case, these circumstances do not exist. No price discrimination will result because the purpose of the delivery agent system was to establish a uniform retail price. Nor, as the district court found, will Star Co.'s forward integration raise barriers to first level entry (publication of daily metropolitan newspapers). The delivery agent contracts expressly allow the delivery agents to deliver for other newspapers as long as such delivery will not disrupt the delivery of Star Co. newspapers. Finally, no argument has been made that Star Co. has undertaken to distribute its own newspapers to avoid government regulation of its first level monopoly profits.

We are not unaware of certain record evidence of two possible anticompetitive effects of the delivery agent system: increased prices and reduced services. There is testimony which tends to show that Star Co. believed at the time of trial that it could not deliver newspapers more efficiently than the contract carriers and that any additional profits would have to come from increased revenues. Indeed, according to the panel majority, most Star Co. readers would pay more for their subscriptions under the announced delivery agent retail prices. While it may be true that many readers initially will have to pay more for their subscriptions, it is also true that many readers will pay less. One of the legitimate business reasons advanced by Star Co. in support of the delivery agent system was the establishment of uniform rates and services for all subscribers, and the record indicates that Star Co.'s proposed uniform rates were lower than the rates charged by some independent contract carriers, although admittedly higher than others....

Concededly, one procompetitive effect that can be eliminated when potential competition is removed from the distribution market is the downward pressure on price. Indeed, it is said that vertical integration frequently is followed by price increases. *See* McGee & Bassett, *Vertical Integration Revisited*, 19 J.L. & Econ. at 27 n.28. And, even if Star Co. is able to achieve distribution economies by vertical integration, such savings may not result in lower retail prices.

Indeed, a price increase is not necessarily inconsistent with the optimum monopoly price theory to the extent that Star Co.'s concern over its circulation and advertising revenue, the monopoly power of the contract carriers, and the individual contract carriers' ability to set varying retail prices may have combined to exert a retardant effect on Star Co.'s wholesale prices, thus robbing Star Co. of its ability to reap the full monopoly profit at the wholesale level.

The monopoly power of the second level monopolist, here the individual contract carrier, is exaggerated by the nature of the newspaper industry. As has been noted, an important source of revenues for a newspaper is advertising revenues. Advertising rates are based on the number of subscriptions. The number of subscriptions is in part a function of price: the lower the retail price, the more subscriptions that are sold. When a contract carrier intends to raise its retail price, the newspaper is threatened with a loss of subscriptions caused by the increased prices. Moreover, the newspaper will not recoup any of the lost advertising revenues through increased sales revenues because the independent contract carrier receives 100% of the increase in the retail price. The newspaper is reluctant to raise its wholesale price to compensate for this loss because any increase in the wholesale price may trigger an additional retail price increase by the contract carrier who wants to maintain a certain level of profit. These conditions create an incentive for the newspaper to "share" even more of the monopoly profit with a contract carrier by lowering its wholesale price in order to head off a retail price increase by the contract carrier.

....

On balance, we agree with the panel dissent that appellees have not borne their burden as plaintiffs of proving that the procompetitive effects generated by optimum monopoly pricing and the unique nature of a newspaper's revenues are outweighed by the minimal anticompetitive effect of eliminating potential competition from the retail market. Again, we emphasize that there is nothing unlawful about the mere possession of monopoly power. Nor is it unlawful *per se* for a monopolist to unilaterally refuse to deal with a former distributor or to vertically integrate. However, a monopolist may be subject to antitrust liability if it misuses its monopoly power to accomplish a vertical integration and a refusal to deal that results in unreasonable anticompetitive effects. Each case must be resolved on its own particular facts. In this case appellees have failed to prove that any anticompetitive effects that might result from Star Co.'s vertical integration and refusal to deal are unreasonable. Accordingly, we reverse the judgment of the district court, dissolve the permanent injunction, and vacate the award of attorney fees.

HEANEY, CIRCUIT JUDGE, with whom LAY, CHIEF JUDGE, and BRIGHT, CIRCUIT JUDGE, join, dissenting.

I would adhere to the majority panel opinion and affirm the district court....

The majority finds that the carriers "have not borne their burden as plaintiffs of proving that the procompetitive effects generated by optimum monopoly pricing and the unique nature of a newspaper's revenues are outweighed by the anticompetitive effect of eliminating potential competition from the retail market." It appears to place primary reliance on the following conclusions in the original dissenting opinion to support this finding:

(1) That while many readers will pay more for their subscriptions, many readers will pay less.

The fact is that 92% of the readers will pay more and only 8% pay less.

(2) That the price increase may be attributable to a general increase in costs unrelated to the Star's decision to vertically integrate.

The fact is that the price comparison was made as of the date that the Star fixed to discontinue dealing with the 250 carriers. There is no evidence in the record that the new price schedule had any relationship to a general increase in costs. To the contrary, the evidence indicates that uniformly higher prices were to be put into effect to increase revenues and profits from circulation.

(3) That the range of services provided to individual readers will be greater than what exists under the contract system.

There is no evidence in the record to support this statement. Rather, many of the divergent services that were being offered to residential, commercial, and rack subscribers were to be curtailed....

What remains then to support the reversal of the district court is the theory developed by the "Chicago school" of economists that absent circumstances not present here, consumers are not harmed when a monopolist extends its monopoly forward into retail distribution — the reasoning being that inasmuch as the monopolist has the power to obtain maximum monopoly profits by charging as much as it chooses at the wholesale level, consumers will not be further harmed if the monopolist takes over distribution. Notwithstanding the Department of Justice's embrace of this theory, we should not be willing to substitute theory for hard evidence in the record. Here, the Star had been unable to maximize its profits under the independent distribution system. The reason is obvious. The Star could not, without violating antitrust laws, control the price at which the independent carriers sold the papers to consumers; and absent a uniform price, the pressure from those paying more than those in an adjacent territory would vent their displeasure on the Star. Thus, notwithstanding the "Chicago" theory, the independent distribution system of 250 carriers operated to hold down prices to the ultimate consumers, and to protect them from the full exercise of unlawfully achieved monopoly power.

One further point deserves emphasis. It was made by Chief Justice Warren in *Brown Shoe Co. v. United States*, 370 U.S. 294, 344 (1962):

> It is competition, not competitors, which the Act protects. But we cannot fail to recognize Congress' desire to promote competition through the protection of viable, small, locally owned businesses. Congress appreciated that occasional higher costs and prices might result from the maintenance of fragmented industries and markets. It resolved these competing considerations in favor of decentralization. We must give effect to that decision.

Here, we should ... show concern for the 250 viable, small, locally owned businesses who are affected by the decision of the Star. For years, they have delivered the newspapers economically and efficiently. They have treated their customers fairly and have given them excellent service. Now they stand to lose their businesses simply because the Star, a highly profitable newspaper, wants to maximize their monopoly prices by establishing a uniformly higher retail price....

NOTES AND QUESTIONS

1. The carriers in the *Kansas City Star* case had exclusive territories, probably because they were natural monopolists. The largest expense of running a newspaper route is the cost of driving the route — that is, the cost of owning and operating a delivery vehicle and paying the driver. The marginal cost of throwing one additional newspaper to a doorstep is very small. Thus it is far cheaper per newspaper for a single carrier to travel down route A-B and deliver 100 newspapers than it is for two carriers to travel down the route and deliver 50 newspapers each. Because the carriers were monopolists, however, they had the power to charge a monopoly price for newspaper subscriptions by reducing their output. Any output reduction would, of course, be a reduction in the *Star*'s circulation. This is why the *Star* was very concerned about the price that the carriers were charging.

2. The district court found that the *Star* was a monopolist in the daily newspaper market in its readership area. A daily newspaper obtains about 80% of its revenue from advertising and about 20% from circulation. The wholesale price of the newspapers is less than the cost of the newsprint and ink used to manufacture them. Furthermore, advertising rates are based on circulation: the more paid subscriptions a newspaper has, the more it can charge for advertising.

A monopoly newspaper has a monopoly in two different markets: newspaper copies and newspaper advertising. In light of the above figures, is it plausible that a newspaper would "monopolize" the market by reducing circulation? Wouldn't it try to keep circulation as high as possible but charge its profit-maximizing price for newspaper advertising? *See* Hovenkamp, *Vertical Integration by the Newspaper Monopolist*, 69 Iowa L. Rev. 451 (1984).

3. Sometimes monopolists may integrate vertically, whether or not integration is economically efficient, in order to avoid a group of antitrust decisions condemning refusals to deal by monopolists. As a basic premise a firm is free to deal or refuse to deal with any other firm as it pleases. In *Eastman Kodak Co. v. Southern Photo Materials Co.*, 273 U.S. 359 (1927), however, the Supreme Court held that it could be illegal monopolization for a firm with monopoly power to refuse to deal with a firm in a different link of the distribution scheme, if the monopolist's purpose was to extend its monopoly. Likewise, in *Otter Tail Power Co. v. United States*, 410 U.S. 366 (1973), the Court held it to be illegal monopolization for a large electric utility to refuse to "wheel" (i.e., transmit) power to community delivery systems if its purpose was to maintain a monopoly of such delivery systems. Most recently, in *Eastman Kodak Co. v. Image Tech. Servs.*, 504 U.S. 451 (1992), the Court held that a firm could "monopolize" a market for its own brand of photocopier by refusing to provide repair parts to independent service technicians. The decision is reprinted in Chapter 4. The Ninth Circuit subsequently approved a finding of unlawful monopolization. *Image Technical Services v. Eastman Kodak Co.*, 125 F.3d 1195, 1203-04 (9th Cir. 1997), *cert. denied*, 118 S. Ct. 1560 (1998). Is *Kodak* inconsistent with *Paschall*?

4. Even the monopolist is ordinarily free to bargain for the best price — i.e., to pay as little as it can for its inputs, and to sell at the highest price possible. *See Kartell v. Blue Shield of Mass., Inc.*, 749 F.2d 922 (1st Cir. 1984), *cert. denied*, 471 U.S. 1029 (1985), holding that it was legal for Blue Shield as health insurer to purchase medical services in behalf of its insureds and to stipulate the maximum price it was willing to pay, even assuming it was a monopolist:

Once one accepts that ... Blue Shield in essence "buys" medical services for the account of others, the reasoning ... indicates that the ban on balance billing is permissible.... Suppose a father buys toys for his son — toys the son picks out. Or suppose a landlord hires a painter to paint his tenant's apartment, to the tenant's specifications. Is it not obviously lawful for the father (the landlord) to make clear to the seller that the father (landlord) is in charge and will pay the bill? Why can he not then forbid the seller to charge the child (the tenant) anything over and above what the father (landlord) pays — at least if the seller wants the buyer's business?

... The relevant antitrust facts are that Blue Shield pays the bill and seeks to set the amount of the charge.

5. In its opinion the Eighth Circuit in *Paschall* noted that the Justice Department presented a brief as amicus curiae in behalf of the defendants. This is one of many briefs submitted by the Justice Department in behalf of defendants during the 1980's. The Justice Department is charged with enforcing the antitrust laws. Does free legal help to defendants constitute "enforcing" the antitrust laws? *See* Litvack, *Government Antitrust Policy: Theory Versus Practice and the Role of the Antitrust Division*, 60 Tex. L. Rev. 649 (1982); Easterbrook, *Is There a Ratchet in Antitrust Law?*, 60 Tex. L. Rev. 705 (1982).

6. The court in *Paschall* opined that the *Star* did not integrate vertically in order to engage in price discrimination, because after integration it switched to a uniform subscription price across all routes. Before integration the independent carriers had set their own prices, which varied considerably from route to route. The court is confusing price discrimination with price differences. Price discrimination occurs when a seller makes a higher *rate of return* in one market than in another. Suppose that it costs much more per newspaper to make deliveries along a rural route than in a concentrated apartment complex. The independent carrier-monopolists each set their own profit-maximizing prices, which would have been higher on the rural route than on the higher density route. By charging the same price on both routes the *Star* was likely engaging in price discrimination: it made a higher rate of profit on the high density routes, where delivery costs were lower. Should this fact change the outcome? See the discussion of the economics of price discrimination in Chapter 8. One likely result of the *Star's* price discrimination scheme was increased circulation along the rural, or high cost, routes.

7. Judge Heaney's dissent cites the Supreme Court's opinion in *Brown Shoe*, reprinted in Chapter 7, *infra*, for the proposition that Congress wanted to protect "viable, small, locally owned business." The Supreme Court was discussing the 1950 Celler-Kefauver amendments to the antimerger statute, section 7 of the Clayton Act, however, and not the Sherman Act. Should the principles established in the legislative history of one antitrust statute be applied to a different statute passed sixty years earlier? Courts do it frequently.

8. In *Weiss v. York Hosp.*, 745 F.2d 786 (3d Cir. 1984), *cert. denied*, 470 U.S. 1060 (1985), the court dismissed monopolization charges brought by a doctor of osteopathy (DO) who claimed that the defendant hospital illegally denied DOs staff privileges. The defendant accounted for 80% of inpatient care in its service area, which was sufficient to give it monopoly power; however, the plaintiff's complaint faltered for failure to explain how the defendant's denial could be anticompetitive:

> York, like any hospital, would maximize its revenues by giving staff privileges to every qualified doctor who applied. Hospitals are in the business of providing facilities (rooms and equipment) and support staff (nurses, administrators, etc.). These resources are fixed in the short run, and the hospital maximizes its revenues by encouraging competition for its hospital beds and operating rooms. Since only physicians with staff privileges can admit and treat patients, York can maximize competition for its facilities by granting staff privileges to every qualified doctor who applies. Excluding DOs on the other hand is likely to weaken York's monopoly position in the long run, since a potential rival ... would have an incentive to provide competing services for the DOs excluded from York.

This tended to support the defendant's theory that it had adequate professional or medical reasons for denying staff privileges to DOs.

PROBLEM 6.8

Dogs'n'Cats, Inc., is a dominant manufacturer of pet supplies for sale in retail stores. Dogs'n'Cats relies on independent distributors to wholesale its supplies to various retail chain stores. Dogs'n'Cats' goal is to have every retail chain in the United States stock its pet supplies exclusively. One of the distributors is Petco. When a chain store complained to Petco about the relatively high cost of Dogs'n'Cats products, Petco began looking about for alternatives and found an Asian supplier, Animals, Inc., which manufactured pet products of equal quality but sold them at a much lower wholesale price. Petco began giving its stores the option of purchasing either Dogs'n'Cats or Animals, Inc., pet supplies. Several chose the latter. Dogs'n'Cats immediately (1) terminated Petco's distributorship and (2) announced that hereafter it would deal only with distributors who sold its supplies exclusively. Has Dogs'n'Cats violated the Sherman Act? *See General Indus. Corp. v. Hartz Mountain Corp.*, 810 F.2d 795 (8th Cir. 1987).

SECTION III. ATTEMPTS TO MONOPOLIZE AND PREDATORY PRICING

A. THE OFFENSE OF ATTEMPT TO MONOPOLIZE

The offense of "attempt" to monopolize is explicit in section 2 of the Sherman Act, which condemns "[e]very person who shall monopolize or attempt to monopolize." Nevertheless, the word "attempt" had a rich common law meaning at the time the Sherman Act was passed, and much of that legacy has been assimilated into the statutory offense of attempt to monopolize. Consider the following seminal definition from Justice Holmes, whose understanding of the common law attempt offense was as sophisticated as that of any legal scholar:

> It is suggested that the several acts charged [in the complaint] are lawful and that intent can make no difference. But they are bound together as the parts of a single plan. The plan may make the parts unlawful. The [Sherman Act] gives this proceeding against combinations in restraint of commerce among the States and against attempts to monopolize the same. Intent is almost essential to such a combination and is essential to such an attempt. Where acts are not sufficient in themselves to produce a result which the law seeks to prevent — for instance, the monopoly, — but require further acts in addition to the mere forces of nature to bring that result to pass, an intent to bring it to pass is necessary in order to produce a dangerous probability that it will happen. But when that intent and the consequent dangerous probability exist, this statute, like many others and like the common law in some cases, directs itself against that dangerous probability as well as against the completed result.

Swift & Co. v. United States, 196 U.S. 375, 396 (1905).

Note the degree to which the following opinion adheres to Swift's common-law attempt formulation.

SPECTRUM SPORTS, INC. V. MCQUILLAN

506 U.S. 447 (1993)

JUSTICE WHITE delivered the opinion of the Court....

I

Sorbothane is a patented elastic polymer whose shock-absorbing characteristics make it useful in a variety of medical, athletic, and equestrian products. BTR, Inc. (BTR) owns the patent rights to sorbothane, and its wholly owned subsidiaries manufacture the product in the United States and Britain. Hamilton-Kent Manufacturing Company (Hamilton-Kent) and Sorbothane, Inc. (S.I.) were at all relevant times owned by BTR....

In 1980, respondents Shirley and Larry McQuillan signed a letter of intent with Hamilton-Kent, which then owned all manufacturing and distribution rights to sorbothane. The letter of intent granted the McQuillans exclusive rights to purchase sorbothane for use in equestrian products. Respondents were designing a horseshoe pad using sorbothane. In 1981, Hamilton-Kent decided to establish five regional distributorships for sorbothane. Respondents were selected to be distributors of all sorbothane products, including medical products and shoe inserts, in the Southwest. Spectrum was selected as distributor for another region.

In January 1982, Hamilton-Kent shifted responsibility for selling medical products from five regional distributors to a single national distributor. In April 1982, Hamilton-Kent told respondents that it wanted them to relinquish their athletic shoe distributorship as a condition for retaining the right to develop and distribute equestrian products.... Respondents refused to sell and continued to distribute athletic shoe inserts. In the fall of 1982, [S.I., Hamilton-Kent's successor] informed respondents that another concern had been appointed as the national equestrian distributor, and that they were "no longer involved in equestrian products." In January 1983, S.I. began marketing through a national distributor a sorbothane horseshoe pad allegedly indistinguishable from the one designed by respondents. In August 1983, S.I. informed respondents that it would no longer accept their orders. Spectrum [was then appointed] national distributor of sorbothane athletic shoe inserts.... Respondents' business failed.

Respondents sued petitioners seeking damages for alleged violations of §§ 1 and 2 of the Sherman Act.... The case was tried to a jury.... All of the defendants were found to have violated § 2 by, in the words of the verdict sheet, "monopolizing, attempting to monopolize, and/or conspiring to monopolize." ... [The jury failed to find a violation of § 1.]

On the § 2 issue that petitioners present here, the Court of Appeals, noting that the jury had found that petitioners had violated § 2 without specifying whether they had monopolized, attempted to monopolize, or conspired to monopolize, held that the verdict would stand if the evidence supported any one of the three possible violations of § 2. The court went on to conclude that a case of attempted monopolization had been established.[4] The court rejected petitioners' argument that attempted monopolization had not been established because respondents had failed to prove that petitioners had a specific intent to monopolize a relevant market. The court also held that in order to show that respondents' attempt to monopolize was likely to succeed it was not necessary to present evidence of the relevant market or of the defendants' market power. In so doing, the Ninth Circuit relied on *Lessig v. Tidewater Oil Co.*, 327 F.2d 459 (9th Cir.), *cert. denied*, 377 U.S. 993 (1964), and its progeny.

The Court of Appeals noted that these cases, in dealing with attempt to monopolize claims, had ruled that "if evidence of unfair or predatory conduct is presented,

---

[4] The District Court's jury instructions were transcribed as follows: "In order to win on the claim of attempted monopoly, the Plaintiff must prove each of the following elements by a preponderance of the evidence: first, that the Defendants had a specific intent to achieve monopoly power in the relevant market; second, that the Defendants engaged in exclusionary or restrictive conduct in furtherance of its specific intent; third, that there was a dangerous probability that Defendants could sooner or later achieve [their] goal of monopoly power in the relevant market; fourth, that the Defendants' conduct occurred in or affected interstate commerce; and, fifth, that the Plaintiff was injured in the business or property by the Defendants' exclusionary or restrictive conduct.... If the Plaintiff has shown that the Defendant engaged in predatory conduct, you may infer from that evidence the specific intent and the dangerous probability element of the offense without any proof of the relevant market or the Defendants' marketing [sic] power."

it may satisfy both the specific intent and dangerous probability elements of the offense, without any proof of relevant market or the defendant's marketpower [sic]." If, however, there is insufficient evidence of unfair or predatory conduct, there must be a showing of "relevant market or the defendant's marketpower [sic]." The court went on to find: "There is sufficient evidence from which the jury could conclude that the S.I. Group and Spectrum Group engaged in unfair or predatory conduct and thus inferred that they had the specific intent and the dangerous probability of success and, therefore, McQuillan did not have to prove relevant market or the defendant's marketing [sic] power."

The decision below, and the *Lessig* line of decisions on which it relies, conflicts with holdings of courts in other Circuits. Every other Court of Appeals has indicated that proving an attempt to monopolize requires proof of a dangerous probability of monopolization of a relevant market. We granted certiorari to resolve this conflict among the Circuits. We reverse.

II

While § 1 of the Sherman Act forbids contracts or conspiracies in restraint of trade or commerce, § 2 addresses the actions of single firms that monopolize or attempt to monopolize, as well as conspiracies and combinations to monopolize. Section 2 does not define the elements of the offense of attempted monopolization. Nor is there much guidance to be had in the scant legislative history of that provision, which was added late in the legislative process. See 1 E. Kintner, Legislative History of the Federal Antitrust Laws and Related Statutes 23-25 (1978); 3 P. Areeda & D. Turner, Antitrust Law ¶ 617, pp. 39-41 (1978)....

... [T]he plaintiff charging attempted monopolization must prove a dangerous probability of actual monopolization, which has generally required a definition of the relevant market and examination of market power. In *Walker Process Equipment, Inc. v. Food Machinery & Chemical Corp.*, 382 U.S. 172, 177 (1965), we found that enforcement of a fraudulently obtained patent claim could violate the Sherman Act. We stated that, to establish monopolization or attempt to monopolize under § 2 of the Sherman Act, it would be necessary to appraise the exclusionary power of the illegal patent claim in terms of the relevant market for the product involved. *Ibid.* The reason was that "[w]ithout a definition of that market there is no way to measure [the defendant's] ability to lessen or destroy competition." ...

Consistent with our cases, it is generally required that to demonstrate attempted monopolization a plaintiff must prove (1) that the defendant has engaged in predatory or anticompetitive conduct with (2) a specific intent to monopolize and (3) a dangerous probability of achieving monopoly power. See Areeda & Turner, *supra*, at ¶ 820, p. 312. In order to determine whether there is a dangerous probability of monopolization, courts have found it necessary to consider the relevant market and the defendant's ability to lessen or destroy competition in that market.

Notwithstanding the array of authority contrary to *Lessig*, the Court of Appeals in this case reaffirmed its prior holdings.... The *Lessig* opinion claimed support from the language of § 2, which prohibits attempts to monopolize "any part" of commerce, and therefore forbids attempts to monopolize any appreciable segment of interstate sales of the relevant product. The "any part" clause, however, applies to charges of monopolization as well as to attempts to monopolize, and it is beyond doubt that the former requires proof of market power in a relevant market. *United States v. Grinnell Corp.*, 384 U.S. 563, 570-571 (1966); *United States v. E.I. du Pont de Nemours & Co.*, 351 U.S. 377, 404 (1956).

In support of its determination that an inference of dangerous probability was permissible from a showing of intent, the *Lessig* opinion cited, and added emphasis to, this Court's reference in its opinion in *Swift* to "intent and the consequent dangerous probability." But any question whether dangerous probability of success requires proof of more than intent alone should have been removed by the subsequent passage in *Swift* which stated that "not every act that may be done with an intent to produce an unlawful result ... constitutes an attempt. It is a question of proximity and degree." ...

It is also our view that *Lessig* and later Ninth Circuit decisions refining and applying it are inconsistent with the policy of the Sherman Act. The purpose of the Act is not to protect businesses from the working of the market; it is to protect the public from the failure of the market. The law directs itself not against conduct which is competitive, even severely so, but against conduct which unfairly tends to destroy competition itself. It does so not out of solicitude for private concerns but out of concern for the public interest.... Thus, this Court and other courts have been careful to avoid constructions of § 2 which might chill competition, rather than foster it. It is sometimes difficult to distinguish robust competition from conduct with long-term anticompetitive effects; moreover, single-firm activity is unlike concerted activity covered by § 1, which "inherently is fraught with anticompetitive risk." *Copperweld*, 467 U.S., at 767-769. For these reasons, § 2 makes the conduct of a single firm unlawful only when it actually monopolizes or dangerously threatens to do so.

The concern that § 2 might be applied so as to further anticompetitive ends is plainly not met by inquiring only whether the defendant has engaged in "unfair" or "predatory" tactics. Such conduct may be sufficient to prove the necessary intent to monopolize, which is something more than an intent to compete vigorously, but demonstrating the dangerous probability of monopolization in an attempt case also requires inquiry into the relevant product and geographic market and the defendant's economic power in that market.

III

We hold that petitioners may not be liable for attempted monopolization under § 2 of the Sherman Act absent proof of a dangerous probability that they would monopolize a particular market and specific intent to monopolize. In this case, the trial instructions allowed the jury to infer specific intent and dangerous probability of success from the defendants' predatory conduct, without any proof of the relevant market or of a realistic probability that the defendants could achieve monopoly power in that market.... [T]he judgment of the Court of Appeals is reversed....

NOTES AND QUESTIONS

1. In order to prove a "dangerous probability" of success an antitrust plaintiff must define a market and show a certain amount of market power. In the absence of such a showing, even fairly egregious conduct is not an antitrust violation. For example, consider the following from *United States v. Empire Gas Corp.*, 537 F.2d 296 (8th Cir. 1976), *cert. denied*, 429 U.S. 1122 (1977):

> ... The record before us establishes that the defendant attempted to use price cuts or threats of price cuts to prevent competitors from soliciting Empire customers. Actions such as these, designed to prevent competitors from increasing their share of the market at the expense of the antitrust defendant, clearly show intent to monopolize....
>
> In addition to the above actions designed to reduce competition from other retailers, the evidence establishes that many of the defendant's price cuts were designed to give Empire *control* over the retail *price* of LP gas.
>
> ... The record shows that the LP gas business is highly competitive in the Lebanon and Wheaton markets as elsewhere. The defendant has many competitors wherever it does business, and new ones spring up frequently. The barriers to entry in this industry are minimal; all that are needed are a supply of LP, a truck, and perhaps a storage tank.

The court then dismissed the complaint.

2. The traditional statement of the attempt offense comes from Justice Holmes's formulation in the *Swift* case, *supra*. It requires the plaintiff to prove three things: (1) the defendant's specific intent to monopolize; (2) some kind of anticompetitive conduct; and (3) a "dangerous probability" that the defendant would have acquired monopoly power. Courts agree that the attempt offense includes these elements. When they interpret the elements, however, all agreement stops. The differences among the circuits go to a wide range of issues: must the intent be subjective, or can it be measured objectively? Must there actually be an intent to monopolize the market (that is, to acquire sufficient market power to engage in monopoly pricing), or must there be merely an intent to engage in conduct that satisfies the conduct requirement of the attempt offense? Will conduct, not sufficient to make one a monopolist, nevertheless convict one of attempt to monopolize? Does proof of a "dangerous probability" of success require a showing that the defendant already has "substantial" market power, or are the power requirements substantially less than they are for monopolization?

One theme underlies the caution that many courts have expressed about using the attempt offense too expansively: the Sherman Act is not a broad statute designed to cover all unfair business practices. Principled use of the statute requires courts to distinguish those questionable business practices that pose a great danger of giving sellers monopoly power from those that do not.

The "intent" requirement in attempt cases reflects in large part the ideology of the various antitrust schools. Economists and Chicago school analysts, for example, are uncomfortable about measuring subjective intent and would prefer to discern intent from pricing behavior. Courts sometimes follow their lead, at least to the point of holding that bad intent cannot be inferred from conduct that has an alternative "legitimate" business explanation. *See Knutson v. Daily Review*, 548 F.2d 795, 814 (9th Cir. 1976), *cert. denied*, 433 U.S. 910 (1977); for discussion of the problem of subjective intent in predatory pricing cases, generally concluding that courts would do well to avoid considering it, *see* 3 P. Areeda & H. Hovenkamp, *Antitrust Law* ¶ 728 (rev. ed. 1996). Courts and commentators generally agree about one thing: the mere "intent" to injure one's rivals by producing a better product at a lower (but nevertheless profitable) price should never violate the antitrust laws. To turn efficiency into an antitrust violation would subvert the most fundamental goal of the antitrust laws, for efficiency is the heart of the competitive process.

Once a relevant market is defined, what is required to establish a "dangerous probability" that the defendant would achieve monopoly power in that market? Must the plaintiff show that the defendant already has some market power, or that it in some other way "dominates" the defined market? Here the case law varies considerably with the kind of conduct at issue. For example, *Lorain Journal Co. v. United States*, 342 U.S. 143 (1951), discussed at some length in the *Aspen* decision, *supra*, condemned a newspaper's policy of not selling advertising to those who also purchased advertising from a competing radio station. Such a claim is plausible only if the newspaper has a large market share. If it did not, a merchant who wanted to advertise in both newspaper and radio would have purchased its newspaper advertising from someone else, unless Lorain Journal compensated the merchant by the amount it valued the radio advertising. By contrast, an attempt to monopolize involving fraudulent patent procurement or badly motivated litigation (see Chapter 9) might be plausible on a much smaller market share. As you might expect, market *share* requirements vary widely in attempt cases. For example, *see Ford v. Stroup*, 1997-1 Trade Cas. ¶ 71838 (6th Cir. 1997, unpublished) (radiologist group's 50-55% share insufficient where entry barriers were not shown to be high; showing of absence of historical entry insufficient when market appeared to be competitive; although a new entrant required an expensive linear accelerator, at least three local facilities having such equipment would have been available to a new entrant); *Springfield Terminal Rwy. Co. v. Canadian Pacific Limited*, 133 F.3d 103 (1st Cir. 1997) (ten percent insufficient); *United States v. Empire Gas Corp.*, *supra* (47% to 50% insufficient); *Twin City Sportservice, Inc. v. Charles O. Finley & Co.*, 676 F.2d 1291 (9th Cir. 1982) (24% sufficient).

3. In *United States v. American Airlines, Inc.*, 743 F.2d 1114 (5th Cir. 1984), the court held that a government complaint stated a claim of attempted monopolization against an airline company accused of attempting to fix prices. The government produced evidence that the president of American (Crandall) called the president of Braniff Airlines (Putnam) and had the following conversation:

> *Crandall*: I think it's dumb as hell ... to sit here and pound the **** out of each other and neither one of us making a ******* dime.
> *Putnam*: Well —
> *Crandall*: ... We can, we can both live here and there ain't no room for Delta. But there's, ah, no reason that I can see, all right, to put both companies out of business.
> *Putnam*: But if you're going to overlay every route of American's on top of ours, on top of every route that Braniff has — I can't just sit here and allow you to bury us without giving our best effort.
> *Crandall*: Oh, sure, but Eastern and Delta do the same thing....
> *Putnam*: Do you have a suggestion for me?
> *Crandall*: Yes. I have a suggestion for you. Raise your ****** fares twenty percent. I'll raise mine the next morning.
>
> ....
>
> *Putnam*: We can't talk about pricing.
> *Crandall*: Oh bull****, Howard. We can talk about any ****** thing we want to talk about.

Putnam, unknown to Crandall, was taping the entire conversation. He turned the tape over to the Department of Justice, which then accused American Airlines of an attempt to monopolize.

The defendant argued, inter alia, that a mere solicitation could not constitute an illegal attempt, and that under the circumstances of this case the attempt would require an actual agreement between the two firms to control price and output. The trial court agreed and dismissed the complaint for failure to state a claim.

In reversing, the Fifth Circuit concluded that if Putnam had accepted Crandall's offer to fix prices "the two airlines, at the moment of acceptance, would have acquired monopoly power. At the same moment, the offense of joint monopolization would have been complete." The court observed that the fact of Crandall's specific intent to monopolize was beyond dispute. Furthermore, Crandall's proposal (a joint price increase by the two dominant firms in the market) was "the most proximate to the commission of the completed offense that Crandall was capable of committing. Considering the alleged market share of American and Braniff, the barriers to entry by other airlines, and the authority of Crandall and Putnam, the complaint sufficiently alleged that Crandall's proposal had a dangerous probability of success."

Finally, the court added:

[The defendant further argues] that price fixing is an offense under section 1 of the Sherman Act and since the government charges that Crandall sought to have American and Braniff fix prices, the government's complaint in reality seeks to have us write an attempt provision into section 1. This argument is meritless. Appellees confuse the section 1 offense of price fixing with the power to control price following acquisition of monopoly power under section 2. Under the facts alleged in the complaint, Crandall wanted both to obtain joint monopoly power and to engage in price fixing. That he was not able to price fix and thus, has no liability under section 1, has no effect on whether his unsuccessful efforts to monopolize constitute attempted monopolization.

Query: The court seems reluctant to "write an attempt provision into section 1" of the Sherman Act. Why should it be? Didn't Holmes simply write the common-law attempt provision into section 2? Or does the fact that section 2 recognizes "attempt to monopolize" *explicitly* suggest that an attempt should not be *implied* with respect to section 1, where it is not made explicit? The Justice Department apparently draws the line by concluding that an *agreement* to fix prices or divide markets constitutes a criminal offense, while an unaccepted solicitation, as in *American Airlines*, is only a civil violation. Joel Klein, Antitrust Division Head, News Conference, May 18, 1998 (explaining why an alleged but unaccepted offer from Microsoft to Netscape to divide the internet browser market would not be treated as a criminal offense).

4. The problem of ambiguous conduct, or conduct that may be both efficient and anticompetitive, is even greater in attempt cases than monopolization cases generally. In thinking this problem through, keep the following principles in mind: (1) conduct that is legal for a monopolist is necessarily legal for the aspiring monopolist as well; (2) as a firm's market share becomes lower, the likelihood that a practice is efficient becomes higher, while the likelihood that it is anticompetitive becomes lower. Can you see why? Consider the following opinion from the Federal Trade Commission:

E.I. DU PONT DE NEMOURS & CO.
96 F.T.C. 653 (1980)

[Du Pont had developed a process for producing titanium dioxide (TiO_2) at a cost significantly lower than any competitor could produce it. Du Pont refused to license this low cost process to any competitor. Rather it built a new plant (the DeLisle Plant) larger than necessary to meet existing demand, and large enough to meet foreseeable future expansion in the market for TiO_2. Du Pont was able to show that the most efficient size for such a plant was one capable of meeting virtually all future expansion in the TiO_2 market. Du Pont sold TiO_2 at a price lower than its short-run profit-maximizing price, but above its cost and sufficiently low to discourage its higher-cost rivals from building new plants themselves.

The Federal Trade Commission staff alleged that these facts — particularly the large plant expansion designed to corner future growth in the TiO$_2$ market — amounted to a violation of section 5 of the Federal Trade Commission Act. The Administrative Law Judge had applied the standards of section 2 of the Sherman Act.]

COMMISSIONER CLANTON....

....

This case raises fundamental questions about the extent to which dominant firms may aggressively pursue competitive opportunities, especially where they enjoy some form of cost or technological advantage over their rivals. More specifically, the crucial issue facing us is not whether such firms may legitimately compete or capitalize on their advantages, but whether those opportunities are exploited in an unreasonable fashion. In other words, how much latitude should be afforded a major, well-established firm when it seizes a competitive edge and attempts to enhance significantly its market position? In the context of this case the question is not so much whether du Pont had the right to expand but whether it did so by measures that went beyond what were justified by its cost advantage.

....

We turn ... to the issue of "specific intent," an elusive aspect of the attempt offense. In this connection, it seems important to bear in mind what the attempt doctrine does not proscribe. As Areeda & Turner put it: "specific intent" clearly cannot include the mere intention to prevail over one's rivals. To declare that intention unlawful would defeat the antitrust goal of encouraging competition on the merits, which is heavily motivated by such an intent. P. Areeda & D. Turner, Antitrust Law ¶ 822a at 314 (1977) (footnote omitted).

....

As a general matter, it seems unwise to find that a firm has the requisite specific intent for anticipating the exclusionary consequences of successful competitive behavior which leads, or may lead, to a monopoly, so long as that behavior is reasonable. To suggest otherwise would be to proscribe all acts in which firms conjure up some thoughts of achieving monopoly irrespective of the actual character of the means employed to gain that end. Perhaps the relationship between intent and conduct is best characterized by the court in *Transamerica*:

> More than an intent to win every sale, even if that would result in the demise of a competitor, is required before it can be concluded a defendant has the type of exclusionary intent condemned by the antitrust law. Intent and conduct are closely related; and there must be some element of unfairness in the conduct before an anticompetitive intent can be found, as distinguished from the benign intent to beat the opposition. (citations omitted) 481 F. Supp. at 1010.

There is no doubt that intent can shed light on questionable conduct and the justifications for the conduct. But the crucial issue is whether du Pont's conduct represents legitimate competitive behavior or an unreasonable effort to propel the firm into a dominant position in the TiO_2 market....

....

As for *Alcoa*, it superficially at least provides a close analogy to the facts of this case. But there are differences, not the least of which is the fact that Alcoa was a monopolist that had maintained its hold over the market through repeated additions to capacity over a long period of time. Moreover, the circumstances and justifications surrounding those increases in output are not detailed. In light of more recent precedents and literature on exclusionary conduct, discussed below, *Alcoa* leaves unanswered a number of important questions that are especially relevant in the context of the attempt case now before us.

For example, *Alcoa* reveals nothing about the scale economies inherent in Alcoa's expansions, nor does the decision specifically address whether Alcoa's additional output conformed to demand estimates or resulted in excess capacity. Furthermore, while the court condemned Alcoa's repeated additions to capacity as preemptive and preservative of monopoly, it gave unclear signals about other aggressive conduct engaged in by the firm, some of which it found to be reasonable and justified by legitimate business reasons....

....

In applying these principles to the facts of this case, it is useful to restate complaint counsel's fundamental objection to du Pont's growth plan. In essence, complaint counsel contend that it was logical for du Pont to do what it did only if monopoly power could be attained in the future. It is argued that du Pont's construction/pricing/non-licensing policy involved a current foregoing of available profits, that du Pont recognized that it could recoup those profits down the road through high volume and higher prices, and that du Pont's policy only made sense if those excess profits would become available at a later date.

....

Turning to the pricing options available to respondent, there is, of course, no evidence that du Pont priced below its costs, since the case was not tried on such a theory. As for the issue of limit pricing, the literature discussed previously suggests that predation may occur even in circumstances where prices are above the dominant firm's costs (whether measured by average variable or average total cost). In this respect, it seems clear that respondent sought to price in a fashion that took account of the propensities and abilities of competitors to expand, although the firm's pricing decisions were affected at least in part by independent economic forces, such as demand conditions. Given this situation, it can be argued that these pricing policies went too far, that they transformed an otherwise legitimate method of expansion into an unlawful course of conduct.

We do not agree. Du Pont's pricing strategy stemmed from its clear cost advantage over competitors and occurred in conjunction with its long-term plan to capture future market growth, a plan which we have pointed out before was consistent with foreseeable demand and scale economies. Thus, this is not a case where du Pont was attempting solely to preserve its market power through selective, temporary price cuts to deter new entry or expansion by existing competitors. Even complaint counsel do not attack respondent's pricing as an independent violation; rather they argue that it is unlawful as part of a broader pattern of behavior. For our part, even if du Pont's pricing can be characterized as a form of limit pricing, we do not find it to be unreasonable, absent at least some evidence of below-cost pricing, in view of the firm's cost advantage, its market position and its legitimate expansion efforts. While there may be circumstances where above cost pricing is unjustifiably exclusionary, those circumstances clearly are not present here....

It may be that du Pont ultimately will achieve a monopoly share of the market. As its share increases, other firms may find it harder to capture the efficiencies enjoyed by du Pont due to the scale economies associated with the ilmenite process. Those effects should be weighed carefully, and we have done so. Antitrust policy wisely disfavors monopoly, but it also seeks to promote vigorous competitive behavior. Indeed, the essence of the competitive process is to induce firms to become more efficient and to pass the benefits of the efficiency along to consumers. That process would be ill-served by using antitrust to block hard, aggressive competition that is solidly based on efficiencies and growth opportunities, even if monopoly is a possible result. Such a view, we believe, is entirely consistent with the "superior skill, foresight and industry" exception in *Alcoa* and subsequent cases, for those decisions clearly indicate that monopolies may be lawfully created by superior competitive ability.

As we have previously indicated, du Pont engaged in conduct consistent with its own technological capacity and market opportunities. It did not attempt to build excess capacity or to expand temporarily as a means of deterring entry. Nor did respondent engage in other conduct that might tip the scales in the direction of liability, such as pricing below cost, making false announcements about future expansion plans, or attempting to lock up customers in requirements contracts to assure the success of its growth plans. In short, we find du Pont's conduct to be reasonable. Accordingly, we affirm the ALJ's dismissal of the complaint.

NOTES AND QUESTIONS

1. Is the *du Pont* decision consistent with Judge Hand's 1945 *Alcoa* decision? Can you find a principled distinction between the two?

2. Suppose that in the future du Pont's share of the titanium dioxide market climbs to near 100%. Nearly all its competitors have been driven from the market, for they are unable to meet du Pont's prices. Du Pont continues to refuse to license its low-cost production process to competitors. Do you suppose the Commission would change its mind? What if, once the last competitor's plant was shut down and dismantled, du Pont raised the price of titanium dioxide by 50%?

3. The Commission makes it clear that the mere subjective "intent" to triumph over one's rivals by being more efficient than they are is not illegal, even if it includes an "intent" to drive the competitors out of business. The real issue, said the Commission, is whether this intent was carried out by "anticompetitive" or "unfair" acts. Doesn't this mean that the question of intent is irrelevant? Does the Commission give much direction on how to distinguish "fair" practices that injure rivals from "unfair" ones?

B. ATTEMPT TO MONOPOLIZE AND ANTICOMPETITIVE CONDUCT: PREDATORY PRICING

Predatory pricing is the offense of driving rivals out of business by selling products at less than their cost, with the expectation of charging a monopoly price in the future when the rivals have either left the market or have been cajoled into raising their own prices. The formulation of an administrable test for predatory pricing has occupied center stage in attempt cases since the mid-1970's. On the one hand, low prices are an important goal of the antitrust laws. Any test designed to make selling at a low price illegal must employ a great deal of caution, or else the antitrust laws will end up subverting the very ends they were designed to achieve. On the other hand, few people have doubted that there are times when sellers attempt to create a monopoly by temporarily charging unreasonably low prices.

When *Standard Oil Co. v. United States*, 221 U.S. 1 (1911), was decided, Progressive Era lawyers generally believed that predatory pricing was easy to pull off, relatively common, and that it represented an important means by which certain large monopolies such as the Standard Oil Company had come into existence. Subsequent argument and evidence suggests that they were wrong, and that Standard generally eliminated rivals from the market by buying them out, not by predating them into bankruptcy. *See* McGee, *Predatory Price Cutting: The Standard Oil (N.J.) Case*, 1 J.L. & Econ. 137 (1958); *but see* Granitz & Klein, *Monopolization by "Raising Rivals' Costs:" the Standard Oil Case*, 39 J.L. & Econ. 1 (1996), arguing that, while Standard may not have used below-cost pricing, it did employ other anticompetitive strategies.

Whether or not Standard used predatory pricing, the popular feeling that price predation was one of the most serious industrial evils of the time inspired Progressive Era lawmakers to devote a great deal of attention to it. Many Progressives were outraged with the rule of reason announced in the *Standard* case. Ignoring the fact that the Supreme Court condemned Standard Oil on virtually every count, critics of Chief Justice White's opinion alleged that the rule of reason would eviscerate the Sherman Act. All three major political parties (Democratic, Republican, and Progressive (Bull Moose)) in the 1912 Presidential election promised stronger antitrust laws. Woodrow Wilson's Democratic administration followed through with the Clayton Act, which was enacted in 1914. Section 2 of the Clayton Act (15 U.S.C. § 13) was concerned with predatory pricing. Today predatory pricing is condemned under both section 1 of the Sherman Act and §2 of the Clayton Act, although the two statutes have traditionally employed different requirements.

Built into §2 of the Clayton Act was its framer's theory about how predatory pricing worked. Today we know that theory as the "subsidy" or "recoupment" theory of predatory pricing. Under the theory, giant trusts like the Standard Oil Company were able to predate smaller rivals out of the market because the trusts operated in many geographic markets, while the smaller rivals operated in only one. The framers of §2 of the Clayton Act believed that the giant companies would engage in below-cost selling in a market in which they had rivals, until the rivals were driven from business. They would finance this below cost selling by raising their prices in other areas where their monopoly position was already secure. By this means they could use a monopoly in one area to leverage a monopoly in a second area. Section 2 of the Clayton Act was designed to reach this perceived practice by making it illegal for the giant companies to charge two different prices in two different markets where the effect of such "discriminatory" pricing was to injure competition.

Today, cases applying §2 of the Clayton Act to predatory pricing are known as "primary-line" price discrimination cases. In 1936 section 2 of the Clayton Act was modified and broadened substantially by the Robinson-Patman amendments to include "secondary-line" injuries, which are injuries that accrue not to the seller's competitors but to its customers. Secondary-line application of the statute is covered in Chapter 8. Today we refer to §2 of the Clayton Act in its entirety as the Robinson-Patman Act, even though predatory pricing is governed by the original 1914 language.

Whether we analyze predatory pricing under the Sherman Act or the Robinson-Patman Act, it is best understood as conduct by which the defendant pays certain higher costs today in order to reap the benefit of supracompetitive monopoly profits tomorrow.

1. STRUCTURAL PREREQUISITES FOR A PREDATORY PRICING CLAIM

BROOKE GROUP LTD. V. BROWN & WILLIAMSON TOBACCO CORP.

509 U.S. 209 (1993)

JUSTICE KENNEDY delivered the opinion of the Court.

This case stems from a market struggle that erupted in the domestic cigarette industry in the mid-1980's. Petitioner Brooke Group, Inc., whom we, like the parties to the case, refer to as Liggett because of its former corporate name, charges that to counter its innovative development of generic cigarettes, respondent Brown & Williamson Tobacco Corporation introduced its own line of generic cigarettes in an unlawful effort to stifle price competition in the economy segment of the national cigarette market. Liggett contends that Brown & Williamson cut prices on generic cigarettes below cost and offered discriminatory volume rebates to wholesalers to force Liggett to raise its own generic cigarette prices and introduce oligopoly pricing in the economy segment. We hold that Brown & Williamson is entitled to judgment as a matter of law.

I

In 1980, Liggett pioneered the development of the economy segment of the national cigarette market by introducing a line of "black and white" generic cigarettes. The economy segment of the market, sometimes called the generic segment, is characterized by its bargain prices and comprises a variety of different products: black and whites, which are true generics sold in plain white packages with simple black lettering describing their contents; private label generics, which carry the trade dress of a specific purchaser, usually a retail chain; branded generics, which carry a brand name but which, like black and whites and private label generics, are sold at a deep discount and with little or no advertising; and "Value-25s," packages of 25 cigarettes that are sold to the consumer some 12.5% below the cost of a normal 20-cigarette pack. By 1984, when Brown & Williamson entered the generic segment and set in motion the series of events giving rise to this suit, Liggett's black and whites represented 97% of the generic segment, which in turn accounted for a little more than 4% of domestic cigarette sales. Prior to Liggett's introduction of black and whites in 1980, sales of generic cigarettes amounted to less than 1% of the domestic cigarette market.

... Cigarette manufacturing has long been one of America's most concentrated industries, ... and for decades, production has been dominated by six firms: R.J. Reynolds, Philip Morris, American Brands, Lorillard, and the two litigants involved here, Liggett and Brown & Williamson. R.J. Reynolds and Philip Morris, the two industry leaders, enjoyed respective market shares of about 28% and 40% at the time of trial. Brown & Williamson ran a distant third, its market share never exceeding 12% at any time relevant to this dispute. Liggett's share of the market was even less, from a low of just over 2% in 1980 to a high of just over 5% in 1984.

The cigarette industry also has long been one of America's most profitable, in part because for many years there was no significant price competition among the rival firms.... List prices for cigarettes increased in lock-step, twice a year, for a number of years, irrespective of the rate of inflation, changes in the costs of production, or shifts in consumer demand. Substantial evidence suggests that in recent decades, the industry reaped the benefits of prices above a competitive level....

By 1980, however, broad market trends were working against the industry. Overall demand for cigarettes in the United States was declining, and no immediate prospect of recovery existed. As industry volume shrank, all firms developed substantial excess capacity. This decline in demand, coupled with the effects of nonprice competition, had a severe negative impact on Liggett. Once a major force in the industry, with market shares in excess of 20%, Liggett's market share had declined by 1980 to a little over 2%. With this meager share of the market, Liggett was on the verge of going out of business.

At the urging of a distributor, Liggett took an unusual step to revive its prospects: It developed a line of black and white generic cigarettes. When introduced in 1980, black and whites were offered to consumers at a list price roughly 30% lower than the list price of full-priced, branded cigarettes. They were also promoted at the wholesale level by means of rebates that increased with the volume of cigarettes ordered. Black and white cigarettes thus represented a new marketing category. The category's principal competitive characteristic was low price. Liggett's black and whites were an immediate and considerable success, growing from a fraction of a percent of the market at their introduction to over 4% of the total cigarette market by early 1984.

As the market for Liggett's generic cigarettes expanded, the other cigarette companies found themselves unable to ignore the economy segment. In general, the growth of generics came at the expense of the other firms' profitable sales of branded cigarettes. Brown & Williamson was hardest hit, because many of Brown & Williamson's brands were favored by consumers who were sensitive to changes in cigarette prices. Although Brown & Williamson sold only 11.4% of the market's branded cigarettes, 20% of the converts to Liggett's black and whites had switched from a Brown & Williamson brand. Losing volume and profits in its branded products, Brown & Williamson determined to enter the generic segment of the cigarette market. In July 1983, Brown & Williamson had begun selling Value-25s, and in the spring of 1984, it introduced its own black and white cigarette.

Brown & Williamson was neither the first nor the only cigarette company to recognize the threat posed by Liggett's black and whites and to respond in the economy segment. R.J. Reynolds had also introduced a Value-25 in 1983. And before Brown & Williamson introduced its own black and whites, R.J. Reynolds had repriced its "Doral" branded cigarette at generic levels....

Brown & Williamson's entry was an even graver threat to Liggett's dominance of the generic category. Unlike R.J. Reynolds' Doral, Brown & Williamson's product was also a black and white and so would be in direct competition with Liggett's product at the wholesale level and on the retail shelf. Because Liggett's and Brown & Williamson's black and whites were more or less fungible, wholesalers had little incentive to carry more than one line. And unlike R.J. Reynolds, Brown & Williamson not only matched Liggett's prices but beat them....

... This precipitated a price war at the wholesale level, in which Liggett five times attempted to beat the rebates offered by Brown & Williamson. At the end of each round, Brown & Williamson maintained a real advantage over Liggett's prices. Although it is undisputed that Brown & Williamson's original net price for its black and whites was above its costs, Liggett contends that by the end of the rebate war, Brown & Williamson was selling its black and whites at a loss.... Liggett's second response was to file a lawsuit....

... Liggett alleged that Brown & Williamson's volume rebates to wholesalers amounted to price discrimination that had a reasonable possibility of injuring competition, in violation of § 2(a). Liggett claimed that Brown & Williamson's discriminatory volume rebates were integral to a scheme of predatory pricing, in which Brown & Williamson reduced its net prices for generic cigarettes below average variable costs. According to Liggett, these below-cost prices were not promotional but were intended to pressure it to raise its list prices on generic cigarettes, so that the percentage price difference between generic and branded cigarettes would narrow. Liggett explained that it would have been unable to reduce its wholesale rebates without losing substantial market share to Brown & Williamson; its only choice, if it wished to avoid prolonged losses on its principal product line, was to raise retail prices. The resulting reduction in the list price gap, it was said, would restrain the growth of the economy segment and preserve Brown & Williamson's supracompetitive profits on its branded cigarettes....

After a 115-day trial involving almost 3,000 exhibits and over a score of witnesses, the jury returned a verdict in favor of Liggett, finding on the special verdict form that Brown & Williamson had engaged in price discrimination that had a reasonable possibility of injuring competition in the domestic cigarette market as a whole. The jury awarded Liggett $49.6 million in damages, which the District Court trebled to $148.8 million. After reviewing the record, however, the District Court held that Brown & Williamson was entitled to judgment as a matter of law on three separate grounds: lack of injury to competition, lack of antitrust injury to Liggett, and lack of a causal link between the discriminatory rebates and Liggett's alleged injury....

The United States Court of Appeals for the Fourth Circuit affirmed. *Liggett Group, Inc. v. Brown & Williamson Tobacco Corp.*, 964 F.2d 335 (1992). The Court of Appeals held that the dynamic of conscious parallelism among oligopolists could not produce competitive injury in a predatory pricing setting, which necessarily involves a price cut by one of the oligopolists.... In the Court of Appeals' view, "[t]o rely on the characteristics of an oligopoly to assure recoupment of losses from a predatory pricing scheme after one oligopolist has made a competitive move is ... economically irrational." ...

II

A

... By its terms, the Robinson-Patman Act condemns price discrimination only to the extent that it threatens to injure competition.... Liggett contends that Brown & Williamson's discriminatory volume rebates to wholesalers threatened substantial competitive injury by furthering a predatory pricing scheme designed to purge competition from the economy segment of the cigarette market.

This type of injury, which harms direct competitors of the discriminating seller, is known as primary-line injury.... We last addressed primary line injury over 25 years ago, in *Utah Pie Co. v. Continental Baking Co.*, 386 U.S. 685

(1967). In *Utah Pie*, we reviewed the sufficiency of the evidence supporting jury verdicts against three national pie companies that had engaged in a variety of predatory practices in the market for frozen pies in Salt Lake City, with the intent to drive a local pie manufacturer out of business. We reversed the Court of Appeals and held that the evidence presented was adequate to permit a jury to find a likelihood of injury to competition.

Utah Pie has often been interpreted to permit liability for primary-line price discrimination on a mere showing that the defendant intended to harm competition or produced a declining price structure. The case has been criticized on the grounds that such low standards of competitive injury are at odds with the antitrust laws' traditional concern for consumer welfare and price competition. See Bowman, *Restraint of Trade by the Supreme Court: The Utah Pie Case*, 77 Yale L.J. 70 (1967); R. Posner, *Antitrust Law: An Economic Perspective* 193-194 (1976); L. Sullivan, *Antitrust* 687 (1977); 3 P. Areeda & D. Turner, *Antitrust Law* ¶ 720c (1978) (hereinafter Areeda & Turner); R. Bork, *The Antitrust Paradox* 386-387 (1978); H. Hovenkamp, *Economics and Federal Antitrust Law* 188-189 (1985). We do not regard the *Utah Pie* case itself as having the full significance attributed to it by its detractors. *Utah Pie* was an early judicial inquiry in this area and did not purport to set forth explicit, general standards for establishing a violation of the Robinson-Patman Act. As the law has been explored since *Utah Pie*, it has become evident that primary-line competitive injury under the Robinson-Patman Act is of the same general character as the injury inflicted by predatory pricing schemes actionable under § 2 of the Sherman Act....

There are, to be sure, differences between the two statutes. For example, we interpret § 2 of the Sherman Act to condemn predatory pricing when it poses "a dangerous probability of actual monopolization," *Spectrum Sports, Inc. v. McQuillan*, [506 U.S. 447 (1993)], whereas the Robinson-Patman Act requires only that there be "a reasonable possibility" of substantial injury to competition before its protections are triggered. *Falls City Industries, Inc. v. Vanco Beverage, Inc.*, 460 U.S. 428, 434 (1983). But whatever additional flexibility the Robinson-Patman Act standard may imply, the essence of the claim under either statute is the same: A business rival has priced its products in an unfair manner with an object to eliminate or retard competition and thereby gain and exercise control over prices in the relevant market.

Accordingly, whether the claim alleges predatory pricing under § 2 of the Sherman Act or primary-line price discrimination under the Robinson-Patman Act, two prerequisites to recovery remain the same. First, a plaintiff seeking to establish competitive injury resulting from a rival's low prices must prove that the prices complained of are below an appropriate measure of its rival's costs.[1]

---

[1] Because the parties in this case agree that the relevant measure of cost is average variable cost, however, we again decline to resolve the conflict among the lower courts over the appropriate measure of cost. See *Cargill, supra,* at 117-118, n. 12; *Matsushita, supra,* at 585, n. 8.

... [W]e have rejected elsewhere the notion that above-cost prices that are below general market levels or the costs of a firm's competitors inflict injury to competition cognizable under the antitrust laws. See *Atlantic Richfield Co. v. USA Petroleum Co.*, 495 U.S. 328, 340 (1990). "Low prices benefit consumers regardless of how those prices are set, and so long as they are above predatory levels, they do not threaten competition.... We have adhered to this principle regardless of the type of antitrust claim involved." *Ibid.* As a general rule, the exclusionary effect of prices above a relevant measure of cost either reflects the lower cost structure of the alleged predator, and so represents competition on the merits, or is beyond the practical ability of a judicial tribunal to control without courting intolerable risks of chilling legitimate price-cutting....

Even in an oligopolistic market, when a firm drops its prices to a competitive level to demonstrate to a maverick the unprofitability of straying from the group, it would be illogical to condemn the price cut: The antitrust laws then would be an obstacle to the chain of events most conducive to a breakdown of oligopoly pricing and the onset of competition. Even if the ultimate effect of the cut is to induce or reestablish supracompetitive pricing, discouraging a price cut and forcing firms to maintain supracompetitive prices, thus depriving consumers of the benefits of lower prices in the interim, does not constitute sound antitrust policy....

The second prerequisite to holding a competitor liable under the antitrust laws for charging low prices is a demonstration that the competitor had a reasonable prospect, or, under § 2 of the Sherman Act, a dangerous probability, of recouping its investment in below-cost prices. See *Matsushita, supra,* at 589; *Cargill, supra,* at 119, n. 15. "For the investment to be rational, the [predator] must have a reasonable expectation of recovering, in the form of later monopoly profits, more than the losses suffered." Recoupment is the ultimate object of an unlawful predatory pricing scheme; it is the means by which a predator profits from predation. Without it, predatory pricing produces lower aggregate prices in the market, and consumer welfare is enhanced. Although unsuccessful predatory pricing may encourage some inefficient substitution toward the product being sold at less than its cost, unsuccessful predation is in general a boon to consumers.

That below-cost pricing may impose painful losses on its target is of no moment to the antitrust laws if competition is not injured.... Even an act of pure malice by one business competitor against another does not, without more, state a claim under the federal antitrust laws....

For recoupment to occur, below-cost pricing must be capable, as a threshold matter, of producing the intended effects on the firm's rivals, whether driving them from the market, or, as was alleged to be the goal here, causing them to raise their prices to supracompetitive levels within a disciplined oligopoly. This requires an understanding of the extent and duration of the alleged predation, the relative financial strength of the predator and its intended victim, and their respective incentives and will....

If circumstances indicate that below-cost pricing could likely produce its intended effect on the target, there is still the further question whether it would likely injure competition in the relevant market. The plaintiff must demonstrate that there is a likelihood that the predatory scheme alleged would cause a rise in prices above a competitive level that would be sufficient to compensate for the amounts expended on the predation, including the time value of the money invested in it....

Evidence of below-cost pricing is not alone sufficient to permit an inference of probable recoupment and injury to competition. Determining whether recoupment of predatory losses is likely requires an estimate of the cost of the alleged predation and a close analysis of both the scheme alleged by the plaintiff and the structure and conditions of the relevant market. *Cf., e.g.,* Elzinga & Mills, *Testing for Predation: Is Recoupment Feasible?*, 34 Antitrust Bull. 869 (1989) (constructing one possible model for evaluating recoupment). If market circumstances or deficiencies in proof would bar a reasonable jury from finding that the scheme alleged would likely result in sustained supracompetitive pricing, the plaintiff's case has failed. In certain situations — for example, where the market is highly diffuse and competitive, or where new entry is easy, or the defendant lacks adequate excess capacity to absorb the market shares of his rivals and cannot quickly create or purchase new capacity — summary disposition of the case is appropriate....

These prerequisites to recovery are not easy to establish, but they are not artificial obstacles to recovery; rather, they are essential components of real market injury. As we have said in the Sherman Act context, "predatory pricing schemes are rarely tried, and even more rarely successful," *Matsushita, supra,* at 589, and the costs of an erroneous finding of liability are high....

B

Liggett does not allege that Brown & Williamson sought to drive it from the market but that Brown & Williamson sought to preserve supracompetitive profits on branded cigarettes by pressuring Liggett to raise its generic cigarette prices through a process of tacit collusion with the other cigarette companies....

In *Matsushita,* we remarked upon the general implausibility of predatory pricing. *Matsushita* observed that such schemes are even more improbable when they require coordinated action among several firms.... In order to succeed, the conspirators must agree on how to allocate present losses and future gains among the firms involved, and each firm must resist powerful incentives to cheat on whatever agreement is reached.

However unlikely predatory pricing by multiple firms may be when they conspire, it is even less likely when, as here, there is no express coordination. Firms that seek to recoup predatory losses through the conscious parallelism of oligopoly must rely on uncertain and ambiguous signals to achieve concerted action. The signals are subject to misinterpretation and are a blunt and imprecise means of ensuring smooth cooperation, especially in the context of changing or unprecedented market circumstances. This anticompetitive minuet is most difficult to compose and to perform, even for a disciplined oligopoly.

... Liggett suggests that these considerations led the Court of Appeals to rule out its theory of recovery as a matter of law....

To the extent that the Court of Appeals may have held that the interdependent pricing of an oligopoly may never provide a means for achieving recoupment and so may not form the basis of a primary-line injury claim, we disagree. A predatory pricing scheme designed to preserve or create a stable oligopoly, if successful, can injure consumers in the same way, and to the same extent, as one designed to bring about a monopoly. However unlikely that possibility may be as a general matter, when the realities of the market and the record facts indicate that it has occurred and was likely to have succeeded, theory will not stand in the way of liability. See *Eastman Kodak Co. v. Image Technical Services, Inc.*, 504 U.S. 451 (1992).

The Robinson-Patman Act, which amended § 2 of the original Clayton Act, suggests no exclusion from coverage when primary-line injury occurs in an oligopoly setting. Unlike the provisions of the Sherman Act, which speak only of various forms of express agreement and monopoly, the Robinson-Patman Act is phrased in broader, disjunctive terms, prohibiting price discrimination "where the effect of such discrimination may be substantially to lessen competition or tend to create a monopoly." ... We decline to create a per se rule of nonliability for predatory price discrimination when recoupment is alleged to take place through supracompetitive oligopoly pricing.

III

Although Liggett's theory of liability, as an abstract matter, is within the reach of the statute, we agree with the Court of Appeals and the District Court that Liggett was not entitled to submit its case to the jury....

A

Liggett's theory of competitive injury through oligopolistic price coordination depends upon a complex chain of cause and effect: Brown & Williamson would enter the generic segment with list prices matching Liggett's but with massive, discriminatory volume rebates directed at Liggett's biggest wholesalers; as a result, the net price of Brown & Williamson's generics would be below its costs; Liggett would suffer losses trying to defend its market share and wholesale customer base by matching Brown & Williamson's rebates; to avoid further losses, Liggett would raise its list prices on generics or acquiesce in price leadership by Brown & Williamson; higher list prices to consumers would shrink the percentage gap in retail price between generic and branded cigarettes; and this narrowing of the gap would make generics less appealing to the consumer, thus slowing the growth of the economy segment and reducing cannibalization of branded sales and their associated supracompetitive profits.

Although Brown & Williamson's entry into the generic segment could be regarded as procompetitive in intent as well as effect, the record contains sufficient evidence from which a reasonable jury could conclude that Brown & Williamson envisioned or intended this anticompetitive course of events.... There is also sufficient evidence in the record from which a reasonable jury could conclude that for a period of approximately 18 months, Brown & Williamson's prices on its generic cigarettes were below its costs, and that this below-cost pricing imposed losses on Liggett that Liggett was unwilling to sustain.... Liggett has failed to demonstrate competitive injury as a matter of law, however, because its proof is flawed in a critical respect: The evidence is inadequate to show that in pursuing this scheme, Brown & Williamson had a reasonable prospect of recovering its losses from below-cost pricing through slowing the growth of generics....

... Recoupment through supracompetitive pricing in the economy segment of the cigarette market is an indispensable aspect of Liggett's own proffered theory, because a slowing of growth in the economy segment, even if it results from an increase in generic prices, is not itself anticompetitive. Only if those higher prices are a product of nonmarket forces has competition suffered. If prices rise in response to an excess of demand over supply, or segment growth slows as patterns of consumer preference become stable, the market is functioning in a competitive manner. Because relying on tacit coordination among oligopolists as a means of recouping losses from predatory pricing is "highly speculative," Areeda & Hovenkamp, [Antitrust Law] ¶ 711.2c, competent evidence is necessary to allow a reasonable inference that it poses an authentic threat to competition. The evidence in this case is insufficient to demonstrate the danger of Brown & Williamson's alleged scheme.

B

Based on Liggett's theory of the case and the record it created, there are two means by which one might infer that Brown & Williamson had a reasonable prospect of producing sustained supracompetitive pricing in the generic segment adequate to recoup its predatory losses: first, if generic output or price information indicates that oligopolistic price coordination in fact produced supracompetitive prices in the generic segment; or second, if evidence about the market and Brown & Williamson's conduct indicate that the alleged scheme was likely to have brought about tacit coordination and oligopoly pricing in the generic segment, even if it did not actually do so.

1

In this case, the price and output data do not support a reasonable inference that Brown & Williamson and the other cigarette companies elevated prices above a competitive level for generic cigarettes. Supracompetitive pricing entails a restriction in output.... In the present setting, in which output expanded at a rapid rate following Brown & Williamson's alleged predation, output in the generic segment can only have been restricted in the sense that it expanded at a slower rate than it would have absent Brown & Williamson's intervention. Such a counterfactual proposition is difficult to prove in the best of circumstances; here, the record evidence does not permit a reasonable inference that output would have been greater without Brown & Williamson's entry into the generic segment.

Following Brown & Williamson's entry, the rate at which generic cigarettes were capturing market share did not slow; indeed, the average rate of growth doubled....

In arguing that Brown & Williamson was able to exert market power and raise generic prices above a competitive level in the generic category through tacit price coordination with the other cigarette manufacturers, Liggett places its principal reliance on direct evidence of price behavior. This evidence demonstrates that the list prices on all cigarettes, generic and branded alike, rose to a significant degree during the late 1980's....

A reasonable jury, however, could not have drawn the inferences Liggett proposes. All of Liggett's data is based upon the list prices of various categories of cigarettes. Yet the jury had before it undisputed evidence that during the period in question, list prices were not the actual prices paid by consumers. As the market became unsettled in the mid-1980s, the cigarette companies invested substantial sums in promotional schemes, including coupons, stickers, and giveways, that reduced the actual cost of cigarettes to consumers below list prices....

Even on its own terms, the list price data relied upon by Liggett to demonstrate a narrowing of the price differential between generic and full-priced branded cigarettes could not support the conclusion that supracompetitive pricing had been introduced into the generic segment....

2

Not only does the evidence fail to show actual supracompetitive pricing in the generic segment, it also does not demonstrate its likelihood. At the time Brown & Williamson entered the generic segment, the cigarette industry as a whole faced declining demand and possessed substantial excess capacity.... The only means by which Brown & Williamson is alleged to have established oligopoly pricing in the face of these unusual competitive pressures is through tacit price coordination with the other cigarette firms. Yet the situation facing the cigarette companies in the 1980's would have made such tacit coordination unmanageable. Tacit coordination is facilitated by a stable market environment, fungible products, and a small number of variables upon which the firms seeking to coordinate their pricing may focus....

The larger number of product types and pricing variables also decreased the probability of effective parallel pricing.... With respect to each product, the net price in the market was determined not only by list prices, but also by a wide variety of discounts and promotions to consumers, and by rebates to wholesalers. In order to coordinate in an effective manner and eliminate price competition, the cigarette companies would have been required, without communicating, to establish parallel practices with respect to each of these variables, many of which, like consumer stickers or coupons, were difficult to monitor....

Liggett argues that the means by which Brown & Williamson signaled its anticompetitive intent to its rivals was through its pricing structure. According to Liggett, maintaining existing list prices while offering substantial rebates to wholesalers was a signal to the other cigarette firms that Brown & Williamson did not intend to attract additional smokers to the generic segment by its entry. But a reasonable jury could not conclude that this pricing structure eliminated or rendered insignificant the risk that the other firms might misunderstand Brown & Williamson's entry as a competitive move.... Without effective signaling, it is difficult to see how the alleged predation could have had a reasonable chance of success through oligopoly pricing....

... We hold that the evidence cannot support a finding that Brown & Williamson's alleged scheme was likely to result in oligopolistic price coordination and sustained supracompetitive pricing in the generic segment of the national cigarette market. Without this, Brown & Williamson had no reasonable prospect of recouping its predatory losses and could not inflict the injury to competition the antitrust laws prohibit. The judgment of the Court of Appeals is

Affirmed.

JUSTICE STEVENS, with whom JUSTICE WHITE and JUSTICE BLACKMUN join, dissenting.

....

[The Sherman Act and the Clayton Act, as amended by the Robinson-Patman Act] differ significantly with respect to one element of the violation, the competitive consequences of predatory conduct.... Section 2 of the Sherman Act ... may be violated when there is a "dangerous probability" that an attempt to achieve monopoly power will succeed. The Clayton Act goes beyond the "dangerous probability" standard to cover price discrimination "where the effect of such discrimination may be to substantially lessen competition or tend to create a monopoly in any line of commerce."

... The Robinson-Patman Act was designed to reach discriminations "in their incipiency, before the harm to competition is effected. It is enough that they 'may' have the proscribed effect."

... Perhaps the Court's most significant error is the assumption that seems to pervade much of the final sections of its opinion: that Liggett had the burden of proving either the actuality of supracompetitive pricing, or the actuality of tacit collusion.... In my opinion, the jury was entitled to infer from the succession of price increases after 1985 ... that B & W's below-cost pricing actually produced supracompetitive prices, with the help of tacit collusion among the players. But even if that were not so clear, the jury would surely be entitled to infer that B & W's predatory plan, in which it invested millions of dollars for the purpose of achieving an admittedly anticompetitive result, carried a "reasonable possibility" of injuring competition.

Accordingly, I respectfully dissent.

NOTES AND QUESTIONS

1. Of what relevance was the fact that the defendant engaged in price "discrimination," as the Robinson-Patman Act defines it? The requirement effectively means that bona fide predatory pricing intended to perpetuate an oligopoly could be defeated if the predator was simply careful to charge the same predatory price to everyone. The Robinson-Patman Act requires not only that the defendant charge two different prices but that the high- and low-priced goods be "of like grade and quality." See Chapter 9, §I.C, *infra*. That requirement often runs contrary to the logic of predatory pricing. For example, in *Brooke* the plaintiff alleged that the defendant's generic and premium cigarettes were "of like grade and quality," thus making the requirement. However, the logic of predatory price discrimination is that the defendant *isolates* buyers of the low price good and prices predatorily only to them, thus making predation less expensive than if it had to charge the predatory price to everyone. If the two classes of cigarettes really were similar, then large numbers of customers buying premium cigarettes would switch to generics, thus undermining the predation scheme.

2. Some circuit decisions have opined that the standard for predatory pricing under the Sherman and Robinson-Patman Acts should be the same. *See, e.g., A. A. Poultry Farms v. Rose Acre Farms*, 881 F.2d 1396 (7th Cir. 1989), *cert. denied*, 494 U.S. 1019 (1990). In *Brooke*, the Supreme Court did not follow that course. Rather, it held that, while the concern of the Sherman Act is with predatory pricing that creates monopoly, the Robinson-Patman Act may be additionally concerned with predation that creates or perpetuates oligopoly.

A. A. Poultry dealt with a different distinction, however. Several lower courts had held that while Sherman Act predatory pricing requires a "dangerous probability of success" in creating a monopoly, Robinson-Patman predation could be proven under a much lighter standard, such as price cutting to below cost with specific intent to harm a rival. This standard originated in the Supreme Court's decision in *Utah Pie Co. v. Continental Baking Co.*, 386 U.S. 685 (1967), where the Court condemned differential price cuts by three national companies in competition with a local company that had the dominant market share. As the *Brooke* case points out, *Utah Pie* has been among the most castigated of Supreme Court antitrust opinions. Its critics have argued that the effect of *Utah Pie* was to prohibit large, but locally nondominant firms from engaging in aggressive price competition against rivals, even if the rivals were larger than the price cutter and there was absolutely no chance that the market would be monopolized. The *Brooke* Court purports to distinguish rather than overrule *Utah Pie*, but the argument is hollow. At the beginning of the complaint period the plaintiff's (Utah Pie's) market share was 66.5%. The market shares of the defendants were: Carnation, 10.3%; Continental, 1.3%; and Pet, 16.4%. By the end of the complaint period the plaintiff's share had dropped to 45.3%, but it was still making a profit. Pet's share had risen to 29.4%. The other two defendants were much smaller. 386 U.S. at 692 n.7. The evidence showed vigorous price competition and widely varying market shares over a period of three or four years. Further, the three defendants actively competed against each other as well as the plaintiff.

3. *Brooke* implicitly overrules several circuit decisions that permit evidence of intent as a substitute for structural evidence in Robinson-Patman Act predatory pricing claims. *See, e.g., Henry v. Chloride, Inc.*, 809 F.2d 1334 (8th Cir. 1987) (requiring below cost prices but recognizing a possible violation upon a showing of price cut plus specific intent to harm a rival). *Accord Double H Plastics v. Sonoco Prods.*, 732 F.2d 351 (3d Cir. 1984).

4. What is the significance of *Brooke*'s conclusion that supracompetitive pricing during the recoupment period "entails" a reduction in output? In the actual case, output during the alleged "recoupment" period was higher than during the period just before predation began. In that set of circumstances, the Court concluded, "output in the generic segment can only have been restricted in the sense that it expanded at a slower rate than it would have absent [the defendant's] intervention." The Court then concluded that this was a "counterfactual" proposition, "difficult to prove in the best of circumstances." 509 U.S. at 233.

What does this mean? That predatory pricing can never be proven in a case where overall market output during the claimed recoupment period is higher than it had been before the alleged predation began? In the "classic" predation story, the market is competitive with an output of, say, 100 units. Then the predator drops price dramatically, and output necessarily rises, perhaps to 125 units. After rivals have been destroyed or disciplined, the market then becomes a monopoly (Sherman Act) or "disciplined oligopoly" (Robinson-Patman Act) with an output of, say, 80 units. By contrast, a "recoupment" output of 110 units would indicate that the price cut was profitable because it produced more sales, not because it was predatory.

Consider a blanket rule that below cost pricing is per se lawful if market output during the alleged recoupment period is higher than output during the period immediately before predation began. Does such a rule go too far? Suppose that the market was already an oligopoly before alleged predation began, as in *Brooke*, and that the purpose of the price cutting was simply to discipline a firm that was no longer adhering to the oligopoly.

5. In one important post-*Brooke* decision the Ninth Circuit held that structural characteristics of the Las Vegas market for retail gasoline necessitated summary judgment on a Sherman Act predatory pricing claim but not on a Robinson-Patman Act claim. *Rebel Oil Co. v. Atlantic Richfield Co (ARCO)*, 51 F.3d 1421, 1434 (9th Cir.), *cert. denied*, 516 U.S. 987 (1995). The Sherman Act claim failed because it

showed that two rivals of defendant ARCO, Texaco and Southland, could readily expand their output of gasoline, thus undermining any attempt by ARCO to effect a monopoly marketwide output reduction. *Id.* at 1441. But while the Sherman Act claim required the defendant to destroy or significantly disable these rivals, the Robinson-Patman oligopoly claim required the defendant to do no more than get the rivals to see that restraining their own output and adhering to an oligopoly price structure was in their own best interests. As the court explained:

> The economic forces at work in an oligopoly are very different than in a monopoly. A predator is able to establish and maintain supracompetitive prices in an oligopoly by making it too painful for its existing competitors to challenge its prices, and thus, "disciplining" them. This distinction between oligopolistic and monopolistic practices is crucial to the survival of Rebel's price discrimination claim. Read in the most favorable light, Rebel's evidence tends to indicate that no new competition can enter the market to challenge ARCO, and that the existing competition, while it may be able to challenge ARCO, lacks the will to do so.

As a general matter, convincing a smaller rival that it is in its own best interest to play the oligopoly game and thus make good profits is far easier than predating that rival into destruction. Indeed, after one or two brief "defections" from the oligopoly, followed by a period of predatory pricing-imposed losses, the maverick firm might learn that cutting price is not a profitable activity and adhere to the oligopoly.

NOTE: WHEN IS PREDATORY PRICING RATIONAL?

Not all markets are conducive to predatory pricing. Consider some of the pitfalls. First of all, it is illegal and can yield substantial damages, and there is at least some risk that the predator will be caught: no one is more likely to file an antitrust lawsuit than a competitor who has been driven out of business by prices that it has been unable to meet.

But legality aside, there are substantial economic difficulties facing any predator. Consider a manufacturer of swidgets, who is in competition with an equally efficient rival. The current (competitive) price of swidgets is $1.00. Suppose the manufacturer decides to destroy its competitor by selling swidgets at 80 cents. First of all, the manufacturer will have to increase its output substantially and many of the victim's customers will flock to the predator. The predator will have to have sufficient output to satisfy all of them. Worse yet, if the market has an average elasticity of demand, when the price of swidgets goes down by 20% the demand for swidgets will increase by 20% or 25%. In other words, the predator will have to sell additional swidgets (at 20 cents loss per swidget) not only to customers stolen from the victim, but also to new customers who enter the market at the lower price. In order to do all of this the predator may have to build a large amount of plant capacity that it does not intend to use permanently — for later, when the rival has been dispatched, the predator intends to charge a monopoly price (say, $1.20), and then demand for swidgets will drop. (The decrease in demand must, of course, be discounted by the amount that capacity in the market will be reduced by the victim's exit.)

What is the purpose of all this? The predator intends to incur all these losses now because it believes that future gains from monopoly pricing will more than offset the losses. First of all, we must consider the time-value of money. The predator sustains the losses immediately; the gains from expected monopoly pricing may be a year or even several years away. These dollars must be discounted to their present value. Secondly, what will happen when the predator eliminates its rival and raises the price to its monopolistic level? The supracompetitive profits will attract new entrants into the market and the predator will have to lower its price all over again.

Furthermore, the predator must consider what will become of the victim's plant. When a firm goes into bankruptcy it does not necessarily cease production. Sometimes it can reorganize; other times it can sell its plant and equipment to an existing company or a new entrant into the market. These possibilities are generally out of the predator's control. If the victim's plant remains in production the entire predation scheme will be frustrated.

It seems clear that before predatory pricing can be expected to succeed, certain prerequisites must be met. For example, barriers to entry in the market must be high enough that the predator can expect a relatively stable period of monopoly returns after the predation has done its work.

Even more importantly, the predator must have a relatively large market share. Consider a market with 10 firms, each with a 10% market share. Suppose that firm A tries to predate against firm D. When A lowers its price it will attract customers not only from D, but from all other competitors as well, and these competitors control 90% of the market. If A doubles its own output (selling every unit at a loss), the result will be to deprive each competitor of a little over 10% of its own sales — hardly enough to drive most firms out of business. And this does not even include the new customers who will enter the market at A's predatory price! Furthermore, suppose that A actually succeeded in driving D out of business. The concentration in the market would decrease from 10 firms to 9, and presumably the remaining 9 firms would share the defunct firm's customers. In that case, A's market share would rise from 10% to 11%. It would hardly be a monopolist.

If A has 90% of the market, however, while a single rival has 10%, then the picture is much different. Now a 10% output increase by A (ignoring customers who enter the market at the predatory price) will almost wipe out firm B. In short, before predatory pricing is likely to succeed the market must be relatively concentrated and conducive to monopolization; secondly, the putative predator must have a relatively large market share in relation to its intended victim. For further discussion of the market structures conducive to predatory pricing, *see* Joskow & Klevorick, *A Framework for Analyzing Predatory Pricing Policy*, 89 Yale L.J. 213 (1979).

Some commentators have gone so far as to argue that predatory pricing is *never* rational. *See Easterbrook, Predatory Strategies and Counterstrategies*, 48 U. Chi. L. Rev. 263 (1981); R. Bork, *The Antitrust Paradox: A Policy at War with Itself* 148-56 (1978). Others are less sure. They note, for example, that if there are legal or economic constraints on new entry into a market, or if the victim has substantially higher capital costs than the predator, predatory pricing might be plausible. Furthermore, predatory pricing might have high strategic values: it might be used, at relatively lower cost, merely to "discipline" rivals rather than drive them out of business. By so punishing one rival in one market, a predator could also "send a message" to other rivals in other markets. *See* R. Posner, *Antitrust Law: An Economic Perspective* 184-96 (1976); 3 P. Areeda & D. Turner, *Antitrust Law* 150-53 (1978). Finally, information about costs in an industry is generally more readily available to incumbents than it is to potential new entrants. If a potential entrant has imperfect information about an incumbent's true costs the challenger might view a predatory price as reflecting lower (but uncertain) costs and conclude that entry would be risky and unprofitable. *See* S.C. Salop, *Strategy, Predation, and Antitrust Analysis* 19-22 (1981).

The *Brooke* decision, *supra*, is not the first instance where the Supreme Court insisted that structural indicators be evaluated carefully in cases claiming predatory pricing. In *Cargill, Inc. v. Monfort of Colo., Inc.*, 479 U.S. 104, 119 n.15 (1986), the plaintiff charged that a merger might facilitate predatory pricing, the Supreme Court suggested that predation was unlikely, given that the defendant's share of market output was only 21% and its share of market capacity only 28.4%. Further, the defendant operated at nearly full capacity, thus making predation more expensive, since it would have to build additional plant capacity in order to enlarge output during the predatory period. In both *Cargill* and *Matsushita Elec. Indus. Co. v. Zenith Radio Corp.*, 475 U.S. 574 (1986), the Court noted that "without barriers to entry it would presumably be impossible to maintain supracompetitive prices for an extended time." *Matsushita*, 475 U.S. at 591-92 n.15; *Cargill, id.* The *Cargill* court also noted:

> In evaluating entry barriers in the context of a predatory pricing claim, ... a court should focus on whether significant entry barriers would exist *after* the merged firm had eliminated some of its rivals, because at that point the remaining firms would begin to charge supracompetitive prices, and the barriers that existed during competitive conditions might well prove insignificant. In this case, for example, although costs of entry into the current competitive market may be high, if Excel [the defendant] and others in fact succeeded in driving competitors out of the market, the facilities of the bankrupt competitors would then be available, and the record shows, without apparent contradiction, that shut-down plants could be producing efficiently in a matter of months and that equipment and a labor force could readily be obtained.

Id. The *Cargill* case is reprinted in Chapter 3, *supra*.

Since most courts deal with predatory pricing as an attempt to monopolize, they examine structural issues under the rubric of "dangerous probability of success" in creating a monopoly, or dominant firm. For example, *see International Distrib. Centers v. Walsh Trucking Co.*, 812 F.2d 786, 788 (2d Cir.), *cert. denied*, 482 U.S. 915 (1987), which rejected the plaintiff's argument that "there can be a dangerous probability that a market will be monopolized where one firm in the market has the specific intent to drive a competitor from the market and has engaged in arguably tortious activity to achieve that objective but does not have significant market power and will not possess such power even if the competitor is driven out of business." The court found entry into the market (shipping of clothing on hangers in trucks) to be extremely easy and noted that new shippers had entered the business even during the alleged predation period. It concluded that it "need not inquire" whether the defendant's prices were below its "reasonably anticipated marginal costs." *See also Shoppin' Bag of Pueblo v. Dillon Cos.*, 783 F.2d 159 (10th Cir. 1986), approving a jury verdict for the defendant where its market share was less than 38 percent.

Likewise, in *ITT Continental*, 104 F.T.C. 280 (1984), the FTC found predatory pricing implausible, given the market structure. The Commission concluded that sales below average variable costs might satisfy the "specific intent" and "anticompetitive conduct" elements of an attempted monopolization claim; but, "without more [they do not] satisfy the 'dangerous probability of success' requirement." 104 F.T.C. at 401-02. The Commission then concluded that "most courts have determined that market shares ranging from 40% to 60% prior to the commencement of a predatory strategy ordinarily must be established in order to prove the requisite dangerous probability of successful monopolization." *Id.* at 412.

The Commission continued:

> [O]ther industry characteristics may help determine whether a given absolute and relative share of the relevant market creates a dangerous probability of monopolization. The absence of substantial entry barriers, *ceteris paribus*, is particularly likely to eliminate that probability. Barriers to entry must be substantial for a predatory pricing strategy to succeed. Otherwise, when the predator attempts to raise prices to supracompetitive levels after the predation period, new firms will enter and/or terminated firms will reenter and force the predator to lower its prices to competitive levels....
>
> The record evidence indicates that barriers to entry into the bread baking industry are not particularly high....

The Seventh Circuit has concluded that unlawful predatory pricing under the Sherman Act is "highly unlikely unless the defendant already has monopoly power." *American Acad. Suppliers v. Beckley-Cardy*, 922 F.2d 1317, 1319 (7th Cir. 1991) (summary judgment for defendant). Likewise, the Fourth Circuit holds:

(1) claims of less than 30% market shares should presumptively be rejected; (2) claims involving between 30% and 50% shares should usually be rejected, except when conduct is very likely to achieve monopoly or when conduct is invidious, but not so much so as to make the defendant per se liable; (3) claims involving greater than 50% share should be treated as attempts at monopolization when the other elements for attempted monopolization are also satisfied.

M&M Med. Supplies & Serv. v. Pleasant Valley Hosp., 981 F.2d 160, 168 (4th Cir. 1992) (en banc). *See also U.S. Anchor Mfg. v. Rule Indus.*, 7 F.3d 986 (11th Cir. 1993) (50% not enough); *Barr Labs. v. Abbott Labs.*, 978 F.2d 98 (3d Cir. 1992) (refusing to find "dangerous probability of success" on a 50% market share, even when this was more than twice as large as nearest competitor).

Suppose that the individual market shares of a group of defendants are quite small, perhaps less than 20% each, but the plaintiff alleges that they have conspired to engage in predatory pricing. Does the allegation of conspiracy make predation on smaller, individual market shares plausible? The Supreme Court thought not in *Matsushita Elec. Indus. Co. v. Zenith Radio Corp.*, 475 U.S. 574 (1986):

> In this case, respondents allege that a large number of firms have conspired over a period of many years to charge below-market prices in order to stifle competition. Such a conspiracy is incalculably more difficult to execute than an analogous plan undertaken by a single predator. The conspirators must allocate the losses to be sustained during the conspiracy's operation, and must also allocate any gains to be realized from its success. Precisely because success is speculative and depends on a willingness to endure losses for an indefinite period, each conspirator has a strong incentive to cheat, letting its partners suffer the losses necessary to destroy the competition while sharing in any gains if the conspiracy succeeds. The necessary allocation is therefore difficult to accomplish. Yet if conspirators cheat to any substantial extent, the conspiracy must fail, because its success depends on depressing the market price for *all* buyers of [the predated product]. If there are too few goods at the artificially low price to satisfy demand, the would-be victims of the conspiracy can continue to sell at the "real" market price, and the conspirators suffer losses to little purpose.

475 U.S. at 590.

In *A. A. Poultry Farms v. Rose Acre Farms*, 881 F.2d 1396 (7th Cir. 1989), *cert. denied*, 494 U.S. 1019 (1990), the court found issues of market structure to be dispositive, making it unnecessary to inquire about the relationship between the defendant's prices and its costs. Further, once structural requirements were not met, the defendant's intent was irrelevant. The industry at issue, egg production, was relatively unconcentrated and had low entry barriers. In such a case, the court held,

> [i]t is much easier to determine from the structure of the market that recoupment is improbable than it is to find the cost a particular producer experiences in the short, middle, or long run (whichever proves pertinent). Market

structure offers a way to cut the inquiry off at the pass.... Only if market structure makes recoupment feasible need a court inquire into the relation between price and cost.

PROBLEM 6.9

For many years Autosound, Inc., has manufactured a highly successful radio sound system that included only an AM/FM receiver. It manufactures about 80% of all such systems. Its only competitor is Car Stereo, Inc., which has the remaining 20%. In recent years the market for car stereo systems having only a radio has declined substantially, for most purchasers prefer a system containing a radio integrated with a cassette tape or even CD player.

Autosound develops a new, integrated AM/FM-cassette-CD system and decides to exit from the market for radio-only car stereos. However, at the time it makes this decision it is stuck with very large inventories of the old system. Autosound decides that these inventories must be cleared out within one year, so it drops the price of the old system dramatically — even lower than the direct cost of parts plus assembly labor. Car Stereo's sales of its competing product plummet, and it sues Autosound, charging predatory pricing. Result? *See Olympia Equip. Leasing Co. v. Western Union Tel. Co.*, 797 F.2d 370 (7th Cir. 1986).

PROBLEM 6.10

For many years AAA Towing has had an exclusive contract with the City of Metropolis to provide towing services for stalled and illegally parked vehicles. Each year this towing franchise is put up for competitive bidding, but no one bids against AAA Towing. Two years ago AAA Towing won with a bid of $60 per tow.

Last year a newcomer, Rainbow Towing, decided to bid against AAA towing, believing it could do the job profitably for much less. Rainbow bid $52 per tow. But when the bids were opened AAA Towing had bid $40, and it retained the franchise. The following year no one bid against AAA, and its bid was $65.

Rainbow believes that the low bid in the single year in which AAA faced competition was predatory. It files suit, arguing that AAA engaged in predatory pricing in order to retain its franchise monopoly. What economic issues should be investigated? Is it significant that: (1) AAA's franchise with Metropolis is exclusive? *See National Reporting Co. v. Alderson Reporting Co.*, 763 F.2d 1020 (8th Cir. 1985); (2) AAA dropped its bid sharply when there was competition, but raised it again when there was none? *See Instructional Sys. Dev. v. Aetna Cas.*, 817 F.2d 639 (10th Cir. 1987).

NOTE: PREDATORY PRICING AND THE ROBINSON-PATMAN ACT

The Robinson-Patman Act, 15 U.S.C. § 13, makes it illegal for someone to sell the same product at two different prices where the effect is to injure "competition" as the statute defines it. The Robinson-Patman Act is commonly called a "price discrimination" statute. That term is a misnomer. Price discrimination occurs when two different sales are made at two different rates of return — that is, when the ratio of price to marginal cost is different in the two sales. The Robinson-Patman Act tags as "discriminatory," however, any two sales made at two different prices. For a fuller discussion of the difference, *see* H. Hovenkamp, *Federal Antitrust Policy*, ch. 14 (2d ed. 1994); E.T. Sullivan & J. Harrison, *Understanding Antitrust and Its Economic Implications*, ch. 8 (2d ed. 1994).

The offense that the framers of the Robinson-Patman Act had in mind was "geographic price-cutting," a particular form of predatory pricing. The framers believed that a large and powerful seller could "finance" predatory pricing by engaging in price discrimination. Their theory went like this: suppose that A and B are competitors in a certain market. B operates in only this market, but A is large and operates in other markets as well, and has monopoly power in some of these markets. A attempts to drive B out of business so that A can also acquire a monopoly in the market shared with B. A does this by pricing its output below cost in B's market. Meanwhile, however, A raises its price in other markets, where it has monopoly power, and uses these increased revenues to pay for the predatory pricing in the market shared with B.

Generally speaking, A's scheme is implausible. First of all, if A is a rational businessman and there are no legal or physical restraints on price discrimination, A is already selling its output in each market at the profit-maximizing price. A cannot simply raise its price in some markets in order to subsidize predatory pricing in a different market. If A raised its price in its monopoly markets to more than the profit-maximizing level, it would produce less, not more, net revenue.

One answer to the above objection, of course, is that the Robinson-Patman Act *is* a law against selling the same product in two different markets at two different prices. As a result, A may not be selling its output in each market at the profit-maximizing price for that market. Because of the Robinson-Patman Act A may be selling at its profit-maximizing price for all markets taken together, but if it could segregate the markets and avoid the law it could obtain higher profits by selling at higher prices in some of them. For example, suppose that A sells in three different markets, Detroit, Atlanta, and Salt Lake City. It has monopoly power in Detroit and Atlanta but faces competition in Salt Lake City. The profit-maximizing monopoly price in Detroit and Atlanta, considered by themselves, would be $1.00. Because of competition, however, A's profit-maximizing price in Salt Lake City is 90 cents. If A prices at more than 90 cents in Salt Lake City most of A's customers there will turn to A's rivals.

If A is legally prohibited from selling its output at different prices in different markets, A must choose either to sell in all three markets at 90 cents, in all three markets at $1.00, or in all three markets at some price between 90 cents and $1.00. Under some circumstances it might be profit-maximizing to sell in all three markets at 90 cents, particularly if Salt Lake City (the competitive market) were much larger than the two monopoly markets.

Suppose that *A* decided that its profit-maximizing price in the three markets taken together is 90 cents, and it has been selling at that price. Now *A* decides to drive *B*, its competitor in Salt Lake City, out of business by lowering its price there to 80 cents. Once *B* has been dispatched, *A* can raise its price in all three markets. Absent any legal sanction, *A* might in fact be able to price its output in Detroit and Atlanta at $1.00 and obtain more revenue, since the profit-maximizing price in each of those markets considered alone is $1.00. The Robinson-Patman Act, however, will require *A* to reduce its price to 80 cents in all three markets.

In short, the statute *can* make predatory pricing more expensive for a seller who operates in many markets but wants to predate only in one. It will have to lower its price in all markets simultaneously. Furthermore, predatory pricing is relatively easy to conceal. One can identify it today only by looking at complex cost figures that may be in the exclusive control of the predator. Under the prevailing judicial tests, predatory pricing is a function either of the alleged predator's marginal costs, or else of its average variable costs. Both are likely to be information generally unavailable to competitors. The former is additionally very difficult to determine even if cost information is made available. See the discussion of the Areeda-Turner test for predatory pricing, *infra.*

In most cases, however, price differences are not so easy to conceal, although sometimes they can be kept secret. *See O. Hommel Co. v. Ferro Corp.*, 659 F.2d 340 (3d Cir. 1981), *cert. denied*, 455 U.S. 1017 (1982).

Thus the Robinson-Patman Act can sometimes make price predation by certain sellers (particularly those that operate in more markets than their victims) much more expensive. The statute might require such a predator to lower its prices in all markets, not merely the predated market. By contrast, if the predator decides to cut prices only in the predated market, the activity will be easier to discover and condemn.

However, the effect of a law against differential pricing in different geographic markets is not as simple as the above illustration suggests. To be sure, the primary-line application of the Robinson-Patman Act may make predatory pricing more expensive. Ironically, however, the statute makes *competitive* pricing in Salt Lake City in the above illustration more expensive too, for exactly the same reason.

Suppose, for example, that *A* has had a monopoly in all three markets for some time and has enjoyed supracompetitive profits from making sales in all three markets at $1.00 each. Now *B* enters Salt Lake City and begins price-cutting to a competitive price of 90 cents. The Robinson-Patman Act may put *A* to the difficult choice of dropping its price to 90 cents in *all three markets* in order to preserve its position in Salt Lake City, or else simply closing its outlets in Salt Lake City, effectively conceding a monopoly to *B*. The latter option may indeed be more attractive, particularly if the Salt Lake City market is relatively small. In short, a statute prohibiting geographic price differences is just as likely to prohibit competitive pricing as it is to prohibit predatory pricing. Which of the two it does more often depends on which of the two (competitive or predatory pricing) occurs more often. Today courts are inclined to think that predatory pricing is extraordinarily difficult to accomplish and that it occurs only infrequently. If that is true it is likely that the Robinson-Patman Act condemns more instances of competitive pricing than of predatory pricing.

One solution to this dilemma is to interpret the Robinson-Patman Act in such a way as to condemn differential pricing when it is predatory, but tolerate it when it is competitive. How does one tell whether a particular instance of differential pricing is competitive or predatory? In general, one must determine if the sales in the market alleged to be predatory are made below cost and with the reasonable expectation that they will dispatch competitors from the market or discipline them in order to permit the predator to price monopolistically later.

This determination is identical with the determination that courts make today in cases alleging predatory pricing under §2 of the Sherman Act. The reason for this similarity of analysis seems clear: the presence or absence of differential pricing or price discrimination in a different geographic market is *absolutely irrelevant* to the question whether a seller is engaging in predatory pricing in a particular market. Although a law against differential pricing makes both predation and intense competition in a single market more expensive for a firm that sells the same product in other markets as well, the presence of differential pricing is of absolutely no help to a court in distinguishing whether the pricing in the low-priced market is predatory or competitive. In order to determine if pricing in the low-priced market is predatory, the court must analyze the relationship between the defendant's prices and its costs in that market. Pricing in the low-priced market is predatory if the only reasonable explanation for the pricing is that the defendant is selling at below cost today in order to drive competitors from the market so that it can price monopolistically tomorrow.

The trend in recent circuit antitrust cases is to treat predatory pricing claims brought under the Robinson-Patman Act in virtually the same way that predatory pricing is analyzed as an attempt to monopolize under section 2 of the Sherman Act. *See, e.g., A. A. Poultry Farms v. Rose Acre Farms*, 881 F.2d 1396 (7th Cir. 1989) (applying the same test under both statutes). *Brooke Group Ltd. v. Brown & Williamson Tobacco Corp.*, reprinted *supra*, illustrates both the similarities and the differences between predatory pricing analysis under the Sherman Act and the Robinson-Patman Act.

2. IDENTIFYING THE PREDATORY PRICE

The *Brooke* decision makes clear that predatory pricing claims can be sustained only under narrowly defined structural conditions that involve either monopoly or oligopoly, high entry barriers, and thus the prospect of a sustained "recoupment" period following the predatory campaign. But the *offense* of predatory pricing consists of the defendant's intentional selection of a particular price for its value in excluding, disciplining, or destroying competition. Identifying that price has been the subject of considerable judicial dispute. The *Brooke* decision provided a little guidance by its dicta suggesting that the defendant's price must be "below an appropriate measure of its rival's costs," and then elaborating:

> [W]e have rejected elsewhere the notion that above-cost prices that are below general market levels or the costs of a firm's competitors inflict injury to competition cognizable under the antitrust laws. See *Atlantic Richfield Co. v. USA Petroleum Co.*, 495 U.S. 328, 340 (1990). "Low prices benefit consumers regardless of how those prices are set, and so long as they are above predatory levels, they do not threaten competition.... We have adhered to this principle regardless of the type of antitrust claim involved." *Ibid.* As a general rule, the exclusionary effect of prices above a relevant measure of cost either reflects the lower cost structure of the alleged predator, and so represents competition on the merits, or is beyond the practical ability of a judicial tribunal to control without courting intolerable risks of chilling legitimate price-cutting....

BARRY WRIGHT CORP. V. ITT GRINNELL CORP.

724 F.2d 227 (1st Cir. 1983)

[Pacific and Barry competed for the business of selling "snubbers" — shock absorbers for nuclear power plants — to ITT Grinnell. Grinnell had a contract with Barry to supply snubbers, but when Barry was unable to meet the production schedule, Grinnell turned to Pacific. Pacific then gave Grinnell a very large discount, as much as 30 percent off its ordinary list price. Barry then sued, alleging that Pacific was engaging, among other things, in predatory pricing.]

BREYER, JUDGE.

Barry first attacks the special 30 percent/25 percent discounts that Pacific granted Grinnell. It argues that Pacific's discounted prices were unreasonably low. This argument founders, however, on the district court finding that these prices, while lower than normal, nonetheless generated revenues more than sufficient to cover the total cost of producing the goods to which they applied. Barry does not attack that finding; but, instead, it argues that price cutting by a monopolist may still prove unlawful, even if prices remain above total cost. While some circuits have accepted a form of Barry's argument, we do not.

To understand the basis of our disagreement, one must ask why the Sherman Act *ever* forbids price cutting. After all, lower prices help consumers. The competitive marketplace that the antitrust laws encourage and protect is characterized by firms willing and able to cut prices in order to take customers from their rivals. And, in an economy with a significant number of concentrated industries, price cutting limits the ability of large firms to exercise their "market power," *see*

J. Bain, *Industrial Organization* ch. 5 (2d ed. 1968); F. Scherer, *Industrial Market Structure and Economic Performance* 56-70, 222-25 (2d ed. 1980); at a minimum it likely moves "concentrated market" prices in the "right" direction — towards the level they would reach under competitive conditions. See 2 P. Areeda & D. Turner, *Antitrust Law* ¶ 404; J. Bain, *supra*, at 118-23; F. Scherer, *supra*, ch. 5. Thus, a legal precedent or rule of law that prevents a firm from unilaterally cutting its prices risks interference with one of the Sherman Act's most basic objectives: the low price levels that one would find in well-functioning competitive markets.

Despite these considerations, courts have reasoned that it is sometimes possible to identify circumstances in which a price cut will make consumers worse off, not better off. Suppose, for example, a firm cuts prices to unsustainably low levels — prices below "incremental" costs. Suppose it drives competitors out of business, and later on it raises prices to levels higher than it could have sustained had its competitors remained in the market. Without special circumstances there is little to be said in economic or competitive terms for such a price cut. Yet, how often firms engage in such "predatory" price cutting, whether they ever do so, and precisely when, is all much disputed — a dispute that is not surprising given the difficulties of measuring costs, discerning intent, and predicting future market conditions.

Despite this dispute, there is general agreement that a profit-maximizing firm might sometimes find it rational to engage in predatory pricing; it might do so if it knows (1) that it can cut prices deeply enough to outlast and to drive away all competitors, and (2) that it can then raise prices high enough to recoup lost profits (and then some) before new competitors again enter the market. *See* Areeda & Turner, *Predatory Pricing and Related Practices Under Section 2 of the Sherman Act*, 88 Harv. L. Rev. 697, 698-99 (1975). There is also general agreement that the antitrust courts' major task is to set rules and precedents that can segregate the economically harmful price-cutting goats from the more ordinary price-cutting sheep, in a manner precise enough to avoid discouraging desirable price-cutting activity.

Barry, of course, suggests that Pacific's price cut is a "goat," arguing that Pacific "intended" to drive Barry from the market place. Some courts have written as if one might look to a firm's "intent to harm" to separate "good" from "bad." *See, e.g., D.E. Rogers Associates, Inc. v. Gardner-Denver Co.*, 718 F.2d 1431, 1435-36 (6th Cir. 1983). But "intent to harm" without more offers too vague a standard in a world where executives may think no further than "Let's get more business," and long-term effects on consumers depend in large measure on competitors' responses. Moreover, if the search for intent means a search for documents or statements specifically reciting the likelihood of anticompetitive consequences or of subsequent opportunities to inflate prices, the knowledgeable firm will simply refrain from overt description. If it is meant to refer to a set of objective economic conditions that allow the court to "infer" improper intent, then, using Occam's razor, we can slice "intent" away. Thus, most courts now find their standard, not in intent, but in the relation of the suspect price to the firm's costs. And, despite the absence of any perfect touchstone, modern antitrust courts look to the relation of price to "avoidable" or "incremental" costs as a way of segregating price cuts that are "suspect" from those that are not.

One can understand the intuitive idea behind this test by supposing, for example, that a firm charges prices that fail to cover these "avoidable" or "incremental" costs — the costs that the firm would save by not producing the additional product it can sell at that price. Suppose further that the firm cannot show that this low price is "promotional," e.g., a "free sample." Nor can it show that it expects costs to fall when sales increase. Then one would know that the firm cannot rationally plan to maintain this low price; if it does not expect to raise its price, it would do better to discontinue production. Moreover, equally efficient competitors cannot permanently match this low price and stay in business. Further, competitive industries are typically characterized by prices that are roughly equal to, not below, "incremental" costs. At a minimum, one would wonder why this firm would cut prices on "incremental production" below its "avoidable" costs unless it later expected to raise its prices and recoup its losses. When prices exceed incremental costs, one cannot argue that they must rise for the firm to stay in business. Nor will such prices have a tendency to exclude or eliminate equally efficient competitors. Moreover, a price *cut* that leaves prices above incremental costs was probably moving prices in the "right" direction — towards the competitive norm. These considerations have typically led courts to question, and often to forbid, price cuts below "incremental costs," (or "avoidable costs"), while allowing those where the resulting price is higher.

In fact, the use of cost-based standards is more complicated than this brief discussion suggests. But, we need not explore here the arguments about how best to measure "incremental" or "avoidable" costs (e.g., whether "average variable cost" is an appropriate surrogate). Nor need we consider the theoretical difficulties that arise when prices fall *between* "incremental costs" and "average (total) costs," a circumstance that can arise either when production is at a level below full capacity and the firm lowers prices to levels that do not cover a "fair share" of fixed costs or when a plant is pushed beyond its "full" capacity at prices that do not cover the specially high costs of the extraordinary production levels.

Here we have a price that exceeds *both* "average cost" and "incremental cost" — that exceeds cost however plausibly measured. And as to those prices, "virtually every court and commentator agrees" that they are lawful, "perhaps conclusively, but at least presumptively." P. Areeda & D. Turner, *Antitrust Law* ¶ 711.1c at 118 (1982 Supp.).

Barry points, however, to a possible exception to this rule — an "exception" created by the Ninth Circuit making certain price cuts unlawful even when the resulting revenues exceed total costs. In *Inglis*, that circuit held that a price cut is unlawful if the anticipated benefits of defendant's price depended on its tendency to discipline or eliminate competition and thereby enhance the firm's long-term ability to reap the benefits of monopoly power.

668 F.2d at 1035. In the Ninth Circuit's view, prices below "average variable costs" (a surrogate for "incremental costs") produce a presumption of "predatory pricing." When prices exceed "average variable cost," but are below average total cost, the plaintiff must prove by a preponderance of the evidence that the defendant's pricing policy depends on its exclusionary or disciplinary tendency. And, in a case like this one — a case that the Ninth Circuit would describe as "prices above average total cost" — the plaintiff can still win if it proves "by clear and convincing evidence — *i.e.*, that it is highly probably true — that the defendant's pricing policy was predatory," in the sense defined in *Inglis. Transamerica Computer Co. v. International Business Machines Corp.*, 698 F.2d at 1388.

The virtue of the Ninth Circuit test is that it recognizes an economic circumstance in which even "above total cost" price cutting might not be procompetitive and might, in theory, hurt the consumer. For instance, if a dominant firm's costs are lower than its competitors', it could use an "above cost" price cut to drive out competition, and then later raise prices to levels higher than they otherwise would be. Moreover, if the price cut meant *less* profit for the firm *unless* (1) it drove out competitors *and* (2) higher prices later followed, the cut might be viewed as lying outside the range of normal, desirable, competitive processes. Even though such a price cut would only injure or eliminate firms that were less efficient than the price-cutter, one could argue that, other things being equal, their continued presence helps the competitive process (say, by constraining price rises) and may lead to greater efficiency in the future. Why should the antitrust laws not forbid this potentially harmful behavior? Indeed, economists have identified this type of pricing behavior (and certain other forms of above-cost pricing behavior) as potentially harmful.

Nonetheless, while technical economic discussion helps to inform the antitrust laws, those laws cannot precisely replicate the economists' (sometimes conflicting) views. For, unlike economics, law is an administrative system the effects of which depend upon the content of rules and precedents only as they are applied by judges and juries in courts and by lawyers advising their clients. Rules that seek to embody every economic complexity and qualification may well, through the vagaries of administration, prove counter-productive, undercutting the very economic ends they seek to serve. Thus, despite the theoretical possibility of finding instances in which horizontal price fixing, or vertical price fixing, are economically justified, the courts have held them unlawful per se, concluding that the administrative virtues of simplicity outweigh the occasional "economic" loss. Conversely, we must be concerned lest a rule or precedent that authorizes a search for a particular type of undesirable pricing behavior end up by discouraging legitimate price competition. Indeed, it is this risk that convinces us not to follow the Ninth Circuit's approach.

Thus, we believe we should not adopt the Ninth Circuit's exception because of the *combined effect* of the following considerations. For one thing, a price cut that ends up with a price exceeding total cost — in all likelihood a cut made by a firm with market power — is almost certainly moving price in the "right" direction (towards the level that would be set in a competitive marketplace). The antitrust laws very rarely reject such beneficial "birds in hand" for the sake of more speculative (future low-price) "birds in the bush." To do so opens the door to similar speculative claims that might seek to legitimate even the most settled unlawful practices. (Should a price-fixer be allowed to argue that a cartel will help weaker firms survive bad times, leaving them as a competitive force when times are good? Suppose the price-fixer offers to "prove it" by "clear and convincing evidence?")

For another thing, the scope of the Ninth Circuit's test is vague. Is it meant to include, for example, "limit pricing" — the common practice of firms in concentrated industries not to price "too high" for fear of attracting new competition? The "anticipated benefits" of such a price arguably depend "on its tendency to discipline or eliminate competition" thereby enhancing "the firm's long-term ability to reap the benefits of monopoly power." Does the test mean to include every common instance of a firm (with market power) deciding not to raise its prices? If it means to include either of these sorts of circumstances, the rule risks making of the antitrust laws a powerful force for price increases. But, if the rule does not mean to include these sorts of circumstance, which prices do, and which do not, fall within the test's proscription?

Further, even were the test more specific, it seems to us as a practical matter most difficult to distinguish in any particular case between a firm that is cutting price to "discipline" or to displace a rival and one cutting price "better to compete." No one would condemn a price cut designed to maximize profits in the short run, *i.e.*, by increasing sales at the lower price, not by destroying competition and then raising prices. But the general troubles surrounding proof of firm costs only hint at the difficulty of deciding whether or not a firm's price cut is profit-maximizing in the short-run, a determination that hinges not only on cost data, but also on elasticity of demand, competitors' responses to price shifts, and changes in unit costs with variations in production volume. Direct statements by firm executives concerning their expectations will probably not be found; and, one might ask, in light of uncertain and changing market conditions, how much will the firm itself know? One can foresee conflicting testimony by economic experts, with the eventual determination made, not by economists or accountants, but by a jury. Of course, one might claim that such are the dangers inherent in many antitrust cases. But the consequence of a mistake here is not simply to force a firm to forego legitimate business activity it wishes to pursue; rather, it is to penalize a procompetitive price cut, perhaps the most desirable activity (from an antitrust perspective) that can take place in a concentrated industry where prices typically exceed costs.

Additionally, if private plaintiffs are allowed to attack the "above total cost disciplinary price," we are unlikely to lack for plaintiffs willing to make the effort. After all, even the most competitive of price cuts may hurt rivals; indeed, such may well be its object....

Finally, we ask ourselves what advice a lawyer ... would have to give a client firm considering procompetitive price-cutting tactics in a concentrated industry. Would he not have to point out the risks of suit — whether ultimately successful or not — by an injured competitor claiming that the cut was "disciplinary?" Price cutting in concentrated industries seems sufficiently difficult to stimulate that we hesitate before embracing a rule that could, in practice, stabilize "tacit cartels" and further encourage interdependent pricing behavior. This risk could be minimized only if the conditions imposed by the words "clear and convincing evidence" were so stringent that the claim could almost never be proved....

In sum, we believe that such above-cost price cuts are typically sustainable; that they are normally desirable (particularly in concentrated industries); that the "disciplinary cut" is difficult to distinguish in practice; that it, in any event, primarily injures only higher cost competitors; that its presence may well be "wrongly" asserted in a host of cases involving legitimate competition; and that to allow its assertion threatens to "chill" highly desirable procompetitive price cutting. For these reasons, we believe that a precedent allowing this type of attack on prices that exceed both incremental and average costs would more likely interfere with the procompetitive aims of the antitrust laws than further them. Hence, we conclude that the Sherman Act does not make unlawful prices that exceed both incremental and average costs.

NOTES AND QUESTIONS

1. *The Areeda-Turner test for predatory pricing.* One of the major doctrinal developments in antitrust has been the proposal of the Areeda-Turner test for predatory pricing and its consideration by various federal circuit courts. The Supreme Court has not yet approved the test, and the Circuit courts, while generally applying it, disagree about many details.

The orthodox statement of the Areeda-Turner test is as follows:

(1) With respect to a monopolist's general (non-discriminatory) pricing in the market in which he has monopoly power:

(A) A short-run profit-maximizing ... price is non-predatory ....

(B) A price at or above full cost is non-predatory ....

(C) A price at or above reasonably anticipated short-run marginal cost is non-predatory ....

(D) Unless at or above full cost, a price below reasonably anticipated short-run marginal cost is predatory, and the monopolist may not defend on the grounds that his price was "promotional" or merely met an equally low price of a competitor.

(2) Recognizing that marginal cost data are often unavailable, we conclude that:

> (A) A price at or above reasonably anticipated average variable cost should be presumed lawful.
>
> (B) A price below reasonably anticipated average variable cost should be conclusively presumed unlawful.

3 P. Areeda & D. Turner, *Antitrust Law* ¶ 711d (1978). Subsequent revisions and the case law are discussed in 3 P. Areeda & H. Hovenkamp, *Antitrust Law* ¶¶ 724c, 735, 739-40 (rev. ed. 1996).

Areeda and Turner reasoned this way: over the long run no firm will stay in business unless it can recover its total costs. Total costs include *fixed* costs (such as plant, property taxes, and most kinds of equipment), which do not vary with output; and *variable* costs (such as most labor costs, raw materials, and utilities) which do vary with output. In order to recover its total costs, a firm must price each unit of its output at average total cost, or "average cost." Average cost is total cost divided by the number of units of output.

Although we would expect a profit-seeking firm to price its output at or above average cost over the long run, there are occasions when firms must sell their output at less than average cost. Sometimes they need money quickly; sometimes they are stuck with excess inventory that may spoil or become obsolete. In short, a price below average total cost can be profit-maximizing (or loss-minimizing) in the short run. For that reason, a rule that condemned pricing at below average total cost would make competitive behavior illegal, and might cause extreme waste of valuable resources. Suppose, for example, that there were a legal rule that forbade a farmer from selling ripe peaches, or a car dealer from selling year-end models, at a reduced price merely because the lower price would be less than the average total cost of producing the product.

But what about pricing at below short-run marginal cost? Short-run marginal cost is the cost incurred by a seller in producing and selling one additional unit of output. Since fixed costs are costs that do not vary with changes in output, short-run marginal cost is a function of variable costs alone. To sell a unit at less than short-run marginal cost is to obtain less money for it than the cost of producing it or — if it is already produced — of bringing it to market. In short, a sale at less than short-run marginal cost produces losses in *both* the short run and the long run. Areeda and Turner conclude that a price below short-run marginal cost is never reasonable unless it can be explained only as an attempt to drive rivals out of business so that the seller can charge a higher (monopoly) price later.

As a result, Areeda and Turner label a price below short-run marginal cost as "predatory." They observe, however, that marginal cost is an artificial concept thrown about largely by economists. Marginal cost measures an incremental change in producer output, but this amount itself varies at differing rates of output. Few businesses have comprehensive knowledge of marginal costs at any particular level of output, and it is virtually impossible to establish in litigation. The same thing is not true of average variable cost, however. Once we have identified certain costs — such as labor and raw materials — as "variable" over a certain period of time, then we can compute average variable cost simply by dividing the sum of those costs by the output during the same time period. Accountants can generally give testimony about a firm's average variable costs, but not about its marginal costs. Areeda and Turner therefore propose using average variable cost as a surrogate for short-run marginal cost. Thus they conclude that a price reasonably anticipated to be above average variable cost should be considered lawful, while a price below reasonably anticipated average variable cost should be conclusively presumed unlawful.

Figure 2

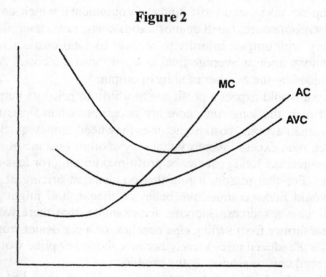

Figure 2 illustrates what is perhaps the greatest problem of the Areeda-Turner average variable cost test. At high levels of output (and predatory pricing generally occurs at high levels of output) marginal cost and average variable cost tend to diverge, with marginal cost higher than average variable cost. The result is that the Areeda-Turner test may excuse many instances of actual price predation. In fact, if a predator knows that its jurisdiction has adopted the Areeda-Turner test it can compute its average variable costs and add to the sales price, thereby engaging in legal predatory pricing — because such pricing at high levels of output would probably be lower than the seller's short-run marginal costs. *See* H. Hovenkamp, *Federal Antitrust Poli*cy § 8.3a (2d ed. 1994). For this reason one commentator has described the Areeda-Turner rule as a "defendant's paradise." *See* Williamson, *Predatory Pricing: A Strategic and Welfare Analysis*, 87 Yale L.J. 284, 305 (1977).

Some courts, such as the Ninth Circuit in the *Inglis* case, have responded to this difficulty in the Areeda-Turner test by accepting the basic Areeda-Turner cost paradigm but minimizing the use to which they put it. In *Inglis*, for example, the Ninth Circuit changed the conclusive presumptions of the Areeda-Turner test into rebuttable presumptions that invited consideration, at least in part, of the defendant's subjective intent. To be sure, such a modification comes with its own difficulties; most importantly, evaluation of subjective intent — the so-called smoking gun — is precisely the kind of thing that Areeda and Turner want to avoid. Their test is designed to enable a court to identify price predation by looking purely at pricing behavior. On the other hand, the Areeda-Turner test runs afoul of the criticism that although it may measure something more accurately than the older subjective tests, the thing that it measures is not really predatory pricing.

In spite of conceptual problems, no one has come up with a better test than average variable cost, and it has its supporters even among economists. *See, e.g.,* W. Baumol, *Predation and the Logic of the Average Variable Cost Test*, 39 J.L. & Econ. 49, 72 (1996) (average variable cost "is really the pertinent criterion, and not merely an inferior proxy for marginal cost").

2. The Areeda-Turner test is a very difficult one for plaintiffs to meet and few have been successful under its orthodox formulation. Among the few victories — and both in courts that have very considerably modified the Areeda-Turner formulation — are *U.S. Philips Corp. v. Windmere Corp.*, 861 F.2d 695 (4th Cir. 1988), *cert. denied*, 490 U.S. 1068 (1989); *D&S Redi-Mix v. Sierra Redi-Mix & Contr'g Co.*, 692 F.2d 1245 (9th Cir. 1982).

Many circuits have accepted the Areeda-Turner test for predatory pricing without substantial qualification. For example, *Northeastern Tel. Co. v. AT&T*, 651 F.2d 76, 88 (2d Cir. 1981): "We agree with Areeda and Turner that in the general case at least, the relationship between a firm's prices and its marginal costs provides the best single determinant of predatory pricing." *National Ass'n of Regulatory Util. Comm'rs v. Federal Commun. Comm'n*, 525 F.2d 630, 638 n.34 (D.C. Cir. 1976); *International Air Indus. v. American Excelsior Co.*, 517 F.2d 714, 724 (5th Cir. 1975).

Other circuits have recognized the value of the average variable cost standard, but have indicated a willingness to consider other factors such as specific intent. *See, e.g., William Inglis & Sons Baking Co. v. ITT Continental Baking Co.*, 668 F.2d 1014 (9th Cir. 1981), *cert. denied*, 459 U.S. 825 (1982):

> [A]lthough we have approved the use of marginal or average variable cost statistics in proving predation, "we have not held that mode of proof to be exclusive." ...
>
> Our approach ... is to focus on what a rational firm would have expected its prices to accomplish.... [A] price should be considered predatory if its anticipated benefits depended on its tendency to eliminate competition. If the justification for a price reduction did not depend upon this anticipated effect, then it does not support a claim of attempted monopolization, even if it had

the actual effect of taking sales from competitors. We emphasize a defendant's rational expectations to avoid penalizing innocent miscalculations that result in anticipated profits being turned into losses, with damaging effects on competitors. Our focus does not require that plaintiffs in all cases come forward with evidence of the defendant's subjective state of mind. Predatory pricing may be proved by examining the relationship between the defendant's prices and costs. But such proof must tend to show that the anticipated benefits of the prices, at the time they were set, depended on their anticipated destructive effect upon competition and the consequent enhanced market position of the defendant. ...

Although pricing below average total cost in the short term may be legitimate, it is less likely that pricing below average variable cost will be. Such pricing, if sustained, will not permit the recovery of any portion of the firm's fixed costs. In addition, the firm, because it cannot recover all its variable costs, has out-of-pocket losses on each unit it sells. The economic case for discontinuance of production is strong.

Although pricing below average total cost and above average variable cost is not inherently predatory, it does not follow, however, that such prices are never predatory. Predation exists when the justification of these prices is based, not on their effectiveness in minimizing losses, but on their tendency to eliminate rivals and create a market structure enabling the seller to recoup his losses. This is the ultimate standard, and not rigid adherence to a particular cost-based rule, that must govern our analysis of alleged predatory pricing.

Guided by these principles, we hold that to establish predatory pricing a plaintiff must prove that the anticipated benefits of defendant's price depended on its tendency to discipline or eliminate competition and thereby enhance the firm's long-term ability to reap the benefits of monopoly power. If the defendant's prices were below average total cost but above average variable cost, the plaintiff bears the burden of showing defendant's pricing was predatory. If, however, the plaintiff proves that the defendant's prices were below average variable cost, the plaintiff has established a prima facie case of predatory pricing and the burden shifts to the defendant to prove that the prices were justified without regard to any anticipated destructive effect they might have on competitors.

3. The *Barry Wright* court expressly disagreed with an earlier Ninth Circuit holding that prices above average total cost can be predatory if predation is established by "clear and convincing" evidence. In that case, *Transamerica Computer Co. v. IBM*, 698 F.2d 1377 (9th Cir. 1983), the Ninth Circuit considered allegations that IBM drove a less efficient rival out of business by price cutting. The Ninth Circuit concluded that the cuts were legal, but also said the following:

[P]rices exceeding average total cost might nevertheless be predatory in some circumstances. The specific example [is] "limit pricing," in which a monopolist sets prices above average total cost but below the short-term profit-maximizing level so as to discourage new entrants and thereby maximize profits over the long run. We [previously] explained that "limit pricing by a monopolist might, on a record which presented the issue, be held an impermissible predatory practice." *CalComp*, 613 F.2d at 743. A similar pricing strategy would be for a monopolist to make *temporary* reductions to a level above average total cost but below the profit-maximizing price whenever a new entrant appears ready to enter the market. One or two such reductions could discourage potential entrants in a market that requires sizable initial investments, leaving the monopolist free to raise his prices to monopoly levels. Such a pricing strategy, like limit pricing, could well be found predatory.

    ... One critic of the Areeda-Turner test points out that a monopolist can employ price strategies that jeopardize consumers' long-run welfare without lowering prices below average total cost and concludes that "it is unrealistic and even analytically wrong to apply a simple short-run price-cost rule for determining whether exclusionary pricing by a monopolist is socially undesirable and therefore predatory." Scherer, *Predatory Pricing and the Sherman Act: A Comment*, 89 Harv. L. Rev. 869, 890 (1976). It may be difficult in many or most instances to assess the long-run consequences of challenged pricing policies. But where those difficulties can be overcome, the law should not prevent plaintiffs from proving antitrust violations....

    For these reasons, we disagree with the district court's conclusion that prices above average total cost should be legal *per se*....

    ... [However,] it is appropriate to impose on the plaintiff a greater burden of proving that prices above average total cost are predatory than the burden imposed by *Inglis* to prove that prices between average variable and average total cost are predatory. We therefore hold that if the challenged prices exceed average total cost, the plaintiff must prove by clear and convincing evidence — i.e., that it is highly probably true — that the defendant's pricing policy was predatory.

However, strong dicta in *Brooke Group*, supra, stated that prices could not be found predatory under the Robinson-Patman Act unless they were below some measure of the defendant's cost. Since the Robinson-Patman Act deals with predatory pricing more aggressively than the Sherman Act does, shouldn't the Sherman Act test be at least as strenuous?

The Eleventh Circuit adheres to an average *total* cost test for predatory pricing. *McGahee v. Northern Propane Gas Co.*, 858 F.2d 1487, 1501 (11th Cir. 1988), reasoned as follows:

    The predatory pricing test requires a cost standard below which it may be inferred that a defendant violated the antitrust statutes. The Sherman Act and its legislative history do not offer guidance as to what measure of cost is relevant, except indicating that, as a codification of the common law, Sherman Act violations could be proven in part through objective evidence. The legislative histories of both the Clayton Act and the Robinson-Patman Act, on the other hand, both offer specific guidance. The Robinson-Patman Act itself uses the word "cost," which should be interpreted as meaning all costs. Moreover, the legislative history specifically explains that a seller cannot sell at average variable cost, without covering any fixed costs, even if he has excess capacity. Furthermore, the Robinson-Patman Act's legislative history refers to "the necessary minimum of profits or of actual costs;" the Clayton Act's legislative history refers to "below cost or without a fair profit." In economic terms, the cost of capital, which can be understood as the expected profit necessary to induce investors to invest, are also costs. Including the cost of capital, expressed by Congress as "a fair profit" and as "the necessary minimum profit," indicates Congress intended all costs to be part of the standard.

Are you convinced that this legislative history unambiguously declares the standard to be average total cost? More importantly, to the extent it suggests that a price below average total cost but above average variable cost cannot be profit maximizing, the legislative history is simply wrong as a matter of economics. When market conditions are so bad that a firm cannot charge enough to cover all its costs, it will nevertheless be better off it can cover all its variable cost plus make some contribution to its fixed costs. For example, if fixed costs in a given month are $1000 and variable costs are $500, a firm would have to obtain $1500 in revenues in order to be fully profitable. However, a firm that obtained $1200 would still be far better off than a firm that did not produce at all. That firm could at least put $700 toward its fixed cost, while the firm that shut down would still have to pay but could contribute nothing at all. For extensive criticism of the *McGahee* holding, *see* 3 P. Areeda & H. Hovenkamp, *Antitrust Law* ¶ 741 (rev. ed. 1996).

4. One of the disappointments of the Areeda-Turner test is the difficulty that courts have had in computing average variable cost. The premise of the test is that in most cases marginal cost is the correct measure of predation, but that average variable cost is a useful surrogate because it is usually close enough and it is much easier to compute. Theoretically, variable costs change with changes in output over a defined time period, while fixed costs do not. But the time period must be defined, and excess capacity does quirky things with cost measurement. For example, if a baker's oven is designed to hold 100 loaves of bread, it may cost no more in fuel to bake 100 loaves than to bake 50. As a result, when increasing from 50 to 100 loaves the baker encounters no fuel cost increase, and this would suggest that fuel is a fixed cost. However, as soon as the baker goes to 101 loaves it will have to run the oven twice (or get a second oven), and this suggests that fuel and perhaps even the oven are variable costs.

In *Inglis, supra,* the Ninth Circuit approached the problem this way:

> It is true, of course, that the fixed production costs of a firm are those costs that do not vary with output and that would remain even if the firm discontinued production. Likewise, variable costs, as the term suggests, are those costs that do vary with output and that the firm is likely to be most concerned with when contemplating a change in price and consequent changes in output. However, to determine whether particular costs are variable, one must evaluate the relationship of the prospective change in output to that level of output which presently exists. For example, some production decisions of great magnitude may entail the substantial retirement or expansion, as the case may be, of productive capacity, in which case costs typically considered fixed become variable. At the other extreme, small expansions of output may entail no change in costs, such as labor or transportation, that are considered typically variable.
>
> In predatory pricing cases the relevant changes in output will be those attributable to the price reduction alleged to be predatory. The reduction of price in such a case no doubt will have resulted in an expansion of output to "clear the market," *i.e.,* to satisfy the increased demand generated by the price reduction. It is those costs that change as a result of the expanded output that appropriately are considered to be variable. Thus, the first step in determining average variable cost in a predatory pricing case will generally be to compare the costs of production before and after the price reduction. The variable costs would then be those expenses that increased as a result of the output expansion attributable to the price reduction. If the new price is below the average of these costs per unit of output there is good reason, as we have said, to infer that the price reduction was predatory....
>
> It follows that the determination of which costs are variable and which fixed will vary with the facts of each case. Moreover, cost categories are solely for the purpose of providing aid in answering the ultimate question: Did the justification for the defendant's price depend upon its anticipated destructive effect on competition or was the price justified as a reasonably calculated means of maximizing profits, minimizing losses, or achieving some other legitimate end? Accordingly, we hold that the determination of fixed and variable costs is a matter for the jury under appropriate instructions.

By contrast, the Areeda-Turner formulation would treat the difference between fixed and variable costs much more categorically, and make it a question of law. Specifically, it would include in fixed costs only (1) capital costs, which include interest on debt and the opportunity cost of equity capital attributable to investment in land, plant, and equipment; (2) property and other taxes unaffected by output; and (3) depreciation on plant. With respect to equipment, the Areeda-Turner formulation would consider "use" depreciation — such as that of a truck that has a generally known life expectancy of, say, 200,000 miles — a variable cost as well. If a piece of equipment does not depreciate with use, its costs would be considered fixed. *See* 3 P. Areeda & H. Hovenkamp, *Antitrust Law* ¶ 740d (rev. ed. 1996).

5. *"Incremental" vs. "fully allocated" costs in predatory pricing cases.* An average cost figure is "fully allocated" when it includes all costs that are encountered in a single firm or plant, however loosely connected to the product under analysis. Consider, for example, a very small store that sells only two items, gasoline and milk. The milk requires a dairy refrigerator and the gasoline requires a tank. Suppose the current fixed costs of each is $10 a month, that the store sells 100 gallons of each product monthly, that it buys each product for $1 per gallon, and that these are its only costs. The firm then "breaks even" by charging $1.10 for each unit of each product. If the store substitutes an improved refrigerator whose fixed costs are $20 per month, with no change in sales, the fully allocated cost (total cost of all inputs divided by all units sold of both products) is now $1.15 per month. The $1.10 price for gasoline now appears to be "below cost."

But this fully allocated cost measure ignores the process by which any firm makes investment decisions. The firm contemplating a new refrigerator asks whether the *incremental* cost of the new equipment will be offset by the anticipated incremental revenue that the new equipment will produce. The new dairy refrigerator may be needed to replace an ailing refrigerator; or perhaps the firm contemplates higher milk volume. A legal rule attributing part of the refrigerator cost to gasoline could perversely force the perfectly competitive firm to maintain artificially high gasoline prices.

Suppose that the store in the previous illustration added a small display case containing cigars and was later accused of predation on that product. The display case is set on empty space that was not previously used. A fully allocated average total cost test would include not only the case itself but also a pro rata share of the property taxes, mortgage payment, payment for the gasoline tanks, and refrigerator. But these costs were already being paid by sales of other products and do not increase simply because the store adds cigars to previously unused space. When the store manager considers the profitability of adding cigars she does not compute a pro rata share of these costs; rather, she considers whether the anticipated additional ("incremental") revenue that the cigars promise to bring in will be sufficient to cover the incremental costs.

Courts taking fixed costs into account using an average total cost test or a long-run incremental cost test have generally concluded that the proper measure of fixed costs is not fully allocated costs, but rather "incremental" costs. The relevant question is how much *additional* fixed cost does the firm encounter in the sale or expansion of sales of the particular product deemed to be predatory. *See, e.g., MCI Communic. Corp. v. AT&T*, 708 F.2d 1081, 1118 (7th Cir. 1983), *cert. denied*, 464 U.S. 891 (1984) ("average total cost" for predatory pricing must refer to "average incremental cost;" fully allocated cost measure arbitrary and incorrect); *Southern Pacific Commun. Co. v. AT&T*, 556 F. Supp. 825, 922

(D.D.C., 1982), *aff'd*, 740 F.2d 980, 1004 (D.C. Cir. 1984), *cert. denied*, 470 U.S. 1056 (1985) ("unlike the concept of average total cost, which has sound economic underpinnings when defined as average incremental cost, the allocation methods used to compute fully distributed cost are inherently arbitrary and have no economic basis"); *William Inglis & Sons Baking Co. v. Continental Baking Co.*, 942 F.2d 1332, 1336 and n.6 (9th Cir. 1991) (may consider only costs "uniquely incurred" in the addition of a new product or output increase in the allegedly predated product).

Consider this example: a major airline has a plane with 100 seats and a flight costs $10,000, or $100 per seat. It sells 60 "full coach" class seats for $200 each, but also sells 40 "supersaver" tickets at $70 each. A competitor in the business of offering discount charter flights sues the airline, claiming predatory pricing in the supersaver seats. What result? *See International Travel Arrangers v. Northwest Airlines*, 991 F.2d 1389, 1396 (8th Cir.), *cert. denied*, 510 U.S. 932 (1993).

6. *Package pricing as predatory.* Suppose an automobile manufacturer is currently selling a particular model for $10,000 without a stereo system. The firm then adds a stereo system that costs $500, but adds only $300 to the car's price. A rival maker of car stereos alleges that the bundled stereo system is being sold at a predatory price. In determining whether the defendant's price is below its cost, what number should the court look at, the "separate" $300 price of the stereo, or the $10,300 price of the car/stereo package? In *Multistate Legal Studies v. Harcourt Brace Jovanovich*, 63 F.3d 1540 (10th Cir. 1995), *cert. denied*, 516 U.S. 1044 (1996), the district court had correctly concluded that the correct price was the package price, which was fully profitable; the Tenth Circuit erroneously reversed on this issue, believing that the relevant question was whether the bundled product itself was offered at an incremental price less than its full cost. (The facts were that the defendant sold a general bar review course and then added a multistate bar exam (MBE) course to the package at no extra charge; although a price of zero was less than the cost of the MBE add-on, the resulting package price was still fully profitable).

Why is the Tenth Circuit's answer incorrect? Think of the problem this way: a firm competes either by cutting a product's price or improving its quality. If the automobile maker cut the car's price by $300, we wouldn't say that the price cut is predatory unless justified by an offsetting $300 in cost reductions, would we? No, the price cut is predatory only if the resulting $9700 price for the car is below cost. The add-on of a $300 radio or some other accoutrement is no different. If the margin on the car was $1000 before the add-on, and $700 after, the resulting package is still fully profitable. Importantly, in that case no "recoupment" is required at all: the price cut is profitable from day one if it yields sufficiently higher output. Even if it does not yield sufficiently higher output, the resulting price is still fully "sustainable" in the sense that the automobile manufacturer earns a current profit.

The real vice of the Tenth Circuit's decision is the scrutiny that may be applied to numerous manufacturers of differentiated products who compete mainly by upgrading their products rather than by cutting price. When the computer manufacturer "competes" by equipping its standard package with a larger disc drive, bigger monitor, or more memory, is it guilty of predatory pricing if the *incremental* price of the package is not sufficient to cover the *incremental* cost of the added or enhanced feature?

PROBLEM 6.11

Fuel for ovens is ordinarily considered a variable cost. Suppose that Breadco has ovens capable of producing 10,000 loaves of bread per day, but they are currently producing only 6,000. At that rate of output, fuel costs $120, or 2 cents per loaf. Breadco then has the opportunity to supply Super Foods, a large supermarket, with 4,000 loaves daily, provided the price is right, and it wins the bid with a price significantly lower than the amount it charges other customers of its bread. Breadco is charged with predatory pricing by a competing bidder for the Super Foods contract.

It takes exactly the same amount of fuel to run a full oven as one that is only 60% full. How should fuel costs be attributed to the sales to Super Foods? Are the costs zero, given that Breadco can increase output from 6,000 to 10,000 loaves without using additional fuel? Or must fuel costs be averaged over the entire output, yielding average variable costs of 1.2 cents per loaf? *See Marsann Co. v. Brammall*, 788 F.2d 611 (9th Cir. 1986), especially at 614 n.2.

PROBLEM 6.12

Gourmet grocery sells 750 items in its medium sized store. Two or three of them, such as milk and bread, are heavily promoted and used to get shoppers inside the door, where they presumably will purchase more. Frequently the promotional prices, widely advertised in the newspapers, are lower than average variable cost. Mom'n'Pop Grocery down the street depends heavily on milk and bread sales for its profits, and it charges predatory pricing in those two items. Gourmet defends by saying that the relevant issue is not whether Gourmet has sold milk and bread at a price lower than AVC; rather, the question is whether Gourmet's entire product line in the aggregate is sold at prices below AVC. Who is correct? *See Lomar Wholesale Grocery, Inc. v. Dieter's Gourmet Foods, Inc.*, 824 F.2d 582 (8th Cir. 1987), *cert. denied*, 484 U.S. 1010 (1988).

Alternatively, Northwest Airlines offers a wide variety of fares on its scheduled flights. The lowest, or "supersaver," fares are substantially below average variable cost. A small regional airline charges predation on those fares. Northwest argues that the relevant question is not whether the "supersaver" fares are lower than AVC, but whether each scheduled flight as a whole produces revenues in excess of AVC. Who is correct? *See International Travel Arrangers v. NWA (Northwest Airlines)*, 991 F.2d 1389 (8th Cir. 1993).

NOTE: CONSPIRACY TO MONOPOLIZE

Section 2 of the Sherman Act condemns not only monopolization and attempts to monopolize, but also "[e]very person who shall ... combine or conspire with any other person or persons, to monopolize ...." There is little separate case law on the offense of conspiracy to monopolize, because any imaginable multi-party "conspiracy" to monopolize would also constitute a combination in restraint of trade under section 1, where the burden of proof is generally much lighter. Most judicial statements of the conspiracy offense come in cases in which the defendants' conduct is also analyzed under section 1 of the Sherman Act. Recent, but inconclusive, discussions are included in *Todorov v. DCH Healthcare Auth.*, 921 F.2d 1438, 1460 n.35 (11th Cir. 1991); *Hudson Valley Asbestos v. Tougher Heating & Plumbing Co.*, 510 F.2d 1140 (2d Cir.), *cert. denied*, 421 U.S. 1011 (1975). *See also International Distrib. Centers v. Walsh Trucking Co.*, 812 F.2d 786 (2d Cir.), *cert. denied*, 482 U.S. 915 (1987), concluding that the conspiracy offense required proof that the alleged conspirators had a specific intent to monopolize, not merely an intent to do the alleged act. Further, a qualifying "agreement" must be proven. *See Seagood Trading Corp. v. Jerrico, Inc.*, 924 F.2d 1555 (11th Cir. 1991) (summary judgment for defendant where there was insufficient evidence of agreement). However, a plaintiff may not have to define a relevant market. *Key Enters. of Del., Inc. v. Venice Hosp.*, 919 F.2d 1550, 1564 (11th Cir. 1990).

INDUSTRIAL CONCENTRATION AND NON-DOMINANT FIRMS: FROM MONOPOLIZATION TO MERGER POLICY

One effect of the "substantial" market power requirement required for monopolization or attempt cases is that §2 of the Sherman Act fails to reach situations where markets perform anticompetitively but there is no dominant firm guilty of unlawful exclusionary practices. For example, in *Dimmitt Agri. Indus. v. CPC Int'l.*, 679 F.2d 516 (5th Cir. 1982), *cert. denied*, 460 U.S. 1082 (1983), the court refused to condemn the practices of a firm that was clearly the price "leader" in a well disciplined oligopoly, but whose own market share was too small to make it guilty of monopolization or attempt. The court concluded:

> We do not dispute Dimmitt's [the plaintiff's] contention that its memoranda evidence, weighed with all reasonable inferences drawn in favor of the jury verdict, supports the conclusion that during 1971-72 CPC [the defendant] exercised a significant degree of control over price.
>
> We conclude, however, that this conduct evidence alone is insufficient to overcome the presumption against monopoly power implied by CPC's indisputably low market shares in the two relevant undifferentiated products, corn syrup and cornstarch. Dimmitt's structural evidence is consistent with the proposition that the corn wet milling industry is only an oligopoly, with

CPC as its price leader. If so, CPC's market power is dependent upon joint action by at least some of its rivals. While we realize that any degree of market power tends to cause economic harm, such as high prices, low output, and underutilized capacity, an interpretation of the completed monopolization offense, to embrace *any* degree of market power, would complicate enforcement, overwhelm the enforcement machinery, and deter arguably legitimate conduct.

See also Brooke Group Ltd. v. Brown & Williamson Tobacco Corp., 509 U.S. 209 (1993), reprinted *supra* (refusing to condemn predatory pricing in a "lockstep" oligopoly where the defendant's market share was only 12%). Likewise, in *Kellogg*, 99 F.T.C. 8 (1982), the Federal Trade Commission refused to recognize a doctrine of "shared monopoly," alleging that the major ready-to-eat breakfast cereal companies had a tacit understanding that they would introduce large numbers of brands in order to dominate grocer shelf space, thus permitting them to raise price to oligopoly levels. *See* H. Hovenkamp, *Federal Antitrust Policy* §§ 4.2-4.6 (2d ed. 1994); Hay, *Oligopoly, Shared Monopoly, and Antitrust Law*, 67 Cornell L. Rev. 439 (1982); Schmalensee, *Entry Deterrence in the Ready-to-Eat Breakfast Cereal Industry*, 9 Bell J. Econ. 305 (1976).

The *Brooke, Dimmitt*, and *Kellogg* decisions suggest a perplexing problem about antitrust policy in highly concentrated markets that do not have a single dominant firm. The first question is *whether* something must be done about apparently unilateral exclusionary practices in such markets (concerted practices are dealt with somewhat more easily under section 1 of the Sherman Act). The second question is: Given an affirmative answer to question one, what is the appropriate method or statute that antitrust policy makers should use?

On the first question, economists have debated the problem of industrial concentration for several decades, and the end of the debate is not in sight. The traditional, centrist view is frequently expressed as the "structure-conduct-performance" paradigm, and holds that highly concentrated markets naturally yield exclusionary and collusive conduct first, and anticompetitive performance second. Thus, the failure of a market to perform competitively is principally one of market structure. Dominance by a single firm may yield an anticompetitive structure, but so might moderately high market shares, on the order of 20% or 25%, held by three or four firms. What determines market concentration? Economies of scale contribute a little, but cannot fully explain very large market shares. Many of the determinants of market share are "stochastic," or random. Thus, high market concentration — because it results in poor performance — is most generally a bad thing. *See* F.M. Scherer & D. Ross, *Industrial Market Structure and Economic Performance*, ch. 4 (3d ed. 1990); L. Weiss, "The Concentration-Profits Relationship and Antitrust," in *Industrial Concentration: The New Learning* (H. Goldschmid, H. Mann & J. Weston eds. 1974) at 184-233. *See also* Schmalensee, *Do Markets Differ Much?*, 75 Am. Econ. Rev. 341 (1985). For a good survey, *see* James W. Meehan, Jr. & Robert J. Larner, "The Structural

School, Its Critics, and Its Progeny: An Assessment," in *Economics and Antitrust Policy* (Robert J. Larner & James W. Meehan, Jr. eds., Quorum 1989), at 182.

In response, the Chicago School has completely rejected the structure-conduct-performance paradigm, arguing that it states the relationship backwards. Performance comes first. Firms grow large because they are innovative and industrious. A firm comes up with a new process or a new product that decreases its costs or makes its offering more attractive in consumers' eyes than the offerings of competitors. As a result, that firm's market share grows very large. In fact, other firms may never catch up. High concentration may be a result of aggressive competition rather than a cause of poor performance. *See* McGee, "Efficiency and Economies of Size," and Demsetz, "Two Systems of Belief About Monopoly," both in *Industrial Concentration: The New Learning, supra*, at 55 & 164; Demsetz, *Industrial Structure, Market Rivalry, and Public Policy*, 16 J.L. & Econ. 1 (1973); Peltzman, *The Gains and Losses From Industrial Concentration*, 20 J.L. & Econ. 229 (1977).

Most of the empirical studies have found correlations between poor industry performance (measured as high price/cost margins) and concentration, but fail to distinguish between high profits in concentrated industries that are a "result" of high concentration and those that are the result of lower costs, higher relative product demand, or some other form of competitive superiority. In this respect, both the centrist and the Chicago School theories seem to be deficient. *See* Clarke, Davies & Waterson, *The Profitability-Concentration Relation: Market Power or Efficiency?*, 32 J. Indus. Econ. 435 (1984).

Other scholarship is inclined to regard both views as half-truths. High concentration may often be the result of competitive prowess, but it may also result in an indefinite period of monopoly returns for the winners. *See* Phillips, *Market Concentration and Performance: A Survey of the Evidence*, 61 Notre Dame L. Rev. 1099 (1986). In such cases a value judgment must be made about whether the monopoly profits are too high a reward for innovative behavior, whether workable solutions to the problem are available, and whether a court is capable of administering these. Some neoclassicists, particularly members of the Chicago School, believe that any policy of forced deconcentration will destroy incentives to innovate. Why bother to innovate and capture a large share of a market if a court will later take it all away from you? The social cost of such a destruction of incentives is likely to be greater than the social value of any efficiencies that result from deconcentration. *E.g.*, Easterbrook, *On Identifying Exclusionary Conduct*, 61 Notre Dame L. Rev. 972 (1986).

The second question — the proper antitrust policy for dealing with the concentration problem — is just as vexing. Because of its requirement of substantial market power held by a single firm, section 2 of the Sherman Act is not an appropriate vehicle for dealing with high market concentration in the absence of a clearly dominant firm. Likewise, section 1 works only when there is a more or less explicit "agreement" among the firms. The principal antitrust device for dealing with industrial concentration has been merger policy under section 7 of the Clayton Act, which historically has accepted the structure-conduct-performance paradigm and was thus directed toward preventing a certain kind of industrial concentration: that which results from combination rather than internal growth. In the last 15 or 20 years this reliance on market structure has been relaxed considerably, and merger policy has increasingly looked at non-structural factors. However, as the subsequent chapter illustrates, a concentrated market structure is still an essential prerequisite to merger illegality.

BIBLIOGRAPHY AND COLLATERAL READINGS

Books

A. Chandler, Scale and Scope: Dynamics of American Capitalism (1991).

H. Hovenkamp, Federal Antitrust Policy, chs. 6-8 (2d ed. 1994).

E.T. Sullivan & J. Harrison, Understanding Antitrust and Its Economics Implications (2d ed. 1994).

Articles

Baumol, Predation and the Logic of the Average Variable Cost Test, 39 J.L. & Econ. 49 (1996).

Brodley & Hay, Predatory Pricing: Competing Economic Theories and the Evolution of Legal Standards, 66 Cornell L. Rev. 738 (1981).

Campbell, Predation and Competition in Antitrust: the Case of Non-fungible Goods, 87 Colum. L. Rev. 1625 (1987).

Cooper, Attempts and Monopolization: A Mildly Expansionary Answer to the Prophylactic Riddle of Section Two, 72 Mich. L. Rev. 375 (1974).

Friedman, Antitrust Analysis and Bilateral Monopoly, 1986 Wis. L. Rev. 873.

Glazer & Lipsky, Unilateral Refusals to Deal under §2 of the Sherman Act, 63 Antitrust L.J. 749 (1995)

Granitz & Klein, Monopolization by "Raising Rivals' Costs": the *Standard Oil* Case, 39 J.L. & Econ. 1 (1996)

Hay, Oligopoly, Shared Monopoly, and Antitrust Law, 67 Cornell L. Rev. 439 (1981).

Kaplow, Extension of Monopoly Power Through Leverage, 85 Colum. L. Rev. 515 (1985).

Kezsbom & Goldman, No Shortcut to Antitrust Analysis: the Twisted Journey of the Essential Facilities Doctrine, 1996 Colum. Bus. L. Rev. 1.

Klein, Market Power in Antitrust: Economic Analysis After *Kodak*, 3 Sup. Ct. Econ. Rev. 43 (1993)

Krattenmaker & Salop, Anticompetitive Exclusion: Raising Rivals' Costs to Achieve Power Over Price, 96 Yale L.J. 209 (1986).

Krattenmaker, Lande & Salop, Monopoly Power and Market Power in Antitrust Law, 76 Geo. L.J. 241 (1987).

Ratner, Should There Be an Essential Facility Doctrine?, 21 U.C. Davis L. Rev. 327 (1988).

Shapiro, Aftermarkets and Consumer Welfare: Making Sense of Kodak, 63 Antitrust L.J. 483 (1995)

Sullivan, Monopolization, the Corporate Strategy, the IBM Cases and the Transformation of the Law, 60 Tex. L. Rev. 587 (1982).

Symposium on Section II of the Sherman Act, 61 Notre Dame L. Rev. 885 (1986).

Werden, The Law and Economics of the Essential Facility Doctrine, 32 St. Louis U. L.J. 433 (1987).

MERGERS AND ACQUISITIONS

Often a firm finds it profitable to expand business by increasing output or moving into a new market or a new distributional level. One way the firm can do this is by new entry — by building a new plant, for example, or by constructing its own chain of retail stores. Another way is by acquisition of a second firm that is already operating in the expansion market. Antitrust policymakers have generally regarded entry by acquisition with more suspicion than so-called "de novo" entry. When a company enters a market de novo it generally increases the capacity in the targeted market, and the result may be higher output and lower prices. When a firm expands by acquisition, however, increased output is not as likely and the possibilities for monopolization, collusion, or other anticompetitive practices may be greater. The law of mergers and acquisitions addresses these concerns.

SECTION I. VERTICAL INTEGRATION THROUGH MERGER

UNITED STATES V. YELLOW CAB CO.

332 U.S. 218 (1947)

JUSTICE MURPHY delivered the opinion of the Court.

The United States filed a complaint ... pursuant to § 4 of the Sherman Anti-Trust Act, to prevent and restrain the appellees from violating §§ 1 and 2 of the Act. ...

The alleged facts, as set forth in the complaint, may be summarized briefly. In January, 1929, one Morris Markin and others commenced negotiations to merge the more important cab operating companies in Chicago, New York and other cities. Markin was then president and general manager, as well as the controlling stockholder, of the Checker Cab Manufacturing Corporation (CCM). That company was engaged in the business of manufacturing taxicabs at its factory in Kalamazoo, Michigan, and shipping them to purchasers in various states.

....

It is said that the appellees have agreed to control the operation and purchase of taxicabs by the principal operating companies in Chicago, New York City, Pittsburgh and Minneapolis, insisting that they purchase their cabs exclusively from CCM. This excludes all other manufacturers of taxicabs from 86% of the Chicago market, 15% of the New York City market, 100% of the Pittsburgh market and 58% of the Minneapolis market. At the same time, the trade of the controlled cab companies is restrained since they are prevented from purchasing cabs from manufacturers other than CCM. The result allegedly is that these companies must pay more for cabs than they would otherwise pay, their other expenditures are increased unnecessarily, and the public is charged high rates for the transportation services rendered.

....

... By excluding all cab manufacturers other than CCM from that part of the market represented by the cab operating companies under their control, the appellees effectively limit the outlets through which cabs may be sold in interstate commerce. Limitations of that nature have been condemned time and again as violative of the Act. In addition, by preventing the cab operating companies under their control from purchasing cabs from manufacturers other than CCM, the appellees deny those companies the opportunity to purchase cabs in a free, competitive market.[5] The Sherman Act has never been thought to sanction such a conspiracy to restrain the free purchase of goods in interstate commerce.

The fact that these restraints occur in a setting described by the appellees as a vertically integrated enterprise does not necessarily remove the ban of the Sherman Act. The test of illegality under the Act is the presence or absence of an unreasonable restraint on interstate commerce. Such a restraint may result as readily from a conspiracy among those who are affiliated or integrated under common ownership as from a conspiracy among those who are otherwise independent. Similarly, any affiliation or integration flowing from an illegal conspiracy cannot insulate the conspirators from the sanctions which Congress has imposed. The corporate interrelationships of the conspirators, in other words, are not determinative of the applicability of the Sherman Act....

And so in this case, the common ownership and control of the various corporate appellees are impotent to liberate the alleged combination and conspiracy from the impact of the Act. The complaint charges that the restraint of interstate trade was not only effected by the combination of the appellees but was the primary object of the combination. The theory of the complaint, to borrow language from *United States v. Reading Co.*, 253 U.S. 26, 57, is that "dominating power" over the cab operating companies "was not obtained by normal expansion to meet the demands of a business growing as a result of superior and enterprising management, but by deliberate, calculated purchase for control." If that theory is borne out in this case by the evidence, coupled with proof of an undue restraint of interstate trade, a plain violation of the Act has occurred.

NOTES AND QUESTIONS

1. The case was remanded for trial, and the District Court found that the defendants had not violated the Sherman Act because they had not intended to restrain competition. The Supreme Court affirmed. 338 U.S. 338 (1949).

2. In *Yellow Cab*, a taxicab manufacturer acquired taxicab companies in Chicago, New York, Pittsburgh, and Minneapolis. The acquisition of a taxicab com-

---

[5] To the extent that the controlled operating companies are charged higher than the open market prices, they are injured.

pany by a taxicab manufacturer is called a "vertical" merger because the two firms stand in a seller-buyer relationship. By acquiring its own taxicab companies, a taxicab manufacturer can eliminate market transactions and perhaps apply its expertise to the care and maintenance of its running cabs. These cost savings are typically realized from vertical integration. The case also involved other kinds of acquisitions, however. Elsewhere in the opinion the court reports that the defendants acquired competing taxicab companies within the same city and operated them as a single business entity. Such a merger between competing firms is called "horizontal." Additionally, the merger brought under common ownership different cab companies in different cities. Such mergers are known as "conglomerate" or "market extension" mergers. How could it be anticompetitive for a taxicab company in Chicago and another one in New York to come under the control of the same owner?

3. The Supreme Court observed that the vertical aspects of the taxicab merger might be bad for two reasons: (1) since most of the taxicabs driven in the cities involved were owned by the defendant's companies, other taxicab manufacturers could not compete for the business of selling cabs to these taxicabs companies; and (2) the acquired taxicab companies would be forced to purchase cabs from their parent company. Why are these restraints bad? The United States alleged that the acquired taxicab companies would be forced to pay more for cabs because of the merger. Does it strike you as plausible that a manufacturer of widgets would buy a business that consumed widgets because it could then force the business to purchase widgets at a greater-than-market price? Wouldn't the profits to the selling company be more than offset by the losses to the buying company?

4. Would your analysis of the anticompetitive effects of the merger change if the cities involved had each established a maximum number of cabs that could be licensed within that city, and the number of cabs had already reached the legal maximum? One of the allegations in the *Yellow Cab* case was that the defendants had conspired to induce city officials to reduce the number of licenses. *See* Kitch, *The Yellow Cab Antitrust Case*, 15 J.L. & Econ. 327 (1972).

Because of the license limit there might be fewer cabs operating in a city than there would be if entry were unregulated. This might enable the cab operators to charge a monopoly price without even coming to an agreement with each other. (Do you see why? Remember, many successful cartels involve explicit limits on output, not explicit agreements about price.) These monopoly profits to the cab operators would permit them to pay a monopoly price for cabs, although competition among cab manufacturers would keep the cab price competitive. In this situation the cab manufacturer might acquire cab operating companies, because then the manufacturer could transfer some of the monopoly profits from the operating companies to itself. It could do this either by charging an inflated price for cabs to the operating companies, or else by simply taking the higher profits from the operating companies directly. But if the operating companies were earning monopoly profits, wouldn't this show up in their stock prices?

5. Would your analysis of the issues in *Yellow Cab* change if taxi fares in the four cities were price-regulated? A price-regulated monopolist can sometimes acquire (or be acquired by) a source of supply and then purchase from the source of supply at an inflated price. The higher price would show up in the price-regulated company's ledger as a higher operating cost, and it could be presented to the rate-making authority as justifying a higher rate. Such price regulation sometimes explains why electric utilities seek to acquire coal mining companies or why price-regulated railroads might wish to manufacture some of their own equipment. In general, vertical integration by a price-regulated firm makes computation of a proper rate base more complex. The more complex the computation of a proper rate base, the greater the chance that the regulated firm can conceal inflated costs. This explains why, when the telephone monopoly was divested, the price-regulated local operating companies were not permitted to manufacture their own terminal equipment. *United States v. AT&T*, 552 F. Supp. 131, 228 (D.D.C. 1982), *aff'd sub nom. Maryland v. United States* (1983). *See* Brennan, *Why Regulated Firms Should Be Kept Out of Unregulated Markets: Understanding the Divestiture in United States v. AT&T*, 32 Antitrust Bull. 741 (1987); W. Viscusi, J. Vernon & J. Harrington, *Economics of Regulation and Antitrust*, ch. 15 (2d ed. 1995).

UNITED STATES V. COLUMBIA STEEL CO.

334 U.S. 495 (1948)

JUSTICE REED delivered the opinion of the Court.

The United States brings this suit under § 4 of the Sherman Act to enjoin United States Steel Corporation and its subsidiaries from purchasing the assets of the largest independent steel fabricator on the West Coast on the ground that such acquisition would violate §§ 1 and 2 of the Sherman Act. The complaint, filed on February 24, 1947, charged that if the contract of sale between United States Steel and Consolidated Steel Corporation were carried out, competition in the sale of rolled steel products and in fabricated steel products would be restrained....

....

The steel production involved in this case may be spoken of as being divided into two stages: the production of rolled steel products and their fabrication into finished steel products. Rolled steel products consist of steel plates, shapes, sheets, bars, and other unfinished steel products and are in turn made from ingots by means of rolling mills. The steel fabrication involved herein may also be divided into structural fabrication and plate fabrication. Fabricated structural steel products consist of building framework, bridges, transmission towers, and similar permanent structures, and are made primarily from rolled steel shapes, although plates and other rolled steel products may also be employed. Fabricated plate products, on the other hand, consist of pressure vessels, tanks, welded pipe, and similar products made principally from rolled steel plates, although shapes and bars are also occasionally used....

The theory of the United States in bringing this suit is that the acquisition of Consolidated constitutes an illegal restraint of interstate commerce because all manufacturers except United States Steel will be excluded from the business of supplying Consolidated's requirements of rolled steel products....

... Over the ten-year period from 1937 to 1946 Consolidated purchased over two million tons of rolled steel products, including the abnormally high wartime requirements. Whatever amount of rolled steel products Consolidated uses in the future will be supplied insofar as possible from other subsidiaries of United States Steel, and other producers of rolled steel products will lose Consolidated as a prospective customer.

The parties are in sharp dispute as to the size and nature of the market for rolled steel products with which Consolidated's consumption is to be compared. The appellees argue that rolled steel products are sold on a national scale, and that for the major producers the entire United States should be regarded as the market. Viewed from this standpoint, Consolidated's requirements are an insignificant fraction of the total market, less than ½ of 1%. The government argues that the market must be more narrowly drawn, and that the relevant market to be considered is the eleven state area in which Consolidated sells its products, and further that in that area by considering only the consumption of structural and plate fabricators a violation of the Sherman Act has been established. If all sales of rolled steel products in the Consolidated market are considered, Consolidated's purchases of two million tons represent a little more than 3% of the total of 60 million tons.... If the comparable market is construed even more narrowly, and is restricted to the consumption of plates and shapes in the Consolidated market, figures for 1937 indicate that Consolidated's consumption of plates and shapes was 13% of the total....

The government realizes the force of appellees' argument that rolled steel products are sold on a national scale, and attempts to demonstrate that during the non-war years 80% of Consolidated's requirements were produced on the West Coast; Consolidated resorts to data not in the record to demonstrate that in fact only 26% of Consolidated's rolled steel purchases were produced in plants located in the Consolidated market area. Whether we accept the government's or Consolidated's figures, however, they are of little value in determining the extent to which West Coast fabricators will purchase rolled steel products in the eastern market in the future, since the construction of new plants at Geneva and Fontana and the creation of new basing points on the West Coast will presumably give West Coast rolled steel producers a far larger share of the West Coast fabricating market than before the war.

Another difficulty is that the record furnishes little indication as to the propriety of considering plates and shapes as a market distinct from other rolled steel products. If rolled steel producers can make other products as easily as plates and shapes, then the effect of the removal of Consolidated's demand for plates and shapes must be measured not against the market for plates and shapes alone, but for all comparable rolled products. The record suggests, but does not conclusively indicate, that rolled steel producers can make other products interchangeably with shapes and plates, and that therefore we should not measure the potential injury to competition by considering the total demand for shapes and plates alone, but rather compare Consolidated's demand for rolled steel products with the demand for all comparable rolled steel products in the Consolidated marketing area.

... We recognize the difficulty of laying down a rule as to what areas or products are competitive, one with another. In this case and on this record we have circumstances that strongly indicate to us that rolled steel production and consumption in the Consolidated marketing area is the competitive area and product for consideration.

....

... A restraint may be unreasonable either because a restraint otherwise reasonable is accompanied with a specific intent to accomplish a forbidden restraint or because it falls within the class of restraints that are illegal *per se*....

A subsidiary will in all probability deal only with its parent for goods the parent can furnish. That fact, however, does not make the acquisition invalid....

The legality of the acquisition by United States Steel of a market outlet for its rolled steel through the purchase of the manufacturing facilities of Consolidated depends not merely upon the fact of that acquired control but also upon many other factors. Exclusive dealings for rolled steel between Consolidated and United States Steel, brought about by vertical integration or otherwise, are not illegal, at any rate until the effect of such control is to unreasonably restrict the opportunities of competitors to market their product. ...

It seems clear to us that vertical integration, as such without more, cannot be held violative of the Sherman Act. It is an indefinite term without explicit meaning. Even in the iron industry, where could a line be drawn — at the end of mining the ore, the production of the pig-iron or steel ingots, when the rolling mill operation is completed, fabrication on order or at some stage of manufacture into standard merchandise? No answer would be possible and therefore the extent of permissible integration must be governed, as other factors in Sherman Act violations, by the other circumstances of individual cases. Technological advances may easily require a basic industry plant to expand its processes into semi-finished or finished goods so as to produce desired articles in greater volume and with less expense.

....

[W]e conclude that the so-called vertical integration resulting from the acquisition of Consolidated does not unreasonably restrict the opportunities of the competitor producers of rolled steel to market their product. We accept as the relevant competitive market the total demand for rolled steel products in the eleven-state area; over the past ten years Consolidated has accounted for only 3% of that demand, and if expectations as to the development of the western steel industry are realized, Consolidated's proportion may be expected to be lower than that figure in the future....

....

Affirmed.

NOTES AND QUESTIONS

1. A firm is "vertically integrated" whenever it does or makes for itself something it would otherwise purchase in the marketplace. A pizza parlor with its own delivery truck is vertically integrated, as is a shoe store owner who washes her own store windows. Obviously, therefore, any notion that there might be a per se rule against vertical integration must be taken with several bags of salt.

2. When will a firm perform or make for itself something it would otherwise purchase? A profit-maximizing firm will generally do so when self-production or self-service is cheaper than purchase of the product or service from others. *See* R. Coase, *The Nature of the Firm,* 4 Economica, New Series 386 (1937). In perfect competition efficiency-creating vertical integration by one firm will have to be matched by the firm's competitors, or else the competitors will lose market share to the more efficient firm. As more firms become vertically integrated competition among the vertically integrated firms will transfer the benefits of the newly-created efficiency to consumers. Clearly, vertical integration by one firm can injure competitors who cannot integrate vertically themselves, or who cannot do so immediately. Under what circumstances, however, can vertical integration injure consumers?

3. If demand for steel remained constant, how would competitors with U.S. Steel be "foreclosed" from the market for fabricated or rolled steel? U.S. Steel might "capture" Consolidated, but it would have to give up other customers, and the result would be simply a realignment of buyers and sellers in the industry. "Foreclosure" of competitors would occur only if U.S. Steel actually ended up selling more steel after the acquisition than it did before — that is, if it retained all its old customers but added Consolidated as a captive customer. Would competition be injured by U.S. Steel's increase in output? Could consumers be injured?

4. Is the "Rule of Reason" for mergers developed in the *Yellow Cab* and *Columbia Steel* cases identical with the rule of reason developed for horizontal restraint cases?

5. Both the *Yellow Cab* and *Columbia Steel* cases were brought under the Sherman Act. Section 7 of the Clayton Act, which forbids mergers, had been passed in 1914, but it applied only to acquisitions of the *stock* of another corporation. The *Columbia Steel* case involved an acquisition of another company's physical assets. Early in the century asset acquisitions were a preferred form of merger for two reasons. First, the original Clayton Act did not reach them; second, stock acquisitions often ran afoul of state corporate law provisions. *See* H. Hovenkamp, *Enterprise and American Law, 1836-1937,* ch. 20 (1991).

As originally passed, section 7 of the Clayton Act also seemed not to apply to vertical acquisitions; it spoke of mergers that eliminated competition "between" the merging firms — that is, mergers of competitors. However, the Supreme Court disagreed in the following case and applied the "policy" of the act to a vertical transaction. One result of the government's defeat in *Columbia Steel* was increased political momentum for expansion of section 7 to include vertical acquisitions as well. The statute was expanded in 1950 to make clear that it applied both to asset acquisitions and to vertical mergers.

The *du Pont* case, reprinted below, was brought under section 7 of the Clayton Act, albeit before the 1950 amendments. Can you tell the difference in the legal standard?

UNITED STATES V. E.I. DU PONT DE NEMOURS & CO.
353 U.S. 586 (1957)

JUSTICE BRENNAN delivered the opinion of the Court.

… The complaint alleged a violation of § 7 of the [Clayton] Act resulting from the purchase by E. I. du Pont de Nemours and Company in 1917-1919 of a 23% stock interest in General Motors Corporation.…

The primary issue is whether du Pont's commanding position as General Motors' supplier of automotive finishes and fabrics was achieved on competitive merit alone, or because its acquisition of the General Motors' stock, and the consequent close intercompany relationship, led to the insulation of most of the General Motors' market from free competition, with the resultant likelihood, at the time of suit, of the creation of a monopoly of a line of commerce.

....

Section 7 is designed to arrest … in their incipiency restraints … in a relevant market which, as a reasonable probability, appear at the time of suit likely to result from the acquisition by one corporation of all or any part of the stock of any other corporation. The section is violated whether or not actual restraints or monopolies, or the substantial lessening of competition, have occurred or are intended.…

....

We hold that any acquisition by one corporation of all or any part of the stock of another corporation, competitor or not, is within the reach of the section whenever the reasonable likelihood appears that the acquisition will result in a restraint of commerce or in the creation of a monopoly of any line of commerce. Thus, although du Pont and General Motors are not competitors, a violation of the section has occurred if, as a result of the acquisition, there was at the time of suit a reasonable likelihood of a monopoly of any line of commerce.…

Appellees argue that there exists no basis for a finding of a probable restraint or monopoly within the meaning of § 7 because the total General Motors market for finishes and fabrics constituted only a negligible percentage of the total market for these materials for all uses, including automotive uses. It is stated in the

General Motors brief that in 1947 du Pont's finish sales to General Motors constituted 3.5% of all sales of finishes to industrial users, and that its fabrics sales to General Motors comprised 1.6% of the total market for the type of fabric used by the automobile industry.

Determination of the relevant market is a necessary predicate to a finding of a violation of the Clayton Act because the threatened monopoly must be one which will substantially lessen competition "within the area of effective competition." Substantiality can be determined only in terms of the market affected. The record shows that automotive finishes and fabrics have sufficient peculiar characteristics and uses to constitute them products sufficiently distinct from all other finishes and fabrics to make them a "line of commerce" within the meaning of the Clayton Act.... Thus, the bounds of the relevant market for the purposes of this case are not coextensive with the total market for finishes and fabrics, but are coextensive with the automobile industry, the relevant market for automotive finishes and fabrics.

The market affected must be substantial. Moreover, in order to establish a violation of § 7 the Government must prove a likelihood that competition may be "foreclosed in a substantial share of ... [that market]." Both requirements are satisfied in this case. The substantiality of a relevant market comprising the automobile industry is undisputed. The substantiality of General Motors' share of that market is fully established in the evidence.

General Motors is the colossus of the giant automobile industry. It accounts annually for upwards of two-fifths of the total sales of automotive vehicles in the Nation.... Expressed in percentages, du Pont supplied 67% of General Motors' requirements for finishes in 1946 and 68% in 1947. In fabrics du Pont supplied 52.3% of requirements in 1946, and 38.5% in 1947. Because General Motors accounts for almost one-half of the automobile industry's annual sales, its requirements for automotive finishes and fabrics must represent approximately one-half of the relevant market for these materials. Because the record clearly shows that quantitatively and percentagewise du Pont supplies the largest part of General Motors' requirements, we must conclude that du Pont has a substantial share of the relevant market.

....

The du Pont Company's commanding position as a General Motors supplier was not achieved until shortly after its purchase of a sizable block of General Motors stock in 1917. At that time its production for the automobile industry and its sales to General Motors were relatively insignificant. General Motors then produced only about 11% of the total automobile production and its requirements, while relatively substantial, were far short of the proportions they assumed as it forged ahead to its present place in the industry.

....

... [T]hat the purchase [of General Motors stock] would result in du Pont's obtaining a new and substantial market, was echoed in the Company's 1917 and 1918 annual reports to stockholders. In the 1917 report appears: "Though this is a new line of activity, it is one of great promise and one that seems to be well suited to the character of our organization. *The motor companies are very large consumers of our Fabrikoid and Pyralin as well as paints and varnishes.*" (Emphasis added.) The 1918 report says: "The consumption of paints, varnishes and fabrikoid in the manufacture of automobiles gives another common interest."

....

In less than four years, by August 1921, Lammot du Pont, then a du Pont vice-president and later Chairman of the Board of General Motors, in response to a query from Pierre S. du Pont, then Chairman of the Board of both du Pont and General Motors, "whether General Motors was taking its entire requirements of du Pont products from du Pont," was able to reply that four of General Motors' eight operating divisions bought from du Pont their entire requirements of paints and varnishes, five their entire requirements of Fabrikoid, four their entire requirements of rubber cloth, and seven their entire requirements of Pyralin and celluloid....

....

Competitors did obtain higher percentages of the General Motors business in later years, although never high enough at any time substantially to affect the dollar amount of du Pont's sales. Indeed, it appears likely that General Motors probably turned to outside sources of supply at least in part because its requirements outstripped du Pont's production, when General Motors' proportion of total automobile sales grew greater and the company took its place as the sales leader of the automobile industry. For example, an undisputed Government exhibit shows that General Motors took 93% of du Pont's automobile Duco production in 1941 and 83% in 1947. ...

We agree with the trial court that considerations of price, quality and service were not overlooked by either du Pont or General Motors. Pride in its products and its high financial stake in General Motors' success would naturally lead du Pont to try to supply the best. But the wisdom of this business judgment cannot obscure the fact, plainly revealed by the record, that du Pont purposely employed its stock to pry open the General Motors market to entrench itself as the primary supplier of General Motors' requirements for automotive finishes and fabrics.

....

The statutory policy of fostering free competition is obviously furthered when no supplier has an advantage over his competitors from an acquisition of his customer's stock likely to have the effects condemned by the statute. We repeat, that the test of a violation of § 7 is whether, at the time of suit, there is a reasonable probability that the acquisition is likely to result in the condemned restraints. The conclusion upon this record is inescapable that such likelihood was proved as to this acquisition. The fire that was kindled in 1917 continues to smolder. It burned briskly to forge the ties that bind the General Motors market to du Pont, and if it has quieted down, it remains hot, and, from past performance, is likely at any time to blaze and make the fusion complete.[36]

JUSTICE BURTON, whom JUSTICE FRANKFURTER joins, dissenting.

... [E]ven assuming the correctness of the Court's conclusion that du Pont's competitors have been or will be foreclosed from General Motors' paint and fabric trade, it is still necessary to resolve one more issue in favor of the Government in order to reverse the District Court. It is necessary to hold that the Government proved that this foreclosure involves a substantial share of the relevant market and that it significantly limits the competitive opportunities of others trading in that market.

The Court holds that the relevant market in this case is the automotive market for finishes and fabrics, and not the total industrial market for these products. The Court reaches that conclusion because in its view "automotive finishes and fabrics have sufficient peculiar characteristics and uses to constitute them products sufficiently distinct from all other finishes and fabrics...." We are not told what these "peculiar characteristics" are. Nothing is said about finishes other than that Duco represented an important contribution to the process of manufacturing automobiles. Nothing is said about fabrics other than that sales to the automobile industry are made by means of bids rather than fixed price schedules....

[T]he types of fabrics used for automobile trim and convertible tops — imitation leather and coated fabrics — are used in the manufacture of innumerable products, such as luggage, furniture, railroad upholstery, books, brief cases, baby carriages, hassocks, bicycle saddles, sporting goods, footwear, belts and table mats. In 1947, General Motors purchased about $9,454,000 of imitation leather and coated fabrics. Of this amount, $3,639,000 was purchased from du Pont (38.5%) and $5,815,000 from over 50 du Pont competitors. Since du Pont produced about 10% of the national market for these products in 1946, 1947 and 1948, and since only 20% of its sales were to the automobile industry, the du Pont sales to the automobile industry constituted only about 2% of the total market. The Court ignores the record by treating this small fraction of the total market as a market of distinct products.

....

NOTES AND QUESTIONS

1. Suppose that General Motors could buy better finishes at a lower price from one of du Pont's competitors. Would it be reasonable for du Pont to force General Motors to buy from itself anyway?

---

[36] The potency of the influence of du Pont's 23% stock interest is greater today because of the diffusion of the remaining shares which, in 1947, were held by 436,510 stockholders; 92% owned no more than 100 shares each, and 60% owned no more than 25 shares each. 126 F. Supp., at 244.

2. In deciding that the relevant market foreclosed by the vertical merger was the market for automobile finishes and fabrics, the Court looked almost exclusively at elasticity of demand. Once made, automotive finishes and fabrics were not particularly useful for manufacturers of other products, such as appliances or furniture. The Court virtually ignored elasticity of supply. The Court conceded that the fabrics used by the automotive industry were of the same "type" as the fabrics used by other large purchasers of fabrics. If the only difference between fabrics used for automobile seat covers and fabrics used for, say, sofas was that the two were cut into different shapes, the cross-elasticity of supply would be very high. In that case the Court erred in its market definition, and Justice Burton's dissent has the better argument. A fabrics manufacturer "foreclosed" from General Motors as a customer could search out a wide variety of alternative customers.

3. Private antitrust damages actions under section 4 of the Clayton Act are governed by a four-year statute of limitation. Criminal antitrust prosecutions are generally governed by a five-year statute, and when the government sues for damages for its own injuries it is generally held to the four-year statute. There is, however, no statute of limitation for civil actions brought by either the government or private parties seeking injunctive relief (although the doctrine of laches may apply).

Does this mean that a firm that acquires another firm is liable forever? In *du Pont*, the acquisition occurred in 1917. The action was brought in 1949. At the time the acquisition occurred General Motors manufactured only 11% of American automobile production, and the effects of the acquisition were not substantial. Should General Motors' growth after the merger occurred, to a size that the Court was willing to recognize as harmful, be relevant to the legality of the merger? Do you suppose the Court was influenced by the fact that the two companies were still distinct from each other? Suppose that in 1917 General Motors had acquired a fabrics and finishes company and completely integrated that company's operations with its own. Should the government be given an injunction requiring divestiture in such circumstances, when the fabrics and finishes company has completely lost its separate identity? The government might argue that the doctrine of laches should not apply, especially if it was only in recent years that the defendant acquired a large enough market share to make the acquisition anticompetitive. In *du Pont*, the Court said that the anticompetitive effects of the acquisition are to be measured "at the time of suit." In 1975 it reiterated that policy. *See United States v. ITT Continental Baking Co.*, 420 U.S. 223 (1975).

BROWN SHOE CO. V. UNITED STATES

370 U.S. 294 (1962)

CHIEF JUSTICE WARREN delivered the opinion of the Court.

This suit was initiated in November 1955 when the Government filed a civil action in the United States District Court for the Eastern District of Missouri alleging that a contemplated merger between the G.R. Kinney Company, Inc. (Kinney) and Brown Shoe Company, Inc. (Brown), through an exchange of Kinney for Brown stock, would violate section 7 of the Clayton Act.

[The proposed merger contained both vertical and horizontal aspects. Brown Shoe Company manufactured approximately 5% of all shoes in the United States, some of which it sold in its own stores. Kinney owned retail stores which accounted for about 1% of all shoes sold in the United States. Before the merger Kinney had not purchased any of its shoes from Brown, but after the merger Brown became Kinney's largest supplier, although Kinney continued to manufacture about half of its retail store requirements itself.]

The District Court found a "definite trend" among shoe manufacturers to acquire retail outlets. For example, International Shoe Company had no retail outlets in 1945, but by 1956 had acquired 130; General Shoe Company had only 80 retail outlets in 1945 but had 526 by 1956; Shoe Corporation of America, in the same period, increased its retail holdings from 301 to 842; Melville Shoe Company from 536 to 947; and Endicott-Johnson from 488 to 540. Brown, itself, with no retail outlets of its own prior to 1951, had acquired 845 such outlets by 1956. Moreover, between 1950 and 1956 nine independent shoe store chains, operating 1,114 retail shoe stores, were found to have become subsidiaries of these large firms and to have ceased their independent operations.

And once the manufacturers acquired retail outlets, the District Court found there was a "definite trend" for the parent-manufacturers to supply an ever increasing percentage of the retail outlets' needs, thereby foreclosing other manufacturers from effectively competing for the retail accounts. Manufacturer-dominated stores were found to be "drying up" the available outlets for independent producers.

....

... The primary vice of a vertical merger or other arrangement tying a customer to a supplier is that, by foreclosing the competitors of either party from a segment of the market otherwise open to them, the arrangement may act as a "clog on competition," *Standard Oil Co. of California v. United States*, 337 U.S. 293, 314, which "deprive[s] ... rivals of a fair opportunity to compete." ... Every extended vertical arrangement by its very nature, for at least a time, denies to competitors of the supplier the opportunity to compete for part or all of the trade of the customer-party to the vertical arrangement. However, the Clayton Act does not render unlawful all such vertical arrangements, but forbids only those whose effect "may be substantially to lessen competition, or to tend to create a monopoly" "in any line of commerce in any section of the country."... The "area of effective competition" must be determined by reference to a product market (the "line of commerce") and a geographic market (the "section of the country").

The outer boundaries of a product market are determined by the reasonable interchangeability of use or the cross-elasticity of demand between the product itself and substitutes for it.[42] However, within this broad market, well-defined submarkets may exist which, in themselves, constitute product markets for antitrust purposes. The boundaries of such a submarket may be determined by examining such practical indicia as industry or public recognition of the submarket as a separate economic entity, the product's peculiar characteristics and uses, unique production facilities, distinct customers, distinct prices, sensitivity to price changes, and specialized vendors. Because § 7 of the Clayton Act prohibits any merger which may substantially lessen competition "in *any* line of commerce" (emphasis supplied), it is necessary to examine the effects of a merger in each such economically significant submarket to determine if there is a reasonable probability that the merger will substantially lessen competition. If such a probability is found to exist, the merger is proscribed.

Applying these considerations to the present case, we conclude that the record supports the District Court's finding that the relevant lines of commerce are men's, women's, and children's shoes. These product lines are recognized by the public; each line is manufactured in separate plants; each has characteristics peculiar to itself rendering it generally noncompetitive with the others; and each is, of course, directed toward a distinct class of customers.

Appellant, however, contends that the District Court's definitions fail to recognize sufficiently "price/quality" and "age/sex" distinctions in shoes. Brown argues that the predominantly medium-priced shoes which it manufactures occupy a product market different from the predominantly low-priced shoes which Kinney sells. But agreement with that argument would be equivalent to holding that medium-priced shoes do not compete with low-priced shoes. We think the District Court properly found the facts to be otherwise. It would be unrealistic to accept Brown's contention that, for example, men's shoes selling below $8.99 are in a different product market from those selling above $9.00.

This is not to say, however, that "price/quality" differences, where they exist, are unimportant in analyzing a merger; they may be of importance in determining the likely effect of a merger. But the boundaries of the relevant market must be drawn with sufficient breadth to include the competing products of each of the merging companies and to recognize competition where, in fact, competition exists. Thus we agree with the District Court that in this case a further division of product lines based on "price/quality" differences would be "unrealistic."

Brown's contention that the District Court's product market definitions should have recognized further "age/sex" distinctions raises a different problem. Brown's sharpest criticism is directed at the District Court's finding that children's shoes constituted a single line of commerce. Brown argues, for example,

---

[42] The cross-elasticity of production facilities may also be an important factor in defining a product market within which a vertical merger is to be viewed.... However, the District Court made but limited findings concerning the feasibility of interchanging equipment in the manufacture of nonrubber footwear. At the same time, the record supports the court's conclusion that individual plants generally produced shoes in only one of the product lines the court found relevant.

that "a little boy does not wear a little girl's black patent leather pump" and that "[a] male baby cannot wear a growing boy's shoes." Thus Brown argues that "infants' and babies'" shoes, "misses' and children's" shoes and "youths' and boys'" shoes should each have been considered a separate line of commerce. Assuming, *arguendo*, that little boys' shoes, for example, do have sufficient peculiar characteristics to constitute one of the markets to be used in analyzing the effects of this merger, we do not think that in this case the District Court was required to employ finer "age/sex" distinctions than those recognized by its classifications of "men's," "women's," and "children's" shoes. Further division does not aid us in analyzing the effects of this merger. Brown manufactures about the same percentage of the Nation's children's shoes (5.8%) as it does of the Nation's youths' and boys' shoes (6.5%), of the Nation's misses' and children's shoes (6.0%) and of the Nation's infants' and babies' shoes (4.9%). Similarly, Kinney sells about the same percentage of the Nation's children's shoes (2%) as it does of the Nation's youths' and boys' shoes (3.1%), of the Nation's misses' and children's shoes (1.9%), and of the Nation's infants' and babies' shoes (1.5%). Appellant can point to no advantage it would enjoy where finer divisions than those chosen by the District Court employed. Brown manufactures significant, comparable quantities of virtually every type of nonrubber men's, women's, and children's shoes, and Kinney sells such quantities of virtually every type of men's, women's, and children's shoes. Thus, whether considered separately or together, the picture of this merger is the same. We, therefore, agree with the District Court's conclusion that in the setting of this case to subdivide the shoe market further on the basis of "age/sex" distinctions would be "impractical" and "unwarranted."

We agree with the parties and the District Court that insofar as the vertical aspect of this merger is concerned, the relevant geographic market is the entire Nation. The relationships of product value, bulk, weight and consumer demand enable manufacturers to distribute their shoes on a nationwide basis, as Brown and Kinney, in fact, do. The anticompetitive effects of the merger are to be measured within this range of distribution.

Once the area of effective competition affected by a vertical arrangement has been defined, an analysis must be made to determine if the effect of the arrangement "may be substantially to lessen competition, or to tend to create a monopoly" in this market.

Since the diminution of the vigor of competition which may stem from a vertical arrangement results primarily from a foreclosure of a share of the market otherwise open to competitors, an important consideration in determining whether the effect of a vertical arrangement "may be substantially to lessen competition, or to tend to create a monopoly" is the size of the share of the market foreclosed. However, this factor will seldom be determinative. If the share of the market foreclosed is so large that it approaches monopoly proportions, the Clayton Act will, of course, have been violated; but the arrangement will also have run afoul of the Sherman Act. And the legislative history of § 7 indicates clearly that the tests for measuring the legality of any particular economic arrangement under the Clayton Act are to be less stringent than those used in applying the Sherman Act. On the other hand, foreclosure of a *de minimis* share of the market will not tend "substantially to lessen competition."

Between these extremes, in cases such as the one before us, in which the foreclosure is neither of monopoly nor *de minimis* proportions, the percentage of the market foreclosed by the vertical arrangement cannot itself be decisive. In such cases, it becomes necessary to undertake an examination of various economic and historical factors in order to determine whether the arrangement under review is of the type Congress sought to proscribe....

... In 1955, the date of this merger, Brown was the fourth largest manufacturer in the shoe industry with sales of approximately 25 million pairs of shoes and assets of over $72,000,000 while Kinney had sales of about 8 million pairs of shoes and assets of about $18,000,000. Not only was Brown one of the leading manufacturers of men's, women's, and children's shoes, but Kinney, with over 350 retail outlets, owned and operated the largest independent chain of family shoe stores in the Nation. Thus, in this industry, no merger between a manufacturer and an independent retailer could involve a larger potential market foreclosure. Moreover, it is apparent both from past behavior of Brown and from the testimony of Brown's President, that Brown would use its ownership of Kinney to force Brown shoes into Kinney stores. Thus, in operation this vertical arrangement would be quite analogous to one involving a tying clause.

Another important factor to consider is the trend toward concentration in the industry. It is true, of course, that the statute prohibits a given merger only if the effect of *that* merger may be substantially to lessen competition. But the very wording of § 7 requires a prognosis of the probable *future* effect of the merger.

The existence of a trend toward vertical integration, which the District Court found, is well substantiated by the record. Moreover, the court found a tendency of the acquiring manufacturers to become increasingly important sources of supply for their acquired outlets. The necessary corollary of these trends is the foreclosure of independent manufacturers from markets otherwise open to them. And because these trends are not the product of accident but are rather the result of deliberate policies of Brown and other leading shoe manufacturers, account must be taken of these facts in order to predict the probable future consequences of this merger. It is against this background of continuing concentration that the present merger must be viewed.

Brown argues, however, that the shoe industry is at present composed of a large number of manufacturers and retailers, and that the industry is dynamically competitive. But remaining vigor cannot immunize a merger if the trend in that industry is toward oligopoly. It is the probable effect of the merger upon the future as well as the present which the Clayton Act commands the courts and the Commission to examine.

Moreover, as we have remarked above, not only must we consider the probable effects of the merger upon the economics of the particular markets affected but also we must consider its probable effects upon the economic way of life sought to be preserved by Congress. Congress was desirous of preventing the formation of further oligopolies with their attendant adverse effects upon local control of industry and upon small business. Where an industry was composed of numerous independent units, Congress appeared anxious to preserve this structure....

NOTES AND QUESTIONS

1. What does a "trend" toward vertical integration in an unconcentrated industry indicate? There was no argument that shoe manufacturers were actually having a hard time finding stores willing to buy their shoes. Nor was there any argument that shoe stores were having a difficult time finding suppliers. In 1963, less than 10% of American shoes were distributed through manufacturer owned or operated stores. *See* Peterman, *The Brown Shoe Case*, 18 J.L. & Econ. 81, 117 (1975). The "trend" thus does not suggest that manufacturers or retailers were trying to avoid foreclosure. Rather, it suggests that vertically integrated firms could produce and resell shoes more cheaply than independent firms could. Both the trial court and the Supreme Court found this to be the case. (See the note, *infra.*) If one firm in a competitive industry integrates vertically and is able to undersell its competitors as a result, a "trend" toward vertical integration will follow when competitors seek to take advantage of the same cost savings.

2. Many vertical mergers have been condemned on rather low "foreclosure" percentages. *E.g.*, *Ash Grove Cement Co. v. FTC*, 577 F.2d 1368 (9th Cir.), *cert. denied*, 439 U.S. 982 (1978) (condemning two different acquisitions, of 10.2% and 3.1%); *United States v. Standard Oil Co. (N.J.)*, 253 F. Supp. 196 (D.N.J. 1966) (condemning firm's acquisition of potash purchaser who had purchased less than 2% of the market).

NOTE: THE ECONOMICS OF VERTICAL MERGERS

Since the early 1980's the number of vertical merger challenges has dropped dramatically, in large part because most of the fears of reduced competition now seem far fetched or at least greatly exaggerated. For example, courts suggested that a company with a monopoly at one distributional level (such as the manufacturing of taxicabs) could "leverage" a second monopoly at a different distributional level (the operating of taxicabs), and thus turn one monopoly into two. Secondly, courts have suggested that by vertical integration a firm can "foreclose" rivals by restricting their markets or source of supply. For example, if a chain of shoe stores acquired a shoe manufacturer, and after the merger the manufacturer refused to sell to competing, independent shoe stores, those competitors would have a more difficult time obtaining shoes. Likewise, if a manufacturer bought many of the retail stores in a particular area, competing manufacturers might find it more difficult to find a market for their products. Thirdly, courts have suggested, as the Supreme Court did in *Yellow Cab, supra*, that a firm could make more money by "forcing" its own subsidiary to sell to it at a lower price.

Most of these theories have either vanished or else they play a very reduced rule in vertical merger analysis today. The implausibility of a firm making money by buying from itself at a lower price or selling to itself at a higher price seems obvious. One exception might be where a firm acquires less than 100% ownership in a firm at a different distributional level, but nevertheless acquires enough to control decisionmaking in the acquired firm. For example, there was evidence in the *du Pont* (GM) case, reprinted *supra*, that du Pont influenced General Motors' decision to buy du Pont products even though du Pont owned only 23% of General Motors' common stock. In that case du Pont might find it profitable to instruct General Motors to do something not in its own interest, such as purchasing materials from du Pont at a supracompetitive price. Although du Pont's gains would be offset by General Motors' losses, du Pont would suffer only 23% of those losses, while the other General Motors stockholders would suffer the balance.

The leverage and foreclosure theories have appeared frequently in decisions involving both vertical mergers and other kinds of vertical restrictions. For example, *see Heatransfer Corp. v. Volkswagenwerk, A.G.*, 553 F.2d 964 (5th Cir. 1977), *cert. denied*, 434 U.S. 1087 (1978) (involving both a vertical merger and a tying arrangement). But both theories have come under broad attack by economists, and courts rely on them less than they once did. Economists commonly argue, for example, that someone with a monopoly at one level of a distributional chain can extract all the monopoly profits available in that chain; the seller cannot enlarge its monopoly profits by acquiring a second monopoly at a different level of distribution. End-use consumers generally pay a single price for a product, and if there is a monopoly mark-up along the distributional chain they are indifferent to (and probably do not even know) whether that monopoly mark-up occurred at the retail level, the distributor level, or the manufacturing level.

Secondly, economists generally note that in markets that are even modestly competitive vertical acquisitions cannot really "foreclose" anyone from the market. Unless someone controls nearly all the sources of supply or outlets, the effect of a vertical acquisition is not foreclosure but a certain amount of reshuffling in the market, and a subsequent new alignment of purchasers and sellers among those firms that are not vertically integrated. For example, if a manufacturer with 20% of a market acquires a retail chain with 10% of the market, the effect may be that the two firms will deal with each other. However, no one will be foreclosed. Competitors of the retailer will buy from a manufacturer who formerly sold to the acquired retailer. Likewise, competitors of the acquiring manufacturer will sell to stores that formerly bought from the manufacturer. The ratio of independent sellers to independent buyers will be the same as it was before the acquisition, although there will be a somewhat different alignment of buyers and sellers. For a general discussion of these theories, *see* 4A P. Areeda & H. Hovenkamp,

Antitrust Law ¶¶ 1003-13 (rev. ed. 1998); H. Hovenkamp, *Federal Antitrust Policy*, ch. 9 (2d ed. 1994).

There are other alleged evils of vertical integration that are more controversial, although virtually all of these require that one of the two firms involved have a substantial amount of market power, or at least a very large market share. For example, it is often said that vertical integration by a monopolist creates "barriers to entry" by requiring a potential new entrant to enter the market at two levels instead of one. For example, if a monopolist in the manufacture of aluminum owns all its own fabricators, then anyone seeking to enter the market at the fabrication level will also have to build its own aluminum plant. Likewise, anyone seeking to enter at the aluminum manufacturing level may have to establish its own fabricating plants.

One answer to the barriers to entry argument is that the vertical integration creates a barrier to entry only if it results in lower cost production of the same product than independent levels of operation would entail. For example, suppose that an independent manufacturer of aluminum has costs of $1.00 per unit, while an independent fabricator has costs of 40 cents per unit. If the vertically integrated firm has total costs of $1.40 per unit for both manufacturing and fabricating, then it is profitable for independent manufacturers and independent fabricators to continue to enter the two separate production levels. However, if because of vertical integration the integrated firm can reduce its costs to $1.35, then the nonintegrated firms will have a difficult time competing unless they can also enter the market at both levels. In short, vertical integration may indeed force potential competitors to enter the market at two levels instead of one — but it is likely to do so only if the vertically integrated operation is more efficient than independent operations are.

It has also been said that vertical integration by a firm with market power can make price discrimination easier, or can hide it from the public and from customers (and law enforcement agents). For example, suppose that a manufacturer makes smidgets and has a large share of the market. Smidgets can be sold in two kinds of stores, discount stores and boutiques. However, smidgets command widely different prices in those two stores. The smidget manufacturer knows that boutique owners are willing to pay $5.00 each for smidgets, but the discount stores will pay only $4.00 each. Both prices are profitable to the smidget manufacturer. Ideally the manufacturer would like to make each set of sales at the profit-maximizing price for that particular set — that is, it would like to sell to the boutiques at $5.00 and to the discount stores at $4.00. However, two things make this difficult. One is arbitrage: eventually the store owners will find out what is happening and the discount store owners will begin reselling smidgets to boutique owners at some price greater than $4.00 but less than $5.00. If that happens the manufacturer will lose its most profitable sales. The other problem is the Robinson-Patman Act, which may prevent this form of differential pricing. (See Chapter 8, *infra.*) Suppose however, that the smidget manufacturer acquires the boutiques. It will then be able to internalize the sales to the boutiques and take advantage of the higher retail price that smidgets command there. At the same time it will continue making sales to discount stores at $4.00.

Although vertical integration may facilitate price discrimination, does that mean it is bad? Unquestionably the manufacturer of smidgets makes more money by price discriminating, or else the manufacturer would not do it. However, it is not at all clear that consumers are worse off. In fact, they may be better off, because the availability of price discrimination may encourage the manufacturer to produce more smidgets than it would otherwise. Whether or not it would depends on what its nondiscriminatory profit-maximizing price would be. For example, if the smidget manufacturer decided (when it did not own the boutiques) that it could maximize its profits by selling only to the boutiques at $5.00, and forgetting about the discount stores, then the price discrimination that resulted from the acquisition of the boutiques would make the discount stores and their customers better off: now they can have smidgets too. By contrast, if the smidget manufacturer could previously maximize its profits by selling to both the discount stores and boutiques at $4.00, then the effect of the vertical merger will be to make the boutique's customers worse off, while the discount store's customers are no better off. In short, once we accept that the smidget manufacturer has market power, it is difficult to tell whether price discrimination is socially preferable to nondiscriminatory pricing.

In general, long-term systematic price discrimination is impossible for a seller without market power. If the seller faces substantial competition then disfavored purchasers (those asked to pay the higher price) will simply buy from a competitor. Of course, it might be socially preferable that the smidget manufacturer not have market power in the first place, but that is not an option that is before us now. For further development of the theory that vertical integration can facilitate or disguise price discrimination, see III P. Areeda & D. Turner, *Antitrust Law* 201-03 (1978); O. Williamson, *Markets and Hierarchies* 82-131 (1975); *The Nature of the Firm: Origins, Evolution, and Development* (O. Williamson & S. Winter eds., 1991).

Another theory of vertical integration is that under certain circumstances it may facilitate horizontal price fixing. For example, one of the most difficult aspects of maintaining a cartel is detection of cheating by cartel members. A member of a manufacturing cartel who wanted to cheat could offer retailers secret rebates if they bought the cartel member's product. By contrast, retail prices are public and are easily policed. If the members of a cartel agree to sell their output only through their own retail stores, cheating will be easier to detect.

The vast majority of vertical acquisitions probably cannot be explained on any of these theories. Most firms integrate vertically in order to reduce costs. Probably the most significant of these are the transaction costs that accrue from the use of the market system itself. As a general rule, a firm can maximize its own profits by dealing with other firms in the distribution chain that are maximally efficient. For example, the aluminum manufacturer is best off if it can obtain bauxite or iron ore at the lowest possible cost. It is likewise better off if it can pay a lower price for transportation services for its finished product. In order to obtain goods or services that are best suited to itself, and at the lowest possible price, a firm may spend a great deal of money in searching for a suitable provider, and additional sums in negotiating a suitable contract. Then it must rely on the other party to the contract to be a stable and financially sound business partner. Firms generally have less information about the financial stability of other firms than they have about themselves; as a result, trusting the financial security of someone else involves more risk than trusting oneself. Often a firm can avoid these costs and risks by obtaining its own source of supply, its own means of transportation, or its own resale outlets.

A firm can also reduce its cost by vertically integrating if another link in the distribution chain is either monopolized or cartelized. For example, suppose that a manufacturer of wash machines purchases electric motors which cost $50 to produce, but are sold to the wash machine manufacturer for $70 because the motor manufacturers are engaged in a successful cartel. In this case the wash machine manufacturer could profit by obtaining its own producer of electric motors: by so doing it could transfer the $20 in monopoly profits away from the cartel and to itself. In fact, even if the wash machine manufacturer were itself a monopolist, it would be better off producing its own motors than it would paying a monopoly price for them. Likewise, consumers would be better off, for when the monopolist's costs go down its profit-maximizing price declines as well.

Figure 1

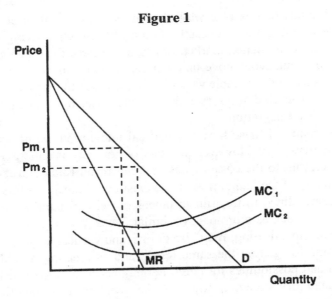

In general, a monopolist who has lower costs will have a lower profit-maximizing price. If the monopolist's marginal cost drops from MC_1 to MC_2, its profit-maximizing price — determined by the intersection of the marginal cost curve and the marginal revenue curve — will drop from Pm_1 to Pm_2. As a result, if one monopolist vertically integrates with another monopolist the integrated firm's profit-maximizing price will be lower than if each firm independently charged its own profit-maximizing price.

Government regulations can also make it cheaper for firms to integrate vertically. For example, when a firm buys or sells a certain good or service, that transaction may have to be accounted for on a tax return. However, if the firm integrates and eliminates the market transaction, then there may not be a purchase or sale that the tax laws recognize. Likewise, many regulations regarding pricing, information disclosure, production restrictions, and market environment apply to exchanges between independent parties, but not to internal exchanges. Suppose, for example, that a state imposes substantial licensing requirements on independent electricians, plumbers, truckers, or engineers, and these requirements increase the cost of providing these services. Often a firm can avoid these costs simply by hiring such providers as full-time employees. Likewise, sometimes governments place entry restrictions on certain businesses that do not apply to vertically integrated firms. A city, for example, might have a legal limit on the number of licensed taxicabs that can be operated in the city. As a result, some hotels might find it difficult to obtain satisfactory taxi service for their patrons. One solution might be for the hotel to acquire and operate its own airport limousine exclusively for its own hotel guests, for such a limousine may be exempt from the entry restrictions.

There are literally hundreds of ways that firms can lower their costs or provide better service by integrating vertically. Some of these cost savings come out of avoidance of the unregulated market, others come out of mechanisms by which integrated firms can avoid governmental regulations. In general, the kinds of particular costs savings available vary greatly from one industry to another — but most industries can find ways to reduce some costs by engaging in a certain amount of vertical integration.

To be sure, many of these forms of vertical integration are not carried out by merger but by new entry. However, whether or not there is a merger may be economically irrelevant to the cost savings that can result (although it may be relevant to the impact of the integration on the existing market). For this reason, most economists are inclined to treat all instances of vertical integration, whether by merger or by contract, as more-or-less similar. Thus, for example, the economist might treat exclusive dealing, franchise tie-ins, and vertical acquisitions as different mechanisms for getting the same result, and as creating roughly equivalent risks of harm and possibilities for good. Largely because of their historical development and statutory structure, however, the antitrust laws view these practices as quite different from each other.

The antitrust literature on vertical integration and vertical mergers is vast. Interested readers might look at 4A P. Areeda & H. Hovenkamp, *Antitrust Law*, ch. 10 (rev. ed. 1998); F. M. Scherer & D. Ross, *Industrial Market Structure and*

Economic Performance, chs. 3 and 4 (3d ed. 1990); R. Blair & D. Kaserman, *Antitrust Economics*, chs. 11 & 12 (1985); H. Hovenkamp, *Federal Antitrust Policy*, ch. 9 (2d ed. 1994); E.T. Sullivan & J. Harrison, *Understanding Antitrust and Its Economic Implications*, chs. 6 and 7 (3d ed. 1998).

SILICON-GRAPHICS

5 Trade Reg Rep. ¶ 23,838 (1995) Federal Trade Commission

Complaint

... Respondent Silicon Graphics, Inc. ("SGI") ... designs and supplies a family of workstation, server and supercomputer systems. SGI develops and markets, among other things, computer hardware incorporating interactive three-dimensional ("3D") graphics, digital media and multiprocessor supercomputing technologies.

Alias Research Inc. ("Alias") ... is a leading producer of workstation-based, 3D and two-dimensional ("2D") computer graphics software, for professional entertainment and industrial customers. Users of Alias' products in the entertainment industry create 3D computer graphic special effects, which may be output to a variety of media, including film and video for use in movies, television, interactive computer games, and other forms of presentation....

Wavefront Technologies, Inc. ("Wavefront") ... is a full-line producer of workstation-based, 3D and 2D computer graphics software, for professional entertainment and industrial customers. Users of Wavefront's products in the entertainment industry create 3D computer graphic special effects, which may be output to a variety of media, including film and video for use in movies, television, interactive computer games, and other forms of presentation....

One relevant line of commerce in which to analyze the effects of the proposed acquisitions is the development, production and sale of entertainment graphics workstations. Entertainment graphics workstations generally are UNIX-based computers with high-speed graphic capability and suitable for use with entertainment graphics software. Personal computers, including Intel-based PCs and Apple MacIntosh computers, are not adequate substitutes for entertainment graphics workstations as platforms for running entertainment graphics software.

Another relevant line of commerce in which to analyze the effects of the proposed acquisitions is the development, production and sale of entertainment graphics software....

The entertainment graphics workstation market is extremely concentrated. SGI is the dominant provider of entertainment graphics workstations, with over 90% of the market. Although various other companies manufacture workstations, most entertainment graphics software was developed for use on SGI workstations and is available only for SGI workstations.

The entertainment graphics software market is highly concentrated and rapidly growing. Alias and Wavefront are two of the three leading developers and sellers of entertainment graphics software. Alias and Wavefront compete principally with SoftImage Inc., a subsidiary of Microsoft Corp....

Prior to the acquisitions described in Paragraph 5, SGI maintained an open software interface for its entertainment graphics workstations, sponsored independent software developer programs, and shared with developers of entertainment graphics software advance information concerning new SGI products to facilitate and promote competitive development of entertainment graphics software. ...

Entry into the entertainment graphics workstation market would not be timely, likely, or sufficient in its magnitude, character, and scope to deter or counteract anticompetitive effects of the acquisitions in the entertainment graphics workstation market. Other manufacturers of computer workstations have graphic engines for their computers that are technically capable of running entertainment graphics software provided a version of the software is written for use with the workstation and its graphic engine. However, without the possibility of having Alias or Wavefront entertainment graphics software developed for those workstations, entry would be unlikely. Marketing a technically comparable or even an improved combination of non-SGI workstations with entertainment graphics software other than that of Alias or Wavefront would be difficult, time consuming and not likely to occur because of the extensive installed user base of SGI workstations with Alias, Wavefront and SoftImage entertainment graphics software.

Entry into the market for the development and sale of entertainment graphics software would not be timely, likely, or sufficient in its magnitude, character, and scope to deter or counteract anticompetitive effects of the acquisitions in the entertainment graphics software market. Developing an entertainment graphics software suite similar to those of Alias and Wavefront is time consuming and unlikely to occur because of extensive installed user bases trained on and using the Alias and Wavefront software programs on SGI entertainment graphics workstations. Combining smaller software developers' niche programs or making smaller producers of entertainment graphics software significant competitors to Alias and Wavefront would be difficult, time consuming and not likely to occur because of the extensive installed user base of SGI workstations with Alias, Wavefront and SoftImage entertainment graphics software. ...

[These] acquisitions .., if consummated, may, individually or in combination, substantially lessen competition and tend to create a monopoly in the relevant markets in violation of Section 7 of the Clayton Act, 15 U.S.C. §18, and Section 5 of the FTC Act, 15 U.S.C. §45, in the following ways, among others:

> a. They may foreclose workstation producers other than SGI from significant, independent sources of entertainment graphics software, reducing competition in the manufacture and sale of entertainment graphics workstations;
>
> b. They may increase costs to workstation producers other than SGI for obtaining entertainment graphics software for their workstation platforms, reducing competition in the manufacture and sale of entertainment graphics workstations;

c. They will facilitate SGI's unilateral exercise of market power in entertainment graphics workstations through price discrimination;

d. They may enable SGI to gain proprietary, competitively sensitive information pertaining to other workstation producers if such workstation producers are able to get Alias or Wavefront entertainment graphics software ported to their workstations, reducing competition in the manufacture and sale of entertainment graphics workstations;

e. They will eliminate Alias and Wavefront as substantial independent competitors, eliminate actual, direct and substantial competition between Alias and Wavefront, and increase the level of concentration in the entertainment graphics software market;

f. They will increase barriers to entry into the relevant markets and make two-level entry necessary;

g. They may foreclose, or increase costs to, competitors to Alias and Wavefront in the entertainment graphics software market in developing software for use in connection with future entertainment graphics workstation products developed by SGI, reducing competition in the development, manufacture and sale of entertainment graphics software.

h. They may cause consumers to pay higher prices for entertainment graphics software and for entertainment graphics workstations;

i. They may reduce innovation competition among producers of entertainment graphics software and among producers of entertainment graphics workstations.

NOTES AND QUESTIONS

1. Silicon Graphics agreed to a consent order requiring it (1) to ensure the continued compatibility of software developed by its newly acquired subsidiaries with the hardware of rivals; and (2) to maintain an "open architecture" policy of publicizing technical information about its own hardware, so that rival manufacturers of graphics software would be able to write products for Silicon Graphics computers and operating systems. *Silicon Graphics*, Dkt. No. C-3626, November 14, 1995.

2. In *Time-Warner*, 5 Trade Reg. Rep. ¶ 24,104 (consent decree, FTC, 1996), the FTC challenged a major cable television system operator's (Time-Warner's) acquisition of a major television programmer (Turner Communications). One of the theories of the complaint was that the acquisition would increase the costs of rival programmers by denying them access to a sufficient number of cable systems. The fixed costs of television programming are very high, but licensing an additional cable system to broadcast an existing program costs very little. As a result, programming is cost effective only if it can be sold to a large number of systems. One claim was that post-acquisition Time-Warner would put Turner's Cable News Network (CNN) on its cable systems exclusively, thus excluding infant rivals such as FoxNews, a competing 24-hour cable news program. The result would be that not enough independent cable systems would remain to enable FoxNews to have sufficient revenue to maintain its program. Time-Warner also entered into a consent decree.

3. In *Fruehauf Corp. v. FTC*, 603 F.2d 345 (2d Cir. 1979), the court refused to enforce an FTC order condemning a truck trailer manufacturer's acquisition of a firm that manufactured wheels and braking devices for such trailers. The court observed:

> Although it has been suggested that a significant percentage of market foreclosure, standing alone, might constitute a sufficient "clog on competition" to amount to a violation of § 7 without more, ... no such *per se* rule has been adopted, except where the share of the market foreclosed reaches monopoly proportions.
>
> ... A showing of some probable anticompetitive impact is still essential (e.g., promotion of a trend toward integration; reduction in number of potential market competitors; entrenchment of a large supplier or purchaser; increase in barriers to entry).

The main theory of the FTC's complaint was that in times of shortages of wheels and brakes Fruehauf would give itself preferred treatment over rival purchasers. The court found no evidence that this would occur, but even if it did, why would it be anticompetitive? *See* 4A P. Areeda & H. Hovenkamp, *Antitrust Law* ¶ 1003b4 (rev. ed. 1998):

> Integrated firms may well prefer their own outlets if there is a permanent fall in supply — for example, the decline of an exhaustible resource. In that case, second level output must also decline, and the number of efficient surviving *B* firms may fall below the number needed for effective competition. But integration is not harmful in that situation and might be beneficial. Assume, for example, that there are five integrated and five unintegrated firms at the *B* level, all of minimum efficient size. If the *A* supply declines, some *B* firms will be eliminated. If the decline is substantial enough, the number may fall to, say, five firms. But all the vertical integration does is to make it probable that the survivors will be integrated firms. If the number of survivors is too few for competitive pricing, it is socially preferable (or at least no worse) that they be integrated.

4. Suppose that a large purchaser of a certain product acquires a supplier. As a result, the purchaser buys exclusively from its new subsidiary, and no longer purchases from *A*, a competing supplier. Should *A* have a damage action for the lost sales under section 7 of the Clayton Act? *See Alberta Gas Chems. v. E.I. du Pont de Nemours & Co.*, 826 F.2d 1235, 1244-46 (3d Cir. 1987):

> A vertically integrated firm seeking to increase profits will engage in self-dealing if the supplying division's output cannot be more profitably sold

elsewhere, or is not more costly or inferior than the product of outside suppliers.... Because of post-merger efficiencies allowing it to purchase the acquiring company's output at a better price than in the marketplace, the acquired
company's purchasing costs would fall — a procompetitive benefit capable
of being passed on via lower prices for its products....

Injuries to competitors of this nature should not be compensable under the
antitrust laws because they do not flow from the anticompetitive effects of a
merger. Far from being caused by any post-merger market power, the competitor's losses would spring from the efficient aspects of the merger....

If the merger were considered unlawful for reasons other than foreclosure
of sales, the question then would become whether damages from the foreclosure flowed from the illegal act.... [P]laintiff must establish that its harm
was caused by that which makes the action unlawful. Assuming the merger
violated the antitrust laws because it concentrated economic power in the
production of methanol — as Alberta [the plaintiff] asserts — any resulting
foreclosure from this concentration is but an incident of, and not a result of,
the unlawful act.

NOTE: MERGER GUIDELINES AND VERTICAL MERGERS

In 1968 the Justice Department first issued Guidelines describing its standards
for challenging mergers under section 7 of the Clayton Act. These Guidelines were
completely rewritten in 1982 to reflect substantial changes in the economic theory
and enforcement policies of the Justice Department's Antitrust Division. These
Guidelines were revised in 1984. They were revised much more substantially and
issued jointly by the Antitrust Division and the Federal Trade Commission in 1992.
The 1992 Guidelines, which are reprinted in Appendix A, pertain only to horizontal mergers, however. In analyzing a vertical merger, these agencies will presumably rely on the market definition, entry barriers, and efficiencies sections of the
1992 Guidelines. The Antitrust Division will then apply the substantive analysis
contained in the 1984 Guidelines. The discussion below briefly contrasts the old
1968 Guidelines with the 1984 Guidelines as they pertain to vertical mergers.

The 1968 Guidelines identified vertical mergers as suspicious largely on the
basis of the market shares of the merging firms. For example, they provided that
the Justice Department would "ordinarily challenge a merger or a series of mergers between a supplying firm, accounting for approximately 10% or more of the
sales in its market, and one or more purchasing firms, accounting in toto for approximately 6% or more of the total purchases in that market, unless it clearly
appears that there are no significant barriers to entry into the business of the purchasing firm or firms." In general, the 1968 Guidelines perceived barriers to entry as the greatest potential danger from vertical mergers, although it recognized
that barriers to entry resulting from economies of scale are "not questionable as
such." The 1968 Guidelines also perceived certain vertical mergers as creating

the danger of a "supply squeeze." Under the supply squeeze theory, a producer could injure its competitors by acquiring an important source of a scarce or technologically complex essential product. In *Fruehauf Corp. v. FTC*, 603 F.2d 345 (2d Cir. 1979), the Federal Trade Commission had relied on a past shortage of heavy duty wheels to apply the supply squeeze theory to Fruehauf's acquisition of Kelsey-Hayes, which manufactured the wheels. The wheels were relatively common foundry items, however, and it is difficult to see how the supply squeeze theory would apply to them.

The 1984 Guidelines for vertical mergers are more explicit and technical than the 1968 Guidelines, and see few occasions for condemning them. First, discussion of the "supply squeeze" has all but disappeared. On the danger that a vertical merger might raise entry barriers, the 1984 Guidelines state the following:

> In certain circumstances, the vertical integration resulting from vertical mergers could create competitively objectionable barriers to entry. Stated generally, three conditions are necessary (but not sufficient) for this problem to exist. First, the degree of vertical integration between the two markets must be so extensive that entrants to one market (the "primary market") also would have to enter the other market (the "secondary market") simultaneously. Second, the requirement of entry at the secondary level must make entry at the primary level significantly more difficult and less likely to occur. Finally, the structure and other characteristics of the primary market must be otherwise so conducive to non-competitive performance that the increased difficulty of entry is likely to affect its performance. The following standards state the criteria by which the Department will determine whether these conditions are satisfied.
>
> If there is sufficient unintegrated capacity in the secondary market, new entrants to the primary market would not have to enter both markets simultaneously. The Department is unlikely to challenge a merger on this ground where post-merger sales (purchases) by unintegrated firms in the secondary market would be sufficient to service two minimum-efficient-scale plants in the primary market. When the other conditions are satisfied, the Department is increasingly likely to challenge a merger as the unintegrated capacity declines below this level.
>
> The relevant question is whether the need for simultaneous entry to the secondary market gives rise to a substantial incremental difficulty as compared to entry into the primary market alone. If entry at the secondary level is easy in absolute terms, the requirement of simultaneous entry to that market is unlikely adversely to affect entry to the primary market....
>
> When entry is not possible under those conditions, the Department is increasingly concerned about vertical mergers as the difficulty of entering the secondary market increases. The Department, however, will invoke this theory only where the need for secondary market entry significantly increases the costs (which may take the form of risks) of primary market entry....

Economies of scale in the secondary market may constitute an additional barrier to entry to the primary market in some situations requiring two-level entry. The problem could arise if the capacities of minimum-efficient-scale plants in the primary and secondary markets differ significantly. For example, if the capacity of a minimum-efficient-scale plant in the secondary market were significantly greater than the needs of a minimum-efficient-scale plant in the primary market, entrants would have to choose between inefficient operation at the secondary level (because of operating an efficient plant at an inefficient output or because of operating an inefficiently small plant) or a larger than necessary scale at the primary level. Either of these effects could cause a significant increase in the operating costs of the entering firm.

1984 Guidelines, § 4.21.

The Guidelines also note that a vertical merger might be used to facilitate collusion at the retail level:

The elimination by vertical merger of a particularly disruptive buyer in a downstream market may facilitate collusion in the upstream market. If upstream firms view sales to a particular buyer as sufficiently important, they may deviate from the terms of a collusive agreement in an effort to secure that business, thereby disrupting the operation of the agreement. The merger of such a buyer with an upstream firm may eliminate that rivalry, making it easier for the upstream firms to collude effectively. Adverse competitive consequences are unlikely unless the upstream market is generally conducive to collusion and the disruptive firm is significantly more attractive to sellers than the other firms in its market.

The Department is unlikely to challenge a merger on this ground unless (1) overall concentration of the upstream market is 1800 HHI or above (a somewhat lower concentration will suffice if one or more of the factors discussed in Section 3.4 indicate that effective collusion is particularly likely), and (2) the allegedly disruptive firm differs substantially in volume of purchases or other relevant characteristics from the other firms in its market. Where the stated thresholds are met or exceeded, the Department's decision whether to challenge a merger on this ground will depend upon an individual evaluation of its likely competitive effect.

1984 Guidelines, § 4.22.

Finally, the 1984 Guidelines note "evasion of rate regulation" as an anticompetitive rationale for some vertical mergers. Recall the discussion of the *Yellow Cab* case at the beginning of this chapter. The Guidelines state:

Non-horizontal mergers may be used by monopoly public utilities subject to rate regulation as a tool for circumventing that regulation. The clearest example is the acquisition by a regulated utility of a supplier of its fixed or variable inputs. After the merger, the utility would be selling to itself and might be able arbitrarily to inflate the prices of internal transactions. Regulators may have great difficulty in policing these practices, particularly if there is no independent market for the product (or service) purchased from the affiliate.

As a result, inflated prices could be passed along to consumers as "legitimate" costs....

1984 Guidelines, § 4.23.

NOTES AND QUESTIONS

1. The acronym "HHI" used in the 1984 Guidelines stands for Herfindahl-Hirschman Index, which is a measure of industrial concentration commonly used by economists and now incorporated into the Guidelines. The HHI and its use are discussed more fully in the Guidelines for horizontal mergers, discussed *infra.* For purposes of understanding the part of the Guidelines dealing with vertical mergers you should know that a concentration of approximately 1800 HHI would be achieved by any of the following markets: (1) a market with two firms of slightly less than 30% share each, and several very small firms; (2) a market containing two firms, each with 25% of the market, and five firms each with 10% of the market; and (3) a market having one firm with 30% of the market, two having 20% each, and several firms having about 5% of the market each.

2. The concern of the Guidelines as applied to vertical mergers is whether the merger will contribute to some kind of horizontal restraint of trade, particularly whether it will facilitate collusion. If there is not such a perceived danger it appears that the Justice Department will not challenge the acquisition, regardless of existing case law. The "foreclosure" theory is all but forgotten. Is it a usurpation of legislative authority for the executive branch to refuse to challenge an acquisition that existing case law suggests is illegal? *See* Easterbrook, *Is There a Ratchet in Antitrust Law?*, 60 Tex. L. Rev. 705 (1982).

3. The Guidelines recognize that price-regulated firms such as electric utilities have a special incentive to integrate vertically into a market that is not price-regulated: the price-regulated firm could charge itself a high price from its subsidiary and use this inflated price to increase its rate base. An example might be an electric utility that acquires its own coal-producing firm. The one problem with the utility's scheme, however, is that coal is bought and sold daily at public prices, and if the utility attempts to charge itself a high price for its own coal the excessive price will be apparent to the rate-making authority. One way the utility might get around this problem, suggests the Guidelines, is by acquiring *all* the available coal and selling it to all buyers at the same inflated price, so that the price appears to be normal. Is this plausible? Would it make a difference if the product was plutonium fuel, which is used only by nuclear power plants?

SECTION II. MERGERS OF COMPETITORS

A. THE DEVELOPMENT OF HORIZONTAL MERGER LAW UNDER THE SHERMAN ACT

NORTHERN SECURITIES CO. V. UNITED STATES

193 U.S. 197 (1904)

[The defendant was a holding company which acquired two large, parallel railroads that ran through the northern United States — the Great Northern Railway and the Northern Pacific Railway. The two lines competed for long hauls, although substantially less so for short ones. The United States charged that the formation of the holding company violated section 1 of the Sherman Act.]

JUSTICE HARLAN delivered the opinion of the Court.

... Necessarily by this combination or arrangement the holding company in the fullest sense dominates the situation in the interest of those who were stockholders of the constituent companies; as much so, for every practical purpose, as if it had been itself a railroad corporation which had built, owned, and operated both lines for the exclusive benefit of its stockholders. Necessarily, also, the constituent companies ceased, under such a combination, to be in active competition for trade and commerce along their respective lines, and have become, practically, one powerful consolidated corporation, by the name of a holding corporation, the principal, if not the sole, object for the formation of which was to carry out the purpose of the original combination, under which competition between the constituent companies would cease. Those who were stockholders of the Great Northern and Northern Pacific and became stockholders in the holding company are now interested in preventing all competition between the two lines, and, as owners of stock or of certificates of stock in the holding company, they will see to it that no competition is tolerated.... This combination is, within the meaning of the act, a "trust;" but if not, it is a *combination in restraint of interstate and international commerce;* and that is enough to bring it under the condemnation of the act. The mere existence of such a combination, and the power acquired by the holding company as its trustee, constitute a menace to, and a restraint upon, that freedom of commerce which Congress intended to recognize and protect, and which the public is entitled to have protected. If such combination be not destroyed, all the advantages that would naturally come to the public under the operation of the general laws of competition, as between the Great Northern and Northern Pacific Railway Companies, will be lost, and the entire commerce of the immense territory in the northern part of the United States between the Great Lakes and the Pacific at Puget Sound will be at the mercy of a single holding corporation, organized in a state distant from the people of that territory.

....

[T]o vitiate a combination such as the act of Congress condemns, it need not be shown that the combination, in fact, results or will result, in a total suppression of trade or in a complete monopoly, but it is only essential to show that, by its necessary operation, it tends to restrain interstate or international trade or commerce or tends to create a monopoly in such trade or commerce and to deprive the public of the advantages that flow from free competition.

....

JUSTICE HOLMES, with whom concurred THE CHIEF JUSTICE, JUSTICE WHITE and JUSTICE PECKHAM, dissenting.

....

Great cases, like hard cases, make bad law. For great cases are called great, not by reason of their real importance in shaping the law of the future, but because of some accident of immediate overwhelming interest which appeals to the feelings and distorts the judgment. These immediate interests exercise a kind of hydraulic pressure which makes what previously was clear seem doubtful, and before which even well settled principles of law will bend. What we have to do in this case is to find the meaning of some not very difficult words....

....

The first section [of the Sherman Act] makes "Every contract, combination in the form of trust or otherwise, or conspiracy in restraint of trade or commerce among the several states, or with foreign nations" a misdemeanor, punishable by fine, imprisonment, or both. Much trouble is made by substituting other phrases assumed to be equivalent, which then are reasoned from as if they were in the act. The court below argued as if maintaining competition were the expressed object of the act. The act says nothing about competition. I stick to the exact words used. The words hit two classes of cases, and only two, — Contracts in restraint of trade and combinations or conspiracies in restraint of trade, — and we have to consider what these respectively are. Contracts in restraint of trade are dealt with and defined by the common law. They are contracts with a stranger to the contractor's business (although, in some cases, carrying on a similar one), which wholly or partially restrict the freedom of the contractor in carrying on that business as otherwise he would. The objection of the common law to them was, primarily, on the contractor's own account. The notion of monopoly did not come in unless the contract covered the whole of England. Of course, this objection did not apply to partnerships or other forms, if there were any, of substituting a community of interest where there had been competition. There was no objection to such combinations merely as in restraint of trade or otherwise unless they amounted to a monopoly. Contracts in restraint of trade, I repeat, were contracts with strangers to the contractor's business, and the trade restrained was the contractor's own.

Combinations or conspiracies in restraint of trade, on the other hand, were combinations to keep strangers to the agreement out of the business. The objection to them was not an objection to their effect upon the parties making the contract, the members of the combination or firm, but an objection to their intended effect upon strangers to the firm and their supposed consequent effect upon the public at large. In other words, they were regarded as contrary to public policy because they monopolized, or attempted to monopolize, some portion of the trade or commerce of the realm. All that is added to the first section by § 2 is that like penalties are imposed upon every single person who, without combination, monopolizes, or attempts to monopolize, commerce among the states; and that the liability is extended to attempting to monopolize any part of such trade or commerce. It is more important as an aid to the construction of § 1 than it is on its own account. It shows that whatever is criminal when done by way of combination is equally criminal if done by a single man. That I am right in my interpretation of words of § 1 is shown by the words "in the form of trust or otherwise." The prohibition was suggested by the trusts, the objection to which, as everyone knows, was not the union of former competitors, but the sinister power exercised or supposed to be exercised by the combination in keeping rivals out of the business and ruining those who already were in. It was the ferocious extreme of competition with others, not the cessation of competition among the partners, that was the evil feared....

I assume that the Minnesota charter of the Great Northern, and the Wisconsin charter of the Northern Pacific, both are valid. Suppose that, before either road was built, Minnesota, as part of a system of transportation between the states, had created a railroad company authorized singly to build all the lines in the states now actually built, owned, or controlled by either of the two existing companies. I take it that that charter would have been just as good as the present one, even if the statutes which we are considering had been in force. In whatever sense it would have created a monopoly, the present charter does. It would have been a large one, but the act of Congress makes no discrimination according to size. Size has nothing to do with the matter. A monopoly of "any part" of commerce among the states is unlawful. The supposed company would have owned lines that might have been competing; probably the present one does. But the act of Congress will not be construed to mean the universal disintegration of society into single men, each at war with all the rest, or even the prevention of all further combinations for a common end.

... [I]t has occurred to me that it might be that when a combination reached a certain size it might have attributed to it more of the character of a monopoly merely by virtue of its size than would be attributed to a smaller one. I am quite clear that it is only in connection with monopolies that size could play any part. But my answer has been indicated already. In the first place, size, in the case of railroads, is an inevitable incident; and if it were an objection under the act, the Great Northern and the Northern Pacific already were too great and encountered the law. In the next place, in the case of railroads it is evident that the size of the combination is reached for other ends than those which would make them monopolies. The combinations are not formed for the purpose of excluding others from the field. Finally, even a small railroad will have the same tendency to exclude others from its narrow area that great ones have to exclude others from the greater one, and the statute attacks the small monopolies as well as the great....

....

A partnership is not a contract or combination in restraint of trade between the partners unless the well known words are to be given a new meaning, invented for the purposes of this act. It is true that the suppression of competition was referred to in *United States v. Trans-Missouri Freight Ass'n* but, as I have said, that was in connection with a contract with a stranger to the defendant's business, — a true contract in restraint of trade. To suppress competition in that way is one thing; to suppress it by fusion is another. The law, I repeat, says nothing about competition, and only prevents its suppression by contracts or combinations in restraint of trade, and such contracts or combinations derive their character as restraining trade from other features than the suppression of competition alone. To see whether I am wrong, the illustrations put in the argument are of use. If I am, then a partnership between two stage drivers who had been competitors in driving across a state line, or two merchants once engaged in rival commerce among the states, whether made after or before the act, if now continued, is a crime. For, again I repeat, if the restraint on the freedom of the members of a combination, caused by their entering into partnership, is a restraint of trade, every such combination, as well the small as the great, is within the act.

NOTES AND QUESTIONS

1. In a concurring opinion Justice Brewer argued as follows: "It must also be remembered that under present conditions a single railroad is, if not a legal, largely a practical, monopoly, and the arrangement by which the control of these two competing roads was merged in a single corporation broadens and extends such monopoly." 193 U.S. at 363. Are you persuaded? If the only electric utility in Minneapolis acquires the only electric utility in St. Paul, has the monopoly been "broadened and extended"?

2. In his dissent Justice Holmes chose sides in a debate that dominated early Sherman Act decision-making: whether the statute merely enacted the common law of trade restraints, or whether it forbade other practices that were legal at common law. Judge Taft addressed the same question in the *Addyston Pipe* case. For an enlightening historical discussion of this issue, *see* H.B. Thorelli, *The Federal Antitrust Policy: Origination of an American Tradition*, 9-53 (1954). *See also* H. Hovenkamp, *Enterprise and American Law, 1836-1937*, chs. 20 and 21 (1991). Holmes certainly knew about the debate, but in the *Northern Securities* case he pretended as if there were not even an issue, and attempted to restrict the phrase "contract in restraint of trade" to its common law meaning.

3. One of Holmes's arguments goes something like this: if one company from the beginning had built both lines consolidated into the Northern Securities holding company, the company would clearly have been legal. Why should it

make a difference that the lines were originally built by two different companies and later consolidated?

One answer might be that if the lines really were in competition, and if railroads are natural monopolies, then no reasonable corporation would have built both lines. However, once the two lines were built, there was excess capacity that would eventually drive one of the lines into bankruptcy. In fact, the Northern Pacific Company had gone bankrupt before the consolidation occurred. One way to eliminate the "ruinous" competition caused by the excess capacity was for the two firms to merge. *See* Hovenkamp, *Regulatory Conflict in the Gilded Age: Federalism and the Railroad Problem*, 88 Yale L.J. 1017 (1988).

But that is not an entirely satisfactory answer to Justice Holmes's question, is it? He could have asked the same question with respect to an industry that was not a natural monopoly. In most merger cases it is clear that the defendant could legally have achieved its size by internal growth. However, since the size came about by merger it runs afoul of the antitrust laws. Is there any reason to believe that a company created by internal growth is more efficient or preferable in some other way than an identical company that has attained its size by merger? Is the latter company more likely to have market power?

4. The *Northern Securities* merger was part of the greatest merger movement in American history, which occurred during the decade 1895-1905. Why should so many mergers occur after, rather than before, the passage of the Sherman Act? One possibility is that economies of scale made business consolidations efficient, that the Sherman Act prevented "loose" consolidations by contract among competing companies, and so they merged as an alternative. *See* A.D. Chandler, Jr., *The Visible Hand: the Managerial Revolution in American Business*, 315-44 (1977). Another argument is that the Sherman Act's prohibition of agreements among competitors was merely an excuse for firms to achieve anticompetitive market positions by merger rather than by contract. *See* N.R. Lamoreaux, *The Great Merger Movement in American Business, 1895-1904* (1985); H. Hovenkamp, *Enterprise, supra*, at ch. 20. As Ms. Lamoreaux notes, only a few of the consolidations of this period succeeded. Most were defeated, not by the federal antitrust laws, but by new competition. What does this suggest about the efficiency of these mergers?

UNITED STATES V. COLUMBIA STEEL CO.

334 U.S. 495 (1948)

[The United States sought to enjoin United States Steel Co. from acquiring certain assets of Consolidated Steel Corp. United States Steel produced about one-third of the national output of rolled steel. Consolidated purchased rolled steel and fabricated it into various steel products. United States Steel also fabricated steel, in competition with Consolidated. Thus the merger was both vertical and horizontal. The Supreme Court's analysis of the vertical aspects appears *supra*.

Until it was amended in 1950, section 7 of the Clayton Act applied only to stock acquisitions, not to asset acquisitions; so this case was brought under sections 1 and 2 of the Sherman Act.]

JUSTICE REED delivered the opinion of the Court.

We turn first to the field of fabricated structural steel products. As in the case of rolled steel, the appellees claim that structural fabricators sell on a national scale, and that Consolidated's production must be measured against all structural fabricators. An index of the position of Consolidated as a structural fabricator is shown by its bookings for the period 1937-1942, as reported by the American Institute of Steel Construction. During that period total bookings in the entire country were nearly 10,000,000 tons, of which Consolidated's share was only 84,533 tons. The government argues that competition is to be measured with reference to the eleven-state area in which Consolidated sells its products. Viewed on that basis, total bookings for the limited area for the six-year period were 1,665,698, of which United States Steel's share was 17% and Consolidated's 5%. The government claims that Consolidated has become a more important factor since that period, and alleges that bookings for 1946 in the Consolidated market were divided among 90 fabricators, of which United States Steel had 13% and Consolidated and Bethlehem Steel each had 11%. The next largest structural fabricators had 9%, 6% and 3% of the total.... The figures on which the government relies demonstrate that at least in the past competition in structural steel products has been conducted on a national scale. Five out of the ten structural fabricators having the largest sales in the Consolidated market perform their fabrication operations outside the area, including United States Steel and Bethlehem Steel. Purchasers of fabricated structural products have been able to secure bids from fabricators throughout the country, and therefore statistics showing the share of United States Steel and Consolidated in the total consumption of fabricated structural products in any prescribed area are of little probative value in ascertaining the extent to which consumers of these products would be injured through elimination of competition between the two companies....

Apart from the question of the geographical size of the market, the appellees urge that the bookings for fabricated structural steel products are of little significance because Consolidated and United States Steel make different types of structural steel products. In view of the fact that structural steel jobs are fabricated on an individual basis, it is difficult to compare the output of United States Steel with that of Consolidated, but the appellees argue that in general Consolidated does only light and medium fabrication, whereas United States Steel does heavy fabrication. The appellees support their argument with an elaborate statistical analysis of bids by the two companies. Those figures show that Consolidated and United States Steel submitted bids for the same project in a very small number of instances.[13]

---

[13] During the ten-year period ending in 1946 United States Steel bid on 2,409 jobs in the Consolidated area and was successful in 839. Consolidated bid on 6,377 jobs and was successful in

Such figures are not conclusive of lack of competition; the government suggests that knowledge that one party has submitted a bid may discourage others from bidding. The government has introduced very little evidence, however, to show that in fact the types of structural steel products sold by Consolidated are similar to those sold by United States Steel. The appellees further urge that only a small proportion of Consolidated's business fell in the category of structural steel products, and that as to plate fabrication and miscellaneous work there was no competition with United States Steel whatsoever. The trial court found on this issue that 16% of Consolidated's business was in structural steel products and 70% in plate fabrication. On the basis of the statistics here summarized, the trial court found that competition between the two companies in the manufacture and sale of fabricated structural steel products was not substantial.

. . . .

The United States makes the point that the acquisition of Consolidated would preclude and restrain substantial potential competition in the production and sale of other steel products than fabricated structural steel and pipe. Force is added to this contention by the fact, adverted to above, that United States Steel does no plate fabrication while Consolidated does. By plate fabrication Consolidated produces many articles not now produced by United States Steel. We mention, as examples, boilers, gas tanks, smoke stacks, storage tanks and barges. Attention is also called to the war activities of Consolidated in steel shipbuilding as indicative of its potentialities as a competitor. We have noted, that this construction was under government direction and financing. We agree that any acquisition of fabricating equipment eliminates some potential competition from anyone who might own or acquire such facilities. We agree, too, with the government's position that potential competition from producers of presently non-competitive articles as well as the possibility that acquired facilities may be used in the future for the production of new articles in competition with others may be taken into consideration in weighing the effect of any acquisition of assets on restraint of trade.

The government's argument, however, takes us into highly speculative situations. Steel ship construction for war purposes was an enterprise undertaken at government expense. We know of nothing from the record that would lead Consolidated or United States Steel to branch out into the peace-time steel ship industry at their own risk. The necessary yards have been sold. It is true that United States Steel might go into plate fabrication. The record shows nothing as to production or demand in the Consolidated trade area for plate fabricated articles.

2,390. There were only 166 jobs, however, on which both companies bid. Forty of these jobs on which both companies bid were awarded to United States Steel, 35 were awarded to Consolidated, and 91 were awarded to competitors. . . .

The above figures indicate that Consolidated customarily bid on lighter types of work; the average tonnage for Consolidated's bids was 90 tons, whereas the average tonnage for United States Steel was 528 tons. The 166 jobs on which both companies submitted bids were considerably larger in volume, averaging 737 tons.

Nothing appears as to the number of producers of such goods in that territory. What we have said in other places in this opinion as to the growing steel industry in this area is pertinent here. Eastern fabricators will find it difficult to meet competition from western fabricators in the western market. Cheaper western rolled steel and freight rates are a handicap to eastern fabricators. Looking at the situation here presented, we are unwilling to hold that possibilities of interference with future competition are serious enough to justify us in declaring that this contract will bring about unlawful restraint.

We conclude that in this case the government has failed to prove that the elimination of competition between Consolidated and the structural fabricating subsidiaries of United States Steel constitutes an unreasonable restraint....

NOTES AND QUESTIONS

1. In *Columbia Steel*, as in *Northern Securities*, the Supreme Court was faced with the fact that most "horizontal" mergers are not perfectly horizontal. The railroads in *Northern Securities* were not perfect competitors because they passed through different cities, and for many customers there was no competitive choice at all. Likewise, the Supreme Court noted in *Columbia Steel* that United States Steel fabricated heavy projects, while Consolidated tended to fabricate lighter ones. The question of proper market definition in merger cases is even more difficult than it is in monopolization cases, because in merger cases we must look at two or more firms simultaneously, rather than one at a time.

In general, defendants in monopolization cases try to argue that the relevant geographic and product markets are actually larger than the plaintiff is alleging. By making the market larger, the defendant's market share becomes smaller. In merger cases defendants sometimes argue that relevant market is larger than alleged, because smaller market shares decrease the likelihood that the court will find an illegal merger. However, sometimes in a merger case it is to the defendant's advantage to argue that certain relevant markets are actually smaller than the plaintiff alleges; this raises the possibility that the acquiring company and the acquired company actually are located in different markets, so their merger would not be a merger of competitors at all.

In *Columbia Steel* the defendants tried to do both things. With respect to the geographic market, they alleged that the market was the entire United States, not merely the American West. This would give both companies a much smaller share in the relevant geographic market. On the other hand, they also argued that the market for "fabricated steel" was too large — that in fact it should have been divided into "heavy fabricated steel" and "light fabricated steel." The adoption of such an argument may have yielded the conclusion that the two companies were not competitors, but in fact produced two different products.

2. In footnote 13 of its opinion the Court noted that United States Steel bid on approximately 2,400 jobs, while Consolidated bid on about 6,400 jobs. Each was successful about one-third of the time. However, both companies bid on the same

job only 166 times. What does this tell you about the extent of the competition between the two firms? Should the relevant product market have been defined as the market for the product involved in those 166 bids? Should one consider the projects the two companies actually built or the ones they bid for, in measuring the competition between them?

3. The Supreme Court termed as "highly speculative" any argument that, although the two firms were not currently competitors, they might be at some future time, but the merger prevented that possibility. Do you regard that argument as speculative?

4. *Columbia Steel* was held to its facts and the Supreme Court resurrected the *Northern Securities* case in *United States v. First Nat'l Bank & Trust Co. of Lexington*, 376 U.S. 665 (1964). The United States sued under sections 1 and 2 of the Sherman Act to enjoin a horizontal merger between two Fayette County, Kentucky, banks. First National, one of the merging partners, was the largest bank in the county, with about 40% of deposits. Security Trust, the other partner, was the fourth largest, with about 12% of deposits. The post-merger bank had more than half the county's assets, deposits, loans, and trust assets. The government brought suit under the Sherman Act because at the time it was unsure whether section 7 of the Clayton Act applied to bank mergers. (In the *Philadelphia Bank* case, reprinted *infra*, the Court held that section 7 did apply to banks, but that decision was reached after the *Lexington* case had been brought.) In *Lexington* the Supreme Court cited *Northern Securities* "for the proposition that where merging companies are major competitive factors in a relevant market, the elimination of significant competition between them, by merger or consolidation, itself constitutes a violation of § 1 of the Sherman Act." It has been widely suggested that the *Lexington* case made the Sherman Act just as expansive as section 7 of the Clayton Act in reaching anticompetitive mergers in their incipiency. This could have proved useful to attack certain mergers, because before 1980 section 7 of the Clayton Act applied only to transactions that were actually in the flow of interstate commerce, not to transactions that merely "affected" interstate commerce. In addition, before 1980, section 7 applied only to corporations, not to natural persons or unincorporated associations. Since the 1980 amendments, however, the subject-matter jurisdiction of section 7 is probably as great as that of the Sherman Act. *See United States v. Rockford Memorial Corp.*, 898 F.2d 1278 (7th Cir.), *cert. denied*, 498 U.S. 920 (1990), which concluded that mergers should be analyzed by the same standard under both statutes. The court characterized the "defendants' argument that section 7 prevents *probable* restraints and section 1 *actual* ones" as "word play." The court found unpersuasive the argument that earlier Supreme Court decisions had condemned large horizontal mergers under Clayton section 7 without a finding that the merger was likely to reduce competition in the post-merger market. Today, both statutes have the same concern: both would condemn "mergers that are likely to 'hurt consumers, as by making it easier for the firms in the market to collude....'"

B. HORIZONTAL MERGERS UNDER SECTION 7 OF THE CLAYTON ACT AND ITS 1950 AMENDMENTS

The Clayton Act was passed in 1914, largely because Congress feared that the "Rule of Reason" developed in *Standard Oil Co. v. United States* would eviscerate the Sherman Act. Congress wanted to make it absolutely clear that certain specific practices, such as the anticompetitive acquisition of competitors, were illegal. Thus, while the language of the Sherman Act is cast very broadly, the Clayton Act is quite specific. The original section 7 of the Clayton Act condemned a corporation's acquisition of "the whole or any part of the stock" of another corporation if the effect was "to substantially lessen competition between the corporation whose stock is so acquired and the corporation making the acquisition."

As enacted in 1914, section 7 of the Clayton Act proved not to be effective in combating mergers. It suffered from three difficulties that were corrected in 1950 by the Celler-Kefauver Amendments to the Act. The first was the split infinitive. In 1950 the Act was amended to read "substantially to lessen competition." Second, the 1914 statute applied to acquisitions of stock, but not to acquisitions of assets. A corporation could avoid the statute simply by purchasing all the property and goodwill of another corporation and leaving the empty shell. *See Thatcher Mfg. Co. v. FTC*, 272 U.S. 554 (1926). The merger in the *Columbia Steel* case, *supra*, was an asset acquisition, not a stock acquisition. Third, as enacted in 1914, section 7 applied only to acquisitions that lessened competition "between" the acquiring and acquired firms. Horizontal mergers eliminate competition "between" the two parties to the merger. Vertical mergers do not, however. If they lessen competition at all, it is competition between the post-merger firm and other businesses that were not parties to the merger. In the *du Pont* (GM) case, the Supreme Court applied old section 7 to a vertical merger. The action had been brought in 1949, before the Celler-Kefauver Amendments were passed. It was decided afterwards, however, and the court applied the "policy" of the new statute. Since 1950 there have been three significant amendments to section 7. In 1976 Congress added § 7A, which requires advance notification and a waiting period for mergers of a specified minimum size. The Antitrust Improvements Act (1980) made the reach of section 7 under the Commerce Clause equal to the reach of the Sherman Act. Formerly the Sherman Act had been interpreted to reach all activities "in or affecting" interstate commerce, but section 7 had been held to reach activities only "in the flow" of interstate commerce. *See United States v. American Bldg. Maint. Indus.*, 422 U.S. 271 (1975). The Improvements Act also replaced the word "corporation" in the old statute with the word "person," so that the statute now covers unincorporated business associations as well as corporations.

The most significant effect of the Celler-Kefauver Amendments to section 7 came not from the changes in the language of the statute but from the extensive legislative history. Both houses of Congress appeared to be alarmed by the "rising tide" of industrial concentration. Their fear, however, was not that concentrated firms would be able to charge supracompetitive prices to consumers, but that mergers were enabling some firms to sell products more cheaply than their nonmerging competitors. As a result many small businesses were either being "gobbled up" by larger companies or else driven into bankruptcy. *See* Hovenkamp, *Derek Bok and the Merger of Law and Economics*, 21 J.L. Reform No. 4 (1988). The following decision is the Supreme Court's first response to the concerns articulated by Congress when it passed the Celler-Kefauver Amendments in 1950.

BROWN SHOE CO. V. UNITED STATES

370 U.S. 294 (1962)

[The United States alleged that a contemplated merger between G.R. Kinney Co. (Kinney) and Brown Shoe Co. (Brown) would violate section 7 of the Clayton Act, as amended in 1950. Both companies were in the business of manufacturing and retailing shoes; so the merger was both vertical and horizontal. The portion of the opinion dealing with the vertical issues is reprinted *supra*.]

CHIEF JUSTICE WARREN delivered the opinion of the Court.

In the District Court, the Government contended that the effect of the merger of Brown — the third largest seller of shoes by dollar volume in the United States, a leading manufacturer of men's, women's, and children's shoes, and a retailer with over 1,230 owned, operated or controlled retail outlets — and Kinney — the eighth largest company, by dollar volume, among those primarily engaged in selling shoes, itself a large manufacturer of shoes, and a retailer with over 350 retail outlets — "may be substantially to lessen competition or to tend to create a monopoly" by eliminating actual or potential competition in the production of shoes for the national wholesale shoe market and in the sale of shoes at retail in the Nation.... The Government argued that the "line of commerce" affected by this merger is "footwear," or alternatively, that the "line[s]" are "men's," "women's," and "children's" shoes, separately considered, and that the "section of the country," within which the anticompetitive effect of the merger is to be judged, is the Nation as a whole, or alternatively, each separate city or city and its immediate surrounding area in which the parties sell shoes at retail.

In the District Court, Brown contended that the merger would be shown not to endanger competition if the "line[s] of commerce" and the "section[s] of the country" were properly determined. Brown urged that not only were the age and sex of the intended customers to be considered in determining the relevant line of commerce, but that differences in grade of material, quality of workmanship, price, and customer use of shoes resulted in establishing different lines of commerce. While agreeing with the Government that, with regard to manufacturing, the relevant geographic market for assessing the effect of the merger upon competition is the country as a whole, Brown contended that with regard to retailing, the market must vary with economic reality from the central business district of a large city to a "standard metropolitan area" for a smaller community. Brown further contended that, both at the manufacturing level and at the retail level, the shoe industry enjoyed healthy competition and that the vigor of this competition would not, in any event, be diminished by the proposed merger because Kinney manufactured less than 0.5% and retailed less than 2% of the Nation's shoes.

[The Court traced the legislative history of the 1950 amendments to section 7 of the Clayton Act. It noted that Congress was concerned, not merely with the fact that the original statute applied only to stock acquisitions, but that it had not been successful in averting the trend toward industrial concentration.]

The dominant theme pervading congressional consideration of the 1950 amendments was a fear of what was considered to be a rising tide of economic concentration in the American economy. Apprehension in this regard was bolstered by the publication in 1948 of the Federal Trade Commission's study on corporate mergers. Statistics from this and other current studies were cited as evidence of the danger to the American economy in unchecked corporate expansions through mergers. Other considerations cited in support of the bill were the desirability of retaining "local control" over industry and the protection of small businesses. Throughout the recorded discussion may be found examples of Congress' fear not only of accelerated concentration of economic power on economic grounds, but also of the threat to other values a trend toward concentration was thought to pose.

What were some of the factors, relevant to a judgment as to the validity of a given merger, specifically discussed by Congress in redrafting § 7?

First, there is no doubt that Congress did wish to "plug the loophole" and to include within the coverage of the Act the acquisition of assets no less than the acquisition of stock.

Second, by the deletion of the "acquiring-acquired" language in the original text, it hoped to make plain that § 7 applied not only to mergers between actual competitors, but also to vertical and conglomerate mergers whose effect may tend to lessen competition in any line of commerce in any section of the country.

Third, it is apparent that a keystone in the erection of a barrier to what Congress saw was the rising tide of economic concentration, was its provision of authority for arresting mergers at a time when the trend to a lessening of competition in a line of commerce was still in its incipiency. Congress saw the process of concentration in American business as a dynamic force; it sought to assure the Federal Trade Commission and the courts the power to brake this force at its outset and before it gathered momentum.

Fourth, and closely related to the third, Congress rejected, as inappropriate to the problem it sought to remedy, the application to § 7 cases of the standards for judging the legality of business combinations adopted by the courts in dealing with cases arising under the Sherman Act, and which may have been applied to some early cases arising under original § 7.

Fifth, at the same time that it sought to create an effective tool for preventing all mergers having demonstrable anticompetitive effects, Congress recognized the stimulation to competition that might flow from particular mergers. When concern as to the Act's breadth was expressed, supporters of the amendments indicated that it would not impede, for example, a merger between two small companies to enable the combination to compete more effectively with larger corporations dominating the relevant market, nor a merger between a corporation which is financially healthy and a failing one which no longer can be a vital competitive factor in the market. The deletion of the word "community" in the original Act's description of the relevant geographic market is another illustration of Congress' desire to indicate that its concern was with the adverse effects of a given merger on competition only in an economically significant "section" of the country. Taken as a whole, the legislative history illuminates congressional concern with the protection of *competition*, not *competitors*, and its desire to restrain mergers only to the extent that such combinations may tend to lessen competition.

Sixth, Congress neither adopted nor rejected specifically any particular tests for measuring the relevant markets, either as defined in terms of product or in terms of geographic locus of competition, within which the anticompetitive effects of a merger were to be judged. Nor did it adopt a definition of the word "substantially," whether in quantitative terms of sales or assets or market shares or in designated qualitative terms, by which a merger's effects on competition were to be measured.

Seventh, while providing no definite quantitative or qualitative tests by which enforcement agencies could gauge the effects of a given merger to determine whether it may "substantially" lessen competition or tend toward monopoly, Congress indicated plainly that a merger had to be functionally viewed, in the context of its particular industry. That is, whether the consolidation was to take place in an industry that was fragmented rather than concentrated, that had seen a recent trend toward domination by a few leaders or had remained fairly consistent in its distribution of market shares among the participating companies, that had experienced easy access to markets by suppliers and easy access to suppliers by buyers or had witnessed foreclosure of business, that had witnessed the ready entry of new competition or the erection of barriers to prospective entrants, all were aspects, varying in importance with the merger under consideration, which would properly be taken into account.

Eighth, Congress used the words "*may be* substantially to lessen competition" (emphasis supplied), to indicate that its concern was with probabilities, not certainties....

....

... [T]he proper definition of the market is a "necessary predicate" to an examination of the competition that may be affected by the horizontal aspects of the merger. The acquisition of Kinney by Brown resulted in a horizontal combination at both the manufacturing and retailing levels of their businesses. Although the District Court found that the merger of Brown's and Kinney's *manufacturing* facilities was economically too insignificant to come within the prohibitions of the Clayton Act, the Government has not appealed from this portion of the lower court's decision. Therefore, we have no occasion to express our views with respect to that finding. On the other hand, appellant does contest the District Court's finding that the merger of the companies' *retail* outlets may tend substantially to lessen competition.

[The Court decided that the relevant lines of commerce (product markets) were men's shoes, women's shoes, and children's shoes.]

... [A]lthough the geographic market in some instances may encompass the entire Nation, under other circumstances it may be as small as a single metropolitan area.... The fact that two merging firms have competed directly on the horizontal level in but a fraction of the geographic markets in which either has operated, does not, in itself, place their merger outside the scope of § 7. That section speaks of "any ... section of the country," and if anticompetitive effects of a merger are probable in "any" significant market, the merger — at least to that extent — is proscribed.[65]

The parties do not dispute the findings of the District Court that the Nation as a whole is the relevant geographic market for measuring the anticompetitive effects of the merger viewed vertically or of the horizontal merger of Brown's and Kinney's manufacturing facilities. As to the retail level, however, they disagree.

The District Court found that the effects of this aspect of the merger must be analyzed in every city with a population exceeding 10,000 and its immediate contiguous surrounding territory in which both Brown and Kinney sold shoes at retail through stores they either owned or controlled. By this definition of the geographic market, less than one-half of all the cities in which either Brown or Kinney sold shoes through such outlets are represented. The appellant recognizes that if the District Court's characterization of the relevant market is proper, the number of markets in which both Brown and Kinney have outlets is sufficiently numerous so that the validity of the entire merger is properly judged by testing its effects in those markets. However, it is appellant's contention that the areas of effective competition in shoe retailing were improperly defined by the District Court. It claims that such areas should, in some cases, be defined so as to include only the central business districts of large cities, and in others, so as to encompass the "standard metropolitan areas" within which smaller communities are found. It argues that any test failing to distinguish between these competitive situations is improper.

---

[65] To illustrate: If two retailers, one operating primarily in the eastern half of the Nation, and the other operating largely in the West, competed in but two mid-Western cities, the fact that the latter outlets represented but a small share of each company's business would not immunize the merger in those markets in which competition might be adversely affected. On the other hand, that fact would, of course, be properly considered in determining the equitable relief to be decreed....

We believe, however, that the record fully supports the District Court's findings that shoe stores in the outskirts of cities compete effectively with stores in central downtown areas, and that while there is undoubtedly some commercial intercourse between smaller communities within a single "standard metropolitan area," the most intense and important competition in retail sales will be confined to stores within the particular communities in such an area and their immediate environs.

We therefore agree that the District Court properly defined the relevant geographic markets in which to analyze this merger as those cities with a population exceeding 10,000 and their environs in which both Brown and Kinney retailed shoes through their own outlets. Such markets are large enough to include the downtown shops and suburban shopping centers in areas contiguous to the city, which are the important competitive factors, and yet are small enough to exclude stores beyond the immediate environs of the city, which are of little competitive significance.

....

... [I]n 32 separate cities, ranging in size and location from Topeka, Kansas, to Batavia, New York, and Hobbs, New Mexico, the combined share of Brown and Kinney sales of women's shoes (by unit volume) exceeded 20%. In 31 cities — some the same as those used in measuring the effect of the merger in the women's line — the combined share of children's shoes sales exceeded 20%; in 6 cities their share exceeded 40%. In Dodge City, Kansas, their combined share of the market for women's shoes was over 57%; their share of the children's shoe market in that city was 49%. In the 7 cities in which Brown's and Kinney's combined shares of the market for women's shoes were greatest (ranging from 33% to 57%) each of the parties alone, prior to the merger, had captured substantial portions of those markets (ranging from 13% to 34%); the merger intensified this existing concentration. In 118 separate cities the combined shares of the market of Brown and Kinney in the sale of one of the relevant lines of commerce exceeded 5%. In 47 cities, their share exceeded 5% in all three lines.

The market share which companies may control by merging is one of the most important factors to be considered when determining the probable effects of the combination on effective competition in the relevant market. In an industry as fragmented as shoe retailing, the control of substantial shares of the trade in a city may have important effects on competition. If a merger achieving 5% control were now approved, we might be required to approve future merger efforts by Brown's competitors seeking similar market shares. The oligopoly Congress sought to avoid would then be furthered and it would be difficult to dissolve the combinations previously approved. Furthermore, in this fragmented industry, even if the combination controls but a small share of a particular market, the fact that this share is held by a large national chain can adversely affect competition. Testimony in the record from numerous independent retailers, based on their actual experience in the market, demonstrates that a strong, national chain of stores can insulate selected outlets from the vagaries of competition in particular locations and that the large chains can set and alter styles in footwear to an extent that renders the independents unable to maintain competitive inventories. A third significant aspect of this merger is that it creates a large national chain which is integrated with a manufacturing operation. The retail outlets of integrated companies, by eliminating wholesalers and by increasing the volume of purchases from the manufacturing division of the enterprise, can market their own brands at prices below those of competing independent retailers. Of course, some of the results of large integrated or chain operations are beneficial to consumers. Their expansion is not rendered unlawful by the mere fact that small independent stores may be adversely affected. It is competition, not competitors, which the Act protects. But we cannot fail to recognize Congress' desire to promote competition through the protection of viable, small, locally owned businesses. Congress appreciated that occasional higher costs and prices might result from the maintenance of fragmented industries and markets. It resolved these competing considerations in favor of decentralization. We must give effect to that decision.

Other factors to be considered in evaluating the probable effects of a merger in the relevant market lend additional support to the District Court's conclusion that this merger may substantially lessen competition. One such factor is the history of tendency toward concentration in the industry. As we have previously pointed out, the shoe industry has, in recent years, been a prime example of such a trend. Most combinations have been between manufacturers and retailers, as each of the larger producers has sought to capture an increasing number of assured outlets for its wares. Although these mergers have been primarily vertical in their aim and effect, to the extent that they have brought ever greater numbers of retail outlets within fewer and fewer hands, they have had an additional important impact on the horizontal plane. By the merger in this case, the largest single group of retail stores still independent of one of the large manufacturers was absorbed into an already substantial aggregation of more or less controlled retail outlets. As a result of this merger, Brown moved into second place nationally in terms of retail stores directly owned. Including the stores on its franchise plan, the merger placed under Brown's control almost 1,600 shoe outlets, or about 7.2% of the Nation's retail "shoe stores" as defined by the Census Bureau, and 2.3% of the Nation's total retail shoe outlets. We cannot avoid the mandate of Congress that tendencies toward concentration in industry are to be curbed in their incipiency, particularly when those tendencies are being accelerated through giant steps striding across a hundred cities at a time. In the light of the trends in this industry we agree with the Government and the court below that this is an appropriate place at which to call a halt.

At the same time appellant has presented no mitigating factors, such as the business failure or the inadequate resources of one of the parties that may have prevented it from maintaining its competitive position, nor a demonstrated need for combination to enable small companies to enter into a more meaningful competition with those dominating the relevant markets. On the basis of the record before us, we believe the Government sustained its burden of proof....

NOTES AND QUESTIONS

1. How did the Supreme Court deal with the lower court's finding that the Brown-Kinney merger created certain efficiencies that would enable the post-merger firm to charge a lower price than before? At one time or another both courts and commentators have taken three different positions on the relationship between efficiency and the legality of a merger:

(a) mergers should be analyzed in terms of their effect on market power, and efficiency considerations are irrelevant;

(b) mergers that create substantial efficiencies should be legal, or there should be at least a limited "efficiency defense" in certain merger cases;

(c) mergers should be condemned *because* they create efficiencies, even if the merger produces no foreseeable effects on the market power of the post-merger firm or increases the likelihood of collusion in the industry.

Does the *Brown Shoe* opinion leave any doubt about the Supreme Court's view in 1962? Perhaps this passage from the District Court's opinion will help:

> [I]ndependent retailers of shoes are having a harder and harder time in competing with company-owned and company-controlled retail outlets. National advertising by large concerns has increased their brand name acceptability and retail stores handling the brand named shoes have a definite advertising advantage. Company-owned and company-controlled retail stores have definite advantages ... in advertising, insurance, inventory control ... and price control. These advantages result in lower prices or in higher quality for the same price and the independent retailer can no longer compete in the low and medium-priced fields and has been driven to concentrate his business in the higher-priced, higher-quality type of shoes — and, the higher the price, the smaller the market. He has been placed in this position, not by choice, but by necessity.

179 F. Supp. at 738 (E.D. Mo. 1959). In fact, the theory under which the government brought the *Brown Shoe* case was not that the Brown-Kinney merger would permit the post-merger firm to price monopolistically or that it would encourage collusion in the industry. Rather, the theory was that, because of efficiencies created by the merger, competitors would either be driven out of business or else they would be forced to merge themselves so that they could compete. This argument forced the defendants to argue that the merger did *not* create any efficiencies and that the post-merger firm would not be able to charge lower prices or produce shoes of a higher quality for the same price. Brief for Petitioner 193-99. For an analysis of the arguments offered in the litigation, *see* Peterman, *The Brown Shoe Case*, 18 J.L. & Econ. 81 (1975).

Was the government's (and the court's) theory that the Brown merger was bad because it created efficiencies wrong? That theory came under severe criticism in the late 1970's and 1980's. *See, e.g.,* R. Bork, *The Antitrust Paradox: A Policy at*

War with Itself, 198-216 (1978). However, the government's theory was quite consistent with the legislative history of the 1950 amendments to section 7 of the Clayton Act. In 1950 the issue foremost on the minds of Congress was not consumer welfare and encouragement of efficiency in the production of goods and services. Rather, it was the protection of small, independent businesses that were being injured by larger, more efficient firms. If it is quite clear that Congress had a particular policy in mind when it passed a statute, should judges (or antitrust scholars) ignore Congressional intent and interpret the statute in a different way, even if the different way is in the best interest of consumers? *See* Hovenkamp, *Antitrust Policy After Chicago*, 84 Mich. L. Rev. 213, 249-55 (1985).

2. The district court found that "independent" shoe retailers were forced by the vertical integration of large firms to deal in higher-quality, higher-priced shoes. Frequently the economies generated by large firms force smaller businesses to find ways of avoiding competition, or of competing in other ways than price. For example, the small grocery store unfortunately located across the street from a large chain store would probably be driven from business if it attempted to match the large store's prices and range of selections. In fact, however, it is quite common to see small stores thriving, even though they are close to much larger stores. The small stores have certain economies of their own that big stores may not have. For example, the small store might be able to stay open longer hours, it might be able to offer very quick service with no waiting, it might offer unique products or services unavailable in the larger stores.

3. The Supreme Court argued that if it approved the Brown Shoe merger now it "might be required" to approve other mergers of similar size companies later, although by then the industry would be much more concentrated and the risks of collusion much higher. Suppose the court approved a merger today which yielded a 10% market share to the post-merger firm, in a market with dozens of competitors. Ten years from now, when the number of competitors in the market has been reduced to five or six, the Court is asked to approve another merger yielding a 10% market share for that post-merger firm. Would fairness, justice, due process, equal protection, or anything else "require" the Supreme Court to approve the second merger? Probably not, if the second proposed merger would have measurable effects on competition in the market, while the first merger did not.

The Supreme Court's "domino theory" argument may have been based not on some concept of fairness, however, but on a particular economic policy. As long as all the competitors in an industry are small, all of them operate under the same set of economic disadvantages. However, if a merger of two of them generates substantial economies, then smaller competitors will immediately be placed at a disadvantage and they will have to merge in order to stay in business. To permit them to go out of business would leave the industry even more concentrated than permitting the merger to go ahead, so the court would have to permit the future mergers as well.

The argument makes sense if one accepts the premise that mergers ought to be condemned because they create efficiency. A wave of mergers in a particular market generally tells us that larger size generates substantial economies in that market. Once one set of firms has achieved these economies other firms must achieve them (either by merger or by internal growth) or they will not be able to compete. In an unrestrained market the firms will gravitate toward the most efficient size and when most of them have reached that size the "wave" of mergers will cease. This is undoubtedly what the Court was observing when it noted a "tendency toward concentration" in the shoe industry.

4. Suppose that the merger between Brown and Kinney had actually been consummated. A few years later a private business person, formerly an independent shoe seller, alleges that she was driven out of business as a result of the illegal merger. Because of the merger, the plaintiff argues, the Brown-Kinney shoe store across the street from her own store was able to sell higher quality shoes at a lower price than she was able to sell them. Should the private entrepreneur have a cause of action for damages? *See Brunswick Corp. v. Pueblo Bowl-O-Mat, Inc.*, reprinted in Chapter 3, *supra*.

UNITED STATES V. PHILADELPHIA NATIONAL BANK

374 U.S. 321 (1963)

JUSTICE BRENNAN delivered the opinion of the Court.

The United States, appellant here, brought this civil action ... to enjoin a proposed merger of the Philadelphia National Bank (PNB) and Girard Trust Corn Exchange Bank (Girard).... The complaint charged violations of § 1 of the Sherman Act, and § 7 of the Clayton Act.... We hold that the merger of appellees is forbidden by § 7 of the Clayton Act and so must be enjoined; we need not, and therefore do not, reach the further question of alleged violation of § 1 of the Sherman Act....

The Philadelphia National Bank and Girard Trust Corn Exchange Bank are, respectively, the second and third largest of the 42 commercial banks with head offices in the Philadelphia metropolitan area, which consists of the City of Philadelphia and its three contiguous counties in Pennsylvania. The home county of both banks is the city itself; Pennsylvania law, however, permits branching into the counties contiguous to the home county, and both banks have offices throughout the four-county area. PNB, a national bank, has assets of over $1,000,000,000, making it (as of 1959) the twenty-first largest bank in the Nation. Girard, a state bank, is a member of the FRS [Federal Reserve System] and is insured by the FDIC; it has assets of about $750,000,000. Were the proposed merger to be consummated, the resulting bank would be the largest in the four-county area, with (approximately) 36% of the area banks' total assets, 36% of deposits, and 34% of net loans. It and the second largest (First Pennsylvania Bank and Trust Company, now the largest) would have between them 59% of the total assets, 58% of deposits, and 58% of the net loans, while after the merger the four largest banks in the area would have 78% of total assets, 77% of deposits, and 78% of net loans.

The present size of both PNB and Girard is in part the result of mergers. Indeed, the trend toward concentration is noticeable in the Philadelphia area generally, in which the number of commercial banks has declined from 108 in 1947 to the present 42. Since 1950, PNB has acquired nine formerly independent banks and Girard six; and these acquisitions have accounted for 59% and 85% of the respective banks' asset growth during the period, 63% and 91% of their deposit growth, and 12% and 37% of their loan growth. During this period, the seven largest banks in the area increased their combined share of the area's total commercial bank resources from about 61% to about 90%.

....

The Government's case in the District Court relied chiefly on statistical evidence bearing upon market structure and on testimony by economists and bankers to the effect that, notwithstanding the intensive governmental regulation of banking, there was a substantial area for the free play of competitive forces; that concentration of commercial banking, which the proposed merger would increase, was inimical to that free play; that the principal anticompetitive effect of the merger would be felt in the area in which the banks had their offices, thus making the four-county metropolitan area the relevant geographical market; and that commercial banking was the relevant product market. The defendants, in addition to offering contrary evidence on these points, attempted to show business justifications for the merger. They conceded that both banks were economically strong and had sound management, but offered the testimony of bankers to show that the resulting bank, with its greater prestige and increased lending limit, would be better able to compete with large out-of-state (particularly New York) banks, would attract new business to Philadelphia, and in general would promote the economic development of the metropolitan area.

We have no difficulty in determining the "line of commerce" (relevant product or services market) and "section of the country" (relevant geographical market) in which to appraise the probable competitive effects of appellees' proposed merger. We agree with the District Court that the cluster of products (various kinds of credit) and services (such as checking accounts and trust administration) denoted by the term "commercial banking," composes a distinct line of commerce. Some commercial banking products or services are so distinctive that they are entirely free of effective competition from products or services of other financial institutions; the checking account is in this category. Others enjoy such cost advantages as to be insulated within a broad range from substitutes furnished by other institutions. For example, commercial banks compete with small-loan companies in the personal-loan market; but the small-loan companies' rates are invariably much higher than the banks', in part, it seems, because the companies' working capital consists in substantial part of bank loans. Finally, there are banking facilities which, although in terms of cost and price they are freely competitive with the facilities provided by other financial institutions, nevertheless enjoy a settled consumer preference, insulating them, to a marked degree, from competition; this seems to be the case with savings deposits. In sum, it is clear that commercial banking is a market "sufficiently inclusive to be meaningful in terms of trade realities."

We part company with the District Court on the determination of the appropriate "section of the country." The proper question to be asked in this case is not where the parties to the merger do business or even where they compete, but where, within the area of competitive overlap, the effect of the merger on competition will be direct and immediate. This depends upon "the geographic structure of supplier-customer relations."...

We recognize that the area in which appellees have their offices does not delineate with perfect accuracy an appropriate "section of the country" in which to appraise the effect of the merger upon competition. Large borrowers and large depositors, the record shows, may find it practical to do a large part of their banking business outside their home community; very small borrowers and depositors may, as a practical matter, be confined to bank offices in their immediate neighborhood; and customers of intermediate size, it would appear, deal with banks within an area intermediate between these extremes. So also, some banking services are evidently more local in nature than others. But that in banking the relevant geographical market is a function of each separate customer's economic scale means simply that a workable compromise must be found: some fair intermediate delineation which avoids the indefensible extremes of drawing the market either so expansively as to make the effect of the merger upon competition seem insignificant, because only the very largest bank customers are taken into account in defining the market, or so narrowly as to place appellees in different markets, because only the smallest customers are considered. We think that the four-county Philadelphia metropolitan area, which state law apparently recognizes as a meaningful banking community in allowing Philadelphia banks to branch within it, and which would seem roughly to delineate the area in which bank customers that are neither very large nor very small find it practical to do their banking business, is a more appropriate "section of the country" in which to appraise the instant merger than any larger or smaller or different area....

We noted in *Brown Shoe* that "[t]he dominant theme pervading congressional consideration of the 1950 amendments [to § 7] was a fear of what was considered to be a rising tide of economic concentration in the American economy." This intense congressional concern with the trend toward concentration warrants dispensing, in certain cases, with elaborate proof of market structure, market behavior, or probable anticompetitive effects. Specifically, we think that a merger which produces a firm controlling an undue percentage share of the relevant market, and results in a significant increase in the concentration of firms in that market, is so inherently likely to lessen competition substantially that it must be enjoined in the absence of evidence clearly showing that the merger is not likely to have such anticompetitive effects.

Such a test lightens the burden of proving illegality only with respect to mergers whose size makes them inherently suspect in light of Congress' design in § 7 to prevent undue concentration. Furthermore, the test is fully consonant with economic theory. That "[c]ompetition is likely to be greatest when there are many sellers, none of which has any significant market share," is common ground among most economists, and was undoubtedly a premise of congressional reasoning about the antimerger statute.

The merger of appellees will result in a single bank's controlling at least 30% of the commercial banking business in the four-county Philadelphia metropolitan area. Without attempting to specify the smallest market share which would still be considered to threaten undue concentration, we are clear that 30% presents that threat. Further, whereas presently the two largest banks in the area (First Pennsylvania and PNB) control between them approximately 44% of the area's commercial banking business, the two largest after the merger (PNB-Girard and First Pennsylvania) will control 59%. Plainly, we think, this increase of more than 33% in concentration must be regarded as significant.

Our conclusion that these percentages raise an inference that the effect of the contemplated merger of appellees may be substantially to lessen competition is not an arbitrary one, although neither the terms of § 7 nor the legislative history suggests that any particular percentage share was deemed critical. The House Report states that the tests of illegality under amended § 7 "are intended to be similar to those which the courts have applied in interpreting the same language as used in other sections of the Clayton Act." Accordingly, we have relied upon decisions under these other sections in applying § 7. In *Standard Oil Co. v. United States*, 337 U.S. 293, this Court held violative of § 3 of the Clayton Act exclusive contracts whereby the defendant company, which accounted for 23% of the sales in the relevant market and, together with six other firms, accounted for 65% of such sales, maintained control over outlets through which approximately 7% of the sales were made.... In the instant case, by way of comparison, the four largest banks after the merger will foreclose 78% of the relevant market.... Doubtless these cases turned to some extent upon whether "by the nature of the market there is room for newcomers." But they remain highly suggestive in the present context, for as we noted in *Brown Shoe* integration by merger is more suspect than integration by contract, because of the greater permanence of the former. The market share and market concentration figures in the contract-integration cases, taken together with scholarly opinion support, we believe, the inference we draw in the instant case from the figures disclosed by the record....

[I]t is suggested that the increased lending limit of the resulting bank will enable it to compete with the large out-of-state banks, particularly the New York banks, for very large loans. We reject this application of the concept of "countervailing power." If anticompetitive effects in one market could be justified by procompetitive consequences in another, the logical upshot would be that every firm in an industry could, without violating § 7, embark on a series of mergers that would make it in the end as large as the industry leader....

NOTES AND QUESTIONS

1. What do you make of the Court's argument that the same market share percentages that trigger liability in a vertical integration-exclusive dealing case ought to suggest liability in a horizontal merger case? Are the issues similar enough to justify this inference?

2. Market power, as you may recall, is a function of both the elasticity of demand in a certain market and the elasticity of supply. What would be the effect of a law that limited the number of banks in a particular community, or that made it very difficult for a new bank to enter? Wouldn't such a law reduce the elasticity of supply in the market? And wouldn't that reduction tend to increase the market power of the banks already in the market?

3. The Supreme Court concluded that a merger between firms controlling an "undue percentage" of a market and which results in a "significant increase" in concentration is "inherently likely to lessen competition." Is this a virtual per se rule banning mergers, once specified market concentration and shares have been reached? Or is it merely a description of the burden a plaintiff must carry in order to establish a prima facie case of illegality in a concentrated market? What if the merger occurred in an unconcentrated market? Would the Court then revert to the *Brown Shoe* test? If so, then doesn't the rule of *Philadelphia Bank* require the defendant to have an "undue" market share?

4. *Philadelphia Bank* involved neither a stock acquisition nor an asset acquisition but a consolidation of two banks into one. At the time *Philadelphia Bank* was decided, it was widely believed that section 7 did not apply to such mergers involving banks. Congress was not pleased with the holding in *Philadelphia Bank* and responded with the Bank Merger Act of 1966. The statute generally exempted bank mergers consummated before the date of the *Philadelphia Bank* decision, and those consummated before the date the statute was passed if they had not yet been challenged by the government. Clayton Act standards continue to apply, however, to bank mergers or consolidations undertaken after the effective date of the statute, and the Clayton Act is incorporated by reference into the Bank Merger Act. The Bank Merger Act additionally provides that the Justice Department can attack a bank merger only during a 30-day period immediately following approval of the merger by the relevant banking authorities (the identity of the authorities depends on the source of the post-merger bank's charter).

Additionally, the Bank Merger Act permits one of the defenses that was raised unsuccessfully in *Philadelphia Bank:* that the merger will not be illegal if the court finds "that the anticompetitive effects [of the consolidation] are clearly outweighed in the public interest by the probable effect of the transaction in meeting the convenience and needs of the community served." 12 U.S.C. § 1828(c) (1987). The Supreme Court has not been particularly tolerant of this defense. *See United States v. First City Nat'l Bank*, 386 U.S. 361 (1967), where the Court remanded for more fact-finding on the competitive benefits of the merger, once it was found to be prima facie illegal under a traditional section 7 approach.

PROBLEM 7.1

Electro and Conductro are two producers of electric cable, which comes in four kinds, insulated and bare aluminum cable, and insulated and bare copper cable. The copper cable costs much more than the aluminum cable, but there are certain places, such as in homes and underground, where only copper can be used. High tension lines are commonly made of aluminum.

The manufacture of bare aluminum cable requires exactly the same equipment as the manufacture of bare copper cable. Once a firm has the machinery, it can make either kind of cable interchangeably. Likewise, the cable is distributed through the same channels, both ending up in independently owned wholesale and retail electric supply outlets.

The manufacturing difference between insulated and bare cable is another matter. Putting insulation on cable requires expensive, sophisticated machinery, and not all cable manufacturers have it.

At the time Electro proposed to acquire all of the assets of Conductro, the market shares of the two firms with respect to each of the above types of cable were as follows:

	Electro	Conductro
Insulated aluminum cable	11.0%	5.0%
Bare aluminum cable	32.0%	0.3%
Bare and insulated aluminum cable	27.8%	1.3%
All insulated cable	0.3%	1.3%
All four types of cable combined	1.8%	1.4%

Which of these are relevant "lines of commerce" for purposes of section 7? Under *Brown Shoe* and *Philadelphia Bank*, is the merger illegal? *See United States v. Aluminum Co. of Am. (Rome Cable)*, 377 U.S. 271 (1964). Note particularly the dissent.

UNITED STATES V. VON'S GROCERY CO.

384 U.S. 270 (1966)

JUSTICE BLACK delivered the opinion of the Court.

On March 25, 1960, the United States brought this action charging that the acquisition by Von's Grocery Company of its direct competitor Shopping Bag Food Stores, both large retail grocery companies in Los Angeles, California, violated § 7 of the Clayton Act....

The record shows the following facts relevant to our decision. The market involved here is the retail grocery market in the Los Angeles area. In 1958 Von's retail sales ranked third in the area and Shopping Bag's ranked sixth. In 1960 their sales together were 7.5% of the total two and one-half billion dollars of retail groceries sold in the Los Angeles market each year. For many years before the merger both companies had enjoyed great success as rapidly growing companies. From 1948 to 1958 the number of Von's stores in the Los Angeles area practically doubled from 14 to 27, while at the same time the number of Shopping Bag's stores jumped from 15 to 34. During that same decade, Von's sales increased fourfold and its share of the market almost doubled while Shopping Bag's sales multiplied seven times and its share of the market tripled. The merger of these two highly successful, expanding and aggressive competitors created the second largest grocery chain in Los Angeles with sales of almost $172,488,000 annually. In addition the findings of the District Court show that the number of owners operating single stores in the Los Angeles retail grocery market decreased from 5,365 in 1950 to 3,818 in 1961. By 1963, three years after the merger, the number of single-store owners had dropped still further to 3,590. During roughly the same period, from 1953 to 1962, the number of chains with two or more grocery stores increased from 96 to 150. While the grocery business was being concentrated into the hands of fewer and fewer owners, the small companies were continually being absorbed by the larger firms through mergers. According to an exhibit prepared by one of the Government's expert witnesses, in the period from 1949 to 1958 nine of the top 20 chains acquired 126 stores from their smaller competitors.... Moreover, a table prepared by the Federal Trade Commission ... shows that acquisitions and mergers in the Los Angeles retail grocery market have continued at a rapid rate since the merger. These facts alone are enough to cause us to conclude contrary to the District Court that the Von's-Shopping Bag merger did violate § 7. Accordingly, we reverse.

....

The facts of this case present exactly the threatening trend toward concentration which Congress wanted to halt. The number of small grocery companies in the Los Angeles retail grocery market had been declining rapidly before the merger and continued to decline rapidly afterwards. This rapid decline in the number of grocery store owners moved hand in hand with a large number of significant absorptions of the small companies by the larger ones....

Appellees' primary argument is that the merger between Von's and Shopping Bag is not prohibited by § 7 because the Los Angeles grocery market was competitive before the merger, has been since, and may continue to be in the future. Even so, § 7 "requires not merely an appraisal of the immediate impact of the merger upon competition, but a prediction of its impact upon competitive conditions in the future; this is what is meant when it is said that the amended § 7 was intended to arrest anticompetitive tendencies in their 'incipiency.'" It is enough for us that Congress feared that a market marked at the same time by both a continuous decline in the number of small businesses and a large number of mergers would slowly but inevitably gravitate from a market of many small competitors to one dominated by one or a few giants, and competition would thereby be destroyed....

JUSTICE STEWART, with whom JUSTICE HARLAN joins, dissenting.

The Court makes no effort to appraise the competitive effects of this acquisition in terms of the contemporary economy of the retail food industry in the Los Angeles area. Instead, through a simple exercise in sums, it finds that the number of individual competitors in the market has decreased over the years, and, apparently on the theory that the degree of competition is invariably proportional to the number of competitors, it holds that this historic reduction in the number of competing units is enough under § 7 to invalidate a merger within the market, with no need to examine the economic concentration of the market, the level of competition in the market, or the potential adverse effect of the merger on that competition. This startling *per se* rule is contrary not only to our previous decisions, but contrary to the language of § 7, contrary to the legislative history of the 1950 amendment, and contrary to economic reality.

....

I believe that even the most superficial analysis of the record makes plain the fallacy ... that competition is necessarily reduced when the bare number of competitors has declined. In any meaningful sense, the structure of the Los Angeles grocery market remains unthreatened by concentration. Local competition is vigorous to a fault, not only among chain stores themselves but also between chain stores and single-store operators. The continuing population explosion of the Los Angeles area, which has outrun the expansion plans of even the largest chains, offers a surfeit of business opportunity for stores of all sizes. Affiliated with co-operatives that give the smallest store the buying strength of its largest competitor, new stores have taken full advantage of the remarkable ease of entry into the market. And, most important of all, the record simply cries out that the numerical decline in the number of single-store owners is the result of transcending social and technological changes that positively preclude the inference that competition has suffered because of the attrition of competitors.

Section 7 was never intended by Congress for use by the Court as a charter to roll back the supermarket revolution. Yet the Court's opinion is hardly more than a requiem for the so-called "Mom and Pop" grocery stores — the bakery and butcher shops, the vegetable and fish markets — that are now economically and technologically obsolete in many parts of the country. No action by this Court can resurrect the old single-line Los Angeles food stores that have been run over by the automobile or obliterated by the freeway. The transformation of American society since the Second World War has not completely shelved these specialty stores, but it has relegated them to a much less central role in our food economy. Today's dominant enterprise in food retailing is the supermarket. Accessible to the housewife's automobile from a wide radius, it houses under a single roof the entire food requirements of the family.

....

Moreover, contrary to the assumption on which the Court proceeds, the record establishes that the present merger itself has substantial, even predominant, market-extension overtones. The District Court found that the Von's stores were located in the southern and western portions of the Los Angeles metropolitan area, and that the Shopping Bag stores were located in the northern and eastern portions. In each of the areas in which Von's and Shopping Bag stores competed directly, there were also at least six other chain stores and several smaller stores competing for the patronage of customers. On the basis of a "housewife's 10-minute driving time" test conducted for the Justice Department by a government witness, it was shown that slightly more than half of the Von's and Shopping Bag stores were not in a position to compete at all with one another in the market.....

Moreover, it is clear that there are no substantial barriers to market entry. The record contains references to numerous highly successful instances of entry with modest initial investments. Many of the stores opened by new entrants were obtained through the disposition of unwanted outlets by chains; frequently the new competitors were themselves chain-store executives who had resigned to enter the market on their own. Enhancing free access to the market is the absence of any such restrictive factors as patented technology, trade secrets, or substantial product differentiation....

The harsh standard now applied by the Court to horizontal mergers may prejudice irrevocably the already difficult choice faced by numerous successful small and medium-sized businessmen in the myriad smaller markets where the effect of today's decision will be felt, whether to expand by buying or by building additional facilities. And by foreclosing future sale as one attractive avenue of eventual market exit, the Court's decision may over the long run deter new market entry and tend to stifle the very competition it seeks to foster.

NOTES AND QUESTIONS

1. Before the merger, Von's was the third largest grocery chain in the relevant market, and Shopping Bag was sixth. Assuming that larger chains were more efficient than smaller ones, how would the largest and second largest chains in Los Angeles be affected by the merger of Von's and Shopping Bag?

2. The Supreme Court characterized the *Von's* case as "two already powerful companies merging in a way which makes them even more powerful than they were before." What do you suppose the Court meant by "powerful"? Was it implying that the post-merger firm, with 7.5% of the relevant market, had substantial market power?

3. No merger is purely "horizontal" in the sense that the two merging firms occupy identical positions in the market. General Motors and Ford, for example, both manufacture automobiles, and if there were a merger between them a court might well decide that "automobiles" was the relevant market. Nevertheless, many customers distinguish between Ford automobiles and General Motors automobiles, and many prefer one over the other. One of the issues in the *Von's* litigation was whether the merger of Von's and Shopping Bag was truly horizontal. By identifying the greater Los Angeles area as the relevant geographic market, a decision that both stores sold the same set of products within this market was enough for the Court to characterize the merger as horizontal. Manifestly, however, some horizontal mergers are more horizontal than others. Los Angeles is more than fifty miles wide at some points. How many people would drive fifty miles across Los Angeles to do their grocery shopping? In fact, the record reveals and the lower court concluded that most shoppers went to a grocery store within ten minutes driving time of their homes. Therefore, with respect to any particular neighborhood, stores that were, say, six or eight miles apart competed with each other. However, some of those stores were closer to other neighborhoods and others were further away. In short, on the demand side the relevant market for retail groceries was not greater Los Angeles, but literally thousands of overlapping circles. In general, no individual store competed with another store more than twenty minutes driving time away.

By contrast, if one looks at elasticity of supply it is perhaps easier to justify a decision that the entire city was the relevant market. Presumably, if Shopping Bag had attempted to raise prices in its stores in the northeastern part of Los Angeles, Von's would have responded by building some stores in the northeastern area as well. Presumably, its existing warehouses, dairies, and other service centers could take care of grocery stores in any part of the city. In short, although this merger did not eliminate competition between the two chains on the demand side, it tended to enhance the market power of the post-merger firm by reducing the elasticity of supply in the market. As we shall find out, however, this is the definition of a conglomerate or market extension merger. In general, courts have been far more lenient toward market extension mergers than they have been toward horizontal mergers.

4. In his dissent, Justice Stewart noted one additional disadvantage of an overly aggressive antimerger law: it could foreclose "future sale as one attractive avenue of eventual market exit." Over the long run, argued Justice Stewart, the knowledge that it might be difficult to find a legal buyer for one's business in the future might deter someone from entering the business in the first place. Justice Stewart's concern may be well founded. Many individual entrepreneurs enter businesses knowing that if they are successful they might be able to sell them at a profit to a larger, established business. Likewise, most individual businessmen eventually want to retire or do something else. Frequently an existing business is a better and more creditworthy potential buyer than a new entrant is. An excessively expansive antimerger law acts as a kind of "restraint on alienation" that might actually injure small businesses more than it helps them — particularly in businesses such as the retail grocery trade, where entry and exit are relatively frequent.

5. In his *Von's* dissent Justice Stewart lamented the lack of consistency in earlier Supreme Court decisions, confessing that the only consistency he could perceive was that "the government always wins." That conclusion does not ring so true today. From 1982 to mid-1988 the Justice Department lost all but one of its contested merger challenges in court. The Federal Trade Commission did much better. For some explanations why, *see* S. Calkins, *Developments in Merger Litigation: the Government Doesn't Always Win*, 56 Antitrust L.J. 855 (1988).

UNITED STATES V. GENERAL DYNAMICS CORP.

415 U.S. 486 (1974)

JUSTICE STEWART delivered the opinion of the Court.

On September 22, 1967, the Government commenced this suit ... challenging as violative of § 7 of the Clayton Act, the acquisition of the stock of United Electric Coal Companies by Material Service Corp. and its successor, General Dynamics Corp....

At the time of the acquisition involved here, Material Service Corp. was a large midwest producer and supplier of building materials, concrete, limestone, and coal. All of its coal production was from deep-shaft mines operated by it or its affiliate, appellee Freeman Coal Mining Corp., and production from these operations amounted to 6.9 million tons of coal in 1959 and 8.4 million tons in 1967. In 1954, Material Service began to acquire the stock of United Electric Coal Companies. United Electric at all relevant times operated only strip or open-pit mines in Illinois and Kentucky; at the time of trial in 1970 a number of its mines had closed and its operations had been reduced to four mines in Illinois and none in Kentucky. In 1959, it produced 3.6 million tons of coal, and by 1967, it had increased this output to 5.7 million tons. Material Service's purchase of United Electric stock continued until 1959. At this point Material's holdings amounted to more than 34% of United Electric's outstanding shares and — all parties are now agreed on this point — Material had effective control of United Electric....

Some months after this takeover, Material Service was itself acquired by the appellee General Dynamics Corp., a large diversified corporation, much of its revenues coming from sales of aircraft, communications, and marine products to Government agencies....

The thrust of the Government's complaint was that the acquisition ... substantially lessened competition in the production and sale of coal in either or both of two geographic markets. It contended that a relevant "section of the country" within the meaning of § 7 was, alternatively, the State of Illinois or the Eastern Interior Coal Province Sales Area, the latter ... comprising Illinois and Indiana, and parts of Kentucky, Tennessee, Iowa, Minnesota, Wisconsin, and Missouri....

As to the relevant product market, the court found that coal faced strong and direct competition from other sources of energy such as oil, natural gas, nuclear energy, and geothermal power which created a cross-elasticity of demand among those various fuels. As a result, it concluded that coal, by itself, was not a permissible product market and that the "energy market" was the sole "line of commerce" in which anticompetitive effects could properly be canvassed.

Similarly, the District Court rejected the Government's proposed geographic markets on the ground that they were "based essentially on past and present production statistics and do not relate to actual coal consumption patterns." The court found that a realistic geographic market should be defined in terms of transportation arteries and freight charges that determined the cost of delivered coal to purchasers and thus the competitive position of various coal producers.... In lieu of the State of Illinois or the Eastern Interior Coal Province Sales Area, the court accordingly found the relevant geographic market to be 10 smaller areas....

[T]he District Court found that the evidence did not support the Government's contention that the 1959 acquisition of United Electric substantially lessened competition in any product or geographic market....

The Government sought to prove a violation of § 7 of the Clayton Act principally through statistics showing that within certain geographic markets the coal industry was concentrated among a small number of large producers; that this concentration was increasing; and that the acquisition of United Electric would materially enlarge the market share of the acquiring company and thereby contribute to the trend toward concentration.

The concentration of the coal market in Illinois and, alternatively, in the Eastern Interior Coal Province was demonstrated by a table of the shares of the largest two, four, and 10 coal-producing firms in each of these areas for both 1957 and 1967 that revealed the following:

	Eastern Interior Coal Province		Illinois	
	1957	1967	1957	1967
Top 2 firms	29.6	48.6	37.8	52.9
Top 4 firms	43.0	62.9	54.5	75.2
Top 10 firms	65.5	91.4	84.0	98.0

These statistics, the Government argued, showed not only that the coal industry was concentrated among a small number of leading producers, but that the trend had been toward increasing concentration. Furthermore, the undisputed fact that the number of coal-producing firms in Illinois decreased almost 73% during the period of 1957 to 1967 from 144 to 39 was claimed to be indicative of the same trend. The acquisition of United Electric by Material Service resulted in increased concentration of coal sales among the leading producers in the areas chosen by the Government, as shown by the following table:

	1959			1967		
	Share of top 2 but for merger	Share of top 2 given merger	Percent increase	Share of top 2 but for merger	Share of top 2 given merger	Percent increase
Province	33.1	37.9	14.5	45.0	48.6	8.0
Illinois	36.6	44.3	22.4	44.0	52.9	20.2

Finally, the Government's statistics indicated that the acquisition increased the share of the merged company in the Illinois and Eastern Interior Coal Province coal markets by significant degrees:

| | Province | | Illinois | |
	Rank	Share (percent)	Rank	Share (percent)
1959				
Freeman	2	7.6	2	15.1
United Electric	6	4.8	5	8.1
Combined	2	12.4	1	23.2
1967				
Freeman	5	6.5	2	12.9
United Electric	9	4.4	6	8.9
Combined	2	10.9	2	21.8

In prior decisions involving horizontal mergers between competitors, this Court has found prima facie violations of § 7 of the Clayton Act from aggregate statistics of the sort relied on by the United States in this case....

The effect of adopting this approach to a determination of a "substantial" lessening of competition is to allow the Government to rest its case on a showing of even small increases of market share or market concentration in those industries or markets where concentration is already great or has been recently increasing, since "if concentration is already great, the importance of preventing even slight increases in concentration and so preserving the possibility of eventual deconcentration is correspondingly great."

While the statistical showing proffered by the Government in this case, the accuracy of which was not discredited by the District Court or contested by the appellees, would under this approach have sufficed to support a finding of "undue concentration" in the absence of other considerations, the question before us is whether the District Court was justified in finding that other pertinent factors affecting the coal industry and the business of the appellees mandated a conclusion that no substantial lessening of competition occurred or was threatened by the acquisition of United Electric. We are satisfied that the court's ultimate finding was not in error.

....

Much of the District Court's opinion was devoted to a description of the changes that have affected the coal industry since World War II.... *First*, it found that coal had become increasingly less able to compete with other sources of energy in many segments of the energy market. Following the War the industry entirely lost its largest single purchaser of coal — the railroads — and faced increasingly stiffer competition from oil and natural gas as sources of energy for industrial and residential uses. Because of these changes in consumption patterns, coal's share of the energy resources consumed in this country fell from 78.4% in 1920 to 21.4% in 1968. The court reviewed evidence attributing this decline not only to the changing relative economies of alternative fuels and to new distribution and consumption patterns, but also to more recent concern with the effect of coal use on the environment and consequent regulation of the extent and means of such coal consumption.

Second, the court found that to a growing extent since 1954, the electric utility industry has become the mainstay of coal consumption. While electric utilities consumed only 15.76% of the coal produced nationally in 1947, their share of total consumption increased every year thereafter, and in 1968 amounted to more than 59% of all the coal consumed throughout the Nation.

Third, and most significantly, the court found that to an increasing degree, nearly all coal sold to utilities is transferred under long-term requirements contracts, under which coal producers promise to meet utilities' coal consumption requirements for a fixed period of time, and at predetermined prices. The court described the mutual benefits accruing to both producers and consumers of coal from such long-term contracts in the following terms:

> This major investment [in electric utility equipment] can be jeopardized by a disruption in the supply of coal. Utilities are, therefore, concerned with assuring the supply of coal to such a plant over its life. In addition, utilities desire to establish in advance, as closely as possible, what fuel costs will be for the life of the plant. For these reasons, utilities typically arrange long-term contracts for all or at least a major portion of the total fuel requirements for the life of the plant....

These developments in the patterns of coal distribution and consumption, the District Court found, have limited the amounts of coal immediately available for "spot" purchases on the open market, since "[t]he growing practice by coal producers of expanding mine capacity only to meet long-term contractual commitments and the gradual disappearance of the small truck mines has tended to limit the production capacity available for spot sales."

Because of these fundamental changes in the structure of the market for coal, the District Court was justified in viewing the statistics relied on by the Government as insufficient to sustain its case. Evidence of past production does not, as a matter of logic, necessarily give a proper picture of a company's future ability to compete....

... The focus of competition in a given time frame is not on the disposition of coal already produced but on the procurement of new long-term supply contracts. In this situation, a company's past ability to produce is of limited significance, since it is in a position to offer for sale neither its past production nor the bulk of the coal it is presently capable of producing, which is typically already committed under a long-term supply contract. A more significant indicator of a company's power effectively to compete with other companies lies in the state of a company's uncommitted reserves of recoverable coal. A company with relatively large supplies of coal which are not already under contract to a consumer will have a more important influence upon competition in the contemporaneous negotiation of supply contracts than a firm with small reserves, even though the latter may presently produce a greater tonnage of coal. In a market where the availability and price of coal are set by long-term contracts rather than immediate or short-term purchases and sales, reserves rather than past production are the best measure of a company's ability to compete.

The testimony and exhibits in the District Court revealed that United Electric's coal reserve prospects were "unpromising." United's relative position of strength in reserves was considerably weaker than its past and current ability to produce. While United ranked fifth among Illinois coal producers in terms of annual production, it was 10th in reserve holdings, and controlled less than 1% of the reserves held by coal producers in Illinois, Indiana, and western Kentucky. Many of the reserves held by United had already been depleted at the time of trial, forcing the closing of some of United's midwest mines. Even more significantly, the District Court found that of the 52,033,304 tons of currently minable reserves in Illinois, Indiana, and Kentucky controlled by United, only four million tons had not already been committed under long-term contracts. United was found to be facing the future with relatively depleted resources at its disposal, and with the vast majority of those resources already committed under contracts allowing no further adjustment in price. In addition, the District Court found that "United Electric has neither the possibility of acquiring more [reserves] nor the ability to develop deep coal reserves," and thus was not in a position to increase its reserves to replace those already depleted or committed.

. . . .

In addition to contending that the District Court erred in finding that the acquisition of United Electric would not substantially lessen competition, the Government urges us to review the court's determinations of the proper product and geographic markets. . . .

While under normal circumstances a delineation of proper geographic and product markets is a necessary precondition to assessment of the probabilities of a substantial effect on competition within them, in this case we nevertheless affirm the District Court's judgment without reaching these questions. By determining that the amount and availability of usable reserves, and not the past annual production figures relied on by the Government, were the proper indicators of future ability to compete, the District Court wholly rejected the Government's prima facie case. Irrespective of the markets within which the acquiring and the acquired company might by viewed as competitors for purposes of this § 7 suit, the Government's statistical presentation simply did not establish that a substantial lessening of competition was likely to occur in any market. . . . Since we agree with the District Court that the Government's reliance on production statistics in the context of this case was insufficient, it follows that the judgment before us may be affirmed without reaching the issues of geo-graphic and product markets.

NOTES AND QUESTIONS

1. Are deep-mined and strip-mined coal the same "line of commerce" for pur-poses of section 7 of the Clayton Act — that is, was the merger in *General Dy-namics* really a horizontal merger? What if customers made no distinction be-tween the two kinds of coal? What if it was much cheaper to produce strip-mined coal than deep-mined coal? How do you evaluate the fact that it takes an entirely different set of equipment to mine deep coal than it takes to strip-mine?

2. In *General Dynamics* the district court decided that the relevant market was not coal but "energy." It based this conclusion on the fact that the cross-elasticity of demand between coal and alternative sources of energy such as natural gas, oil, nuclear and geothermal power was very high. Did the court make the same error that the Supreme Court made in *du Pont* (cellophane)? Probably not. There were many coal producers (39 in the Eastern Interior Coal Province alone), which would suggest that coal was selling at a competitive price. At that com-petitive price, the cross-elasticity of demand between coal and other energy sources was very high. This would suggest that even were coal to come under the control of a monopolist, the monopolist would be held to the competitive price by competition from alternative energy sources.

3. Does the *General Dynamics* case discard any "per se" rule against mergers that may have been developed in the *Philadelphia Bank* case? By suggesting that in "prior decisions" the Supreme Court had found "prima facie violations" based on statistical evidence of concentration, was the Court overruling *Philadelphia Bank*? A few recent decisions have suggested that the *Philadelphia Bank* pre-sumption either no longer applies or else must be considerably weakened. As a result, market concentration becomes little more than one of many factors that the court must consider. Barriers to entry have become *at least* as important as market concentration in merger analysis. *See, e.g., United States v. Baker Hughes*, 908 F.2d 981, 991-92 (D.C. Cir. 1990), in which the court approved a merger even though the post-merger HHI exceeded 4000. It then noted:

> [A] defendant seeking to rebut a presumption of anticompetitive effect must show that the *prima facie* case inaccurately predicts the relevant transaction's probable effect on future competition. The more compelling the *prima facie* case, the more evidence the defendant must present to rebut it successfully. A defendant can make the required showing by affirmatively showing why a given transaction is unlikely to substantially lessen competition, or by discred-iting the data underlying the initial presumption in the government's favor.

However,

> [i]mposing a heavy burden of production on a defendant would be particu-larly anomalous where, as here, it is easy to establish a *prima facie* case.

The government, after all, can carry its initial burden of production simply by presenting market concentration statistics. To allow the government virtually to rest its case at that point, leaving the defendant to prove the core of the dispute, would grossly inflate the role of statistics in actions brought under section 7. The Herfindahl-Hirschman Index cannot guarantee litigation victories.

908 F.2d at 991-92. Is the latter paragraph consistent with *Philadelphia Bank*? with *General Dynamics*?

The 1992 Horizontal Merger Guidelines, discussed *infra*, continue to use market concentration as a starting point, but they give much higher regard to non-market share factors as well.

4. In earlier cases the Supreme Court tended to view long-term requirements contracts as enhancing the market power of the selling firm, by enabling it to "foreclose" a certain market. *See, e.g., Standard Oil of Cal. v. United States*, 337 U.S. 293 (1949) *(Standard Stations)*. In *General Dynamics*, however, the Court viewed the coal companies as victims of their own requirements contracts. In the Court's eyes, sale of coal under requirements contracts did "not represent the exercise of competitive power but rather the obligation to fulfill previously negotiated contracts at a previously fixed price." Is the situation in *General Dynamics* that much different, or has the Court's attitude toward vertical integration by contract changed?

5. Suppose that a company is currently producing 10% of the coal being produced in some market, but it has only 2% of the reserves in that market. It merges with another company that is currently producing 10% of the coal but that owns only 2% of the reserves. What are the relevant percentages for determining each party's share of the relevant market? The answer to that question is more complex than first appears. If coal reserves are large enough to satisfy the demand for coal for the next 1,000 years, then a company with 2% of the reserves might go on producing 10% of production for a long time. By contrast, if reserves are being rapidly depleted and are likely to run out within the next few decades, then a company with 10% of current output but only 2% of the reserves is in trouble and will have to reduce production or find additional reserves in the near future. As a result there cannot be a general rule that one must look at either reserves or at current output in determining relevant market shares of nonrenewable natural resources. Sand, for example, may be a nonrenewable natural resource. However, an electronics company that made silicon chips from sand and owned .001% of the world's sand would probably have sufficient sand to corner 100% of the silicon chip market for the next 1,000 years.

6. How would the Supreme Court treat a merger of two coal companies that have very small shares of current output (say, 2-3%), but very large shares of available reserves (say, 25% each)?

NOTE: PARTIAL ACQUISITIONS

Section 7 of the Clayton Act applies to the acquisition of the "whole or any part" of the stock or assets of another firm. When the Supreme Court decided *General Dynamics*, Material Service Corp. had acquired 34% of the outstanding shares of United Electric. In the vertical acquisition at issue in the *du Pont (GM)* case, du Pont owned 23% of General Motors' outstanding common stock. No one disputed that these acquisitions were not covered by the statute because they involved less than all or even half of the acquired firm's equity. Clearly, under the literal language of the statute if a firm purchases a single share of another firm's stock, section 7 could be applied. Since section 7 applies to asset acquisitions as well, presumably if du Pont had purchased a single General Motors truck for delivery purposes it would come within the statute. After all, a truck is part of the "assets" of General Motors. How broadly must the statute be read?

One answer to the problem of defining an appropriate lower limit to partial acquisitions for section 7 purposes is that an acquisition is not illegal unless it substantially lessens competition or "tends to" create a monopoly. However, the determination that a particular acquisition lessens competition requires a great deal of sophisticated economic analysis. Would it not be far better to have some threshold below which a partial stock or asset acquisition would be considered *per se* legal? After all, every firm that deals with other firms (and all firms do) is involved daily in asset acquisitions.

One such threshold is explicit in the statute. Section 7 creates an exception for "persons purchasing ... stock solely for investment and not using the same by voting or otherwise to bring about ... the substantial lessening of competition." How does one determine whether a particular stock purchase was "solely for investment"? The courts have been consistent about one thing: if the purchase has any anticompetitive effect, then it will not be considered "solely for investment," regardless of the intent of the purchasing party. *See Gulf & W. Indus. v. Great Atl. & Pac. Tea Co.*, 476 F.2d 687, 693 (2d Cir. 1973). The result is that the "solely for investment" exception is no exception at all. Any stock purchase may be challenged on the grounds that it may substantially lessen competition or tend to create a monopoly, and if it does so the investment exception will not provide a defense.

It is also no answer that we need not worry about stock acquisitions unless the stock purchaser acquires enough shares to control the corporation in which it is a shareholder. First of all, how many shares must one purchase in order to "control" a corporation? To control everything perhaps one needs 51% of the shares. But a large shareholder with substantially less than 51% can have considerable influence on a firm's decisionmaking. The 23% interest in the *du Pont* case, for example, was enough. In *General Dynamics*, the parties agreed that the 34% acquisition was enough to give the acquiring firm "effective control."

But to focus on "control" provides an incomplete answer, because ownership affects people's attitudes in other ways. The extreme case is ownership of the stock of a competitor. Suppose that corporations A, B, and C are all intense competitors in a certain market. The competitive game being what it is, each of them would like nothing better than to drive one of the other two (or perhaps both) out of business. Now suppose that A acquires 10% of the shares of B. Suppose further that B has several larger shareholders, and there is no plausible way that A, with its 10% ownership, can control B's operations. A's purchase of B may be intended "solely" for investment. For example, A as a competitor of B might have good knowledge about B's financial stability, or about the expanding market for the product that both A and B manufacture. As a result, A might conclude that B's shares are a good investment. Clearly, however, the "competition" between A and B has taken on a new characteristic. It is clear that A now has a large stake in B's survival and profitability. Will A and B continue to compete just as strongly as they did before? Might C have some cause for concern about A's stock acquisition of B?

The problems presented by partial acquisitions of assets are generally different than those presented by partial stock acquisitions. For example, if A purchased an unused plant or fleet of trucks from its competitor B, that purchase would not give A a continuing interest in B's welfare. In fact, a very substantial asset acquisition might not affect competition at all. Suppose for example that A and B were the only competitors in a market and that A operated two plants and B three. Then A purchases one of B's plants. The result is that now A operates three plants and B two. Under what circumstances could such a transaction lessen competition?

Market efficiency considerations urge relatively free exchange of productive assets between competitors. Relatively technical industries in particular are apt to employ a great deal of specialized equipment that has little use in other markets. If a company is not using a large, specialized plant or piece of equipment and puts it on the market, the highest bidder (or perhaps the only bidders) for the asset are often competitors. A rule that forbade too many such transactions could cause a great amount of social waste.

On the other hand, it is clear that when a company purchases a plant from a competitor there is a danger of precisely the kind of anticompetitive results that amended section 7 was designed to prevent. Presumably such a sale will not take place unless the plant is more valuable to the buyer than it is to the seller, and that suggests that the buyer may produce more from it than the seller would produce if the seller kept the plant. Under what circumstances would the purchase of a plant give the new owner more market power to raise prices by *reducing* output? It is possible, of course, that the purchaser of the plant does not intend to use it, but is buying it in order to remove it from the market — i.e., so that neither the seller nor some other competitor could use it either. Is this a plausible scheme for creating market power?

If A's rival operates only one plant, and A purchases it, and the rival exits from the market, the transaction is likely to be just as anticompetitive as a merger between the two firms. This was a common mechanism by which firms avoided application of section 7 of the Clayton Act before its 1950 amendments. Since the statute then applied only to stock acquisitions, a firm could purchase nearly all the assets of a corporation and leave nothing behind except the corporate charter.

In general, courts have not developed any easy threshold for determining when a partial stock or asset acquisition raises an issue under section 7. Unless a claim is implausible on its face, the plaintiff will generally be given an opportunity to show that any partial stock or asset acquisition may substantially lessen competition or tend to create a monopoly. For an excellent discussion of the problem of partial acquisitions, *see* 5 P. Areeda & D. Turner, *Antitrust Law* 295-358 (1980).

1. THE 1992 HORIZONTAL MERGER GUIDELINES

In 1992 the Department of Justice and the Federal Trade Commission jointly issued new Guidelines describing the standards that the two antitrust enforcement agencies will apply in analyzing horizontal mergers. The 1992 Guidelines are reprinted in this book as Appendix A, *infra*. Vertical and conglomerate (potential competition) mergers continue to be analyzed under older Guidelines printed in 1984. The 1992 Guidelines are the first Guidelines to be issued jointly by the Department of Justice and the Federal Trade Commission. It is important to remember that the merger Guidelines are merely guidelines, designed to aid firms in predicting Justice Department response to prospective acquisitions. The courts are not bound by them except to the extent that an appellate court adopts the Guidelines' position as the law.

NOTES AND QUESTIONS

1. How would some of the big 1960's merger cases decided by the Supreme Court fare under the new merger Guidelines? For some the answer is clear, assuming one accepts the market definitions adopted in those cases. In *Von's*, for example, Von's Grocery commanded 4.7% of the market, Shopping Bag 4.2% of the market, and the top four firms before the merger controlled about 25% of the market. This suggests a pre-merger HHI of less than 300 and a post-merger HHI of about 40 points higher. The *Von's* merger would certainly not be challenged under the new Guidelines.

The situation in *Brown Shoe* is a little more complex. The district court found that the merger of Brown's and Kinney's manufacturing plants was not illegal, and that finding was not challenged on appeal. Brown manufactured about 4% of the nation's shoes and Kinney about 0.5%. The 24 largest shoe manufacturers in the United States manufactured about 35% of the shoes. This certainly indicates that the industry was very diffuse.

Both the district court and the Supreme Court condemned the merger at the retail level, however. At the retail level the relevant markets were found to be citywide, consisting of cities (including their suburbs) having a population of more than 10,000 and including one or more Brown retail stores and one or more

Kinney retail stores. The Supreme Court condemned the merger in all such cities. However, the court's opinion reveals that the combined retail market shares of Brown and Kinney exceeded 20% in only 30 or so cities. It exceeded 30% in only a dozen cities, and 40% in only 6 cities. Although the opinion does not provide enough information to compute the HHI in each city, it is unlikely that the merger would be challenged in more than a dozen or so cities, even though there were well over 100 cities in which both Brown and Kinney operated retail stores. Under the "fix it first" rule that the agencies often employ, the merger would probably be permitted to proceed, but only after the company sold off the offending stores in those cities in which the post-merger concentration was too great.

2. The 1992 Guidelines clearly abandon any notion that mergers should be condemned because they create efficiency — that is, because they enable the post-merger firm to undersell its rivals, do they not?

3. How workable is a litigation strategy of defining a relevant market by hypothesizing a "small but significant and nontransitory increase in price," and then considering the number of customer defections and extent of entry by competitors? How accurately do you suppose an economist can "hypothesize" a "small but significant" increase — say, 5% — in the price of typewriters and predict how many typewriter customers will refuse to buy? Is this form of analysis any more accurate than the kind undertaken in *Brown Shoe* or *Philadelphia Bank?* For critiques, *see* Stigler & Sherwin, *The Extent of the Market*, 28 J.L. & Econ. 555, 582 (1985); Scheffman, *Merger Policy and Enforcement at the Federal Trade Commission: the Economist's View*, 54 Antitrust L.J. 117, 119 (1985); Harris & Jorde, *Market Definition in the Merger Guidelines: Implications for Antitrust Enforcement*, 71 Cal. L. Rev. 464, 481 (1983).

Some courts have been skeptical about the DOJ's approach to market definition, and refused to follow it. *E.g., Monfort of Colo., Inc. v. Cargill, Inc.*, 761 F.2d 570 (10th Cir. 1985), *rev'd on other grounds*, 479 U.S. 104 (1986), concluding that the Guidelines "are more useful for setting prosecutorial policy than delineating judicial standards," and then accepting the district court's traditional market/submarket analysis. (The Supreme Court's opinion is reprinted in Chapter 3, *supra.*) Other cases refusing to follow the Guidelines' approach to market definition include: *Laidlaw Acquisition Corp. v. Mayflower Group, Inc.*, 636 F. Supp. 1513 (S.D. Ind. 1986); *Tasty Baking Co. v. Ralston Purina, Inc.*, 653 F. Supp. 1250 (E.D. Pa. 1987); *Christian Schmidt Brewing Co. v. G. Heileman Brewing Co.*, 600 F. Supp. 1326 (E.D. Mich.), *aff'd*, 753 F.2d 1354 (6th Cir.), *cert. dismissed*, 469 U.S. 1200 (1985).

4. *Facilitation of Collusion.* Notice the not-so-subtle shift in the focus of merger policy as expressed in the Guidelines. Traditionally, American merger policy was concerned with the merger that created the very large single firm. The earliest cases involved mergers that created dominant firms. But even in the 1960's the most frequently articulated concern was single-firm dominance. That concern was often unrealistic, given a standard that condemned mergers creating market shares of as little as 5%.

One important difference between a focus on single-firm dominance and a focus on collusion is the perceived impact of the merger on competitors. Both single large firms and cartels can charge monopoly prices, but single large firms are probably more effective at exclusionary practices, because it is difficult for a cartel to orchestrate them while disguising their concerted action. The Supreme Court made this observation in *Matsushita Elec. Indus. Co. v. Zenith Radio Corp.*, 475 U.S. 574, 590 (1986), when it opined that predatory pricing by a group of firms acting in concert was highly unlikely.

Thus an important result of the Guidelines is that concern about injury to competitors has virtually dropped out of merger policy. Is this consistent with the legislative history of the Clayton Act? With the 1950 Amendments? (See the *Brown Shoe* case, *supra*.)? Collusion, when it occurs, benefits rivals.

A more subtle shift between the 1982/1984 Guidelines and the 1992 Guidelines is that, while both are concerned with facilitation of collusion, the 1992 Guidelines speak of "coordinated interaction" rather than collusion. Why? Because the term "collusion" suggests price fixing, while "coordinated interaction" refers to *both* explicit price fixing and tacit oligopoly behavior. Many of the market conditions that make collusion easier also facilitate oligopolistic behavior — e.g., a small number of firms, high entry barriers, and homogenous products. The Guidelines' new usage suggests an increased role for "game theory" in future merger analysis. The relevant game theory deals with a firm's rational responses to the behavior of other firms when they are unable to reach an explicit "agreement." Often game theory suggests collusion-like outcomes that can be more stable than cartels, and hence are more likely to be socially damaging. *See* H. Hovenkamp, *Federal Antitrust Policy* § 4.2 (2d ed. 1994).

5. In 1987 the National Association of Attorneys General (NAAG) of the fifty states adopted an alternative set of Guidelines for horizontal mergers. These Guidelines were substantially revised in 1993. The Guidelines were designed to apply to decisions by state attorneys general to enforce section 7 of the Clayton Act, an authority which they have been held to have. *Georgia v. Pennsylvania R.R.*, 324 U.S. 439 (1945). However, the Guidelines also apply to decisions by state attorneys general to enforce the state merger statutes of their own respective states. At least tacitly, the Supreme Court has approved state challenges to mergers under federal law under standards that are inconsistent with the standards employed by the federal enforcement agencies. In *California v. American Stores Co.*, 495 U.S. 271 (1990), the Court held that a private person (in this case, the State of California, which is a "private" enforcer of the federal antitrust laws) may obtain divesture in a merger case. Importantly, the California challenge to the merger came after the Federal Trade Commission had already approved it.

The principal differences between the federal Guidelines and the Guidelines of the state attorneys general are in basic ideology and market definition. The state Guidelines argue that the purpose of merger enforcement is not necessarily to make markets more efficient, but rather to prevent wealth transfers from consumers to suppliers. As a result, they would presumably challenge any merger that threatened to yield a price increase, whether or not it produced compensating efficiencies. Respecting market definition, the state attorneys general reject the federal government's "five per cent" rule and simply look from the consumers' perspective to the range of products that consumers in general consider to be adequate substitutes. "A comparably priced substitute will be deemed suitable and thereby expand the product market definition if, and only if, considered suitable by customers accounting for 75% of the purchases."

See Harris & Jorde, *Antitrust Market Definition: An Integrated Approach*, 72 Cal. L. Rev. 1 (1984), upon which the NAAG Guidelines relied for their relevant market analysis. *See also* Barnes, *Federal and State Philosophies in the Antitrust Law of Mergers*, 56 Geo. Wash. L. Rev. 263 (1988).

Why would political officials representing the states be more concerned about mergers than those representing the federal government?

6. The *"Cellophane" Fallacy in the Federal Merger Guidelines.* The *Cellophane* fallacy, you may recall from Chapter 6, is the error of concluding that a firm is not a monopolist because it cannot profitably raise prices higher than the current level. In the *du Pont* (Cellophane) case, reprinted in Chapter 6, the Supreme Court concluded that cellophane was not a relevant market capable of being monopolized, for if du Pont increased cellophane prices by only a small amount, large numbers of customers would substitute waxed paper, glassine, or some other flexible packaging material. Quite possibly, however, this high cross-elasticity of demand existed between cellophane and its substitutes because du Pont was already charging its profit-maximizing price for cellophane, and could not profitably charge more.

The 1982/84 Merger Guidelines and the 1992 revisions do something quite similar to what the Supreme Court did in the *du Pont* case. The Guidelines define markets in merger cases by beginning with the output of the merging firm, starting with current market prices, and then asking how many customers will walk away or how many new firms will enter in response to a "small but significant and nontransitory increase in price," often around 5%.

But what if the market is already subject to collusion? The effect may be that too large a market will be drawn. For example, the dominant firm in the market for electronic watches, which are cheap to produce, might face its principal competition from manufacturers of mechanical watches, which cost more to produce. As a result, the dominant electronic watch maker — with a share of the electronic watch market of, say, 80% — is able to charge prices well above its marginal costs. The mechanical watch makers have plenty of capacity but they have high costs. The smaller competing electronic watch makers have roughly the same costs as the dominant firm, but they do not have the additional capacity and will not have it for several years. The dominant maker of electronic watches may set its price very close to the price currently charged by the mechanical watch makers.

In this market, by beginning with current market prices and then positing a "small but significant and nontransitory" price increase, the Department of Justice is likely to end up grouping the electronic and mechanical watches into the same market. The result is that it might permit the dominant electronic watch manufacturer to purchase its largest rival. If the market were correctly identified as electronic watches, the merger would be challenged.

Is the *Cellophane* fallacy in the Merger Guidelines a drafting error? Probably not, for two reasons. First of all, use of current market prices as a predicate for delineating markets is essential in any "quick look" market definition scheme (in fact, it may be essential in *all* market definition schemes). Current market prices are all that we have to go by. For example, if we knew what the competitive price (marginal cost) was, we could already see how much market power is being exercised in the market by comparing the competitive and actual prices. The *Cellophane* fallacy consists not in using current market prices as a basis for delineating markets, but in not understanding the limitations that such a use imposes.

Second, and more problematic, is the Antitrust Division's argument that the purpose of section 7 is to condemn mergers that enhance or enlarge market power beyond the present level, not to minimize the amount of market power already being exercised. *See* Baxter, *Responding to the Reaction: The Draftsman's View*, 71 Cal. L. Rev. 618, 623 and n.35 (1983). If collusion or monopoly pricing is already occurring in a market, as this argument goes, a merger among two of the participants will not make competition any worse than it already is, so the merger will not "lessen" competition.

But isn't this view somewhat naive about cartel behavior? Markets are functional, dynamic creatures. For many cartels the biggest threat is not new entry by outsiders (which the Guidelines take into account in their discussion of entry barriers), but rather "cheating" by cartel members. Cartel cheating is unlikely to show up in the "prevailing market price" that the Antitrust Division uses under the Guidelines, for one very good reason: the cheating, in order to be pulled off, must be disguised from fellow cartel members. If the cheater can hide it from fellow cartel members he can probably hide it from the Antitrust Division as well. Perhaps the most direct form of cheating is secret rebates paid to buyers who choose a particular cartel member. But such rebates are probably not common today because they signal to customers that the market is cartelized. In a competitive, unregulated market we do not expect sellers to say "the price of widgets is $10, but if you buy them from me I will secretly give you $2 back for each one you purchase." Rather, the cheating takes more subtle forms that do not show up in the price at all — principally, the provision of extra services. Manufacturers engaged in collusion may provide advertising services, delivery services, investment in retail stores, or may even redesign the product, or at least install add-ons, in order to convince a customer to purchase from them rather than a different cartel member. The result, of course, is that although the cartel price remains high many of the profits are frittered away. A merger among cartel members in such a case can then facilitate collusion, not by increasing the prevailing price, but rather by decreasing the amount of such costly extras. The cartel with the costly extras is bad, but the cartel without them is worse. Such a merger facilitates collusion even though the prevailing market price does not change by one cent.

The same thing is generally true of tacit collusion, or oligopoly behavior. There is ample reason today for thinking that firms in oligopolized markets are quite inflexible about competing on price, but much more willing to compete by offering — often on a discriminatory basis — various kinds of services. A merger in such a market may likewise not affect prevailing prices very much, but may enable the firms in the market to avoid some of this service competition.

In short, a merger in a concentrated market where the dominant firms already have substantial power can make the market far more stable, even though it has little short run impact on the dominant firms' profit maximizing price. When mergers shrink a concentrated market from five firms to four, or from six firms to five, collusion becomes easier to manage, the chance of detection by customers or enforcers is diminished, and long run stability becomes easier to achieve. Analysis of market power in merger cases should look very carefully at markets where the *Cellophane* fallacy is a possibility for the simple reason that these are markets that have demonstrated a capacity to perform anticompetitively at the current level of concentration; they are likely to become even more anticompetitive at higher concentration levels.

Language in the 1992 revisions of the Guidelines suggests that the government is having second thoughts about its use of current market prices for merger analysis. The 1992 Guidelines note that if the pre-merger behavior of the firms is "strongly suggestive of coordinated interaction," the Agency may attempt to base its price increase critique not on current market prices but rather on "a price more reflective of the competitive price." How this price will be determined is not entirely clear. Isn't this a fairly explicit rejection of the position under which the 1984 Guidelines were defended that one need not worry about express or tacit collusion that is already occurring? What kinds of evidence will the agencies use in determining whether "coordinated interaction" is already occurring? *See* 2A Areeda, Hovenkamp, & Solow, *Antitrust Law* ¶ 536, 538c (rev. ed. 1995); and 4 P. Areeda & H. Hovenkamp, *id.* at ¶ 929a (rev. ed. 1998).

7. The 1984 Guidelines had stated that the relevant question for determining market boundaries was whether a single firm that controlled all sales in a provisional market could profitably impose a "small but significant and nontransitory" increase in price. The 1992 Guidelines (see Appendix A of this casebook) state the question differently, as "whether a hypothetical profit-maximizing firm ... that was the only present and future producer or seller of those products in that area likely would impose at least a 'small but significant and nontransitory' increase in price...." § 1.0. This difference becomes important when a 5% price increase would not be profitable to a monopolist or cartel but a much larger price increase would be.

For example, suppose a cartel of sellers A, B, and C is currently charging $1.00 per unit. It sells to two classes of buyers: a "high elasticity" class that is very sensitive at the current price level and will shift to different suppliers X, Y, and Z if the price rises above $1.02; a "low elasticity" class that does not have an adequate substitute for the product and is willing to pay any price up to $1.40. The former class accounts for 10 sales per period and the latter accounts for 90. This is a common situation. For example, an automobile maker may consider a heavy steel part as an adequate substitute for an aluminum part, but an aircraft maker would not.

In this case, assuming zero costs, a 5% price increase would be unprofitable to cartel ABC: pre-increase revenue is $100.00. If cartel ABC increases the price to $1.05 it will sell ninety units and total revenue will be $94.50. Further, this 5% price increase is unprofitable *because* the high elasticity customers shifted their purchases to X, Y, and Z; so the apparent result is that X, Y, and Z must be included in the relevant market.

However, if cartel ABC should raise its price to $1.40 the firms will also lose precisely the same ten sales, but total revenue would go from $100.00 to $90 \times$ $1.40, or $126.00, making this 40% price increase quite profitable. As a result, inclusion of X, Y, and Z in the market would be a serious error, and might result in approval of a merger involving A, B, or C, depending on their relative sizes compared to X, Y, and Z.

The new Guidelines correctly delineate the relevant market as the output of A, B, and C, excluding X, Y, and Z, on the principle that the profit-maximizing price for an ABC cartel is 5% *or more*.

Although this approach is technically more correct, it is more difficult to produce the relevant data. The economic expert must consider not only the profitability of a price increase of 5% above current levels, but of all possible price increases of 5% or more. As the hypothesized price increase departs further from current prices, estimates about customer responses become increasingly speculative.

8. Do the 1992 Guidelines suggest that the enforcement agencies are abandoning the *Philadelphia Bank* presumption (see the discussion *supra*, this chapter) that mergers achieving a certain level of concentration or post-merger market share are presumptively illegal, and the burden then shifts to the defendants to show that the merger will not be anticompetitive? The 1992 Guidelines seem extraordinarily reluctant to assign burdens of proof on most issues. *See* § 0.1.

Many factors other than market structure and the market share of the merging firms may be relevant to the precise prediction of a merger's competitive consequence. These include ease of entry, buyer concentration and sophistication, product durability, product differentiation, sales methods, presence or absence of collusion facilitating devices, number and size of sales, extent of vertical integration, and history of collusion. The rationale of the *Philadelphia Bank* presumption is that courts are not particularly good institutions for assessing the relevance of each of these factors, assigning weights to them, and balancing them against one another. As a consequence, the approach designed to simplify litigation and also to produce the fewest errors is to identify mergers in markets where concentration levels and participant market share are sufficiently high to warrant a judgment that collusion or tacit coordination of prices poses a threat.

But don't the 1992 Guidelines suggest that market concentration/market share data and numerous pieces of non-market share information will all be thrown into the same pot and evaluated in a more *Gestalt* fashion? *See* § 0.2. First, the Agency will determine the post-merger market concentration and the concentration impact of the merger. Second, the agency will look for signals of adverse competitive effects. Third, it will attempt to find out whether entry would discipline any attempt at monopoly pricing.

2. JUDICIAL RESPONSES TO THE MERGER GUIDELINES

FTC V. STAPLES, INC.

United States District Court, Dist. of Columbia, 970 F. Supp. 1066 (1997)

THOMAS F. HOGAN, DISTRICT JUDGE.

Plaintiff, the Federal Trade Commission ("FTC" or "Commission"), seeks a preliminary injunction pursuant to Section 13(b) of the Federal Trade Commission Act, 15 U.S.C. § 53(b), to enjoin the consummation of any acquisition by defendant Staples, Inc., of defendant Office Depot, Inc....

Defendants are both corporations which sell office products — including office supplies, business machines, computers and furniture — through retail stores, commonly described as office supply superstores, as well as through direct mail delivery and contract stationer operations. Staples is the second largest office superstore chain in the United States with approximately 550 retail stores located in 28 states and the District of Columbia, primarily in the Northeast and California. In 1996 Staples' revenues from those stores were approximately $4 billion through all operations. Office Depot, the largest office superstore chain, operates over 500 retail office supply superstores that are located in 38 states and the District of Columbia, primarily in the South and Midwest. Office Depot's 1996 sales were approximately $6.1 billion. OfficeMax, Inc., is the only other office supply superstore firm in the United States. ...

Whenever the Commission has reason to believe that a corporation is violating, or is about to violate, Section 7 of the Clayton Act, the FTC may seek a preliminary injunction to prevent a merger pending the Commission's administrative adjudication of the merger's legality.... However, in a suit for preliminary relief, the FTC is not required to prove, nor is the Court required to find, that the proposed merger would in fact violate Section 7.... Federal Trade Commission Act, 15 U.S.C. §53(b), provides that "[u]pon a proper showing that, weighing the equities and considering the Commission's likelihood of ultimate success, such action would be in the public interest...." Courts have interpreted this to mean that a court must engage in a two-part analysis in determining whether to grant an injunction.... (1) First, the Court must determine the Commission's likelihood of success on the merits in its case under Section 7 of the Clayton Act, and (2) Second, the Court must balance the equities. *See FTC v. Freeman Hospital*, 69 F.3d 260, 267 (8th Cir. 1995)....

Likelihood of success on the merits in cases such as this means the likelihood that the Commission will succeed in proving, after a full administrative trial on the merits, that the effect of a merger between Staples and Office Depot "may be substantially to lessen competition, or to tend to create a monopoly" in violation of Section 7 of the Clayton Act.... It is not enough for the FTC to show merely that it has a "fair and tenable chance" of ultimate success on the merits as has been argued and rejected in other cases. *See FTC v. Freeman Hospital*, 69 F.3d 260, 267 (8th Cir. 1995).... However, the FTC need not prove to a certainty that the merger will have an anti-competitive effect. That is a question left to the Commission after a full administrative hearing. Instead, in a suit for a preliminary injunction, the government need only show that there is a "reasonable probability" that the challenged transaction will substantially impair competition....

One of the few issues about which the parties to this case do not disagree is that metropolitan areas are the appropriate geographic markets for analyzing the competitive effects of the proposed merger. A geographic market is that geographic area "to which consumers can practically turn for alternative sources of the product and in which the antitrust defendant faces competition." *Morgenstern v. Wilson*, 29 F.3d 1291, 1296 (8th Cir. 1994), *cert. denied*, 513 U.S. 1150 (1995). In its first amended complaint, the FTC identified forty-two such metropolitan areas as well as future areas which could suffer anti-competitive effects from the proposed merger. Defendants have not challenged the FTC's geographic market definition in this proceeding. Therefore, the Court will accept the relevant geographic markets identified by the Commission.

In contrast to the parties' agreement with respect to the relevant geographic market, the Commission and the defendants sharply disagree with respect to the appropriate definition of the relevant product market or line of commerce.... The Commission defines the relevant product market as "the sale of consumable office supplies through office superstores," with "consumable" meaning products that consumers buy recurrently, i.e., items which "get used up" or discarded. For example, under the Commission's definition, "consumable office supplies" would not include capital goods such as computers, fax machines, and other business machines or office furniture, but does include such products as paper, pens, file folders, post-it notes, computer disks, and toner cartridges. The defendants characterize the FTC's product market definition as "contrived" with no basis in law or fact, and counter that the appropriate product market within which to assess the likely competitive consequences of a Staples-Office Depot combination is simply the overall sale of office products, of which a combined Staples-Office Depot accounted for 5.5% of total sales in North America in 1996....

The consumable office products at issue here are identical whether they are sold by Staples or Office Depot or another seller of office supplies. A legal pad sold by Staples or Office Depot is "functionally interchangeable" with a legal pad sold by Wal-Mart. A post-it note sold by Staples or Office Depot is "functionally interchangeable" with a post-it note sold by Viking or Quill....

The Court recognizes that it is difficult to overcome the first blush or initial gut reaction of many people to the definition of the relevant product market as the sale of consumable office supplies through office supply superstores. The products in question are undeniably the same no matter who sells them, and no one denies that many different types of retailers sell these products. After all, a combined Staples-Office Depot would only have a 5.5% share of the overall market in consumable office supplies. Therefore, it is logical to conclude that, of course, all these retailers compete, and that if a combined Staples-Office Depot raised prices after the merger, or at least did not lower them as much as they would have as separate companies, that consumers, with such a plethora of options, would shop elsewhere.... However, the mere fact that a firm may be termed a competitor in the overall marketplace does not necessarily require that it be included in the relevant product market for antitrust purposes. The Supreme Court has recognized that within a broad market, "well-defined submarkets may exist which, in themselves, constitute product markets for antitrust purposes." *Brown Shoe....* There is a possibility, therefore, that the sale of consumable office supplies by office superstores may qualify as a submarket within a larger market of retailers of office supplies in general....

[T]he FTC presented evidence comparing Staples' prices in geographic markets where Staples is the only office superstore, to markets where Staples competes with Office Depot or OfficeMax, or both. Based on the FTC's calculations, in markets where Staples faces no office superstore competition at all, something which was termed a one firm market during the hearing, prices are 13% higher than in three firm markets where it competes with both Office Depot and OfficeMax. The data which underly this conclusion make it compelling evidence.... Similarly, the evidence showed that Office Depot's prices are significantly higher — well over 5% higher, in Depot-only markets than they are in three firm markets....

There is similar evidence with respect to the defendants' behavior when faced with entry of another competitor. The evidence shows that the defendants change their price zones[1] when faced with entry of another superstore, but do not do so for other retailers. For example, Staples changed its price zone for Cincinnati to a lower priced zone when Office Depot and OfficeMax entered that area.... There are numerous additional examples of zones being changed and prices falling as a result of superstore entry. There is no evidence that zones change and prices fall when another non-superstore retailer enters a geographic market.

Though individually the FTC's evidence can be criticized for looking at only brief snapshots in time or for considering only a limited number of [areas], taken

---

[1] [The record showed that the merger participants placed each store into a pre-designated price "zone" depending on the identity and amount of competition it faced in that area — ed.]

together, however, the Court finds this evidence a compelling showing that a small but significant increase in Staples' prices will not cause a significant number of consumers to turn to non-superstore alternatives for purchasing their consumable office supplies. Despite the high degree of functional interchangeability between consumable office supplies sold by the office superstores and other retailers of office supplies, the evidence presented by the Commission shows that even where Staples and Office Depot charge higher prices, certain consumers do not go elsewhere for their supplies. This further demonstrates that the sale of office supplies by non-superstore retailers are not responsive to the higher prices charged by Staples and Office Depot in the one firm markets. This indicates a low cross-elasticity of demand between the consumable office supplies sold by the superstores and those sold by other sellers....

When assessing key trends and making long range plans, Staples and Office Depot focus on the plans of other superstores. In addition, when determining whether to enter a new metropolitan area, both Staples and Office Depot evaluate the extent of office superstore competition in the market and the number of office superstores the market can support. When selecting sites and markets for new store openings, defendants repeatedly refer to markets without office superstores as "non-competitive," even when the new store is adjacent to or near a warehouse club, consumer electronics store, or a mass merchandiser such as Wal-Mart. In a monthly report entitled "Competitor Store Opening/Closing Report" which Office Depot circulates to its Executive Committee, Office Depot notes all competitor store closings and openings, but the only competitors referred to for its United States stores are Staples and OfficeMax....

After accepting the Commission's definition of the relevant product market, the Court next must consider the probable effect of a merger between Staples and Office Depot in the geographic markets previously identified. One way to do this is to examine the concentration statistics and HHIs within the geographic markets. If the relevant product market is defined as the sale of consumable office supplies through office supply superstores, the HHIs in many of the geographic markets are at problematic levels even before the merger. Currently, the least concentrated market is that of Grand Rapids-Muskegon-Holland, Michigan, with an HHI of 3,597, while the most concentrated is Washington, D.C. with an HHI of 6,944. In contrast, after a merger of Staples and Office Depot, the least concentrated area would be Kalamazoo-Battle Creek, Michigan, with an HHI of 5,003, and many areas would have HHIs of 10,000. The average increase in HHI caused by the merger would be 2,715 points. The concentration statistics show that a merged Staples-Office Depot would have a dominant market share in 42 geographic markets across the country. The combined shares of Staples and Office Depot in the office superstore market would be 100% in 15 metropolitan areas. It is in these markets the post-merger HHI would be 10,000. In 27 other metropolitan areas, where the number of office superstore competitors would drop from three to two, the post-merger market shares would range from 45% to 94%, with post-merger

HHIs ranging from 5,003 to 9,049. Even the lowest of these HHIs indicates a "highly concentrated" market....

Barriers to Entry

The defendants argued during the hearing and in their briefs that the rapid growth in overall office supply sales has encouraged and will continue to encourage expansion and entry. One reason for this, according to Dr. Hausman's declaration, is that entry is more attractive when an industry is growing, because new entrants can establish themselves without having to take all of their sales away from existing competitors. In addition, the defendants' impressive retailing expert, Professor Maurice Segall, testified at the hearing that there are "no barriers to entry in retailing," and defendants pointed to the fact that all office superstore entrants have entered within the last 11 years....

There are problems with the defendants' evidence, however, that prevent the Court from finding in this case that entry into the market by new competitors or expansion into the market by existing firms would likely avert the anti-competitive effects from Staples' acquisition of Office Depot. For example, while it is true that all office superstore entrants have entered within the last 11 years, the recent trend for office superstores has actually been toward exiting the market rather than entering. Over the past few years, the number of office superstore chains has dramatically dropped from twenty-three to three. All but Staples, Office Depot, and OfficeMax have either closed or been acquired. The failed office superstore entrants include very large, well-known retail establishments such as Kmart, Montgomery Ward, Ames, and Zayres. A new office superstore would need to open a large number of stores nationally in order to achieve the purchasing and distribution economies of scale enjoyed by the three existing firms. Sunk costs would be extremely high. Economies of scale at the local level, such as in the costs of advertizing and distribution, would also be difficult for a new superstore entrant to achieve since the three existing firms have saturated many important local markets. For example, according to the defendants' own saturation analyses, Staples estimates that there is room for less than two additional superstores in the Washington, D.C. area and Office Depot estimates that there is room for only two more superstores in Tampa, Florida....

For the reasons discussed above, the Court finds it extremely unlikely that a new office superstore will enter the market and thereby avert the anti-competitive effects from Staples' acquisition of Office Depot....

Efficiencies

Whether an efficiencies defense showing that the intended merger would create significant efficiencies in the relevant market, thereby offsetting any anti-competitive effects, may be used by a defendant to rebut the government's prima facie case is not entirely clear. The newly revised efficiencies section of the Merger Guidelines recognizes that, "mergers have the potential to generate significant efficiencies by permitting a better utilization of existing assets, enabling the combined firm to achieve lower costs in producing a given quality and quantity than either firm could have achieved without the proposed transaction." See Merger Guidelines §4. This coincides with the view of some courts that "whether an acquisition would yield significant efficiencies in the relevant market is an important consideration in predicting whether the acquisition would substantially lessen competition.... [T]herefore, ... an efficiency defense to the government's prima facie case in section 7 challenges is appropriate in certain circumstances." *FTC v. University Health*, 938 F.2d 1206, 1222 (11th Cir. 1991). The Supreme Court, however, in *FTC v. Procter & Gamble Co.*, 386 U.S. 568, 579, 87 S. Ct. 1224, 1230, 18 L. Ed. 2d 303 (1967), stated that "[p]ossible economics cannot be used as a defense to illegality in section 7 merger cases." There has been great disagreement regarding the meaning of this precedent and whether an efficiencies defense is permitted. Compare *RSR Corp. v. FTC*, 602 F.2d 1317, 1325 (9th Cir. 1979) (finding that the efficiencies argument has been rejected repeatedly), *cert. denied*, 445 U.S. 927 (1980) with *University Health*, 938 F.2d at 1222 (recognizing the defense).... Assuming that it is a viable defense, however, the Court cannot find in this case that the defendants' efficiencies evidence rebuts the presumption that the merger may substantially lessen competition or shows that the Commission's evidence gives an inaccurate prediction of the proposed acquisition's probable effect.

The Court agrees with the defendants that where, as here, the merger has not yet been consummated, it is impossible to quantify precisely the efficiencies that it will generate. In addition, the Court recognizes a difference between efficiencies which are merely speculative and those which are based on a prediction backed by sound business judgment. Nor does the Court believe that the defendants must prove their efficiencies by "clear and convincing evidence" in order for those efficiencies to be considered by the Court. That would saddle Section 7 defendants with the nearly impossible task of rebutting a possibility with a certainty, a burden which was rejected in *United States v. Baker Hughes, Inc.*, 908 F.2d 981, 992 (D.C. Cir. 1990). Instead, like all rebuttal evidence in Section 7 cases, the defendants must simply rebut the presumption that the merger will substantially lessen competition by showing that the Commission's evidence gives an inaccurate prediction of the proposed acquisition's probable effect. See id. at 991. Defendants, however, must do this with credible evidence, and the Court with respect to this issue did not find the defendants' evidence to be credible.

Defendants submitted an "Efficiencies Analysis" which predicated that the combined company would achieve savings of between $4.9 and $6.5 billion over the next five years. In addition, the defendants argued that the merger would also generate dynamic efficiencies. For example, defendants argued that as suppliers become more efficient due to their increased sales volume to the combined

Staples-Office Depot, they would be able to lower prices to their other retailers. Moreover, defendants argued that two-thirds of the savings realized by the combined company would be passed along to consumers.

... [T]he cost savings estimate of $4.947 billion over five years which was submitted to the Court exceeds by almost 500% the figures presented to the two Boards of Directors in September 1996, when the Boards approved the transaction. The cost savings claims submitted to the Court are also substantially greater than those represented in the defendants' Joint Proxy Statement/Prospectus "reflecting the best currently available estimate of management," and filed with the Securities and Exchange Commission on January 23, 1997....

There are additional examples of projected savings, such as the projected savings on employee health insurance, which are not merger specific, but the Court need not discuss every example here. However, in addition to the non-merger specific projected savings, Mr. Painter also revealed problems with the defendants' methodology in making some of the projections. For example, in calculating the projected cost savings from vendors, Staples estimated cost savings for a selected group of vendors, and then extrapolated these estimated savings to all other vendors. Mr. Painter testified that, although Hewlett Packard is Staples' single largest vendor, it was not one of the vendors used for the savings estimate. In addition, the evidence shows that Staples was not confident that it could improve its buying from Hewlett Packard. Yet, Staples' purchases and sales of Hewlett Packard products were included in the "all other" vendor group, and defendants, thereby, attributed cost savings in the amount of $207 million to Hewlett Packard even though Staples' personnel did not believe that they could, in fact, achieve cost savings from Hewlett Packard.

In addition to the problems that the Court has with the efficiencies estimates themselves, the Court also finds that the defendants' projected pass through rate — the amount of the projected savings that the combined company expects to pass on to customers in the form of lower prices — is unrealistic. The Court has no doubt that a portion of any efficiencies achieved through a merger of the defendants would be passed on to customers. Staples and Office Depot have a proven track record of achieving cost savings through efficiencies, and then passing those savings to customers in the form of lower prices. However, in this case the defendants have projected a pass through rate of two-thirds of the savings while the evidence shows that, historically, Staples has passed through only 15-17%. Based on the above evidence, the Court cannot find that the defendants have rebutted the presumption that the merger will substantially lessen competition by showing that, because of the efficiencies which will result from the merger, the Commission's evidence gives an inaccurate prediction of the proposed acquisition's probable effect.

[The court then concluded that the private losses from temporary prohibition of the merger failed to outweigh the threat of public injury if it occurred; thus the equities favored granting the preliminary injunction.]

NOTES AND QUESTIONS

1. The defendants subsequently scrapped their merger plans.

2. *Submarkets in Merger Cases.* Ever since *Brown Shoe Co. v. United States,* 370 U.S. 294 (1962), so-called "submarkets" have played an important role in merger litigation. As *Brown Shoe* explained:

> The outer boundaries of a product market are determined by the reasonable interchangeability of use or the cross-elasticity of demand between the product itself and substitutes for it. However, within this broad market, well-defined submarkets may exist which, in themselves, constitute product markets for antitrust purposes. The boundaries of such a submarket may be determined by examining such practical indicia as industry or public recognition of the submarket as a separate economic entity, the product's peculiar characteristics and uses, unique production facilities, distinct customers, distinct prices, sensitivity to price changes, and specialized vendors.

Id. at 325-26.

At this time you should reread the note on submarkets in monopolization cases, reprinted *supra* Chapter 6 following the *Aspen* decision. As that discussion observes, the concept of a "submarket" is contradictory to the existence of a larger market. To say that a grouping of sales is a "market" implies a high degree of consumption or production substitutability among them. To say that some segment of this grouping constitutes a "submarket" is to say that there is not sufficiently high substitutability between the market sales inside the submarket and the market sales outside the submarket. In short, if a grouping of sales is really a "market," it can logically contain no submarket. Antitrust would be far better off had we never heard of submarkets.

The 1992 Guidelines apparently reject the concept of submarkets, for they fail to mention them. Since the Federal Trade Commission is a joint issuer of the Guidelines, it has presumably rejected submarket analysis as well. Nevertheless, the FTC has continued to rely on them, as the Staples decision indicates. *See also* Calkins, *Developments in Merger Litigation: the Government Doesn't Always Win,* 56 Antitrust L.J. 855, 875 (1988), which argues that the FTC, unlike the DOJ, is more interested in winning its cases than in educating courts about economics. In any event, the *Staples* analysis makes clear that the court was not talking about "submarkets" at all; rather it concluded that sales of office supplies through superstores was a relevant *market,* for the grouping would be able profitably to sustain a price increase to profitable levels. On the use of submarkets in antitrust analysis, *see* 2A P. Areeda, H. Hovenkamp and J. Solow, *Antitrust Law* ¶ 533 (rev. ed. 1995).

NOTE: THE HERFINDAHL-HIRSCHMAN INDEX

For more than a half century economists have been using "indexes" to measure the relative size, or concentration, of firms in a particular market. The 1968

Merger Guidelines issued by the Antitrust Division selected the Four-Firm Concentration Ratio (CR4) as an index for merger policy. The CR4, which is nothing more than the sum of the market shares of the four largest firms in the market, came to have a powerful influence on judicial treatment of mergers. It may still be the most widely used index in antitrust litigation.

One of the most dramatic changes in the 1982/84 Merger Guidelines, continued in the 1992 Guidelines, is the abandonment of the CR4 in favor of the Herfindahl-Hirschman Index (HHI). The HHI consists of the sums of the squares of the market shares of all participants in the market.

There are important differences between the CR4 and the HHI. The most obvious have to do with use of data and scope of conclusions. On the one hand, the CR4 is easier to use than the HHI, for the CR4 requires market share information only about the four largest firms (although information about a few other firms may be necessary in order to determine which four are the largest). By contrast, the HHI requires market share information about every firm in the market, except perhaps for very small firms, whose impact on the HHI is very small. For this same reason, however, the HHI purports to "say" more about market concentration than the CR4. Since the data used in generating the HHI covers the entire market, the conclusion may be somehow more valid than a conclusion drawn from an examination of only four firms.

The HHI always responds to a particular merger in the same way. For example, a merger of a 10% firm and a 5% firm will always increase the HHI by 100. The effect of such a merger on the CR4 depends on how the two firms were ranked. If both firms were among the top four, they will become one and the CR4 will increase by the size of what had been the fifth firm. If neither firm was among the top four, the CR4 will remain unchanged, unless the post-merger firm becomes one of the top four. If the 10% firm was among the top four but the 5% firm was not, the CR4 will increase by five. Is the HHI's consistency superior? Probably not. The CR4 may be telling us that mergers by firms whose absolute size is the same, but whose relative size in relation to the rest of the market is greater, pose a greater anticompetitive threat.

The HHI is much more sensitive to errors in market share measurement, at least if a very large firm is measured incorrectly. This is so because the squaring of market shares tends to exaggerate such errors. For example, if a 35% firm is incorrectly measured as 40%, the CR4 increases by only five. The HHI will increase by 375. This makes accurate market definition particularly important when the HHI is used.

But there are other differences between the two indexes that go much further. The HHI is much more sensitive than the CR4 to disparities *among* the sizes of the largest firms. For example, a market whose four largest firms each have 10% shares and one whose largest firm has a 37% share and whose second, third, and fourth firms have 1% each have the same CR4: 40. But the first market has an HHI of 400 (plus a 100or 200 to account for other firms), while the second market has an HHI of 1,370 (plus 60 or 70 to account for other firms).

Why the large difference? The HHI is predicated on a "market dominance" model that weighs large firms very heavily into the calculus. For this reason, the choice of the HHI as a concentration index for the Merger Guidelines strikes some people as peculiar. The principal concern of merger policy expressed in the Guidelines is not monopolization but rather facilitation of express or tacit collusion (oligopoly). Is such collusion more likely to occur when a market is dominated by three or four firms of roughly equal size, or when it has one large firm and several smaller ones? That may depend on the type of collusion. Express collusion may work best when firms have more-or-less equal market shares and similar cost functions (which are more likely when the firms are about the same size). Certain forms of oligopoly "price leadership," by contrast, may work best when there is a single dominant firm large enough to discipline price-cutting rivals. Depending on the anticompetitive threat posed by a particular industry, the CR4 may actually predict performance more reliably. At least one study has found the CR4 to be superior in this as well as other respects. *See* Kwoka, *The Effect of Market Share Distribution on Industry Performance*, 61 Rev. Econ. & Statistics 101 (1979). For a summary of findings comparing the two indexes, *see* 4 P. Areeda & H. Hovenkamp, *Antitrust Law* ¶¶ 930-31 (rev. ed. 1998); Kwoka, *The Herfindahl Index in Theory and Practice*, 30 Antitrust Bull. 915 (1985).

This discussion should suggest to you that the CR4 and the HHI are not "equivalent" indexes. In a general sense, they both respond to increases in concentration, but at the margin they do so in very different ways. For example, an HHI reading of 1,000 can describe markets with CR4's ranging from 33.5 to 62. An HHI of 1,800 can describe markets with CR4's from 44.73 to 84.48. *See* Weinstock, *Some Little-Known Properties of the Herfindahl-Hirschman Index: Problems of Translation and Specification*, 29 Antitrust Bull. 705, 707 (1984).

Finally, and most importantly, there is no single "correct" index. A particular index is based on a particular theory about the relationship between structure and competition. There are a variety of such theories and they often conflict with each other. Furthermore, the CR4 may work better in some markets, while the HHI may be superior in others.

PROBLEM 7.2

Nine firms currently manufacture billups. Last year the billup revenue of each of the firms was as follows: Firm A = $8,000,000; Firm B = $5,500,000; Firm C = $5,000,000; Firm D = $4,000,000; Firm E = $3,000,000; Firm F = $1,500,000; Firm G = $1,000,000; Firm H = $1,000,000; Firm I = $1,000,000. Billups are undifferentiated, unbranded products, and all the firms have more-or-less the same costs. In response to a "small but significant and nontransitory increase in price," it would take at least four years for a new firm to begin manufacturing billups, but firms G, H, and I all have fairly substantial excess capacity. Customers have no good substitutes for billups. The firms are widely dispersed spatially, and transportation costs are relatively high. There is no known history of collusion or other anticompetitive behavior in the market, and it currently appears to be performing competitively. Firm *C* proposes to acquire Firm *H*. Analyze the merger under the DOJ Guidelines.

HOSPITAL CORP. OF AMERICA V. FTC

807 F.2d 1381 (7th Cir. 1986), *cert. denied*, 481 U.S. 1038 (1987)

POSNER, CIRCUIT JUDGE.

Hospital Corporation of America, the largest proprietary hospital chain in the United States, asks us to set aside the decision by the Federal Trade Commission that it violated section 7 of the Clayton Act by the acquisition in 1981 and 1982 of two corporations, Hospital Affiliates International, Inc. and Health Care Corporation. Before these acquisitions (which cost Hospital Corporation almost $700 million), Hospital Corporation had owned one hospital in Chattanooga, Tennessee. The acquisitions gave it ownership of two more. In addition, pursuant to the terms of the acquisitions it assumed contracts, both with four-year terms, that Hospital Affiliates International had made to manage two other Chattanooga-area hospitals. So after the acquisitions Hospital Corporation owned or managed 5 of the 11 hospitals in the area....

If all the hospitals brought under common ownership or control by the two challenged acquisitions are treated as a single entity, the acquisitions raised Hospital Corporation's market share in the Chattanooga area from 14 percent to 26 percent. This made it the second largest provider of hospital services in a highly concentrated market where the four largest firms together had a 91 percent market share compared to 79 percent before the acquisitions....

....

When an economic approach is taken in a section 7 case, the ultimate issue is whether the challenged acquisition is likely to facilitate collusion. In this perspective the acquisition of a competitor has no economic significance in itself; the worry is that it may enable the acquiring firm to cooperate (or cooperate better) with other leading competitors on reducing or limiting output, thereby pushing up the market price....

The acquisitions reduced the number of competing hospitals in the Chattanooga market from 11 to 7....

The reduction in the number of competitors is significant in assessing the competitive vitality of the Chattanooga hospital market. The fewer competitors there are in a market, the easier it is for them to coordinate their pricing without committing detectable violations of section 1 of the Sherman Act, which forbids price fixing. This would not be very important if the four competitors eliminated by the acquisitions in this case had been insignificant, but they were not; they accounted in the aggregate for 12 percent of the sales of the market. As a result of the acquisitions the four largest firms came to control virtually the whole market, and the problem of coordination was therefore reduced to one of coordination among these four.

Moreover, both the ability of the remaining firms to expand their output should the big four reduce their own output in order to raise the market price (and, by expanding, to offset the leading firms' restriction of their own output), and the ability of outsiders to come in and build completely new hospitals, are reduced by Tennessee's certificate-of-need law. Any addition to hospital capacity must be approved by a state agency.... Should the leading hospitals in Chattanooga collude, a natural consequence would be the creation of excess hospital capacity, for the higher prices resulting from collusion would drive some patients to shorten their hospital stays and others to postpone or reject elective surgery. If a noncolluding hospital wanted to expand its capacity so that it could serve patients driven off by the high prices charged by the colluding hospitals, the colluders would have not only a strong incentive to oppose the grant of a certificate of need but also substantial evidence with which to oppose it — the excess capacity (in the market considered as a whole) created by their own collusive efforts. At least the certificate of need law would enable them to delay any competitive sally by a noncolluding competitor....

All this would be of little moment if, in the event that hospital prices in Chattanooga rose above the competitive level, persons desiring hospital services in Chattanooga would switch to hospitals in other cities, or to nonhospital providers of medical care. But this would mean that the Chattanooga hospital market, which is to say the set of hospital-services providers to which consumers in Chattanooga can feasibly turn, includes hospitals in other cities plus nonhospital providers both in Chattanooga and elsewhere; and we do not understand Hospital Corporation to be challenging the Commission's market definition, which is limited to hospital providers in Chattanooga. Anyway, these competitive alternatives are not important enough to deprive the market shares statistics of competitive significance. Going to another city is out of the question in medical emergencies; and even when an operation or some other hospital service can be deferred, the patient's doctor will not (at least not for reasons of price) send the patient to another city, where the doctor is unlikely to have hospital privileges. Finally, although hospitals increasingly are providing services on an out-patient basis, thus competing with nonhospital providers of the same services (tests, minor surgical procedures, etc.), most hospital services cannot be provided by nonhospital providers; as to these, hospitals have no competition from other providers of medical care....

All these considerations, taken together, supported — we do not say they compelled — the Commission's conclusion that the challenged acquisitions are likely to foster collusive practices, harmful to consumers, in the Chattanooga hospital market. Section 7 does not require proof that a merger or other acquisition has caused higher prices in the affected market. All that is necessary is that the merger create an appreciable danger of such consequences in the future....

But of course we cannot just consider the evidence that supports the Commission's prediction. We must consider all the evidence in the record. We must therefore consider the significance of the facts, pressed on us by Hospital Corporation, that hospital services are complex and heterogeneous, that the sellers in this market are themselves heterogeneous because of differences in the services provided by the different hospitals and differences in the corporate character of the hospitals (some are publicly owned, some are proprietary, and some are private but nonprofit), that the hospital industry is undergoing rapid technological and economic change, that the payors for most hospital services (Blue Cross and other insurance companies, and the federal government) are large and knowledgeable, and that the FTC's investigation which led to this proceeding was touched off by a complaint from a competitor of Hospital Corporation. Most of these facts do detract from a conclusion that collusion in this market is a serious danger, but it was for the Commission — it is not for us — to determine their weight.

The first fact is the least impressive. It is true that hospitals provide a variety of different services many of which are "customized" for the individual patient, but the degree to which this is true seems no greater than in other markets. Although collusion is more difficult the more heterogeneous the output of the colluding firms, there is no established threshold of complexity beyond which it is infeasible and Hospital Corporation made no serious effort to show that hospital services are more complex than products and services in other markets, such as steel, building materials and transportation, which collusion has been frequent.

The heterogeneity of the sellers has two aspects: the hospitals in Chattanooga offer different mixtures of services; and they have different types of ownership — private for-profit ("proprietary"), private not-for-profit, public. The significance of these features is unclear. Concerning the first, if one assumes that collusion is practiced on a service-by-service basis, the fact that hospitals provide different mixtures of service seems irrelevant to the feasibility of collusion. True, since different types of service may not be substitutable — open-heart surgery is not a substitute for setting a broken leg — specialized hospitals might not compete with one another. But that is not Hospital Corporation's argument. Its argument is that the different mixture of services in the different hospitals would make it difficult for their owners to fix prices of competing services, and this we don't understand.

Different ownership structures might reduce the likelihood of collusion but this possibility is conjectural and the Commission was not required to give it conclusive weight.... Nonprofit status affects the method of financing the enterprise (substituting a combination of gift and debt financing for equity and debt financing) and the form in which profits (in the sense of the difference between revenue and costs) are distributed, and it may make management somewhat less beady-eyed in trying to control costs. But no one has shown that it makes the enterprise unwilling to cooperate in reducing competition — which most enterprises dislike and which nonprofit enterprises may dislike on ideological as well as selfish grounds....

....

Hospital Corporation's most telling point is that the impetus for the Commission's complaint came from a competitor — a large nonprofit hospital in Chattanooga. A rational competitor would not complain just because it thought that Hospital Corporation's acquisitions would facilitate collusion. Whether the competitor chose to join a cartel or stay out of it, it would be better off if the cartel were formed than if it were not formed. For the cartel would enable this seller to raise its price, whether or not to the cartel level. By staying out of the cartel and by pricing just below the cartel price, the competitor might, as we noted earlier, do even better than by joining the cartel.

The hospital that complained to the Commission must have thought that the acquisitions would lead to lower rather than higher prices — which would benefit consumers, and hence, under contemporary principles of antitrust law, would support the view that the acquisitions were lawful. But this is just one firm's opinion. It was not binding on the Commission, which having weighed all the relevant facts concluded that the acquisitions had made collusion in this market significantly more likely than before. Since, moreover, the complainant was a nonprofit hospital, in attributing the complaint to fear of lower prices Hospital Corporation is contradicting its argument that the non-profit sector of the hospital industry does not obey the laws of economic self-interest.

....

The Commission's order is affirmed and enforced. 15 U.S.C. § 21(c).

NOTE

1. The *Hospital* case generally looks at much simpler indicia of injury to competition than the Merger Guidelines suggest. *See also FTC v. Elders Grain*, 868 F.2d 901 (7th Cir. 1989), where the court dwelt mainly on the fact that the merger would reduce the number of large firms in the market from six to five, thus facilitating collusion. The court concluded:

> The penalties for price-fixing are now substantial, but they are brought into play only where sellers actually agree on price or output or other dimensions of competition; and if conditions are ripe, sellers may not have to communicate or otherwise collude overtly in order to coordinate their price and output decisions; at least they may not have to collude in a readily detectable manner.

Contrast this with the approach of the Federal Trade Commission in *B.F. Goodrich Co.*, 5 Trade Reg. Rep. (CCH) ¶ 22,519 (F.T.C. 1988), which required the fact finder to estimate the increased likelihood of collusion that might result from a merger by determining whether there were

> (1) relatively high barriers or impediments to entry; (2) a relatively high level of concentration; (3) a low level of product differentiation, and a low

level of geographic differentiation occasioned by transportation cost differences; (4) a relatively inelastic demand for industry output at competitive price levels; (5) insignificant intra-industry differences in cost functions; (6) a large number of small buyers; (7) a high degree of transaction frequency and visibility; and (8) relatively stable and predictable demand and supply conditions.

Which approach seems best calculated to produce accurate merger decisions?

NOTE: AN EFFICIENCY DEFENSE IN MERGER CASES?

The *Staples* court, *supra*, considered, but ultimately rejected, the defendant's claim that the challenged merger generated significant efficiencies that would offset any anticompetitive effects. The court concluded (1) the defendants greatly exaggerated the scope of "merger-specific" efficiencies — that is, efficiencies uniquely attributable to the merger that could not be achieved by other means; and (2) there was little evidence that these efficiencies, even if realized, would be "passed on" to consumers.

Courts have had a difficult time determining the proper role that efficiency considerations should play in merger law. Today few people doubt that mergers can create substantial efficiencies. The transactional efficiencies that can be created by vertical mergers are discussed *supra*. In the *Brown Shoe* case, both the district court and the Supreme Court noted that the post-merger Brown-Kinney firm would be more efficient than the two companies had been before the merger, and more efficient than many of their competitors. In his dissent in *Von's*, Justice Stewart observed that the "supermarket revolution" was making small, independent grocery stores "economically and technologically obsolete."

Nevertheless, despite an outpouring of literature, an "efficiency defense" has never played a significant role in merger cases. In *Brown Shoe* the Supreme Court condemned the merger *because* it produced certain efficiencies that would injure competitors of the post-merger firm, although they would benefit consumers. Leading representatives of the Chicago School of antitrust believe that there should not be a general efficiency defense in merger cases. *See* R. Bork, *The Antitrust Paradox: A Policy at War with Itself*, 124 (1978); R. Posner, *Antitrust Law: An Economic Perspective*, 112 (1976). Both former Judge Bork and Judge Posner conclude that there should be no efficiency defense because relevant efficiencies simply cannot be measured in litigation. It is relatively easy to conclude in a generalized way that vertical integration saves the cost of contracting, but it is very difficult to compute the amount of the savings. Likewise, it is often obvious that horizontal mergers can create certain multi-plant economies, but it is very difficult to determine in litigation how much these economies will reduce the cost of production. An "efficiency defense" would have to begin with a merger that is prima facie illegal (or otherwise the defense is unnecessary) and then attempt to balance the potential for inefficiency created by the increased market power of the merging firms against the efficiency created by the merger. Neither of those things is particularly easy to measure; balancing them against each other can be extraordinarily difficult. However, several commentators have argued for an efficiency defense in merger cases. *See* Williamson, *Economies as an Antitrust Defense Revisited*, 125 U. Pa. L. Rev. 699 (1977); Fisher and Lande, *Efficiency Considerations in Merger Enforcement*, 71 Cal. L. Rev. 1580 (1983); Muris, *The Efficiency Defense Under Section 7 of the Clayton Act*, 30 Case W. Res. L. Rev. 381 (1980).

At the same time, the view that mergers in general produce substantial efficiencies has come under broad attack, with several authors finding that firms who have experienced recent mergers actually perform more poorly than other firms in the same market. *See* D. Ravenscraft and F.M. Scherer, *Mergers, Sell-Offs, and Economic Efficiency* (1987); D. Ravenscraft and F.M. Scherer, *The Long-Run Performance of Mergers and Takeovers*, 17-18 (1986); W. Adams & J. Brock, *The Bigness Complex* (1986); D. Mueller, "The United States, 1962-1972" and "A Cross-National Comparison of Results," in *The Determinants and Effects of Mergers: An International Comparison* (D. Mueller, ed. 1980). Assuming these authors are correct, should such a discovery affect merger policy? Won't the market itself discipline firms for transacting unprofitable mergers?

The efficiency statement in the 1992 Merger Guidelines (§ 4 of the Guidelines, reprinted as Appendix A) was significantly revised in 1997. It is nevertheless quite conservative about efficiencies and requires strict proof. Before the DOJ will approve on efficiency grounds a presumptively illegal merger, the defendant must prove the existence of significant efficiencies that cannot reasonably be achieved by other means. The Guidelines term these "merger specific" efficiencies.

The entire notion of an "efficiencies defense" raises an additional problem that has as much to do with the political ideology of antitrust as with its economic content. To the economist all efficiency gains are good ones, regardless of where they go. Is that necessarily true for antitrust policy? Some people have argued that efficiency should be the exclusive goal of antitrust policy. *See, e.g.*, R. Posner, *Antitrust Law: An Economic Perspective*, 8-22 (1976). Suppose that two competing firms, each with 30% of the blivet market, should merge. Such a merger would be prima facie illegal under the new merger guidelines. Before the merger the market behaved fairly competitively, the marginal cost of producing blivets was $1.00 and they sold for $1.05. After the merger, however, the post-merger firm has substantial market power and is able to reduce the output of blivets to a level lower than the pre-merger output had been. It now sells blivets at a profit-maximizing price of $1.10. Should it be a defense that the merger has enabled the firm to reduce the marginal cost of manufacturing blivets to 90 cents? In that case the merger has produced a great deal of efficiency, but most of the efficiency shows up as increased profits for the post-merger firm. Consumers pay a higher price after the merger than they did before. Pure economic analysis suggests that we balance the efficiency gains from the merger against the efficiency losses that result from the increase in market power. If the gains exceed the losses the merger is efficient. The economist is not concerned with the identity of the people who benefit from the increase in efficiency, for that is a purely distributive question.

Nevertheless, this distributive question may be very important to antitrust policy. The antitrust laws are democratically passed statutes. Their legislative histories are peppered with concerns for fairness, wealth distribution, and protection for small businesses or consumers. On the other hand, there is little evidence that any member of Congress believed that all efficiency gains were good ones, regardless of who pocketed them. *See* Hovenkamp, *Antitrust's Protected Classes*, 88 Mich. L. Rev. 1 (1989).

Thus, one controversial issue in merger policy is whether firms asserting the efficiency defense must show that the resulting efficiencies will be "passed on" to consumers. Several courts have suggested such a requirement. *See FTC v. University Health*, 938 F.2d 1206, 1222-23 (11th Cir. 1991) (defendant asserting efficiency defense "must demonstrate that the intended acquisition would result in significant economies and that these economies ultimately would benefit competition and, hence, consumers"); *United States v. United Tote*, 768 F. Supp. 1074, 1084-85 (D. Del. 1991) (rejecting efficiency defense in part because there was "no guarantee that these benefits will be passed along" to consumers); *American Medical Int'l*, 104 F.T.C. 1, 213-20 (1984) (similar).

But is the requirement realistic? First, contrary to popular belief, in a competitive market efficiencies are *never* passed on, at least not in the short run. Take the example of two farmers who merge, enabling the larger post-merger farm to use less equipment and labor per acre. While the larger farm has lower costs, its corn is sold in a competitive market and the farm's output is much too small to have any impact on the market price. The post-merger farmer responds to the cost reduction by producing more, but *not* by charging less than the market price. *See* P. Yde & M. Vita, *Merger Efficiencies: Reconsidering the "Passing-on" Requirement*, 64 Antitrust L.J. 735 (1996); G. Werden, *An Economic Perspective on the Analysis of Merger Efficiencies*, 11 Antitrust 12 (Summer, 1997).

Of course, if *all* farmers could take advantage of these efficiencies, competition would drive the price down and efficiency gains would be substantially passed on to consumers. But that would be an extraordinarily rare case: for example, suppose a market contained 50 perfectly competitive firms and they paired off in mergers to create 25 firms that were still in perfect competition but had lower costs.

In contrast to the perfectly competitive farmers, the firm with market power (whether previously held or acquired by the merger) responds to reduced costs by lowering its price, but not to the same extent as the efficiency gains. This, of course, is the case that concerns merger policy. A requirement that efficiency gains be *entirely* passed on would eviscerate the efficiency defense.

A weaker but more realistic requirement is not that efficiencies be entirely passed on, but that they offer cost reductions sufficient to offset any likely price increases. As a result, the merger will not produce higher prices. For example, if a merger is likely to result in a five percent price increase when efficiencies are ignored, the amount of efficiencies passed through to consumers must be roughly five percent as well, with the result that market output remains just as high as it was before the merger, and prices just as low. This is essentially the position taken by the 1997 revisions to the 1992 Horizontal Merger Guidelines.

A similar statement is contained in the horizontal merger guidelines issued by the state attorneys general:

> [E]fficiencies will only be considered when the merging parties can demonstrate by clear and convincing evidence that the merger will lead to significant efficiencies. Moreover, the merging parties must demonstrate that the efficiencies will ensure that consumer prices will not increase despite any increase in market power due to the merger. In highly concentrated markets, even a merger which produces efficiencies will tend to create or enhance market power and will likely increase consumer prices.

Horizontal Merger Guidelines of the National Association of Attorneys General § 5.3 (1993).

One interesting conclusion of the efficiency analysis is that if one considers only economic welfare, a small efficiency gain is sufficient to offset a significant increase in market power. In such a case, a merger that produced an actual price increase would be regarded as efficient if the efficiency gains equalled or exceeded the economic losses that result from inefficient monopoly pricing. However, if one considers wealth transfers from consumers as the relevant policy criterion, then it takes a very large efficiency gain to offset relatively modest gains in market power. *See* Fisher, Johnson & Lande, *Price Effects of Horizontal Mergers*, 77 Cal. L. Rev. 777 (1989).

Does this mean that the potential of mergers to create certain efficiencies is irrelevant? No it does not. If we totally ignored the efficiencies created by mergers, and operated from the assumption that the only economic effect that can come from mergers is increased market power, we could have a per se rule against all mergers. The per se rule is built on the premise that certain practices are highly likely to have bad consequences, and almost certain not to have any good ones. We do not have a per se rule against mergers, however, and today most mergers are approved by the Justice Department or simply ignored. We recognize the potential of mergers to create efficiencies by a rule that condemns mergers only when their potential to create market power or to permit its exercise is apparent.

Many of the mergers found illegal under current law create substantial efficiencies. They are nevertheless condemned because no court is capable of balancing the increase in market power or the potential for its exercise against the economies achieved, and then determining whether the post-merger firm is more likely to raise its prices or lower them. Judges must find ways to simplify. When a merger involves companies having a small share of the market we can infer that the potential for increased market power is simply not present; therefore, the merger must be calculated to increase the efficiency of the post-merger firm. By contrast, if the merger involves firms sufficiently large that the impact on market power is real, then the dangers are too great — in spite of possible economies that are incapable of measurement. In that case we condemn the merger rather than take the risk.

UNITED STATES V. WASTE MANAGEMENT, INC.

743 F.2d 976 (2d Cir. 1984)

WINTER, CIRCUIT JUDGE:

....

We summarize those facts that are not in dispute. WMI is in the solid waste disposal business. It provides services in twenty-seven states and had revenues of approximately $442 million in 1980. At the time of the acquisition, EMW was a diversified holding company that owned a subsidiary by the name of Waste Resources, which was in the waste disposal business in ten states and had revenues of $54 million in 1980.

WMI and Waste Resources each had subsidiaries that operated in or near Dallas. WMI has one subsidiary, American Container Service ("ACS") in Dallas, and another, Texas Waste Management, in the Dallas suburb of Lewisville. Waste Resources had a Dallas subsidiary called Texas Industrial Disposal, Inc. ("TIDI"). WMI now operates TIDI as a WMI sub.

Waste collection involves several different types of equipment and serves the needs of various types of customers. For present purposes, it is important to distinguish between "non-containerized" and "containerized" equipment. "Non-containerized" refers to trucks with compactors into which trash cans and bags are loaded by hand. "Containerized" equipment consists of two types of receptacles, "dumpsters" and "roll off," each emptied by different kinds of trucks. Dumpsters typically have a volume of one to eight cubic yards and are emptied by "front-load" trucks that pick the dumpsters up with clamps and empty them into a hopper. Roll-off containers range up to 50 cubic yards in volume and are carried to a dump, emptied and then returned. Trucks that transport roll-off containers are known, not surprisingly, as roll-off trucks. If the customer desires containerized service, the waste hauler provides the dumpster or roll-off container.

There are various relevant classes of customers: (i) single or multiple dwelling residential customers; (ii) apartment complexes of varying size, (iii) "business" customers — stores, restaurants, etc., and (iv) "industrial" customers — construction sites, factories, etc. Customers choose among the kinds of services according to their individual needs, the quantity of trash produced being a critical factor.

The parties strenuously disagree over the proper definition of the relevant product and geographic markets. The government contended in the district court that the product market should be defined in terms of equipment type and that front-load and roll-off waste collection service each constitutes a separate product market. WMI argued that the market includes all forms of waste collection. The district court adopted a definition of the relevant product market that differed from the positions of both parties. Judge Griesa concluded that the product market included all trash collection, except for collection at single-family or at multiple family residences or small apartment complexes. Rejecting WMI's contentions as to the relevant geographic market, the district court excluded Tarrant County, which includes Fort Worth, thus limiting the market to Dallas County plus a small fringe area.

Based on revenue data, Judge Griesa found that the combined market share of TIDI and ACS was 48.8%. He viewed that market share as *prima facie* illegal under *United States v. Philadelphia National Bank*, 374 U.S. 321, 364-66 (1963). Agreeing with appellants that entry into the product market is easy — indeed, individuals operating out of their homes can compete successfully "with any other company" — Judge Griesa nevertheless held that proof of ease of entry did not rebut the *prima facie* showing of illegality. The district court therefore ordered WMI to divest itself of TIDI. Because we conclude that potential entry into the relevant Dallas market by new firms or by firms now operating in Fort Worth is so easy as to constrain the prices charged by WMI's subs, we reverse on the grounds that the merged firm does not substantially lessen competition.

....

A post-merger market share of 48.8% is sufficient to establish *prima facie* illegality under *United States v. Philadelphia National Bank* and its progeny.

WMI does not claim that 48.8% is too small a share to trigger the *Philadelphia National Bank* presumption. Rather, it argues that the presumption is rebutted by the fact that competitors can enter the Dallas waste hauling market with such ease that the finding of a 48.8% market share does not accurately reflect market power. WMI argues that it is unable to raise prices over the competitive level because new firms would quickly enter the market and undercut them.

In discussing ease of entry, Judge Griesa stated:

> Defendants in the present case urge that even if the Government has made a prima facie showing on the basis of market share statistics, there are circumstances which undermine the significance of these statistics. Among the arguments in this regard are:
>
> (1) It is so easy to enter the trash collection market that the relative competitive strength of a company cannot properly be measured solely with respect to the existing companies in the market, but must take into account potential new entrants.
> (2) Over the past several years there has been a trend toward deconcentration, involving steady entry into the market by new companies.
> ....

[T]he Court agrees that entry into the trash collection business is relatively easy, and the barriers to entry not great. A person wanting to start in the trash collection business can acquire a truck, a few containers, drive the truck himself, and operate out of his home. A great deal depends on the individual's personal initiative, and whether he has the desire and energy to perform a high quality of service. If he measures up well by these standards, he can compete successfully with any other company for a portion of the trade, even though a small portion. If he does not measure up, he is less successful or fails.

Over the last 10 years or so a number of companies have started in the commercial trash collection business, performing containerized service. A few, including TIDI and ACS, have grown to substantial size, presumably because of good management and service, and also as a result of acquiring other companies. The majority of new entrants have either remained relatively small or disappeared as independent entities by going out of business or being acquired by larger companies.

There is no showing of any circumstance, related to ease of entry or the trend of the business, which promises in and of itself to materially erode the competitive strength of TIDI and ACS. With regard to the legal effect of low entry barriers and potential competition in a § 7 case, there is no persuasive authority for allowing such factors to overcome a strong prima facie showing of concentration in the *existing* competitive structure.

....

Finally, the *Merger Guidelines* issued by the government itself not only recognize the economic principle that ease of entry is relevant to appraising the impact upon competition of a merger but also state that it may override all other factors. Where entry is "so easy that existing competitors could not succeed in raising prices for any significant period of time," the government has announced that it will usually not challenge a merger. *United States Department of Justice 1984 Merger Guidelines*, 46 Antitrust & Trade Reg. Rep. (BNA) No. 1169 Spec. Supp. § 3.3, at S-6. If the Department of Justice routinely considers ease of entry as relevant to determining the competitive impact of a merger, it may not argue to a court addressing the same issue that ease of entry is irrelevant. We conclude, therefore, that entry by potential competitors may be considered in appraising whether a merger will "substantially lessen competition."

Turning to the evidence in this case, we believe that entry into the relevant product and geographic market by new firms or by existing firms in the Fort Worth area is so easy that any anti-competitive impact of the merger before us would be eliminated more quickly by such competition than by litigation....

....

Given Judge Griesa's factual findings, we conclude that the 48.8% market share attributed to WMI does not accurately reflect future market power. Since that power is in fact insubstantial, the merger does not, therefore, substantially lessen competition in the relevant market and does not violate Section 7.

Reversed.

NOTES AND QUESTIONS

1. Section 3.3 of the 1982 Guidelines, which were used in *Waste Management*, states that "[i]f entry into a market is so easy that existing competitors could not succeed in raising price for any significant period of time, the Department is unlikely to challenge mergers in that market." But in arguing the *Waste Management* case on appeal the Department of Justice concluded:

> While high "entry barriers amplify the anticompetitive price effects caused by seller concentration," this does not mean that a merger which produces a 50 percent aggregate share of the merged firms in a concentrated market is legal if entry barriers are low. At bottom, ease of entry is but one of a number of structural factors relevant to the likely competitive impact of a merger...."

DOJ Waste Management Appeal Brief at 49. Is this statement consistent with the statement on entry barriers in the DOJ Guidelines at that time? Should a federal agency that has issued such Guidelines be prevented from taking a position inconsistent with them? For an argument that the 1984 Guidelines failed to take entry barriers seriously enough, *see* Schmalensee, *Ease of Entry: Has the Concept Been Applied Too Readily?*, 56 Antitrust L.J. 41 (1987). At this time you might wish to reread the note on entry barriers in monopolization and merger cases, reprinted in Chapter 6, Section II.C1, *supra*.

Assuming that *Waste Management* is correct, and that no merger should be condemned even in a concentrated market if entry barriers are very low, what kind of evidence is necessary to show low entry barriers? In *United States v. Baker Hughes*, 908 F.2d 981, 983 (D.C. Cir. 1990), the post-merger HHI in the market for the defendant's drilling equipment was above 4000. The defendant sought to show low entry barriers, and the government argued that such proof must establish that new entry would be "quick and effective" at disciplining any possible post-merger monopoly pricing. The court rejected the government's proposed test, noting that it

> would require of defendants a degree of clairvoyance alien to section 7, which ... deals with probabilities, not certainties. Although the government disclaims any attempt to impose upon defendants the burden of proving that entry actually will occur, ... we believe that an inflexible "quick and effective" entry requirement would tend to impose precisely such a burden. A defendant cannot realistically be expected to prove that new competitors will "quickly" or "effectively" enter unless it produces evidence regarding specific competitors and their plans. Such evidence is rarely available....

In response to its losses in *Waste Management*, *Baker Hughes*, and other cases, the government drafted a much more rigorous entry barrier analysis into the 1992

Horizontal Merger Guidelines than was contained in the 1984 Guidelines. *See 1992 Guidelines*, Appendix A, §§ 3.0-3.4.

Note how the Guidelines distinguish potential production that is to be counted as "in the market" (that is, those whose output would be brought to bear in response to a 5% price increase) and that which is to be treated in estimating barriers to entry. The Guidelines distinguish between "committed" and "uncommitted" entrants. A firm is an "uncommitted" entrant if it could quickly expand its output in response to the merging parties' price increase, if this output expansion did not entail the expenditure of significant irreversible or "sunk" costs, and if the new expansion "could be quickly terminated without significant loss." The output of such a firm will be counted as "in the market."

By contrast, a "committed" entrant is a firm that will encounter significant irreversible or sunk costs and may not even be in existence at the time the market is analyzed. In order for a market to be counted as having sufficiently low entry barriers that anticompetitive concerns are not raised, new entry must require sufficiently small commitment that entry can be expected in two years' time, but if the commitment is too small the firms making the entry will already have been counted in the relevant market. Markets that can be entered *de novo* without substantial commitment, perhaps by firms that do not even exist at the time of analysis, will also be counted as having low entry barriers.

Finally, note that the likelihood of entry is evaluated in terms of *post*-entry prices. A firm considering a new market wants to know, not whether the market is profitable today, but whether it will be profitable after its own output is added to that of the market. The more concentrated the market, and the more extensive the scale economies, the more questionable post-entry profits become. For example, if minimum efficient scale is 30% of market output and the elasticity of demand is one, post-entry prices could be 30% lower than current prices. Does this analysis mean that economies of scale count as an entry barrier in the Guidelines?

2. In *Waste Management* the court defined a "relevant market," but then concluded that entry into this market was so easy that no firm in it could maintain price at monopoly levels. But you may recall that a "relevant market" for antitrust purposes is a grouping of sales such that a firm controlling these sales *could* raise price to unacceptable levels. Shouldn't the court simply have defined the market more broadly? No. The analysis is proper under the established law of horizontal mergers, which requires markets to be defined by reference to firms that already operate in the same or related product or geographic areas. In *Waste Management*, however, the court recognized that a substantial limit on the defendant's power to charge monopoly prices would come from firms that had not yet entered the market at all. For this reason, no relevant market could be defined so as to include them.

3. The Justice Department also lost several merger cases to the argument that courts need not be too concerned about the anticompetitive effects of a merger if buyers from the post-merger firm are powerful and sophisticated. Such buyers will either force the post-merger firms to behave competitively or else they will integrate vertically into the post-merger market themselves or set up new independent firms that will restore competition. *See United States v. Baker Hughes*, 908 F.2d 981, 983 (D.C. Cir. 1990); *United States v. Country Lake Foods*, 754 F. Supp. 669, 677 (D. Minn. 1990); *United States v. Syufy Enters.*, 903 F.2d 659 (9th Cir. 1990). In *Country Lake* the court approved a merger among milk producers in a highly concentrated market, noting that milk distributors, who purchased from the producers, were even more concentrated. These buyers

> would recognize price increases that are not based on normal market conditions. They declared that a substantial increase in milk prices would prompt them to aggressively negotiate a reduction or to seek a substitute or replacement supplier of fluid milk. If competitive prices could not be found within the [relevant geographic market], the purchasers would seek supplies from outside dairies.

The Coase Theorem tells us that firms forced to deal with each other will strike a bargain that maximizes their joint profits. *See* Coase, *The Problem of Social Cost*, 3 J.L. & Econ. 1 (1960). Which is a more profitable situation for two monopolists (or oligopolies) forced to deal with each other: vertically integrating into each other's market and restoring competition at both levels, or preserving the monopoly but dividing the profits? If the latter, then we cannot always trust vertically related firms to discipline monopoly, no matter how sophisticated and powerful they are. *See* Hovenkamp, *Mergers and Buyers*, 77 Va. L. Rev. 1369 (1991).

PROBLEM 7.3

Personal compact disc players are high tech devices that are manufactured in a market which is highly product-differentiated and highly concentrated. World output is controlled by three firms, one of which is Japanese and two of which are American. Kasawa, the Japanese firm, makes a high quality player that commands a high price. Last year its revenues from personal compact disc player sales were $125,000,000, and it sold about 250,000 units. Sound, Inc., is the larger of the two American firms, manufacturing a medium-quality player that commands a lower price. Last year it sold about 125,000 units, for total revenues of $50,000,000. Sonic, the second American company, makes a low quality unit that sells for the lowest price. Last year it sold about 100,000 units, for total revenues of $30,000,000.

None of the three firms manufacture components for personal compact disc players. They merely assemble them, and assembly does not require any particular skills. The components are traded freely in an unrestricted market. Sound now proposes to acquire Sonic. Analyze the proposed merger under the 1992 Guidelines.

NOTE: "UNILATERAL" ANTITCOMPETITIVE EFFECTS OF HORIZONTAL MERGERS

One important change in the 1992 Guidelines is the notion that mergers in product-differentiated markets may enable certain firms to increase prices *unilaterally. 1992 Guidelines* § 2.2. The theory originated in a famous article by Harold Hotelling. Hotelling, *Stability in Competition*, 39 Econ. J. 41 (1929).

Consider a row of hot dog vendors arrayed across a beach 50 yards apart. The hot dogs and their vendors are physically identical but the differentiation applies to the variable distances that bathers must walk in order to reach a hot dog stand. Assume further that the pre-merger price of each vendor is a dollar, and that bathers, who are the potential customers, are willing to pay as much as two dollars less one cent for each yard they must walk. Thus, when all vendors charge the same price the customers maximize their value by walking to the closest vendor, but they would be willing to walk to any vendor who is as far as 100 yards away. The 100-yard remote vendor produces value to the customer of precisely the hot dog's cost, and no customer will walk to a vendor who is 101 yards or further away. The vendors are called *A, B, C, D ... N.*

FIGURE A

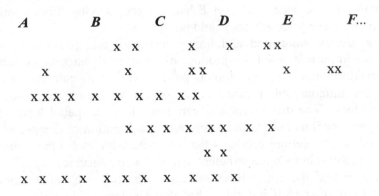

In this setting a potential customer would be willing to purchase a hot dog from as many as five vendors. For example, if she were sunbathing precisely at the location of vendor *D*, then vendors *C* and *E* would be 50 yards away in either direction, and vendors *B* and *F* would be 100 yards away in either direction. Ordinarily the customer would prefer to purchase from *D*, which gives her value of $2.00 for a price of $1.00. Since she must walk 50 yards to either *C* or *E*, these vendors give her value of $1.50 ($2.00 - 50 cents for 50 yards) for $1.00; and vendors *B* and *F* give her value of $1.00 ($2.00 - $1.00 for 100 yards) for her $1.00, thus depriving her of all consumers' surplus, but nevertheless leaving her willing to purchase a hot dog.

Also observe that each of the vendors has a range of "captured" or preferred customers of 50 yards, or 25 yards on either side, which is half way to the next vendor. That is, a customer located 20 yards to the left of vendor B would be 30 yards from vendor A. To that customer vendor B could charge a price as much as 10 cents higher than vendor A and still make the sale. However, the vendors are unable to price discriminate; they must charge the same price to all. In this "equilibrium" situation they all charge a price of $1.00.

Suppose that vendors C and D should merge, while leaving their stands (or "plants") in the same location. The two vendors together will be able to charge a significantly higher price than they were when they were competing. For example, considering the customers sunbathing between C and D, the new firm CD has at least a 50-cent (50-yard) advantage over vendors B and E, both of which are at least 50 yards more remote. Considering this group of customers alone, CD could increase its price to $1.50 without losing any of them to either B or E. And further, the range of customers located between former C and D is a full 50 yards, the same as the range of individual firms' preferred customers before the merger. In sum, this merger would very likely facilitate a significant price increase, perhaps by as much as 30 or 40 cents.

Also, observe that the significant increase in power occurs only because the CD merger united two firms that were *adjacent* in the beach/hot dog market. If two remote firms, such as A and E had merged, leaving three competitors between them, these price effects would not occur.

While greatly simplified and highly artificial, this illustration nevertheless makes an important point. In product differentiated markets mergers between firms making "adjacent," or similar, product variations can have a much more significant anticompetitive effect than mergers between firms making more remote products. The differentiations can apply to both spatial location, as in the hot dog vendor illustration, and to product specification or design, as in the case of manufacturers selling products that compete with each other (such as BMW and Oldsmobile) but are nevertheless distinctive in consumers' minds.

Note also that the competitive effects of the hot dog vendor merger would quickly be dissipated if individual hot dog vendors could cheaply and quickly relocate their stands — for example, if all were mobile carts that could be moved at the vendor's will. In that case, when firms C and D merged and attempted a price increase of, say, 30 percent, we would expect firms A, B, E, F, and perhaps others to move their carts closer into the CD territory in order to participate in these price increases. The effect would be to drive the prices back down towards the $1.00 level. Thus the threat of such a merger to produce anticompetitive results depends on the inability of other firms to respond by innovating or relocating *into* that portion of the market that has now become more competitive as a result of the merger.

Before a merger of adjacent sellers can be anticompetitive, the product differentiation in question must be "significant," going to fairly fundamental differences in product design, manufacturing costs, technology, or use of inputs. While most markets exhibit some degree of product differentiation, not all product differentiation is significant. For example, today even agricultural products are subject to branding, such as Chiquita and Del Monte bananas. Other products, such as ready-to-eat breakfast cereals, seem far more different on first appearance than they are in fact. While Kellogg's Frosted Flakes and Post's Alphabits might appear quite distinctive they are in fact made with common ingredients and common technology, with equipment that can be reconfigured to extrude different shapes or designs. And, of course, they are promoted differently. Leaving aside intellectual property rights, a firm making one could quite easily switch its production facilities to the manufacturing of the other. To this extent, costs are more-or-less the same and collusion might be quite possible.

As the hot dog vendor illustration suggests, a merger in a product differentiated market is more likely to result in a unilateral price increase as:

(1) the products of the two merger participants are more similar to one another;

(2) the products of the two merger participants are more different from the products produced by nonparticipants; and

(3) nonparticipants are unable to alter or reconfigure their products to make them more nearly like the products of the merger participants.

To the extent that such a merger enables the post-merger firm profitably to assess a significant price increase without losing sales to other firms, we would say that the merger facilitates the emergence of a new grouping of sales in which the merging firms have either a monopoly or else a dominant share.

In *United States v. Interstate Bakers Corp.*, 1996-1 Trade Cas. ¶ 71272 (N.D. Ill. 1995), the court approved a consent decree requiring the merging wholesale bakers, Interstate and Continental, to divest certain brand labels:

The Complaint alleges that Interstate's acquisition of Continental would likely lead to an increase in price charged to consumers for white pan bread. Following the acquisition, Interstate likely would unilaterally raise the price of its own brands.... Because Interstate and Continental's brands are perceived by consumers as close substitutes, Interstate could pursue such a pricing strategy without losing so much in sales to competing white pan bread brands or to private labels that the price increase would be unprofitable. Interstate could, for instance, profitably impose a significant increase in the price of Wonder white pan bread, since a substantial portion of any sales lost for that product would be recaptured by increased sales of Interstate's other brands.

Since many consumers consider Interstate and Continental brands to be closer substitutes than most other branded or private label white breads, the competitive discipline provided by rivals after the acquisition would be insufficient to prevent Interstate from significantly increasing the prices now being charged for Interstate and Continental branded white pan bread. Moreover, in response to Interstate's price increases, competing bakers would likely increase their prices of white pan bread.

See also United States v. Kimberly-Clark Corp., 1996-1 Trade Cas. ¶ 71405 (N.D. Tex.), a judgment on a consent decree terminating a challenge to a merger that included two out of three major manufacturers of facial tissue. The acquiring firm, Kimberly-Clark, produced Kleenex, which dominated the market with a 48.5 percent share and was a lower priced tissue. The acquired firm, Scott, produced Scotties, which had only a seven percent share but was also aggressively priced, forcing Kleenex to be priced lower than it otherwise would be. Under the decree Kimberly-Clark agreed to divest the Scotties brand and two out of four tissue mills.

For more on unilateral anticompetitive effects of horizontal mergers, *see* 4 P. Areeda, H. Hovenkamp & J. Solow, *Antitrust Law* ¶ 914 (rev. ed. 1998); Baker, *Contemporary Empirical Merger Analysis*, 5 Geo. Mason L. Rev. 347 (1997); Baker, *Unilateral Competitive Effects Theories in Merger Analysis*, 11 Antitrust 21 (Spring, 1997); Shapiro, *Mergers with Differentiated Products*, 10 Antitrust 23, 24 (Spring, 1996). *See also* Vellturo, *Evaluating Mergers with Differentiated Products*, 11 Antitrust 16 (Spring, 1997). As Vellturo notes, often the data necessary to estimate the rate at which customers respond to a price increase in product A by switching to product B, are more readily obtained than the data necessary to measure a relevant market and compute overall demand effects. To that extent such analysis can be more reliable than traditional market concentration analysis.

SECTION III. MERGERS OF POTENTIAL COMPETITORS

UNITED STATES V. SIDNEY W. WINSLOW

227 U.S. 202 (1913)

JUSTICE HOLMES delivered the opinion of the Court.

This is a writ of error to determine whether two counts in an indictment ... charge offenses under the Sherman Act....

The facts alleged are as follows: For the last twenty-five years practically all the shoes worn in the United States have been made by the help of machines, grouped as lasting machines, welt-sewing machines and outsole-stitching machines, heeling machines and metallic fastening machines.... Before and up to February 7, 1899, the defendants Winslow, Hurd and Brown, through the Consolidated and McKay Lasting Machine Company, under letters patent, made sixty per cent of all the lasting machines made in the United States; the defendants Barbour and Howe, through the Goodyear Shoe Machinery Company, in like manner made eighty per cent of all the welt-sewing machines and outsole-stitching machines, and ten per cent of all the lasting machines; and the defendant Storrow, through the McKay Shoe Manufacturing Company, made seventy per cent of all the heeling machines and eighty per cent of all the metallic fastening machines made in the United States....

On February 7, 1899, the three groups of defendants above named, up to that time separate, organized the United Shoe Machinery Company and turned over to that company the stocks and business of the several corporations that they respectively controlled. The new company now makes all the machines that had been made in different places, at a single new factory at Beverly, Massachusetts, and directly, or through subsidiary companies, carries on all the commerce among the States that had been carried on independently by the constituent companies before.... The defendants are alleged to have done the acts recited with intent unreasonably to extend their monopolies, rights and control over commerce among the States; to enhance the value of the same at the expense of the public, and to discourage others from inventing and manufacturing machines for the work done by those of the defendants. The organization of the new company and the turning over of the stocks and business to it are alleged to constitute a breach of the Sherman Act.

....

.... On the face of it the combination was simply an effort after greater efficiency. The business of the several groups that combined, as it existed before the combination, is assumed to have been legal. The machines are patented, making them is a monopoly in any case, the exclusion of competitors from the use of them is of the very essence of the right conferred by the patents, and it may be assumed that the success of the several groups was due to their patents having been the best. As ... they did not compete with one another, it is hard to see why the collective business should be any worse than its component parts. It is said that from seventy to eighty per cent of all the shoe machinery business was put into a single hand. This is inaccurate, since the machines in question are not alleged to be types of all the machines used in making shoes, and since the defendants' share in commerce among the States does not appear. But taking it as true we can see no greater objection to one corporation manufacturing seventy per cent of three noncompeting groups of patented machines collectively used for making a single product than to three corporations making the same proportion of one group each. The disintegration aimed at by the statute does not extend to reducing all manufacture to isolated units of the lowest degree. It is as lawful for one corporation to make every part of a steam engine and to put the machine together as it would be for one to make the boilers and another to make the wheels....

NOTES AND QUESTIONS

1. Justice Holmes's short opinion amounts to little more than a rhetorical question: when two people who do not compete with each other merge, how much competition do they eliminate? Clearly, in Holmes's mind, none.

Justice Holmes never considered the possibility that a manufacturer of lasting machines might someday want to expand its business to include heeling machines,

and that its experience in the lasting machine business might give it some expertise and goodwill that would make its entry into the heeling machine business
easier. In short, Justice Holmes never considered the fact that, although the defendants were not actual competitors, they were *potential* competitors. Each of
them was a likely entrant into the businesses run by the others.

The entire notion of potential competition must be considered carefully. Few
people may be actual competitors in any practical sense, but *everyone* is a "potential" competitor with everyone else. The relevant question for merger policy is
how much does a particular person "potentially compete" with someone else?

In large part this is a question of cross-elasticity of supply. If a seller attempts to raise its prices, the higher profits will attract new entry into the
seller's market. This new entry may come from persons operating in the same
geographic market but manufacturing a slightly different product, or it may
come from someone manufacturing the same product but in a different geographic market. The new entry may, of course, come from someone who is
presently not manufacturing anything in any market. If a particular merger
eliminates the most likely entrant into a market, the reduction in cross-elasticity
of supply can be far more substantial than if it eliminates someone who was
really not likely to enter. In general, the greater the reduction in the cross-
elasticity of supply generated by a merger (or by any other exclusionary practice, for that matter), the greater will be the increase in market power of those
persons operating in the relevant market. At the outer limit, a person manufacturing 100% of a certain product may have no market power, because a minuscule price increase would invite large-scale entry by someone sitting on the
"edge" of the market. The elimination of that potential entrant by merger
could greatly increase the market power of the post-merger firm. The theory
illustrates that market power is a function not only of market share, but also
of demand and supply elasticities. If a firm making 70% of the heeling machines in the country (the relevant market) merges with a firm that makes
70% of the lasting machines, the post-merger firm's market share is exactly
the same as it was before the merger: 70% of the heeling machines and 70% of
the lasting machines. Nevertheless, if each of the firms had been a potential
entrant into the business of the other, the increase in market power could be
substantial.

2. The other side of the story, of course, is that after the merger the newly
formed United Shoe Machinery Company consolidated all its operations into a
single plant and was able to offer a full line of shoe machinery and related products to people who wanted to manufacture shoes. The efficiencies produced by a
potential competition merger can be just as large as the efficiencies produced by
a horizontal or vertical merger, particularly if the merger partners produce complementary products, as they did in the *Sidney Winslow* case. As Justice Holmes
observes, it is as lawful for one corporation to manufacture an entire steam engine as it is for a group of corporations to make each individual part — and it is
probably a lot cheaper.

UNITED STATES V. CONTINENTAL CAN CO.

378 U.S. 441 (1964)

JUSTICE WHITE delivered the opinion of the Court.

In 1956, Continental Can Company, the Nation's second largest producer of metal containers, acquired all of the assets, business and good will of Hazel-Atlas Glass Company, the Nation's third largest producer of glass containers, in exchange for 999,140 shares of Continental's common stock and the assumption by Continental of all the liabilities of Hazel-Atlas. The Government brought this action seeking a judgment that the acquisition violated § 7 of the Clayton Act and requesting an appropriate divestiture order. Trying the case without a jury, the District Court found that the Government had failed to prove reasonable probability of anticompetitive effect in any line of commerce, and accordingly dismissed the complaint at the close of the Government's case....

The industries with which this case is principally concerned are ... the metal can industry, the glass container industry and the plastic container industry, each producing one basic type of container made of metal, glass, and plastic, respectively.

Continental Can is a New York corporation organized in 1913 to acquire all the assets of three metal container manufacturers. Since 1913 Continental has acquired 21 domestic metal container companies as well as numerous others engaged in the packaging business, including producers of flexible packaging; a manufacturer of polyethylene bottles and similar plastic containers; 14 producers of paper containers and paperboard; four companies making closures for glass containers; and one — Hazel-Atlas — producing glass containers. In 1955, the year prior to the present merger, Continental, with assets of $382 million, was the second largest company in the metal container field, shipping approximately 33% of all such containers sold in the United States. It and the largest producer, American Can Company, accounted for approximately 71% of all metal container shipments. National Can Company, the third largest, shipped approximately 5%, with the remaining 24% of the market being divided among 75 to 90 other firms.

....

Hazel-Atlas was a West Virginia corporation which in 1955 had net sales in excess of $79 million and assets of more than $37 million. Prior to the absorption of Hazel-Atlas into Continental the pattern of dominance among a few firms in the glass container industry was similar to that which prevailed in the metal container field. Hazel-Atlas, with approximately 9.6% of the glass container shipments in 1955, was third. Owens-Illinois Glass Company had 34.2% and Anchor-Hocking Glass Company 11.6%, with the remaining 44.6% being divided among at least 39 other firms.

....

We deal first with the relevant market. It is not disputed here, and the District Court held, that the geographical market is the entire United States. As for the product market, the court found, as was conceded by the parties, that the can industry and the glass container industry were relevant lines of commerce. Beyond these two product markets, however, the Government urged the recognition of various other lines of commerce, some of them defined in terms of the end uses for which tin and glass containers were in substantial competition. These end-use claims were containers for the beer industry, containers for the soft drink industry, containers for the canning industry, containers for the toiletry and cosmetic industry, containers for the medicine and health industry, and containers for the household and chemical industry.

... The court, nevertheless, with one exception — containers for beer — rejected the Government's claim that existing competition between metal and glass containers had resulted in the end-use product markets urged by the Government: "The fact that there is inter-industry or inter-product competition between metal, glass and plastic containers is not determinative of the metes and bounds of a relevant product market." In the trial court's view, the Government failed to make "appropriate distinctions ... between inter-industry or overall commodity competition and the type of competition between products with reasonable interchangeability of use and cross-elasticity of demand which has Clayton Act significance." The interindustry competition, concededly present, did not remove this merger from the category of the conglomerate combination, "in which one company in two separate industries combined with another in a third industry for the purpose of establishing a diversified line of products."

... The District Court's findings having established the existence of three product markets — metal containers, glass containers and metal and glass beer containers — the disputed issue on which that court erred is whether the admitted competition between metal and glass containers for uses other than packaging beer was of the type and quality deserving of § 7 protection and therefore the basis for defining a relevant product market. In resolving this issue we are instructed on the one hand that "[f]or every product, substitutes exist. But a relevant market cannot meaningfully encompass that infinite range." On the other hand it is improper "to require that products be fungible to be considered in the relevant market." In defining the product market between these terminal extremes, we must recognize meaningful competition where it is found to exist. Though the "outer boundaries of a product market are determined by the reasonable interchangeability of use or the cross-elasticity of demand between the product itself and substitutes for it," there may be "within this broad market, well-defined submarkets ... which, in themselves, constitute product markets for antitrust purposes."...

It is quite true that glass and metal containers have different characteristics which may disqualify one or the other, at least in their present form, from this or that particular use; that the machinery necessary to pack in glass is different from that employed when cans are used; that a particular user of cans or glass may pack in only one or the other container and does not shift back and forth from day to day as price and other factors might make desirable; and that the competition between metal and glass containers is different from the competition between the can companies themselves or between the products of the different glass companies. These are relevant and important considerations but they are not sufficient to obscure the competitive relationships which this record so compellingly reveals.

Baby food was at one time packed entirely in metal cans. Hazel-Atlas played a significant role in inducing the shift to glass as the dominant container by designing "what has become the typical baby food jar." According to Continental's estimate, 80% of the Nation's baby food now moves in glass containers. Continental has not been satisfied with this contemporary dominance by glass, however, and has made intensive efforts to increase its share of the business at the expense of glass. In 1954, two years before the merger, the Director of Market Research and Promotion for the Glass Container Manufacturers Institute concluded, largely on the basis of Continental's efforts to secure more baby food business, that "the can industry is beginning to fight back more aggressively in this field where it is losing ground to glass." In cooperation with some of the baby food companies Continental carried out what it called a Baby Food Depth Survey in New York and Los Angeles to discover specific reasons for the preference of glass-packed baby food. Largely in response to this and other in-depth surveys, advertising campaigns were conducted which were designed to overcome mothers' prejudices against metal containers.

In the soft drink business, a field which has been, and is, predominantly glass territory, the court recognized that the metal can industry had "[a]fter considerable initial difficulty ... developed a can strong enough to resist the pressures generated by carbonated beverages" and "made strenuous efforts to promote the use of metal cans for carbonated beverages as against glass bottles." Continental has been a major factor in this rivalry. It studied the results of market tests to determine the extent to which metal cans could "penetrate this tremendous market," and its advertising has centered around the advantages of cans over glass as soft drink containers, emphasizing such features as convenience in stacking and storing, freedom from breakage and lower distribution costs resulting from the lighter weight of cans.

The District Court found that "[a]lthough at one time almost all packaged beer was sold in bottles, in a relatively short period the beer can made great headway and may well have become the dominant beer container." Regardless of which industry may have the upper hand at a given moment, however, an intense competitive battle on behalf of the beer can and the beer bottle is being waged both by the industry trade associations and by individual container manufacturers....

In the food canning, toiletry and cosmetic, medicine and health, and household and chemical industries the existence of vigorous competition was also recognized below. In the case of food it was noted that one type of container has supplanted the other in the packing of some products and that in some instances similar products are packaged in two or more different types of containers. In the other industries "glass container, plastic container and metal container manufacturers are each seeking to promote their lines of containers at the expense of other lines, … all are attempting to improve their products or to develop new ones so as to have a wider customer appeal," the result being that "manufacturers from time to time may shift a product from one type of container to another."

In the light of this record and these findings, we think the District Court employed an unduly narrow construction of the "competition" protected by § 7 and of "reasonable interchangeability of use or the cross-elasticity of demand" in judging the facts of this case….

… In our view there is and has been a rather general confrontation between metal and glass containers and competition between them for the same end uses which is insistent, continuous, effective and quantitywise very substantial. Metal has replaced glass and glass has replaced metal as the leading container for some important uses; both are used for other purposes; each is trying to expand its share of the market at the expense of the other; and each is attempting to preempt for itself every use for which its product is physically suitable, even though some such uses have traditionally been regarded as the exclusive domain of the competing industry….

Moreover, price is only one factor in a user's choice between one container or the other. That there are price differentials between the two products or that the demand for one is not particularly or immediately responsive to changes in the price of the other are relevant matters but not determinative of the product market issue. Whether a packager will use glass or cans may depend not only on the price of the package but also upon other equally important considerations. The consumer, for example, may begin to prefer one type of container over the other and the manufacturer of baby food cans may therefore find that his problem is the housewife rather than the packer or the price of his cans. This may not be price competition but it is nevertheless meaningful competition between interchangeable containers.

....

Based on the evidence thus far revealed by this record we hold that the interindustry competition between glass and metal containers is sufficient to warrant treating as a relevant product market the combined glass and metal container industries and all end uses for which they compete….

....

Continental occupied a dominant position in the metal can industry. It shipped 33% of the metal cans shipped by the industry and together with American shipped about 71% of the industry total. Continental's share amounted to 13 billion metal containers out of a total of 40 billion and its $433 million gross sales of metal containers amounted to 31.4% of the industry's total gross of $1,380,000,000. Continental's total assets were $382 million, its net sales and operating revenues $666 million….

Continental's major position in the relevant product market — the combined metal and glass container industries — prior to the merger is undeniable. Of the 59 billion containers shipped in 1955 by the metal ($39^3/_4$ billion) and glass ($19^1/_3$

billion) industries, Continental shipped 21.9%, to a great extent dispersed among all of the end uses for which glass and metal compete. Of the six largest firms in the product market, it ranked second.

When Continental acquired Hazel-Atlas it added significantly to its position in the relevant line of commerce. Hazel-Atlas was the third largest glass container manufacturer in an industry in which the three top companies controlled 55.4% of the total shipments of glass containers. Hazel-Atlas' share was 9.6%, which amounted to 1,857,000,000 glass containers out of a total of $19^1/_3$ billion industrial total....

... It is not at all self-evident that the lack of current competition between Continental and Hazel-Atlas for some important end uses of metal and glass containers significantly diminished the adverse effect of the merger on competition. Continental might have concluded that it could effectively insulate itself from competition by acquiring a major firm not presently directing its market acquisition efforts toward the same end uses as Continental, but possessing the potential to do so. Two examples will illustrate. Both soft drinks and baby food are currently packed predominantly in glass, but Continental has engaged in vigorous and imaginative promotional activities attempting to overcome consumer preferences for glass and secure a larger share of these two markets for its tin cans. Hazel-Atlas was not at the time of the merger a significant producer of either of these containers, but with comparatively little difficulty, if it were an independent firm making independent business judgments, it could have developed its soft drink and baby food capacity. The acquisition of Hazel-Atlas by a company engaged in such intense efforts to effect a diversion of business from glass to metal in both of these lines cannot help but diminish the likelihood of Hazel-Atlas realizing its potential as a significant competitor in either line.... It would make little sense for one entity within the Continental empire to be busily engaged in persuading the public of metal's superiority over glass for a given end use, while the other is making plans to increase the Nation's total glass container output for that same end use. Thus, the fact that Continental and Hazel-Atlas were not substantial competitors of each other for certain end uses at the time of the merger may actually enhance the long-run tendency of the merger to lessen competition.

NOTES AND QUESTIONS

1. Are a manufacturer of glass bottles and a manufacturer of metal cans "actual" competitors, "potential" competitors — or is this simply a question of degree? Suppose that brewers are absolutely indifferent whether their beer is placed in bottles or in cans, provided that the two sell for the same price. Assume, however, that the cost of producing a bottle is 7 cents, while the cost of producing a can is 8 cents. As long as bottles are sold at the competitive price, the beer bottlers will prefer bottles and the competition from cans will be, at best, "potential."

But should the bottle industry ever be cartelized or come under the control of a monopolist, the bottle seller's power to sell at a supracompetitive price will be limited by the existence of the can market. If the bottle sellers attempt to charge more than 8 cents, beer bottlers will switch to cans.

2. The *Continental Can* decision makes one thing clear: our definition of a particular merger as a "conglomerate" or "potential competition" merger is entirely a function of our definition of the relevant markets. To say that two firms operate in the same product and geographic markets is to say that they compete; to say that one or both of the markets are different, however, is to conclude that their competition is only "potential." Sometimes the question whether two firms operate in the same market is controversial, as it was in *Continental Can*. In that case, the conclusion that they are in the same market, plus the application of the fixed market share rules of *Brown Shoe, Von's Grocery,* or *Philadelphia Bank* can yield a certain amount of over-reaching, can they not? This is so because, although the level of competition that exists between any two firms is a continuum, antitrust analysis has tended to group all pairs of firms into two categories: they are either competitors or they are not. As Justice Harlan's dissent suggests, although Continental Can and Hazel-Atlas "compete," they probably do not compete as much as did the parties in *Brown Shoe, Von's Grocery,* or *Philadelphia Bank.* In that case, does it make sense to use the same kind of market share analysis? *See* Werden, *Section 7 of the Clayton Act and the Analysis of Semihorizontal Mergers,* 27 Antitrust Bull. 135 (1982); Areeda & Turner, *Conglomerate Mergers: Extended Interdependence and Effects of Interindustry Competition as Grounds for Condemnation,* 127 U. Pa. L. Rev. 1082 (1979).

It seems clear however, that the degree of *actual* competition in *Continental Can* is significantly higher than it was in *Sidney W. Winslow,* does it not? In the *Winslow* case, the merger partners produced complementary products. The elasticity of demand between them was very low. Someone who wanted to manufacture shoes would need to have both a lasting machine and a heeling machine. If the price of lasting machines rose dramatically the entrant might decide not to manufacture shoes at all, or she might do her lasting by hand — but she could not reasonably substitute a heeling machine for a lasting machine. In *Continental Can,* by contrast, the cross-elasticity of demand between the two products is substantially higher. A beer bottler currently using glass bottles and suddenly facing a large price increase for bottles might consider switching to cans.

3. The Court observed that before the merger the glass container companies were competing vigorously, both to develop new uses for glass bottles and to convince customers that they would be better off with glass. The metal container companies carried on similar research and development. The Court assumed that once Continental Can and Hazel-Atlas come under common control they would lose the incentive to do this, for gains in the can market would come only at the expense of losses in the glass bottle market, and vice versa. Is the Court correct? Hazel-Atlas manufactured approximately 10% of the market's glass containers. Suppose that the "Can" division of the post-merger firm developed a superior can

that stole 1,000,000 units per year away from glass manufacturers. Since Hazel-Atlas/Continental is the developer of this new can, it will get all the 1,000,000 sales of the new can, at least initially, until it is copied by competitors. However, the Glass division, which has 10% of the productive capacity for glass containers, will suffer only 10% of the loss in sales. Thus the post-merger firm would realize a net gain of 900,000 units. On the other hand, if a competing firm developed the new can Hazel-Atlas/Continental would lose all 1,000,000 sales. Wouldn't the post-merger firm have just as much incentive to innovate after the merger as it did before?

4. The 1992 Merger Guidelines, reprinted as Appendix A in this book, are relevant only to horizontal mergers. Conglomerate mergers continue to be addressed under earlier Guidelines issued in 1984. But is *Continental Can* a horizontal or a conglomerate merger case? If it is simply a horizontal merger case in a product differentiated market, then both the 1984 and 1992 Guidelines provide that the government would be less likely to challenge the merger, because collusion in product differentiated markets is more difficult to accomplish.

If there is any difference in consumer preference for the output of colluding firms, then the cartel members will not be able to fix the same price. For example, if a manufacturer of cheap, low-quality personal computers and a manufacturer of expensive, high-quality computers fixed the same price, all the customers would flock to the second manufacturer. As a result, when products are differentiated, the cartel members will have to agree on a price "scale," not merely on a price. How easy would it be for a can manufacturer and a glass bottle manufacturer to fix prices, given the fact that each serves dozens of different types of customers? *See* H. Hovenkamp, *Federal Antitrust Policy* § 4.1 (2d ed. 1994).

5. *In United States v. El Paso Nat. Gas Co.*, 376 U.S. 651 (1964), the Supreme Court condemned El Paso's acquisition of Pacific Northwest. El Paso was a natural gas company located in the southwest and selling natural gas into the southern California market. Pacific Northwest was located in the northwest and had attempted unsuccessfully to sell gas into southern California. It had bid against El Paso numerous times but had lost the bids. There was evidence, however, that El Paso had adjusted its bids downward in order to account for Pacific Northwest's competition. The Court reasoned as follows:

> Pacific Northwest, though it had no pipeline into California, is shown by this record to have been a substantial factor in the California market at the time it was acquired by El Paso. At that time El Paso was the only actual supplier of out-of-state gas to the vast California market....
>
> At that time Pacific Northwest was the only other important interstate pipeline west of the Rocky Mountains. Though young, it was prospering and appeared strong enough to warrant a "treaty" with El Paso that protected El Paso's California markets.

Edison's [a power company's] search for a firm supply of natural gas in California ... illustrates what effect Pacific Northwest had merely as a potential competitor in the California market. Edison took its problem to Pacific Northwest and, as we have seen, a tentative agreement was reached for Edison to obtain Pacific Northwest gas. El Paso responded, offering Edison a firm supply of gas and substantial price concessions. We would have to wear blinders not to see that the mere efforts of Pacific Northwest to get into the California market, though unsuccessful, had a powerful influence on El Paso's business attitudes within the State....

This is not a field where merchants are in a continuous daily struggle to hold old customers and to win new ones over from their rivals. In this regulated industry a natural gas company (unless it has excess capacity) must compete for, enter into, and then obtain Commission approval of sale contracts in advance of constructing the pipeline facilities. In the natural gas industry pipelines are very expensive; and to be justified they need long-term contracts for sale of the gas that will travel them. Those transactions with distributors are few in number. For example, in California there are only two significant wholesale purchasers — Pacific Gas & Electric in the north and the Southern Companies in the south. Once the Commission grants authorization to construct facilities or to transport gas in interstate commerce, once the distributing contracts are made, a particular market is withdrawn from competition. *The competition then is for the new increments of demand that may emerge with an expanding population and with an expanding industrial or household use of gas.*

The effect on competition in a particular market through acquisition of another company is determined by the nature or extent of that market and by the nearness of the absorbed company to it, that company's eagerness to enter that market, its resourcefulness, and so on. Pacific Northwest's position as a competitive factor in California was not disproved by the fact that it had never sold gas there. Nor is it conclusive that Pacific Northwest's attempt to sell to Edison failed....

Unsuccessful bidders are no less competitors than the successful one. The presence of two or more suppliers gives buyers a choice. Pacific Northwest was no feeble, failing company; nor was it inexperienced and lacking in resourcefulness. It was one of two major interstate pipelines serving the trans-Rocky Mountain States; it had raised $250 million for its pipeline that extended 2,500 miles through rugged terrain. It had adequate reserves and managerial skill. It was so strong and militant that it was viewed with concern, and coveted, by El Paso. If El Paso can absorb Pacific Northwest without violating § 7 of the Clayton Act, that section has no meaning in the natural gas field. For normally there is no competition — once the lines are built and the long-term contracts negotiated — except as respects the incremental needs.

The amount of actual competition in *El Paso Natural Gas* was greater than it was in *Continental Can*, was it not? Customers probably did not distinguish between natural gas delivered by El Paso and gas delivered by Pacific Northwest. The only reason that Pacific Northwest had not been operating in California was that it had not yet made a successful bid there. Unless Pacific Northwest operated at a substantial cost disadvantage with respect to the California market, the two firms were actual competitors.

But was California the relevant geographic market? The Supreme Court assumed that it was, and noted elsewhere in the opinion that El Paso's share of current sales in that market was about 50%. Since Pacific Northwest's sales in California were zero, the Court could not easily treat this as a horizontal merger and simply determine the amount by which El Paso's share of the California market increased as a result. It did not increase at all. In short, if El Paso had more market power in the California market after the merger than it did before, it was not because the merger handed El Paso a larger share of the California market. It was because the elasticity of supply facing El Paso was lower after the merger than it had been before.

An alternative would have been to take the total uncommitted capacity of all gas companies capable of delivering gas into the California market, plus all gas actually being sold in California, and treat the merger as horizontal. Then El Paso's share of the relevant market would drop dramatically, but the acquisition would have enlarged its actual market share. This latter method has the advantage that it would account for the fact that other very large gas companies, such as Westcoast Transmission Company of Canada, were capable of selling gas into the California market. Presumably any attempt by El Paso to increase the price for new gas could be met by an increase in production by such companies, up to the limit of their productive capacity.

FTC V. PROCTER & GAMBLE CO.

386 U.S. 568 (1967)

JUSTICE DOUGLAS delivered the opinion of the Court.

This is a proceeding initiated by the Federal Trade Commission charging that respondent, Procter & Gamble Co., had acquired the assets of Clorox Chemical Co. in violation of § 7 of the Clayton Act.... The charge was that Procter's acquisition of Clorox might substantially lessen competition or tend to create a monopoly in the production and sale of household liquid bleaches.

....

At the time of the merger, in 1957, Clorox was the leading manufacturer in the heavily concentrated household liquid bleach industry. It is agreed that household liquid bleach is the relevant line of commerce. The product is used in the home as a germicide and disinfectant, and, more importantly, as a whitening agent in washing clothes and fabrics. It is a distinctive product with no close substitutes. Liquid bleach is a low-price, high-turnover consumer product sold mainly through grocery stores and supermarkets. The relevant geographical market is the

Nation and a series of regional markets. Because of high shipping costs and low sales price, it is not feasible to ship the product more than 300 miles from its point of manufacture. Most manufacturers are limited to competition within a single region since they have but one plant. Clorox is the only firm selling nationally; it has 13 plants distributed throughout the Nation. Purex, Clorox's closest competitor in size, does not distribute its bleach in the northeast or mid-Atlantic States; in 1957, Purex's bleach was available in less than 50% of the national market.

At the time of the acquisition, Clorox was the leading manufacturer of household liquid bleach, with 48.8% of the national sales — annual sales of slightly less than $40,000,000. Its market share had been steadily increasing for the five years prior to the merger. Its nearest rival was Purex, which manufactures a number of products other than household liquid bleaches, including abrasive cleaners, toilet soap, and detergents. Purex accounted for 15.7% of the household liquid bleach market. The industry is highly concentrated; in 1957, Clorox and Purex accounted for almost 65% of the Nation's household liquid bleach sales, and, together with four other firms, for almost 80%. The remaining 20% was divided among over 200 small producers. Clorox had total assets of $12,000,000; only eight producers had assets in excess of $1,000,000 and very few had assets of more than $75,000.

In light of the territorial limitations on distribution, national figures do not give an accurate picture of Clorox's dominance in the various regions. Thus, Clorox's seven principal competitors did no business in New England, the mid-Atlantic States, or metropolitan New York. Clorox's share of the sales in those areas was 56%, 72%, and 64% respectively. Even in regions where its principal competitors were active, Clorox maintained a dominant position. Except in metropolitan Chicago and the west-central States Clorox accounted for at least 39%, and often a much higher percentage, of liquid bleach sales.

Since all liquid bleach is chemically identical, advertising and sales promotion are vital. In 1957 Clorox spent almost $3,700,000 on advertising, imprinting the value of its bleach in the mind of the consumer. In addition, it spent $1,700,000 for other promotional activities. The Commission found that these heavy expenditures went far to explain why Clorox maintained so high a market share despite the fact that its brand, though chemically indistinguishable from rival brands, retailed for a price equal to or, in many instances, higher than its competitors.

Procter is a large, diversified manufacturer of low-price, high-turnover household products sold through grocery, drug, and department stores. Prior to its acquisition of Clorox, it did not produce household liquid bleach. Its 1957 sales were in excess of $1,100,000,000 from which it realized profits of more than $67,000,000; its assets were over $500,000,000. Procter has been marked by rapid growth and diversification. It has successfully developed and introduced a number of new products. Its primary activity is in the general area of soaps, detergents, and cleansers; in 1957, of total domestic sales, more than one-half (over $500,000,000) were in this field. Procter was the dominant factor in this area. It accounted for 54.4% of all packaged detergent sales. The industry is heavily concentrated — Procter and its nearest competitors, Colgate-Palmolive and Lever Brothers, account for 80% of the market.

In the marketing of soaps, detergents, and cleansers, as in the marketing of household liquid bleach, advertising and sales promotion are vital. In 1957, Procter was the Nation's largest advertiser, spending more than $80,000,000 on advertising and an additional $47,000,000 on sales promotion. Due to its tremendous volume, Procter receives substantial discounts from the media. As a multiproduct producer Procter enjoys substantial advantages in advertising and sales promotion. Thus, it can and does feature several products in its promotions, reducing the printing, mailing, and other costs for each product. It also purchases network programs on behalf of several products, enabling it to give each product network exposure at a fraction of the cost per product that a firm with only one product to advertise would incur.

Prior to the acquisition, Procter was in the course of diversifying into product lines related to its basic detergent-soap-cleanser business. Liquid bleach was a distinct possibility since packaged detergents — Procter's primary product line — and liquid bleach are used complementarily in washing clothes and fabrics, and in general household cleaning. As noted by the Commission:

> Packaged detergents — Procter's most important product category — and household liquid bleach are used complementarily, not only in the washing of clothes and fabrics, but also in general household cleaning, since liquid bleach is a germicide and disinfectant as well as a whitener. From the consumer's viewpoint, then, packaged detergents and liquid bleach are closely related products.... Since products of both parties to the merger are sold to the same customers, at the same stores, and by the same merchandising methods, the possibility arises of significant integration at both the marketing and distribution levels.

... The Commission found that the substitution of Procter with its huge assets and advertising advantages for the already dominant Clorox would dissuade new entrants and discourage active competition from the firms already in the industry due to fear of retaliation by Procter. The Commission thought it relevant that retailers might be induced to give Clorox preferred shelf space since it would be manufactured by Procter, which also produced a number of other products marketed by the retailers. There was also the danger that Procter might underprice Clorox in order to drive out competition, and subsidize the underpricing with revenue from other products. The Commission carefully reviewed the effect of the acquisition on the structure of the industry, noting that "[t]he practical tendency of the ... merger ... is to transform the liquid bleach industry into an arena of big business competition only, with the few small firms that have not disappeared through merger eventually falling by the wayside, unable to compete with their giant rivals." Further, the merger would seriously diminish potential competition by eliminating

Procter as a potential entrant into the industry. Prior to the merger, the Commission found, Procter was the most likely prospective entrant, and absent the merger would have remained on the periphery, restraining Clorox from exercising its market power. If Procter had actually entered, Clorox's dominant position would have been eroded and the concentration of the industry reduced....

....

The anticompetitive effects with which this product-extension merger is fraught can easily be seen: (1) the substitution of the powerful acquiring firm for the smaller, but already dominant, firm may substantially reduce the competitive structure of the industry by raising entry barriers and by dissuading the smaller firms from aggressively competing; (2) the acquisition eliminates the potential competition of the acquiring firm.

The liquid bleach industry was already oligopolistic before the acquisition, and price competition was certainly not as vigorous as it would have been if the industry were competitive. Clorox enjoyed a dominant position nationally, and its position approached monopoly proportions in certain areas. The existence of some 200 fringe firms certainly does not belie that fact. Nor does the fact, relied upon by the court below, that, after the merger, producers other than Clorox "were selling more bleach for more money than ever before." In the same period, Clorox increased its share from 48.8% to 52%. The interjection of Procter into the market considerably changed the situation. There is every reason to assume that the smaller firms would become more cautious in competing due to their fear of retaliation by Procter. It is probable that Procter would become the price leader and that oligopoly would become more rigid.

The acquisition may also have the tendency of raising the barriers to new entry. The major competitive weapon in the successful marketing of bleach is advertising. Clorox was limited in this area by its relatively small budget and its inability to obtain substantial discounts. By contrast, Procter's budget was much larger; and, although it would not devote its entire budget to advertising Clorox, it could divert a large portion to meet the short-term threat of a new entrant. Procter would be able to use its volume discounts to advantage in advertising Clorox. Thus, a new entrant would be much more reluctant to face the giant Procter than it would have been to face the smaller Clorox.[3]

---

[3] The barriers to entry have been raised both for entry by new firms and for entry into new geographical markets by established firms. The latter aspect is demonstrated by Purex's lesson in Erie, Pennsylvania. In October 1957, Purex selected Erie, Pennsylvania — where it had not sold previously — as an area in which to test the salability, under competitive conditions, of a new bleach. The leading brands in Erie were Clorox, with 52%, and the "101" brand, sold by Gardner Manufacturing Company, with 29% of the market. Purex launched an advertising and promotional campaign to obtain a broad distribution in a short time, and in five months captured 33% of the Erie market. Clorox's share dropped to 35% and 101's to 17%. Clorox responded by offering its bleach at reduced prices, and then added an offer of a $1-value ironing board cover for 50 cents with each purchase of Clorox at the reduced price. It also increased its advertising with television spots. The result was to restore Clorox's lost market share and, indeed, to increase it slightly. Purex's share fell to 7%.

Possible economies cannot be used as a defense to illegality. Congress was aware that some mergers which lessen competition may also result in economies but it struck the balance in favor of protecting competition.

The Commission also found that the acquisition of Clorox by Procter eliminated Procter as a potential competitor. The Court of Appeals declared that this finding was not supported by evidence because there was no evidence that Procter's management had ever intended to enter the industry independently and that Procter had never attempted to enter. The evidence, however, clearly shows that Procter was the most likely entrant. Procter had recently launched a new abrasive cleaner in an industry similar to the liquid bleach industry, and had wrested leadership from a brand that had enjoyed even a larger market share than had Clorox. Procter was engaged in a vigorous program of diversifying into product lines closely related to its basic products. Liquid bleach was a natural avenue of diversification since it is complementary to Procter's products, is sold to the same customers through the same channels, and is advertised and merchandised in the same manner. Procter had substantial advantages in advertising and sales promotion, which, as we have seen, are vital to the success of liquid bleach. No manufacturer had a patent on the product or its manufacture, necessary information relating to manufacturing methods and processes was readily available, there was no shortage of raw material, and the machinery and equipment required for a plant of efficient capacity were available at reasonable cost. Procter's management was experienced in producing and marketing goods similar to liquid bleach. Procter had considered the possibility of independently entering but decided against it because the acquisition of Clorox would enable Procter to capture a more commanding share of the market.

It is clear that the existence of Procter at the edge of the industry exerted considerable influence on the market. First, the market behavior of the liquid bleach industry was influenced by each firm's predictions of the market behavior of its competitors, actual and potential. Second, the barriers to entry by a firm of Procter's size and with its advantages were not significant. There is no indication that the barriers were so high that the price Procter would have to charge would be above the price that would maximize the profits of the existing firms. Third, the number of potential entrants was not so large that the elimination of one would be insignificant. Few firms would have the temerity to challenge a firm as solidly entrenched as Clorox. Fourth, Procter was found by the Commission to be the most likely entrant. These findings of the Commission were amply supported by the evidence.

NOTES AND QUESTIONS

1. What did Justice Douglas mean in *Procter & Gamble* when he wrote that "[p]ossible economies cannot be used as a defense to illegality." Did he mean, as *Brown Shoe* suggested, that the merger was bad *because* it produced certain economies and therefore injured competitors of the post-merger firm? Or did Justice Douglas mean merely that once a merger was shown to have sufficient anticompetitive effects to justify condemnation the Court would not recognize the creation of economies as an affirmative defense? The difference between the two views can be quite significant. See the note on efficiency defenses in merger cases, *supra*, Section II.B1 of this chapter.

2. Justice Douglas said that Procter's acquisition of Clorox was bad because it raised "barriers to entry" in the bleach industry. He then cited economies in advertising as such an entry barrier: the fact that a large firm like P&G can obtain advertising cheaply makes it more difficult and expensive for a smaller firm to enter the market. Under this usage, isn't the phrase "barrier to entry" simply a synonym for efficiency? Every cost-reducing practice of a firm already in the market makes entry by others more difficult. See the note on entry barriers in monopolization and merger cases, Chapter 6, *supra*.

One problem with the term as Justice Douglas used it is that it fails to distinguish barriers to persons outside the market who want to get in and barriers to persons who are already inside the market. P&G's advertising economies injured existing rivals just as much as prospective entrants. A true barrier to entry should *protect* incumbents while it excludes outsiders.

3. Justice Douglas believed that Procter's presence as a potential entrant into the bleach industry made the bleach industry more competitive, even though Procter was not manufacturing bleach. This "potential entrant" argument has taken two forms. One version is that an acquisition is bad if one firm would have entered the other firm's market anyway had the merger not occurred. If the alternative way is less anticompetitive than the merger, the merger ought to be condemned. This is known as the "actual potential entrant" doctrine. It is in effect an argument, not that a market is less competitive as a result of a merger, but that the market could have been more competitive if the acquiring firm had entered in a different way.

The second version of the argument appeared in both *Procter* and *El Paso Natural Gas*. It is that the acquiring firm was *perceived* as an entrant by the firms already selling in the market. Because they feared entry, they behaved more competitively. However, if the "perceived potential entrant" should actually acquire one of the firms in the market, then its status as a perceived potential entrant would disappear and the market would become less competitive. Unlike the actual potential entrant doctrine, the perceived potential entrant doctrine does argue that a particular merger lessens competition, not merely that it diminishes the chances for increased competition in the future. For that reason, courts have been somewhat more willing to accept the perceived potential entrant doctrine than they have the actual potential entrant doctrine.

For example, *United States v. Falstaff Brewing Corp.*, 410 U.S. 526 (1973), involved the acquisition by Falstaff Brewing of Narragansett Brewing Co. Falstaff was a very large brewer, but it did not sell beer in the Northeastern United States. Narragansett was a regional brewer which had the largest share of the New England market, about 20%. The government argued the case under the actual potential entrant doctrine. The government said that Falstaff should have entered the New England market *de novo* or else by means of a "toehold" acquisition — that is, by acquiring a small company in New England rather than the largest seller there. Entry by either of these means, argued the government, would have increased competition in the New England market. Entry by the mechanism that Falstaff chose, however, did not.

The Supreme Court held that the merger might violate section 7, but the Court relied on the perceived potential entrant doctrine rather than the actual potential entrant doctrine. It held that Falstaff might have been perceived by New England beer sellers as a potential entrant into their market. This perception caused them to price beer more competitively, because they knew that Falstaff would be attracted into the market by high profits. Once Falstaff acquired Narragansett, however, it was already in the market and no longer exercised a downward pressure on prices. Thus it was possible that Falstaff's presence on the edge of the market made the market more competitive, and the market became less competitive as a result of Falstaff's entry. The court remanded for determination whether Falstaff was actually perceived as a potential entrant by firms already inside the market. The district court decided that it was not and dismissed the complaint. *United States v. Falstaff Brewing Corp.*, 383 F. Supp. 1020 (D.R.I. 1974). The government did not appeal.

4. During the 1980's the lower courts considered several merger challenges under both the perceived and actual potential entrant doctrines. In *Yamaha Motor Co. v. FTC*, 657 F.2d 971 (8th Cir. 1981), *cert. denied*, 456 U.S. 915 (1982), the court enforced a divestiture order, based on the actual potential entrant doctrine. Yamaha and Brunswick had formed a joint venture for making small outboard motors. Both firms manufactured motors, but they had always sold them in different countries, although Yamaha had once tried unsuccessfully to market a small motor in the United States. The FTC concluded that Yamaha was a potential entrant into the American market, and if it had entered without a joint venture with Brunswick, Yamaha and Brunswick would have been competitors in the American market. Because the joint venture included an agreement allocating sales territories, however, such competition would never occur under the joint venture agreement.

In general, however, the circuit courts have looked at the potential competition doctrines with a great deal of skepticism. For example, *Tenneco, Inc. v. FTC*, 689 F.2d 346 (2d Cir. 1982), rejected a challenge to a merger between a major automobile parts manufacturer (excluding shock absorbers) and a major automobile shock absorber manufacturer. The shock absorber market was highly concentrated, with a CR4 exceeding 90, and entry barriers were found to be very high. Nevertheless, the Second Circuit disagreed with the FTC's decision condemning the merger:

> To establish a violation of section 7 in this case based upon the elimination of actual potential competition, .. the Commission must show: (1) that

the relevant market is oligopolistic; (2) that absent its acquisition of Monroe, Tenneco would likely have entered the market in the near future either *de novo* or through toehold acquisition; and (3) that such entry by Tenneco carried a substantial likelihood of ultimately producing deconcentration of the market or other significant procompetitive effects....

The record establishes that the structure, history and probable future of the market for replacement shock absorbers are all consistent with the Commission's finding. The extraordinarily high concentration ratios have remained stable over many years with the same firms occupying the top four positions since at least the late 1960s. Substantial barriers to entry severely limit the number of firms likely to provide additional competition. The industry has been highly profitable, and despite recent indications that profit margins may be decreasing, industry experts, including Tenneco executives, foresee a bright future. ...

Nevertheless, we reject the Commission's finding that Tenneco was an actual potential entrant likely to increase competition in the market for replacement shock absorbers. The record lacks substantial evidence supporting the Commission's finding that Tenneco was likely to have entered the market for replacement shock absorbers in the near future either *de novo* or through toehold acquisition. ...

We also conclude that the record contains inadequate evidence to support the Commission's conclusion that Tenneco's acquisition of Monroe violated section 7 by eliminating Tenneco as a perceived potential competitor in the market for replacement shock absorbers. ...

There is abundant evidence that the oligopolists in the market for replacement shock absorbers perceived Tenneco as a potential entrant. Industry executives testified that they considered Tenneco one of very few manufacturers with both the incentive and the capability to enter the market. This perception was based on Tenneco's financial strength and on the compatibility of shock absorbers with exhaust system parts produced by Tenneco's Walker Division. This testimony was enhanced by evidence that the negotiations between Tenneco and DeCarbon were initiated by an independent broker and that the negotiations that eventually led to the Tenneco-Monroe merger were initiated by Monroe, indicating that those in the industry were aware of Tenneco's interest. This, especially when combined with the fact that industry participants were apparently not privy to the lack of success in Tenneco's toehold acquisition negotiations, is more than sufficient to satisfy the substantial evidence requirement with respect to industry perceptions of Tenneco as a potential entrant.

However, the analysis does not end here. The Commission's conclusion that the perception of Tenneco as a potential entrant actually tempered the conduct of oligopolists in the market must also be supported by substantial evidence. It is not.

... [The Commission] must produce at least circumstantial evidence that Tenneco's presence probably directly affected competitive activity in the market.... [But the] testimony constitutes direct evidence that Tenneco had no direct effect on Maremont's business decisions or competitive activity. In the face of this contrary and unchallenged direct evidence, the substantiality of circumstantial evidence arguably suggesting an "edge effect" vanishes....

The court then dismissed the complaint. For further discussion of the potential competition doctrine, *see* 5 P. Areeda & D. Turner, *Antitrust Law* ¶¶ 1116-1126 (1980); H. Hovenkamp, *Federal Antitrust Policy* §§ 13.4-13.5 (2d ed. 1994); E.T. Sullivan & J. Harrison, *Understanding Antitrust and Its Economic Implications*, ch. 7 (3d ed. 1998).

5. In *United States v. Penn-Olin Chem. Co.*, 378 U.S. 158 (1964), the Supreme Court held that the potential competition doctrine applied to a joint venture, in this case by the formation of a new corporation owned jointly by Pennsalt and Olin to make sodium chlorate in the southeastern United States. One parent corporation, Pennsalt, made sodium chlorate in the Northwest. The other, Olin, was both a purchaser and a distributor of sodium chlorate and had patented certain uses of the product. The court acknowledged that a joint venture can in fact create a new actual competitor in a market, as it did in this case, while a merger generally eliminates an actual or potential competitor. Nevertheless, it held that the same considerations applied to section 7 analysis of a joint venture as to a potential competition merger:

> Just as a merger eliminates actual competition, this joint venture may well foreclose any prospect of competition between Olin and Pennsalt in the relevant sodium chlorate market.... The existence of an aggressive, well equipped and well financed corporation engaged in the same or related lines of commerce waiting anxiously to enter an oligopolistic market would be a substantial incentive to competition which cannot be underestimated.... This same situation might well have come about had either Olin or Pennsalt entered the relevant market alone and the other remained aloof watching developments.
>
> Here the evidence shows beyond question that the industry was rapidly expanding; the relevant southeast market was requiring about one-half of the national production of sodium chlorate; few corporations had the inclination, resources and know-how to enter this market; both parent corporations of Penn-Olin had great resources; each had long been identified with the industry, one owning valuable patent rights while the other had engaged in sodium chlorate production for years; each had other chemicals, the production of which required the use of sodium chlorate; right up to the creation of Penn-Olin, each had evidenced a long-sustained and strong interest in entering the relevant market area; each enjoyed a good reputation and business connection with the major consumers of sodium chlorate in the relevant

markets ... ; and, finally, each had the know-how and capacity to enter that market and could have done so individually at a reasonable profit. Moreover, each company had compelling reasons for entering the southeast market. Pennsalt needed to expand its sales to the southeast, which it could not do economically without a plant in that area. Olin was motivated by "the fact that [it was] already buying and using a fair quantity [of sodium chlorate] for the production of sodium chlorite...." Unless we are going to require subjective evidence, this array of probability certainly reaches the prima facie stage. As we have indicated, to require more would be to read the statutory requirement of reasonable probability into a requirement of certainty. This we will not do.

The court then remanded for determination whether either Pennsalt or Olin would have entered the southeast market independently. If they would have, the merger violated the potential competition doctrine. For thoughtful analysis of the problem of joint ventures and merger policy, *see* Brodley, *Joint Ventures and Antitrust Policy*, 95 Harv. L. Rev. 1521, 1523-38 (1982).

POTENTIAL COMPETITION MERGERS UNDER THE 1984 JUSTICE DEPARTMENT MERGER GUIDELINES

Although horizontal mergers are governed by the 1992 Horizontal Merger Guidelines, reprinted in Appendix A, potential competition mergers continue to be governed by the substantive standards articulated in the 1984 Justice Department Merger Guidelines. In all likelihood, however, questions pertaining to market definition and entry barriers will be resolved under the 1992 Guidelines. Respecting potential competition mergers, the 1984 Guidelines note the following:

§ 4.111. Harm to "Perceived Potential Competition"

By eliminating a significant present competitive threat that constrains the behavior of the firms already in the market, the merger could result in an immediate deterioration in market performance. The economic theory of limit pricing suggests that monopolists and groups of colluding firms may find it profitable to restrain their pricing in order to deter new entry that is likely to push prices even lower by adding capacity to the market. If the acquiring firm had unique advantages in entering the market, the firms in the market might be able to set a new and higher price after the threat of entry by the acquiring firm was eliminated by the merger.

§ 4.112. Harm to "Actual Potential Competition"

By eliminating the possibility of entry by the acquiring firm in a more procompetitive manner, the merger could result in a lost opportunity for improvement in market performance resulting from the addition of a significant competitor. The more procompetitive alternatives include both new entry and entry through a "toehold" acquisition of a present small competitor.

§ 4.12. Relation Between Perceived and Actual Competition

If it were always profit-maximizing for incumbent firms to set price in such a way that all entry was deterred and if information and coordination were sufficient to implement this strategy, harm to perceived potential competition would be the only competitive problem to address. In practice, however, actual potential competition has independent importance. Firms already in the market may not find it optimal to set price low enough to deter all entry; moreover, those firms may misjudge the entry advantages of a particular firm and, therefore, the price necessary to deter its entry.

§ 4.13. Enforcement Standards

....

The factors that the Department will consider are as follows:

§ 4.131. Market Concentration

Barriers to entry are unlikely to affect market performance if the structure of the market is otherwise not conducive to monopolization or collusion. Adverse competitive effects are likely only if overall concentration, or the largest firm's market share, is high. The Department is unlikely to challenge a potential competition merger unless overall concentration of the acquired firm's market is above 1800 HHI (a somewhat lower concentration will suffice if one or more of the factors discussed in Section 3.4 indicate that effective collusion in the market is particularly likely). Other things being equal, the Department is increasingly likely to challenge a merger as this threshold is exceeded.

§ 4.132. Conditions of Entry Generally

If entry to the market is generally easy, the fact that entry is marginally easier for one or more firms is unlikely to affect the behavior of the firms in the market. The Department is unlikely to challenge a potential competition merger when [entry is easy].

§ 4.133. The Acquiring Firm's Entry Advantage

If more than a few firms have the same or a comparable advantage in entering the acquired firm's market, the elimination of one firm is unlikely to have any adverse competitive effect. The other similarly situated firm(s) would continue to exert a present restraining influence, or, if entry would be profitable, would recognize the opportunity and enter. The Department is unlikely to challenge a potential competition merger if the entry advantage ascribed to the acquiring firm (or another advantage of comparable importance) is also possessed by three or more other firms. Other things being equal, the Department is increasingly likely to challenge a merger as the number of other similarly situated firms decreases below three and as the extent of the entry advantage over non-advantaged firms increases.

If the evidence of likely actual entry by the acquiring firm is particularly strong, however, the Department may challenge a potential competition merger, notwithstanding the presence of three or more firms that are objectively similarly situated. In such cases, the Department will determine the likely scale of entry, using either the firm's own documents or the minimum efficient scale in the industry. The Department will then evaluate the merger much as it would a horizontal merger between a firm the size of the likely scale of entry and the acquired firm.

§ 4.134. The Market Share of the Acquired Firm

Entry through the acquisition of a relatively small firm in the market may have a competitive effect comparable to new entry. Small firms frequently play peripheral roles in collusive interactions, and the particular advantages of the acquiring firm may convert a fringe firm into a significant factor in the market.

The Department is unlikely to challenge a potential competition merger when the acquired firm has a market share of five percent or less. Other things being equal, the Department is increasingly likely to challenge a merger as the market share of the acquired firm increases above that threshold. The Department is likely to challenge any merger satisfying the other conditions in which the acquired firm has a market share of 20 percent or more.

PROBLEM 7.4

Alpha Corp. is an American firm that manufactures and sells Responders in the United States. A Responder is a piece of high-tech hardware used in American defense applications. There are no known substitutes. Alpha proposes to acquire all the stock of Beta Corp., a Japanese firm that manufactures Responders for foreign defense applications. Currently, however, Beta Corp. does not sell Responders to the United States government, or in the United States at all. Alpha is the largest supplier of Responders in the United States, accounting for about 25% of United States sales. Beta is much larger than Alpha and provides 40% of world demand for Responders outside the United States. If Beta wished to make sales in the United States, it would take at least 18 months for it to establish sufficient distribution facilities. Thus, assume that the relevant geographic market is the United States.

SECTION IV. THE FAILING COMPANY DEFENSE

CITIZEN PUBLISHING CO. V. UNITED STATES

394 U.S. 131 (1969)

JUSTICE DOUGLAS delivered the opinion of the Court.

Tucson, Arizona, has only two daily newspapers of general circulation, the Star and the Citizen.... Prior to 1940 the two papers vigorously competed with each other. While their circulation was about equal, the Star sold 50% more advertising space than the Citizen and operated at a profit, while the Citizen sustained losses. Indeed the Star's annual profits averaged about $25,825, while the Citizen's annual losses averaged about $23,550.

In 1936 the stock of the Citizen was purchased by one Small and one Johnson for $100,000 and they invested an additional $25,000 of working capital. They sought to interest others to invest in the Citizen but were not successful. Small increased his investment in the Citizen, moved from Chicago to Tucson, and was prepared to finance the Citizen's losses for at least awhile from his own resources. It does not appear that Small and Johnson sought to sell the Citizen; nor was the Citizen about to go out of business. The owners did, however, negotiate a joint operating agreement between the two papers which was to run for 25 years from March 1940, a term that was extended in 1953 until 1990. By its terms the agreement may be canceled only by mutual consent of the parties.

The agreement provided that each paper should retain its own news and editorial department, as well as its corporate identity. It provided for the formation of Tucson Newspapers, Inc. (TNI), which was to be owned in equal shares by the Star and Citizen and which was to manage all departments of their business except the news and editorial units. The production and distribution equipment of each paper was transferred to TNI. The latter had five directors — two named by the Star, two by the Citizen, and the fifth chosen by the Citizen out of three named by the Star.

The purpose of the agreement was to end any business or commercial competition between the two papers and to that end three types of controls were imposed. First was *price fixing*. The newspapers were sold and distributed by the circulation department of TNI; commercial advertising placed in the papers was sold only by the advertising department of TNI; the subscription and advertising rates were set jointly. Second was *profit pooling*. All profits realized were pooled and distributed to the Star and the Citizen by TNI pursuant to an agreed ratio. Third was a *market control*. It was agreed that neither the Star nor the Citizen nor any of their stockholders, officers, and executives would engage in any other business in Pima County — the metropolitan area of Tucson — in conflict with the agreement. Thus competing publishing operations were foreclosed.

All commercial rivalry between the papers ceased. Combined profits before taxes rose from $27,531 in 1940 to $1,727,217 in 1964.

....

The case went to trial on ... a charge brought under § 7 of the Clayton Act. The ... charge arose out of the acquisition of the stock of the Star by the shareholders of the Citizen pursuant to an option in the joint operating agreement. Arden Publishing Company was formed as the vehicle of acquisition and it now publishes the Star.

....

The only real defense of appellants was the "failing company" defense — a judicially created doctrine.... That defense was before the Court in *International*

Shoe Co. v. FTC, 280 U.S. 291, where § 7 of the Clayton Act was in issue. The evidence showed that the resources of one company were so depleted and the prospect of rehabilitation so remote that "it faced the grave probability of a business failure." There was, moreover, "no other prospective purchaser." It was in that setting that the Court held that the acquisition of that company by another did not substantially lessen competition within the meaning of § 7.

In the present case the District Court found:

> At the time Star Publishing and Citizen Publishing entered into the operating agreement, and at the time the agreement became effective, Citizen Publishing was not then on the verge of going out of business, nor was there a serious probability at that time that Citizen Publishing would terminate its business and liquidate its assets unless Star Publishing and Citizen Publishing entered into the operating agreement.

The evidence sustains that finding. There is no indication that the owners of the Citizen were contemplating a liquidation. They never sought to sell the Citizen and there is no evidence that the joint operating agreement was the last straw at which the Citizen grasped. Indeed the Citizen continued to be a significant threat to the Star. How otherwise is one to explain the Star's willingness to enter into an agreement to share its profits with the Citizen? Would that be true if as now claimed the Citizen was on the brink of collapse?

The failing company doctrine plainly cannot be applied in a merger or in any other case unless it is established that the company that acquires the failing company or brings it under dominion is the only available purchaser. For if another person or group could be interested, a unit in the competitive system would be preserved and not lost to monopoly power. So even if we assume, arguendo, that in 1940 the then owners of the Citizen could not long keep the enterprise afloat, no effort was made to sell the Citizen; its properties and franchise were not put in the hands of a broker; and the record is silent on what the market, if any, for the Citizen might have been.

Moreover, we know from the broad experience of the business community since 1930, the year when the *International Shoe* case was decided, that companies reorganized through receivership, or through Chapter X or Chapter XI of the Bankruptcy Act often emerged as strong competitive companies. The prospects of reorganization of the Citizen in 1940 would have had to be dim or nonexistent to make the failing company doctrine applicable to this case.

The burden of proving that the conditions of the failing company doctrine have been satisfied is on those who seek refuge under it. That burden has not been satisfied in this case.

NOTES AND QUESTIONS

1. Both the House and Senate Reports on the 1950 amendments to section 7 of the Clayton Act contemplated some kind of "failing company" defense. On the surface at least, such a defense is attractive: if a firm is on the verge of bankruptcy and is not a viable competitor to begin with, then how much competition can a merger eliminate? Furthermore, the defense has an appeal to those who believe that antitrust should occasionally protect small business, inefficiency notwithstanding. It provides small businesses with a "parachute" in case things go bad.

Clearly the failing company defense gives a certain amount of protection to small businesses when they are the partners to the prospective merger. However, it may injure small businesses when they are competitors with the failing company that is being acquired, for one result of the acquisition may be that the failing company will be a better competitor than it was before. *See Brunswick Corp. v. Pueblo Bowl-O-Mat, Inc.*, 429 U.S. 477 (1977), for one instance when a small business was injured by a merger that might have been legal because of the failing company defense.

Can the failing company defense be justified on the alternative grounds that it is efficient? Suppose that a market contains five firms of equal market shares and that Firm *C* is certainly failing. If it goes out of business altogether, total output in the market is likely to decline, because capacity has declined. Suppose Firm *A* acquires Firm *C*. *A* is not likely to acquire *C* merely to close *C*'s plant; *C*'s imminent failure would do that. Rather, *A* intends to operate *C*'s plant, thus suggesting that total market output will be greater with the acquisition than without it. As a general rule, a firm with large capacity maximizes its profit at a higher rate of output than a firm with a small capacity, even if it is a monopolist, provided that price is higher than average variable cost. In that case the acquisition will yield an output increase by *A*, and output increases are generally good. So a tradeoff would have to be computed between (1) any increase in market power or likelihood of collusion that may result from the merger; and (2) resulting efficiencies, including the effects of maintaining a larger amount of productive capacity on the market. For rival views about how these competing concerns should be evaluated, *see* Campbell, *The Efficiency of the Failing Company Defense*, 63 Tex. L. Rev. 251 (1984); McChesney, *Defending the Failing-Firm Defense*, 65 Neb. L. Rev. 1 (1985); Friedman, *Untangling the Failing Company Doctrine*, 64 Tex. L. Rev. 1375 (1986).

The failing company defense can operate so as to legalize some very anticompetitive mergers. For example, if a market contains four competitors of roughly equal size and one is on the verge of bankruptcy, the failing company defense might result in the acquisition of one of the remaining competitors of 50% of the market, while the other two have 25% each. Absent the defense we would expect the three remaining firms to divide the failing firm's customers among themselves, and each would end up with about one-third of the market.

Courts today generally agree that before the failing company defense will apply, the target company must be shown to be unable to recover through bankruptcy — that is, but for the merger the target company's assets will be scrapped or sold to the highest bidder.

The failing company defense is an affirmative defense: it becomes necessary only after we have decided that a merger poses a sufficient threat to competition that it would otherwise be enjoined under section 7.

For general discussions of the defense, *see* 4A P. Areeda, H. Hovenkamp, & J. Solow, *Antitrust Law* ¶¶ 951-54 (rev. ed. 1998); H. Hovenkamp, *Federal Antitrust Policy* § 12.8 (2d ed. 1994).

2. In 1970 Congress passed the Newspaper Preservation Act, 15 U.S.C. § 1801 (1988), which permits "joint newspaper operating arrangements" similar to the one disapproved in the *Citizen Publishing* case. The act permits two or more newspapers to enter into an agreement or joint venture for the purpose of sharing production facilities, distribution mechanisms, solicitation of advertising, and circulation, and even for setting joint advertising and circulation rates. It expressly prohibits the member newspapers from having joint editorial or reportorial staffs, or from creating joint editorial policies. In order to qualify under the act the joint operating arrangement must have the prior written consent of the United States Attorney General, and it must show that all or all but one of the member newspapers were "failing newspapers" — that is, that each was unlikely "to remain or become a financially sound publication." Finally, the Act provides that parties to a joint newspaper operating arrangement will be subject to antitrust liability for activities not expressly exempted by the Newspaper Preservation Act. Today several large cities have pairs of daily newspapers that operate pursuant to such joint newspaper operating arrangements.

In *Michigan Citizens for an Independent Press v. Thornburgh*, 493 U.S. 38 (1989), an equally divided Supreme Court affirmed a decision by the District of Columbia Circuit which interpreted the Newspaper Preservation Act phrase "probable danger of financial failure" to mean that one of two newspapers seeking permission to enter a joint operating agreement must be suffering losses that more than likely cannot be reversed by unilateral action. While the Attorney General must approve the initial joint venture, she apparently does not need to approve subsequent amendments. *See Mahaffey v. Detroit Newspaper Agency*, 969 F. Supp. 446 (E.D. Mich. 1997) (because the Newspaper Preservation Act contained no procedure for amending a JOA or any statement of the consequences of such an amendment, an amendment to an existing JOA did not lose its antitrust immunity simply because the Justice Department had not approved the amendment). On the Newspaper Preservation Act, *see* Areeda, Hovenkamp & Solow, *id.* at ¶ 955.

3. The 1992 Horizontal Merger Guidelines recognize a "failing division" defense as well as the failing company defense. See § 5.2 of the Guidelines, Appendix A. That defense, unlike the failing company defense, has no precedent in the statute, legislative history, or case law. Should the Attorney General unilaterally create a "defense" not mentioned in a statute or commanded by the case law, and then announce publicly that she will not enforce the statute in cases where the "defense" can successfully be raised?

SECTION V. PRIVATE ENFORCEMENT OF SECTION 7

Congress unquestionably intended that private persons should sometimes be permitted to enforce the antimerger laws. Section 4 of the Clayton Act, 15 U.S.C. § 15, creates a private action for treble damages plus attorneys' fees for injuries caused by "anything forbidden in the antitrust laws," and section 1 of the Clayton Act, 15 U.S.C. § 12, includes the Clayton Act in "antitrust laws." Congress is even more explicit in section 16 of the Clayton Act, 15 U.S.C. § 26, which creates a private right of injunctive relief from antitrust violations and expressly includes section 7 in its coverage.

Nevertheless, private actions under section 7 pose some problems not generally shared by private actions under the other antitrust statutes. First of all, section 7 is an "incipiency" statute. Courts condemn mergers because of their tendency to create market power in the post-merger firm, or to facilitate collusion in the market affected by the merger. However, even the relatively tolerant Horizontal Merger Guidelines condemn mergers long before they give the post-merger firm substantial market power. As a result there are few private cases alleging, for example, that a horizontal merger enabled the post-merger firm to price monopolistically and that the plaintiff was injured by being required to pay a monopoly overcharge. The private injuries caused by mergers are much more subtle.

Unquestionably mergers that are marginally illegal under the incipiency test or the new Merger Guidelines do cause substantial private injuries. Often, however, these injuries are caused by the increased efficiency of the post-merger firm, not by its increased market power. The efficiencies that result from mergers are present in all mergers, whether legal or illegal. Present, measurable market power, however, comes only from mergers that are far beyond the threshold for legality. Furthermore, mergers are "public" offenses: as a general matter, merging firms cannot conceal their merger either from the general public or from enforcement agencies. As a result, the vast majority of mergers occur only after at least one of the parties to the merger has made some kind of calculation that the merger will not be found illegal in court. Mergers that give the post-merger firm measurably increased market power do not often occur unless someone has made a rather serious miscalculation.

Since all mergers can create efficiencies, but only some of them increase measurably the post-merger firm's market power, the danger of overdeterrence in private merger litigation is high. The threat of treble damage lawsuits plus attorney's fees might encourage many firms to forego a merger that would in fact provide large efficiency gains and have relatively insignificant effects on market power. This danger of overdeterrence makes it very important for courts to distinguish the private costs created by mergers from the social costs.

Anyone who is injured by a merger suffers a private cost. This may include persons who are charged a monopoly price because the merger has created monopoly power. However, it may also include the management of a company which is the target of a tender offer from another firm. Likewise it may include a business which has a difficult time competing with a firm that has become more efficient as the result of a merger, or it may include an independent distributor whose contract is terminated because a firm has vertically integrated by merger.

The social costs of mergers accrue not from the post-merger firm's greater efficiency, but from its increased market power. If the post-merger firm is able to reduce market output and charge a higher price than the participating firms did before the merger, and if these losses are not outweighed by efficiency gains, then the merger is socially costly. By contrast, if the result of the merger is that the post-merger firm can sell a better product at a lower price — as was the case, for example, in *Brown Shoe* — then the merger is socially useful, even though it may injure certain people, such as the competitors of the post-merger firm, or people whose business services to the firm become unnecessary as a result of the merger.

Although there is no general "efficiency defense" in merger cases, the danger of overdeterrence requires that private plaintiffs alleging injuries from mergers be able to show that they are injured by the post-merger firm's increased market power, not by its increased efficiency. This, in large part, is the lesson of the Supreme Court in *Brunswick Corp. v. Pueblo Bowl-O-Mat, Inc.*, 429 U.S. 477 (1977), reprinted in Chapter 3, Section I.A3g, *supra*. In *Brunswick*, the plaintiff was a competitor of a merging firm who alleged that it was injured because its competitor was more efficient after the merger than it had been before. In fact, the plaintiff argued that the competitor would have gone out of business but for the merger, and that as a result of the merger the plaintiff was forced to continue to be a competitor where it otherwise would have been a monopolist.

When the facts are stated as boldly as they are above, something immediately strikes us as wrong. The merger laws were designed to encourage competition and decrease monopoly, not vice versa. In fact, however, many damages actions alleging illegal mergers are much more ambiguous, and it takes a fair amount of analysis to discern whether the plaintiff was injured by the post-merger firm's market power or its increased efficiency. For example, how would you deal with a competitor's charge that as a result of a merger a firm engaged in predatory pricing? Perhaps the plaintiff 's theory is that predatory pricing requires a predator with a deep pocket, and the relatively large parent company that acquired the competitor had the necessary funds to finance a long period of below marginal cost selling.

Such a theory might be plausible. (See the discussion of predatory pricing in Chapter 6.) One thing seems clear, however. Whether or not such price predation was facilitated by an illegal merger, the plaintiff is complaining about predatory pricing, not about an illegal merger. The merger may be absolutely illegal under current law; but a plaintiff claiming that it was injured by predatory pricing financed by a merger must nevertheless prove that the pricing was truly predatory. How does it do this? Probably by employing the same test that courts apply generally in predatory pricing cases. Many times a price reduction following a merger will appear "predatory" from a competitor's view. Such a price reduction may be a function of nothing more than the increased efficiency of the firm that went through the merger.

One way to solve this problem is to restrict private damages actions in merger cases to "overcharge" injuries or injuries that are directly attributable to a post-merger firm's reduction of output. An alternative is to eliminate the damages action arising immediately under section 7, on the theory that private injuries that result from mergers are the result of some kind of post-merger exclusionary practice, and we already have a barrage of antitrust laws to protect private plaintiffs from such activities. For example, the competitor complaining that a merger facilitated predatory pricing must prove predatory pricing — and as a general rule it will not be able to collect additional damages because it can show that the defendant was guilty of both predatory pricing and an illegal merger. Likewise a distributor who has been terminated because of a post-merger output reduction may have a cause of action for monopolization under section 2 of the Sherman Act. If it cannot prove monopolization (perhaps because it cannot prove that the post-merger defendant has market power), that is good evidence that the termination was the result of the post-merger firm's increased efficiency, not of monopolistic practices. *See* Hovenkamp, *Merger Actions for Damages*, 35 Hastings L.J. 937 (1984).

CARGILL, INC. V. MONFORT OF COLORADO, INC.

479 U.S. 104 (1986) (This decision is reprinted in Chapter 3)

NOTES AND QUESTIONS

1. In *Chrysler Corp. v. General Motors Corp.*, 589 F. Supp. 1182 (D.D.C. 1984), the court decided that Chrysler Motor Co., a competitor, had standing to challenge a joint venture created by General Motors Corp. and Toyota Motor Corp. for the manufacture of automobiles. (A month earlier the Federal Trade Commission had approved the joint venture.) The court did not suggest how Chrysler might be injured by the venture. The case was later settled out of court. The settlement shortened the period of "active cooperation" between G.M. and Toyota from 12 to 8 years.

How is a firm injured by a merger or joint venture of two or more of its competitors? If the joint venture between General Motors and Toyota reduces competition in the automobile industry and enables the post-merger firm to charge a higher price, Chrysler will be better off, will it not? It will be able to charge a higher price too, protected by the "umbrella" created by the larger firm. By contrast, if the merger creates efficiencies that permit General Motors and Toyota to charge *lower* prices, Chrysler will be injured. What would you think of a rule that a competitor may *never* have standing to challenge a horizontal merger? *See* Easterbrook, *The Limits of Antitrust*, 63 Tex. L. Rev. 1 (1984); Markovits, *The*

Limits to Simplifying Antitrust: A Reply to Professor Easterbrook, 63 Tex. L. Rev. 41 (1984).

2. Just as problematic as the private action for damages resulting from an illegal merger is the private injunctive action seeking divestiture. Once a merger has taken place, the entire market reorients itself to the structure of the new firm. As a result, divestiture can cause repercussions throughout the economy and create an entire new set of private injuries. Furthermore, it is often impossible for divestiture to restore the market to anything resembling the pre-merger situation. In *California v. American Stores Co.*, 495 U.S. 271 (1990), the Supreme Court held that the remedy of divestiture was available to a private party (in this case, the state of California acting as parens patriae). The Court found no evidence in the legislative history that Congress intended to exclude divestiture from the scope of section 16 of the Clayton Act, granting "injunctive relief " to private antitrust plaintiffs. The issue is discussed further in Chapter 3.

3. Suppose that Firm *A* attempts to acquire Firm *B* through a tender offer for Firm *B*'s shares. Firm *B*'s managers are opposed to the takeover however, fearing that they will lose their jobs. They file a suit seeking a preliminary injunction, alleging that the merger would be illegal under section 7 of the Clayton Act. Should tender offer targets have standing to bring such actions? The courts are divided. Among those granting standing are *Marathon Oil Co. v. Mobil Corp.*, 669 F.2d 378, 383-84 (6th Cir. 1981), *cert. denied*, 455 U.S. 982 (1982); *Grumman Corp. v. LTV Corp.*, 665 F.2d 10, 11 (2d Cir. 1981). Those denying standing include *Central Nat'l Bank v. Rainbolt*, 720 F.2d 1183 (10th Cir. 1983), holding that injury alleged by the takeover target that "is not the result of diminution in competition but rather the effect of change in … control" does not come within the "ambit of the antitrust laws." In *Carter Hawley Hale Stores v. The Limited, Inc.*, 587 F. Supp. 246 (C.D. Cal. 1984), the plaintiff Carter Hawley Hale (CHH) objected that a planned tender offer would (1) result in lessened competition in the apparel market; (2) produce "disruption and uncertainty" in CHH's business affairs, and (3) permit the defendant to learn CHH's trade secrets. As to the second and third allegations the court replied:

> [E]ach of these alleged injuries does not result from the possibility of substantially lessened competition, but rather derives from the fact that after a successful, albeit unfriendly, merger, two corporate entities become one. Put another way, each of these "injuries" to CHH would occur in the event of a merger, whether or not the merger would substantially lessen competition. Thus, CHH has not alleged an "antitrust injury"….

Id. at 250. But even with respect to the allegation that the merger would lessen competition between the two firms, the court found that CHH lacked standing to raise the issue. "If the proposed merger is completed, CHH will be a part of the very entity it claims will have a supercompetitive advantage, i.e., it suffers no antitrust harm." As a result, "it is inconsistent for CHH to complain of this outcome on *antitrust* grounds." *Id.*

PROBLEM 7.5

Ten firms sell pre-wrapped dessert snacks (such as Twinkies and Hostess Buns) in the Philadelphia area. Of these, Alpha, the largest, sells 18%, and Beta, the second largest, sells 10%. Delta, the fourth largest firm, sells 5%. Total revenue of all firms selling dessert snacks is far smaller than the total revenue of firms selling bread, and about equal to the total revenue of yet another group of firms that sell pre-wrapped bakery fresh cookies. Most stores in Philadelphia have shelf space to display only three brands of dessert snacks, and competition among the ten firms is keen to acquire this shelf space.

In 1988 Alpha Co. acquires Beta Co. The acquisition is approved by the Justice Department. However, Delta Company challenges the acquisition, alleging that (1) the merger will facilitate collusion in the Philadelphia dessert snack market; (2) the post-merger Alpha-Beta Co. will engage in predatory pricing against its rivals, and has already cut price by 25% to selected Philadelphia stores; (3) Alpha-Beta Co. now insists that in order to get either Alpha brand dessert snacks or Beta brand dessert snacks, stores must stock and display both; as a result, competitors face a much more limited opportunity to obtain shelf access.

SECTION VI. INTERLOCKING DIRECTORATES UNDER SECTION 8 OF THE CLAYTON ACT

Section 8 of the Clayton Act forbids a person from serving as a director or other corporate officer on two different corporations, where the prerequisites of the act are satisfied. First, the statute applies only "if such corporations are or shall have been theretofore, by virtue of their business and location of operation, competitors, so that the elimination of competition by agreement between them would constitute a violation of any of the provisions of any of the anti-trust laws." 15 U.S.C. § 19. Second, the statute applies to companies with more than ten million dollars each in capital, surplus, and undivided profits. 1990 amendments to the statute provide "safe harbors" even if the ten million dollar threshold is met: (1) if the competitive sales of either corporation are less than one million dollars, (2) if the competitive sales of either corporation are less than 2% of that corporation's total sales, or (3) if the competitive sales of each corporation are less than 4% of that corporation's sales.

Banks and related associations and common carriers are generally exempted from section 8. In 1983 the Supreme Court decided that this exemption applies if *either* of two interlocked directorates is a bank. As a result, section 8 did not apply to an interlock between a bank and an insurance company. *BankAmerica Corp. v. United States*, 462 U.S. 122 (1983).

The statute explicitly requires that the two corporations be "competitors." Thus it does not apply to so-called "vertical interlocks" — in which a common director or officer sits on the board of, say, a manufacturer and one of the manufacturer's independent distributors or retailers. On the other hand, if the two corporations are in fact competitors, then a common director or officer violates the statute, even if each corporation is sufficiently small that a merger between them would be legal, provided that the relationship does not qualify for one of the safe harbor exemptions outlined above. *See United States v. Sears, Roebuck & Co.*, 111 F. Supp. 614 (S.D.N.Y. 1953).

SECTION VII. SHOULD WE REGULATE BIGNESS?

From the time the Sherman Act was passed up to the present day people have been concerned with business bigness, or, as they have sometimes put it, "the rising tide of concentration" in industry. The expressed concerns with raw business size have been both economic and noneconomic — although if one looks at the attitudes of Congress and antitrust policy makers throughout the twentieth century, noneconomic concerns appear to dominate. People have argued that bigness in business is bad for a host of reasons, some of which contradict each other: big business is able to take advantage of certain cost savings and drive smaller businesses into bankruptcy; big business is too large to be efficient; big business places too much political power in relatively few hands; and big business makes too much money.

At various times both Congress and the Executive Branch have considered legislation to control business bigness. These proposals have taken widely different forms. Some have been directed against mergers, but some would force large corporations to divest certain assets even if all their growth had been internal. For a survey of such proposals, *see* H. Blake, "Legislative Proposals for Industrial Deconcentration," in H. Goldschmid, H.M. Mann & J.F. Weston, *Industrial Concentration: The New Learning*, 340-59 (1974).

The proponents of some kind of legislation regulating industrial concentration have relied on two rather controversial empirical conclusions. The first is that large corporations make more money than smaller ones, and that there is a positive correlation between industrial concentration and profitability. The second conclusion, which is more controversial than the first, is that many firms today are far larger than the minimum size necessary to take advantage of all available economies of scale.

In 1951 Professor Joe S. Bain published a pioneering study of the relationship between profitability and market concentration in 42 industries. Bain, *Relation of Profit Rate to Industry Concentration: American Manufacturing, 1936-1940*, 65 Q. J. Econ. 293-324 (1951); for a critique, see Phillips, *A Critique of Empirical Studies of Relations Between Market Structure and Profitability*, 24 J. Indus. Econ. 241-49 (1976). Professor Bain found that in general the more highly concentrated the industry, the higher its profit rates. In the last thirty years Bain's findings have been subjected to a number of criticisms and a number of people have rallied to Bain's support. Most economists have concluded that there *is* a positive correlation between concentration and high profits — although they disagree about the numbers. After thirty years of debate we do not have a very precise view of the relationship that exists between profitability and concentration, but economists rather persistently find that firms in highly concentrated industries generally make higher profits than firms in unconcentrated industries. A survey of the literature on the relationship between concentration and profitability is contained in Goldschmid, Mann & Weston, *supra*, at 162-245; and F.M. Scherer & D. Ross, *Industrial Market Structure and Economic Performance*, 440-44 (3d ed. 1990).

How do we explain persistent high profits in concentrated industries? The way that comes immediately to mind when we think about industries that have relatively few competitors is either express or tacit collusion, or oligopolistic interdependence. If the collusion is express and we can catch the conspirators in the act, our problem would be simple. Unfortunately that is not often the case. The problem of judicial remedy in cases of oligopoly pricing has been often analyzed and considered insoluble (see the discussion of oligopoly, *supra*). Courts cannot force firms in concentrated industries simply to ignore the pricing behavior of their competitors. Put more simply, reduction of output and pricing at above marginal cost may be inherent in oligopoly situations, especially where there are fewer than four or so firms in the market, and any other kind of pricing behavior would be irrational. To some antitrust theorists, such as those who proposed the statutes described above, this has justified structural relief: forced divestiture until the market is sufficiently diffuse that oligopolistic interdependence is no longer likely to occur. *See, e.g.*, C. Kaysen & D. Turner, *Antitrust Policy*, 27 (1959).

This kind of structural relief comes with one immense problem of its own, however: what if certain markets are concentrated because the most efficient size for firms in that market is very large? If that is the case, forced divestiture could impose costs in the form of diseconomies of size that far outweigh any inefficiency caused by the oligopolistic pricing itself. For one concise argument to this effect, *see* Peltzman, *The Gains and Losses from Industrial Concentration*, 20 J.L. & Econ. 229 (1977); *and see the responses in* 22 J.L. & Econ. 183-211 (1979). *See also* Meehan & Larner, "The Structural School, Its Critics, and Its Progeny: An Assessment," in *Economics and Antitrust Policy* 179 (R. Larner & J. Meehan, eds. 1989).

For this reason proponents of forced deconcentration generally rely on a second empirical premise. This premise — that most big firms in concentrated industries are far larger than economies require — is much more controversial. The biggest problem is that the word "economies" applies to a wide range of phenomena that differ substantially from one industry to the next. One must determine the most efficient size of the single plant, whether a firm can realize certain multi-plant economies, and whether there are transactional economies that can be achieved by integration of operations. For example, it is probable that a plant capable of producing 5% to 10% of the American market for automobiles is large enough to realize all available economies of plant size. However, certain multi-plant economies, such as advertising, can be achieved at much larger outputs.

The cost of developing an advertisement or slogan is the same, whether one's production of automobiles is 1,000 units per year or 10,000,000. However, such economies become less significant as one reaches very high outputs, because the cost as distributed per unit of output becomes quite small. For some of the problems involved in measuring the economies that industries can achieve by size and integration, *see* Scherer & Ross, *supra*, at 97-151; for a somewhat different approach, *see* G. Stigler, *The Economies of Scale*, 1 J.L. & Econ. 54-71 (1958).

F.M. Scherer and others have made several studies of representative American industries and have concluded that a few firms are as much as ten times as large as the "Minimum Efficient Size" (MES) required for their particular industry, and that many firms are about four times as large as the MES. The MES represents a firm large enough to take advantage of all available economies. Thus, if MES is properly computed a firm larger than MES would not be more efficient than an MES firm, but it could be less efficient if a larger plant size generated diseconomies. That is, if a certain plant or firm becomes too large it will operate inefficiently and its cost of production will begin to rise. The findings and the literature are surveyed in Scherer & Ross, *supra*, at 97-151; and in Goldschmid, Mann & Weston, *supra*, at 15-113, which includes an insightful dialogue between Professor Scherer and Professor John S. McGee.

Critics have faulted Scherer and his followers for failing to make exhaustive lists of the efficiencies that large size can generate. As John S. McGee puts it, "a so-called minimum optimum size that does not exhaust all of the economies is simply not a minimum-cost size." McGee may have pointed to a serious flaw in the MES approach: no list of available economies can really be exhaustive, for technology is constantly changing the list, and the list is already very long and complex. To understand fully the kinds of economies that can be achieved in, say, automobile production, one must consider engineering, transportation costs, market location, availability of natural resources and other materials, labor, federal, state and local tax laws and regulations, and management, to name only a few things.

Furthermore, the establishment of a minimum plant size for optimal efficiency does not necessarily mean that larger firms cannot be equally efficient. If the MES in a particular market is a plant capable of producing 2% of market demand, but firms do not begin to suffer from diseconomies of excessive size until they occupy a 30% share or greater, we would not expect to find an industry full of identical firms occupying 2% of the market. We would expect to find firms operating in the entire range from 2% to 30%. In the real world not all firms behave in the same way, not all have equally effective management, and not all have the same run of good or bad luck. If all firms in the 2% to 30% range are capable of being equally efficient, we would expect some of them to grow far beyond the 2% minimum size, some to stay there, and some to go broke even though they are within the efficiency range (that is to say, not all firms of an efficient size are necessarily efficient firms). Additionally, if our computation of MES overlooked just one nontrivial economy it might be profitable for two firms in that market whose combined share was less than 30% to merge. In short, in the natural course of things we expect firms to be larger than MES, right up to the maximum size they can be without suffering from diseconomies of large size.

Some of the proponents of forced industrial deconcentration have gone even further than the argument that many American firms are larger than MES. They have argued that some American firms, particularly conglomerates, are too large to be efficient, and that they could actually operate at reduced cost if they were smaller. Conglomerates have been accused of continuing to produce certain products after demand for them disappeared, but subsidizing the losses from profits earned in other sectors. They have been accused of exhibiting managerial "sluggishness," because top management is deluged with too much information from too many different sources. They have been accused of purchasing and selling among their own subsidiaries not because the transactions were most efficient, but because necessary information was so readily available. Finally, large conglomerates have often been accused of being poor innovators. These arguments and others are summarized in Scherer & Ross, *supra*, at 668-72. For generally conflicting views, *see* the essays collected in *Antitrust, Innovation, and Competitiveness* (T. Jorde & D. Teece, eds. 1992). In recent years there has been a great revival of the work of Joseph A. Schumpeter, who argued forcefully that large firms (or joint ventures) innovate more than small ones, and that the gains from giving innovation free rein far exceed any losses from the industrial concentration that results. *See, e.g.*, J. Schumpeter, *Capitalism, Socialism, and Democracy*, chs. 7-8 (1942).

In any event, there are persuasive arguments that not many profitable, ongoing American businesses suffer from substantial diseconomies of excessively large size. Such diseconomies will generally not come about except by miscalculation. Suppose that there are three possible sizes and configurations of plants for producing widgets. Plant *A* will produce 250,000 widgets annually at a price of $1.00, when it is running at optimal capacity. Plant *B* will produce 500,000 widgets per year at a price of 90 cents. Plant *C* will produce 1,000,000 per year at a price of $1.10. If a manufacturer believes it has a market for 1,000,000 widgets per year, it will build two plants of size *B* — not one plant of size *C*. On the other hand, if it is already operating a plant of size *A* and selling 250,000 widgets annually but believes it could increase its market to 500,000, the manufacturer has two choices. It might build another plant of size *A*, or it might close *A* and produce a plant of size *B*. Facing this choice, with *A* already in operation, the firm might conclude that it is profit-maximizing to build a second plant of size *A*, simply because the first plant's costs are sunk. It may not be able to recover those costs if it builds plant *B*. Likewise, if the manufacturer is starting out in the business and believes its market will not exceed 250,000 widgets per year, it would probably build plant *A* even though it knows that a plant of size *B* could produce widgets more cheaply. Plant *B* may not deliver them more cheaply if it is running at only 50% of its capacity.

In short, we sometimes expect to find plants that are smaller than optimal for the manufacture of a particular product. However, we do not expect to find plants of larger than optimal size unless there has been a miscalculation. For example, someone might think that a market for 500,000 widgets will maintain itself indefinitely, and build a plant of size B. A few years later, however, demand drops to 250,000 and the firm is stuck with an excessively large plant.

The above argument applies not only to plant size, but to every aspect of running a firm: people might sometimes plan to do things at less than their most efficient rate, but they seldom plan to do them at more. One possible exception is a dominant firm's building of excess capacity for strategic purposes. See the discussion, *supra*. Even du Pont, which was accused by the Federal Trade Commission of monopolization for building an excessively large plant (see the *du Pont* (*Titanium*) case, *supra*) built a plant only large enough to take care of its anticipated rate of production. Furthermore, the arguments that American firms are too big are not arguments that they have grossly excess capacity (some do and some do not, but their raw size has little to do with that fact). The argument is that they are doing things on a scale that is inefficient because it is too large.

The argument above is only an extension of an argument we have seen in a different context. Faced with a choice between buying something in the marketplace or doing something for itself (vertical integration), a profit-maximizing firm will choose the cheapest course. If integration will produce substantial diseconomies of size, the firm will be more likely to purchase the service in the market. Thus, there might be some basis for concluding that firms are larger than the minimum size necessary to achieve optimal efficiency. However, there is little basis in either logic or evidence to conclude that firms are larger than the maximum size that will permit them to operate efficiently.

It seems reasonable to conclude that most American firms do not suffer from diseconomies caused by large size. We are much less sure, however, about the proposition that firms are substantially larger than their minimum efficient size. As a result, forced divestiture is not likely to produce efficiency gains (except perhaps a reduction of monopoly pricing) but may very well produce substantial losses in efficiency. The American economy could pay a large price if firms were divided in the absence of specific evidence of inefficient practices. If large businesses have no economic advantage over smaller rivals, then they will be able to maintain high rates of profit only by means of inefficient exclusionary practices. If we have no evidence of such practices, then we have at least a basis for an inference that the large size is a result of efficiency. In that case forced divestiture could cost American consumers heavily. Worse yet, it could mean that American business could lose its competitive position in world markets, at least if other countries are inclined to permit businesses to seek out their most efficient size in unrestrained markets.

American antitrust policy has always been guided by a concern for bigness. However, the law itself has always tempered that concern by establishing various bad conduct requirements. The reasons for this are clear. It is extraordinarily difficult — perhaps impossible — to look at an established business of a given size and pronounce that business as too big to be efficient. Economists have debated such questions for decades and have failed to reach agreement. To believe that we can perform such a task in litigation is questionable.

By contrast, we have more confidence about specific practices that we have labeled exclusionary or monopolistic. To be sure, some of these practices are more obviously inefficient than others. For example, we have a great deal of confidence about industrial sabotage, price-fixing, patent fraud, and perhaps predatory pricing at below marginal cost. We have less confidence about tying arrangements, reciprocity, and intentional building of excess capacity. This suggests strongly that antitrust policy should focus heavily on issues of conduct, not merely on issues of structure.

By establishing bad conduct requirements for antitrust liability, however, we at least increase the chances that we are really attacking inefficient rather than efficient practices, and that American consumers will come out gainers as a result.

To be sure, this may leave us with the uncomfortable situation that firms in concentrated industries make more money than we would like them to make. Consumers would be better off if they would price their output more competitively — that is, if they behaved more like competitors. But, as we have noted before, there are good reasons to believe that the deadweight loss that results from supracompetitive pricing in oligopolistic markets is far less than the loss that would result if we forced firms to operate at less than their most efficient size.

BIBLIOGRAPHY AND COLLATERAL READINGS

Books

4-4A P. Areeda, H. Hovenkamp, & J. Solow, Antitrust Law, chs. 9-10 (rev. ed. 1998); 5 P. Areeda & D. Turner, Antitrust Law, ch. 11 (1980).

T. Freyer, Regulating Big Business: Antitrust in Great Britain and America, 1880-1990 (1992).

H. Hovenkamp, Enterprise and American Law: 1836-1937, at ch. 20 (1991).

H. Hovenkamp, Federal Antitrust Policy, chs. 9, 12, and 13 (2d ed. 1994).

N. Lamoreaux, The Great Merger Movement in American Business, 1895-1904 (1985).

E.T. Sullivan & J. Harrison, Understanding Antitrust and Its Economic Implications (3d ed. 1998).

Articles

Baker, Contemporary Empirical Merger Analysis, 5 Geo. Mason L. Rev. 347 (1997).

Baker, Unilateral Competitive Effects Theories in Merger Analysis, 11 Antitrust 21 (Spring, 1997).

Baker & Bresnahan, The Gains from Merger or Collusion in Product-Differentiated Industries, 33 J. Indus. Econ. 427 (1985).

Bittlingmayer, Did Antitrust Policy Cause the Great Merger Wave?, 28 J.L. & Econ. 77 (1985).

Bok, Section 7 of the Clayton Act and the Merging of Law and Economics, 74 Harv. L. Rev. 226 (1960).

Brodley, Proof of Efficiencies in Mergers and Joint Ventures, 64 Antitrust L.J. 575 (1996).

Brodley, Potential Competition Mergers: A Structural Synthesis, 87 Yale L.J. 1 (1977).

Calkins, The New Merger Guidelines and the Herfindahl-Hirschman Index, 71 Cal. L. Rev. 402 (1983).

Fisher, Johnson, & Lande, Price Effects of Horizontal Mergers, 77 Cal. L. Rev. 777 (1989).

Fisher, Lande, & Vandaele, Efficiency Considerations in Merger Enforcement, 71 Cal. L. Rev. 1580 (1983).

Hovenkamp, Derek Bok and the Merger of Law and Economics, 21 J.L. Reform 515 (1988).

Hovenkamp, Mergers and Buyers, 77 Va. L. Rev. 1369 (1991).

Kattan, Efficiencies and Merger Analysis, 62 Antitrust L.J. 518 (1994).

Kwoka & Warren-Boulton, Efficiencies, Failing Firms, and Alternatives to Merger: A Policy Synthesis, 31 Antitrust Bull. 431 (1986).

Pitofsky, Proposals for Revised United States Merger Enforcement in a Global Economy, 81 Geo. L.J. 195 (1993).

Shapiro, Mergers with Differentiated Products, 10 Antitrust 23 (Spring, 1996).

Vellturo, Evaluating Mergers with Differentiated Products, 11 Antitrust 16 (Spring, 1997).

Werden, Simulating Unilateral Competitive Effects from Differentiated Products Mergers, 11 Antitrust 27 (Spring, 1997).

Williamson, Economies as an Antitrust Defense: the Welfare Trade-Offs, 58 Am. Econ. Rev. 18 (1968).

Yde & Vita, Merger Efficiencies: Reconsidering the "Passing-on"Requirement, 64 Antitrust L.J. 735 (1996).

Chapter 8

SECONDARY-LINE DIFFERENTIAL PRICING AND THE ROBINSON-PATMAN ACT

SECTION I. INTRODUCTION

The Robinson-Patman Act — sometimes called the "Wrong-way Corrigan" of antitrust[1] — is the most controversial of the federal antitrust laws. It has been described as subverting the very competition the antitrust laws are designed to protect, as protecting small business at the expense of consumers, and as dictating standards of conduct that virtually force companies to break other antitrust laws in order to avoid violating the Robinson-Patman Act.

The basic liability-creating section of the Robinson-Patman Act, section 2(a), 15 U.S.C. § 13(a), makes it unlawful "to discriminate in price between different purchasers of commodities of like grade and quality … where the effect of such discrimination may be substantially to lessen competition or tend to create a monopoly in any line of commerce, or to injure, destroy, or prevent competition with any person who either grants or knowingly receives the benefit of such discrimination, or with customers of either of them."

The Robinson-Patman Act is frequently called a "price discrimination" statute, but that is a misnomer. The statute as interpreted by the courts is directed at price *differences*, not at price discrimination. Economic price discrimination occurs when a seller has different rates of return on sales to two different customers. In more technical language, price discrimination occurs when the ratio of price to marginal cost is different in different sales. Thus sales of widgets at $1 each to two different customers can in fact be price discrimination if the seller's marginal cost is lower for one customer than for another. Such a pair of sales would not violate the Robinson-Patman Act, however, because both buyers pay the same price. As a result many instances of actual economic price discrimination fall outside the Act — for example, where a manufacturer charges the same delivered price to customers located varying distances from the seller's plant. On the other hand, the Act has frequently been used to condemn nondiscriminatory differential pricing: instances where a higher price to one buyer reflects no more than the higher costs incurred by the seller. The Robinson-Patman Act provides a "cost justification" defense which sometimes permits differential pricing that is economically nondiscriminatory. The courts have been so restrictive in their interpretation of the cost justification defense, however, that many instances of non-discriminatory price difference may violate the statute. The ironic result is that

---

[1] On July 18, 1938, Douglas "Wrong Way" Corrigan took off from New York City intending to fly to Los Angeles, but landed twenty hours later in Dublin, Ireland.

the statute actually forces sellers to engage in economic price discrimination by selling to different purchasers at the same price, even though the marginal costs incurred by the seller are higher for one purchaser than for another.

The statute is not necessarily bad, however, simply because it condemns differential pricing rather than economically discriminatory pricing. That is a value judgment we can make only after we have decided whether either discriminatory pricing or differential pricing ought to be condemned.

A. THE ECONOMICS OF PRICE DISCRIMINATION

In order to engage in persistent price discrimination, a seller must have a certain amount of market power. In a perfectly competitive market all sales will be made at economic cost, and a disfavored seller (one asked to pay more than cost) will simply buy from someone else. The one general exception to the market power requirement is when the price discrimination is the result of a seller's below cost pricing. For example, a seller may attempt to sell below cost in order to drive competitors out of business, or to encourage them to price oligopolistically. If the seller operates in more than one geographic market, and if it predates in only one market, then the seller will also be engaged in economic price discrimination: it is selling at cost in the nonpredated markets, but at below cost in the predated market.

Persistent, nonpredatory price discrimination requires market power, however, and it often requires that the seller have some mechanism for preventing "arbitrage." Arbitrage occurs when a favored purchaser resells the product to a disfavored purchaser at some price greater than the favored purchaser paid for the product but less than the price that the original seller would have charged to the disfavored purchaser. Often the transaction costs of arbitrage are greater than the amount of price difference between the purchasers, and arbitrage will not occur. For example, suppose that a wholesaler sells salt in large quantities to a large grocery store for $10 per carton but in small quantities to a small store for $12 per carton. The small grocer might be willing to pay the larger grocer $11 per carton for salt, and the larger grocer might be willing to resell the salt at that price. However, if the costs of bargaining and redelivery of the salt are greater than $2 per carton, arbitrage will not occur.

Assume, however, that a particular seller has market power and that arbitrage will not defeat a price discrimination scheme. In that case the seller can either sell its output at its nondiscriminatory profit-maximizing price, or perhaps obtain greater profits by engaging in price discrimination. Given the existence of the market power, is there any reason that society ought to prefer the "evil" of nondiscriminatory monopolistic pricing to the "evil" of price discrimination?

One thing is clear: *both* monopoly pricing and price discrimination can make sellers richer and buyers as a group poorer than competitive pricing does. Absent legal sanctions, a profit-maximizing seller who has the requisite market power will choose the alternative that transfers the larger amount of wealth away from consumers and to itself. Any antitrust policy of favoring purchasers over sellers might suggest that both price discrimination and monopoly pricing are bad, not because they are inefficient but because they redistribute wealth in a way that we find politically or morally displeasing.

From an efficiency standpoint, however, the problem is conceptually more difficult. One of the ironies of price discrimination is that while it can make sellers even richer than nondiscriminatory monopolistic pricing, it can also make some buyers better off, and it can increase total market output.

1. PERFECT PRICE DISCRIMINATION

Figure 1 illustrates the differences between competitive pricing, nondiscriminatory monopolistic pricing, and perfect price discrimination. The figure shows the demand curve (D) of either an entire market, or else of a single firm with sub-

Figure 1

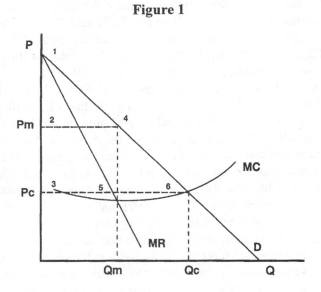

stantial market power. It also shows marginal cost (MC) and marginal revenue (MR) curves. If this were a competitive industry, prices would be driven to marginal cost and the price of each unit of output would be determined by the point where marginal cost is equal to demand. This is the competitive price, P_c on the vertical axis. In such a market a purchaser willing to pay the marginal cost of producing the product will be able to buy it. Many of these customers, of course, would have been willing to pay more than the competitive price, and triangle 1-3-6 represents the "consumers' surplus" — the amount of wealth created by the fact that many consumers can purchase the product for less than the value they place on it. For example, if a consumer would have been willing to pay as much as $3.00 for a product, but is able to purchase it for $2.50, the transaction creates a consumers' surplus of 50 cents. The consumer is 50 cents wealthier: she has a product she values at $3.00 but is out of pocket only $2.50.

Perfect competition maximizes the size of the consumers' surplus. However, in perfect competition there is *no* producers' surplus. Producers' surplus represents the amount of money obtained in the sale of a product in excess of the smallest amount that the seller would have been willing to accept for the sale. Since sellers are generally willing to make sales at marginal cost (which includes a fair rate of return), any price in excess of marginal cost creates producers' surplus in the amount of the excess. For example, if the marginal cost of producing and delivering a widget to a customer is $1.00, but the seller obtains a price of $1.10, the seller has received a producers' surplus of 10 cents. Many market transactions simultaneously generate consumers' and producers' surplus.

A profit-maximizing seller would naturally like to turn as much consumers' surplus as possible into producers' surplus. If the marginal cost of producing a blivet is $1.00, but a particular consumer values the blivet at $2.00 then a sale could be consummated at any price between $1.00 and $2.00. If the sale is consummated at $1.10, then 10 cents is producers' surplus and 90 cents is consumers' surplus. However, that same customer would have been willing to pay $1.90, which would have generated a producers' surplus of 90 cents.

The same demand, cost, and revenue curves of Figure 1 can also describe a single firm with substantial market power. One way the seller with market power can enlarge its producers' surplus, thereby increasing its profits, is by pricing its product at its profit-maximizing price, determined by the intersection between the marginal cost and marginal revenue curves on the graph. If the seller sells at its nondiscriminatory profit-maximizing price, P_m on the price axis of Figure 1, then the seller has created for itself a producers' surplus equal to rectangle 2-3-5-4, which represents revenues in excess of marginal cost. By contrast, consumers' surplus has been reduced to triangle 1-2-4. More seriously, however, triangle 4-5-6 represents deadweight loss, which is value that accrues to *neither* consumers nor producers. Triangle 4-5-6 represents value lost because customers unwilling to pay price P_m have chosen not to buy but to substitute an alternative that would have been less attractive to them in a competitive market. They lose the consumers' surplus that they could have had by purchasing at price P_c. However, this lost value does not go to the producer either, for it receives no revenues from sales that it does not make.

Suppose that the seller is able to determine precisely what every purchaser in the market is willing to pay for a blivet. If the seller can identify each purchaser willing to pay $1.00, each purchaser willing to pay $1.10, etc., and make every sale at the largest price that a buyer is willing to pay, then the seller would be able to turn *all* of triangle 1-3-6 into *producers'* surplus. Furthermore, the seller would make even the sales at price P_c, because those sales are profitable. In short, under *perfect* price discrimination output is the same as it would be in a competitive market: the seller would sell to every customer willing to pay marginal cost or more. The chief difference between perfect competition and perfect price discrimination is that in the former all of 1-3-6 would be consumers' surplus. In the latter, all of triangle 1-3-6 would be producers' surplus.

Theoretically, perfect price discrimination allocates resources in the same way that perfect competition does. Output is the same as it would be under competition. No customers make inefficient substitutions for another product, because everyone willing to pay the marginal cost of a blivet will be able to purchase one. The chief difference between perfect price discrimination and perfect competition is that in the former the price-discriminating seller is better off and its customers are worse off.

By contrast, the difference between perfect price discrimination and non-discriminatory monopoly pricing is that monopoly pricing reduces output in the monopolized market, forces customers to make inefficient substitutions for other products, and thereby distorts the market in those products as well. However, some customers are better off in the monopoly-priced market than in the discriminatory market. These are the customers who would have paid price P_m in the monopoly-priced market, but who actually value blivets more than P_m, and under perfect price discrimination therefore pay more. These purchasers would be located along the demand curve in Figure 1 between points 1 and 4.

2. IMPERFECT PRICE DISCRIMINATION

The differing effects of perfect price discrimination and nondiscriminatory monopoly pricing are easily described. But no seller can engage in anything approaching perfect price discrimination. First of all, 100 different customers might individually place 100 different values on a particular product. The seller, however, must generally be content to identify two or three different groups of customers — perhaps a high preference group, a medium preference group, and a low preference group. Further, if the cost of identifying these three groups, determining the profit-maximizing price for each group, and preventing arbitrage from one group to another is higher than the additional revenues that the seller can obtain by price discriminating, then discrimination will be unprofitable.

In addition, if price discrimination is not perfect it no longer follows that discriminatory pricing results in a higher output than nondiscriminatory monopoly pricing. Suppose, for example, that a monopolist determines that its nondiscriminatory profit-maximizing price is $1.50, although its marginal cost at that rate of output is only $1.00. Suppose further that it is able to segregate three groups of potential purchasers. One group values the product at $1.00, another at $1.50 and another at $2.00. Perhaps the monopolist could reach these three groups of buyers by putting the product in three different boxes, marked "good," "better," and "best." Suppose, however, that the monopolist discovers that the middle group is quite cost conscious and most of them will buy the $1.00 product if it is available, even though they would be willing to pay $1.50 otherwise. The seller might conclude that it is more profitable to sell the product only in $1.50 and $2.00 versions.

After all, the $1.00 sales are not particularly profitable, but the $1.50 sales are very profitable. In short, the monopolist might price discriminate, but only *within* the group of customers who are willing to pay the profit-maximizing price or more. In that case, the lowest-price sales would be made at the profit-maximizing price, not at marginal cost. Output would be no greater than under nondiscriminatory monopoly pricing, and monopoly deadweight loss would be just as high. Furthermore, price discrimination within this group is not perfect either. Some disfavored customers will refuse to pay more than the nondiscriminatory profit-maximizing price. In that case, output under price discrimination would be even less than it would be under nondiscriminatory monopoly pricing.

The idea that price discrimination does not cause any socially costly deadweight loss evaporates when we give up the illusion of "perfect" price discrimination. Furthermore, it is quite possible that the entire value to a seller of engaging in price discrimination will be eaten up by the costs of acquiring and maintaining the requisite market power, and the cost of obtaining the information necessary for the seller to engage in price discrimination. For example, if price discrimination is worth $1,000,000 per year to a seller, it will be willing to spend any amount up to $1,000,000 in acquiring and maintaining the requisite market power, identifying the groups of customers who place differential values on the product, and disguising or marketing the product so as to prevent arbitrage. Many of these expenses are likely to be socially wasteful. (See the discussion of the deadweight loss of monopoly in Chapter 2, *supra*.) The result is that nearly all of triangle 1-3-6 in Figure 1 may not be producers' surplus at all, but deadweight loss. For a fuller discussion of these problems, *see* H. Hovenkamp, *Federal Antitrust Policy*, ch. 14 (2d ed. 1994); E.T. Sullivan & J. Harrison, *Understanding Antitrust and Its Economic Implications*, ch. 8 (3d ed. 1998).

In contrast to the monopolist's persistent price discrimination, purely sporadic price discrimination is frequently a sign of healthy competition. Competitive markets are rarely in perfect equilibrium. Supply and demand are always fluctuating, and even in a market with one thousand sellers we expect to see continual, daily adjustments in prices. Suppose, for example, that on a particular day the demand for blivets has dropped in relation to the supply. On the previous day a seller sold blivets for $1.00 each. When she opens for business on this morning she does not know of the change in market conditions. The first customer walks in and, not knowing of the market change either, purchases blivets from her at $1.00. The second and third customers walk away, however, and the fourth customer tells the seller that he can buy blivets across the street for 90 cents. When the seller learns of the change in the market she will likely drop her price to 90 cents, and we would not want a legal policy preventing her from doing so, even though the result is that she will be engaging in price discrimination as between her first customer in the morning and other customers later in the day. In all markets information is less than perfect, and different sellers respond to changes in the market in slightly different ways and at different times. The result is sporadic, short-term price discrimination which is not anti-competitive at all, but evidence of hard, vigorous competition. If there is a cartel, on the other hand, we would expect each seller to hold to the agreed-upon price in spite of short-term fluctuations in demand.

B. ANTITRUST POLICY AND THE ROBINSON-PATMAN ACT

The "fit" between the practices condemned by the Robinson-Patman Act and the kind of price discrimination which is inefficient is very poor. The Robinson-Patman Act has been used to condemn the kind of sporadic price discrimination which is really evidence of hard competition. Likewise, the Act has been used to condemn many instances of nondiscriminatory, differential pricing, simply because the defendant was unable to meet the "cost justification" defense that the statute creates. Likewise, many sellers engaged in persistent price discrimination are not covered by the statute because they make all sales at the same "price." For example, consider the variable proportion tying arrangement. Suppose a seller of a mimeograph machine requires purchasers to use its ink as a condition of obtaining the machine. The seller earns a 5% rate of return on the machine but a 20% rate of return on the ink. The seller will obtain a much higher net rate of return from high-volume users of the machine than from low-volume users, for the former use more ink. Nevertheless, all sales of machines are made at the same price, and all sales of ink are made at the same price per unit. The seller has not violated the Robinson-Patman Act. See the discussion of tie-ins and price discrimination in Chapter 5.

Why has such a poorly designed statute managed to survive for so long? Largely because no one lobbies Congress for allocative efficiency. Many interest groups have become highly effective lobbyists for their own interests, however, and among the most successful of these have been small businesses and retailers. The legislative history of the Robinson-Patman Act is filled with vituperative comments aimed at the "chain stores" — large, integrated merchandisers who were destroying the fortunes of many small businesses, mainly as a result of their efficiency of distribution. The one "evil" most explicitly targeted by the Act was price discounting of large quantity wholesale purchases, which gave large retailers an advantage over smaller ones. To this day, it seems, Robinson-Patman survives because the owners of small and medium-sized businesses believe that the statute protects them from larger competitors, by preventing suppliers from treating the larger competitors more favorably than themselves. In fact, small distributors have not fared so well under the Robinson-Patman Act. The statute has been used frequently to prevent associations of small merchants or manufacturers from using volume buying to obtain lower prices. *See, e.g., Mid-South Distribs. v. FTC*, 287 F.2d 512 (5th Cir.), *cert. denied*, 368 U.S. 838 (1961); *Standard Motor Prods. v. FTC*, 265 F.2d 674 (2d Cir.), *cert. denied*, 361 U.S. 826 (1959).

In 1977 the United States Department of Justice issued a report sharply critical of the Robinson-Patman Act (Report on the Robinson-Patman Act (1977)). Since then it has not enforced the statute. Today the great majority of cases are brought by private plaintiffs.

C. THE TECHNICAL COVERAGE OF THE ROBINSON-PATMAN ACT

The Robinson-Patman Act is a maze of technical requirements that often operate to hide or subvert the statute's basic purpose. Much litigation has been devoted to questions such as the meaning of "commodities of like grade and quality" under the statute, or the meaning of its requirement that the commodities must be "sold for use, consumption, or resale within the United States."

Unlike the Sherman Act, which applies to all transactions "affecting commerce," up to the full Constitutional power of Congress to regulate interstate commerce, the Robinson-Patman Act requires that the seller be "engaged in" interstate commerce and that one of the discriminatory sales itself be made in interstate commerce. This has frequently meant that at least one of the transactions alleged to violate the statute must involve commodities, negotiations, or parties that crossed a state boundary. *See Cliff Food Stores v. Kroger*, 417 F.2d 203 (5th Cir. 1969). As a practical matter, this may mean that retail transactions never violate the Act, since buyer and seller are located in the same state. *E.g.*, *Indiana Grocery v. Super-Valu Stores*, 647 F. Supp. 254 (S.D. Ind. 1986).

The statute applies to "sales" and not leases even though, as the discussion of tying arrangements suggests (see Chapter 5, *supra*), leases are often used to facilitate price discrimination. The statute applies only to the sale of "commodities," and therefore does not cover labor or business services — even though price discrimination in service markets is commonly easier to pull off than it is in the sale of goods. For example, the doctor who charges wealthy patients more than poor ones need not worry about arbitrage.

Section 2(a) of the Robinson-Patman Act explicitly covers "indirect" as well as "direct" price discrimination. Within the statute, "indirect" price discrimination refers to a seller's differential treatment of different classes of customers — for example, if the seller gives the favored buyer delivery, stocking or storage, advertising, brokerage allowances, return privileges, or any other favorable terms which put one buyer in a better position than another buyer.

When courts analyze "indirect" price discrimination they generally do so from the buyer's point of view, not from the seller's. Thus, for example, if a seller provides "free" delivery in carload lots but requires buyers of less than carloads to pay their own delivery, courts will not generally look at the seller's marginal cost of servicing these two classes of customers in this way. Rather courts will ask whether the carload lot buyer is effectively obtaining the commodity at a lower price than the small buyer is. If the answer is yes, the burden shifts to the defendant seller to show that the free delivery of carload lots was "cost justified."

The statute has been held to require that there actually be two different sales, to two different purchasers, at two different prices. One sale and one offer to sell at a higher or lower price is not a violation of the statute. Furthermore, the two sales must be consummated within a reasonable time of each other. The question whether a parent and its subsidiary, or affiliated corporations, are two "different" purchasers has perplexed the court, although recent authority suggests that closely related corporations are not "different" and therefore that sales to them do not fall within the statute. Is the Supreme Court's decision in *Copperweld Corp. v. Independence Tube Corp.*, 467 U.S. 752 (1983) (reprinted in Chapter 4) that a parent and its subsidiary cannot be "conspiring entities" under the Sherman Act relevant to this issue? *See Caribe BMW v. Bayerische Motoren Werke Aktiengesellschaft*, 19 F.3d 745 (1st Cir. 1994) (defendant and its wholly owned subsidiary were a single "seller," and thus Robinson-Patman Act applies).

Sales to agencies of the federal government are not covered by the Robinson-Patman Act. In 1983, however, the Supreme Court decided that the Act applies when the low price sale is made to a state or local government agency, if the agency resells the commodity in competition with the disfavored purchasers. *Jefferson Cty. Pharm. Ass'n v. Abbott Labs.*, 460 U.S. 150 (1983). The Supreme Court assumed without deciding that a sale to a state or local government agency for internal consumption would be exempt from the Act, at least if the product was being used for some "traditional governmental function." Four dissenters argued that application of the Robinson-Patman Act to purchases by state and local governmental agencies was inconsistent with the intent of the Act's framers.

For more comprehensive treatment of the Act's technical coverage, *see* F. Rowe, *Price Discrimination Under the Robinson-Patman Act* (1962); H. Hovenkamp, *Federal Antitrust Policy* § 14.6 (2d ed. 1994).

SECTION II. PRIMARY-LINE DISCRIMINATION

The original section 2 of the Clayton Act was enacted in 1914, but substantially amended and renamed the "Robinson-Patman Act" in 1936. The original 1914 provision was concerned chiefly with injuries that could accrue to the competitors of a seller engaged in price discrimination. We call these "primary-line" injuries. Today courts treat such injuries as a form of predatory pricing, and for that reason we have included primary-line actions in the section on predatory pricing (Chapter 6, *supra*).

SECTION III. SECONDARY-LINE DISCRIMINATION

The 1936 Amendments to section 2 were concerned chiefly with injuries that can accrue to the price discriminator's disfavored customers (that is, the customers forced to pay the higher price). These are called "secondary-line" injuries. In secondary-line price discrimination the perceived victims are customers of the defendant, not its competitors. If, for example, someone sells widgets to A at $1.00 and to B at 90 cents, then A is the victim of price discrimination as defined by the Robinson-Patman Act.

A. "PRICE DISCRIMINATION" AND "INJURY TO COMPETITION" UNDER THE ROBINSON-PATMAN ACT

FTC V. MORTON SALT CO.

334 U.S. 37 (1948)

JUSTICE BLACK delivered the opinion of the Court.

Respondent manufacturers several different brands of table salt and sells them directly to (1) wholesalers or jobbers, who in turn resell to the retail trade, and (2) large retailers, including chain store retailers. Respondent sells its finest brand of table salt, known as Blue Label, on what it terms a standard quality discount system available to all customers. Under this system the purchasers pay a delivered price and the cost to both wholesale and retail purchasers of this brand differs according to the quantities brought. These prices are as follows, after making allowance for rebates and discounts:

	Per case
Less-than-carload purchases	$1.60
Carload purchases	1.50
5,000-case purchases in any consecutive 12 months	1.40
50,000-case purchases in any consecutive 12 months	1.35

Only five companies have ever bought sufficient quantities of respondent's salt to obtain the $1.35 per case price. These companies could buy in such quantities because they operate large chains of retail stores in various parts of the country. As a result of this low price these five companies have been able to sell Blue Label salt at retail cheaper than wholesale purchasers from respondent could reasonably sell the same brand of salt to independently operated retail stores, many of whom competed with the local outlets of the five chain stores.

....

.... Respondent's basic contention, which it argues this case hinges upon, is that its "standard quantity discounts, available to all on equal terms, as contrasted, for example, to hidden or special rebates, allowances, prices or discounts, are not discriminatory within the meaning of the Robinson-Patman Act." Theoretically, these discounts are equally available to all, but functionally they are not. For as the record indicates (if reference to it on this point were necessary) no single independent retail grocery store, and probably no single wholesaler, bought as many as 50,000 cases or as much as $50,000 worth of table salt in one year. Furthermore, the record shows that, while certain purchasers were enjoying one or more of respondent's standard quantity discounts, some of their competitors made purchases in such small quantities that they could not qualify for any of respondent's discounts, even those based on carload shipments. The legislative history of the Robinson-Patman Act makes it abundantly clear that Congress considered it to be an evil that a large buyer could secure a competitive advantage over a small buyer solely because of the large buyer's quantity purchasing ability. The Robinson-Patman Act was passed to deprive a large buyer of such advantages except to the extent that a lower price could be justified by reason of a seller's diminished costs due to quantity manufacture, delivery or sale, or by reason of the seller's good faith effort to meet a competitor's equally low price.

....

... It is argued that the findings fail to show that respondent's discriminatory discounts had in fact caused injury to competition. There are specific findings that such injuries had resulted from respondent's discounts, although the statute does not require the Commission to find that injury has actually resulted. The statute requires no more than that the effect of the prohibited price discriminations "may be substantially to lessen competition ... or to injure, destroy, or prevent competition." After a careful consideration of this provision of the Robinson-Patman Act, we have said that "the statute does not require that the discriminations must in fact have harmed competition, but only that there is a reasonable possibility that they 'may' have such an effect." Here the Commission found what would appear to be obvious, that the competitive opportunities of certain merchants were injured when they had to pay respondent substantially more for their goods than their competitors had to pay....

Apprehension is expressed in this Court that enforcement of the Commission's order against respondent's continued violations of the Robinson-Patman Act might lead respondent to raise table salt prices to its carload purchasers. Such a conceivable, though, we think, highly improbable, contingency, could afford us no reason for upsetting the Commission's findings and declining to direct compliance with a statute passed by Congress.

....

NOTES AND QUESTIONS

1. Why was Morton Salt's "price discrimination" scheme not frustrated by arbitrage? Couldn't a buyer simply purchase 50,000 cases at $1.35 per case and resell them to small purchasers at $1.55 per case — lower than the $1.60 Morton Salt charged purchasers of less than a carload? If Morton Salt were truly price discriminating, such a scheme would cost it many of its most profitable sales.

There are several possible explanations. Most likely, Morton Salt did not care whether someone resold its salt, because it made just as much money per case from a 50,000 case sale as it did from a 100 case sale; that is, although the price per case of a 100 case sale was higher, costs were also higher. If Morton Salt did not care whether there was such arbitrage, that is good evidence that it was not engaged in true price discrimination.

Another possibility, however, is that Morton Salt was engaged in price discrimination, but that the additional transaction costs of arbitrage were greater than the amount of the discrimination. Someone seeking to purchase salt at $1.35 and resell it at $1.55 would have to buy the salt, store it, possibly advertise it, and then engage in individual sales and perhaps deliveries to smaller purchasers. If these operations cost more than 20 cents per case, arbitrage would be unprofitable. As a general rule, a seller's ability to price discriminate is limited by the costs of arbitrage. If arbitrage costs 20 cents per unit, then a price differential of less than 20 cents between favored and disfavored customers will preclude arbitrage from occurring.

2. The Supreme Court noted that the legislative history of the Robinson-Patman Act made it "abundantly clear" that "Congress considered it to be an evil that a large buyer could secure a competitive advantage over a small buyer solely because of the large buyer's quantity purchasing ability." If that is true, then doesn't the legislative policy of the Robinson-Patman Act require the court to dispense with economic efficiency and use the statute to protect small businesses from larger, more efficient competitors? Isn't that precisely what the Court does when it defines "injury to competition" under the statute as injury to the "competitive opportunities" of small businesses who had to pay more than their larger competitors did? Isn't the Court confusing "injury to competition" with "injury to competitors"?

3. Is there any evidence in the opinion that Morton Salt had market power in the wholesale salt market? A manufacturer can generally not engage in systematic price discrimination unless it has market power. If Morton Salt's $1.60 price to small buyers were really a monopoly price, but Morton Salt had no market power, small buyers would simply find a seller willing to sell to them at a competitive price. Thus, persistent price differentials have one of two explanations: (1) either the seller has a certain amount of market power; or (2) the price differential is in fact nondiscriminatory and merely reflects the higher costs of dealing with one set of customers. The case law on secondary-line price discrimination under the Robinson-Patman Act generally fails to discuss market power. It is simply not an issue. The absence of a market power requirement in secondary-line Robinson-Patman cases is economically irrational. However, there may be some explanations for the case law.

First of all, the legislative history of the Robinson-Patman amendments makes clear that the framers of the 1936 statute believed the real villains in secondary-line cases were large buyers, such as chain stores, and not large sellers. The theory was that big buyers somehow managed to force sellers to grant them discounts so large that the sales were effectively below cost. In order to cover these losses the sellers had to raise the price to smaller buyers. Is the theory plausible? Can any buyer, no matter how great its monopsony power, force a seller to make long-term, below cost sales? Wouldn't a seller be better off simply to make the sales to the small buyers at the profit-maximizing price, and refuse to sell to the large buyers except at some price in excess of its marginal costs? This "subsidy" theory in the legislative history of the 1936 amendments is simply another version of the "recoupment" theory of predatory pricing, discussed *supra*. About the only thing that could explain the theory is a giant conspiracy between large buyers (the chain stores) and sellers to force small retailers out of business. Evidence of such a conspiracy has not surfaced. Furthermore, not even the conspiracy theory would explain why it would be profitable for sellers to make below-cost sales to large buyers, or why sellers would benefit from forcing their smaller customers out of business.

Another possible explanation for the absence of a market power requirement in secondary-line cases is that the "cost justification" defense, discussed *infra*, serves the same function. If price differences cannot be cost justified, then there is an inference of price discrimination, without the need of a showing that the defendant has market power.

In fact, however, it is probably easier for a plaintiff to show that the defendant has market power than it is for a defendant to justify price differentials under the rules that courts have created for the cost justification defense. Almost no seller knows its marginal costs with respect to each sale, and it is very difficult to compute such costs even for various categories of sales. Nevertheless, courts have generally required defendants to produce this kind of data in order to meet the affirmative defense of cost justification. *See United States v. Borden Co.*, this chapter, *infra*. *See generally* Hovenkamp, *Market Power and Secondary-Line Differential Pricing*, 71 Geo. L.J. 1157 (1983).

TEXACO, INC. V. HASBROUCK

496 U.S. 543 (1990)

JUSTICE STEVENS delivered the opinion of the Court.

... Respondents are 12 independent Texaco retailers. They displayed the Texaco trademark, accepted Texaco credit cards, and bought their gasoline products directly from Texaco. Texaco delivered the gasoline to respondents' stations. The retail gasoline market in Spokane was highly competitive throughout the damages period, which ran from 1972 to 1981. Stations marketing the nationally advertised Texaco gasoline competed with other major brands as well as with stations featuring independent brands. Moreover, although discounted prices at a nearby Texaco station would have the most obvious impact on a respondent's trade, the cross-city traffic patterns and relatively small size of Spokane produced a city-wide competitive market....

The respondents tried unsuccessfully to increase their ability to compete with lower priced stations. Some tried converting from full service to self-service stations. Two of the respondents sought to buy their own tank trucks and haul their gasoline from Texaco's supply point, but Texaco vetoed that proposal.

While the independent retailers struggled, two Spokane gasoline distributors supplied by Texaco prospered. Gull Oil Company (Gull) had its headquarters in Seattle and distributed petroleum products in four western States under its own name. In Spokane it purchased its gas from Texaco at prices that ranged from six to four cents below Texaco's RTW price. Gull resold that product under its own name; the fact that it was being supplied by Texaco was not known by either the public or the respondents. In Spokane, Gull supplied about 15 stations....

The Dompier Oil Company (Dompier) started business in 1954 selling Quaker State Motor Oil. In 1960 it became a full line distributor of Texaco products, and by the mid-1970's its sales of gasoline represented over three-quarters of its business. Dompier purchased Texaco gasoline at prices of 3.95 cents to 3.65 cents below the RTW price. Dompier thus paid a higher price than Gull, but Dompier, unlike Gull, resold its gas under the Texaco brand names. It supplied about eight to ten Spokane retail stations....

Like Gull, Dompier picked up Texaco's product at the Texaco bulk plant and delivered directly to retail outlets. Unlike Gull, Dompier owned a bulk storage facility, but it was seldom used because its capacity was less than that of many retail stations. Again unlike Gull, Dompier received from Texaco the equivalent of the common carrier rate for delivering the gasoline product to the retail outlets. Thus, in addition to its discount from the RTW price, Dompier made a profit on its hauling function.

... There was ample evidence that Texaco executives were well aware of Dompier's dramatic growth and believed that it was attributable to "the magnitude of the distributor discount and the hauling allowance." In response to complaints from individual respondents about Dompier's aggressive pricing, however, Texaco representatives professed that they "couldn't understand it."

II

At the ... trial, Texaco contended that the special prices to Gull and Dompier were justified by cost savings, were the product of a good faith attempt to meet competition, and were lawful "functional discounts."

III

It is appropriate to begin our consideration of the legal status of functional discounts[11] by examining the language of the Act. Section 2(a) provides in part:

> It shall be unlawful for any person engaged in commerce, in the course of such commerce, either directly or indirectly, to discriminate in price between different purchasers of commodities of like grade and quality, .. where the effect of such discrimination may be substantially to lessen competition or tend to create a monopoly in any line of commerce, or to injure, destroy, or prevent competition with any person who either grants or knowingly receives the benefit of such discrimination, or with customers of either of them....

15 U.S.C. § 13(a).

---

[11] In their brief filed as amici curiae, the United States and the Federal Trade Commission suggest the following definition of "functional discount," which is adequate for our discussion: "A functional discount is one given to a purchaser based on its role in the supplier's distributive system, reflecting, at least in a generalized sense, the services performed by the purchaser for the supplier." Brief for United States et al. as Amici Curiae 10.

The Act contains no express reference to functional discounts. It does contain two affirmative defenses that provide protection for two categories of discounts — those that are justified by savings in the seller's cost of manufacture, delivery or sale, and those that represent a good faith response to the equally low prices of a competitor.... As these come to us, neither of those defenses is available to Texaco.

In order to establish a violation of the Act, respondents had the burden of proving four facts: (1) that Texaco's sales to Gull and Dompier were made in interstate commerce; (2) that the gasoline sold to them was of the same grade and quality as that sold to respondents; (3) that Texaco discriminated in price as between Gull and Dompier on the one hand and respondents on the other; and (4) that the discrimination had a prohibited effect on competition. 15 U.S.C. § 13(a).... The first two elements of respondents' case are not disputed in this Court, and we do not understand Texaco to be challenging the sufficiency of respondents' proof of damages. Texaco does argue, however, that although it charged different prices, it did not "discriminate in price" within the meaning of the Act, and that, at least to the extent that Gull and Dompier acted as wholesalers, the price differentials did not injure competition. We consider the two arguments separately.

IV

Texaco's first argument would create a blanket exemption for all functional discounts. Indeed, carried to its logical conclusion, it would exempt all price differentials except those given to competing purchasers. The primary basis for Texaco's argument is the following comment by Congressman Utterback, an active sponsor of the Act:

> In its meaning as simple English, a discrimination is more than a mere difference. Underlying the meaning of the word is the idea that some relationship exists between the parties to the discrimination which entitles them to equal treatment, whereby the difference granted to one casts some burden or disadvantage upon the other. If the two are competing in the resale of the goods concerned, that relationship exists. Where, also, the price to one is so low as to involve a sacrifice of some part of the seller's necessary costs and profit as applied to that business, it leaves that deficit inevitably to be made up in higher prices to his other customers; and there, too, a relationship may exist upon which to base the charge of discrimination. But where no such relationship exists, where the goods are sold in different markets and the conditions affecting those markets set different price levels for them, the sale to different customers at those different prices would not constitute a discrimination within the meaning of this bill.

80 Cong. Rec. 9416 (1936).

We have previously considered this excerpt from the legislative history, and have refused to draw from it the conclusion which Texaco proposes. *FTC v.*

Anheuser-Busch, Inc., 363 U.S. 536, 547-551 (1960). Although the excerpt does support Texaco's argument, we remain persuaded that the argument is foreclosed by the text of the Act itself. In the context of a statute that plainly reveals a concern with competitive consequences at different levels of distribution, and carefully defines specific affirmative defenses, it would be anomalous to assume that the Congress intended the term "discriminate" to have such a limited meaning. In *Anheuser-Busch* we rejected an argument identical to Texaco's....

Since we have already decided that a price discrimination within the meaning of § 2(a) "is merely a price difference," we must reject Texaco's first argument.

V

In *FTC v. Morton Salt Co.*, 334 U.S. 37, 46-47 (1948), we held that an injury to competition may be inferred from evidence that some purchasers had to pay their supplier "substantially more for their goods than their competitors had to pay."... Texaco, supported by the United States and the Federal Trade Commission as amici curiae, (the Government), argues that this presumption should not apply to differences between prices charged to wholesalers and those charged to retailers. Moreover, they argue that it would be inconsistent with fundamental antitrust policies to construe the Act as requiring a seller to control his customers' resale prices. The seller should not be held liable for the independent pricing decisions of his customers. As the Government correctly notes, Brief for United States et al. as Amici Curiae 21-22 (filed Aug. 3, 1989), this argument endorses the position advocated 35 years ago in the Report of the Attorney General's National Committee to Study the Antitrust Laws (1955).

After observing that suppliers ought not to be held liable for the independent pricing decisions of their buyers, and that without functional discounts distributors might go uncompensated for services they performed, the Committee wrote:

> The Committee recommends, therefore, that suppliers granting functional discounts either to single-function or to integrated buyers should not be held responsible for any consequences of their customers' pricing tactics. Price cutting at the resale level is not in fact, and should not be held in law, "the effect of "a differential that merely accords due recognition and reimbursement for actual marketing functions. The price cutting of a customer who receives this type of differential results from his own independent decision to lower price and operate at a lower profit margin per unit.

Id., at 208....

The hypothetical predicate for the Committee's entire discussion of functional discounts is a price differential "that merely accords due recognition and reimbursement for actual marketing functions." Such a discount is not illegal. In this case, however, both the District Court and the Court of Appeals concluded that even without viewing the evidence in the light most favorable to the respondents, there was no substantial evidence indicating that the discounts to Gull and Dompier constituted a reasonable reimbursement for the value to Texaco of their actual marketing functions. Indeed, Dompier was separately compensated for its hauling function, and neither Gulf nor Dompier maintained any significant storage facilities.

... Nor should any reader of the commentary on functional discounts be much surprised by today's result. Commentators have disagreed about the extent to which functional discounts are generally or presumptively allowable under the Robinson-Patman Act. They nevertheless tend to agree that in exceptional cases what is nominally a functional discount may be an unjustifiable price discrimination entirely within the coverage of the Act.... F. Rowe, Price Discrimination Under the Robinson-Patman Act 174, n.7 (1962); *id.*, at 195-205.

... Both Gull and Dompier received the full discount on all their purchases even though most of their volume was resold directly to consumers. The extra margin on those sales obviously enabled them to price aggressively in both their retail and their wholesale marketing. To the extent that Dompier and Gull competed with respondents in the retail market, the presumption of adverse effect on competition recognized in the *Morton Salt* case becomes all the more appropriate. Their competitive advantage in that market also constitutes evidence tending to rebut any presumption of legality that would otherwise apply to their wholesale sales.

The evidence indicates, moreover, that Texaco affirmatively encouraged Dompier to expand its retail business and that Texaco was fully informed about the persistent and marketwide consequences of its own pricing policies. Indeed, its own executives recognized that the dramatic impact on the market was almost entirely attributable to the magnitude of the distributor discount and the hauling allowance. Yet at the same time that Texaco was encouraging Dompier to integrate downward, and supplying Dompier with a generous discount useful to such integration, Texaco was inhibiting upward integration by the respondents: two of the respondents sought permission from Texaco to haul their own fuel using their own tankwagons, but Texaco refused. The special facts of this case thus make it peculiarly difficult for Texaco to claim that it is being held liable for the independent pricing decisions of Gull or Dompier.

... [I]ndirect competitive effects surely may not be presumed automatically in every functional discount setting, and, indeed, one would expect that most functional discounts will be legitimate discounts which do not cause harm to competition. At the least, a functional discount that constitutes a reasonable reimbursement for the purchasers' actual marketing functions will not violate the Act. When a functional discount is legitimate, the inference of injury to competition recognized in the *Morton Salt* case will simply not arise. Yet it is also true that not every functional discount is entitled to a judgment of legitimacy, and that it will sometimes be possible to produce evidence showing that a particular functional discount caused a price discrimination of the sort the Act prohibits. When such anticompetitive effects are proved — as we believe they were in this case — they are covered by the Act....

The judgment is affirmed....

[The concurring opinions of JUSTICES WHITE and SCALIA are omitted.]

NOTES AND QUESTIONS

1. The Court notes that the retail gasoline market at issue was "highly competitive," and Texaco was losing market share to other major gasoline companies. If that is so, how could there be an injury to competition? Was the plaintiff a victim of "antitrust injury?" If not, how do you harmonize *Hasbrouck* with the Supreme Court's *J. Truett Payne* decision, reprinted *infra*, requiring antitrust injury in Robinson-Patman Act cases? Isn't this a major inconsistency in recent Supreme Court decisions applying the Robinson-Patman Act in secondary-line and primary-line (predatory pricing) situations? Compare *Hasbrouck* with the Supreme Court's 1993 decision in *Brooke Group Ltd. v. Brown & Williamson Tobacco Corp.*, 509 U.S. 209 (1993), reprinted in Chapter 6, *supra*.

2. In *Chroma Lighting v. GTE Products Corp.*, 111 F.3d 653 (9th Cir.), *cert. denied*, 118 S. Ct. 357 (1997), the court held that "in a secondary-line Robinson-Patman case, the ... inference that competitive injury to individual buyers harms competition generally may not be overcome by proof of no harm to competition." The plaintiff was a distributor of certain Sylvania lighting products and went out of business after Sylvania gave discounts to larger distributors in competition with the plaintiff. The court relied mainly on the Supreme Court's holding in *Morton Salt* for the proposition that

> competitive injury in a secondary-line Robinson-Patman case may be inferred from evidence of injury to an individual competitor. More specifically, *Morton Salt* permits a fact finder to infer injury to competition from evidence of a substantial price difference over time, because such a price difference may harm the competitive opportunities of individual merchants, and thus create a "reasonable possibility" that competition itself may be harmed.

FTC v. Morton Salt, 334 U.S. 37, 46-47 (1948).

The plaintiff attempted to rebut this presumption by showing that "competition in the relevant market remains healthy," but the court found such a showing inadequate. Other circuits are divided on the issue. *Boise Cascade Corp. v. FTC*, 837 F.2d 1127, 1144 (D.C. Cir. 1988) (no competitive harm unless competition in the relevant market is injured); *J.F. Feeser v. Serv-A-Portion*, 909 F.2d 1524, 1532-33 (3d Cir. 1990), *cert. denied*, 499 U.S. 921 (1991) (harm to competitor is all that is required).

The relevant statutory language makes it unlawful to charge competing purchaser/resellers different prices

> where the effect of such discrimination may be substantially to lessen competition or tend to create a monopoly in any line of commerce, *or to injure,*

> *destroy, or prevent competition with any person who either grants or know-*
> *ingly receives the benefits of such discrimination, or with customers of either*
> *of them ...*

15 U.S.C. §13(a) (emphasis added).

The Ninth Circuit agreed with the Third Circuit's *Feeser* and with Judge Mikva's dissent in the D.C. Circuit's *Boise Cascade* decision that the italicized portion of that statute permits a secondary-line violation to be shown on the basis of injury to a competitor alone rather than injury to competition. This language, as the court paraphrased Judge Mikva, "shifts the focus of the statute from protecting competition to protecting individual disfavored buyers from the loss of business to favored buyers."

But does the statutory language really have that meaning? While the distributors or dealers of a common manufacturer "compete" in the resale of the manufacturer's product, they also compete to be the best seller of that manufacturer's product. Price incentives are a typical reward of such competition. For example, a manufacturer might reward a dealer for its success with various rebates or discounts that lower its wholesale price. A dealer who knowingly attempts to receive such a reward is not "injuring," "destroying," or "preventing" such competition. Rather, he is furthering such competition.

The Ninth Circuit seemed to read the italicized statutory language as if it condemned price discriminations that "injure ... any person...." But the language reaches only those price discriminations that "injure ... *competition* with any person." The injury that a less effective dealer receives when a more effective dealer is rewarded with a rebate is not an injury to competition, but an inducement to competition.

The Third Circuit also noted in *Feeser*, *supra*, that the first portion of the statutory language ("may be substantially to lessen competition or tend to create a monopoly") was contained in the original 1914 Clayton Act formulation. This language, the Third Circuit opined, "refers generally to broad impacts on competition." By contrast, the language added by the 1936 "Robinson-Patman" amendments ("to injure, destroy, or prevent competition with any person who either grants or knowingly receives the benefits of such discrimination") was intended "specifically to protect the ability of individual companies to compete." But does protecting "the ability of individual companies *to compete*" have to mean insulating them from all incentives programs rewarding dealers with larger sales by giving them lower effective prices?

To be sure, the secondary-line provisions of the Robinson-Patman Act were intended to give smaller rivals a certain element of protection against larger rivals. But the Supreme Court has also insisted that these provisions be interpreted in such a way so as to make them, to the extent possible, consistent with the overall goals of the antitrust laws. *See, e.g., Great A. & P. Tea Co. v. FTC*, 440 U.S. 69, 80 n.13 (1979), reprinted *infra*; *United States v. United States Gypsum*

Co., 438 U.S. 422, 458 (1978), reprinted *infra*. Just as in *Chroma Lighting*, those decisions involved secondary line applications of the Robinson-Patman Act.

PROBLEM 8.1

Steel, Inc. manufactures steel which is sold to various fabricators for a variety of purposes. Steel, Inc. also owns some fabrication plants itself. Some of these plants are carried in Steel, Inc.'s organizational structure as unincorporated divisions. Others are separately incorporated and listed as wholly-owned subsidiaries. Like most large firms, Steel, Inc. supplies steel to its divisional and subsidiary fabricators through a transfer pricing mechanism. That is, the steel is sold from Steel, Inc., to the division or subsidiary that will fabricate it, even though the division or subsidiary is wholly owned by Steel, Inc.

One of the unincorporated divisional plants fabricates steel into bridge girders. Bridge Co. is also a fabricator of steel bridge girders in competition with Steel, Inc.'s divisional fabricator. Steel, Inc. sells its own divisional plant steel for $4.00 per unit, while it charges Bridge Co. $5.00 per unit. Bridge Co. brings an action charging Steel, Inc. with violating the Robinson-Patman Act by discriminating in price in favor of its divisional plant. What outcome?

One of Steel, Inc.'s separately incorporated but wholly owned subsidiaries is called Hunter Chassis Co. Hunter makes automobile chassis out of steel in competition with an independent company, Bodyworks, Inc. Once again, Steel, Inc. sells its own subsidiary, Hunter, steel for $4.00 per unit, while it charges Bodyworks $5.00 per unit. Bodyworks also brings a Robinson-Patman case against Steel, Inc. What outcome? Should the outcome in the second case be the same as or different from that in the first case? Why? Is the Supreme Court's decision interpreting the Sherman Act in *Copperweld Corp. v. Independence Tube Corp.*, 467 U.S. 752 (1984) (reprinted in Chapter 4, *supra*) relevant? Why or why not? *See Russ' Kwik Car Wash v. Marathon Petroleum Co.*, 772 F.2d 214 (9th Cir. 1985), especially Judge Kennedy's dissent. Suppose that Hunter Chassis was only partly owned by Steel, Inc.? For example, suppose Steel, Inc. owned 60% of Hunter's shares while the remaining 40% were owned by others? Suppose Steel, Inc. owned only 20% of Hunter's shares? *See Danko v. Shell Oil Co.*, 115 F. Supp. 886 (E.D.N.Y. 1953); *Parrish v. Cox*, 586 F.2d 9 (6th Cir. 1978); *City of Mt. Pleasant v. Associated Elec. Coop.*, 838 F.2d 268, 278-79 (8th Cir. 1988); Shelanski, Comment, *Robinson-Patman Act Regulation of Intra-Enterprise Pricing*, 80 Calif. L. Rev. 247 (1992).

J. TRUETT PAYNE CO. V. CHRYSLER MOTORS CORP.

451 U.S. 557 (1981)

JUSTICE REHNQUIST delivered the opinion of the Court.

The question presented in this case is the appropriate measure of damages in a suit brought under § 2(a) of the Clayton Act, as amended by the Robinson-Patman Act.

Petitioner, for several decades a Chrysler-Plymouth dealer in Birmingham, Ala., went out of business in 1974. It subsequently brought suit against respondent in the United States District Court for the Northern District of Alabama, alleging that from January 1970 to May 1974 respondent's various "sales incentive" programs violated § 2(a). Under one type of program, respondent assigned to each participating dealer a sales objective and paid to the dealer a bonus on each car sold in excess of that objective. Under another type of program, respondent required each dealer to purchase from it a certain quota of automobiles before it would pay a bonus on the sale of automobiles sold at retail. The amount of the bonus depended on the number of retail sales (or wholesale purchases) made in excess of the dealer's objective, and could amount to several hundred dollars. Respondent set petitioner's objectives higher than those of its competitors, requiring it to sell (or purchase) more automobiles to obtain a bonus than its competitors. To the extent petitioner failed to meet those objectives and to the extent its competitors met their lower objectives, petitioner received fewer bonuses. The net effect of all this, according to petitioner, was that it paid more money for its automobiles than did its competitors. It contended that the amount of the price discrimination — the amount of the price difference multiplied by the number of petitioner's purchases — was $81,248. It also claimed that the going-concern value of the business as of May 1974 ranged between $50,000 and $170,000.

....

Petitioner first contends that once it has proved a price discrimination in violation of § 2(a) it is entitled at a minimum to so-called "automatic damages" in the amount of the price discrimination. Petitioner concedes that in order to recover damages it must establish cognizable injury attributable to an antitrust violation and some approximation of damage. It insists, however, that the jury should be permitted to infer the requisite injury and damage from a showing of a substantial price discrimination. Petitioner notes that this Court has consistently permitted such injury to be inferred in injunctive actions brought to enforce § 2(a), *e.g.,* *FTC v. Morton Salt Co.,* 334 U.S. 37 (1948), and argues that private suits for damages under § 4 should be treated no differently. We disagree.

By its terms § 2(a) is a prophylactic statute which is violated merely upon a showing that "the effect of such discrimination *may be* substantially to lessen competition." (Emphasis supplied.) As our cases have recognized, the statute does not "require that the discriminations must in fact have harmed competition." Section 4 of the Clayton Act, in contrast, is essentially a remedial statute. It provides treble damages to "[a]ny person who *shall be injured* in his business or property by reason of anything forbidden in the antitrust laws ...." (Emphasis supplied.) To recover treble damages, then, a plaintiff must make some showing of actual injury attributable to something the antitrust laws were designed to prevent....

Our decision here is virtually governed by our reasoning in *Brunswick Corp. v. Pueblo Bowl-O-Mat, Inc.,* 429 U.S. 477 (1977). There we rejected the contention that the mere violation of § 7 of the Clayton Act, which prohibits mergers which *may* substantially lessen competition, gives rise to a damages claim under § 4. We explained that "to recover damages [under § 4] respondents must prove more than that the petitioner violated § 7, since such proof establishes only that injury may result." *Id.*, at 486. Likewise in this case, proof of a violation does not mean that a disfavored purchaser has been actually "injured" within the meaning of § 4.

....

Petitioner next contends that even though it may not be entitled to "automatic damages" upon a showing of a violation of § 2(a), it produced enough evidence of actual injury to survive a motion for a directed verdict. That evidence consisted primarily of the testimony of petitioner's owner, Mr. Payne, and an expert witness, a professor of economics. Payne testified that the price discrimination was one of the causes of the dealership going out of business....

Neither Payne nor petitioner's expert witness offered documentary evidence as to the effect of the discrimination on retail prices. Although Payne asserted that his salesmen and customers told him that the dealership was being undersold, he admitted he did not know if his competitors did in fact pass on their lower costs to their customers. Petitioner's expert witness took a somewhat different position. He believed that the discrimination would ultimately cause retail prices to be held at an artificially high level since petitioner's competitors would not reduce their retail prices as much as they would have done if petitioner received an equal bonus from respondent. He also testified that petitioner was harmed by the discrimination even if the favored purchasers did not lower their retail prices, since petitioner in that case would make less money per car.

Even construed most favorably to petitioner, the evidence of injury is weak. Petitioner nevertheless asks us to consider the sufficiency of its evidence in light of our traditional rule excusing antitrust plaintiffs from an unduly rigorous standard of proving antitrust injury....

... In the first place, it is a close question whether petitioner's evidence would be sufficient to support a jury award even under our relaxed damages rules. In those cases where we have found sufficient evidence to permit a jury to infer antitrust injury and approximate the amount of damages, the evidence was more substantial than the evidence presented here. In *Zenith* [*Radio Corp. v. Hazeltine Research, Inc.*, 395 U.S. 100], for example, plaintiff compared its sales in Canada, where it was subject to a violation, with its sales in the United States, where it was not. And in *Bigelow* [*v. RKO Radio Pictures, Inc.*, 327 U.S. 251], plaintiff adduced evidence not only comparing its profits with a competitor not subject to the violation but also comparing its profits during the time of the violation with the period immediately preceding the violation.

But a more fundamental difficulty confronts us in this case. The cases relied upon by petitioner all depend in greater or lesser part on the inequity of a wrongdoer defeating the recovery of damages against him by insisting upon a rigorous standard of proof. In this case, however, we cannot say with assurance that respondent is a "wrongdoer." Because the court below bypassed the issue of liability and went directly to the issue of damages, we simply do not have the benefit of its views as to whether respondent in fact violated § 2(a). Absent such a finding, we decline to apply to this case the lenient damages rules of our previous cases. Had the court below found a violation, we could more confidently consider the adequacy of petitioner's evidence.

Accordingly, we think the proper course is to remand the case so that the Court of Appeals may pass upon respondent's contention that the evidence adduced at trial was insufficient to support a finding of violation of the Robinson-Patman Act.... We emphasize that even if there has been a violation of the Robinson-Patman Act, petitioner is not excused from its burden of proving antitrust injury and damages. It is simply that once a violation has been established, that burden is to some extent lightened.

NOTES AND QUESTIONS

1. Is *J. Truett Payne* consistent with *Morton Salt* (decided earlier) and *Hasbrouck* (decided later)? In *Brunswick Corp. v. Pueblo Bowl-O-Mat, Inc.*, 429 U.S. 477 (1977), the Supreme Court held that in order to recover damages a private antitrust plaintiff must show "antitrust injury" — that is, "injury of the type that the antitrust laws were intended to prevent and that flows from that which makes the defendants' acts unlawful." However, in *Morton Salt* did not the Supreme Court identify the fact that small grocers had to pay a higher price for salt than large grocers as the lessening of competition that the Robinson-Patman Act was aimed at? Didn't it do the same thing in *Hasbrouck*?

2. On remand the Fifth Circuit noted that the plaintiff 's sales actually increased during the period in which it was allegedly the victim of its supplier's price discrimination. It dismissed the complaint, concluding that there was no injury to competition among dealers. In fact, the competition became more intense. The Fifth Circuit virtually required that in order to show antitrust injury in a secondary-line price discrimination case, the plaintiff must show that it lost substantial sales or was driven from business as a result of the defendant's price discrimination scheme. Is it plausible that a manufacturer of cars would want to use a price discrimination scheme such as incentive rebates in order to drive a poorly performing dealership out of business? Why not simply terminate the dealership?

3. The "Dealer Incentive Plan" at issue in *J. Truett Payne* is part of a scheme of partial vertical integration, designed by Chrysler to make its dealers operate more efficiently. If Chrysler owned and operated its retail dealerships, then it could hire, fire, and generally supervise retail operations. A manufacturer that sells through independent dealers must find more indirect mechanisms, however, for ensuring the efficiency of its outlets. Chrysler's answer was to reward its dealers who performed well and penalize the ones who did not. Dealers who met their sales quotas or exceeded them paid a lower net cost per car than dealers who failed to meet their quotas. That does not necessarily mean, however, that the different net prices charged to efficient and inefficient dealers were discriminatory.

Perhaps it cost Chrysler more money to sell through inefficient dealers: they are more likely to go out of business; they may be slower in paying for cars; they may produce more dissatisfied customers who will not come back to Chrysler for another car. The question whether a dealer incentive program is actually discriminatory illustrates the enormous difficulty of determining a seller's true marginal costs with respect to any transaction.

FTC V. HENRY BROCH & CO.

363 U.S. 166 (1960)

JUSTICE DOUGLAS delivered the opinion of the Court.

Section 2(c) of the Clayton Act ... makes it unlawful for "any person" to make an allowance in lieu of "brokerage" to the "other party to such transaction." The question is whether that prohibition is applicable to the following transactions by respondent.

Respondent is a broker or sales representative for a number of principals who sell food products. One of the principals is Canada Foods Ltd., a processor of apple concentrate and other products. Respondent agreed to act for Canada Foods for a 5% commission. Other brokers working for the same principal were promised a 4% commission. Respondent's commission was higher because it stocked merchandise in advance of sales. Canada Foods established a price for its 1954 pack of apple concentrate at $1.30 per gallon in 50-gallon drums and authorized its brokers to negotiate sales at that price.

The J. M. Smucker Co., a buyer, negotiated with another broker, Phipps, also working for Canada Foods, for apple concentrate. Smucker wanted a lower price than $1.30 but Canada Foods would not agree. Smucker finally offered $1.25 for a 500-gallon purchase. That was turned down by Canada Foods, acting through Phipps. Canada Foods took the position that the only way the price could be lowered would be through reduction in brokerage. About the same time respondent was negotiating with Smucker. Canada Foods told respondent what it had told Phipps, that the price to the buyer could be reduced only if the brokerage were cut; and it added that it would make the sale at $1.25 — the buyer's bid — if respondent would agree to reduce its brokerage from 5% to 3%. Respondent agreed and the sale was consummated at that price and for that brokerage. The reduced price of $1.25 was thereafter granted Smucker on subsequent sales. But on sales to all other customers, whether through respondent or other brokers, the price continued to be $1.30 and in each instance respondent received the full 5% commission. Only on sales through respondent to Smucker were the selling price and the brokerage reduced.

The customary brokerage fee of 5% to respondent would have been $2,036.84. The actual brokerage of 3% received by respondent was $1,222.11. The reduction of brokerage was $814.73 which is 50% of the total price reduction of $1,629.47 granted by Canada Foods to Smucker.

....

The Robinson-Patman Act was enacted in 1936 to curb and prohibit all devices by which large buyers gained discriminatory preferences over smaller ones by virtue of their greater purchasing power. A lengthy investigation revealed that large chain buyers were obtaining competitive advantages in several ways other than direct price concessions and were thus avoiding the impact of the Clayton Act. One of the favorite means of obtaining an indirect price concession was by setting up "dummy" brokers who were employed by the buyer and who, in many cases, rendered no services. The large buyers demanded that the seller pay "brokerage" to these fictitious brokers who then turned it over to their employer. This practice was one of the chief targets of § 2(c) of the Act. But it was not the only means by which the brokerage function was abused and Congress in its wisdom phrased § 2(c) broadly, not only to cover the other methods then in existence but all other means by which brokerage could be used to effect price discrimination....

It is urged that the seller is free to pass on to the buyer in the form of a price reduction any differential between his ordinary brokerage expense and the brokerage commission which he pays on a particular sale because § 2(a) of the Act permits price differentials based on savings in selling costs resulting from differing methods of distribution. From this premise it is reasoned that a seller's broker should not be held to have violated § 2(c) for having done that which is permitted under § 2(a). We need not decide the validity of that premise, because the fact that a transaction may not violate one section of the Act does not answer the question whether another section has been violated. Section 2(c), with which we are here concerned, is independent of § 2(a) and was enacted by Congress because § 2(a) was not considered adequate to deal with abuses of the brokerage function.

....

The fact that the buyer was not aware that its favored price was based in part on a discriminatory reduction in respondent's brokerage commission is immaterial. The Act is aimed at price discrimination, not conspiracy. The buyer's intent might be relevant were he charged with receiving an allowance in violation of § 2(c). But certainly it has no bearing on whether the respondent has violated the law. The powerful buyer who demands a price concession is concerned only with getting it. He does not care whether it comes from the seller, the seller's broker, or both.

Congress enacted the Robinson-Patman Act to prevent sellers and sellers' brokers from yielding to the economic pressures of a large buying organization by granting unfair preferences in connection with the sale of goods. The form in which the buyer pressure is exerted is immaterial and proof of its existence is not required. It is rare that the motive in yielding to a buyer's demands is not the "necessity" for making the sale. An "independent" broker is not likely to be independent of the buyer's coercive bargaining power. He, like the seller, is constrained to favor the buyers with the most purchasing power. If respondent merely paid over part of his commission to the buyer, he clearly would have violated the Act. We see no distinction of substance between the two transactions. In each case the seller and his broker make a concession to the buyer as a consequence of his economic power. In both cases the result is that the buyer has received a discriminatory price. In both cases the seller's broker reduces his usual brokerage fee to get a particular contract. There is no difference in economic effect between the seller's broker splitting his brokerage commission with the buyer and his yielding part of the brokerage to the seller to be passed on to the buyer in the form of a lower price.

....

It is suggested that reversal of this case would establish an irrevocable floor under commission rates. We think that view has no foundation in fact or in law. Both before and after the sales to Smucker, respondent continued to charge the usual 5% on sales to other buyers. There is nothing in the Act, nor is there anything in this case, to require him to continue to charge 5% on sales to all customers. A price reduction based upon alleged savings in brokerage expenses is an "allowance in lieu of brokerage" when given only to favored customers. Had respondent, for example, agreed to accept a 3% commission on all sales to all buyers there plainly would be no room for finding that the price reductions were violations of § 2(c).

....

NOTES AND QUESTIONS

What does the *Henry Broch* decision do to the concept of the independent broker, whose job is to bring a buyer and seller together, sometimes, if necessary, by reducing her own commission in order to reach a net price that is acceptable to both buyer and seller?

The legislative history of the Robinson-Patman Act reveals that the Congress that passed it may have been anticompetitive; however, was it as anticompetitive as the Supreme Court's decision in *Broch*? The legislative history reveals that section 2(c) was designed to deal with "phony" brokerage allowances, given when there was no real broker at all, but when a large buyer performed certain services traditionally performed by the independent broker. In such cases, the seller might charge a uniform price but subtract a 5% "brokerage allowance" even though no broker participated. Justice Whittaker's dissent, not reprinted here, contains a long analysis of the legislative history of section 2(c). Clearly, Justice Whittaker noted, the statute does not forbid brokerage allowances for brokerage services actually performed. In this case, not only were brokerage services actually performed, but there was a real independent broker actually performing them!

B. COMMODITIES OF "LIKE GRADE AND QUALITY"

FTC V. BORDEN CO.

383 U.S. 637 (1966)

JUSTICE WHITE delivered the opinion of the Court.

The Borden Company, respondent here, produces and sells evaporated milk under the Borden name, a nationally advertised brand. At the same time Borden packs and markets evaporated milk under various private brands owned by its customers. This milk is physically and chemically identical with the milk it distributes under its own brand but is sold at both the wholesale and retail level at prices regularly below those obtained for the Borden brand milk. The Federal Trade Commission found the milk sold under the Borden and the private labels to be of like grade and quality as required for the applicability of § 2(a) of the Robinson-Patman Act .... The Court of Appeals set aside the Commission's order on the sole ground that as a matter of law, the customer label milk was not of the same grade and quality as the milk sold under the Borden brand....

... Here, because the milk bearing the Borden brand regularly sold at a higher price than did the milk with a buyer's label, the court considered the products to be "commercially" different and hence of different "grade" for the purposes of § 2(a), even though they were physically identical and of equal quality. Although a mere difference in brand would not in itself demonstrate a difference in grade, decided consumer preference for one brand over another, reflected in the willingness to pay a higher price for the well-known brand, was, in the view of the Court of Appeals, sufficient to differentiate chemically identical products and to place the price differential beyond the reach of § 2(a).

We reject this construction of § 2(a), as did both the examiner and the Commission in this case....

Obviously there is nothing in the language of the statute indicating that grade, as distinguished from quality, is not to be determined by the characteristics of the product itself, but by consumer preferences, brand acceptability or what customers think of it and are willing to pay for it. Moreover, what legislative history there is concerning this question supports the Commission's construction of the statute rather than that of the Court of Appeals.

....

The Commission's construction of the statute also appears to us to further the purpose and policy of the Robinson-Patman Act. Subject to specified exceptions and defenses, § 2(a) proscribes unequal treatment of different customers in comparable transactions, but only if there is the requisite effect upon competition, actual or potential. But if the transactions are deemed to involve goods of disparate grade or quality, the section has no application at all and the Commission never reaches either the issue of discrimination or that of anticompetitive impact. We doubt that Congress intended to foreclose these inquiries in situations where a single seller markets the identical product under several different brands, whether his own, his customers' or both. Such transactions are too laden with potential discrimination and adverse competitive effect to be excluded from the reach of § 2(a) by permitting a difference in grade to be established by the label alone or by the label and its consumer appeal.

If two products, physically identical but differently branded, are to be deemed of different grade because the seller regularly and successfully markets some quantity of both at different prices, the seller could, as far as § 2(a) is concerned, make either product available to some customers and deny it to others, however discriminatory this might be and however damaging to competition. Those who were offered only one of the two products would be barred from competing for those customers who want or might buy the other. The retailer who was permitted to buy and sell only the more expensive brand would have no chance to sell to those who always buy the cheaper product or to convince others, by experience or otherwise, of the fact which he and all other dealers already know — that the cheaper product is actually identical with that carrying the more expensive label.

The seller, to escape the Act, would have only to succeed in selling some unspecified amount of each product to some unspecified portion of his customers, however large or small the price differential might be. The seller's pricing and branding policy, by being successful, would apparently validate itself by creating a difference in "grade" and thus taking itself beyond the purview of the Act.

Our holding neither ignores the economic realities of the marketplace nor denies that some labels will command a higher price than others, at least from some portion of the public. But it does mean that "the economic factors inherent in brand names and national advertising should not be considered in the jurisdictional inquiry under the statutory 'like grade and quality' test."…

NOTES AND QUESTIONS

1. The Court's opinion sees something "illegitimate" about using advertising to create differential consumer preferences. Suppose that Borden's cost of producing milk was $1.00 per gallon, excluding advertising. Assume further that the only difference between the name brand and the private brand milk was that Borden spent 25 cents per gallon advertising the former, but nothing advertising the latter. Borden then sells the name brand for $1.25 and the private brand for $1.00. In this case Borden has not engaged in economic price discrimination: its ratio of price to marginal cost is the same in both sets of sales. However, under the reasoning of the majority opinion the advertising costs are irrelevant to the question whether or not the products are of "like grade or quality," even though the apparent result of the advertising is that consumers differentiate between the products.

Ultimately the Supreme Court's opinion forces us to some decision about how much consumers need to be protected from their own choices. The Chicago School of antitrust analysis generally regards the consumer as free and able to make his or her own choices in the marketplace. If the consumer wishes to pay 25 cents more for an advertised product than for a chemically identical but unadvertised product, that is the consumer's business. But what if the advertising created the impression that Borden's name brand milk was somehow better than its house brand milk? One way to solve that problem, of course, is to regulate the content of advertising, and the Federal Trade Commission does that extensively. Another way, however, might be to force Borden to charge the same price for its advertised milk as for its unadvertised milk. However, the latter remedy goes too far, does it not? The result would be to eliminate *all* advertising of Borden milk, not just false or misleading advertising.

2. In *A. A. Poultry Farms v. Rose Acre Farms*, 881 F.2d 1396, 1407-08 (7th Cir. 1989), *cert. denied*, 494 U.S. 1019 (1990), the court concluded that the "like grade and quality" requirement was not met with respect to two sets of transactions. In the first set, the seller picked the sizes; in the second set, the buyer picked them. In effect, the defendant boxed random-sized eggs as the chickens laid them. If a customer was willing to take such a box, it paid the lower price. But if a customer insisted on having only "extra large," it paid a higher price. In comparing these two transactions the court said "they are not fundamentally the same good, for the same reason that a seat on the 6:00 a.m. flight from Chicago to New York is not the same as a seat on the 5:00 p.m. flight, and a seat ... reserved two weeks in advance is not the same as a seat on that flight for which the passenger had to stand by."

C. DEFENSES

The Robinson-Patman Act explicitly recognizes two affirmative defenses. Section 2(a) (15 U.S.C. § 13(a)) exempts price "differentials which make only due allowance for differences in the cost of manufacture, sale, or delivery resulting from the differing methods or quantities in which such commodities are to such purchasers sold or delivered." Section 2(b) (15 U.S.C. § 13(b)) permits a seller to rebut a prima facie case of violation "by showing that his lower price or the furnishing of services or facilities to any purchaser or purchasers was made in good faith to meet an equally low price of a competitor, or the services or facilities furnished by a competitor."

The defenses are generally called the "cost justification" defense and the "meeting competition" defense, respectively. Both are affirmative defenses: they are raised after the plaintiff has made out a prima facie case, and in claiming the defenses the defendant has the burden of proof.

1. THE "COST JUSTIFICATION" DEFENSE

The cost justification language of section 2(a) of the Robinson-Patman Act has the potential to turn the Act at least halfway into a price discrimination statute, rather than a price difference statute. It explicitly permits a defendant to avoid liability by showing that differential price treatment to two buyers was cost justified — i.e., that the seller had a higher marginal cost with respect to the disfavored buyer than he did for the favored buyer.

In fact, however, the courts have been quite restrictive in their interpretation of the "cost justification" defense. It has not rescued many defendants.

UNITED STATES V. BORDEN CO.

370 U.S. 460 (1962)

JUSTICE CLARK delivered the opinion of the Court.

This is a direct appeal from a judgment dismissing the Government's Section 2(a) Clayton Act suit in which it sought an injunction against the selling of fluid milk products by the appellees, The Borden Company and Bowman Dairy Company, at prices which discriminate between independently owned grocery stores and grocery store chains. The District Court in an unreported decision found the pricing plan of each dairy to be a prima facie violation of § 2(a) but concluded that these discriminatory prices were legalized by the cost justification proviso of § 2(a), which permits price differentials as long as they "make only due allowance for differences in the cost of manufacture, sale, or delivery resulting from the differing methods or quantities in which such commodities are to such purchasers sold or delivered."...

....

... Both appellees are major distributors of fluid milk products in metropolitan Chicago. The sales of both dairies to retail stores during the period in question were handled under plans which gave most of their customers — the independently owned stores — percentage discounts off list price which increased with the volume of their purchases to a specified maximum while granting a few customers — the grocery store chains — a flat discount without reference to volume and substantially greater than the maximum discount available under the volume plan offered independent stores. These discounts were made effective through schedules which appeared to cover all stores; however, the schedules were modified by private letters to the grocery chains confirming their higher discounts. Although the two sets of discounts were never officially labeled "independent" and "chain" prices, they were treated, called, and regarded as such throughout the record.

....

The Borden pricing system produced two classes of customers. The two chains, A & P and Jewel, with their combined total of 254 stores constituted one class. The 1,322 independent stores, grouped in four brackets based on the volume of their purchases, made up the other. Borden's cost justification was built on comparisons of its average cost per $100 of sales to the chains in relation to the average cost of similar sales to each of the four groups of independents. The costs considered were personnel (including routemen, clerical and sales employees), truck expenses, and losses on bad debts and returned milk. Various methods of cost allocation were utilized: Drivers' time spent at each store was charged directly to that store; certain clerical expenses were allocated between the two general classes; costs not susceptible of either of the foregoing were charged to the various stores on a per stop, per store, or volume basis.

Bowman's cost justification was based on differences in volume and methods of delivery. It relied heavily upon a study of the cost per minute of its routemen's time. It determined that substantial portions of this time were devoted to three operations, none of which were ever performed for the 163 stores operated by its two major chain customers. These added work steps arose from the method of collection, *i.e.*, cash on delivery and the delayed collections connected therewith, and the performance of "optional customer services." The customer services, performed with varying frequency depending upon the circumstances, included "services that the driver may be requested to do, such as deliver the order inside, place the containers in a refrigerator, rearrange containers so that any product remaining unsold from yesterday will be sold first today, leave cases of products at different spots in the store, etc." The experts conducting the study calculated as to these elements a "standard" cost per unit of product delivered: the aggregate time required to perform the services, as determined by sample time studies, was divided by the total number of units of product delivered. In essence, the Bowman justification was merely a comparison of the cost of these services in relation to the disparity between the chain and independent prices. Although it was shown that the five sample independents in the Government's prima facie case received the added services, it was not shown or found that all 2,500 independents supplied by Bowman partook of them. On the basis of its studies Bowman estimated that about two-thirds of the independent stores received the "optional customer services" on a daily basis and that "most store customers pay the driver in cash daily."

    ... The Government candidly recognizes in its briefs filed in the instant case that "[a]s a matter of practical necessity ... when a seller deals with a very large number of customers, he cannot be required to establish different cost-reflecting prices for each customer." In this same vein, the practice of grouping customers for pricing purposes has long had the approval of the Federal Trade Commission. We ourselves have noted the "elusiveness of cost data in a Robinson-Patman Act proceeding." *Automatic Canteen Co. v. Federal Trade Comm'n*, 346 U.S. 61, 68 (1953). In short, to completely renounce class pricing as justified by class accounting would be to eliminate in practical effect the cost justification proviso as to sellers having a large number of purchasers, thereby preventing such sellers from passing on economies to their customers. It seems hardly necessary to say that such a result is at war with Congress' language and purpose.

    But this is not to say that price differentials can be justified on the basis of arbitrary classifications or even classifications which are representative of a numerical majority of the individual members. At some point practical considerations shade into a circumvention of the proviso. A balance is struck by the use of classes for cost justification which are composed of members of such selfsameness as to make the averaging of the cost of dealing with the group a valid and reasonable indicium of the cost of dealing with any specific group member. High on the list of "musts" in the use of the average cost of customer groupings under the proviso of § 2(a) is a close resemblance of the individual members of each group on the essential point or points which determine the costs considered.

In this regard we do not find the classifications submitted by the appellees to have been shown to be of sufficient homogeneity. Certainly, the cost factors considered were not necessarily encompassed within the manner in which a customer is owned. Turning first to Borden's justification, we note that it not only failed to show that the economies relied upon were isolated within the favored class but affirmatively revealed that members of the classes utilized were substantially unlike in the cost saving aspects considered. For instance, the favorable cost comparisons between the chains and the larger independents were for the greater part controlled by the higher average volume of the chain stores in comparison to the average volume of the 80-member class to which these independents were relegated. The District Court allowed this manner of justification because "most chain stores do purchase larger volumes of milk than do most independent stores." However, such a grouping for cost justification purposes, composed as it is of some independents having volumes comparable to, and in some cases larger than, that of the chain stores, created artificial disparities between the larger independents and the chain stores. It is like averaging one horse and one rabbit. As the Federal Trade Commission said in *In the Matter of Champion Spark Plug Co.*, 50 F.T.C. 30, 43 (1953): "A cost justification based on the difference between an estimated average cost of selling to one or two large customers and an average cost of selling to all other customers cannot be accepted as a defense to a charge of price discrimination." This volume gap between the larger independents and the chain stores was further widened by grouping together the two chains, thereby raising the average volume of the stores of the smaller of the two chains in relation to the larger independents. Nor is the vice in the Borden class justification solely in the paper volumes relied upon, for it attributed to many independents cost factors which were not true indicia of the cost of dealing with those particular consumers. To illustrate, each independent was assigned a portion of the total expenses involved in daily cash collections, although it was not shown that all independents paid cash and in fact Borden admitted only that a "large majority" did so.

Likewise the details of Bowman's cost study show a failure in classification. Only one additional point need be made. Its justification emphasized its costs for "optional customer service" and daily cash collection with the resulting "delay to collect." As shown by its study these elements were crucial to Bowman's cost justification. In the study the experts charged all independents and no chain store with these costs. Yet, it was not shown that all independents received these services daily or even on some lesser basis. Bowman's studies indicated only that a large majority of independents took these services on a daily basis. Under such circumstances the use of these cost factors across the board in calculating independent store costs is not a permissible justification, for it possibly allocates costs to some independents whose mode of purchasing does not give rise to them. The burden was upon the profferer of the classification to negate this possibility, and this burden has not been met here. If these factors control the cost of dealing, then their presence or absence might with more justification be the password for admission into the various price categories.

....

In sum, the record here shows that price discriminations have been permitted on the basis of cost differences between broad customer groupings, apparently based on the nature of ownership but in any event not shown to be so homogeneous as to permit the joining together of these purchasers for cost allocations purposes. If this is the only justification for appellees' pricing schemes, they are illegal....

NOTES AND QUESTIONS

1. All classification schemes contain a certain amount of arbitrariness, do they not? Borden serviced about 1,300 stores and Bowman about 2,500. In all likelihood neither dairy had identical marginal costs for servicing any two stores. Each one was a slightly different distance from the storage facility, and each needed a slightly different combination of services. Simple differences, such as whether the delivery agent had to walk up a flight of stairs, affected the marginal cost of selling milk to a particular grocery store. In order to justify its costs, therefore, Borden must either produce its precise marginal cost for each of its 1,300 stores — certainly an impossible task — or else it must group together stores that impose relatively close, although not identical, marginal costs.

2. If Borden and Bowman are competitors, both with each other and with other dairies, would it be to their advantage to set truly discriminatory price schedules (i.e., schedules in which the price differentials could not be cost justified)? Any particular grocer would buy from the dairy that gave it the best price. In a competitive market, the price lists would naturally tend toward the cost of servicing the buyers who fell within a particular category. Any class of buyers charged a price above marginal cost would switch to another seller.

3. Because of the difficulties imposed by the Supreme Court in *Borden*, the cost justification defense has proved somewhat illusive. Courts have frequently rejected expensive studies undertaken by defendants to show cost justification. The courts have generally held either that the studies did not account for all elements of cost, or that the studies grouped buyers who were not sufficiently homogeneous. In many of these cases the defendant clearly had no market power. *See, e.g., Allied Accessories & Auto Parts Co. v. General Motors Corp.*, 825 F.2d 971, 977 (6th Cir. 1987). The defendant GM had one low-priced buyer of filters who had agreed not to obtain promotional brochures, catalogs, field representative services, or GM-sponsored incentive programs normally offered to automobile parts distributors. GM then averaged the costs of giving these services to all the other distributors (about 2000 in number) and asserted that this average was no greater than the discrimination in price. The court rejected the methodology because: (1) the high-priced set of customers was never offered the option of foregoing the same set of services as well; (2) there was a great deal of diversity in the services given to the various 2000 customers, none of which was accounted for in GM's "average" figures; and (3) although the additional services were *offered* to most customers in the larger class, many did not claim them and the others claimed them in varying degrees. What would GM have to do in order to satisfy these objections?

Nevertheless, a few defendants have been able to assert the defense successfully. *See, e.g., Acadia Motors, Inc. v. Ford Motor Co.*, 44 F.3d 1050 (1st Cir. 1995) (differential warranty reimbursement rates found to be cost justified); *Americom Distrib. Corp. v. ACS Communications, Inc.*, 990 F.2d 223 (5th Cir.), *cert. denied*, 510 U.S. 867 (1993) (lower price on larger order cost justified).

2. THE "MEETING COMPETITION" DEFENSE

Section 2(b) of the Robinson-Patman Act, 15 U.S.C. § 13(b), provides that a defendant seller can rebut a prima facie case of unlawful price discrimination "by showing that his lower price or the furnishing of services or facilities to any purchaser or purchasers was made in good faith to meet an equally low price of a competitor, or the services or facilities furnished by a competitor." Case law developing the defense has become entangled in many complexities, such as what constitutes "good faith," and whether someone who actually bids lower than a competitor has merely "met" competition or has beaten it and thus falls outside the protection of the defense. For some of these complexities *see* Kuenzel & Schiffres, *Making Sense of Robinson-Patman: The Need to Revitalize Its Affirmative Defenses*, 62 Va. L. Rev. 1211 (1976).

In recent years the United States Supreme Court has substantially restructured the "Meeting Competition" defense, in the following two opinions.

UNITED STATES V. UNITED STATES GYPSUM CO.
438 U.S. 422 (1978)

[The first part of this opinion is reprinted in Chapter 4.]

[In *FTC v. A. E. Staley Mfg. Co.*, 324 U.S. 746 (1945), the Supreme Court held that in order to justify a low-price sale under the meeting competition defense, a seller had to rely on more than rumors about a competitor's prices. The Court concluded that discriminatory bids "made in response to verbal information received from salesmen, brokers or intending purchasers, without supporting evidence" were not made with sufficient "good faith" to qualify for the defense.

[The defendants in *United States Gypsum* were competitors who exchanged price information in violation of *United States v. Container Corp. of Am.*, 393 U.S. 333 (1969); see Chapter 4. The defendants argued that under the *Staley* holding the information exchanges were necessary for them to "investigate or verify" a competitor's price so that they could meet its competition in good faith.]

CHIEF JUSTICE BURGER delivered the opinion of the Court.

....

Staley's "investigate or verify" language coupled with *Corn Products'* focus on "personal knowledge of the transactions" have apparently suggested to a number of courts that, at least in certain circumstances, direct verification of discounts between competitors may be necessary to meet the burden-of-proof requirements of the § 2(b) defense....

A good-faith belief, rather than absolute certainty, that a price concession is being offered to meet an equally low price offered by a competitor is sufficient to satisfy the § 2(b) defense. While casual reliance on uncorroborated reports of buyers or sales representatives without further investigation may not, as we noted earlier, be sufficient to make the requisite showing of good faith, nothing in the language of § 2(b) or the gloss on that language in *Staley* and *Corn Products* indicates that direct discussions of price between competitors are required....

The so-called problem of the untruthful buyer which concerned the Court of Appeals does not in our view call for a different approach to the § 2(b) defense. The good-faith standard remains the benchmark against which the seller's conduct is to be evaluated, and we agree with the Government and the FTC that this standard can be satisfied by efforts falling short of interseller verification in most circumstances where the seller has only vague, generalized doubts about the reliability of its commercial adversary — the buyer. Given the fact-specific nature of the inquiry, it is difficult to predict all the factors the FTC or a court would consider in appraising a seller's good faith in matching a competing offer in these circumstances. Certainly, evidence that a seller had received reports of similar discounts from other customers; or was threatened with a termination of purchases if the discount were not met, would be relevant in this regard. Efforts to corroborate the reported discount by seeking documentary evidence or by appraising its reasonableness in terms of available market data would also be probative as would the seller's past experience with the particular buyer in question.

There remains the possibility that in a limited number of situations a seller may have substantial reasons to doubt the accuracy of reports of a competing offer and may be unable to corroborate such reports in any of the generally accepted ways. Thus the defense may be rendered unavailable since unanswered questions about the reliability of a buyer's representations may well be inconsistent with a good-faith belief that a competing offer had in fact been made. As an abstract proposition, resort to interseller verification as a means of checking the buyer's reliability seems a possible solution to the seller's plight, but careful examination reveals serious problems with the practice.

Both economic theory and common human experience suggest that interseller verification — if undertaken on an isolated and infrequent basis with no provision for reciprocity or co-operation — will not serve its putative function of corroborating the representations of unreliable buyers regarding the existence of competing offers. Price concessions by oligopolists generally yield competitive advantages only if secrecy can be maintained; when the terms of the concession are made publicly known, other competitors are likely to follow and any advantage to the initiator is lost in the process.... Thus, if one seller offers a price concession for the purpose of winning over one of his competitor's customers, it is unlikely that the same seller will freely inform its competitor of the details of the concession so that it can be promptly matched and diffused. Instead, such a seller would appear to have at least as great an incentive to misrepresent the existence or size of the discount as would the buyer who received it. Thus verification, if undertaken on a one-shot basis for the sole purpose of complying with the § 2(b) defense, does not hold out much promise as a means of shoring up buyers' representations.

The other variety of interseller verification is, like the conduct charged in the instant case, undertaken pursuant to an agreement, either tacit or express, providing for reciprocity among competitors in the exchange of price information. Such an agreement would make little economic sense, in our view, if its sole purpose were to guarantee all participants the opportunity to match the secret price concessions of other participants under § 2(b). For in such circumstances, each seller would know that his price concession could not be kept from his competitors and no seller participating in the information-exchange arrangement would, therefore, have any incentive for deviating from the prevailing price level in the industry. See *United States v. Container Corp.* Regardless of its putative purpose, the most likely consequence of any such agreement to exchange price information would be the stabilization of industry prices. Instead of facilitating use of the § 2(b) defense, such an agreement would have the effect of eliminating the very price concessions which provide the main element of competition in oligopolistic industries and the primary occasion for resort to the meeting-competition defense.

Especially in oligopolistic industries such as the gypsum board industry, the exchange of price information among competitors carries with it the added potential for the development of concerted price-fixing arrangements which lie at the core of the Sherman Act's prohibitions. The Department of Justice's 1977 Report on the Robinson-Patman Act focused on the growing use of the Act as a cover for price fixing; former Antitrust Division Assistant Attorney General Kauper discussed the mechanics of the process:

> And thus you find in some industries relatively extensive exchanges of price information for the purpose, at least the stated purpose, of complying with the Robinson-Patman Act ....
>
> Now, the mere exchange of price information itself may tend to stabilize prices. But I think it is also relatively common that once that exchange process begins, certain understandings go along with it — that we will exchange prices, but it will be understood, for example, you will not undercut my prices.
>
> And from there it is a rather easy step into a full-fledged price-fixing agreement. I think we have seen that from time to time, and I suspect we will

continue to see it as long as there continues to be a need to justify particular price discriminations in the terms of the Robinson-Patman Act.

We are left, therefore, on the one hand, with doubts about both the need for and the efficacy of interseller verification as a means of facilitating compliance with § 2(b), and, on the other, with recognition of the tendency for price discussions between competitors to contribute to the stability of oligopolistic prices and open the way for the growth of prohibited anticompetitive activity. To recognize even a limited "controlling circumstance" exception for interseller verification in such circumstances would be to remove from scrutiny under the Sherman Act conduct falling near its core with no assurance, and indeed with serious doubts, that competing antitrust policies would be served thereby. In *Automatic Canteen Co. v. FTC*, 346 U.S. 61, 74 (1953), the Court suggested that as a general rule the Robinson-Patman Act should be construed so as to insure its coherence with "the broader antitrust policies that have been laid down by Congress"; that observation buttresses our conclusion that exchanges of price information — even when putatively for purposes of Robinson-Patman Act compliance — must remain subject to close scrutiny under the Sherman Act.

NOTES AND QUESTIONS

1. Why would any seller ever ask a price of $1.00 instead of $1.25? Because he believes that if he asks $1.25 of a particular customer the customer will buy somewhere else? Aren't *all* prices calculated to "meet competition"? Even the monopolist is unable to charge an infinite price. If there is no legal impediment to price discrimination, a monopoly seller would size up each individual buyer, take a guess at the largest amount that the buyer would be willing to pay based on the information available to the seller, and ask a price in that amount. That entire process is the meeting of competition. Would it matter if a buyer, asked to pay too high a price, decided not to buy any product at all? To buy a somewhat different product? Does the good faith meeting competition defense apply only when a seller is attempting to meet the competition of a particular, known seller?

2. Won't the *Gypsum* case encourage buyers to lie to sellers about competing offers?

FALLS CITY INDUSTRIES V. VANCO BEVERAGE, INC.

460 U.S. 428 (1983)

JUSTICE BLACKMUN delivered the opinion of the Court.

Section 2(b) of the Clayton Act, as amended by the Robinson-Patman Act, provides that a defendant may rebut a prima facie showing of illegal price discrimination by establishing that its lower price to any purchaser or purchasers "was made in good faith to meet an equally low price of a competitor." The United States Court of Appeals for the Seventh Circuit has concluded that the "meeting-competition" defense of § 2(b) is available only if the defendant sets its lower price on a customer-by-customer basis and creates the price discrimination by lowering rather than by raising prices....

From July 1, 1972, through Nov. 30, 1978, petitioner Falls City Industries, Inc., sold beer f.o.b. its Louisville, Ky., brewery to wholesalers throughout Indiana, Kentucky, and 11 other States. Respondent Vanco Beverage, Inc., was the sole wholesale distributor of Falls City beer in Vanderburgh County, Ind. That county includes the city of Evansville. Directly across the state line from Vanderburgh County is Henderson County, Ky., where Falls City's only wholesale distributor was Dawson Springs, Inc. The city of Henderson, Ky., located in Henderson County, is less than 10 miles from Evansville. The two cities are connected by a four-lane interstate highway. The two counties generally are considered to be a single metropolitan area.

Vanco and Dawson Springs each purchased beer from Falls City and other brewers and resold it to retailers in Vanderburgh County and Henderson County, respectively. The two distributors did not compete for sales to the same retailers. This was because Indiana wholesalers were prohibited by state law from selling to out-of-state retailers, and Indiana retailers were not permitted to purchase beer from out-of-state wholesalers. Indiana law also affected beer sales in two other ways relevant to this case. First, Indiana required brewers to sell to all Indiana wholesalers at a single price. Second, although it was ignored and virtually unenforced, state law prohibited consumers from importing alcoholic beverages without a permit.

In December 1976, Vanco sued Falls City in the United States District Court for the Southern District of Indiana, alleging, among other things, that Falls City had discriminated in price against Vanco, in violation of § 2(a) of the Clayton Act, as amended by the Robinson-Patman Act, by charging Vanco a higher price than it charged Dawson Springs....

... The [district] court held, however, that Vanco had made out a prima facie case of price discrimination under the Robinson-Patman Act. The District Court found that Vanco competed in a geographic market that spanned the state border and included Vanderburgh and Henderson Counties. Although Vanco and Dawson Springs did not sell to the same retailers, they "competed for sale of [Falls City's] beer to ... consumers of beer from retailers situated in [that] market area." Falls City charged a higher price for beer sold to Indiana distributors than it charged for the same beer sold to distributors in other States, including Kentucky. This pricing policy resulted in lower retail prices for Falls City beer in Kentucky than in Indiana, because Kentucky distributors passed on their savings to retailers who in turn passed them on to consumers. Finding that many customers living in the Indiana portion of the geographic market ignored state law to purchase cheaper Falls City beer from Henderson County retailers, the court concluded that Falls City's pricing policies prevented Vanco from competing effectively with Dawson Springs, and caused it to sell less beer to Indiana retailers.

The District Court rejected Falls City's § 2(b) meeting-competition defense. The court reasoned that, instead of reducing its prices to meet those of a competitor, Falls City had created the price disparity by raising its prices to Indiana wholesalers more than it had raised its Kentucky prices. Instead of "adjusting prices on a customer to customer basis to meet competition from other brewers," Falls City charged a single price throughout each State in which it sold beer. The court concluded that Falls City's higher Indiana price was not set in good faith; instead, it was raised "for the sole reason that it followed the other brewers ... for its profit."

The United States Court of Appeals for the Seventh Circuit, by a divided vote, affirmed the finding of liability....

....

When proved, the meeting-competition defense of § 2(b) exonerates a seller from Robinson-Patman Act liability. This Court consistently has held that the meeting-competition defense "'at least requires the seller, who has knowingly discriminated in price, to show the existence of facts which would lead a reasonable and prudent person to believe that the granting of a lower price would in fact meet the equally low price of a competitor.'" The seller must show that under the circumstances it was reasonable to believe that the quoted price or a lower one was available to the favored purchaser or purchasers from the seller's competitors. Neither the District Court nor the Court of Appeals addressed the question whether Falls City had shown information that would have led a reasonable and prudent person to believe that its lower Kentucky price would meet competitors' equally low prices there; indeed, no findings whatever were made regarding competitors' Kentucky prices, or the information available to Falls City about its competitors' Kentucky prices....

On its face, § 2(b) requires more than a showing of facts that would have led a reasonable person to believe that a lower price was available to the favored purchaser from a competitor. The showing required is that the "lower price ... *was made* in good faith *to meet*" the competitor's low price. Thus, the defense requires that the seller offer the lower price in good faith *for the purpose* of meeting the competitor's price, that is, the lower price must actually have been a good faith response to that competing low price. In most situations, a showing of facts giving rise to a reasonable belief that equally low prices were available to the favored purchaser from a competitor will be sufficient to establish that the seller's lower price was offered in good faith to meet that price. In others, however, despite the availability from other sellers of a low price, it may be apparent that the defendant's low offer was not a good faith response.

... The Court of Appeals explicitly relied on two ... factors in rejecting Falls City's meeting-competition defense: the price discrimination was created by raising rather than lowering prices, and Falls City raised its prices in order to increase its profits. Neither of these factors is controlling. Nothing in § 2(b) requires a seller to *lower* its price in order to meet competition. On the contrary,

§ 2(b) requires the defendant to show only that its "lower price ... was made in good faith to meet an equally low price of a competitor." A seller is required to justify a price difference by showing that it reasonably believed that an equally low price was available to the purchaser and that it offered the lower price for that reason; the seller is not required to show that the difference resulted from subtraction rather than addition.

A different rule would not only be contrary to the language of the statute, but also might stifle the only kind of legitimate price competition reasonably available in particular industries. In a period of generally rising prices, vigorous price competition for a particular customer or customers may take the form of smaller price increases rather than price cuts. Thus, a price discrimination created by selective price increases can result from a good faith effort to meet a competitor's low price.

... A seller need not choose between "ruinously cutting its prices to all its customers to match the price offered to one, [and] refusing to meet the competition and then ruinously raising its prices to its remaining customers to cover increased unit costs." *Standard Oil Co. v. FTC*, 340 U.S., at 250. Nor need a seller choose between keeping all its prices ruinously low to meet the price offered to one, and ruinously raising its prices to all customers to a level significantly above that charged by its competitors. A seller is permitted "to retain a customer by realistically meeting in good faith the price offered to that customer, without necessarily changing the seller's price to its other customers." The plain language of § 2(b) also permits a seller to retain a customer by realistically meeting in good faith the price offered to that customer, without necessarily freezing his price to his other customers.

Section 2(b) does not require a seller, meeting in good faith a competitor's lower price to certain customers, to forgo the profits that otherwise would be available in sales to its remaining customers. The very purpose of the defense is to permit a seller to treat different competitive situations differently. The prudent businessman responding fairly to what he believes in good faith is a situation of competitive necessity might well raise his prices to some customers to increase his profits, while meeting competitors' prices by keeping his prices to other customers low.

....

The Court of Appeals also relied on *Staley* for the proposition that the meeting-competition defense "'places emphasis on individual [competitive] situations, rather than upon a general system of competition,'" and "does not justify the maintenance of discriminatory pricing among classes of customers that results merely from the adoption of a competitor's discriminatory pricing structure." The Court of Appeals was apparently invoking the District Court's findings that Falls City set prices statewide rather than on a "customer to customer basis," and the District Court's conclusion that this practice disqualified Falls City from asserting the meeting-competition defense....

There is no evidence that Congress intended to limit the availability of § 2(b) to customer-specific responses. Section 2(b)'s predecessor, § 2 of the original

Clayton Act, stated that "nothing herein contained shall prevent ... discrimination in price in the same or different communities made in good faith to meet competition." The Judiciary Committee of the House of Representatives, which drafted the clause explained the new section's anticipated function: "It should be noted that while the seller is permitted to meet *local* competition, [§ 2(b)] does not permit him to cut *local* prices until his competitor has first offered lower prices, and then he can go no further than to meet those prices." Congress intended to allow reasonable pricing responses on an area-specific basis where competitive circumstances warrant them. The purpose of the amendment was to "restric[t] the proviso to price differentials occurring in actual competition." We conclude that Congress did not intend to bar territorial price differences that are in fact responses to competitive conditions.

Section 2(b) specifically allows a "lower price ... to any purchaser or purchasers" made in good faith to meet a competitor's equally low price. A single low price surely may be extended to numerous purchasers if the seller has a reasonable basis for believing that the competitor's lower price is available to them. Beyond the requirement that the lower price be reasonably calculated to "meet not beat" the competition, Congress intended to leave it a "question of fact ... whether the way in which the competition was met lies within the latitude allowed." Once again, this inquiry is guided by the standard of the prudent businessman responding fairly to what he reasonably believes are the competitive necessities.

A seller may have good reason to believe that a competitor or competitors are charging lower prices throughout a particular region.... In such circumstances, customer-by-customer negotiations would be unlikely to result in prices different from those set according to information relating to competitors' territorial prices. A customer-by-customer requirement might also make meaningful price competition unrealistically expensive for smaller firms such as Falls City, which was attempting to compete with larger national breweries in 13 separate States.

... Territorial pricing, however, can be a perfectly reasonable method — sometimes the most reasonable method — of responding to rivals' low prices. We choose not to read into § 2(b) a restriction that would deny the meeting-competition defense to one whose area-wide price is a well tailored response to competitors' low prices.

NOTES AND QUESTIONS

1. The court noted that distributors in the low-price market (Kentucky) and those in the high-price market (Indiana) did not sell to the same retailers because an Indiana statute prohibited Indiana distributors from selling to out-of-state retailers, and Indiana retailers from buying from out-of-state distributors. Thus the favored and disfavored distributors did not compete for immediate customers at all. On the other hand, the differential pricing forced distributors in Indiana to sell to Indiana retailers at a higher price than Kentucky distributors sold to Kentucky retailers. The injury caused by the differential pricing was therefore shared by the disfavored distributors and their retailers. Presumably the Indiana retailers were losing sales to customers who crossed the state line to buy cheaper beer in Kentucky. Because the Indiana retailers sold less beer, they purchased less from Indiana distributors. Doesn't this create a "passing-on" problem analogous to that in *Illinois Brick v. Illinois, supra,* Chapter 3. Does *J. Truett Payne v. Chrysler Motor Corp., supra,* this chapter, holding that secondary-line plaintiffs are not entitled to automatic damages in the amount of the overcharge, suggest a rule for allocating damages between direct and indirect purchasers? In general, courts have permitted indirect purchasers to proceed under the Robinson-Patman Act, even after *Illinois Brick. See, e.g., Paceo, Inc. v. Ishi Kawajma-Harima Heavy Indus. Co.,* 468 F. Supp. 256 (N.D. Cal. 1979).

2. The decision of the Supreme Court in the *Vanco Beverage* case modifies considerably the accepted definition of the "meeting competition" defense as the Supreme Court described it nearly forty years earlier in *FTC v. A.E. Staley Mfg. Co.,* 324 U.S. 746 (1945). In *Staley,* the defendant attempted to raise the meeting competition defense by showing that they had attempted to meet their competitors' entire price schedule. The competitors' price schedule, however, had itself already been found illegal under the Robinson-Patman Act. *Corn Prods. Ref. Co. v. FTC,* 324 U.S. 726 (1945). Thus, *Staley* could stand for either or both of two propositions: (1) one cannot meet competition by meeting a competitor's entire price schedule; competition must be met on a customer-by-customer basis; or (2) one cannot meet competition when the competitor's pricing is itself illegal under the Robinson-Patman Act. In *Vanco,* the Supreme Court has effectively told us that *Staley* stood for the second proposition but not the first.

Is this a sensible rule? What if Falls City's competitors in Kentucky were also violating the Robinson-Patman Act. Suppose, for example, that they were selling beer at a lower (or higher) price in Henderson County Kentucky than they were in some other county. Would that have any bearing on Falls City's need to compete with their prices in Henderson County? What if Falls City did not know that the competitors were themselves violating the Robinson-Patman Act? Should a seller seeking to "meet competition" in a certain market be put on notice whether the competitor's price is itself a violation of the Robinson-Patman Act? *See Standard Oil Co. v. Brown,* 238 F.2d 54 (5th Cir. 1956); *Knoll Assocs.,* 70 F.T.C. 311 (1966).

Compare Falls City with Coastal Fuels of Puerto Rico, Inc. v. Caribbean Petroleum Corp., 79 F.3d 182 (1st Cir.), *cert. denied,* 117 S. Ct. 294 (1996), holding that while one can meet competition on a regional basis rather than customer-by-customer, there must nevertheless be evidence that someone else in the region is actually making sales at the lower price. Suppose that a defendant's lower price actually ends up meeting a rival's competition, but the seller did not know that fact at the time it offered the lower price. Can one be acting in "good faith," as the statute requires, without knowing about the rival's lower price? *See Nichols Motorcycle Supply, Inc. v. Dunlop Tire Corp.*, 913 F. Supp. 1088 (N.D. Ill. 1995).

3. Seller *A* and seller *B* both sell widgets in St. Paul and Minneapolis. Each sells them for $1.00 in St. Paul and 80 cents in Minneapolis. Each is charged separately with a Robinson-Patman Act violation. *A* defends the low price in Minneapolis by arguing that it was a good faith effort to meet *B*'s competition. *B* defends its low price as a good faith effort to meet *A*'s competition. Will the defense succeed? What will happen to *B*'s defense if *A* has already been cleared? If *A* has already been condemned?

PROBLEM 8.2

Fred's Chocolates is a growing candy manufacturer selling to local distributors located in various parts of the country. Fred's principal rival is Anna Belle's Sweets, which also sells through distributors scattered across the country. Fred's experience is that any time an Anna Belle's distributor is in the geographic area, it must cut its price in order to meet Anna Belle's competition. Fred's has two distributors located in southern California, one in Los Angeles and one in San Diego. Their customers, retail stores, overlap a great deal. One day the San Diego distributor informs Fred's that an Anna Belle's distributor has come into San Diego for the first time. Fred's immediately cuts the price to the San Diego distributor, without actually inquiring whether the Anna Belle's distributor is selling cheaper. Is Fred's experience in other geographic areas sufficient to warrant his claim of the "meeting competition" defense? *See Rose Confections, Inc. v. Ambrosia Chocolate Co.*, 816 F.2d 381, 391-93 (8th Cir. 1987).

D. ROBINSON-PATMAN VIOLATIONS BY BUYERS

Section 2(f) of the Robinson-Patman Act (15 U.S.C. § 13(f)) makes it "unlawful for any person engaged in commerce ... knowingly to induce or receive a discrimination which is prohibited by this section."

GREAT ATLANTIC & PACIFIC TEA CO. V. FTC

440 U.S. 69 (1979)

JUSTICE STEWART delivered the opinion of the Court.

The question presented in this case is whether the petitioner, the Great Atlantic & Pacific Tea Co. (A&P), violated § 2(f) of the Robinson-Patman Act, by knowingly inducing or receiving illegal price discriminations from the Borden Co. (Borden).

The alleged violation was reflected in a 1965 agreement between A&P and Borden under which Borden undertook to supply "private label" milk to more than 200 A&P stores in a Chicago area that included portions of Illinois and Indiana. This agreement resulted from an effort by A&P to achieve cost savings by switching from the sale of "brand label" milk (milk sold under the brand name of the supplying dairy) to the sale of "private label" milk (milk sold under the A&P label).

To implement this plan, A&P asked Borden, its longtime supplier, to submit an offer to supply under private label certain of A&P's milk and other dairy product requirements. After prolonged negotiations, Borden offered to grant A&P a discount for switching to private-label milk provided A&P would accept limited delivery service. Borden claimed that this offer would save A&P $410,000 a year compared to what it had been paying for its dairy products. A&P, however, was not satisfied with this offer and solicited offers from other dairies. A competitor of Borden, Bowman Dairy, then submitted an offer which was lower than Borden's.

At this point, A&P's Chicago buyer contacted Borden's chain store sales manager and stated: "I have a bid in my pocket. You [Borden] people are so far out of line it is not even funny. You are not even in the ball park." When the Borden representative asked for more details, he was told nothing except that a $50,000 improvement in Borden's bid "would not be a drop in the bucket."

Borden was thus faced with the problem of deciding whether to rebid. A&P at the time was one of Borden's largest customers in the Chicago area. Moreover, Borden had just invested more than $5 million in a new dairy facility in Illinois. The loss of the A&P account would result in underutilization of this new plant. Under these circumstances, Borden decided to submit a new bid which doubled the estimated annual savings to A&P from $410,000 to $820,000. In presenting its offer, Borden emphasized to A&P that it needed to keep A&P's business and was making the new offer in order to meet Bowman's bid. A&P then accepted Borden's bid after concluding that it was substantially better than Bowman's.
....

An Administrative Law Judge found, after extended discovery and a hearing that lasted over 110 days, that A&P had acted unfairly and deceptively in accepting the second offer from Borden and had ... violated § 2(f)....
....

The Robinson-Patman Act was passed in response to the problem perceived in the increased market power and coercive practices of chainstores and other big buyers that threatened the existence of small independent retailers. Notwithstanding this concern with buyers, however, the emphasis of the Act is in § 2(a), which prohibits price discriminations by sellers. Indeed, the original Patman bill as reported by Committees of both Houses prohibited only seller activity, with no mention of buyer liability. Section 2(f), making buyers liable for inducing or receiving price discriminations by sellers, was the product of a belated floor amendment near the conclusion of the Senate debates.

As finally enacted, § 2(f) provides: "That it shall be unlawful for any person engaged in commerce, in the course of such commerce, knowingly to induce or receive a discrimination in price *which is prohibited by this section*." (Emphasis added.) Liability under § 2(f) thus is limited to situations where the price discrimination is one "which is prohibited by this section." While the phrase "this section" refers to the entire § 2 of the Act, only subsections (a) and (b) dealing with seller liability involve discriminations in price. Under the plain meaning of § 2(f), therefore, a buyer cannot be liable if a prima facie case could not be established against a seller or if the seller has an affirmative defense. In either situation, there is no price discrimination "prohibited by this section." ...

The derivative nature of liability under § 2(f) was recognized by this Court in *Automatic Canteen Co. of America v. FTC*, 346 U.S. 61. In that case, the Court stated that even if the Commission has established a prima facie case of price discrimination, a buyer does not violate § 2(f) if the lower prices received are either within one of the seller's defenses or not known by the buyer not to be within one of those defenses. The Court stated:

> Thus, at the least, we can be confident in reading the words in § 2(f), "a discrimination in price which is prohibited by this section," as a reference to the substantive prohibitions against discrimination by sellers defined elsewhere in the Act. It is therefore apparent that the discriminatory price that buyers are forbidden by § 2(f) to induce cannot include price differentials that are not forbidden to sellers in other sections of the Act .... For we are not dealing simply with a "discrimination in price"; the "discrimination in price" in § 2(f) must be one "which is prohibited by this section." Even if any price differential were to be comprehended within the term "discrimination in price," § 2(f), which speaks of prohibited discriminations, cannot be read as declaring out of bounds price differentials within one or more of the "defenses" available to sellers, such as that the price differentials reflect cost differences, fluctuating market conditions, or bona fide attempts to meet competition, as those defenses are set out in the provisos of §§ 2(a) and 2(b).

346 U.S., at 70-71 (footnotes omitted). The Court thus explicitly recognized that a buyer cannot be held liable under § 2(f) if the lower prices received are justified by reason of one of the seller's affirmative defenses.

The petitioner, relying on this plain meaning of § 2(f) and the teaching of the *Automatic Canteen* case, argues that it cannot be liable under § 2(f) if Borden had a valid meeting-competition defense. The respondent, on the other hand, argues that the petitioner may be liable even assuming that Borden had such a defense. The meeting-competition defense, the respondent contends, must in these circumstances be judged from the point of view of the buyer. Since A&P knew for a fact that the final Borden bid beat the Bowman bid, it was not entitled to assert the meeting-competition defense even though Borden may have honestly believed that it was simply meeting competition. Recognition of a meeting-competition defense for the buyer in this situation, the respondent argues, would be contrary to the basic purpose of the Robinson-Patman Act to curtail abuses by large buyers.

The short answer to these contentions of the respondent is that Congress did not provide in § 2(f) that a buyer can be liable even if the seller has a valid defense. The clear language of § 2(f) states that a buyer can be liable only if he receives a price discrimination "prohibited by this section." If a seller has a valid meeting-competition defense, there is simply no prohibited price discrimination.

....

In the *Automatic Canteen* case, the Court warned against interpretations of the Robinson-Patman Act which "extend beyond the prohibitions of the Act and, in so doing, help give rise to a price uniformity and rigidity in open conflict with the purposes of other antitrust legislation." Imposition of § 2(f) liability on the petitioner in this case would lead to just such price uniformity and rigidity.[13]

In a competitive market, uncertainty among sellers will cause them to compete for business by offering buyers lower prices. Because of the evils of collusive action, the Court has held that the exchange of price information by competitors violates the Sherman Act. *United States v. Container Corp.*, 393 U.S. 333. Under the view advanced by the respondent, however, a buyer, to avoid liability, must either refuse a seller's bid or at least inform him that his bid has beaten competition. Such a duty of affirmative disclosure would almost inevitably frustrate competitive bidding and, by reducing uncertainty, lead to price matching and anticompetitive cooperation among sellers.

Ironically, the Commission itself ... recognized the dangers inherent in a duty of affirmative disclosure:

> The imposition of a duty of affirmative disclosure, applicable to a buyer whenever a seller states that his offer is intended to meet competition, is contrary to normal business practice and, we think, contrary to the public interest.
>
> ....
>
> We fear a scenario where the seller automatically attaches a meeting competition caveat to every bid. The buyer would then state whether such bid meets, beats, or loses to another bid. The seller would then submit a second, a third, and perhaps a fourth bid until finally he is able to ascertain his competitor's bid.

....

As in the *Automatic Canteen* case, we decline to adopt a construction of § 2(f) that is contrary to its plain meaning and would lead to anticompetitive results. Accordingly, we hold that a buyer who has done no more than accept the lower of two prices competitively offered does not violate § 2(f) provided the seller has a meeting-competition defense.

Because both the Commission and the Court of Appeals proceeded on the assumption that a buyer who accepts the lower of two competitive bids can be liable under § 2(f) even if the seller has a meeting-competition defense, there was not a specific finding that Borden did in fact have such a defense. But it quite

---

[13] More than once the Court has stated that the Robinson-Patman Act should be construed consistently with broader policies of the antitrust laws. *United States v. United States Gypsum Co.*, 438 U.S. 422; *Automatic Canteen Co. of America v. FTC* [346 U.S. 61].

clearly did.... "A good-faith belief, rather than absolute certainty, that a price concession is being offered to meet an equally low price offered by a competitor is sufficient to satisfy the § 2(b) defense." *United States v. United States Gypsum Co.* Since good faith, rather than absolute certainty, is the touchstone of the meeting-competition defense, a seller can assert the defense even if it has unknowingly made a bid that in fact not only met but beat his competition.

Under the circumstances of this case, Borden did act reasonably and in good faith when it made its second bid. The petitioner, despite its longstanding relationship with Borden, was dissatisfied with Borden's first bid and solicited offers from other dairies....

... Borden was informed by the petitioner that it was in danger of losing its A&P business in the Chicago area unless it came up with a better offer. It was told that its first offer was "not even in the ball park" and that a $50,000 improvement "would not be a drop in the bucket." In light of Borden's established business relationship with the petitioner, Borden could justifiably conclude that A&P's statements were reliable and that it was necessary to make another bid offering substantial concessions to avoid losing its account with the petitioner.

Borden was unable to ascertain the details of the Bowman bid. It requested more information about the bid from the petitioner, but this request was refused. It could not then attempt to verify the existence and terms of the competing offer from Bowman without risking Sherman Act liability. *United States v. United States Gypsum Co.* Faced with a substantial loss of business and unable to find out the precise details of the competing bid, Borden made another offer stating that it was doing so in order to meet competition. Under these circumstances, the conclusion is virtually inescapable that in making that offer Borden acted in a reasonable and good-faith effort to meet its competition, and therefore was entitled to a meeting-competition defense.

Since Borden had a meeting-competition defense and thus could not be liable under § 2(b), the petitioner who did no more than accept that offer cannot be liable under § 2(f).

JUSTICE MARSHALL, dissenting in part.
....

I agree with the Court's suggestion that we must resolve the dilemma confronting a buyer who properly invites a seller to meet a competitor's price and then fortuitously obtains a lower bid. Congress could not have expected the buyer to choose between asking the seller to increase the bid to a specific price or accepting the lower bid and facing liability under § 2(f). Rather, it must have intended some accommodation for buyers who act in good faith yet receive bids that beat competition. This does not mean, however, that a buyer should be liable under § 2(f) only if his seller also would be liable. That solution to the buyer's dilemma would enable him to manufacture his own defense by misrepresenting to a seller the response needed to meet a competitor's bid and then allowing the seller to rely in good faith on incorrect information. The Court purports to reserve this "lying buyer" issue, but the derivative standard it adopts today belies the reservation. If "prohibited by this section" means that a buyer's liability depends on that of the seller, then absent seller liability, the buyer's conduct and bad faith are necessarily irrelevant.

I would hold that under § 2(f), the Robinson-Patman Act defenses must be available to buyers on the same basic terms as they are to sellers. To be sure, some differences in the nature of the defenses would obtain because of the different bargaining positions of sellers and buyers. With respect to the meeting-competition defense at issue here, a seller can justify a price discrimination by showing that his lower price was offered in "good faith" to meet that of a competitor. In my view, a buyer should be able to claim that defense — independently of the seller — if he acted in good faith to induce the seller to meet a competitor's price, regardless of whether the seller's price happens to beat the competitor's. But a buyer who induces the lower bid by misrepresentation should not .escape Robinson-Patman Act liability. This definition of the meeting-competition defense both extricates buyers from an impossible dilemma and respects the congressional intent to prevent buyers from abusing their market power to gain competitive advantage.

NOTES AND QUESTIONS

1. Does the *A&P* case effectively sabotage section 2(f) of the Robinson-Patman Act? Under the Supreme Court's decision in *United States Gypsum*, 438 U.S. 422 (1978), reprinted *supra*, price information exchanges between competitors are illegal, and it is no defense that the sellers exchanged information in order to make out a "meeting competition" defense. Furthermore, said the court, it is not necessary for a seller to obtain information from a competitor about a reputed lower price; the seller will not be in violation of the statute as long as the seller acted in good faith. Suppose that *A* and *B* are competitors in the sale of Gadgets and the market price has been hovering around $1.00. Now *X*, a buyer, comes to *A*, with whom he has been doing business for some time. *X* tells *A* that *B* has offered to sell all the Gadgets *X* wants at 80 cents. In fact, *X* is lying and has really never corresponded with *B* at all. Under the *Gypsum* doctrine, *A* cannot call *B* to verify the offer. Not having any reason to doubt *X*, *A* decides to make the sale to *X* at 80 cents. Under the holding in *A & P*, *X* has not violated the statute, because *A* would probably be able to raise the defense of "good faith" meeting of competition, even though *A* was not *really* meeting competition. Furthermore, *X* knows that *A* is not actually meeting competition.

The virtual effect of the *A & P* decision is that a buyer cannot unilaterally "induce" a price discrimination. There must virtually be a conspiracy between the buyer and seller to engage in illegal price discrimination — or, at the very least, both the buyer and the seller must somehow independently decide to enter into a transaction in violation of the statute. The language of section 2(f) seems clear, however, that Congress did not mean to restrict buyer's liability to situations involving a conspiracy between the buyer and the seller. The statute is cast entirely in terms of single-firm conduct.

The suggestion in Justice Marshall's dissent makes much more sense if the integrity of section 2(f) is to be preserved. Justice Marshall would make the Act's affirmative defenses available to both buyer and seller on the "same terms." Under Justice Marshall's rule the seller could take advantage of the "meeting competition" defense if the seller acted in good faith, and the buyer could have the defense if the buyer acted in good faith. However, the buyer would not be able to take advantage of the seller's good faith if the buyer itself were acting in bad faith.

Would Justice Marshall's rule be any more anti-competitive than the majority's rule? It might be if a bit of bad faith is good for competition. Perhaps hard, healthy competition requires a buyer to be able to say "I can get it cheaper somewhere else," even though they know that in fact they cannot. The statement gives the seller the choice of making the sale at a lower price or not making it at all. Presumably the seller will not make the sale unless it is profitable for it to do so. In short, the majority's rule would seem to do a better job of encouraging marginal cost pricing, although sometimes little white lies help reduce prices to marginal cost.

SECTION IV. CRIMINAL VIOLATIONS OF THE ROBINSON-PATMAN ACT

Section 3 of the Robinson-Patman Act (15 U.S.C. § 13a (1976)) makes it a crime for any seller knowingly to discriminate in price or to sell goods at an unreasonably low price "for the purpose of destroying competition or eliminating a competitor." The statute provides a maximum fine of $5,000 or imprisonment up to one year, or both. The statute has seldom been used. It is not an "antitrust law" for the purposes of section 4 of the Clayton Act, and there is no private right of action under section 3. *Nashville Milk Co. v. American Distilling Co.*, 570 F.2d 848, 854 (9th Cir. 1977), *cert. denied*, 439 U.S. 829 (1978). In general, however, activity that would violate section 3 would also violate the general provisions of section 2a of the Robinson-Patman Act, or else section 2 of the Sherman Act.

The small amount of section 3 litigation that has reached the Supreme Court had dwelt on the statute's intent requirements. Because the statute is criminal, it has generally been held to require specific intent. In *United States v. National Dairy Prods. Corp.*, 372 U.S. 29 (1963), the Supreme Court held that the statute's prohibition of "unreasonably low prices" was not unconstitutionally vague. Nevertheless, the Department of Justice has not enforced the statute since the early 1960's. Repeal has often been proposed, but has never passed.

BIBLIOGRAPHY AND COLLATERAL READINGS

Books

H. Hovenkamp, Federal Antitrust Policy, ch. 14 (2d ed. 1994).

R. Posner, The Robinson-Patman Act: Federal Regulation of Price Differences (1976).

F.M. Rowe, Price Discrimination Under the Robinson-Patman Act (1962).

E.T. Sullivan & J. Harrison, Understanding Antitrust and Its Economic Implications (3d ed. 1998).

United States Department of Justice, Report on the Robinson-Patman Act (1977).

Articles

Baxter, A Parable, 23 Stan. L. Rev. 973 (1971).

Calvani, Government Enforcement of the Robinson-Patman Act, 53 Antitrust L.J. 921 (1985).

Hansen, Robinson-Patman Law: A Review and Analysis, 51 Fordham L. Rev. 1113 (1983).

Hovenkamp, Market Power and Secondary Line Differential Pricing, 71 Geo. L.J. 1157 (1983).

O'Brien & Shaffer, The Welfare Effects of Forbidding Discriminatory Discounts: A Secondary Line Analysis of Robinson-Patman, 10 J.L. Econ. & Org. 296 (1994).

Chapter 9

ANTITRUST AND OTHER FORMS OF REGULATION

"Regulation" is government intervention in the marketplace. Government price controls, output controls, quality controls, and restrictions on entry are all common forms of regulation. The federal antitrust laws themselves are a form of regulation, as are common law rules and the litigation process itself.* This chapter briefly examines the relationship between the federal antitrust laws and these other forms of regulation.

The relationship between antitrust and regulation is complicated by the fact that, not only does regulation come in many varieties, it is also imposed by a variety of sovereigns. Federal, state, and local governments all regulate. The potential for conflict between antitrust and other forms of regulation arises at all three levels.

This chapter is divided into three sections. Section I considers the relationship between the antitrust laws and the classical "regulated industries" generally. Section II considers questions about private liability for "petitions" to the government (the *Noerr-Pennington* doctrine). These petitions can take the form of requests for regulation, but they can also take the form of litigation before a court or regulatory agency. Section III considers the special problems of federalism that arise in the case of conflict between federal antitrust policy and regulation imposed by state or local government.

SECTION I. ANTITRUST AND AGENCY REGULATION

A. OVERVIEW

Broadly defined, a "regulated industry" is one whose behavior is controlled in part by legislative or governmental agency decision rather than by free market forces. Virtually all American industries are regulated to some degree. Today the term "regulated industry" refers more specifically to a collection of industries in which pricing, entry and exit, or method of operation are determined substantially by a regulatory agency rather than by the market. The agencies include (among others) the Federal Communications Commission, the Federal Energy Regulatory Commission, the Surface Transportation Board (formerly the Interstate Commerce Commission), the Securities and Exchange Commission, the Commodity Futures Trading Commission, the Federal Reserve System, and the Federal Maritime Commission. In addition, there are a host of state and local regulatory agencies that

---

* On the "regulatory" role of the Antitrust Division of the Justice Department, *see* Sullivan, *The Antitrust Division as a Regulatory Agency: An Enforcement Policy in Transition,* 64 Wash. U. L.Q. 996 (1986).

control everything from the price of taxicab rides to the cost of trash collection. *See generally* S. Breyer, *Regulation and Its Reform* (1982); C. Sunstein, *After the Rights Revolution: Reconceiving the Regulatory State* (1990).

Just as there are almost no American industries completely free of statutory regulation, there are also few regulated markets in which competitive forces are unimportant. Businesses are extraordinarily creative in their ability to compete with one another. If a regulatory agency determines the retail price in a certain market, the sellers in that market will concentrate on nonprice competition. For example, when air fares were price-regulated several years ago, the airlines competed vigorously in different ways: by offering cabin services, movies, stereo music, more frequent flights, "free" ground transportation, or other amenities. Other industries are no exception. It would be impossible for a legislature or regulatory agency to develop a regulatory scheme so comprehensive and detailed that it eliminated all forms of competition among providers in the same market in the regulated industry.

As a result, antitrust enforcement has found a place in most of the regulated industries. The common law nature of federal antitrust permits a certain amount of "after the fact" judgment of a particular firm's activity that even the most comprehensive of regulatory schemes could not foresee. Today there is substantial antitrust litigation in the communications, interstate transportation, and public utility industries, all of which remain subject to agency regulation.

B. THEORIES OF REGULATION AND THE MOVEMENT TOWARD DEREGULATION

Industries have generally become regulated for one of five reasons: (1) they are (or are thought to be) natural monopolies; (2) some other form of "market failure" prevents the competitive processes from allocating resources properly within a certain market; (3) some scarce natural resource is thought to require allocation in a way the unregulated market is unlikely to yield; (4) the market itself is thought to be unable to provide consumers with adequate information about the product; or (5) some interest group has successfully persuaded a legislative body that its particular industry should be protected from competitive forces by means of a regulatory scheme. *See* S. Breyer, *Regulation and Its Reform*, 13-35 (1982).

Two developments have produced and sustained a hearty skepticism about regulation and the large-scale recent move toward deregulation in many markets. The first is a growing belief that many industries have been regulated for political rather than economic reasons, and that often regulation results in the protection of inefficiency, higher product prices, and extraordinarily high public costs in running the regulatory process itself. The second development is a major uprising in the economic theory of competition and natural monopoly.

1. THE IDEOLOGY OF REGULATION

The era of federal regulation dates back to the late nineteenth century. The Interstate Commerce Commission was the first federal agency created to supplant competition with various forms of regulation in a large American industry: the railroads. At that time and throughout the first half of the nineteenth century, the prevailing theory of regulation was that it was passed in the "public interest" to protect American consumers from price gouging or other unfair practices that would prevail in certain industries if they were not restrained by regulatory agencies.

Eventually many economists, historians, and political scientists began to argue, however, that the biggest beneficiaries of the regulatory process were the regulated industries themselves. In the period before the Interstate Commerce Commission was created in 1887, and during the early years of its operation, railroads had been subject to serious overdevelopment. Excess capacity had led to giant rate wars that had driven many of them into bankruptcy. One effect of state and federal regulation of railroads was to limit new entry into the industry, and eventually guarantee them a "fair" profit. *See* G. Kolko, *Railroads and Regulation, 1877-1916*, at 64-83 (1965); *Regulation in Perspective: Historical Essays* (T. McCraw ed. 1981); T. McCraw, *Prophets of Regulation* (1984); Hovenkamp, *Regulatory Conflict in the Gilded Age: Federalism and the Railroad Problem*, 98 Yale L.J. 1017 (1988).

More recently, there has been a growing skepticism about both the rationales for government regulation and its effects. On one hand, price regulation may put a ceiling on a firm's power to price monopolistically. On the other hand, today many people perceive regulation as protecting inefficiency in business by guaranteeing a fair rate of return which is calculated from cost data most often submitted by the regulated firms themselves. This attitude is sometimes borne out by the political process. For example, when the movement for price deregulation in the interstate trucking industry began, the loudest objections were raised by members of the trucking industry themselves — good evidence, it seems, that the chief danger of deregulation was not monopoly pricing, which would benefit the deregulated firms, but more intense competition.

In addition, we have become aware that the regulatory process itself imposes enormous costs, often larger than the costs of the competitive marketplace. If every rate change, every decision to enter or withdraw from a particular market, or every significant change in the service to be delivered must be approved by an agency after a fact-finding procedure, the costs of regulation can be enormous, perhaps larger than the costs that would result from unregulated monopoly pricing. *See* S. Breyer, *supra*, at 184-284; Posner, *Natural Monopoly and Its Regulation*, 21 Stan. L. Rev. 548, 619 (1969).

2. NATURAL MONOPOLY, CONTESTABILITY, AND DEREGULATION

The second reason for the growing trend toward deregulation is a major change in the economic theory of competition and natural monopoly. This change has been brought about by one rather general development in the economic theory of property rights, and one quite specific development.

The general development is the Coase theorem, which states that two parties bargaining over a legal entitlement will reach the efficient, or joint-maximizing result, assuming transaction costs are low. *See* Coase, *The Problem of Social Cost*, 3 J.L. & Econ. 1 (1960). Importantly, the Coase theorem does not depend on the existence of competitive or even moderately competitive markets. Indeed, most of the illustrations in Coase's famous article (such as the rancher and farmer bargaining over damage done by grazing cattle) were bilateral monopolies — situations where a monopoly seller faces a monopoly buyer. In law and economics, the Coase theorem serves greatly to weaken the premise that only "perfect competition" yields competitive results. One result has been a great deal of interest in institutional settings designed to make competition work better by lowering transaction costs.

The more specific development is the theory of franchise bidding and its more technical offspring, the doctrine of contestable markets. These theories call into question the robustness of the traditional economic theory of natural monopoly. A "natural" monopoly is a market that can be served most efficiently by a single incumbent firm. In more technical terminology, a natural monopoly is a market where costs decline as output increases through the entire range in which profitable sales can be made. Figure 1 illustrates such a market. The market demand curve (D) crosses the average total cost curve (AC) to the left of the lowest point on the AC curve. Over the long run a single firm operating in this market would have to recover its total costs, which it could do by setting its price at the intersection of D and AC. This would yield a price of P_c and output of Q_c. Technically speaking, this is not the "competitive" price and output, for price is well above marginal cost. However, it is the price that most regulatory agencies strive to achieve and is one way of identifying the lowest price consistent with profitability.

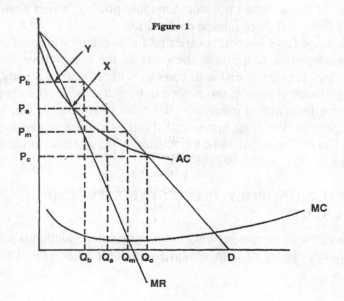

Figure 1

Because the average cost curve in Figure 1 slopes downward through the entire relevant range, any firm that produced less than Q_c would be less efficient and would face higher costs. Suppose, for example, that two equally efficient and equal-sized sellers shared the market in Figure 1. Each would fill half the demand, so their joint output would lie on a point along the average cost curve midway between the vertical axis and the demand curve: point X. At that point each firm could sell one half the output in the market at a price equal to its average total costs. However, the combined output of the firms would be lower than the output of a single firm in the market would be, and the price would be higher. Two equal sized firms would have a combined output of Q_a and they would charge a price of P_a. If three identical firms shared this market, the loss of efficiency would be even more severe, output would be even lower, and prices would be higher. In that case each firm would have costs equal to the point on the AC curve one third of the distance between the vertical axis and the demand curve — point Y. The three firms would have a total output of Q_b and each would charge a price of P_b. The more firms that occupied the market, the lower total output would be and the higher the market price would be. Such a market behaves most favorably to consumers when it is occupied by a single seller which sets its price equal to its average costs. *See generally* R. Schmalensee, *The Control of Natural Monopolies* (1979).

The last part of the preceding sentence is critical to the theory of regulation. A natural monopolist is a monopolist. Although the natural monopoly behaves optimally when it is occupied by a single seller pricing at average cost, there is little reason to believe that a monopolist in such a market will price at average cost. Unless restricted, the monopolist will set its price at the intersection of its marginal cost and marginal revenue curves, just like any other monopolist. In Figure 1 the unregulated monopolist would sell at P_m and produce at a rate of Q_m. Whether P_m is above or below P_a or P_b varies from situation to situation. By contrast, if the industry were regulated a single incumbent (such as an electric utility) would be given the entire market but a regulatory agency would try to ensure that the price approached P_c rather than P_m.

The theory of natural monopoly has justified price regulation by federal, state, or local governments in many markets — electricity, natural gas, water, telephone and telegraph, cable television, the railroad industry, and — quite inappropriately — even commercial air traffic and trucking. In recent years, however, the natural monopoly model has been challenged by the theory of contestable markets. This attack formed an important justification for the deregulation movement of the 1980's, particularly in commercial air traffic.

The theories of franchise bidding and contestable markets view the traditional economic model for natural monopoly as flawed in one very important way: although it describes competition (or the lack of it) *within* the market very well, it completely ignores the question of competition *for* the market. Assuming that the market in Figure 1 is operated most efficiently by a monopolist, how do we determine who that monopolist will be? One way is by taking competitive bids, with the bid being awarded to the firm that agrees to sell in the market for, say, two years at the lowest bid price. If there were no collusion among the bidders, we would expect the bids to come in at around price P_c.

Once a firm is in the market and operating, however, what incentive does it have to continue to price competitively? No firm can be expected to charge the same price forever. Any requirement that it can pass increased costs on to its customers will amount to little more than the creation of a regulatory agency that will supervise the firm's request for price increases and make sure that they are reasonable in comparison with its increased costs.

One solution would be to renew the bidding periodically. For example, if Firm A wins the initial bid it will operate as a monopolist in the market and charge the bid price for two years. Then there will be a new round of bids in which A can attempt to remain in the market by submitting the most favorable bid, and potential competitors can attempt to steal the market away from A by bringing in a lower bid.

The initial bid might well yield a competitive price for the first two-year period. A may have a substantial advantage over potential competitors, however, in the second and all subsequent bids. Suppose that A is a gas pipeline company that was successful in an original bid to supply natural gas from Nevada to Los Angeles. After winning the bid, company A builds a pipeline from Nevada to Los Angeles and for two years provides natural gas at the bid price. At the end of the two-year period the market is opened for new bidding. Now, however, A already owns the pipeline. All potential competitors must calculate the costs of building a pipeline into their bids. These additional costs, which must be borne by A's competitors but not by A itself, give A considerable latitude for monopolistic pricing. For example, if A knows that any competitor must face \$1,000,000 in entry costs that have already been "sunk" by A itself, then A will be able to add any amount short of \$1,000,000 in monopoly profits to a competitive price and still win the bid. A's sunk costs (that is, money that A has already invested and that it is unlikely to recover if it leaves the market) become the means by which it can engage in monopolistic pricing.

The higher A's relative sunk costs, the more power A will have to price monopolistically in a particular natural monopoly market. A natural monopoly such as a gas pipeline, where sunk costs are very high, contains a great deal of room for monopoly pricing. In other markets sunk costs are far lower. For example, a city might award a single trash hauling contract each year to bidders who already own a fleet of trucks. In that case, the incumbent may not have a significant advantage over newcomers, and can retain its position only by bidding a competitive price.

A perfectly contestable natural monopoly market will behave just as competitively as a perfectly competitive market with 100 identical incumbents. As soon as the incumbent in the perfectly contestable market raises its price above cost it becomes a target for entry by another firm which can undercut the monopolist by a slight amount, reap the profits, and impose large losses on the incumbent. In theory, *all* natural monopoly markets can be made into contestable markets. Even the natural gas pipeline, for example, could become contestable if the pipeline itself were owned by the State, which periodically took bids for its operation. In that case, the incumbent would not have the advantage of having large sunk costs in the pipeline. It would have to bid competitively or lose the market to a lower bid. The theory of contestable markets and its implications for industry regulation have produced a gigantic literature. Perhaps the most seminal historical contribution is Demsetz, *Why Regulate Utilities?*, 11 J.L. & Econ. 55 (1968). The general formulation of the theory is contained in W. Baumol, J. Panzar & R. Willig, *Contestable Markets and the Theory of Industry Structure* (1982), which is highly technical. For a discussion of some of the implications for antitrust policy in particular markets, *see* Brodley, *Antitrust Policy Under Deregulation: Airline Mergers and the Theory of Contestable Markets*, 61 B.U.L. Rev. 823 (1981); Bailey, *Contestability and the Design of Regulatory and Antitrust Policy*, 71 Am. Econ. Rev. 178 (1981). For a less optimistic view of contestability, *see* Williamson, *Franchise Bidding for Natural Monopolies — In General and with Respect to CATV*, 7 Bell J. Econ. & Mgmt. Sci. 73 (1976).

The theory of contestable markets has come under a good deal of criticism, largely because there appear to be no markets that approach perfect contestability. That is to say, although there is a robust "pure" theory of contestability, the "applied" theory of contestability leaves much to be desired. For example, protagonists of contestability presented the passenger airline industry as the paradigm example of a contestable market. But a host of airline mergers in the mid- and late 1980's revealed that when the number of actual, incumbent competitors on an airline route declines, prices go up. Why should this be true in a "contestable" market? Probably because, although airplanes themselves are highly mobile across markets, other parts of the airlines' "plant" are not. For example, gate space is in short supply at most airports; as a result new carriers either cannot get in, have a long wait, or may have to pay someone else a premium. Further, one cannot easily enter such markets offering a single flight, but must offer convenient connecting flights as well — customers may be willing to pay a premium for the convenience of not having to change carriers en route. Finally, although airplanes are very mobile pieces of equipment, ground service and labor are not. One thinks twice before uprooting and transferring personnel, or training new personnel for a new market. Several studies have concluded that airlines are either imperfectly contestable or not particularly contestable at all. *See* Borenstein, *The Evolution of U.S. Airline Competition*, 6 J. Econ. Perspectives 45 (1992), a readable article concluding that contestability is "no substitute for actual competition," and that airport concentration is the culprit. Equally critical is Dempsey, *Flying Blind: the Failure of Airline Deregulation* (1990).

In general, the process of deregulation has been concentrated in those industries where sunk costs are low, and where contestability appears to work quite well without the need for major restructuring of the industries themselves. Such deregulation has been substantial in the commercial airline industry and the trucking industry, for example. *See* Airline Deregulation Act of 1978, 49 U.S.C. § 1301, P.L. No. 95-504, 92 Stat. 1705 (codified at scattered sections of 49 U.S.C.; Motor Carrier Deregulation Act of 1980, 49 U.S.C. § 11101 P.L. No. 96-296, 94 Stat. 793 (codified at scattered sections of tit. 18 & 49 U.S.C.). Significant price regulation remains, however, in natural monopolies where sunk costs are high, such as pipelines, electric utilities at the retail level, and most forms of communication that depend on wire or cable connections between the communicating parties. But the world is changing quickly.

The general thrust of contestability theory and the deregulation movement is to take markets that were once considered to be regulated natural monopolies and treat them instead as competitive. To the extent that they are less regulated and more competitive, traditional regulatory concerns give way to antitrust concerns. The result is growing room for antitrust enforcement in these industries. *See* H. Hovenkamp, *Federal Antitrust Policy*, ch. 19 (2d ed. 1994).

C. JURISDICTIONAL PROBLEMS OF ANTITRUST ENFORCEMENT IN REGULATED INDUSTRIES

MCI COMMUNICATIONS CORP. V. AT&T

708 F.2d 1081 (7th Cir.), *cert. denied*, 464 U.S. 891 (1983).

JUDGE CUDAHY. American Telephone and Telegraph Company ("AT&T") appeals from a judgment in the amount of $1.8 billion, entered on a jury verdict, in a treble damage suit brought by plaintiffs MCI Communications Corporation and MCI Telecommunication Corporation (collectively "MCI") under section 4 of the Clayton Act, 15 U.S.C. §15 (1976).

I.

Facts

MCI's original complaint, filed March 6, 1974, contained four separate counts: monopolization, attempt to monopolize, and conspiracy to monopolize — all under section 2 of the Sherman Act — and conspiracy in restraint of trade — under section 1 of the Sherman Act. MCI alleged that AT&T had committed twenty-two types of misconduct, classifiable into several categories including predatory pricing, denial of interconnections, negotiation in bad faith and unlawful tying....

....

A. *Background and Initial Entry of MCI*

Prior to 1969, the telecommunications industry was regulated as a lawful monopoly. Local exchange service was and still is provided exclusively by one of the twenty-three Bell System operating companies or by one of some 1600 independent telephone companies, depending upon the geographical area involved. Long distance service was provided by the Long Lines Department of

AT&T in partnership with these operating companies. The network of long distance transmission facilities was owned in substantial part by Long Lines; however, the interexchange facilities of the local telephone companies, including both transmission and switching facilities, were used in conjunction with Long Lines facilities whenever efficiency required. The local exchange facilities and switching machines belonging to the local companies were also used at each end of a regular long distance call.

....

In 1963 ... MCI requested permission from the Federal Communications Commission ("FCC") to construct and operate a long distance telephone system between Chicago and St. Louis. The proposed system consisted of a terminal in each city and microwave radio relay towers connecting the terminals. Through this system, MCI intended to provide long distance, private line telephone service to business and industrial subscribers whose needs justified the exclusive or semi-exclusive use of a long distance telephone line. MCI also sought interconnections from its terminals to ordinary local telephone facilities, principally telephone wires running in conduits beneath the street. These interconnections were essential to MCI's ability to do business, since they provided the telephone or computer linkage between MCI's terminals and its individual customers in each city.

In 1969, after lengthy administrative proceedings in which AT&T and the other general service carriers opposed MCI's application, the FCC approved MCI's proposal. The *MCI* decision resulted in a deluge of new applications to the FCC for authority to construct and operate facilities for specialized common carrier services. MCI filed applications for authority to provide specialized services among more than 100 cities. Other companies filed similar applications....

In September 1971, AT&T entered into interim contracts with MCI defining the kinds of interconnections that AT&T would provide for MCI's initial Chicago-St. Louis route and establishing the price for those interconnections....

Through a series of informal complaints and conferences with FCC staff, MCI charged that AT&T was treating it unfairly, on the question of interconnections, in at least three respects:

> (1) MCI claimed that AT&T was unlawfully denying it interconnections ... for point-to-point service to customers located outside a local distribution area, including multi-point service;
>
> (2) MCI claimed that it was being charged excessive and discriminatory prices for the local distribution facilities provided by the Bell System; and
>
> (3) MCI claimed that if was being harassed by Bell System employees in the provision of local distribution facilities through delays, improper installation, improper maintenance and other similar practices.

AT&T denied each of these charges.... AT&T also contended that it was providing MCI with all the interconnections to which MCI was entitled and that the prices it was charging for those interconnections were not excessive or unfair.

In August 1973, with negotiations still pending, and without informing MCI, AT&T decided to file with forty-nine of the state utility commissions interconnection tariffs that would be equally applicable to all carriers — including MCI and Western Union. By filing interconnection tariffs with the state commissions rather than the FCC, AT&T made it more difficult for MCI to oppose the tariffs, since, in the words of one AT&T official, the interconnection "controversy would spread to 49 jurisdictions." Even after making this unilateral tariff decision, AT&T continued to "negotiate" with MCI. After MCI accidentally learned of the state tariff plan, however, AT&T formally broke off all contract negotiations.

... On November 2, 1973, MCI filed a complaint in federal district court under section 406 of the Communications Act asking that AT&T be ordered to provide interconnections ....

[T]he United States District Court for the Eastern District of Pennsylvania issued a preliminary injunction ordering AT&T to provide all of the interconnections sought by MCI, on the theory that such interconnections were contemplated and required by the FCC's ... decision....

From the time of MCI's entry into the telecommunications field, AT&T's prices for specialized long distance services had been a significant source of controversy....

....

Concurrent with MCI's entry into the telecommunications field, AT&T ... initiated studies to consider nationwide deaveraging of its rates for individual private line service. Pursuant to these studies, AT&T formulated a plan known as the Hi-Lo tariff, which provided for the deaveraging of AT&T's individual private line service into two principal rate categories. Under Hi-Lo, AT&T would *lower* its rates on certain "high density" long distance routes, many of which MCI planned to serve. At the same time, AT&T would increase its rates between so-called "low-density" cities, most of which MCI was not planning to serve. [MCI alleged that AT&T's opposition and delaying in the provision of interconnect services was illegal monopolization. It also alleged that AT&T's Hi-Lo tariff was illegal predatory pricing.]

... AT&T contends that the district court should have dismissed this suit on its motion because the FCC's regulatory control over AT&T's conduct renders AT&T immune from antitrust liability. Judge Grady traced the legislative history of the Federal Communications Act, and concluded that while AT&T is subject to considerable regulatory control and supervision, there is no indication that the Act was meant to immunize a carrier such as AT&T from the antitrust laws. Moreover, he concluded, the regulatory scheme to which AT&T is subject is not so wholly inconsistent with the antitrust laws as to require immunity. AT&T is not subject to conflicting requirements, nor would it be held liable for decisions which were not its own business judgment. The district court noted that the FCC did not sanction AT&T's conduct with regard to interconnections nor dictate its tariffs. Thus, while certain actions might ultimately have been subject to agency review, the initial decisions were the product of

AT&T's private business judgment, and were not so heavily regulated as to remove them from AT&T's control.

On appeal, AT&T contends that the district court's decision incorrectly focused on blanket immunity rather than immunity for the particular actions of which MCI complained. Thus, AT&T argues that the critical question left unconsidered by the district court is "whether the charges in this case do in fact relate to matters basic to the pervasive regulatory scheme to which AT&T is subject."

...

As the district court recognized, the Communications Act of 1934 does not expressly grant AT&T immunity from the antitrust laws for the conduct challenged in the instant case. Nor does the legislative history of the Communications Act indicate how Congress intended that the Act and the antitrust laws were to be reconciled. "Repeal of the antitrust laws by implication is not favored and not casually to be allowed. Only where there is a 'plain repugnancy between the antitrust and regulatory provisions' will repeal be implied." As a further limitation, repeal is to be regarded as implied only where necessary to make the regulatory scheme work, and even then, only to the minimum extent necessary.

Application of these general principles to a particular claim of implied immunity requires an evaluation of the specific regulatory scheme involved and the administrative authority exercised pursuant to that scheme. Thus, in our case, the inquiry must focus upon (1) whether the activities that are the subject of MCI's complaint were required or approved by the Federal Communications Commission, pursuant to its statutory authority, in a way that is incompatible with antitrust enforcement, or (2) whether these activities are so pervasively regulated "that Congress must be assumed to have forsworn the paradigm of competition."

With respect to interconnections, we conclude, as did the district court, that the FCC's regulatory authority under the Communications Act does not preclude application of the Sherman Act. The mere pervasiveness of a regulatory scheme does not immunize an industry from antitrust liability for conduct that is voluntarily initiated. Although the FCC has authority to compel interconnection under section 201(a) of the Act, the initial decision whether to interconnect rests with the utility, and the record shows that the FCC did not control or approve of AT&T's actions here. Nor has the FCC supervised AT&T's interconnection practices so closely that the FCC's approval could be inferred.

....

AT&T relies heavily on *Hughes Tool Co. v. Trans World Airlines, Inc.*, 409 U.S. 363 (1973), to support its claim that "matters at the heart of a pervasive scheme of common carrier, or public utility, regulation [here, presumably, AT&T's interconnection and pricing policies] are immune from antitrust liability." In [that case] however, the Supreme Court ... held that where the Civil Aeronautics Board (CAB) had specifically authorized certain transactions between a parent and its subsidiary, those transactions were immunized from antitrust liability by section 414 of the Federal Aviation Act, 49 U.S.C. § 1378 (1976).... In the instant case, by contrast, neither AT&T's interconnection decisions nor its price structure policies are dictated, in the first instance, by the FCC (although, of course, AT&T's overall rate of return is subject to continuing surveillance)....

AT&T also cites the case of *FCC v. RCA Communications, Inc.*, 346 U.S. 86 (1953), for the proposition that the public interest standard embodied in the Communications Act is inconsistent and thus presumably irreconcilable with the policy of the antitrust laws favoring competition. However, the Third Circuit, in *Sound, Inc. v. AT&T*, 631 F.2d 1324 (3d Cir. 1980), recently rejected precisely this irreconcilability argument. In *Sound, Inc.*, AT&T argued that it was exempt, by virtue, *inter alia*, of the public interest standard contained in the Communications Act, from antitrust liability arising out of its rate structure and marketing practices for terminal telephone equipment. In rejecting AT&T's assertion that the public interest standard of the Communications Act was necessarily inconsistent with the pro-competition standard of the antitrust laws, the Third Circuit noted that the FCC had exercised its supervisory authority so as to *encourage* rather than discourage competition in the terminal equipment market. In light of this policy, the court concluded that "the maintenance of an antitrust suit will not conflict with the operation of the regulatory scheme authorized by Congress but will supplement that scheme." Similarly, in the instant case, the interconnection policies adopted by the FCC during the time period relevant to this litigation appear designed to promote, rather than inhibit competition in the specialized telecommunications field. Thus, the allowance of antitrust liability is likely to complement rather than undermine the applicable statutory scheme.

AT&T's assertion of implied immunity with respect to MCI's predatory pricing allegations presents a closer question.... Although the Communications Act grants the FCC potentially broad authority over interstate and foreign telephone rates, in practice, this authority is considerably more circumscribed. First, as the district court in this case noted, the Act gives the carrier sole responsibility for filing a tariff, and a carrier may file a new or revised tariff at any time. Thus, it is AT&T, not the FCC, that has the primary responsibility for initiating and setting both regular and private line telephone rates. "When [such decisions] are governed in the first instance by business judgment and not regulatory coercion, courts must be hesitant to conclude that Congress intended to override the fundamental national policies embodied in the antitrust laws." ...

The less than comprehensive nature of the FCC's authority over tariffs is further reinforced by the huge volume of tariff filings received by the Commission. During the twelve month period between September 1974 and August 1975, for example, the FCC received 1,371 tariff filings, totaling 11,491 pages. Because of this volume, it was able to investigate only a small percentage of the tariffs filed. We thus conclude that where, as here, the ... pricing decisions complained of are more the result of business judgment than regulatory coercion, and the FCC has neither dictated nor approved of those decisions, the challenged rate filings are not immune from antitrust scrutiny....

Our conclusion that AT&T is not entitled to antitrust immunity in the instant case does not mean that AT&T's status as a regulated common carrier is irrelevant to our evaluation of AT&T's conduct. On the contrary, an industry's regulated status is an important "fact of market life," the impact of which on pricing and other competitive decisions "is too obvious to be ignored." For this reason, the Supreme Court has repeatedly recognized that consideration of federal and state regulation may be proper even after the issue of antitrust immunity has been resolved. *United States v. Marine Bancorporation*, 418 U.S. 602, 627 (1975) (application of antitrust doctrine to bank mergers "must take into account the unique federal and state restraints on [defendant's conduct]."

... As Professors Areeda & Turner have stated:

> [A]ntitrust courts can and do consider the particular circumstances of an industry and therefore adjust their usual rules to the existence, extent, and nature of regulation. Just as the administrative agency must consider the competitive premises of the antitrust laws, the antitrust court must consider the peculiarities of an industry as recognized in a regulatory statute.

1 P. Areeda & D. Turner, *Antitrust Law* ¶ 223d (1978).

In its broad outline, the offense of monopolization is well understood. Most recently, the Supreme Court has stated:

> The offense of monopoly under §2 of the Sherman Act has two elements: (1) the possession of monopoly power in the relevant market and (2) the willful acquisition or maintenance of that power as distinguished from growth or development as a consequence of a superior product, business acumen, or historic accident.

Cases dealing with non-regulated industries have developed a number of analytic tools designed to aid courts in identifying each of these elements. In many instances, however, these tools are of only limited value in resolving monopolization charges against regulated monopolies. In particular, the presence of a substantial degree of regulation, although not sufficient to confer antitrust immunity, may effect both the shape of "monopoly power" and the precise dimensions of the "willful acquisition or maintenance" of that power.

According to the Supreme Court, monopoly power may be defined as "the power to control prices or exclude competition" in a relevant market. *United States v. E. I. duPont De Nemours & Co.*, 351 U.S. 377, 391 (1956). In many cases involving unregulated industries, however, courts have eschewed examination of the ostensible monopolist's actual degree of control over prices or competition, and have relied solely on statistical data concerning the accused firm's share of the market. Where that data reveals a market share of more than seventy to eighty percent, the courts have inferred the existence of monopoly power.

Such a heavy reliance on market share statistics is likely to be an inaccurate or misleading indicator of "monopoly power" in a regulated setting. In many regulated industries, each purveyor of service, regardless of absolute size, is in a mono-poly position with regard to its customers. Indeed, while a regulated firm's dominant share of the market typically explains *why* it is subject to regulation, the firm's statistical dominance may also be the *result* of regulation. For these reasons, the size of a regulated company's market share should constitute, at most, a point of departure in assessing the existence of monopoly power. Ultimately, that analysis must focus directly on the ability of the regulated company to control prices or exclude competition — an assessment which, in turn, requires close scrutiny of the regulatory scheme in question.

In the instant case, the district court properly instructed the jury that, in determining whether AT&T possessed monopoly power in the relevant market,

> you may consider the effect of the FCC's exercise of regulatory authority over prices and entry, including interconnection. Similarly, you may consider the effect of the exercise by state regulatory agencies of regulatory authority over prices and entry in connection with the provision of local services and facilities. That AT&T may have had the largest share or the entire share of the telephone business in certain areas would not be sufficient to establish that AT&T possessed monopoly power if in fact regulation by regulatory agencies prevented AT&T from having the power to restrict entry or control prices.

Although the district court's instructions in this area might have been more helpful if they had described, in more detail, the specific regulatory scheme to which AT&T was subject, we believe the instructions, taken as a whole, adequately apprised the jury of its duty "to take into account the unique federal and state regulatory restraints" to which AT&T was subject....

AT&T's status as a regulated public utility also bears on the second element of a monopolization offense: the willful acquisition or maintenance of monopoly power. The precise dimensions of the "willfulness" standard have been the subject of considerable litigation and varying formulations even in cases involving unregulated industries. Some courts, building upon Judge Learned Hand's noted opinion in *United States v. Aluminum Co. of America*, 148 F.2d 416 (2d Cir. 1945), have concluded that monopolistic conduct can be presumed from the possession of monopoly power unless the accused firm affirmatively demonstrates that its monopoly position has been "thrust upon it." Under this analysis, if the ordinary business conduct of a dominant firm leads to the acquisition or maintenance of monopoly power, that conduct is presumed to reflect the requisite willful monopolistic intent. Whatever merit this presumption may have in other contexts, we believe it is a particularly inappropriate means of identifying monopolistic conduct by a regulated utility or common carrier. For these industries, anticipating and meeting all reasonable demands for services is often an explicit statutory obligation. To apply the *Alcoa* presumption to such conduct would be tantamount to holding that adherence to a firm's regulatory obligation could, by itself, constitute improper willfulness in a section 2 monopolization case.

....

The impact of regulation was also an important element of AT&T's defense in the instant case. Particularly with regard to the interconnection controversy, AT&T argued that its dealings with MCI were reasonable and that they represented a good faith attempt to comply with AT&T's regulatory obligations under section 201 of the Communications Act. AT&T claims that the trial court's instructions improperly prevented the jury from considering this defense, in that the instructions were fatally "silent concerning the overall structure of the Communications Act, the public interest standards under which the provisions of that Act are administered by the FCC and to which common carriers are required to conform their conduct, and the requirements set forth in the Act relating to the particular interconnection and pricing controversies presented to the jury for resolution."

NOTES AND QUESTIONS

1. Many federal statutes creating regulatory regimes say little or nothing about the impact of agency regulation on possible antitrust scrutiny of the regulated firms. As a result the courts have had to develop rules for determining when antitrust actions can proceed or must give way. Under the doctrine of "primary jurisdiction" the antitrust laws, which are general, must give way to the more specific provisions of a federal regulatory statute when it is clear that enforcement of the antitrust laws would frustrate the specific regulatory scheme. This generally means that allegedly anticompetitive conduct in these industries is evaluated initially by some federal agency other than the Department of Justice, the Federal Trade Commission, or the courts. If the particular activity alleged to be an antitrust violation is mandated by the regulatory agency, or if it has been approved by the agency after a full consideration of the consequences for competition, then the antitrust laws have been preempted. *See Hughes Tool Co. v. Trans World Airlines*, 409 U.S. 363 (1973). If the agency's approval of activity initiated by the firm is merely pro forma, however, or if the agency did not fully evaluate the activity in order to determine the effects on competition, then there will be considerable room for antitrust enforcement. *See* 1A P. Areeda & H. Hovenkamp, *Antitrust Law* ¶¶ 240-46 (rev. ed. 1997).

When analyzing the scope of antitrust coverage in regulated industries the courts generally begin with the proposition that "[r]epeals of the antitrust laws by implication from a regulatory statute are strongly disfavored, and have only been found in cases of plain repugnancy between the antitrust and regulatory provisions." *United States v. Philadelphia Nat'l Bank*, 374 U.S. 321, 350-51 (1963) (bank merger approved by Comptroller of the Currency was not immunized, since regulation of banking is not "so comprehensive that enforcement of the antitrust laws would be either unnecessary ... or disruptive"). The standard is difficult to meet, but not impossible. *See, e.g., Pan Am. World Airways v. United States*, 371 U.S. 296 (1962) (CAB's authority to regulate "unfair or deceptive practice or unfair methods of competition" gave it primary authority over injunctive relief against most anticompetitive acts).

An interesting case where "repugnancy" was found is *Gordon v. New York Stock Exch.*, 422 U.S. 659 (1975). The Securities and Exchange Commission had been given power under the Securities Exchange Act to alter or supplement stock exchange rules that fixed "reasonable rates of commission." The Court held that this authority, coupled with the SEC's history of actively regulating commissions, immunized the exchange's rate-setting from antitrust scrutiny. The Court was concerned that having a court impose requirements on the exchange different from those that the SEC imposed would interfere with the proper functioning of the Act.

In *Finnegan v. Campeau Corp.*, 915 F.2d 824 (2d Cir. 1990), the court held that "the antitrust laws are inconsistent with the Williams Act [Securities Law take-over disclosure requirement] and implied repeal is necessary to make the securities regulations work." Campeau had commenced an unsolicited tender offer for all the shares of Federated Department Stores. Federated agreed to be acquired by Macy. Discussions among Campeau, Macy, and Federated resulted in a settlement, in which Campeau and Macy agreed to stop bidding against one another. Campeau agreed to acquire Federated and to sell to Macy certain Federated assets. Disgruntled Federated shareholders sued, alleging that the agreement between Campeau and Macy to refrain from bidding violated § 1 of the Sherman Act. Clearly, an agreement among bidders in an unregulated auction that one would stop bidding so that the second could obtain a lower price would be illegal price fixing.

The Second Circuit stated that "disclosure is the means by which Congress sought to protect target shareholders [and] that once information regarding an agreement between rival bidders has been revealed in a filing, the target company's shareholders have received the protection Congress and the SEC designed for them." The court also noted that "the application of the antitrust laws [to joint bidding arrangements] would upset the balance among incumbent management, target shareholders and bidders which Congress sought to achieve through the Williams Act."

2. In *Square D Co. v. Niagara Frontier Tariff Bur.*, 476 U.S. 409 (1986), the Supreme Court reaffirmed the so-called *Keogh* doctrine, established in *Keogh v. Chicago & Nw. R.R.*, 260 U.S. 156 (1922), that a rate which has been filed and approved by the Interstate Commerce Commission cannot form the basis of a treble damage action based on the theory that those proposing the rate were engaged in price fixing.

Keogh's rationale, as Justice Brandeis explained in the Court's opinion, was to honor "the paramount purpose of Congress — prevention of unjust discrimination...." In fact, a principal purpose of regulated rates in the late nineteenth and early twentieth centuries was to defeat the attempts of large companies to drive smaller firms out of business by obtaining discriminatorily low rates from railroad companies. For example, Standard Oil Co. was alleged to have acquired its monopoly in this way.

The regulatory world has changed a great deal since *Keogh*, however. First, the principal stated purpose of rate regulation today is not to prohibit price discrimination but rather to force efficient pricing in monopoly markets (although many regulated markets are not monopolies). In fact, a certain amount of price discrimination is actually encouraged. Second, procedural devices such as class action suits and offensive collateral estoppel tend to make antitrust damages awards against regulated firms nondiscriminatory — i.e., all firms who paid a cartel rate would be in an equally good position to collect damages. Finally, and perhaps most significantly, one of the most important consequences of the deregulation movement has been to inject more antitrust into the regulated industries. The law against cartelization, whose anticompetitive effects are most easily recognized, would seem to be a good place to start.

Nevertheless, the Supreme Court ruled in *Square D* that *Keogh* "represents a longstanding statutory construction that Congress has consistently refused to disturb, even when revisiting this specific area of law." For example, when Congress passed the Motor Carrier Act of 1980, which greatly deregulated the trucking industry, it made no attempt to change the doctrine. "If there is to be an overruling of the *Keogh* rule, it must come from Congress, rather than from this Court." The Court noted, however, that *Keogh* did not confer antitrust *immunity* on the defendants; it merely held that they could not be liable for treble damages. They could still be found liable in a civil or criminal government action.

Suppose that a private plaintiff alleges not that a filed rate is the result of price fixing but that the rate is predatory, designed to exclude a rival from the market? The circuit courts do not agree about whether a *competitor* can challenge a filed rate. *See In re Lower Lake Erie Iron Ore Antitrust Litig.*, 998 F.2d 1144 (3d Cir. 1993) (permitting a competitor challenge); *Barnes v. Arden Mayfair*, 759 F.2d 676 (9th Cir. 1985) (same); *City of Kirkwood v. Union Elec. Co.*, 671 F.2d 1173, 1178 (8th Cir.), *cert. denied*, 459 U.S. 1170 (1983) (same). *But see Pinney Dock & Transp. Co. v. Penn Cent. Corp.*, 838 F.2d 1445 (6th Cir. 1988), interpreting *Keogh* to require that the regulatory commission be "the sole source of the rights not only of shippers, but of the entire public, including competitors." On the filed rate doctrine, *see* 1A P. Areeda & H. Hovenkamp, *Antitrust Law*, at ¶ 247.

3. The *MCI* case suggests the strong relationship that exists between technology and the economics of regulation. When telecommunications required overhead or underground lines linking all buildings provided with telephone service, the entire telephone system (except for the instruments) was arguably a natural monopoly. The cost of two or more competing systems, when one was sufficient to carry the entire load, would be very high, particularly if a substantial cost of providing telephone services is the installation of the physical system itself, while marginal costs (the cost of one additional phone call) are very low. Once microwave and other forms of wireless communication became a part of the system, however, the system's status as a natural monopoly began to erode. For example it might be economic for two or more firms in competition to provide wireless communication between distant cities. These changes in technology are the principle economic reason for the divestiture of the telephone company, in which the local operating companies were separated from American Telephone & Telegraph Co., which provides long distance services. *United States v. AT&T*, 552 F. Supp. 131 (D.D.C. 1982), *aff'd sub nom. Maryland v. United States*, 460 U.S. 1001 (1983). *See* S. Breyer, *Regulation and Its Reform*, 285-314 (1982).

If the costs of pervasive agency regulation are higher than the costs of competition (and many economists believe they are significantly higher), then the most efficient regulatory scheme will permit price-regulated monopolies to exist only to the extent that they are bona fide natural monopolies: that is, only in those areas where competition of incumbents would not produce lower prices and higher output. The telephone companies once took the position that not only the lines, but even the manufacture and sale or lease of telephone instruments should be a monopoly. For many years it was either impossible or else very expensive for a customer to lease a phone line from the telephone company without obtaining telephone instruments from the company as well. The telephone companies generally argued that a monopoly in the instruments was necessary because improperly designed instruments could damage the telephone lines themselves. Both the FCC and the courts eventually rejected that argument. *See Litton Sys. v. AT&T*, 700 F.2d 785 (2d Cir. 1983), *cert. denied*, 464 U.S. 1073 (1984); *Phonetele, Inc. v. AT&T*, 664 F.2d 716 (9th Cir. 1981), *cert. denied*, 459 U.S. 1145 (1983); *Hush-A-Phone Corp. v. United States*, 238 F.2d 266 (D.C. Cir. 1956). *See also* Brennan, *Why Regulated Firms Should Be Kept Out of Unregulated Markets: Understanding the Divestiture in United States v. AT&T*, 32 Antitrust Bull. 741 (1988).

The Federal Telecommunications Act of 1996 significantly deregulates telecommunications. In particular:

1. The Act contemplates increased competition in all parts of the telecommunications system, including even the (traditionally) hard-wired local telephone service, which has always been a price regulated monopoly subject to only modest competition, but which the framers of the statute no longer regard as a natural monopoly.

2. The new legislation severely limits the power of states to regulate and thus create "state-action" antitrust immunities for activities within their state. (On the "state action" exemption, see *infra*, Section III, Part B.) The 1996 Telecommunications Act provides that:

No State or local statute or regulation, or other State or local legal requirement, may prohibit or have the effect of prohibiting the ability of any entity to provide any interstate or intrastate telecommunications service.

47 U.S.C. § 253(a). However, the statute also expressly permits states to compel universal service and to govern consumer protection, to manage the process of creating, protecting, and compensating for easements and rights

of way for utilities, and to determine eligibility to serve rural markets. Conceivably, any one of these provisions could be employed so as to protect incumbent telephone companies from entry by outsiders. *See* P. Huber, M. Kellogg, & J. Thorne, *The Telecommunications Act of 1996* § 1.1.1 (1996). But the Federal Communications Commission has broad authority to set aside any state law or rule that is deemed inconsistent with the Act's purpose. *See* 47 U.S.C. § 261.

3. The general policy of the Telecommunications Act is to require "interconnection" between various telecommunications providers on reasonable terms at virtually every point in the telecommunications network where interconnection is possible. 47 U.S.C. § 251(a) of the statute provides that "each telecommunications carrier has the duty ... to interconnect directly or indirectly with the facilities and equipment of other telecommunications carriers; and ... not to install network features, functions, or capabilities that do not comply with the guidelines and standards established ...." This requirement effectively compels local telephone firms (1) to permit resale of services; (2) to provide telephone number portability and "equality" in dialing access; (3) to afford access to physical interconnection points including switches, poles, conduits, and rights of way, and even the right to place switching and interconnection equipment within the buildings of a competing local carrier; and (4) to provide all necessary interconnection services, including information services.

To the extent any one of these interconnection or cooperation requirements is not specifically compelled by an FCC rule, antitrust may have a role in determining the proper dealing requirements and perhaps even the price under which dealing transactions are to be made. Meanwhile, the FCC is obliged to promulgate and implement regulations determining the appropriate terms and conditions for such cooperation. Importantly, the interconnection obligations in the Act do not depend on a prior finding of market power or monopoly power on the part of the firm from whom the interconnection is sought. Whether power or exclusive control will become an element in FCC regulations remains to be seen.

4. While mergers among covered telephone carriers were formerly governed by the Federal Communications Act, which permitted the FCC to immunize the merger from antitrust scrutiny, that statute is now repealed and such mergers will fall within the jurisdiction of the antitrust laws.

5. Finally, the Telecommunications Act contains a provision that "... nothing in this Act or the Amendments made by this Act shall be construed to modify, impair or supersede the applicability of any antitrust laws." 47 U.S.C. § 601(b)(1). The Conference Committee reporting on the final bill observed:

> ... in the future, the conferees anticipate that cable companies will be providing local telephone service and the BOC's will be providing cable

service. Mergers between these kinds of companies should not be allowed to go through without a thorough antitrust review .... By returning review of mergers in a competitive industry to the DOJ, this repeal would be consistent with one of the underlying themes of the bill — to get both agencies back to their proper roles and to end government by consent decree.... The repeal would not affect the [Federal Communications] Commission's ability to conduct any review of a merger for Communications Act purposes, e.g., transfer of licenses. Rather, it would simply end the Commission's ability to confer antitrust immunity.

Joint Explanatory Statement of the Committee of Conference, § 601, Telecommunications Act of 1996, PL 104-104.

4. Does a statutory monopolist have market power? In most cases the answer is yes. Not only does it have 100% of a defined market, but elasticity of supply is very low: other firms are prohibited by law from entering the market. Furthermore, with respect to many of the services rendered by regulated monopolists the elasticity of demand at current prices is quite low too: most people would be willing to pay more for electricity, water, telephone service, or natural gas, for example, than they pay under a regime of price regulation. If that were not the case — if the firm's profit-maximizing price were very close to the regulated price — then the value of price regulation would be questionable.

The offense of monopolization requires two elements, however, market power and some exclusionary or anticompetitive act. Why would a statutory monopolist commit an "exclusionary" act? After all, it already has the protection of a statute that effectively excludes everyone. As in the *MCI* case, the allegation is generally that the statutory monopolist attempted to monopolize some market closely related to the statutory monopoly, but not necessarily a part of it. In other words, the defendant attempted to turn one (legal) monopoly into two. By requiring all telephone line lessees to rent their instruments from itself, for example, American Telephone and Telegraph can effectively extend a phone line monopoly into a phone-line-and-instrument monopoly: the independent market for instruments vanishes if all users of AT&T's monopoly lines must also use its instruments.

But can a monopolist enlarge its monopoly profits by acquiring a second monopoly of an integrally related product? As both the discussion of vertical integration and tying arrangements indicates, generally it cannot. A monopolist of a single part of any process or integrated product can usually extract all the monopoly profits available. This is so because customers are interested only in the final output price, not in the price of each component. For example, when a residential customer pays $10.00 per month for residential telephone service, he is generally indifferent whether that service is billed out at $2.00 for the lines and $8.00 for the instrument, or $5.00 for the lines and $5.00 for the instrument, etc. His bill is the same no matter how the costs are divided between the telephone and the lines.

The exception to this rule is when the monopolist is prevented by a regulatory agency from charging its profit-maximizing price for its monopoly service. In that case, the regulated monopolist might want to obtain a second monopoly in a product or service that is not price-regulated. For example, if customers are willing to pay $8.00 monthly for phone service, but the price is set by the regulatory agency at $5.00, which is sufficient to give the telephone company a competitive rate of return, the company might require customers to lease its telephones as a condition of subscribing to its lines, and charge $3.00 more than the competitive price for the telephones. This is a common form of rate regulation evasion when regulated firms are permitted to operate in vertically-related, unregulated markets. *See* H. Hovenkamp, *Federal Antitrust Policy* §§ 9.5c, 10.6c (2d ed. 1994).

5. Another problem that occurs when regulated firms operate in unregulated markets is "cross-subsidization," which can occur when a firm attributes costs in one market to a different market. For example, suppose that the long distance telecommunications market is competitive, while the local telephone exchanges are price regulated monopolies. However, one firm both operates the local exchanges and competes in the long distance market. If that firm can convince the regulatory agency to attribute to local service costs that really apply to long distance service, it can charge a lower price for long distance service than its competitors, who do not operate in a regulated market. Precise cost attribution as between long distance and local telephone service is virtually impossible (when you call from a telephone in San Francisco to one in New York, what percentage of the cost is borne by the local San Francisco exchange, and what part by the "long lines," permitting long distance communication?). This explains why the AT&T divestiture required the price regulated local operating companies to get out of the competitively operated long distance telecommunications market, and vice-versa.

6. In *Town of Concord v. Boston Edison Co.*, 915 F.2d 17, 25 (1st Cir. 1990), the court considered charges of a price "squeeze" by a regulated electric utility. The utility was accused of selling wholesale power at a high price to smaller municipal power companies, but of charging a low retail price for its own electricity. This allegedly made it difficult for the smaller utilities to compete with the defendant for new customers along the common boundaries of their service areas. Without finding a regulatory exemption, the court dismissed the complaint, holding that the presence of comprehensive regulation greatly undermined the plausibility of the plaintiffs' claims. In this case, regulation of both utility prices and of new entry by others

> diminishes the likelihood of "entry barrier" harm, namely the risk that (1) prices will rise because (2) new firms will hesitate to enter a market and compete after (3) a squeeze has driven pre-existing independent competitors from the marketplace. All three propositions are made doubtful by regulation.

Further, the court noted, any rule forbidding such price squeezes would add a new dimension to the problem of determining the utility's optimal rates. Regulatory agencies are generally incapable of making any more than rough judgments about the optimal rate for a regulated company to charge. Further, any kind of innovative pricing technique could injure competing firms not undertaking the innovation:

> [C]ourt involvement in the rate-setting process could easily discourage utilities from proposing, and commissions from considering, such innovative, economically based, energy-conserving pricing systems as off-peak pricing (charging higher prices for electricity used during peak periods), incremental-cost pricing (charging prices for certain services reflecting the higher costs of hypothetical new construction, or even traditional Ramsey pricing (tailoring rates to reflect the comparative likelihood that higher rates will force customers to discontinue service) ....

D. ANTITRUST EXEMPTIONS

1. LABOR ORGANIZATIONS

At common law, courts considered labor unions to be nothing more than cartels. Combinations of sellers of labor were dealt with in the same way as combinations of sellers of products. This judicial hostility toward labor unions increased after the Sherman Act was passed, largely because the statute contained no exception for labor organizations. *See* H. Hovenkamp, *Enterprise and American Law, 1836-1937*, chs. 18-19 (1991). But in 1914 Congress created the first labor exemption in the Clayton Act.

Section 6 of the Clayton Act provides that the antitrust laws shall not be construed to "forbid the existence and operation" of labor organizations, or to "forbid or restrain individual members of such organizations from lawfully carrying out" their "legitimate objects." In addition, labor organizations are not to be construed as illegal combinations or conspiracies in restraint of trade under the antitrust laws. 15 U.S.C. § 17. Section 20 of the Clayton Act provides that strikes and other specified labor activities are not to be considered "violations of any law of the United States."

Originally, the Supreme Court read this labor exemption narrowly. Section 6 immunizes only activities "lawfully carrying out" a union's "legitimate objects." The Court reasoned that since a secondary boycott by a labor union was neither "lawful" nor a "legitimate object," it was not protected by the Clayton Act. *Duplex Printing Press Co. v. Deering*, 254 U.S. 443, 468-69 (1921).

In 1932, Congress passed the Norris-LaGuardia Act, which deprived federal courts of the power to issue injunctions in most labor disputes, including secondary boycotts. This Act, which ostensibly had nothing to do with antitrust law, nonetheless triggered reconsideration of the labor exemption by the Supreme Court. In *United States v. Hutcheson*, 312 U.S. 219 (1941), the Court gave a new, and much broader, reading to the exemption. The Court read what it termed the "interlacing" statutes — the Sherman Act, the Clayton Act, and the Norris-LaGuardia Act — as the equivalent of a single, unified provision, and concluded that conduct protected by the Clayton and Norris-LaGuardia Acts would not violate the Sherman Act. Under this new formulation,

> [i]f the facts ... come within the conduct enumerated in § 20 of the Clayton Act they do not constitute a crime within the general terms of the Sherman Law .... So long as a union acts in its self-interest and does not combine with non-labor groups, the licit and the illicit under § 20 are not to be distinguished by any judgment regarding the wisdom or unwisdom, the rightness or wrongness, the selfishness or unselfishness of the end of which the particular union activities are the means.

Id. at 232.

The statutory exemption for labor organizations does not apply when a union enters into an agreement with a nonlabor group. Agreements or arrangements between unions and employers are neither expressly barred nor expressly permitted by the Clayton or Norris-LaGuardia Acts. *See United Mine Workers v. Pennington*, 381 U.S. 657, 662 (1965). The statutory exemption thus applies to unilateral acts by unions, but not to agreements with employers.

The difficulty with this formulation is obvious: the labor policy of the United States favors collective bargaining and the formation of contracts between employers and employees. These contracts necessarily are agreements "in combination with" employers, who are a nonlabor group. Many of these contracts contain provisions that can restrain trade. To resolve this conflict between labor and antitrust policy, the courts have created a "limited nonstatutory exemption from antitrust sanctions" for employer-union agreements. *See Connell Constr. Co. v. Plumbers Local 100*, 421 U.S. 616, 622 (1975).

If the court finds a combination with a nonlabor group, the next question becomes whether the union is acting in its self-interest. The line drawing is problematic. Agreements affecting wages, for example, are plainly matters of direct interest to labor unions. It is permissible for a union to bargain with a multi-employer unit — a group of employers who bargain together as a single unit — and sign contracts that fix wages for many competitors. A union is free to fix a wage scale and attempt to force each employer it bargains with to adhere to that scale. But when a union agrees with one group of employers to impose a certain wage scale on other employers without bargaining with the latter group, it forfeits its exemption — at least where there is evidence of intent to drive other employers out of business. *United Mine Workers v. Pennington*, 381 U.S. 657, 665-66 (1965) (three justice plurality).

The nonstatutory exemption also requires that the challenged agreement must affect principally only the bargaining parties. In *Continental Maritime v. Pacific Coast Metal*, 817 F.2d 1391 (9th Cir. 1987), the Ninth Circuit approved an agreement between a union and two Portland, Oregon shipbuilders to work temporarily for lower wages. The agreement was challenged by a competing shipbuilder from San Francisco, with whom the unions refused to negotiate a similar agreement, who alleged a combination among the parties to injure its business. As the court suggested, however, the requirement that the agreement affect principally the bargaining parties applies to effects made explicit in the agreement itself, not generally to effects that an agreement may have on the market.

The means chosen by the union to implement its self interest must not restrict the market more than is necessary to achieve legitimate union goals. *H.A. Artists & Assocs. v. Actors' Equity Ass'n*, 451 U.S. 704, 722 (1981). Agreements between unions and employers to deny other competitors entry into the market are not exempt from antitrust sanctions, for they restrict the market more than is necessary. For example, a union-employer agreement that contractors will buy only from local union manufacturers, and that manufacturers will sell only to local union contractors, violates the antitrust laws. *Allen Bradley Co. v. Local Union No. 3*, 325 U.S. 797, 809 (1945) (union's involvement was only part of a general conspiracy among local businesses to restrain trade). The Court reached a similar result in *Connell Constr. Co. v. Plumbers Local 100*, 421 U.S. 616 (1975) (union and employer with whom union had no relationship could not agree to subcontract work only to contractors who had contracts with local union). But unions legitimately may be concerned about preserving work traditionally done by union members, and agreements restricting the employer's ability to deal may be the key to such job preservation. *National Woodwork Mfrs. Ass'n v. NLRB*, 386 U.S. 612 (1967). A union-employer agreement that all goods produced by the employers must be delivered by union drivers has therefore been held permissible. *Grandad Bread, Inc. v. Continental Baking Co.*, 612 F.2d 1105, 1110-11 (9th Cir. 1979) (preservation of union jobs is "a matter properly considered in the collective bargaining agreement"), *cert. denied*, 449 U.S. 1076 (1981).

Other conditions of employment are also proper subjects for agreement. For example, a union may agree with grocery stores to set fixed hours for sales of meat for all stores in a metropolitan area, since the union had a significant interest in the hours worked by its butchers. *Amalgamated Meat Cutters Local 189 v. Jewel Tea Co.*, 381 U.S. 676 (1965) (plurality opinion). The issue is whether the restriction is "intimately related to wages, hours and working conditions" and is not undertaken "at the behest of or in combination with nonlabor groups." *Id.* at 689-90.

In *Brown v. Pro Football, Inc.*, 116 S. Ct. 2116 (1996), the Supreme Court interpreted the nonstatutory labor exemption to immunize a horizontal agreement among a group of employers — in this case, professional football teams seeking to cap the salaries of certain classes of players. Importantly, the action was taken in response to ongoing collective bargaining that had reached an impasse. The Court wrote:

> As a matter of logic, it would be difficult, if not impossible, to require groups of employers and employees to bargain together, but at the same time to forbid them to make among themselves or with each other any of the competition-restricting agreements potentially necessary to make the process work or its results mutually acceptable. Thus, the implicit exemption recog-

nizes that, to give effect to federal labor laws and policies and to allow meaningful collective bargaining to take place, some restraints on competition imposed through the bargaining process must be shielded from antitrust sanctions....

Consequently, the question before us is one of determining the exemption's scope: Does it apply to an agreement among several employers bargaining together to implement after impasse the terms of their last best good-faith wage offer? We assume that such conduct, as practiced in this case, is unobjectionable as a matter of labor law and policy. On that assumption, we conclude that the exemption applies....

Although the caselaw we have cited focuses upon bargaining by a single employer, no one here has argued that labor law does, or should, treat multiemployer bargaining differently in this respect. Indeed, Board and court decisions suggest that the joint implementation of proposed terms after impasse is a familiar practice in the context of multiemployer bargaining....

Multiemployer bargaining itself is a well-established, important, pervasive method of collective bargaining, offering advantages to both management and labor. See Appendix (multi-employer bargaining accounts for more than 40% of major collective-bargaining agreements, and is used in such industries as construction, transportation, retail trade, clothing manufacture, and real estate, as well as professional sports).... The upshot is that the practice at issue here plays a significant role in a collective-bargaining process that itself comprises an important part of the Nation's industrial relations system.

In these circumstances, to subject the practice to antitrust law is to require antitrust courts to answer a host of important practical questions about how collective bargaining over wages, hours and working conditions is to proceed — the very result that the implicit labor exemption seeks to avoid. And it is to place in jeopardy some of the potentially beneficial labor-related effects that multi-employer bargaining can achieve. That is because unlike labor law, which sometimes welcomes anticompetitive agreements conducive to industrial harmony, antitrust law forbids all agreements among competitors (such as competing employers) that unreasonably lessen competition among or between them in virtually any respect whatsoever....

For these reasons, we hold that the implicit ("nonstatutory") antitrust exemption applies to the employer conduct at issue here. That conduct took place during and immediately after a collective-bargaining negotiation. It grew out of, and was directly related to, the lawful operation of the bargaining process. It involved a matter that the parties were required to negotiate collectively. And it concerned only the parties to the collective-bargaining relationship.

Our holding is not intended to insulate from antitrust review every joint imposition of terms by employers, for an agreement among employers could be sufficiently distant in time and in circumstances from the collective-bargaining process that a rule permitting antitrust intervention would not significantly interfere with that process.... We need not decide in this case whether, or where, within these extreme outer boundaries to draw that line. Nor would it be appropriate for us to do so without the detailed views of the Board, to whose "specialized judgment" Congress "intended to leave" many of the "inevitable questions concerning multi-employer bargaining bound to arise in the future."

For comprehensive treatment of the labor exemption, *see* 2A P. Areeda & H. Hovenkamp, *Antitrust Law* ¶¶ 255-57 (rev. ed. 1997).

PROBLEM 9.1

The Detroit Auto Dealers Association entered into an agreement that new car dealers in Detroit would limit showroom hours by closing on Saturday and on three weekday evenings. When the Federal Trade Commission sought an injunction, the defendants, 90 auto dealers and their trade association, argued that the conduct was exempted from the Sherman Act by the labor exemption. Defendants asserted that the closing restrictions were an attempt to defend themselves against the possibility of unionization of sales people and against the threats (and acts) of violence which often accompanied unionization attempts in the Detroit area. Does the labor exemption apply to defendants' agreement? Would your answer change if the unions were also parties to the agreement that restricted hours? *See Detroit Auto Dealers Ass'n v. FTC*, 955 F.2d 457 (6th Cir. 1991), *cert. denied*, 506 U.S. 972 (1992).

2. EXPORT ASSOCIATIONS

Fostering competition is a major goal of American antitrust policy. But American companies operating on a world-wide scale often are faced with competition from foreign cartels, which may not be restricted by such laws. Congress has on two occasions provided an exemption from the Sherman Act for American businesses engaged in the export trade. The Webb-Pomerene Act was passed in 1918 to "aid and encourage" American manufacturers to extend the nation's foreign trade. "Congress felt that American firms needed the power to form joint export associations in order to compete with foreign cartels. But ... the exemption created was carefully hedged to avoid substantial injury to domestic interests." *United States v. Concentrated Phosphate Export Ass'n*, 393 U.S. 199, 206 (1968). Section 2 of the Webb-Pomerene Act, 15 U.S.C. § 62, exempts any "association" whose "sole purpose" is engaging in export trade, so long as (1) its actions do not restrain trade within the United States or restrain the export trade of its domestic competitors; and (2) it does nothing that "artificially or intentionally enhances or depresses the prices" or substantially lessens competition or restrains trade *within* the United States. The "unfair methods of competition" provisions of the FTC Act *are* applicable to export associations, however. *Id.* § 64.

To qualify for the exemption, export associations must file a number of documents with the Federal Trade Commission, and must make annual reports to the FTC. *Id.* § 65. The FTC has the power to investigate the association. If it finds a prohibited restraint, it may issue "recommendations" to the association for "readjustment" of its business. If the association fails to comply, the FTC may refer the case to the Attorney General for prosecution. Since, in this event, the association has forfeited its exemption, it also leaves itself open to ordinary antitrust remedies. *See United States Alkali Export Ass'n v. United States*, 325 U.S. 196 (1945).

Because of the antitrust liability uncertainties surrounding the interpretation of the law governing export trade, Congress in 1982 passed the Export Trading Company Act. 15 U.S.C. §§ 4001-4021. Its purpose was to encourage exports by facilitating the formation and operation of export trading companies, export trade associations, and the expansion of export trade service. *Id.* § 4001(b). Under the 1982 Act, the Department of Commerce has the authority, with the concurrence of the Department of Justice, to certify export trading companies.

Four antitrust standards must be met before certification can be granted. Section 4013(a) requires the applicant to show that the proposed conduct will

> (1) result in neither a substantial lessening of competition or restraint of trade within the United States nor a substantial restraint of the export trade of any competitor of the applicant;
>
> (2) not unreasonably enhance, stabilize, or depress prices within the United States ... ;
>
> (3) not constitute unfair methods of competition against competitors engaged in the export of goods, wares, merchandise, or services of the class exported by the applicant; and
>
> (4) not ... reasonably be expected to result in the sale for consumption or resale within the United States of the goods, wares, merchandise, or services exported of the class by the applicant.

Once the export trading company obtains a certificate, it is immunized from antitrust suits brought by federal or state enforcement officials "whenever the conduct that forms the basis of the action is specified in, and complies with, the terms of the certificate. Conduct which falls outside the scope of, or violates the terms of, the certificate is 'ultra vires' and would not be protected." H.R. Rep. No. 924, 97th Cong., 2d Sess. 7 (1982).

Section 4016 provides for private antitrust actions for injunctive relief or actual damages against the export certificate-holder if specific antitrust standards set out in section 4013 have been violated. The statute of limitations for a private action is two years from notice of the violation. The certificate itself creates a presumption of legality for conduct specified in the certificate. A successful defendant is entitled to recover reasonable costs and attorney's fees.

Finally, Title IV of the Act (the Foreign Trade Antitrust Improvements of 1982, 96 Stat. 1246), which supplements the antitrust certification provisions of

Title III, amended the Sherman Act and the FTC Act to require that before they can serve as a jurisdictional threshold for enforcement actions against exporting entities, such conduct must have a "direct, *substantial*, and reasonably foreseeable effect" on commerce in the United States, or on the export commerce of a United States resident. 15 U.S.C. § 6a; *Id.* § 45(a)(3). *See also National Bank of Canada v. Interbank Card Ass'n*, 666 F.2d 6, 8 (2d Cir. 1981). The statute also permits the Secretary of Commerce to issue a certificate regarding specific export trading practices, the effect of which insulates, under certain circumstances, the holder of the certificate from treble damage suits.

3. INSURANCE

The McCarran-Ferguson Act, 15 U.S.C. §§ 1011-1012, specifically provides that the Sherman Act, the Clayton Act, and the FTC Act are only "applicable to the business of insurance to the extent that such business is not regulated by State law." A particular practice that under normal circumstances would violate the antitrust laws (e.g., price fixing), is immune from attack if it is done in the course of activities authorized and regulated by state law. There are two requirements for application of the exemption: (1) the questioned activity must be part of the "business of insurance," and (2) it must be authorized and regulated by the state.

The first requirement demands a definition of "business of insurance." An "indispensable characteristic of insurance" is the "spreading and underwriting of a policyholder's risk," which "strongly suggest[s] that Congress understood the business of insurance to be the underwriting and spreading of risk." *Group Life & Health Ins. Co. v. Royal Drug Co.*, 440 U.S. 205, 211-12, 220-21 (1979). *Royal Drug* held that agreements entered into by an insurance company, under which it set the maximum price it would pay for drugs, and which enabled it to "minimize costs and maximize profits," were outside the "business of insurance" and were therefore not immunized by the McCarran-Ferguson Act. *Id.* at 214. The relationship of insurer to insured ("the 'business of insurance'"), not that of insurer to non-insureds ("the business of insurance companies"), was the subject that Congress intended to immunize. *Id.* at 215-17. The primary concern of Congress, said the Court, was that "cooperative ratemaking efforts be exempt." *Id.* at 221.

In *Union Labor Life Ins. Co. v. Pireno*, 458 U.S. 119 (1982), the Supreme Court distilled the *Royal Drug* holding into a three-prong test for determining whether a particular practice was part of the "business of insurance":

> *[F]irst*, whether the practice has the effect of transferring or spreading a policyholder's risk; *second*, whether the practice is an integral part of the policy relationship between the insurer and the insured; and *third*, whether the practice is limited to entities within the insurance industry. None of these criteria is necessarily determinative in itself....

Id. at 129. At issue in *Pireno* was an insurance company's use of a physician peer review panel to determine whether a particular physician's treatments and rates were "reasonable." Since the peer review panel served only to keep the insurer's costs (and, therefore, the insureds' premiums) down, but played no part in the spreading and underwriting of a policyholder's risk, it was not exempt from antitrust attack. *Id.* at 130-31. *See also United States v. Title Ins. Rating Bur. of Ariz.,* 700 F.2d 1247 (9th Cir. 1983), holding that an agreement among title insurers to fix escrow fees was not exempt because many other businesses, such as banks and escrow companies, offered the same services, and the services themselves were unrelated to the spreading of any risk.

The second requirement of the statute is normally easier to satisfy. The actual setting of rates and regulation of insurer-insured relations is normally done by state insurance commissions. The activities of insurance rate bureaus (which set rates for policies) are exempt from antitrust attack if they are licensed and supervised by the state. *See North Little Rock Transp. Co. v. Casualty Reciprocal Exch.,* 181 F.2d 174 (8th Cir. 1950). But this analysis is not free from problems. For example, suppose state *A*'s prohibition on insurance company "agreements ... in restraint of trade" and "arrangements ... which tend to lessen ... competition," cannot be enforced against a company which is not qualified to do business in *A*. When that company acquires a state *A* insurance company, *A* has not "regulated" the acquisition, and it is not exempted by the McCarran-Ferguson Act from antitrust attack. *See United States v. Chicago Title & Trust Co.,* 242 F. Supp. 56 (N.D. Ill. 1965).

The McCarran-Ferguson exemption does not apply to acts of "boycott, coercion, or intimidation." In *St. Paul Fire & Marine Ins. Co. v. Barry,* 438 U.S. 531 (1978), the Supreme Court found that an agreement among insurers to insure medical malpractice only if it occurred during the period covered by the policy constituted a "boycott." The ruling seems odd in one respect: joint drafting of insurance policies is protected by the Act, and any such drafting is effectively a refusal to deal or "boycott" of buyers unwilling to accept the terms of a policy. Suppose a group of insurers agree with each other not to insure people with two or more drunk driving convictions? Other kinds of "boycotts" are less problematic. For example, *Malley-Duff & Assocs. v. Crown Life Ins. Co.,* 734 F.2d 133 (3d Cir. 1984), held that an agreement between an insurance company and one agent to terminate a second agent was a nonexempt boycott. Likewise, *In re Workers Compensation Ins.,* 867 F.2d 1552 (8th Cir.), *cert. denied,* 492 U.S. 920 (1989), found a boycott in an insurers' agreement to exclude from a trade association other insurers who charged lower prices than the defendants.

In its most recent decision on the McCarran exemption, the Supreme Court found that qualifying "boycotts" had been alleged but narrowed the meaning of that term. In *Hartford Fire Ins. Co. v. California,* 509 U.S. 764 (1993), several state attorneys general alleged that primary insurers unlawfully agreed to reduce their policy coverages so as to eliminate losses that occurred outside the policy period, or upon which claims were made outside the policy period, and losses caused by certain forms of "sudden and accidental" pollution. Although a simple agreement to develop a new insurance form with reduced coverage was exempt "business of insurance," the plaintiffs alleged that the defendants entered collateral agreements with two other entities. The first was an agreement with Insurance Services Office (ISO) that the latter would not supply risk data for risks that the conspirators no longer wished to cover. Several nonconspiring insurers would have continued to write the larger risks, but they could not do so without adequate risk data. Secondly, the defendant insurers allegedly agreed with foreign sellers of *re*insurance that the reinsurers would not provide their services to the nonconspiring insurers either. Reinsurers sell insurance to primary insurers, enabling the latter to reduce their own risk from catastrophic losses. In finding a boycott the Court noted:

> It is ... important ... to distinguish between a conditional boycott and a concerted agreement to seek particular terms in particular transactions. A concerted agreement to terms (a "cartelization") is "a way of obtaining and exercising market power by concertedly exacting terms like those which a monopolist might exact." The parties to such an agreement (the members of a cartel) are not engaging in a boycott, because: "They are not coercing anyone, at least in the usual sense of that word; they are merely (though concertedly) saying "we will deal with you only on the following trade terms."

The critical issue was whether the agreement covered only the terms of the contract under negotiation, or whether it reached further. For example, if a group of tenants agreed with each other that they would not renew their leases unless they received lower rents from the landlord, they would be negotiating the contract at hand. They would not be "boycotting" anyone. However, if the tenants also refused to engage in unrelated transactions — for example, if they refused to sell their landlord food or other supplies until he lowered the rents — this latter agreement would be a boycott. "[T]his expansion of the refusal to deal beyond the targeted transaction ... gives great coercive force to a commercial boycott: unrelated transactions are used as leverage to achieve the terms desired." Applying this definition, the Court found that the plaintiffs' allegations contained several qualifying "boycotts." For example, the reinsurers allegedly refused to write reinsurance on any policy given by a firm that also wrote a policy containing the coverages that the defendants wanted removed from the market.

Recently Congress has entertained proposals to repeal the McCarran-Ferguson antitrust exemption for insurance, or reduce its scope. Would such an action greatly increase insurers' antitrust exposure? Insurance is heavily regulated by state law, and some of the activities now exempted by McCarran-Ferguson would probably also be exempted under the "state action" doctrine. (See Section III, below). The principal difference between the "state action" doctrine and the insurance exemption is that the former contains an "active state supervision" requirement while the latter does not. As a result, many insurer activities that are not effectively supervised by the state are nonetheless exempt from the antitrust laws. Would repeal of the special exemption for insurance be a good idea?

For further discussion of the insurance exemption, *see* 1 P. Areeda & H. Hoven-kamp, *Antitrust Law* ¶¶ 219, 220 (rev. ed. 1997).

4. AGRICULTURAL ORGANIZATIONS

Section 6 of the Clayton Act exempts from the antitrust laws "agricultural [and] horticultural organizations, instituted for the purpose of mutual help, and not having capital stock or conducted for profit." The Capper-Volstead Act of 1922, 7 U.S.C. § 291, extended the exemption to capital stock agricultural cooperatives, which had not been covered under the Clayton Act. The exemption authorizes persons engaged in the production of agricultural products, such as farmers, ranchers, planters, dairymen, or nut or fruit growers, to act together in cooperatives, collectively processing, preparing for market, handling, and marketing agricultural products.

The purpose of the exemption is to allow farmers to act together in cooperatives, like a corporation, within the framework of the antitrust laws. *Maryland & Va. Milk Producers Ass'n v. United States*, 362 U.S. 458 (1960). Thus, while the creation and internal operations of a farmer cooperative are immune from attack, the external activities of the cooperative are judged by the same standards as any other business. These cooperatives may, however, voluntarily combine to fix prices at which they will sell their products, provided that no nonfarmer or other organization is a party to the combination. *United States v. Maryland Coop. Milk Producers, Inc.*, 145 F. Supp. 151 (D.D.C. 1956).

The cooperative is subject to other traditional antitrust prohibitions. For example, a cooperative may not use its legal monopoly power to suppress competition among independent producers and processors. *Maryland & Va. Milk Producers Ass'n v. United States*, 362 U.S. 458 (1960) (purchase of independent dairy with intent to suppress competition). Nor may it coerce individual producers to join it, or coerce other organizations into complying with its demands. *North Texas Producers Ass'n v. Metzger Dairies*, 348 F.2d 189 (5th Cir. 1965).

The Secretary of Agriculture is given authority to issue cease and desist orders whenever he finds that an organization is monopolizing or restraining trade "to such an extent that the price of any agricultural product is unduly enhanced." 7 U.S.C. § 292.

5. PROFESSIONAL SPORTS

Professional sports are big business in America. The very nature of the business requires mutual dependence among the teams that make up the sport. It would be difficult for a professional team to survive without operating in a league, and the members of a league *must* cooperate on a wide variety of issues that in other industries might well be serious restraints of trade. Moreover, professional sports teams, while they compete with each other on the field, arguably are not competing with each other in a business sense; they compete with other forms of entertainment in their own communities. The hybrid nature of professional sports leagues — half business, half sport — has forced courts to deal with the issue of how to promote competition within the business without damaging the sport.

Professional baseball is in a unique position relative to other sports. As the result of an early case, *Federal Baseball Club of Baltimore, Inc. v. National League of Prof. Baseball Clubs*, 259 U.S. 200 (1922), the national pastime is exempt from the antitrust laws. Although the Supreme Court has recognized that *Federal Baseball* was decided on highly questionable grounds (the Court actually found no interstate commerce involved in the game of baseball), it has refused to repeal the judicial exemption. *See Flood v. Kuhn*, 407 U.S. 258 (1972). Congress arguably gave implied approval to the exception in 1961, by providing that nothing contained in an act relating to telecasting of sporting events "shall be deemed to change, determine, or otherwise affect the applicability or nonapplicability of the antitrust laws to ... football, baseball, basketball, or hockey." 15 U.S.C. § 1294.

The Supreme Court has refused to extend the judicial exemption to any other sport. *See Haywood v. National Basketball Ass'n*, 401 U.S. 1204 (1971); *Radovich v. National Football League*, 352 U.S. 445 (1957). Thus, professional sports other than baseball are generally covered by the antitrust laws. A federal court, for example, has enjoined enforcement of National Football League rules barring N.F.L. owners from acquiring teams in other sports. *See North Am. Soccer League v. National Football League*, 465 F. Supp. 665 (S.D.N.Y. 1979). The draft rules of various sports leagues have also been attacked, and have frequently been found unreasonable. *See Smith v. Pro Football, Inc.*, 593 F.2d 1173 (D.C. Cir. 1978); *Mackey v. National Football League*, 543 F.2d 606 (8th Cir. 1976), *cert. denied*, 434 U.S. 801 (1977).

SECTION II. PETITIONS TO THE GOVERNMENT

A. POLITICAL PROCESS, "RENT-SEEKING," AND THE ANTITRUST LAWS

Perhaps the world's greatest creator of monopoly is government itself. For example, the surest way for a firm to maintain its exclusive position in some market is to convince the sovereign to pass a statute forbidding others from entering. At common law a "monopoly" was not a firm that had simply come to dominate a market; rather, it was someone with an exclusive grant, or franchise, from the state.

The political process in a democratic country becomes a means by which firms attempt to earn monopoly profits. They engage in "rent-seeking" by urging governments to guarantee profit margins, give them exclusive privileges to operate in a market, authorize their own innovations for sale, or refuse to authorize the innovations of their competitors (see the *Allied Tube* case reprinted below). Many of the things that private firms request from government are downright anticompetitive.

Worse yet, government often obliges them. *See* D. Farber & P. Frickey, *Law and Public Choice: A Critical Introduction* (1991); Hovenkamp, *Legislation, Well-Being and Public Choice*, 57 U. Chi. L. Rev. 63 (1990).

But the purpose of the antitrust laws is not to prevent people from asking the government for what they want. The purpose of antitrust is not even to prohibit the government from granting anticompetitive requests. Ever since its decision in *Eastern R.R. Presidents Conf. v. Noerr Motor Freight, Inc.*, 365 U.S. 127 (1961), the Supreme Court has recognized that individuals have a right, grounded in the First Amendment, to petition the government. This right is protected no matter how anticompetitive the petitioners' intent, and whether they conduct the petitioning singly or in concert. *Noerr* held that the antitrust laws proscribe only trade restraints that result from private action, not those that result from valid government action.

The conduct challenged in *Noerr* was a concerted campaign by railroads to lobby for legislation restricting competition from the trucking industry. *Id.* at 136. The Court's conclusion, which rested not on the First Amendment but on the Sherman Act itself, was that the antitrust laws do not prohibit two or more persons from associating together in an attempt to persuade the government to take a certain regulatory action, no matter how anticompetitive. "[N]o violation of the [Sherman] Act can be predicated upon mere attempts to influence the passage or enforcement of laws." Further,

> We think it equally clear that the Sherman Act does not prohibit two or more persons from associating together in an attempt to persuade the legislature or the executive to take particular action with respect to a law that would produce a restraint or a monopoly. Although such associations could perhaps, through a process of expansive construction, be brought within the general proscription of "combination[s] ... in restraint of trade," they bear very little if any resemblance to the combinations normally held violative of the Sherman Act....
>
> In a representative democracy such as this, these branches of government act on behalf of the people and, to a very large extent, the whole concept of representation depends upon the ability of the people to make their wishes known to their representatives. To hold that the government retains the power to act in this representative capacity and yet hold, at the same time, that the people cannot freely inform the government of their wishes would impute to the Sherman Act a purpose to regulate, not business activity, but political activity, a purpose which would have no basis whatever in the legislative history of that Act. Secondly, and of at least equal significance, such a construction of the Sherman Act would raise important constitutional questions. The right of petition is one of the freedoms protected by the Bill of Rights, and we cannot, of course, lightly impute to Congress an intent to invade these freedoms....

Further,

> The right of the people to inform their representatives in government of their desires with respect to the passage or enforcement of laws cannot properly be made to depend upon their intent in doing so. It is neither unusual nor illegal for people to seek action on laws in the hope that they may bring about an advantage to themselves and a disadvantage to their competitors.... A construction of the Sherman Act that would disqualify people from taking a public position on matters in which they are financially interested would thus deprive the government of a valuable source of information and, at the same time, deprive the people of their right to petition in the very instances in which that right may be of the most importance to them....

The court reiterated this conclusion in *UMW v. Pennington*, 381 U.S. 657 (1965). In *California Motor Transp. Co. v. Trucking Unlimited*, 404 U.S. 508 (1972), it held that the First Amendment required such a limitation on the Sherman Act. The *California Motor* case is discussed further below.

ALLIED TUBE & CONDUIT CORP. V. INDIAN HEAD, INC.
486 U.S. 492 (1988)

JUSTICE BRENNAN delivered the opinion of the Court.

....

I

The National Fire Protection Association (Association) is a private, voluntary organization with more than 31,500 individual and group members representing industry, labor, academia, insurers, organized medicine, firefighters, and government. The Association, among other things, publishes product standards and codes related to fire protection through a process known as "consensus standard making." One of the codes it publishes is the National Electrical Code, which establishes product and performance requirements for the design and installation of electrical wiring systems. Revised every three years, the National Electric Code (Code) is the most influential electrical code in the nation. A substantial number of state and local governments routinely adopt the Code into law with little or no change; private certification laboratories, such as Underwriters Laboratories, normally will not list and label an electrical product that does not meet Code standards; many underwriters will refuse to insure structures that are not built in conformity with the Code; and many electrical inspectors, contractors, and distributors will not use a product that falls outside the Code.

Among the electrical products covered by the Code is electrical conduit, the hollow tubing used as a raceway to carry electrical wires through the walls and floors of buildings. Throughout the relevant period, the Code permitted using electrical conduit made of steel, and almost all conduit sold was in fact steel conduit. Starting in 1980, respondent began to offer plastic conduit made of polyvinyl chloride. Respondent claims its plastic conduit offers significant competitive advantages over steel conduit, including pliability, lower installed cost, and lower susceptibility to short circuiting. In 1980, however, there was also a scientific basis for concern that, during fires in high-rise buildings, polyvinyl chloride conduit might burn and emit toxic fumes.

Respondent initiated a proposal to include polyvinyl chloride conduit as an approved type of electrical conduit in the 1981 edition of the Code. Following approval by one of the Association's professional panels, this proposal was scheduled for consideration at the 1980 annual meeting, where it could be adopted or rejected by a simple majority of the members present. Alarmed that, if approved, respondent's product might pose a competitive threat to steel conduit, petitioner, the nation's largest producer of steel conduit, met to plan strategy with, among others, members of the steel industry, other steel conduit manufacturers, and its independent sales agents. They collectively agreed to exclude respondent's product from the 1981 Code by packing the upcoming annual meeting with new Association members whose only function would be to vote against the polyvinyl chloride proposal.

Combined, the steel interests recruited 230 persons to join the Association and to attend the annual meeting to vote against the proposal. Petitioner alone recruited 155 persons — including employees, executives, sales agents, the agents' employees, employees from two divisions that did not sell electrical products, and the wife of a national sales director. Petitioner and the other steel interests also paid over $100,000 for the membership, registration, and attendance expenses of these voters. At the annual meeting, the steel group voters were instructed where to sit and how and when to vote by group leaders who used walkie-talkies and hand signals to facilitate communication. Few of the steel group voters had any of the technical documentation necessary to follow the meeting. None of them spoke at the meeting to give their reasons for opposing the proposal to approve polyvinyl chloride conduit. Nonetheless, with their solid vote in opposition, the proposal was rejected and returned to committee by a vote of 394 to 390. Respondent appealed the membership's vote to the Association's Board of Directors, but the Board denied the appeal on the ground that, although the Association's rules had been circumvented, they had not been violated.[1]

In October 1981, respondent brought this suit in Federal District Court, alleging that petitioner and others had unreasonably restrained trade in the electrical conduit market in violation of § 1 of the Sherman Act. 26 Stat. 209, 15 U.S.C. § 1....
....

II

Concerted efforts to restrain or monopolize trade by petitioning government officials are protected from antitrust liability under the doctrine established by *Noerr*. The scope of this protection depends, however, on the source, context,

---

[1] ... The Association subsequently approved use of polyvinyl chloride conduit for buildings of less than four stories in the 1984 Code, and for all buildings in the 1987 Code.

and nature of the anticompetitive restraint at issue. "[W]here a restraint upon trade or monopolization is the result of valid governmental action, as opposed to private action," those urging the governmental action enjoy absolute immunity from antitrust liability for the anticompetitive restraint. In addition, where, independent of any governmental action, the anticompetitive restraint results directly from private action, the restraint cannot form the basis for antitrust liability if it is "incidental" to a valid effort to influence governmental action. The validity of such efforts, and thus the applicability of *Noerr* immunity, varies with the context and nature of the activity. A publicity campaign directed at the general public, seeking legislation or executive action, enjoys antitrust immunity even when the campaign employs unethical and deceptive methods. But in less political arenas, unethical and deceptive practices can constitute abuses of administrative or judicial processes that may result in antitrust violations.

In this case, the restraint of trade on which liability was predicated was the Association's exclusion of respondent's product from the Code, and no damages were imposed for the incorporation of that Code by any government. The relevant context is thus the standard-setting process of a private association. Typically, private standard-setting associations, like the Association in this case, include members having horizontal and vertical business relations. See generally 7 P. Areeda, Antitrust Law ¶ 1477, p. 343 (1986) (trade and standard-setting associations routinely treated as continuing conspiracies of their members). There is no doubt that the members of such associations often have economic incentives to restrain competition and that the product standards set by such associations have a serious potential for anticompetitive harm. Agreement on a product standard is, after all, implicitly an agreement not to manufacture, distribute, or purchase certain types of products. Accordingly, private standard-setting associations have traditionally been objects of antitrust scrutiny. When, however, private associations promulgate safety standards based on the merits of objective expert judgments and through procedures that prevent the standard-setting process from being biased by members with economic interests in stifling product competition, those private standards can have significant procompetitive advantages. It is this potential for procompetitive benefits that has led most lower courts to apply rule of reason analysis to product standard-setting by private associations.

Given this context, petitioner does not enjoy the immunity accorded those who merely urge the government to restrain trade. We agree with the Court of Appeals that the Association cannot be treated as a "quasi-legislative" body simply because legislatures routinely adopt the Code the Association publishes. Whatever *de facto* authority the Association enjoys, no official authority has been conferred on it by any government, and the decisionmaking body of the Association is composed, at least in part, of persons with economic incentives to restrain trade. "We may presume, absent a showing to the contrary, that [a government] acts in the public interest. A private party, on the other hand, may be presumed to be acting primarily on his or its own behalf." The dividing line between restraints resulting from governmental action and those resulting from private action may not always be obvious. But where, as here, the restraint is imposed by persons unaccountable to the public and without official authority, many of whom have personal financial interests in restraining competition, we have no difficulty concluding that the restraint has resulted from private action.

Noerr immunity might still apply, however, if, as petitioner argues, the exclusion of polyvinyl chloride conduit from the Code, and the effect that exclusion had of its own force in the marketplace, were incidental to a valid effort to influence governmental action. Petitioner notes that the lion's share of the anticompetitive effect in this case came from the predictable adoption of the Code into law by a large number of state and local governments. Indeed, petitioner argues that, because state and local governments rely so heavily on the Code and lack the resources or technical expertise to second-guess it, efforts to influence the Association's standard-setting process are the most effective means of influencing legislation regulating electrical conduit. This claim to *Noerr* immunity has some force. The effort to influence governmental action in this case certainly cannot be characterized as a sham given the actual adoption of the 1981 Code into a number of statutes and local ordinances. Nor can we quarrel with petitioner's contention that, given the widespread adoption of the Code into law, any effect the 1981 Code had in the marketplace of its own force was, in the main, incidental to petitioner's genuine effort to influence governmental action. And, as petitioner persuasively argues, the claim of *Noerr* immunity cannot be dismissed on the ground that the conduct at issue involved no "direct" petitioning of government officials, for *Noerr* itself immunized a form of "indirect" petitioning. See *Noerr*, 365 U.S. 127 (1961) (immunizing a publicity campaign directed at the general public on the ground that it was part of an effort to influence legislative and executive action).

Nonetheless, the validity of petitioner's actions remains an issue. We cannot agree with petitioner's absolutist position that the *Noerr* doctrine immunizes every concerted effort that is genuinely intended to influence governmental action.... We ... conclude that the *Noerr* immunity of anticompetitive activity intended to influence the government depends not only on its impact, but also on the context and nature of the activity.

Here petitioner's actions took place within the context of the standard-setting process of a private association. Having concluded that the Association is not a "quasi-legislative" body, we reject petitioner's argument that any efforts to influence the Association must be treated as efforts to influence a "quasi-legislature" and given the same wide berth accorded legislative lobbying. That rounding up supporters is an acceptable and constitutionally protected method of influencing elections does not mean that rounding up economically interested persons to set private standards must also be protected. ...

... Unlike the publicity campaign in *Noerr*, the activity at issue here did not take place in the open political arena, where partisanship is the hallmark of decisionmaking, but within the confines of a private standard-setting process. The validity of conduct within that process has long been defined and circumscribed by the antitrust laws without regard to whether the private standards are likely to be adopted into law. Indeed, because private standard-setting by associations comprising firms with horizontal and vertical business relations is permitted at all under the antitrust laws only on the understanding that it will be conducted in a nonpartisan manner offering procompetitive benefits, the standards of conduct in this context are, at least in some respects, more rigorous than the standards of conduct prevailing in the partisan political arena or in the adversarial process of adjudication. The activity at issue here thus cannot, as in *Noerr*, be characterized as an activity that has traditionally been regulated with extreme caution, or as an activity that "bear[s] little if any resemblance to the combinations normally held violative of the Sherman Act." And petitioner did not confine itself to efforts to persuade an independent decisionmaker; rather, it organized and orchestrated the actual exercise of the Association's decisionmaking authority in setting a standard. Nor can the setting of the Association's Code be characterized as merely an exercise of the power of persuasion, for it in part involves the exercise of market power. The Association's members, after all, include consumers, distributors, and manufacturers of electrical conduit, and any agreement to exclude polyvinyl chloride conduit from the Code is in part an implicit agreement not to trade in that type of electrical conduit. Although one could reason backwards from the legislative impact of the Code to the conclusion that the conduct at issue here is "political," we think that, given the context and nature of the conduct, it can more aptly be characterized as commercial activity with a political impact. Just as the antitrust laws should not regulate political activities "simply because those activities have a commercial impact," so the antitrust laws should not necessarily immunize what are in essence commercial activities simply because they have a political impact.

....

... Although we do not here set forth the rules of antitrust liability governing the private standard-setting process, we hold that at least where, as here, an economically interested party exercises decision-making authority in formulating a product standard for a private association that comprises market participants, that party enjoys no *Noerr* immunity from any antitrust liability flowing from the effect the standard has of its own force in the marketplace.

This conclusion does not deprive state and local governments of input and information from interested individuals or organizations or leave petitioner without ample means to petition those governments. Petitioner, and others concerned about the safety or competitive threat of polyvinyl chloride conduit, can, with full antitrust immunity, engage in concerted efforts to influence those governments through direct lobbying, publicity campaigns, and other traditional avenues of political expression. To the extent state and local governments are more difficult to persuade through these other avenues, that no doubt reflects their preference for and confidence in the nonpartisan consensus process that petitioner has undermined. Petitioner remains free to take advantage of the forum provided by the standard-setting process by presenting and vigorously arguing accurate scientific evidence before a nonpartisan private standard-setting body. And petitioner can avoid the strictures of the private standard-setting process by attempting to influence legislatures through other forums. What petitioner may not do (without exposing itself to possible antitrust liability for direct injuries) is bias the process by, as in this case, stacking the private standard-setting body with decisionmakers sharing their economic interest in restraining competition.

The judgment of the Court of Appeals is

Affirmed.

NOTES

The Causation Problem in Noerr-Pennington *Cases.* Observe that Indian Head was not seeking damages for injuries caused when state and local governments enacted codes prohibiting the use of plastic conduit. Rather, it complained about the chilling effect that the restrictions in the model National Electric Code had on contractor decisions to stick with steel conduit. The first form of injury was very likely protected by *Noerr-Pennington. See Sessions Tank Liners v. Joor Mfg.,* 827 F.2d 458 (9th Cir. 1987), where the court found *Noerr* protection for a petition to a private body when the injury was caused by subsequent legislative enactment of the private body's proposal. In this case the injury "resulted from the act of public officials, ... not the ... action of defendants," whose proposal "had no legal force and little injurious effect until it was adopted by local legislatures or enforced by local fire officials." *Id.* at 464.

This analysis suggests that the First Amendment may not be an integral part of the *Noerr-Pennington* exemption. Every plaintiff must show that the defendant's antitrust violation caused its injury. (See Chapter 3, *supra.*). Suppose that Firms *A, B,* and *C* petition a state agency for a regulation that burdens a competitor, Firm *D.* The agency passes the regulation and *D* sues *A, B,* and *C* under the antitrust laws. Can *D* prove causation? Although *A, B,* and *C* asked the government to do something, the government officials presumably had discretion to do it or not do it. They may have passed the regulation without the intervention of *A, B,* and *C.* What must *D* show in order to establish that *A, B,* and *C* "caused" its injury?

FTC V. SUPERIOR COURT TRIAL LAWYERS ASS'N

493 U.S. 411 (1990)

JUSTICE STEVENS delivered the opinion of the Court.

Pursuant to a well-publicized plan, a group of lawyers agreed not to represent indigent criminal defendants in the District of Columbia Superior Court until the District of Columbia government increased the lawyers' compensation. The questions presented are whether the lawyers' concerted conduct violated § 5 of the Federal Trade Commission Act and if so, whether it was nevertheless protected by the First Amendment to the Constitution.

I

The burden of providing competent counsel to indigent defendants in the District of Columbia is substantial. During 1982, court-appointed counsel represented the defendant in approximately 25,000 cases. In the most serious felony cases, representation was generally provided by full-time employees of the District's Public Defender System (PDS). Less serious felony and misdemeanor cases constituted about 85 percent of the total caseload. In these cases, lawyers in private practice were appointed and compensated pursuant to the District of Columbia Criminal Justice Act (CJA).

Although over 1,200 lawyers have registered for CJA appointments, relatively few actually apply for such work on a regular basis. In 1982, most appointments went to approximately 100 lawyers who are described as "CJA regulars." These lawyers derive almost all of their income from representing indigents. In 1982, the total fees paid to CJA lawyers amounted to $4,579,572....

Bar organizations began as early as 1975 to express concern about the low fees paid to CJA lawyers. Beginning in 1982, respondents, the Superior Court Trial Lawyers Association (SCTLA) and its officers, and other bar groups sought to persuade the District to increase CJA rates to at least $35 per hour. Despite what appeared to be uniform support for the bill, it did not pass. It is also true, however, that nothing in the record indicates that the low fees caused any actual shortage of CJA lawyers or denied effective representation to defendants.

At an SCTLA meeting, the CJA lawyers voted to form a "strike committee." The eight members of that committee promptly met and informally agreed "that the only viable way of getting an increase in fees was to stop signing up to take new CJA appointments, and that the boycott should aim for a $45 out-of-court and $55 in-court rate schedule."

On August 11, 1983, about 100 CJA lawyers met and resolved not to accept any new cases after September 6 if legislation providing for an increase in their fees had not passed by that date. Immediately following the meeting, they prepared (and most of them signed) a petition stating:

> We, the undersigned private criminal lawyers practicing in the Superior Court of the District of Columbia, agree that unless we are granted a substantial increase in our hourly rate we will cease accepting new appointments under the Criminal Justice Act.

On September 6, 1983, about 90 percent of the CJA regulars refused to accept any new assignments. Thereafter, SCTLA arranged a series of events to attract the attention of the news media and to obtain additional support. These events were well publicized and did engender favorable editorial comment, but the trial examiner found that "there is no credible evidence that the District's eventual capitulation to the demands of the CJA lawyers was made in response to public pressure, or, for that matter, that this publicity campaign actually engendered any significant measure of public pressure."...

Within 10 days, the key figures in the District's criminal justice system "became convinced that the system was on the brink of collapse because of the refusal of CJA lawyers to take on new cases." On September 15, they hand-delivered a letter to the mayor describing why the situation was expected to "reach a crisis point" by early next week and urging the immediate enactment of a bill increasing all CJA rates to $35 per hour. The mayor promptly met with members of the strike committee and offered to support an immediate temporary increase to the $35 level as well as a subsequent permanent increase to $45 an hour for out-of-court time and $55 for in-court time.

At noon on September 19, 1983, over 100 CJA lawyers attended a SCTLA meeting and voted to accept the $35 offer and end the boycott....

II

The Federal Trade Commission (FTC) filed a complaint against SCTLA and four of its officers (respondents) alleging that they had "entered into an agreement among themselves and with other lawyers to restrain trade by refusing to compete for or accept new appointments under the CJA program beginning on September 6, 1983, unless and until the District of Columbia increased the fees offered under the CJA program." The complaint alleged that virtually all of the attorneys who regularly compete for or accept new appointments under the CJA program had joined the agreement. The FTC characterized respondents' conduct as "a conspiracy to fix prices and to conduct a boycott" and concluded that they were engaged in "unfair methods of competition in violation of § 5 of the FTC Act."

... [T]he FTC rejected each of respondents' defenses. It held that their "coercive, concerted refusal to deal" had the "purpose and effect of raising prices" and was illegal per se.... [T]he FTC refused to conclude that the boycott was harmless, noting that the "boycott forced the city government to increase the CJA fees from a level that had been sufficient to obtain an adequate supply of CJA lawyers to a level satisfactory to the respondents. The city must, as a result of the boycott, spend an additional $4 million to $5 million a year to obtain legal services for indigents. We find that these are substantial anticompetitive effects resulting from the respondents' conduct."...

The Court of Appeals vacated the FTC order and remanded for a determination whether respondents possessed "significant market power." It concluded ... that "the SCTLA boycott did contain an element of expression warranting First Amendment protection." It noted that boycotts have historically been used as a dramatic means of expression and that respondents intended to convey a political message to the public at large. It therefore concluded that under *United States v. O'Brien*, 391 U.S. 367 (1968), a restriction on this form of expression could not be justified unless it is no greater than is essential to an important governmental interest. This test, the Court reasoned, could not be satisfied by the application of an otherwise appropriate per se rule, but instead required the enforcement agency to "prove rather than presume that the evil against which the Sherman Act is directed looms in the conduct it condemns."...

III

... We may assume that the preboycott rates were unreasonably low, and that the increase has produced better legal representation for indigent defendants. Moreover, given that neither indigent criminal defendants nor the lawyers who represent them command any special appeal with the electorate, we may also assume that without the boycott there would have been no increase in District CJA fees at least until the Congress amended the federal statute. These assumptions do not control the case, for it is not our task to pass upon the social utility or political wisdom of price-fixing agreements.

As the ALJ, the FTC, and the Court of Appeals all agreed, respondents' boycott "constituted a classic restraint of trade within the meaning of Section 1 of the Sherman Act." As such, it also violated the prohibition against unfair methods of competition in § 5 of the FTC Act.... Prior to the boycott CJA lawyers were in competition with one another, each deciding independently whether and how often to offer to provide services to the District at CJA rates. The agreement among the CJA lawyers was designed to obtain higher prices for their services and was implemented by a concerted refusal to serve an important customer in the market for legal services and, indeed, the only customer in the market for the particular services that CJA regulars offered. "This constriction of supply is the essence of "price-fixing," whether it be accomplished by agreeing upon a price, which will decrease the quantity demanded, or by agreeing upon an output, which will increase the price offered." The horizontal arrangement among these competitors was unquestionably a "naked restraint" on price and output....

It is of course true that the city purchases respondents' services because it has a constitutional duty to provide representation to indigent defendants. It is likewise true that the quality of representation may improve when rates are increased. Yet neither of these facts is an acceptable justification for an otherwise unlawful restraint of trade. As we have remarked before, the "Sherman Act reflects a legislative judgment that ultimately competition will produce not only lower prices, but also better goods and services." *National Society of Professional Engineers v. United States.* This judgment "recognizes that all elements of a bargain — quality, service, safety, and durability — and not just the immediate cost, are favorably affected by the free opportunity to select among alternative offers." That is equally so when the quality of legal advocacy, rather than engineering design, is at issue....

Our decision in *Noerr* in no way detracts from this conclusion. In *Noerr* we "considered whether the Sherman Act prohibited a publicity campaign waged by railroads" and "designed to foster the adoption of laws destructive of the trucking business, to create an atmosphere of distaste for truckers among the general public, and to impair the relationships existing between truckers and their customers." Interpreting the Sherman Act in the light of the First Amendment's Petition Clause, the Court noted that "at least insofar as the railroads' campaign was directed toward obtaining governmental action, its legality was not at all affected by any anticompetitive purpose it may have had."

It of course remains true that "no violation of the Act can be predicated upon mere attempts to influence the passage or enforcement of laws," even if the defendants' sole purpose is to impose a restraint upon the trade of their competitors. But in the *Noerr* case the alleged restraint of trade was the intended consequence of legislation; in this case the boycott was the *means* by which respondents sought to obtain favorable legislation. The restraint of trade that was implemented while the boycott lasted would have had precisely the same anticompetitive consequences during that period even if no legislation had been enacted. In *Noerr*, the desired legislation would have created the restraint on the truckers' competition; in this case the emergency legislative response to the boycott put an end to the restraint.

....

The lawyers' association argues that if its conduct would otherwise be prohibited by the Sherman Act and the Federal Trade Act, it is nonetheless protected by the First Amendment rights recognized in *Claiborne Hardware*. That case arose after black citizens boycotted white merchants in Claiborne County, Miss. The white merchants sued under state law to recover losses from the boycott. We found that the "right of the States to regulate economic activity could not justify a complete prohibition against a nonviolent, politically motivated boycott designed to force governmental and economic change and to effectuate rights guaranteed by the Constitution itself." We accordingly held that "the nonviolent elements of petitioners' activities are entitled to the protection of the First Amendment."

The lawyers' association contends that because it, like the boycotters in *Claiborne Hardware*, sought to vindicate constitutional rights, it should enjoy a similar First Amendment protection. It is, of course, clear that the association's efforts to publicize the boycott, to explain the merit of its cause, and to lobby District officials to enact favorable legislation — like similar activities in *Claiborne Hardware* — were activities that were fully protected by the First Amendment. But nothing in the FTC's order would curtail such activities, and nothing in the FTC's reasoning condemned any of those activities.

The activity that the FTC order prohibits is a concerted refusal by CJA lawyers to accept any further assignments until they receive an increase in their compensation; the undenied objective of their boycott was an economic advantage for those who agreed to participate. It is true that the *Claiborne Hardware* case also involved a boycott. That boycott, however, differs in a decisive respect. Those who joined the *Claiborne Hardware* boycott sought no special advantage for themselves. They were black citizens in Port Gibson, Mississippi, who had been the victims of political, social, and economic discrimination for many years. They sought only the equal respect and equal treatment to which they were constitutionally entitled. They struggled "to change a social order that had consistently treated them as second class citizens." As we observed, the campaign was not intended "to destroy legitimate competition." Equality and freedom are preconditions of the free market, and not commodities to be haggled over within it.

The same cannot be said of attorney's fees. As we recently pointed out, our reasoning in *Claiborne Hardware* is not applicable to a boycott conducted by business competitors who "stand to profit financially from a lessening of competition in the boycotted market." *Allied Tube Corp. v. Indian Head*. No matter how altruistic the motives of respondents may have been, it is undisputed that their immediate objective was to increase the price that they would be paid for their services. Such an economic boycott is well within the category that was expressly distinguished in the *Claiborne Hardware* opinion itself....

V

Respondents' concerted action in refusing to accept further CJA assignments until their fees were increased was thus a plain violation of the antitrust laws. The exceptions derived from *Noerr* and *Claiborne Hardware* have no application to respondents' boycott....

The Court of Appeals, however, crafted a new exception to the per se rules, and it is this exception which provoked the FTC's petition to this Court. The Court of Appeals derived its exception from *United States v. O'Brien*, 391 U.S. 367 (1968). In that case O'Brien had burned his Selective Service registration certificate on the steps of the South Boston Courthouse. He did so before a sizable crowd and with the purpose of advocating his antiwar beliefs. We affirmed his conviction. We held that the governmental interest in regulating the "nonspeech element" of his conduct adequately justified the incidental restriction on First Amendment freedoms. Specifically, we concluded that the statute's incidental restriction on O'Brien's freedom of expression was no greater than necessary to further the Government's interest in requiring registrants to have valid certificates continually available.

However, the Court of Appeals held that, in light of *O'Brien*, the expressive component of respondents' boycott compelled courts to apply the antitrust laws "prudently and with sensitivity," with a "special solicitude for the First Amendment rights" of respondents. The Court of Appeals concluded that the governmental interest in prohibiting boycotts is not sufficient to justify a restriction on the communicative element of the boycott unless the FTC can prove, and not merely presume, that the boycotters have market power. Because the Court of Appeals imposed this special requirement upon the Government, it ruled that per se antitrust analysis was inapplicable to boycotts having an expressive component.

There are at least two critical flaws in the Court of Appeals' antitrust analysis: it exaggerates the significance of the expressive component in respondents' boycott and it denigrates the importance of the rule of law that respondents violated. Implicit in the conclusion of the Court of Appeals are unstated assumptions that most economic boycotts do not have an expressive component, and that the categorical prohibitions against price fixing and boycotts are merely rules of "administrative convenience" that do not serve any substantial governmental interest unless the price-fixing competitors actually possess market power.

It would not much matter to the outcome of this case if these flawed assumptions were sound. *O'Brien* would offer respondents no protection even if their boycott were uniquely expressive and even if the purpose of the per se rules were purely that of administrative efficiency. We have recognized that the Government's interest in adhering to a uniform rule may sometimes satisfy the *O'Brien* test even if making an exception to the rule in a particular case might cause no serious damage. *United States v. Albertini*, 472 U.S. 675, 688 (1985) ("The First Amendment does not bar application of a neutral regulation that incidentally burdens speech merely because a party contends that allowing an exception in the particular case will not threaten important government interests"). The administrative efficiency interests in antitrust regulation are unusually compelling. The per se rules avoid "the necessity for an incredibly complicated and prolonged economic investigation into the entire history of the industry involved, as well as related industries, in an effort to determine at large whether a particular restraint has been unreasonable." *Northern Pac. R. Co. v. United States*, 356 U.S. 1, 5 (1958). If small parties "were allowed to prove lack of market power, all parties would have that right, thus introducing the enormous complexities of market definition into every price-fixing case." R. Bork, The Antitrust Paradox 269 (1978). For these reasons, it is at least possible that the *Claiborne Hardware* doctrine, which itself rests in part upon *O'Brien*, exhausts *O'Brien*'s application to the antitrust statutes.

In any event, however, we cannot accept the Court of Appeals' characterization of this boycott or the antitrust laws. Every concerted refusal to do business with a potential customer or supplier has an expressive component. At one level, the competitors must exchange their views about their objectives and the means of obtaining them. The most blatant, naked price-fixing agreement is a product of communication, but that is surely not a reason for viewing it with special solicitude. At another level, after the terms of the boycotters' demands have been agreed upon, they must be communicated to its target: "we will not do business until you do what we ask." That expressive component of the boycott conducted by these respondents is surely not unique. On the contrary, it is the hallmark of every effective boycott.

At a third level, the boycotters may communicate with third parties to enlist public support for their objectives; to the extent that the boycott is newsworthy, it will facilitate the expression of the boycotters' ideas. But this level of expression is not an element of the boycott. Publicity may be generated by any other activity that is sufficiently newsworthy. Some activities, including the boycott here, may be newsworthy precisely for the reasons that they are prohibited: the harms they produce are matters of public concern. Certainly that is no reason for removing the prohibition.

In sum, there is thus nothing unique about the "expressive component" of respondents' boycott. A rule that requires courts to apply the antitrust laws "prudently and with sensitivity" whenever an economic boycott has an "expressive component" would create a gaping hole in the fabric of those laws. Respondents' boycott thus has no special characteristics meriting an exemption from the per se rules of antitrust law.

Equally important is the second error implicit in respondents' claim to immunity from the per se rules. In its opinion, the Court of Appeals assumed that the antitrust laws permit, but do not require, the condemnation of price fixing and boycotts without proof of market power. The opinion further assumed that the per se rule prohibiting such activity "is only a rule of 'administrative convenience and efficiency,' not a statutory command." This statement contains two errors. The per se rules are, of course, the product of judicial interpretations of the Sherman Act, but the rules nevertheless have the same force and effect as any other statutory commands. Moreover, while the per se rule against price fixing and boycotts is indeed justified in part by "administrative convenience," the Court of Appeals erred in describing the prohibition as justified only by such concerns. The per se rules also reflect a long-standing judgment that the prohibited practices by their nature have "a substantial potential for impact on competition."...

Of course, some boycotts and some price-fixing agreements are more pernicious than others; some are only partly successful, and some may only succeed when they are buttressed by other causative factors, such as political influence. But an assumption that, absent proof of market power, the boycott disclosed by this record was totally harmless — when overwhelming testimony demonstrated that it almost produced a crisis in the administration of criminal justice in the District and when it achieved its economic goal — is flatly inconsistent with the clear course of our antitrust jurisprudence. Conspirators need not achieve the dimensions of a monopoly, or even a degree of market power any greater than that already disclosed by this record, to warrant condemnation under the antitrust laws.

The judgment of the Court of Appeals is accordingly reversed insofar as that court held the per se rules inapplicable to the lawyers' boycott. The case is remanded for further proceedings consistent with this opinion.

NOTES AND QUESTIONS

1. Of what significance is the fact that the lawyers' boycott was "well publicized"? Should the per se rule be reserved for secret practices, such as price fixing? Wouldn't that encourage people to bring dubious practices into the open?

2. Normally, the Federal Trade Commission has only the power to obtain a "cease and desist" order barring further antitrust violations. But the District of Columbia in this case may have an antitrust damages action under § 1 of the Sherman Act. How would the damages be measured?

3. After the *Trial Lawyers* decision, what is the status of *Missouri v. National Organization for Women*, reprinted in Chapter 4? Was that boycott more like the one in *Trial Lawyers*, or like the one in *Claiborne Hardware*?

4. Does *Trial Lawyers* suggest a "commercial" exception to *Noerr* when the government acts as a purchaser of services rather than as a policy maker in the more abstract sense? Some courts have found such an exception, suggesting that in such cases "the government ... is not acting as a political body but as a participant in the marketplace." *General Aircraft Corp. v. Air Am.*, 482 F. Supp. 3, 7 (D.D.C. 1979). Most lower courts have refused to recognize a commercial exception. For example, in *Airport Car Rental Antitrust Litig.*, 693 F.2d 84 (9th Cir. 1982), the Ninth Circuit found no exception for a transaction in which the antitrust defendants, car rental companies, attempted to convince state airport officials to restrict the leasing of airport space to themselves and not make it available to their competitors. However, weakly stated dicta in the Supreme Court's decision in *City of Columbia & Columbia Outdoor Advertising, Inc. v. Omni Outdoor Advertising, Inc.*, 499 U.S. 365, 375 (1991), reprinted *infra*, suggested that "immunity does not necessarily obtain where the State acts not in a regulatory capacity but as a commercial participant in a given market."

What if the antitrust plaintiff alleges that the antitrust defendant bribed a government official to take some action that worked to the plaintiff's disadvantage? On the one hand, the injury was caused by governmental, not by private, action. On the other hand, the legal political process does not include bribery, and the First Amendment does not protect it. Many plaintiffs have alleged that public officials were somehow "co-conspirators" with the antitrust defendant in creating the statutory scheme that injured the plaintiffs. *E.g., Affiliated Capital Corp. v. City of Houston*, 735 F.2d 1555 (5th Cir. 1984) (en banc), *cert. denied*, 474 U.S. 1053 (1986). *See* Calkins, *Developments in Antitrust and the First Amendment: The Disaggregation of* Noerr, 57 Antitrust L.J. No. 2 (1988). The Supreme Court's *Columbia* decision, reprinted *infra*, suggests that even bribery is protected.

5. In *Mass. School of Law at Andover v. ABA*, 107 F.3d 1026 (3d Cir.), *cert. denied*, 118 S. Ct. 264 (1997), the plaintiff, a law school which was denied accreditation by the ABA, alleged that many states prevented graduates from unaccredited law schools from taking the state's bar examination. The court responded that *Noerr* protected the ABA's presentation of accrediting recommendations to state governments, with the result that the government itself rather than the ABA decided which law school graduates were eligible for bar admissions.

However, the plaintiff also alleged that "independent of any bar examination requirements, it was injured by the stigmatic effect in the market place of the denial of accreditation." *Id.* at 1037. The court concluded that such injury was merely incidental to the ABA's legitimate petitioning efforts and thus protected under *Noerr* as well:

> Discussing the quality and competence of its decisions is a legitimate, although somewhat indirect, way of petitioning the states to continue to follow its guidance. Yet, such activity is no more indirect than the public relations campaign held to be petitioning in *Noerr*.

B. THE "SHAM" EXCEPTION

In *Eastern R.R. Presidents Conf. v. Noerr Motor Freight, Inc.*, 365 U.S. 127 (1961), the Supreme Court suggested an exception to its rule insulating petitions to the government from antitrust liability:

> There may be situations in which a publicity campaign, ostensibly directed toward influencing governmental action, is a mere sham to cover what is actually nothing more than an attempt to interfere directly with the business relationships of a competitor and the application of the Sherman Act would be justified.

A decade later in *California Motor Transp. Co. v. Trucking Unlimited*, 404 U.S. 508 (1972), the Court found that such a "sham" might have existed. The antitrust defendants and antitrust plaintiffs were competing trucking companies. The plaintiffs challenged that the defendants filed a variety of administrative and judicial actions before state and federal tribunals in order to deny the plaintiffs the right to operate in parts of the California trucking market. In distinguishing the *Noerr* and *Pennington* decisions the Court said:

> In the present case ... the allegations are not that the conspirators sought "to influence public officials," but that they sought to bar their competitors from meaningful access to adjudicatory tribunals and so to usurp that decision-making process. It is alleged that petitioners "instituted the proceedings and actions ... with or without probable cause, and regardless of the merits of the cases." The nature of the views pressed does not, of course, determine whether First Amendment rights may be invoked; but they may bear upon a purpose to deprive the competitors of meaningful access to the agencies and courts....
>
> ... [U]nethical conduct in the setting of the adjudicatory process often results in sanctions. Perjury of witnesses is one example. Use of a patent obtained by fraud to exclude a competitor from the market may involve a violation of the antitrust laws, as we held in *Walker Process Equipment v. Food Machinery & Chemical Corp.*, 382 U.S. 172, 175-177 [1965]. Conspiracy with a licensing authority to eliminate a competitor may also result in an antitrust transgression. *Continental Ore Co. v. Union Carbide & Carbon Corp.*, 370 U.S. 690, 707 [1962].... Similarly, bribery of a public purchasing agent may constitute a violation of § 2(c) of the Clayton Act, as amended by the Robinson-Patman Act....

There are many other forms of illegal and reprehensible practice which may corrupt the administrative or judicial processes and which may result in antitrust violations. Misrepresentations, condoned in the political arena, are not immunized when used in the adjudicatory process. Opponents before agencies or courts often think poorly of the other's tactics, motions, or defenses and may readily call them baseless. One claim, which a court or agency may think baseless, may go unnoticed; but a pattern of baseless, repetitive claims may emerge which leads the factfinder to conclude that the administrative and judicial processes have been abused.... Insofar as the administrative or judicial processes are involved, action of that kind cannot acquire immunity by seeking refuge under the umbrella of "political expression."

The "sham" exception is most often invoked by antitrust plaintiffs challenging improperly motivated litigation, as in the following case, or complaints before administrative agencies as antitrust violations.

PROFESSIONAL REAL ESTATE INVESTORS, INC. V. COLUMBIA PICTURES INDUSTRIES, INC.

508 U.S. 49 (1993)

JUSTICE THOMAS delivered the opinion of the Court.

This case requires us to define the "sham" exception to the doctrine of antitrust immunity first identified in *Eastern R. Presidents Conference v. Noerr Motor Freight, Inc.*, 365 U.S. 127 (1961), as that doctrine applies in the litigation context. Under the sham exception, activity "ostensibly directed toward influencing governmental action" does not qualify for *Noerr* immunity if it "is a mere sham to cover ... an attempt to interfere directly with the business relationships of a competitor." We hold that litigation cannot be deprived of immunity as a sham unless the litigation is objectively baseless....

I

Petitioners Professional Real Estate Investors, Inc., and Kenneth F. Irwin (collectively, PRE) operated La Mancha Private Club and Villas, a resort hotel in Palm Springs, California. Having installed videodisc players in the resort's hotel rooms and assembled a library of more than 200 motion picture titles, PRE rented videodiscs to guests for in-room viewing.... Respondents, Columbia Pictures Industries, Inc., and seven other major motion picture studios (collectively, Columbia), held copyrights to the motion pictures recorded on the videodiscs that PRE purchased. Columbia also licensed the transmission of copyrighted motion pictures to hotel rooms through a wired cable system called Spectradyne. PRE therefore competed with Columbia not only for the viewing market at La Mancha but also for the broader market for in-room entertainment services in hotels. In 1983, Columbia sued PRE for alleged copyright infringement through the rental of videodiscs for viewing in hotel rooms. PRE counterclaimed, charging Columbia with violations of §§ 1 and 2 of the Sherman Act.... In particular, PRE alleged that Columbia's copyright action was a mere sham that cloaked underlying acts of monopolization and conspiracy to restrain trade....

Columbia did not dispute that PRE could freely sell or lease lawfully purchased videodiscs under the Copyright Act's "first sale" doctrine, see 17 U.S.C. § 109(a).... [S]ummary judgment depended solely on whether rental of videodiscs for in-room viewing infringed Columbia's exclusive right to "perform the copyrighted work[s] publicly." § 106(4). Ruling that such rental did not constitute public performance, the District Court entered summary judgment for PRE. The Court of Appeals affirmed on the grounds that a hotel room was not a "public place" and that PRE did not "transmit or otherwise communicate" Columbia's motion pictures. 866 F.2d 278 (9th Cir. 1989).

On remand, Columbia sought summary judgment on PRE's antitrust claims, arguing that the original copyright infringement action was no sham and was therefore entitled to immunity under [Noerr].... [T]he District Court granted the motion: "It was clear from the manner in which the case was presented that [Columbia was] seeking and expecting a favorable judgment...." The Court of Appeals affirmed ... , [reasoning] that the existence of probable cause "preclude[d] the application of the sham exception as a matter of law" because "a suit brought with probable cause does not fall within the sham exception to the *Noerr-Pennington* doctrine." Finally, the court observed that PRE's failure to show that "the copyright infringement action was baseless" rendered irrelevant any "evidence of [Columbia's] subjective intent." It accordingly rejected PRE's request for further discovery on Columbia's intent....

II

PRE contends that "the Ninth Circuit erred in holding that an antitrust plaintiff must, as a threshold prerequisite ..., establish that a sham lawsuit is baseless as a matter of law." It invites us to adopt an approach under which either "indifference to ... outcome," *ibid.*, or failure to prove that a petition for redress of grievances "would ... have been brought but for [a] predatory motive," would expose a defendant to antitrust liability under the sham exception. We decline PRE's invitation. Those who petition government for redress are generally immune from antitrust liability. We first recognized in *Noerr* that "the Sherman Act does not prohibit ... persons from associating together in an attempt to persuade the legislature or the executive to take particular action with respect to a law that would produce a restraint or a monopoly."... In light of the government's "power to act in [its] representative capacity" and "to take actions ... that operate to restrain trade," we reasoned that the Sherman Act does not punish "political activity" through which "the people ... freely inform the government of their wishes." *Noerr*, 365 U.S., at 137. Nor did we "impute to Congress an intent to invade" the First Amendment right to petition. *Id.*, at 138. *Noerr*, however, withheld immunity from "sham" activities because "application of the Sherman Act would be justified" when petitioning activity, "ostensibly directed toward influencing governmental action, is a mere sham to cover ... an attempt to interfere directly with the business relationships of a competitor." *Id.*, at 144. In *Noerr* itself, we found that a publicity campaign by railroads seeking legislation harmful to truckers was no sham in that the "effort to influence legislation" was "not only genuine but also highly successful." *Ibid.* In *California Motor Transport Co. v. Trucking Unlimited*, 404 U.S. 508 (1972), we elaborated on *Noerr* in two relevant respects. First, we extended *Noerr* to "the approach of citizens ... to administrative agencies ... and to courts." Second, we held that the complaint showed a sham not entitled to immunity when it contained allegations that one group of highway carriers "sought to bar ... competitors from meaningful access to adjudicatory tribunals and so to usurp that decisionmaking process" by "institut[ing] ... proceedings and actions ... with or without probable cause, and regardless of the merits of the cases." We left unresolved the question presented by this case — whether litigation may be sham merely because a subjective expectation of success does not motivate the litigant. We now answer this question in the negative and hold that an objectively reasonable effort to litigate cannot be sham regardless of subjective intent.

Our original formulation of antitrust petitioning immunity required that unprotected activity lack objective reasonableness. *Noerr* rejected the contention that an attempt "to influence the passage and enforcement of laws" might lose immunity merely because the lobbyists' "sole purpose ... was to destroy [their] competitors."... "*Noerr* shields from the Sherman Act a concerted effort to influence public officials regardless of intent or purpose." *Pennington*, 381 U.S., at 670.

Nothing in *California Motor Transport* retreated from these principles. Indeed, we recognized that recourse to agencies and courts should not be condemned as sham until a reviewing court has "discern[ed] and draw[n]" the "difficult line" separating objectively reasonable claims from "a pattern of baseless, repetitive claims ... which leads the factfinder to conclude that the administrative and judicial processes have been abused." Our recognition of a sham in that case signifies that the institution of legal proceedings "without probable cause" will give rise to a sham if such activity effectively "bar[s] ... competitors from meaningful access to adjudicatory tribunals and so ... usurp[s] th[e] decisionmaking process." Since *California Motor Transport*, we have consistently assumed that the sham exception contains an indispensable objective component. We have described a sham as "evidenced by repetitive lawsuits carrying the hallmark of *insubstantial* claims." *Otter Tail Power Co. v. United States*, 410 U.S. 366, 380 (1973) (emphasis added). We regard as sham "private action that is not genuinely aimed at procuring favorable government action," as opposed to "a valid effort to influence government action." *Allied Tube & Conduit Corp. v. Indian Head, Inc.*, 486 U.S. 492, 500, n. 4 (1988). And we have explicitly observed that a successful "effort to influence governmental action ... certainly cannot be characterized as a sham."...

... In *Columbia v. Omni Outdoor Advertising, Inc.*, 499 U.S. 365 (1991), we similarly held that challenges to allegedly sham petitioning activity must be resolved according to objective criteria. We dispelled the notion that an antitrust plaintiff could prove a sham merely by showing that its competitor's "purposes were to delay [the plaintiff's] entry into the market and even to deny it a meaningful access to the appropriate ... administrative and legislative fora."...

III

We now outline a two-part definition of "sham" litigation. First, the lawsuit must be objectively baseless in the sense that no reasonable litigant could realistically expect success on the merits. If an objective litigant could conclude that the suit is reasonably calculated to elicit a favorable outcome, the suit is immunized under *Noerr*, and an antitrust claim premised on the sham exception must fail. Only if challenged litigation is objectively meritless may a court examine the litigant's subjective motivation. Under this second part of our definition of sham, the court should focus on whether the baseless lawsuit conceals "an attempt to interfere directly with the business relationships of a competitor," *Noerr*, *supra*, at 144....

Of course, even a plaintiff who defeats the defendant's claim to *Noerr* immunity by demonstrating both the objective and the subjective components of a sham must still prove a substantive antitrust violation. Proof of a sham merely deprives the defendant of immunity; it does not relieve the plaintiff of the obligation to establish all other elements of his claim....

IV

We conclude that the Court of Appeals properly affirmed summary judgment for Columbia on PRE's antitrust counterclaim. Under the objective prong of the sham exception, the Court of Appeals correctly held that sham litigation must constitute the pursuit of claims so baseless that no reasonable litigant could realistically expect to secure favorable relief. The existence of probable cause to institute legal proceedings precludes a finding that an antitrust defendant has engaged in sham litigation. The notion of probable cause, as understood and applied in the common law tort of wrongful civil proceedings, requires the plaintiff to prove that the defendant lacked probable cause to institute an unsuccessful civil lawsuit and that the defendant pressed the action for an improper, malicious purpose.... Probable cause to institute civil proceedings requires no more than a "reasonabl[e] belie[f] that there is a chance that [a] claim may be held valid upon adjudication" (internal quotation marks omitted). *Hubbard v. Beatty & Hyde, Inc.*, 343 Mass. 258, 262, 178 N.E.2d 485, 488 (1961); Restatement (Second) of Torts § 675, Comment e, pp. 454-455 (1977). Because the absence of probable cause is an essential element of the tort, the existence of probable cause is an absolute defense.... Just as evidence of anticompetitive intent cannot affect the objective prong of *Noerr*'s sham exception, a showing of malice alone will neither entitle the wrongful civil proceedings plaintiff to prevail nor permit the factfinder to infer the absence of probable cause. When a court has found that an antitrust defendant claiming *Noerr* immunity had probable cause to sue, that finding compels the conclusion that a reasonable litigant in the defendant's position could realistically expect success on the merits of the challenged lawsuit. Under our decision today, therefore, a proper probable cause determination irrefutably demonstrates that an antitrust plaintiff has not proved the objective prong of the sham exception and that the defendant is accordingly entitled to *Noerr* immunity.... Columbia enjoyed the "exclusive righ[t] ... to perform [its] copyrighted" motion pictures "publicly." 17 U.S.C. § 106(4). Regardless of whether it intended any monopolistic or predatory use, Columbia acquired this statutory right.... Indeed, to condition a copyright upon a demonstrated lack of anticompetitive intent would upset the notion of copyright as a "limited grant" of "monopoly privileges" intended simultaneously "to motivate the creative activity of authors" and "to give the public appropriate access to their work product." *Sony Corp. of America v. Universal City Studios, Inc.*, 464 U.S. 417, 429 (1984).

When the District Court entered summary judgment for PRE on Columbia's copyright claim in 1986, it was by no means clear whether PRE's videodisc rental activities intruded on Columbia's copyrights. At that time, the Third Circuit and a District Court within the Third Circuit had held that the rental of video cassettes for viewing in on-site, private screening rooms infringed on the copyright owner's right of public performance. *Columbia Pictures Industries, Inc. v. Redd Horne, Inc.*, 749 F.2d 154 (1984); *Columbia Pictures Industries, Inc. v. Aveco, Inc.*, 612 F. Supp. 315 (MD Pa. 1985), *aff 'd*, 800 F.2d 59 (3d Cir. 1986). Although the District Court and the Ninth Circuit distinguished these decisions by reasoning that hotel rooms offered a degree of privacy more akin to the home than to a video rental store, ... copyright scholars criticized both the reasoning and the outcome of the Ninth Circuit's decision, see 1 P. Goldstein, Copyright: Principles, Law and Practice § 5.7.2.2, pp. 616-619 (1989); 2 M. Nimmer & D. Nimmer, Nimmer on Copyright § 8.14[C][3], pp. 8-168 to 8-173 (1992). The Seventh Circuit expressly "decline[d] to follow" the Ninth Circuit and adopted instead the Third Circuit's definition of a "public place." *Video Views, Inc. v. Studio 21, Ltd.*, 925 F.2d 1010, 1020, *cert. denied*, 502 U.S. (1991). In light of the unsettled condition of the law, Columbia plainly had probable cause to sue. Any reasonable copyright owner in Columbia's position could have believed that it had some chance of winning an infringement suit against PRE. Even though it did not survive PRE's motion for summary judgment, Columbia's copyright action was arguably "warranted by existing law" or at the very least was based on an objectively "good faith argument for the extension, modification, or reversal of existing law." Fed. Rule Civ. Proc. 11.... A court could reasonably conclude that Columbia's infringement action was an objectively plausible effort to enforce rights. Accordingly, we conclude that PRE failed to establish the objective prong of *Noerr*'s sham exception.

Finally, the Court of Appeals properly refused PRE's request for further discovery on the economic circumstances of the underlying copyright litigation. As we have held, PRE could not pierce Columbia's *Noerr* immunity without proof that Columbia's infringement action was objectively baseless or frivolous. Thus, the District Court had no occasion to inquire whether Columbia was indifferent to the outcome on the merits of the copyright suit, whether any damages for infringement would be too low to justify Columbia's investment in the suit, or whether Columbia had decided to sue primarily for the benefit of collateral injuries inflicted through the use of legal process. Such matters concern Columbia's economic motivations in bringing suit, which were rendered irrelevant by the objective legal reasonableness of the litigation. The existence of probable cause eliminated any "genuine issue as to any material fact," Fed. Rule Civ. Proc. 56(c), and summary judgment properly issued. We affirm the judgment of the Court of Appeals.

So ordered.

JUSTICE STEVENS, with whom JUSTICE O'CONNOR joins, concurring in the judgment.

... I disagree with the Court's equation of "objectively baseless" with the answer to the question whether any "reasonable litigant could realistically expect success on the merits." There might well be lawsuits that fit the latter definition but can be shown to be objectively unreasonable, and thus shams....

... The label "sham" [might] apply to a plaintiff who had some reason to expect success on the merits but because of its tremendous cost would not bother to achieve that result without the benefit of collateral injuries imposed on its competitor by the legal process alone. Litigation filed or pursued for such collateral purposes is fundamentally different from a case in which the relief sought in the litigation itself would give the plaintiff a competitive advantage or, perhaps, exclude a potential competitor from entering a market with a product that either infringes the plaintiff's patent or copyright or violates an exclusive franchise granted by a governmental body. The case before us today is in the latter, obviously legitimate, category. There was no unethical or other improper use of the judicial system; instead, respondents invoked the federal court's jurisdiction to determine whether they could lawfully restrain competition with petitioners. The relief they sought in their original action, if granted, would have had the anticompetitive consequences authorized by federal copyright law....

Repetitive filings, some of which are successful and some unsuccessful, may support an inference that the process is being misused. *California Motor Transport Co. v. Trucking Unlimited*, 404 U.S. 508 (1972). In such a case, a rule that a single meritorious action can never constitute a sham cannot be dispositive. Moreover, a simple rule may be hard to apply when there is evidence that the judicial process has been used as part of a larger program to control a market and to interfere with a potential competitor's financing without any interest in the outcome of the lawsuit itself, see *Otter Tail Power Co. v. United States*, 410 U.S. 366, 379, n. 9 (1973); *Westmac, Inc. v. Smith*, 797 F.2d 313, 322 (6th Cir. 1986) (Merritt, C. J., dissenting). It is in more complex cases that courts have required a more sophisticated analysis — one going beyond a mere evaluation of the merits of a single claim. In one such case Judge Posner made the following observations about the subtle distinction between suing a competitor to get damages and filing a lawsuit only in the hope that the expense and burden of defending it will make the defendant abandon its competitive behavior:

> But we are not prepared to rule that the difficulty of distinguishing lawful from unlawful purpose in litigation between competitors is so acute that such litigation can never be considered an actionable restraint of trade, provided it has some, though perhaps only threadbare, basis in law. Many claims not wholly groundless would never be sued on for their own sake; the stakes, discounted by the probability of winning, would be too low to repay the investment in litigation. Suppose a monopolist brought a tort action against its single, tiny competitor; the action had a colorable basis in law; but in fact the monopolist would never have brought the suit — its chances of winning, or the damages it could hope to get if it did win, were too small compared to what it would have to spend on the litigation — except that it wanted to use pretrial discovery to discover its competitor's trade secrets; or hoped that the competitor would be required to make public disclosure of its potential liability in the suit and that this disclosure would increase the interest rate that the competitor had to pay for bank financing; or just wanted to impose heavy legal costs on the competitor in the hope of deterring entry by other firms. In these examples the plaintiff wants to hurt a competitor not by getting a judgment against him, which would be a proper objective, but just by the maintenance of the suit, regardless of its outcome.... [W]e think it is premature to hold that litigation, unless malicious in the tort sense, can never be actionable under the antitrust laws. The existence of a tort of abuse of process shows that it has long been thought that litigation could be used for improper purposes even when there is probable cause for the litigation; and if the improper purpose is to use litigation as a tool for suppressing competition in its antitrust sense, ... it becomes a matter of antitrust concern.

Grip-Pak, Inc. v. Illinois Tool Works, Inc., 694 F.2d 466, 472 (1982).

NOTES AND QUESTIONS

1. In a footnote, the Court added the following:

> We need not decide here whether and, if so, to what extent *Noerr* permits the imposition of antitrust liability for a litigant's fraud or other misrepresentations (citing *Walker Process Equipment, Inc. v. Food Machinery & Chemical Corp.*, 382 U.S. 172, 176-177 (1965)).

Professional Real Estate thus seems to apply only to decisions where the underlying claim was based on a dubious *legal* theory. This considerably narrows the impact of the decision. For example, one of the most commonly litigated areas involving the "sham" exception is wrongfully-based patent or copyright infringement suits, such as *Walker Process, ibid*. But most claims of "sham" in that context refer to the patentee's factual misrepresentations in the patent application, its knowledge that the patent was in fact unenforceable, or that the defendant in the infringement action (now the antitrust plaintiff) was not really infringing. In such cases, the element of bad faith is that the antitrust defendant knew of *facts* that undermined its own legal claim. *Professional Real Estate* appears not to apply to such cases. See *Nobelpharma v. Implant Innovations*, 141 F.3d 1059 (Fed. Cir. 1998), *cert. petition filed*, *****, which upheld a jury instruction that if a patentee had committed "a knowing, willful and intentional act, misrepresentation or omission" before the Patent and Trademark Office in applying for its patent, and thus knew that the patent was unenforceable, then its subsequent infringement suit could constitute the basis for an antitrust violation. The court then found that the patentee brought its infringement suit "knowing that the '891 patent was either invalid or unenforceable and with the intent of interfering directly with 3I's ability to compete in the relevant market." The appellate court agreed, concluding that

> if the evidence shows that the asserted patent was acquired by means of either a fraudulent misrepresentation or a fraudulent omission and that the party asserting the patent was aware of the fraud when bringing suit, such conduct can expose a patentee to liability under the antitrust laws.

Thus, as the court noted, infringement suits can be attacked as antitrust violations in two different ways. If a patent is valid but an infringement suit is *objectively* baseless — perhaps because the infringement defendant is clearly not infringing — then PRE would permit an attack on the baseless legal claim. By contrast, if the patent is invalid or unenforceable and the patentee knows this, then the infringement suit can be attacked as an antitrust violation even if the legal theory of the lawsuit is objectively sound.

2. In stating possible criteria for determining whether an *improperly* motivated infringement suit is a "sham," the Court suggests the factor "whether any damages for infringement would be too low to justify Columbia's investment in the suit." Suppose that the damages for infringement were $100,000, but Columbia predicted only a 25% chance of collecting $200,000, thus making the case worth about $50,000. Would that suggest "sham?" Suppose that 100 hotel and resort operators around the country were doing exactly what PRE was doing, and that the suit would "send a message" to these operators as well. In that case, what is the expected value of the suit?

3. Suppose a dominant firm that owns several patents threatens to sue a rival for patent infringement unless the rival abandons a certain production process that competes with the dominant firm's patented process. The suit, if filed, would be a baseless "sham." (For the relationship between patent law and antitrust, see the note in Chapter 6, Section II.C2, *supra*.) Should a mere threat to sue, as opposed to a lawsuit itself, receive *Noerr-Pennington* protection?

A threat to sue is not a "petition" to the sovereign the way that an actual lawsuit is. But consider the consequences of holding that a threat to sue is not protected. Firms might then be forced to sue immediately rather than writing demand letters or making other threats to sue. The threat to sue, whether in the form of a demand letter or something else, is an important device for getting people to stop doing unlawful things without the need for a lawsuit. Most courts that have addressed the issue have held that a legitimate threat to sue is protected just as the lawsuit itself. As the Fifth Circuit put it, "[t]he litigator should not be protected only when he strikes without warning. If litigation is in good faith, a token of that sincerity is a warning that it will be commenced and a possible effort to compromise the dispute." *Virginia Panel Corp. v. Mac Panel Co.*, 133 F.3d 860 (Fed. Cir. 1997), *cert. denied*, 119 S. Ct. 52 (1998) (threats to file infringement suit protected). However, just as legitimate threats are protected by *Noerr*, unjustified threats can fall within the "sham" exception. *See CVD v. Raytheon Co.*, 769 F.2d 842, 851 (1st Cir. 1985), *cert. denied*, 475 U.S. 1016 (1986).

Suppose a dominant firm not only threatens a competitor with a lawsuit but also writes a letter to the competitor's customers, telling them their supplier is behaving illegally and warning them of the consequences of subsequent legal action. Is the letter protected under *Noerr*? *See Alexander v. National Farmers Org.*, 687 F.2d 1183, 1200-03 (8th Cir. 1982), *cert. denied*, 461 U.S. 937 (1983).

4. What happens if the petitioning activities are found to be a "sham?" From that point, the antitrust plaintiff must still prove the remaining elements of its claim. That is, the "sham" petition is not itself the entire violation. For example, sham petitioning by a single firm could be monopolization or an attempt to monopolize only if the requisite market power and dangerous probability of success elements were established as well. The *Professional Real Estate* opinion makes this clear: "Proof of a sham merely deprives the defendant of immunity; it does not relieve the plaintiff of the obligation to establish all other elements of his claim...." Previously, not all courts had gotten it right. *See Rickards v. Canine Eye Registration Fund*, 783 F.2d 1329 (9th Cir.), *cert. denied*, 479 U.S. 851 (1986), which found that a group of antitrust defendants lacked market power but nevertheless that their "sham" petition constituted an antitrust violation.

5. The term "sham" applies not only to improperly motivated litigation or administrative actions, but also to certain improperly motivated requests for legislative action. In *City of Columbia & Columbia Outdoor Advertising, Inc. v. Omni Outdoor Advertising, Inc.*, 499 U.S. 365 (1991), reprinted *infra*, the Supreme Court accepted both a "state action" and a *Noerr* defense to a claim that an influential private firm's request for an ordinance injuring the plaintiff's business violated the antitrust laws. Here, the plaintiff's purpose in petitioning the government was to obtain passage of the anticompetitive ordinance, and the ordinance was actually passed. The portion of the opinion finding a "state action" exemption is reprinted later in this chapter. The Court also refused to find that the request for the ordinance fell within *Noerr*'s "sham" exception, stating:

> The "sham" exception to *Noerr* encompasses situations in which persons use the governmental process as opposed to the outcome of that process as an anticompetitive weapon. A classic example is the filing of frivolous objections to the license application of a competitor, with no expectation of achieving denial of the license but simply in order to impose expense and delay. ...
>
> Neither of the Court of Appeals' theories for application of the "sham" exception to the facts of the present case is sound. The court reasoned, first, that the jury could have concluded that COA's interaction with city officials "was actually nothing more than an attempt to interfere directly with the business relations of a competitor." This analysis relies upon language from *Noerr*, but ignores the import of the critical word "directly." Although COA indisputably set out to disrupt Omni's business relationships, it sought to do so not through the very process of lobbying, or of causing the city council to consider zoning measures, but rather through the ultimate product of that lobbying and consideration, viz., the zoning ordinances. The Court of Appeals' second theory was that the jury could have found "that COA's purposes were to delay Omni's entry into the market and even to deny it a meaningful access to the appropriate city administrative and legislative fora." But the purpose of delaying a competitor's entry into the market does not render lobbying activity a "sham," unless (as no evidence suggested was true here) the delay is sought to be achieved only by the lobbying process itself, and not by the governmental action that the lobbying seeks. "If *Noerr* teaches anything it is that an intent to restrain trade as a result of government action sought ... does not foreclose protection." Sullivan, *Developments in the Noerr Doctrine*, 56 Antitrust L.J. 361, 362 (1987). As for "deny[ing] ... meaningful access to the appropriate city administrative and legislative fora," that may render the manner of lobbying improper or even unlawful, but does not necessarily render it a "sham." We did hold in *California Motor Transport, supra*, that a conspiracy among private parties to monopolize trade by excluding a competitor from participation in the regulatory process did not enjoy *Noerr* protection. But *California Motor Transport* involved a context in which the conspirators' participation in the governmental process was itself claimed to be a "sham," employed as a means of imposing cost and delay. ("It is alleged that petitioners 'instituted the proceedings and actions ... with or without probable cause, and regardless of the merits of the cases.'" 404 U.S., at 512.) The holding of the case is limited to that situation. To extend it to a context in which the regulatory process is being invoked genuinely, and not in a "sham" fashion, would produce precisely that conversion of antitrust law into regulation of the political process that we have

sought to avoid. Any lobbyist or applicant, in addition to getting himself heard, seeks by procedural and other means to get his opponent ignored. Policing the legitimate boundaries of such defensive strategies, when they are conducted in the context of a genuine attempt to influence governmental action, is not the role of the Sherman Act. In the present case, of course, any denial to Omni of "meaningful access to the appropriate city administrative and legislative fora" was achieved by COA in the course of an attempt to influence governmental action that, far from being a "sham," was if anything more in earnest than it should have been. If the denial was wrongful there may be other remedies, but as for the Sherman Act, the *Noerr* exemption applies.

PROBLEM 9.2

Hospitals in many states cannot be built or enlarged unless the operators can acquire a "Certificate of Need." The Certificate of Need is granted only after a government agency determines that patient load in a community is sufficient to support the new hospital space. The purpose of the Certificate of Need requirement is to keep hospital costs low.

Regis and Alegis are large proprietary hospitals in a medium-sized town. Together they account for 75% of hospital capacity in the area. When their only competitor, St. Francis, a Catholic hospital, sought to add a large wing, Regis and Alegis jointly objected to the regulatory agency that there was already plenty of hospital capacity. When the agency requested Regis and Alegis to supply proof, they submitted false information about patient demand over the preceding five years. The agency denied St. Francis' request for the new wing, and St. Francis sued Regis and Alegis, charging a conspiracy to monopolize the hospital market. Regis and Alegis raise *Noerr-Pennington* as a defense. Outcome? *See St. Joseph's Hosp. v. Hospital Corp. of Am.*, 795 F.2d 948 (11th Cir. 1986).

Alternatively, suppose that when St. Francis applied for its Certificate of Need, the agency requested it to supply information justifying more hospital space. In response, St. Francis submitted false information which exaggerated patient demand for the previous five years. The existing hospitals then sue St. Francis under the antitrust laws. Outcome?

SECTION III. PROBLEMS OF FEDERALISM: PREEMPTION AND THE "STATE ACTION" DOCTRINE

All state and local government regulation is subject to the limitation imposed by the Supremacy Clause of the Constitution that it will be trumped, or preempted, by inconsistent federal legislation. The preemption doctrine in the antitrust context simply considers whether such regulation is so inconsistent with federal antitrust policy that one must give way to the other. Ordinarily, the state or local regulation gives way. But the "State Action" doctrine, developed in Part

B of this Section, notes an important exception where federal antitrust policy actually defers to state and local regulation.

A. PREEMPTION

FISHER V. CITY OF BERKELEY
475 U.S. 260 (1986)

JUSTICE MARSHALL delivered the opinion of the Court.

The question presented here is whether a rent control ordinance enacted by a municipality pursuant to popular initiative is unconstitutional because pre-empted by the Sherman Act.

I

In June 1980, the electorate of the City of Berkeley, California, enacted an initiative entitled "Ordinance 5261-N. S., Rent Stabilization and Eviction for Good Cause Ordinance," (hereafter Ordinance).... [T]he Ordinance establishes a base rent ceiling reflecting the rents in effect at the end of May 1980. A landlord may raise his rents from these levels only pursuant to an annual general adjustment of rent ceilings by a Rent Stabilization Board of appointed commissioners or after he is successful in petitioning the Board for an individual adjustment. A landlord who fails to register with the Board units covered by the Ordinance or who fails to adhere to the maximum allowable rent set under the Ordinance may be fined by the Board, sued by his tenants, or have rent legally withheld from him. If his violations are willful, he may face criminal penalties.

....

Although fully briefed on the question whether the Berkeley Ordinance constitutes state action exempt from antitrust scrutiny, ... the California Supreme Court noted that consideration of this issue would become necessary only were there to be "'truly a conflict between the Sherman Act and the challenged regulatory scheme.'" Such a conflict would exist, the Supreme Court concluded, only if the Ordinance on its face mandated conduct prohibited by either § 1 or § 2 of the Sherman Act....

We begin by noting that appellants make no claim under either § 4 or § 16 of the Clayton Act, 15 U.S.C. §§ 15 and 26, that the process by which the Rent Stabilization Ordinance was passed renders the Ordinance the product of an illegal "contract, combination ... , or conspiracy." Appellants instead claim that, regardless of the manner of its enactment, the regulatory scheme established by the Ordinance, on its face, conflicts with the Sherman Act and therefore is preempted.

Recognizing that the function of government may often be to tamper with free markets, correcting their failures and aiding their victims, this Court noted in *Rice v. Norman Williams Co.*, that a "state statute is not pre-empted by the federal antitrust laws simply because the state scheme may have an anticompetitive effect." See *Exxon Corp. v. Governor of Maryland*, 437 U.S. 117, 133 (1978).

We have therefore held that a state statute should be struck down on pre-emption grounds "only if it mandates or authorizes conduct that necessarily constitutes a violation of the antitrust laws in all cases, or if it places irresistible pressure on a private party to violate the antitrust laws in order to comply with the statute." 458 U.S., at 661.

While *Rice* involved a state statute rather than a municipal ordinance, the rule it established does not distinguish between the two. As in other pre-emption cases, the analysis is the same for the acts of both levels of government. Only where legislation is found to conflict "irreconcilably" with the antitrust laws, does the level of government responsible for its enactment become important. Legislation that would otherwise be pre-empted under *Rice* may nonetheless survive if it is found to be state action immune from antitrust scrutiny under *Parker v. Brown*, 317 U.S. 341 (1943). The ultimate source of that immunity can be only the State, not its subdivisions.

Appellants argue that Berkeley's Rent Stabilization Ordinance is pre-empted under *Rice* because it imposes rent ceilings across the entire rental market for residential units. Such a regime, they contend, clearly falls within the *per se* rule against price fixing, a rule that has been one of the settled points of antitrust enforcement since the earliest days of the Sherman Act. That the prices set here are ceilings rather than floors and that the public interest has been invoked to justify this stabilization should not, appellants argue, save Berkeley's regulatory scheme from condemnation under the *per se* rule.

Certainly there is this much truth to appellants' argument: Had the owners of residential rental property in Berkeley voluntarily banded together to stabilize rents in the city, their activities would not be saved from antitrust attack by claims that they had set reasonable prices out of solicitude for the welfare of their tenants. Moreover, it cannot be denied that Berkeley's Ordinance will affect the residential housing rental market in much the same way as would the philanthropic activities of this hypothetical trade association. What distinguishes the operation of Berkeley's Ordinance from the activities of a benevolent landlords' cartel is not that the Ordinance will necessarily have a different economic effect, but that the rent ceilings imposed by the Ordinance and maintained by the Stabilization Board have been unilaterally imposed by government upon landlords to the exclusion of private control.

The distinction between unilateral and concerted action is critical here. Adhering to the language of § 1, this Court has always limited the reach of that provision to "unreasonable restraints of trade effected by a 'contract, combination ... , or conspiracy' between *separate* entities." *Copperweld Corp. v. Independence Tube Corp.*, 467 U.S. 752, 768 (1984) (emphasis in original). We have therefore deemed it "of considerable importance" that independent activity by a single entity be distinguished from a concerted effort by more than one entity to fix prices or otherwise restrain trade, *Monsanto Co. v. Spray-Rite Service Corp.*, 465 U.S. 752, 763 (1984). Even where a single firm's restraints directly affect prices and have the same economic effect as concerted action might have, there can be no liability under § 1 in the absence of agreement. *Id.*, at 760-761; *United States v. Parke, Davis & Co.*, 362 U.S. 29, 44 (1960). Thus, if the Berkeley Ordinance stabilizes rents without this element of concerted action, the program it establishes cannot run afoul of § 1.

Recognizing this concerted action requirement, appellants argue that the Ordinance "forms a combination between [the City of Berkeley and its officials], on the one hand, and the property owners on the other. It also creates a horizontal combination among the landlords." In so arguing, appellants misconstrue the concerted action requirement of § 1. A restraint imposed unilaterally by government does not become concerted action within the meaning of the statute simply because it has a coercive effect upon parties who must obey the law. The ordinary relationship between the government and those who must obey its regulatory commands whether they wish to or not is not enough to establish a conspiracy. Similarly, the mere fact that all competing property owners must comply with the same provisions of the Ordinance is not enough to establish a conspiracy among landlords. Under Berkeley's Ordinance, control over the maximum rent levels of every affected residential unit has been unilaterally removed from the owners of those properties and given to the Rent Stabilization Board. While the Board may choose to respond to an individual landlord's petition for a special adjustment of a particular rent ceiling, it may decide not to. There is no meeting of the minds here. The owners of residential property in Berkeley have no more freedom to resist the city's rent controls than they do to violate any other local ordinance enforced by substantial sanctions.

Not all restraints imposed upon private actors by government units necessarily constitute unilateral action outside the purview of § 1. Certain restraints may be characterized as "hybrid," in that nonmarket mechanisms merely enforce private marketing decisions. See *Rice v. Norman Williams Co.*, 458 U.S., at 665 (STEVENS, J., concurring in the judgment). Where private actors are thus granted "a degree of private regulatory power," the regulatory scheme may be attacked under § 1. Indeed, this Court has twice found such hybrid restraints to violate the Sherman Act. See *Schwegmann Bros. v. Calvert Distillers Corp.*, 341 U.S. 384 (1951); *California Retail Liquor Dealers Assn. v. Midcal Aluminum, Inc.*, 445 U.S. 97 (1980).

In *Schwegmann*, a Louisiana statute authorized a distributor to enforce agreements fixing minimum retail prices not only against parties to such contracts, but also against retailers who sold the distributor's products without having agreed to the price restrictions. After finding that the statute went far beyond the now-repealed Miller-Tydings Act, which offered a limited antitrust exemption to certain "'contracts or agreements prescribing minimum prices for the resale'" of specified commodities, the Court held that two liquor distributors had violated § 1 when they attempted to hold a retailer to the price-fixing terms of a contract it had refused to sign. In so holding, the Court noted that "when a state compels retailers to follow a parallel price policy, it demands private conduct which the

Sherman Act forbids." 341 U.S., at 389. However, under the Louisiana statute, both the selection of minimum price levels and the exclusive power to enforce those levels were left to the discretion of distributors. While the petitioner-retailer in that case may have been legally required to adhere to the levels so selected, the involvement of his suppliers in setting those prices made it impossible to characterize the regulation as unilateral action by the State of Louisiana.

The trade restraint condemned in *Midcal* entailed a similar degree of free participation by private economic actors. That case presented an antitrust challenge to California's requirement that all wine producers, wholesalers, and rectifiers file fair trade contracts or price schedules with the State. If a wine producer did not set prices, wholesalers had to post a resale price schedule for that producer's brands. No state-licensed wine merchant could sell wine to a retailer at other than those prices. The Court found that "California's system for wine pricing plainly constitutes resale price maintenance in violation of the Sherman Act .... The wine producer holds the power to prevent price competition by dictating the prices charged by wholesalers." Here again, the mere existence of legal compulsion did not turn California's scheme into unilateral action by the State. The Court noted: "The State has no direct control over wine prices, and it does not review the reasonableness of the prices set by wine dealers."

The hybrid restraints condemned in *Schwegmann* and *Midcal* were thus quite different from the pure regulatory scheme imposed by the Berkeley's Rent Stabilization Ordinance. While the Ordinance does give tenants — certainly a group of interested private parties — some power to trigger the enforcement of its provisions, it places complete control over maximum rent levels exclusively in the hands of the Rent Stabilization Board. Not just the controls themselves but also the rent ceilings they mandate have been unilaterally imposed on the landlords by the city.

There may be cases in which what appears to be a state- or municipality-administered price stabilization scheme is really a private price-fixing conspiracy, concealed under a "gauzy cloak of state involvement," *Midcal*, *supra*, at 106. This might occur even where prices are ostensibly under the absolute control of government officials. However, we have been given no indication that such corruption has tainted the rent controls imposed by Berkeley's Ordinance. Adopted by popular initiative, the Ordinance can hardly be viewed as a cloak for any conspiracy among landlords or between the landlords and the municipality. Berkeley's landlords have simply been deprived of the power freely to raise their rents. That is why they are here. And that is why their role in the stabilization program does not alter the restraint's unilateral nature.

Because under settled principles of antitrust law, the rent controls established by Berkeley's Ordinance lack the element of concerted action needed before they can be characterized as a *per se* violation of § 1 of the Sherman Act, we cannot say that the Ordinance is facially inconsistent with the federal antitrust laws. We therefore need not address whether, even if the controls were to mandate § 1 violations, they would be exempt under the state-action doctrine from antitrust scrutiny.

The judgment of the California Supreme Court is

Affirmed.

[JUSTICE BRENNAN's dissenting opinion is omitted.]

NOTES AND QUESTIONS

1. How broad is the antitrust immunity created by *Fisher*? Does *Fisher* hold that local governments are immune from federal antitrust challenge under section one of the Sherman Act when there is no allegation or proof of concerted conduct between government officials and private parties? Is this the meaning of the Court's use of the term "unilateral"? Would such a rationale create immunity under section two of the Sherman Act?, or section two or three of the Clayton Act? *See* D. Mandelker, J. Gerard & E.T. Sullivan, *Federal Land Use Law* § 11.08 (1999). *See generally Westborough Mall v. City of Cape Girardeau*, 693 F.2d 733 (8th Cir. 1982).

2. The substantive allegations in the *Boulder* decision, to which the Court refers, were that the City passed an ordinance delaying expansion by one cable television firm in order to study the possibilities of entry by a second or perhaps more cable television firms. The city itself was not a competitor in the market for providing cable television services, but is rather best seen as a purchaser of those services on behalf of its citizens. How must such an antitrust violation be characterized? Monopolization or attempt? In that case it falls under the rule of reason and would not be preempted. Was Boulder's offense a vertical restraint? If so, it was certainly a nonprice restraint, and in that case it would be analyzed under the rule of reason even if there were an "agreement" between the city and those who may have benefitted from the statute. Once again, the *Fisher* standard would not require preemption. Perhaps Boulder and one or more cable television firms conspired to exclude another firm part of the market, and thus engaged in a concerted refusal to deal. However, the case for per se treatment is very weak, particularly given the fact that the City of Boulder itself is not a supplier of cable television services; thus, this would be concerted agreement among noncompeting firms.

In short, does not the disposition of *Fisher* demand a similar result in *Boulder*?

3. In *Exxon Corp. v. Governor of Md.*, 437 U.S. 117 (1978), the Supreme Court held that the mere fact that a statute was anticompetitive and inconsistent with the general policies of the Sherman Act did not mandate preemption unless the law actually forced private parties to violate the Sherman Act. It approved a state statute compelling the vertical disintegration of oil companies within the state.

4. Liquor price posting statutes have often been found to be preempted by the Sherman Act. For example, see the *Midcal* and *Schwegmann* cases, both discussed in the *Fisher* opinion. The statutes are preempted for compelling resale price maintenance, which is illegal per se.

But this creates a conceptual problem. Where is the "agreement" between two persons? If a statute orders wholesalers to post a price and retailers to sell at the posted price, it is not compelling the wholesalers and retailers to "agree" with each other. To be sure, they may discuss the price and agree about it before it is posted, but that is quite a different matter. As *Fisher* makes clear, the mere compliance with the statute is likewise not an agreement between the private citizen and the state.

In order to solve this conceptual difficulty, courts in price-posting cases have developed the concept of the "hybrid" restraint. For example, in *324 Liquor Corp. v. Duffy*, 479 U.S. 335 (1987), the Supreme Court struck down a statute requiring liquor wholesalers to post wholesale prices and retailers to set their prices at 112% or more of the posted wholesale price, but permitted wholesalers to sell cases of liquor at less than the posted price. This was a "hybrid" restraint, the court explained, because the statute granted the wholesalers the power to force the retailers to set a price independently of the price that the wholesalers actually charged. For example, a wholesaler could post a price of $100 a case, thus requiring the retailer to charge a per-bottle price totaling at least $112 per case. But under the statute the wholesaler was then free to sell the case at any price it pleased. This, as the court observed, was merely compelling a form of resale price maintenance. *See* 1 P. Areeda & H. Hovenkamp, *Antitrust Law* ¶ 217 (rev. ed. 1997).

B. THE "STATE ACTION" DOCTRINE

The principal purpose of the antitrust laws is to regulate private conduct, not to second guess regulatory decisions made by state and local government. If a particular restraint is authorized or compelled by a governmental regulation, it may be exempt from federal antitrust liability under the "state action" doctrine.

The state action exemption from the antitrust laws must be distinguished from the very broad concept of "state action" used in litigation under the fourteenth amendment and the federal civil rights statutes. The fourteenth amendment concept of state action is expansive and applies to public officials at every governmental level other than federal, and sometimes even to private persons acting under color of state law. *See* L. Tribe, *American Constitutional Law* §§ 18-1 to 18-7 (2d ed. 1988). By contrast, the antitrust "state action" exemption is strictly construed and applies only to legislation and regulations of the state itself, or of governmental subdivisions whose authority to regulate comes explicitly from a state.

In 1943, the Supreme Court announced the state action doctrine in *Parker v. Brown*, 317 U.S. 341 (1943), a case which challenged California's agricultural marketing regulation which restricted competition among raisin growers and permitted the fixing of prices at which growers could sell the raisins. The defendants named in *Parker* were state officials who had administrative responsibility for approving the "production zones" and "proration programs" for raisin producers.

In rejecting the Sherman Act challenge, the Supreme Court's unanimous opinion stated that "nothing in the language of the Sherman Act or in its history ... suggests that its purpose was to restrain a state or its officers or agents from activities directed by its legislature." *Id.* at 350-51. The result suggested that state conduct authorized by the state legislature was immune from antitrust challenge regardless of the degree of anticompetitiveness. The state, in other words, was free to substitute its judgment for that of the federal statutory scheme as to how competition was to be regulated. But the conduct had to be clearly that of the state. Private conduct which was merely encouraged or perhaps authorized by the state was not immunized under *Parker. Id.* at 352. Lower courts interpreted the *Parker v. Brown* exemption to cover Clayton Act violations as well. *See, e.g., Feldman v. Gardner*, 661 F.2d 1295, 1304 n.76 (D.C. Cir. 1981).

Thirty-two years after *Parker*, the Supreme Court was confronted with the issue whether the setting of minimum prices by lawyers, implicitly sanctioned but not mandated by a state supreme court rule, was protected from antitrust challenge. The Court reasoned in *Goldfarb v. Virginia State Bar*, 421 U.S. 773 (1975), that the state action defense could be invoked only if the state, through a sovereign act, *required* the challenged practice. *Id.* at 791. Applying this test to the facts in *Goldfarb*, the Court found that the minimum-fee schedule was not required by the state supreme court. Thus the price fixing arrangement was not exempt from the antitrust laws. For a time, therefore, it appeared that the exemption applied only to private activities that were "compelled" by state law.

In a plurality opinion in *Cantor v. Detroit Edison Co.*, 428 U.S. 579 (1976), the Court then held that the *Parker* defense was available only for official state action taken by state officials. *Id.* at 591-92. The implication was that conduct engaged in by private individuals subject to state mandate was not protected. The Michigan Public Service Commission approved Detroit Edison's practice of furnishing "free" light bulbs to customers. The cost was included in the monthly electric fee. The action by a local druggist alleged that the utility was exercising monopoly power in one market (electricity) to suppress competition in another (light bulbs). Focusing on the lack of an explicit state policy to replace competition in the retail light bulb market and the minor state involvement in the distribution scheme of the utility, the Court held the state action doctrine inapplicable. *Id.* at 593-96. Implicitly, the emerging state action defense required evidence of (1) a state policy to replace the competition mandated by the federal antitrust laws, (2) state supervision of the new policy, and (3) a degree of state compulsion for the challenged practice. *See* Areeda, *Antitrust Immunity for "State Action" After Lafayette*, 95 Harv. L. Rev. 435, 438 (1981).

In *Bates v. State Bar*, 433 U.S. 350 (1977), the Supreme Court clarified these requirements. It held that a rule prohibiting advertising by attorneys, which was approved and supervised by the Arizona Supreme Court under its constitutional authority to enforce disciplinary rules, was exempt from antitrust scrutiny. The restraint was compelled, the Court reasoned, at the direction of the state acting as sovereign.

The Court has frequently considered the scope of the state action doctrine when a political subdivision such as a city, acting in its authorized capacity, is charged with an antitrust violation. In rejecting the defense generally as applied to cities, the Court in *City of Lafayette v. Louisiana Power & Light Co.*, 435 U.S. 389 (1978), held that "the *Parker* doctrine exempts only anticompetitive conduct engaged in as an act of government by the state as sovereign, or, by its subdivisions, pursuant to state policy to displace competition with regulation or monopoly public service." *Id.* at 413. *Lafayette* addressed the issue whether a city, which operated an electric power company and which was charged with "various antitrust offenses in the conduct" of the utility, could seek a dismissal of the antitrust charges under the *Parker* doctrine. The plurality opinion interjected federalism as the basis for holding that cities should not automatically be treated the same as states.

> Cities are not themselves sovereign; they do not receive all the federal deference of the States that create them.... *Parker*'s limitation of the exemption to "official action directed by a state," ... is consistent with the fact that the States' subdivisions generally have not been treated as equivalents of the States themselves. In light of the serious economic dislocation which could result if cities were free to place their own parochial interests above the Nation's economic goals reflected in the antitrust laws, ... we are especially unwilling to presume that Congress intended to exclude anticompetitive municipal action from their reach.

Id. at 412-13.

The Court then opined that cities could come within the state action immunity if evidence demonstrated that the state intended to displace a competition policy by authorizing the anticompetitive practices. 435 U.S. at 414.

CALIFORNIA RETAIL LIQUOR DEALERS ASS'N V. MIDCAL ALUMINUM, INC.

445 U.S. 97 (1980)

JUSTICE POWELL delivered the opinion of the Court.

In a state-court action, respondent Midcal Aluminum, Inc., a wine distributor, presented a successful antitrust challenge to California's resale price maintenance and price posting statutes for the wholesale wine trade. The issue in this case is whether those state laws are shielded from the Sherman Act by ... the "state action" doctrine of *Parker v. Brown*....

Under § 24866 (b) of the California Business and Professions Code, all wine producers, wholesalers, and rectifiers must file fair trade contracts or price schedules with the State. If a wine producer has not set prices through a fair trade contract, wholesalers must post a resale price schedule for that producer's brands. No state-licensed wine merchant may sell wine to a retailer at other than the price set "either in an effective price schedule or in an effective fair trade contract...."

... A licensee selling below the established prices faces fines, license suspension, or outright license revocation. The State has no direct control over wine prices, and it does not review the reasonableness of the prices set by wine dealers.

Midcal Aluminum, Inc., is a wholesale distributor of wine in southern California. In July 1978, the Department of Alcoholic Beverage Control charged Midcal with selling 27 cases of wine for less than the prices set by the effective price schedule of the E. & J. Gallo Winery.... Midcal stipulated that the allegations were true .... Midcal then filed a writ of mandate in the California Court of Appeal for the Third Appellate District asking for an injunction against the State's wine pricing system.

The Court of Appeal ruled that the wine pricing scheme restrains trade in violation of the Sherman Act.

....

California's system for wine pricing plainly constitutes resale price maintenance in violation of the Sherman Act. The wine producer holds the power to prevent price competition by dictating the prices charged by wholesalers. As Mr. Justice Hughes pointed out in *Dr. Miles*, [see Casebook, p. 421] such vertical control destroys horizontal competition as effectively as if wholesalers "formed a combination and endeavored to establish the same restrictions ... by agreement with each other." ...

[Our earlier] decisions establish two standards for antitrust immunity under *Parker v. Brown*. First, the challenged restraint must be "one clearly articulated and affirmatively expressed as state policy"; second, the policy must be "actively supervised" by the State itself. *City of Lafayette v. Louisiana Power & Light Co.*, 435 U.S. 389, 410 (1978) (opinion of Brennan, J.). The California system for wine pricing satisfies the first standard. The legislative policy is forthrightly stated and clear in its purpose to permit resale price maintenance. The program, however, does not meet the second requirement for *Parker* immunity. The State simply authorizes price setting and enforces the prices established by private parties. The State neither establishes prices nor reviews the reasonableness of the price schedules; nor does it regulate the terms of fair trade contracts. The State does not monitor market conditions or engage in any "pointed reexamination" of the program. The national policy in favor of competition cannot be thwarted by casting such a gauzy cloak of state involvement over what is essentially a private price-fixing arrangement....

NOTES AND QUESTIONS

1. The "state action" doctrine is judicially created. Is it justified by the legislative history of the Sherman Act? It is difficult to conceive how the framers of the Sherman Act in 1890 could have imagined such a doctrine. Under the prevailing interpretations of the Commerce Clause there was an absolute line between interstate activities, which only the federal government could regulate (*see*, *for example*, *Wabash, St. L. & Pac. Ry. v. Illinois*, 118 U.S. 557 (1886)), and intrastate activities, which only the states could control (*for example*, *United States v. E.C. Knight Co.*, 156 U.S. 1 (1895). Furthermore, state judicial jurisdiction was absolutely limited to persons and activities within the state. *E.g.*, *Pennoyer v. Neff*, 95 U.S. 714 (1877). As a result, in 1890 a state statute could constitutionally be applied only to activities entirely within that state's borders. At the same time, the Sherman Act, which was passed under the Commerce Clause, could not reach wholly intrastate activities. In such a regime the "state action" doctrine simply had no place. *Parker v. Brown* was decided in 1943, one year after the Supreme Court had greatly expanded federal jurisdiction under the commerce clause to reach intrastate activities if they merely "affected" interstate commerce. *Wickard v. Filburn*, 317 U.S. 111 (1942). Only then did the modern "state action" doctrine become possible and, perhaps, necessary. *See* Hovenkamp & MacKerron, *Municipal Regulation and Federal Antitrust Policy*, 32 UCLA L. Rev. 719 (1985).

2. In *Hoover v. Ronwin*, 466 U.S. 558 (1984), the plaintiff, who had taken the Arizona bar examination and failed, alleged that the Committee on Examination and Admissions, responsible for administering and grading the bar examination, "had set the grading scale ... with reference to the number of new attorneys they thought desirable [to be admitted to the bar], rather than with reference to some 'suitable' level of competence." Ronwin claimed unlawful monopolization, but the Supreme Court found that the "state action" doctrine precluded liability. The Committee on Examination and Admissions was completely controlled by the state supreme court, which was a part of the state itself. Once the principal actor was identified as the state itself, no authorization from any other part of the state was needed, nor was "active supervision" required, since no private conduct was being challenged.

In a dissenting opinion Justice Stevens, joined by Justices White and Blackmun, complained that Ronwin had alleged that the Committee on Examination and Admissions (composed largely of lawyers), not the state supreme court itself, had made the anticompetitive decisions. They reasoned that the Court should look behind the "official" act to determine who the real decision makers were. Responding to the dissent, the Court's opinion stated:

> The reasoning adopted by the dissent would allow Sherman Act plaintiffs to look behind the actions of state sovereigns and base their claims on perceived conspiracies to restrain trade among the committees, commissions, or others who necessarily must advise the sovereign. Such a holding would emasculate the *Parker v. Brown* doctrine. For example, if a state legislature enacted a law based on studies performed, or advice given, by an advisory committee, the dissent would find the state exempt from Sherman Act liability but not the committee. A party dissatisfied with the new law could circumvent the state action doctrine by alleging that the committee's advice reflected an

undisclosed collective desire to restrain trade without the knowledge of the legislature. The plaintiff certainly would survive a motion to dismiss — or even summary judgment — despite the fact that the suit falls squarely within the class of cases found exempt from Sherman Act liability in *Parker*.

In a footnote, the court added:

> The dissent suggests that it is "pretense" to say that the Arizona Supreme Court is the relevant "decision-maker." The dissent also surmises that "it appears that the court *always* follows [the Committee's] recommendations" (emphasis in original). There is no evidence to support this statement. Under Arizona law, the responsibility is on the court — and only on it — to admit or deny admission to the practice of law. This Court certainly cannot assume that the Arizona court, in the exercise of its specifically reserved power under its Rules, invariably agrees with its committee. Even if it did, however, it would be action of the sovereign.

Does *Hoover* clarify when an agency is the "state" and when it is not? Consider the following cases, all decided after *Hoover*.

In *Southern Motor Carriers Rate Conf. v. United States*, 471 U.S. 48 (1985), the Court found the "state action" exemption to apply, but it appeared to hold that state rate-making agencies are not part of the state itself but, rather, separate entities requiring clearly articulated authorization from the state legislature, just as a municipality would. (See the discussions of the *Boulder*, *Hallie*, and *Columbia* decisions, *infra*.) However, in *Charley's Taxi Radio Dispatch v. SIDA of Haw.*, 810 F.2d 869 (9th Cir. 1987), the court held that the director of the state's Department of Transportation was part of the state itself, and needed no independent authorization from the legislature. In *Cine 42nd St. Theater Corp. v. Nederlander Org.*, 790 F.2d 1032 (2d Cir. 1986), the court held that the New York Urban Development Corporation, an incorporated public agency, was not the "state" for purposes of the "state action" doctrine, because it had been designed to facilitate urban development without the bureaucratic delays that had frustrated other projects. As a result, the court concluded, the Corporation should be considered distinct from ordinary state agencies.

NOTE: FEDERALISM AND THE "STATE ACTION" DOCTRINE

Midcal's outcome notwithstanding, the "state action" doctrine is highly deferential toward state and local regulation, is it not? Under *Fisher*, the *Parker* doctrine applies only to state or local regulation found to be preempted by the antitrust laws. In most areas of federal-state conflict that is the end of the matter. Once a state or local regulation is found to be preempted by a valid federal statute, the regulation cannot be enforced. E.T. Sullivan & J. Harrison, *Understanding Antitrust and Its Economic Implications*, 65-69 (3d. ed. 1998).

Midcal not only permits continued enforcement of regulations that are preempted by the federal antitrust laws, it gives state governments virtual *carte blanche* to exempt any type of regulation they choose, no matter how anticompetitive. The record of antitrust litigation involving local governments suggests that counties and municipalities often pass inefficient, "special interest" legislation designed to benefit a relatively small constituency at the expense of the community as a whole. Commentators have made the same point. *See, e.g.,* Kitch, Isaacson & Kasper, *The Regulation of Taxicabs in Chicago,* 14 J.L. & Econ. 285 (1971). Query: why doesn't the electoral process keep inefficient, special interest legislation from being passed? *See* Farber & Frickey, *The Jurisprudence of Public Choice,* 65 Tex. L. Rev. 873 (1987); Sunstein, *Interest Groups in American Public Law,* 38 Stan. L. Rev. 29 (1985). Assuming that local governments or states are prone to pass inefficient legislation, is there any reason for thinking that Congress or a federal court interpreting the antitrust laws would do any better?

Some commentators have argued that a little less deference to state or local regulation would be a good idea. For example, see Wiley, *A Capture Theory of Antitrust Federalism,* 99 Harv. L. Rev. 713 (1986), arguing that less federal deference is in order if the state or local regulation is an obvious example of special interest "capture" of the regulatory process, and the activity is not protected by a specific federally-created exemption. *See also* Cirace, *An Economic Analysis of the "State-Municipal Action" Antitrust Cases,* 61 Tex. L. Rev. 481 (1982), arguing that federal law should preempt any local legislation that is not justified by a perceived market failure. *And see* Hovenkamp & MacKerron, *Municipal Regulation and Federal Antitrust Policy,* 32 UCLA L. Rev. 719 (1985), arguing that federal deference is in order only if the state or local government is a better regulator of the conduct at issue than the federal government is. The federal government is likely to be the superior regulator when the regulation has substantial effects, or "spillovers," outside the geographic territory controlled by the sovereign. These and other proposals are discussed more fully in H. Hovenkamp, *Federal Antitrust Policy* §§ 20.2 to 20.3 (2d ed. 1994).

1. THE AUTHORIZATION REQUIREMENT AND THE PROBLEM OF LOCAL GOVERNMENT ANTITRUST LIABILITY

Midcal articulated a concise two-part test for the "state action" exemption. First, the restraint had to be "clearly articulated and affirmatively expressed," or *authorized,* in state regulatory policy. Second, any private conduct performed under the state scheme had to be "actively supervised" by the state. Interpreting these requirements required several additional decisions.

One of the most important authorization issues pertains to the regulatory power of municipalities. Throughout this discussion the term "municipal" refers to some unit of local government. It could be a municipality, county, township, or even a school or water district. The *Lafayette* decision, discussed *supra,* first considered whether a municipality may itself "authorize" anticompetitive activity. The answer was no; authorization must come from the state. Next, in *Community Commun. Co. v. City of Boulder*, 455 U.S. 40 (1982), the Court considered what it would take for a state to authorize a municipality to regulate in such a way as to meet the "clear articulation" requirement.

Boulder was an antitrust challenge to a municipal ordinance that delayed the further development of the plaintiff's cable television system for three months, pending the city's study of its needs. The City of Boulder was a "home rule" municipality, which under the Colorado constitution was "entitled to exercise 'the full right of self-government in both local and municipal matters,' and with respect to such matters the City Charter and ordinances supersede the laws of the State." The city claimed that its "home rule" status provided adequate state authorization for its ordinance. The Supreme Court disagreed, saying:

> [In *City of Lafayette* we recognized] that a State may frequently choose to effect its policies through the instrumentality of its cities and towns. It was stressed, however, that the "state policy" relied upon would have to be "clearly articulated and affirmatively expressed." ...
>
> Respondent [argues] that through the Home Rule Amendment the people of the State of Colorado have vested in the city of Boulder "*every power thereofore possessed by the legislature* ... in local and municipal affairs.'" The power thus possessed by Boulder's City Council assertedly embraces the regulation of cable television, which is claimed to pose essentially local problems. Thus, it is suggested, the city's cable television moratorium ordinance is an "act of government" performed by the city *acting as the State* in local matters, which meets the "state action" criterion of *Parker*.
>
> We reject this argument: it both misstates the letter of the law and misunderstands its spirit. The *Parker* state-action exemption reflects Congress' intention to embody in the Sherman Act the federalism principle that the States possess a significant measure of sovereignty under our Constitution. But this principle contains its own limitation: Ours is a "*dual* system of government," which has no place for sovereign cities. As this Court stated long ago, all sovereign authority "within the geographical limits of the United States" resides either with the Government of the United States, or [with] the States of the Union. *There exist within the broad domain of sovereignty but these two.* There may be cities, counties, and other organized bodies with limited legislative functions, but they are all derived from, or exist in, subordination to one or the other of these....
>
> [P]lainly the requirement of "clear articulation and affirmative expression" is not satisfied when the State's position is one of mere *neutrality* respecting the municipal actions challenged as anticompetitive. A State that allows its municipalities to do as they please can hardly be said to have "contemplated" the specific anticompetitive actions for which municipal liability is sought. Nor can those actions be truly described as "comprehended within the powers *granted*," since the term, "granted," necessarily implies an affirmative

addressing of the subject by the State. The State did not do so here: The relationship of the State of Colorado to Boulder's moratorium ordinance is one of precise neutrality.

The *Boulder* decision created numerous problems for the relationship between state and local government. In several states, for example, large cities have authority to regulate under a general home rule provision that effectively permits the city to displace state law within its boundaries. Smaller cities in the same states, however, were perceived to require less overall regulatory authority. They regulate under specific statutory grants of power, such as zoning enabling acts, rent control enabling acts, acts permitting the cities to provide their own electric power, and so on. One of *Boulder*'s ironies is that in such states the small towns, whose grants of regulatory authority are "market specific," may have substantially more power to regulate than larger cities that regulate under a home-rule provision. Most troubling of all was the specter of treble damages actions against municipalities (although no municipality was ever actually required to pay damages).

Responding to these concerns, Congress passed the Local Government Antitrust Act, codified at 15 U.S.C. §§ 35, 36. The statute provides that no "damages, interest on damages, costs or attorney's fees may be recovered" in private damages actions under the federal antitrust laws "from any local government, or official or employee thereof acting in an official capacity." The statute permits a prevailing plaintiff to obtain an injunction and attorney's fees in injunction actions. While the Act says nothing about when local government conduct violates the antitrust laws, its damage exclusion has reduced substantially the number of antitrust complaints filed against municipalities.

Shortly after Congress passed the Local Government Antitrust Act, Supreme Court thinking about municipal antitrust liability changed. After reading the *Hallie* and *Columbia* decisions, *infra*, consider how much of *Lafayette* and *Boulder* remains. Has the Local Government Antitrust Act become superfluous?

HALLIE V. CITY OF EAU CLAIRE

471 U.S. 34 (1985)

JUSTICE POWELL delivered the opinion of the Court.

This case presents the question whether a municipality's anticompetitive activities are protected by the state action exemption to the federal antitrust laws ... when the activities are authorized, but not compelled, by the State, and the State does not actively supervise the anticompetitive conduct.

I

Petitioners — Town of Hallie, Town of Seymour, Town of Union, and Town of Washington (the Towns) — are four Wisconsin unincorporated townships located adjacent to respondent, the City of Eau Claire (the City). Town of Hallie is located in Chippewa County, and the other three towns are located in Eau Claire County. The Towns filed suit against the City in United States District Court for the Western District of Wisconsin seeking injunctive relief and alleging that the City violated the Sherman Act, 15 U.S.C. § 1 *et seq.*, by acquiring a monopoly over the provision of sewage treatment services in Eau Claire and Chippewa Counties, and by tying the provision of such services to the provision of sewage collection and transportation services. [T]he City had obtained federal funds to help build a sewage treatment facility within the Eau Claire Service Area, that included the Towns; the facility is the only one in the market available to the Towns. The City has refused to supply sewage treatment services to the Towns. It does supply the services to individual landowners in areas of the Towns if a majority of the individuals in the area vote by referendum election to have their homes annexed by the City, and to use the City's sewage collection and transportation services.

Alleging that they are potential competitors of the City in the collection and transportation of sewage, the Towns contended in the District Court that the City used its monopoly over sewage treatment to gain an unlawful monopoly over the provision of sewage collection and transportation services, in violation of the Sherman Act. They also contended that the City's actions constituted an illegal tying arrangement and an unlawful refusal to deal with the Towns.

II

....

Municipalities ... are not beyond the reach of the antitrust laws by virtue of their status because they are not themselves sovereign. *City of Lafayette v. Louisiana Power & Light Co.*, 435 U.S. 389, 412 (1978) (opinion of BRENNAN, J.). Rather, to obtain exemption, municipalities must demonstrate that their anticompetitive activities were authorized by the State "pursuant to state policy to displace competition with regulation or monopoly public service." ...

It is therefore clear from our cases that before a municipality will be entitled to the protection of the state action exemption from the antitrust laws, it must demonstrate that it is engaging in the challenged activity pursuant to a clearly expressed state policy. We have never fully considered, however, how clearly a state policy must be articulated for a municipality to be able to establish that its anticompetitive activity constitutes state action. Moreover, we have expressly left open the question whether action by a municipality — like action by a private party — must satisfy [*Midcal*'s] "active state supervision" requirement.

III

....

A

Wisconsin Stat. § 62.18(1) (1982) grants authority to cities to construct, add to, alter, and repair sewerage systems. The authority includes the power to "describe with reasonable particularity the district to be [served]." *Ibid.* This grant of authority is supplemented by Wis. Stat. Ann. § 66.069(2)(c) (Supp. 1984), providing that a city operating a public utility

> "may by ordinance fix the limits of such service in unincorporated areas. Such ordinance shall delineate the area within which service will be provided and the municipal utility shall have no obligation to serve beyond the area so delineated."

With respect to joint sewerage systems, § 144.07(1) provides that the State's Department of Natural Resources may require a city's sewerage system to be constructed so that other cities, towns, or areas may connect to the system, and the Department may order that such connections be made. Subsection (1m) provides, however, that an order by the Department of Natural Resources for the connection of unincorporated territory to a city system shall be void if that territory refuses to become annexed to the city.

B

The Towns contend that these statutory provisions do not evidence a state policy to displace competition in the provision of sewage services because they make no express mention of anticompetitive conduct. As discussed above, the statutes clearly contemplate that a city may engage in anticompetitive conduct. Such conduct is a foreseeable result of empowering the City to refuse to serve unannexed areas. It is not necessary, as the Towns contend, for the state legislature to have stated explicitly that it expected the City to engage in conduct that would have anticompetitive effects. Applying the analysis of *City of Lafayette*, 435 U.S. 389 (1978), it is sufficient that the statutes authorize the City to provide sewage services and also to determine the areas to be served. We think it is clear that anticompetitive effects logically would result from this broad authority to regulate. ...

Nor do we agree with the Towns' contention that the statutes at issue here are neutral on state policy. The Towns attempt to liken the Wisconsin statutes to the Home Rule Amendment involved in *City of Boulder*, arguing that the Wisconsin statutes are neutral because they leave the City free to pursue either anticompetitive conduct or free-market competition in the field of sewage services. The analogy to the Home Rule Amendment involved in *City of Boulder* is inapposite. That Amendment to the Colorado Constitution allocated only the most general authority to municipalities to govern local affairs. We held that it was neutral and did not satisfy the "clear articulation" component of the state action test. The Amendment simply did not address the regulation of cable television. Under Home Rule the municipality was to be free to decide every aspect of policy relating to cable television, as well as policy relating to any other field of regulation of local concern. Here, in contrast, the State has specifically authorized Wisconsin cities to provide sewage services and has delegated to the cities the express authority to take action that foreseeably will result in anticompetitive effects. No reasonable argument can be made that these statutes are neutral in the same way that Colorado's Home Rule Amendment was.

The Towns' argument amounts to a contention that to pass the "clear articulation" test, a legislature must expressly state in a statute or its legislative history that it intends for the delegated action to have anticompetitive effects. This contention embodies an unrealistic view of how legislatures work and of how statutes are written. No legislature can be expected to catalog all of the anticipated effects of a statute of this kind. ...

In sum, we conclude that the Wisconsin statutes evidence a "clearly articulated and affirmatively expressed" state policy to displace competition with regulation in the area of municipal provision of sewerage services. These statutory provisions plainly show that "'the legislature contemplated the kind of action complained of.'" *City of Lafayette, supra.* This is sufficient to satisfy the clear articulation requirement of the state action test.

C

The Towns further argue that the "clear articulation" requirement of the state action test requires at least that the City show that the State "compelled" it to act. In so doing, they rely on language in *Cantor v. Detroit Edison Co.*, 428 U.S. 579 (1976), and *Goldfarb v. Virginia State Bar*, 421 U.S. 773 (1975). We disagree with this contention for several reasons. *Cantor* and *Goldfarb* concerned private parties — not municipalities — claiming the state action exemption. This fact distinguishes those cases because a municipality is an arm of the State. We may presume, absent a showing to the contrary, that the municipality acts in the public interest. A private party, on the other hand, may be presumed to be acting primarily on his or its own behalf.

None of our cases involving the application of the state action exemption to a municipality has required that compulsion be shown. Both *City of Boulder*, 455 U.S., at 56-57, and *City of Lafayette*, 435 U.S., at 416-417, spoke in terms of the State's direction *or authorization* of the anticompetitive practice at issue. This is so because where the actor is a municipality, acting pursuant to a clearly articulated state policy, compulsion is simply unnecessary as an evidentiary matter to prove that the challenged practice constitutes state action. In short, although compulsion affirmatively expressed may be the best evidence of state policy, it is by no means a prerequisite to a finding that a municipality acted pursuant to clearly articulated state policy.

IV

Finally, the Towns argue that as there was no active state supervision, the City may not depend on the state action exemption. The Towns rely primarily on language in *City of Lafayette.* It is fair to say that our cases have not been entirely clear. The plurality opinion in *City of Lafayette* did suggest, without elaboration and without deciding the issue, that a city claiming the exemption must show that its anticompetitive conduct was actively supervised by the State. 435 U.S., at 410. In *California Retail Liquor Dealers Assn. v. Midcal Aluminum, Inc.*, a unanimous Court held that supervision is required where the anticompetitive conduct is by private parties. In *City of Boulder*, however, the most recent relevant case, we expressly left this issue open as to municipalities. 455 U.S., at 51-52, n. 14. We now conclude that the active state supervision requirement should not be imposed in cases in which the actor is a municipality.[10]

As with respect to the compulsion argument discussed above, the requirement of active state supervision serves essentially an evidentiary function: it is one way of ensuring that the actor is engaging in the challenged conduct pursuant to state policy. In *Midcal*, we stated that the active state supervision requirement was necessary to prevent a State from circumventing the Sherman Act's proscriptions "by casting ... a gauzy cloak of state involvement over what is essentially a private price-fixing arrangement." Where a private party is engaging in the anticompetitive activity, there is a real danger that he is acting to further his own interests, rather than the governmental interests of the State. Where the actor is a municipality, there is little or no danger that it is involved in a *private* price-fixing arrangement. The only real danger is that it will seek to further purely parochial public interests at the expense of more overriding state goals. This danger is minimal, however, because of the requirement that the municipality act pursuant to a clearly articulated state policy. Once it is clear that state authorization exists, there is no need to require the State to supervise actively the municipality's execution of what is a properly delegated function.

V

We conclude that the actions of the City of Eau Claire in this case are exempt from the Sherman Act. They were taken pursuant to a clearly articulated state policy to replace competition in the provision of sewerage services with regulation. We further hold that active state supervision is not a prerequisite to exemption from the antitrust laws where the actor is a municipality rather than a private party. We accordingly affirm the judgment of the Court of Appeals for the Seventh Circuit.

NOTES AND QUESTIONS

1. In *Hallie*, the Supreme Court held that in order to qualify for the "state action" exemption a municipality's activities do not need to be either "compelled" by the state or "actively supervised" by the state. The Court justifies both of these

---

[10] In cases in which the actor is a state agency, it is likely that active state supervision would also not be required, although we do not here decide that issue. Where state or municipal regulation of a private party is involved, however, active state supervision must be shown, even where a clearly articulated state policy exists.

conclusions with the observation that a municipality will presumably act in the "public interest" rather than its own interest, and therefore would not consider anything as self-serving as participation in a private price-fixing agreement. If that is the case, then why should municipalities *ever* be held liable under the antitrust laws? But more to the point, do you believe what the Court says about municipalities. Doesn't a municipality have some of the same profit incentives that a private firm has? If so, might it not be tempted to participate in a private price fixing agreement? *See Affiliated Capital Corp. v. City of Houston*, 735 F.2d 1555 (5th Cir. 1984) (en banc), which may have involved a municipality's participation in a private territorial division scheme.

2. The *Hallie* opinion left unanswered the question whether a private defendant, rather than a municipality, must be "compelled" to act by the State, rather than merely "permitted" to act. However, in *Southern Motor Carriers Rate Conf. v. United States*, 471 U.S. 48 (1985), which was decided the same day, it answered that question in the negative. The Court held that the activities of a legislatively authorized "rate bureau" (a legalized cartel in which price-regulated common carriers jointly draft and propose rates to a regulatory agency) qualified for the "state action" exemption, even though the state legislation merely authorized, and did not compel, the activities. The Court made clear, however, that its holding did not amount to a blanket rule that state compulsion is unnecessary in state action cases involving private defendants. Rather it looked closely at the joint rate-making activities in question and found a good reason for individual firms to be given the option whether to set rates jointly or separately:

> Most common carriers probably will engage in collective ratemaking, as that will allow them to share the cost of preparing rate proposals. If the joint rates are viewed as too high, however, carriers individually may submit lower proposed rates to the commission in order to obtain a larger share of the market. Thus, through the self-interested actions of private common carriers, the States may achieve the desired balance between the efficiency of collective ratemaking and the competition fostered by individual submissions. Construing the Sherman Act to prohibit collective rate proposals eliminates the free choice necessary to ensure that these policies function in the manner intended by the States.

In effect, the Court is arguing that a "compulsion" requirement in this case would make the states prevent the carriers from cheating on their own cartel. Are you convinced by the Court's "efficiency" argument? Would it not have been useful to discern how often a disruptive carrier requested to deviate downward from the rate set by the legal cartel?

PROBLEM 9.3

Euclid, like most municipalities, has a comprehensive land-use planning (zoning) scheme which regulates both residential and commercial land uses. Euclid's authority for this regulation is a standard Zoning Enabling Act, which authorizes municipalities within the state to "establish and regulate land uses and building construction within their limits." Jack has a parcel of land which is zoned residential, but he wishes to construct a retail vegetable market on it. He petitions the Euclid city council for a reclassification of the land from residential to retail. Ron currently owns a grocery store across the street from Jack's parcel, and the only grocery store within a two-mile radius. Ron (1) makes $1,500 contributions to each of the city council members for their next campaign; (2) objects vociferously at the city council meeting to Jack's request for a reclassification of his property; and (3) secretly bribes two of the council members. The city council votes 5-2 to deny Jack's request.

Jack files an antitrust complaint naming both the city council and Ron as defendants, seeking $250,000 in damages. What arguments should each defendant make? Outcome? *See Pendleton Constr. Corp. v. Rockbridge Cty., Va.*, 652 F. Supp. 312 (W.D. Va. 1987); *Whitworth v. Perkins*, 559 F.2d 378 (5th Cir. 1977). Now, consider the impact of the following decision.

CITY OF COLUMBIA & COLUMBIA OUTDOOR ADVERTISING, INC. V. OMNI OUTDOOR ADVERTISING, INC.

499 U.S. 365 (1991)

JUSTICE SCALIA delivered the opinion of the Court.

This case requires us to clarify the application of the Sherman Act to municipal governments and to the citizens who seek action from them.

I

Petitioner Columbia Outdoor Advertising, Inc. (COA), a South Carolina corporation, entered the billboard business in the city of Columbia, South Carolina (also a petitioner here), in the 1940's. By 1981 it controlled more than 95% of what has been conceded to be the relevant market. COA was a local business owned by a family with deep roots in the community, and enjoyed close relations with the city's political leaders. The mayor and other members of the city council were personal friends of COA's majority owner, and the company and its officers occasionally contributed funds and free billboard space to their campaigns. According to respondent, these beneficences were part of a "longstanding" "secret anticompetitive agreement" whereby "the City and COA would each use their [sic] respective power and resources to protect ... COA's monopoly position," in return for which "City Council members received advantages made possible by COA's monopoly."

In 1981, respondent Omni Outdoor Advertising, Inc., a Georgia corporation, began erecting billboards in and around the city. COA responded to this competition in several ways. First, it redoubled its own billboard construction efforts and modernized its existing stock. Second, according to Omni, it took a number of anticompetitive private actions, such as offering artificially low rates, spreading untrue and malicious rumors about Omni, and attempting to induce Omni's customers to break their contracts. Finally (and this is what gives rise to the issue we address today), COA executives met with city officials to seek the enactment of zoning ordinances that would restrict billboard construction. COA was not alone in urging this course; a number of citizens concerned about the city's recent explosion of billboards advocated restrictions, including writers of articles and editorials in local newspapers.

In the spring of 1982, the city council passed an ordinance requiring the council's approval for every billboard constructed in downtown Columbia. This was later amended to impose a 180 day moratorium on the construction of billboards throughout the city, except as specifically authorized by the council. A state court invalidated this ordinance on the ground that its conferral of unconstrained discretion upon the city council violated both the South Carolina and Federal Constitutions. The city then requested the State's regional planning authority to conduct a comprehensive analysis of the local billboard situation as a basis for developing a final, constitutionally valid, ordinance. In September 1982, after a series of public hearings and numerous meetings involving city officials, Omni, and COA (in all of which, according to Omni, positions contrary to COA's were not genuinely considered), the city council passed a new ordinance restricting the size, location, and spacing of billboards. These restrictions, particularly those on spacing, obviously benefitted COA, which already had its billboards in place; they severely hindered Omni's ability to compete.

In November 1982, Omni filed suit against COA and the city in Federal District Court, charging that they had violated §§ 1 and 2 of the Sherman Act.... Omni contended, in particular, that the city's billboard ordinances were the result of an anticompetitive conspiracy between city officials and COA that stripped both parties of any immunity they might otherwise enjoy from the federal antitrust laws. In January 1986, after more than two weeks of trial, a jury returned general verdicts against the city and COA on both the federal and state claims. It awarded damages, before trebling, of $600,000 on the § 1 Sherman Act claim, and $400,000 on the § 2 claim.[2] The jury also answered two special interrogatories, finding specifically that the city and COA had conspired both to restrain trade and to monopolize the market. Petitioners moved for judgment notwithstanding the verdict, contending among other things that their activities were outside the scope of the federal antitrust laws. In November 1988, the District Court granted the motion.

A divided panel of the United States Court of Appeals for the Fourth Circuit reversed the judgment of the District Court and reinstated the jury verdict on all counts.

---

[2] The monetary damages in this case were assessed entirely against COA, the District Court having ruled that the city was immunized by the Local Government Antitrust Act of 1984, 98 Stat. 2750, as amended, 15 U.S.C. §§ 34-36, which exempts local governments from paying damages for violations of the federal antitrust laws.

II

... In recent years, we have held that *Parker* immunity does not apply directly to local governments.... We have recognized, however, that a municipality's restriction of competition may sometimes be an authorized implementation of state policy, and have accorded *Parker* immunity where that is the case.

The South Carolina statutes under which the city acted in the present case authorize municipalities to regulate the use of land and the construction of buildings and other structures within their boundaries. It is undisputed that, as a matter of state law, these statutes authorize the city to regulate the size, location, and spacing of billboards. It could be argued, however, that a municipality acts beyond its delegated authority, for *Parker* purposes, whenever the nature of its regulation is substantively or even procedurally defective. On such an analysis it could be contended, for example, that the city's regulation in the present case was not "authorized" by S.C. Code § 5-23-10 (1976), if it was not, as that statute requires, adopted "for the purpose of promoting health, safety, morals or the general welfare of the community." As scholarly commentary has noted, such an expansive interpretation of the *Parker* defense authorization requirement would have unacceptable consequences.

> To be sure, state law "authorizes" only agency decisions that are substantively and procedurally correct. Errors of fact, law, or judgment by the agency are not "authorized." Erroneous acts or decisions are subject to reversal by superior tribunals because unauthorized. If the antitrust court demands unqualified "authority" in this sense, it inevitably becomes the standard reviewer not only of federal agency activity but also of state and local activity whenever it is alleged that the governmental body, though possessing the power to engage in the challenged conduct, has actually exercised its power in a manner not authorized by state law. We should not lightly assume that *Lafayette*'s authorization requirement dictates transformation of state administrative review into a federal antitrust job. Yet that would be the consequence of making antitrust liability depend on an undiscriminating and mechanical demand for "authority" in the full administrative law sense.

P. Areeda & H. Hovenkamp, *Antitrust Law* ¶ 212.3b, p. 145 (Supp. 1989).

We agree with that assessment, and believe that in order to prevent *Parker* from undermining the very interests of federalism it is designed to protect, it is necessary to adopt a concept of authority broader than what is applied to determine the legality of the municipality's action under state law.... It suffices for the present to conclude that here no more is needed to establish, for *Parker* purposes, the city's authority to regulate than its unquestioned zoning power over the size, location, and spacing of billboards.

Besides authority to regulate, however, the *Parker* defense also requires authority to suppress competition more specifically, "clear articulation of a state policy to authorize anticompetitive conduct" by the municipality in connection with its regulation. *Hallie*, 471 U.S., at 40. We have rejected the contention that this requirement can be met only if the delegating statute explicitly permits the displacement of competition. It is enough, we have held, if suppression of competition is the "foreseeable result" of what the statute authorizes, *id.*, at 42. That condition is amply met here. The very purpose of zoning regulation is to displace unfettered business freedom in a manner that regularly has the effect of preventing normal acts of competition, particularly on the part of new entrants. A municipal ordinance restricting the size, location, and spacing of billboards (surely a common form of zoning) necessarily protects existing billboards against some competition from newcomers.

The Court of Appeals was therefore correct in its conclusion that the city's restriction of billboard construction was *prima facie* entitled to *Parker* immunity. The Court of Appeals upheld the jury verdict, however, by invoking a "conspiracy" exception to *Parker* that has been recognized by several Courts of Appeals.... That exception is thought to be supported by two of our statements in *Parker*: "[W]e have no question of the state or its municipality becoming a *participant in a private agreement or combination by others* for restraint of trade, *cf. Union Pacific R. Co. v. United States*, 313 U.S. 450." *Parker*, 317 U.S., at 351-352 (emphasis added). "The state in adopting and enforcing the prorate program made no contract or agreement and entered into no conspiracy in restraint of trade or to establish monopoly but, as sovereign, imposed the restraint as an act of government which the Sherman Act did not undertake to prohibit." *Parker* does not apply, according to the Fourth Circuit, "where politicians or political entities are involved as conspirators" with private actors in the restraint of trade.

There is no such conspiracy exception. The rationale of *Parker* was that, in light of our national commitment to federalism, the general language of the Sherman Act should not be interpreted to prohibit anticompetitive actions by the States in their governmental capacities as sovereign regulators. The sentences from the opinion quoted above simply clarify that this immunity does not necessarily obtain where the State acts not in a regulatory capacity but as a commercial participant in a given market. That is evident from the citation of *Union Pacific R. Co. v. United States*, 313 U.S. 450 (1941), which held unlawful under the Elkins Act certain rebates and concessions made by Kansas City, Kansas, in its capacity as the owner and operator of a wholesale produce market that was integrated with railroad facilities. These sentences should not be read to suggest the general proposition that even governmental regulatory action may be deemed private and therefore subject to antitrust liability when it is taken pursuant to a conspiracy with private parties. The impracticality of such a principle is evident if, for purposes of the exception, "conspiracy" means nothing more than an agreement to impose the regulation in question. Since it is both inevitable and desirable that public officials often agree to do what one or another group of private citizens urges upon them, such an exception would virtually swallow up the *Parker* rule: All anticompetitive regulation would be vulnerable to a "conspiracy" charge. See

Areeda & Hovenkamp, *supra*, ¶ 203.3b; Elhauge, *The Scope of Antitrust Process*, 104 Harv. L. Rev. 667, 704-705 (1991).

Omni suggests, however, that "conspiracy" might be limited to instances of governmental "corruption," defined variously as "abandonment of public responsibilities to private interests," "corrupt or bad faith decisions," and "selfish or corrupt motives." Ultimately, Omni asks us not to define "corruption" at all, but simply to leave that task to the jury: "At bottom, however, it was within the jury's province to determine what constituted corruption of the governmental process in their community." Omni's amicus eschews this emphasis on "corruption," instead urging us to define the conspiracy exception as encompassing any governmental act "not in the public interest."

A conspiracy exception narrowed along such vague lines is similarly impractical. Few governmental actions are immune from the charge that they are "not in the public interest" or in some sense "corrupt." The California marketing scheme at issue in *Parker* itself, for example, can readily be viewed as the result of a "conspiracy" to put the "private" interest of the State's raisin growers above the "public" interest of the State's consumers. The fact is that virtually all regulation benefits some segments of the society and harms others; and that it is not universally considered contrary to the public good if the net economic loss to the losers exceeds the net economic gain to the winners. *Parker* was not written in ignorance of the reality that determination of "the public interest" in the manifold areas of government regulation entails not merely economic and mathematical analysis but value judgment, and it was not meant to shift that judgment from elected officials to judges and juries. If the city of Columbia's decision to regulate what one local newspaper called "billboard jungles" ... is made subject to *ex post facto* judicial assessment of "the public interest," with personal liability of city officials a possible consequence, we will have gone far to "compromise the States' ability to regulate their domestic commerce," *Southern Motor Carriers Rate Conference, Inc. v. United States*, 471 U.S. 48, 56 (1985). The situation would not be better, but arguably even worse, if the courts were to apply a subjective test: not whether the action was in the public interest, but whether the officials involved thought it to be so. This would require the sort of deconstruction of the governmental process and probing of the official "intent" that we have consistently sought to avoid....

The foregoing approach to establishing a "conspiracy" exception at least seeks (however impractically) to draw the line of impermissible action in a manner relevant to the purposes of the Sherman Act and of *Parker*: prohibiting the restriction of competition for private gain but permitting the restriction of competition in the public interest. Another approach is possible, which has the virtue of practicality but the vice of being unrelated to those purposes. That is the approach which would consider *Parker* inapplicable only if, in connection with the governmental action in question, bribery or some other violation of state or federal law has been established. Such unlawful activity has no necessary relationship to whether the governmental action is in the public interest. A mayor is guilty of accepting a bribe even if he would and should have taken, in the public interest, the same action for which the bribe was paid. (That is frequently the defense asserted to a criminal bribery charge and though it is never valid in law, it is often plausible in fact.) When, moreover, the regulatory body is not a single individual but a state legislature or city council, there is even less reason to believe that violation of the law (by bribing a minority of the decisionmakers) establishes that the regulation has no valid public purpose. To use unlawful political influence as the test of legality of state regulation undoubtedly vindicates (in a rather blunt way) principles of good government. But the statute we are construing is not directed to that end. Congress has passed other laws aimed at combatting corruption in state and local governments. See, e.g., 18 U.S.C. § 1951 (Hobbs Act). "Insofar as [the Sherman Act] sets up a code of ethics at all, it is a code that condemns trade restraints, not political activity." *Eastern Railroad Presidents Conference v. Noerr Motor Freight, Inc.*, 365 U.S. 127, 140 (1961).

For these reasons, we reaffirm our rejection of any interpretation of the Sherman Act that would allow plaintiffs to look behind the actions of state sovereigns to base their claims on "perceived conspiracies to restrain trade." We reiterate that, with the possible market participant exception, any action that qualifies as state action is "ipso facto ... exempt from the operation of the antitrust laws." This does not mean, of course, that the States may exempt private action from the scope of the Sherman Act; we in no way qualify the well established principle that "a state does not give immunity to those who violate the Sherman Act by authorizing them to violate it, or by declaring that their action is lawful."

[That portion of the opinion dealing with the "sham" exception to the Noerr-Pennington doctrine is reprinted *supra*.]

The judgment of the Court of Appeals is reversed, and the case is remanded for further proceedings consistent with this opinion.

It is so ordered.

JUSTICE STEVENS, with whom JUSTICE WHITE and JUSTICE MARSHALL join, dissenting....

Today the Court adopts a significant enlargement of the state action exemption. The South Carolina statutes that confer zoning authority on municipalities in the State do not articulate any state policy to displace competition with economic regulation in any line of commerce or in any specific industry. As the Court notes, the state statutes were expressly adopted to promote the "health, safety, morals or the general welfare of the community." Like Colorado's grant of "home rule" powers to the city of Boulder, they are simply neutral on the question whether the municipality should displace competition with economic regulation in any industry. There is not even an arguable basis for concluding that the State authorized the city of Columbia to enter into exclusive agreements with any person, or to use the zoning power to protect favored citizens from competition. Nevertheless, under the guise of acting pursuant to a state legislative grant to regulate health, safety, and welfare, the city of Columbia in this case enacted an ordinance that amounted to economic regulation of the billboard market; as the Court recognizes, the ordinance "obviously benefitted COA, which already had its billboards in place ... [and] severely hindered Omni's ability to compete."...

In this case, the jury found that the city's ordinance, ostensibly one promoting health, safety, and welfare, was in fact enacted pursuant to an agreement between city officials and a private party to restrict competition. In my opinion such a finding necessarily leads to the conclusion that the city's ordinance was fundamentally a form of economic regulation of the billboard market rather than a general welfare regulation having incidental anticompetitive effects. Because I believe our cases have wisely held that the decision to embark upon economic regulation is a nondelegable one that must expressly be made by the State in the context of a specific industry in order to qualify for state action immunity, ... I would hold that the city of Columbia's economic regulation of the billboard market pursuant to a general state grant of zoning power is not exempt from antitrust scrutiny.

NOTES AND QUESTIONS

1. Has the Supreme Court effectively overruled its *Boulder* decision, as the dissent suggests? Suppose a state passes a very general "welfare" statute that gives municipalities virtual *carte blanche*. *Wall v. City of Athens*, 663 F. Supp. 747 (M.D. Ga. 1987), involved the following state statute:

> It is declared by the General Assembly of Georgia that in the exercise of powers specifically granted to [home rule municipalities] by law, local governing authorities of cities and counties are acting pursuant to state policy ....

And:

> This chapter is intended to articulate clearly and express affirmatively the policy of the State of Georgia that in the exercise of such powers, such local governing authorities shall be immune from antitrust liability to the same degree and extent as enjoyed by the State of Georgia. O.C.G.A. § 36-19-1 (April 4, 1984).

The court found the attempt ineffectual. The decision seems to be consistent with *Boulder*. If the state enacts a detailed list of activities in which municipalities may engage, then *Parker* exempts those activities from antitrust attack. But if the state attempts to exempt all at once with a blanket statement, no exemption is conferred. In any event, a later decision found that the same language did qualify a municipality for the exemption. *McCallum v. City of Athens*, 976 F.2d 649 (11th Cir. 1992). Which decision is more consistent with *Boulder*? with *Hallie*? with *Columbia*?

Does a state statute that authorizes a municipality to engage in a certain kind of activity implicitly authorize the municipality to prevent private parties from competing? For example, does a statute authorizing a city to operate a hospital also authorize it to forbid any privately owned hospital from being built in the city limits? Should it matter whether the authorized service is a natural monopoly, such as retail electric power? *See Lancaster Community Hosp. v. Antelope Valley Hosp.*, 940 F.2d 397 (9th Cir. 1991), *cert. denied*, 502 U.S. 1094 (1992).

2. The *Columbia* decision also refused to recognize a "co-conspiracy" exception to *both* the *Parker* and *Noerr* doctrines, reasoning:

> Omni urges that we should use this case to recognize a "conspiracy" exception [to *Noerr*], which would apply when government officials conspire with a private party to employ government action as a means of stifling competition. We have left open the possibility of such an exception, see, e.g., *Allied Tube, supra*, at 502, n. 7....
>
> Giving full consideration to this matter for the first time, we conclude that a "conspiracy" exception to *Noerr* must be rejected. We need not describe our reasons at length, since they are largely the same as those set forth in Part II above for rejecting a "conspiracy" exception to *Parker*. As we have described, *Parker* and *Noerr* are complementary expressions of the principle that the antitrust laws regulate business, not politics; the former decision protects the States' acts of governing, and the latter the citizens' participation in government. Insofar as the identification of an immunity destroying "conspiracy" is concerned, *Parker* and *Noerr* generally present two faces of the same coin. The *Noerr* invalidating conspiracy alleged here is just the *Parker* invalidating conspiracy viewed from the standpoint of the private sector participants rather than the governmental participants. The same factors which, as we have described above, make it impracticable or beyond the purpose of the antitrust laws to identify and invalidate lawmaking that has been infected by selfishly motivated agreement with private interests likewise make it impracticable or beyond that scope to identify and invalidate lobbying that has produced selfishly motivated agreement with public officials. "It would be unlikely that any effort to influence legislative action could succeed unless one or more members of the legislative body became ... 'coconspirators'" in some sense with the private party urging such action. And if the invalidating "conspiracy" is limited to one that involves some element of unlawfulness (beyond mere anticompetitive motivation), the invalidation would have nothing to do with the policies of the antitrust laws. In *Noerr* itself, where the private party "deliberately deceived the public and public officials" in its successful lobbying campaign, we said that "deception, reprehensible as it is, can be of no consequence so far as the Sherman Act is concerned."...

PROBLEM 9.4

Consider the following under the Supreme Court's *Columbia* decision:

1. Three members of a five-person city council are the owners of an ambulance company. They pass an ordinance on a 3-2 vote that gives the company a monopoly of all police ambulance calls in the region. A competing ambulance company sues under the antitrust laws. A state statute authorizes the municipality to regulate local ambulance service. Are the three city council members liable as private defendants? Is the municipality liable?

2. A municipality owns a hot dog and soft drink vending service, from which it makes a great deal of money. It gives its own service the exclusive right to sell prepared food on municipal beaches, in municipal parks, and in municipal stadiums. A state statute authorizes the municipality to regulate health, safety, and vending of goods in these facilities. The municipality is sued by a competing vendor. Has it violated the antitrust laws?

2. THE "ACTIVE SUPERVISION" REQUIREMENT

The Supreme Court's *Midcal* decision, as you recall, assessed two requirements for the "state action" exemption. First, the challenged activity must be adequately authorized in state policy. Second, any private conduct carried out pursuant to this regulatory regime must be "actively supervised" by the state or one of its agencies.

In *Patrick v. Burget*, 486 U.S. 94 (1988), the Supreme Court found that private conduct pursuant to a state regulatory policy did not qualify for the state action exemption because it was inadequately supervised. Patrick was a surgeon with staff privileges at Columbia Memorial Hospital. Most of the supervisory staff at the hospital were partners in nearby Astoria Clinic. Patrick refused to join the clinic but established an independent practice in competition with the clinic. The clinic then treated him with hostility, giving him no referrals. When Patrick was later charged with negligence, the defendant hospital and its supervisory staff hastily voted to terminate his staff privileges. Patrick challenged the dismissal under the antitrust laws, contending that "the Clinic partners had initiated and participated in the hospital peer-review proceedings to reduce competition from petitioner rather than to improve patient care...." In refusing to find that the dismissal was exempt under *Parker*, the Supreme Court said the following:

> In this case, we need not consider the "clear articulation" prong of the *Midcal* test, because the "active supervision" requirement is not satisfied. The active supervision requirement stems from the recognition that "[w]here a private party is engaging in the anticompetitive activity, there is a real danger that he is acting to further his own interests, rather than the governmental interests of the State." The requirement is designed to ensure that the state action doctrine will shelter only the particular anticompetitive acts of private parties that, in the judgment of the State, actually further state regulatory policies. To accomplish this purpose, the active supervision requirement mandates that the State exercise ultimate control over the challenged anticompetitive conduct. The mere presence of some state involvement or monitoring does not suffice. The active supervision prong of the *Midcal* test

requires that state officials have and exercise power to review particular anti-competitive acts of private parties and disapprove those that fail to accord with state policy. Absent such a program of supervision, there is no realistic assurance that a private party's anticompetitive conduct promotes state policy, rather than merely the party's individual interests.

The defendants had alleged that three government agencies supervised private peer review actions: the Oregon Health Division, the Oregon Board of Medical Examiners (BOME), and the Oregon court system. The Court concluded that each failed to meet the standard. The Health Division had some supervisory powers over hospital peer review, but it was largely limited to ensuring that hospitals had an active peer review process in place. "The Health Division has no power to review private peer review decisions and overturn a decision that fails to accord with state policy. Thus, the activities of the Health Division under Oregon law cannot satisfy the active supervision requirement of the state action doctrine."

Likewise, the main function of the BOME was to license physicians, but it also lacked the "power to disapprove private privilege decisions." Rather, its only role in a termination was to determine whether additional action was appropriate, such as revocation or suspension of a physician's license.

That left the state judiciary. Said the Court:

> This Court has not previously considered whether state courts, acting in their judicial capacity, can adequately supervise private conduct for purposes of the state action doctrine. All of our prior cases concerning state supervision over private parties have involved administrative agencies or state supreme courts with agency-like responsibilities over the organized bar, see *Bates v. State Bar of Arizona*, 433 U.S. 350 (1977). This case, however, does not require us to decide the broad question whether judicial review of private conduct ever can constitute active supervision, because judicial review of privilege-termination decisions in Oregon, if such review exists at all, falls far short of satisfying the active supervision requirement.
>
> As an initial matter, it is not clear that Oregon law affords any direct judicial review of private peer-review decisions. Oregon has no statute expressly providing for judicial review of privilege terminations. Moreover, we are aware of no case in which an Oregon court has held that judicial review of peer-review decisions is available....
>
> Moreover, the Oregon courts have indicated that even if they were to provide judicial review of hospital peer-review proceedings, the review would be of a very limited nature. The Oregon Supreme Court, in its most recent decision addressing this matter, stated that a court "should [not] decide the merits of plaintiff's dismissal" and that "[i]t would be unwise for a court to do more than to make sure that some sort of reasonable procedure was afforded and that there was evidence from which it could be found that plaintiff's conduct posed a threat to patient care." *Straube* [*supra*]. This kind of review would fail to satisfy the state action doctrine's requirement of active supervision.

FTC V. TICOR TITLE INSURANCE CO.

504 U.S. 621 (1992)

JUSTICE KENNEDY delivered the opinion of the Court.

The Federal Trade Commission filed an administrative complaint against six of the nation's largest title insurance companies, alleging horizontal price fixing in their fees for title searches and title examinations.… The Commission charged the title companies with violating § 5(a)(1) of the Federal Trade Commission Act, 38 Stat. 719, 15 U.S.C. § 45(a)(1), which prohibits "[u]nfair methods of competition in or affecting commerce." One of the principal defenses the companies assert is state-action immunity from antitrust prosecution, as contemplated in the line of cases beginning with *Parker v. Brown*.…

I

Title insurance is the business of insuring the record title of real property for persons with some interest in the estate, including owners, occupiers, and lenders. A title insurance policy insures against certain losses or damages sustained by reason of a defect in title not shown on the policy or title report to which it refers. Before issuing a title insurance policy, the insurance company or one of its agents performs a title search and examination. The search produces a chronological list of the public documents in the chain of title to the real property. The examination is a critical analysis or interpretation of the condition of title revealed by the documents disclosed through this search. The title search and examination are major components of the insurance company's services.…

… Four of respondents are the nation's largest title insurance companies: Ticor Title Insurance Co., with 16.5 percent of the market; Chicago Title Insurance Co., with 12.8 percent; Lawyers Title Insurance Co., with 12 percent; and Safeco Title Insurance Co. (now operating under the name Security Union Title Insurance Co.), with 10.3 percent. Stewart Title Guarantee Co., with 5.4 percent of the market, is the country's eighth largest title insurer, with a strong position in the West and Southwest.

… The Commission did not challenge the insurers' practice of setting uniform rates for insurance against the risk of loss from defective titles, but only the practice of setting uniform rates for the title search, examination, and settlement, aspects of the business which, the Commission alleges, do not involve insurance. Before the Administrative Law Judge (ALJ), the respondents defended against liability on [the ground that] their activities are entitled to state-action immunity, which permits anticompetitive conduct if authorized and supervised by state officials.… [After numerous dismissals] four States remain in which violations were alleged: Connecticut, Wisconsin, Arizona, and Montana. The ALJ held that the rates for search and examination services had been fixed in these four States.…

Rating bureaus are private entities organized by title insurance companies to establish uniform rates for their members. The ALJ found no evidence that the collective setting of title insurance rates through rating bureaus is a way of pooling risk information. Indeed, he found no evidence that any title insurer sets rates according to actuarial loss experience. Instead, the ALJ found that the usual practice is for rating bureaus to set rates according to profitability studies that focus on the costs of conducting searches and examinations. Uniform rates are set notwithstanding differences in efficiencies and costs among individual members.

The ALJ described the regulatory regimes for title insurance rates in the four States still at issue. In each one, the title insurance rating bureau was licensed by the State and authorized to establish joint rates for its members. Each of the four States used what has come to be called a "negative option" system to approve rate filings by the bureaus. Under a negative option system, the rating bureau filed rates for title searches and title examinations with the state insurance office. The rates became effective unless the State rejected them within a specified period, such as 30 days. Although the negative option system provided a theoretical mechanism for substantive review, the ALJ determined, after making detailed findings regarding the operation of each regulatory regime, that the rate filings were subject to minimal scrutiny by state regulators. In Connecticut the State Insurance Department has the authority to audit the rating bureau and hold hearings regarding rates, but it has not done so. The Connecticut rating bureau filed only two major rate increases, in 1966 and in 1981. The circumstances behind the 1966 rate increase are somewhat obscure. The ALJ found that the Insurance Department asked the rating bureau to submit additional information justifying the increase, and later approved the rate increase although there is no evidence the additional information was provided. In 1981 the Connecticut rating bureau filed for a 20 percent rate increase. The factual background for this rate increase is better developed though the testimony was somewhat inconsistent. A state insurance official testified that he reviewed the rate increase with care and discussed various components of the increase with the rating bureau. The same official testified, however, that he lacked the authority to question certain expense data he considered quite high. In Wisconsin the State Insurance Commissioner is required to examine the rating bureau at regular intervals and authorized to reject rates through a process of hearings. Neither has been done. The Wisconsin rating bureau made major rate filings in 1971, 1981, and 1982.... The 1982 rate increase received but a cursory reading at the office of the Insurance Commissioner. The supporting materials were not checked for accuracy, though in the absence of an objection by the agency, the rate increase went into effect. In Arizona the Insurance Director was required to examine the rating bureau at least once every five years. It was not done.... In Montana the rating bureau made its only major rate filing in 1983. In connection with it, a representative of the rating bureau met with officials of the State Insurance Department. He was told that the filed rates could go into immediate effect though further profit data would have to be provided. The ALJ found no evidence that the additional data were furnished.

... [T]he Commission held that none of the four states had conducted sufficient supervision, so that the title companies were not entitled to immunity in any of those jurisdictions. The Court of Appeals for the Third Circuit disagreed with the Commission....

II

... Our decisions make clear that the purpose of the active supervision inquiry is not to determine whether the State has met some normative standard, such as efficiency, in its regulatory practices. Its purpose is to determine whether the State has exercised sufficient independent judgment and control so that the details of the rates or prices have been established as a product of deliberate state intervention, not simply by agreement among private parties. Much as in causation inquiries, the analysis asks whether the State has played a substantial role in determining the specifics of the economic policy. The question is not how well state regulation works but whether the anticompetitive scheme is the State's own....

The respondents contend that principles of federalism justify a broad interpretation of state-action immunity, but there is a powerful refutation of their viewpoint in the briefs that were filed in this case. The State of Wisconsin, joined by Montana and 34 other States, has filed a brief as *amici curiae* on the precise point. These States deny that respondents' broad immunity rule would serve the States' best interests. We are in agreement with the amici submission.

If the States must act in the shadow of state-action immunity whenever they enter the realm of economic regulation, then our doctrine will impede their freedom of action, not advance it. The fact of the matter is that the States regulate their economies in many ways not inconsistent with the antitrust laws. For example, Oregon may provide for peer review by its physicians without approving anticompetitive conduct by them. See *Patrick, supra*, at 105. Or Michigan may regulate its public utilities without authorizing monopolization in the market for electric light bulbs. See *Cantor v. Detroit Edison Co.*, 428 U.S. 579, 596 (1976). So we have held that state-action immunity is disfavored, much as are repeals by implication. *Lafayette v. Louisiana Power & Light Co.*, 435 U.S. 389, 398-399 (1978). By adhering in most cases to fundamental and accepted assumptions about the benefits of competition within the framework of the antitrust laws, we increase the States' regulatory flexibility.

States must accept political responsibility for actions they intend to undertake. It is quite a different matter, however, for federal law to compel a result that the States do not intend but for which they are held to account. Federalism serves to assign political responsibility, not to obscure it. Neither federalism nor political responsibility is well served by a rule that essential national policies are displaced by state regulations intended to achieve more limited ends. For States which do choose to displace the free market with regulation, our insistence on real compliance with both parts of the *Midcal* test will serve to make clear that the State is responsible for the price fixing it has sanctioned and undertaken to control.

The respondents contend that these concerns are better addressed by the requirement that the States articulate a clear policy to displace the antitrust laws with their own forms of economic regulation. This contention misapprehends the close relation between *Midcal*'s two elements. Both are directed at ensuring that particular anticompetitive mechanisms operate because of a deliberate and intended state policy. In the usual case, *Midcal*'s requirement that the State articulate a clear policy shows little more than that the State has not acted through inadvertence; it cannot alone ensure, as required by our precedents, that particular anticompetitive conduct has been approved by the State.

It seems plain, moreover, in light of the amici curiae brief to which we have referred, that sole reliance on the requirement of clear articulation will not allow the regulatory flexibility that these States deem necessary. For States whose object it is to benefit their citizens through regulation, a broad doctrine of state-action immunity may serve as nothing more than an attractive nuisance in the economic sphere. To oppose these pressures, sole reliance on the requirement of clear articulation could become a rather meaningless formal constraint.

III

In the case before us, the Court of Appeals relied upon a formulation of the active supervision requirement articulated by the First Circuit: "'Where ... the state's program is in place, is staffed and funded, grants to the state officials ample power and the duty to regulate pursuant to declared standards of state policy, is enforceable in the state's courts, and demonstrates some basic level of activity directed towards seeing that the private actors carry out the state's policy and not simply their own policy, more need not be established,'" quoting *New England Motor Rate Bureau, Inc. v. FTC*, 908 F.2d 1064, 1071 (1st Cir. 1990). Based on this standard, the Third Circuit ruled that the active supervision requirement was met in all four states, and held that the respondents' conduct was entitled to state-action immunity from antitrust liability.

While in theory the standard articulated by the First Circuit might be applied in a manner consistent with our precedents, it seems to us insufficient to establish the requisite level of active supervision.... [W]e must conclude that there was no active supervision in either Wisconsin or Montana.

The respondents point out that in Wisconsin and Montana the rating bureaus filed rates with state agencies and that in both States the so-called negative option rule prevailed. The rates became effective unless they were rejected within a set time. It is said that as a matter of law in those States inaction signified substantive approval. This proposition cannot be reconciled, however, with the detailed findings, entered by the ALJ and adopted by the Commission, which demonstrate that the potential for state supervision was not realized in fact. The ALJ found, and the Commission agreed, that at most the rate filings were checked for mathematical accuracy. Some were unchecked altogether. In Montana, a rate filing became effective despite the failure of the rating bureau to provide additional requested information. In Wisconsin, additional information was provided after a lapse of seven years, during which time the rate filing remained in effect. These findings are fatal to respondents' attempts to portray the state regulatory regimes as providing the necessary component of active supervision. The findings demonstrate that, whatever the potential for state regulatory review in Wisconsin and Montana, active state supervision did not occur. In the absence of active supervision in fact, there can be no state-action immunity for what were otherwise private price fixing arrangements....

This case involves horizontal price fixing under a vague imprimatur in form and agency inaction in fact. No antitrust offense is more pernicious than price fixing. *FTC v. Superior Court Trial Lawyers Assn.*, 493 U.S. 411, 434, n.16 (1990). In this context, we decline to formulate a rule that would lead to a finding of active state supervision where in fact there was none. Our decision should be read in light of the gravity of the antitrust offense, the involvement of private actors throughout, and the clear absence of state supervision. We do not imply that some particular form of state or local regulation is required to achieve ends other than the establishment of uniform prices.... [W]e do not here call into question a regulatory regime in which sampling techniques or a specified rate of return allow state regulators to provide comprehensive supervision without complete control, or in which there was an infrequent lapse of state supervision. Cf. *324 Liquor Corp. v. Duffy*, 479 U.S. 335, 344, n.6 (1987) (a statute specifying the margin between wholesale and retail prices may satisfy the active supervision requirement). In the circumstances of this case, however, we conclude that the acts of the respondents in the States of Montana and Wisconsin are not immune from antitrust liability.*

JUSTICE SCALIA, concurring.

The Court's standard is in my view faithful to what our cases have said about "active supervision." On the other hand, I think the Chief Justice and Justice O'Connor are correct that this standard will be a fertile source of uncertainty and (hence) litigation, and will produce total abandonment of some state programs because private individuals will not take the chance of participating in them. That is true, moreover, not just in the "negative-option" context, but even in a context such as that involved in *Patrick v. Burget*, 486 U.S. 94 (1988): Private physicians invited to participate in a state-supervised hospital peer review system may not know until after their participation has occurred (and indeed until after their trial has been completed) whether the State's supervision will be "active" enough.

I am willing to accept these consequences because I see no alternative within the constraints of our "active supervision" doctrine, which has not been challenged here; and because I am skeptical about the *Parker v. Brown* exemption for state-programmed private collusion in the first place.

---

* As to Connecticut and Arizona, the Court remanded for consideration whether the Third Circuit had given adequate regard to the FTC's fact findings. — Eds.

CHIEF JUSTICE REHNQUIST, with whom JUSTICE O'CONNOR and JUSTICE THOMAS join, dissenting.

In each instance since *Midcal* in which we have concluded that the active supervision requirement for state action immunity was not met, the state regulators lacked authority, under state law, to review or reject the rates or action taken by the private actors facing antitrust liability. Our most recent formulation of the "active supervision" requirement was announced in *Patrick v. Burget*, 486 U.S. 94 (1988), where we concluded that to satisfy the "active supervision" requirement, "state officials [must] have and exercise power to review particular anticompetitive acts of private parties and disapprove those that fail to accord with state policy." Until today, therefore, we have never had occasion to determine whether a state regulatory program which gave state officials authority — "power" — to review and regulate prices or conduct, might still fail to meet the requirement for active state supervision because the state's regulation was not sufficiently detailed or rigorous.

... In the States at issue here, the particular conduct was approved by a state agency. The agency manifested this approval by raising no objection to a required rate filing by the entity subject to regulation. This is quite consistent with our statement that the active supervision requirement serves mainly an "evidentiary function" as "one way of ensuring that the actor is engaging in the challenged conduct pursuant to state policy...." *Hallie v. Eau Claire*, 471 U.S. 34, 46 (1985).

The Court insists that its newly required "active supervision" will "increase the States' regulatory flexibility." But if private actors who participate, through a joint rate filing, in a State's "negative option" regulatory scheme may be liable for treble damages if they cannot prove that the State approved the specifics of a filing, the Court makes it highly unlikely that private actors will choose to participate in such a joint filing. This in turn lessens the States' regulatory flexibility, because as we have noted before, joint rate filings can improve the regulatory process by ensuring that the state agency has fewer filings to consider, allowing more resources to be expended on each filing....

... The Court maintains that the proper state action inquiry does not determine whether a State has met some "normative standard" in its regulatory practices. But the Court's focus on the actions taken by state regulators, i.e., the way the State regulates, necessarily requires a judgment as to whether the State is sufficiently active — surely a normative judgment.

The Court of Appeals found — properly, in my view — that while the States at issue here did not regulate respondents' rates with the vigor the petitioner would like, the States' supervision of respondents' conduct was active enough so as to provide for immunity from antitrust liability. The Court of Appeals, having concluded that the Commission applied an incorrect legal standard, reviewed the facts found by the Commission in light of the correct standard and reached a different conclusion. This does not constitute a rejection of the Commission's factual findings. I would therefore affirm the judgment below.

[An additional dissenting opinion by JUSTICE O'CONNOR, joined by JUSTICE THOMAS, is omitted.]

NOTES AND QUESTIONS

1. As noted in *Hallie, supra,* the "active supervision" requirement applies to the conduct of private parties. It does not apply to municipalities. But suppose that the municipality gives economic decisionmaking power to a private party. Must the private conduct be supervised? If so, who must supervise it? In footnote 10 of the *Hallie* opinion the Supreme Court suggested that "[w]here state or municipal regulation of a private party is involved, however, active *state* supervision must be shown, even where a clearly articulated state policy exists." Was this merely a slip of the pen, or did the Court really mean to suggest that the *state* must supervise private decisionmaking in regulatory schemes created by municipalities? Courts addressing the issue have held that if municipalities create regulatory schemes requiring supervision, the municipalities themselves must do the supervising. *See Englert v. City of McKeesport,* 637 F. Supp. 930 (W.D. Pa. 1986) (requiring active municipal supervision over municipally authorized private electrical inspections). *See* 1 P. Areeda & H. Hovenkamp, *Antitrust Law* ¶ 226 (rev. ed. 1997).

2. The Health Care Quality Improvement Act, 42 U.S.C. §§ 11101-11152, exempts medical peer review from the antitrust laws if the review was undertaken in the "reasonable belief" that it would further quality health care. The statute "does not change other immunities under the law" — so presumably the states are free to create even larger "state action" exemptions, provided the conduct is actively supervised. Under the statute, physicians' conduct in the peer review process is subjected to an *objective* standard of good faith. As a result, if physicians conduct peer review proceedings in an orderly fashion, give due notice and opportunity to be heard to the subject, and act deliberately, a disciplined or excluded physician will not be permitted to inquire into their actual state of mind. *See, e.g., Austin v. McNamara,* 979 F.2d 728 (9th Cir. 1992) (if there was an objective basis for the dismissal, statute's standard was met, even though some review board members may subjectively have been hostile toward the plaintiff); *Fobbs v. Holy Cross Health Sys. Corp.,* 29 F.3d 1439 (9th Cir. 1994), *cert. denied,* 513 U.S. 1127 (1995) (same); *Bryan v. James E. Holmes Regional Medical Center,* 33 F.3d 1318 (11th Cir. 1994) (HCQIA exempted physician disciplinary action prompted by reasonable belief that plaintiff had acted unprofessionally; numerous complaints of abusive behavior directed at subordinates; staff had made numerous attempts to control the problem by other means). *And see Imperial v. Suburban Hospital Assn.,* 37 F.3d 1026 (4th Cir. 1994) (hospital and staff immune from antitrust liability when all procedural requirements of HCQIA met); *Smith v. Ricks,* 31 F.3d 1478 (9th Cir. 1994) (HCQIA immunized hospital providing adequate notice and opportunity to be heard in physician discipline process and conducting thorough review).

3. *Hass v. Oregon State Bar*, 883 F.2d 1453 (9th Cir. 1989), held that a statutorily created state bar association, like a municipality, was a governmental agency that did not need to be supervised in order for its activities to qualify for the "state action" exemption. But the bar association was made up of lawyers, and the principal interests that the bar association protected were those of the lawyers themselves. A dissenting judge objected that

> the Bar's regulatory authority is simply not constrained by the same degree of public scrutiny typically governing other state agencies. While state agencies may not operate as democratically as municipal governments, they usually provide some opportunity for public participation in regulatory decisions.... The Bar, however, is not required to submit *any* of its Fund decisions for public scrutiny. Requiring active supervision of the Bar would serve the salutary purpose of ensuring that the public, either directly or through publicly accountable state officials, would have an opportunity to participate in a delegated regulatory decisionmaking process of significant public importance.

Do you agree with the majority or with the dissent?

4. In *Hardy v. City Optical*, 39 F.3d 765 (7th Cir. 1994), the Seventh Circuit held that optometrists' requirement that patients obtaining their eye examinations also obtain their contact lenses in the same place could have been an unlawful tying arrangement. The requirement did not enjoy a *Parker* exemption by virtue of a statute requiring that only certain eye care professionals such as optometrists could recommend and fit contact lenses. The statute seemed to contemplate that the person conducting the eye examination could *either* supply the contact lenses herself or else write a prescription so that the patient could procure them elsewhere. Suppose that the statute *forbad* the consumer from purchasing contact lenses from anyone other than the person who performed the eye examination? Would there be any private conduct left to supervise?

In *Massachusetts School of Law at Andover v. ABA*, 107 F.3d 1026 (3d Cir.), *cert. denied*, 118 S. Ct. 264 (1997), the Third Circuit examined states' policies of adopting the accreditation recommendations of the American Bar Association and excluding graduates from unaccredited law schools from the states' bar exam. The plaintiff was a law school that the ABA refused to accredit after it was found not to be in compliance with several of the ABA's accreditation standards. The court noted that it was not the ABA itself that forbad the plaintiff's graduates from taking the bar exam. Rather, "[e]ach state retains" that authority. Further,

> to the extent that [the plaintiff's] alleged injury arises from the inability of its graduates to take the bar examination in most states, the injury is the result of state action and thus is immune from antitrust action .... The ABA does not decide who can take the bar examinations. Rather, it makes an accreditation decision which it conveys to the states, but the states make the decisions

as to bar admissions. Without state action, the ABA's accreditation decisions would not affect state bar admissions requirements. Because the states are sovereign in imposing the bar admission requirements, the clear articulation and active supervision requirements urged by MSL are inapplicable.

PROBLEM 9.5

Kansas has a liquor price-posting statute which requires liquor distributors to post their wholesale liquor prices monthly. But the statute differs from most other price-posting statutes in one respect: wholesale transactions must be made at the posted price. The state's Alcoholic Beverage Control Board establishes a minimum markup percentage for retail sales, which is published quarterly. Retailers may charge more than the posted wholesale price plus the minimum markup, but they may not charge less. The minimum markup percentages have been changed only once in the preceding ten years. Is the statute preempted under *Fisher*? If so, is it saved by the "state action" exemption? *See Kansas ex rel. Stephan v. Lamb*, 1987-1 Trade Cas. ¶ 67521 (D. Kan. 1987), which will give you the wrong answer. Why?

PROBLEM 9.6

A state statute (1) defines the exclusive service areas for privately-owned electric utilities in the state, and (2) instructs the utilities that when large new customers that straddle a utility boundary apply for service, the utility entitled to the customer is the one in whose area the customer has the largest number of square feet of space. So, for example, if a new subdivision is located 60 percent in utility A's territory and 40 percent in utility B's territory, utility A would provide the service. No agency of the state supervises the operation of this customer assignment process. Have the "state action" requirements respecting private firm conduct been met? Does it matter that the "supervisory" activity consists merely in calculating the number of square feet in each utility's territory? Would the state have to have a mechanism for resolving disputes? *See Municipal Utils. Bd. of Albertville v. Alabama Power*, 934 F.2d 1493 (11th Cir. 1990).

————————

BIBLIOGRAPHY AND COLLATERAL READINGS

Books

1 & 1A P. Areeda & H. Hovenkamp, Antitrust Law (rev. ed. 1997)
S. Breyer, Regulation and Its Reform, ch. 12 (1982).
H. Hovenkamp, Federal Antitrust Policy, chs. 18-20 (2d ed. 1994).
T. McCraw, Prophets of Regulation (1984).

E.T. Sullivan & J. Harrison, Understanding Antitrust and Its Economic Implications (3d ed. 1998).

C. Sunstein, After the Rights Revolution: Reconceiving the Regulatory State (1990).

Articles

Areeda, Antitrust Immunity for "State Action" After Lafayette, 95 Harv. L. Rev. 435 (1981).

Breyer, Antitrust, Deregulation, and the Newly Liberated Marketplace, 75 Calif. L. Rev. 1005 (1987).

Calkins, Developments in Antitrust and the First Amendment: The Disaggregation of Noerr, 57 Antitrust L.J. No. 2 (1988).

Easterbrook, Antitrust and the Economics of Federalism, 26 J.L. & Econ. 23 (1983).

Elhauge, Making Sense of Antitrust Petitioning Immunity, 80 Calif. L. Rev. 1177, 1184 (1992).

Elhauge, The Scope of Antitrust Process, 104 Harv. L. Rev. 667, 704-05 (1991).

Garland, Antitrust and State Action, Economic Efficiency and the Political Process, 96 Yale L.J. 486 (1987).

Jorde, Antitrust and the New State Action Doctrine: a Return to Deferential Economic Federalism, 75 Calif. L. Rev. 227 (1987).

Lopatka, State Action and Municipal Antitrust Immunity: An Economic Approach, 53 Fordham L. Rev. 23 (1984).

Note, The Use of Hypothetical Rates in Antitrust Damages Calculations: Reforming the Keogh Doctrine, 38 Stan. L. Rev. 1141 (1986).

Page, Interest Groups, Antitrust, and State Regulation: Parker v. Brown in the Economic Theory of Legislation, 1987 Duke L.J. 618.

Wiley, A Capture Theory of Antitrust Federalism, 99 Harv. L. Rev. 713 (1986).

DEPARTMENT OF JUSTICE AND FEDERAL TRADE COMMISSION HORIZONTAL MERGER GUIDELINES, APRIL 2, 1992

CONTENTS

0. PURPOSE, UNDERLYING POLICY ASSUMPTIONS AND OVERVIEW

These Guidelines outline the present enforcement policy of the Department of Justice and the Federal Trade Commission (the "Agency") concerning horizontal acquisitions and mergers ("mergers") subject to § 7 of the Clayton Act,[1] to § 1 of the Sherman Act,[2] or to § 5 of the FTC Act.[3] They describe the analytical framework and specific standards normally used by the Agency in analyzing mergers.[4] By stating its policy as simply and clearly as possible, the Agency hopes to reduce the uncertainty associated with enforcement of the antitrust laws in this area.

Although the Guidelines should improve the predictability of the Agency's merger enforcement policy, it is not possible to remove the exercise of judgment from the evaluation of mergers under the antitrust laws. Because the specific standards set forth in the Guidelines must be applied to a broad range of possible factual circumstances, mechanical application of those standards may provide misleading answers to the economic questions raised under the antitrust laws. Moreover, information is often incomplete and the picture of competitive conditions that develops from historical evidence may provide an incomplete answer to the forward-looking inquiry of the Guidelines. Therefore, the Agency will apply the standards of the Guidelines reasonably and flexibly to the particular facts and circumstances of each proposed merger.

0.1 Purpose and Underlying Policy Assumptions of the Guidelines

The Guidelines are designed primarily to articulate the analytical framework the Agency applies in determining whether a merger is likely substantially to

---

[1] 15 U.S.C. § 18 (1988).

[2] 15 U.S.C. § 1 (1988). Mergers subject to § 1 are prohibited if they constitute a "contract, combination ..., or conspiracy in restraint of trade."

[3] 15 U.S.C. § 45 (1988). Mergers subject to § 5 are prohibited if they constitute an "unfair method of competition."

[4] These Guidelines update the Merger Guidelines issued by the U.S. Department of Justice in 1984. The Merger Guidelines may be revised from time to time as necessary to reflect any significant changes in enforcement policy or to clarify aspects of existing policy.

lessen competition, not to describe how the Agency will conduct the litigation of cases that it decides to bring. Although relevant in the latter context, the factors contemplated in the Guidelines neither dictate nor exhaust the range of evidence that the Agency must or may introduce in litigation. Consistent with their objective, the Guidelines do not attempt to assign the burden of proof, or the burden of coming forward with evidence, on any particular issue. Nor do the Guidelines attempt to adjust or reapportion burdens of proof or burdens of coming forward as those standards have been established by the courts.[5] Instead, the Guidelines set forth a methodology for analyzing issues once the necessary facts are available. The necessary facts may be derived from the documents and statements of both the merging firms and other sources.

Throughout the Guidelines, the analysis is focused on whether consumers or producers "likely would" take certain actions, that is, whether the action is in the actor's economic interest. References to the profitability of certain actions focus on economic profits rather than accounting profits. Economic profits may be defined as the excess of revenues over costs where costs include the opportunity cost of invested capital.

Mergers are motivated by the prospect of financial gains. The possible sources of the financial gains from mergers are many, and the Guidelines do not attempt to identify all possible sources of gain in every merger. Instead, the Guidelines focus on the one potential source of gain that is of concern under the antitrust laws: market power.

The unifying theme of the Guidelines is that mergers should not be permitted to create or enhance market power or to facilitate its exercise. Market power to a seller is the ability profitably to maintain prices above competitive levels for a significant period of time.[6] In some circumstances, a sole seller (a "monopolist") of a product with no good substitutes can maintain a selling price that is above the level that would prevail if the market were competitive. Similarly, in some circumstances, where only a few firms account for most of the sales of a product, those firms can exercise market power, perhaps even approximating the performance of a monopolist, by either explicitly or implicitly coordinating their actions. Circumstances also may permit a single firm, not a monopolist, to exercise market power through unilateral or non-coordinated conduct — conduct the success of which does not rely on the concurrence of other firms in the market or on coordinated responses by those firms. In any case, the result of the exercise of market power is a transfer of wealth from buyers to sellers or a misallocation of resources.

Market power also encompasses the ability of a single buyer (a "monopsonist"), a coordinating group of buyers, or a single buyer, not a monopsonist, to depress the price paid for a product to a level that is below the competitive price and thereby

---

[5] For example, the burden with respect to efficiency and failure continues to reside with the proponents of the merger.

[6] Sellers with market power also may lessen competition on dimensions other than price, such as product quality, service, or innovation.

depress output. The exercise of market power by buyers ("monopsony power") has adverse effects comparable to those associated with the exercise of market power by sellers. In order to assess potential monopsony concerns, the Agency will apply an analytical framework analogous to the framework of these Guidelines.

While challenging competitively harmful mergers, the Agency seeks to avoid unnecessary interference with the larger universe of mergers that are either competitively beneficial or neutral. In implementing this objective, however, the Guidelines reflect the congressional intent that merger enforcement should interdict competitive problems in their incipiency.

0.2 Overview

The Guidelines describe the analytical process that the Agency will employ in determining whether to challenge a horizontal merger. First, the Agency assesses whether the merger would significantly increase concentration and result in a concentrated market, properly defined and measured. Second, the Agency assesses whether the merger, in light of market concentration and other factors that characterize the market, raises concern about potential adverse competitive effects. Third, the Agency assesses whether entry would be timely, likely and sufficient either to deter or to counteract the competitive effects of concern. Fourth, the Agency assesses any efficiency gains that reasonably cannot be achieved by the parties through other means. Finally the Agency assesses whether, but for the merger, either party to the transaction would be likely to fail, causing its assets to exit the market. The process of assessing market concentration, potential adverse competitive effects, entry, efficiency and failure is a tool that allows the Agency to answer the ultimate inquiry in merger analysis: whether the merger is likely to create or enhance market power or to facilitate its exercise.

1. MARKET DEFINITION, MEASUREMENT AND CONCENTRATION

1.0 Overview

A merger is unlikely to create or enhance market power or to facilitate its exercise unless it significantly increases concentration and results in a concentrated market, properly defined and measured. Mergers that either do not significantly increase concentration or do not result in a concentrated market ordinarily require no further analysis.

The analytic process described in this section ensures that the Agency evaluates the likely competitive impact of a merger within the context of economically meaningful markets — i.e., markets that could be subject to the exercise of market power. Accordingly, for each product or service (hereafter "product") of each merging firm, the Agency seeks to define a market in which firms could effectively exercise market power if they were able to coordinate their actions.

Market definition focuses solely on demand substitution factors — i.e., possible consumer responses. Supply substitution factors — i.e., possible production responses — are considered elsewhere in the Guidelines in the identification of firms that participate in the relevant market and the analysis of entry. See Sections 1.3 and 3. A market is defined as a product or group of products and a geographic area in which it is produced or sold such that a hypothetical profit-maximizing firm, not subject to price regulation, that was the only present and future producer or seller of those products in that area likely would impose at least a "small but significant and nontransitory" increase in price, assuming the terms of sale of all other products are held constant. A relevant market is a group of products and a geographic area that is no bigger than necessary to satisfy this test. The "small but significant and non-transitory" increase in price is employed solely as a methodological tool for the analysis of mergers: it is not a tolerance level for price increases.

Absent price discrimination, a relevant market is described by a product or group of products and a geographic area. In determining whether a hypothetical monopolist would be in a position to exercise market power, it is necessary to evaluate the likely demand responses of consumers to a price increase. A price increase could be made unprofitable by consumers either switching to other products or switching to the same product produced by firms at other locations. The nature and magnitude of these two types of demand responses respectively determine the scope of the product market and the geographic market.

In contrast, where a hypothetical monopolist likely would discriminate in prices charged to different groups of buyers, distinguished, for example, by their uses or locations, the Agency may delineate different relevant markets corresponding to each such buyer group. Competition for sales to each such group may be affected differently by a particular merger and markets are delineated by evaluating the demand response of each such buyer group. A relevant market of this kind is described by a collection of products for sale to a given group of buyers.

Once defined, a relevant market must be measured in terms of its participants and concentration. Participants include firms currently producing or selling the market's products in the market's geographic area. In addition, participants may include other firms depending on their likely supply responses to a "small but significant and nontransitory" price increase. A firm is viewed as a participant if, in response to a "small but significant and nontransitory" price increase, it likely would enter rapidly into production or sale of a market product in the market's area, without incurring significant sunk costs of entry and exit. Firms likely to make any of these supply responses are considered to be "uncommitted" entrants because their supply response would create new production or sale in the relevant market and because that production or sale could be quickly terminated without significant loss.[7] Uncommitted entrants are capable of making such quick and

---

[7] Probable supply responses that require the entrant to incur significant sunk costs of entry and exit are not part of market measurement, but are included in the analysis of the significance of entry. See Section 3. Entrants that must commit substantial sunk costs are regarded as "committed"

uncommitted supply responses that they likely influenced the market premerger, would influence it post-merger, and accordingly are considered as market participants at both times. This analysis of market definition and market measurement applies equally to foreign and domestic firms.

If the process of market definition and market measurement identifies one or more relevant markets in which the merging firms are both participants, then the merger is considered to be horizontal. Sections 1.1 through 1.5 describe in greater detail how product and geographic markets will be defined, how market shares will be calculated and how market concentration will be assessed.

1.1 Product Market Definition

The Agency will first define the relevant product market with respect to each of the products of each of the merging firms.[8]

1.11 General Standards

Absent price discrimination, the Agency will delineate the product market to be a product or group of products such that a hypothetical profit-maximizing firm that was the only present and future seller of those products ("monopolist") likely would impose at least a "small but significant and nontransitory" increase in price. That is, assuming that buyers likely would respond to an increase in price for a tentatively identified product group only by shifting to other products, what would happen? If the alternatives were, in the aggregate, sufficiently attractive at their existing terms of sale, an attempt to raise prices would result in a reduction of sales large enough that the price increase would not prove profitable, and the tentatively identified product group would prove to be too narrow.

Specifically, the Agency will begin with each product (narrowly defined) produced or sold by each merging firm and ask what would happen if a hypothetical monopolist of that product imposed at least a "small but significant and nontransitory" increase in price, but the terms of sale of all other products remained constant. If, in response to the price increase, the reduction in sales of the product would be large enough that a hypothetical monopolist would not find it profitable to impose such an increase in price, then the Agency will add to the product group the product that is the next-best substitute for the merging firm's product.[9]

---

entrants because those sunk costs make entry irreversible in the short term without foregoing that investment; thus the likelihood of their entry must be evaluated with regard to their long-term profitability.

[8] Although discussed separately, product market definition and geographic market definition are interrelated. In particular, the extent to which buyers of a particular product would shift to other products in the event of a "small but significant and nontransitory" increase in price must be evaluated in the context of the relevant geographic market.

[9] Throughout the Guidelines, the term "next best substitute" refers to the alternative which, if available in unlimited quantities at constant prices, would account for the greatest value of diversion of demand in response to a "small but significant and nontransitory" price increase.

In considering the likely reaction of buyers to a price increase, the Agency will take into account all relevant evidence, including, but not limited to, the following:

(1) evidence that buyers have shifted or have considered shifting purchases between products in response to relative changes in price or other competitive variables;

(2) evidence that sellers base business decisions on the prospect of buyer substitution between products in response to relative changes in price or other competitive variables;

(3) the influence of downstream competition faced by buyers in their output markets; and

(4) the timing and costs of switching products.

The price increase question is then asked for a hypothetical monopolist controlling the expanded product group. In performing successive iterations of the price increase test, the hypothetical monopolist will be assumed to pursue maximum profits in deciding whether to raise the prices of any or all of the additional products under its control. This process will continue until a group of products is identified such that a hypothetical monopolist over that group of products would profitably impose at least a "small but significant and nontransitory" increase, including the price of a product of one of the merging firms. The Agency generally will consider the relevant product market to be the smallest group of products that satisfies this test.

In the above analysis, the Agency will use prevailing prices of the products of the merging firms and possible substitutes for such products, unless premerger circumstances are strongly suggestive of coordinated interaction, in which case the Agency will use a price more reflective of the competitive price.[10] However, the Agency may use likely future prices, absent the merger, when changes in the prevailing prices can be predicted with reasonable reliability. Changes in price may be predicted on the basis of, for example, changes in regulation which affect price either directly or indirectly by affecting costs or demand.

In general, the price for which an increase will be postulated will be whatever is considered to be the price of the product at the stage of the industry being examined.[11] In attempting to determine objectively the effect of a "small but significant and nontransitory" increase in price, the Agency, in most contexts, will use a price increase of five percent lasting for the foreseeable future. However,

---

[10] The terms of sale of all other products are held constant in order to focus market definition on the behavior of consumers. Movements in the terms of sale for other products, as may result from the behavior of producers of those products, are accounted for in the analysis of competitive effects and entry. See Sections 2 and 3.

[11] For example, in a merger between retailers, the relevant price would be the retail price of a product to consumers. In the case of a merger among oil pipelines, the relevant price would be the tariff — the price of the transportation service.

what constitutes a "small but significant and nontransitory" increase in price will depend on the nature of the industry, and the Agency at times may use a price increase that is larger or smaller than five percent.

1.12 Product Market Definition in the Presence of Price Discrimination

The analysis of product market definition to this point has assumed that price discrimination — charging different buyers different prices for the same product, for example — would not be profitable for a hypothetical monopolist.

A different analysis applies where price discrimination would be profitable for a hypothetical monopolist. Existing buyers sometimes will differ significantly in their likelihood of switching to other products in response to a "small but significant and nontransitory" price increase. If a hypothetical monopolist can identify and price differently to those buyers ("targeted buyers") who would not defeat the targeted price increase by substituting to other products in response to a "small but significant and nontransitory" price increase for the relevant product, and if other buyers likely would not purchase the relevant product and resell to targeted buyers, then a hypothetical monopolist would profitably impose a discriminatory price increase on sales to targeted buyers. This is true regardless of whether a general increase in price would cause such significant substitution that the price increase would not be profitable. The Agency will consider additional relevant product markets consisting of a particular use or uses by groups of buyers of the product for which a hypothetical monopolist would profitably and separately impose at least a "small but significant and nontransitory" increase in price.

1.2 Geographic Market Definition

For each product market in which both merging firms participate, the Agency will determine the geographic market or markets in which the firms produce or sell. A single firm may operate in a number of different geographic markets.

1.21 General Standards

Absent price discrimination, the Agency will delineate the geographic market to be a region such that a hypothetical monopolist that was the only present or future producer of the relevant product at locations in that region would profitably impose at least a "small but significant and nontransitory" increase in price, holding constant the terms of sale for all products produced elsewhere. That is, assuming that buyers likely would respond to a price increase on products produced within the tentatively identified region only by shifting to products produced at locations of production outside the region, what would happen? If those locations of production outside the region were, in the aggregate, sufficiently attractive at their existing terms of sale, an attempt to raise price would result in a reduction in sales large enough that the price increase would not prove profitable, and the tentatively identified geographic area would prove to be too narrow.

In defining the geographic market or markets affected by a merger, the Agency will begin with the location of each merging firm (or each plant of a multiplant firm) and ask what would happen if a hypothetical monopolist of the relevant product at that point imposed at least a "small but significant and nontransitory" increase in price, but the terms of sale at all other locations remained constant. If, in response to the price increase, the reduction in sales of the product at that location would be large enough that a hypothetical monopolist producing or selling the relevant product at the merging firm's location would not find it profitable to impose such an increase in price, then the Agency will add the location from which production is the next-best substitute for production at the merging firm's location.

In considering the likely reaction of buyers to a price increase, the Agency will take into account all relevant evidence, including, but not limited to, the following:

(1) evidence that buyers have shifted or have considered shifting purchases between different geographic locations in response to relative changes in price or other competitive variables;

(2) evidence that sellers base business decisions on the prospect of buyer substitution between geographic locations in response to relative changes in price or other competitive variables;

(3) the influence of downstream competition faced by buyers in their output markets; and

(4) the timing and costs of switching suppliers.

The price increase question is then asked for a hypothetical monopolist controlling the expanded group of locations. In performing successive iterations of the price increase test, the hypothetical monopolist will be assumed to pursue maximum profits in deciding whether to raise the price at any or all of the additional locations under its control. This process will continue until a group of locations is identified such that a hypothetical monopolist over that group of locations would profitably impose at least a "small but significant and nontransitory" increase, including the price charged at a location of one of the merging firms.

The "smallest market" principle will be applied as it is in product market definition. The price for which an increase will be postulated, what constitutes a "small but significant and nontransitory" increase in price, and the substitution decisions of consumers all will be determined in the same way in which they are determined in product market definition.

1.22 Geographic Market Definition in the Presence of Price Discrimination

The analysis of geographic market definition to this point has assumed that geographic price discrimination — charging different prices net of transportation costs for the same product to buyers in different areas, for example — would not be profitable for a hypothetical monopolist. However, if a hypothetical monopolist can identify and price differently to buyers in certain areas ("targeted buyers") who would not defeat the targeted price increase by substituting to more distant sellers in response to a "small but significant and nontransitory" price increase for the relevant product, and if other buyers likely would not purchase the relevant product and resell to targeted buyers,[12] then a hypothetical monopolist would profitably impose a discriminatory price increase. This is true even where a general price increase would cause such significant substitution that the price increase would not be profitable. The Agency will consider additional geographic markets consisting of particular locations of buyers for which a hypothetical monopolist would profitably and separately impose at least a "small but significant and nontransitory" increase in price.

1.3 Identification of Firms that Participate in the Relevant Market

1.31 Current Producers or Sellers

The Agency's identification of firms that participate in the relevant market begins with all firms that currently produce or sell in the relevant market. This includes vertically integrated firms to the extent that such inclusion accurately reflects their competitive significance in the relevant market prior to the merger.

To the extent that the analysis under Section 1.1 indicates that used, reconditioned or recycled goods are included in the relevant market, market participants will include firms that produce or sell such goods and that likely would offer those goods in competition with other relevant products.

1.32 Firms That Participate Through Supply Response

In addition, the Agency will identify other firms not currently producing or selling the relevant product in the relevant area as participating in the relevant market if their inclusion would more accurately reflect probable supply responses. These firms are termed "uncommitted entrants." These supply responses must be likely to occur within one year and without the expenditure of significant sunk costs of entry and exit, in response to a "small but significant and nontransitory" price increase. If a firm has the technological capability to achieve such an uncommitted supply response, but likely would not (e.g., because difficulties in achieving product acceptance, distribution, or production would render such a response unprofitable), that firm will not be considered to be a market participant. The competitive significance of supply responses that require more time or that require firms to incur significant sunk costs of entry and exit will be considered in entry analysis. See Section 3.[13]

---

[12] This arbitrage is inherently impossible for many services and is particularly difficult where the product is sold on a delivered basis and where transportation costs are a significant percentage of the final cost.

[13] If uncommitted entrants likely would also remain in the market and would meet the entry tests of timeliness, likelihood and sufficiency, and thus would likely deter anticompetitive mergers or

Sunk costs are the acquisition costs of tangible and intangible assets that cannot be recovered through the redeployment of these assets outside the relevant market, i.e., costs uniquely incurred to supply the relevant product and geographic market. Examples of sunk costs may include market-specific investments in production facilities, technologies, marketing (including product acceptance), research and development, regulatory approvals, and testing. A significant sunk cost is one which would not be recouped within one year of the commencement of the supply response, assuming a "small but significant and nontransitory" price increase in the relevant market. In this context, a "small but significant and nontransitory" price increase will be determined in the same way in which it is determined in product market definition, except the price increase will be assumed to last one year. In some instances, it may be difficult to calculate sunk costs with precision. Accordingly, when necessary, the Agency will make an overall assessment of the extent of sunk costs for firms likely to participate through supply responses.

These supply responses may give rise to new production of products in the relevant product market or new sources of supply in the relevant geographic market. Alternatively, where price discrimination is likely so that the relevant market is defined in terms of a targeted group of buyers, these supply responses serve to identify new sellers to the targeted buyers. Uncommitted supply responses may occur in several different ways: by the switching or extension of existing assets to production or sale in the relevant market; or by the construction or acquisition of assets that enable production or sale in the relevant market.

1.321 Production Substitution and Extension: The Switching or Extension of Existing Assets to Production or Sale in the Relevant Market

The productive and distributive assets of a firm sometimes can be used to produce and sell either the relevant products or products that buyers do not regard as good substitutes. Production substitution refers to the shift by a firm in the use of assets from producing and selling one product to producing and selling another. Production extension refers to the use of those assets, for example, existing brand names and reputation, both for their current production and for production of the relevant product. Depending upon the speed of that shift and the extent of sunk costs incurred in the shift or extension, the potential for production substitution or extension may necessitate treating as market participants firms that do not currently produce the relevant product.[14]

---

deter or counteract the competitive effects of concern (see Section 3, *infra*), the Agency will consider the impact of those firms in the entry analysis.

[14] Under other analytical approaches, production substitution sometimes has been reflected in the description of the product market. For example, the product market for stamped metal products such as automobile hub caps might be described as "light metal stamping," a production process rather than a product. The Agency believes that the approach described in the text provides a more clearly focused method of incorporating this factor in merger analysis. If production substitution

If a firm has existing assets that likely would be shifted or extended into production and sale of the relevant product within one year, and without incurring significant sunk costs of entry and exit, in response to a "small but significant and nontransitory" increase in price for only the relevant product, the Agency will treat that firm as a market participant. In assessing whether a firm is such a market participant, the Agency will take into account the costs of substitution or extension relative to the profitability of sales at the elevated price, and whether the firm's capacity is elsewhere committed or elsewhere so profitably employed that such capacity likely would not be available to respond to an increase in price in the market.

1.322 Obtaining New Assets for Production or Sale of the Relevant Product

A firm may also be able to enter into production or sale in the relevant market within one year and without the expenditure of significant sunk costs of entry and exit, in response to a "small but significant and nontransitory" increase in price for only the relevant product, even if the firm is newly organized or is an existing firm without products or productive assets closely related to the relevant market. If new firms, or existing firms without closely related products or productive assets, likely would enter into production or sale in the relevant market within one year without the expenditure of significant sunk costs of entry and exit, the Agency will treat those firms as market participants.

1.4 Calculating Market Shares

1.41 General Approach

The Agency normally will calculate market shares for all firms (or plants) identified as market participants in Section 1.3 based on the total sales or capacity currently devoted to the relevant market together with that which likely would be devoted to the relevant market in response to a "small but significant and nontransitory" price increase. Market shares can be expressed either in dollar terms through measurement of sales, shipments, or production, or in physical terms through measurement of sales, shipments, production, capacity, or reserves.

Market shares will be calculated using the best indicator of firms' future competitive significance. Dollar sales or shipments generally will be used if firms are distinguished primarily by differentiation of their products. Unit sales generally will be used if firms are distinguished primarily on the basis of their relative advantages in serving different buyers or groups of buyers. Physical capacity or reserves generally will be used if it is these measures that most effectively distinguish firms.[15] Typically, annual data are used, but where individual sales are

---

among a group of products is nearly universal among the firms selling one or more of those products, however, the Agency may use an aggregate description of those markets as a matter of convenience.

[15] Where all firms have, on a forward-looking basis, an equal likelihood of securing sales, the Agency will assign firms equal shares.

large and infrequent so that annual data may be unrepresentative, the Agency may measure market shares over a longer period of time.

In measuring a firm's market share, the Agency will not include its sales or capacity to the extent that the firm's capacity is committed or so profitably employed outside the relevant market that it would not be available to respond to an increase in price in the market.

1.42 Price Discrimination Markets

When markets are defined on the basis of price discrimination (Sections 1.12 and 1.22), the Agency will include only sales likely to be made into, or capacity likely to be used to supply, the relevant market in response to a "small but significant and nontransitory" price increase.

1.43 Special Factors Affecting Foreign Firms

Market shares will be assigned to foreign competitors in the same way in which they are assigned to domestic competitors. However, if exchange rates fluctuate significantly, so that comparable dollar calculations on an annual basis may be unrepresentative, the Agency may measure market shares over a period longer than one year.

If shipments from a particular country to the United States are subject to a quota, the market shares assigned to firms in that country will not exceed the amount of shipments by such firms allowed under the quota.[16] In the case of restraints that limit imports to some percentage of the total amount of the product sold in the United States (i.e., percentage quotas), a domestic price increase that reduced domestic consumption also would reduce the volume of imports into the United States. Accordingly, actual import sales and capacity data will be reduced for purposes of calculating market shares. Finally, a single market share may be assigned to a country or group of countries if firms in that country or group of countries act in coordination.

1.5 Concentration and Market Shares

Market concentration is a function of the number of firms in a market and their respective market shares. As an aid to the interpretation of market data, the Agency will use the Herfindahl-Hirschman Index ("HHI") of market concentration. The HHI is calculated by summing the squares of the individual market shares of all the participants.[17] Unlike the four-firm concentration ratio, the HHI

---

[16] The constraining effect of the quota on the importer's ability to expand sales is relevant to the evaluation of potential adverse competitive effects. See Section 2.

[17] For example, a market consisting of four firms with market shares of 30 percent, 30 percent, 20 percent and 20 percent has an HHI of 2600 ($30^2 + 30^2 + 20^2 + 20^2 = 2600$). The HHI ranges from 10,000 (in the case of a pure monopoly) to a number approaching zero (in the case of an atomistic market). Although it is desirable to include all firms in the calculation, lack of information about

reflects both the distribution of the market shares of the top four firms and the composition of the market outside the top four firms. It also gives proportionately greater weight to the market shares of the larger firms, in accord with their relative importance in competitive interactions.

The Agency divides the spectrum of market concentration as measured by the HHI into three regions that can be broadly characterized as unconcentrated (HHI below 1000), moderately concentrated (HHI between 1000 and 1800), and highly concentrated (HHI above 1800). Although the resulting regions provide a useful framework for merger analysis, the numerical divisions suggest greater precision than is possible with the available economic tools and information. Other things being equal, cases falling just above and just below a threshold present comparable competitive issues.

1.51 General Standards

In evaluating horizontal mergers, the Agency will consider both the post-merger market concentration and the increase in concentration resulting from the merger.[18] Market concentration is a useful indicator of the likely potential competitive effect of a merger. The general standards for horizontal mergers are as follows:

   a) *Post-Merger HHI Below 1000.* The Agency regards markets in this region to be unconcentrated. Mergers resulting in unconcentrated markets are unlikely to have adverse competitive effects and ordinarily require no further analysis.

   b) *Post-Merger HHI Between 1000 and 1800.* The Agency regards markets in this region to be moderately concentrated. Mergers producing an increase in the HHI of less than 100 points in moderately concentrated markets post-merger are unlikely to have adverse competitive consequences and ordinarily require no further analysis. Mergers producing an increase in the HHI of more than 100 points in moderately concentrated markets post-merger potentially raise significant competitive concerns depending on the factors set forth in Sections 2-5 of the Guidelines.

   c) *Post-Merger HHI Above 1800.* The Agency regards markets in this region to be highly concentrated. Mergers producing an increase in the HHI of less than 50 points, even in highly concentrated markets post-merger, are unlikely to have adverse competitive consequences and ordinarily require no further analysis. Mergers producing an increase in the HHI of more than 50

---

small firms is not critical because such firms do not affect the HHI significantly.

[18] The increase in concentration as measured by the HHI can be calculated independently of the overall market concentration by doubling the product of the market shares of the merging firms. For example, the merger of firms with shares of 5 percent and 10 percent of the market would increase the HHI by 100 ($5 \times 10 \times 2 = 100$). The explanation for this technique is as follows: In calculating the HHI before the merger, the market shares of the merging firms are squared individually: $(a)^2 + (b)^2$. After the merger, the sum of those shares would be squared: $(a + b)^2$, which equals $a^2 + 2ab + b^2$. The increase in the HHI therefore is represented by $2ab$.

points in highly concentrated markets post-merger potentially raise significant competitive concerns, depending on the factors set forth in Sections 2-5 of the Guidelines. Where the post-merger HHI exceeds 1800, it will be presumed that mergers producing an increase in the HHI of more than 100 points are likely to create or enhance market power or facilitate its exercise. The presumption may be overcome by a showing that factors set forth in Sections 2-5 of the Guidelines make it unlikely that the merger will create or enhance market power or facilitate its exercise, in light of market concentration and market shares.

1.52 Factors Affecting the Significance of Market Shares and Concentration

The post-merger level of market concentration and the change in concentration resulting from a merger affect the degree to which a merger raises competitive concerns. However, in some situations, market share and market concentration data may either understate or overstate the likely future competitive significance of a firm or firms in the market or the impact of a merger. The following are examples of such situations.

1.521 Changing Market Conditions

Market concentration and market share data of necessity are based on historical evidence. However, recent or ongoing changes in the market may indicate that the current market share of a particular firm either understates or overstates the firm's future competitive significance. For example, if a new technology that is important to long-term competitive viability is available to other firms in the market, but is not available to a particular firm, the Agency may conclude that the historical market share of that firm overstates its future competitive significance. The Agency will consider reasonably predictable effects of recent or ongoing changes in market conditions in interpreting market concentration and market share data.

1.522 Degree of Difference Between the Products and Locations in the Market and Substitutes Outside the Market

All else equal, the magnitude of potential competitive harm from a merger is greater if a hypothetical monopolist would raise price within the relevant market by substantially more than a "small but significant and nontransitory" amount. This may occur when the demand substitutes outside the relevant market, as a group, are not close substitutes for the products and locations within the relevant market. There thus may be a wide gap in the chain of demand substitutes at the edge of the product and geographic market. Under such circumstances, more market power is at stake in the relevant market than in a market in which a hypothetical monopolist would raise price by exactly five percent.

2. THE POTENTIAL ADVERSE COMPETITIVE EFFECTS OF MERGERS

2.0 Overview

Other things being equal, market concentration affects the likelihood that one firm, or a small group of firms, could successfully exercise market power. The smaller the percentage of total supply that a firm controls, the more severely it must restrict its own output in order to produce a given price increase, and the less likely it is that an output restriction will be profitable. If collective action is necessary for the exercise of market power, as the number of firms necessary to control a given percentage of total supply decreases, the difficulties and costs of reaching and enforcing an understanding with respect to the control of that supply might be reduced. However, market share and concentration data provide only the starting point for analyzing the competitive impact of a merger. Before determining whether to challenge a merger, the Agency also will assess the other market factors that pertain to competitive effects, as well as entry, efficiencies and failure.

This section considers some of the potential adverse competitive effects of mergers and the factors in addition to market concentration relevant to each. Because an individual merger may threaten to harm competition through more than one of these effects, mergers will be analyzed in terms of as many potential adverse competitive effects as are appropriate. Entry, efficiencies, and failure are treated in Sections 3-5.

2.1 Lessening of Competition Through Coordinated Interaction

A merger may diminish competition by enabling the firms selling in the relevant market more likely, more successfully, or more completely to engage in coordinated interaction that harms consumers. Coordinated interaction is comprised of actions by a group of firms that are profitable for each of them only as a result of the accommodating reactions of the others. This behavior includes tacit or express collusion, and may or may not be lawful in and of itself.

Successful coordinated interaction entails reaching terms of coordination that are profitable to the firms involved and an ability to detect and punish deviations that would undermine the coordinated interaction. Detection and punishment of deviations ensure that coordinating firms will find it more profitable to adhere to the terms of coordination than to pursue short-term profits from deviating, given the costs of reprisal. In this phase of the analysis, the Agency will examine the extent to which post-merger market conditions are conducive to reaching terms of coordination, detecting deviations from those terms, and punishing such deviations. Depending upon the circumstances, the following market factors, among others, may be relevant: the availability of key information concerning market conditions, transactions and individual competitors; the extent of firm and product heterogeneity; pricing or marketing practices typically employed by firms in the market; the characteristics of buyers and sellers; and the characteristics of typical transactions. Certain market conditions that are conducive to reaching terms of coordination also may be conducive to detecting or punishing deviations from those terms. For example, the extent of information available to firms in the market, or the extent of homogeneity, may be relevant to both the ability to reach terms of coordination and to detect or punish deviations from those terms. The extent to which any specific market condition will be relevant to one or more of the conditions necessary to coordinated interaction will depend on the circumstances of the particular case.

It is likely that market conditions are conducive to coordinated interaction when the firms in the market previously have engaged in express collusion and when the salient characteristics of the market have not changed appreciably since the most recent such incident. Previous express collusion in another geographic market will have the same weight when the salient characteristics of that other market at the time of the collusion are comparable to those in the relevant market. In analyzing the effect of a particular merger on coordinated interaction, the Agency is mindful of the difficulties of predicting likely future behavior based on the types of incomplete and sometimes contradictory information typically generated in merger investigations. Whether a merger is likely to diminish competition by enabling firms more likely, more successfully or more completely to engage in coordinated interaction depends on whether market conditions, on the whole, are conducive to reaching terms of coordination and detecting and punishing deviations from those terms.

2.11 Conditions Conducive to Reaching Terms of Coordination

Firms coordinating their interactions need not reach complex terms concerning the allocation of the market output across firms or the level of the market prices but may, instead, follow simple terms such as a common price, fixed price $ differentials, stable market shares, or customer or territorial restrictions. Terms of coordination need not perfectly achieve the monopoly outcome in order to be harmful to consumers. Instead, the terms of coordination may be imperfect and incomplete — inasmuch as they omit some market participants, omit some dimensions of competition, omit some customers, yield elevated prices short of monopoly levels, or lapse into episodic price wars — and still result in significant competitive harm. At some point, however, imperfections cause the profitability of abiding by the terms of coordination to decrease and, depending on their extent, may make coordinated interaction unlikely in the first instance.

Market conditions may be conducive to or hinder reaching terms of coordination. For example, reaching terms of coordination may be facilitated by product or firm homogeneity and by existing practices among firms, practices not necessarily themselves antitrust violations, such as standardization of pricing or product variables on which firms could compete. Key information about rival firms and the market may also facilitate reaching terms of coordination. Conversely, reaching terms of coordination may be limited or impeded by product heterogeneity or by firms having substantially incomplete information about the conditions and prospects of their rivals' businesses, perhaps because of important differences among their current business operations. In addition, reaching terms of coordination may be limited or impeded by firm heterogeneity, for example, differences in vertical integration or the production of another product that tends to be used together with the relevant product.

2.12 Conditions Conducive to Detecting and Punishing Deviations

Where market conditions are conducive to timely detection and punishment of significant deviations, a firm will find it more profitable to abide by the terms of coordination than to deviate from them. Deviation from the terms of coordination will be deterred where the threat of punishment is credible. Credible punishment, however, may not need to be any more complex than temporary abandonment of the terms of coordination by other firms in the market.

Where detection and punishment likely would be rapid, incentives to deviate are diminished and coordination is likely to be successful. The detection and punishment of deviations may be facilitated by existing practices among firms, themselves not necessarily antitrust violations, and by the characteristics of typical transactions. For example, if key information about specific transactions or individual price or output levels is available routinely to competitors, it may be difficult for a firm to deviate secretly. If orders for the relevant product are frequent, regular and small relative to the total output of a firm in a market, it may be difficult for the firm to deviate in a substantial way without the knowledge of rivals and without the opportunity for rivals to react. If demand or cost fluctuations are relatively infrequent and small, deviations may be relatively easy to deter.

By contrast, where detection or punishment is likely to be slow, incentives to deviate are enhanced and coordinated interaction is unlikely to be successful. If demand or cost fluctuations are relatively frequent and large, deviations may be relatively difficult to distinguish from these other sources of market price fluctuations, and, in consequence, deviations may be relatively difficult to deter.

In certain circumstances, buyer characteristics and the nature of the procurement process may affect the incentives to deviate from terms of coordination. Buyer size alone is not the determining characteristic. Where large buyers likely would engage in long-term contracting, so that the sales covered by such contracts can be large relative to the total output of a firm in the market, firms may have the incentive to deviate. However, this only can be accomplished where the duration, volume and profitability of the business covered by such contracts are sufficiently large as to make deviation more profitable in the long term than honoring the terms of coordination, and buyers likely would switch suppliers.

In some circumstances, coordinated interaction can be effectively prevented or limited by maverick firms — firms that have a greater economic incentive to deviate from the terms of coordination than do most of their rivals (e.g., firms that are unusually disruptive and competitive influences in the market). Consequently, acquisition of a maverick firm is one way in which a merger may make coordinated interaction more likely, more successful, or more complete. For example, in a market where capacity constraints are significant for many competitors, a firm is more likely to be a maverick the greater is its excess or divertable capacity in relation to its sales or its total capacity, and the lower are its direct and opportunity costs of expanding sales in the relevant market.[19] This is so because a firm's incentive to deviate from price-elevating and output-limiting terms of coordination is greater the more the firm is able profitably to expand its output as a proportion of the sales it would obtain if it adhered to the terms of coordination and the smaller is the base of sales on which it enjoys elevated profits prior to the price cutting deviation.[20] A firm also may be a maverick if it has an unusual ability secretly to expand its sales in relation to the sales it would obtain if it adhered to the terms of coordination. This ability might arise from opportunities to expand captive production for a downstream affiliate.

2.2 Lessening of Competition Through Unilateral Effects

A merger may diminish competition even if it does not lead to increased likelihood of successful coordinated interaction, because merging firms may find it profitable to alter their behavior unilaterally following the acquisition by elevating price and suppressing output. Unilateral competitive effects can arise in a variety of different settings. In each setting, particular other factors describing the relevant market affect the likelihood of unilateral competitive effects. The settings differ by the primary characteristics that distinguish firms and shape the nature of their competition.

2.21 Firms Distinguished Primarily by Differentiated Products

In some markets the products are differentiated, so that products sold by different participants in the market are not perfect substitutes for one another. Moreover, different products in the market may vary in the degree of their substitutability for one another. In this setting, competition may be non-uniform (i.e., localized), so that individual sellers compete more directly with those rivals selling closer substitutes.[21]

---

[19] But excess capacity in the hands of non-maverick firms may be a potent weapon with which to punish deviations from the terms of coordination.

[20] Similarly, in a market where product design or quality is significant, a firm is more likely to be an effective maverick the greater is the sales potential of its products among customers of its rivals, in relation to the sales it would obtain if it adhered to the terms of coordination. The likelihood of expansion responses by a maverick will be analyzed in the same fashion as uncommitted entry or committed entry (see Sections 1.3 and 3) depending on the significance of the sunk costs entailed in expansion.

[21] Similarly, in some markets sellers are primarily distinguished by their relative advantages in

A merger between firms in a market for differentiated products may diminish competition by enabling the merged firm to profit by unilaterally raising the price of one or both products above the premerger level. Some of the sales loss due to the price rise merely will be diverted to the product of the merger partner and, depending on relative margins, capturing such sales loss through merger may make the price increase profitable even though it would not have been profitable premerger. Substantial unilateral price elevation in a market for differentiated products requires that there be a significant share of sales in the market accounted for by consumers who regard the products of the merging firms as their first and second choices, and that repositioning of the non- parties' product lines to replace the localized competition lost through the merger be unlikely. The price rise will be greater the closer substitutes are the products of the merging firms, i.e., the more the buyers of one product consider the other product to be their next choice.

2.211 Closeness of the Products of the Merging Firms

The market concentration measures articulated in Section 1 may help assess the extent of the likely competitive effect from a unilateral price elevation by the merged firm notwithstanding the fact that the affected products are differentiated. The market concentration measures provide a measure of this effect if each product's market share is reflective of not only its relative appeal as a first choice to consumers of the merging firms' products but also its relative appeal as a second choice, and hence as a competitive constraint to the first choice.[22] Where this circumstance holds, market concentration data fall outside the safeharbor regions of Section 1.5, and the merging firms have a combined market share of at least thirty-five percent, the Agency will presume that a significant share of sales in the market are accounted for by consumers who regard the products of the merging firms as their first and second choices. Purchasers of one of the merging firms' products may be more or less likely to make the other their second choice than market shares alone would indicate. The market shares of the merging firms' products may understate the competitive effect of concern, when, for example, the products of the merging firms are relatively more similar in their various attributes to one another than to other products in the relevant market. On the

---

serving different buyers or groups of buyers, and buyers negotiate individually with sellers. Here, for example, sellers may formally bid against one another for the business of a buyer, or each buyer may elicit individual price quotes from multiple sellers. A seller may find it relatively inexpensive to meet the demands of particular buyers or types of buyers, and relatively expensive to meet others' demands. Competition, again, may be localized: sellers compete more directly with those rivals having similar relative advantages in serving particular buyers or groups of buyers. For example, in open outcry auctions, price is determined by the cost of the second lowest-cost seller. A merger involving the first and second lowest-cost sellers could cause prices to rise to the constraining level of the next lowest-cost seller.

[22] Information about consumers' actual first and second product choices may be provided by marketing surveys, information from bidding structures, or normal course of business documents from industry participants.

other hand, the market shares alone may overstate the competitive effects of concern when, for example, the relevant products are less similar in their attributes to one another than to other products in the relevant market. Where market concentration data fall outside the safeharbor regions of Section 1.5, the merging firms have a combined market share of at least thirty-five percent, and where data on product attributes and relative product appeal show that a significant share of purchasers of one merging firm's product regard the other as their second choice, then market share data may be relied upon to demonstrate that there is a significant share of sales in the market accounted for by consumers who would be adversely affected by the merger.

2.212 Ability of Rival Sellers to Replace Lost Competition

A merger is not likely to lead to unilateral elevation of prices of differentiated products if, in response to such an effect, rival sellers likely would replace any localized competition lost through the merger by repositioning their product lines.[23]

In markets where it is costly for buyers to evaluate product quality, buyers who consider purchasing from both merging parties may limit the total number of sellers they consider. If either of the merging firms would be replaced in such buyers' consideration by an equally competitive seller not formerly considered, then the merger is not likely to lead to a unilateral elevation of prices.

2.22 Firms Distinguished Primarily by Their Capacities

Where products are relatively undifferentiated and capacity primarily distinguishes firms and shapes the nature of their competition, the merged firm may find it profitable unilaterally to raise price and suppress output. The merger provides the merged firm a larger base of sales on which to enjoy the resulting price rise and also eliminates a competitor to which customers otherwise would have diverted their sales. Where the merging firms have a combined market share of at least thirty-five percent, merged firms may find it profitable to raise price and reduce joint output below the sum of their premerger outputs because the lost markups on the foregone sales may be outweighed by the resulting price increase on the merged base of sales.

This unilateral effect is unlikely unless a sufficiently large number of the merged firm's customers would not be able to find economical alternative sources of supply, i.e., competitors of the merged firm likely would not respond to the price increase and output reduction by the merged firm with increases in their own outputs sufficient in the aggregate to make the unilateral action of the merged firm unprofitable. Such non-party expansion is unlikely if those firms

---

[23] The timeliness and likelihood of repositioning responses will be analyzed using the same methodology as used in analyzing uncommitted entry or committed entry (see Sections 1.3 and 3), depending on the significance of the sunk costs entailed in repositioning.

face binding capacity constraints that could not be economically relaxed within two years or if existing excess capacity is significantly more costly to operate than capacity currently in use.[24]

3. ENTRY ANALYSIS

3.0 Overview

A merger is not likely to create or enhance market power or to facilitate its exercise, if entry into the market is so easy that market participants, after the merger, either collectively or unilaterally could not profitably maintain a price increase above premerger levels. Such entry likely will deter an anticompetitive merger in its incipiency, or deter or counteract the competitive effects of concern.

Entry is that easy if entry would be timely, likely, and sufficient in its magnitude, character and scope to deter or counteract the competitive effects of concern. In markets where entry is that easy (i.e., where entry passes these tests of timeliness, likelihood, and sufficiency), the merger raises no antitrust concern and ordinarily requires no further analysis.

The committed entry treated in this Section is defined as new competition that requires expenditure of significant sunk costs of entry and exit.[25] The Agency employs a three step methodology to assess whether committed entry would deter or counteract a competitive effect of concern.

The first step assesses whether entry can achieve significant market impact within a timely period. If significant market impact would require a longer period, entry will not deter or counteract the competitive effect of concern.

The second step assesses whether committed entry would be a profitable and, hence, a likely response to a merger having competitive effects of concern. Firms considering entry that requires significant sunk costs must evaluate the profitability of the entry on the basis of long-term participation in the market, because the underlying assets will be committed to the market until they are economically depreciated. Entry that is sufficient to counteract the competitive effects of concern will cause prices to fall to their premerger levels or lower. Thus, the profitability of such committed entry must be determined on the basis of premerger market prices over the long term.

A merger having anticompetitive effects can attract committed entry, profitable at premerger prices, that would not have occurred premerger at these same prices. But following the merger, the reduction in industry output and increase in prices associated with the competitive effect of concern may allow the same entry to occur without driving market prices below premerger levels. After a merger that results in decreased output and increased prices, the likely sales opportunities

---

[24] The timeliness and likelihood of non-party expansion will be analyzed using the same methodology as used in analyzing uncommitted or committed entry (see Sections 1.3 and 3) depending on the significance of the sunk costs entailed in expansion.

[25] Supply responses that require less than one year and insignificant sunk costs to effectuate are analyzed as uncommitted entry in Section 1.3.

available to entrants at premerger prices will be larger than they were premerger, larger by the output reduction caused by the merger. If entry could be profitable at premerger prices without exceeding the likely sales opportunities — opportunities that include pre-existing pertinent factors as well as the merger-induced output reduction — then such entry is likely in response to the merger.

The third step assesses whether timely and likely entry would be sufficient to return market prices to their premerger levels. This end may be accomplished either through multiple entry or individual entry at a sufficient scale. Entry may not be sufficient, even though timely and likely, where the constraints on availability of essential assets, due to incumbent control, make it impossible for entry profitably to achieve the necessary level of sales. Also, the character and scope of entrants' products might not be fully responsive to the localized sales opportunities created by the removal of direct competition among sellers of differentiated products. In assessing whether entry will be timely, likely, and sufficient, the Agency recognizes that precise and detailed information may be difficult or impossible to obtain. In such instances, the Agency will rely on all available evidence bearing on whether entry will satisfy the conditions of timeliness, likelihood, and sufficiency.

3.1 Entry Alternatives

The Agency will examine the timeliness, likelihood, and sufficiency of the means of entry (entry alternatives) a potential entrant might practically employ, without attempting to identify who might be potential entrants. An entry alternative is defined by the actions the firm must take in order to produce and sell in the market. All phases of the entry effort will be considered, including, where relevant, planning, design, and management; permitting, licensing, and other approvals; construction, debugging, and operation of production facilities; and promotion (including necessary introductory discounts), marketing, distribution, and satisfaction of customer testing and qualification requirements.[26] Recent examples of entry, whether successful or unsuccessful, may provide a useful starting point for identifying the necessary actions, time requirements, and characteristics of possible entry alternatives.

3.2 Timeliness of Entry

In order to deter or counteract the competitive effects of concern, entrants quickly must achieve a significant impact on price in the relevant market. The Agency generally will consider timely only those committed entry alternatives that can be achieved within two years from initial planning to significant market impact.[27] Where the relevant product is a durable good, consumers, in response to

---

[26] Many of these phases may be undertaken simultaneously.

[27] Firms which have committed to entering the market prior to the merger generally will be included in the measurement of the market. Only committed entry or adjustments to pre-existing

a significant commitment to entry, may defer purchases by making additional investments to extend the useful life of previously purchased goods and in this way deter or counteract for a time the competitive effects of concern. In these circumstances, if entry only can occur outside of the two year period, the Agency will consider entry to be timely so long as it would deter or counteract the competitive effects of concern within the two year period and subsequently.

3.3 Likelihood of Entry

An entry alternative is likely if it would be profitable at premerger prices, and if such prices could be secured by the entrant.[28] The committed entrant will be unable to secure prices at premerger levels if its output is too large for the market to absorb without depressing prices further. Thus, entry is unlikely if the minimum viable scale is larger than the likely sales opportunity available to entrants.

Minimum viable scale is the smallest average annual level of sales that the committed entrant must persistently achieve for profitability at premerger prices.[29] Minimum viable scale is a function of expected revenues, based upon premerger prices,[30] and all categories of costs associated with the entry alternative, including an appropriate rate of return on invested capital given that entry could fail and sunk costs, if any, will be lost.[31]

Sources of sales opportunities available to entrants include: (a) the output reduction associated with the competitive effect of concern,[32] (b) entrants' ability to capture a share of reasonably expected growth in market demand,[33] (c) entrants' ability securely to divert sales from incumbents, for example, through vertical integration or through forward contracting, and (d) any additional anticipated contraction in incumbents' output in response to entry.[34] Factors that reduce the

---

entry plans that are induced by the merger will be considered as possibly deterring or counteracting the competitive effects of concern.

[28] Where conditions indicate that entry may be profitable at prices below premerger levels, the Agency will assess the likelihood of entry at the lowest price at which such entry would be profitable.

[29] The concept of minimum viable scale ("MVS") differs from the concept of minimum efficient scale ("MES"). While MES is the smallest scale at which average costs are minimized, MVS is the smallest scale at which average costs equal the premerger price.

[30] The expected path of future prices, absent the merger, may be used if future price changes can be predicted with reasonable reliability.

[31] The minimum viable scale of an entry alternative will be relatively large when the fixed costs of entry are large, when the fixed costs of entry are largely sunk, when the marginal costs of production are high at low levels of output, and when a plant is underutilized for a long time because of delays in achieving market acceptance.

[32] Five percent of total market sales typically is used because where a monopolist profitably would raise price by five percent or more across the entire relevant market, it is likely that the accompanying reduction in sales would be no less than five percent.

[33] Entrants' anticipated share of growth in demand depends on incumbents' capacity constraints and irreversible investments in capacity expansion, as well as on the relative appeal, acceptability and reputation of incumbents' and entrants' products to the new demand.

[34] For example, in a bidding market where all bidders are on equal footing, the market share of incumbents will contract as a result of entry.

sales opportunities available to entrants include: (a) the prospect that an entrant will share in a reasonably expected decline in market demand, (b) the exclusion of an entrant from a portion of the market over the long term because of vertical integration or forward contracting by incumbents, and (c) any anticipated sales expansion by incumbents in reaction to entry, either generalized or targeted at customers approached by the entrant, that utilizes prior irreversible investments in excess production capacity. Demand growth or decline will be viewed as relevant only if total market demand is projected to experience long-lasting change during at least the two year period following the competitive effect of concern.

3.4 Sufficiency of Entry

Inasmuch as multiple entry generally is possible and individual entrants may flexibly choose their scale, committed entry generally will be sufficient to deter or counteract the competitive effects of concern whenever entry is likely under the analysis of Section 3.3. However, entry, although likely, will not be sufficient if, as a result of incumbent control, the tangible and intangible assets required for entry are not adequately available for entrants to respond fully to their sales opportunities. In addition, where the competitive effect of concern is not uniform across the relevant market, in order for entry to be sufficient, the character and scope of entrants' products must be responsive to the localized sales opportunities that include the output reduction associated with the competitive effect of concern. For example, where the concern is unilateral price elevation as a result of a merger between producers of differentiated products, entry, in order to be sufficient, must involve a product so close to the products of the merging firms that the merged firm will be unable to internalize enough of the sales loss due to the price rise, rendering the price increase unprofitable.

4. EFFICIENCIES

[Editor's note: This statement on horizontal merger efficiencies, which was issued April 8, 1997, replaces §4.0 of the 1992 Horizontal Merger Guidelines as originally issued.]

Competition usually spurs firms to achieve efficiencies internally. Nevertheless, mergers have the potential to generate significant efficiencies by permitting a better utilization of existing assets, enabling the combined firm to achieve lower costs in producing a given quantity and quality than either firm could have achieved without the proposed transaction. Indeed, the primary benefit of mergers to the economy is their potential to generate such efficiencies.

Efficiencies generated through merger can enhance the merged firm's ability and incentive to compete, which may result in lower prices, improved quality, enhanced service, or new products. For example, merger-generated efficiencies may enhance competition by permitting two ineffective (e.g., high cost) competitors to become one effective (e.g., lower cost) competitor. In a coordinated interaction context (see Section 2.1), marginal cost reductions may make coordination less likely or effective by enhancing the incentive of a maverick to lower price or by creating a new maverick firm. In a unilateral effects context (see Section 2.2), marginal cost reductions may reduce the merged firm's incentive to elevate price. Efficiencies also may result in benefits in the form of new or improved products, and efficiencies may result in benefits even when price is not immediately and directly affected. Even when efficiencies generated through merger enhance a firm's ability to compete, however, a merger may have other effects that may lessen competition and ultimately may make the merger anticompetitive.

The Agency will consider only those efficiencies likely to be accomplished with the proposed merger and unlikely to be accomplished in the absence of either the proposed merger or another means having comparable anticompetitive effects. These are termed merger-specific efficiencies.[1] Only alternatives that are practical in the business situation faced by the merging firms will be considered in making this determination; the Agency will not insist upon a less restrictive alternative that is merely theoretical.

Efficiencies are difficult to verify and quantify, in part because much of the information relating to efficiencies is uniquely in the possession of the merging firms. Moreover, efficiencies projected reasonably and in good faith by the merging firms may not be realized. Therefore, the merging firms must substantiate efficiency claims so that the Agency can verify by reasonable means the likelihood and magnitude of each asserted efficiency, how and when each would be achieved (and any costs of doing so), how each would enhance the merged firm's ability and incentive to compete, and why each would be merger-specific. Efficiency claims will not be considered if they are vague or speculative or otherwise cannot be verified by reasonable means.

Cognizable efficiencies are merger-specific efficiencies that have been verified and do not arise from anticompetitive reductions in output or service. Cognizable efficiencies are assessed net of costs produced by the merger or incurred in achieving those efficiencies.

The Agency will not challenge a merger if cognizable efficiencies are of a character and magnitude such that the merger is not likely to be anticompetitive in any relevant market.[2] To make the requisite determination, the Agency considers

---

[1] The Agency will not deem efficiencies to be merger-specific if they could be preserved by practical alternatives that mitigate competitive concerns, such as divestiture or licensing. If a merger affects not whether but only when an efficiency would be achieved, only the timing advantage is a merger-specific efficiency.

[2] Section 7 of the Clayton Act prohibits mergers that may substantially lessen competition "in any line of commerce ... in any section of the country." Accordingly, the Agency normally assesses competition in each relevant market affected by a merger independently and normally will challenge the merger if it is likely to be anticompetitive in any relevant market. In some cases, however, the Agency in its prosecutorial discretion will consider efficiencies not strictly in the relevant market, but so inextricably linked with it that a partial divestiture or other remedy could

whether cognizable efficiencies likely would be sufficient to reverse the merger's potential to harm consumers in the relevant market, e.g., by preventing price increases in that market. In conducting this analysis,[3] the Agency will not simply compare the magnitude of the cognizable efficiencies with the magnitude of the likely harm to competition absent the efficiencies. The greater the potential adverse competitive effect of a merger — as indicated by the increase in the HHI and post merger HHI from Section 1, the analysis of potential adverse competitive effects from Section 2, and the timeliness, likelihood, and sufficiency of entry from Section 3 — the greater must be cognizable efficiencies in order for the Agency to conclude that the merger will not have an anticompetitive effect in the relevant market. When the potential adverse competitive effect of a merger is likely to be particularly large, extraordinarily great cognizable efficiencies would be necessary to prevent the merger from being anticompetitive.

In the Agency's experience, efficiencies are most likely to make a difference in merger analysis when the likely adverse competitive effects, absent the efficiencies, are not great. Efficiencies almost never justify a merger to monopoly or near-monopoly.

The Agency has found that certain types of efficiencies are more likely to be cognizable and substantial than others. For example, efficiencies resulting from shifting production among facilities formerly owned separately, which enable the merging firms to reduce the marginal cost of production, are more likely to be susceptible to verification, merger-specific, and substantial, and are less likely to result from anticompetitive reductions in output. Other efficiencies, such as those relating to research and development, are potentially substantial but are generally less susceptible to verification and may be the result of anticompetitive output reductions. Yet others, such as those relating to procurement, management, or capital cost are less likely to be merger-specific or substantial, or may not be cognizable for other reasons.

5. FAILURE AND EXITING ASSETS

5.0 Overview

Notwithstanding the analysis of Sections 1-4 of the Guidelines, a merger is not likely to create or enhance market power or to facilitate its exercise, if imminent

---

not feasibly eliminate the anticompetitive effect in the relevant market without sacrificing the efficiencies in the other market(s). Inextricably linked efficiencies rarely are a significant factor in the Agency's determination not to challenge a merger. They are most likely to make a difference when they are great and the likely anticompetitive effect in the relevant market(s) is small.

[3] The result of this analysis over the short term will determine the Agency's enforcement decision in most cases. The Agency also will consider the effects of cognizable efficiencies with no short-term, direct effect on prices in the relevant market. Delayed benefits from efficiencies (due to delay in the achievement of, or the realization of consumer benefits from, the efficiencies) will be given less weight because they are less proximate and more difficult to predict.

failure, as defined below, of one of the merging firms would cause the assets of that firm to exit the relevant market. In such circumstances, post-merger performance in the relevant market may be no worse than market performance had the merger been blocked and the assets left the market.

5.1 Failing Firm

A merger is not likely to create or enhance market power or facilitate its exercise if the following circumstances are met: 1) the allegedly failing firm would be unable to meet its financial obligations in the near future; 2) it would not be able to reorganize successfully under Chapter 11 of the Bankruptcy Act;[34] 3) it has made unsuccessful good-faith efforts to elicit reasonable alternative offers of acquisition of the assets of the failing firm[35] that would both keep its tangible and intangible assets in the relevant market and pose a less severe danger to competition than does the proposed merger; and 4) absent the acquisition, the assets of the failing firm would exit the relevant market.

5.2 Failing Division

A similar argument can be made for "failing" divisions as for failing firms. First, upon applying appropriate cost allocation rules, the division must have a negative cash flow on an operating basis. Second, absent the acquisition, it must be that the assets of the division would exit the relevant market in the near future if not sold. Due to the ability of the parent firm to allocate costs, revenues, and intracompany transactions among itself and its subsidiaries and divisions, the Agency will require evidence, not based solely on management plans that could be prepared solely for the purpose of demonstrating negative cash flow or the prospect of exit from the relevant market. Third, the owner of the failing division also must have complied with the competitively-preferable purchaser requirement of Section 5.1.

---

[34] 11 U.S.C. §§ 1101-1174 (1988).

[35] Any offer to purchase the assets of the failing firm for a price above the liquidation value of those assets — the highest valued use outside the relevant market or equivalent offer to purchase the stock of the failing firm — will be regarded as a reasonable alternative offer.

SELECTED ANTITRUST STATUTES

SHERMAN ACT

Section 1 [15 U.S.C. § 1]

Every contract, combination in the form of trust or otherwise, or conspiracy, in restraint of trade or commerce among the several States, or with foreign nations, is hereby declared to be illegal. Every person who shall make any contract or engage in any combination or conspiracy hereby declared to be illegal shall be deemed guilty of a felony, and, on conviction thereof, shall be punished by fine not exceeding $10,000,000 if a corporation, or, if any other person, $350,000, or by imprisonment not exceeding three years, or by both said punishments, in the discretion of the court.

Section 2 [15 U.S.C. § 2]

Every person who shall monopolize, or attempt to monopolize, or combine or conspire with any other person or persons, to monopolize any part of the trade or commerce among the several States, or with foreign nations, shall be deemed guilty of a felony, and, on conviction thereof, shall be punished by fine not exceeding $10,000,000 if a corporation, or, if any other person, $350,000, or by imprisonment not exceeding three years, or by both said punishments, in the discretion of the court.

Section 4 [15 U.S.C. § 4]

The several district courts of the United States are invested with jurisdiction to prevent and restrain violations of sections 1 to 7 of this title; and it shall be the duty of the several United States attorneys, in their respective districts, under the direction of the Attorney General, to institute proceedings in equity to prevent and restrain such violations. Such proceedings may be by way of petition setting forth the case and praying that such violation shall be enjoined or otherwise prohibited. When the parties complained of shall have been duly notified of such petition the court shall proceed, as soon as may be, to the hearing and determination of the case; and pending such petition and before final decree, the court may at any time make such temporary restraining order or prohibition as shall be deemed just in the premises.

Section 8 [15 U.S.C. § 7]

The word "person", or "persons", wherever used in sections 1 to 7 of this title shall be deemed to include corporations and associations existing under or authorized by the laws of either the United States, the laws of any of the Territories, the laws of any State, or the laws of any foreign country.

CLAYTON ACT

Section 1 [15 U.S.C. § 12]

"Commerce," as used herein, means trade or commerce among the several States and with foreign nations, or between the District of Columbia or any Territory of the United States and any State, Territory, or foreign nation, or between any insular possessions or other places under the jurisdiction of the United States, or between any such possession or place and any State or Territory of the United States or the District of Columbia or any foreign nation, or within the District of Columbia or any Territory or any insular possession or other place under the jurisdiction of the United States: *Provided*, That nothing in this Act contained shall apply to the Philippine Islands.

The word "person" or "persons" wherever used in this Act shall be deemed to include corporations and associations existing under or authorized by the laws of either the United States, the laws of any of the Territories, the laws of any State, or the laws of any foreign country.

(b) This Act may be cited as the "Clayton Act".

Section 2 [15 U.S.C. § 13, as Amended by Robinson-Patman Act]

(a) Price; selection of customers

It shall be unlawful for any person engaged in commerce, in the course of such commerce, either directly or indirectly, to discriminate in price between different purchasers of commodities of like grade and quality, where either or any of the purchases involved in such discrimination are in commerce, where such commodities are sold for use, consumption, or resale within the United States or any Territory thereof or the District of Columbia or any insular possession or other place under the jurisdiction of the United States, and where the effect of such discrimination may be substantially to lessen competition or tend to create a monopoly in any line of commerce, or to injure, destroy, or prevent competition with any person who either grants or knowingly receives the benefit of such discrimination, or with customers of either of them: *Provided*, That nothing herein contained shall prevent differentials which make only due allowance for differences in the cost of manufacture, sale, or delivery resulting from the differing methods or quantities in which such commodities are to such purchasers sold or delivered: *Provided, however*, That the Federal Trade Commission may, after due investigation and hearing to all interested parties, fix and establish quantity limits, and revise the same as it finds necessary, as to particular commodities or classes of commodities, where it finds that available purchasers in greater quantities are so few as to render differentials on account thereof unjustly discriminatory or promotive of monopoly in any line of commerce; and the foregoing shall then not be construed to permit differentials based on differences in quantities greater than those so fixed and established: *And provided further*, That nothing herein contained shall prevent persons engaged in selling goods, wares, or merchandise in commerce from selecting their own customers in bona fide transactions and not in restraint of trade: *And provided further*, That nothing herein contained shall prevent price changes from time to time where in response to changing conditions affecting the market for or the marketability of the goods concerned, such as but not limited to actual or imminent deterioration of perishable goods, obsolescence of seasonal goods, distress sales under court process, or sales in good faith in discontinuance of business in the goods concerned.

(b) Burden of rebutting prima-facie case of discrimination

Upon proof being made, at any hearing on a complaint under this section, that there has been discrimination in price or services or facilities furnished, the burden of rebutting the prima-facie case thus made by showing justification shall be upon the person charged with a violation of this section, and unless justification shall be affirmatively shown, the Commission is authorized to issue an order terminating the discrimination: *Provided, however*, That nothing herein contained shall prevent a seller rebutting the prima-facie case thus made by showing that his lower price or the furnishing of services or facilities to any purchaser or purchasers was made in good faith to meet an equally low price of a competitor, or the services or facilities furnished by a competitor.

(c) Payment or acceptance of commission, brokerage, or other compensation

It shall be unlawful for any person engaged in commerce, in the course of such commerce, to pay or grant, or to receive or accept, anything of value as a commission, brokerage, or other compensation, or any allowance or discount in lieu thereof, except for services rendered in connection with the sale or purchase of goods, wares, or merchandise, either to the other party to such transaction or to an agent, representative, or other intermediary therein where such intermediary is acting in fact for or in behalf, or is subject to the direct or indirect control, of any party to such transaction other than the person by whom such compensation is so granted or paid.

(d) Payment for services or facilities for processing or sale

It shall be unlawful for any person engaged in commerce to pay or contract for the payment of anything of value to or for the benefit of a customer of such person in the course of such commerce as compensation or in consideration for any services or facilities furnished by or through such customer in connection with the processing, handling, sale, or offering for sale of any products or commodities manufactured, sold, or offered for sale by such person, unless such payment or consideration is available on proportionally equal terms to all other customers competing in the distribution of such products or commodities.

(e) Furnishing services or facilities for processing, handling, etc.

It shall be unlawful for any person to discriminate in favor of one purchaser against another purchaser or purchasers of a commodity bought for resale, with or without processing, by contracting to furnish or furnishing, or by contributing to the furnishing of, any services or facilities connected with the processing, handling, sale, or offering for sale of such commodity so purchased upon terms not accorded to all purchasers on proportionally equal terms.

(f) Knowingly inducing or receiving discriminatory price

It shall be unlawful for any person engaged in commerce, in the course of such commerce, knowingly to induce or receive a discrimination in price which is prohibited by this section.

Section 3 [15 U.S.C. § 14]

It shall be unlawful for any person engaged in commerce, in the course of such commerce, to lease or make a sale or contract for sale of goods, wares, merchandise, machinery, supplies, or other commodities, whether patented or unpatented, for use, consumption, or resale within the United States or any Territory thereof or the District of Columbia or any insular possession or other place under the jurisdiction of the United States, or fix a price charged therefor, or discount from, or rebate upon, such price, on the condition, agreement, or understanding that the lessee or purchaser thereof shall not use or deal in the goods, wares, merchandise, machinery, supplies, or other commodities of a competitor or competitors of the lessor or seller, where the effect of such lease, sale, or contract for sale or such condition, agreement, or understanding may be to substantially lessen competition or tend to create a monopoly in any line of commerce.

Section 4 [15 U.S.C. § 15]

… [A]ny person who shall be injured in his business or property by reason of anything forbidden in the antitrust laws may sue therefor in any district court of the United States in the district in which the defendant resides or is found or has an agent, without respect to the amount in controversy, and shall recover threefold the damages by him sustained, and the cost of suit, including a reasonable attorney's fee.

Section 4 [15 U.S.C. § 15c]

(a) Parens patriae; monetary relief; damages; prejudgment interest

(1) Any attorney general of a State may bring a civil action in the name of such State, as parens patriae on behalf of natural persons residing in such

State, in any district court of the United States having jurisdiction of the defendant, to secure monetary relief as provided in this section for injury sustained by such natural persons to their property by reason of any violation of sections 1 to 7 of this title. The court shall exclude from the amount of monetary relief awarded in such action any amount of monetary relief (A) which duplicates amounts which have been awarded for the same injury, or (B) which is properly allocable to (i) natural persons who have excluded their claims pursuant to subsection (b)(2) of this section, and (ii) any business entity.

(2) The court shall award the State as monetary relief threefold the total damage sustained as described in paragraph (1) of this subsection, and the cost of suit, including a reasonable attorney's fee....

Section 5 [15 U.S.C. § 16]

A final judgment or decree heretofore or hereafter rendered in any civil or criminal proceeding brought by or on behalf of the United States under the antitrust laws to the effect that a defendant has violated said laws shall be prima facie evidence against such defendant in any action or proceeding brought by any other party against such defendant under said laws as to all matters respecting which said judgment or decree would be an estoppel as between the parties thereto: *Provided*, That this section shall not apply to consent judgments or decrees entered before any testimony has been taken. Nothing contained in this section shall be construed to impose any limitation on the application of collateral estoppel, except that, in any action or proceeding brought under the antitrust laws, collateral estoppel effect shall not be given to any finding made by the Federal Trade Commission under the antitrust laws or under section 45 of this title which could give rise to a claim for relief under the antitrust laws.

Section 6 [15 U.S.C. § 17]

The labor of a human being is not a commodity or article of commerce. Nothing contained in the antitrust laws shall be construed to forbid the existence and operation of labor, agricultural, or horticultural organizations, instituted for the purposes of mutual help, and not having capital stock or conducted for profit, or to forbid or restrain individual members of such organizations from lawfully carrying out the legitimate objects thereof; nor shall such organizations, or the members thereof, be held or construed to be illegal combinations or conspiracies in restraint of trade, under the antitrust laws.

Section 7 [15 U.S.C. § 18]

No person engaged in commerce or in any activity affecting commerce shall acquire, directly or indirectly, the whole or any part of the stock or other share capital and no person subject to the jurisdiction of the Federal Trade Commission shall acquire the whole or any part of the assets of another person engaged also in commerce or in any activity affecting commerce, where in any line of commerce or in any activity affecting commerce in any section of the country, the effect of such acquisition may be substantially to lessen competition, or to tend to create a monopoly.

No person shall acquire, directly or indirectly, the whole or any part of the stock or other share capital and no person subject to the jurisdiction of the Federal Trade Commission shall acquire the whole or any part of the assets of one or more persons engaged in commerce or in any activity affecting commerce, where in any line of commerce or in any activity affecting commerce in any section of the country, the effect of such acquisition, of such stocks or assets, or of the use of such stock by the voting or granting of proxies or otherwise, may be substantially to lessen competition, or to tend to create a monopoly.

This section shall not apply to persons purchasing such stock solely for investment and not using the same by voting or otherwise to bring about, or in attempting to bring about, the substantial lessening of competition. Nor shall anything contained in this section prevent a corporation engaged in commerce or in any activity affecting commerce from causing the formation of subsidiary corporations for the actual carrying on of their immediate lawful business, or the natural and legitimate branches or extensions thereof, or from owning and holding all or a part of the stock of such subsidiary corporations, when the effect of such formation is not to substantially lessen competition. ...

Nothing contained in this section shall apply to transactions duly consummated pursuant to authority given by the Secretary of Transportation, Federal Power Commission, Surface Transportation Board, the Securities and Exchange Commission in the exercise of its jurisdiction under section 79j of this title, the United States Maritime Commission, or the Secretary of Agriculture under any statutory provision vesting such power in such Commission, Board, or Secretary.

Section 8 [15 U.S.C. § 19]

(a) (1) No person shall, at the same time, serve as a director or officer in any two corporations (other than banks, banking associations, and trust companies) that are —

  (A) engaged in whole or in part in commerce; and
  (B) by virtue of their business and location of operation, competitors, so that the elimination of competition by agreement between them would constitute a violation of any of the antitrust laws;

  if each of the corporations has capital, surplus, and undivided profits aggregating more than $10,000,000 as adjusted pursuant to paragraph (5) of this subsection.

  (2) Notwithstanding the provisions of paragraph (1), simultaneous service as a director or officer in any two corporations shall not be prohibited by this section if —

(A) the competitive sales of either corporation are less than $1,000,000, as adjusted pursuant to paragraph (5) of this subsection;

(B) the competitive sales of either corporation are less than 2 per centum of that corporation's total sales; or

(C) the competitive sales of each corporation are less than 4 per centum of that corporation's total sales.

For purposes of this paragraph, "competitive sales" means the gross revenues for all products and services sold by one corporation in competition with the other, determined on the basis of annual gross revenues for such products and services in that corporation's last completed fiscal year. For the purposes of this paragraph, "total sales" means the gross revenues for all products and services sold by one corporation over that corporation's last completed fiscal year.

(3) The eligibility of a director or officer under the provisions of paragraph (1) shall be determined by the capital, surplus and undivided profits, exclusive of dividends declared but not paid to stockholders, of each corporation at the end of that corporation's last completed fiscal year.

(4) For purposes of this section, the term "officer" means an officer elected or chosen by the Board of Directors.

(5) For each fiscal year commencing after September 30, 1990, the $10,000,000 and $1,000,000 thresholds in this subsection shall be increased (or decreased) as of October 1 each year by an amount equal to the percentage increase (or decrease) in the gross national product, as determined by the Department of Commerce or its successor, for the year then ended over the level so established for the year ending September 30, 1989. As soon as practicable, but not later than January 31 of each year, the Federal Trade Commission shall publish the adjusted amounts required by this paragraph.

(b) When any person elected or chosen as a director or officer of any corporation subject to the provisions hereof is eligible at the time of his election or selection to act for such corporation in such capacity, his eligibility to act in such capacity shall not be affected by any of the provisions hereof by reason of any change in the capital, surplus and undivided profits, or affairs of such corporation from whatever cause, until the expiration of one year from the date on which the event causing ineligibility occurred.

FEDERAL TRADE COMMISSION ACT

Section 1 [15 U.S.C. § 41]

A commission is created and established, to be known as the Federal Trade Commission (hereinafter referred to as the Commission), which shall be composed of five Commissioners, who shall be appointed by the President, by and with the advice and consent of the Senate. Not more than three of the Commissioners shall be members of the same political party.... No Commissioner shall engage in any other business, vocation, or employment. Any Commissioner may be removed by the President for inefficiency, neglect of duty, or malfeasance in office. A vacancy in the Commission shall not impair the right of the remaining Commissioners to exercise all the powers of the Commission.

Section 5 [15 U.S.C. § 45]

(1) Unfair methods of competition in or affecting commerce, and unfair or deceptive acts or practices in or affecting commerce, are hereby declared unlawful.

(2) The Commission is hereby empowered and directed to prevent persons, partnerships, or corporations, except banks, savings and loan institutions described in section 57a(f)(3) of this title, Federal credit unions described in section 57a(f)(4) of this title, common carriers subject to the Acts to regulate commerce, air carriers and foreign air carriers subject to part A of subtitle VII of Title 49, and persons, partnerships, or corporations insofar as they are subject to the Packers and Stockyards Act, 1921, as amended [7 U.S.C.A. § 181 et seq.], except as provided in section 406(b) of said Act [7 U.S.C.A. § 227(b)], from using unfair methods of competition in or affecting commerce and unfair or deceptive acts or practices in or affecting commerce.

(b) Whenever the Commission shall have reason to believe that any such person, partnership, or corporation has been or is using any unfair method of competition or unfair or deceptive act or practice in or affecting commerce, and if it shall appear to the Commission that a proceeding by it in respect thereof would be to the interest of the public, it shall issue and serve upon such person, partnership, or corporation a complaint stating its charges in that respect and containing a notice of a hearing upon a day and at a place therein fixed at least thirty days after the service of said complaint. The person, partnership, or corporation so complained of shall have the right to appear at the place and time so fixed and show cause why an order should not be entered by the Commission requiring such person, partnership, or corporation to cease and desist from the violation of the law so charged in said complaint. Any person, partnership, or corporation may make application, and upon good cause shown may be allowed by the Commission to intervene and appear in said proceeding by counsel or in person. The testimony in any such proceeding shall be reduced to writing and filed in the office of the Commission. If upon such hearing the Commission shall be of the opinion that the method of competition or the act or practice in question is prohibited by this subchapter, it shall make a report in writing in which it shall state its findings as to the facts and shall issue and cause to be served on such person, partnership, or corporation an order requiring such person, partnership, or corporation to cease and desist from using such method of competition or such act or practice.

PATENT ACT (35 U.S.C. § 1-293)

35 U.S.C § 271

...

(d) No patent owner otherwise entitled to relief for infringement or contributory infringement of a patent shall be denied relief or deemed guilty of misuse or illegal extension of the patent right by reason of his having done one or more of the following: (1) derived revenue from acts which if performed by another without his consent would constitute contributory infringement of the patent; (2) licensed or authorized another to perform acts which if performed without his consent would constitute contributory infringement of the patent; (3) sought to enforce his patent rights against infringement or contributory infringement; (4) refused to license or use any rights to the patent; or (5) conditioned the license of any rights to the patent or the sale of the patented product on the acquisition of a license to rights in another patent or purchase of a separate product, unless, in view of the circumstances, the patent owner has market power in the relevant market for the patent or patented product on which the license or sale is conditioned....

Table Of Cases

Reference are to pages. Principal cases and the pages
where they appear are in italics.

Index

A

B

BAINIAN DEFINITION OF ENTRY BARRIERS, pp. 670 to 672.

BARRIERS TO ENTRY, pp. 659 to 674.
Horizontal merger guidelines, pp. 874, 875.

BASEBALL EXEMPTION, p. 1000.

BASE-POINT PRICING, pp. 288 to 298.

BLOCK-BOOKING.
Tying arrangements, pp. 582 to 587.

BOYCOTTS AND OTHER CONCERTED REFUSALS TO DEAL, pp. 368
    to 415.
Competitors targeted, pp. 368 to 383.
Customer dealings targeted, pp. 383 to 388.
Data dissemination, pp. 385, 386.
Limited balancing approach, pp. 383 to 388.
Naked and ancillary refusals to deal, pp. 404 to 409.
Non-commercial boycotts, pp. 161, 409 to 415.
Per se analysis, pp. 368 to 383.
Politically motivated boycotts, pp. 161, 409 to 415.
Self-regulation and disciplinary actions, pp. 388 to 404.
Vertical restraint of trade.
    Unilateral refusals to deal, pp. 437 to 440.

BUNDLING.
Tying arrangements, pp. 582 to 587.

BURDEN OF PROOF.
Horizontal arrangements, pp. 325 to 345.
Private actions to enforce law, p. 76.

BUSINESS OR PROPERTY REQUIREMENT.
Private enforcement actions, pp. 111 to 114.

BUSINESS REVIEW LETTERS, pp. 151, 152.

BUYER PRICE DISCRIMINATION, pp. 961 to 967.

C

CARTELS.
Boycotts and other concerted refusals to deal, pp. 368 to 415. (*See* BOYCOTTS
    AND OTHER CONCERTED REFUSALS TO DEAL).
Conspiracy to monopolize, p. 773.
Development of analytical and evidentiary rules, pp. 187 to 189.
Market allocation, pp. 345 to 368.

D

I

O

OFFENSE OF MONOPOLIZATION.
Monopolies. (*See* MONOPOLIES).

OLIGOPOLY PRICING, pp. 298 to 310.

OPTIMAL DETERRENCE MODEL, pp. 170 to 175.

OUTPUT RESTRICTIONS.
Price fixing, pp. 201 to 209.

OVERBROAD REMEDIAL ORDERS, pp. 161 to 163.

P

PACKAGE LICENSING.
Tying arrangements, pp. 582 to 587.

PACKAGE PRICING.
Predatory pricing, pp. 771, 772.

PARENS PATRIAE, pp. 150, 151.

PARTIAL ACQUISITIONS, pp. 844 to 846.

PASS-ON THEORY.
Direct purchaser requirement in private enforcement actions, pp. 96 to 111.

PATENTS.
Joint ventures and patent licensing, pp. 349, 350.
Monopolies.
    Patent abuses as monopolization, pp. 706 to 712.
Text of Patent Act, Appx. B
Tying arrangements.
    Intellectual property licensing, pp. 582 to 587.

PERCEIVED POTENTIAL ENTRANT DOCTRINE, pp. 896 to 899.

PERFECT COMPETITION.
Economic theories and implications, pp. 55 to 58.

PERFECT PRICE DISCRIMINATION, pp. 921 to 923.

PER SE ILLEGALITY.
Boycotts, pp. 368 to 383.
Horizontal arrangements, pp. 188, 189.
Price fixing, p. 209.
Tying arrangements, pp. 519 to 531.

S

W